Exploring
Child Development

Second Edition

Exploring
Child Development

Richard Fabes
Arizona State University

Carol Lynn Martin
Arizona State University

Boston   New York   San Francisco
Mexico City   Montreal   Toronto   London   Madrid   Munich   Paris
Hong Kong   Singapore   Tokyo   Cape Town   Sydney

Executive Editor: *Carolyn O. Merrill*
Editorial Assistant: *Kate Edwards*
Developmental Editors: *Tom Pauken and Mary Connell*
Marketing Manager: *Brad Parkins*
Editorial-Production Administrator: *Anna Socrates*
Composition and Prepress Buyer: *Linda Cox*
Manufacturing Buyer: *Megan Cochran*
Cover Administrator: *Linda Knowles*
Cover Designer: *Studio Nine*
Text Designer: *Glenna Collett*
Editorial Production Services: *Lifland et al., Bookmakers*
Photo Researcher: *Helane M. Prottas/Posh Pictures*
Illustrations: *Jay Alexander, Susan Avishai, and LMY Studios*
Electronic Composition: *Omegatype Typography, Inc.*

For related titles and support materials, visit our online catalog at www.ablongman.com

Library of Congress Cataloging-in-Publication Data
Fabes, Richard A.
    Exploring child development / Richard Fabes, Carol Lynn Martin.—2nd ed.
      p.   cm.
    Includes bibliographical references and index.
    ISBN 0-205-34808-4
    1. Child development. I. Martin, Carol Lynn. II. Title.

HQ767.9 .F33 2002
305.231—dc21   2002022802

Brief Contents

To the Student   xxi
To the Instructor   xxiii

PART 1 *Introduction to Child Development*   1

    1 Introduction to the Study of Children's Development   2

    2 Understanding Development   25

PART 2 *Prenatal and Neonatal Development*   59

    3 Genetics and Prenatal Development   60

    4 Birth and Neonatal Development   96

PART 3 *Infant and Toddler Development*   133

    5 Cognitive, Language, and Physical Development in Infancy and Toddlerhood   134

    6 Social and Emotional Development in Infancy and Toddlerhood   175

PART 4 *Early Childhood Development*   211

    7 Cognitive, Language, and Physical Development in Early Childhood   212

    8 Social and Emotional Development in Early Childhood   244

PART 5 *Late Childhood Development*   283

    9 Cognitive, Language, and Physical Development in Late Childhood   284

    10 Social and Emotional Development in Late Childhood   317

PART 6 *Early Adolescent Development*   351

    11 Cognitive and Physical Development in Early Adolescence   352

    12 Social and Emotional Development in Early Adolescence   383

PART 7 *Late Adolescent Development*   411

    13 Cognitive and Physical Development in Late Adolescence   412

    14 Social and Emotional Development in Late Adolescence   439

Glossary   469
References   477
Name Index   529
Subject Index   545

Contents

To the Student   xxi
To the Instructor   xxiii
Supplements   xxviii
Acknowledgments   xxx
About the Authors   xxxi

PART 1

Introduction to Child Development   **1**

1 Introduction to the Study of Children's Development   2

What Is Child Development?   4
What Are Some Critical Issues in the Study of Child Development?   4
    Influences on Child Development   5
    Teasing Out the Roles of Nature and Nurture   7
    Continuity versus Discontinuity   9
    Critical and Sensitive Periods   9
    Individual Differences in Development—Stability and Change   10
What Are the Historical Roots of the Study of Child Development?   11
    Children of Antiquity   11
    Children as Miniature Adults: Medieval Children   11
    Early Philosophical Roots of Childhood   12
    Charles Darwin: Evolution and Child Development   13
    G. Stanley Hall: Pioneer in the Study of Development   13
What Changes in Contemporary American Life Influence the Study of Child Development?   14
    Changes in Family Structure   14

THE PRACTICAL IMPACT Trends in US Family Values Since 1950   15
    Children of Lesbian and Gay Parents   17
    Ethnic and Racial Diversity   18

THE SOCIAL IMPACT What Is the Impact of Immigration on American Life?   19

THE SCIENTIFIC IMPACT Is Development Different for Children of Color?   20

Can We Capture the Diversity of Children's Development?   21

Try It Out   23
Sum It Up   24
Key Terms and Concepts   24

2   Understanding Development   **25**

How Do Theories Explain Child Development?   26
    Scientific Theories   26
    Evaluating Theories of Development   27
What Are the Major Biology-Based Theories of Child Development?   27
    Evolutionary Theories   28
    Ethological Theory   28
    Attachment Theory   29
    Neurodevelopmental Approaches   29
What Are the Major Psychoanalytic Theories of Child Development?   30
    Freud's Psychosexual Theory   30
    Erikson's Psychosocial Theory   31
What Are the Major Environment-Based Theories of Child Development?   32
    Classical Conditioning   32
    Operant Conditioning   33
    Social Learning Theory   35
What Are the Major Cognition-Based Theories of Child Development?   35
    Piaget's Cognitive Developmental Theory   35
    Vygotsky's Theory of Cognitive Development   38
    Information Processing Theory   39
What Are the Major Contextual Theories of Child Development?   40
    Bronfenbrenner's Ecological Theory   40
    Dynamic Systems Theory   41
How Is Child Development Studied?   43
    Scientific Reasoning and the Scientific Method   43

THE PRACTICAL IMPACT)   Assessing Your Personal Beliefs   44
    Topics in Developmental Science   45
    Research Strategies   46

THE SCIENTIFIC IMPACT)   What Are the Ethical Concerns
    in Studying Child Development?   49
    Measuring Change over Time   50

THE SOCIAL IMPACT)   Do Gifted Children Become
    Well-Adjusted Adults?   51
    Measuring Children's Behavior   51
Try It Out   53
Sum It Up   54
Key Terms and Concepts   55
See the Impact   56
    Benchmarks in Child Development   56
    National Hotlines for Child Development   56
    Impact Report on Child Development   57
    Recommended Websites   57

PART 2

Prenatal and Neonatal Development   **59**

3   Genetics and Prenatal Development   **60**

How Do Genes Influence Development?   61
Hunting for Genes: The Human Genome Project   61
Genes and Chromosomes   62
Genetic Transmission Patterns   64

THE SOCIAL IMPACT   Should the Sex of a Child
Be Preselected?   65

THE SCIENTIFIC IMPACT   Genes, Attention Disorders,
and Thrill-Seeking   67

How Do Genes and Environments Work Together?   68
Genomes to Life Project   69
What Are Common Chromosomal Abnormalities?   69
Down Syndrome   69
Sex Chromosome Abnormalities   70
How Are Genetic Diseases Detected?   71
Genetic Technology   71

THE PRACTICAL IMPACT   Treating a Diseased Fetus   72

Genetic Counseling   72
How Does Prenatal Development Proceed?   73
Ovulation   73
Spermatogenesis   74
Fertilization   74
Overcoming Infertility   75
Overview of Prenatal Development   76
The Germinal Stage   77
The Embryonic Stage   78
The Fetal Stage   82
What Conditions Influence Pregnancy and Prenatal Development?   83
Diseases   85
Drugs   86
Environmental Hazards   90
Maternal Conditions   91
Protective Factors   92
Cultural Influences on Pregnancy   93
Try It Out   94
Sum It Up   94
Key Terms and Concepts   95

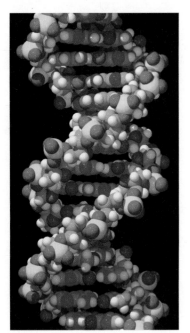

4 Birth and Neonatal Development   96

How Is a Baby Born?   97
The Birth Process   97
Birthing Methods   100
Birth Complications and Related Procedures   102

How Is Childbirth Experienced?   103
The Mother's Perspective   104
The Father's Perspective   105
The Newborn's Perspective   105
Parent-Newborn Bonding   106
Cultural Differences in the Experience of Childbirth   107

What Are the Characteristics of a Newborn?   108
Physical Appearance   108
Neonatal Reflexes   109
Neonatal States   111
Neonatal Sleep Patterns   112
Neonatal Imitation   113
Behavioral Assessment of Neonates   113

How Does Early Brain Development Proceed?   114
Progressive Events in Brain Development   115
Brain Plasticity   117
Regressive Events in Brain Development   117
Environmental Effects on Brain Development   117

How Do Neonates Perceive Their Worlds?   118
The Visual World of the Newborn   118
The Newborn's World of Sound   119

THE SCIENTIFIC IMPACT Do Newborns Prefer to Hear Their
Own Language?   120
The Newborn's World of Taste, Smell, and Touch   120
The "Dance of Perception"   121

Why Are Some Newborns At Risk?   121
Consequences of Low Birthweight and Prematurity   123
Neonatal Intensive Care   124
Caregiving and High-Risk Infants   125

THE SOCIAL IMPACT Should There Be Limits
to Neonatal Treatment?   126

THE PRACTICAL IMPACT Preventing SIDS   126
Infant Mortality   127

Try It Out   127
Sum It Up   128
Key Terms and Concepts   129
See the Impact   130
Benchmarks in Prenatal and Neonatal Development   130
National Hotlines for Pregnancy and Prenatal
and Neonatal Development   130
Impact Report on Prenatal and Neonatal Development   131
Recommended Websites   131

PART 3

Infant and Toddler Development　　**133**

5　Cognitive, Language, and Physical Development in Infancy and Toddlerhood　　**134**

How Do Infants and Toddlers Develop Physically?　135
　Growth Patterns in Infants and Toddlers　135
　Brain Development　135
　Motor Development in Infants and Toddlers　137

THE PRACTICAL IMPACT　Why Babies Aren't Crawling　139
　Bowel and Bladder Control　140

What Factors Influence Infant Health and Safety?　140
　Promoting Healthy Development and Growth　140
　Avoiding Accidents　141
　Infant Nutrition　141

THE SOCIAL IMPACT　Should Babies Be Taught to Swim?　141
　Weaning and Feeding Infants and Toddlers　143
　Failure-to-Thrive Infants　144

How Do Infants' Perceptual Abilities Develop?　144
　Perception of Colors, Patterns, and Faces　144
　Perception of Moving Objects　145
　Depth Perception　145

How Do Infants and Toddlers Learn and Remember?　146
　Learning Through Contingency and Association　146
　Learning What's Familiar: Habituation and Novelty Responses　147
　Long-Term Memory　147

How Do Cognitive Abilities Develop During Infancy and Toddlerhood?　149
　Stage I: Using Reflexive Schemes (Birth to 1 Month)　149
　Stage II: Exploring Movements of the Body (1 to 4 Months)　150
　Stage III: Exploring Objects (4 to 8 Months)　150
　Stage IV: Active Problem Solving (8 to 12 Months)　151
　Stage V: Creative Problem Solving (12 to 18 Months)　151
　Stage VI: Using Symbols to Represent Reality
　　(18 to 24 Months)　151
　Infants' Understanding of the Permanence of Objects　152
　Infants' Understanding of Number Concepts　155
　Perception and Early Cognitive Development　155
　Understanding Differences Among People: Emerging
　　Understanding of Desires　157
　The Social Contexts of Early Learning and Cognitive
　　Development　157
　The Cultural Contexts of Early Learning and Cognitive
　　Development　158

How Do Infants and Toddlers Develop Language Skills?　159
　Before the First Words　160
　First Words　161
　Development of Vocabulary　161

THE SCIENTIFIC IMPACT) Can Babies Communicate
    Through Hand Signals?   162
        Solving the Mystery of Word Meaning   162
        First Sentences   165
        Early Talkers and Late Talkers   165
How Is Children's Language Acquisition Explained?   166
        Innate Theories: Biological Influences on Language Acquisition   166
        Learning-Based Theories of Language Acquisition   168
        Social Interaction Theories of Language Acquisition   169
        Genie's Outcomes   170
        The Resilient and Fragile Aspects of Language Development   171
Try It Out   172
Sum It Up   173
Key Terms and Concepts   174

6 Social and Emotional Development in Infancy
and Toddlerhood   **175**

How Do Emotions Develop During Infancy and Toddlerhood?   176
        Smiling and Laughter   176
        Crying   178
        Anger and Temper Tantrums   180
        Self-Awareness and Emotions   181
        Play and Emotional Development   182
How Does Temperament Influence Development During Infancy
    and Toddlerhood?   182
        The Structure of Temperament   182
        Contributions of Temperament to Infant Development   184

THE SCIENTIFIC IMPACT)   What Are the Early Roots of Shyness?   185
How Do Parent-Infant Attachments Influence Development?   185
        Attachment Theory   186
        The Development of Attachment   187
        Assessing Patterns of Attachment in the Strange Situation   188
        Caregiver and Child Factors Affecting Attachment   192
        The Role of Culture in Attachment   193
        Consequences of Attachment   194
        Attachment to Fathers   194
How Does Day Care Influence Infants' and Toddlers' Development?   195
        Patterns of Day Care Use   195
        Effects of Day Care   197

THE PRACTICAL IMPACT)   What Day Care Teachers Earn   198
        Culture and Day Care   199

THE SOCIAL IMPACT)   How Does Mom's Working Affect
    Children's Development?   200
Why Are Children Abused and Neglected?   200
        Definitions of Child Abuse and Neglect   201
        Incidence of Child Abuse and Neglect   201
        Characteristics of Victims of Child Abuse and Neglect   202
        Characteristics of Child Abusers   202
        Effects of Child Abuse and Neglect   205
        Preventing Child Abuse and Neglect   205

Try It Out   206
Sum It Up   206
Key Terms and Concepts   207
See the Impact   208
    Benchmarks in Infant and Toddler Development   208
    National Hotlines for Infants and Toddlers   208
    Impact Report on Infants and Toddlers   209
    Recommended Websites   209

PART 4

Early Childhood Development   **211**

7   Cognitive, Language, and Physical Development
    in Early Childhood   **212**

**How Do Children's Bodies and Motor Skills Develop
    During Early Childhood?**   213
    Changing Body Size and Appearance   213
    Brain Development   213
    Gross Motor Skills   214
    Fine Motor Skills   215
    Cultural and Racial Influences on Motor Development   216
What Are the Nutritional and Health Issues for Young Children?   216
    Undernourishment and Malnourishment   217
    Accidents and Diseases   218
How Do Young Children Think and Solve Problems?   220
    Piaget's View of Preoperational Thinking   220
    Evaluating Piaget's Theory of Preoperational Development   223
    Young Children's Memory   224
    Young Children's Understanding of Everyday Events   225
    Young Children as Experts   226
    Theory of Mind: Young Children's Understanding of Mental Events   226

THE SOCIAL IMPACT Can Young Children's Eyewitness
    Testimony Be Believed?   227

    Young Children's Understanding of Pretend and Real   228
    The Social Context of Cognitive Development   229
    Cultural Influences on Young Children's Thinking   230
    Educating Young Children   231

THE SCIENTIFIC IMPACT When Are Young Children Prepared
    to Start School?   234

    Early Intervention and Young Children's Cognitive
        Development   234
    Sesame Street   236
**What Changes Occur in Young Children's Language Development
    During Early Childhood?**   237
    Vocabulary   237
    Young Children's Language Styles   238

Beyond Two-Word Sentences   238
Understanding Conversational Rules   239
The Social Context of Language Development   239

THE PRACTICAL IMPACT) Helping Children to Learn Language   240
Language Development in Bilingual Children   241
Try It Out   241
Sum It Up   242
Key Terms and Concepts   243

8   Social and Emotional Development in Early Childhood   **244**

How Does Self-Awareness Change During Early Childhood?   245
Developing Self-Concept   245
Developing Self-Esteem   246
Influences on Young Children's Perception of Self   247
How Do Young Children Develop a Concept of Gender?   248

THE SCIENTIFIC IMPACT)   Is Self-Esteem Lower in African American
and Hispanic Children?   249
Young Children's Gender Stereotypes   250
Young Children's Gender-Typed Play Preferences   251
Similarities and Differences Between Young Girls and Boys   251
What Are the Contemporary Theories of Gender Development?   252
Biological Theories   252
Social Learning Theories   253
Cognitive Theories   253
How Do Emotions Develop During Early Childhood?   254
Dealing with Conflict, Anger, and Aggression   255
Developing Caring Feelings and Actions   257
How Do Parenting Behaviors Influence Young Children's Development?   258
Disciplining Young Children   259
Influences on Parents' Use of Discipline   260
Parenting Styles   262
How Does Divorce Affect Young Children's Development?   263
Young Children's Understanding of Divorce   264
Effects of Divorce on Young Children's Behavior and Adjustment   265
Factors That Affect Young Children's Adjustment to Divorce   266
Child Custody Arrangements   267
Young Children's Adjustment to Remarriage   267

THE SOCIAL IMPACT)   Does Custody Make a Difference?   269
How Do Peer and Sibling Relationships Develop During Early Childhood?   269
Young Children's Friendships   270
Young Children at Play   271
Young Children's Sibling Relationships   273
How Does Television Influence Young Children's Emotional and Social
Development?   275
Effects of Television on Family Life   275
Effects of Television Violence on Children's Aggression   276

THE PRACTICAL IMPACT)   Supervising Children's Television
Viewing   277
Effects of Television on Children's Prosocial Behavior   277
Try It Out   278

Sum It Up   278
Key Terms and Concepts   279
See the Impact   280
    Benchmarks in Early Childhood Development   280
    National Hotlines for Preschool Children   280
    Impact Report on Early Childhood   281
    Recommended Websites   281

PART 5

Late Childhood Development   283

9 Cognitive, Language, and Physical Development in Late Childhood   284

How Do Children Develop Physically During Late Childhood?   285
    Brain Development   285
    Body Size and Appearance   285
    Motor Development   285
    Physical Fitness and Sports   286
    Nutrition   287
    Obesity   287
How Do School-Age Children Think and Solve Problems?   288
    Children's Logical Problem Solving   288
    Children's Understanding of Categories and Concepts   290
    Children's Understanding of Seriation   290

THE SCIENTIFIC IMPACT   Are There Cultural Differences in Children's Reasoning?   291
    Culture as a Context for Children's Cognitive Development   291
    Information Processing in School-Aged Children   292
What Characteristics Define Children's Intelligence and Creativity?   293
    Measuring Intelligence   293
    Understanding the Limits of IQ Scores   294
    Identifying the Components of Intelligence   295
    Creativity in Children   296
How Do Language and Literacy Develop During the School Years?   297
    Development of Syntax   298
    Development of Semantics   298
    Development of Pragmatics   299
    Children's Literacy   299
How Do School-Age Children Understand the Social World?   301
    Social Perspective Taking: Communicating with Others   301
    Children's Understanding of Others' Beliefs and Feelings   302
    Children's Understanding of Race and Prejudice   303

THE PRACTICAL IMPACT   Reducing Prejudice in Children   304
How Does Schooling Influence Children's Cognitive Development?   304
    Opportunities for Active Learning   305

Multicultural and Multilingual Education   305

THE SOCIAL IMPACT How Successful Is Bilingual Education?   306
Teachers' Bias in Achievement Expectations   306
How Do Schools Address Students' Special Needs?   307
Children with Physical Disabilities   308
Children with Attention-Deficit Hyperactivity Disorders   308
Children with Mental Retardation   310
Gifted and Talented Children   312
How Do Family and Culture Influence Children's Intellectual
Development?   312
Impact of Poverty on Children's Intellectual Development   313
Role of the Family in Children's Giftedness   313
Roles of Parental Involvement and Cultural Beliefs
in Academic Achievement   314
Try It Out   315
Sum It Up   315
Key Terms and Concepts   316

10 Social and Emotional Development in Late Childhood   **317**

How Do Emotions Develop During Late Childhood?   318
Stress and Coping   318

THE PRACTICAL IMPACT Helping Children Cope with Disaster   320
Children's Responses to Community Violence   321
What Emotional and Psychological Disturbances Affect Children
in Late Childhood?   323
Antisocial Behavior   324
Childhood Depression   326
Children's Fears   328
How Do Children's Family Relationships Change During Late Childhood?   329
Reduced Parent-Child Interaction   329
Reduced Parental Supervision   330
Increased Importance of Sibling Relationships   331
Only Children   331

THE SCIENTIFIC IMPACT How Can Public Policy Affect
Children and Families?   332
What Factors Influence School-Age Children's Peer Relationships?   332
Peer Rejection   333
Development of Social Competence   334
How Does School Affect Social and Emotional Development
in Late Childhood?   335
Influence of the School Environment   335

THE SOCIAL IMPACT Are Schools Safe?   337
Influence of Teacher-Child Relationships   337
What Changes Take Place in Moral Development During Late Childhood?   338
Piaget's Theory of Moral Development   338
Kohlberg's Theory of Moral Development   341
Culture and Morality   345
Gender and Morality   346
Try It Out   346
Sum It Up   346

Key Terms and Concepts   347
See the Impact   348
    Benchmarks in Late Childhood Development   348
    National Hotlines for School-Age Children   348
    Impact Report on Late Childhood   349
    Recommended Websites   349

PART 6

Early Adolescent Development   **351**

11   Cognitive and Physical Development in Early Adolescence   **352**

What Is Early Adolescence?   353
    Historical Perspectives on Adolescence   353
    Cultural Perspectives on Adolescence   354
    Terminology Used in Defining Adolescence   355
**How Do Physical Growth and Sexual Maturation Occur
    During Early Adolescence?**   356
    Brain Development in Early Adolescence   356
    The Adolescent Growth Spurt   356
    The Process of Puberty   357
    Young Adolescents' Responses to Physical and Sexual
        Maturation   361
    Psychological Reactions to Pubertal Events   364

THE SOCIAL IMPACT)   Do Gender Roles Intensify When
    Adolescents Reach Puberty?   366
What Are the Health Concerns for Young Adolescents?   366
    Nutrition   367
    Exercise and Sports Participation   367
    Eating Disturbances and Disorders   368
How Do Young Adolescents Think and Solve Problems?   373
    Reaching Cognitive Maturity: Formal Operational Thinking   373

THE SCIENTIFIC IMPACT)   What Do Boys Do When They Find
    a Real Gun?   374
    Adolescent Egocentrism   375
How Does School Influence Early Adolescent Development?   376
    Adaptation to a Change in Schools   377

THE PRACTICAL IMPACT)   Developmentally Appropriate
    Middle Schools   378
    Perceptions of Academic Competence   378
    Academic Achievement and Cultural Diversity   379
Try It Out   381
Sum It Up   381
Key Terms and Concepts   382

12 Social and Emotional Development in Early Adolescence **383**

How Do Young Adolescents View Themselves? 384
Self-Concept During Early Adolescence 384
Self-Esteem During Early Adolescence 385
Gender and the Self During Early Adolescence 385
How Do Adolescents Form an Identity? 386
Erikson's Theory of Adolescent Identity Development 386
Marcia's Theory of Adolescent Identity Development 387
Ethnic Identity 388
How Do Family Relationships Change During Early Adolescence? 390
Parenting and Early Adolescent Development 390
The Bidirectionality of Parent-Adolescent Relationships 392
Parent-Adolescent Conflict 392

THE SCIENTIFIC IMPACT   What Roles Do Mothers and Fathers Play in
Teens' Peer Relationships? 393

What Are the Characteristics of Early Adolescent Peer Relationships? 394
The Adolescent Peer Culture 394

THE SOCIAL IMPACT   Do Friends Lead Adolescents into Trouble? 395
Friendships During Early Adolescence 397
Peer Popularity and Rejection 398
Dating and Romantic Relationships 398
Emerging Sexuality During Early Adolescence 399
Deviant Peer Groups: Adolescent Gangs 400

THE PRACTICAL IMPACT   Gang Prevention 402

How Do Mass Media Influence Young Adolescents' Development? 403
Popular Music 403
Computers 404
Try It Out 406
Sum It Up 406
Key Terms and Concepts 407
See the Impact 408
Benchmarks in Early Adolescence 408
National Hotlines for Young Teens 408
Impact Report on Young Adolescents 409
Recommended Websites 409

PART 7

*Late Adolescent
Development*   **411**

13 Cognitive and Physical Development in Late Adolescence **412**

How Does Physical Develement Occur During Late Adolescence? 413
Physical Growth and Development During Late Adolescence 413
Brain Development and Behavior in Late Adolescence 413

What Are the Health and Safety Issues in Late Adolescence?   414
 Accidents   414
 Homicides   415
 Suicide   416
 Sexually Transmitted Diseases   417
 AIDS   417
 Diseases and Chronic Illnesses   418

THE PRACTICAL IMPACT   Adolescent AIDS: The Legacy
 of Ryan White   419
 Fitness and Exercise   420

THE SOCIAL IMPACT   Should Schools Start Later for Teens?   421
 Sports and Development in Late Adolescence   421

THE SCIENTIFIC IMPACT   How Does Athletic Performance Influence
 Girls' Development?   422
What Changes Occur in Older Adolescents' Thinking and Reasoning?   422
 Social Cognition: Thinking About People and Relationships   423
 Understanding Other People's Perspectives   424
 Moral Reasoning and Moral Education in Late Adolescence   425
 Political and Religious Thinking   427
**What Gender Differences Are Found in Adolescents' Cognitive Abilities
 and Achievement?   428**
 Gender Differences in Verbal Skills   428
 Gender Differences in Spatial-Visual Skills   429
 Gender Differences in Math and Science Skills   430
 Explaining Gender Differences in Cognitive Abilities
 and Achievement   431
What Factors Contribute to Dropping Out of School?   434
 Characteristics of High School Dropouts   434
 Preventing High School Dropout   436
Try It Out   436
Sum It Up   437
Key Terms and Concepts   438

14 Social and Emotional Development in Late Adolescence   **439**

How Do Older Adolescents Develop Autonomy?   440
 Forms of Autonomy   440
 Factors That Contribute to Adolescent Autonomy   440
How Does Sexuality Change During Late Adolescence?   441
 Sexual Attitudes and Behaviors of Older Adolescents   441
 Correlates of Adolescent Sexual Attitudes and Behaviors   442
 The Social-Psychological Context of Adolescent Sexuality   443
 Adolescent Contraceptive Use   444
 Teen Pregnancy   445

THE SOCIAL IMPACT   Is Childhood Sexual Abuse Related
 to Teen Pregnancy?   445
 Adolescent Parenting   447
 Adolescent Sex Education   448
 Gay and Lesbian Youth   449

What Types of Behavior Problems Occur During Late Adolescence?   450
    Antisocial Behavior   451
    Depression   452

THE SCIENTIFIC IMPACT   What Family Factors Relate to Violence
Among Minority Youths?   453
    Substance Use and Abuse   453

THE PRACTICAL IMPACT   Preventing Teenage Drug Use   456
How Does Employment Affect Older Adolescents?   458
What Factors Influence Adolescents' Vulnerability and Resiliency?   460
Try It Out   462
Sum It Up   464
Key Terms and Concepts   465
See the Impact   466
    Benchmarks in Late Adolescence   466
    National Hotlines for Late Adolescent Development   466
    Impact Report on Older Adolescents   467
    Recommended Websites   467

Photo Credits   468
Glossary   469
References   477
Name Index   529
Subject Index   545

To the Student

Our goal in writing this book was to explain how children develop, from conception through adolescence, and to explore the impact that individual characteristics, biological factors, personal relationships, social policies, and cultural values and beliefs have on a child's development. We do this by focusing on scientific research that examines the relationships children have with people and with their environments and how these relationships influence a child's cognitive, physical, social, and emotional development.

One of the best ways to understand what this book teaches is to first analyze the facts and issues that are presented and then apply them to your own life. Understanding the central role of relationships in development may lead you to new insights about your own childhood, as well as those of infants, children, and adolescents around you. Not only will you find the study of child development more meaningful; you will also be in a position to make better-informed decisions about issues related to children and their development.

Richard Fabes
Carol Lynn Martin

To the Instructor

In this second edition of *Exploring Child Development,* we have retained the philosophy and approach of the first edition, while adding new features and enhancing existing ones.

THEMES AND GOALS

This textbook focuses on the many ways in which children are affected by their environments. The underlying goals of *Exploring Child Development* remain the same as those of the first edition:

◆ To show how children are unique and the impact that people, contexts, and experiences have on how they develop;

◆ To encourage students to think critically about research and issues in child development and see how these relate to real-life experiences.

To accomplish these goals, the text uses a transactional approach. The conceptual foundation of the text is that development is shaped by the continuous interplay between individuals and their ever-changing environments.

Infants, children, and adolescents are influenced not only by personal relationships, but also by social policies and cultural environments. Also, children play an active role in their own development: Their characteristics and actions cause others to react in certain ways, and these reactions then influence their development. This text focuses on the influences these intertwined interactions have on the cognitive, physical, social, and emotional development of infants, children, and adolescents.

Diversity

Given the diversity and variability that exist in children, families, and their environments, we believe that the best way to understand children and their development is to consider development within different biological, familial, social, and cultural backgrounds. The dynamic interplay among diverse individual and environmental characteristics means that children's developmental outcomes (such as their physical and psychological health) are influenced by many factors.

Scientific Inquiry and Critical Thinking

Though written in a personal, accessible style, this is a research-based text that takes a scientific approach to exploring child development. It teaches students how to use objective, replicable procedures to try to root out subjective and biased assumptions. Knowing how developmental scientists conduct research is essential to understanding infants, children, and adolescents, and it provides a framework through which hypotheses concerning development can be tested and verified, sometimes revealing evidence that is contrary to popular belief.

ORGANIZATION OF THE TEXTBOOK

The textbook is divided into seven parts, based on the sequence of developmental changes from conception through adolescence.

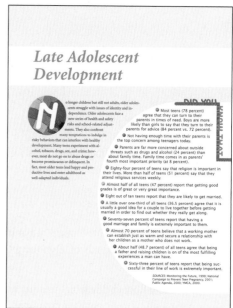

The Parts

Part 1 introduces the transactional approach to development and issues related to diversity and change. Part 2 discusses the origins of development, including heredity and genetics; how life begins; prenatal development; and childbirth. Part 3 focuses on the astonishing changes and accomplishments of infants and toddlers. Special attention is given to understanding these accomplishments within the context of early relationships, especially caregiving relationships. Part 4 focuses on early childhood and includes perspectives on cognitive, physical, social, and emotional development during the preschool years. Part 5 covers the period of childhood from the time children enter school until they begin puberty. The chapters in Parts 4 and 5 highlight the abilities that expand and develop during childhood and their links to the broadening scope of relationships found in peer and school environments.

NEW!

One of the unique features of this book is that we distinguish between early and late adolescence. Although a 13-year-old and an 18-year-old are both adolescents, their developmental tasks are very different. Part 6 provides in-depth coverage of early adolescent development, and Part 7 focuses on later adolescence. The chapters in Parts 6 and 7 discuss in detail the dramatic cognitive, physical, social, and emotional changes that accompany the transitions of early and late adolescence. Emphasis is given to the changing nature of interpersonal relationships during these stages.

Integration and Application

Each of the seven parts weaves the themes of the book into a visual and personal synthesis of developmental trends, illustrating the continuity of development. Each part begins with a new feature called *Did You Know That,* a set of statistical "grabbers" that relate to social policies and other issues concerning children. These statistics are designed to get students thinking about the material that follows.

Child development involves complex changes in related processes and behaviors; it is not a product of isolated transformations. Cognitive, physical, social, and emotional development are intimately interrelated. To help students synthesize and integrate this information, each part ends with *See the Impact,* a section that brings together the different aspects of development presented in separate chap-

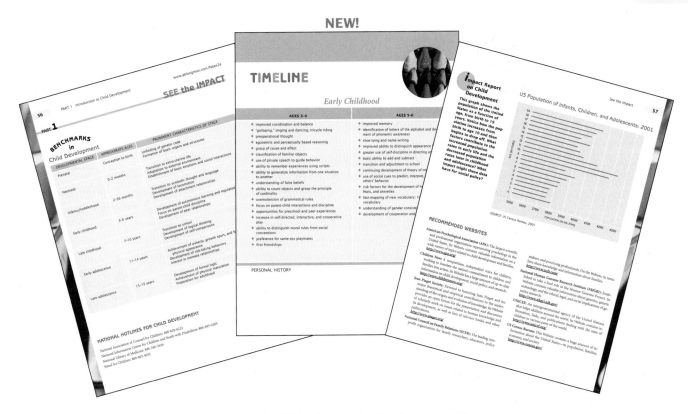

ters. This section also features a *Benchmarks* chart, which relates to the *Developmental Time-line.* The timeline is a unique new feature, packaged with each copy of the textbook, that is designed to personalize the material presented in the text and make it more meaningful to students. The major developmental milestones for each age period are identified, with a blank area below where students can describe their own developmental milestones or those of their child or sibling. Students can then plot their own development and compare it to the milestones on the timeline. By asking students to talk about their own developmental milestones, instructors can emphasize the diversity and individuality of developmental trajectories.

Also at the end of each part is an *Impact Report,* which presents statistics regarding the current status of the age group discussed in that part with respect to some critical issues. Students are asked to reflect on the report, which is followed by suggestions for obtaining more information about the issues discussed in the chapters. Included are Web addresses and national hotline numbers.

Chapter Organization and Features

Each chapter begins with a **Chapter Outline,** which corresponds to the main chapter headings. The headings are framed as key questions, which are answered in the paragraphs that follow.

Key terms are boldfaced in the narrative where they first appear and then are defined in the margin. The key terms are also listed at the end of the chapter with page references and included in an end-of-book glossary. Figures, tables, and photos are designed to increase comprehension and concept integration. To enhance students' appreciation of how the science of child development relates to everyday life, many examples of **practical applications** are included.

Try It Out, the chapter-closing activities, provide meaningful opportunities for relating chapter content to firsthand experience. These applications and activities are designed to make the material more personally and professionally relevant. *Sum It Up,* the end-of-chapter summary points, synthesizes the information presented in the chapter.

Along with the pedagogical elements embedded in each chapter are features that highlight the impact of several important influences on a child's development.

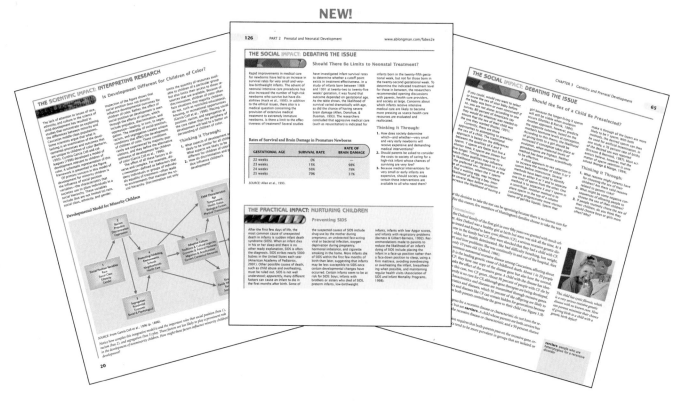

NEW!

◆ *The Practical Impact: Nurturing Children* suggests ways of making decisions and solving problems within the context of personal relationships. The direct applications to the areas of education, parenting, health, and safety will be particularly relevant to students who are pursuing careers working with children, as well as to those who become parents.

◆ *The Scientific Impact: Interpreting Research* presents findings from current scientific research in child development, highlighting the ways scientists tackle issues related to infants, children, and adolescents. The research is presented in an engaging and informative style and is followed by *Thinking It Through* questions, which call for critical thinking.

◆ *The Social Impact: Debating the Issue* focuses on contemporary debates concerning child development. The issues represent points of controversy in the field. *Thinking It Through* questions encourage students to analyze and express opinions on these issues in order to gain a better understanding of them and to develop the skills needed to evaluate research, policy, and media pronouncements related to child and adolescent development.

New Content

Drawing on the most recent information and research available, this second edition of *Exploring Child Development* features expanded coverage of many areas, an enhanced focus on cognitive development, and increased emphasis on the diversity of factors influencing child development. Among the new topics and those given revised coverage are the following:

Chapter 1: Introduction to the Study of Child Development
◆ Developmental outcomes for the children with working mothers
◆ Interrelationships between developmental domains
◆ Influence of social policy on children's development

Chapter 2: Understanding Development
◆ Emerging developmental research
◆ Evolutionary theories
◆ Physiological measures of children's behavior

Chapter 3: Genetics and Prenatal Development
◆ Human Genome Project
◆ Genes and the environment
◆ Genes, attention disorders, and thrill-seeking behavior
◆ Assisted reproduction
◆ Caffeine as a teratogen
◆ Influence of nutrition on prenatal development

Chapter 4: Birth and Neonatal Development
◆ Men's perspectives on fatherhood
◆ Childbirth in other cultures
◆ Changing views on critical periods

Chapter 5: Cognitive, Language, and Physical Development in Infancy and Toddlerhood
◆ Brain development
◆ Resiliency of language development
◆ Identifying problems in language acquisition
◆ Variations in language development

Chapter 6: Social and Emotional Development in Infancy and Toddlerhood
◆ Temperament
◆ Cultural influences and the role of the father in temperament and attachment

Chapter 7: Cognitive, Language, and Physical Development in Early Childhood
◆ Nutrition and health issues
◆ Language development
◆ Bilingual children

Chapter 8: Social and Emotional Development in Early Childhood
◆ Cultural differences in parenting
◆ Effects of divorce and stepfamilies on children

Chapter 9: Cognitive, Language, and Physical Development in Late Childhood
◆ Influence of nutrition on development
◆ Information processing

Chapter 10: Social and Emotional Development in Late Childhood
◆ Culture and morality
◆ Helping children cope with disaster

Chapter 11: Cognitive and Physical Development in Early Adolescence
◆ Brain development
◆ Health, diet, and exercise
◆ Guns and children

Chapter 12: Social and Emotional Development in Early Adolescence
◆ Role of mothers and fathers in teens' peer relationships

Chapter 13: Cognitive and Physical Development in Late Adolescence
◆ Brain development and behavior
◆ Sports and development
◆ Gender differences in cognitive abilities and achievement

Chapter 14: Social and Emotional Development in Late Adolescence
◆ Gay and lesbian youth
◆ Substance abuse

Supplements

SUPPLEMENTS FOR STUDENTS

For this second edition of *Exploring Child Development,* we have streamlined our supplements for students, placing all materials in one printed supplement and one on-line resource.

- **Grade Aid,** a comprehensive interactive workbook written by Denise Bodman of Arizona State University, guides students through each chapter, with a chapter introduction (Before you read . . .), guided activities (As you read . . .), Apply It sections, 1-minute quizzes, crossword puzzles, and practice tests (After you read . . .).
- **On-line study and research materials** at the Website that accompanies *Exploring Child Development* include a wide range of resources for both instructors and students. Students will find practice tests specific to this new edition, plus a link to Allyn & Bacon's *Human Development SuperSite,* which contains an array of learning activities, flashcards, research studies and summaries, and annotated research Web links.
- **i-search: Human Development** is a booklet designed to help students select and evaluate research from the Web to find the best and most credible information available. It contains a practical and to-the-point discussion of search engines, detailed information on evaluating online sources, citation guidelines for Web resources, Web activities for human development, Web links for human development, and a detailed guide to ContentSelect.

Also available with the purchase of a new book is access to *ContentSelect,* our customized research database of on-line content from leading academic publications and journals. The collection contains high-quality, peer-reviewed material that is keyword searchable, providing accurate and relevant articles to you and your students.

SUPPLEMENTS FOR INSTRUCTORS

Supplemental material designed to enhance classroom lectures and discussions accompanies this second edition of *Exploring Child Development.* The ancillary material has been created to offer students and instructors information based on the transactional approach to child development.

- **The Instructor's Resource Manual,** written by Pamela Guerra-Schmidt and Deborah Laffran Chini of Modesto Junior College, is an invaluable resource for instructors. For each chapter, it contains an overview/summary; learning objectives; a listing of transparencies; additional lecture topics; classroom demonstrations and projects; and suggested videos, readings, and Websites.
- **The Test Bank,** written by Richard Fabes and Carol Lynn Martin, contains an extensive array of test questions. Each chapter includes multiple-choice, true/false, fill-in, and essay questions. Each question is page-referenced to the textbook, coded by level of difficulty (easy, medium, or difficult), and classified (factual, conceptual, or applied).

◆ **The Computerized Test Bank** is available with Tamarack's easy-to-use *TestGen* software, which lets you prepare tests for printing as well for network and on-line testing. The software provides full editing capability for Windows and Macintosh.

◆ **The Transparency Package,** designed to enhance your classroom presentations, contains 70 color acetate transparencies drawn from the text and other relevant sources.

◆ **The PowerPoint Presentation,** developed by Gary Levy of the University of Utah specifically for *Exploring Child Development,* provides a comprehensive lecture outline. This outline can be displayed to the entire class using a computer and an overhead projector with an LCD panel, printed and made into overhead transparencies, or printed and distributed individually to students. The Instructor's Manual is also available on the PowerPoint CD-ROM.

◆ **The Allyn and Bacon Interactive Video for Child Development** illustrates real-life applications of the textbook topics and provides a springboard from which to start classroom discussions, facilitated by on-screen critical thinking questions. An accompanying video guide is also available, to make classroom use of the video even more effective.

Acknowledgments

We would once again like to thank the reviewers of the first edition:

Sharon Antonelli, *San Jose City College*
Harry Avis, *Sierra Community College*
Phoebe Baker, *Tulsa Community College*
Daniel Bellack, *Trident Community College*
Michael Bergmire, *Jefferson College*
Linda Dersheid, *Northern Illinois University*
Martha M. Ellis, *Collin Community College*
Linda Estes, *St. Charles Community College*
Linda E. Flickinger, *St. Clair County Community College*
Tom Frangicetto, *Northampton Community College*
Janet Fuller, *Mansfield University*
Thomas Gerry, *Columbia Green Community College*
Debra L. Hollister, *Valencia Community College*
Kevin Keating, *Broward Community College*
John S. Klein, *Castleton State College*
Kevin MacDonald, *California State University–Long Beach*
Barbara Matthews, *Palm Beach Community College*
Mary Ann McLaughlin, *Clarion University of Pennsylvania*
Shana Pack, *Kentucky Wesleyan College*
Rob Palkovitz, *University of Delaware*
Maribeth Palmer-King, *Broome Community College*
Richard Passman, *University of Wisconsin–Milwaukee*
Peggy Perkins, *University of Nevada–Las Vegas*
Randall J. Russac, *University of North Florida*
Marcia Rysztak, *Lansing Community College*
Michael F. Shaughnessy, *Eastern New Mexico University*
Patricia D. Stanley, *Louisiana State University–Shreveport*
Susan Troy, *Northeast Iowa Community College*
James Turcott, *Kalamazoo Valley Community College*
Patty Wilhite, *Northeast Louisiana University*
Peggy Wroten, *Northeast Mississippi Community College*

In addition, we want to express our appreciation to the reviewers of the second edition:

Tena Carr, *San Joaquin Delta College*
Denise Davidson, *Loyola University–Chicago*
Christyn Dundorf, *Portland Community College*
Diane K. Feibel, *University of Cincinnati–Raymond Walters College*
Janet Fuller, *Mansfield University*
Leslie B. Minor-Evans, *Central Oregon Community College*
Sherri Addis Palmer, *Truman State University*
Thomas G. Reio, Jr., *University of Maryland*
Michael Sonntag, *Lander University*

About the Authors

Richard A. Fabes, Ph.D., is professor of child development at Arizona State University, where he has been for more than 15 years. He is the Chair of the Department of Family and Human Development and is a member of the Society for Research in Child Development, National Council on Family Relations, American Psychological Association, and American Psychological Society. He is Associate Editor of *Merrill-Palmer Quarterly* and has been a member of the editorial boards of several widely known scientific journals, including *Developmental Psychology* and *Psychological Bulletin.* Author of over 100 articles, book chapters, and edited books, he co-authored a chapter in the latest edition of the *Handbook of Child Psychology.* Most of his publications are in the area of socio-emotional development of young children. He is married to Carol Martin, and away from work he enjoys tennis, traveling, and music.

Carol Lynn Martin, Ph.D., is professor of child development at Arizona State University, where she has been for more than 10 years. She is a member of the Society for Research in Child Development, National Council on Family Relations, and American Psychological Society and a fellow of the American Psychological Association. She is Associate Editor for *Developmental Psychology* and has been a member of the editorial boards of several widely known scientific journals, including *Child Development.* Author of over 50 articles and book chapters, she co-authored a chapter in the latest edition of the *Handbook of Child Psychology.* Most of her publications are in the area of gender-role development and the cognitive processes underlying it. Away from work she enjoys tennis, traveling, pottery, reading, and swimming.

DEVELOPMENTAL

Late Childhood

AGES 7–8	AGES 9–10
✦ increasing organization of brain	✦ increasing organization of brain
✦ blooming and pruning of neuronal connections	✦ blooming and pruning of neuronal connections
✦ marked skeletal growth	✦ start of growth spurt for girls
✦ permanent teeth	✦ improved coordination, balance, and reaction times
✦ increased nutritional, health, and safety risks	✦ cursive writing
✦ improvements in jumping, throwing, catching, kicking, and batting	✦ drawing three-dimensionally and in perspective
✦ participation in school life	✦ greater metacognitive awareness
✦ achievement of literacy and legible printing	✦ use of memory strategies in learning
✦ concrete operational thinking	✦ understanding of metaphors, double meanings, and humor
✦ knowledge of conservation and decentration	✦ interest in social comparisons of self with others
✦ development of logic and reversible thinking	✦ greater self-regulation
✦ increased skills in hierarchical classification and seriation	✦ ability to adapt conversations to needs of others
✦ appearance of heteronomous morality	✦ morality based on external qualities
✦ involvement in organized games and activities	
✦ peer group identification	
✦ increased prosocial behavior	
✦ higher-level development of friendships	
✦ academic, social, and physical self-esteem based on attributions of success and failure	

PERSONAL HISTORY

TIMELINE

Early Childhood

AGES 3–4	AGES 5–6
✦ growth spurt for right hemisphere of brain	✦ development of more efficient connections between left and right hemispheres of brain
✦ blooming and pruning of neuronal connections	✦ blooming and pruning of neuronal connections
✦ improved coordination and balance	✦ increase in myelination of brain
✦ "galloping," singing and dancing, tricycle riding	✦ improved memory
✦ preoperational thought	✦ identification of letters of the alphabet and development of phonemic awareness
✦ egocentric and perceptually based reasoning	✦ shoe tying and name writing
✦ grasp of cause and effect	✦ improved ability to distinguish appearance from reality
✦ classification of familiar objects	✦ greater use of self-discipline in directing attention
✦ use of private speech to guide behavior	✦ basic ability to add and subtract
✦ ability to remember experiences using scripts	✦ transition and adjustment to school
✦ ability to generalize information from one situation to another	✦ continuing development of theory of mind
✦ understanding of false beliefs	✦ use of social cues to predict, interpret, and influence others' behavior
✦ ability to count objects and grasp the principle of cardinality	✦ risk factors for the development of health problems, fears, and anxieties
✦ overextension of grammatical rules	✦ fast-mapping of new vocabulary; 10,000-word vocabulary
✦ focus on parent-child interactions and discipline	✦ understanding of gender consistency
✦ opportunities for preschool and peer experiences	✦ development of cooperation and aggression
✦ increase in self-directed, interactive, and cooperative play	
✦ ability to distinguish moral rules from social conventions	
✦ preference for same-sex playmates	
✦ first friendships	

DEVELOPMENTAL

Infancy and Toddlerhood

2–12 MONTHS	12–24 MONTHS	24–36 MONTHS
◆ critical brain development	◆ critical brain development	◆ critical brain development: rapid growth of left hemisphere
◆ blooming of neuronal connections, especially in visual areas of brain	◆ blooming and pruning of neuronal connections, especially in language parts of brain	◆ blooming and pruning of neuronal connections
◆ rapid growth in size	◆ cruising, walking, and climbing	◆ running
◆ voluntary reaching and grasping	◆ stacking and sorting toys; scribbling	◆ negotiating stairs
◆ preference for hearing own language	◆ ability to search for hidden objects	◆ throwing and catching a ball
◆ sensorimotor cognitive development: circular reactions and goal-directed behavior	◆ problem solving through active experimentation	◆ bowel and bladder control
◆ expression of temperament	◆ rapid language acquisition and growth of vocabulary	◆ self-dressing and self-feeding
◆ development of attachment	◆ evidence of attachment	◆ development of self-concept and self-esteem
◆ color, pattern, face, motion, and depth perception	◆ separation anxiety	◆ pretend play, parallel play, and social play
◆ understanding of basic principles of objects and motions	◆ self-recognition and self-reference	◆ development of gender stereotypes and gender-typed preferences
◆ control of trunk; rolling over	◆ categorization of self and others on the basis of age and sex	◆ egocentrism, animism, and preoperational thinking
◆ crawling, sitting, and standing	◆ gender-typed toy play	◆ two- and three-word sentences
◆ imitation and deferred imitation	◆ development of self-conscious emotions	◆ development of multiple attachments
◆ memory for familiar people, places, and objects	◆ emergence of compliance and self-control	◆ beginning literacy and media exposure
◆ habituation	◆ ability to play turn-taking games	◆ development of empathy
◆ social smiling and laughter		
◆ stranger anxiety		
◆ use of gestures to communicate		
◆ cooing and babbling		
◆ first words; holophrases		

PERSONAL HISTORY

TIMELINE

Early Adolescence

AGES 11–12	AGES 13–14
✦ development of limbic system	✦ development of limbic system
✦ increasing organization of brain	✦ increasing organization of brain
✦ pubertal and hormonal changes	✦ end of girls' growth spurt; beginning of boys' growth spurt
✦ evidence of sex differences in physical development and motor performance	✦ greater self-consciousness and focus on self
✦ emergence of formal operational thinking	✦ adjustment to middle or junior high school
✦ development of stronger academic subject preferences	✦ concern with appearance and peer approval
✦ greater interest in and time spent on hobbies and collections	✦ appearance of conventional morality
✦ emergence of idealism and critical thinking	✦ peer pressure to conform
✦ emergence of religious faith or spirituality	✦ greater commitment of time to peer group
✦ greater grasp of abstract concepts, irony, and sarcasm	✦ formation of friendships on the basis of intimacy and loyalty
✦ increased ability to adjust language and speech to suit different situations	✦ improved self-regulation of cognitive performance
✦ increase in moodiness and parent-child conflict	✦ risk factors for delinquency, substance abuse, and eating disorders
✦ risk factors for accidents, homicide, depression, and suicide	

PERSONAL HISTORY

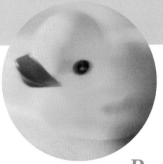

Prenatal and Neonatal Development

CONCEPTION AND PRENATAL DEVELOPMENT	BIRTH	NEONATAL PERIOD (0–2 MONTHS)
GERMINAL STAGE ✦ aligning of maternal and paternal chromosomes ✦ genetic transmission of physical characteristics ✦ sex determination ✦ basic intelligence ✦ basic personality and behavioral traits **EMBRYONIC STAGE** ✦ development of nervous system and major organs ✦ development of basic physical structures ✦ cephalocaudal and proximodistal growth ✦ serious teratogenic effects on growth and development **FETAL STAGE** ✦ rapid growth in size and weight ✦ rapid brain development ✦ viability and preparation for birth ✦ transfer of immunities from mother to child	✦ labor and dilation of cervix ✦ crowning and molding of baby's head ✦ delivery of baby ✦ delivery of placenta ✦ Apgar testing of health status ✦ cultural and social expectations for birth	✦ adaptation to extrauterine environment ✦ reflex responses ✦ rapid brain development ✦ short-term, context-bound memory ✦ expression of basic emotions ✦ states of arousal ✦ ability to imitate ✦ importance of caregiving

PERSONAL HISTORY

Late Adolescence

AGES 15–16	AGES 17–19
✦ increasing organization of brain	✦ increasing organization of brain
✦ development of prefrontal cortex	✦ development of prefrontal cortex
✦ achievement of sexual maturity	✦ physical and athletic maturity
✦ development of personal autonomy	✦ greater risk for STDs and AIDS
✦ identity formation; integration of organized self-concept	✦ possible development of postconventional moral reasoning
✦ development of greater responsibility and character	✦ elaboration of religious and political thinking
✦ dating; sexual activity and interpersonal intimacy	✦ greater community involvement and societal perspective taking
✦ greater autonomy in day-to-day planning	✦ refinement of gender role expectations and gender behavior
✦ evaluation of vocational options in terms of interests, abilities, and values	✦ preparation for college, career, or the world of work
✦ opportunities for paid work experience	✦ development of life skills
✦ adjustment to high school	✦ planning for independence
✦ risk of dropping out of school	

PERSONAL HISTORY

Exploring
Child Development

Introduction to Child Development

I f you are not aware of these shocking statistics, you should be. At a time when wealth in the United States is near an all-time high, it is easy to overlook the fact that many children find themselves in situations that put their healthy development at risk.

For most people, caring for a child is one of life's most rewarding experiences—there is nothing more important than nurturing and understanding children. The statistics listed here emphasize the need for caring adults in children's lives. One of the purposes of this textbook is to give you a better understanding of this need. In this text, you will find a wide range of scientifically based information that will be both personally and professionally valuable. Even if you already have children of your own or have experience in caring for children, there is still much to learn about them. By devoting some time and effort, you can become better informed about the changing needs of children and the role that caring adults can play in helping them develop and reach their potential. It is our hope that, in becoming so informed, you will help to ensure that these statistics change for the better.

DID YOU KNOW THAT

In the United States,

● 2 children under 5 are murdered every day?

● 12 children and youths die from firearms every day?

● 77 babies die every day?

● 399 children are arrested for drug abuse every day?

● 1,352 babies are born to teen mothers every day?

● 2,140 babies are born into poverty every day?

● 2,806 high school students drop out every day?

● 5,044 children are arrested every day?

● 17,297 students are suspended from school every day?

● 1 out of 2 children lives in a single-parent family at some point in his or her childhood?

● 1 out of 2 children never completes a single year of college?

● 1 out of 3 children will be poor at some point in his or her childhood (and 1 out of 5 is poor now)?

● 1 out of 3 children is hungry or at risk for going hungry?

● 1 out of 6 children has no health insurance?

● each year, an estimated 826,000 children are victims of abuse and neglect?

SOURCES: Children's Defense Fund, 2000; National Child Abuse and Neglect Data System, 2001.

Introduction to the Study of Children's Development

CHAPTER OUTLINE

✦ What Is Child Development?

✦ What Are Some Critical Issues in the Study of Child Development?

✦ What Are the Historical Roots of the Study of Child Development?

✦ What Changes in Contemporary American Life Influence the Study of Child Development?

✦ Can We Capture the Diversity of Children's Development?

think he enjoyed school. He was a good student, although he never got the marks that he was capable of getting, I don't think. In high school he got an award when he graduated for never missing a day. In four years, he never missed a day of school. The first time he worked I think was the beginning of his senior year. He went to work at Burger King. After he was out, he got a New York State—$500 New York State Regents Scholarship. He went to Brian and Stratton. It's a business school. And he didn't feel he was learning more than he already knew, so he decided to go back to work. And then after that, he got a job at the Burger King in Lockport. He worked for Burger King—I don't know—maybe a year—and after that he got a job for Park Security, driving an armored car. He got the job there because he had a pistol permit. Tim graduated, and he said at the graduation that quite a few of the kids were going into the military. He come home one day and said he was going in the service. That's about all I can tell you about when he went in the service, or over to the Persian Gulf. He didn't seem to mind going, and he was ready to go when the time come, and they went to Kuwait. And I believe it was right around the end of '91, Christmastime in '91 or so. And he come back, he seemed to be happy when he come home.

> —*Bill McVeigh* (father of Tim McVeigh, the
> individual found guilty of and executed for
> the 1995 bombing of the federal office
> building in Oklahoma City, Oklahoma, in
> which 168 men, women, and children were
> killed), testifying at his son's sentencing
> hearing, June 11, 1997

What motivates people to carry out horrendous acts of violence and destruction? Many movies, books, and documentaries have tried to answer this question. Often people look to a person's childhood to get clues about what must have "gone wrong" to lead him or her to be so callous and murderous. But in his testimony about his son's background and life, Tim McVeigh's father reveals nothing unusual or special about his son's development. His testimony also included the playing of a videotaped compilation of old home movies made when Tim was a small boy in New York, where he grew up, went to school and church, and did many of the same things millions of other children of his generation did.

But were there clues? Tim McVeigh was socially awkward and fascinated by guns. He found in the military an order and a purpose that were lacking in his life in upstate New York. His mother and two sisters had moved to Florida when Tim was 15, leaving him and his father to fend for themselves. He was smart, but disengaged. As a teen, he dropped out of community college and became obsessed with survivalism, storing weapons and supplies in the basement.

Research tells us that children who have difficulties relating to others, who feel isolated and negative, or who are abused and treated poorly are at risk for developing behavior problems, such as delinquency, criminal behavior, and depression, later in life (Brendgen, Vitaro, Bukowski, Doyle, & Markiewicz, 2001; Eisenberg et al., 2000), but predicting which children will grow up to be criminals and terrorists is virtually impossible because these individuals are so rare. Nevertheless, trying to figure out how they became this way is intriguing. Like many people, scientists and practitioners who study and work with children are interested in these kinds of questions. What effects do people's environments have on them? How important are early experiences in predicting later behavior? Can children's development and behavior be changed? Developmental scientists also focus on successful development, such as the development of competence and wisdom (Masten & Curtis, 2000; Pasupathi, Staudinger, & Baltes, 2001). But development is complex, and many factors influence who we are and what we become. What we understand about this process is the essence of this book. Devoting time to studying and understanding the broad and diverse influences on children's development, although they are complex, can be very rewarding. And the endeavor has relevance and meaning! Adults can make a difference in children's lives. Understanding children, their development, and the factors that can lead to positive and negative outcomes allows us to help them reach their potential and be successful, productive, and happy individuals.

WHAT IS CHILD DEVELOPMENT?

Child development involves changes in physical, social, emotional, and intellectual functioning over time, from conception through adolescence. Changes include alterations in size, shape, and function, and these alterations can be either progressive or regressive (Magnusson, 1995). Time and change work in concert to shape who we are.

In this book, child development is presented in terms of functionally defined age-related stages: prenatal, infancy and toddlerhood, early and late childhood, and early and late adolescence. These stages reflect a contemporary view of development and are helpful in conceptualizing the complex interdependent changes that take place across childhood.

In each stage of development, **developmental domains** provide a basis for focusing on specific areas of development. **Physical development** involves growth and change in a person's body and bodily functions. Included in this developmental domain is the study of physiological and motor development, as well as the impacts of illness, nutrition, and health. **Cognitive development** involves mental processes used to process information, become aware, solve problems, and gain knowledge. This developmental domain encompasses the study of brain functioning, perception, memory, learning, thinking, and language. **Social-emotional development** involves processes related to one's interactions with others. Included in this domain is the study of relationships, emotions, personality, and moral development.

Is any one of these domains more important than the others? Some people might think so. For example, many parents and educators believe that being smart and doing well in school (the cognitive domain) are the most important aspects of successful development (Zill, 1999). Parents are much less certain about the roles of social and emotional development in healthy development (Zero to Three, 1997). But are these attitudes accurate? Consider the story of William James Sidis—a child prodigy whose intellectual gifts were "off the charts." William, who was born in 1898, learned to read when he was 18 months of age. By the age of 6, he could read several languages. At that point, he was required by law to go to school, where he moved through all seven grades of elementary school in just six months. Over the next couple of years, he was taught at home until he went to high school, from which he graduated in three months. At the age of 11, William entered Harvard University, and a few months later he delivered a brilliant speech to the Harvard Math Club.

You may think that things looked pretty good for William at this point in his life. Unfortunately, however, this was the high point of his life. Although he received his bachelor's degree from Harvard at the age of 16, he never put it to use. He went to graduate school for a year and then went to law school, but never received a degree from either. He taught at a university for a short period of time and then turned against the schooling and accomplishments he had obtained. He spent the rest of his life working at mindless, low-paying jobs, moving from one job to another. He never married, and he was filled with bitterness and loneliness. When he died at the age of 46, William was alone, obscure, penniless, and miserably maladjusted (Montour, 1977).

The story of William Sidis reveals that no single developmental domain is more important than another. Each domain is important at all stages of development, and this book examines each stage in terms of these three broad developmental domains and the interrelationships among them. Development is multifaceted and complex, with domains and processes operating simultaneously.

WHAT ARE SOME CRITICAL ISSUES IN THE STUDY OF CHILD DEVELOPMENT?

The study of child development is filled with issues that are central to a complete understanding of how children change and become who they are. Scientists agree on the need to

child development changes in physical, social, emotional, and intellectual functioning over time, from conception through adolescence

developmental domains the three categories established to provide a basis for focusing on the specific areas of physical, cognitive, and social-emotional development

physical development involves growth and change in a person's body and bodily functions

cognitive development involves development of mental processes used to process information, become aware, solve problems, and gain knowledge

social-emotional development involves development of processes related to one's interactions with others

address these critical issues but disagree about the answers to the questions they raise. These issues also capture the attention of the general public and media. For example, in a series of tragic events that occurred between December 1997 and April 1999, young students in Kentucky, Arkansas, Oregon, and Colorado opened fire on classmates. In the worst of these cases—the tragedy in Littleton, Colorado, in the spring of 1999—thirteen people were killed, booby traps and bombs were planted, and the teens took their own lives. Immediately, local and national media gathered the experts to discuss the events. Laypeople also tried to make sense of the tragedy. The questions were the same as they had been before: "How could this happen?" "What caused these kids to do these terrible deeds?" "Was it something in their upbringing or something within them?" The answers to these questions are elusive, but to begin to answer them we must understand children and adolescents and the influences that affect their development.

INFLUENCES ON CHILD DEVELOPMENT

Developmental changes are brought about by a variety of different mechanisms. Some changes occur largely as a result of the unfolding of one's genetic code. These changes are referred to as **maturation,** and they involve a series of preprogrammed transformations in the form, structure, or function of an individual. One vivid example of maturation is the physical changes associated with puberty; these changes result from genetically inherited instructions that guide development of the adolescent's nervous system. Associated with maturational changes are changes in other domains of development (such as social and intellectual changes) and in other aspects of life such as diet, exercise, or stress.

Environmental factors also influence human development (Harris, 1995). Because environmental stimuli bombard children every moment of every day, their potential for influencing development is great. The influence of the environment begins very early: Some aspects of the environment to which a pregnant woman is exposed (such as toxins or radiation) can affect her unborn child and influence the child's development. The effects of these early environmental exposures can be devastating and permanent.

The environment also influences behavior through **learning,** which occurs as the result of observation, experience, instruction, or practice. Learning affects a wide range of activities, behaviors, and attitudes—sports, attitudes toward people of different races, achievement in school, and aggressiveness, to name only a few. Learning also influences the process by which children become members of a social group, a family, a community, a tribe, or a team. The process by which children learn social roles and become members of groups is referred to as **socialization.** By teaching them the values, beliefs, customs, and expectations of their society, socialization helps most children to get along cooperatively in the social and cultural contexts in which they find themselves.

Some developmental changes are relatively permanent, such as the development of the skeletal system, whereas other changes may be more fleeting, such as the use of a particular cognitive strategy to add numbers. Many people make the mistake of assuming that changes caused by biological agents (such as drugs or hormones) are irreversible, whereas those caused by social agents (such as family interactions or schooling) can be modified. However, some changes brought about by biological agents can be reversed. For example, the very serious brain damage caused by the genetic disease phenylketonuria (PKU) can be prevented by altering the child's diet. On the other hand, a child may never overcome the intellectual deficits caused by parents who are too depressed to interact with her or him. Table 1.1 lists some helpful ways to think about developmental change.

The extent to which biological/genetic and environmental factors influence development has been, and continues to be, hotly debated in the field of child development. This controversy is often referred to as the **nature versus nurture debate.** The nature side of the debate emphasizes the role of biological/genetic factors, whereas the nurture side emphasizes the role of the environment.

These students were evacuated from Columbine High School in Littleton, Colorado after two adolescents went on a shooting rampage, killing 13 students. It is difficult to answer questions about why these boys killed their classmates. How might the study of child development help to answer these kinds of questions?

maturation changes brought about largely as a result of the unfolding of one's genetic code

learning changes that occur as the result of observation, experience, instruction, or practice

socialization the process by which children learn social roles and become members of groups

nature versus nurture debate controversy over the extent to which biological/genetic and environmental factors influence development

TABLE 1.1
Thinking about Developmental Change

LOCUS OF CHANGE	CAUSE OF CHANGE	EXAMPLES OF CHANGE
A. Change occurs within the individual	1. Individual characteristics	Brain development Puberty
	2. Environmental factors	Prenatal exposure to X rays causes physical deformities Exposure to tennis instructor improves tennis skills
B. Change occurs outside the individual	1. Individual characteristics	Parents express more emotion when infant begins to walk Adolescent's relationship with parents changes because of the onset of puberty
	2. Environmental factors	Child's relationship with parents changes because of divorce Child becomes withdrawn because of peer rejection

In this photo from the 1970 movie L'Enfant Sauvage, *the Wild Boy of Aveyron is being trained to speak. Why did Itard attempt to socialize the boy? What questions does this case raise about the study of child development?*

The Wild Boy of Aveyron: A Case for Nurture?

One way to examine the effects of biology and the environment on development is to study children who are deprived of human contact. Do these children develop like children who have contact with others? If so, then genetic inheritance is the major factor in their development and the role of the social environment in producing normal behavior is small. Or, does their behavior become more human after contact with other humans? Of course, conducting such an experiment by design is out of the question. But there are rare instances in which children are abandoned early in development and left to survive on their own.

The Wild Boy of Aveyron stands out as one of the most famous and well-documented cases of a child abandoned in the wild. The Wild Boy was captured by hunters in 1798 and placed in a hospital in Aveyron (in the countryside outside Paris), where he was diagnosed as a "congenital idiot." At the time of his capture, the boy was about 12 years old and probably had been living alone in the wild since the age of 3 or 4.

Initial descriptions of the boy's behavior aroused much curiosity; he was described as a savage, subject to fits of anger, nervous spasms, and convulsions. He slept according to the sun; was restless, shy, and wild; sought escape at every opportunity; did not talk but growled and grunted; bit and scratched; and showed little affection. He disliked sleeping in a bed; was not bothered by cold temperatures or foul smells; ate berries, roots, and raw chestnuts; and disliked sweets. In short, the Wild Boy, who came to be known as Victor, lacked all elements of "civilized" human behavior (Malson, 1972).

Eventually Victor was brought under the care of Jean Itard, a French physician. Itard argued that Victor's retardation was the result of lack of experience and contact with humans. He believed that if Victor was given proper remedial experience he would become normal and civilized. Itard set out to provide educational experiences for Victor and show that the environment is the major influence on development.

Under Itard's care, Victor's behavior did change. He lost some of his wildness and made important intellectual strides. He learned to dress himself, to use table utensils to eat, and to express basic emotions. Although he never learned to speak, he learned to identify various letters. Interestingly, he learned to express simple wants and needs through writing. By the end of five years with Itard, however, Victor's behavior was by no means "normal." Compared to children his own age, Victor was still severely intellectually and socially retarded. Itard stopped the experiment because he felt that not enough progress had been made (Itard, 1972a/1801, 1972b/1806). Victor lived out his life with the woman who had been caring for him at the hospital, and he died in 1828.

Scientifically, there is little we can conclude about Itard's natural experiment. Certainly, Victor's condition improved, but the best we can say is that the results are inconclusive. We do not know enough about Victor prior to the time he was captured to answer the nature versus nurture question: Perhaps Victor had some biological condition that impaired his ability to learn and become socialized. His tendency toward "fits of convulsions and spasms" may have been the reason he was abandoned in the first place (Frith, 1989).

Medical Wonders: A Case for Nature?

Itard tried to use the unusual case of Victor to study the extent to which environmental influences contribute to development. Other cases of unusual circumstances have been used to explore the degree to which biological processes contribute to development. Such is the case of Brandi Bender, who, when she was 6 years old, had the entire right side of her cortex (the outer layer of the brain) removed because of severe epileptic seizures. Because the right side of the cortex controls the muscles on the left side of the body, she lost motor control over half of her body. After seven years of intensive therapy in motor skills, math, and music, however, Brandi became talented in skills that ordinarily are associated with the right cortex of the brain. Thus, Brandi's brain was plastic enough to compensate for the loss of half of her cortex. Brandi's brain rearranged many of its connections to allow her to be skilled in areas normally controlled by the right brain. Unfortunately, not all areas regained function—she still cannot use her left arm (Nash, 1997).

Cases like Brandi's tell us that if there is a way to compensate for severe damage, the brain will find it and attempt to restore things to normal. But, like the case of Victor, Brandi's case provides only limited help in answering the nature versus nurture question. Brandi's recovery proves that biology and physiology are not the sole or dominant influences on early development. Without such environmental factors as the experiences provided by her intense therapy (ranging from leg lifts to musical drills), Brandi would never have recovered to the extent that she did. The environmental experiences she had may have determined how her brain rewired itself (Jacobs, 1997).

TEASING OUT THE ROLES OF NATURE AND NURTURE

Modern child development researchers use sophisticated techniques and strategies, such as adoption and twin studies, to address questions of nature and nurture. Additionally, the essence of the nature versus nurture debate has changed somewhat: Now the debate is not over whether nature or nurture has an influence—we know that both do—but over how nature and nurture work together to influence development (Gottlieb, 1997; Rutter et al., 1997).

Determining the genetic and environmental bases for characteristics and behaviors is challenging, particularly for complex human characteristics such as intelligence, mental illness, or **personality** (a person's unique behavioral, motivational, and mental styles of responding). Much of our knowledge about the genetic transmission of physical characteristics has been acquired by studying insects and animals, but they provide poor models for studying complex behaviors and characteristics in humans. Another problem is that the environment is difficult to assess or control. Despite the difficulties, behavioral genetics researchers use a variety of techniques to assess the roles that genetics and the environment play in human behavior.

Adoption Studies

An adopted child carries the genetic inheritance of his or her biological parents but is raised by parents who are genetically unrelated to him or her. This situation provides a natural opportunity to study genetic influences. If an adopted child behaves more similarly to the parents who raised him or her, this suggests that the family environment plays a strong role in the behavior being studied. In contrast, if an adopted child behaves more similarly to the biological parents, this suggests that genetic factors play a strong role in that behavior (Plomin, Fulker, Corley, & DeFries, 1997).

personality a person's unique behavioral, motivational, and mental styles of responding

Identical twins share the same genetic structure. Even so, they often are very different from each other. What does this tell us about nature versus nurture?

Twin Studies

Another way to tease out the roles that nature and nurture play in development is to study twins. **Monozygotic (MZ) twins,** often called *identical twins,* share the same genetic code because they developed from one fertilized egg, which divided into two separate individuals. **Dizygotic (DZ) twins,** often called *fraternal twins,* develop from two separate eggs fertilized by two separate sperm cells. DZ twins may be very similar or very different genetically, just like any two siblings. On average, about 50 percent of their genetic code is shared. Both kinds of twins experience the same prenatal environment, are born at the same time, and usually live in the same family, so they share many similarities in environmental factors. Because MZ and DZ twins differ in the degree to which they share genetic codes but tend to have similar environments, they provide a way to estimate how genes and environment interact to influence development (Wachs, 1992).

If a characteristic has a strong environmental component and a weak genetic component, MZ twins should be no more alike than DZ twins on that characteristic. If a characteristic has a strong genetic component, then MZ twins should be more alike on that characteristic than DZ twins. Geneticists determine **heritability**—an estimate of the degree to which variation of a characteristic in a population is influenced by genetic factors— by comparing the degrees of similarity of MZ and DZ twins (Plomin, 1994).

Studies of twins have shown that height, for example, is largely genetically determined. MZ twins are quite similar in height, usually differing by only about ⅓ inch. DZ twins are less similar in height, usually differing by about 1½ inches (Mange & Mange, 1994). The heritability estimate suggests that 90 percent of the variation in height is due to genetic factors. Twins' weights vary much more than their heights do, suggesting that environmental factors play a larger role in determining one's weight.

Such findings suggest that the correspondence of certain physical traits increases as the degree of genetic relatedness increases. But does this relationship apply to complex human characteristics? The answer seems to be yes. For example, the risk of a person's developing schizophrenia—a serious mental illness—increases when close family members have the disorder (Gottesman, 1991). The closer the relative, the greater the risk. The risk of developing schizophrenia is greatest when an MZ twin has developed the disorder, but this risk does not reach 100 percent. This finding suggests that, although genetic factors may predispose someone to schizophrenia, nongenetic factors (such as family experiences or stress-related factors) may need to be present for the illness to occur (Gottesman, 1991). Findings such as these reinforce the importance of exploring how genes and the environment work together to influence development.

Twin and Adoption Methods Combined

Sometimes researchers combine the twin and adoption methods, looking at the similarity or dissimilarity of twins who are reared apart. From these studies, researchers have concluded that many aspects of personality have a sizable genetic component, with roughly 50 percent of the variability in personality accounted for by heredity (Tellegen, 1988). The remaining 50 percent of the variability in personality is attributable to environmental factors, including shared experiences (such as experience in the same family) and non-shared experiences (such as influences of different teachers or friends). MZ twins raised together tend to be no more alike than MZ twins reared apart, suggesting that non-shared environments influence personality development to a greater extent than do shared experiences.

Shared environments, however, play a greater role in the development of intelligence (Plomin, Fulker et al., 1997). Studies conducted on twins raised together and apart have shown that intelligence test scores are most closely related for MZ twins who are raised together. About 50 percent of the variability in intelligence can be attributed to genetic inheritance and 50 percent to environmental influences. Even the shared prenatal environment of twins contributes to their similarities and may partly explain why DZ twins have higher resemblance in intelligence than do ordinary siblings (Devlin, Daniels, & Roeder, 1997).

monozygotic (MZ) twins twins who share the same genetic code because they developed from one fertilized egg, which divided into two separate individuals; identical twins

dizygotic (DZ) twins twins who develop from two separate eggs fertilized by two separate sperm cells; fraternal twins

heritability an estimate of the degree to which variation of a characteristic in a population is influenced by genetic factors

Twin and adoption studies help us understand that genes and the environment are complexly interwoven. For instance, genes may influence exposure and susceptibility to different kinds of environments. Children who are genetically predisposed to be active will search out peers who are active, thereby affecting their development by changing the quality of their environment (Rutter et al., 1997).

CONTINUITY VERSUS DISCONTINUITY

Another major issue in child development concerns the course of development: Does it occur gradually and smoothly or in a series of abrupt and separate changes? Some developmental scientists focus on gradual changes and view development as *continuous*—like the development of vocabulary (see Figure 1.1a). Other scientists view development as *discontinuous* and focus on the acquisition of qualitatively new patterns of behavior—such as the transition from crawling to walking (see Figure 1.1b). These qualitatively different patterns in development are called *stages,* and, as you will see, many theories of development (such as Piaget's) are stage theories.

The advantage of using stages to represent development is that they help organize information in a meaningful way. The disadvantage of stage theories is that they gloss over the inconsistencies, complexities, and irregularities of development (Aylward, 1997; Flavell, 1982). Changes that seem abrupt, such as a child's first step, may actually be the culmination of a long gradual process rather than a sudden shift (Thelen, 1989). For instance, infants increasingly kick their legs in rhythm until they begin to crawl and walk. These early leg kicks reveal a continuity in development, setting the stage for what appears to be a rather abrupt change in the infant's development—namely, the beginning of upright self-movement (Thelen & Smith, 1998). When viewed in this manner, development is best conceived of as a dynamic and complex pattern of both gradual and abrupt changes (see Figure 1.1c).

CRITICAL AND SENSITIVE PERIODS

Another important issue is whether there exist **critical periods** of development—periods during which specific biological or environmental events must occur if development is to proceed normally. According to the critical period view, individuals are unusually sensitive

FIGURE 1.1

Views on the Nature of Developmental Change

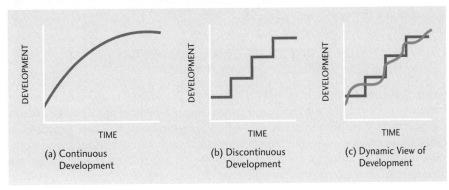

Some developmentalists view change as a smooth trajectory (a), whereas others view it as a series of discrete stages (b). Still others believe that change consists of both discrete stages and smooth trajectories (c). Which of these models best fits your view of developmental change?

critical periods periods during which specific biological or environmental events must occur if development is to proceed normally

Ducklings follow the first moving object they see. Here, they follow Konrad Lorenz, who used ethological theory to explain development. What role do critical and sensitive periods play in human development?

to specific types of stimulation at certain times during development. If the stimulation is received during the critical time period, development proceeds normally; if the stimulation is not received, normal development is altered. If the needed stimulation is received at the wrong time, it is not likely to have the same impact it would have had if it had occurred during the critical period (Wachs, 1992).

Evidence for critical periods has been well documented in many animals. For example, a critical period immediately after birth has been established for imprinting in ducklings—they follow the first moving object they see right after birth, which usually is the mother duck. The strongest evidence for critical periods in child development comes from studies of language development. Children who do not have sufficient exposure to language before the age of 6 or 7 years, like Victor, may never acquire a language (Newport, 1991).

For most aspects of development, however, the concept of critical periods appears to be too narrow (Bornstein, 1989). Brandi Bender's case shows that children are remarkably resilient and can compensate for inadequate or inappropriate stimulation during important times in development. Many developmentalists use the term **sensitive periods** to refer to times that are optimal for the development of certain behaviors or functions but, unlike critical periods, are not necessary (Shavinina, 1997). The concept of sensitive periods acknowledges that it is possible for development to occur later, although it is more difficult for it to do so and recovery may be incomplete (Wachs, 1992).

INDIVIDUAL DIFFERENCES IN DEVELOPMENT— STABILITY AND CHANGE

Another vital issue in the field of child development is sorting out universal versus individual developmental characteristics and events. Because children are all members of the same species, they are alike in many ways—they have similar basic forms, functions, and abilities. However, as soon as children are born (and even before), differences among them are noticeable. Also, although children share biological and cultural characteristics, every child is unique. Even identical twins, who share identical genetic information, are different in many respects. The question is, are individual differences stable and permanent or do they change over time? Do fussy children grow up to be fussy adolescents and adults? Do shy children grow up to be shy adolescents and adults? As you will learn, individual differences

sensitive periods periods of time that are optimal for the development of certain behaviors or functions

tend to be consistent, but human behavior is amazingly flexible and subject to change over time and situations.

WHAT ARE THE HISTORICAL ROOTS OF THE STUDY OF CHILD DEVELOPMENT?

The desire to understand children is not new, but the science of child development is. It is only about 100 years old. Cultural and social factors in Western civilization limited scientific inquiry into child development. In addition, the study of child development has been influenced by views concerning the nature, role, and status of children in society. Historically, conceptualizations of children and developmental stages were affected by these views.

CHILDREN OF ANTIQUITY

In ancient Greece and Rome, children were viewed as helpless and incapable of caring for themselves. Because children were considered to be lacking in self-control and prone to disobedience, a heavy emphasis was placed on discipline (Borstelmann, 1983). Children were meant to serve the interests of the gods through their families and society; they had no status independent of such considerations.

Children also were viewed as naive and easily susceptible to corruption. In ancient Greece, Plato's (808 BC) concerns about this susceptibility led him to propose drastic measures. Plato was convinced that the citizens of Athens had succumbed to the decadence of the society and were unfit to rear children. He proposed that children be separated from their parents early in life and reared under state control. Selective screening would ensure that only those individuals of the highest moral character were allowed to rear and train children. Plato believed that socialization and the environment are critical factors in influencing development and that development is a continuous process. Although his contention that children should be reared by professional caregivers rather than parents seems undesirable by today's standards, it reflects the belief that children are important to the future of a society—a view held by most people today.

CHILDREN AS MINIATURE ADULTS: MEDIEVAL CHILDREN

During the European Middle Ages, children were not recognized as distinct from adults. As soon as a child could live without the constant attention and help of her or his caregiver (about the age of 6 or 7), she or he belonged to adult society (Aries, 1962). Evidence of this lack of distinction between children and adults is seen often in the art of the times, in which children were depicted as miniature adults. Medieval artists did not represent physical differences other than size in the bodies and dress of adults and children.

This lack of a distinction between children and adults did not mean that children were neglected or forsaken. It simply reflected the historical context of the Middle Ages: Children's labor was considered a necessity, and because infant mortality was so high—one-half to two-thirds of all children died during infancy—adults were reluctant to recognize children as special individuals (Jaffe, 1997). Children worked liked adults, dressed like adults, and could legally be married, crowned, or hanged like adults. Distinctions were not made between activities appropriate for children and for adults, because it was believed that children generally did not have needs beyond those of adults. Although this view has been challenged (Elkind, 1986; Pollock, 1983), compared to our lives, the lives of children and families during this historical period were harsh and difficult, and the attitudes toward children reflected this harshness. These attitudes exemplify the fact that how children are perceived and treated is intricately bound to the historical context in which children are raised.

Notice how the children in this painting are depicted as if they were miniature adults. What differences would you expect to see if they were accurately portrayed? What does this tell us about the conceptualization of children during this period?

EARLY PHILOSOPHICAL ROOTS OF CHILDHOOD

A more enlightened view of childhood began to appear during the Renaissance (late fourteenth and early fifteenth century) and the Reformation (fifteenth and sixteenth centuries). More children were living to adulthood, and helping them acquire knowledge and skills at an early age became more important. Between the sixteenth and eighteenth centuries, a new conception of childhood emerged, based on the philosophy of humanism. In particular, two philosophers, writing about 100 years apart, took an interest in the welfare of children and recognized that children have needs that are different from those of adults. The two philosophers, John Locke and Jean-Jacques Rousseau, argued that childhood is a period of importance and that early development sets the stage for what one becomes later in life. But at the same time, Locke's and Rousseau's views on the primary influence and process of development differed, reflecting the nature versus nurture debate.

John Locke: *Tabula Rasa*

John Locke (1632–1704) proposed that a child is like a blank slate, or *tabula rasa*, upon which experiences in life write their story. Through interactions with people and objects in the environment, each child develops his or her unique character and abilities. Locke emphasized the long-term impact of early experiences and the responsibility parents bear for their children's character formation.

> The great mistake I have observed in people's breeding their children . . . is that the mind has not been made obedient to discipline and pliant to reason when it was most tender, most easy to be bowed.
>
> —*John Locke* (1690/1964)

This quote reflects Locke's belief that the environment is the driving force in development. By promoting children's obedience and curiosity, parents encourage their children to develop into rational, attentive, and affectionate people. Through the experiences provided by parents, children are socialized into their culture.

Jean-Jacques Rousseau: Innate Morality

Jean-Jacques Rousseau (1712–1778) also challenged the notion that children are merely miniature and inferior adults. In contrast to Locke, however, Rousseau emphasized the importance of internal, or innate, forces. He believed that, from the time they are born, children possess an intrinsic character that is perfect and good. The role of adults, in Rousseau's view, is to let the natural positive forces in children emerge without restraint:

God makes all things good; man meddles with them and they become evil.
—*Jean-Jacques Rousseau* (1762/1911)

Because of his emphasis on letting the natural qualities of the child dictate his or her development, Rousseau is humorously referred to as the "grandfather of permissive parenting." Children should be allowed to naturally unfold, with little pressure from adults (although he did sometimes advocate that parents carefully regulate their children's experiences). In emphasizing the inborn, natural qualities of development, Rousseau placed greater importance on internal (nature) rather than external (nurture) processes (Synnott, 1988).

Locke and Rousseau set the stage for the modern scientific study of child development. They assigned children a special status and argued that experiences early in development shape later development.

CHARLES DARWIN: EVOLUTION AND CHILD DEVELOPMENT

With his theory of evolution, Charles Darwin (1809–1882) radically changed the way scientists thought about child development. In his *Origin of Species* (published in 1859), Darwin proposed the revolutionary ideas that various species had a common ancestor and that species either die out or change to meet the demands of their changing environments. Darwin's views challenged the ingrained theological view that child behavior is created in a fixed and perfect form. Instead, Darwin believed that human behavior evolved slowly over time.

Darwin's theory is based on the concept of **natural selection**—the idea that, in nature, individuals who are best adapted to their surroundings survive and reproduce, and the adaptive characteristics of those individuals are passed on to the next generation. After many generations, the traits of these individuals become increasingly prevalent in the population (Darwin, 1859).

The impact of Darwin's work continues to be dramatic and pervasive. The possibility that human behavior reflects evolutionary adaptation and selection is a part of many theories of development. Theories such as ethology and sociobiology have been developed based specifically on Darwin's propositions (Wilson, 1978). Furthermore, Darwin's emphasis on common ancestors has led to comparisons between the development of human behavior and the development of similar behaviors in other species (Berman, Rasmussen, & Suomi, 1994).

G. STANLEY HALL: PIONEER IN THE STUDY OF DEVELOPMENT

Up to 100 years ago, most studies of child development consisted of philosophical treatises (such as those written by Locke and Rousseau) and biographical diaries written by parents about their infant children (Darwin, 1877). Then, at the beginning of the twentieth century, G. Stanley Hall (1844–1924) pioneered the application of scientific procedures to the study of child development. For example, he was the first to use questionnaires with children. Although his early attempts were somewhat haphazard, his research illustrated how scientific methods can be used to understand children.

Hall was the first scientist to focus attention on adolescent development and was the first to define adolescence as a separate period of life. He also wrote one of the first developmental textbooks. Thus, Hall's work directly stimulated significant areas of contemporary developmental study—scientific aspects of the study of development, adolescence, and early childhood education (Cairns, 1998).

natural selection the process, in nature, whereby individuals who are best adapted to their surroundings survive and reproduce, and the adaptive characteristics of those individuals are passed on to the next generation

Locke, Rousseau, Darwin, and Hall all had important influences on the early study and conceptualization of child development. Can you identify their contributions? Can you discuss their views on nature versus nurture?

WHAT CHANGES IN CONTEMPORARY AMERICAN LIFE INFLUENCE THE STUDY OF CHILD DEVELOPMENT?

Just as historical changes affected the study of children, contemporary changes in American population and culture have an impact on the study of child development. This impact reminds us that the study of child development is influenced by the contexts in which researchers work. Changes in family composition and increasing cultural diversity, for example, are influences that have stimulated new research.

CHANGES IN FAMILY STRUCTURE

Family life in the United States has been changing dramatically. Even the concept of "family" is changing. The prevalence of the traditional **nuclear family,** in which the biological mother and father and their children live together, has been declining for some years. In 1960, 73 percent of all children lived with their biological parents who had been married only once; by 1996, this figure had dropped to 56 percent (US Census Bureau, 2001b).

The fastest growing family type in the United States in recent years is the **single-parent family,** in which children live with only their mother or their father. The primary cause of single-parent families is divorce, and 90 percent of single-parent families are headed by women. In 1960, only 9 percent of children under the age of 18 lived with a single parent. By 1996, the proportion of single-parent children had jumped to nearly one-quarter of all US children (US Census Bureau, 2001b), and, with the exception of Asian American children, the proportion was even larger for minority children (see Figure 1.2). As you can see from Figure 1.2, the percentage of minority children living in single-parent families is especially high for African American children. This is due primarily to the higher rate of African American children living with mothers who were never married.

Another family type that has become increasingly common is the **blended family**—formed when a widowed or divorced person remarries. If the remarried husband or wife or both have children from a former marriage, a **stepfamily** is formed. About 29 percent of African American children, 15 percent of Hispanic children, and 17 percent of Caucasian American children live in stepfamilies; almost all of these children live with their biological mother (US Census Bureau, 2001b). Census estimates suggest that by 2007 stepfamilies will outnumber traditional nuclear families. It is estimated that about one-third of all children can expect to live with a biological parent and a stepparent for at least one year before the age of 18 (Dainton, 1993; DeLongis & Preece, 2002).

An **extended family** consists of one or more parents, one or more of the parents' children, and one or more other relatives (grandparents, aunts, uncles, etc.) living together

nuclear family family structure in which the biological mother and father and their children live together

single-parent family family structure in which children live with only their mother or their father

blended family family structure formed when a widowed or divorced person remarries

stepfamily family structure formed when a person who has children from a former marriage remarries

extended family family structure consisting of one or more parents, one or more of the parents' children, and one or more other relatives living together in one household

FIGURE 1.2

Children Living in Different Types of Families, by Race: 1995

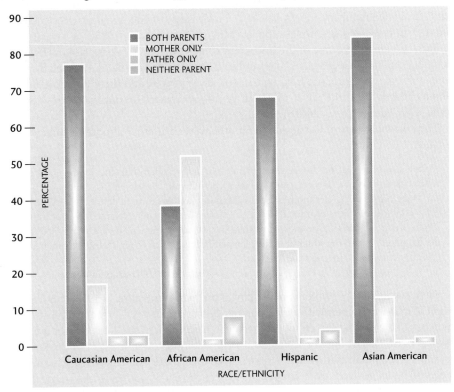

Legend:
- BOTH PARENTS
- MOTHER ONLY
- FATHER ONLY
- NEITHER PARENT

Y-axis: PERCENTAGE (0–90)
X-axis: RACE/ETHNICITY — Caucasian American, African American, Hispanic, Asian American

SOURCE: US Census Bureau, 2001b.

Notice the dramatic differences between the graphs for African American children and those for Caucasian American, Asian American, and Hispanic children. What are the major differences, and what factors might account for these differences?

THE PRACTICAL IMPACT: NURTURING CHILDREN

Trends in US Family Values Since 1950

The last half of the twentieth century saw important changes in US family values. These changes, which influenced children's development by affecting the customs, values, and environments they were exposed to, can be described in terms of three patterns (Whitehead, 1993):

1. 1950 to mid-1960s: Traditional familism
The nuclear family dominated.
Birth rates were high.
Divorce rates were low.
The economy was strong; the standard of living was high.
Relatively low numbers of women were in the work force.

Men and women had traditional gender roles.

2. Mid-1960s to mid-1980s: Individualism
The population became more diverse.
Marriage was more often postponed, and increased attention was paid to the single lifestyle.
Birth rates declined.
Birth control became more available.
Divorce rates increased.
Participation of women in the work force increased.
Self-expression was emphasized.
Feminism developed, and gender role stereotypes declined.

3. Mid-1980s to present: New familism
Birth rates and the incidence of multiple births increased.
Advances occurred in biotechnology and fertility treatment.
Family structure became more diverse.
Divorce rates leveled off.
Increased attention was paid to the aging population.
The discrepancy between the poor and the affluent increased.
With Internet communication came increased globalism.

in one household. This type of family is more common among certain ethnic groups. For example, sharing a residence with extended family members has long been a characteristic of African American families (Garcia Coll, 1990). Similarly, many Mexican American families include aunts and uncles, grandparents, cousins, in-laws, and sometimes even close friends. Extended family members exchange a wide range of goods and services, including child care, nursing, and emotional support (Muller & Espenshade, 1985).

Table 1.2 identifies some of the important changes that have taken place in US households since 1970 and are projected to occur by 2010. Fewer households are headed by a married couple, the average household consists of fewer people, and there are more families without children under the age of 18. These trends are expected to continue throughout this decade (US Census Bureau, 2001b).

The following story of Cassie and her mother reveals another important change in the structure of US families:

> At 7:40 A.M., four-year-old Cassie sidles in, her hair half-combed, a blanket in one hand, a fudge bar in the other. "Pleeese, can't you take me with you?" Cassie pleads. "You know I can't take you to work," her mother replies. Cassie's shoulders drop in defeat . . . and she is resigned to her mother's imminent departure. As her mother later explained, she continually feels that she owes Cassie more time than she actually gives her. She has a time-debt to her daughter . . . and she sometimes finds herself indulging Cassie with treats or softened rules in exchange for missed time together.
>
> —*Hochschild* (1997, adapted from pp. 3–4)

Parents, particularly mothers, are working more than ever before. In 1950, only about 13 percent of married mothers with children under 17 worked for pay. Currently, almost 70 percent do so, and about 56 percent of mothers who have children age 1 or younger are in the work force (US Department of Labor, 2001b). In addition, the number of hours that both men and women put in at work has increased since 1980; more women particularly are working over 40 hours per week. For example, in 1979, 14 percent of women worked more than 40 hours per week. Today, that figure has increased over 50 percent—to about 21.5 percent (Bureau of Labor Statistics, 1999). Moreover, women moving into the workforce are less likely than ever to move out of it. And parents feel the pressure of this time drain—57 percent of fathers and 55 percent of mothers reported feeling guilty that they spent too little time with their children (Hochschild, 1997).

With the increased number of families in which parents work outside the home, young children are spending more time with non-parental caregivers. Figure 1.3 outlines the changes in enrollments in preschool programs since 1965 for 3- and 4-year-old children. As you can see, there has been a steady increase. Today, more than 4 million children under the age of 6 are enrolled in some type of preschool program. These findings strongly suggest that preschool enrollments are large, growing, and here to stay (National Research Council, 2001).

These changes in US households reflect changes in values, technology, and demographics that have occurred since 1970. Together, these trends have important effects on the

TABLE 1.2

Household Comparisons: 1970 versus 2000 versus 2010 (projected)

	1970	2000	2010
Percent of households made up of married couples with children	40%	24%	20%
People per household	3.14	2.59	2.53
Families headed by women with no husband present	5.6 million	12.3 million	13.9 million
Families headed by men with no wife present	1.2 million	3.9 million	4.7 million
Families with no children under 18 at home	44%	54%	59%

SOURCE: US Census Bureau, 2001b.

environments in which children find themselves. Scientists interested in the study of child development must be attentive to these changes in order to understand the complex factors that influence the course of development.

CHILDREN OF LESBIAN AND GAY PARENTS

Historically, people in Western cultures believed that the most favorable home environments were those provided by traditional two-parent families. Although rarely stated explicitly, it is most often assumed that the parents in such families are heterosexual (Patterson, 1992). In the contemporary United States, this is not always the case—many children grow up in homes where the parent or parents are gay or lesbian.

Estimates of the number of gay and lesbian parents in the United States range from 2 to 8 million, and estimates of the number of children of gay and lesbian parents range from 4 to 14 million (Savin-Williams & Esterberg, 2000). The exact figures are difficult to determine because many gay and lesbian parents conceal their sexual orientation out of fear of discrimination and prejudice (Saffron, 1996). In most cases, children are born as a result of a heterosexual relationship between biological parents. After one parent acknowledges her or his sexual orientation, separation or divorce may occur, and the children are then raised in a gay or lesbian home (Falk, 1989).

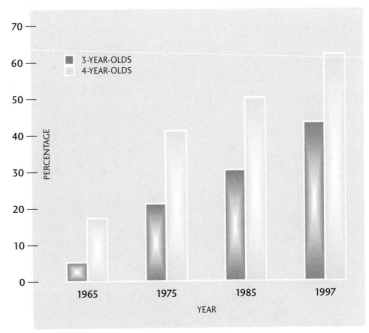

FIGURE 1.3

Percent of 3- and 4-Year-Old Children Enrolled in Preschool Programs: 1965–1997

SOURCE: National Center for Educational Statistics, 1998.

Notice the consistent increase in preschool enrollments from 1965 to 1997. What factors contributed to this change?

However, an increasing number of children, conceived through donor insemination, are now being born into lesbian homes (Chan, Raboy, & Patterson, 1998). Whatever the precise figures and contexts of conception, it is clear that the number of children of gay and lesbian parents has increased and is substantial.

Much of the research on children reared in homosexual households has been generated in the last twenty years, often because of custody disputes. Concerns about children's sexual development, the quality of the parenting provided by gay and lesbian parents, and the stress and ridicule these children might face have been raised by those who believe that children in these families are at risk and that homosexuals should be denied the rights and privileges of having a family (Focus on the Family, 1992). The scientific evidence presents a different picture, however.

Research on children from gay and lesbian homes suggests that they are no different from children reared by heterosexual parents (Fitzgerald, 1999; Golombok & Tasker, 1996; Patterson, 1995). Children's performance on standard developmental and psychological tests gives no indication as to whether they have a homosexual parent or a heterosexual parent. Thus, children raised by gay and lesbian parents appear to be just as healthy and well adjusted as those raised by heterosexual couples (Tasker & Golombok, 1997); there is no evidence to suggest that the development of children of gay men or lesbians is compromised in any respect (Patterson & Chan, 1999). The evidence to date indicates that the home environments provided by gay and lesbian parents are as likely as those provided by heterosexual parents to support and enable children's growth and development.

Of course, lesbian and gay parents are as diverse in their backgrounds, personalities, and values as are heterosexual parents. Having addressed the negative assumptions and popular prejudices that underlie the concerns about gay and lesbian parenting, researchers now

These two mothers are interacting with their child. What does the research on children from gay and lesbian homes show about their psychological health and adjustment? In what ways is developmental research able to dispel misconceptions about parenting?

FIGURE 1.4

Percent Increase in Population, by Race: 1990 to 2000

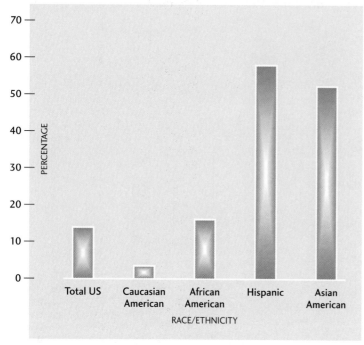

SOURCE: US Census Bureau, 2001c.

Notice the large percentage increases over the decade of the 1990s in His-panic and Asian American individuals in the US population. What factors contributed to these changes and what impact are they likely to have on children and families in the United States?

are exploring issues raised by the emergence of different kinds of lesbian and gay families with children (Patterson & Chan, 1999).

ETHNIC AND RACIAL DIVERSITY

In addition to paying more attention to the changing family structure, researchers have become more sensitive to cultural and ethnic influences on child development. This adjustment in part reflects the fact that the US population is more diverse than ever before. According to current and projected data collected by the US Census Bureau (2001c), Caucasian Americans are the slowest growing segment of the US population and their contribution to the total population growth in this country is becoming smaller (see Figure 1.4). From 1990 to 2030, the percentage of total population growth accounted for by Caucasian Americans is expected to decrease. By the year 2050, Caucasian Americans will represent only a slight majority. As seen in Figure 1.4, the Hispanic population is the fastest growing group, and by the year 2025 it will be the largest minority group in the United States. Similarly, the Asian population in the United States is expected to increase at a considerable pace through the year 2050.

Although birth rates generally are higher for minority groups than for Caucasian Americans, almost one-third of the current growth in minority groups is caused by immigration. By 2050, the net increase in population due to immigration is projected to be 82 million (US Census Bureau, 2001d).

Increased diversity in the US population demands greater sensitivity to human variety and the culturally diverse environments in which children are raised. However, relatively few studies have been conducted on minority children, adults, and families (Arms, Davidson, & Moore, 1992).

The task of researching the impact of diversity is complicated by the considerable variation that exists within, as well as between, minority groups (McAdoo, 1993). For example, Hispanics from Puerto Rico reside primarily in cities of the Northeast, are a relatively young group (median age is 23.3 years), and have not done well economically in the United States. In contrast, Hispanics from Cuba reside primarily in urban areas of the Southeast, particularly Florida, are relatively older (median age is 39.1 years), and generally have done well economically, particularly those who immigrated prior to 1980 (Ortiz, 1995). As a result, the development of individuals in these two Hispanic groups is influenced in different ways by the backgrounds, experiences, values, and beliefs of their different subcultures.

A further complication in researching the role of diversity in development is the lack of agreement on the terminology used to identify groups. For example, in one poll 30 percent of respondents indicated that they wished their race to be identified as "African American," whereas the majority listed "black" as their choice (Roper Organization, 1993). These findings reflect a difference not only in label preference but also in the meanings of *race* and *ethnicity*. Although there are no clear, unambiguous definitions of these terms, **race** primarily refers to a group whose members share a genetic heritage (Curran & Renzetti, 1996). **Ethnicity** primarily refers to a group whose members share a common cultural heritage and a sense of belonging (Yetman, 1991). Although there is some overlap in the two terms, ethnicity is considered to be a social construct whereas race is considered to be relatively less so. For example,

race a group whose members share a genetic heritage

ethnicity a group whose members share a common cultural heritage and a sense of belonging

THE SOCIAL IMPACT: DEBATING THE ISSUE

What Is the Impact of Immigration on American Life?

No group of children in America is expanding more rapidly than children from immigrant families (Zhou, 1997). In the last two decades, the number of immigrant children in public schools has grown by nearly 8 million. From 1990 to 1997, the number of children from immigrant families grew by 47 percent, compared with only 7 percent for US-born children of US-born parents (National Research Council, 1998). Today, there are approximately 12 million children in the US who are immigrants or who were born to immigrant parents. Most immigrant children come from Central and South America, the Caribbean, and Asia (Camarota, 2001). These children come to the United States with or to join other family members.

It is not surprising that immigrants and their impact on US society have caught the attention of the public, as well as that of government officials (National Research Council, 1998). In a 1993 poll, 75 percent of American citizens supported some kind of limitation on immigration (*Time,* 1993). Their concerns may be based on public anxiety about the high cost of providing services to new immigrants. But is this concern justified?

Although legal immigrants and refugees may receive benefits such as food stamps and health care, the average household incomes of legal immigrants and refugees who enter the United States generally are *higher* than those of US-born Americans (Fix & Passell, 1994). Considering the taxes that an immigrant and his or her dependents are likely to pay over a lifetime, the United States actually gains revenue from immigrants (Glastris, 1997). However, the economic status of *undocumented* immigrants is so poor that when the immigrant population in the United States is examined as a whole, the immigrants are less well off than US-born Americans. Thus, many beliefs about immigrant children and their families are based on those immigrants who are in the United States *illegally.*

Another misconception about immigrants is that they are at risk for poor educational outcomes because of their limited proficiency in English. Research shows that immigrant children do well in school and often stay in school longer than their US-born peers with similar backgrounds (McDonnell & Hill, 1993). The academic performance of many immigrant children exceeds that of the average US-born child, despite the fact that immigrant children often come from disadvantaged or war-torn backgrounds.

In the future, the United States will be even more racially, ethnically, and culturally diverse (Castex, 1997). With increased research, other negative beliefs and stereotypes about immigrants may be dispelled. Far from being a fringe element of the American population, immigrant children and their families are an increasingly large core of US society (Future of Children, 1995).

Thinking It Through:

1. What factors contribute to negative views about the impact of immigrants on US society?
2. What do you think US immigration policy should be? Should the United States accept many immigrants into the country? Why or why not?
3. How does immigration influence theory and research about child and adolescent development?

most (but not all) Americans of African descent are grouped racially as black; however, the term *African American* refers to an ethnic group, most often to people whose ancestors experienced slavery in the United States (Soberon, 1996). Thus, not all blacks in the United States are African American (for example, some are from Haiti and others from the Caribbean).

Similar confusion exists over the terminology used to refer to people of Mexican or Spanish descent. Consider the following terms (Campos, 1996; Office of Management and Budget, 1995; Soberon, 1996):

- **Spanish.**   Used to refer indiscriminately to any person who speaks Spanish. This term is imprecise because it includes people from many different countries and continents (America, the Caribbean, Europe).
- **Latino/Latina.**   Used to refer to people in the United States originating from or having a heritage related to Latin America (Central or South American). Because *Latin* refers to the fact that a romance language (Spanish, Portuguese, French) is the native tongue of the majority of Latin Americans, this term may not be appropriate for people from that region who do not speak a romance language (such as native Indians).
- **Mexican.**   Used to refer to the inhabitants of Mexico. The term may be appropriate for Mexican citizens working in or visiting the United States, but it is not appropriate for people of Mexican descent who are citizens of the United States.
- **Mexican American.**   Commonly used to recognize US citizens who are descendants of Mexicans. The term may be inappropriate for those who identify them-

Is Development Different for Children of Color?

The lack of attention to issues of race, ethnicity, and culture in the science of child development has resulted in studies that concentrate on explaining the differences between minority and Caucasian middle-class populations. Some scientists argue that what is lacking is an examination of the developmental processes and outcomes that are unique to children of color (Barbarin, 1993). Cynthia Garcia Coll and colleagues (1996) developed a model of development relevant to children of color. A schematic representation of this framework is presented in the figure.

Of primary concern in this model of development for minority children is the influence of social position variables—the characteristics that societies use to place individuals in a social hierarchy. These variables include (but are not limited to) race, social class, ethnicity, and gender.

Inspection of the figure shows that social position does not directly influence developmental outcomes for children of color. Rather, the effect of social position on development is seen through the effects of racism, which include prejudice, discrimination, and oppression—leading, in turn, to segregation. The interplay of social position, racism, and segregation creates unique conditions that affect the development of children of color. These conditions rarely are experienced by majority populations, and they define the alternative pathways of development for children of color (Garcia Coll et al., 1996).

The effect of all these factors is diverse and complex. For example, *discrimination*—defined as behaviors that deny individuals or groups of individuals equality of treatment—often leads to environments that maintain the social hierarchy. Discrimination not only

limits the quantity of resources available to children of a particular group but also limits their access to those resources that are available. Because of discrimination, children of color often face situations that majority children do not, such as restricted educational, housing, or recreational opportunities (Garcia Coll et al., 1996). Placing social position, racism, and segregation at the core rather than the periphery of development will lead to a better understanding of children of color.

Thinking It Through:

1. What aspects of development are likely to be similar for all children? What aspects are likely to be different for children of color?
2. How do discrimination and prejudice influence children's development?

Developmental Model for Minority Children

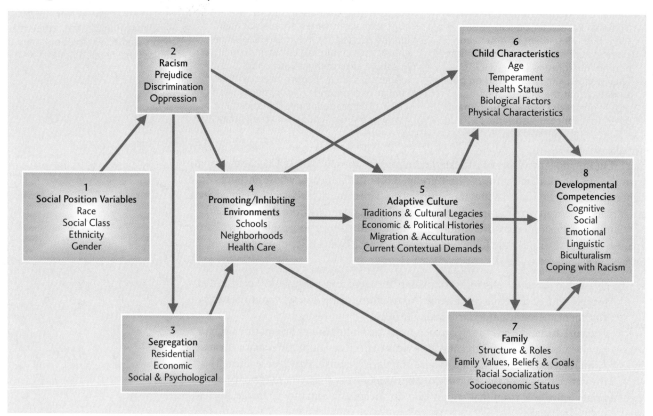

SOURCE: From Garcia Coll et al., 1996 (p. 1896).

Notice how complex this integrative model is and the important roles that social position (box 1), racism (box 2), and segregation (box 3) play. These factors are less likely to play a prominent role in the development of nonminority children. How might these factors influence minority children's development?

selves as having a Spanish rather than a Mexican heritage or for those who do not view themselves as Americans by choice.

✦ **Chicano/Chicana.**   Used to refer to descendants of inhabitants of Mexico. Preferred by political activists and those who seek to create a new identity, it is reflective of a unique culture.

✦ **Hispanic.**   Used to refer to people of Mexican, Puerto Rican, Cuban, Central and South American, and other Spanish culture or origin, regardless of race. This term is used by the US Census Bureau as an encompassing ethnic classification with many subgroups. Because of its broadness, this is the term used most often in this book.

Another controversy concerns how to classify persons who identify with more than one race. Consider, for example, the case of Tiger Woods, who, in 1997, became the youngest golfer ever (at age 21) to win the Masters golf tournament. Tiger's father is African American (but also part Native American and Caucasian), and his mother is Asian American (from Thailand). Tiger caused a stir when he refused to identify himself as a black. Instead, he coined a term, saying he was "Cablinasian"—a mixture of Caucasian, African American, Native American, and Asian (Padilla, 1997).

Tiger's situation points out an increasing dilemma for many: What do people of mixed races call themselves? For the most part, the term **multiracial** has been used to refer to people like Tiger who are of two or more races. And there are more multiracial individuals today than in the past. In 1960, there were about 150,000 interracial marriages, compared with 1.5 million in 1990 (OMB, 1995). Today, about 2.4 percent of the US population (about 7 million people) can be considered multiracial (US Census Bureau, 2001c). For these individuals, a single category often does not reflect how they think of themselves.

The amazing diversity of people has only just begun to be recognized in theories and research on child development (Spencer, 1990). Although many developmental processes (such as motor or language development) probably emerge in similar fashion across racially and ethnically diverse populations, our understanding of child development needs to be expanded to consider factors and situations that may be unique to a particular group (such as lifestyle or food choices). For instance, for children of color, more explicit attention needs to be paid to the unique circumstances they face (such as racism and stereotyping). Clearly, the "one size fits all" model of development is inadequate, and identifying and integrating the experiences and circumstances that are not shared by the majority population will provide the basis for a fuller and more inclusive understanding of child development (Garcia Coll et al., 1996).

Tiger Woods created a controversy when he declined to identify himself as being of one race or another. Many individuals are, like Tiger, multiracial, and their increasing numbers reflect the fact that the population of the United States is becoming more diverse.

CAN WE CAPTURE THE DIVERSITY OF CHILDREN'S DEVELOPMENT

Given the diversity and variability that exist in children, families, and their environments, the best way to study and understand children and their development is to focus specifically on this diversity. Thus, development can be best viewed from a **transactional perspective,** which holds that development occurs as the result of the interplay between the diversity of qualities individuals bring to their environments and the diversity of environments individuals experience. Development is a product of the continuous interactions between the child and his or her social context (Sameroff, 1989). Although it has long been recognized that children's environments significantly affect their development, equal emphasis must be given to the effects that children have on their environments.

An example of dynamic transactions between children and their environments is provided in Figure 1.5 (Sameroff, 1987). According to this model, a complicated childbirth may make a mother anxious and nervous about her fragile newborn child. The mother's anxiety during the first months of the infant's life may cause her to be uncertain and inappropriate

multiracial a term used to describe people who are of two or more races

transactional perspective the view that development occurs as the result of the interplay between the diversity of qualities individuals bring to their environments and the diversity of environments individuals experience

FIGURE 1.5

Example of Transactional Model

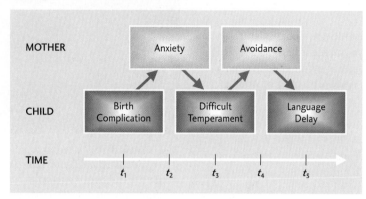

SOURCE: Sameroff, 1987 (p. 278). Copyright © 1987. This material is used by permission of John Wiley & Sons, Inc.

By considering this transactional model, you can see that the relationship between birth complications and language delay is more complex than it appears. The model depicts different transactions that may occur between birth and the subsequent delay of language.

in her interactions with the infant. In response to such inconsistency, the infant may develop some irregularities in feeding and sleeping patterns. These irregularities might decrease the pleasure the mother obtains from the relationship and, as a result, cause her to spend less time with her infant. One outcome of her withdrawal may be that the infant is exposed to less language, which hinders the acquisition of language. In this example, the developmental outcome (delayed language of the child) is not caused by the complicated birth or by the mother's subsequent anxiety; the most direct cause is the mother's avoidance. But you can see from this example that such a conclusion would be a serious oversimplification of a complex sequence of transactions that occurred over time.

Our understanding of the complex interaction of individuals and their environments is still rudimentary (Bronfenbrenner & Ceci, 1994), but the diversity of individual and environmental factors makes it likely that development is multiply determined. No single influence determines the outcomes of development, and similar developmental outcomes can be produced in a variety of ways. Additionally, individual and environmental factors, and their interaction, change as children mature. For example, the interactions of infants and their environments are qualitatively different depending on whether or not the infant has developed the ability to crawl or walk (Campos, Kermoian, & Zumbahlen, 1992). The ability to crawl or walk creates a sense of control, as well as increasing the risk of falling and getting hurt. Thus, infants who can move about their environments have different experiences than those who cannot.

Because the transactional model emphasizes the divergent nature of development, it leads us to expect that parents belonging to a particular ethnic or cultural group share beliefs and practices that overlap with, but differ in some respects from, those of parents from other cultures. Thus, children in minority families might be exposed to caregiving environments characterized by unique cultural beliefs and caregiving practices that differ from those of the Caucasian American culture. For example, Hispanic mothers engage in predominantly nonverbal interactions with their infants, whereas Caucasian American mothers engage in more verbally oriented interactions (Hurtado, 1995). Whereas Caucasian American mothers are likely to emphasize parenting goals that relate to the development of children's confidence and independence, Hispanic mothers are more likely to value parenting goals that emphasize respectful, obedient behavior (Harwood et al., 1996). These differences reflect the fact that parental belief systems are influenced by cultural values regarding what constitutes desirable behavior.

Differences in parental beliefs also are found in other cultures. For example, the Digo and Kikuyu are two East African cultures that have different beliefs about infant capacities (DeVries & Sameroff, 1984). The Digo believe that infants can learn within a few months after birth, and they begin to teach their infants at that time. The Kikuyu, in contrast, believe that serious education is not possible before the second year of life, and they delay education until that time. Thus, caregivers from different cultures and subcultures have different beliefs, goals, reactions, and expectations about their children, and these beliefs uniquely influence children's development.

Understanding the complexity of issues related to children's development also has important implications for social policy. Individuals concerned about children's welfare and well being can make a difference by formulating and influencing policies that affect children's development. For example, in the United States, nearly 60,000 children have been adopted from foreign countries since 1992, and the number of adoptions increases annually by about 18 percent. Many of these children come from countries where they were institutionalized for at least eight months and where they likely experienced some combination of adverse conditions and malnutrition (Johnson, 2001; US State Department, 2000). Many of these children reach their adoptive families in poor medical health and with varying degrees of developmental problems. Despite these experiences and problems, many internationally adopted children make excellent progress. Unfortunately, many do not. To address this issue, developmental scientists have begun to focus their studies on the factors that make a difference in these children's lives (Gunnar, Bruce, & Grotevant, 2000). Their research is resulting in important findings that are relevant for policies related to international adoptions. For example, their research points to the need for these children and families to have access to psychological and health services both before and after adoption. However, internationally adopted children are not eligible for federal funding to subsidize the cost of these services. Thus, the adoptive parents of internationally adopted children must rely on personal funds and private health insurance, which may be limited. Individuals interested in improving outcomes for these children and families can use research findings to advocate for removal of the barriers to obtaining these much needed services.

In this book, you will learn about the complex mechanisms, patterns, and issues related to child and adolescent development. For organizational and presentational effectiveness, the chapters are broken into the domains of physical, cognitive, and social-emotional development. These developmental domains are, however, intimately interrelated; that is, children's development consists of a process of continuous interaction among all three domains.

Throughout the book, we focus on the transactions that children have with their environments. We include a wide variety of transactions, ranging from close interactions with other people to the impact of broad influences such as schools, neighborhoods, and culture. Implicit in these discussions is our emphasis on the role that human relationships play in influencing development. It is through their relationships that children develop and learn about themselves.

Finally, although we emphasize the scientific study of child development, the study of how children develop also is influenced by values and goals. Researchers, caregivers, communities, and societies observe, interpret, and respond to developmental processes according to their values and goals (Fabes, Martin, & Smith, 1994). You are encouraged to analyze the facts and issues of child and adolescent development in terms of your own life and values. By doing so, you will find the study of child development more meaningful and interesting. The information in this book will help you make better-informed decisions about issues related to children and their development and, it is hoped, will foster your development of caring attitudes and behaviors.

TRY IT OUT
Activities Relating to Child Development

1. Interview your parents, uncles, aunts, or grandparents about their childhoods. Compare their development to your own, and identify differences and similarities in the factors, environments, and relationships that likely influenced their and your development. What historical, social, cultural, and individual factors might account for some of the differences?

2. Which do you believe is the more important influence on children's development—nature or nurture? Why? What might be some developmental examples of the interplay between genes and environment?

3. Gather information on children and families in another historical era or country or in a religious or ethnic group different from your own. Identify differences in values, customs, and beliefs about children and childrearing. How might these differences influence the children's development?

SUM IT UP

What is child development?

✦ Child development involves changes in characteristics and behavior, from conception through adolescence.

What are some critical issues in the study of child development?

✦ Child development is a continuous, complex process influenced by a variety of mechanisms. The extent to which these mechanisms reflect biological versus environmental effects is the subject of a debate central to the study of development.

✦ Adoption, twin, and case studies have been used to examine influences on child development. Although fascinating, these cases point out the difficulty of separating biological and environmental influences on development.

✦ Recent evidence suggests that development consists of both gradual and sudden changes over time.

✦ The notion of critical periods implies that a specific event must occur at a specific point if development is to proceed normally. The concept of sensitive periods provides a more flexible view of development.

✦ The study of child development includes investigating how individuals come to be different from one another and the stability of these differences.

What are the historical roots of the study of child development?

✦ The science of child development is only about 100 years old.

✦ Children of antiquity were viewed as helpless and incapable of caring for themselves. Plato believed that most parents were too corrupt to care for their children and advocated state control of child rearing.

✦ In the Middle Ages, there was no concept of childhood separate from adulthood. Children were viewed as miniature adults.

✦ John Locke and Jean-Jacques Rousseau described how early experiences influence later development. Their views differed as to whether nature (Locke's *tabula rasa*) or nurture (Rous-

seau's "innate morality") was the more important influence on development.

✦ By tying development to the evolution of the species, Charles Darwin changed the way scientists thought about development.

✦ G. Stanley Hall was a pioneer in the scientific study of development and adolescence.

What changes in contemporary American life influence the study of child development?

✦ The percentage of people living in traditional nuclear families has decreased, whereas the number of people living in alternative types of families (stepfamilies, extended families) has increased.

✦ The number of children growing up in gay and lesbian households has increased. Research finds no differences between these children and those raised in heterosexual households.

✦ Because of immigration, the US population is more racially and ethnically diverse than ever before, and this trend will continue. By 2050, Caucasian Americans will represent only a slight majority.

✦ Understanding the role of diversity in the US population is complicated by changing terminology, variation among and within ethnic and racial groups, and the lack of theories relevant to minority groups.

Can we capture the diversity of children's development?

✦ Development can best be viewed from a transactional perspective, emphasizing the interplay between the qualities children bring to their environments and the environments they experience.

✦ The emphasis on understanding development in the context of human relationships reflects the belief that children learn about themselves through their relationships with others.

✦ Recognizing your own goals and values makes the study of child development and its application more meaningful.

KEY TERMS and CONCEPTS

blended family (*14*)
child development (*4*)
cognitive development (*4*)
critical periods (*9*)
developmental domains (*4*)
dizygotic (DZ) twins (*8*)
ethnicity (*18*)
extended family (*14*)
heritability (*8*)

learning (*5*)
maturation (*5*)
monozygotic (MZ) twins (*8*)
multiracial (*21*)
natural selection (*13*)
nature versus nurture debate (*5*)
nuclear family (*14*)
personality (*7*)
physical development (*4*)

race (*18*)
sensitive periods (*10*)
single-parent family (*14*)
social-emotional development (*4*)
socialization (*5*)
stepfamily (*14*)
transactional perspective (*21*)

Understanding Development

CHAPTER 2

CHAPTER OUTLINE

✦ How Do Theories Explain Child Development?

✦ What Are the Major Biology-Based Theories of Child Development?

✦ What Are the Major Psychoanalytic Theories of Child Development?

✦ What Are the Major Environment-Based Theories of Child Development?

✦ What Are the Major Cognition-Based Theories of Child Development?

✦ What Are the Major Contextual Theories of Child Development?

✦ How Is Child Development Studied?

People frequently wonder about the causes of their own and others' behavior. As you learned in Chapter 1, questions about the origins of behavior have long fascinated developmental scientists. To what extent is our behavior due to biological factors or to the ways we are raised in our families? Can a poor family environment be overcome by positive experiences with friends and in school? To design studies about development, developmental scientists formulate theories about the causes of behavior.

HOW DO THEORIES EXPLAIN CHILD DEVELOPMENT

Babies delivered by cocaine-addicted mothers are exposed to drugs before they are born. They are likely to be raised in disorganized homes with drug-abusing parents who probably will not have the ability to provide them with warmth, shelter, food, and nurturance. What is the best way to improve the lives of these children? Are these infants' brains permanently damaged by drug exposure during critical periods of development? Should children born in this situation be taken away from their mothers? Should the children receive social support within their families to help them overcome the problems of being raised in a disadvantaged environment? Think about your response to the problem of how to improve crack babies' lives. What would you do first? What priorities would you set for providing support for these children?

Theories of child development help developmental scientists decide what to focus on when they study or work with children. Each theory provides a framework for investigating development and suggests the factors that are the most central in the investigation. Recall from Chapter 1 the story of Victor, the Wild Boy of Aveyron. Faced with the challenge of explaining and treating the Wild Boy's behavior, Itard relied on a theory for guidance. Itard believed that development is shaped by the environment and that Victor's savage behavior was due to the savage environment he grew up in. Without a theory, Itard would have had no way to explain what caused Victor's behavior, nor would he have been able to plan ways to help Victor become civilized. Theories are important because they provide the tools researchers need to organize and understand the complexities of development.

Theories are not just for researchers. In everyday life, people develop implicit theories to help them understand and explain other people's behavior. For instance, people all over the United States have tried to understand why people like Timothy McVeigh (see Chapter 1) commit terroristic acts or why school children murder other children. These personal theories influence interactions with others and guide major decisions that people make in their everyday lives.

SCIENTIFIC THEORIES

The implicit theories that we use every day are simply smaller versions of the formal theories that scientists use. Some people believe that scientific theories are elaborate ideas developed with little relevance to the real world. But this belief is wrong—theories are the backbone of developmental research and are very much connected to the real world. A scientific **theory** is a structured set of ideas that attempts to organize and explain facts. In contrast, a **fact** is a statement, based on observation, with which many people would agree (Miller, 1993). Facts may be single observations or summaries of many observations. For instance, your height is a fact with which any physician would agree.

Theories organize and give meaning to facts by describing how they fit together. Theories also guide future research by suggesting which investigative leads scientists should pursue. As noted earlier, it is a fact that many unborn children are exposed to crack cocaine. Should scientists focus their research on the effects of the drug on the child or on the child's later experiences in a drug-abusing family? Research based on biological theories might assess how biochemical changes associated with drugs influence development (Holzman & Paneth, 1994). Research based on environmental theories might focus on the stressful

theory a structured set of ideas that attempts to organize and explain facts

fact a statement, based on observation, with which many people would agree

TABLE 2.1

Categorization of Theories of Human Development

CATEGORY	DESCRIPTION	THEORIES INCLUDED
Biology-based theories	Emphasis on inherited biological factors and processes	Evolutionary theories Ethological theories Attachment theory Neurodevelopmental theories
Psychoanalytic theories	Emphasis on unconscious internal drives and interactions with others	Freud's psychosexual theory Erikson's psychosocial theory
Environment-based theories	Emphasis on the role of the external world	Classical conditioning Operant conditioning Social learning theory
Cognition-based theories	Emphasis on the role of cognition and processing of information	Piaget's theory Vygotsky's theory Information processing theory
Contextual theories	Emphasis on the interaction between individuals and their environments	Ecological theory Dynamic systems theory

conditions associated with living in drug-addicted families (Black et al., 1994). Both kinds of theories—biological and environmental—have proved important in understanding that early drug exposure does not necessarily cause permanent, irreversible damage. We now know that supportive family environments can buffer children from the devastating effects of early drug exposure (Leventhal et al., 1997).

Different theories provide different frames of reference for interpreting facts, and there is a tendency to interpret facts in ways that fit the theory. As you will soon learn, there are many theories of human development, each of which presents a unique perspective on development. Because human behavior is so complex, it is unlikely that any single theory will be able to explain all behavior (Miller, 1993).

EVALUATING THEORIES OF DEVELOPMENT

Developmental scientists consider whether a theory explains the available facts about the real world of child development. The more facts it explains, the better the theory is. A good theory also is understandable, predicts future events, provides practical guidance, and stimulates new knowledge. A good theory is **empirically based,** meaning that it is based on observation and experimentation. Thus, a good theory is testable—researchers are able to determine whether its propositions are correct. If a theory is untestable, its usefulness and accuracy cannot be determined (Thomas, 1996).

Theories of development can be distinguished from one another in terms of their perspective on the developmental issues discussed in Chapter 1 (such as nature versus nurture and continuity versus discontinuity). The major theories and approaches used to study child development are categorized in terms of these issues in Table 2.1 and in the following sections.

WHAT ARE THE MAJOR BIOLOGY-BASED THEORIES OF CHILD DEVELOPMENT?

Many theories focus on the biological factors that underlie development—including both evolutionary processes and physiological development, such as the functioning of

empirically based based on observation and experimentation

F IGURE 2.1
Infant and Adult Faces

Notice how infants of many different species have similar facial features, such as a small nose, a large forehead, and big eyes. Ethologists believe that these features are cues that evolved to elicit caregiving behavior from parents. These facial features make infants appear lovable and attractive to caregivers.

evolutionary theories
explanations of development that focus on how behaviors promote the survival of the individual and the species

ethological theory explanation of development that focuses on the causes and adaptive value of behavior, considering both the evolutionary history of the species and the social context

the brain. Biology-based theories assume that powerful organic or inherited forces influence behavior.

EVOLUTIONARY THEORIES

As you learned in Chapter 1, Darwin's theory of evolution is based on the idea that individuals who have characteristics that promote survival and reproduction are more likely to pass these characteristics on to future generations. For instance, early primates who had physical characteristics such as opposable thumbs and an upright stance had increased chances of surviving because they were better able to adapt to their environment and gather food than individuals without those characteristics. Likewise, the ability to communicate, reason, and cooperate increased their chances for survival. Thus, the capacities for social behavior and reasoning, along with physical characteristics, underwent natural selection (Darwin, 1877).

Today, **evolutionary theories** influence many areas of research on development, including studies of social behavior and mate selection (Buss, 1998). In these studies, researchers focus on the behaviors they believe promote the survival of the species. Likewise, evolutionary developmental theorists consider the aspects of child development that promote survival (Bjorklund & Pellegrini, 2000; Geary & Bjorklund, 2000). For instance, evolutionary developmental theorists speculate that the limited capacity of children's memory is advantageous for language acquisition because it helps children focus on the most essential features of language. Computer simulations of language learning confirm this speculation (Elman, 1991; Newport, 1994). Furthermore, evolutionary theorists explain children's play activities, aggression, and lack of inhibition by focusing on the survival value each has (Bjorklund & Pellegrini, 2000).

ETHOLOGICAL THEORY

Ethological theory, derived from Darwin's ideas about evolution, focuses on the causes and adaptive value of behavior, considering both the evolutionary history of the species and the social context. Ethologists have been influential in proposing that there are critical periods in development during which a specific type of learning occurs rapidly. For example, as you learned in Chapter 1, newborn ducklings have a critical period during which they learn to follow the first moving object they see. Because this object usually is their mother, this inherited tendency (called imprinting) increases their chances of survival.

Ethological research has focused on questions such as how adults become attached to infants, why infants prefer to look at human faces, and how facial expressions communicate emotions and intentions. For instance, developmental ethologists are concerned with why infants of many different species have similar facial features, such as a small nose, a large forehead, and big eyes (see Figure 2.1). Ethologists proposed that these features are visual cues that have evolved to elicit caregiving behavior from parents. Research has confirmed

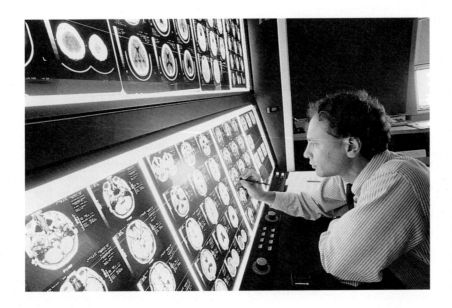

Neurodevelopmental theories focus on how the brain influences behavior and development. These theories also emphasize the importance of early experience and how early experiences influence the organization and functioning of the brain.

this idea with respect to human infants (Zebrowitz, Kendall-Tackett, & Fafel, 1991); even adults who have a "baby face" are perceived by others as being more childlike in their behavior (Zebrowitz & Montepare, 1992).

ATTACHMENT THEORY

Based on ethological principles, John Bowlby (1907–1990) developed an influential theory about the importance of early relationships for the developing child. According to Bowlby's **attachment theory,** all children become emotionally attached to their caregivers, regardless of the treatment they receive from them. Attachments form as infants give cues to which caregivers respond, increasing the likelihood of infant survival.

Research today focuses on the quality of the attachment that forms. Over the first few years of life, children develop inner working models about themselves and others, based on the kind of care they have received. For example, a child who receives sensitive and consistent caregiving comes to view himself or herself as worthy. Children's inner working models become internalized views or expectations about relationships with others and provide a basic roadmap for subsequent interactions with people (Crittenden & Claussen, 2000).

Recent research on attachment theory supports the idea that inner working models are influential in later development. Infants who have strong emotional ties with their caregivers are more likely than other children to explore their environments readily, to maintain contact with their caregivers, to become independent, and to have good self-esteem (Thompson, 1998). Researchers also are exploring how these early attachments influence dating, marriage, friendships, and parenting later in life (Crowell & Treboux, 2001).

NEURODEVELOPMENTAL APPROACHES

Neurodevelopmental approaches to the study of development focus on the relationship of brain development to behavior and thinking. How the brain develops and how the different parts of the brain function provide a broad basis for understanding how biology and environment both contribute to development. Studies of brain development point to the importance of the early years of children's lives (MacLean, 1985). For instance, early in development, the brain depends on environmental input to fine-tune itself so that it is maximally sensitive to its environment (Jacobs, 1997). That is, the kinds of experiences a child has help to determine the patterns of connections in the brain (Elbert, Heim, & Rockstroh,

attachment theory explanation of development that focuses on the quality of the early emotional relationships developed between children and their caregivers

neurodevelopmental approaches explanations of development that focus on the relationship of brain development to behavior and thinking

2001). Early experiences, then, have a crucial role in determining how the brain wires itself, which in turn influences how the individual later responds to stimuli.

WHAT ARE THE MAJOR PSYCHOANALYTIC THEORIES OF CHILD DEVELOPMENT?

Psychoanalytic theories of development have their origins in the belief that the most important causes of behavior are rooted in the unconscious drives and forces that develop within the mind of an individual. Although today psychoanalytic theories are not often used to guide research, they continue to influence the ways people think about human behavior. Freudian notions underlie much of the thinking about developmental issues.

FREUD'S PSYCHOSEXUAL THEORY

Sigmund Freud (1856–1939) was a physician whose training stressed biological determinism—the view that all human activity has biological or neurological causes. Freud also was influenced by Darwin's theory of evolution and Newton's law of physics (that energy cannot be created or destroyed). These influences led Freud to postulate that human behavior arises from the dynamic, internal energy that is the result of our evolutionary heritage (Green, 1989). Freud called this fixed pool of energy the **libido**—the source of action and sexual desire.

According to Freud, the human personality, or psyche, consists of three structures: the id, the ego, and the superego. The **id** represents the primitive and instinctual components of the psyche that are unconscious, irrational, and uncontrolled. The id is driven by the pleasure principle—it seeks immediate gratification and avoids pain and distress (Freud, 1923/1960). Because the demands of the id are irrational, they often do not match what the environment provides. For example, because infants cannot feed themselves when they become hungry, immediate gratification may not be available. Infants may seek gratification by crying, sucking, and maybe even hallucinating. However, the reality of the world eventually forces changes in the id. It transforms a portion of itself into a new personality structure—the ego.

The **ego** is the source of reason and operates according to the reality principle, which is based on the conditions and demands of the real world. The ego seeks to fulfill the demands of the id in ways that are acceptable to society. The ego does not, however, represent an internalized set of social rules. This aspect of the psyche develops out of the ego and becomes the superego.

The **superego,** which represents one's conscience and morals and social conventions, demands strict adherence with cultural expectations. When its demands are disobeyed, the superego punishes the individual by producing guilt, shame, and fear.

An individual's behavior depends on the dynamic interactions of these three structures. The ego continually negotiates settlements between the demands of the id and the constraints of the superego.

Freud's theory of **psychosexual development** is a stage theory of development, based on how the libido is transformed into different structures and modes of expression (see Table 2.2). During each stage, the increased sensitivity of a particular area of the body makes it an erogenous zone where libidinal energy is invested and pleasure is experienced (Freud, 1920/1965). Different erogenous zones are activated over the course of development as the child's genetic blueprint unfolds.

The ideas put forth by Freud on the importance of early development and the role that parents play in influencing children's personalities have become ingrained in our culture. One of his most enduring contributions is his concept of the unconscious—the idea that there are influences on our behavior of which we generally are not aware. His notion that there are defense mechanisms—such as repression and projection—that protect

psychoanalytic theories explanations of development that focus on the unconscious drives and forces that develop within the mind

libido the source of action and sexual desire

id the part of the psyche that is primitive and instinctual

ego the part of the psyche that is the source of reason and operates within the conditions and demands of the real world

superego the part of the psyche that represents one's conscience and morals and social conventions

psychosexual development Freud's stage theory of development, based on how the libido is transformed into different structures and modes of expression

TABLE 2.2

Freud's Theory of Psychosexual Development

STAGE	AGES	PSYCHIC DEVELOPMENT
Oral	Birth–1 year	Id is the only psychic structure operating. Pleasure principle operates unconsciously. Erogenous zone is the mouth.
Anal	1–3 years	Ego develops as the result of conflicts with the social world. Reality principle operates. Erogenous zone is the anus.
Phallic	3–6 years	Superego develops as the result of the conflict over the sexual desire for the opposite-sex parent and the rivalry of the same-sex parent. Erogenous zone is the genital region.
Latency	6 years–puberty	Libido becomes dormant. Focus is on the development of skills necessary for adult functioning. There is no particular erogenous zone.
Genital	Puberty–adulthood	Focus is on mature sexual functioning and reproduction. Erogenous zone is the genital area.

individuals from anxiety and fear also has become widely accepted. His belief that early experiences and patterns of social interactions can produce mental illness led him to develop psychoanalysis—a form of therapy designed to help individuals recover their memories of the early interactions that have influenced their behavior.

Notwithstanding the contributions, there are serious problems with Freud's theory. The most important criticism is that the theory is not based on solid scientific evidence. In fact, although Freud proposed a developmental theory, he never really studied children; he obtained his evidence from his patients' recollections, during psychoanalysis, of their childhoods. Furthermore, many aspects of Freud's theory are unmeasurable and therefore untestable—how does one measure libidinal energy or identify the source of the superego? Inherent in Freud's discussion of the libido and its source of gratification is the notion that infants and young children are sexual beings and derive erotic pleasure from their interactions. This notion was (and still is) very controversial. Freud developed his theory during a period in history when society was very restrictive in its views about sexuality. Other Freudian concepts reflect cultural biases, such as the implication that male sexuality has a superiority that makes it a source of envy and jealousy for females (Horney, 1967).

ERIKSON'S PSYCHOSOCIAL THEORY

Erik Erikson (1902–1994) was a German-born psychoanalyst who extended and refined Freud's theory of development. Erikson accepted Freud's theory of psychosexual development but believed that, for several reasons, it was incomplete:

◆ It gave too little recognition to social and cultural influences.
◆ It failed to recognize developmental changes beyond adolescence.
◆ It did not give enough emphasis to ego development.
◆ It focused primarily on the development of neurotic and maladaptive behavior and did not give enough consideration to *healthy* development.

Sigmund Freud developed a psychosexual theory of development based on the idea that internal forces and energy play an important role in development. What contributions has Freud's theory made to today's thinking about child development?

TABLE 2.3
Erikson's Psychosocial Theory of Development

STAGE (CRISIS)	RESULTS OF POSITIVE RESOLUTION OF CRISIS	AGES
Trust vs. Mistrust	Ability to predict and depend on one's own behavior and the behavior of others	0–1 year
Autonomy vs. Shame/Doubt	Ability to do things for oneself	2–3 years
Initiative vs. Guilt	High and realistic sense of ambition and independence	3–6 years
Industry vs. Inferiority	Active and satisfying involvement in activities	7–12 years
Identity vs. Identity Diffusion	Determination of one's identity	12–18 years
Intimacy vs. Isolation	Ability to commit to another and establish a close, loving relationship	20s
Generativity vs. Stagnation	Incorporation of the needs of others into one's personal life	20s–50s
Integrity vs. Despair	Healthy adjustment to aging and mortality	50s and beyond

SOURCE: Adapted from Erikson, 1959.

Erikson argued that, during development, individuals go through a series of eight **psychosocial crises** that reflect a struggle between two conflicting personality characteristics. These crises represent critical periods in personality development (Erikson, 1968). The sequence and type of crisis at each stage are fixed; individuals can do nothing to prevent a crisis from occurring or to change or speed up the sequence of crises. Erikson believed, however, that these crises manifest themselves differently from person to person. For example, although all infants experience the natural conflict between Trust and Mistrust during the first year of life, individual circumstances affect the outcome of the crisis. Imagine how differently trust is experienced by an infant who has warm clothing and adequate food and by an infant who is left alone for hours with only a bottle or who is constantly hungry and ignored by caregivers. Thus, the levels of attention given to infants may affect their development of basic trust (Wallerstein & Goldberger, 1998). What kind of trust did Victor, the Wild Boy, develop when he was abandoned at a young age? What kind of autonomy did he develop?

Erikson's major contribution was the detailed definitions he provided of psychosocial stages and the crisis associated with each stage, shown in Table 2.3. In addition, Erikson recognized cultural differences (Erikson, 1963) and contributed significantly to the study of adolescence, especially the process by which adolescents form personal identities (Erikson, 1968). Unfortunately, though, apart from research on adolescent identity, there is little research on childhood and adult psychosocial crises. Moreover, many of Erikson's theoretical propositions, like other psychoanalytic ideas, are difficult, if not impossible, to test (Green, 1989).

WHAT ARE THE MAJOR ENVIRONMENT-BASED THEORIES OF CHILD DEVELOPMENT?

Environment-based theories maintain that the environment in which people live and the experiences they have are major determinants of behavior. According to this view, people are relatively passive in responding to the environments they are exposed to during their lives. Behavioral changes occur only when the environment is changed. Environment-based studies focus on factors that determine how behavior changes in response to everyday events.

CLASSICAL CONDITIONING

Ivan Pavlov (1849–1936), a Russian physiologist, was the founder of modern learning theory. While studying dogs' digestive systems, he made an important accidental discovery. When

psychosocial crises in Erikson's lifespan theory, the struggles that occur at the various stages of development between two conflicting personality characteristics

food was placed on a dog's tongue, the dog salivated as a reflex response to the food. Pavlov noticed that, after a while, dogs also salivated when they saw the food coming. For this to happen, the dogs must have learned to associate the sight of food with the taste of the food. Thus, they learned a conditioned response to a previously neutral stimulus. Many people have noticed a similar pattern of conditioning in their pets—cats often come running at the sound of a can opener because they have associated the sound of the can opener with food (Crain, 1992).

In Pavlov's studies, the typical **classical conditioning** procedure was to present, over several trials, a *conditioned stimulus*—for example, a bright light—paired with an unconditioned stimulus, such as food. The food is an *unconditioned stimulus* because it automatically elicits a response, the *unconditioned response* of salivation. The light begins as a neutral stimulus, but with repeated pairings the dog learns to associate it with the food, thereby producing a *conditioned response*—salivating at the sight of the light (Kehoe & Macrae, 1998).

The principles of classical conditioning were first applied to humans by John Watson (1878–1958). Watson argued that infants naturally respond with fear to only two events: suddenly losing support (fear of falling) and sudden loud noises. How, then, do children develop fear of snakes or dogs or the dark? Freud would have argued that a child's fear of snakes reflects his or her repressed, unconscious drives and instincts. For Watson, the answer was that children learn to be fearful through classical conditioning.

To test this idea, Watson and colleagues conditioned an 11-month-old boy named Albert to fear a white rat (Watson & Raynor, 1920). At first, Albert was not afraid of the rat. But then Albert was shown the rat while a loud noise was made. After four pairings, Albert was shown the rat by itself, and he whimpered and withdrew from it. A few days later, Albert was tested to see whether he had generalized his fear to other objects or animals. He had indeed become fearful of all kinds of furry animals and objects such as rabbits and fur coats (Crain, 1992). Classical conditioning can thus be used to explain children's development of common fears such as that of going to visit the doctor (see Figure 2.2).

Watson also found a method to decondition fears. He used *systematic desensitization* to decondition the fears of a young child named Peter. Peter was afraid of many animals, furry things, and mechanical objects. When Peter was relaxed and eating in his highchair, Watson would bring in a caged animal and leave it visible in the distance. The animal was gradually brought closer, allowing Peter to associate the pleasant feelings of eating with the presence of the animal. Over repeated and gradual exposures, Peter eventually lost his fear of the animal.

OPERANT CONDITIONING

B. F. Skinner (1905–1990) was concerned with how the environment shapes people's behaviors. **Operant conditioning** focuses on how the consequences of a behavior affect the likelihood that the behavior will be repeated. For instance, if an infant is praised when he or she takes a first step, the infant will be more motivated to take another step.

The principles of operant conditioning have been studied extensively and applied effectively to many kinds of human behavior. Behavior is more likely to occur after the presentation of **positive reinforcement** (such as food or praise). Behavior also is more likely to occur with **negative reinforcement,** which consists of removing a negative, or aversive, condition. Seat belt alarms are an example of an effective negative reinforcer: Once the seat belt is hooked, the annoying buzzing stops, thereby increasing the chances that one will use seat belts in the future.

In contrast, **punishment** is the application of unpleasant consequences to decrease the likelihood that a behavior will be repeated. Some parents use scolding or spanking as punishment, in the hope that these consequences will reduce undesirable behaviors. Punishment also may take the form of extra work, revoking privileges, or disapproval. Studies show, however, that punishment often is effective for only a short time and may have unintended negative side effects (such as increasing anxiety and timidity). A more effective strategy for reducing unwanted behavior may be **extinction,** in which all positive consequences are withheld (Crain, 1992).

Have you ever wondered how animals in the movies or on television learn to do difficult routines on cue? The answer lies in the fact that animal trainers use the principles of

B. F. Skinner theorized that behaviors are conditioned as the result of the consequences associated with a particular behavior. His model of operant conditioning was extremely influential in identifying the environmental factors that control and modify behavior. Can you describe the operant processes through which such environmental factors influence behavior and development?

classical conditioning
Pavlov's theory of how responses to neutral stimuli become conditioned

operant conditioning
learning based on the principle that the consequences of a behavior affect the likelihood that the behavior will be repeated

positive reinforcement presentation of stimuli that increase the likelihood that a behavior will recur

negative reinforcement removal of a negative or aversive stimulus, which increases the likelihood that a behavior will recur

punishment application of unpleasant consequences to decrease the likelihood that a behavior will be repeated

extinction reducing unwanted behavior by withholding all positive consequences

IGURE 2.2

An Example of Classical Conditioning

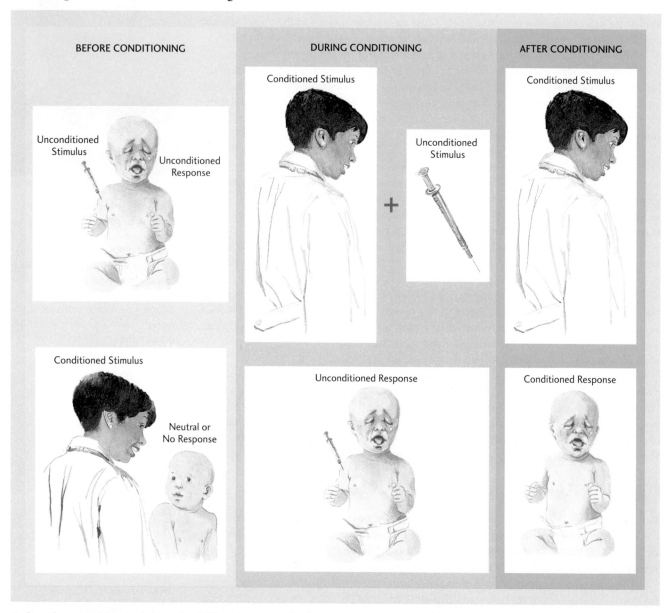

At first, the pain of the vaccination the child receives naturally elicits crying, but the sight of the doctor does not. After the child associates the doctor with the vaccination, the sight of the doctor elicits fear and crying. Thus, the child is classically conditioned to fear the doctor. Using classical conditioning principles, how might you recondition and eliminate the child's fear of the doctor?

shaping the process of rewarding behaviors that approximate the desired behavior

operant conditioning to train them. Complex strings of behaviors are learned through **shaping**—a process of rewarding behaviors that approximate the desired behavior. A small step toward a larger goal is rewarded a few times, and then the next step is rewarded. For example, getting children to put their toys away can be shaped by rewarding them first when they approach the toys, then when they pick them up, and then when they attempt to put them away (Green, 1989). Similarly, animals are rewarded for performing small tasks, which are eventually developed into a complex string of behaviors.

SOCIAL LEARNING THEORY

Four-year-old Todd watches as his friend Ian puts on high heels and a fancy dress. Several children begin to comment about Ian's appearance, telling him he shouldn't dress up in girls' clothes. They tease him and won't play with him for the rest of the day.

In this story, Ian may have learned a hard lesson; the consequences of dressing in girls' clothing can be severe, and he may be unlikely to do it again in the future. But what does Todd learn from observing Ian? Does Todd need to experience the teasing to recognize that putting on "girls' clothes" might lead to negative consequences? According to Albert Bandura (1925–present), much of children's learning occurs by watching the consequences that others experience for their behaviors, through a process called **vicarious reinforcement.** From his observation of Ian, Todd learns that boys shouldn't dress up in girls' clothes. Knowledge of response consequences guides children's and adults' future behavioral choices (Bandura, 1977).

Bandura's **social learning theory** is based on his idea that individuals are greatly influenced by other people. In addition to being influenced by vicarious reinforcement, Bandura believes that children and adults imitate, or model, the behavior of other people. Through *modeling,* individuals learn new behaviors, the contexts appropriate for those behaviors, and their consequences. Consider how children often mimic the behaviors of superheroes from movies and television. How are they able to do this?

Four processes are involved in modeling the behavior of others:

- ✦ **Attention.**   A child must pay attention to models to be able to imitate their behavior. The models most likely to capture attention are those with power, prestige, or charisma.
- ✦ **Retention.**   To imitate another person's behavior later on, a child must have a way to represent the behavior in her or his memory so that it can be retrieved when necessary.
- ✦ **Motor reproduction.**   To successfully reproduce another's behavior, a child must have the motor control or abilities to carry out the action. Imitation provides the pattern for a behavior but not the actual skill to accomplish it.
- ✦ **Reinforcement and motivation.**   Successful imitation requires that the behavior have the desired consequences, causing the child to want to repeat it.

Social learning theory often has been used to explain the impact of television on children's behavior. Popular television characters attract children's attention, and children may learn to act inappropriately by observing the behaviors of these powerful models (American Medical Association, 1996). Based on the four processes described above, what might be effective strategies for reducing children's modeling of inappropriate behavior? What might be effective strategies for increasing their modeling of positive behaviors?

WHAT ARE THE MAJOR COGNITION-BASED THEORIES OF CHILD DEVELOPMENT?

Cognition-based theories emphasize the role of mental processes such as memory, decision making, and information processing in influencing development. Studies of cognitive development focus on how thinking and reasoning change over time and the effects of these changes on development. Cognition-based theories assume that an essential feature of development is that individuals strive for greater understanding of the world around them.

PIAGET'S COGNITIVE DEVELOPMENTAL THEORY

Jean Piaget (1896–1980) was a Swiss scientist who became interested in the question of how we come to know and understand the world around us. While administering intelligence tests to French school children, Piaget noticed a pattern in the reasons children gave for

Imitation and modeling are powerful ways to learn or alter behavior. In this picture, the young sibling is trying to imitate the behavior of her older brother. What factors contribute to whether or not a child imitates or models someone else's behavior?

vicarious reinforcement
learning by watching the consequences to others of their behaviors

social learning theory
Bandura's theory that individuals are greatly influenced by observing and imitating other people

correct and incorrect answers on the tests. He speculated that children of different ages use different kinds of thought processes. Piaget also observed the development of his own children and became convinced that children's thinking is very different from that of adolescents and adults (Crain, 1992; Miller, 1993). This idea became the central tenet of his theory.

Piaget's View of Intelligence

Piaget defined intelligence as an active process in which people acquire information by interacting with objects, ideas, and other people. From these interactions, individuals develop better ways of adapting to life's challenges. According to Piaget, cognitive development is a process of developing the intellectual means to adapt to the environment (Langer & Killen, 1998).

When children interact with people and objects in the world, changes occur in their conceptions of the world. Children's abilities to interact with the environment are based on their **schemes**—cognitive guides, or blueprints, for processing information. A child gathers information about an object or person by applying a scheme and using it to sort and organize the information. The schemes that children use change over time. Infants use schemes, such as sucking and grasping, that are based on their senses. Young children use schemes that are based on the appearances of objects. As children grow older, they develop more complex and abstract schemes. For instance, a high school student may have a scheme for solving algebraic equations.

Changes occur rapidly when information is being processed about the world. For instance, an infant who first holds a rattle has to apply schemes to the rattle to try to solve the problem of what this object is. Children develop their problem-solving abilities through two continually occurring processes of adaptation: **assimilation,** or directly processing information that fits a scheme, and **accommodation,** or changing the scheme to fit the new information from the environment. For example, the infant holding a rattle for the first time may assimilate it into an existing scheme for smooth, round objects by sucking on it. He or she may then accommodate and develop a scheme for "rattle" after shaking it and realizing that some things make sounds when shaken. The interplay of assimilation and accommodation helps children adapt to their ever-changing environment (Piaget, 1952).

Piaget believed that intelligence undergoes dramatic changes over time. These changes are so clear-cut that Piaget referred to them as stages of cognitive development (see Table 2.4). Each stage is marked by specific types of thinking and problem solving that differ qualitatively from those of other stages. Furthermore, the stages are sequential and nonreversible—children do not return to earlier stages of thinking (Zigler & Gilman, 1998).

Piaget's Stages of Cognitive Development

Piaget's first stage, the **sensorimotor stage,** begins at birth and lasts until about 2 years of age. The sensorimotor child relates to objects and people through his or her senses and motor skills, hence the name of the stage. The means for interacting with objects are innate reflexive behaviors, such as sucking and grasping, that change as children gain experience. Give an infant a small block, for example, and he or she will try to suck it. Infants use sensorimotor schemes to allow them to learn about the qualities of objects—their shapes, textures, and tastes.

A major accomplishment of the child's first two years is coming to understand that objects continue to exist even when she or he cannot see them—the concept of *object permanence*. During the first two years of life, children also begin to show signs of purposeful behavior, and by the end of this time, they understand how to use symbols (such as language) to represent their thoughts.

The second stage in Piaget's theory, the **preoperational stage,** lasts from about 2 to 7 years of age. Preoperational children think in symbols, which permit more flexibility and planning in their problem solving. Preoperational children are egocentric in their thinking—they believe that everyone sees the world as they do. A child who hides only her

schemes cognitive guides, or blueprints, for processing information about the world

assimilation directly processing information that fits a scheme

accommodation changing a scheme to fit new information from the environment

sensorimotor stage Piaget's first stage of cognitive development (0 to 2 years), in which the child relates to objects and people through his or her senses and motor skills

preoperational stage Piaget's second stage of cognitive development (2 to 7 years), in which children begin to think in symbols but are egocentric and perceptually bound in their thinking

TABLE 2.4

Piaget's Stages of Cognitive Development

STAGE	APPROXIMATE AGES (IN YEARS)	MAJOR FEATURES
Sensorimotor stage	0–2	Motoric knowledge Lack of understanding that objects continue to exist when not in view Present orientation
Preoperational stage	2–7	Symbolic representation Planning Thinking and problem solving guided by perception and appearances Egocentric thinking
Concrete operational stage	7–11	Logic used in problem solving Logic applied only to concrete objects and events
Formal operational stage	11 and beyond	Logic applied to hypothetical and abstract problems Concern with concepts like justice, equality, and fairness

Vygotsky proposed a theory about the important role that social interactions and caregivers have in facilitating learning in their children. How do you think the father in this photograph is helping the son to put this puzzle together?

or his face behind a curtain and then yells, "Come and find me," is exhibiting egocentric thinking: If I can't see you, you can't see me! Preoperational children are fooled by the appearance of an object, and their thinking is based on that appearance. For example, to a preoperational child, a half pint of milk poured into a tall, thin glass is more than the same half pint poured into a short, wide glass.

The third stage, the **concrete operational stage,** lasts from 7 to about 11 years of age. The major accomplishment of this stage is using logic to solve problems. This basic logic involves understanding that things maintain their identity even though their outward appearance may be changed. For instance, a concrete operational child recognizes that a half pint of milk poured from a tall, thin glass into a short, wide one is still a half pint of fluid because nothing has been added or taken away.

The final stage of Piaget's theory, the **formal operational stage,** begins around the age of 11. The major accomplishment of this stage is applying the logical principles first used in the concrete operational stage to more hypothetical and abstract situations. Because of this newly attained level of understanding, older children and adolescents become interested in and concerned about broad social issues and abstract concepts such as justice, equality, and fairness (Zigler & Gilman, 1998).

Literally thousands of studies have been done to test Piaget's ideas. His theory also has been expanded and refined by others, labeled *neo-Piagetians.* Neo-Piagetians (Case & Edelstein, 1993; Fischer & Bidell, 1998) have proposed theories based on the idea of stages of cognitive development, but they give more emphasis than Piaget did to the way information is processed in the brain. For instance, Case argues that children's thinking is organized into central conceptual structures—networks of concepts that allow for thinking about a variety of situations (Case & Okamoto, 1996). These structures change during development with increasing connections between different parts of the brain, which, in turn, increase memory capacity.

VYGOTSKY'S THEORY OF COGNITIVE DEVELOPMENT

Lev Vygotsky (1896–1934) was a Russian psychologist whose work with children with disabilities gave him an interest in issues of development (Rieber & Hall, 1998). He proposed a theory of development based on the idea that children use psychological tools such as language, numbering systems, and maps to develop higher levels of thinking. Language is particularly important to development because it allows children to develop new ideas and to regulate their behavior. Vygotsky argued that people use language to engage in internal dialogues that help them solve difficult tasks. For instance, you may say to yourself that when you finish reading this section you will take a break. Through the self-direction of your internal dialogue, you continue reading, thereby regulating your behavior and promoting the learning of the material. Vygotsky regarded this internal, or private, speech as a critical element in cognitive development and learning.

More than Piaget, Vygotsky emphasized the influence of social interaction on development. A 3-year-old boy, for example, may be unable to discuss a trip he took to the zoo, but, given a series of prompts by his mother, he can describe the animals he saw and the foods he ate during his trip. The mother acts as a skilled helper in using language to describe experiences. Similarly, a teacher may provide the information and support a student needs to carry out long division. The distance between what a child can do unaided and what a child can do through interaction with skilled helpers is called the **zone of proximal development.** It is within this zone that a person's potential for new learning is strongest.

The idea that children learn through social interactions with skilled helpers suggests that everyday experiences play a crucial role in children's development. Through their routine interactions, caregivers and teachers provide meaningful assistance to children in developing cognitive, social, and emotional skills (Stringer, 1998). For instance, caregivers often describe problem-solving strategies to children to help them guide their own behavior. As they grow older, children repeat these guidance messages to themselves, out loud at first. These messages later become the silent inner speech that is used to guide behavior (Vygotsky, 1934/1986).

concrete operational stage Piaget's third stage of cognitive development (7 to 11 years), in which children begin to use logic to solve problems

formal operational stage Piaget's fourth stage of cognitive development (begins around the age of 11), in which individuals are capable of applying logical principles to hypothetical and abstract situations

zone of proximal development Vygotsky's term for the distance between what a child can do unaided and what a child can do through interaction with skilled helpers

INFORMATION PROCESSING THEORY

Can you remember learning to walk? Do you remember the first word you spoke? Most people cannot remember experiences from their early childhood. Why do we remember so little from our lives before the age of 5? This question is one of many that intrigue information processing theorists.

Studies of cognitive development have stimulated efforts to understand how people take in, remember, and use information from their experiences (Keil, 1998). **Information processing theory** is based on a model in which people have limited capacities for learning but can flexibly apply strategies to find ways around those limitations (Munakata, 1998; Siegler, 1996, 1998).

The human information processing model, shown in Figure 2.3, has three parts. The **sensory register** allows people to very briefly retain visual, auditory, and other information taken in through the senses. **Short-term memory** holds information long enough for the person to evaluate and selectively act on inputs. The capacity of short-term memory is limited: Only a few bits of information can be remembered (Bjorklund, 1995). **Long-term memory,** however, has an unlimited capacity for storing information over long periods of time. In long-term memory, information becomes linked to earlier memories, associations, and visual representations, creating networks that aid in recall. Individuals consciously link or classify ideas and use memory aids (such as rehearsal) to retrieve information.

Information processing theory has been particularly useful for understanding why children and adults remember information differently. For instance, 4-year-old children are less likely than adults to use memory aids and thus are less likely to process information so that it is retained in long-term memory. The theory also is helpful in understanding other changes, such as increased attention to relevant features, that occur in information processing as we grow older.

IGURE 2.3

Information Processing System

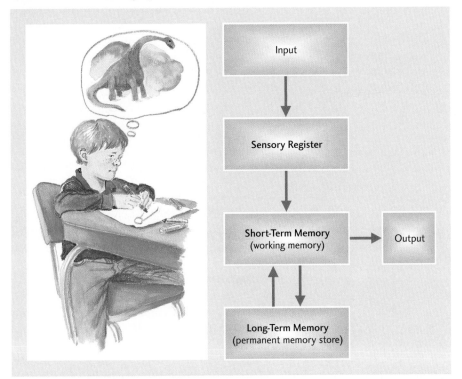

This diagram depicts the three parts of the information processing system. Can you explain what these parts are and how they work together?

information processing theory explanations for development that are based on a model in which people have limited capacities for learning but can flexibly apply strategies to find ways around those limitations

sensory register the part of the information processing system that allows people to very briefly retain information taken in through the senses

short-term memory the part of the information processing system that holds information long enough for the person to evaluate and selectively act on the input

long-term memory the part of the information processing system that has an unlimited capacity for storing information over long periods of time

WHAT ARE THE MAJOR CONTEXTUAL THEORIES OF CHILD DEVELOPMENT?

Contextual theories emphasize the interaction between the biological and environmental forces that influence behavior and development in particular contexts. Although these theories are diverse, each is based on the idea that, to truly understand child development, one must study children in their historical, social, and cultural contexts. Development occurs when a child acts within the environment to produce change.

BRONFENBRENNER'S ECOLOGICAL THEORY

What happens to children raised in neighborhoods with drive-by shootings, drug dealing, and poor access to health care? How do societal values influence children's development? Urie Bronfenbrenner (1917–present) used a concept from earth science—ecology—to outline the interplay between the child and his or her immediate social and physical environment. As shown in Figure 2.4, the child's experiences are viewed as subsystems within larger systems, or a set of nested structures (Bronfenbrenner, 1979).

FIGURE 2.4
Bronfenbrenner's Ecological Model

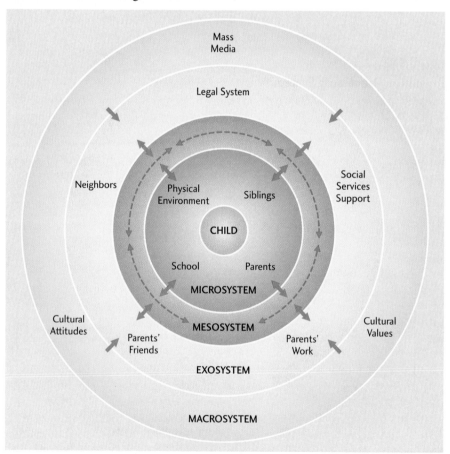

Notice that the different spheres contain different types of influences. Bronfenbrenner believed that these different levels of influence interact to affect a person's development and behavior. This model depicts the complexity of contextual theories of development.

The innermost circle in the **ecological model** in Figure 2.4 represents the child's **microsystem** (immediate environment) and includes influences such as physical objects (toys and technology), the structure of the environment, and the roles of and relationships among family members (Bronfenbrenner & Morris, 1998). This immediate environment has important effects on development. In a classic series of studies of the microsystem, Caldwell and colleagues (Bradley & Caldwell, 1976; Elardo, Bradley, & Caldwell, 1975) found that the quality of 6-month-old infants' physical and intellectual environments (such as the presence of appropriate play materials and opportunities for daily stimulation) related to their intellectual performance four years later. Similar results have been obtained in more recent studies (Brooks-Gunn, 1995).

The middle sphere of the ecological model is the **mesosystem,** which encompasses the connections among settings including the child and how these connections influence the child—for example, how a child's relationships at school affect her or his relationships with extended family members. In one of the first studies of mesosystem influences, it was found that children whose parents were actively involved in their hospital care were less emotionally distressed (both while in the hospital and at home up to a year later) than were children whose parents were allowed only brief visits (Prugh et al., 1953). Introducing people from one of the children's settings (the family) into another (the hospital) helped ease the transition between them.

The next circle, the **exosystem,** represents the linkages among settings, one of which does not include the child, and how these influence development. External settings include parents' social worlds, such as their employment, church attendance, and friends, and the physical environment beyond the immediate setting, such as neighborhood conditions. Researchers studying the exosystem have found, for instance, that children who live in violent neighborhoods have difficulty sleeping, have impaired cognitive performance, and often are aggressive, depressed, and fearful (Gorman-Smith & Tolan, 1998; Horn & Trickett, 1998). The outermost circle, the **macrosystem,** represents larger societal values, historical changes, and social policies (Bronfenbrenner, 1986).

Bronfenbrenner's ecological model is based on his assumption that the environment plays a decisive role in development. But the child and his or her environment are not separate. The child interacts with the environment of which he or she is a part, and these interactions are the engine of development (Bronfenbrenner & Evans, 2000; Bronfenbrenner & Morris, 1998). Children meet their environment most directly in everyday situations (micro- or mesosystem interactions), but these are embedded in the larger physical, social, and cultural contexts (the exosystem), which also affect their development (Magnusson, 1995).

DYNAMIC SYSTEMS THEORY

One of the newest theories in the study of development is **dynamic systems theory** (Thelen & Smith, 1998). The basic ideas of dynamic systems come from research done outside of the social sciences, largely in physics and biology. Dynamic systems theorists assume that complex systems form from basic and simple conditions without requiring a master plan for development (Thelen & Smith, 1994, 1998). This is a new way of thinking about development. Rather than unfolding from a master plan coded by the genes, development is believed to involve self-organization, in which systems change as a result of their interactions. The individual parts of a system, called **control parameters,** interact in ways that eventually lead to advancement to a new level or a new form. Control parameters can include external as well as internal factors. In this way, dynamic systems theory emphasizes the strong interconnections between children and their environments.

Consider the development of walking as a dynamic system (see Figure 2.5). Walking is a motion of coordinated leg movements that is performed easily by most people. Walking also is highly variable and complex because it requires constant readjustments to allow for different surfaces and different speeds. How does a child develop these coordinated motions and learn to adjust them as needed? A child has acquired many components of walking before she or he actually walks—balance, coordination of the legs, stepping abilities, and leg strength. At

ecological model Bronfenbrenner's model of the different spheres of influence

microsystem the inner sphere of the ecological model, which represents the immediate environment and includes influences such as physical objects, the structure of the environment, and the roles of and relationships among family members

mesosystem the middle sphere of the ecological model, which encompasses the connections among settings including the child and how these connections influence the child

exosystem the part of the ecological model that represents the linkages among settings, one of which does not include the child, and how these influence development

macrosystem the outermost sphere of the ecological model, which represents societal values and attitudes

dynamic systems theory a theory based on the idea that complex systems form from basic and simple conditions without requiring a master plan for development

control parameters the individual parts of a dynamic system

FIGURE 2.5

A Dynamic Systems Model of Walking

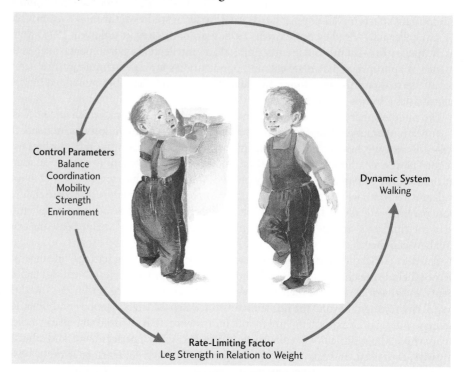

In this model, the different elements involved in walking are considered to be control parameters. The slowest-developing aspect is the rate-limiting component, which limits the speed at which the behavior is acquired. Once this aspect develops, the system evolves into a new form—walking.

some point, these separate pieces all come together and the child is able to propel herself or himself across the floor for a few steps, usually with great concentration and little grace.

The slowest, or last-developing, part of a system is called the **rate-limiting component;** when it develops, the system evolves into a new form (Thelen, 1989). For many chil-

Dynamic systems approaches are based on the idea that complex behaviors arise from simple components. What components are involved in a toddler's taking his or her first steps? How might these components vary from one child to another?

dren, the last part of the "walking puzzle," the rate-limiting component, is leg strength. When their legs develop adequate strength, balance improves, enabling them to shift their weight back and forth on one leg as they take a step. If assistance is provided to reduce the input of the rate-limiting (leg strength) component, such as by putting children into a walker, they can easily walk earlier than development normally would allow. Once children are walking unaided, practice at using all the parts of the system together leads to smoother and better performance. As you can see from this example, a new behavior—walking— emerges out of several different systems that eventually work together to produce this new ability. Later, with further adjustments and development of individual pieces of the motor system, brain, and body, the child will move to another new form—running.

Although the dynamic systems approach is based on ideas formed outside the developmental sciences, the theory fits very well with the idea that development involves transactional experiences, from which universal developmental domains are constructed (Horowitz, 2000).

HOW IS CHILD DEVELOPMENT STUDIED

Theories guide researchers by helping them to identify interesting and important questions. Once a question has been identified, scientists set out to answer it using a well-defined approach, called the scientific method.

Consider 4-year-old Bridget. She is a typical preschooler. Her best friend is Ivanna, and she seldom plays with boys. Bridget, like many other children, prefers to play with children who are the same sex as she. Scientists have been trying to discover why children prefer same-sex playmates (Maccoby, 1998; Martin, 1994; Martin & Fabes, 2001), but how do they investigate a question like this? Finding an answer requires application of scientific reasoning and use of the scientific method.

SCIENTIFIC REASONING AND THE SCIENTIFIC METHOD

Scientific reasoning is similar to good everyday problem solving. When you need to solve a problem, you apply logical reasoning to minimize the number of possible explanations, with the ultimate goal of finding one probable explanation (Overton, 1998). Scientific reasoning is designed to produce results that are objective (they are measurable and observable by others), reliable (they can be replicated repeatedly), and valid (they accurately describe the phenomenon in question).

To solve the many mysteries of child development, researchers use the scientific method. The scientific method involves four steps:

1. **Formulating a hypothesis.**   Through observation and study, a scientist develops an educated expectation, or hypothesis, about the phenomenon or behavior he or she is interested in.
2. **Designing a study.**   The scientist strategically designs a study that tests the hypothesis. The study may involve many different methods, such as structured interviews, observations, or experiments in the laboratory.
3. **Collecting evidence.**   The scientist uses the strategy that he or she has designed to collect information to test the accuracy of the hypothesis.
4. **Interpreting and reporting the evidence.**   The scientist analyzes the data and interprets the patterns of the findings as they relate to the hypothesis.

Consider the hypothesis that children play with same-sex peers because they have common interests. If this hypothesis is accurate, we would expect children to play more often with same-sex peers during gender-typed activities. For instance, a girl would be more likely to play with other girls when playing with a kitchen set than when swinging, a non-gender-typed activity. To test this hypothesis, a scientist might design a study in which a team of observers watches certain children while they play and notes the sex of the children who play

rate-limiting component
the slowest, or last-developing, part of a dynamic system

THE PRACTICAL IMPACT: NURTURING CHILDREN

Assessing Your Personal Beliefs

For some people, one theory "reso-nates" more than another—it makes more sense to them and just feels right. Which of the theories resonates with you? On each continuum, mark where your beliefs about the basic is-sues of human development fall. Then compare your answers with those that match different theoretical perspec-tives, as shown in the table below.

Dominant Influence: To what extent do you think biological and internal factors account for development?

Biological and Internal Influences

Minor ———————————— Major

To what extent do you think environ-mental factors account for development?

Environmental Influences

Minor ———————————— Major

Importance of Early Experience: Do you think that the experiences of early childhood are especially important to development?

Yes ———————————— No

Continuity/Discontinuity: Do you think development proceeds smoothly?

Yes ———————————— No

Now compare your responses to those that follow, given by theorists from different perspectives.

Issues in Development from Each Theoretical Perspective

	EMPHASIS ON BIOLOGICAL FACTORS	EMPHASIS ON ENVIRONMENTAL FACTORS	EMPHASIS ON EARLY EXPERIENCE	EMPHASIS ON CONTINUITY
Biology-Based Theories				
Evolutionary	Major	Minor	No	No
Ethology	Major	Minor	Yes	No
Attachment	Major	Major	Yes	No
Neurodevelopmental	Major	Major	Yes	No
Psychoanalytic Theories				
Freud	Major	Minor	Yes	No
Erikson	Major	Minor	No	No
Environment-Based Theories				
Classical Conditioning	Minor	Major	No	Yes
Operant Conditioning	Minor	Major	No	Yes
Social Learning	Minor	Major	No	Yes
Cognition-Based Theories				
Piaget	Major	Major	Yes	No
Vygotsky	Major	Major	Yes	No
Information Processing	Major	Some	No	Yes
Contextual Theories				
Ecological	Minor	Major	No	No
Dynamic Systems	Major	Major	No	No

This picture depicts a common scene: boys playing with other boys. Although the tendency of boys to play with other boys and girls to play with other girls is widely recognized, the reasons for it remain unclear. Can you identify the steps in the scientific method that would allow researchers to test their ideas about the reasons for these play preferences?

with them and what they are doing at that time. After some amount of time, the scientist summarizes and analyzes the observations. The scientist then interprets the findings to determine whether the children were more likely to play with same-sex peers when they were involved in gender-typed activities than when they were involved in non-gender-typed activities. When Maccoby (1988) investigated this hypothesis, she did not find support for it. Instead, children played with same-sex playmates regardless of the type of activity. Thus, this same-sex preference appears to be due to factors other than shared interests. When a hypothesis is not confirmed, scientists often learn interesting new information, which may change theories and help them formulate different hypotheses to test.

TOPICS IN DEVELOPMENTAL SCIENCE

Think about some of the headlines that you have seen related to child development or some of the issues that you have discussed with your friends. Should children go to preschool? How do teen gangs form? Can babies learn before they are born? Developmental scientists are interested in these questions and many more. What determines the areas or topics they choose to study?

The topics that are studied by developmental scientists have changed over time, and the "hot" topics of developmental science also change over time (Horowitz, 2000). The scientific study of child development grew out of concerns about the welfare of children, and very practical questions were the initial focus of research efforts. Research trends then changed for many years, becoming more focused on topics related to children's learning (Schwebel, Plumert, & Pick, 2000).

Just as topics have changed over time, so too have the ways they are evaluated by both the lay public and other scientists. Recently, there has been an increasing emphasis on topics that have practical and everyday importance in the lives of children (Lerner, Fisher, & Weinberg, 2000; McCall & Groark, 2000). The newsworthiness of the topic, the severity of the issue (e.g., HIV infection in babies), and the number of people whose lives are touched by the issue also are factors in how topics are evaluated (Fabes, Martin, Hanish, & Updegraff, 2000).

Traditionally, research topics have been described as falling into one of two camps— basic developmental research and applied developmental research. Basic developmental research is designed to answer broad, fundamental questions about development, such as the following:

◆ What are the causes of developmental disabilities?
◆ How is language acquired?
◆ What emotions are infants born with?

Applied developmental research is designed to solve practical problems, such as

◆ how to treat children with developmental delays
◆ how to improve the language skills of children who suffer head injuries
◆ how to help parents cope with chronically ill infants

Both types of research are necessary for understanding child development. Basic research lays the foundation for the applied research that follows. Additionally, applied research often produces questions that can be answered only through basic research (Herrmann, 1998).

Today, there is a movement toward integrating the basic and applied approaches. Basic researchers can consider the implications of their research for applied issues. Applied scientists can ground their research on applied problems in basic research findings. And, basic research can be conducted within the context of an applied problem. For instance, research on children's high accident rates when driving ATVs led to the development of the idea that children's understanding of their own abilities varies depending on their familiarity with the demands of a situation. Children are most at risk for making errors (and possibly injuring themselves) when they are learning a new skill or acting within a new environment (Schewebel et al., 2000). When research is done in this way, the complementary roles of applied and basic research become even more apparent.

RESEARCH STRATEGIES

For both basic and applied developmental research, scientists have developed methods, or research designs, to help them determine whether their hypotheses are correct. No single research design is perfect, and each research design has advantages and disadvantages. The following qualities vary according to the design of the study:

◆ Degree of control and structure
◆ Degree to which cause and effect can be determined
◆ Degree to which the findings of the study generalize to other people or settings
◆ Degree to which the findings directly apply to real-life events and processes

Table 2.5 outlines how these qualities apply to the six different types of research designs discussed in this chapter.

How do scientists select the methods they believe will be most useful in investigating a problem? First, the theory that guides their research may lead them to choose a particular method. Ethologists, for instance, choose methods that allow them to collect data in natural settings, because they are interested in observing the adaptive functions of behaviors as they

TABLE 2.5

Comparing Different Research Strategies

METHOD	CONTROL AND STRUCTURE	DETERMINATION OF CAUSALITY	GENERALIZES WELL	DIRECT APPLICATION TO REAL LIFE
Case studies	No	No	No	Yes
Clinical interviews	No	No	Possibly	Possibly
Survey studies	No	No	Possibly	No
Naturalistic studies	No	No	Possibly	Yes
Correlational studies	No	No	Possibly	Possibly
Experimental studies	Yes	Yes	Possibly	Possibly

occur in everyday situations. Learning theorists are more likely to choose controlled settings, such as laboratory experiments, where they can manipulate conditions to study the effects of reinforcement on specific behaviors.

Second, the research question may dictate the best methods, leading scientists to adopt different methods at different times. For example, when first investigating a question, a scientist might examine behaviors in a natural setting. After formulating a testable hypothesis, he or she may then move into a more controlled environment where cause and effect can be tested.

Case Studies

In a **case study,** the researcher collects information about aspects of a person's life, such as medical history, family background, school grades, friendships and relationships, intelligence and achievement, personality characteristics, or dreams and desires. The advantage of this design is that it allows an in-depth view of the person. The disadvantage is that the information may not generalize to other people because of unique features of the person (Yin, 1994).

Jean Piaget developed a comprehensive theory about how children move through different stages in their cognitive development. Many of his studies involved using the clinical interview method. What is this method and how can it produce useful information about children's development?

One of the earliest case studies was Charles Darwin's detailed diary study of his infant son's behavior (Darwin, 1877). Other important case studies have been based on the lives of famous people such as Mahatma Gandhi (Erikson, 1969). Case studies may feature people who are unusual or who have a noteworthy condition, such as Victor (Chapter 1). More recently, a case study of a severely neglected and abused child named Genie provided insights into how development proceeds under extremely harsh conditions (Curtiss, 1977).

Clinical Interviews

In a **clinical interview,** the researcher asks detailed questions in interaction with the participant. The goal of the clinical interview is to identify how the individual thinks about some topic. In the following example of a clinical interview (Piaget, 1946/1969, p. 207), the researcher is exploring the child's understanding of age. This interview reveals a common misunderstanding that young children have about age: that it is directly related to size.

Experimenter:	Are you the same age? (as his older sister)
Filk (boy, age 5):	No, because we weren't born at the same time.
Experimenter:	Who was born first?
Filk:	She was.
Experimenter:	Will you be the same age as her one day or will the two of you never be the same age?
Filk:	Soon I will be bigger than her, because men are bigger than women. Then I shall be older.

The data obtained in a clinical interview may be biased by participants' telling the experimenter what they believe the experimenter wants to hear (Garbarino & Stott, 1992). Also, the method can be used only with language-proficient participants and thus is not useful with very young children or with children who have language problems. The advantage of this method is its flexibility. The clinical interview can be used to probe for new information or to gain insights into people's thoughts and feelings.

Survey Studies

A **survey study** is used to determine how a number of people respond to a set of structured questions. A survey may be conducted by phone, in person, or by mail. An advantage is that

case study method in which the researcher collects information about aspects of a person's life

clinical interview method in which the researcher asks detailed questions while interacting with the participant

survey study method in which a number of people respond to a set of structured questions

Examples of Correlational Relationships

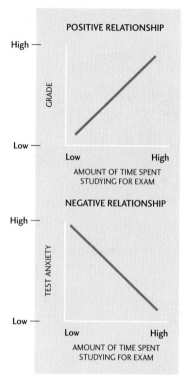

Correlations provide evidence of the type of relationship between two variables. The top graph depicts a positive correlation—as students study more, their grades improve. The bottom graph depicts a negative correlation—as students study more, their anxiety about test performance decreases. Correlational research, however, cannot tell us the reasons for these relationships.

naturalistic study method in which researchers observe the behavior of people in their natural environments

correlational study method in which researchers compare participants on two variables to determine whether the variables relate to each other

correlation coefficients calculated measures of the relations between variables

data for many people can be obtained easily, but a disadvantage is that people often respond inaccurately as they try to present themselves in the most positive way (Fowler, 1993).

If you have answered questions for a telephone poll, you have been involved in a survey study. Survey studies are popular for gathering data about demographics (age, income, marital status), beliefs and attitudes, leisure activities, political beliefs, and consumer choices. Several large-scale surveys have been done on adults. One is the General Social Survey, which covers topics such as attitudes, life satisfaction, health, religion, sex, and race. Another is the National Health Interview Survey, designed to obtain information about eating and health habits. The National Survey of Children is one of the few large-scale studies of a broad range of topics done on children (Cozby, Worden, & Kee, 1989). Every decade, the US Census Bureau conducts one of the largest surveys, encompassing almost the entire US population, and the results have important consequences for funding and political representation for cities and states.

Naturalistic Studies

In a **naturalistic study,** researchers observe the behavior of people in their natural environments—homes, schools, malls, or parks. Because researchers are watching people in their familiar everyday settings, the people tend to behave normally. A disadvantage of naturalistic studies is the difficulty of generalizing from one setting to another setting. In addition, the researcher has no control over the naturalistic setting, making it virtually impossible to determine cause and effect.

Thorne (1993) conducted a year-long naturalistic study in public school classrooms in California and Michigan. She observed children's social behavior in the lunchrooms, hallways, and playgrounds. From these observations, she described how boys and girls interact. For instance, she concluded that both sexes tend to play in same-sex groups but that children cross gender lines for certain games such as "chase and kiss." Thorne's data did not enable her to draw cause-and-effect conclusions, though, because she could not systematically control for variables that might explain why children behaved as they did.

Correlational Studies

Are children who watch more television more aggressive? The important research hypothesis that they tend to be more aggressive has been difficult to test. Because so many children watch television, it is difficult to find children who do not watch television to serve as a comparison group. In such cases, researchers use correlational studies. A **correlational study** compares participants (children, in this case) on two variables to determine whether the variables relate to each other: Are children who watch more television more likely to be aggressive than children who watch less television?

To uncover patterns in variables, researchers use **correlation coefficients**—calculations of the relations between variables. Correlation coefficients range from +1.0 to −1.0. A positive score represents a positive relationship between variables (a high score on one variable is related to a high score on the other). Zero represents no relationship between variables, and a negative score represents an inverse relationship between variables (a high score on one variable is related to a *low* score on the other). Figure 2.6 illustrates positive and negative correlations.

Although correlational studies demonstrate how variables are related, they cannot reveal whether one of the variables causes the other one. In the example of television viewing and aggression, for instance, it is impossible to know whether television viewing causes children to be more aggressive. It may be that children who are aggressive are more inclined to watch television than are less aggressive children. Or, television viewing and aggression may each be related to a third variable that has not been considered, such as parental supervision. Perhaps when parents do not supervise their children closely, the children watch more television and are also more aggressive, even though the two are not directly linked (Cozby et al., 1989).

Sometimes correlational studies provide the only ethical way to study a topic. For example, the most scientifically sound way to study the effects of spanking on children would be to have one group of parents spank their children and another group not spank theirs.

THE SCIENTIFIC IMPACT: INTERPRETING RESEARCH

What Are the Ethical Concerns in Studying Child Development?

Scientists who study child development follow strict guidelines for the ethical treatment of the participants in their studies. Before running a study, scientists submit a plan for the study to the institutional review board at their college or university. This board is responsible for granting approval for and overseeing studies that involve human participants. To obtain approval, scientists must comply with the American Psychological Association's guidelines for research with human participants and the guidelines for children developed by the Society for Research in Child Development. Special care is taken with children because they are assumed to be more vulnerable to stress and less able to evaluate what participation in a research program may mean. The guidelines for research with children include the following:

- **Protection from harm.** Each child must be protected from potential physical and psychological harm. No treatment or experimental condition can cause harm.
- **Protection of well-being.** If, in the course of research, information that may seriously affect a child's well-being comes to the researcher's attention, the investigator has a responsibility to discuss the information with experts in the field so that the parents may arrange necessary assistance for their child.
- **Informed consent.** Each child and his or her parents have the right to know the procedures that will be used in the study and decide whether or not to be involved in the study. Informed consent also requires a description of the risks and benefits of the study.
- **Privacy.** Children involved in studies have the right to maintain their privacy. This is accomplished by allowing children to remain anonymous when they participate in studies, typically by assigning iden-tification numbers rather than using names and by analyzing data at a group rather than an individual level.
- **Right to beneficial treatments.** Children have the right to receive any treatment that is found to be effective when used in a study. If a child is a member of a nontreated control group, she or he has the option of receiving the treatment as soon as the treatment is found to be successful.

Thinking It Through:

1. What special protections must be in place for children who participate in research, over and above those extended to adults?
2. What scientific risk is there in informing research participants about the specific nature of the study, the hypotheses, and the methods before the study begins?

But this would not be ethical. A correlational study allows researchers to ask parents about spanking practices and examine the data in relation to their children's behavior.

Experimental Studies

How do scientists investigate whether television viewing causes aggression? To answer the question of causality, scientists must use an **experimental study,** in which people are brought into a laboratory where the situation is manipulated and the effects of the manipulation are noted. The causes of behavior are easier to determine with experimental methods than with correlational methods because the scientist controls the sequence of events and any extraneous variables that may influence the findings in unexpected ways.

Scientists gain control over extraneous variables in several ways. One way is by trying to hold constant all other factors that may influence behavior. For instance, in a study of television violence, a scientist might hold constant the characteristics of the experimenter, the ages of the participants, the lighting, and the time of day participants are tested.

Not all variables can be easily controlled, however, especially characteristics of people. Scientists want to ensure that the effects of uncontrollable variables are randomly distributed across the groups involved in the study. For instance, a child's upbringing may influence his or her likelihood of being aggressive with other people, but it is impossible to identify and control all the variables related to a child's upbringing in any one study. To minimize the effects of these variables, scientists use randomization. They select participants at random, called **random sampling,** and they randomly assign people to groups, called **random assignment.** In this way, the effects of upbringing and other uncontrolled variables will be approximately the same for all groups in the study.

Scientists design experimental studies by determining which variable they want to test the effects of. This is the **independent variable,** which is assumed to be the cause of the behavior and is manipulated by the scientist. If the independent variable is exposure to violent programming, one group of children watches a violent program and the other

experimental study method in which scientists bring people into a laboratory where the situation is manipulated and the effects of the manipulation are noted

random sampling selecting participants for a study at random

random assignment randomly assigning people to groups in a study so that the effects of uncontrolled variables will be the same for all groups in the study

independent variable condition that is assumed to be the cause of the behavior and is manipulated by the scientist

watches a nonviolent program. The children who watch the violent program are considered to be in the **experimental group,** whereas the children watching the nonviolent program are in the **control group.** All other variables are kept the same for both groups. The researcher then assesses whether children who received the independent variable (exposure to violent programming) differ from those who did not. The behavior thought to be affected by the independent variable is the **dependent variable**—in this case, aggressive behavior following the television viewing. Thus, in experimental studies, the "cause" is the independent variable and the "effect" is the dependent variable (Cozby et al., 1989).

Although the experimental method allows scientists to determine cause and effect, it has disadvantages. The major disadvantage is that laboratory situations often are not realistic. People may respond quite differently in a laboratory setting than in real life. Findings from experimental studies may be very relevant for real life, but care must be taken in interpreting them if the experimental manipulation is not realistic.

MEASURING CHANGE OVER TIME

Many of the most interesting questions in child development involve change over time. Is an outgoing and affectionate toddler likely to grow up to be a teenager who has many friends? Do active children become active adults? To answer these questions, scientists use methods that assess change over time.

One method for assessing change is the **cross-sectional study.** As Figure 2.7 illustrates, in cross-sectional studies, individuals of different ages are tested at the same point in time, and the results from each age group are compared. For instance, a researcher interested in developmental changes in memory capacity might test children who are 4, 8, 12, and 16 years old. Children at each age would be shown a group of objects and later asked what they remembered about the objects. By averaging the memory scores for children at each age, researchers could get an idea how memory capacity changes.

 **IGURE 2.7**

Cross-Sectional Design

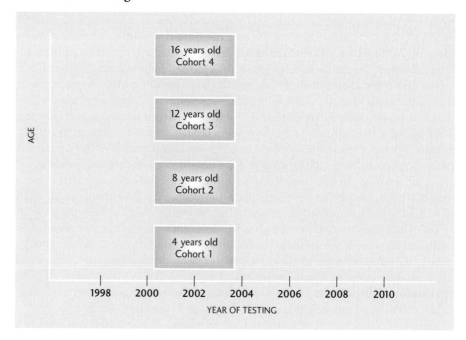

The cross-sectional design involves testing groups of people of different ages at the same point in time. What are the strengths and weaknesses of this design?

experimental group group that receives the independent variable

control group comparison group that is treated in the same way as the experimental group but does not receive the independent variable

dependent variable the behavior thought to be affected by the independent variable

cross-sectional study method in which individuals of different ages are tested at the same point in time and the results from each age group are compared

THE SOCIAL IMPACT: DEBATING THE ISSUE

Do Gifted Children Become Well-Adjusted Adults?

Remember the case of William James Sidis, the child prodigy discussed in Chapter 1? Many people believe that gifted children are like William—odd and socially awkward. But is this perception true? One attempt to examine this issue was launched in 1920, when Lewis Terman (1877–1956) began a longitudinal study of gifted children. He was interested in discovering the origins and outcomes of being a genius. He was particularly interested in testing the popular belief that geniuses grow up to be maladjusted. This study is one of the classic longitudinal studies (Terman, 1925). Over 1000 highly intelligent (IQ scores of 140 and above, or 40 points over the average) children from California were followed from school age through the rest of their lives. Terman was involved in the study until the children were in their 40s and 50s (Terman & Oden, 1959), and then new researchers took over the study to continue following Terman's

"Termites," as the participants called themselves.

Terman's participants were successful at all stages of their lives. As children, they did well in school, had satisfactory peer relationships, and showed early and intense interests in science and literature. Many more of the gifted participants finished college and obtained graduate degrees than did members of comparison groups with normal-range IQ scores. With respect to social adjustment and maturity, the gifted participants were similar to comparison groups of non-gifted people. Almost all of them married, and many had children. In their 40s, the gifted participants were at the peak of their careers.

The Termites included many distinguished scientists, doctors, lawyers, and inventors. One participant learned fifteen languages, and two others were awarded over a hundred patents. Generally, the participants seemed contented with their lives. The gifted

participants did not grow up to be criminals or alcoholics; in fact, their rates of criminal behavior and alcoholism were much lower than those for the general population. Even in their 70s, many of the participants had active and intellectually stimulating lives (Shurkin, 1992).

Thinking It Through:

1. Why is it important to test common-sense beliefs? In what ways does Terman's study dispel the myth that geniuses are eccentric?

2. If you were designing a study of the psychological adjustment of gifted children, what kinds of measures would you consider including in your study? Why is it difficult to measure adjustment?

3. Why are longitudinal studies difficult to conduct? What factors make them expensive? How do you keep participants interested in being in the study?

Cross-sectional studies are limited in their ability to identify age-related changes. In these studies, the children in each age group make up a **cohort,** or unique birth group. The scientist may be unaware of important systematic ways in which cohorts differ. For instance, suppose a comparison of computer skills in 10-year-olds and 60-year-olds reveals that more of the 10-year-olds are highly skilled. The scientist might be tempted to conclude that as people grow older they lose computer skills. However, these two cohorts have experienced different historical times, which affected the amount of their exposure to computers in the first place.

Another method for assessing change over time is the **longitudinal study** (see Figure 2.8), in which the same group of individuals is tested at different points in time. When the results at the different points in time are compared, developmental changes become apparent. Problems of longitudinal studies include a tendency for some individuals to drop out and for test scores to improve because of repeated testing. Longitudinal studies also are limited in their ability to identify age-related changes. Any changes that occur may be due to the particular cohort studied rather than to age changes. These studies also are expensive and time-consuming (Willett, Singer, & Martin, 1998).

To minimize problems with cross-sectional and longitudinal designs, scientists may use a combination of the two strategies, called a **cohort-sequential research design.** In this design, illustrated in Figure 2.9 on page 53, a cross-sectional study is expanded so that data are collected from the same cohorts at different points in time. New participants can be added at each time point to prevent the problems of repeated testing and attrition.

MEASURING CHILDREN'S BEHAVIOR

Developmental scientists have devised many ways to measure variables of interest, such as aggression, memory, intelligence, and stress. Four broad categories of measures are used. *Physiological measures* record responses of the body, such as heart rate, hormone production, and galvanic skin response (sweating), which are used to assess arousal and anxiety. Activity

longitudinal study method in which the same group of individuals is tested at different points in time

cohort a group of individuals who are the same age or who experience similar events at the same time

cohort-sequential research design a cross-sectional study expanded so that data are collected from the same cohorts at different points in time

Longitudinal Design

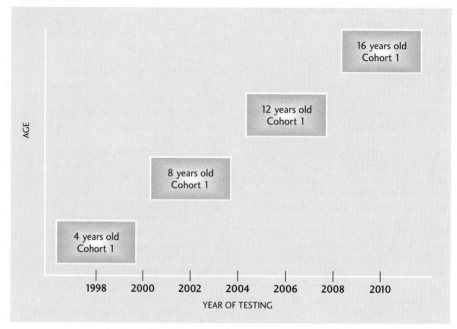

The longitudinal design involves testing the same people repeatedly at several different points in time. What are some limitations of longitudinal designs?

To examine the influence of television on children, researchers often use experimental procedures. What are the strengths and weaknesses of the experimental method? How might a researcher examine television's influences using naturalistic procedures?

in different parts of the brain can be assessed by recording electrical activity in the brain. Brain cell activity is recorded through sensitive electrodes placed at various locations on the person's head and scalp. Many of these methods are used with infants and young children.

Behavioral measures involve the direct assessment of behavior through observation. To investigate whether children have preferences for certain toys, observers watch them play to see if they choose one type of toy over another. To assess whether mothers and fathers respond to their children differently, observers watch and record how parents play with their children.

Self-reports are a third type of measure. Rather than observing children as they play with dolls or cars, a scientist might ask them which toy they prefer. Self-reports include questionnaires in which people respond to questions about their behavior, attitudes, beliefs, values, and habits. Self-report measures are the easiest type of information to gather, but people may not be accurate in reporting or may not remember the information they are asked to report on.

Projective measures indirectly assess individuals' psychological states. The typical strategy is to show a participant an ambiguous scene, such as a picture of a boy standing by a fireplace looking sad. The participant is then asked to make up a story about the boy. Or a child may be asked to draw a person or a family. From these stories and drawings, researchers infer the person's thinking and feelings. This method yields only subjective data, however, which might vary in interpretation from researcher to researcher.

Consider, too, the special challenges involved in testing hypotheses relevant to infants and young children. Many of the techniques used with older children and adults, such as questionnaires and projective measures, are impossible to use with young children. Infants and young children do not have the verbal skills necessary to answer questions. Whereas older children can provide some insight into their own thinking and experience, this kind of insight is very difficult for younger children to provide, even when they have some verbal skills. Testing infants, in particular, is difficult because they are often crying, asleep, or drowsy, making them unresponsive to any kind of testing. Adhering to ethical guidelines also is problematic when testing young children and infants, because it is difficult to assess a nonverbal child's refusal to participate.

Cohort-Sequential Design

The cohort-sequential research design minimizes the problems of both cross-sectional and longitudinal designs. The same children are tested at several points in time, but new participants are added at each time point to prevent the problems of repeated testing and attrition.

As you can see, developmental scientists face many challenges as they choose a research question, a theoretical basis, a set of methods, and the types of measures. But studying how behavior develops and changes over time can be rewarding and meaningful work.

TRY IT OUT

Activities Relating to Child Development

1. Where do you stand in the nature versus nurture debate? What evidence, experiences, and observations can you cite to support your position? How do your ideas on the respective roles of biology and environment in development compare with those of your classmates?

2. Think about your own behavior. Can you think of examples of behaviors that you learned through operant conditioning? Through social learning? Describe how you might have acquired these behaviors.

3. Consider the development of a child born to a drug-addicted mother. Think about the kinds of microsystem, exosystem, and macrosystem influences that could potentially play a role in the

child's development. Now consider how interventions could be used at each of these levels to improve the developmental outcome for the child.

4. Design an individual or collaborative research project using one of the research strategies described in this chapter. Begin by posing a question that you wish to answer about child development. Try to formulate a hypothesis. Now, what methods will you use to test this hypothesis? Who will your participants be and how many will there be? What information will you need, where and how will you get it, and in what form will you record it? What ethical issues will you need to consider? What might be the outcomes of applications of your findings?

SUM IT UP

How do theories explain child development?

✦ Scientific theories are structured sets of ideas that help explain the complexities of child development, organize existing evidence, and provide guidance for future research.

✦ Developmental theories attempt to explain how behavior changes over time.

✦ Theories are judged by their usefulness, testability, ability to provide practical guidance, and ability to stimulate new research.

What are the major biology-based theories of child development?

✦ Evolutionary theory focuses on the idea that development of the individual is the result of the inheritance of characteristics that promote survival of the species.

✦ Ethological theory focuses on the evolutionary causes and adaptive value of behavior. Ethologists propose that there are critical and sensitive periods in development.

✦ Attachment theorists argue that early emotional ties with caregivers provide a child with an inner working model on which future relationships are based, and that attachment behaviors increase an infant's likelihood of survival.

✦ Neurodevelopmental theory focuses on how the brain develops and how experience influences this development.

What are the major psychoanalytic theories of child development?

✦ Psychoanalytic theories stress the role of unconscious internal drives as the major influences on development.

✦ Freud's psychosexual theory emphasized the development of sexual energy (the libido) and how the libido becomes focused on different erogenous zones over five stages (oral, anal, phallic, latency, genital) of development.

✦ Erikson's psychosocial theory is based on crises that individuals undergo at different stages of development. How individuals resolve these crises influences their development.

What are the major environment-based theories of child development?

✦ Classical conditioning was discovered by Pavlov, who found that pairing a neutral stimulus with an unconditioned stimulus eventually elicits a conditioned response to the neutral, or conditioned, stimulus.

✦ Watson applied classical conditioning to the study of children's emotions and found that emotions such as fear often result from the pairing of a once-neutral stimulus with an unconditioned stimulus that naturally elicits fear.

✦ Skinner focused on learning that occurs because of the consequences that follow a response (operant conditioning). Behaviors that lead to positive consequences are more likely to be repeated than those that lead to aversive consequences.

✦ Social learning theory emphasizes the roles of observation and imitation. Individuals develop new patterns of behavior by observing others and then modeling their behaviors.

What are the major cognition-based theories of child development?

✦ Piaget's theory of cognitive development maintains that children's thinking is qualitatively different from that of adolescents or adults. Cognitive development involves adapting to one's environment, using the processes of assimilation and accommodation.

✦ Vygotsky's theory of cognitive development emphasizes the importance of psychological tools, such as language, in development. Vygotsky also places great emphasis on the role of the social context and how social interactions support development in a learner's zone of proximal development.

✦ Information processing theory focuses on both environmental input and the processing of information in the brain. The individual has limited but flexible capacities for processing information from the environment. These capacities change over time.

What are the major contextual theories of child development?

✦ Bronfenbrenner's ecological theory features the interplay of the individual and his or her social and physical environment. The interactions between the child and the environment are the engine of development.

✦ Dynamic systems theory is a theoretical approach to understanding development that focuses on self-organization. Separate components of behavior develop at different times and then come together to produce new forms of action and behavior.

How is child development studied?

✦ The goals of scientific research are to produce findings that are objective, reliable, and valid. The scientific method involves four steps: formulating a hypothesis, designing a study, collecting evidence, and interpreting and reporting the evidence.

✦ Basic research is designed to investigate broad core developmental issues, whereas applied research is designed to solve practical problems.

✦ Many research strategies are available for testing hypotheses, and each has advantages and disadvantages. Case studies involve collecting information from individuals. Survey studies are used to determine how a number of people respond to structured questions. Naturalistic studies involve observing behavior in natural settings. Correlational studies assess the relationships between variables. Experimental studies investigate cause and effect.

✦ Change over time is measured through the use of developmental designs. In cross-sectional studies, individuals of different ages are tested at the same time. In longitudinal studies, the same group of individuals is followed and tested over time. In cohort-sequential studies, multiple groups of individuals are followed and tested over time.

✦ Different measures are used to study children's development. Physiological measures assess activity in the body, such as heart rate and electrical activity in the brain. Behavioral measures require direct observation of people's behavior. Self-reports involve asking people to answer questions about their behavior or attitudes. Projective measures use people's responses to ambiguous scenes or pictures to measure their psychological states indirectly. Special challenges are involved in testing nonverbal infants and toddlers.

KEY TERMS and CONCEPTS

accommodation (*36*)

assimilation (*36*)

attachment theory (*29*)

case study (*47*)

classical conditioning (*33*)

clinical interview (*47*)

cohort (*51*)

cohort-sequential research design (*51*)

concrete operational stage (*38*)

control group (*50*)

control parameters (*41*)

correlational study (*48*)

correlation coefficients (*48*)

cross-sectional study (*50*)

dependent variable (*50*)

dynamic systems theory (*41*)

ecological model (*41*)

ego (*30*)

empirically based (*27*)

ethological theory (*28*)

evolutionary theories (*28*)

exosystem (*41*)

experimental group (*50*)

experimental study (*49*)

extinction (*33*)

fact (*26*)

formal operational stage (*38*)

id (*30*)

independent variable (*49*)

information processing theory (*39*)

libido (*30*)

long-term memory (*39*)

longitudinal study (*51*)

macrosystem (*41*)

mesosystem (*41*)

microsystem (*41*)

naturalistic study (*48*)

negative reinforcement (*33*)

neurodevelopmental approaches (*29*)

operant conditioning (*33*)

positive reinforcement (*33*)

preoperational stage (*36*)

psychoanalytic theories (*30*)

psychosexual development (*30*)

psychosocial crises (*32*)

punishment (*33*)

random assignment (*49*)

random sampling (*49*)

rate-limiting component (*42*)

schemes (*36*)

sensorimotor stage (*36*)

sensory register (*39*)

shaping (*34*)

short-term memory (*39*)

social learning theory (*35*)

superego (*30*)

survey study (*47*)

theory (*26*)

vicarious reinforcement (*35*)

zone of proximal development (*38*)

PART 1

SEE the IMPACT

BENCHMARKS in Child Development

DEVELOPMENTAL STAGE	APPROXIMATE AGES	PROMINENT CHARACTERISTICS OF STAGE
Prenatal	Conception to birth	Unfolding of genetic code Formation of basic organs and structures
Neonatal	0–2 months	Transition to extra-uterine life Adaptation to external environment Establishment of basic emotions and social interactions
Infancy/toddlerhood	2–36 months	Transition to symbolic thought and language Development of locomotion Development of attachment relationships
Early childhood	3–6 years	Development of autonomous learning and regulated actions Focus on parent-child discipline Development of peer relationships
Late childhood	7–10 years	Transition to school Development of logical thinking Development of self-comparisons
Early adolescence	11–14 years	Achievement of puberty, growth spurt, and focus on physical appearance Development of risk-taking behaviors Interest in intimate relationships
Late adolescence	15–19 years	Development of formal logic Achievement of physical maturation Preparation for adulthood

NATIONAL HOTLINES FOR CHILD DEVELOPMENT

National Association of Counsel for Children: 888-828-6222

National Information Center for Children and Youth with Disabilities: 800-695-0285

National Library of Medicine: 888-346-3656

Stand for Children: 800-663-4032

*i*mpact Report on Child Development

This graph shows the population of the United States as a function of age, from birth to 19 years. Notice how the population increases from birth to age 10 and then begins to drop off. What factors contribute to the increased population rates in early life and the decreased population rates later in childhood and adolescence? What impact might these data have for social policy?

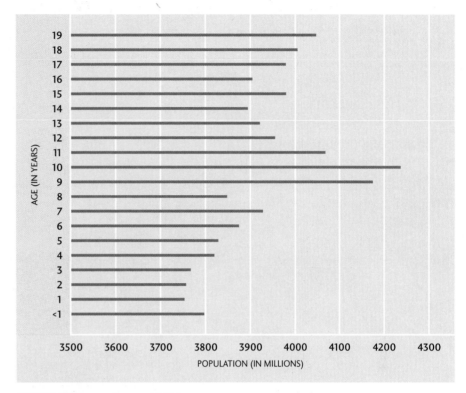

US Population of Infants, Children, and Adolescents: 2001

SOURCE: US Census Bureau, 2001d.

RECOMMENDED WEBSITES

American Psychological Association (APA): The largest scientific and professional organization representing psychology in the United States. Its Website contains valuable information on a wide variety of topics related to child development and families. http://www.apa.org/

Children Now: A nonpartisan, independent voice for children, working to translate the nation's commitment to children and families into action. Its Website has a large amount of up-to-date information on child development, social policy, and research. http://www.childrennow.org/

Jean Piaget Society: Devoted to honoring Jean Piaget and his major theoretical and empirical contributions to the understanding of the origins and evolution of knowledge. Its Website provides an open forum for the presentation and discussion of scholarly work on issues related to human knowledge and its development, as well as lists of relevant books and other publications. http://www.piaget.org/

National Council on Family Relations (NCFR): The leading nonprofit organization for family researchers, educators, policy makers, and practicing professionals. On the Website, its members share knowledge and information about families. http://www.ncfr.com/

National Human Genome Research Institute (NHGRI): Established to take a lead role in the Human Genome Project. Its Website contains valuable information about genetics, genetic technology, and the ethical, legal, and social implications of genetics research. http://www.nhgri.nih.gov/

UNICEF: An intergovernmental agency of the United Nations that helps children around the world. Its Website contains information, links, and publications dealing with the state of children in various parts of the world. http://www.unicef.org/

US Census Bureau: This Website contains a huge amount of information about the United States—its population, families, economy, and society. http://www.census.gov/

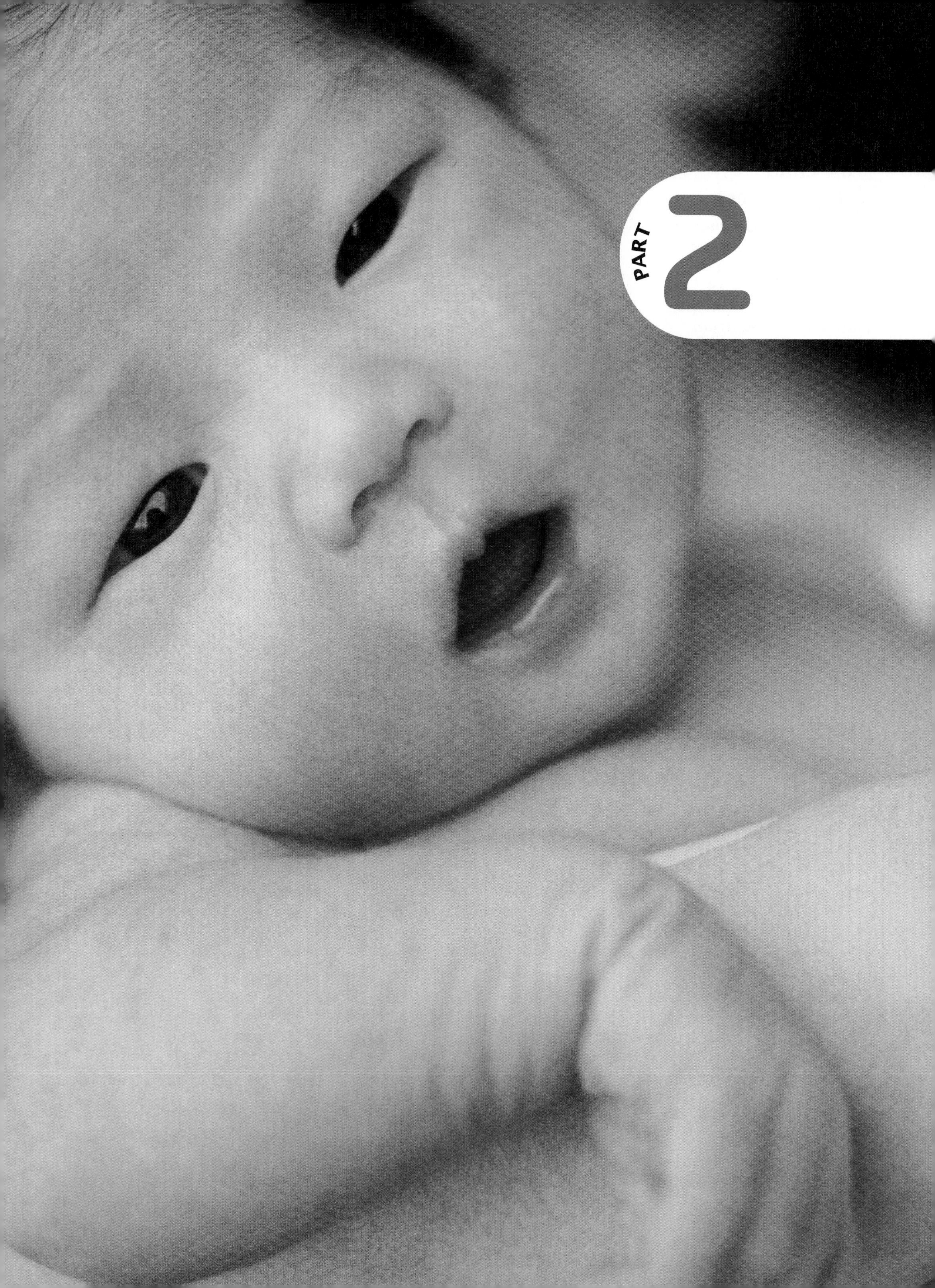

PART 2

Prenatal and Neonatal Development

The miracle of life and its development captures the attention, fancy, and amazement of parents, as well as poets, writers, and scientists. From a single fertilized cell, a complex individual made up of trillions of cells develops. Parents-to-be all over the world wonder whether their unborn child is a boy or girl and whether the child is healthy. Most children are born healthy, but some are born with serious disorders due to genetic or environmental factors. As the statistics here reveal, the costs associated with complicated births and pregnancies are considerable—for parents, children, and society as a whole.

Once children are born, the demands of parenting and caregiving begin. Growth and development are rapid in the early years of life, and many changes occur as the result of the birth of a child. Newborns are not as helpless and passive as we once thought them to be. Thanks to new research, our ideas of newborns have changed. Babies actively strive to meet their needs for food, comfort, and social interactions.

● Nearly 4 million babies are born in the United States each year. There are high costs associated with poor outcomes of pregnancy, and many of these outcomes are preventable.

● Costs for complicated births range from $20,000 to $400,000 per baby, compared to about $6400 for a "normal" uncomplicated delivery. Cesarean delivery costs an average of $11,450.

● Each year in the United States, preterm deliveries cost an estimated $460 million more than full-term deliveries.

● The average treatment cost for delivery of very-low-birthweight infants (less than 1500 grams) is almost $50,000, ranging from $32,000 for infants weighing 1251–1500 grams to almost $90,000 for those weighing 501–750 grams. This is more than $1000 per day, with an average hospital stay of forty-nine days.

● The lifetime medical costs for one premature baby are conservatively estimated at $500,000.

● Low birthweight accounts for 10 percent of all health care costs for children.

● Health care, education, and child care from birth to 15 years for the 3.5 to 4 million children born at low birthweight cost between $5.5 and $6 billion more than they would if those children had been born at normal birthweight.

● The estimated lifetime cost for eighteen of the most clinically significant birth defects in the United States is about $8–10 billion.

● Conditions with the highest costs per case include those with high levels of long-term activity limitations: cerebral palsy ($503,000), Down syndrome ($451,000), and spina bifida ($294,000).

SOURCE: March of Dimes, 2000.

CHAPTER 3

Genetics and Prenatal Development

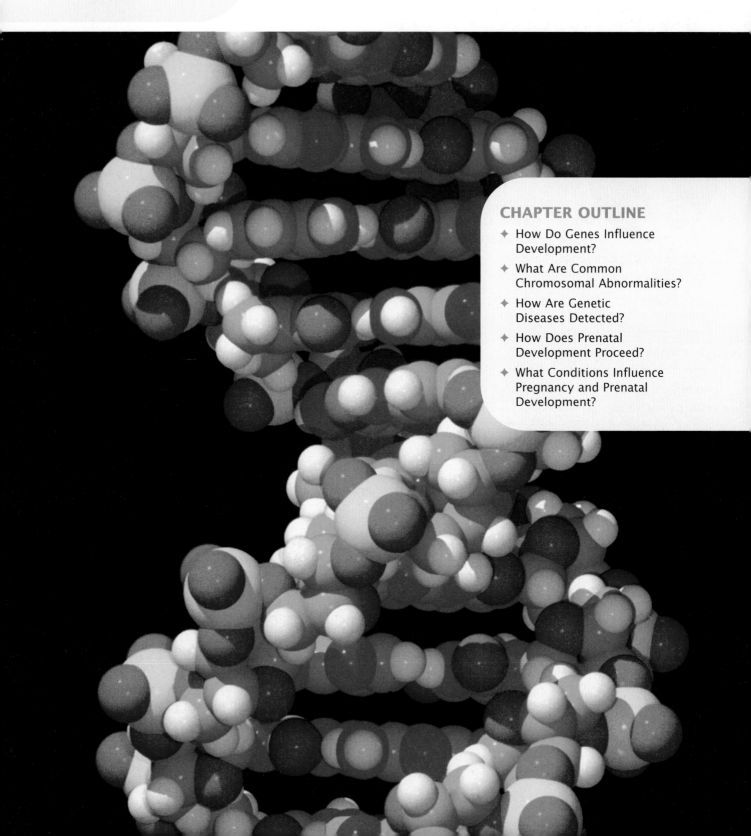

CHAPTER OUTLINE

- ◆ How Do Genes Influence Development?
- ◆ What Are Common Chromosomal Abnormalities?
- ◆ How Are Genetic Diseases Detected?
- ◆ How Does Prenatal Development Proceed?
- ◆ What Conditions Influence Pregnancy and Prenatal Development?

M ost parents have very vivid memories of when they discovered that a baby was on the way. When couples receive the good news about pregnancy, thoughts generally focus on the excitement and joy of having a child and on the external signs of the pregnancy. And all the while, their developing child's genetic endowment, transmitted at conception, is guiding prenatal development as the child grows from a single cell into a complex, functioning human being.

HOW DO GENES INFLUENCE DEVELOPMENT?

After a second child is born, parents often wonder how their two children could be so different from each other, especially since they were raised with similar expectations and goals. One possibility is that children inherit different genetic patterns. Like many parents, scientists are interested in these differences, and they study inheritance to learn how people develop in their appearance, thinking, and behavior.

HUNTING FOR GENES: THE HUMAN GENOME PROJECT

We are fortunate to live in the twenty-first century, which is being called the biology century. Never have so many exciting findings about genetics been made in such a short time. Over the last decade, the *Human Genome Project* (HGP), involving the coordinated efforts of many scientists all over the world, has had as its goal the massive job of mapping the human genome. One day in February 2001, in a room packed with reporters, scientists from the HGP gave a press conference. During this important media event, they announced that they had succeeded in developing the first initial sequencing of the human genome (International Human Genome Sequencing Consortium, 2001). They also announced a major surprise—that the human genome had been found to contain around 30,000 genes, considerably below the initial estimate of 100,000 (Baltimore, 2001).

By mapping genes, scientists can begin to examine how genes code for development. This knowledge can be used in many ways—for instance, in developing more effective treatments for diseases.

What is the human genome? Virtually every human cell carries a genetically programmed blueprint for development. The blueprint is coded by the **genes,** which reside on thin structures called **chromosomes.** The number of chromosomes varies dramatically across species. In normal humans, each cell contains forty-six chromosomes that work together in pairs: One chromosome of the pair is inherited from the mother and the other from the father.

The human genome is essentially a book of instructions. In this book are twenty-three chapters, called chromosomes. Each chapter has several thousand stories, called genes. Each story consists of paragraphs, called exons, which are interrupted by advertisements, called introns. The **exons** provide protein-coding information; they are the coding parts of DNA. The noncoding parts are the **introns,** whose functions have not yet been determined. Each paragraph is made up of words, called **codons,** which provide specific information about what amino acids should be added to make up the specific protein. Each word is written in letters, called bases. So the genetic code is a series of codons that specify which amino acids are required to make up specific proteins, which are the building blocks of our bodies. In the human genome book there are 1 billion words, making it about the length of 5000 books the size of this textbook! This gigantic recipe for human life is contained within the microscopic nucleus of a tiny cell that would fit easily into the period at the end of this sentence (Ridley, 1999).

The HGP began in 1990, when the Department of Energy and the National Institutes of Health proposed a joint project to the US Congress, in which a sixteen-nation group of scientists would completely map the human genome in fifteen years. At the time, the task seemed formidable. Nonetheless, as you can see from the timeline in Figure 3.1, the initial working draft of the human genome was completed earlier than expected, and the new target date for completion of the project is 2003.

genes the structures containing the code that provides the blueprint for development

chromosomes the structures on which genes reside

exons the parts of DNA providing protein-coding information

introns the noncoding parts of DNA

codons the parts of exons that provide coding information for amino acids in DNA

FIGURE 3.1

Timeline for the Development of the Human Genome Project

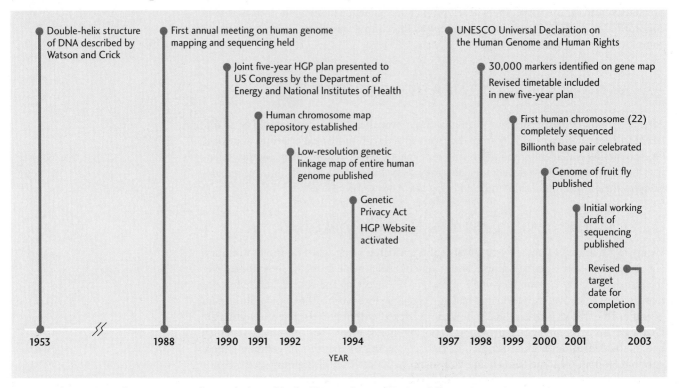

Various advances over the past 50 years have culminated in the Human Genome Project. What ethical issues arise as the project nears completion?

Whose genes are being mapped in this project? DNA was extracted from twenty individuals, but the DNA of only five of these individuals has been used as the prototypic genome. You may wonder whether it makes sense to unravel the code of just a few specific individuals. Individuals share 99.99 percent of their genetic code with other individuals, and people of different sexes, races, and national descents may have more in common genetically than people of the same sex or race or national descent. The categories of sex and race that are so important culturally reflect only a very tiny portion of our genes. For these reasons, knowing the genetic map of one individual provides insights into the genetics of all humans.

GENES AND CHROMOSOMES

To understand the actions of genes, consider how a child comes to have his or her specific complement of genes. The process begins as sex cells—ova and sperm—develop within the child's mother and father. Most cells multiply by creating exact duplicates of themselves through **mitosis,** which involves one duplication of chromosomes and one cell division (see Figure 3.2a). Each of the resulting cells contains the full complement of twenty-three pairs of chromosomes. Ova and sperm, however, undergo a process called **meiosis,** which involves one duplication of chromosomes and two cell divisions. Each of the resulting four cells contains half the complement of chromosomes: one member of each pair of chromosomes (see Figure 3.2b). Once conception occurs, the chromosomes of the ovum and sperm align so that the newly developing child has half his or her genes from each parent. Thus, genes provide a unique plan for development, incorporating genetic information from each parent.

mitosis the process of cell replication involving one duplication of chromosomes and one cell division, resulting in twenty-three pairs of chromosomes (forty-six total)

meiosis the process of cell replication undergone by ova and sperm, involving one duplication of chromosomes and two cell divisions, resulting in twenty-three chromosomes

FIGURE 3.2
Mitosis and Meiosis

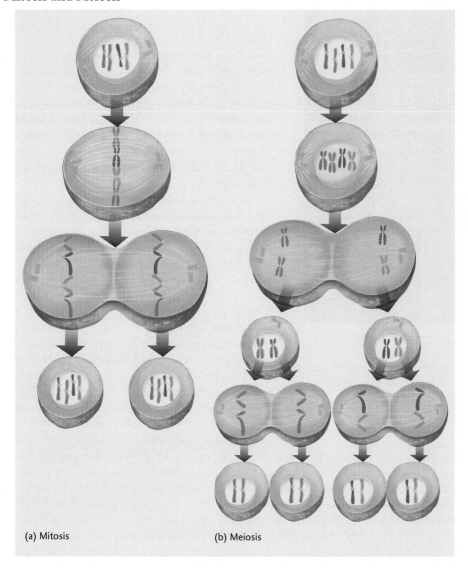

(a) Mitosis   (b) Meiosis

Mitosis and meiosis are processes involved in the creation of new cells. Notice that meiosis, which produces sex cells, involves an extra cell division. Why is an extra cell division needed?

Chromosomes vary in size, with some containing more genetic material than others. In a **karyotype** analysis, a geneticist photographs chromosomes and then aligns each chromosome with the other member of its pair, and the pairs are ordered by size and structure. The first twenty-two pairs of chromosomes, called **autosomes,** account for most aspects of development. The twenty-third pair, called the **sex chromosomes,** is unique in that the members may not match. For human females, the sex chromosomes normally consist of two X chromosomes. For males, the sex chromosomes normally consist of an X and a Y chromosome, which are given different labels because they look and function differently (Mange & Mange, 1994). The X chromosome is quite large; it contains about 2000 genes. The Y chromosome is very small, with only about 40 genes, and most of these code for male-specific characteristics (Tilford et al., 2001). The blueprint for development is outlined by the genes that are arranged in specific locations on the "arms" or "legs" of chromosomes. For

karyotype a photograph of chromosomes, used by geneticists to align each chromosome with the other member of its pair

autosomes the first twenty-two pairs of chromosomes, which account for most of the body cells

sex chromosomes the twenty-third pair of chromosomes, which accounts for a person's sex

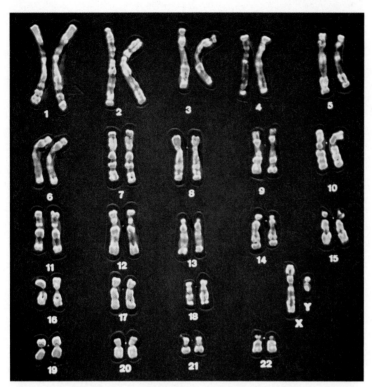

In a karyotype analysis, geneticists align the chromosomes by pairs and identify them by number. Notice that the first pairs of autosomes tend to be larger than the higher numbered pairs. You can see that, in the sex chromosomes for this male (the twenty-third pair), the X chromosome is much larger than the Y chromosome. What factors determine whether a boy or a girl is conceived?

instance, researchers have located a gene on chromosome 10 involved in hormone production whose presence increases the risk of breast cancer for women.

GENETIC TRANSMISSION PATTERNS

How likely is it that a child will be tall like his father or have the same color eyes as his mother? Certain physical characteristics, such as a cleft chin, and hundreds of diseases are determined by the action of a single gene, making it possible to predict whether they will occur in offspring. Other characteristics and diseases have genetic components, but the transmission patterns are more complex and difficult to determine because they are caused by multiple genes.

A person's **genotype,** or genetic code, influences his or her **phenotype,** which is the outward expression of the genotype. But not all the information in one's genotype is expressed in one's phenotype. Because genes work in pairs, certain types of genes are more likely to be expressed than others. Both parents may contribute identical copies of a gene to their child, in which case the child is **homozygous** for the trait. Or each parent may contribute a different copy of the gene to their child, in which case the child is **heterozygous** for the trait.

As an illustration of the action of genes, consider a girl who is heterozygous for a cleft chin, having received the gene for a cleft chin from her dad and a "normal," non-cleft chin gene from her mother. This girl will have a cleft chin, because the gene for that trait is dominant. A gene whose code is expressed is called a **dominant gene.** For dominant genes to be expressed, only one copy needs to be present. A gene that is not expressed in the presence of a dominant gene is a **recessive gene,** such as the gene for a non-cleft chin. For a recessive characteristic to be expressed, both genes in the pair must be recessive. For instance, if a child inherits the homozygous pattern of a non-cleft chin gene from her mother and a non-cleft chin gene from her father, she will not have a cleft chin.

Until recently, it was assumed that characteristics such as eye color, hair color, and height were the result of the action of a single gene. Today, however, geneticists believe that each of these characteristics is determined by multiple genes. Although dark eye colors tend to be dominant over light eye colors, it is possible for two blue-eyed parents to give birth to a brown-eyed child (Eiberg & Mohr, 1987).

Dominant Transmission

Most serious genetic diseases are not transmitted through a dominant gene, because diseased offspring would not survive long enough to transmit the characteristics to their own children. But some genetic diseases, like Huntington's chorea (a degenerative neurological disease), are transmitted by a single dominant gene (on the fourth chromosome) and are maintained in the population because they often do not strike until middle-age.

Dominant transmission poses serious problems for those who carry the dominant gene for a disease. For example, suppose a woman learns that her mother had Huntington's chorea. Consideration of the possible combinations of genetic pairs contributed by her parents reveals that the woman has a 50 percent chance of having the dominant gene for Huntington's (see Figure 3.3a on page 66). In the past, this woman would have had to decide about having children before she knew whether or not she had the gene. Now she can be tested for Hunt-

genotype a person's genetic code

phenotype the outward expression of the genotype

homozygous describes a child's condition with respect to a trait when both parents have contributed identical copies of the gene for that trait to their child

heterozygous describes a child's condition with respect to a trait when each parent has contributed a different copy of the gene for that trait to their child

dominant gene a gene whose code is expressed when only one copy of the gene is present

recessive gene a gene whose code is not expressed in the presence of a dominant gene

THE SOCIAL IMPACT: DEBATING THE ISSUE

Should the Sex of a Child Be Preselected?

If you could, would you want to select or know the sex of your baby before the baby was born or even conceived? If so, you are not alone: according to one survey, 80 percent of Americans say they would do whatever was needed to ensure that the sex of their child was the one they wanted (Pooler, 1991).

Currently, there are three approaches to attempting to preselect the sex of a child. The traditional approach is based on the differences between the qualities of X and Y sperm. Y sperm are faster but live a shorter time; X sperm are slower but live longer. Timing intercourse to match these qualities may influence the likelihood of giving birth to a child of the preferred sex. Intercourse at the time of ovulation, when the Y sperm will find a waiting egg, may increase the likelihood of having a boy. Intercourse several days before ovulation may increase the likelihood of having a

girl because the longer-living X sperm will still be viable when ovulation occurs (Shettles & Rorvik, 1984). Another approach, however, predicts the opposite outcome, based on the mother's hormone levels at conception. According to this theory, the likelihood of giving birth to a girl should be increased if conception takes place at ovulation, when maternal levels of gonadotropins are highest. Neither method has been proven scientifically to be effective.

A third approach to sex selection is to increase the number of either X or Y sperm before intercourse. Several methods have been used to identify sperm as either X or Y and to separate one kind of sperm from the other. One method is to separate X and Y sperm in a centrifuge. Another method is to place sperm in the top of a column containing progressively more viscous layers of gel-like liquids. Sperm that

make it through all the layers are more likely to be Y sperm. With both methods, the desired sperm can then be used for artificial insemination. In one study, a 76 percent rate of births of the desired sex was reported (Ericsson & Beernink, 1987). Most scientists believe, however, that the matter of sperm selection is unresolved (Mange & Mange, 1994).

Thinking It Through:

1. What reasons might parents have for choosing the sex of their children? Are there valid reasons related to genetic risks?
2. What might be some negative consequences of allowing people to choose the sex of their children?
3. If people routinely chose the sex of their children, do you think they would choose boys or girls more often? Why?

ington's, but the decision to take the test can be agonizing because there is no known cure for the disease. For this reason, few members of Huntington's families choose to take the test.

Recessive Transmission

The birth into the Deford family of the first girl in over fifty years was greeted with much celebration and joy. Alex Deford was a healthy girl at birth but soon was sick all the time. At 4 months, Alex was tested and found to have *cystic fibrosis (CF),* a serious recessive genetic disease. Because no one in the family had CF, they were shocked that they had a child with CF.

As Alex grew older, her health deteriorated. She had difficulty breathing, lost weight, and developed heart and liver problems. She was continually in and out of the hospital. Alex died when she was only 10 years old (Deford, 1986).

CF is the most common autosomal recessive disease among Caucasians, affecting about 1 in 2000 newborns. It is the leading genetic cause of childhood death. About 1 in 20 people are heterozygous for CF: they have one copy of the disease gene but also have the normal, dominant gene that masks the effect of the recessive gene. A child with the disease has identical recessive genes—in this case, two CF genes. About 50 percent of people with CF die by the age of 24. There currently is no cure for CF, although gene therapies are being developed.

Approximately 500 characteristics and diseases are transmitted through recessive genes. Unlike dominant characteristics and diseases, which 50 percent of the offspring are likely to have, recessive characteristics and diseases like CF can remain hidden for generations because they are not expressed unless both parents contribute the gene to their child (see Figure 3.3b on page 66).

People who are heterozygous for a recessive disease or characteristic do not have the recessive disease or characteristic but are **carriers.** A child whose parents are both carriers has a 25 percent chance of having the recessive disease or characteristic and a 50 percent chance of being a carrier.

Because recessive transmission requires that both parents pass on the recessive gene, recessive diseases and characteristics tend to be more prevalent in groups that are isolated or

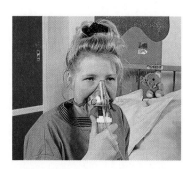

This child has cystic fibrosis, which is a very serious recessive genetic disease with no known cure. How can parents minimize their chance of giving birth to a child with a genetic birth defect?

carriers people who are heterozygous for a recessive disorder

Transmission Patterns

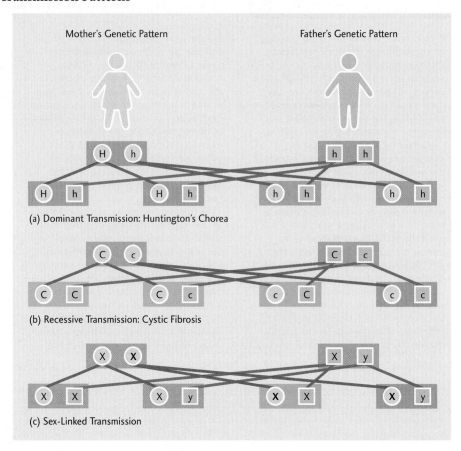

Part (a): The father is homozygous, with two healthy copies (h) of the gene, but the mother is diseased because she has one diseased copy (H) of the dominant Huntington's gene. As you can see, the offspring of these two parents have a 50 percent chance of being healthy and a 50 percent chance of being diseased. *Part (b):* The father and mother are carriers because they each have one copy of the cystic fibrosis gene (c). Their offspring have a 25 percent chance of being healthy, a 50 percent chance of being carriers, and a 25 percent chance of having the disease, because it takes two copies of the cystic fibrosis gene (cc) to have the disease. *Part (c):* The mother carries the gene for a sex-linked disease on one of her X chromosomes (**X**). The daughters have a 50 percent chance of not being carriers of the disease gene and a 50 percent chance of being carriers, with one disease copy and one normal copy of the gene. None of the daughters will have the disease, because those with a disease copy (**X**X) will have one normal copy of the gene to mask the disease copy. The sons have a 50 percent chance of being normal and a 50 percent chance of being diseased, because those with a disease copy (**X**Y) will not have a normal gene on their Y chromosome to suppress the disease gene.

that intermarry. For instance, people of Mediterranean origin are more at risk for *beta thalassemia,* an untreatable but prenatally detectable disease that accounts for hundreds of thousands of childhood deaths a year worldwide. Jewish people from Central and Eastern Europe and certain groups of French Canadians are more at risk for *Tay Sachs disease,* which is a serious and untreatable illness that often leads to death within the first two years of life. The risk for Jewish and French Canadian groups is about 1 in 6000 births, as compared to 1 in 550,000 births among non–Jewish American and non–French Canadian populations. Individuals with African heritage, especially those from West Africa, are more at risk for *sickle cell anemia,* a disease of the blood that causes painful joint swelling, anemia, and

THE SCIENTIFIC IMPACT: INTERPRETING RESEARCH

Genes, Attention Disorders, and Thrill-Seeking

In the mid-1990s, Dean Hamer set out to discover the difference between an adventurer, like Lawrence of Arabia, and a non–thrill seeker, such as Queen Victoria. Hamer believed that dopamine, a neurotransmitter in the brain, was a key to thrill-seeking behavior. The first person to confirm this idea was Richard Ebstein, who identified a gene called D4DR on chromosome 11. This gene has a variable repeat sequence in the middle, which is repeated between two and eleven times. Most people have from four to seven copies of this sequence, but some people have fewer and some have many more. Hamer and his colleagues were interested in whether the individual variations in the number of repeats would relate to the level of novelty-seeking. They suspected that the more repeats a person had—the longer his or her D4DR genes—the more ineffective the dopamine receptor would be at capturing dopamine. So for this person to feel dopamine effects, he or she would have to engage in more novelty-seeking behavior. In contrast, a person with a more effective dopamine receptor—with shorter D4DR genes—would need less stimulation to experience dopamine effects. In several studies, a relation was found between D4DR length and personality, but Hamer and his colleagues decided that very little of the variation in the thrill-seeking aspect of personality really depended on this gene (Greenberg et al., 2000; Hamer & Copeland, 1998; Osher, Hamer, & Benjamin, 2000; Ridley, 1999).

Thinking It Through:

1. What difficulties do genetic researchers face in trying to investigate the links between genes and behavior?
2. Describe how individual variations in thrill-seeking might relate to developmental problems later in childhood and adolescence.
3. What are the legal implications in finding a genetic link to behavior?

---

infections and may lead to an early death. For African Americans, the risk of having both genes for the disease is about 1 in 500 (Mange & Mange, 1994).

The genes that cause diseases such as sickle cell anemia do not die out of the population because they confer genetic advantages as well as disadvantages, thus favoring a kind of genetic diversity called **balanced polymorphism.** For example, although few individuals with sickle cell anemia survive to reproduce, those who are heterozygous for the disease are resistant to malaria. Because they increase the likelihood of survival for those who are heterozygous, genes like those for sickle cell anemia are preserved in a population (Plomin, DeFries, McClearn, & Rutter, 1997).

Sex-Linked Transmission

Hemophilia causes excessive bleeding because of failures in blood clotting. This genetic disease was frequently observed among members of European royalty. The pattern of transmission is recessive, but with a twist. In this case, as is true for virtually all cases of sex-linked transmission, the gene for the disease is found on the X chromosome. Recessive transmission is different on the sex chromosomes than on the autosomes. On the autosomes, two recessive copies of the gene must be present for the characteristic to be expressed. This is not true on the sex chromosomes. Because the Y chromosome is smaller than the X, it does not carry as much genetic material. A single recessive gene on the unmatched segment of the X chromosome may express itself, because there is no corresponding gene on the Y to suppress it. Figure 3.3c shows how sex-linked transmissions of such conditions as hemophilia, baldness, and color-blindness occur. With sex-linked transmission, females are more likely to be carriers and males are about three times more likely to have the disease. For example, **fragile X syndrome**—a common cause of mild to moderate mental retardation—occurs in 1 in 1250 males and 1 in 2500 females (Plomin, DeFries et al., 1997). Fragile X syndrome stems from a mutated region near the tip of the long arm of the X chromosome. At this point on the chromosome, the more copies there are of a particular amino acid (trinucleotide, CGG), the more severe the retardation. Individuals with fragile X syndrome may have protruding ears, a prominent jaw, unusual speech, and poor eye contact.

Polygenic Transmission

Dominant, recessive, and sex-linked patterns are the most straightforward mechanisms for transferring genetic information from one generation to the next. However, many

balanced polymorphism a kind of genetic diversity in which the genes that cause diseases provide certain genetic advantages as well as disadvantages

fragile X syndrome a condition passed on by sex-linked transmission and characterized by protruding ears, prominent jaw, unusual speech, poor eye contact, and mild to moderate retardation

characteristics, such as a predisposition for colon cancer or diabetes, are coded by multiple genes and may require an environmental stimulus for the disease to be manifested.

HOW DO GENES AND ENVIRONMENTS WORK TOGETHER?

The nature-nurture issue is well illustrated by considering how genes and environments work together to produce human development. A child's phenotype unfolds during development, when genes and gene products interact with each other and with environmental factors. The interesting issue is how genes and environmental factors interact to produce the many variations we can observe among different people.

With all the discussion about how single genes can cause disorders, it is easy to think that genes determine development. However, from what is known about genes in animals and plants, it is clear that possession of a gene is not a guarantee that it will be expressed the same way in every individual. Remember that virtually all the cells in our bodies contain the same genetic material, but a cell in the brain does not function the same way as a cell in the liver. This is because different genes are being "turned on" in different cells, producing different proteins, which then lead to different functions. When a gene is expressed—"turned on"—its chemical products are produced, and these products interact with the elements of the internal environment (e.g., other gene products) and external environment (e.g., nutrition, climate, exercise). Some genes, such as those determining blood types, are directly expressed in essentially the same way regardless of the context or outside conditions. Other genes may be expressed fully, partially, or not at all, depending on outside conditions. Furthermore, some genes do not express themselves except under particular circumstances. Siamese cats have a gene that expresses itself differently depending on the environmental conditions, especially temperature—the lower the temperature, the darker the fur and the more extensive the dark areas. Apparently, the enzyme that produces the pigment to darken the fur (which is coded by the gene) works more effectively at lower temperatures, farther from the center of the body. Thus, Siamese cats vary in how much dark fur is on their paws, ears, and faces. Similarly, many human dominant traits for diseases are variable in their expression, allowing some individuals to have a very mild form of a disease while others have more serious forms.

Scientists are focusing attention on finding out when and how different genes express themselves so that they can better control and intervene in faulty genes. The environment plays an important role in how and when genes are expressed. Also, the particular genes that are expressed vary depending on the developmental stage of the organism. Researchers have discovered, for instance, that out of 1800 genes in strawberries, about 200 change their expression depending on whether the strawberry is green or fully ripe (Aharoni et al., 2000).

Although single genes can be the cause of certain diseases or characteristics, most physical features, disorders, and behaviors are likely influenced by multiple genes and by genes in interaction with environmental agents, as discussed earlier. Many characteristics, such as skin color, are due to polygenic inheritance. Also, **gene-environment (G-E) interactions,** in which the influence of a gene varies depending on its environment, account for many aspects of development. Consider, for example, a gene-gene-environment interaction involved in bladder cancer. Leslie inherits the two genes (NAT1 and NAT2) and smokes. Compared to her smoker friend, Jerry, who did not inherit NAT1 and NAT2, Leslie has a much greater chance of developing bladder cancer. This is because the NAT2 gene reduces Leslie's ability to metabolize carcinogens and the NAT1 gene transforms compounds into carcinogens more rapidly than normal—and tobacco smoke provides the chemicals that become transformed into carcinogens (Taylor & Bell, 1998). If Leslie never smoked, her NAT1 and NAT2 genes might not cause her any serious problems. In this case, the environmental input—smoking—is as central to getting cancer as are the genes, and neither, by itself, can be accurately labeled the cause of bladder cancer.

Investigating the causes for a child's behavior is complicated by the fact that there are various types of G-E interactions influencing development (Scarr & McCartney, 1983). Parents, because they share genetic material with their child, often provide a rearing environ-

gene-environment (G-E) interaction a situation in which the influence of a gene varies depending on its environment

ment that matches the child's genotype, creating a **passive G-E interaction.** Because the parents' own behavior is influenced by their genetic inheritance, this inheritance then influences the kind of environment in which the child is raised. Parents who enjoy reading are likely to provide their child with a rearing environment that encourages reading. Children's genotypes also draw responses from others, giving rise to an **evocative G-E interaction.** For instance, a child who smiles at people is likely to be treated positively. The third type is an **active G-E interaction,** created when people seek out environments compatible with their genotype. Children who are relatively inactive may seek out others who are quiet and studious, while avoiding sports. This behavior is called *niche-building,* because it involves selecting for oneself the aspects of the environment that are most comfortable and then learning from exposure to those environments.

GENOMES TO LIFE PROJECT

Identifying the sequence of the human genome is a crucial step in understanding human development. Once sequencing is complete, the next step is even more far-reaching—namely, to develop a fundamental, comprehensive, and systemic understanding of life. This is the goal of the most ambitious biological program yet proposed, called the Genomes to Life Project. Rather than concentrating on the individual life components, such as genes and other DNA sequences, this new program intends to consider an integrated view of biology at a whole-systems level. The plan for this ten-year program is to use DNA sequences as the starting point for tackling questions about the most fundamental and essential processes of life. How do organisms develop, survive, carry out their normal lives, and reproduce? Scientists will consider how biology and environmental factors interact over time in dynamic and transactional ways to produce development.

WHAT ARE COMMON CHROMOSOMAL ABNORMALITIES?

The chances that a healthy mother will give birth to a healthy infant are high. Nonetheless, 3 to 5 percent of newborns have some type of genetic or chromosomal abnormality. Genetic disorders are due to flaws in one or two genes. In contrast, chromosomal abnormalities occur when a child is born with missing or extra chromosomes. Most embryos with genetic or chromosomal abnormalities do not survive until birth—they are spontaneously aborted, or miscarried, before the mother even knows she is pregnant.

DOWN SYNDROME

A common chromosomal abnormality is *Down syndrome,* which occurs in about 1 in 900 live births (March of Dimes, 2000). About 90 percent of children with Down syndrome have forty-seven chromosomes rather than the normal forty-six, with an extra number 21 chromosome (referred to as *trisomy 21*). This excess genetic material results from the failure of chromosomes to separate during meiosis. About 5000 children are born each year with Down syndrome, and more than 350,000 people in the United States currently have Down syndrome (National Down Syndrome Society, 2000).

Most children with Down syndrome have certain physical characteristics, including wide-spaced eyes, a large protruding tongue, short stature, a round face, folds in the corners of their eyes, and unusual creases on the palms of their hands (Hassold & Patterson, 1998). Children with Down syndrome also often have heart and eye defects and may have immunological problems that make them susceptible to diseases. These physical problems account for the lower life expectancy for Down syndrome individuals, but life expectancy has increased from an average of 15 years in the 1940s to 55 or more years today (March of Dimes, 2000).

passive G-E interaction a situation in which parents provide a rearing environment that matches the child's own genotype

evocative G-E interaction a situation in which the child's genotype draws responses from others

active G-E interaction a situation in which the child seeks out environments compatible with his or her genotype

Down syndrome children tend to be identifiable by their facial features, such as a large tongue, wide-spaced eyes, and a round face. What risk factors increase a couple's chance of giving birth to a child with Down syndrome?

Down syndrome children have mental retardation, with intelligence scores ranging from 20 to 80 (100 is an average score), but most are in the mild to moderate retardation range (Plomin, DeFries, et al., 1997; Robinson, Goodman, & O'Brien, 1984). Language skills are severely impaired (Fowler, Gelman, & Gleitman, 1994). By adolescence, language skills remain at the level of a 3-year-old (Plomin, DeFries, et al., 1997). About 50 percent of children with Down syndrome have visual or hearing impairments, some of which are correctable with glasses or surgery. About 50 percent of Down syndrome children develop behavioral problems as they grow older, especially boys with limited or no language skills (Tager-Flusberg, 1994).

Young mothers have little risk of giving birth to Down syndrome infants—only 1 in 2400 live births of Down syndrome infants are to mothers under 20 years of age. By age 35, the risk increases to 1 in every 365 births; and by age 40, the risk is 1 in 110 live births (National Down Syndrome Society, 2000). The most common cause of Down syndrome is a failure of sex cell division during the formation of ova (Mange & Mange, 1994; Plomin, DeFries et al., 1997).

SEX CHROMOSOME ABNORMALITIES

Sex chromosome abnormalities include having an extra X or Y chromosome and lacking an X chromosome. Through karyotype analyses, many more cases of sex chromosome abnormalities can now be identified.

Turner's Syndrome

Girls born with *Turner's syndrome* are missing either the second X chromosome (XO) or part of the second X chromosome, usually as a result of cell division abnormalities in the father's sperm (Mange & Mange, 1994). Estimates vary, but there may be 1 case of Turner's syndrome in every 2500 births (Plomin, DeFries, et al., 1997). Girls with Turner's syndrome lack ovaries and have immature external genitalia. They tend to be short, with broad chests and wide (webbed) necks. This condition often can be identified at birth, but many girls are not identified until they reach puberty and fail to menstruate. Early identification is useful because hormone therapy can help. Girls with Turner's syndrome have normal verbal skills but often have poor spatial skills, difficulty sustaining attention and remembering information, and delayed social skills (McCauley, Kay, Ito, & Treder, 1987). They are also prone to heart, kidney, and thyroid problems (Turner Syndrome Society of the US, 2001).

Trisomy-X Syndrome

The chromosome disorder 47,XXX, in which girls are born with an extra X chromosome, occurs in approximately 1 out of 1000 female births. These females are phenotypically normal but may have a slightly lower intelligence level than 46,XX females (Hartl, 1994). They often are quiet and passive, and they may have delayed development of speech and motor skills. Females with 47,XXX are usually fertile, although they may reach menopause at an earlier age than 46,XX females.

Klinefelter's Syndrome

Boys born with an extra X chromosome have *Klinefelter's syndrome* (XXY). This is probably the most common chromosomal variation found in humans (Klinefelter Syndrome & Associates, 2001). The likelihood of this disorder is 1 or 2 cases per 1000 births (Plomin, DeFries, & McClearn, 1990). Boys with Klinefelter's syndrome are sterile and tend to have long limbs and immature testes (Sotos, 1997). Because they lack adequate male hormones, they do not develop masculine characteristics at puberty, such as facial and body hair, and may have femalelike breast development. Early hormone replacement therapy can produce a more typical male pattern of development. Mental retardation may occur (Jones & Cahill, 1994). Klinefelter's boys often have language deficits, attention problems, and reading difficulties (Rovet et al., 1996).

XYY Syndrome

Boys born with *XYY syndrome,* characterized by one or more extra Y chromosomes, appear normal (Jones & Cahill, 1994). XYY boys are tall, have severe acne during adolescence, are poorly coordinated, and may exhibit impulsive behaviors and lower intelligence (Kumra et al., 1998). The more Y chromosomes a boy has, the lower his intelligence is likely to be.

XYY patterns are caused by cell division problems during sperm production. About 1 in 1000 births is a boy with extra Y chromosomes (Plomin, DeFries, & McClearn, 1990).

In the 1960s, researchers identified a higher-than-expected frequency of the XYY pattern in inmates of a maximum security prison. The hypothesis was proposed that having an extra Y chromosome produces aggressive and antisocial behavior. Later studies revealed, however, that this hypothesis is wrong: male prisoners in general, regardless of the nature of their crime, are likely to have XYY patterns. These findings suggest that lower intelligence and impulsive behavior, rather than aggressiveness, may land XYY men in prison (Sutton, 1988).

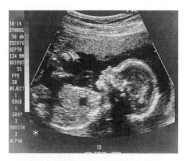

In this ultrasound image of a fetus, features such as the head, arms, and legs are easily identifiable. Physicians use these images to look for physical abnormalities such as neural tube defects or missing arms or legs. Can you explain how an ultrasound works?

HOW ARE GENETIC DISEASES DETECTED

In the past, family planning was limited to the ability to choose whether or not to have a child. Today, with tremendous advances in the ability to detect genetic and chromosomal abnormalities, more options are available to help families plan for the future. Fortunately, in most cases the outcome of genetic testing is favorable, and families can be assured that they will have a child who is no more at risk for health problems than other children (Mange & Mange, 1994).

GENETIC TECHNOLOGY

Genetic and chromosomal disorders account for many problems that affect the health and well-being of infants. Because of the significance of these disorders for infant health, many technologies have been developed to assess the status of infants even before they are born. Some of these technologies, such as ultrasound imaging, involve visual examination of the unborn child to determine physical defects. Other technologies, such as amniocentesis, require obtaining genetic material that is used to test for genetic and chromosomal problems.

Ultrasound Imaging

A painless and virtually risk-free procedure for identifying some developmental problems is **ultrasound,** in which video images of the fetus and its internal organs are produced from the echoes of sound waves. Ultrasound can detect heart conditions and physical deformities. Ultrasound is used with other techniques when an accurate image of the fetus's location is needed. Studies show that ultrasound helps identify possible birth defects when performed by physicians with extensive training in fetal diagnosis (Crane et al., 1994), and many women want an ultrasound as part of their routine pregnancy exams (Stephens, Montefalcon, & Lane, 2000).

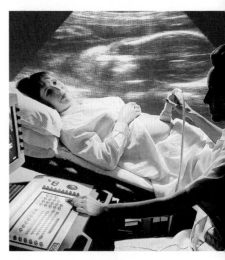

This woman is undergoing an ultrasound procedure. What advantages are associated with this procedure compared to other prenatal tests?

Chorionic Villus Sampling

Since the 1980s, **chorionic villus sampling (CVS)** has been successfully used to assess genetic material in fetal cells. Either by inserting a needle through the mother's abdominal wall or by inserting a catheter through the mother's cervix, cells are removed from the projections on the chorionic membrane (a layer of protective cells surrounding the fetus); these are then analyzed for genetic defects (Wapner, 1997).

CVS can be done during the first trimester of pregnancy, usually nine to twelve weeks after conception. The risk of problems associated with CVS is very low (Salihu, Boos, & Schmidt, 1997), particularly when it is performed after the eighth week of pregnancy by experienced medical personnel (Wilson, 2000). The early detection CVS affords gives couples more time to consider their options—such as whether to continue or terminate the pregnancy.

ultrasound a procedure used to identify some developmental problems, in which video images of the fetus and the fetus's internal organs are produced from the echoes of sound waves

chorionic villus sampling (CVS) a procedure used to assess genetic material in fetal cells, in which cells are removed from the projections on the chorionic membrane

THE PRACTICAL IMPACT: NURTURING CHILDREN

Treating a Diseased Fetus

Their first son died when he was only 7 months old. He died of an X-linked recessive disease called *severe combined immunodeficiency,* which strikes approximately 1 out of every 100,000 babies. Because it is X-linked, it strikes boys more often than girls. The disease produces a very weak immune system, increasing the child's susceptibility to infections. Most infants born with this disease die within the first year of life. When the woman became pregnant again, she was concerned that her second child would also have the disease. Using chorionic villus sampling, doctors tested the unborn child's DNA. The child, another son, was affected. In a medical first, the child was treated for the disease in utero by Dr. Alan Flake, a pediatric surgeon at Children's Hospital of Philadelphia. Using the unaffected father's bone marrow, Flake gave the fetus three transplants of cells by ultrasound-guided injections at 16, 17½, and 18½ weeks. At birth, the child seemed normal except for an easily treated rash. At 11 months, he showed no signs of the immune disease and was healthy.

Medical treatment for unborn children, or *fetology,* is a relatively new medical specialty. To date, medical treatments such as blood and bone marrow transfusions, insertion of drainage tubes, and surgical repairs have been performed in utero. Although there are risks to these prenatal treatments, early treatment can prevent symptoms of a disease and may even eliminate the disease entirely (Flake et al., 1996). Similar techniques may soon be used to treat other genetic disorders such as sickle cell anemia. With improvements in technology and medical science, it is likely that fetologists will be able to treat more and more cases in the future.

Amniocentesis

A common method of detecting genetic problems during prenatal development is **amniocentesis,** in which a long, thin needle is inserted through the mother's abdominal wall into the fluid-filled amniotic sac surrounding the fetus. The amniotic fluid contains some skin cells of the fetus; some fluid is removed, and then these cells are examined to determine whether genetic defects are present. In addition, the analysis determines whether biochemical or metabolic imbalances are present. The sex of the child also may be identified.

Studies show that the risk of amniocentesis for the unborn child is small (Simpson & Elias, 1994). The major drawback is that the test is done relatively late in pregnancy (fifteen to nineteen weeks) and obtaining the results takes several weeks. The advantage is that it is a very accurate method of identifying a variety of prenatal developmental problems (Wilson, 2000).

Detection of Alpha Fetoprotein

The mother's blood contains *alpha fetoproteins,* which can be used to screen for several developmental problems during pregnancy. If the mother has a high level of alpha fetoproteins, the fetus may have a neural tube defect (such as spina bifida), which then can be confirmed through ultrasound. If the mother's alpha fetoprotein level is low, the fetus may have a chromosomal abnormality (such as Down syndrome), which must be confirmed through genetic testing (Akbas et al., 2001).

GENETIC COUNSELING

Despite the many advances that science has made in detecting genetic and chromosomal abnormalities, tens of thousands of children are born each year with birth defects. Birth defects occur in 1 of every 33 births and are the leading cause of infant death, accounting for about 22 percent of all infant deaths (March of Dimes, 2000). Table 3.1 lists the incidence of the most common types of birth defects.

Genetic counselors help couples determine the likelihood of having children with birth defects, assist them in making decisions about conception, and provide counseling for families who have given birth to infants with genetic problems. Genetic counseling is recommended of individuals in the following situations (Mange & Mange, 1994):

✦ Individuals who have children with a genetic disorder

amniocentesis a procedure used to determine whether genetic defects are present, in which amniotic fluid is collected

TABLE 3.1

Incidence of Common Birth Defects

BIRTH DEFECT	ESTIMATED INCIDENCE
Structural/Metabolic	
Heart and circulation	1 in 115 births
Muscles and skeleton	1 in 130 births
Genital and urinary tract	1 in 135 births
Nervous system and eyes	1 in 235 births
Chromosomal disorders	1 in 600 births
Down syndrome	1 in 900 births
Respiratory tract	1 in 900 births
Cleft lip/palate	1 in 930 births
Spina bifida	1 in 2000 births
Metabolic disorders	1 in 3500 births
Congenital Infections	
Syphilis	1 in 2000 births
HIV infection	1 in 2700 births
Rubella	1 in 100,000 births
Other	
Fetal alcohol syndrome	1 in 1000 births
Rh blood incompatibility	1 in 1400 births

NOTE: All numbers are based on the best available estimates, which underestimate the incidence of many birth defects.
SOURCE: March of Dimes, 2000.

   ◆ Individuals with a known genetic disorder who would like to start families
   ◆ Women who have had repeated miscarriages
   ◆ Older pregnant women
   ◆ Couples at risk for genetic diseases because of their ethnicity or ancestry
   ◆ Couples at risk for genetic diseases because they are related to each other

Genetic counseling begins with an accurate medical history and diagnosis. Karyotype analyses may be done to determine the genetic patterns of the parents, and a pedigree analysis may be carried out to determine genetic diseases of other family members. Genetic counselors use this information to help families make difficult decisions about conception, pregnancy, and birth.

HOW DOES PRENATAL DEVELOPMENT PROCEED

From the time the sperm and egg unite, miraculous changes occur that culminate in the birth of an infant. How these changes are brought about, what influences them, and how to maximize optimal outcomes are questions that confront parents and scientists. In this section, you will learn that prenatal development is made up of many complex and interrelated processes working together to produce a human infant.

OVULATION

For pregnancy to occur, a human egg, or **ovum,** and a sperm cell must meet and share their genetic material. This process begins with ovulation. Each month, a woman releases at least

ovum a human egg

one ovum from her ovaries during ovulation. Ovulation occurs as a normal part of the woman's menstrual cycle. In addition to ensuring that ovulation takes place, the menstrual cycle initiates changes in the uterus that prepare it to receive a fertilized ovum.

The average menstrual cycle is approximately equal to a lunar month but can vary greatly, from twenty-five to thirty-five days. At birth, females have approximately 400,000 to 500,000 immature ova in each ovary, and no new ova develop after birth. With an average cycle of twenty-eight days, a women ovulates about 13 ova per year, or 481 ova in the thirty-seven years of her reproductive life (Jones, 1997). How these ova are selected from the thousands contained in a woman's ovary remains a mystery.

Each menstrual cycle is divided into three main phases. The first is the *menstrual phase* (lasting four to five days), when menstruation (the "period") takes place. Menstruation occurs because the lining of the uterus degenerates and is expelled in a bloody discharge.

The second phase is the *follicular phase,* in which the lining of the uterus grows back and thickens, influenced by the female hormone estrogen. This phase continues until ovulation, which occurs on about day 14 of a 28-day cycle or day 16 of a 30-day cycle (Rathus, Nevid, & Fichner-Rathus, 1993). This is the time of the month when a woman is most likely to get pregnant.

The last phase is the *luteal phase,* lasting from ovulation until the beginning of the next menstruation (usually about fourteen days). During this phase, different hormones are secreted (such as progesterone) that prepare the uterus for the arrival of a fertilized ovum. If fertilization does not occur, the ovum disintegrates and is washed out of the body in the menstrual flow. If fertilization does occur, the fertilized ovum embeds itself in the uterine lining; menstrual cycles usually stop during pregnancy (Jones, 1997).

SPERMATOGENESIS

After puberty, men produce sperm in their testes on a daily basis throughout their lives (about 100 sperm are produced per second). Sperm develop in a process called **spermatogenesis,** which requires about seventy-two days to produce a mature sperm cell (Rathus et al., 1993). In early stages, sperm are called **spermatocytes,** and each contains forty-six chromosomes, including one X and one Y sex chromosome. These spermatocytes divide into two **spermatids,** each of which has twenty-three chromosomes, including either an X or a Y sex chromosome. Mature spermatids, called **spermatozoa,** are fully functional and capable of fertilizing a human ovum.

Approximately 200 to 500 million sperm are released at each ejaculation (Wong & Perry, 1998). A man is considered fertile if there are approximately 60 million sperm in a normal ejaculation, 60 percent are normal in shape and size, and 40 percent of these sperm are mobile (Institute of Medicine, 1990).

FERTILIZATION

The mature ovum is one of the largest cells in the human body, with a diameter of approximately 190 micrometers (about the size of a period printed on this page). As shown in Figure 3.4a, the two primary layers are an outer protective layer of cells and an inner nucleus that contains twenty-three chromosomes—the genetic material of the woman. Each month during her reproductive lifetime, a woman releases an ovum during ovulation. Once released, the ovum enters the fallopian tube and is moved toward the uterus by cilia, small hairlike structures lining the tube. The ovum cannot propel itself and so is dependent on the cilia to move it to the uterus (Glass, 1994). For fertilization to occur, an ovum must be penetrated by a sperm cell within 24 to 48 hours after ovulation.

A healthy sperm cell is about .0002 inch long and is composed of a head, body, and tail (see Figure 3.4, b and c). The head contains the genetic material, and the tail moves the sperm through the woman's reproductive system. The body contains the energy production system for moving the tail (Wong & Perry, 1998).

spermatogenesis the process by which sperm develop

spermatocytes sperm in the early stages of development, at which time each one contains forty-six chromosomes, including one X and one Y sex chromosome

spermatids the result of the division of spermatocytes, each one containing twenty-three chromosomes and including either an X or a Y sex chromosome

spermatozoa mature spermatids, which are fully functional and capable of fertilizing a human ovum

F IGURE 3.4

Ovum and Sperm

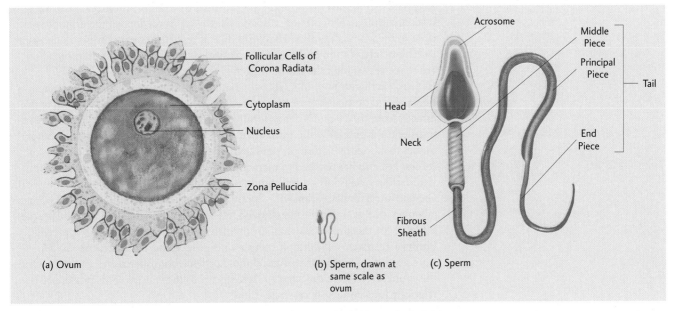

(a) Ovum

(b) Sperm, drawn at same scale as ovum

(c) Sperm

The ovum is much larger than the sperm. The chromosomal material is in the nucleus of the ovum and in the head of the sperm. Can you explain the processes by which ova and sperm are produced?

As noted earlier, males produce X and Y sperm. If an X sperm fertilizes the ovum, a girl is conceived; if a Y sperm fertilizes the ovum, the child will be a boy. Thus, it is the father's sperm that determines the child's sex (the mother contributes only X chromosomes).

Once ejaculated, the sperm begin a long journey through the female reproductive tract. Of the millions of sperm that are ejaculated, only 100 to 1000 actually reach the ovum. Thus, there is a "survival of the fittest" test that eliminates many damaged or weak sperm. For fertilization to occur, sperm must reach and penetrate the ovum within about three days of ejaculation. After this time, the fertilizing abilities of sperm decline, although in rare cases sperm can survive longer than six days (Jones, 1997).

Fertilization begins when a sperm penetrates the outer layer of an ovum. Once this happens, the ovum releases a secretion that thickens its outer layer, preventing other sperm from penetrating it. After penetration, the head of the sperm sinks into the nucleus of the ovum and the corresponding chromosomes align in pairs. Fertilization is complete once the chromosomes from the sperm and ovum combine to form twenty-three pairs that carry unique genetic instructions (Moore, 1998).

OVERCOMING INFERTILITY

About 8.5 percent of couples who want children are unsuccessful in their efforts. Infertility is defined as being unable to conceive after twelve months of unprotected intercourse or being unable to carry a fetus to term (Institute of Medicine, 1990; Keel, May, & DeJonge, 2000). For about 50 percent of infertile couples, the conditions that complicate conception are related to the mother; abnormal ovulation, damaged ovaries, and endometriosis are a few. Another 30 percent of infertile couples have conception problems that are attributed to the father—low sperm count, hormone deficiency, and sperm antibodies. For the remaining 20 percent, there are complications involving both parents (Mange & Mange, 1994). Parents who are having difficulty conceiving, however, have many options, including surgery, hormone therapy, and artificial insemination, to remedy their situation.

Couples spend almost $3 billion each year trying to overcome fertility problems. In addition to surgery, traditional medical procedures, and adoption, several new procedures for "assisted reproduction" are now available.

- **Artificial Insemination.**   Sperm are provided by a donor, and near the time when the woman is ovulating, a doctor uses a syringe to deposit the donor's sperm close to the woman's uterus. This procedure is repeated as many times as necessary to achieve fertilization and is often successful. About 8000 US children each year are conceived though the use of artificial insemination.
- **In Vitro Fertilization.**   In 1978, baby Louise, a normal baby girl, was born in England after fertilization in a test tube. The basic procedure is to obtain an ovum directly from the woman's ovary, fertilize it with sperm in a culture dish, and then transfer the zygote(s) to the woman's uterus. Women are usually treated with hormones to induce ovulation of more than one egg, which increases the chances of success but also has resulted in many multiple pregnancies. The success rate for in vitro fertilization is low—only about 10 percent of such attempts end in a live birth.
- **Gamete Intrafallopian Transfer.**   Sperm and an ovum are deposited into the woman's fallopian tube, and then fertilization occurs as it would normally. The rate of success is higher for this procedure than for in vitro fertilization (16 versus 10 percent).
- **Embryo Transfer.**   If both partners are infertile, embryo transfer may be a suitable option. In this procedure, donors provide both sperm and an ovum. Once the ovum is fertilized, the zygote is transferred to the woman. This procedure is relatively rare, and its success rate is low.
- **Surrogate Mothers.**   A surrogate mother is artificially inseminated with sperm from the man, carries the fertilized egg through pregnancy and birth, and then gives up the child.

Although it is possible for infertile couples to have children through these assisted reproductive techniques, they are not a solution for all couples. Procedures can be lengthy, expensive, and physically and emotionally demanding. Most physicians recommend that couples begin with the less expensive and less invasive procedures, progressing to the more aggressive methods later (Keel et al., 2000). Furthermore, these techniques have generated important ethical and moral questions that are as yet unanswered. For example, what happens to their frozen embryos when a couple divorce? What happens when a surrogate mother decides that she cannot give up the baby after having carried it for nine months? Until these questions are resolved, interested couples need to be aware that uncertainties exist and take steps to minimize undesired consequences (Robertson, 1996).

OVERVIEW OF PRENATAL DEVELOPMENT

In most Western cultures, birth is considered the beginning of a person's lifetime (Rosenblith, 1992). At birth, however, infants already have been influenced by their genetic makeup and the qualities of their prenatal environment. An understanding of the changes that take place during prenatal development is needed to fully understand later development.

Prenatal development, which begins at conception and ends at birth, proceeds through three stages.

germinal stage the first stage of prenatal development, which begins at conception and lasts until the fertilized egg implants itself in the uterine wall

embryonic stage the second stage of prenatal development, which begins at implantation and lasts until about eight weeks

fetal stage the third and final stage of prenatal development, which begins at about eight weeks and lasts until birth

- The **germinal stage** begins at conception and lasts until the fertilized egg implants itself in the uterine wall (usually about two weeks). Cell division and differentiation are the main qualities of this stage.
- The **embryonic stage** begins at implantation and lasts until about eight weeks. The developing child is referred to as an *embryo*. During this stage, the major organs and body parts develop almost daily. This stage is the most critical time in prenatal development; it is when environmental damage is most likely to occur.
- The **fetal stage** begins at about eight weeks and lasts until birth. The developing child is referred to as a *fetus*. During this stage, elaboration of the existing organs and structures occurs and the brain develops rapidly.

TABLE 3.2

Early Timetable of Prenatal Development

DAY	MILESTONE
0	Ovulation occurs (ovum lasts up to 24 hours; sperm last up to
1	6 days).
6	Fertilization occurs.
7	Zygote adheres to uterine wall.
10	Implantation begins.
14	Implantation is complete.
15	Amnion, chorion, placenta, and umbilical cord begin to develop. First menstrual period is missed.

SOURCE: Adapted from Jones, 1997.

THE GERMINAL STAGE

The fertilized ovum, called the **zygote,** takes two to three days to reach the uterus. During this time, the zygote divides several times through mitosis, producing cells that are identical to the zygote. The first cell division occurs within about twenty-four hours after fertilization. By the time the zygote reaches the uterus, it consists of twelve to sixteen cells that are beginning to separate into two layers. The inner layer of cells develops into the infant, and the outer mass of cells eventually forms the structures that support the developing infant, such as the umbilical cord and placenta (Wong & Perry, 1998). Table 3.2 outlines the major changes of early prenatal development.

After two or three days of floating freely in the uterus, the zygote implants itself in the wall of the uterus. The cells of the outer layers of the zygote develop hairlike projections that burrow into the lining of the uterus. Eventually, these hairlike structures will transfer nutrients to the zygote. The connections established by implantation provide a source of nutrients for the zygote until the support structures are fully functional. This process is complete during the second week, and the zygote, measuring no more than 1 millimeter in diameter, now consists of a few thousand cells. Implantation also triggers hormonal changes that prevent menstruation and provide the woman with some of the first noticeable signs that she is pregnant.

Ectopic Pregnancies

Usually implantation takes place in the uterus, but sometimes it occurs outside the uterus—most commonly in a fallopian tube, but occasionally in the abdomen or ovary. This condition, known as an **ectopic pregnancy** (outside the uterus), occurs in about 1 in every 100 pregnancies (Wong & Perry, 1998). The main cause of ectopic pregnancies is damaged fallopian tubes. Ectopic pregnancies cause abdominal pain and irregular vaginal bleeding and are dangerous to the health of the mother if not terminated.

Multiple Pregnancies

Another complication of fertilization occurs when multiple pregnancies (such as twins) develop. In the United States, twins occur in about 1 in every 80 pregnancies, but in other parts of the world, the incidence varies, with a much higher rate in West Africa, for example, and a much lower rate in Japan. The incidence of twin pregnancies is up to four times greater than the rate of twin births, though, because often one of the embryos spontaneously aborts early in development (Jones, 1997).

Rates of twin births generally are greater than they were ten years ago. As you can see in Figure 3.5, as the age of the mother increases, the rates of twin births increase, becoming particularly high for mothers who are 45 to 49 years of age (National Center for Health

zygote the fertilized ovum

ectopic pregnancy a pregnancy that occurs outside the uterus

FIGURE 3.5

Rates of Twin Births by Age of Mother: 1990 vs. 1999

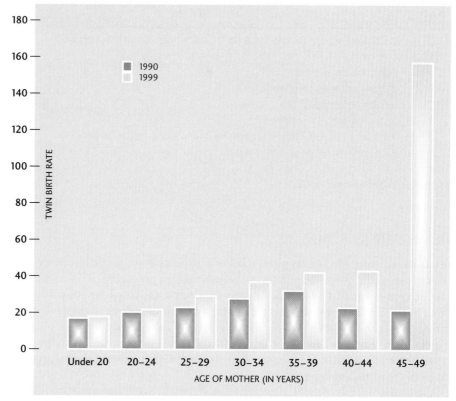

NOTE: Birth rate = twin births per 1000 live births.

SOURCE: National Center for Health Statistics, 2001a.

Notice that the rate of twins increases with the age of the mother only for those giving birth in 1999. Also notice the dramatic increase for the oldest mothers in 1999. What factors likely contributed to these increases?

Early in embryonic development, the human embryo is indistinguishable from embryos of other species. In this photo, the 5-week-old embryo is floating within the amniotic sac. How might the resemblance of embryos of different species at this stage be used to support an evolutionary view of development?

Statistics, 2001a). Notice the dramatic increase in twin births to older mothers since 1990—almost 600 percent. More than one-third (34 percent) of all births to mothers aged 45 to 49 were twin births. This high rate of twins among older women likely results from the use of fertility drugs by women who decided to delay pregnancy and then needed to overcome the greater difficulty in getting pregnant.

Multiple pregnancies involving more than two children are even rarer than twins. Triplets occur once in every 8000 to 9000 pregnancies, and quadruplets occur once in every 700,000 pregnancies (Grant, 1993). Because of the increased use of fertility drugs, the incidence of giving birth to 3 or more babies has quadrupled since 1980. The higher rates of multiple pregnancies among Caucasian American women likely result from the use of fertility drugs (see Figure 3.6). With increasing numbers of fetuses, the chance of survival and good outcomes decreases. But today's medical technology makes it more probable that multiple infants will survive—as in the case of Bobbi McCaughey, who, in 1997, gave birth to seven babies after she took fertility drugs to get pregnant.

THE EMBRYONIC STAGE

Once implantation occurs, the embryo and its support structures take shape and begin to function. Table 3.3 on page 80 identifies the major accomplishments of prenatal development. From the inner mass of cells, two membranes form that surround and protect the

FIGURE 3.6

Rates of Births Greater Than Twins, by Race

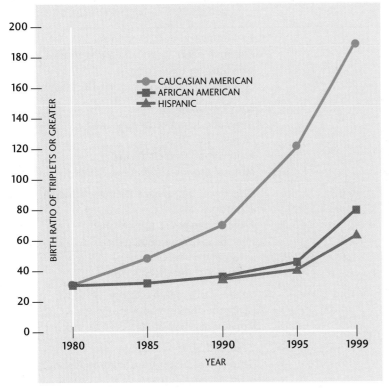

NOTE: Birth ratio = live births of 3 or more babies per 100,000 total live births. Data on Hispanic births available only from 1990 on.

SOURCE: National Center for Health Statistics, 2001a.

Notice that the rates of births greater than twins increased for all ethnic groups, but increased more for Caucasian American mothers than for minority mothers. What factors might explain the general increase in rates and the greater increase for Caucasian American mothers?

embryo. The first is the **amnion,** which grows over the embryo and becomes filled with *amniotic fluid.* The amount of amniotic fluid is about 5 to 10 milliliters after eight weeks of development and increases through pregnancy to a maximum of 1000 to 1200 milliliters (Wong & Perry, 1998). This sac and its fluid provide the developing embryo with shock-absorbing protection.

The second membrane is the **chorion,** which grows to surround the embryo after about one month of development. The chorion helps form the **placenta,** a mass of tissue through which nutrients and waste products are exchanged between the mother and the developing embryo. The placenta is made up of fine blood vessels (called *capillaries*) from the mother's and embryo's circulatory systems. The mother's blood does not directly mix with that of her developing child. The developing embryo is connected to the placenta by the **umbilical cord,** the lifeline of the embryo, which consists of two arteries and one vein.

The third week of prenatal development begins with the formation of three layers of cells. The outer layer is the *ectoderm,* which later becomes the skin and nervous system. The middle layer is the *mesoderm,* which becomes the muscles, bones, and circulatory system. The inner layer is the *endoderm,* which becomes the digestive system and lungs. The formation of these layers reveals the remarkable nature of early development. Early development involves not only the change from a single cell into a creature that ultimately consists of several trillion cells but also increasing cell differentiation. Our many different types of cells—hair cells, liver cells, brain cells, and so on—all form from a single cell.

amnion a membrane that grows over the embryo and becomes filled with amniotic fluid, which protects the embryo

chorion a membrane that grows to surround the embryo after about one month of development and helps form the placenta

placenta the structure through which nutrients and waste products are exchanged between the mother and the developing embryo

umbilical cord the lifeline of the embryo, consisting of two arteries and one vein

TABLE 3.3
Milestones and Characteristics of Prenatal Development

AGE (MONTHS)	LENGTH (INCHES)	WEIGHT	MILESTONES AND CHARACTERISTICS
1	.17		Backbone and vertebrae form. Primitive heart forms and starts to beat. Arm and leg buds form. Embryo is not yet distinguishable as human.
2	1.25	1 g	Bone cells appear. Arms and legs become distinct. Fingers and toes form. Major blood vessels form. Internal organs continue to develop.
3	3	28 g	Eyes form, but eyelids are fused closed. Ears form. Arms and legs are fully formed. Heartbeat can be detected. External genitalia develop. Fingernails and toenails form.
4	6.5–7	113 g (4 oz)	Head is large relative to rest of body. Face takes on human features. Movements may be detected by mother.
5	10–12	227–454 g (.5–1 lb)	Head and body hair are visible. Head is less disproportionate to rest of body. Brain develops rapidly. Periods of sleep alternate with periods of alertness.
6	11–14	567–681 g (1.25–1.5 lb)	Layers of the cortex of the brain develop. Skin is wrinkled. Skin is pink because blood in vessels is visible.
7	13–17	1135–1362 g (2.5–3 lb)	Fetus becomes viable. Eyelids open and eyelashes form. Teeth form.
8	16.5–18	2100 g (6 lb)	Fat deposits form. Body is more rounded. Skin unwrinkles. Testes in boys descend into scrotum sac.
9	20	3178–3405 g (7–7.5 lb)	Body hair is shed. Nails reach tips of fingers and toes. Growth rate slows down. Fetus moves into position for birth.

SOURCE: Bennett and Brown, 1993; Jones, 1997; Moore, 1993.

About twenty-one days after fertilization, the ectoderm begins to form a groove that develops into the *neural tube.* This tube eventually becomes the central nervous system. The front portion of the tube becomes the brain, and the back forms the spinal cord.

Within a few weeks, the embryo is about ½ inch long and looks more like a salamander than a human being. In fact, early in development it is almost impossible to distinguish embryos of different species. By the end of the embryonic period (at about eight weeks), however, human embryos look distinctively different than embryos of other species.

During the embryonic period, the brain, nervous system, circulatory system, and sensory organs develop. At four weeks, the heart, although still just a tube, begins to flutter and then beat. Arms and legs appear, first as buds and later as limbs. The liver, pancreas, and major divisions of intestines develop around this time and the embryo's face begins to form, although at this age the face is still unrecognizable. By eight weeks, the fingers and toes are visible and are noticeably webbed. At the end of eight weeks, the embryo weighs about .03 ounce and is slightly over 1 inch in length.

Development during the embryonic period proceeds according to two important principles. The first is that growth occurs from the head downwards—a principle referred to as **cephalocaudal development** (see Figure 3.7). The second is that body parts closer to the central axis of the body develop first, while those that are farther away from the center of the body (such as the hands) develop later. This principle is referred to as **proximodistal development.**

By the end of the embryonic period, 95 percent of the major body structures are developed and some are even functioning, although they are incapable of sustaining the

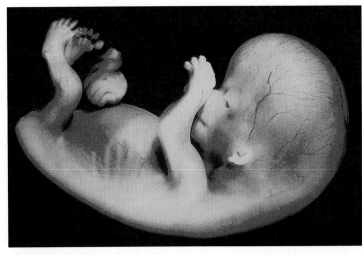

The 8-week-old embryo is beginning to look more human in its physical features. Why is the embryo most susceptible to damaging environmental influences during this time period?

IGURE 3.7

Changes in Body Proportion During Prenatal Development

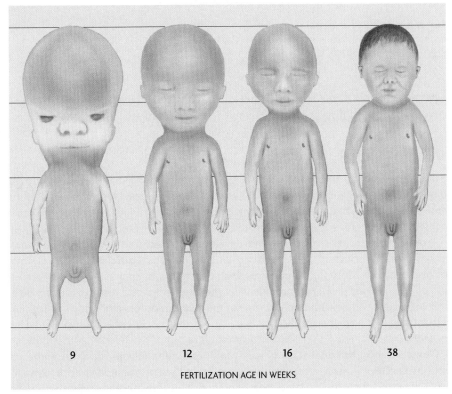

9   12   16   38

FERTILIZATION AGE IN WEEKS

SOURCE: Moore, 1998.

Notice that, as the embryo and fetus grow, the size of the head relative to the rest of the body changes. What other aspects of developmental change can you identify in this figure?

cephalocaudal development the principle that growth occurs from the head downwards

proximodistal development the principle that body parts closer to the central axis of the body develop first, while those farther away from the center of the body develop later

FIGURE 3.8

Growth and Change of Fetus and Mother

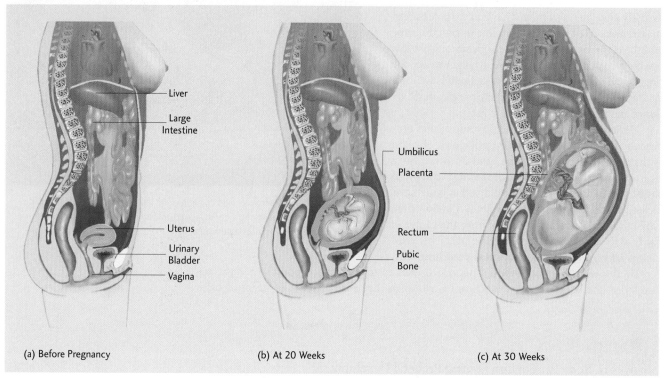

(a) Before Pregnancy   (b) At 20 Weeks   (c) At 30 Weeks

SOURCE: Moore, 1998.

Early in pregnancy, the embryo is small and causes few noticeable physical changes in the mother. Later in pregnancy, the physical changes in the mother increase as the baby grows larger. Can you describe how the mother's and the embryo's systems are connected?

embryo independent of the mother. Because the organs and body systems are forming, the embryonic period is a time of great vulnerability to environmental influences.

THE FETAL STAGE

The transition from an embryo to a fetus is gradual and signifies that the developing child is unquestionably recognizable as human. The fetal stage is marked by growth and elaboration of the structures that developed earlier. This is the final and longest phase of prenatal development—extending from about the ninth week after fertilization until birth.

Around the sixteenth week of prenatal development, many mothers first feel the movements of their unborn child. These fetal movements, known as **quickening,** are dramatic signs of pregnancy. More than a positive pregnancy test, a bulging abdomen, or even the sound of the fetal heartbeat, the movements of the fetus signal and confirm the presence of the life inside the woman. Quickening is one of the greatest sources of joy during pregnancy, and lack of fetal movements can be a source of great anxiety (Eisenberg, Murkoff, & Hathaway, 1999).

Growth during the fetal stage is very rapid, especially during the third and fourth months. The rate of growth is greater than at any other time before or after birth. By sixteen weeks, the fetus is three to four times larger and over a hundred times heavier than it was at the end of the embryonic period. It is 6 to 7 inches long and weighs about 4 ounces (Jones, 1997). As the fetus enlarges, the mother's uterus, or womb, grows; as a result, it is around the sixteenth week that her condition becomes obvious to others (see Figure 3.8).

quickening fetal movements during pregnancy

Important body changes occur during the third and fourth months. The fetus develops a penis or vagina at the beginning of the third month. In males, the process begins when the testes secrete the male hormone testosterone, which causes a group of cells to develop into the penis, scrotum, and seminal vesicles. In females, because testosterone is not secreted, these cells develop into the fallopian tubes, uterus, and vagina. Thus, boys' and girls' sex organs have the same origins but develop differently depending on the presence or absence of testosterone (Wong & Perry, 1998).

The nervous system also develops rapidly during the early part of the fetal period. By the fifth month, the cells of the brain have migrated to their proper locations and formed connections with other brain cells. These connections allow brain cells to communicate with one another and to control some bodily functions. The fetus displays simple reflexes such as

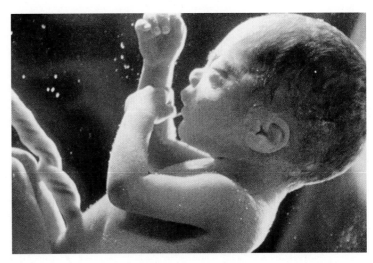

Notice that the 8-month-old fetus is quite well developed at this point. What major changes occur during the last trimester?

sucking and swallowing and can react to disturbances of its environment, such as loud noises made outside but near the mother's uterus (Jones, 1997). Such reactions indicate that the fetus is not simply an unreactive mass of tissue but is a responsive being, capable of learning (Joseph, 2000).

An important milestone is reached as the fetus enters the last trimester of prenatal development. Prior to this point, a fetus born prematurely has a poor chance of surviving. At about seven months, survival is possible with intensive care because the fetus's lungs and nervous system are developed enough to support breathing. Thus, the seventh month marks the **age of viability**—the point at which postnatal survival is likely (Moore, 1998).

During the last three months, the finishing touches of prenatal development are completed. At thirty weeks, the eyelids open to reveal fully formed eyes with pupils that respond to light. By thirty-five weeks, the hands have a firm grasp and the hair is growing. Increased production of fat makes the body more rounded and less wrinkled (Sadler, 2000). This increase in fat improves control of body temperature. By the end of the last trimester, the average newborn is about 20 inches long and weighs 7 to 7½ pounds.

WHAT CONDITIONS INFLUENCE PREGNANCY AND PRENATAL DEVELOPMENT?

Although genetic and chromosomal disorders cause some birth defects, about 80 percent of birth defects are caused by environmental problems during prenatal development. The unborn child has at least two lines of protection from environmental influences. The first is the amniotic fluid, which protects the fetus from physical injuries. The second line of protection is the **placental barrier,** created by blood vessel walls that separate the maternal and fetal circulatory systems. This barrier acts as a filter, blocking many harmful agents from entering the blood supply of the child. The placental barrier effectively blocks large agents, such as bacteria, but not smaller agents, such as viruses. The mother's hormones, any alcohol she drinks, and the nicotine from any cigarettes she smokes are among the substances that can cross the placental barrier. Thus, the protection provided by the placental barrier is incomplete.

Alcohol and cigarettes are examples of **teratogens**—agents that cross the placental barrier and cause or increase the incidence of physical malformations and behavioral and cognitive deficits in children. Many teratogens have been identified, including diseases such

age of viability the point at which postnatal survival is likely

placental barrier a line of protection for the unborn child, created by blood vessel walls that separate the maternal and fetal circulatory systems

teratogens agents that cross the placental barrier and cause or increase the incidence of physical malformations and behavioral and cognitive deficits

as smallpox and HIV, environmental agents such as X rays and pesticides, and drugs such as cocaine and alcohol. Although the effects of teratogens vary, the severity of these effects depends on at least three factors:

♦ **When the teratogenic exposure occurs.**   A particular teratogen will affect a zygote, an embryo, and a fetus differently. If the zygote is exposed to a teratogen, a spontaneous abortion may occur. As you can see in Figure 3.9, teratogenic exposure during the embryonic period is particularly harmful. During the embryonic stage, organs and body structures, which are undergoing rapid development, are likely to be damaged. Teratogenic exposure at the fetal stage, when the brain is developing quickly, may damage the nervous system and brain, affecting later behavior or intelligence.

♦ **Amount of teratogenic exposure.**   Some teratogens, especially alcohol and drugs, are dosage dependent; that is, the more the mother takes, the greater the likelihood

FIGURE 3.9
Critical Periods for Teratogenic Effects

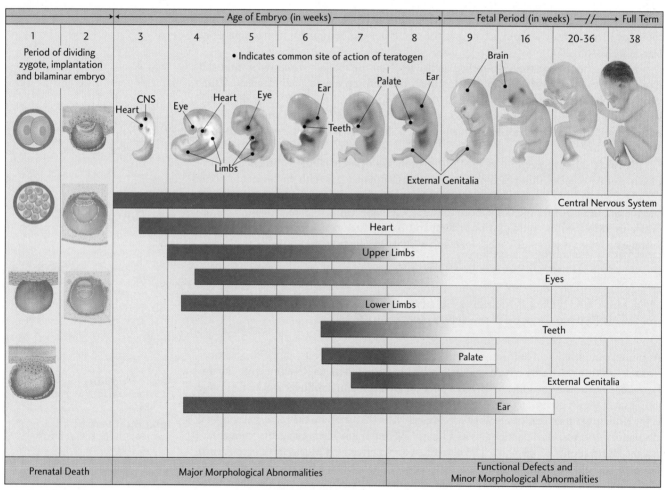

NOTE: Dark portions denote highly sensitive periods; light portions denote less sensitive periods.
SOURCE: Moore, 1998.

The timing of teratogen exposure is crucial. Notice that teratogens have the most impact during the embryonic stage, except on certain body parts such as the brain and ears, which continue to be at risk for teratogenic effects because they continue to grow and develop during the fetal period.

that the developing child will be affected. Similarly, the longer the exposure to teratogens, the greater the likelihood that development will be disrupted.

✦ **Fetal characteristics.**   Important individual differences occur in fetal reactions to a teratogen. Depending on constitution, some fetuses will perish under the influence of a particular teratogen, while others may suffer severe or mild complications.

These three factors operate together to determine the degree to which teratogens influence the developing child. Some effects are direct (for example, the fetus is exposed to alcohol when the mother drinks), and some are indirect (for example, the fetus receives less oxygen while the mother is smoking). Because many teratogenic effects occur before women even know they have conceived, a good strategy to ensure healthy offspring is for women to avoid teratogens if there is any possibility that they may be pregnant—that is, if they have had unprotected intercourse.

DISEASES

About 3 to 5 percent of birth defects are caused by infectious diseases transmitted to the developing child (Thorogood, 1997). Several diseases have a dramatic impact on the developing child, even when they produce only mild symptoms in the mother. The diseases most likely to influence prenatal development are caused by viruses. Approximately 5 percent of women who are pregnant are affected by viral diseases (Gibbs & Sweet, 1994).

Rubella

The placental barrier does not provide complete protection for the developing child. During a mini-epidemic of rubella—a form of measles—in the 1960s, 30,000 fetuses and newborns died and over 16,000 children were born deaf or blind (Rosenblith, 1992). Rubella causes flu-like symptoms so mild that pregnant women may not even realize they are ill. Nonetheless, rubella crosses the placental barrier and interferes with normal development during early pregnancy. If the mother has rubella during the first twelve weeks of pregnancy, the child has about an 80 percent chance of showing some effects. At thirteen to fourteen weeks, the risk drops to about 50 percent; by the end of the second trimester, the risk is 25 percent (Cunningham, MacDonald, & Gant, 1993).

As many as 2 in 10 women of childbearing age are susceptible to rubella, but the dangers of rubella can be prevented through immunization prior to pregnancy. Although preventive efforts have reduced rubella-related defects in infants, an increase has occurred in the last decade (National Center for Health Statistics, 1996). Today, about 1 in 100,000 infants has birth defects caused by rubella (March of Dimes, 2000). The incidence of rubella-related defects is especially high among Hispanic Americans and African Americans because of lower immunization rates (Office of Minority Health, 1998).

Syphilis

Unlike most other bacteria, the bacteria that cause syphilis can cross the placental barrier and damage the developing child. Before effective treatments, syphilis accounted for about one-third of stillborn children. Unlike most teratogens, syphilis is more dangerous in later prenatal development, especially after the eighteenth week. Syphilis causes lesions on the eyes, leading to blindness, and on the skin and mucous membranes. Children who were exposed prenatally to syphilis also suffer retarded growth, liver damage, and problems with their nervous systems (Fletcher & Gordon, 1990).

In most states, prenatal health care includes testing for syphilis and other sexually transmitted diseases. Although antibiotics reduced the rates of new cases of syphilis in the 1960s, prenatal syphilis infection continues to be a problem (National Center for Health Statistics, 2001). About 1 in 2000 newborns is affected by syphilis (March of Dimes, 2000), and most of these children are born to low-income women who do not receive adequate prenatal care (Gibbs & Sweet, 1994).

Pediatric AIDS

Pregnant women infected with the human immunodeficiency virus (HIV) often transmit the disease to their developing children. In the United States, most children with HIV are born to drug-addicted mothers, although the number of women infected through hetero-sexual transmission is rapidly increasing (Centers for Disease Control, 2001b). HIV is usually transmitted to the fetus through the placental barrier but also may be transmitted during delivery because of the infant's exposure to vaginal fluids and during breast-feeding (Committee on Pediatric AIDS, 1998). HIV-infected infants are likely to have impaired brain growth (Epstein et al., 1986), bacterial and viral infections, cognitive deficits, and weak muscles (Byers, 1989).

The first case of AIDS in the United States was reported in 1981; now, there are almost 800,000 AIDS sufferers (Centers for Disease Control, 2001b). Thus, more and more children are being exposed to this disease prenatally. Today, about 1 in 2700 newborns is affected by HIV (March of Dimes, 2000). Studies suggest that mothers with AIDS who take AZT during pregnancy are much less likely to transmit the virus to their newborns (Morris, 1998).

DRUGS

In the United States, 90 percent of pregnant women take some type of drug during pregnancy (Cunningham et al., 1993), including over-the-counter medications, prescriptions, and illicit drugs. Drugs influence the mother's entire body and are transmitted to the developing child during pregnancy.

Thalidomide

> During her pregnancy, my mother was prescribed thalidomide to alleviate severe morning sickness symptoms. My mother took thalidomide twice, two teaspoons total. Thalidomide caused my birth disabilities, necessitating thirty-two operations over my life and nine years accumulated time spent in the hospital before I was 16, in a different city from where my parents lived.
>
> —*Randy Warren* (founder and CEO of the Thalidomide Victims Association of Canada, Thalidomide Workshop), 1997

The negative consequences of drugs are best illustrated by the thalidomide tragedy. In Europe in the 1950s, over 10,000 children were born with arms or legs missing, hands growing from their shoulders, or feet growing from their hips. Medical researchers pinpointed the cause of these defects: The mothers had taken a mild sedative called thalidomide, prescribed to them by their doctors during early pregnancy to control nausea and insomnia. The US Food and Drug Administration had not approved the use of thalidomide because of lack of testing, so most families in the United States were spared its tragic consequences (Bower, 1995).

The timing of thalidomide ingestion was significant (Beckman & Brent, 1986). Because thalidomide interferes with development of the skeletal system, its effects are most obvious during the late embryonic period, when arms and legs are forming. As Randy Warren's story illustrates, even a very small amount of a teratogen can have very serious consequences during this time. Once developed, the embryo's arms and legs are not affected by thalidomide.

Although it was banned worldwide, thalidomide has been discovered to be effective in treating a variety of diseases. In a controversial move, the Food and Drug Administration in 1998 approved the use of thalidomide to treat leprosy. To avoid the tragic consequences of thalidomide on developing embryos, a number of safeguards have been instituted. Men who take thalidomide must practice birth control and cannot donate blood or semen. Women can begin taking thalidomide only after a negative pregnancy test. Then they are tested every week for the first month and every two to four weeks after that. In addition, they must use two forms of effective birth control at the same time for at least one month before receiving thalidomide and must continue until one month after their last dose (Center for the Evaluation of Risks to Human Reproduction, 1999b).

Alcohol

Over 5 million women in the United States drink alcohol during pregnancy, and each year more than 50,000 babies are born with some degree of alcohol-related damage (March of Dimes, 2000). When a pregnant woman drinks, her unborn child is exposed to the teratogen ethanol—the active ingredient in alcoholic beverages. Because the fetus is less able to metabolize ethanol than the mother, the fetus's exposure may be longer and more intense. Women who drink heavily during pregnancy (five or six drinks a day) are more likely to miscarry or have low-birthweight infants (Andres & Jones, 1994). Heavy drinkers and binge drinkers also have a much higher risk of giving birth to a child with **fetal alcohol syndrome (FAS),** a constellation of problems marked by physical deformities and intellectual deficits. Characteristics of FAS include the following (Streissguth, 1997):

This 8-year-old child has fetal alcohol syndrome. He has the typical facial abnormalities associated with the syndrome, including a flat nose and small, narrow head. In some states, mothers who drink or take drugs during pregnancy are charged with child abuse. Do you agree or disagree with this policy? Why?

+ Abnormally flat face and nose
+ Narrow head
+ Delayed and retarded physical growth
+ Heart defects
+ Cognitive deficits
+ Hyperactivity

The most serious and consistent feature of FAS is mental retardation. In a longitudinal study of 500 FAS children followed until age 7, the children were found to have an average IQ score of 65, compared with a normal score of about 100 (Streissguth, Sampson, & Barr, 1989). Women who drink alcohol moderately (one or two drinks per day) may be at risk for giving birth to children with **fetal alcohol effects (FAE).** These children have slightly retarded physical development and may have learning disabilities (Kerns, Don, Mateer, & Streissguth, 1997), and these effects may be long term (Streissguth et al., 1999).

Binge drinking may be more injurious than consistent low levels of drinking (Abel, 1996). The timing of fetal exposure to ethanol also is important. For example, facial anomalies and mental retardation are more likely to occur if the mother drinks early in pregnancy (Coles, 1994; Maier, Chen, & West, 1996). Some evidence suggests that women who quit drinking during pregnancy may prevent FAS or FAE in their newborns (Coles, 1994). No one knows how much alcohol consumed during pregnancy is *too* much, so physicians recommend total abstinence.

But even this precaution may not be enough—children may suffer effects from alcohol that was consumed *before* the woman became pregnant. For example, children born to abstaining mothers who previously had been drinkers had lower IQ scores than children whose mothers did not drink before or after becoming pregnant (Russell, Czarnecki, Cowan, & McPherson, 1991).

Caffeine

Until recently, it was difficult to determine whether caffeine consumed by a pregnant woman acted as a teratogen. Some studies suggested that just two cups of coffee could increase the risk of miscarriage; others found no effect, even when large amounts were consumed. Part of the difficulty in assessing the effects of caffeine arose from researchers' need to rely on participants' own reports of caffeine use, which often are faulty. A new method is now available, in which assessments are made of the blood levels of a substance produced when caffeine is broken down by the liver. This method is assumed by researchers to be a more accurate barometer of caffeine consumption. When this method was used in a large study involving over 40,000 women and the risks associated with other factors likely to increase the risk of miscarriage (e.g., smoking) were taken into account, the results showed that only large amounts of caffeine increased miscarriage risk for women. Two cups of coffee a day did not increase miscarriage risk. But women who consumed five or more cups of coffee a day were more than twice as likely to miscarry as women who consumed less caffeine or none at all (Klebanoff et al., 1999). Thus, women should monitor the amount of caffeine they ingest during pregnancy, remembering that caffeine is found in a variety of foods, including coffee, tea, chocolate, and many carbonated beverages.

fetal alcohol syndrome (FAS) a constellation of problems, including physical deformities and intellectual deficits, that may occur if a mother drinks heavily during pregnancy

fetal alcohol effects (FAE) the effects, including mildly retarded physical development and learning disabilities, that may occur if a mother drinks moderately during pregnancy

Cigarettes

Despite the warnings about the dangers of cigarette smoking, an estimated 3.4 million mothers smoke during pregnancy (National Center for Health Statistics, 2001a), or approximately 13 percent of pregnant women (March of Dimes, 2000). The highest rates generally are found among mothers 15 to 25 years of age. Caucasian mothers are more likely to smoke during pregnancy than are minority mothers, especially at younger ages (National Center for Health Statistics, 2001a). With each puff, they expose themselves and their unborn children to toxic substances. Even secondhand smoke puts a fetus at risk and should be avoided (Dollberg et al., 2000).

Smokers ingest over 3000 chemicals in each cigarette, including known carcinogens. Some of these chemicals pass through the placenta and influence the unborn child. For example, carbon monoxide and nicotine deprive the child of oxygen, adversely influencing brain development. The danger to fetuses is especially severe when mothers smoke a pack or more a day.

Males who smoke may decrease their sperm production, making conception less likely. Women who smoke during pregnancy increase their risk of having a spontaneous abortion, premature birth, and complications in delivery (deHass, Harlow, & Cramer, 1991; Taylor & Sanderson, 1995). Infants born to smokers are smaller and less likely to survive.

Some studies report that children of smokers have deficits in motor coordination, brain development, physical growth, and spatial and reading abilities, as well as increased irritability (Brook, Brook, & Whiteman, 2000; Kallen, 2000). However, these outcomes also are influenced by related lifestyle factors such as alcohol use, socioeconomic status, and nutrition (Barr, Streissguth, Darby, & Sampson, 1990). Smoking also has long-term effects (Fergusson, Horwood, & Lynskey, 1993; Lassen & Oei, 1998). As indicated in Figure 3.10, children whose mothers smoked during pregnancy were more likely to fail in school and have learning deficiencies than children whose mothers did not smoke. Notice that the more a mother smoked, the more likely the child was to fail at school (Newman & Buka, 1991).

Because the effects of smoking are dosage related, they can be minimized if mothers reduce the number of cigarettes they smoke and reduce their exposure to secondhand smoke. Smokers who enroll in smoking cessation programs and reduce their smoking tend to give birth to normal-birthweight babies, but this does not prevent all smoking-related deficits (Lindley, Becker, Gray, & Herman, 2000). Ideally, women should stop smoking before they become pregnant.

Cocaine

The impact of illicit drug abuse and addiction on children in the United States is particularly devastating. About 5.5 percent of women use some illicit drug during pregnancy, translating into approximately 221,000 babies who have the potential to be born drug exposed (National Institute for Drug Abuse, 1999). The full extent of the effects of prenatal drug exposure on a child is still not known completely, but science has shown that babies born to mothers who use drugs during pregnancy are often delivered prematurely, have low birthweights and smaller head circumferences, and are often shorter in length than infants not exposed in utero to drugs. Estimating the actual consequences of maternal drug use is difficult, and determining the specific hazard of a particular drug to the unborn child is even more problematic, given that more than one substance is typically used.

Cocaine is one of the most commonly used illicit drugs. In a study of 400,000 admissions of women to drug treatment facilities in 1993, the second most common reason for admission (following alcohol use, at 44 percent) was use of cocaine, especially crack cocaine, at 26 percent (National Center for Health Statistics, 1996). About 1.7 million Americans currently use cocaine at least once per month, and over 45,000 pregnant women smoke crack cocaine each year. Although overall use of cocaine has decreased somewhat in the last few years, rates among inner-city and minority groups have increased (National Institute on Drug Abuse, 1999). Federal law mandates drug testing of all newborns.

FIGURE 3.10

Smoking Among Mothers During Pregnancy and School Failure and Learning Problems for Children at Age 7

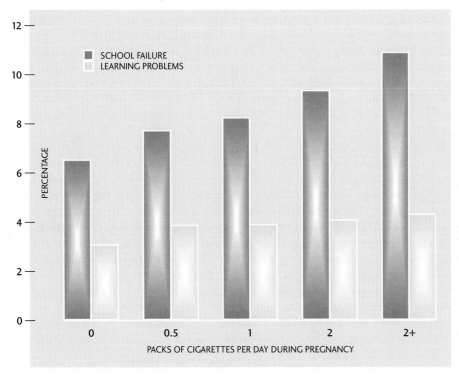

SOURCE: Adapted from Newman and Buka, 1991.

Notice that the rates of school failure and learning problems in children depend on whether and how much the mother smoked during pregnancy. School failure seems to be more influenced by maternal smoking than learning problems are. What can be done to decrease the rates of smoking among pregnant women?

Women who use cocaine during pregnancy have more miscarriages and stillbirths and lower-birthweight babies than do other women (Kuhn et al., 2000; Mastrogiannis, Decavalas, Verma, & Tejani, 1990), and this is especially true for mothers who use crack cocaine (Richardson, Hamel, Goldschmidt, & Day, 1999). Infants born to cocaine-using mothers are more at risk for physical deformities, especially of the heart and circulatory system (Chasnoff, Chisum, & Kaplan, 1988), and their brain development may be adversely affected (Scher, Richardson, & Day, 2000).

The effects of cocaine on prenatal development occur for two reasons (Lester, Freier, & LaGasse, 1995). First, the fetus is exposed to significant amounts of cocaine for long periods because it passes through the placental barrier and then metabolizes slowly in the fetus (Keller & Snyder-Keller, 2000). This exposure interferes with information processing within the brain, increases blood pressure, and produces heart seizures. Second, cocaine affects the mother's system, in turn influencing the environment of her unborn child. For instance, cocaine decreases oxygen and blood flow in the mother, interfering with normal prenatal development (Bingol et al., 1987). Importantly, cocaine use rarely occurs alone. Only 2 percent of mothers reported using just cocaine during pregnancy; women were 49 times more likely to use another drug too if they used cocaine (Lester et al., 2001).

After birth, infants exposed to cocaine prenatally seldom experience withdrawal from the drug, but they may be irritable and have attention-span and motor-development problems (Chasnoff, Burns, Schnoll, & Burns, 1985; Lester, Freier, & LaGasse, 1995). They also

This 38-year-old woman is having her first child. What factors contribute to the increase in the number of older women starting families?

may show less interest in learning than other infants (Alessandri, Sullivan, Imaizumi, & Lewis, 1993). Although research suggests that some children who were exposed to cocaine prenatally may have cognitive deficits, these deficits greatly depend on the family environment (Azuma & Chasnoff, 1993; Griffith, Azuma, & Chasnoff, 1994). For example, children born to mothers who use cocaine also are at greater risk of abuse and neglect than children of nonusers, and abuse and neglect, in turn, are linked to cognitive deficits (Leventhal et al., 1997). Some studies suggest that the home environment (Hurt et al., 2001) and poverty are the major risks for young children (Van Beveren, Little, & Spence, 2000). The long-term effects that can be attributed directly to a mother's cocaine use are difficult to pinpoint because, as noted previously, cocaine use is associated with many other risk factors (Mayes, Granger, Bornstein, & Zuckerman, 1992).

Heroin

Heroin (and other narcotics such as morphine and codeine) crosses the placental barrier, and infants of mothers who use heroin are born addicted to the drug and undergo withdrawal (Yanai et al., 2000). Addicted newborns experience sleep disturbances, hyperactivity, convulsions, fever, sweating, vomiting, diarrhea, and even death (D'Apolito, 1998). Heroin-exposed infants are small and have behavioral problems such as irritability and excessive crying. These effects are evident at four months after birth, but research has not consistently found narcotic effects on behavior after about 1 year of age (Fabris, Prandi, Perathoner, & Soldi, 1998).

Because drug-addicted parents expose their children to many risk factors, it is difficult to disentangle the effects due solely to prenatal exposure to the drug. In an interesting study, Wilson (1989) compared heroin-exposed infants with unexposed infants raised by addicted parents. Intelligence in the children related to the home environment, with the lowest IQ children being those raised by addicted parents. Thus, the effects of prenatal drug exposure may be exacerbated by caregivers who continue to use drugs and tend to have disorganized and chaotic lifestyles (Eyler & Behnke, 1999).

ENVIRONMENTAL HAZARDS

Lead, pesticides, radiation, and chemicals are environmental agents that may cross the placental barrier and affect the developing fetus. These environmental agents may be hazardous to people of any age and increase the risk of cancer later in life. However, they are particularly hazardous to prenatal development.

Radiation

Radiation is a powerful teratogen. Over thirty types of birth defects, many involving the central nervous system, have been related to prenatal exposure to high levels of radiation. The most common effects are microencephaly (abnormally small brain and skull) and mental retardation. The severity and type of effect depend on the amount of radiation received and on the timing of the exposure. Following World War II, Japanese women survivors who had been closest to the sites of the atomic bomb explosions and had received high levels of radiation gave birth to physically deformed and mentally retarded children (Otake & Schull, 1984). Although diagnostic X-ray procedures involve much less radiation, a risk for birth defects remains, especially for fetuses at between 8 and 15 weeks (Cunningham et al., 1993).

Chemical Hazards

Every day we are surrounded by potentially dangerous chemicals in our air, water, and food and in the products we use. Unfortunately, pregnant women may not even be aware that they have been exposed to harmful chemicals. For example, in the 1950s, an industrial plant in Japan dumped mercury waste into the ocean, polluting the water and fish. Children born to mothers living nearby suffered severe retardation and irreversible physical and neurological impairments. Pregnant women often unknowingly expose their unborn children to high levels of lead, contained in paint, auto emissions, and coatings on blinds and shades;

this is especially true for poor women (Rothenberg et al., 1999). Research now suggests that many common products, ranging from food preservatives to insecticides and even some cosmetics, pose risks to unborn children.

MATERNAL CONDITIONS

In addition to biological and teratogenic factors that affect the developing child, characteristics of the mother can pose risks to the unborn child. A mother's physical, psychological, and social characteristics can affect the fetus by influencing her health or by altering the chemistry of her blood.

Maternal Age

More than ever before, women are delaying having their first child. As shown in Figure 3.11, birth rates have been dropping among women in their early 20s, but increasing among women in their early 30s and early 40s—particularly Caucasian American and Asian American women (National Center for Health Statistics, 2001a). Today, it is not uncommon for a woman to have her first child or start a second family after 40.

Pregnancy risks increase as the mother gets older (Reichman & Pagnini, 1997). Mothers over 35 are at increased risk for having a child with Down syndrome. They also risk developing high blood pressure, gestational diabetes, and cardiovascular disease, all of which are usually controllable. Additionally, older mothers are somewhat more likely to miscarry (Astolfi & Zonta, 1999). When an older mother eliminates as many risk factors as possible and undergoes extensive prenatal testing, however, her chances of delivering a healthy newborn are virtually as good as those for a younger mother (Yagel et al., 1998).

IGURE 3.11

Changes in Birth Rates, by Age and Race/Ethnicity of Mother

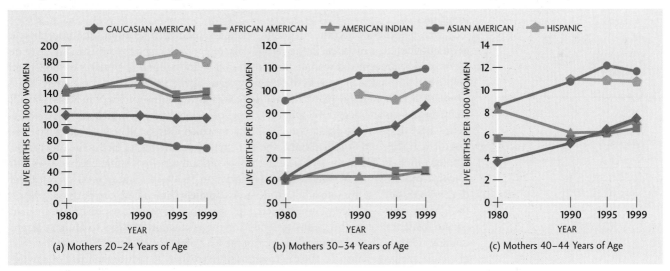

NOTE: Data for Hispanic mothers were not available until 1990.
SOURCE: National Center for Health Statistics, 2001a.

Notice how the birth rates vary for women of different races/ethnicities. For young mothers, birth rates have been relatively steady; more Hispanic American women have babies at a young age than do women of other ethnicities. In both groups of older mothers, there are more Asian American women than women of other ethnicities. Changes over time are seen mainly for older Caucasian American and Asian American mothers. What factors have contributed to these changes in birth rates?

Maternal Stress

A pregnant woman's psychological condition influences the health of her unborn child. Like any other major life transition, pregnancy and delivery produce a moderate amount of stress, as parents-to-be must adjust to new demands and responsibilities. Stress can cause changes in the mother's blood chemistry. Research has shown that mothers who are stressed or emotionally upset produce hormones that cross the placental barrier and affect the fetus (Monk et al., 2000). Extreme and prolonged conditions of stress increase the risk for miscarriage, difficult labor and delivery, and prematurity (Glover, 1997).

Parity

Parity, or the number and spacing of children a woman bears, also affects prenatal development. Generally, a woman's endocrine system takes four years to return to prepregnancy condition (Cunningham et al., 1993). Infants born before the endocrine system recovers may be at a disadvantage; a pregnancy within three months of delivery is classified as a high-risk pregnancy (Eisenberg, Murkoff, & Hathaway, 1999). Infants conceived after the period of recuperation have a better prenatal environment than do firstborn children. Blood circulation is richer after a first pregnancy, and later-born children suffer fewer birth defects and complications. Furthermore, labor and delivery are quicker and less demanding for later-born children. However, the advantages of this enhanced prenatal environment are lost if later births follow too closely.

PROTECTIVE FACTORS

What can a couple do to increase their chances of giving birth to a healthy baby? Good nutrition during pregnancy is essential. Proper nutrition and weight gain increase the likelihood of giving birth to a healthy baby (Cnattingius, Bergstrom, Lipworth, & Kramer, 1998). Women need not "eat for two"; usually a woman needs only about 300 additional calories (American College of Obstetricians and Gynecologists, 2000). Pregnant women have some special nutritional needs, though. To produce more blood, they need increased levels of iron, protein, and folic acid; to help fetal bones grow, they need more calcium and phosphorus. Ideally, women of average weight should gain approximately 30 pounds during pregnancy.

Even before they become pregnant, women should keep in mind the importance of good nutrition. For instance, in the early 1990s, researchers recognized that many birth defects could be prevented if women took folate, a B vitamin found in a variety of foods, both before and during the first weeks of pregnancy. During the early weeks of pregnancy, before women know they are pregnant, the neural tube is forming. If supplies of folate are insufficient, the child is at risk of developing two types of serious and common birth defects called neural tube defects. One defect is anencephaly, in which most or all of the brain tissue does not form. If the child is not stillborn, she or he will die shortly after birth. The other defect is spina bifida, in which the spinal column does not fully enclose. Spina bifida causes neurological problems and may cause mental retardation. Its effects range in severity; most children with this defect live into adulthood. Approximately 2500 infants are born each year in the United States with neural tube defects, and about half of these cases are caused by inadequate folate intake by the mother (Center for the Evaluation of Risks to Human Reproduction, 1999a). The recommendation from the US Public Health Service is that all women of childbearing age consume 400 micrograms of folate daily to reduce their risk of having a child with these neural defects. For pregnant women, the recommended amount is 800 micrograms daily. Folate is found in liver, dark leafy vegetables, broccoli, citrus fruits and juices, wheat germ, and dried beans and peas. Since 1998, folic acid has been added to breads and other grain products. Many multivitamins contain folate.

Exercise also provides important benefits, especially to the mother and her well being. Regular exercise gives pregnant women more energy, builds bones and muscles, and generally improves health. It may also improve women's ability to cope with childbirth pain (American College of Obstetricians and Gynecologists, 2000).

parity the number and spacing of children a woman bears

One of the most important ways women can protect their unborn children is to have regular prenatal checkups. Regular checkups allow complications to be prevented or dealt with promptly and effectively. The number of women who receive prenatal care has steadily increased, and prenatal care has been associated with lower rates of birth complications (March of Dimes, 2001). Unfortunately, not every woman receives adequate prenatal care. Caucasian American women are more likely than many other women to receive prenatal care (National Center for Health Statistics, 2001a).

Pregnancy is a family affair. A supportive and nurturing environment protects a pregnant woman and her unborn child by creating favorable conditions for them. Having a sympathetic partner, relatives, or friends helps minimize the negative effects of stress. Additionally, having a source of social support helps a woman deal with the physical demands or complications that arise during pregnancy.

CULTURAL INFLUENCES ON PREGNANCY

In every culture, reproduction and pregnancy are fundamental issues of human existence. Although reproduction and pregnancy are biological events that are similar all over the world, the experience and treatment of these events differ dramatically across cultures. In most Western cultures, pregnancy represents a major transition into adult life. Unlike marriage, pregnancy and birth are irreversible processes and mark a break from childhood (Fogel, 1997). But other cultures view pregnancy and birth differently. For example, West Africans view pregnancy as a divine gift, primarily signifying a couple's purity and strength (Nsamenang, 1992). Infertility among West African couples is interpreted as proof that the couple is being punished by their ancestors (Nsamenang, 1987). Most West Africans indicate that they would prefer to die in poverty and be survived by children than to die rich and childless (Nsamenang & Laosebikan, 1981).

Women's Responses

Culture also affects the impact of pregnancy and the changes it brings for the parents-to-be. The fact that responses to pregnancy differ for different cultures and subcultures tells us that this biological condition is interpreted through the lens of cultural values and beliefs and institutions. In North America, many women become preoccupied with their weight gain and physical appearance during the later stages of pregnancy because of the emphasis the culture places on slenderness. North American women report feeling that they had lost control of their bodies and become embarrassingly conspicuous. Some pregnant women believe they look less attractive sexually and worry about being attractive to their partners (Fogel, 1997). In contrast, on the island of Yap in Micronesia, females are desired for their fertility, and the largeness of a pregnant woman is a symbol of her ability to produce children. In the Yap culture, the increased size associated with pregnancy is highly valued, so women do not worry about looking too big during pregnancy (Lingenfelter, 1993).

Men's Responses

In the United States, men and women differ somewhat in their reactions to pregnancy. In one study, the majority of mothers and fathers reported that they anticipated and were curious about the upcoming birth, but fathers expressed less anxiety and less pleasure about the pregnancy than did mothers. Mothers were more likely to say they talked to or loved the unborn child (Mercer et al., 1988).

Pregnancy and birth are biological events that occur similarly worldwide. However, the changes that occur during pregnancy and birth are viewed differently depending on cultural expectations. In this photo, Australian Aboriginal women are performing a "baby smoking" ceremony. What might be the purpose of this ceremony?

Some expectant fathers experience a sympathetic pregnancy, known by the French term *couvade*. During his partner's pregnancy, the father may suffer symptoms for which there is no recognized physiological basis, including increased or decreased appetite, weight gain, diarrhea or constipation, and headaches or toothaches. Onset is usually during the third gestational month, and the symptoms usually go away after childbirth (Holditch-Davis, Harris, Sandelowski, & Edwards, 1994). In most Western cultures, *couvade* is seen as an expression of anxiety about the pregnancy, ambivalence about being a father, or envy over the attention the expectant mother receives during her pregnancy (Klein, 1991).

In some non-Western cultures, *couvade* refers to a custom whereby expectant fathers identify with their mates and make sacrifices of their own during the pregnancy. In India, for example, when the wife of a Brahman becomes pregnant, the husband traditionally stops chewing betel palm leaves until his wife gives birth. In the Philippines, an expectant father stops eating sour fruit a week before the delivery to prevent the newborn from being born with stomach problems. An expectant father in the Ifugao tribe of the Philippines is not supposed to disturb his unborn child by cutting wood during his wife's pregnancy (Meltzer, 1981).

Unfortunately, not all men share the feelings of their pregnant partners. The likelihood of extramarital sex increases during pregnancy (Thorpe, Dragonas, & Golding, 1992), and about 1 in 6 pregnant adult women is physically abused by her partner (Parker, McFarlane, & Socken, 1994). Thus, in addition to cultural differences, there are individual differences in how men (and women and children) react to pregnancy (Clinton, 1986).

TRY IT OUT

Activities Relating to Pregnancy and Prenatal Development

1. Interview a woman who is pregnant with her first baby. Ask her how she feels about the pregnancy. How does she feel about her own physical and emotional condition? Are any of her concerns based on cultural beliefs and attitudes? To what extent does she engage in behaviors that promote healthy development of the unborn child? What concerns does she express about the health of the baby? After your interview, consider what conditions in the baby's total environment might influence prenatal development.

2. Review how you are similar to and different from your grandparents, parents, and siblings. To what extent do you think genes versus family environment contributed to those differ-ences? Discuss with your family members the genetic factors in your family history that might be relevant to your medical history. What might you do to offset genetically related health risks?

3. What factors contribute to a couple's ability to conceive? How do these factors differ for women and men? Collect information on techniques that help couples who have trouble conceiving. Which of these procedures would you consider if you had trouble conceiving?

4. Collaborate with classmates on a research project to identify (a) factors that can prevent conception, (b) ethical dilemmas in genetic counseling, or (c) optimal nutrition during pregnancy.

SUM IT UP

How do genes influence development?

✦ Many exciting new discoveries regarding human genetics have been made in the last decade, largely as a result of the Human Genome Project.

✦ The human genome is the book of instructions for human life, written by genes on chromosomes. Genes provide information about how proteins, the building blocks of the body, are to be constructed.

✦ Humans have twenty-three pairs of chromosomes. Sex is determined by the twenty-third pair, the sex chromosomes.

✦ Many physical characteristics and diseases result from information coded by a single gene, which can be expressed through a dominant, recessive, or sex-linked pattern.

✦ Most personality, behavioral, and intellectual traits are complexly determined by multiple genes.

✦ The focus of much recent genetics research has been the expression of genes: What causes certain genes to turn on? Why do some genes express themselves while others do not? Under what conditions do genes become expressed?

✦ Gene-environment interactions account for many aspects of development. There is passive G-E interaction, evocative G-E interaction, and active G-E interaction.

What are common chromosomal abnormalities?

✦ One of the most common chromosomal abnormalities is Down syndrome, which results from an extra chromosome on the twenty-first pair.

✦ Sex-linked chromosomal abnormalities are those characterized by extra or missing sex chromosomes. Children with these disorders usually have abnormal development of sexual organs and often have behavioral problems.

How are genetic diseases detected?

✦ Genetic disorders can be detected by using ultrasound imaging, chorionic villus sampling, and amniocentesis. Genetic counselors help couples determine their risks for genetic disorders.

How does prenatal development proceed?

✦ Fertilization occurs when an egg and sperm cell meet and share their genetic material. The window of time for fertilization is only a few days around ovulation.

✦ Each menstrual cycle is divided into three phases—the menstrual, follicular, and luteal phases. Ovulation occurs in the middle of the woman's menstrual cycle.

✦ Sperm cells undergo a process of development, called spermatogenesis, in which cells initially containing forty-six chromosomes divide until they contain only twenty-three.

✦ New procedures for "assisted reproduction" include artificial insemination, in vitro fertilization, and gamete intrafallopian transfer, embryo transfer, and surrogate mothers. Rates of success vary.

✦ The first stage of prenatal development is the germinal stage, which begins at fertilization and lasts until the egg implants in the mother's uterus. Cell division and differentiation are the hallmarks of this stage.

✦ The second stage is the embryonic stage, which begins at implantation and lasts until eight weeks. Because 95 percent of the organs and body parts develop during this stage, the embryo is most vulnerable to environmental damage.

✦ The third stage, the fetal stage, lasts from eight weeks until the end of pregnancy. During this stage, elaboration of the existing organs and structures occurs and the brain develops rapidly.

✦ Development is directional. Parts of the body close to the head develop first, and those farther away from the head develop later (cephalocaudal development). Additionally, growth occurs from the center of the body outward (proximodistal development).

✦ The seventh month of prenatal development marks a critical juncture—the age of viability. A child born during this stage is likely to survive.

What conditions influence pregnancy and prenatal development?

✦ Teratogens are agents that cross the placental barrier and harm the developing child. Teratogens include certain kinds of diseases, drugs, and environmental toxins. The effects of teratogens depend on their timing and amount and on the characteristics of the fetus.

✦ About 5 percent of birth defects are due to infectious diseases transmitted by the mother to the developing child. Diseases such as rubella, syphilis, and AIDS can seriously affect the health and well-being of the developing child.

✦ Many women take drugs during pregnancy. Alcohol, cigarettes, cocaine, prescription drugs, and illicit drugs cross the placental barrier and can harm the developing child.

✦ Environmental hazards such as radiation and chemicals and maternal characteristics such as age and stress can affect the conditions of both the mother and the developing child.

✦ Eating well, getting exercise, undergoing regular prenatal checkups, and having support from family and friends increase a woman's chances of having a healthy child.

✦ Although reproduction and pregnancy are biological events that are similar all over the world, the *experience* of pregnancy varies according to the culture one lives in.

KEY TERMS and CONCEPTS

active G–E interaction (69)
age of viability (83)
amniocentesis (72)
amnion (79)
autosomes (63)
balanced polymorphism (67)
carriers (65)
cephalocaudal development (81)
chorion (79)
chorionic villus sampling (71)
chromosomes (61)
codons (61)
dominant gene (64)
ectopic pregnancy (77)
embryonic stage (76)
evocative G–E interaction (69)
exons (61)

fetal alcohol effects (FAE) (87)
fetal alcohol syndrome (FAS) (87)
fetal stage (76)
fragile X syndrome (67)
gene–environment (G–E)
   interactions (68)
genes (61)
genotype (64)
germinal stage (76)
heterozygous (64)
homozygous (64)
introns (61)
karyotype (63)
meiosis (62)
mitosis (62)
ovum (73)
parity (92)

passive G–E interaction (69)
phenotype (64)
placenta (79)
placental barrier (83)
proximodistal development (81)
quickening (82)
recessive gene (64)
sex chromosomes (63)
spermatogenesis (74)
spermatids (74)
spermatocytes (74)
spermatozoa (74)
teratogens (83)
ultrasound (71)
umbilical cord (79)
zygote (77)

Birth and Neonatal Development

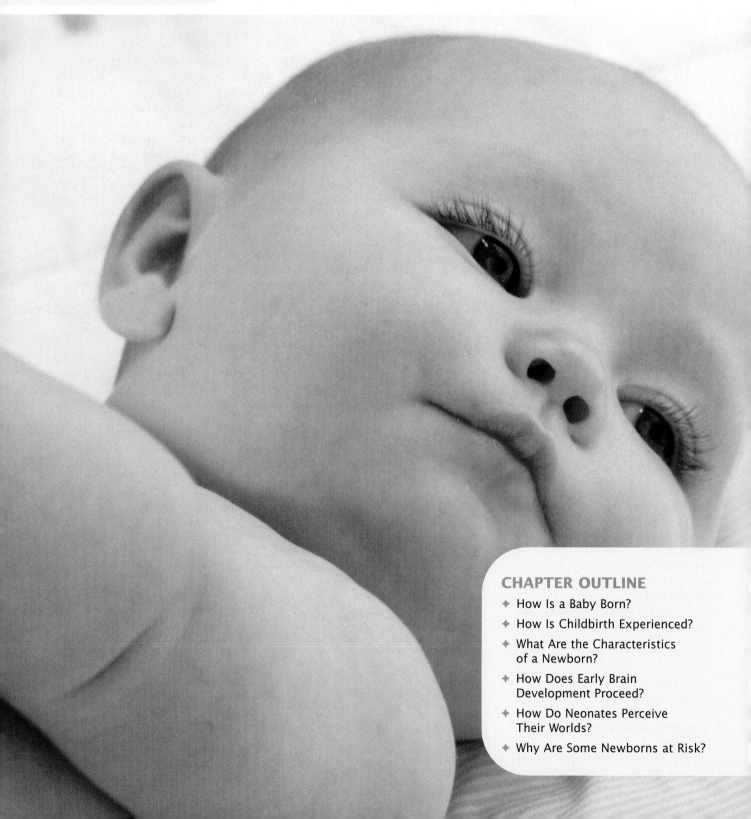

CHAPTER OUTLINE

✦ How Is a Baby Born?

✦ How Is Childbirth Experienced?

✦ What Are the Characteristics of a Newborn?

✦ How Does Early Brain Development Proceed?

✦ How Do Neonates Perceive Their Worlds?

✦ Why Are Some Newborns at Risk?

For most individuals, the birth of a child into the family is an unforgettable and mysterious event, and family members continue to tell stories about the birth of their babies long after the children have grown up. Even children marvel at the birth of a baby and the early changes that occur. Most people's family and personal lifestyles are altered dramatically by the arrival of a newborn.

How is a Baby Born

The birth of a child is a complex and exciting event. For approximately nine months, the expecting parents, family members, and friends anticipate the event. During that time, the unborn child has been developing in preparation for life outside the mother's womb. Even with nine months' notice, many expecting parents are caught off guard by the events associated with birth.

THE BIRTH PROCESS

When a woman finds out she is pregnant, her doctor will count 280 days from the first day of her last period and pronounce this to be her due date. Only about 3 percent of all women give birth on their due date, but over 45 percent give birth within one week before or after

that date. Although most children are delivered at between thirty-seven and forty-one weeks' gestation, a sizable number are delayed or are preterm (see Figure 4.1), and the proportion is greater for minorities (especially African American children) than for Caucasians. Girls tend to be born a few days earlier than boys, and women who have shorter menstrual cycles tend to have shorter pregnancies, although the reasons for these differences are not clear (Jones, 1997).

One of the many mysteries surrounding childbirth is what causes it to begin. Much of our present understanding of how labor begins comes from observations of sheep. For some time, sheepherders in Idaho had noticed that pregnant ewes grazing in certain pastures failed to give birth on time. Looking for the causes of this delay, researchers discovered that the newborn lambs had underdeveloped adrenal and pituitary glands. These abnormalities occurred because the pregnant ewes were eating plants containing high levels of a chemical that crossed the placenta and harmed the glandular development of the fetus. As a result, the fetus secreted lower-than-normal levels of adrenal steroid hormones. Subsequent research confirmed that fetal steroids initiate labor. Injections of fetal hormones into pregnant ewes any time during the second half of their pregnancy resulted in early delivery (Nathanieisz, 1995).

Like the sheep, human newborns who are delivered early tend to have larger adrenal glands and those delivered late tend to have underdeveloped glands. However, the mother's body also may trigger labor by releasing prostaglandins, a group of fatty acids widely distributed throughout body tissues (Nathanieisz, 1995). Other evidence suggests that

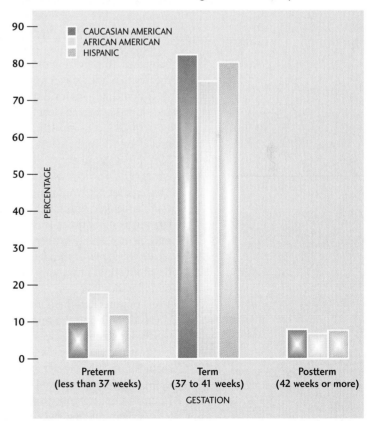

FIGURE 4.1

Distribution of Gestation Among US Women, by Race

SOURCE: Adapted from National Center for Health Statistics, 2001a.

What conclusions can you draw about the likelihood that a mother will give birth on or close to her due date?

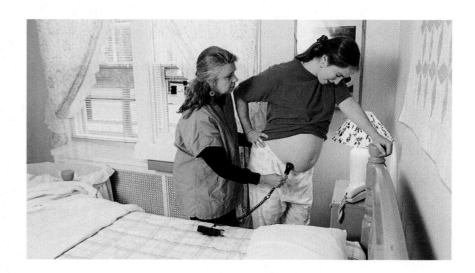

Here a woman in labor is attended by a midwife. What are the symptoms of true labor? What factors influence when labor starts and how long it lasts?

oxytocin, a hormone secreted by the mother's pituitary glands, stimulates uterine contractions and hastens labor. In fact, many women are given synthetic oxytocin (pitocin) to hasten labor contractions. Other evidence indicates that, along with hormones, maturation of the placenta controls the onset of labor (Jones, 1997). The variety of possible causes of birth suggests that we still have much to learn about the factors that determine when birth occurs.

Women all over the world experience the same general biological changes associated with birth. About two to three weeks before birth, many women report that they suddenly can breathe more easily and feel more comfortable. This relief is referred to as **lightening** and occurs when the fetus drops into the pelvic cavity, decreasing pressure on the mother's diaphragm. In a few hours to a week before the onset of labor, the baby's head moves further down into the mother's pelvis in preparation for birth.

The birth process is divided into three stages: (1) dilation of the cervix, (2) birth of the baby, and (3) expulsion of the placenta, or "afterbirth." The first stage lasts the longest, but the length of each stage varies considerably from birth to birth. For mothers who are having their first child—**primiparous women**—the entire birth process usually lasts from 10 to 16 hours. The average length of time is shorter (6 to 11 hours) for women who have previously given birth—**multiparous women.** Any duration up to 24 hours is considered normal (Wong & Perry, 1998).

Stage 1: Dilation of the Cervix

Throughout pregnancy, and especially during the last month or two, women experience mild, irregular contractions of the uterus, called **Braxton-Hicks contractions.** During late pregnancy, women sometimes experience **false labor** in the form of contractions that may be moderately intense and rhythmic. The contractions associated with false labor decrease over time, especially when women exercise. The true contractions of labor mark the beginning of the first stage of the birth process. Early contractions last about 30 to 60 seconds and occur at 5- to 20-minute intervals. By the end of labor, the interval is only about 1 to 3 minutes and the duration and intensity of contractions are greater (Cassidy, 1993).

Early in labor, the muscle contractions of the uterus pull the sides of the uterus upwards, increasing the size of the opening of the uterus, called the *cervix.* Dilation of the cervix is necessary for the fetus to move through the birth canal. The cervix dilates from a diameter of .3 centimeter at the beginning of labor to about 10 centimeters at the end. The entire dilation takes about 8 to 14 hours in a primiparous woman, but takes only 4 to 6 hours in a multiparous woman because her cervix is more pliable.

Early in the first stage, the mucous plug that ordinarily blocks the cervix is dislodged and some blood from the vagina is produced (often referred to as the "bloody show"). Also during this first stage, a small tear usually appears in the amniotic sac and the fluid trickles or gushes from the sac through the vagina. This tearing of the sac is often called "breaking

lightening when the fetus drops into the pelvic cavity, decreasing pressure on the mother's diaphragm

primiparous women women who are having their first child

multiparous women women who have previously given birth

Braxton-Hicks contractions mild, irregular contractions of the uterus experienced throughout pregnancy, especially during the last month or two

false labor moderately intense, rhythmic contractions late in the pregnancy

water," and it is one of the sure signs that labor is beginning. Sometimes, however, the sac remains intact after labor has advanced, and the doctor will puncture the amnion to release the fluid (this does not hurt the mother or fetus). Ideally, to avoid infection, birth should occur within 12 hours of breaking the sac. Parents are often instructed to start timing the contractions when the water breaks. Once contractions are about 5 minutes apart, the woman needs to move to the birthing area.

The last part of dilation, called *transition*, is the most difficult part—the severity of the contractions is greatest and the pain is the worst. Women often have an urge to push the baby out, but at this point it is too early to push because the cervix is still dilating. Transition is the time when most women receive some kind of medication to cope with the pain. Until recently, sedatives and general anesthesia were widely given to women in labor to help them sleep, rest, and manage the pain. Unfortunately, these medications cross the placenta and affect the baby. If large dosages of sedatives or anesthetics are used, the baby may be restless and withdrawn for days after birth (Brazelton, Nugent, & Lester, 1987). Heavy use of drugs during birth is related to learning disorders among school children (Brackbill, McManus, & Woodward, 1985); however, most evidence indicates that low levels of medication used during birth do not significantly affect healthy babies (Walker & O'Brien, 1999).

Instead of anesthesia and sedatives, which affect the mother's whole body, regional pain control is used for most births in the United States today. A common method for controlling the pain of labor is the **epidural block,** in which a local anesthetic is delivered to block pain in the region from the waist to the feet (Thorp & Breedlove, 1996). Recent innovations in the form of smaller needles, new medications, and a new delivery method, which includes a drip epidural on a wheeled cart, provide pregnant women with fewer side effects, more mobility, and more soothing effects while in labor (Shute, 1997).

> . . . the nurse checked my cervix and informed me that I was 4 cm and asked me if I wanted an anesthetic. I said that I didn't want any yet and might not ever want it. Then the next contraction hit, and I said the magic word—"epidural." Honestly, I was not crazy about the idea of taking drugs for this, but I wasn't sure how I would get through the next few hours without it.
>
> —Anonymous mother's on-line birth story

In deciding whether they want to receive medications during labor, mothers must weigh the benefits of pain relief against their concerns about drug effects. Many mothers, like the one in the story above, feel ambivalent about taking medication, although over 80 percent of women in childbirth in the United States receive some form of pain medication.

Transition is the period of time that is most difficult for the fetus as well. In order to assess how the fetus is managing, its heart rate is monitored by placing small box-shaped sensors on the mother's abdomen. If the heart rate goes too high or too low, emergency procedures may be needed to quickly remove the baby (Cassidy, 1993).

Stage 2: Expulsion of the Fetus

In the second stage of the birth process, the tempo of activity changes. During the first stage, the mother was relatively passive; she experienced uncomfortable contractions for many hours while waiting for the cervix to open completely. In the second stage, the mother begins the intense physical effort of pushing the baby through the birth passage (Sleep, 1993).

The second stage begins when the cervix is fully dilated and ends with the baby's birth. Contractions now help push the baby through the birth canal. The contractions decrease in intensity a bit and last about 60 seconds, with 1- to 3-minute rest periods in between. The second stage can be quite quick (as short as 5 minutes) for some mothers, particularly multiparous women, but it usually lasts about 1 to 2 hours for primiparous women.

As the fetus moves through the cervix and vagina, the mother may feel some urge to push and will be encouraged to do so by the doctor or midwife. To push, the mother applies pressure using her diaphragm. **Crowning** occurs when the top of the baby's head becomes visible. The baby's head is large and difficult to deliver. To help the fetus pass through the birth canal, the baby's head undergoes **molding,** in which the bones of the baby's skull,

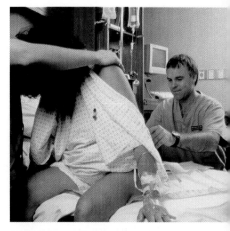

Many women choose to have an epidural block during childbirth. What is this type of pain conrol, and why is it preferable to having sedatives?

epidural block a common method for controlling the pain of labor, in which a local anesthetic is delivered to block pain in the region from the waist to the feet

crowning when the top of the baby's head becomes visible

molding when the bones of the baby's skull, which are not yet fused, press together and even overlap to accommodate passage through the birth canal

episiotomy a small incision made in the skin below the vagina to prevent tearing of the vaginal tissues as the baby emerges

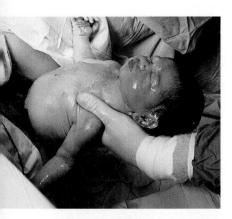

In this picture, the second stage of birth has just occurred; a healthy newborn was just delivered. Can you describe the other two stages and the events that take place in all three stages?

which are not yet fused, press together and may even overlap. Molding gives the newborn's head an elongated shape, which usually disappears soon after delivery. To create a larger opening for the head, the doctor may perform an **episiotomy**—that is, make a small incision in the skin below the vagina. This procedure is used to prevent tearing of the vaginal tissues as the baby emerges. Although almost half of all women who give birth in the United States have an episiotomy, debate about its effectiveness in reducing trauma persists, and its systematic use has been questioned (Eason & Feldman, 2000).

Once the baby's head emerges, with the face toward the mother's back, the doctor or nurse suctions out the fluids in the air passages and checks to see if the umbilical cord is around the baby's neck—a common occurrence that poses no special danger if detected at this time (Jones, 1997). The baby then turns so that the shoulders can fit through the vaginal opening. After the shoulders are delivered, the rest of the baby slides out, and he or she takes a first breath and usually emits a rousing cry. The old tradition of slapping the back side of the newborn to stimulate breathing usually is not necessary. The umbilical cord is then clamped about 3 inches from the baby's abdomen and cut. Because there are no nerve endings in the umbilical cord, neither the mother nor the infant feels this happen.

Stage 3: Expulsion of the Placenta

Contractions continue after the baby is born, helping the placenta move through the birth canal. About 15 to 30 minutes after the baby has been delivered, the placenta is expelled. The doctor checks the placenta to ensure that it is intact, because any remaining pieces may lead to uterine infections.

BIRTHING METHODS

Birth is a significant event in every culture, but social customs and birthing methods vary widely across cultures and at different times in history. Women in Nepal, for example, are rubbed with oil to make them more comfortable, and they wear a waist cloth tied above their stomachs to "prevent the child from going up to the mother's mouth" (Escarce, 1989). In some cultures, women give birth alone, but the more common pattern is for a group of people to assist. Nepalese women are assisted by other women who have had children but not by men or children. In contrast, in Laos, women's primary helpers are the husband and mother-in-law (Muret-Wagstaff & Moore, 1989).

Practices in the United States have varied over time. In the nineteenth century, most women gave birth at home with midwives. By the 1950s, the trend had reversed, with most women giving birth at a hospital and almost all newborns being delivered by physicians. Modern practices have reduced the risks that women and infants face during birth. Many fewer women and children die in childbirth than did in the past (see Figure 4.2).

In the United States, a wide range of settings and options are available for childbirth. Ninety-nine percent of births occur at the hospital (National Center for Health Statistics, 2001a), although many families choose a hospital birthing room that looks more like a bedroom than a traditional hospital room. Some families select a specially designed bathtub filled with warm water as the site for delivery.

FIGURE 4.2

Historical Trends in US Infant and Maternal Mortality Rates

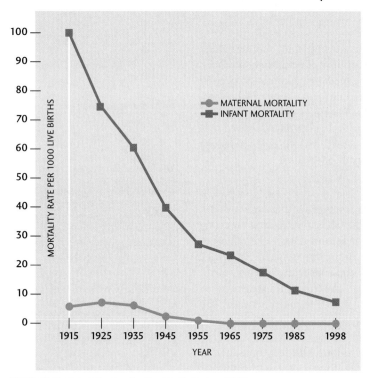

SOURCE: National Center for Health Statistics, 2001a.

What factors have contributed to the decreasing rates of infant and maternal mortality in the United States?

The range of options depends on the mother's risk factors—her age, weight, and general health. Certain women are at risk for complications during delivery:

- Adolescent girls
- Older women, particularly those over 35 or 40 who are having their first child
- Women who have certain conditions or diseases
- Women carrying twins, triplets, or other multiple fetuses

Women who are at risk have limited options because they must have the full range of support systems available in case of an emergency.

To provide couples with more choices in birthing methods, birthing centers have been developed. These centers provide an out-of-hospital, family-centered setting where labor and delivery are treated as normal life events to be shared with whomever the mother likes. Many centers encourage mothers to walk, eat, drink, and get into positions that are comfortable for them during labor and delivery. Certified nurse-midwives provide most of the care, but many centers have close connections with hospitals in case of an emergency. Only women with low-risk pregnancies are accepted at birthing centers.

Modern practices also influence when and how mothers give birth. In Figure 4.3, for example, notice how many more children are born on weekdays, when physicians are more available and hospitals have more staff on duty. Consider also the fact that rates for surgical births are greater on weekdays than on weekends (National Center for Health Statistics, 2001a), again suggesting that patterns of births and birth procedures reflect trends in staffing and practices of modern health care providers.

Lamaze Childbirth

During World War II, Russian doctors were faced with a problem; they did not have any pain medication they could administer to women who were giving birth. To help these women through labor and delivery, they applied the principles of classical conditioning (see Chapter 2). Through breathing and muscular relaxation, they conditioned the women to respond positively to their contractions (Wong & Perry, 1998). These techniques were adopted by Dr. Fernand Lamaze and introduced around the world.

Lamaze classes usually involve six weekly sessions in which the participants prepare for birth by learning

- how the childbirth process works
- how to breathe during labor and delivery to control pain and discomfort
- how to focus on relaxing thoughts and feelings
- how fathers or other partners can help in labor and delivery

The goal of the classes is to help women manage the pain of labor and delivery and to maximize the enjoyment of the parents of the birth of their children.

Leboyer: Birth Without Violence

A complementary birth approach was developed by Dr. Frederick Leboyer, a French physician. The focus of this technique is on the infant's, rather than the parents', birth experience.

FIGURE 4.3

Average Number of Births, by Day of the Week

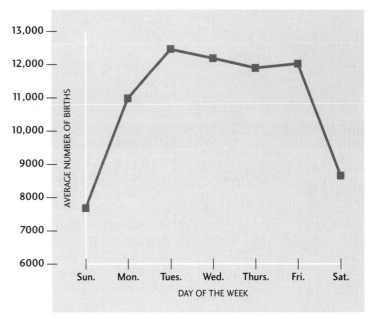

SOURCE: Adapted from National Center for Health Statistics, 2001a.

Examine the graph and notice the large dropoff in births on Saturdays and Sundays. What do you think might explain these differences?

This woman has just given birth in a tub filled with warm water. What factors must be taken into account when women decide about birthing options?

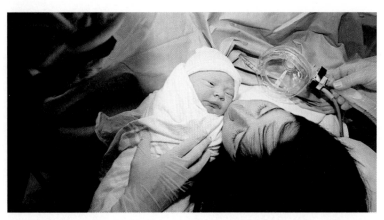

If there were potential complications with the birth of your child, would you lean toward choosing a c-section to be safe or waiting and trying alternative approaches?

TABLE 4.1

Conditions Most Commonly Associated with the Use of Cesarean Sections

1. Unfavorable shape of pelvis
2. Breech presentation
3. Placenta previa (placenta is attached near the opening of the cervix)
4. Cord prolapse (compressed or ruptured umbilical cord)
5. Fetal distress (significant increase or decrease in fetal heart rate)
6. Eclampsia (pregnancy-induced hypertension)
7. Prolonged labor
8. Diabetes

Source: Adapted from National Center for Health Statistics, 2001a.

cesarean section procedure by which the fetus is delivered through an incision in the mother's abdomen

Leboyer developed techniques that minimize the infant's trauma of being born by mimicking the conditions of the mother's womb. The bright lights of the operating room are replaced with dim, indirect lighting; the temperature of the usually cool delivery room is raised so that it is closer to the mother's body temperature. After delivery and before the umbilical cord is cut, the naked infant is placed on the mother's bare belly, providing direct physical contact. The infant is then given a warm bath, in an effort to re-create the experience of the prenatal environment.

How well do the Lamaze and Leboyer methods meet their goals? The existing evidence is conflicting. Some research reports that when parents are Lamaze trained, mothers experience less pain and parents have more positive feelings about the birth experience (Leventhal, Leventhal, Shacham, & Easterling, 1989; Mackey, 1990). Other research fails to find such differences (Copstick, Taylor, Hayes, & Morris, 1986; Hodnett & Osborn, 1989). Part of the reason for these different findings is that parents are individuals with different needs and no program will consistently meet the needs of all parents.

Some couples who try the Lamaze or the Leboyer childbirth technique do not succeed in having unmedicated births (Shute, 1997). When this happens, they often feel guilty for not being tough enough or angry because they were not told how much it would hurt.

Despite the conflicting evidence, it appears that alternative birthing techniques, if properly supervised, can be safe, enjoyable, and satisfying (Galotti, Pierce, Reimer, & Luckner, 2000). The best advice for parents-to-be is to choose a birth method carefully—obtain all available information on the method, just as you would when choosing a physician or hospital.

BIRTH COMPLICATIONS AND RELATED PROCEDURES

The experience of childbirth is usually positive for family members, as they celebrate the entry of a healthy newborn into the world. But childbirth can be stressful and frightening for some families. Many complications can occur during delivery.

Cesarean Sections

Although most births involve the fetus descending through the mother's vagina, many do not. In a nonvaginal birth, known as a **cesarean section,** the fetus is delivered through an incision in the mother's abdomen. In general, a cesarean section is used whenever it is believed that further delay in delivery would seriously compromise the health of the fetus. Table 4.1 lists some of the conditions most commonly associated with cesarean sections.

Although the conditions for performing cesarean sections have not changed much in recent years, the number of cesarean sections performed in the United States has increased dramatically since the 1970s. Figure 4.4 shows that cesarean deliveries accounted for about 5 percent of all deliveries in 1970 but about 22 percent in 1999 (National Center for Health Statistics, 2001a). About 900,000 cesarean deliveries are performed each year in the United States, making it the most common type of major surgery performed. European rates are about one-fourth to one-half the US rates (Korte & Scaer, 1992).

Many factors account for the rise in cesarean births. By the 1960s, increasing emphasis was being placed on the health of the fetus. At the same time, advances in medical care had made cesarean deliveries safer to perform. As a safe alternative to normal deliveries, cesarean sections became a practical way to improve the outcome of difficult pregnancies. Another contributing factor was the rising number of repeat cesareans. More than 98 percent of women in the United States who have had a cesarean delivery undergo cesareans for subsequent pregnancies (National Center for Health Statistics, 2001a). Furthermore, doctors' concerns about being sued for malpractice, should something go wrong with the delivery, increased the likelihood that a cesarean section would be used at the slightest indication of fetal distress (Korte & Scaer, 1992).

Today, most parents and doctors are urged to exercise caution in the use of cesarean sections. A cesarean section represents major surgery. Compared to a normal delivery, it is costly, involves a longer recovery period, has a higher risk of infection, and may be more likely to make infants or their mothers ill (Haynes de Reght, Minkoff, Feldman, & Schwartz, 1986). Even women who have had previous cesarean sections can usually have subsequent vaginal deliveries. Alternative methods are available for dealing with fetal distress and prolonged labor, and these can be tried before moving forward with surgery. However, when the mother or her unborn child is at risk, complications can be avoided with early and aggressive surgical intervention.

Induced Labor

During some pregnancies, situations arise in which the prolongation of the pregnancy is not in the best interests of either the mother or the fetus. In these situations, labor may be induced. Almost 20 percent of women who delivered in 1999 had induced labor, twice the 1990 level. The rate of induction has increased every year since 1989 (National Center for Health Statistics, 2001a). Pitocin or other medications may be given to start labor and delivery. These drugs have been found to be effective (Prysak & Castronova, 1998), and studies show no higher chances that infants delivered after labor is induced will develop physical problems (Alexander, Bloom, McIntire, & Leveno, 1999). However, because labor may signal the maturity of the fetus, its absence may indicate that the fetus is not quite ready for life outside the mother's womb. Although there clearly are times when allowing a pregnancy to continue is dangerous for mother or child, decisions to induce labor must be made carefully.

Breech and Transverse Presentations

In 95 percent of all births, the fetus is delivered in the head-down position. In about 4 percent of births, however, the fetus is positioned with buttocks or feet leading the way (National Center for Health Statistics, 2001a). This position is referred to as the **breech presentation.** Breech deliveries usually involve longer periods of labor but often occur with no difficulties. Sometimes, however, breech presentation requires cesarean delivery. In 1 out of 200 births, the fetus is positioned with shoulders and arms leading the way—known as the **transverse presentation.** In these cases, a cesarean delivery almost always is necessary (Cunningham et al., 1993).

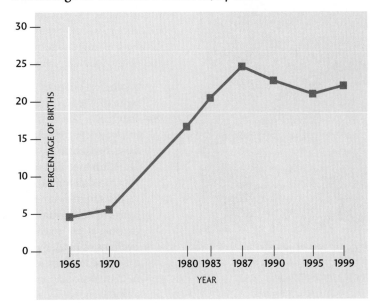

FIGURE 4.4

Percentage of Cesarean Deliveries, by Year

SOURCE: Adapted from National Center for Health Statistics, 2001a; Taffel, Placek, & Moien, 1989.

What factors have contributed to the increased rates of cesarean deliveries since 1970? What factors should a mother and her doctor consider before deciding on a cesarean delivery?

HOW IS CHILDBIRTH EXPERIENCED

Mothers, fathers, and newborns experience childbirth differently. As with all the major life events, the birth of a child has a lasting impact on the family, and mothers, fathers, and newborns each face a different set of challenges as they adjust to the changes brought about by birth.

breech presentation fetal position in which the buttocks or feet lead the way

transverse presentation fetal position in which the shoulders and arms lead the way

What factors do families have to consider when deciding about the setting for childbirth?

THE MOTHER'S PERSPECTIVE

The experience of birth is intense and mixed. Although having a baby is a joyous time for most women, many new mothers feel anxious, fragile, and overwhelmed after giving birth. The "baby blues" are not an inevitable part of having a baby, but they are very common, affecting about 70 to 80 percent of women giving birth. New mothers often cry unexpectedly and feel sad or angry without knowing why. A number of factors contribute to these blues, including the following (Eisenberg, Murkoff, & Hathaway, 1999):

- **Biological changes.**   The postpartum period is a time of great changes in a woman's body. Levels of female hormones drop sharply after childbirth.
- **Fatigue.**   The strains of labor, delivery, and care of the newborn, combined with a loss of sleep, contribute to mothers' feeling overwhelmed and exhausted.
- **Loss of attention.**   The baby takes center stage, and mothers no longer receive the attention they had while pregnant.
- **Increased demands at home.**   New mothers may feel overwhelmed by the responsibilities at home, particularly if there are other children in the family.
- **Sense of anticlimax.**   After the long pregnancy and all the excitement generated, the "big event" may not live up to the mother's expectations.
- **Feelings of inadequacy.**   Concern about her ability to care for the newborn may raise the mother's levels of confusion, guilt, and anxiety. In addition, changes in her physical appearance and body may raise the mother's doubts about her attractiveness.

For most mothers, these feelings usually begin a day or so after birth and peak three or four days later, but they rarely last more than a week or two and go away without the need for treatment.

> I knew I had to leave until I could come to terms with what was happening to me. I couldn't let my children continue to see me this way. I walked down the stairs and put my precious newborn baby into the nanny's arms. I put three blank checks and my credit cards in her hand, saying, "Please understand that I couldn't do this if I didn't have you here. I can't stay. There is something wrong, really wrong with me, and I have to leave until I figure it out." . . . My body was racked with hysterical crying, and I began to understand for the first time why a person would want to take her own life.
> —*Marie Osmond,* 2001

In these words you hear the despair that about 10 percent of new mothers experience. For 39-year-old Marie Osmond, known for her signature smile and upbeat attitude, the "blue" feelings associated with birth did not subside quickly or easily. Beautiful, talented, and happily married, she was living what seemed to be the picture-perfect life, co-hosting the successful *Donny and Marie Show.* What could go so wrong that it would send her on a tearful flight away from her children? In Marie's case, she was suffering from postpartum depression.

In contrast to the baby blues, **postpartum depression** is marked by intense feelings of sadness, anxiety, or despair that disrupt the new mother's ability to function and interact with her child (Epperson, 1999). Postpartum depression can affect the newborn child. In one study, newborns of mothers who experienced postpartum depression showed poor motor activity and were more irritable (Abrams, Field, Scafidi, & Prodromidis, 1995).

It is not known why some women become depressed after childbirth and others do not. One important factor is biology. Because some women are more sensitive to the biological changes that accompany birth, they may be more prone to postpartum depression. Stressful life events (unwanted pregnancy, single parenthood, lack of social support) and delivery complications also increase the chances of postpartum depression (Hagen, 1999; Logsdon, McBride, & Birkimer, 1994). Not surprisingly, lack of sleep and problems with the newborn's sleeping patterns are associated with postpartum depression (Hiscock & Wake, 2001). If depression and anxiety do not go away and begin to interfere with the mother's functioning, treatment may be needed.

postpartum depression intense feelings of sadness, anxiety, or despair experienced by a mother after the birth of a child

Research findings tell us that, all in all, it is common for mothers to experience a brief period of fear and anxiety after childbirth. Such feelings are quite common and do not mean that the new mother is a failure or that she is mentally ill. For the most part, these feelings are the result of the changes, both physical and psychological, brought about by the birth of a child.

THE FATHER'S PERSPECTIVE

> Probably one of the most memorable moments with Jeremy . . . was being able to be there for his birth and to hold him for the first time right after he was born. To cradle a newborn life in your arms that you know is yours and that you created—you really can't describe it. You don't want to put him down. You don't want to let him go. . . . A lot of other experiences have come since then, but that has got to be one of the most enjoyable.
>
> —Anonymous father's on-line story of the birth of his son

As this birth story reveals, for most contemporary fathers, experiencing the birth of their children does not mean pacing the hospital hallway with a pocketful of cigars to hand out as soon as word comes down. Today, many fathers take an active role in the birth process. In childbirth classes, fathers frequently serve as coaches for their partners, providing both physical and emotional support.

How a father experiences the birth of his child is strongly influenced by his emotional reactions and the degree to which he believes he is able to support his partner. Many men report that assisting in the birth of their child was a wonderful experience but at the same time made them feel helpless, particularly in dealing with their partner's labor. The more involved fathers become in the birth process, the more often they report feelings of closeness to their spouse and to their newborn child (Doherty, 1997).

Compared with fathers of the past, today's fathers show a high level of expectation of participating in the care of their newborns and a high degree of confidence in their ability to do so (Fox, Bruce, & Combs-Orne, 2000). Even before they become fathers, men have considerable expectations about fatherhood. In one study (Marsiglio, Hutchinson, & Cohan, 2000), men who were not yet fathers were asked about their perceptions of becoming a father. Most of the men were receptive to the idea (fatherhood readiness) and had relatively clear visions about what to expect once they became fathers (fatherhood visions).

Having a baby has a significant effect on fathers' concepts of themselves. In a classic study in which new fathers were compared to men who were not yet fathers, Cowan et al. (1985) found that several aspects of the new fathers' self-concepts changed in the direction of becoming more mature. These new fathers described themselves as being more aware of their personal relationships and using more tact and skill in managing family problems. Additionally, new fathers place more importance on their role as father and less on their role as spouse (Strauss & Goldberg, 1999). Of course, not all fathers "mature"—some regress, becoming jealous over the loss of attention and freedom, and some suffer from a type of postpartum depression (Antonucci & Mikus, 1988). Importantly, men's interactions with their partners and other family members contribute to their perceptions of themselves as fathers and influence how they respond to the birth of a child (Marsiglio et al., 2000). Thus, men's attitudes and beliefs about fatherhood are influenced by those individuals who are most meaningful in their lives.

The involvement of the father in the birth also influences how mothers feel about the birth experience. Fathers who are supportive during birth and labor have partners who are less anxious and distressed and are not as likely to need medication (Biller, 1993). Although the determinants of a father's level of involvement in the birth process and with his very young child are complex, fathers with greater psychological, social, and economic resources tend to be more involved and more satisfied with their involvement (Daly, 1993; Woodworth, Belsky, & Crnic, 1996).

THE NEWBORN'S PERSPECTIVE

How does the newborn experience birth? Most of us would imagine that birth is a grueling and frightening experience. The baby is squeezed through the birth canal for several hours,

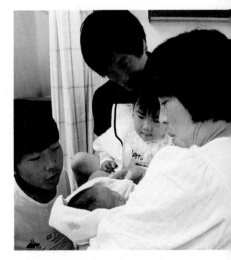

The birth of a baby influences the whole family. Describe how fathers and siblings are influenced by the birth of a child into the family.

FIGURE 4.5

Comparison of Stress Hormone Levels

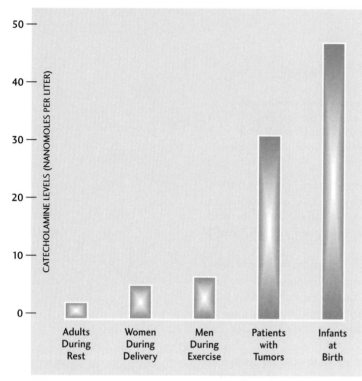

SOURCE: Adapted from Lagercrantz and Slotkin, 1986.

Why are stress hormone levels so high at birth? Notice that women giving birth have relatively low stress hormone levels.

during which time his or her head is compressed and put under considerable pressure. Then, the baby is delivered from the warm, moist, and protected environment of the womb into a bright, loud, and chaotic world. As Figure 4.5 shows, newborns produce "stress" hormones, called *catecholamines*, at levels 20 times higher than those found in adults—levels higher even than those found in adults who have serious medical conditions (Lagercrantz & Slotkin, 1986).

Despite these conditions, the stress of a normal delivery usually is not harmful (Gunnar, 1989). Evidence suggests that the fetus is well equipped to withstand this stress and that the chemicals produced by the stress may prepare the newborn to survive outside the mother's womb. For example, the surge in stress hormones helps clear the newborn's lungs and promotes normal breathing. Additionally, the surge in hormones increases the newborn's metabolism and energy supply (Slotkin, Kudlacz, Hou, & Seidler, 1990). One result of the increased metabolism and energy supply is that the newborn is born alert and aroused. By causing the newborn to be alert, the hormonal surge may promote the development of emotional ties between parents and their newborn during the first hours of life (Slotkin & Seidler, 1989). Birth by cesarean section does not lead to the surge in stress hormones, raising another concern about the overuse of this procedure.

PARENT-NEWBORN BONDING

Touching or holding their newborn for the first time is an emotional event for most parents. But human parents are not the only ones who experience this. Tender scenes between parents and newborns occur in many species—chimps and gorillas are just two examples (Bard, 1994). Parents' early contact behaviors may be part of intuitive parenting, some aspects of which may be determined by genetically driven responsiveness to infants.

When mothers and newborns spend time together right after birth, do they create a special bond that then helps the baby to develop? Conversely, are children who are deprived of early bonding, because they were adopted or sick, at risk for later developmental problems or even child abuse? These questions arose in the 1960s, after two decades during which mothers generally gave birth in cold and sterile hospital rooms, usually after taking pain medications that decreased their awareness of the birth process. Once the baby was born, she or he was whisked away to a nursery. Every 4 hours or so during the four or five days that mother and child stayed in the hospital, a nurse would bring in the baby for mom to feed. Thus, early contact between mother and child was limited.

Because of their concerns about these childbirth procedures, Klaus and colleagues (Klaus, Kennell, Plumb, & Zeuhlke, 1970) compared mothers and newborns who went through this typical procedure to a group of mothers and newborns who had extended contact immediately after birth. After one month, the mothers with extended contact were more likely to be responsive to their newborns. Based on these results, Klaus and Kennell (and others) proposed that there is a sensitive period immediately following birth during which mothers and infants bond through close physical contact. When bonding is interrupted, parenting failures are more likely and the child is at greater risk for abuse, neglect, and poor parenting.

As a result of these findings, there have been many positive changes in birthing practices, such as allowing babies to room in with their mothers. The scientific basis for bonding has not held up over time, however. Studies conducted since the 1970s have not supported the original findings (Goldberg, 1983; Lamb, 1982a, 1982b; Myers, 1984). For mothers who may be at risk for developing poor relationships with their newborns, however, having extra time with their infants may promote healthy interactions (Perusse, Neale, Heath, & Eaves, 1994).

No one denies the importance of parents' and infants' spending time together. Establishing a healthy parent-child relationship has many phases; spending the first hours together may be one of these phases. If parents miss this first step, they still have many other opportunities to develop healthy parent-child relationships. There is no evidence of a critical period for human bonding—success or failure in the parent-child relationship does not hinge on a few brief moments in time (Goldberg, 1983). The emotional tie between infants and their significant caregivers develops over a long period of time and is not dependent only on the early interactions.

CULTURAL DIFFERENCES IN THE EXPERIENCE OF CHILDBIRTH

Societies have unique responses to the event of birth, based on their beliefs, values, and customs. Even labor and labor pain vary from culture to culture, as do women's physiological reactions to childbirth (Mander, 2000; Scopesi, Zanobini, & Carossino, 1997). In the United States, birth generally is considered a very private affair, with only a few people involved. Until recently, this meant that mothers went through almost the entire birth process in the presence of only medical personnel. Only in the last twenty years or so have fathers and other close family members or friends attended births. At the other extreme, the Jahara of South America believe that the birth of a child is an event of interest to the entire community. They celebrate birth as a public event—mothers give birth under a shelter and in full view of the entire village, even small children (Fogel, 1997).

In Holland, midwives play a much greater role in childbirth than they do in the United States. In fact, midwives in Holland are part of the medical establishment and have belonged to the medical profession since 1972, along with general practitioners, dentists, pharmacists, and obstetricians. Midwifery training in Holland has always been of very high quality, with strict criteria for entry into the profession. These criteria have given midwives a more professional status than they have in the United States. This status is reflected in the Dutch word for *midwife,* which translates to mean "wise woman" (Smulders, 1999).

In developing countries, about two-thirds of all births take place outside of health care facilities. In almost half of the births, mothers deliver alone or are attended by untrained traditional birth attendants or family members. A wide variety of traditional beliefs are associated with birth. For example, in many countries, people believe that all life from the placenta must be transferred to the newborn; otherwise, the baby may die. Therefore, the cord is cut only after pulsations stop or after the delivery of the placenta. In some areas, the cord is milked, especially if the baby is not breathing, in order to bring the baby's soul back from the mother (World Health Organization, 1999).

In Turkey, after a mother gives birth, she receives presents of gold and the child receives various gifts. The mother is not supposed to go out from her house for forty days. If she works, she has a holiday of forty days automatically. Relatives, friends, and neighbors are all helpful. During the first three days, only close relatives come to visit; but in the following days, others come also, bearing presents. In Anatolia (the peninsula of land that constitutes the Asiatic portion of Turkey), there is a custom of planting trees in the names of newly born children. Chestnut, mulberry, or apple trees are planted for girls, poplar or pine trees for boys. Planting trees is a kind of investment for them, as the trees can be used in negotiating their marriages when they grow up (Yenen, 1997).

In many cultures, specific ceremonies surrounding birth reflect the traditions and values of the culture. Morris Opler (1981) describes one interesting example of such a ceremony for children born into the Jicarilla Apache Indian tribe. This event usually is con-

Notice how comfortable the father in this photo appears to be in holding his newborn and how alert the baby is. How do fathers experience birth? How has fathers' experience of birth changed in the past fifty years?

ducted within four days of birth, to bond the child both to the family and to protective supernatural powers. Called "water has been put on the top of his head," the ceremony marks the first time water touches the baby. Only water mixed from sacred "male" and "female" rivers is used. The newborn is bathed in the sacred water and songs are sung. The parents' and siblings' faces are painted with red ochre. This face painting is like a prayer and is considered a blessing in Jicarilla culture. When all have been painted, the singer presents the newborn to the father, saying "This is your baby." This announcement publicly establishes the sacred obligation of the father to his newborn child and his mate. The father then gives the baby to the mother.

Birth rituals and traditions illustrate how one's culture attributes meaning to birth. Because birth is such a powerful and profound event in most people's lives, many customs have developed that link it to the fabric of culture. These customs signify that birth is a social as well as a physical event and highlight the significance a culture places on bringing forth new life. Perhaps the remarkable thing is the ability of parents and newborns to adapt to the diversity of rituals different cultures prescribe.

WHAT ARE THE CHARACTERISTICS OF A NEWBORN

The adjustments a newborn must make to a new world are complex and demanding. After nine months as a protected and dependent being inside the mother's womb, the newborn must adapt to life outside the womb. The term **neonate** refers to infants who are making this adjustment—usually within their first one to two months. To survive, newborns must accomplish four major tasks:

- **Breathing on their own.**   The newborn's first challenge is to obtain the oxygen necessary for survival. To do this, the infant must switch from relying on oxygen provided by the blood in the umbilical cord to breathing on his or her own. A newborn's mouth and nose are filled with fluid before birth, and this shift requires that the fluid be drained and the airways opened for breathing. Childbirth itself forces some of the fluid out during the tight squeeze through the birth canal. The doctor or nurse clears out the remaining fluid to help the baby breathe.
- **Changing blood circulation.**   The infant's circulation pattern must also change to allow for breathing. Before birth, the placenta supports the infant. When the link to the mother is severed, circulation changes so that blood flows, for the first time, to the lungs. This change shifts the pressure of blood in the heart, which then changes the direction of blood flow. This is why newborns have irregular heartbeats and unstable blood pressure.
- **Controlling body temperature.**   Unlike the uterine environment, which has a steady, warm temperature, the environment outside the womb is susceptible to extreme changes in temperature. To survive, infants must control their body temperature and adjust to shifting temperatures.
- **Ingesting food.**   During prenatal development, the fetus obtains nutrients through the placenta. After birth, the newborn must obtain nourishment a different way—through his or her mouth. Normally, infants quickly adapt to oral feeding because they are capable of sucking when they are born and their digestive systems are developed enough to process the nutrients they need.

PHYSICAL APPEARANCE

Many parents are surprised by the appearance of their newborn child—he or she does not look like the babies they've seen on television! Newborns on average range in length from 19 to 21 inches, and their length at birth depends more on the size of the mother's uterus than on genetic inheritance. This is why a small mother can carry the child of a very large father. The average weight for newborns is 7 to 7½ pounds. After a vaginal delivery, the

neonate an infant who is in the first one to two months of life

baby's head often is misshapen, the face swollen, and the nose flattened from the pressures of moving through the birth canal. The newborn also may be covered in a white, waxy covering, called the **vernix caseosa,** which provides protection from bacteria. Many infants have uneven coloring, often having bluish or grayish fingers, nose, and feet as a result of poor blood circulation. Because of the presence of maternal hormones, the newborn may have enlarged genitalia.

> She had microscopic fingernails, a scrawny, funny ducktail hairdo, and tiny replicas of a wizened old man's hands. . . . She had weighed six pounds, fifteen ounces at birth, and had been twenty-one-and-one-half inches long. . . . I leaned over and started whispering to her and stroking her head. She looked up at me and I kept whispering. . . . Amazing. Forty-eight hours ago she hadn't even been born.
>
> —*Bob Greene* (1984, pp. 11–12)

Like most new parents, Bob Greene began his assessment of his newborn with a quick examination of her size, fingers, and head. Medical personnel also do a quick examination of the general well-being of the infant, to determine whether any type of emergency intervention is needed. The most commonly used procedure was developed by an anesthesiologist, Dr. Virginia Apgar. The **Apgar Scale** is a simple and effective method of diagnosing potential problems in full-term and preterm newborns (Hegyi et al., 1998). At 1 minute and 5 minutes after birth, the baby is examined for five vital signs: respiration, reflex responsiveness, muscle tone, color, and heart rate (see Table 4.2).

To test her new system, Dr. Apgar attended hundreds of births and meticulously recorded her findings. Newborns who scored from 8 to 10 usually emerged from the birth canal with a lusty cry and adjusted on their own. Babies who scored from 4 to 7 needed help or close observation until their scores improved. Those who scored from 0 to 3 were limp and unresponsive. To survive, they needed CPR. For example, a child who has been oxygen deprived during labor and delivery is likely to have blue- or gray-colored skin, may have arms and legs that droop because of lack of muscle tone, and may not be breathing immediately after birth. Fortunately, only 1.4 percent of newborns have Apgar scores of less than 7, although the rate is twice as high for African American babies as it is for Caucasian babies (2.4 vs. 1.2 percent; National Center for Health Statistics, 2001a).

NEONATAL REFLEXES

Infants are born with simple, coordinated, unlearned responses, called **reflexes,** that provide limited ways for them to interact with their environment. Some reflexes aid survival because they orient the infant toward food or protection. Protective reflexes include coughing, sneezing, blinking, and muscle withdrawal (see Table 4.3).

TABLE 4.2

Apgar Scoring System

SIGN	0 RATING	1 RATING	2 RATING
Heart rate	Absent	Slow (below 100)	Over 100
Respiration	Absent	Slow and irregular	Good, crying
Skin color	Blue or pale	Extremities blue, trunk pink	Completely pink
Muscle tone	Limp	Some flexion of extremities	Active movements
Reflex response	No response	Grimace	Vigorous crying

SOURCE: Adapted from Apgar, 1953.

vernix caseosa a white, waxy covering that provides the infant with protection from bacteria

Apgar Scale a method of diagnosing potential problems in newborns, in which five vital signs are examined: respiration, reflex responsiveness, muscle tone, color, and heart rate

reflexes simple, coordinated, unlearned responses

TABLE 4.3

Some Neonatal Reflexes

NAME	STIMULUS	RESPONSE	DEVELOPMENTAL COURSE
Blink	Puff air at baby	Closes eyes	Permanent
Sucking	Place object in infant's mouth	Sucks rhythmically	Changes to voluntary sucking by 2 months
Stepping	Hold baby under the arms in upright position, with feet on the ground; move baby forward	Steps by alternating legs	Disappears at 2 to 3 months
Babkin	Gently squeeze baby's palms with baby lying on back	Closes eyes, opens mouth, and turns head to middle of body	Disappears around 3 to 4 months
Rooting	Tickle baby's cheek with finger or nipple	Turns head toward finger or nipple and tries to suck	Disappears around 3 to 4 months
Tonic neck	Lay baby down flat	Turns head to one side, with arm and leg extended on that side and other arm and leg bent inward	Disappears around 3 to 4 months
Palmar grasp	Press finger against baby's palm	Grasps the finger	Declines after 3 to 4 months

(Continued)

TABLE 4.3
(*Continued*)

NAME	STIMULUS	RESPONSE	DEVELOPMENTAL COURSE
Moro	Make sudden loud noise or let infant's head drop slightly	Arches back, throws arms out, and then draws them in, legs extended	Disappears around 5 to 6 months
Swimming	Place infant face down in water	Moves arms and legs rhythmically, exhales through mouth	Disappears around 6 months
Babinski	Gently stroke sole of baby's foot from heel to toe	Spreads out and curls toes, turns foot inward	Changes at 12 months

SOURCE: Adapted from Prectl and Beintema, 1965.

Feeding reflexes include the rooting and sucking reflexes. The *rooting reflex* is seen when you rub your finger against a newborn's cheek: The baby turns toward the stimulation in search of a nipple to suck. The *sucking reflex* is seen whenever something touches an infant's lips: The baby tries to suck on it. Sucking is a surprisingly complex behavior that involves coordinating breathing and swallowing as well as coordinating the movements of the tongue, lips, and jaw to create a vacuum.

Other reflexes include the *Moro reflex,* a startle reaction to loud noises in which infants fling their arms out and then draw them in, arch their backs, and extend their legs. The *palmar grasping reflex* is elicited by touching the inside of the baby's hand, which causes the fingers to curl around the object. Parents of newborns are often surprised at how powerful this grasp reflex is—newborns can be lifted by using their grasping reflex.

Because reflexes help a newborn survive, an assessment of reflexes provides important insights into problems that some babies may face. An infant's reflexes can be used as indicators of the development of the nervous system. Reflexes that are too strong or too weak or that do not show expected developmental changes may indicate that the child has a problem. Babies who have been exposed to medications during delivery may fail to show some of the reflexes, such as sucking, but catch up soon after birth. As the infant's brain develops, the infant begins to take over voluntary control of actions and some reflexes disappear, usually between 4 and 8 months. The normal development of reflexes has been charted, and deviations from this pattern may signal that an infant has neurological problems. For instance, infants who have brain damage caused by cerebral palsy may continue to show a reflex after it should have disappeared (Allen, 1996).

NEONATAL STATES

If you have ever spent time with a young infant, you have probably observed rapid changes in her or his **state of arousal**—the degree to which the infant is alert, attentive, and awake. Infants rapidly drift in and out of wakefulness, excitement, drowsiness, and sleep. As shown in Table 4.4, these different states can be described in terms of six major categories, from high to low arousal: fussing/crying, nonalert waking, alert waking, drowsiness/sleep-wake transition, active sleep, and quiet sleep (Thoman & Whitney, 1990).

state of arousal the degree to which an infant is alert, attentive, and awake

TABLE 4.4

Infant States of Arousal

STATE	DESCRIPTION	TIME IN STATE (WHILE ALONE)
Fussing/crying	Low-intensity fussing or higher intensity crying	3%
Nonalert awake	Eyes open but unfocused, body movements, isolated fussing	3%
Alert awake	Attentive, looking around, eyes open	7%
Drowsiness/sleep-wake transition	Little motor activity, eyes closing and opening	7%
Active sleep	Eyes closed, uneven breathing, rapid eye movements, smiling, grimacing	50%
Quiet sleep	Eyes closed, regular and slow respiration, limited activity	30%

SOURCE: Adapted from Thoman and Whitney, 1990.

Understanding states of arousal is important for several reasons:

✦ States of arousal influence infants' interactions with others and with their environment. In a quiet alert state, infants learn better and seem particularly tuned in to the environment.

✦ Infant states of arousal provide information about individual differences. Some infants sleep more than others whereas some are more alert, and these differences are seen even during prenatal development (Groome et al., 1997). These differences in states of arousal also provide insight into the behavioral traits of young infants. As you will learn, some infants are passive and react little to their environment, whereas others are more responsive and easily irritated.

✦ The regularity of states of arousal provides a window on the maturity of the nervous system. Neonates who are very irregular in their states of arousal are at risk for later developmental problems (Thoman, 1990).

Infant states vary depending on the qualities of the caregiving they receive. In a classic study, Sander and colleagues (1972) found that newborns cried more and showed altered arousal patterns when they were introduced to new caregivers who responded differently than their previous caregivers had. These findings suggest that infant states of arousal develop through an interaction between their biological tendencies, such as the maturation level of the nervous system, and their environment, such as the quality of caregiving they receive.

NEONATAL SLEEP PATTERNS

You get so tired. In the middle of the night something interrupts your sleep; it is that cry again, and you don't know how you're going to make it out of bed to hold the baby.
—*Bob Greene* (1984, p. 21)

A newborn child averages about 16 hours of sleep a day. Nonetheless, as Bob Greene's diary entry reveals, parents of newborns often are bleary-eyed and tired because they do not get enough sleep. This is because newborns do not sleep 16 hours all at one time. In Figure 4.6, you can see that the typical adult sleeps for one long period of about 7 to 8 hours and is

The newborn's ability to nurse involves many complex skills. What reflexes of a newborn are involved in nursing? Can you identify some of the protective reflexes?

awake for the rest of the day. In contrast, the typical newborn sleeps six or seven times a day for about 2 to 3 hours at a time (Thoman & Whitney, 1989). Even this figure is somewhat misleading, because newborns may fall asleep for a few minutes or a few hours at almost any time of the day. By the end of two weeks, neonates begin to sleep somewhat longer during the night than during the day, and parents use a wide variety of techniques to help infants fall asleep (Toselli, Farneti, & Salzarulo, 1998).

Young infants awaken because they are hungry or uncomfortable and often fall asleep soon after being fed or changed. As they grow older, the time they spend sleeping decreases. The timing of sleep also changes as they get older. Older infants sleep more hours at night and fewer hours during the day, matching adult patterns more closely.

The length of time an infant sleeps at night may be an indicator of brain development (Zaiwalla & Stein, 1993). Indices of brain activity show that changes in sleeping and waking occur in the first months of life (Hoppenbrouwers et al., 1988). For instance, the brain activity patterns associated with drowsiness are not found in very young infants but are found in infants 5 to 8 months of age (Berg & Berg, 1987). The changes in sleep-wake cycles may signal important changes in the brain's ability to process information, which increase the infant's responsiveness to his or her environment (Sigman, Beckwith, Cohen, & Parmelee, 1989).

FIGURE 4.6
Sleep Patterns Across the Lifespan

Newborn —
One Year —
Four Years —
Ten Years —
Adult —

6 PM   Midnight   6 AM   Noon   6 PM

The shaded areas represent sleep in this schematic representation of the basic rest-activity cycle superimposed on the sleep-wake cycle.

SOURCE: Bornstein and Lamb, 1992. Reproduced with permission of the authors.

Notice how the sleep patterns of newborns are different from those of older children and adults. What factors contribute to these differences?

NEONATAL IMITATION

One of the most surprising capabilities of newborns is that they can imitate facial expressions (Heimann, 2001). Stick out your tongue at a newborn and the child probably will stick her or his tongue out too. Although this sounds easy, it is quite an amazing and difficult accomplishment. Think about trying to imitate a scary facial expression. You can try to match the face you have seen, but you cannot know for sure that you have copied that scary face. Unless you have a mirror, there is no way to monitor the imitation process visually.

Despite this difficulty, neonates are capable of imitating facial expressions such as pursed lips. Even 1- and 3-day-old infants can imitate simple expressions and head movements, and will continue to imitate them for a short time after the display stops (Maratos, 1998). Cross-cultural studies provide additional evidence: In rural Nepal, 1-hour-old newborns imitate lip-widening and lip-pursing (Reissland, 1988). It appears that neonates have an internal code that they use to match what they see with what they do. This code is not programmed at birth; instead, neonates use others' behaviors as a guide to help them construct their responses (Ullstadius, 2000).

By 6 weeks of age, infants not only imitate those in their immediate presence but also show evidence of **deferred imitation**—imitation of behaviors that occurred in the past (Meltzoff & Moore, 1994). Infants' ability to imitate someone after a delay indicates that they remember something about that individual, which sets the stage for additional interactions.

BEHAVIORAL ASSESSMENT OF NEONATES

A neonate's behavior provides insight into his or her development and health. For this reason, many instruments have been developed to assess their behavior. The most widely used instrument is the **Neonatal Behavioral Assessment Scale,** developed by a pediatrician,

In this photo, the young infant is imitating an adult (off camera) who is pursing his lips. The infant tries several times before she is successful. What kind of information about newborns' capabilities is gained from the fact that newborns can imitate basic facial expressions?

deferred imitation imitation of behaviors that occurred in the past

Neonatal Behavioral Assessment Scale a measure commonly used to assess a newborn's responses to the environment

TABLE 4.5
Brazelton's Neonatal Behavioral Assessment Scale (Revised)

REFLEX ACTIONS ASSESSED	BEHAVIORS ASSESSED
palmar grasp	orientation to a visual stimulus
Babinski	orientation to an auditory stimulus
standing	alertness
automatic walking	pull-to-sit
tonic neck reflex	cuddliness
Moro	irritability
rooting	activity
sucking	smiling
	self-quieting activity

Babinski

irritability

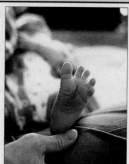

tonic neck reflex

smiling

SOURCE: Adapted from Brazelton, Nugent, and Lester, 1987.

Dr. T. Berry Brazelton, to measure a newborn's responses to the environment, especially reactions to others. The assessment is conducted with simple equipment by a trained examiner, who reviews the newborn's reflexes, motor capabilities, abilities to control attention and behavior, and responses to interaction with others (see Table 4.5). For instance, to assess cuddliness, the examiner holds the baby close and assesses to what extent the baby relaxes or curls up to cuddle. To assess self-quieting abilities, the examiner observes the actions a baby takes after he or she has become fussy: Does the baby suck his or her thumb to settle down?

The scale is used to identify newborns who have difficulties adjusting to their new environment outside the womb. After difficulties are identified, appropriate interventions can be developed. For instance, a neonate with impaired brain development may be hypersensitive to stimulation and react in a disorganized manner. Better control over the kinds of stimulation the infant receives may help the baby develop the ability to organize responses to the environment. The scale provides useful information even for infants who are not at risk, because it helps identify each baby's capacity for receiving and using stimulation from the environment (Brazelton, Nugent, & Lester, 1987).

HOW DOES EARLY BRAIN DEVELOPMENT PROCEED

About half of all human genes are involved in building the brain by providing the codes for its basic structures and functions (Robinson, 1996). Once brain development has been set in motion, the genetic code goes only so far before the child's environment makes a tremendous impact on the brain's development. An infant who has an enriched environment, in which she or he is exposed to many people, to music, to language, and to play opportunities, develops under optimum conditions.

neurons the nerve cells that make up the communication system of the brain

dendrites parts of a neuron that are located on the cell body and receive messages from other neurons

axon long part of a neuron that is located at the cell base and sends messages to other neurons

synapses small gaps, or spaces, between the cells through which information is transmitted from one neuron to the next

PROGRESSIVE EVENTS IN BRAIN DEVELOPMENT

By the time a baby is born, the parts of the brain that control many important survival-related functions, such as breathing, swallowing, sucking, and maintaining a heartbeat, are functioning. The sensory areas of the brain also develop early, allowing newborns to smell, taste, feel, see, and hear things going on around them. Only later do areas of the brain develop that are thought to be involved in regulating emotions, acquiring language, and reasoning. During early infancy, the size of the brain increases dramatically and it becomes capable of controlling more and more complex behaviors.

A newborn's nervous system is formed from the neural tube (see Chapter 3). Very early in prenatal development, the neural tube generates **neurons,** which are the nerve cells that make up the communication system of the brain (Begley, 1996). These brain cells migrate outward to specific areas of the brain, to form its structure. At birth, a newborn's brain has over 100 billion neurons (Nash, 1997).

As you can see in Figure 4.7, a neuron is composed of a cell body, many **dendrites** for receiving messages, and a long **axon** for sending messages. After migrating to their appropriate locations in the nervous system, neurons spin out axons and dendrites that allow for the transmission of information among them. At this point, each neuron produces many different connections with other neurons. Information is transmitted through electrical impulses that travel down the length of a neuron, causing it to produce a chemical response to the impulse. This chemical messenger then transmits the information from one neuron to the next through small gaps, or spaces, between the cells, called **synapses.** With the wealth of new sensory information that is available to the newborn, neurons form synaptic connections at a very fast rate (see Figure 4.8 on page 116).

Progressive events involved in early brain development, such as the proliferation and migration of neurons, add structure to the developing brain. Unfavorable environments

GURE 4.7

Brain Cell and Synaptic Connections

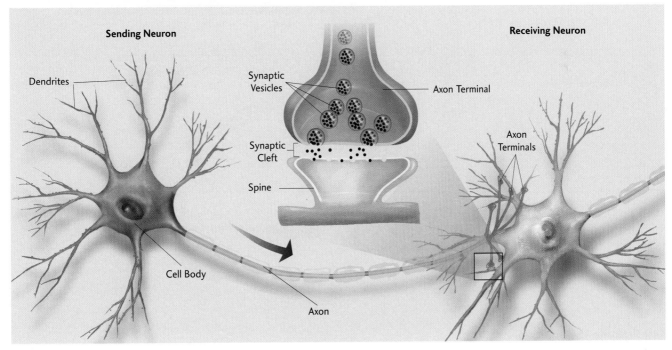

The dendrites of the neuron receive messages, and the axons send messages. How are these messages sent?

FIGURE 4.8

Development of Neural Connections, from Birth Through 15 Months of Age

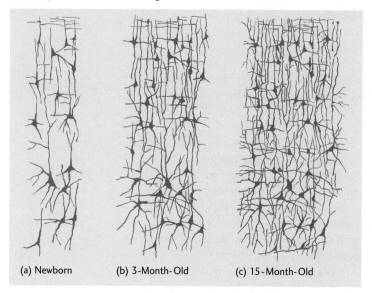

(a) Newborn   (b) 3-Month-Old   (c) 15-Month-Old

What differences are apparent in the depictions of the neural connections of young children at different ages? What factors contribute to these differences?

(such as prenatal exposure to drugs or alcohol) can disrupt these early progressive events (see Figure 4.9).

Another process that occurs in the early years of brain development is **myelination,** in which the neurons are sheathed in smooth layers of fatty proteins (myelin). Electrical impulses travel about three times faster along myelinated pathways. Myelination begins during prenatal development for parts of the spinal cord. In the brain, myelination occurs first in parts that control reflexes and later in parts that control voluntary movements (Cratty, 1999). After birth, those parts of the brain that are used to process sensory information (such as the visual system) myelinate first, and the parts that control attention, memory, self-control, and learning myelinate later. The most dramatic changes in myelination occur before 2 years of age, although some continue into adulthood (Sampaio & Truwit, 2001). Research has linked myelination to behavioral and cognitive development. For instance, particular brain locations in the cortex (the outer layer of the brain) are myelinated at 15 to 24 months of age, which corresponds to the time when children make tremendous advances in their cognitive and language skills (Konner, 1991).

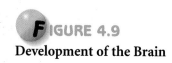

FIGURE 4.9

Development of the Brain

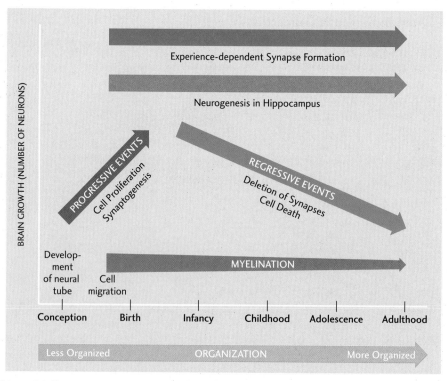

myelination the process in which a neuron is sheathed in a smooth layer of fatty proteins (myelin)

This model illustrates different events in brain development. How does this model help you understand the impact that children's environment can have on their development?

BRAIN PLASTICITY

Infant brains are more flexible than adult brains. The flexibility, or plasticity, of the brain allows it to fine-tune through interaction with its environment. Because of this plasticity, infant brains adjust to many different situations and are able to recover from serious assaults. We know about the benefits of brain plasticity from clinical cases. Recall from Chapter 1 the case of Brandi Binder, who, because of severe epileptic seizures, had the entire right side of her cortex removed when she was 6 years old but still managed to become talented in art, math, and music. With age, some of the brain's plasticity is lost. Adults who have the operation Brandi had lose much more functioning (Goodman & Whitaker, 1985).

REGRESSIVE EVENTS IN BRAIN DEVELOPMENT

During early development, the brain generates about two to three times more neurons and connections between neurons than are needed to survive and function. *Pruning* then takes place to decrease the number of cells and connections. Although cells and connections are lost, those that are maintained are strengthened and the brain becomes increasingly organized.

Pruning is influenced by both genetic and environmental factors, but the connections lost during pruning are those that are not reinforced by the child's environment. That is, connections that a child does not use disappear. Early experiences play a crucial role, therefore, in the formation of neural pathways (Greenough & Alcantara, 1993; Greenough, Black, & Wallace, 1987).

The timing of progressive and regressive events involved in brain development varies for different parts of the brain. In the first year, the visual and auditory parts of the brain undergo synaptogenesis and pruning. During the second to fifth years, the areas of the brain involved in language understanding and speech production undergo their most rapid changes. Over most of early childhood and into the adolescent years, the parts of the brain responsible for higher cognitive functioning undergo rapid changes in both progressive and regressive events.

ENVIRONMENTAL EFFECTS ON BRAIN DEVELOPMENT

The story of brain development suggests how our genetic inheritance sets up sensitive periods that act as windows of opportunity for learning from early experiences. These early experiences actually change the structure and functioning of the brain. In fact, experience may be the chief architect of the brain (Nash, 1997).

Because of the rapid growth of the brain during the early years of life, children are vulnerable to the effects of the environment during this time (Nelson & Bloom, 1997). Unfavorable conditions such as poor nutrition or exposure to drugs or diseases increase the risk of problems in brain development. Disruptions of growth and development during the brain's growth spurt can have a variety of serious outcomes:

- ✦ Permanent reduction in brain size
- ✦ Reduction in the number of neurons
- ✦ Reduced myelination of cells
- ✦ Decreased numbers of synaptic connections

Damage or disruption in the development of the brain during the early years may increase the likelihood that a child will have difficulties in school, lack the ability to handle stress well, and have poor motor and sensory functioning (Cratty, 1986). One source of this type of disruption is inadequate stimulation during sensitive periods. For example, infants who have depressed mothers and who receive less social interaction have brains that are less active (Nash, 1997). Animal studies support the idea that environmental stimulation has a strong effect on brain development. Animals that live in enriched environments—with playmates and toys to interact with—have 25 percent more connections between neurons than do animals in impoverished environments (Greenough, Black, & Wallace, 1987).

Research on brain development in rats, cats, and humans has popularized the idea that the first three years of life are the most critical for brain development. Although focusing the lay public's attention on the critical events of early life may be beneficial in that parents, teachers, and others become more aware of potentially damaging events in young children's lives, this increased attention also has a downside. First, there are other times of life when the brain is susceptible to influence—in particular, during prenatal development. For example, during cell migration (six to twenty-four weeks prenatal), the brain is highly vulnerable to teratogens, drug and alcohol exposure, and malnutrition (Thompson & Nelson, 2001). Second, there are few truly critical periods in human development. Instead, most are best characterized as being sensitive periods, in that the time periods are broader and more flexible (Bornstein, 1989). Third, recent research suggests that brain development and brain plasticity continue in important ways into adolescence and adulthood, and these time periods should not be ignored (Greenough & Black, 1992; Gould, 1999).

The implications of the newest research on brain development are profound. The idea that the environment is central in fine-tuning the brain suggests that experience may be even more important than previously thought in influencing both healthy and unhealthy developmental outcomes.

HOW DO NEONATES PERCEIVE THEIR WORLDS

Neonates perceive sights, sounds, textures, smells, and tastes, but their abilities to experience these sensations are not as fully developed as adults'. Newborns' senses of taste and smell are more developed after birth than their senses of vision and hearing are. Because their sensory systems are not yet fully developed, low-intensity stimuli, such as pale colors and soft sounds, may not be noticed at all. High-intensity stimuli, such as bright light or loud noise, may cause newborns to withdraw. Stimuli that are moderately intense are the "gentle magnets" that draw the attention of neonates (Stern, 1992).

THE VISUAL WORLD OF THE NEWBORN

Because the womb is a dark place, fetuses have little exposure to visual information before birth. Until the 1960s, people did not really know what or how newborns could see. Many parents have noticed that their newborns stare at them right after birth and sometimes follow movements with their eyes. But just what does the world look like to a newborn?

Newborns have poor visual acuity; what they see at 20 feet is what an adult with good vision sees at 300 to 800 feet (Aslin, 1987). The optic nerve and parts of the brain that process visual information are not fully developed at birth. Furthermore, the newborn's eye is shorter in length than an adult's eye, leading to less detailed information encoding (Dannemiller, 2001). Visual acuity improves rapidly, within six months, but it does not reach adult levels until 4 to 6 years of age (Maurer & Lewis, 2001). You may wonder how scientists determine what a young infant can see. Developing methods that allow for the assessment of nonverbal infants has been a challenge. A variety of methods have been designed, all of which tap into the kinds of behaviors that infants can perform: look at objects, suck on pacifiers, and turn their heads. In studying visual acuity, Fantz and his colleagues developed a clever method that capitalizes on infants' preferences for looking at patterns rather than solid colors (Fantz, Ordy, & Udelf, 1962). Infants are presented with two stimuli—one is a solid gray block of color, and the other is a pattern of black-and-white stripes varying systematically in width. Fantz assumed that when infants stopped showing a preference for the striped pattern (as the presented stripes got narrower), the limits of their visual acuity had been reached. Imagine what this test might look like to a very young infant: In the first presentation, the stripes are quite wide, and so the infant focuses on the striped pattern. As the stripes become very narrow, however, they no longer appear to be stripes to the infant's eye; instead, they are seen as the same gray as the other stimulus. So, both stimuli look the same to the infant, and neither attracts more interest than the other.

Look at the picture of the flag. What aspects of the photo draw your attention? How would a newborn visually scan this picture?

Soon after birth, although their vision is blurry, neonates can see and track slow-moving objects within their visual range—about 7 inches in front of the face. While tracking an object, newborns move their eyes with jerky motions, which are gradually replaced with smoother movements as they gain control of their eye muscles.

When adults visually scan objects, their eyes make very small and rapid movements to shift from one point of fixation to another. These movements allow them to take in visual information about the whole object, collecting enough small images that they recognize an object for what it is.

Just as adults do, newborns systematically scan objects, especially faces. A few simple rules sum up how neonates visually scan the world around them (Kellman & Banks, 1998):

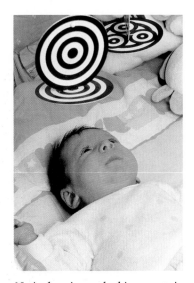

Notice how intensely this neonate is looking at the mobile. What features of the mobile make it effective in catching the visual attention of the newborn?

 ✦ They look for edges, using broad, jerky sweeps across their visual field.
 ✦ If they find an edge, they keep looking at it.
 ✦ They sweep their eyes across the edge again and again.
 ✦ If they cannot continue scanning one edge, they look for another.

As infants grow older, their scanning moves from the external edges to the more internal parts. Generally, younger infants attend to the most striking aspect of an object—the part that is moving, the brightest part, or the largest part. This is why mobiles that are bright and feature high-contrast colors are the ones young infants find most attractive. Parents holding a newborn often notice that she or he seems to look above their eyes. This is due to the newborn's fascination with areas of highest contrast—the hairline or eyebrows. However, newborns often look right into a caregiver's eyes because the eyes are very striking and appealing.

Important changes occur in the development of the eye and of the visual pathways to the brain over the first months of life, all of which improve the visual capabilities of young infants (Dannemiller, 2001). Additionally, as newborns develop greater control over the movements of their eyes, they are able to seek out and fix their attention on objects that appeal to them. This increased control occurs as the result of the maturation of the neonate's nervous system. Importantly, caregivers respond to these changes with increased attention and affection toward the infant. Caregivers often report that their infant is looking at them "for the first time" and that this is an expression of affection on the part of the infant. Caregivers find this immensely appealing. They cannot tell you what has changed, but are aware that something is different. This interplay shows how changes in the maturation of the infant's nervous system bring about changes in the infant's social and emotional relationships (Bertenthal, 1996).

Infants are born with capacities that direct them to learn about and orient to people and events that are crucial for their survival. Infants are especially attentive to faces, particularly when held close. They prefer curved lines and moderate complexity, as found in faces, and areas of high contrast, as found in eyes and mouths. Caregivers elicit the infant's attention by holding their face close to the infant's face in the same orientation and by interacting with the infant. The infant's visual capabilities combine with the caregivers' tendencies to interact with the baby in ways that provide mutually rewarding visual interactions.

THE NEWBORN'S WORLD OF SOUND

The structures needed for hearing are more developed at birth than the structures needed for vision are. By 1 year of age, an infant's auditory system generally is similar to an adult's (Kellman & Banks, 1998). But what do newborns hear? From birth, babies can hear sounds that are whispered, but not sounds softer than that; adults can hear much softer sounds (Nozza, 1995). Newborns cannot hear sounds of short duration as well as adults can, and they prefer relatively high-pitched sounds, such as the sound of a woman's voice (Fernald, 1985). Even newborns can localize sounds; for instance, they can identify the location of a rattle by hearing that the sound is coming from the left side rather than the right side (Aslin, Jusczyk, & Pisoni, 1998). Newborns' localization ability is relatively crude at birth but improves dramatically between birth and 6 months of age (Aslin & Hunt, 2001). Infants seem particularly attuned to human voices, especially the sound of their own mother's voice (DeCasper & Spence, 1986).

THE SCIENTIFIC IMPACT: INTERPRETING RESEARCH

Do Newborns Prefer to Hear Their Own Language?

As you have learned, newborns have preferences for certain sounds; they like to listen to their mother's voice, heartbeats, and stories that they listened to while they were still in the womb. Do unborn children also pay attention to the language that they hear spoken? Can they distinguish it from another language? If a mother and father speak only English during pregnancy, will their newborn prefer to listen to English rather than another language?

Eight 2-day-old infants who were born into monolingual English homes and eight 2-day-old infants who were born into monolingual Spanish homes were tested to determine whether they could discriminate between their own and another language. A contingent reinforcement procedure was used, in which infants learned to control the presentation of audio recordings of women speaking in either Spanish or English by sucking on a pacifier that was connected to a computer. The harder and longer the infants sucked, the longer they could control the length of time they heard the voices. After spending about 12 minutes learning how to control the voices through sucking, twelve of the sixteen infants showed the expected pattern: They activated the recordings in their native language for longer periods than they did the recordings in the foreign language (Moon, Cooper, & Fifer, 1993). The two days over which the infants were exposed to their native language after birth may have influenced their preferences, but the researchers believe that it is more likely that their prenatal experiences determined their preferences for their native language.

Thinking It Through:

1. Why would newborns have a preference for their own language?
2. What differences would you expect in the pattern of findings if 2-*month*-old infants were studied instead of 2-*day*-old infants? Would it be more difficult to determine when the infants' preferences developed?
3. Why did the researchers use infant sucking behavior to answer their research questions? What other behaviors could they have measured as indicators of preferences?

Newborns prefer the sounds they were exposed to during prenatal development. Within two days of birth, infants show a preference for hearing their own language rather than another language. They tend to prefer to listen to speech sounds, even in languages other than their own, rather than to nonspeech sounds (Werker & Vouloumanos, 2001). They also prefer the sounds of intrauterine heartbeats to many other sounds, and they prefer melodies their mother sang during pregnancy to other melodies. Prenatal exposure to sounds appears to "set" infants' preferences for sounds after they are born (Aslin, 1987).

THE NEWBORN'S WORLD OF TASTE, SMELL, AND TOUCH

Neonates have well-developed senses of taste, touch, and smell. Newborns can distinguish among tastes that are sweet, salty, bitter, and sour. They prefer sweet solutions over all other tastes, and they show disgust or distress when tasting something bitter or sour (Rosenstein & Oster, 1988). Although their numbers increase after birth, taste buds form early in prenatal development, suggesting that this sensory system functions even before birth. Early in life, babies have a wider distribution of taste buds than adults do—taste buds are found even on the tonsils and in the back of the throat. Further confirmation of the early functioning of the sense of taste comes from the findings that premature newborns pucker their lips when they taste something sour (Tatzer, Schubert, Timischl, & Simbruner, 1985) and premature and full-term neonates are calmed by sweet-tasting substances (Smith & Blass, 1996; Zeifman, Delany, & Blass, 1996). Recently, scientists have confirmed that flavors from the mother's diet during pregnancy are transmitted to the amniotic fluid and swallowed by the fetus. Exposure to flavors prenatally and through breast milk enhances infants' enjoyment of solid foods with those flavors during weaning (Mennella, Jagnow, & Beauchamp, 2001).

Newborns can distinguish between smells such as vinegar and alcohol. They turn away and make faces when presented with strong or unpleasant smells (vinegar) and turn toward more pleasant smells (Lipsitt, Engen, & Kaye, 1963).

Smells may be one of the first and most basic connections between neonates and their caregivers (Fabes & Filsinger, 1988). Within six days after birth, infants will turn their heads toward the smell of their mother's breast milk rather than that of other mothers (MacFarlane, 1975). Breast-fed infants show particular sensitivity to their mother's smells, such as her perfume and underarm odor (Cernoch & Porter, 1985; Porter, Makin, Davis, & Christensen, 1992). Mothers have a similar sensitivity for their infant's smells and can identify the smell of their infant soon after birth. When presented with clothing worn by their own baby and identical clothing worn by other babies, mothers are most likely to pick the clothing of their own baby by the smell (Porter, Cernoch, & McLaughlin, 1983).

Early in prenatal development, the fetus responds to a light touch—moving, for instance, when touched by an instrument. The parts of the nervous system that process information about touch develop very early. At birth, the presence of reflex responses to touch suggests that the newborn is particularly sensitive on the face, hands, soles of the feet, and abdomen (Reisman, 1987). Newborns are sensitive to changes in temperature and respond to cooling temperatures by waking up and moving around, which increases their heat production. A full-term newborn may sweat when the temperature is hot, but a preterm infant does not, suggesting that the cooling mechanism of sweating matures more slowly than other responses to temperature (Harpin, Chellappah, & Rutter, 1983). When infants are hungry, they will root toward warmth. For example, when warm glass tubes are held close to their cheeks, they move their heads and open their mouths toward the tubes (Reisman, 1987). This finding suggests that temperature cues are used by infants to locate nourishment.

The extent to which newborns experience pain has important consequences for their treatment. For many years, medical personnel assumed that infants were buffered from pain, at least for a short time after birth. Because of this assumption, they avoided giving newborns anesthesia or pain medication for surgical procedures, to reduce the risk of complications. Today, however, we know that newborns do experience pain. When they are circumcised or receive injections, newborns become distressed. They hold their breath and cry, their arms and legs and bodies become rigid, their faces show "pain" expressions, and they have difficulty sleeping (Anand & Hickey, 1987). Neonates' bodies respond to surgical procedures by producing more stress hormones (Gunnar, Fisch, Korsvik, & Donhowe, 1981). When newborns need to undergo surgical procedures, the American Academy of Pediatrics (1989) recommends that physicians use anesthesia and analgesics, following the same guidelines as for other high-risk groups. These procedures effectively and safely reduce the pain and distress experienced during surgery (Stang et al., 1997).

THE "DANCE OF PERCEPTION"

Newborns respond to meaningful stimuli, and their responses facilitate the development of close relationships. Babies curl up in their caregivers' arms, look at their caregivers and appear interested in what they see, and respond to their caregivers' touch. When an infant cries, the mother's breasts respond with increased blood flow, facilitating milk production. In turn, caregivers' responses reinforce and shape the infant's subsequent responses. Thus, as in a dance, each partner mutually leads and follows the other's responses.

Additionally, caregivers respond to babies in ways that facilitate interactions. By holding a baby in the crook of their arm, they place the baby at just the right distance for the baby's eyes to focus. By speaking in a high-pitched, melodious voice, they draw the baby's attention and soothe his or her distress. As this "dance of perception" between the young infant and the caregivers continues, each partner in the dance fine-tunes his or her responses to adapt to the other's nuances.

WHY ARE SOME NEWBORNS AT RISK?

Although most babies are born healthy, some newborns face risky health situations right from the start. For example, children who are born too early or too small may have difficulty

What is this mother doing to facilitate interaction with her baby? What do babies do to contribute to interactions?

making the adjustment from the prenatal environment to the postnatal world. An important distinction is made between infants who are **preterm** (or **premature**)—those born prior to 37 weeks' gestation—and infants who are **low birthweight**—those born after 37 weeks' gestation but weighing less than 5½ pounds. Low birthweight usually is a more significant risk factor than prematurity, accounting for 75 percent of the poor postnatal outcomes (Fanaroff, Martin, & Miller, 1994). Prematurity is a risk factor largely because of the many disabilities often associated with it (Allen, 1993). A baby born at thirty weeks takes eight weeks to reach the same developmental level as a baby born at thirty-eight weeks. The combination of being both preterm and low-birthweight places a newborn at the greatest risk for negative outcomes (Bardin, Zelkowitz, & Papageorgious, 1997).

Rates of low-birthweight and premature babies vary by racial/ethnic group (National Center for Health Statistics, 2001a). As depicted in Figure 4.10, African American mothers

FIGURE 4.10

Low-Birthweight and Preterm Births, by Race/Ethnicity

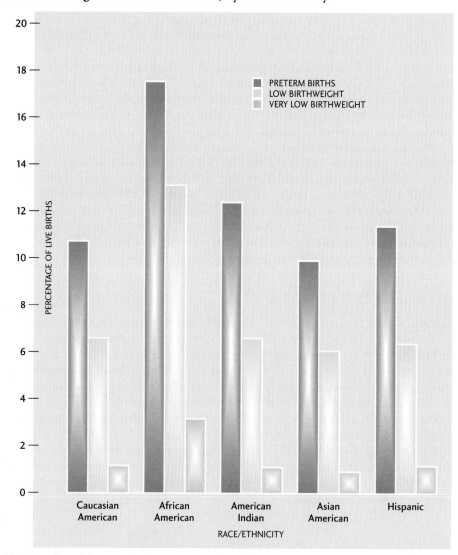

SOURCE: Adapted from National Center for Health Statistics, 2001a.

What factors contribute to differences among the groups in the percentages of low-birthweight and preterm births?

preterm or **premature** term describing infants born prior to 37 weeks' gestation

low birthweight term describing infants born after 37 weeks' gestation but weighing less than 5½ pounds

TABLE 4.6
Factors That Place Newborns at Risk for Poor Developmental Outcomes

BIOLOGICAL RISK FACTORS	ENVIRONMENTAL RISK FACTORS
Prematurity	Poverty/unemployment
Intracranial hemorrhage	No medical insurance
Growth retardation	Teenage mother
Brain abnormalities	Mental retardation or emotional disturbance
Biochemical abnormalities	in parent or caregiver
Infections	Substance abuse by caregiver
Lung disease	History of child abuse or neglect in family
Neonatal seizures	Family dysfunction
Maternal substance abuse during	Lack of parenting skills
pregnancy	Parent-child separation (divorce, maternal
	incarceration)

SOURCE: Adapted from Allen, 1993.

have a higher incidence of low-birthweight, very-low-birthweight (less than 3.3 pounds), and premature deliveries than any other ethnic group. The reason for this difference is unclear, but some factors that increase the likelihood of African American mothers' delivering low-birthweight and premature infants seem not to affect other ethnic groups, even other minority groups. A list of the factors that place a newborn at risk for poor developmental outcomes appears in Table 4.6.

Over the past decade, annual rates of preterm births in the United States have increased almost 14 percent, from 10.2 to 11.6 percent of all births. The current preterm birth rate is over 50 percent higher than the Healthy People 2010 objective set by the US Department of Health and Human Services. Had the target been attained, more than 150,000 of the over 540,000 cases of prematurity that year would have been prevented. About 23,000 of the preterm infants born in 1999 were born two to three months premature and weighed less than 1000 grams (2.3 pounds). These infants are referred to as "kilogram kids," and they spend their first few months fighting for their lives. In the past, virtually all of these newborns died. Today, almost 9 out of every 10 infants who weigh less than 500 grams at birth do not live, whereas about 75 percent of those who weigh 1000 grams survive (National Center for Health Statistics, 2001a). However, poor postnatal development remains a concern, particularly for those weighing less than 600 grams (Lemons et al., 2001).

Prematurity and low birthweight interact with cultural and social variations in caregiving environments to influence children's developmental outcomes. For instance, Bradley and colleagues (1994) found that the percentage of low-birthweight children living in poverty who were adaptive and resilient was very low (about 10 percent). This percentage is considerably lower than the 40 percent of preterm children from more affluent, nonpoverty households who were adaptive and resilient. These findings are particularly noteworthy given that the researchers did not include children with serious chronic medical problems (such as cerebral palsy). The odds that a premature, low-birthweight child living in poverty will show early evidence of the ability to tolerate adverse conditions are "for all practical purposes, nil" (Bradley et al., 1994, p. 357). These findings provide evidence that certain environmental conditions, such as poverty, can increase the vulnerability of an already vulnerable child (Fang, Madhavan, & Alderman, 1999).

CONSEQUENCES OF LOW BIRTHWEIGHT AND PREMATURITY

Most infants who are born too early or weigh too little at birth develop normally and become healthy and thriving children. The positive outcomes for many of these children relate to the plasticity of an infant's nervous system, which recovers from early trauma more quickly and easily than an adult's nervous system. Nonetheless, as a group, these infants are more likely to show a variety of physical problems, including the following (Hack, Klein, & Taylor, 1995):

✦ Subnormal growth
✦ Mental retardation
✦ Blindness
✦ Deafness
✦ Cerebral palsy (a brain disorder involving loss of control over motor functions)
✦ Health problems (asthma, kidney dysfunction, diabetes)

The smallest infants are at a higher risk for having low intelligence scores and deficits in cognitive abilities when they grow up, even when neurological and social risk factors are taken into account (Doussard-Roosevelt et al., 1997). Very-low-birthweight babies (weighing less than 3½ pounds) are particularly at risk for problems in specific areas, such as memory and fine motor skills, with verbal abilities being less impaired (Hack, Taylor, Klein, & Eiben, 1994; Schothorst & van Engeland, 1996).

Low-birthweight babies also have more difficulties in school, and the number of difficulties seems to increase as the weight of the child at birth decreases. Very-low-birthweight children are particularly vulnerable to problems in mathematics and specific learning disabilities (Koller et al., 1997; Taylor, Klein, & Hack, 1994); in addition, they have an increased risk of needing special education classes (Hack, Klein, & Taylor, 1995). Very-low-birthweight children who are premature show the greatest impairments in intelligence, motor performance, and attention (Korkman, Liikanen, & Fellman, 1996).

Very-low-birthweight children also may have more behavior problems than other children, and the lower the birthweight, the more problems reported (McCormick, Gortmaker, & Sobol, 1990). The problems include hyperactivity, poor social skills, and conduct disorders (Young, 1996).

NEONATAL INTENSIVE CARE

Most preterm newborns with developmental problems are put in a neonatal intensive care unit. The first step is to stabilize the newborn's body temperature and place her or him in an isolette to prevent loss of warmth. If respiratory problems are evident, the newborn is given oxygen. Heart, respiration, and other vital signs are closely monitored. Treatment for apnea or infection is given. After the infant is stabilized, she or he can be moved to an intermediate-level care facility. Upon reaching 5½ pounds, babies graduate from their special care facilities and can go home.

Approximately 2 to 9 percent of newborns require intensive care, and most of these are very-low-birthweight infants (Hack et al., 1995; Widerstrom, Mowder, & Sandall, 1991). Most of these newborns spend between fifteen and fifty days receiving special care in the neonatal intensive care unit, with the longest stays for the lightest babies (Gottfried, 1985). Changes in medical care, especially neonatal intensive care, have dramatically improved the survival rates for very-low-birthweight infants (Hobar & Lucey, 1995).

Not long ago, newborns in intensive care units experienced the frantic pace of hospital life and continuous monitoring, without concern for their special developmental needs or their families' needs (Young, 1996). Today, medical personnel are more sensitive to these newborns' special requirements and attempt to provide an environment that mimics the conditions of the prenatal environment. Lights are turned down, infants are swaddled in hammocks, and medical personnel know when to encourage or limit interactions with the infants. Importantly, parents are encouraged to be involved in their infant's care (Gottwald & Thurman, 1990). Breast-feeding and supplemental touching and caressing appear to be particularly valuable for premature and low-birthweight babies (Bier et al., 1997; Browne,

Notice that this infant is in an incubator, which helps keep him warm. How has technology improved the survival chances of newborns needing intensive care? What ethical issues does this technology raise?

2000). These interventions are effective in shortening the length of the premature infant's stay in intensive care.

CAREGIVING AND HIGH-RISK INFANTS

Even in the best of circumstances, adjusting to the birth of a child is difficult and stressful for parents and other family members. Adjusting to the birth of a high-risk infant means additional emotional, psychological, and physical challenges. Seeing an infant in an intensive care unit can be frightening and overwhelming, and parents often are not prepared for this. Preterm and very-low-birthweight babies look different than healthy, full-term babies; the tubes, machines, and isolettes are foreign and unsettling to most parents (Fleming et al., 1994; Singer et al., 1999). Even in well-functioning families, parents who give birth to fragile children experience chronic or recurrent stress (Clubb, 1991; DeMeir et al., 2000).

Once a high-risk infant is taken home, the family faces many new challenges. The baby may have short-term health care needs, such as a need for someone to monitor apnea episodes, or long-term needs, such as a need for a ventilator. High-risk newborns require a great deal of parents' time and energy, and many parents report that family life deteriorates: Spouses have less time for each other and parents have less time to attend to the needs of their other children (Diehl, Moffitt, & Wade, 1991). Family functioning also can be affected by financial concerns, which mount as the care for the fragile child continues. For families with high-risk infants, problems with finances are a common source of stress (Wegener & Aday, 1989).

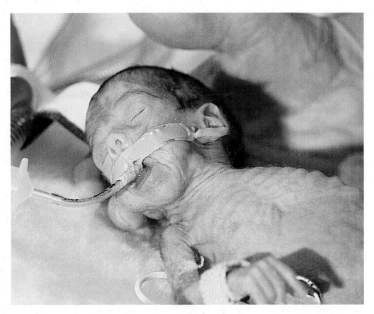

Preterm infants often have difficulty breathing and may experience short periods when they stop breathing. Can you describe the ways in which this preterm baby looks different from a full-term baby?

THE SOCIAL IMPACT: DEBATING THE ISSUE

Should There Be Limits to Neonatal Treatment?

Rapid improvements in medical care for newborns have led to an increase in survival rates for very small and very-low-birthweight infants. The advent of neonatal intensive care procedures has also increased the number of high-risk newborns who survive but have disabilities (Hack et al., 1995). In addition to the ethical issues, there also is a medical question concerning the provision of extensive medical treatment to extremely immature newborns. Is there a limit to the effectiveness of treatment? Several studies

have investigated infant survival rates to determine whether a cutoff point exists in treatment effectiveness. In a study of infants born between 1988 and 1991 at twenty-two to twenty-five weeks' gestation, it was found that outcome depended on gestational age. As the table shows, the likelihood of survival varied dramatically with age, as did the chance of having severe brain damage (Allen, Donohue, & Dusman, 1993). The researchers concluded that aggressive medical care (such as resuscitation) is indicated for

infants born in the twenty-fifth gestational week, but not for those born in the twenty-second gestational week. To determine the indicated treatment level for those in between, the researchers recommended opening discussions with parents, health care providers, and society at large. Concerns about which infants receive intensive medical care are likely to become more pressing as scarce health care resources are evaluated and reallocated.

Thinking It Through:

1. How does society determine which—and whether—very small and very early newborns will receive expensive and demanding medical interventions?
2. Should parents be asked to consider the costs to society of caring for a high-risk infant whose chances of surviving are very low?
3. Because medical interventions for very small or early infants are expensive, should society make certain these interventions are available to all who need them?

Rates of Survival and Brain Damage in Premature Newborns

GESTATIONAL AGE	SURVIVAL RATE	RATE OF BRAIN DAMAGE
22 weeks	0%	—
23 weeks	15%	98%
24 weeks	56%	79%
25 weeks	79%	31%

SOURCE: Allen et al., 1993.

THE PRACTICAL IMPACT: NURTURING CHILDREN

Preventing SIDS

After the first few days of life, the most common cause of unexpected death in infants is sudden infant death syndrome (SIDS). When an infant dies in his or her sleep and there is no other ready explanation, SIDS is often the diagnosis. SIDS strikes nearly 5000 babies in the United States each year (American Academy of Pediatrics, 2001). Other possible causes of death, such as child abuse and overheating, must be ruled out. SIDS is not well understood; apparently, many different factors can cause an infant to die in the first months after birth. Some of

the suspected causes of SIDS include drug use by the mother during pregnancy, an undetected fast-acting viral or bacterial infection, oxygen deprivation during pregnancy, hormonal imbalance, and cigarette smoking in the home. More infants die of SIDS within the first few months of birth than later, suggesting that infants may be less susceptible to SIDS once certain developmental changes have occurred. Certain infants seem to be at risk for SIDS: boys, infants with brothers or sisters who died of SIDS, preterm infants, low-birthweight

infants, infants with low Apgar scores, and infants with respiratory problems (Barness & Gilbert-Barness, 1992). Recommendations made to parents to reduce the likelihood of an infant's dying of SIDS include placing the infant in a face-up position rather than a face-down position to sleep, using a firm mattress, avoiding overdressing or overheating the infant, breastfeeding when possible, and maintaining regular health visits (Association of SIDS and Infant Mortality Programs, 1998).

In interactions with their parents, preterm infants are less responsive, alert, and active than their full-term peers. Yet parents of preterm infants take a *more* active role in interactions than parents of full-term infants do (Goldberg & DiVitto, 1995). For example, parents of preterm infants stay closer, hold and touch more, and provide more stimulation. These findings suggest that parents of a preterm infant sometimes compensate for the low responsiveness of their infant by taking more direct action to engage the infant. This compensation provides a basis for secure parent-infant relationships as the preterm infant gets older and healthier. Nonetheless, parents of very-low-birthweight infants or of preterm infants who have a lasting illness (such as a heart defect) are more likely to have difficulties establishing secure relationships with their newborn (Feldman et al., 1999; Plunkett et al., 1986).

INFANT MORTALITY

Many infants worldwide do not live long enough to celebrate their first birthday. In 2001, Angola and Afghanistan had two of the highest rates of infant mortality in all the world. In the United States, the infant mortality rate was relatively low, with only 7 children out of 1000 not surviving until their first birthday. However, despite the excellent medical facilities in the United States, the US infant mortality rate is still higher than that of many other developed countries—twenty countries have lower rates (UNICEF, 2001).

Within the United States, some groups have much higher rates of infant mortality than others. Compared with the mortality rate for Caucasian American infants—6.0 deaths per 1000 live births—mortality rates are 136 percent higher for African American infants and 45 percent higher for Native American Indian infants. The mortality rate for Hispanic infants is comparable to that for Caucasian American infants, whereas Asian American infants have a mortality rate that is 16 percent lower (National Center for Health Statistics, 2001a). Why the infant mortality rates for these groups differ is as yet unknown, but one likely reason is differences in access to and use of prenatal and postnatal care. Cultural values and family support are important, too, as evidenced by the lower rates of infant mortality among Hispanic infants, despite lower socioeconomic status and less prenatal care (Balcazar, Peterson, & Krull, 1997).

TRY IT OUT
Activities Relating to Birth and Neonates

1. How have birthing practices changed over time? Talk to your parents and their friends about their childbirth experiences, and compare them to those of parents who have given birth within the last ten years. What changes have occurred in attitudes, practices, and technology? How have these changes altered the experience of childbirth? What type of birth method would you choose? Why?

2. Arrange to observe a newborn, and watch for the characteristics of a neonate identified in this chapter. Design a rating chart on which to record the characteristics you observe. You might also attempt to assess the newborn's behavior, using information in this chapter. On the basis of your observations, develop a research question on a topic in neonatal development that interests you.

3. Use your imagination and the information in this chapter to try to experience a physical and social environment the way a newborn would. What is your visual world like? What do you hear, taste, smell, and feel? How do others' interactions with you influence your "dance of perception"? How do you interact with the world?

4. Re-read the section on low-birthweight and at-risk newborns. Consider the impact that having an at-risk baby would have on a family. Try thinking about how parents' expectations of having a healthy, cuddly baby would contribute to the difficulties of dealing with an at-risk newborn. What factors might influence how parents respond to this situation and how they cope with the demands of caring for a fragile baby?

SUM IT UP

How is a baby born?

◆ There are three stages of labor. In the first stage, contractions of the uterus cause the cervix to dilate.

◆ In the second stage, the baby is born. The baby moves through the birth canal and is expelled through the vaginal opening.

◆ In the third stage, the placenta is expelled.

◆ There are many birthing methods to choose among, including the Lamaze method, which focuses on educating the parents and teaching relaxation techniques, and the Leboyer method, which focuses on lessening the trauma of childbirth for the infant by using quiet and dimly lit rooms.

◆ Infrequently, birth complications occur, for a variety of reasons. A woman may require a surgical method of birth (cesarean section) to safeguard her baby's health, a fetus may be in an unusual position, or birth may have to be induced.

How is childbirth experienced?

◆ A mother's experience of childbirth encompasses both positive and negative feelings. The mother feels excitement and the pain of labor and also may experience baby blues or post-partum depression due to biological changes, fatigue, loss of attention, and the increased stresses on family life.

◆ A father's experience of childbirth depends on whether or not he feels confident of his ability to support his partner. Today, many more fathers are present when their children are born; they feel closer to their partners and children for having shared the experience.

◆ Newborns produce high levels of stress hormones during birth, but they are well equipped to manage the birth process. These hormones cause infants to be alert and attentive immediately following birth.

◆ Parents may feel a special closeness to their child after birth, but the scientific evidence does not support the idea that there is a critical period for initial bonding.

What are the characteristics of a newborn?

◆ Newborns face four challenges after birth: breathing on their own, changing their blood circulation, controlling their body temperature, and ingesting food.

◆ Newborns' physical characteristics differ from those of older infants: they have misshapen heads and faces, uneven coloring, and enlarged genitalia.

◆ The Apgar scale is used to assess whether newborns need emergency medical care.

◆ Newborns have automatic behaviors, called reflexes, some of which help them to survive. Assessment of reflexes provides information about the condition of the baby's nervous system.

◆ Newborns shift among states of arousal. These states influence the quality of interactions between caregivers and newborns.

◆ Newborns sleep 16 hours a day, spread out over the day and night. Sleep and wake cycles may indicate brain development.

◆ The ability of newborns to imitate facial expressions indicates that they have some internal code that allows them to match what they see with what they do.

◆ Brazelton's Neonatal Behavioral Assessment Scale allows medical personnel to evaluate the development and health of newborns.

How does early brain development proceed?

◆ Progressive events in brain development—cell generation and the formation of billions of synaptic connections—are largely genetically controlled.

◆ Neurons allow communication among the various areas of the brain. Myelination of neurons helps them send and receive information more quickly and efficiently.

◆ Regressive events include cell death and the loss of connections between neurons. Which connections are lost and which develop more fully depend on experiences.

◆ Susceptibility to brain damage is particularly high during prenatal and early infant development.

How do neonates perceive their worlds?

◆ Newborns' vision is blurry compared to that of adults. Newborns like to look at areas of high contrast, especially edges of things, and they like to look at faces.

◆ Newborns can hear fairly well at birth. They like to listen to familiar and high-pitched voices and sounds.

◆ The senses of smell, taste, and touch are well developed by the time the child is born. Newborns can distinguish many tastes and smells, and they prefer sweet tastes and pleasant smells.

◆ Newborns feel pain and show signs of distress when they are in pain.

Why are some newborns at risk?

◆ Preterm, or premature, babies are born too early—before 37 weeks. Low-birthweight babies weigh too little—less than 5.5 pounds—when they are born. The combination of these two risk factors is more serious than either alone.

◆ Some newborns require intensive medical care, which is usually provided in neonatal intensive care units.

◆ High-risk infants usually develop into healthy children, but some have physical and cognitive problems. These problems are more likely to occur if the infant is of very low birthweight.

◆ Taking care of high-risk infants is challenging and, depending on the nature of the infant's problems, can be very stressful for families.

◆ In the United States, infants have a good chance of surviving their first year of life, but in many countries and for some groups within the United States, the infant mortality rate is high.

KEY TERMS and CONCEPTS

Apgar Scale (*109*)
axon (*115*)
Braxton-Hicks contractions (*98*)
breech presentation (*103*)
cesarean section (*102*)
crowning (*99*)
deferred imitation (*113*)
dendrites (*115*)
epidural block (*99*)
episiotomy (*100*)

false labor (*98*)
lightening (*98*)
low birthweight (*122*)
molding (*99*)
multiparous women (*98*)
myelination (*116*)
Neonatal Behavioral Assessment Scale (*113*)
neonate (*108*)
neurons (*115*)

postpartum depression (*104*)
preterm (*122*)
premature (*122*)
primiparous women (*98*)
reflexes (*109*)
state of arousal (*111*)
synapses (*115*)
transverse presentation (*103*)
vernix caseosa (*109*)

BENCHMARKS in
Prenatal and Neonatal Development

	PHYSICAL/MOTOR DEVELOPMENT	COGNITIVE DEVELOPMENT	SOCIAL/EMOTIONAL DEVELOPMENT
Conception	Genetic transmission Sex determination	Genetic basis of intelligence	Genetic basis of personality and behavioral traits
Prenatal Germinal	Development of zygote Cell division and differentiation Development of placenta and umbilicus Implantation		
Embryonic	Critical time for teratogenic effects Cephalocaudal and proximodistal growth Development of sensory and internal organs	Beginning of brain and central nervous system development	Pregnancy confirmed Parental excitement about pregnancy Feelings of concern for health of child
Fetal	Rapid growth of body and brain Development of external genitalia Age of viability Preparation for birth Reflexes functioning	All senses functioning to some degree Well-defined stages of arousal REM sleep	Mother's condition becoming obvious Family preparing for arrival of new child
Birth	Labor and dilation of cervix Crowning and molding Afterbirth Beginning of breathing and body temperature control	Exposure to sensations from world outside the uterus	Parental, societal, and cultural expectations for birth Addition of new family member
Neonate	Reflexes Rapid brain development Continuation of perceptual development Cycling through states of arousal Initial weight loss followed by weight gain	Innate preferences Perceptual memory Ability to learn simple contingencies Ability to imitate facial expressions	Parent-newborn bonding Caregiving Individual differences in behavioral traits becoming evident

NATIONAL HOTLINES FOR PREGNANCY AND PRENATAL AND NEONATAL DEVELOPMENT

SIDS Alliance: 800-221-7437

March of Dimes Birth Defects Foundation: 888-663-4637

Crisis Pregnancy Helpline: 888-467-8466

*i*mpact Report on Prenatal and Neonatal Development

Countries vary tremendously in their infant mortality rates. What are some factors that may account for these differences?

Worldwide Rates of Infant Mortality

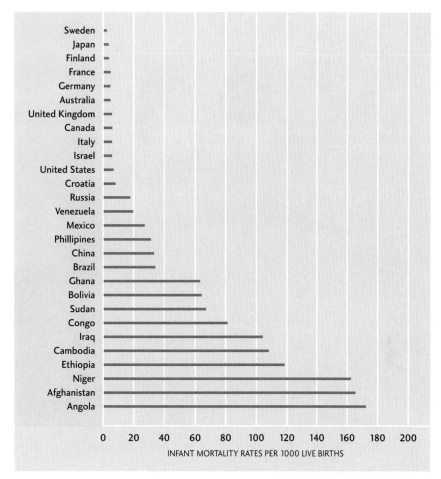

INFANT MORTALITY RATES PER 1000 LIVE BIRTHS

NOTE: Rates reflect the number dying between birth and 1 year of age per 1000 live births.

SOURCE: UNICEF, 2001.

RECOMMENDED WEBSITES

The Baby Center: This comprehensive site for parents and family care workers is reviewed by a medical advisory board.
http://www.babycenter.com/

Childbirth: Designed to help readers become good consumers with respect to pregnancy and childbirth, this Website has many links to educational, informational, and personal resources.
http://www.childbirth.org/

IVF Net: This comprehensive site, dedicated to the science of reproductive medicine, provides information on fertility and pregnancy for both scientists and parents.
http://www.ivf.net/

NOAH on Pregnancy: The New York Online Access to Health (NOAH) Website gives consumers high-quality health information that is accurate, timely, relevant, and unbiased. NOAH currently supports English and Spanish.
http://www.noah-health.org/

OBGYN Net: Run by the Association of Labor Assistants and Childbirth Educators, the OBGYN site offers up-to-the-minute reference information, an events calendar, clinical reference collections, powerful search tools, discussion forums, electronic journals, and recent articles.
http://www.obgyn.net/

On-Line Birth Center: Abstracts, articles, and resources appear on midwifery, pregnancy, birth, and breast-feeding.
http://www.moonlily.com/obc/

SIDS Network: A growing collaborative effort, this site offers up-to-date information as well as support for those who have been touched by SIDS.
http://www.sids-network.org/

Infant and Toddler Development

From the moment they are born, infants are bombarded by sights, sounds, smells, and tactile sensations. A major task of the first two years of life is to develop ways of making sense of and organizing these sensations. As the brain develops and infants gain experience, they increasingly acquire abilities to integrate and understand the world around them. Eventually they learn to understand words and to coordinate their eyes and hands so that they can reach out to grab something they want.

Infants also face the task of developing ways of interacting with their social world. Parents, caregivers, siblings, other family members, and friends interact with infants, and the quality of these interactions has important implications for infants' development. In turn, infants' actions and responses affect how others interact with them. This reciprocal interaction forms the basis for much of the development that occurs during this stage of life. Unfortunately, as the statistics indicate, very young children also are at risk for accidental injury, illness, and maltreatment.

Cognitive, Language, and Physical Development in Infancy and Toddlerhood

CHAPTER OUTLINE

✦ How Do Infants and Toddlers Develop Physically?

✦ What Factors Influence Infant Health and Safety?

✦ How Do Infants' Perceptual Abilities Develop?

✦ How Do Infants and Toddlers Learn and Remember?

✦ How Do Cognitive Abilities Develop During Infancy and Toddlerhood?

✦ How Do Infants and Toddlers Develop Language Skills?

✦ How Is Children's Language Acquisition Explained?

Twenty years ago, little was known about the capabilities of infants. Most people assumed that their worlds were filled with confusion—they could not see or hear very well, nor could they learn very easily. That picture has changed dramatically. Today, we recognize that infants are actively learning about the people and objects they encounter, and much of this learning occurs in the context of routine interactions with those people. For example, by 2 months of age, infants stare intensely at new toys or objects. This behavior shows us that young infants selectively attend to things that interest them.

HOW DO INFANTS AND TODDLERS DEVELOP PHYSICALLY?

Growth in height and weight and dramatic changes in motor skills occur rapidly during the first two years of life, more rapidly than for older children. Infants' proportions are different from those of older children and adults. Their heads are much larger relative to the size of their bodies. A newborn's head is about one-quarter of his or her body size, whereas an adult's head makes up about 12 percent of his or her body size. Relative to head size, infants have a large forehead, small flat nose, and large eyes. They have a distinctive body shape as well, with a protruding stomach; short, bowed legs; and relatively high amounts of fat (Cratty, 1999).

Growth is an indication of children's health. Pediatricians use growth charts to follow changes in children's height and weight over time and to compare one child's growth to that of other children. Each curved line on the charts in Figure 5.1 represents a different growth pattern. The bottom line represents a child who is growing more slowly than other children. This child is ranked in the 5th percentile, meaning that only 5 percent of children of the same age are shorter (or weigh less). The blue line in the middle represents an average growth pattern. If a child is in the 50th percentile, half of the other children are taller and half shorter. The top line represents the growth of a child in the 95th percentile, who is taller (or heavier) than almost all other children. For most children, growth patterns remain similar over time, so a child who is average in height at age 3 is likely to be average at age 5.

GROWTH PATTERNS IN INFANTS AND TODDLERS

By their first birthday, most children gain 15 pounds and grow 9 inches. After prenatal growth, there is no other period of life in which children grow as quickly as they do during the first year. As you can see in Figure 5.1, infant boys and girls continue to grow rapidly during the first three years, and their growth patterns are similar. By age 2, boys reach about 50 percent and girls 53 percent of their adult height. Birth weight usually doubles by 5 months, triples by the end of the first year, and quadruples by about 30 months of age. It takes ten years for children to reach half their adult weight.

Genetic factors play a major role in determining a child's growth pattern, especially for height and body type and to a lesser extent for weight. Generally, tall parents have children who are tall and short parents have children who are short.

The conditions in which a child is raised also influence growth patterns. Children who do not receive adequate nutrition during their early years do not achieve optimal height. Changes in diet can alter trends, however. For example, because of improved diets, Japanese children born after World War II grew too large to fit into the school desks that their parents had used as children. Americans, too, are taller than their ancestors because of improved diets; children born after World War II tend to be about 1 inch taller than their parents (Roche, 1979).

BRAIN DEVELOPMENT

The brain develops very quickly during the first few years of life (see Chapter 4). When a baby is 6 months of age, her or his brain weighs approximately half what an adult brain

Growth Charts for Height and Weight (birth to 36 months)

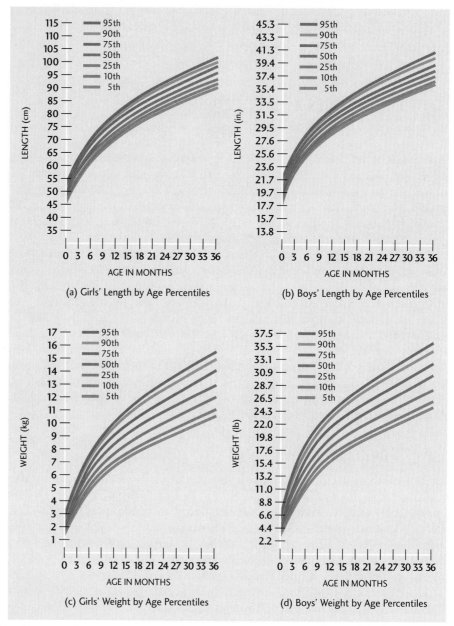

(a) Girls' Length by Age Percentiles

(b) Boys' Length by Age Percentiles

(c) Girls' Weight by Age Percentiles

(d) Boys' Weight by Age Percentiles

SOURCE: National Center for Health Statistics, 1976.

Notice that infants tend to grow very rapidly in both weight and height. Girls and boys show similar growth patterns in the first two years of life. See http://www.cdc.gov/growthcharts.

weighs; by the time she or he reaches 2 years of age, the weight of the baby's brain is almost 80 percent of that of an adult brain.

The largest part of the brain is the cerebral cortex, which has many folds, or convolutions, throughout its surface. The cerebral cortex controls higher thought processes such as problem solving, consciousness, and language. The cortex is the last part of the brain to finish growing. Because of its slower rate of growth, the cortex is more susceptible to environmental influences than other parts of the brain. The cerebral cortex is divided into two halves, called hemispheres, each of which has areas specialized for certain functions. For most people, the left hemisphere is specialized for language processing, whereas the right hemisphere is specialized for recognizing spatial relationships (reading maps, for instance). Hemispheric development occurs unevenly. The left hemisphere develops rapidly around the age of 2; the right hemisphere develops later. Also, the two hemispheres are not fully connected until later (see Chapter 7).

The timing of the "blooming" and later "pruning" of neuronal connections varies according to the region of the brain (Huttenlocher, 1979; Huttenlocher & Dabholkar, 1997). Connections for the visual areas of the brain bloom during the first months of life; pruning starts in the infant and toddler years and lasts until the preschool period. In the auditory and language parts of the brain, blooming and pruning occur somewhat later, with peak overproduction occurring late in the first year of life and pruning occurring through young childhood. For the areas of higher cognitive functioning, blooming of connections occurs at approximately 1 year of age, but it is not until later in adolescence that the number of connections has been pruned to match adult levels.

Because of the rapid growth of the brain, children's experiences during infancy and toddlerhood play an important role in helping to "wire" the brain. Early experiences may be particularly influential because the nature of those experiences helps to determine how many and which types of neuronal connections are maintained during synaptic pruning. As a consequence of the child's experiences, the brain fine-tunes itself through its neuronal connections to be responsive to the child's environment. Remember, though, that these early experiences are not the only experiences that matter. As discussed earlier (see Chapter 2), the brain has the ability to adapt to many changing environments. Thus, brain development is a life-long process (Thompson & Nelson, 2001).

MOTOR DEVELOPMENT IN INFANTS AND TODDLERS

Tickle a newborn's foot and the baby will move his or her whole body in response, but tickle a preschooler's foot and the child will move only his or her leg. This difference illustrates how infants' movements become more localized and specialized during the first few years of life. Major developments in motor activity occur during the first year or two as infants acquire the abilities to sit, crawl, stand, and walk. But before they can acquire these abilities, infants must gain control over their muscles and learn to cope with the forces of gravity.

During the first year, infants' reflexes become inhibited as the brain develops and they gain voluntary control over many of their movements. The process is complex, and the rate at which they develop motor skills depends on many factors. After the first year, motor development mainly involves practicing and mastering previously learned skills. Infants gain greater control and precision in movement as their ability to integrate information from the senses and the muscles increases. But there are dramatic individual differences in motor development. Some infants are advanced and others are delayed in demonstrating skills, and the "normal" range is broad.

Lifting the Head and Sitting

Infants raise their head before they learn to stand up. The cephalocaudal trend—by which development proceeds from head to tail—is apparent in the development of motor control and stability (see Table 5.1). Infants first gain control over their head, later their trunk, and even later their balance, enabling them to stand and walk.

Caregivers often are cautioned to support the head when they hold a newborn. There are good reasons for this. At birth, infants have little control over their head and neck muscles and cannot hold up their head. Within a month, most infants can hold up their head if someone supports the base of the neck. Three-month-old Kirra can raise her chest off the floor when placed on her stomach. In another two to three months, she gains enough control over her upper trunk to be able to sit with support. By the time she is 7 or 8 months old, Kirra's control extends to her lower trunk, and she can sit erect (Gallahue & Ozmun, 1995).

TABLE 5.1

Major Milestones of Motor Development in Infancy

ABILITY	APPROXIMATE AGE OF ONSET
Turns head to one side	One week
Holds head with support	First month
Lifts head and chest	Second month
Supports head well when lying on stomach	Third month
Sits with support	
Crawls	Sixth month
Stands with support	
Rolls over from front to back	Eighth month
Sits alone	
Creeps	Ninth month
Stands alone	Twelfth month
Walks alone	Twelfth to fifteenth month

SOURCE: Adapted from Gallahue and Ozmun, 1995.

This baby can stand, but only while being held up. How has her ability to control her muscles changed thus far? What other motor skills does she need to begin to stand on her own?

Crawling, Creeping, and Standing

Five-month-old Manuel is lying on his stomach. When he reaches for a toy in front of him, this motion causes his head and chest to rise, and then his outstretched arm pulls him forward. In a month or so, depending on his sleeping position (see the Practical Impact box), these motions will turn into crawling, in which he will move with his stomach on the floor. Several months later, when he is stronger and more coordinated, Manuel's crawling will change into creeping, in which he will move on his hands and knees without his stomach's touching the floor. Like most infants, Manuel will be able to stand at about 6 months, but only while someone holds him up under the arms. He will then begin to stand by holding onto furniture and pulling himself up. By 11 to 13 months, Manuel will stand well on his own.

Walking

Most families respond to an infant's first steps with excitement, recognizing that walking is the most spectacular feat of early motor development. The increased mobility infants gain when they learn to walk leads to many new opportunities for learning, as well as danger. The relationship between infants and their caregivers changes once this important developmental milestone is reached.

Learning to walk progresses in stages. Not long after infants start to creep and pull themselves to a standing position, they begin to **cruise**—moving around while holding onto things for support. At 10 to 15 months, children make tentative and unsteady efforts to walk unassisted, usually with their arms held shoulder high and their feet spread apart and pointed outward. This first walking motion involves wobbly movements as children shift their weight from one foot to the other to move forward, giving them an unsteady toddling motion. Gradually, they lower their arms, turn their feet forward, and narrow their stance (Cratty, 1999). During their second year, children try many variations in their movements, including walking sideways, backwards, and on their toes.

Children's motor development, especially with respect to walking, is well described by a dynamic systems perspective (see Chapter 2). Recall that this perspective focuses on how each action is made up of bits and pieces of experience and how an action is dynamic because it changes every time it is performed (Adolph, 1997; Fogel, 1997). For instance, infants can walk on smooth floors as well as carpets because the complex actions required for each step are subtly adjusted to accommodate the different types of floor (Thelen & Smith, 1994). Rather than assuming that advances in motor development are accounted for solely by

cruise in infant development, to move around while holding onto things for support

THE PRACTICAL IMPACT: NURTURING CHILDREN

Why Babies Aren't Crawling

Developmental "milestones" are used by parents and caregivers to determine whether their child is on track for a healthy developmental outcome. Surprisingly, some of these developmental markers are changing.

If you were raising a child even ten years ago, you would have expected to see your child begin crawling around 6 to 8 months of age. Today, many infants are not crawling at all, or, if they are, they begin much later than babies did in the past. Many babies are not turning over when they usually did either. Should parents be concerned?

Not according to developmental specialists who have conducted several studies of this change in infant motor development. The change is apparently an unexpected consequence of the public health campaign started in 1994 to reduce sudden infant death syndrome (SIDS) by teaching parents to place infants on their backs when they sleep (see Chapter 4). This campaign has been effective: SIDS deaths have dropped by about 40 percent since the program began.

Are the babies who are sleeping on their backs experiencing slower than normal development? Will their development be delayed? When researchers studied the slower-to-crawl babies, they found that these babies were normal in every other way; they sat up and walked when they were expected to do so. Pediatricians, caregivers, and parents need to be aware that today crawling and turning over are not good markers of developmental status. Instead, language skills are considered to be superior indicators of whether a baby's development is on track or is delayed (Davis, Moon, Sachs, & Ottolini, 1998).

---

maturation of the brain, dynamic systems theory assumes that the components leading to motor actions act in concert to produce changes, with each component important and necessary for producing change.

Research shows that infants have many of the motor capabilities involved in walking long before they put them all together and begin to walk. But why don't infants walk earlier? One reason is that they are unable to support their weight on one leg. Watch as adults walk and you will see that they shift all their weight from one leg to the other. Thus, each leg must be able to support the weight of the body, which requires muscle strength and balance. As infants' fat-to-muscle ratio changes over the first year, they achieve a critical combination of strength and balance that enables them to put the necessary components together to walk (Fogel & Thelen, 1987). Because infants' fat-to-muscle ratios vary, the timing of walking varies from one child to the next. Dynamic systems theory is useful for explaining how a minor change in balance and strength results in the reorganization of capabilities to develop a much more complex behavior—walking.

Implications of Walking for Infants and Families

When infants begin to walk, new worlds open up to them. At the same time, a new emotional climate develops in the home. For example, once they can move about by themselves, infants react with increased frustration and anger when they cannot quite reach an attractive goal or an object they set out to get (Campos, Kermoian, & Zumbahlen, 1992). Their increased ability to locomote also heightens infants' sensitivity to the presence of caregivers. Infants who can walk show greater levels of distress when separated from caregivers and greater affection when in their presence.

Parents, too, change their emotional reactions once infants begin to walk. The expression of anger increases; some parents report that the onset of walking coincides with the first time they express anger toward their infants. As they see their infants develop independence, parents increasingly hold them responsible for their actions, expecting the infants to comply when told "No, stop that!" Parents also express more affection toward their walking infants, as a result of the pride they feel in their infants' new accomplishments (Campos et al., 1992).

Walking provides a good example of the transactional and interrelated nature of the domains of development. To be able to walk, children must accomplish a series of complex motor and physical tasks involving coordination, balance, and strength. Moving about freely changes children's expectations about what they can do, thereby changing their emotional

When do you think this infant will begin walking? What factors contribute to an infant's developing the motor skill of walking? Why do some infants walk before others?

When infants begin walking, their movements are unsteady. Many toddlers direct their movements by leaning in the direction they want to go. What are the other differences between toddlers who have just started walking and those who have been walking for months?

responses. The new level of independence children achieve as walkers changes their parents' expectations about them. Thus, changes in childrens' physical development can bring about changes in their social and emotional relationships with others.

BOWEL AND BLADDER CONTROL

During the first year of life, infants have no control over the muscles involved in elimination and have little, if any, awareness of the physical signs that signal elimination. In the middle of the second year, many children make the connection between the feelings of impending elimination and their outcome (Leach, 1997). The potential to be toilet trained increases at the end of the second year or the beginning of the third year, once toddlers can anticipate elimination. Control over bowel movements usually is accomplished earlier than bladder control.

When to start toilet training is a serious concern for many parents. Junko was very anxious because her son, who had just turned 3, was not yet toilet trained. She wondered what she should do about this. Research shows that there are large individual differences in when children become toilet trained (Taubman, 1997). Most children learn to control their bladders and bowels when they are ready, just as they learn to sit and walk. For example, shortly after Junko voiced her concerns, her son seemed to spontaneously become toilet trained.

When Junko's son was ready for toilet training, he responded positively and quickly to it. Starting to train him earlier would have lengthened the process and probably not produced earlier bowel or bladder control. Four percent of children are toilet trained by age 2, 60 percent are trained by age 3, and only 2 percent are not trained by age 4. Boys generally take longer to be trained than girls. If a child is not trained by 42 months, caregivers may want to seek the advice of a pediatrician (Blum, Taubman, & Osborne, 1997).

WHAT FACTORS INFLUENCE INFANT HEALTH AND SAFETY?

Infants' health issues vary depending on their age, genetic inheritance, condition at birth, and living conditions. The leading causes of death for children under 1 year of age are congenital anomalies, sudden infant death syndrome (SIDS), and disorders related to low birthweight or premature birth (see Chapter 4). After children learn to walk, the leading cause of death is physical injuries, which account for about one-third of all deaths for children 1 to 4 years of age (Brenner et al., 2001; National Center for Health Statistics, 2001c). Many health problems that children experience can be prevented through the use of vaccines to ward off diseases and safety devices to protect them from injuries. Another health issue for young children is exposure to environmental hazards, such as lead and radon gas. Children who live in impoverished environments are most at risk for health and safety problems because of a lack of health care and the unsafe conditions in which they live (Bellinger & Adams, 2001).

PROMOTING HEALTHY DEVELOPMENT AND GROWTH

In order to promote children's healthy development and growth, the American Academy of Pediatrics (1991) recommends six "well-child" visits during the first year of life, six visits over the next four years, and then a visit every other year until the age of 20.

In the United States, all states require that children receive basic immunizations before entering school. However, approximately 20 percent of children under 3 do not receive immunizations, and inner city, low-income children are least likely to be immunized (National Center for Health Statistics, 2001b). Unfortunately, many US children lack access to health care, and the number of children without any form of health insurance has increased over the last twenty-five years (US Census Bureau, 2002). Hispanic children are less likely to have health insurance than Caucasian American or African American children (US Census Bureau, 2001c). The lack of health insurance among Hispanic children may be due to cultural factors—because of social and cultural barriers (such as limited English proficiency or fear of deportation), immigrant families may not seek health coverage.

AVOIDING ACCIDENTS

As you learned in the introduction to this section, infants and toddlers are at risk for many kinds of accidents. Before they crawl, infants may fall off changing tables or beds or get caught in crib rails; they can suffocate on soft bedding materials or on pillows. Baby appliances such as walkers, rockers, and jumpers can cause injuries if used improperly (Smith, Bowman, Luria, & Shields, 1997). Unsupervised crawling and walking infants may hurt themselves by falling down stairs, falling into swimming pools, or walking out into the street. Infants and toddlers also may be hurt or killed in car accidents. Caregivers need to be particularly cautious about car safety; babies should be restrained in car seats attached to the back seat. Infants and toddlers also may be poisoned by dangerous chemicals in the house. Because these very young children are prone to explore, caregivers should babyproof and toddlerproof their homes.

What types of accidents are most commonly experienced by toddlers? What steps can caregivers take to prevent accidents?

INFANT NUTRITION

In the 1940s and early 1950s, pediatricians recommended that parents feed their infants on a rigid 4-hour schedule, with the idea that this routine would increase infants' self-regulation of hunger. Today, most pediatricians recommend feeding "on demand"—that is, feeding infants whenever they are hungry. Feeding on demand allows infants to control their own nutritional intake and satisfaction (Drewett, 1993).

Infants grow most rapidly in the first year, so adequate nutrition during that period is essential. Most infants obtain adequate nutrition from breast milk or formula. Human milk has evolved to provide the best nutrition for an infant, and it changes in composition to match the infant's needs. Even a mother who is malnourished produces milk that is sufficient to meet her infant's nutritional needs for the first few months of life (Brown, Robertson, & Akhtar, 1986).

THE SOCIAL IMPACT: DEBATING THE ISSUE

Should Babies Be Taught to Swim?

Drowning is one of the most common accidents of childhood. In addition to falling into swimming pools, rivers, and lakes, children have drowned by toppling into toilets or buckets with just a few inches of water in them. In an effort to "drownproof" them, some parents enroll their children in infant swimming programs. Other parents enroll their infants in these programs because they believe that there is a critical period for learning to swim.

These programs should be viewed with caution for several reasons. First, parents must realize that their children will never be "drownproofed" because no one, regardless of age or skill, is completely safe around water (Langen-

dorfer, 1987). Second, scientific evidence does not support the idea of a critical period for acquiring swimming skills. Third, although few experience this rare condition, some babies will suffer hyponatremia (water intoxication) if they ingest large quantities of water during swimming. Symptoms of hyponatremia are lethargy, weakness, vomiting, and seizures, and victims may die (Burd, 1986). A more common problem is that children may catch giardia, an intestinal parasite that causes severe diarrhea. Because of these concerns, the YMCA Division of Aquatics (1984) and the American Academy of Pediatrics (1999) recommend that parents

wait until children are 3 years old before enrolling them in organized aquatic programs (Gallahue & Ozmun, 1995).

Thinking It Through:

1. Why might people think that infancy is an ideal time to teach swimming skills?
2. What were your experiences in and around water as a baby or young child? If you can swim, when and under what circumstances did you learn to swim?
3. What guidelines might you follow to prevent the accidental drowning of an infant or toddler in your care?

Benefits of Breast-Feeding to Infants

Human milk provides all the protein needed by a baby for the first six months of life. It also contains a balance of amino acids and minerals that differs from that in other nutritional sources. Human milk contains more cholesterol than cow's milk or formulas, and cholesterol is essential for promoting myelination within the brain (Uauy & Peirano, 1999). Also important for brain development is human milk's higher concentration of lactose, which provides the fuel needed by the infant's rapidly growing brain. Although human and cow's milk are both low in iron, the iron in human milk is absorbed better, reducing the likelihood of iron deficiencies. Human milk also is more digestible than cow's milk.

Breast milk also provides an array of protective benefits to infants. Breast-fed infants are more resistant to infections than bottle-fed infants. One reason is cleanliness. Contaminants are more likely to be a problem with bottle-feeding, especially in countries that have very hot climates (which promote bacteria growth) or that have contaminated water (Lifshitz, Finch, & Lifshitz, 1991). Another reason is that breast milk contains substances that fight off infections. Breast-feeding is especially useful in transferring the mother's immunities to the infant in the first weeks of life and stimulating the infant's own immune system. During the first few days of the baby's life, the mother's breasts produce **colostrum,** a pre-milk substance containing antibodies from the mother that protect the baby from infections. The advantages of breast-feeding may last a long time; breast-fed infants have less risk of some diseases later in life, including coronary artery disease, allergies, and diabetes (Lifshitz et al., 1991).

Findings from several studies suggest that breast-feeding helps to minimize the risk of obesity in children. In a study of 15,000 children aged 9 to 14, children who were breast-fed as babies were found to be less likely to grow up to be overweight than were formula-fed babies, even when potential confounding influences (such as the amount of time spent watching television, physical activity, and maternal weight) were controlled (Gillman et al., 2001). Also, the influence of breast-feeding on weight may become evident in early childhood, although the research evidence to support this trend is less clear-cut (Hediger, Overpeck, Kuczmarski, & Ruan, 2001; von Kries et al., 1999).

Breast-fed newborns tend to be more irritable, reactive, and physiologically adaptive than bottle-fed babies. Research shows that this is an optimal pattern of responsiveness (DiPietro, Larson, & Porges, 1987). Longer term effects of breast-feeding include scoring slightly higher on intelligence tests, even when family economic backgrounds are taken into account (Fergusson, Beautrais, & Silva, 1982). Babies breast-fed longer than eight months show increases in IQ and reading comprehension scores at 8 and 18 years of age as well (Horwood & Fergusson, 1998). It is unclear, however, whether it is the composition of breast milk or the interpersonal interactions involved in breast-feeding that affects later cognitive development (Doyle, Rickards, Kelly, Ford, & Callanan, 1992; Lucas, Morely, Cole, Lister, & Leeson-Payne, 1992). One study suggests that the association between breast-feeding and parental characteristics (such as IQ) explains why children's intelligence scores improve with breast-feeding. As well as being more likely to provide breast-feeding opportunities, mothers who have higher IQs provide more educational opportunities and enrichment for their children. Thus, their children are more likely to perform well on IQ tests (Jacobson, Chiodo, & Jacobson, 1999). These findings do not detract from the many health advantages associated with breast-feeding. And the possible intellectual benefits of breast-feeding do not mean that caregivers should be overly concerned if they cannot or do not breast-feed. As you will learn, many other factors, such as providing an enriching intellectual environment, play important roles in influencing children's intellectual growth.

Benefits of Breast-Feeding to Mothers

In addition to conveying nutritional and protective benefits to infants, breast-feeding also has benefits for mothers. Many women enjoy breast-feeding their infants because of the pleasure and closeness they experience during feeding sessions. Women who breast-feed lose more weight and experience nonpainful uterine contractions, which help them to recover from childbirth more quickly than women who do not breast-feed. Breast-feeding

colostrum a pre-milk substance containing antibodies from the mother that protect the baby from infections also delays ovulation, which is beneficial for mothers who do not use or have limited access to birth control. Convenience also is a factor. Breast milk does not need to be heated up or cooled down; it is portable and usually plentiful. And breast-feeding is less expensive: In the United States, breast-feeding saves $400 in food purchases in the first year (Smolin & Grosnevor, 2000). In developing countries, families attempting to bottle-feed may spend 50 percent of their income on infant formula (Lifshitz et al., 1991). Also, parents do not have to worry about the potentially fatal consequences if formula is limited or water is contaminated.

For women who find breast-feeding to be difficult and painful, trained lactation consultants can improve the likelihood of success. However, breast-feeding is not an option for all women. For example, it is difficult to maintain while working outside the home, although breast pumps allow women to express their milk for later use. Some women are advised not to breast-feed because of the medication they are taking or diseases they might transfer to their infants through breast milk. Mothers with AIDS, for instance, may pass the disease on to their infants through their milk (Sizer & Whitney, 1997). Additionally, breast-feeding can be demanding on mothers—using a bottle allows other family members to help and participate in the care of the infant. Bottle-feeding requires less energy from infants and so may be preferable for weak babies.

When caregivers decide to use bottle-feeding, it is very important that they select a specially formulated infant formula. Using cow's milk or other types of milk can lead to serious nutritional deficiencies (Smolin & Grosnevor, 2000).

Notice that the mother is holding the infant and gazing at him. Beyond providing infants with optimal nutrition, what aspects of breast-feeding may be pleasant for mothers and encourage attachment for infants?

Prevalence of Breast-Feeding

In the 1970s, only about 25 percent of new mothers in the United States breast-fed their babies; today, about 60 percent of mothers breast-feed (Ryan, 1997). Breast-feeding has become especially popular among college-educated, higher income women (Life Science Research Office, 1995). Mothers also are breast-feeding for longer periods of time than they did in the 1970s. Today, 20 percent more mothers breast-feed for 5 or 6 months (Ryan, 1997). Experts on nutrition would like to increase to 75 percent the number of mothers who breast-feed for the first few weeks and increase to 50 percent the number who continue until the babies are 4 to 6 months old (Sizer & Whitney, 1997).

WEANING AND FEEDING INFANTS AND TODDLERS

The recommended timing for introducing solid foods into an infant's diet has changed since the 1970s, when mothers were encouraged to offer cereal to infants as young as 6 weeks of age. Pediatricians now recommend delaying solid foods until the child has reached at least 13 to 14 pounds (double the average birth weight) or is between 4 and 6 months old. Before that time, infants' digestive systems are not sufficiently developed to digest starchy foods. Undigested solid foods may sensitize the child to proteins that cause food allergies and may result in kidney malfunction. Infants signal their readiness for solid foods by demanding to be fed more frequently than every 2 hours and by drinking large quantities of milk (Lifshitz et al., 1991). Although "baby teeth" begin to erupt between 5 and 9 months of age and most infants have six teeth by their first birthday, their first foods need to be soft because infants are unable to chew well until their second year.

Children need high-calorie foods because they have high energy needs for rapid growth. Most parents start by introducing cereals, which are digested easily and rarely cause food allergies. Later, fruits and vegetables are added to an infant's diet. Protein foods such as cheese, yogurt, egg yolks, and pureed meats can be introduced at 6 to 8 months. Whole eggs, milk, and more table foods can be introduced when babies are 1 year old (Sizer & Whitney, 1997).

Throughout the toddler years, children make a gradual transition to their family's regular diet and develop more mature eating habits and skills. Toddlers need to eat frequently, and their diet must include nutrient-dense foods to ensure that their nutritional needs are met while they are growing rapidly. For example, low-fat milk is not appropriate

Notice that this baby has smeared his face with food. Why should infants be allowed to feed themselves? When should caregivers begin to let infants feed themselves?

for an infant. Reducing fat and cholesterol in the diet, restricting high-calorie foods, and limiting between-meal snacks may be recommended for many older children and adults, but for infants such restrictions can contribute to inadequate nutrition and failure to thrive (Smolin & Grosvenor, 2000).

FAILURE-TO-THRIVE INFANTS

Failure to thrive (FTT) is a term used to describe infants and children who do not appear to be ill or abnormal but who do not grow at the expected rates (Casey, 1992). Children whose growth is below normal or whose growth rate slows down drastically may be FTT infants (Lifshitz et al., 1991).

The most common causes of FTT are *undernutrition,* in which children do not have enough food to eat, and *malnutrition,* in which children do not receive the appropriate nutrients. The quality of the interactions children have with their caregivers also may be a factor (Powell, Low, & Speers, 1987). Once treated with adequate nutrition and calories, FTT children return to normal growth patterns (Bithoney & Newberger, 1987), although children with FTT generally are shorter and lighter than those without FTT, even fourteen years after the initiation of treatment (Oates, Peacock, & Forrest, 1985).

Failure to thrive is more than a growth problem. Children with FTT also are likely to show abnormal behaviors; be passive, inactive, and withdrawn; show little expression of emotion; avoid close physical contact and cuddling; and show unusual eating behaviors (Powell et al., 1987).

Mothers of FTT children may be depressed or may have serious psychological problems that interfere with caregiving activities, including feeding. Families of children with FTT often have disorganized homes and experience social isolation or multiple stressors (Casey, 1992).

Several studies show that FTT children lag behind their peers in language development, reading, verbal intelligence, and social maturity, even years after treatment. The outcomes for the individual child depend on how long the child had FTT, the ongoing quality of caregiving, and the child's home environment (Casey, 1992).

HOW DO INFANTS' PERCEPTUAL ABILITIES DEVELOP

Infants are bombarded by sights, sounds, smells, tastes, and tactile sensations. From this array of stimuli, they perceive and make sense of their world by selecting some types of information and ignoring others. Selective perception requires interpreting sensory information by actively sorting and organizing the information into meaningful units. Making meaning is an innate capability in humans, and many of the changes that occur in perception are due to the maturation of the nervous system and brain (Kellman & Banks, 1998).

PERCEPTION OF COLORS, PATTERNS, AND FACES

In Chapter 4, you read how newborns are attracted to high-contrast stimuli that are moderately intense, complex, and sharply defined. With increased visual acuity, development of their visual system, and better control of eye movements, infants between 2 and 4 months expand the range of their attention to include stimuli that are colorful, meaningful, and patterned.

By 2 months of age, infants discriminate red, blue, and green (Adams, 1989). They perceive patterns in place of the simple lines and shapes seen by newborns; that is, they observe the relationships among the lines and shapes. Several studies indicate that by 3 months of age infants take notice of patterns that are "different" or misaligned, but 1-month-old infants do not (Van Griffin & Haith, 1984). These findings suggest that be-

failure to thrive (FTT) a term used to describe infants and children who do not grow at the expected rates

tween 1 and 3 months infants begin to see the organization of visual displays rather than only their details.

As you learned in Chapter 4, newborns like looking at contrasting areas of faces. Infants' preferences for faces increase as they grow older and learn to recognize how a whole face should look. By 12 weeks of age, infants prefer faces over nonface stimuli, even when the complexity of the two pictures is equal (Dannemiller & Stephens, 1988; see Figure 5.2). By 5 months, infants treat their own faces as familiar, social stimuli (Legerstee, Anderson, & Schaffer, 1998), suggesting that they recognize themselves through facial cues.

When shown schematic drawings of faces, infants exhibit a preference for looking at typical faces rather than faces with distorted features (Maurer & Barrerra, 1981). Surprisingly, even infants as young as 3 months prefer attractive adult faces over less attractive faces (Langlois et al., 1987; Samuels & Ewy, 1985), and by 6 months they prefer attractive faces of infants and adults of diverse races (Langlois, Ritter, Roggman, & Vaughn, 1991).

Although young infants recognize and prefer to look at faces, they are not very good at reading emotions displayed on faces. Until they are about 6 months old, they recognize only simple and clearly displayed emotional expressions. For instance, they recognize a smile only if it is broad and open-mouthed (Kuchuk, Vibbert, & Bornstein, 1986). Not until they are 18 to 24 months old do infants understand that facial expressions reflect others' emotional states (Repacholi & Gropnik, 1997; Saarni, Mumme, & Campos, 1998).

PERCEPTION OF MOVING OBJECTS

Infants prefer to watch moving objects rather than stationary ones. When shown moving and stationary objects or patterns, infants prefer to look at patterns or objects that move at a moderate rate. Infants' abilities to detect motion improve in the first three months; by about 6 months of age, infants are good at coordinating their movements with the movements of objects (Aslin, 1987). For instance, they will grasp at a moving object within a twentieth of a second of the moment it touches their hand (von Hofsten, 1983).

Infants also recognize and prefer complex patterns of motion made by people (such as walking or running). To test infants' abilities in this area, researchers devised an unusual experiment in which a person was outfitted with small lights to mark the locations of the major joints (such as shoulders and hips). The outfitted person was then filmed running and walking in a very dark room so that only the points of lights were visible on the film. When shown these moving light displays along with computer-generated lights moving in nonhumanlike patterns, infants from 3 to 5 months of age preferred to watch the human patterns of motion (Bertenthal, Proffitt, Kramer, & Spetner, 1987).

DEPTH PERCEPTION

Does an infant recognize that stairs drop off? Will he or she try to crawl down the stairs or be afraid of falling? The classic study of depth perception involved placing infants on a **visual cliff apparatus,** which uses a checkerboard pattern covered with Plexiglas to create an illusion of depth. On the "cliff" end, the checkerboard pattern drops off several feet but the Plexiglas continues level. If an infant can detect height, will she or he crawl over the "edge" of the cliff?

By 7 months, most infants avoid the cliff area of the apparatus, even when their mother calls them from across the "abyss." This suggests that infants of this age respond to changes in depth (Walk & Gibson, 1961). Prior to this age, infants often show interest in the cliff but may or may not avoid it. Seven-month-old crawling babies begin to show fear of heights, and infants who push themselves around in walkers also develop a fear of the cliff (Bertenthal & Campos, 1984).

Infants detect depth and distance before they can crawl, probably because of changes that occur in the visual system between 3 and 7 months of age. Depth and distance are

FIGURE 5.2

Face and Nonface Stimuli Used to Study Infants' Face Preferences

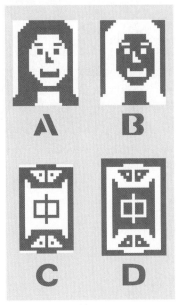

SOURCE: Dannemiller and Stephens, 1988.

Early studies of face preferences compared infants' responses to faces and to other patterns, but it was unclear whether the complexity of the stimuli influenced their responses. To ensure that the amount and complexity of visual information did not bias their results, Dannemiller and Stephens (1988) controlled for the amount of dark and light areas in each figure that infants were shown. Infants show face preferences even when the information is controlled.

visual cliff apparatus a checkerboard pattern covered with Plexiglas, used to create an illusion of depth

Why will this infant avoid crawling over the "cliff"? What changes must take place in the visual system for an infant to be able to detect depth?

better perceived when the viewer is able to compare images from both eyes. At birth, the visual system receives input from both eyes in the same part of the brain, but by 6 or 7 months, separate locations develop for input from each eye (Kellman & Banks, 1998).

Researchers use looming and zooming objects to assess infants' responses to distance. Around 3 months of age, infants respond to looming objects—those that seem to be coming toward them—by blinking. When an object is zooming away from them, they do not blink (Banks, 1988). Seven-month-old infants begin to use visual cues to determine depth (Kellman & Banks, 1998). The relative size of an object, for example, provides information about whether the object is close or far away.

How Do Infants and Toddlers Learn and Remember?

The motor and perceptual changes that infants undergo in their first two years expand their foundations for learning. Infants have many more opportunities to learn about their world as they gain increased access to it by walking. Changes in their nervous system and increased tendencies to organize information into patterns also give them ways to represent and store information in more useful and memorable units. Infants are able to learn associations even at birth, and their memories improve as they grow older.

Not all associations are learned. When newborn Patrick searched for the nipple after being tickled on the cheek, he was exhibiting a reflex, not a learned behavior. By 7 months of age, he shows evidence of learning when he becomes excited and attentive when placed in his high chair. Patrick has learned and remembers the contingency "When I am put in this chair, I get food," and he acts accordingly. Many behaviors that older infants and toddlers exhibit, such as playing pat-a-cake or peek-a-boo, result from learning to associate one event with another.

LEARNING THROUGH CONTINGENCY AND ASSOCIATION

In Chapter 2, you learned about Albert, the young boy who was conditioned to be afraid of a white rat. Albert initially was unafraid of the rat, but when researchers paired a loud, unpleasant noise with the rat, Albert learned to associate the two. After making that association, he responded to the sight of the rat with fear, even when no noise occurred.

Human newborns as young as 2 hours old can be trained through classical conditioning methods to expect a contingency. In one study, newborns were gently stroked on the head for 10 seconds before they were fed sweetened water. Initially, the stroking had no effect on sucking behavior, but once infants learned the association, stroking caused them to orient their head, pucker their lips, and suck more than infants who had not been provided with the same contingency (Blass, Ganchrow, & Steiner, 1984). When the infants in the contingency group were given a different contingency—they were stroked, but the feeding was stopped—they often cried, became angry, or whimpered, indicating that their expectancies had been violated.

Infants also learn through operant conditioning, in which they associate their actions with particular consequences (see Chapter 2). When a baby experiences a pleasant or rewarding consequence for a behavior, he or she is likely to act in the same way again. In studies of infants, the actions most commonly measured are sucking, kicking, gazing, and head turning. Infants are particularly quick to learn about consequences that have to do with feeding or that allow them to hear their mother. For instance, infants have been taught that if they suck longer or harder, they can listen to a sound they like, such as their mother's voice (DeCasper & Fifer, 1987). They have learned to associate their behavior (sucking) with a positive consequence (hearing mother's voice).

LEARNING WHAT'S FAMILIAR: HABITUATION AND NOVELTY RESPONSES

When infants find something fascinating, they turn their attention to this stimulus and gaze intently at it. Beyond sensing objects and perceiving their forms, what do infants gain from such focused attention? Scientists who use information processing theories to explore cognitive changes in children are interested in whether there are differences in the ways infants and children pay attention to stimuli and what kinds of information they acquire while they focus so attentively.

To gain her infant's attention, Marta repeatedly dangles a stuffed bear in front of her daughter and then removes it. At first, her daughter Celina stares at the bear for a long time, but with continued presentations, Celina looks at the bear for shorter periods of time, as if she is getting bored. This behavior provides evidence of **habituation**—a decrease in attention to a stimulus that has been presented repeatedly (Bornstein & Ludemann, 1989). Now Marta replaces the bear with a clown, and Celina shows renewed interest. Celina's increase in attention to this new stimulus after habituation to a previous stimulus, a response called **dishabituation,** shows that she distinguishes between the two stimuli, the bear and the clown.

When babies habituate and then dishabituate, they demonstrate that they remember, at least for a short time, an object they have been shown and can compare that memory with a new stimulus (Schneider & Bjorklund, 1998). To assess infants' short-term memories, researchers use habituation-dishabituation tasks and measure visual behavior, sucking rates, and heart and respiration rates. Because infants cannot use words to tell us about their perceptions, thoughts, and memories, the habituation task is important in assessing these abilities.

Evidence of habituation is found very early in life: newborns habituate to repeated visual presentations (Slater, Mattock, Brown, & Bremner, 1991). The fact that habituation occurs so early allows researchers to test what kinds of things infants discriminate, including social categories. For example, in one study, infants habituated to faces of men and dishabituated when presented with faces of women. This finding suggests that by 9 months of age infants distinguish between the appearances of men and women (Leinbach & Fagot, 1993).

As infants grow older, they habituate to new stimuli more quickly. A newborn might take 5 to 10 minutes to habituate, but a 6-month-old habituates in 30 seconds (Bornstein, 1985). Among infants of the same age, the rate of habituation varies, and these differences are stable over the first three years. Faster habituation may reflect an ability to process information more effectively, which may be critical to memory later in life (Schneider & Bjorklund, 1998).

LONG-TERM MEMORY

Fetuses can learn associations in the last months of prenatal development and remember them after birth. Newborns are capable of learning basic survival-related information, such as the sources of nourishment and the smells and sounds of their mother. However, young infants have fragile memories—they are unlikely to remember information for very long, and their memories are constrained by the context of learning. Marked improvements occur at 2 to 3 months and at 6 to 10 months of age. These improvements are linked to increased myelination of the neurons, the increased number of synapses formed in the brain, development of the frontal cortex, and increased attention span. Another improvement occurs at around 18 to 20 months of age, when babies use language to aid memory.

habituation a decrease in attention to a stimulus that has been presented repeatedly

dishabituation an increase in attention to a new stimulus after an infant has habituated to a previous stimulus

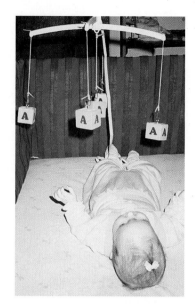

Notice that this infant has a ribbon tied to her foot and to the mobile. She has learned that when she kicks she turns the mobile. Why is this method useful for assessing infants' memories? What factors influence whether infants will remember the contingency?

The day after watching his father make cookies, this child pretends to make cookies. What does deferred imitation tell us about children's memory capabilities?

infantile amnesia inability to recall events that occurred very early in life

Try to remember experiences that occurred during the first three years of your life. Few people, if any, can do this. The inability to recall events that occurred very early in life is called **infantile amnesia.** Why do we remember so little from our earliest years? Initial research on this question suggested that young infants need repeated exposure to ensure memory that lasts for even a few days. In one study, mothers repeated phrases to their 2-week-old infants sixty times a day for two weeks. After over 800 exposures, infants remembered the information for almost two days (Ungerer, Brody, & Zelazo, 1978). If it takes this many exposures to learn something for two days, it is no wonder that we remember so few childhood experiences! Encouraging them to reenact events or parts of events, though, can remind very young children of past experiences and inoculate them against forgetting these experiences over long periods of time (Hudson & Sheffield, 1998).

Research has shown that memory is improved when the procedures are more familiar to children. Consider 6-month-old Yi Ling, who participates in an experiment in which one end of a ribbon is tied to her leg and the other end to an interesting mobile above the crib. After 5 minutes, Yi Ling recognizes the contingency: when she kicks, the mobile turns (Rovee-Collier & Fagen, 1981). Two weeks later, Yi Ling returns to the laboratory, and the mobile-and-string set-up is tried again. Will Yi Ling remember that kicking her foot makes the mobile move? Unlike many of the testing situations used in early research to assess infants' long-term memory, this situation closely resembles her everyday experiences, and she remembers the contingency.

When infants are placed in familiar situations and are motivated to remember, they learn with less repetition (or fewer exposures) and remember for longer periods of time. For instance, in a series of studies, 2- and 3-month-old infants were trained in two 9-minute sessions to learn the contingency that leg-kicking will make a mobile turn. When their memories were tested within one or two weeks of learning the contingency, most babies remembered it, but the longer the time between learning and testing, the less likely they were to remember. Generally, 2-month-old infants remembered the contingency when tested one week after learning it. The 3-month-old infants remembered it two weeks later, but after that time they acted as though they had never seen the mobile (Rovee-Collier, Enright, Lucas, Fagen, & Gekoski, 1981). Other studies show that older infants, like Yi Ling (6 months), can remember the contingency up to seven weeks later when reminders are given (Rovee-Collier & Shyi, 1992).

Infants, like all learners, remember best when the testing conditions are similar to the original learning situation. Thus, infants' memories are context-bound—that is, strongly tied to situational cues. The importance of situational cues in infant memory has been confirmed by another series of leg-kicking studies. In these studies, some infants were shown a reminder (a moving mobile) on day 13 after they first learned the kicking contingency—one day before they were likely to completely forget it. The "reminded" infants remembered the contingency better the next day than infants who had not been reminded about their earlier learning or those who had been shown only a still mobile or a ribbon (Hayne & Rovee-Collier, 1995). Similarly, when infants were tested in an environment that differed from the one in which learning took place, such as a crib with a different colored bumper, they were less likely to remember the contingency than when tested in the same environment (Butler & Rovee-Collier, 1989; Hayne, Rovee-Collier, & Perris, 1987).

Deferred imitation, in which there is a delay between seeing an action and imitating it (see Chapter 4), provides evidence of infants' long-term memory, because it requires that the infant have a way of representing an observed action in memory and recalling it. A child who watches his father make cookies and the next day pretends to make cookies is showing that he remembered the previous day's cookie-making actions. Research indicates that infants' abilities to engage in deferred imitation improve during their first two years. Infants from 11 to 20 months old show deferred imitation of novel actions for up to twelve months (Meltzoff, 1995).

Longitudinal studies support the finding that infants are capable of long-term memory. In one study, 6-month-old infants were trained to reach for a toy whenever it made a noise. The training took place in a laboratory room under two situations—with the lights on and with the lights off. Two years later, the same children and other children serving as a control group were asked if they remembered being in the earlier study. None of them did. Some of the children were reminded of the earlier study by being shown the toys that had been used. Then, while sitting with their mothers, the children were tested in the dark and in the light to see whether they would reach for the toy that made the sound, as they had done two years before. The children who had participated in the earlier study were much more likely than the other children to reach for the toy (Perris, Myers, & Clifton, 1990).

This study shows that unusual situations may be memorable to young children for a long period of time, especially when the events are novel and involve smells, sounds, and movements. Infantile amnesia may occur because adults are seldom in the same situations as they were when infants, because adults and infants represent information differently, and because brain development and cognitive abilities are different for adults and infants (Hayne & Rovee-Collier, 1995; Schneider & Bjorklund, 1998).

HOW DO COGNITIVE ABILITIES DEVELOP DURING INFANCY AND TODDLERHOOD

Important changes occur in purposeful behavior during infancy. At 2 months, infants do not reach out to grab a rattle, but by 18 months, they experiment with problem solving. During the first two years of life, infants move from narrow and repetitive reflex actions to the flexible use of symbols to represent objects and people. During this time, infants and toddlers also come to recognize that other people and objects are separate from themselves. At 8 to 12 months, infants begin to show the first signs of truly intelligent behavior; for example, they plan and try out different actions to obtain a goal. According to Piaget, these changes characterize the first period of cognitive development: the *sensorimotor period* (see Chapter 2). Piaget described the rapid changes that infants and toddlers undergo in terms of six stages (Piaget, 1936/1963). Each stage builds on the skills acquired in the previous ones (see Table 5.2).

STAGE I: USING REFLEXIVE SCHEMES (BIRTH TO 1 MONTH)

In stage I, neonates spend their time using the reflexive behaviors that they were able to perform at birth. As you learned in Chapter 4, many neonatal reflexes, such as grasping, looking, and sucking, help them survive. Piaget viewed these reflexes as the basic schemes, called *sensorimotor schemes*, that provide children with ways to interact with and know about the

TABLE 5.2
Stages in the Sensorimotor Period

STAGE	AGE	CHARACTERISTICS
Stage I	Birth to 1 month	Practices reflex actions
Stage II	1 to 4 months	Engages in primary circular reactions—repetitive actions centered on the infant's body
Stage III	4 to 8 months	Uses visually guided reaching for greater exploration Engages in secondary circular reactions—repetitive actions centered on objects
Stage IV	8 to 12 months	Shows first signs of intelligence by using intentional behavior to solve problems
Stage V	12 to 18 months	Engages in tertiary circular reactions—modified repetitive actions designed to explore qualities of objects
Stage VI	18 to 24 months	Achieves greater flexibility in problem solving by using symbols to represent objects

What do children learn when parents play games like peek-a-boo with them?

world around them. Infants' first knowledge of the world is derived from these schemes. For example, through their experiences in applying their "sucking" scheme, infants come to know the shape of a nipple. By grasping a toy, infants come to know its shape. In Piagetian terms, infants assimilate information by using schemes.

Although sensorimotor schemes are repetitive and automatic behaviors, they are not applied rigidly: infants make them fit the situation, such as by changing the shape of their lips to fit around a differently shaped nipple. According to Piaget, infants accommodate their schemes to meet the demands of different situations. At this point, however, infants' behavior is not purposeful—they do not have goals in mind while exercising reflex actions.

STAGE II: EXPLORING MOVEMENTS OF THE BODY (1 TO 4 MONTHS)

In stage II, infants act somewhat more purposefully. By 2 to 3 months, many infants recognize that their actions have specific effects, as seen in the foot-kicking studies described earlier. They discover these effects through repetitive actions, which Piaget described as primary circular reactions. **Primary circular reactions** are repetitive actions that are centered on an infant's own body and motions. These actions, such as thumbsucking, first occur accidentally, but infants find them pleasurable and so continue the actions. For example, Piaget described how his son Laurent began sucking his thumb. Laurent's hand accidentally landed near his mouth while he was being held. Seeing this interesting object, Laurent tried to suck on it, but his arm slipped away. After many tries, Laurent moved his arm so that his thumb was near his mouth, and he began sucking his thumb (Piaget, 1936/1963).

STAGE III: EXPLORING OBJECTS (4 TO 8 MONTHS)

At around 4 months, stage III infants begin to combine primary circular reactions into more coordinated patterns. For instance, they coordinate schemes so that they can grasp objects they see. To do this, infants must make the connection among what they see, the movements of their arms, and the movements of their hands. The coordination of vision and movement schemes allows infants much more flexibility to explore.

During a meal, 7-month-old Noah drops a spoon off the edge of his tray onto the floor. He finds the sound interesting, so he repeats this action each time his mother puts the spoon back on his tray. Noah's behavior indicates that he is exploring the qualities of objects—in this case, the spoon. Noah, like other stage III infants, demonstrates that he can use a new type of circular reaction, called a secondary circular reaction. **Secondary circular reactions** are repetitive actions focused on the qualities of objects, such as the noises they make or their shapes and colors. Like primary circular reactions, these reactions begin accidentally, but through them infants explore the characteristics of objects rather than those of their own body. The sound a spoon makes when it hits the floor or the sound a plastic duck makes when squeezed becomes the focus of attention, and infants will repeat the action time and time again to reproduce this interesting property.

Infants in this stage want to make appealing sights and sounds continue. Piaget (1936/1963) describes how, at 7 months, his son Laurent used all his skills to make an interesting event happen again. After watching his father drum on a tin box, Laurent turned toward the box, shook his arm in front of the box, and shook his head, trying out all of his movements to make the phenomenon reoccur.

primary circular reactions repetitive actions that are centered on an infant's own body and motions

secondary circular reactions repetitive actions focused on the qualities of objects, such as the noises they make or their shapes and colors

These actions illustrate how infants become goal-oriented and more tuned in to their environments as they mature cognitively. Because of these changes, everyday activities become increasingly challenging and interesting. The highly repetitive, structured, and predictable games that caregivers and infants often engage in during feeding, bathing, and diapering provide infants with opportunities to learn contingencies and elicit smiles of obvious pleasure. In turn, caregivers respond positively to the increased pleasure displayed by infants, creating a mutually rewarding context for interactions.

STAGE IV: ACTIVE PROBLEM SOLVING (8 TO 12 MONTHS)

According to Piaget, infants in stage IV show the first signs of intelligence, marked by the intentional application of schemes to reach a goal. Like stage III infants, stage IV infants use familiar schemes, but they are now purposeful in applying those schemes. Older infants set out to accomplish a task and often have a goal in mind before starting an action. One indication of purposeful behavior in infants is the desire to complete activities they begin. Unlike a younger infant, who might be easily distracted by other interesting objects, an infant in stage IV who fails to accomplish his or her task is likely to be upset. For instance, 10-month-old Stacie becomes upset after her father picks her up and moves her away from the cat she is trying to catch. A few months earlier, Stacie would have been easily distracted by this movement and would have happily lost interest in the cat. Unfortunately for the cat, Stacie now has a pre-set goal, and her actions are based on achieving this goal.

STAGE V: CREATIVE PROBLEM SOLVING (12 TO 18 MONTHS)

Infants in stage V are creative problem solvers. For the first time, they are capable of applying entirely new strategies to solve problems rather than simply using combinations of previously learned schemes. Infants' creativity during this stage stems from their use of **tertiary circular reactions,** in which infants systematically modify their behaviors in subtle ways to explore the effects of those modifications. Noah, who earlier dropped a spoon off his high chair to explore the qualities of the spoon, begins to explore these qualities in a new way as he grows older. He now experiments with different trajectories of the spoon: dropping it, throwing it gently, and flinging it across the room. Noah acts as a budding scientist, interested in finding out how variations in his behavior influence the qualities of the spoon. Now he might squeeze a toy duck to make it quack, then sit on it, and finally bite it to find out what happens.

The ability to conduct tertiary circular actions provides children with the means to learn from their actions. Because stage V infants are capable of trying many ways to solve a problem, they are more likely to hit upon a successful solution than are younger infants who use more rigidly applied schemes.

STAGE VI: USING SYMBOLS TO REPRESENT REALITY (18 TO 24 MONTHS)

After 18 months of age, toddlers develop a new and important ability that changes the way they approach and solve problems. Stage VI toddlers begin to use mental symbols to represent objects, called **symbolic representation.** They no longer need to act out a sequence of events to discover the outcome—they can imagine the actions beforehand. Thus, problem solving now can take place inside the child's mind before he or she takes any action.

Piaget described how his daughter Lucienne solved a problem using mental symbols. Piaget inserted a metal chain into a matchbox and then handed the matchbox to Lucienne. The matchbox was left partially open, and Lucienne began exploring the box by turning it over. She then tried to grasp the chain through the opening. When those actions were unsuccessful, she tried a new way to solve the problem: she inserted her index finger into the opening, grabbed a small part of the chain, and then pulled the whole chain out. Piaget

tertiary circular reactions subtle modifications infants make in their behavior so as to explore the effects of those modifications

symbolic representation the use of mental symbols to represent objects

How do infants explore the qualities of objects during play? Why is play so important for cognitive development?

then repeated this experiment, this time leaving a smaller opening in the matchbox. Lucienne tried to solve the problem the same way she did before, but this time her solution did not work because the opening was too small. She then paused and seemed to think about how to solve the problem. During this pause, Piaget noticed that Lucienne was opening her mouth, at first a little and then wider and wider. This indicated to him that Lucienne recognized that she needed to increase the size of the opening in the matchbox so that her finger would fit in it. Lucienne then used her finger to widen the opening and successfully applied her previous scheme of grasping the chain. She did not have to try many different actions before finding a solution; Lucienne "thought" through the problem, using symbols for the object and actions, and decided which actions were most likely to be successful.

Stage VI toddlers thus rely less on motor actions and more on symbols for solving many everyday problems. With their increased use of symbols, toddlers are more capable than infants of thinking about the past and future, thinking about problems quickly and flexibly, and remembering actions to use in new situations.

INFANTS' UNDERSTANDING OF THE PERMANENCE OF OBJECTS

There was that first long stage when she didn't pick anything up at all, and everything had to be handed to her. . . . Now it's different. If she is playing with a toy, and it slips out of her hand, she will follow it with her eyes; we can see her wondering what has become of it. A month ago it would have stayed on the floor, no longer a part of her consciousness; now, most of the time, she will return to it and pick it up again. She understands that even though it's out of her hand for the moment, it's still a part of her world.

—*Bob Greene;* journal entry about Amanda
at 8 months (1984, p. 229)

Knowing that people and objects have an independent existence beyond one's own perception of them is called understanding **object permanence**. Infants are not born with an understanding of object permanence; they have no idea that objects or people continue to exist outside of their own perception of them. When Bob Greene's daughter was younger, she did not bother to look for objects she dropped because they were no longer part of her consciousness. This lack of understanding of object permanence extends to infants' bodies: they are unaware that the objects flying in front of their face are their own arms and hands.

Over the first two years of life, infants gradually develop an understanding of object permanence by coming to realize that objects have form and depth and that they are solid. Toward the end of the sensorimotor period, infants become capable of acting on that knowledge by actively searching for objects that have disappeared.

Searching for Hidden Objects

Piaget assumed that an important indicator of infants' understanding of object permanence was whether they tried to find a hidden object. Based on the studies he conducted on infants' searching strategies, Piaget outlined how infants develop an understanding of object permanence and how this understanding relates to the stages of sensorimotor cognitive development.

In stages I and II (0 to 4 months), infants show no evidence of realizing the independent existence of objects. An infant who drops a rattle outside her or his field of vision will not cry in frustration or even look for the toy. If someone covers a toy with a cloth while a stage I or II infant watches, the infant does not try to uncover it; as far as the infant is concerned, the toy has disappeared.

In stage III (4 to 8 months), infants search for an object that is partially in view but not one that is completely hidden. Because infants at this age do not search for hidden objects, Piaget suggested that they still do not realize the permanence of objects.

Infants' behavior during stage IV (8 to 12 months) is puzzling and intriguing. They show some understanding of object permanence, but their understanding is far from com-

object permanence the concept that people and objects have an independent existence beyond one's own perception of them

plete. Vonnie's mother hides a doll under a washcloth several times, and Vonnie finds it. Then, Vonnie watches her mother hide the doll under a washcloth and, from there, under a blanket. Where will Vonnie look for the doll? You might guess that she would look under the blanket, assuming that the last hiding place is the best bet for finding the toy. Stage IV infants, however, show a surprising pattern: they look in the first place the object was hidden. Thus, Vonnie looks under the washcloth. The tendency to search in the first hiding place (A) while ignoring the second (B) is called the **A-not-B error.**

Why would an infant like Vonnie search in the first hiding spot? This question has intrigued researchers for years. According to Piaget, infants remember the object as an "object + action"—that is, the object takes on the characteristics of the action performed on it. In this case, the doll becomes doll-under-a-washcloth, and an infant with this concept is unlikely to search for doll-under-a-washcloth by looking under a blanket. Research shows that this error may be due to infants' inability to inhibit actions they have performed before (such as searching in the A hiding place) until a certain level of brain development has occurred (Diamond, 1991).

By the time they reach stage V, infants are capable of searching for hidden objects that have been moved several times. The only limit to their understanding is that they must see each movement of the object to be able to find it. By 18 months, stage VI toddlers have overcome this limitation and have a fully developed concept of object permanence. They now can follow multiple movements of objects, even when the movements cannot be seen. For instance, when Sean watches his mother place a toy cow in a plastic cup and then place the plastic cup under a blanket, he still knows where the cow is. Although Sean does not see that the cow is hidden under the blanket, he infers that the cow continues to exist even though it is hidden in the cup and then infers that the cow must still be wherever the cup is, which in this case is under the blanket.

Remembering the Location of Hidden Objects

The search task requires that infants coordinate several schemes, including their vision and reaching schemes, to find a hidden object. Maybe infants younger than 18 months understand object permanence but cannot master the coordination of schemes well enough to demonstrate what they understand. The issue of children's *performance versus competence* is a recurring one in developmental research. Researchers often have to infer what infants or children know from what they do; if their actions are limited, inferences about their knowledge may be inaccurate. A solution to this problem is to simplify the tasks that infants and children are asked to perform. Rather than having infants search for hidden objects, an alternative approach is to examine their visual attention to different objects. Remember that infants pay more attention to surprising and novel experiences than to familiar ones. Based on this preference, researchers have devised clever visual attention studies that allow them to assess infants' understanding of objects without the performance demands involved in Piaget's search studies.

In one of these studies (Baillargeon & Graber, 1988), 7- to 8-month-old infants were shown objects that appeared and disappeared. During one of these presentations, however, the sequence of events was "impossible." As depicted in Figure 5.3 on page 154, infants first saw an object located on one of two placemats. Next, a screen was pushed in front of each placemat, hiding the object from the infants' view. Fifteen seconds later, a hand reached behind one of the two screens and pulled out the object. For one event, the object was pulled from behind the screen that covered the placemat on which the infant had seen the object—the "possible sequence." For the other event, the object was pulled out from behind the screen that had *not* hidden the object—the "impossible sequence." Infants stared longer at, and were more surprised by, the impossible sequence than the possible one. This result indicates that the infants remembered the location of the hidden object and were surprised when it was not where it was supposed to be.

By using simplified methods, researchers have found evidence of object permanence in even younger infants (Haith & Benson, 1998; Munakata, McClelland, Johnson,

A-not-B error infants' tendency to search in the first hiding spot (A) while ignoring the second (B)

Baillargeon and Graber's Possible and Impossible Events

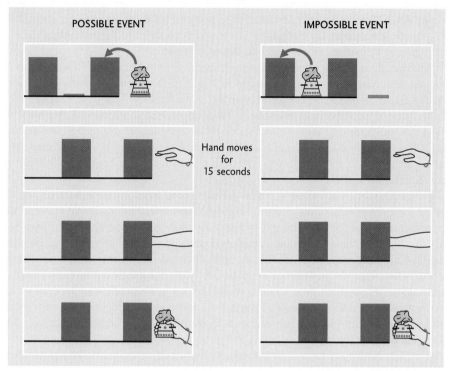

SOURCE: Baillargeon and Graber, 1988. Copyright © 1988 by the American Psychological Association. Adapted with permission.

Infants in this study were shown possible and impossible events to determine whether they had an understanding of object permanence. In the possible event, the screen on the right covers the object, and a hand reaches behind the screen and removes the object. In the impossible event, the screen on the left covers the object, but the hand reaches behind the screen on the right and removes the object. Infants were surprised by and paid more attention to the impossible event. How can we use this reaction to determine what infants know?

& Siegler, 1997). Additionally, 5-month-old infants were more surprised and paid more attention when a wall appeared to move *through* a solid object than when the wall stopped upon coming into contact with the object (Baillargeon, Spelke, & Wasserman, 1985). Other studies have shown that 3- and 4-month-old infants understand basic principles of objects and motions, such as gravity and inertia (Spelke, Breinlinger, Macomber, & Jacobson, 1992). These studies suggest that, very early in life, children develop basic concepts about the world that are then expanded and elaborated later in development (see Table 5.3). Piaget, however, was accurate in describing how infants act on objects around them. By 6 to 12 months, infants begin to demonstrate in their actions what they know about objects (Goubet & Clifton, 1998). This change is likely due to development of the frontal cortex of the brain (Diamond, 1991). It is not until the end of their second year, however, that infants can completely integrate their knowledge of objects with their actions (Small, 1990).

Thousands of studies have tested Piaget's ideas about cognitive development. Although much of his work has been substantiated, some findings have led to conclusions different from those Piaget originally suggested. For example, infants' abilities are more variable and context-dependent than Piaget initially proposed. Also, as you have seen, infants' understanding of object permanence is more complex and cumulative than Piaget thought.

TABLE 5.3

Stages in Understanding of Object Permanence

STAGE	AGE	KNOWLEDGE	ACTION OR LIMITATION
Stages I & II	0 to 4 months	Loses awareness of objects when they disappear By 3 to 4 months, understands inertia and gravity	Loses interest and does not search
Stage III	4 to 8 months	Recognizes continued existence of hidden objects Understands solidity of objects	Cannot find completely hidden objects
Stage IV	8 to 12 months	Remembers last location of a hidden object	Shows A-not-B error—will search for object in the first hiding place but not the second
Stages V & VI	12 to 24 months	Coordinates knowledge and performance Recognizes complex hiding patterns	Can search for and find hidden objects, even if they are hidden in two places

INFANTS' UNDERSTANDING OF NUMBER CONCEPTS

Infants' cognitive accomplishments include more than problem solving and understanding objects. Research has demonstrated something few people thought possible: Infants have a basic understanding of the concept of number. Wynn (1992) used a version of the possible-impossible event procedure to explore infants' understanding of numbers. After being habituated to displays of one or two items, one group of 5-month-old infants watched an "addition situation," in which one object was added to another, and another group watched a "subtraction situation," in which one of two objects was removed (see Figure 5.4 on page 156). In both situations, one outcome was a possible event and one was impossible. In the addition situation, for instance, a screen was lifted to hide one Mickey Mouse doll. Infants then saw a hand place another identical mouse doll behind the screen. In the possible event, the screen dropped to reveal two dolls (1 + 1 = 2). In the impossible version, the screen dropped to reveal only one doll (1 + 1 = 1). Infants spent more time looking at the impossible event; that is, they stared longer at 1 + 1 = 1 than at 1 + 1 = 2. These findings suggest that even 5-month-old infants have a basic understanding of addition and subtraction. However, more recent studies have not consistently supported Wynn's original findings. In some cases, infants were unable to show numerical competencies by adding and subtracting small numbers of objects (Wakeley, Rivera, & Langer, 2000a). The discrepant findings may suggest that the numerical abilities of young infants are more fragile and inconsistent than Wynn's initial study (Wakeley et al., 2000a, b) demonstrated, or they may be due to the use of different methods to assess infants' abilities (Wynn, 2000). Furthermore, very young infants may simply have basic visual concepts of what a small number of objects looks like and exhibit surprise when objects do not match these expectations (Haith & Benson, 1998).

PERCEPTION AND EARLY COGNITIVE DEVELOPMENT

Piaget theorized that infants form concepts from their direct experience with objects. Other researchers, however, believe that infants may develop basic concepts about the world around them from perceptual knowledge alone (Mandler, 1992). According to this view, infants' early concepts come from their perceptions of objects rather than their direct physical actions on them.

Infants as young as 6 months spend a great deal of time looking back and forth between two new objects, as if they are contemplating similarities and differences between them

 **IGURE 5.4**

Wynn's Possible and Impossible Events

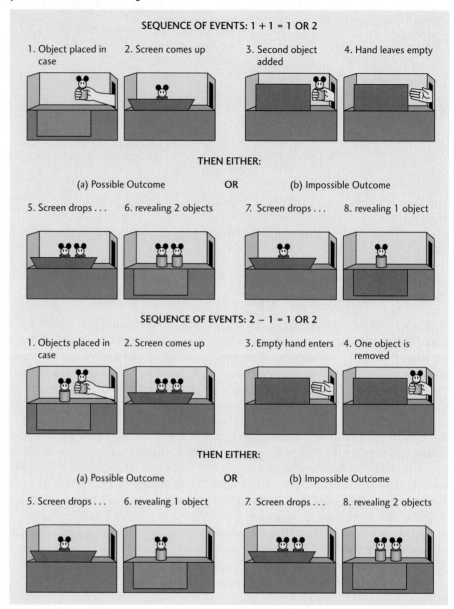

SOURCE: Wynn, 1992.

To test their understanding of addition and subtraction, Wynn showed infants possible events (1 + 1 = 2; 2 − 1 = 1) and impossible events (1 + 1 = 1; 2 − 1 = 2). In both cases, the infant paid more attention to the impossible event. Do you think that infants can subtract and add? If so, how else might these accomplishments be tested? If not, how do you explain Wynn's results?

(Ruff, 1986). This visual scrutiny increases as they grow older (Mandler, 1990). What are infants doing during these intense visual inspections of objects? Mandler believes that infants may be comparing similarities and differences between objects and forming **image schemas**—primitive notions, based on the visual appearance of objects, that lay a foundation for thinking about them. For instance, infants may have an up-down schema, a container schema, and a part-whole schema. A container schema has an interior, an exterior, and a boundary; infants with a container schema understand that containers hold things

image schemas primitive notions, based on the visual appearance of objects, that lay a foundation for thinking about them

and are surprised if they do not. Infants may use image schemas to develop perception-based concepts that help them quickly learn about the world without requiring actions on their part.

By 10 months of age, infants begin to understand the relationships between objects such as a lid and a pot. Evidence of this understanding comes from **relational play,** in which children perform actions that demonstrate their understanding of the relationship between two objects (Fenson, Kagan, Kearsley, & Zelazo, 1976)—for example, a child might place a spoon in a cup or a lid on a box. Perception of objects plays a part in this aspect of cognitive development in that babies are more likely to recognize the roles of objects when the objects are more perceptually distinct, such as when a lid and a box are different colors (Bates, Carlson-Luden, & Bretherton, 1980).

Babies also are capable of understanding categories when the members are perceptually distinct. And by 10 months, infants show abilities to form categories similar to those used by adults (e.g., gender categories for male and female faces) (Younger & Fearing, 1999). By 15 months of age, infants will pick up objects that belong to the same category before they pick up objects belonging to another category—for example, first picking up pictures of cats and then pictures of dogs (Mandler & Bauer, 1988; Levy, 1999; Oakes, Plumert, Lansink, & Merryman, 1996). By 18 to 24 months, toddlers can sort objects from two categories into spatially distinct groups (Gopnik & Metlzoff, 1992).

UNDERSTANDING DIFFERENCES AMONG PEOPLE: EMERGING UNDERSTANDING OF DESIRES

Like the understanding that objects differ from one another, the understanding that people differ from one another emerges during the first few years of life. One method of assessing infants' understanding of differences among people is to determine whether they recognize that not all people have the same preferences or desires. Researchers who investigated this problem used a simple food preference task in which infants had placed in front of them a bowl of delicious goldfish crackers and a bowl of raw broccoli (Repacholi & Gopnick, 1997). All the babies preferred the crackers to the broccoli. Then an adult reached over and tasted each food. With some babies, the adult showed a preference for the broccoli over the crackers. Then the adult placed the bowls near the infant and asked for some food. How did the infant determine which food to give to the adult? If the infant understood that some people, including this particular adult, like broccoli, the infant would hand her or him more broccoli. If, instead, the baby assumed that all people like what the baby likes, then the baby would hand crackers to the adult. Repacholi and Gopnik (1997) found that 14-month-old babies handed the adult crackers, thereby showing no evidence of understanding differences among people in their desires, whereas 18-month-olds did distinguish people by their desires.

THE SOCIAL CONTEXTS OF EARLY LEARNING AND COGNITIVE DEVELOPMENT

Much of infants' knowledge of the world is gained through their many daily interactions with others, particularly caregivers. The Russian scientist Lev Vygotsky believed that social interactions are essential for learning and that infants develop cognitive skills through interactions with others more skilled than themselves (Vygotsky, 1978). Older children and adults serve as role models for thinking, provide stimulating environments for children, and encourage children's learning by guiding them to solutions.

In Vygotsky's view, children develop their cognitive abilities through socially mediated learning. As you learned in Chapter 2, Vygotsky used the concept of the *zone of proximal development* to represent the range in learning that a child is capable of with help from more skilled and experienced partners (Rogoff, 1990). Through interactions with skilled partners, children expand their cognitive competencies.

Children's cognitive development is influenced by daily interactions within a cultural community (Rogoff, 1990). Parents and other adults in the community involve children in

relational play actions demonstrating an understanding of the relationship between two objects

Parents in rural areas differ from parents in urban areas in their methods of scaffolding. How might this Guatemalan parent provide scaffolding for her daughter?

guided participation in everyday activities, which become the context for an "apprenticeship in thinking." Through these apprenticeships, children learn about their own culture and develop enhanced cognitive skills. Adults from all over the world use many of the same methods to guide their children's participation in daily events.

Caregivers provide structure and support for children's thinking through informal teaching methods, called **scaffolding.** Just as steel and wooden scaffolding provides the support needed to construct a building, caregivers' cognitive scaffolding provides the support children need to extend their current skills to a higher level of competence. The type of scaffolding used by caregivers changes as infants' understanding increases, and it varies according to the caregiver's preferences (Bruner, 1983). For instance, caregivers often help infants interpret situations through their actions, emotions, and tone of voice. With older children, some mothers prefer a social style of scaffolding in which they draw attention to themselves ("watch me do it"), whereas other mothers use an activity-oriented method in which they draw attention to objects or events ("find the piece of the puzzle that matches the color of the one next to it") (Bornstein & Tamis-LeMonda, 1990).

Mothers and fathers are equally effective in their ability to supply scaffolding for their children's emerging skills (Connor, Knight, & Cross, 1997), and they begin these interactions soon after the child's birth. By 2 months of age, infants already have developed a basic understanding of what patterns to expect in these interactions. In one study (Murray & Trevarthen, 1986), mothers and their 2-month-old infants were videotaped, and the babies were given the chance to watch the live interactions with their mothers on a video monitor. The babies responded positively by making eye contact and moving their mouths. When the live video was replaced with a taped replay of their mothers' reactions in a former exchange, the babies were distressed and looked away. Although the mothers were responding as they had before, their responses were not contingent on their infants' actions—they were not in synchrony—and this was distressing to the babies.

Like synchrony, joint attention between "teacher" and "learner" facilitates cognitive development. Because they share a focus of attention, caregivers and infants have a common ground for interpreting and understanding interactions (Rogoff, 1998). By about 6 months, infants and their caregivers begin to share and negotiate learning tasks during play. Ten- to 12-month-old infants and their caregivers work out the details of interactions quite well and are well practiced in their routine interactions (Corkum & Moore, 1998; Rogoff, 1990). The ability of parents to successfully engage their children in joint attention on a task influences their children's later cognitive development. Toddlers whose mothers engage them in effective joint attention at 6 and 12 months have comparatively higher IQs (Hunter, McCarthy, MacTurk, & Vietze, 1987). In general, caregivers who are responsive and sensitive to their children's interactions encourage cognitive development (Bornstein & Tamis-LeMonda, 1997).

THE CULTURAL CONTEXTS OF EARLY LEARNING AND COGNITIVE DEVELOPMENT

Do caregivers all over the world use scaffolding to encourage their children's cognitive development? To answer this question, Rogoff and colleagues (Rogoff, Mistry, Goncu, & Mosier, 1993) examined the use of scaffolding by middle-class parents in cities in Utah and Turkey and by parents in small communities in India and Guatemala. In all four communities, the two parents and their children jointly took part in structuring learning situations.

scaffolding informal teaching methods that guide children's participation in daily events

Striking cultural variations in the use of scaffolding were found. In Utah and Turkey, parents were more likely to provide verbal instructions and activity lessons that were removed from the ordinary context of adult life. For instance, parents in these communities interacted with their children around toys and games but did not take their toddlers into their workplaces. In India and Guatemala, however, children were less likely to receive direct instruction during play but were more likely to be observant of, and take primary responsibility for, learning and participating in adult activities. These differences relate to the expectations and demands of the children's communities. In communities in which children spend most of their time with their parents, the children are expected to learn the specific economic skills of their parents, such as weaving, and their training involves watching and participating in these activities. In communities in which children spend less time with their parents, the children are expected to learn varied skills and to spend years in school. The focus is on motivating children to learn through praise and verbal instruction. Both methods of scaffolding produce the desired result of socializing children to become effective members of the community in which they are raised (Rogoff et al., 1993).

How do infants and toddlers develop language skills?

Language is a social tool consisting of a complex set of rules for using symbols (Owens, 1996). With a limited number of words, we can generate an infinite number of different messages. Thus, language is creative and flexible, and children show evidence of this when they generate words to say things they probably have never heard. For example, when 24-month-old Brandon experienced his first snowfall, he referred to it as "milk rain"— generating his own unique description of the event. Language also can be used to refer to events that happened in the past or to describe future events.

Infants are exposed to language during social interactions, even before they understand what individual words mean. When adults carry on a conversation in front of a young infant, the infant is likely to hear them speaking around 150 words a minute, making 12 to 30 sounds per second (Lieberman, 1984). From these exchanges, infants learn to recognize speech sounds, words, and what words mean. Before they even utter a word, children practice many skills that relate to mastering language. During the first year, infants' language production consists of cooing, babbling, and gesturing—using sounds and motions to communicate their desires. In the second year, the range and flexibility of infants' language abilities expand rapidly as they begin to use their first words and phrases to express themselves. By the time they are 5 years old, most children are competent speakers of their native language.

To become speakers of a language, children must be able to master four language-related domains (Gleason, 1993):

+ **Distinguish sounds and sound patterns.** A child who is a competent speaker of a language recognizes and distinguishes the basic sounds of that language, or **phonemes.** In English, phonemes include the /sh/ sound, which is distinct from the /s/ sound. Competence in language also involves being able to produce these sounds so that others can understand them.
+ **Learn the meanings of words.** **Semantics** refers to the meanings associated with words. Children accomplish an amazing feat when they learn how to use cues from others and from the environment to make sense of a sound and associate it with a particular word.
+ **Learn to put words together.** **Syntax** is the grammar, or rules, of a language. Competent speakers of English realize that "I store am going" is not a grammatical sentence. As part of mastering their language, children must learn to arrange words in meaningful order and use the parts of speech as prescribed by the rules of the language.

phonemes the sounds of a language that are the basis for word construction

semantics the meanings associated with words

syntax the grammar, or rules, of a language

◆ **Learn to use language in a social context.**   **Pragmatics** refers to the practical rules guiding the use of verbal and nonverbal communication in differing situations. A child who commands his grandmother to take him to the playground has not yet learned that in this situation the polite use of language is more likely to bring success than a command is. To become competent speakers, children must learn the rules of using language with others, such as waiting for pauses in conversations to speak and taking turns in a discussion.

BEFORE THE FIRST WORDS

Infants are actively engaged in learning language. Before they utter words, infants must become proficient in distinguishing and producing the sounds of their native language, and they need to identify individual words and their meanings from the streams of sounds they hear spoken around them.

Distinguishing the Sounds of Speech

Children must be able to discriminate the sounds of language before they can put sounds together in a meaningful way. Each language uses a subset of the 100 to 150 possible phonemes; for instance, English uses about forty-five phonemes (Owens, 1996). Languages differ in terms of the number and types of phonemes they contain (Menyuk, 1988).

Because each language involves only some of the sounds that are possible, scientists have asked whether infants learn to hear only the sounds from their native language or have the ability to hear all sounds. Research has demonstrated a surprising pattern—newborns are able to discriminate and attend to the sounds from all languages, but by 10 months of age, infants no longer attend to phonemes unless the phonemes occur in the speech they hear every day (Werker & Tees, 1984). Infants therefore appear to have a sensitive period in which their capabilities are fine-tuned to the particular language (or languages) they are exposed to in early life (Best, 1995). The processes underlying this fine-tuning and the extent to which it occurs have yet to be determined (Aslin, Jusczyk, & Pisoni, 1998; Jusczyk, 1997).

Children also acquire **phonemic awareness**—knowledge of permissible and nonpermissible strings of sounds in their native language. For instance, English combines *s* + *p* in words such as *speak* and *spring* but not *s* + *r*. As they listen to the language around them, infants and toddlers are exposed to the many sound combinations of their native language (Menyuk, 1988). From this exposure, children learn the statistical regularities in speech—the sounds that occur together—and this helps them extract information about words and their boundaries (Saffran, Aslin, & Newport, 1996). Infants also achieve phonemic and semantic competence through their attention to the rhymes and rhythms of language. For example, *intonation*—rising and falling speech patterns—gives clues about meaning. Universally, adults tend to use exaggerated intonation and a higher pitch when speaking to infants. Caregivers use rising intonations when they want infants to pay attention to something (Fernald, 1989).

Producing the Sounds of Speech

By 2 months of age, many infants make their first noncrying sounds. They begin **cooing,** making soft, repetitive vowel sounds such as "aah" and "ooh." Around 6 months of age, infants begin to produce sounds combining consonants and vowels, such as "ba" and "da." Between 6 and 10 months of age, they begin **babbling,** repeating consonant-vowel combinations such as "mama" and "dada." Many caregivers interpret these babbles as words, but at this age infants do not associate these sounds with particular meanings.

Intentional Communication

Ten-month-old Ray looks at his father, points to a teddy bear, and grunts. The message is clear: he wants his father to hand him the teddy bear. Even before they utter a word, infants communicate their needs through gestures and vocalizations. As they grow older, children add verbal interactions as another way to communicate (Owens, 1996).

pragmatics the practical rules guiding the use of verbal and nonverbal communication in differing situations

phonemic awareness knowledge of permissible and nonpermissible strings of sounds in one's native language

cooing making soft, repetitive vowel sounds such as "aah" and "ooh"

babbling repeating consonant-vowel combinations, such as "mama" or "dada," two or more times

Infants' abilities to communicate develop in concert with their cognitive abilities and based on the responses they receive to their communication attempts. For instance, the cognitive ability to understand cause-and-effect relationships goes hand in hand with realizing that behavior can be used to achieve an effect or a goal. A 10-month-old infant understands cause and effect and uses gestures to communicate needs and desires. In response, caregivers demand more precise communication from their older infants: they expect them to communicate more directly, such as by pointing to objects.

FIRST WORDS

Children's understanding of language, called **receptive language,** precedes their ability to produce language, or **expressive language.** For example, long before they can utter the word *cat,* infants respond to "Where's the cat?" by looking at the cat. Many children understand single words at around 8 to 9 months of age (Owens, 1996). This is most reliably demonstrated by their response to being called by their name or to being told "No!"

When infants cannot say what they want, they use gestures. How does this infant's pointing at an object indicate that she understands cause-and-effect relationships?

Although infants communicate through gestures and produce and respond to wordlike sounds during the first year, they usually do not begin to say real words until they are about 12 months old (Bloom, 1998). Children's first attempts to speak real words are important because they signal that the child understands the symbolic significance of words. Speaking words is not an easy task. To produce a word, children must be able to recognize the sounds that make up the word and the order in which these sounds need to be produced. They must remember the sounds and integrate them into a smooth-flowing word.

First words usually are the names of common objects or people. The importance of children's social environment as a setting for language development is apparent: Their first words often describe the important people and objects with which they are most familiar, such as *mama, dada,* names of pets, or names of categories (*hat, doggie*). For some children, first words include action words (*bye-bye, all gone*) and, of course, the word *no* (Bloom, 1994; Nelson, 1981).

The ability to say words indicates a remarkable increase in children's level of abstract thinking—they now understand the correspondence between a mental concept and the set of sounds (the word) that has been assigned to that mental concept (Woodward & Markman, 1998). In addition, their first words are packed with meaning. A child's first words are **holophrases,** individual words that convey as much meaning as sentences. For instance, a child is likely to say "doggie" to announce that the dog is entering the room or to convey her desire that the dog come play with her. *Doggie* means much more than simply "the dog."

DEVELOPMENT OF VOCABULARY

Once children understand the sound-word connection (between 12 and 18 months), they add around three words per month to their vocabulary. After 18 to 24 months, a vocabulary explosion often occurs, in which children quickly acquire a large number of words at a rapid rate (Bates, O'Connell, & Shore, 1987; see Figure 5.5 on page 163). They also begin to use words for social rituals, such as saying "bye-bye" (Gopnick, 1988). Around age 2, children include words that indicate an understanding of success ("hooray") and failure ("uh-oh") (Gopnick & Meltzoff, 1986). Because children's vocabularies are limited, they invent new words by, for instance, changing a noun to a verb. A child who sits in a rocker chair might say "Rocker me, mommy" (Clark, 1997).

receptive language
children's understanding of language

expressive language
children's ability to produce language

holophrases individual words that convey as much meaning as whole sentences

THE SCIENTIFIC IMPACT: INTERPRETING RESEARCH

Can Babies Communicate Through Hand Signals?

Most 1-year-olds are limited in their ability to express their desires because they know only a few words. Does this mean that infants are unable to let their caregivers know when they are cold or what they want to eat? For most infants, these would be difficult messages to convey. Some babies, however, have learned how to communicate complex messages through the use of simple gestures, called *baby signs.*

Baby signing as an area of study arose from Linda Acredolo's experience with her 1-year-old daughter Kate, who began to sign for flowers by wrinkling her nose and sniffing. With encouragement, Kate learned twenty-nine signs in the next six months and became able to communicate many complex ideas. As she grew older and her verbal skills developed, she stopped using signs.

Because of her experience with Kate, Acredolo and her colleague, Susan Goodwyn, began a study of baby signs in 140 families. They found that children who used signs were helped in their language development rather than hindered, and that their parents responded more positively toward them because of their increased ability to communicate their needs to sleep or eat or have a book read to them. They also found that girls were more likely to develop signs than boys and that parent-child interactions were important in helping children to learn signs. By 16 to 18 months of age, children averaged about four signs that they used frequently (Acredolo & Goodwyn, 1988). Infants who use signs may be less frustrated because their needs can be addressed more quickly. For example, one child in the study who was afraid of dogs could easily signal this fear to parents and be comforted promptly.

Infants can be encouraged to use signs they invent themselves, or caregivers can teach signs to children. For instance, *noisy* can be represented by pointing a finger to the child's ear, *go out* by pretending to turn a doorknob, and *cold* by hugging the arms to the body (see the figure). Acredolo and Goodwyn recommend that caregivers start with a few simple physical signs, say the words as they make the signs, and repeat the signs often to increase likelihood of the child's using them (Acredolo & Goodwyn, 1996).

Thinking It Through:

1. Why might effective nonverbal communication benefit infants and toddlers and their relationships with parents?
2. How might effective nonverbal communication promote the development of language and thinking?
3. What signs and signals did you learn and use as a young child? What five signs would you regard as the most important to teach a baby?

Baby Signs

Drink/Bottle
Description:
Thumb to mouth, tilting up
Mimics a drinking motion
Possible Situations:
To request a bottle;
to request juice or water

Food/Eat
Description:
Fingertips to lips
Depicts putting food in mouth
Possible Situations:
To request something to eat;
to label food or someone eating

Sleep
Description:
Head tilted,
hands against cheek
Mimics head on pillow
Possible Situations:
Request to take a nap;
request to go to bed

SOURCE: Acredolo and Goodwyn, 1996.

Baby signs are often related to the activities and immediate needs of the infant. Many of the signs are made by performing the action to be communicated or by indicating a part of the body (for example, noisy might be indicated by pointing to the ear). Which signs do you think infants are most likely to use?

SOLVING THE MYSTERY OF WORD MEANING

Every time children hear a new word, they must act like detectives, trying to solve the mystery of the meaning that is intended by the word. Young children are smart word learners and understand the meanings of novel nouns quickly (Akhtar, Carpenter, & Tomasello, 1996). One way children learn word meanings is through **fast mapping,** in which they learn to associate the sound of the word with the concept the word stands for, sometimes in a single exposure (Markson & Bloom, 1997). Mappings are more likely to occur, and are

fast mapping associating the sound of a word with the concept the word stands for, sometimes in a single exposure

FIGURE 5.5

Growth of Young Children's Vocabulary

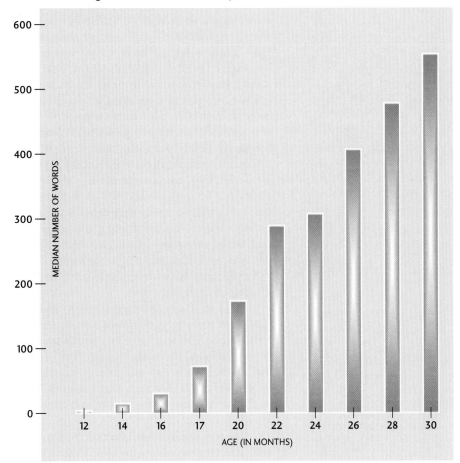

NOTE: Data for 8 to 16 months and for 18 to 30 months came from different samples of children.
SOURCE: Fenson et al., 1994.

Notice that after children learn about fifty words, they tend to show a spurt in vocabulary learning. How do you think children learn so many words so quickly? What role do caregivers play in children's word learning?

more accurate, for concrete objects than for abstract information (Rice, 1990). Children's abilities to attend and remember enhance their ability to learn new words (Samuelson & Smith, 1998). Children also use cues from social interactions to attach meaning to new words (Tomasello, Strosberg, & Akhtar, 1996).

The speed of the mapping process increases with age, such that preschoolers are more likely than toddlers to learn words in a single exposure. In one study, children were asked to play a hiding game with a puppet. They were shown three objects—two familiar objects and one new object called a *koob*—and three hiding places. The children were asked to hide each object in a designated spot. After hiding the two familiar toys, the children were directed to "hide the koob under the bowl." They were then asked questions about the objects and the objects' names. The results revealed that almost all of the children fast mapped the name *koob* to the new object (Dollaghan, 1985).

Although fast mapping helps children learn new words, it does not provide solutions to more subtle aspects of the word meaning mystery (Woodward & Markman, 1998). Listen to young children's speech and you will note that their use of words is often quite different

FIGURE 5.6

Examples of Children's Mapping of Words to Categories

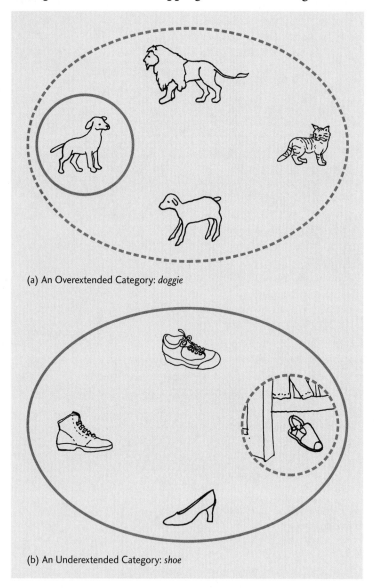

(a) An Overextended Category: *doggie*

(b) An Underextended Category: *shoe*

When children overextend, their use of a word extends beyond the category named by the word. In (a), the child has extended "doggie" to mean any animal with hair. When children underextend, their use of a word is narrower than the category named by the word. In (b), the child has narrowed the meaning of "shoe" to only shoes in closets—not shoes on people's feet.

overextension the use of words to refer to objects or things that are outside the bounds of the category named by the word

underextension the use of words to refer to a smaller group than the word actually names

from adults'—especially the way they relate a word to a class of objects. Sometimes children use words to refer to objects or things that are outside the bounds of the category named by the word, in a process called **overextension** (Anglin, 1985). A child who uses the word *doggie* to refer to all furry animals with four legs—a cat, a dog, a lamb—is overextending the bounds of the meaning of the word. The child is nonetheless demonstrating the ability to map a set of sounds (doggie) to a meaningful grouping (small furry animals). The tendency to overextend words is very common among young children (Woodward & Markman, 1998). When children use words to refer to a smaller group than the word actually names, they are exhibiting **underextension** (MacWhinney, 1989). For instance, a child who uses *shoe* to refer only to the shoes in the closet but not to the shoes he or she wears is underextending the range of the meaning of *shoe* (Clark, 1981) (see Figure 5.6). Children pay particular attention to the forms of objects and their functions when trying to solve the mystery of word meaning.

Children also must determine the level of meaning intended by a word (Woodward & Markman, 1998). When Kurt was 2 and first met his friend's cat, Simon, he heard the labels "Simon," "cat," and "animal." Each label is correct, but each has a different level of meaning. How does Kurt know which word stands for the individual animal and which stands for the whole category of small and furry creatures?

One way children learn the meanings associated with alternative words for the same object is through cues that others provide in their speech. When children hear the cue word *the*, they know that the following word refers to a category of objects rather than a single unique object (Callanan, 1989). When Kurt heard "See the cat," he had a way to recognize that *cat* must refer to the category rather than a name. In contrast, when he heard "This is Simon," the preceding words acted as a cue that *Simon* was the proper name of the object (Gelman & Taylor, 1984).

Another way children resolve the category-level problem is through certain assumptions they make about words and objects. Around age 2, children make the assumption that only one name applies to each object. When they hear a new word associated with an object, they assume that word is the name of the object (Merriman & Bowman, 1989). Given another word, they are unlikely to think it is also the name of the object. Instead, they assume that it refers to another aspect of the object. Children show an order of preference for mapping new words to objects and attributes. They first assume the new word is an object name. If it is not an object name, they then assume the new word refers to a part of the object. If that is not correct either, they assume the word refers to an unusual aspect of the object, such as its texture or shape (Marcus et al., 1992). Using these assumptions and the cues others give, children eventually learn that multiple labels can be used to represent people and objects (Deak & Maratsos, 1998; Hall & Graham, 1998).

As you might suspect, it is difficult for children to understand the meanings of words that refer to abstract concepts—such as *tall* and *short, high* and *low*—because these words are not associated with any particular object (Woodward & Markman, 1998). Think about a child who hears the word *tall* associated with a building and with a person. What will this child likely infer about the meaning of the word *tall?* A person may be tall relative to a chair but is short in comparison to a building. *Tall* is not associated with a person in the same way that *adult* might be. So it is not surprising that children have difficulty mastering these descriptive terms.

FIRST SENTENCES

At about 18 months, many children begin to produce sequences of words, usually separated by long pauses. By the end of the second year, these sequences give way to true sentences (Bloom, 1998). The shift from using holophrases to actually producing sentences marks another tremendous accomplishment of the toddler years. In true sentences, children do not randomly string words together. Instead, the order of the words represents their first application of grammar—the use of rules to convey meaning. Constructing sentences is taxing and requires much effort for young children; this probably explains why early sentences are produced haltingly and why children often repeat the same sentence over and over with only minor changes (Cartwright & Brent, 1997).

Two-word sentences contain the information that is available in each word as well as the information implied in the order of the words (Braine, 1963). Children's early sentences emphasize meaning and usually refer to actions or objects (Bloom, 1998). When discussing actions, children talk about who performs the action, where it is done, and the object used to perform the action. When discussing objects, children talk about the names and characteristics of the objects, their locations, and their ownership. A construction that children commonly use is an agent and its action, such as "daddy go" or "doggie bark." Examples of 2-year-olds' two-word sentences are shown in Table 5.4.

Children's earliest sentences are called **telegraphic speech** because they contain only the most essential and informative words and seldom include less informative words, such as *a, an,* or *the.* Telegraphic speech gradually becomes elaborated as children develop more sophisticated language skills.

EARLY TALKERS AND LATE TALKERS

Early talkers are children between 11 and 20 months of age who are in the top 10 percent for vocabulary production (Bates, Dale, & Thal, 1995). The variations in when children begin to talk relate to language competence five years later, although long-term studies beyond this

At about what age did Kurt realize that "Simon" is the name of this particular cat? What cues would Kurt have used to understand that the word "Simon" is this cat's name rather than a label for the category?

ABLE 5.4

Examples of Children's Two-Word Sentences

SEMANTIC RELATION	ENGLISH	GERMAN	SAMOAN
agent–action	teddy fall	puppe kommt (doll comes)	pa'u pepe (fall doll)
action–object	hit ball	tur aufmachen (door open)	tapale 'oe (hit you)
possessor–possession	mama dress	mein ball (my ball)	lol a'u (candy my)
rejection–action	no wash	nicht blasen (not blow)	le 'ai (not eat)

SOURCE: Adapted from de Villiers and de Villiers, 1992.

telegraphic speech early language in which only highly informative words are used and less informative words are neglected

time frame have yet to be conducted. Interestingly, early-talking children can be described as "saying everything they know." Whereas most children have significantly better comprehension of information than production of speech, early-talkers are normal in comprehension but exceedingly high in their production of speech (Bates et al., 1995).

In contrast, children who are at the bottom of the vocabulary production scale relative to their peers have mixed developmental outcomes. Many of these children will appear normal in language development within about a year or so; for that reason, language specialists have not wanted to label them as having any type of language disorder. Instead, they are labeled as being "late talkers" (Paul, 1991; Rescorla & Schwartz, 1990). About half of late talkers continue to show delayed language development, especially those in families with lower socioeconomic status, those with the greatest delays, and those with the smallest expressive vocabularies (Paul, Spangle-Looney, & Dahm, 1991). Nonetheless, the long-term outcome for these children is unclear: Many show normal-range language development later in childhood, but some continue to show evidence of delayed language development (Bates et al., 1995).

How is children's language acquisition explained?

How do most children quickly and easily develop the skills needed to speak sentences and understand the rules of a language? Many different explanations have been proposed. Some emphasize the special role of the human brain in interpreting language, whereas others emphasize the role of rewards for grammatical speech. To better understand the issues of language development, consider the case of Genie, a girl who was denied exposure to language, along with satisfaction of her other basic needs, during eleven years of her life.

One day in 1970, a slumped and disheveled child weighing approximately 60 pounds entered a welfare office in Los Angeles with her almost blind mother. What social workers thought might be an autistic child of 5 or 6 years turned out to be a 13-year-old who had been hidden away in a back room since the age of 2. Genie's father believed she was brain damaged and forced her to live virtually alone for her whole life. Genie's only contacts with humans were brief and unpleasant: her father would sometimes bark at her, but little was ever said to her directly. She was strapped into a crib at night and onto a potty chair for most of her days.

Genie was immediately removed from this horrible environment and admitted to a children's hospital. She was weak, unable to walk very well, and not toilet trained. Psychologists, social workers, linguists, and therapists all worked with Genie, trying to assess her capabilities and help her develop the social, emotional, and intellectual skills that should have been a natural part of her upbringing. In addition to her physical problems, Genie could not utter more than a few sounds. Would she be able to learn language and adapt to her new environment? The following sections explore the theoretical stances on language acquisition and how these theories might predict outcomes for Genie.

INNATE THEORIES: BIOLOGICAL INFLUENCES ON LANGUAGE ACQUISITION

Biological theories suggest that a special capacity for understanding language resides within the human brain. The dominant biological theory was proposed by Noam Chomsky (1965, 1986), who argued that children are born with a **language acquisition device (LAD)** in their brain that allows them to understand the properties—the universal grammar—of all human languages. The LAD acts as a guide, or blueprint, for recognizing language input and detects the regularities in language. Children develop a sense of universal grammar merely by being exposed to language.

Some indirect evidence in support of Chomsky's ideas comes from the similarities in the ways children all over the world acquire language. Scientific evidence supports Chom-

language acquisition device (LAD) in biological theory, a part of the brain that allows children to understand the properties of all human languages

sky's assumptions about the importance of the brain in language acquisition. Although the LAD part of the brain has not been identified, people with various kinds of brain damage show very specific language disorders, which suggests that different aspects of language are processed in specific locations in the left hemisphere of the brain. For instance, people with damage to Broca's area of the brain (see Figure 5.7) can express meaning but are unable to produce sentences with grammatical rules. Damage to Wernicke's area does not prevent people from forming grammatically correct sentences, but they convey nothing meaningful in their sentences. Recent studies suggest that the brain is involved in very complex ways in processing language (Maratsos, 1998; Seidenberg, 1997). For instance, studies using brain imaging techniques show that different sites within the brain are activated for processing nouns and for processing verbs (Damasio & Damasio, 1992). None of these studies, however, has addressed the question of whether humans are born with a special capacity for understanding language.

Biological factors, specifically brain development, may play a powerful role in language acquisition. According to Lenneberg (1967), there is a critical period for language development, from about the age of 2 to puberty, during which the brain is primed for processing language. Without exposure to language during this critical period, a person will never develop language, because thereafter the brain loses its ability to acquire language through simple exposure.

Evidence in support of Lenneberg's critical period hypothesis has been obtained in studies of immigrants' language abilities. When people move to the United States from other countries, they are placed in a new environment and need to learn a new language to function effectively. How easily do non-English-speaking immigrants learn to speak English?

FIGURE 5.7

Language-Related Areas of the Brain

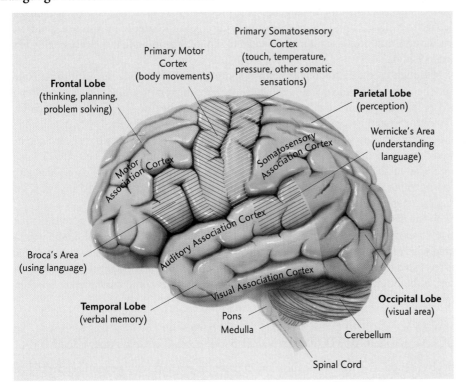

The figure shows the areas of the brain that are thought to be heavily involved in processing language-related information. What does recent research tell us about the complexity of language processing?

Research on second language learning suggests that age at arrival in a foreign country relates to mastery of the language, even after decades of practice with the language. In one study, Korean children who arrived in the United States before age 7 mastered English as well as native English-speaking children; those who arrived here between 8 and 15 years of age were less capable; and adolescents and adults who arrived between 17 and 39 years of age did not master English very well at all (Johnson & Newport, 1989). These findings suggest that learning a new language is easier for children than it is for adults.

Biologically based theories have dominated much of the scientific thinking about language development. Although these theories explain many of the interesting features of language development, they may not provide the whole explanation. Language development occurs more gradually than is implied by innate theories, and the universal features that Chomsky believes underlie all languages have been difficult to identify (Moerk, 1989).

The case of Genie was a natural test of innate biological theory, because Genie was not exposed to language during the critical period. According to biologically based theories, the prognosis for Genie would be pessimistic. Genie might be unable to acquire language, even with rigorous training.

LEARNING-BASED THEORIES OF LANGUAGE ACQUISITION

In contrast to theories of biological influences on language development, learning-based theories emphasize a child's environment as the key to developing language skills. The leading proponent of this theory was Skinner (1957), who suggested that children learn language through reinforcement of correct and grammatical forms of speech. Other behaviorists suggest that language is learned through observation—by watching and listening to others (see Chapter 2).

Rewards and punishment are involved in important ways in language development: Caregivers encourage infants to talk and reinforce their talking with praise, affection, and attention. Thus, reinforcement motivates children's communication efforts (Owens, 1996). Imitation also is important to language acquisition in that children grow up speaking the language they hear around them; they imitate idioms and dialects. For instance, children in parts of the South might say "I'm fixin' to go to school," meaning that they are getting ready to go to school.

Although they are useful in explaining some aspects of language acquisition, learning-based theories do not adequately explain the development of grammar. Parents seldom reward or punish grammaticality in children's speech; they are more likely to reinforce children for *what* they say than *how* they say it (deVilliers & deVilliers, 1992). Also, children produce so many new and unusual sentences that it is unlikely that they have heard and borrowed them from others or have been reinforced for these sentences (Clark, 1997). For instance, after taking a bath, 30-month-old Jake told his mother that he was "barefoot all over," referring to the fact that he was naked. It is unlikely that Jake had ever heard anyone refer to being naked in this way.

To the extent that observational learning, rewards, and punishments account for language development, the prognosis for Genie would be somewhat hopeful. If she was presented with many instances of speech from all the concerned people trying to help her and was rewarded for producing grammatically correct sentences, she might slowly acquire language, although it could take years of training for her to become a competent speaker of English.

SOCIAL INTERACTION THEORIES OF LANGUAGE ACQUISITION

Caregivers support language acquisition in many important ways beyond rewarding children and providing models for language use. Social interaction theories of language development suggest that the social context of language is a fundamental part of language development (Bohannon & Warren-Leubecker, 1989). Thus, children acquire language in interaction with parents and other skilled speakers of the language. Many studies confirm the importance of social interaction in language acquisition. For instance, a child may watch foreign-language television for hours a day but will not learn the language unless he or she interacts with others using that language. Simple exposure to language is not enough to allow one to learn it (Bloom, 1998).

Children's active participation in social interactions is also vital to their developing complex forms of language. Language acquisition seems to require children's participation in the activities that the language is helping to create (Cole, 1992). For children to acquire anything more than the basics of language, they must actively participate in everyday social interactions using language.

Another way in which caregivers foster children's language acquisition is through exposure. By talking to them, caregivers expose infants to the rules, contexts, and patterns of language. Early in language development, mere exposure makes a critical difference (Owens, 1996). In a two-year longitudinal study of US families with toddlers, Hart and Risley (1995) found that the average family spent 28 minutes an hour interacting with their child when he or she was very young and even more time when the child began to speak words. Parents addressed their children an average of 325 times per hour, although the rate varied from 56 to 793 times per hour (Hart & Risley, 1995). Thus, in a 14-hour day, one child may hear about 700 utterances while another hears over 11,000 utterances! Over several years, the language environments of these two children will grow even more discrepant. It is no wonder that the researchers found that, by age 3, children exposed to more utterances a day knew more words than children exposed to fewer utterances a day (Hart & Risley, 1995). The powerful message of this research is that the sheer quantity of language interactions to which a child is exposed in her or his social environment makes a difference in early language development.

Another role of caregivers is in providing many examples of language near the child's own level of understanding. They talk to and interact with their children in specific ways that seem to facilitate language development (Vygotsky, 1986). The version of language that caregivers use with their children has been termed **child-directed speech** or *motherese;* it consists of simple, repetitive sentences spoken in attention-getting ways. Child-directed speech is spoken in a loud, high-pitched voice and uses exaggerated intonations to direct and maintain the child's attention. Child-directed speech has a simple vocabulary, is repetitious, and focuses on present events. Many studies indicate that not only caregivers but also older children use child-directed speech (Hoff-Ginsberg, 1986). Even mothers of deaf infants use child-directed sign language (Masataka, 1996, 1998).

In child-directed speech, words that may be difficult for the child to understand are modified; for instance, a parent might say "tummy" for "stomach" and "grandpa" for "grandfather." Caregivers also simplify the grammar in sentences and use active constructions, such as "baby eats carrots" rather than "the carrots are going to be eaten by the baby." In these ways, child-directed speech exposes children to simplified language that is still more complex than what they may already understand and use (Bruner, 1983).

Studies suggest that use of child-directed speech is related to enhanced language skills in children (Gleitman, Newport, & Gleitman, 1984). Further, studies show that infants whose mothers try to elicit language from them ("Tell me what this is called" and "Is that a horse or a cow?") develop larger vocabularies than many of their peers do (Jones & Adamson, 1987). A longitudinal study of language development in the first three years of life indicated that children whose mothers allow them to take turns in conversations learn language more rapidly (Menyuk, Liebergott, & Schultz, 1995).

Caregivers differ in their use of child-directed speech. Compared to older mothers, adolescent mothers speak fewer words to their infants, and their infants vocalize less than those of older mothers (Culp, Osofsky, & O'Brien, 1996). Additionally, children of depressed mothers, who do not use exaggerated intonation patterns when talking to their infants and who are less responsive, verbalize less than children of non-depressed mothers (Bettes, 1988). Although caregivers all over the world use child-directed speech, cultural differences are apparent in its specific forms (Ingram, 1989). For instance, Korean mothers emphasize

Why are social interactions so important in language development? What do caregivers do to simplify their speech?

child-directed speech a special version of language that caregivers use with their children; also called motherese

action-oriented speech rather than object-oriented speech with their infants. Korean infants understand more verbs than do English-speaking infants (Choi & Gopnick, 1995).

Caregivers use subtle methods to illustrate complex forms of grammar—for instance, **expansion** of the child's own utterances. When an infant says "cup," a caregiver is likely to respond by saying "Yes, that is your cup." By expanding the child's one or two words to a complete sentence, the caregiver is presenting the child with an opportunity to understand and acquire the complexities of the language.

Caregivers' use of expansions and child-directed speech acts as scaffolding for learning language. The scaffolding changes as parents offer ever more advanced versions of the language, thereby providing an optimal language-learning environment for children. The social context, especially active interactions with caregivers, provides children with a learning environment that supports their language development. However, it is unlikely that the social context provides a full explanation for all aspects of language development. Not all children have optimal social interactions, and yet most children learn language.

According to social interaction theories, Genie's prognosis would be somewhat hopeful. Genie had little exposure to people during her early years and so had few opportunities to engage in language within a social context. Over time, Genie might gradually gain language skills through intensive social interactions with concerned caregivers if they provide motivation and appropriate levels of child-directed language and expansions of her speech.

GENIE'S OUTCOMES

Soon after Genie appeared in the welfare office, she began working with Susan Curtiss, a graduate student in linguistics. Curtiss kept records of Genie's vocalizations and conducted testing of her language skills (Curtiss, 1977). At first, Genie's vocalizations were high-pitched, monotone whimpers or squeaks. After many outings with Curtiss, Genie acquired new words that represented some of her favorite things, such as *pail* for the plastic containers she liked to play with and *store* for the places she liked to visit.

Genie quickly developed a variety of social skills, and she learned a number of new vocabulary words in a relatively short time. One year after Genie was admitted to the hospital, her grammar resembled that of an 18-month-old child; six months later, she was using plurals and could produce some two- and three-word sentences. The linguists working with Genie were excited about the possibility that she would learn grammar despite being beyond the critical period, but in three more years Genie's speech did not improve very much. Unlike most 3-year-olds, Genie could not correctly form complex sentences using *why, where,* or *what*. For example, she produced word strings such as "Where is may I have a penny?" or "I where is graham cracker on top shelf" (Rymer, 1993). Genie also had difficulty recognizing how to use grammatical markers such as *-ed* and *-s*.

In tests conducted to assess Genie's brain functioning, researchers discovered an abnormality: Her left hemisphere, which in most people is involved in processing language, did not function at all. Her right hemisphere processed language. Genie's brain could not handle language input normally.

After living with a string of researchers and foster parents, Genie today lives in a home for adults with mental impairments. Now in her forties and without the special attention researchers provided, Genie seems to have lost her hard-won social skills along with her battle to acquire language (Rymer, 1993).

How can we explain Genie's developmental successes and failures? It is difficult to draw firm conclusions because of the severe physical and emotional abuse and neglect she suffered at the hands of her parents. The abuse, including malnourishment, may have interfered with her ability to learn language. Or, she may have been brain damaged in some way before the abuse started, the brain damage hampering her ability to learn language and causing her father to think she was mentally retarded. Despite developing cognitive and social skills, Genie may have found it hard to learn grammar and syntax because of her brain dysfunction. In addition, Genie missed the early years of language learning, possibly limiting her ability to ever acquire language skills. Genie's story suggests that exposure to language may be important for

expansion taking young children's simplified language and adding complexity and completeness to it

normal brain development, as well as for language acquisition. For many years Genie lacked the stimulus of social interaction and appropriate language models to observe and follow. She was never reinforced for using language, and she never heard child-directed speech. Thus, in the triumph and ultimate tragedy of Genie's story, you can see how each theory of language acquisition provides insights about how children acquire and learn to use language.

THE RESILIENT AND FRAGILE ASPECTS OF LANGUAGE DEVELOPMENT

Genie's case is useful for illustrating that, despite horrifying early conditions, some aspects of language development can be resilient whereas others are not. Rather than assuming that there is a strictly controlled critical period in learning language, most researchers today understand that aspects of language development vary in their vulnerability to environmental conditions.

Most deaf children are born to hearing parents. What kind of language input do they receive? How do these children learn language?

In general, language learning is remarkably resilient, even under extreme conditions. Although Genie had difficulty with syntax—especially understanding and using grammatical markers correctly—she developed a large vocabulary, even of words that were unusual for a child first developing language (such as words for emotions or for many variations in color hues) (Curtiss, 1977). Language need not be spoken to be acquired. Children who are exposed from birth to conventional sign languages (such as American Sign Language) learn language at the same rate and in the same pattern as children acquiring spoken language (Lillo-Martin, 1999; Newport & Meier, 1985).

Unfortunately, not all children have exposure to a rich and varied linguistic environment. About 90 percent of deaf children are born to hearing parents and thus are not exposed to a signed language early in life. With no exposure to sign language until much later in life, these children have no usable linguistic input. But even with such limited language exposure, these children find a way to communicate, using gestures to express their desires. The gestures these children use, called "home signs," are more complex than those used by hearing children to supplement their spoken language, and they are not imitations of the gestures used by the hearing parents; home signs follow the patterns expected for early language use (Goldin-Meadow, 1997).

Deaf children who have not been exposed to sign language and who cannot use speech have been studied in Taiwan and the United States (Golding-Meadow & Mylander, 1998). Both the Taiwanese and the US children used gestures to communicate in various ways with their hearing parents—to make requests and comments, to talk about past and present, and to ask questions. Children in both countries tended to develop series of gestures akin to sentences, and the order of the gestures followed neither Mandarin nor English word order. The findings concerning deaf children's development of home signing suggests that some linguistic properties are not transmitted from one generation to another but instead result from attempts to communicate with others (National Research Council and Institute of Medicine, 2000).

Language learning is resilient to even relatively extreme variations in the amount of input to the language learner. Hearing children raised by deaf parents lack the usual spoken language input but typically acquire spoken language with only about 5 to 10 hours a week of exposure to hearing speakers. Furthermore, these children do not mimic idiosyncracies of their deaf parents' speech but instead regularize their language to map onto the norms of the spoken language they are learning. Although blind children lack the means to visually associate objects with the spoken words they hear, they do not experience difficulties in language development (Schiff-Myers, 1988). Apparently, language development does not depend on a mapping of words onto the physical world.

Even variations in biological conditions may not deter language development. As important as the brain is for language development, children who experience major brain damage may still acquire language. Surprisingly, children who have damage to the left cortex of the brain may recover language use as long as the damage occurs early in life (Feldman, 1994). When both hemispheres are damaged, speech and language difficulties are more likely to result (National Research Council and Institute of Medicine, 2000).

Genie's case also demonstrates, however, that not all aspects of language development are resilient. Evidence concerning the timing of linguistic exposure suggests that there are some aspects of language development that are more fragile and vulnerable to environmental conditions. Generally, exposure to a language early in life results in better proficiency in the language than does later exposure, supporting the idea that there is a critical or sensitive period for language input. For instance, deaf children of hearing parents who receive no linguistic input until later in life are typically greatly impaired in their use of syntax, just as Genie was, even when these children do not experience the same sorts of physical and social deprivation that Genie did (Curtiss, 1989; Newport, 1991). Similarly, even after 30 years of exposure to American Sign Language, native signers (exposed at birth) outperform early learners, and early learners (before age 6) outperform late learners (after age 12).

Second-language learning also is affected by the timing of input. Children who are exposed to a second language early in life (before the age of 7 or so) master the complexities of the language more easily than those who learn later in life, even when the speakers have many years of practice with the second language (Newport, 1991). Research has illustrated that the influence of early input on language development is not tightly time-bound, however. This sensitive period is not a window that closes at 6 or 7, but rather one that seems to close more gradually over many years' time. Furthermore, unlike the resilient aspects of language, which are learned in consistent patterns across individuals, the fragile aspects of language are much more variable. Some individuals master the complexities of a second language even relatively late in life; many others do not. The conclusion that can be drawn from the evidence on deaf isolates, second-language learning, and cases like Genie's is that the ability to acquire language diminishes with age (Stromswold, 2000).

Studies of brain activity provide support for the fragility of some aspects of language development. When studies have been done to assess event-related brain potentials (called ERPs), which provide indications about the processing of information in the brain, different patterns have been found for early- versus late-language learners. Among Chinese-English bilingual speakers, the parts of the brain that deal with semantic aspects of language (e.g., nouns and verbs) were relatively unaffected by delays in exposure, but the parts of the brain that process grammatical markers of language (e.g., prepositions and conjunctions) were markedly different depending on the delay in exposure to the second language (Weber-Fox & Neville, 1996). This finding suggests that the parts of the brain that deal with grammar are more modifiable, and thus more vulnerable to variations in language exposure, than the parts that deal with meaning (National Research Council and Institute of Medicine, 2000).

TRY IT OUT

Activities Relating to Infants and Toddlers

1. At what age did you first walk unassisted? In what physical environment and social context did you accomplish this feat? At what age did you first use words to communicate? What were your first words and sentences, and in what social and cultural contexts did you say them? Did your family members use child-directed language with you? Do you use child-directed language with children or pets today? What does it sound like?

2. Observe an infant or toddler to identify his or her perceptual abilities. You might interact with or test the baby informally to try to determine perception of colors, patterns, faces, movement, or depth. Try to identify the baby's stage of sensori-

motor development. What perceptual, motor, and cognitive abilities characterize this stage? For example, does the baby understand object permanence? number concepts? How could you tell when the baby entered the next stage of sensorimotor development? How could you or others best stimulate this development?

3. Investigate and report on a nutrition, health, or safety issue concerning infants or toddlers. For example, you might research a topic such as immunizations, baby foods, SIDS, lead exposure, baby toys, furniture and appliances for babies, infant car seats, or FTT babies.

Sum It Up

How do infants and toddlers develop physically?

✦ Growth in height and weight is more rapid during infancy than at any other time in the lifespan, except for prenatal development. Infants' growth is influenced by genetics and their living conditions.

✦ Infants gain control over muscles in a cephalocaudal pattern, beginning with the neck and head and moving down toward the feet.

✦ By about 6 months (depending on their sleeping position), most infants crawl. At 8 or 9 months, infants creep and cruise, holding onto furniture for balance. By 10 to 15 months, most infants begin unassisted walking. Walking is the major motor milestone of infancy and is one of the last major motor skills that infants master.

✦ Children do not have control or awareness of the physical symptoms associated with elimination until the middle of their second year. Most children are toilet trained by the age of 3.

What factors influence infant health and safety?

✦ Many accidents and health problems of infants can be prevented with proper safety precautions and immunizations.

✦ Because of their rapid growth, infants require a healthy and nutritious diet. Breast milk is the ideal food for young infants and protects them from diseases.

✦ Failure-to-thrive infants have slower than normal growth because of undernutrition or malnutrition. Given adequate diets, these children grow normally. Failure-to-thrive children experience many difficulties with family interactions and with their behavior and cognitive functioning.

How do infants' perceptual abilities develop?

✦ At around 3 months of age, infants begin to discriminate colors; recognize patterns; prefer faces, especially attractive ones; and recognize human-generated motion.

✦ By 5 to 7 months of age, infants begin to recognize depth and distance by using visual cues.

How do infants and toddlers learn and remember?

✦ Infants learn about the world through associations with existing behaviors, as in classical conditioning, or through associations of their actions with particular consequences, as in operant conditioning.

✦ Infants have fragile memories. Infants generally remember better when given reminders and visual cues that mimic the original learning situation.

How do cognitive abilities develop during infancy and toddlerhood?

✦ From birth to 2 years of age, infants are in Piaget's sensorimotor period of cognitive development, which is further divided into six stages.

✦ In stage I (0 to 1 month), infants practice their reflex actions.

✦ In stage II (1 to 4 months), infants demonstrate that they can repeat interesting actions centering on their body, called primary circular reactions.

✦ In stage III (4 to 8 months), infants coordinate schemes so that they can reach for interesting objects that they see. They also demonstrate secondary circular reactions, in which their repetitive actions focus on the noises or shapes of objects rather than on their own body.

✦ In stage IV (8 to 12 months), infants show the first signs of true intelligence by intentionally applying a scheme to reach a goal.

✦ In stage V (12 to 18 months), infants are creative in their problem solving—they vary their strategies and assess the outcomes of the variations. These systematic variations are tertiary circular reactions.

✦ In stage VI (18 to 24 months), infants begin to use symbols for the first time. Symbols allow them much greater flexibility in problem solving—they can mentally consider outcomes without having to act them out.

✦ Children's understanding of objects undergoes dramatic changes during infancy and toddlerhood. Infants move from having no concept of the permanence of objects to having a partial understanding. Only later in infancy do they acquire a full understanding of object permanence.

✦ Mandler proposed that infants develop concepts from their perceptions of objects rather than from their direct experiences with them, as Piaget suggested.

✦ By 18 months of age, infants show a basic understanding that people differ from one another.

✦ Social interactions, especially with knowledgeable adults, expand the range of children's cognitive abilities, as indicated by Vygotsky's zone of proximal development. Parents use scaffolding to maintain children's attention on a task and to structure tasks so that children can successfully complete them.

How do infants and toddlers develop language skills?

✦ To become speakers of a language, children must master four domains: (1) phonemes—the sounds of the language; (2) semantics—the understanding of word meaning; (3) syntax—the rules for forming sentences; and (4) pragmatics—the practical applications of language in different situations.

◆ Even before they utter their first words, infants engage in many language-related activities, including cooing, babbling, and intentional communication through gesturing.

◆ During the first year, experience with language helps fine-tune children's abilities to distinguish phonemes.

◆ Infants' first words, spoken around 12 months, are usually words that label important and familiar people or objects. These words are called holophrases because they convey a sentence's worth of meaning.

◆ Children use fast mapping to learn new vocabulary. The meaning they assign to words may over- or underextend the category of meaning typically associated with the word.

◆ Infants begin to form two-word sentences when they are around 2 years old. First sentences are grammatical and telegraphic (only the most important and informative words are included).

◆ Early-talking children have better language competence later in childhood; outcomes for late-talking children range from normal to delayed language development.

How is children's language acquisition explained?

◆ Chomsky's innate theory of language acquisition emphasizes that humans are specially equipped with a language acquisition device that allows them to understand and process the regularities of language. Lenneberg's innate theory assumes that there is a critical period in language development during which children must be exposed to language. Innate theories best account for the creativity and universal features of language.

◆ Learning theories emphasize the roles of modeling and reinforcement in language development. Learning theories best account for idioms, first words, and dialects.

◆ Social interactions in everyday life play an important role in children's language development by providing a rich language-learning environment.

◆ Some aspects of language development (e.g., grammar) are more vulnerable to environmental conditions.

KEY TERMS and CONCEPTS

A-not-B error (*154*)
babbling (*160*)
child-directed speech (*169*)
colostrum (*142*)
cooing (*160*)
cruise (*138*)
dishabituation (*147*)
expansion (*170*)
expressive language (*161*)
failure-to-thrive (FTT) (*144*)
fast mapping (*162*)

habituation (*147*)
holophrases (*161*)
image schemas (*156*)
infantile amnesia (*148*)
language acquisition device (LAD) (*166*)
object permanence (*152*)
overextension (*164*)
phonemes (*159*)
phonemic awareness (*160*)
pragmatics (*160*)
primary circular reactions (*150*)

receptive language (*161*)
relational play (*157*)
scaffolding (*158*)
semantics (*159*)
secondary circular reactions (*150*)
symbolic representation (*151*)
syntax (*159*)
telegraphic speech (*165*)
tertiary circular reactions (*151*)
underextension (*164*)
visual cliff apparatus (*145*)

Social and Emotional Development in Infancy and Toddlerhood

CHAPTER 6

CHAPTER OUTLINE

- How Do Emotions Develop During Infancy and Toddlerhood?
- How Does Temperament Influence Development During Infancy and Toddlerhood?
- How Do Parent-Infant Attachments Influence Development?
- How Does Day Care Influence Infants' and Toddlers' Development?
- Why Are Children Abused and Neglected?

The period of infancy and toddlerhood is a time when children make major strides in the development of social and emotional competencies (Saarni, Mumme, & Campos, 1998). Infants and toddlers must develop the social and emotional skills that allow them to get and hold the attention of adults and other important figures in their lives, express affection and annoyance when appropriate, establish relationships, and adapt to the demands of increasingly complex environments. Establishing trust and some measure of independence are important outcomes (Erikson, 1968). The characteristics infants and toddlers bring to these environments—and the ways significant people treat them—have important consequences for their development. For some children, the period of infancy and toddlerhood is an exciting time of growth, change, and challenge. For other children, however, this period often is fraught with insecurity and uncertainty—and sometimes even victimization.

HOW DO EMOTIONS DEVELOP DURING INFANCY AND TODDLERHOOD?

For many years, people believed that newborns and young infants expressed only one emotional state—general excitement (Bridges, 1932)—and that other emotions appeared gradually with age and experience. New research suggests, however, that many of the basic emotions are present at birth. As you can see from Table 6.1, the basic emotions of interest, sadness, and disgust are present at birth, and joy, anger, surprise, and fear develop during the first eight months. Although researchers sometimes disagree as to the precise timetable for the development of emotions (Malatesta, 1990), it is clear that by the end of the first year of life infants have a wide range of emotional capacities and express emotions in increasingly complex ways (Kochanska, Coy, Tjebkes, & Husarek, 1998).

Children also become more social and independent over the first two years of life—the clingy behavior of infants eventually is replaced by more mature forms of social behavior, such as making a verbal request or moving about to get something one wants. Children's behavior also changes in response to the demands of their environments. Very young infants often get the attention of their parents by crying, but older infants use other means, such as showing a toy to a parent or expressing affection, as they face increased expectations for age-appropriate behavior.

SMILING AND LAUGHTER

> When you're drawing up your list of life's miracles, you might place near the top the first moment your baby smiles at you. . . . Today, she looked right at me. And she smiled. . . . Her toothless mouth opened, and she scrunched her face up and it really was a grin. . . . The sleepless nights, the worries, the crying—all of a sudden it was all worth it. . . . She is no longer just something we are nursing and carrying along—somewhere inside, part of her knows what's going on, and that part of her is telling us that she's with us.
> —*Bob Greene;* journal entry about Amanda at 7 weeks of age (1984, pp. 33–34)

As Bob Greene's journal entry suggests, an infant's smile not only conveys a sense of well-being and pleasure but also reminds us that young infants have meaningful internal states (Greenspan & Greenspan, 1985). In fact, smiling may be one of the most significant aspects of social and emotional development during the first six months of life. Similar to many other aspects of early development, smiling develops through a series of maturational changes (Super & Harkness, 1991). Table 6.2 outlines these changes. As you can see, newborn children sometimes smile, but their smiles are not enduring or strong and occur most often while they are asleep. Such a smile is called an **endogenous smile** because it is triggered by changes in nervous system activity. Endogenous smiles are reflexive and involve only the lower face muscles.

TABLE 6.1

The Appearance of Emotions in the First Year of Life

EMOTION	AGE
Interest	Birth
Sadness	Birth
Disgust	Birth
Joy	Months 1–2
Anger	Months 2–3
Surprise	Months 3–4
Shyness	Months 4–5
Fear	Months 6–8

SOURCE: Adapted from Izard and Malatesta, 1987.

endogenous smile smile that is triggered by changes in nervous system activity and involves only the lower face muscles

exogenous smile smile that is triggered by external stimuli

social smile smile that is triggered by social stimuli (such as the mother's face)

TABLE 6.2
The Development of Smiling and Laughing

AGE	RESPONSE	STIMULATION	TIME TO ONSET	CONDITIONS
Smiling				
Neonate	Corners of mouth	No external stimulation		Due to nervous system fluctuations
Week 1	Corners of mouth	Low-level, modulated sound	6–8 sec	During sleep, boosting of tension
Week 2	Mouth pulled back	Low-level, modulated voices		When drowsy, satiated
Week 3	Grin, includes eyes	Moderate-level voices	4–5 sec	When alert, attentive (nodding head with voices)
Week 4	Grin, active smile	Moderate or moderately intense sounds	Reduced	Vigorous tactile stimulation effective
Weeks 5–8	Grin, active smile, cooing	Active stimulation, first visual stimulation	Less than 3 sec	Nodding head, flicking lights, stimulation that must be followed
Weeks 9–12	Grin, active smile, cooing	Inactive visual stimulation, moderately intense	Short	Trial-by-trial effects, recognition
Laughter				
Month 4	Laughter	Multisensory, vigorous stimulation	1–2 sec	Touch, tickling, auditory
Months 5–6	Laughter	Intense auditory stimulation and touch	Immediate	Items that may previously have caused crying
Months 7–9	Laughter	Social, visual stimulation	Immediate	Tactile, auditory decline
Months 10–12	Laughter	Visual, social	Immediate or anticipatory	Visual incongruities, active participation

SOURCE: Sroufe and Waters, 1976. Copyright © 1976 by the American Psychological Association. Adapted with permission.

By 2 to 3 weeks, infants smile when gently stimulated by high-pitched sounds or by soft stroking of their abdomens. This gentle stimulation increases the level of nervous system excitement and elicits a tiny reflex smile (Sroufe, 1977). This reflex smile is labeled an **exogenous smile** because it is triggered by external stimuli (Wolff, 1963).

Over the next few weeks, infants smile when they are fully awake and attentive. These alert smiles are fuller and more expressive than the earlier smiles and may be a response to a combination of visual, tactile, and auditory stimulation (Stack & LePage, 1996). Playing pat-a-cake, for example, might elicit twenty to thirty smiles, whereas auditory or visual stimuli alone might elicit only eight to ten smiles (Rosenblith, 1992).

By 6 to 8 weeks, an important change takes place—the **social smile** first appears. Now, the infant smiles upon seeing mother's or father's face or hearing her or his voice. Social smiles are longer lasting and involve the entire face; the grin goes from cheek to cheek, and the eyes widen and brighten (Izard & Malatesta, 1987).

At about 10 weeks of age, infants' smiling becomes *instrumental*—they use their smiles to achieve a goal, such as getting mom, dad, or other caregivers to smile back (Bower, 1982). Smiles are powerful social reinforcers for both infants and caregivers. When an infant smiles, the caregiver tends to smile back and repeat the behavior that elicited the smile. Infants learn about the power of their smiles, and they begin to use their smiles to gain control over their environment (Brazelton, 1991). For example, 10-month-old infants are more likely to

This 1-month-old infant's reflex smile involves just the muscles of her lower face. Notice that only her mouth is smiling—her eyes are not. To get a sense of this, cover half the picture with your finger. What does the mouth convey to you? What do the eyes convey?

The social smile of this 3-month-old child involves the entire face—the grin is from cheek to cheek, and the eyes are bright and wide open. What changes occur in the parents' responses when their infant begins to smile like this?

smile at their mother when the mother is attentive to them than when she is not, suggesting that infant smiling is responsive to the social context (Jones, Collins, & Hong, 1991; Schneider, 1997). Additionally, the mutually reinforcing smiles between an infant and his or her caregiver foster the development of attachment. Thus, consistent with ethological theory, smiling appears to be a genetic adaptation that promotes close contact and emotional ties between infants and their caregivers.

Infants' laughter appears at about 4 months of age. At first, laughing occurs in response to physical stimulation, such as tickling or being swooped up high in mom's or dad's arms (Sroufe & Waters, 1976). After 6 months of age, infants increasingly laugh at visual and social stimuli, such as playing peek-a-boo or seeing sister make a funny face. As toddlers, children laugh at events that earlier made them cry, such as seeing dad wear a mask. These milestones reflect the child's developmental progression from laughter based on physical stimulation to laughter based on cognitive interpretations (Snow, 1989). Laughing also is mutually reinforcing and fosters positive feelings and interactions between the infant and others in the social environment.

Although the development of smiling and laughter is similar across cultures, the behaviors used by parents in different cultures to elicit smiling vary. For example, American mothers rely largely on toys and objects to elicit smiling in their infants, whereas Japanese mothers are likely to engage infants in social stimulation. Mothers in both cultures are equally effective in eliciting smiles in their infants, but they do it in different ways (using toys versus using touch or physical contact) because of different culture-based parenting goals. In the United States, mothers place high value on promoting autonomy and independent exploration of the object world. Japanese mothers, in contrast, place high value on strengthening mutual dependency and making the infant an extension of themselves. Thus, they engage their infants differently (Bornstein, Tal, & Tamis-LeMonda, 1991).

CRYING

Crying is an infant's most effective way of communicating. This is true from the moment the child is born—the cries of the newborn tell the mother, doctor, and nurse that the newborn's lungs have filled with air. The cries also tell something about the status of the newborn's nervous system. Differences in pitch, duration, or pattern of crying may reveal abnormalities in a newborn's functioning. For example, newborns with high-pitched, shrill cries may have *cri du chat* (cry of a cat) syndrome, indicating brain damage or other nervous system disorders (Baird, Campbell, Ingram, & Gomez, 2001). Crying is the mechanism by which infants communicate their needs. Infants who are placid and rarely cry may be at risk of poor growth because their parents are not always made aware of the need to feed them (Skuse, Wolke, & Reilly, 1992).

Crying begins as a reflex response that has survival value and progressively becomes more controllable. Moreover, the significance of crying changes over the course of infancy and toddlerhood (Barr, Hopkins, & Green, 2000).

Characteristics of Cries

Mothers frequently report that they can distinguish different types of cries their infants make. Researchers also have identified different characteristics of infants' crying (Wasz-Hockert, Michelsson, & Lind, 1985; Wolff, 1969). The basic cry is a rhythmic pattern of crying followed by a brief silence, a short inhalation whistle, and then another brief silence. Anger cries differ from the basic cry in that excess air forced through the vocal cords gives the cry a more breathy sound. The pain cry is distinguishable through its sudden and loud onset and duration, followed by a period of breath holding. A fourth cry—the hunger cry—is similar to the basic cry, but it tends to be rhythmic, have a braying sound, and be accompanied by kicking in the same rhythm as the crying (Wolff, 1969). Despite the fact that many caregivers and some researchers believe that it is possible to tell, from the sound alone, the specific cause of an infant's cry, the research evidence is mixed (Gustafson, Wood, & Green, 2000).

The amount of crying varies dramatically from infant to infant and from day to day (St. James-Roberts & Plewis, 1996). Crying increases over the first six weeks of life and then decreases. Figure 6.1 shows that crying peaks in the first three months and then decreases by about half by the end of the first year. On the average, infants cry more in the first three months of life than at any other time, averaging about 2 hours of crying each day. Although some babies cry more than others, what most infants have in common is a period of fussiness late in the day, beginning at 3 to 12 weeks (McGlaughlin & Grayson, 2001; Zeskind, 1985). Figure 6.1 also reveals that infant crying initially is greatest in the evening, when the infant's nervous system overloads (Amato, 1997) and then shifts toward feeding times as the infant gets older (St. James-Roberts & Halil, 1991). These patterns of infant crying are similar across different Western cultures (St. James-Roberts, 1993).

As with the development of smiling, crying progresses from internal to external sources of stimulation (Snow, 1989). During the neonatal period, infants cry primarily because of physical needs—because they are hungry, in pain, or physically uncomfortable. Additionally, there are periods when infants cry for no apparent reason. As infants get older, their crying gradually becomes more related to cognitive and emotional conditions than to physical ones (Lester, 1985). For example, older infants might cry because they are scared or angry or because they do not want to be left alone. Caregivers' perceptions of infant crying change with the infants' age—as infants get older, caregivers perceive more complex and individualized needs and motives in the cries they hear (Leger, Thompson, Merritt, & Benz, 1996).

From birth, crying is an infant's most effective way of communicating. How should caregivers respond to infants' crying? What consequences might be associated with such responses?

FIGURE 6.1

Patterns of Crying at Different Times of Day

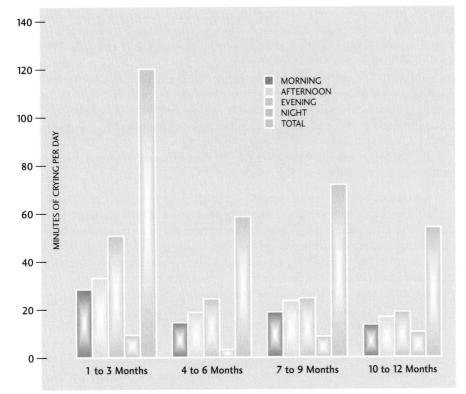

SOURCE: St. James-Roberts and Halil, 1991. Reprinted with the permission of Cambridge University Press.

Both the total amount of crying and the times of day during which crying occurs change over the course of the first year of life. What developmental changes take place that might account for these differences?

To keep children calm and to minimize their crying, Navajo caregivers confine them on a cradleboard. Notice how the infant is tightly swaddled to reduce movement and decrease the chance of becoming upset and aroused.

Culture and Infant Crying

People in different cultures, and in the same culture at different times, have contrary ideas about appropriate responses to a crying infant. In some cultures, crying is thought to be good for the infant. Some Mexican mothers believe that crying cleanses the child of illness or disease and that letting the child cry strengthens the child's lungs and nervous system (Atkin, Olvera, Givaudan, & Landeros, 1989). In other cultures, caregivers believe that infants should not cry and that their needs should be constantly and consistently attended to. For example, traditional Navajo caregivers believe that infants should be kept calm and quiet. To prevent crying, they often wrap Navajo infants onto a cradleboard for the first 10 months of life. These swaddled infants, who are in a lower state of arousal, sleep longer and cry less (Chisholm, 1989).

ANGER AND TEMPER TANTRUMS

Although there is some debate as to when infants first express anger, it is clear that by the end of the first year children can and do become angry (Buss & Goldsmith, 1998). At about 9 months of age, infants begin to develop a sense of control, and angry crying and temper tantrums are signals of their frustration when things are not to their liking (Wolf, 1996). As infants move beyond the first year of life, they become aware of, and are frustrated by, the limits they experience. For example, 14-month-old Ethan used to play happily in his high chair and car seat, but he now cries and flails his arms and legs when put in either one. Ethan is a physically active infant who is mobile and agile. The restrictiveness of the car seat and high chair is frustrating, and he reacts angrily to it. Similarly, 16-month-old Josephina enjoys playing with her mother's car keys. But her smiles turn to screams of protest when her mother needs the keys and takes them from her. Josephina becomes rigid, throws herself to the ground, and kicks and yells. These behaviors give an infamous reputation to the toddler years, commonly referred to as the "terrible twos and threes."

Three important changes take place during the toddler years that contribute to the defiant reputation toddlers have (Hoyt, 1996; Schaefer & DiGeronimo, 1995):

- ◆ **Increased ability to express anger.** As toddlers' communication skills increase, so does their ability to express anger and frustration. Their vocabulary increases dramatically, although they have not yet learned to censor themselves. They now are more capable of telling caregivers when things are not to their liking. The amount of angry crying decreases, but defiant language increases (Kopp, 1992).
- ◆ **Limitations in social understanding.** Although toddlers have many increased capacities, they do not yet understand concepts such as waiting, sharing, or patience. Thus, hunger, boredom, or fatigue can cause angry outbursts.
- ◆ **Strivings toward autonomy.** Toddlers increasingly strive to express their newfound abilities and their desire to be individuals (Erikson, 1968). This independence often conflicts with what is required of them or what is best for them. For example, 30-month-old Dori constantly struggles with her mother over getting dressed. Dori only wants to wear her red skirt and cries angrily when she has to wear anything else.

As most parents know, young children's angry reactions sometimes become intense and escalate into temper tantrums (Portegal, Kororok, & Davidson, 1996). Two types of temper tantrums have been identified (Turecki & Tonner, 1985): **manipulative tantrums,** in which children use the tantrum to manipulate others into giving them what they want, and **temperamental tantrums,** in which children respond with anger because some aspect of their style of interacting has been violated. For example, Reese, who has a low tolerance for change, threw several temper tantrums when household routines were disrupted during his grandparents' visit. The best ways to respond to the two types of tantrums differ. It is important not to give in to manipulative tantrums, but it is important to help the child cope with situations giving rise to temperamental tantrums (Brooks, 1998).

SELF-AWARENESS AND EMOTIONS

By 18 to 24 months of age, children understand that emotions are connected with what one wants or does not want (Wellman & Woolley, 1990). Toddlers' temper tantrums illustrate that young children can and do use an emotional reaction to try to get what they want. Thus, children's first understanding of emotions is based on associations with their desired goals and outcomes (Stein & Trabasso, 1989).

Toddlers also begin to express **self-conscious emotions,** such as pride, shame, embarrassment, and guilt. Self-conscious emotions are those that involve injury to or enhancement of one's sense of self (Tangney, 1999). For example, at about 24 months, children show signs of embarrassment when they are caught violating a rule—they may lower their eyes, hang their head, and hide their face with their hands.

Self-conscious emotions require several important advances in self-awareness and cognitive development. For these emotions to develop, children must have the following characteristics (Lewis, 1993):

Notice the look of shame and guilt on this 2-year-old's face. Once children understand that there are standards for their behavior, self-conscious emotions appear. What other changes bring about the development of self-conscious emotions?

- A conscious awareness of themselves as distinct from others
- A recognition that there are certain rules to be followed and standards or expectations to be met
- The ability to evaluate their behavior in relation to these standards
- A sense of responsibility for meeting or not meeting these standards

When children see themselves as responsible for success in meeting a standard, they experience pride. When they view themselves as responsible for failing to meet a standard or follow a rule, they may feel guilt, embarrassment, or shame. Thus, at about age 2, children have a rudimentary understanding that their behaviors lead to others' approval or disapproval, and they feel emotions that reflect this anticipation (Frolund, 1997). After age 3, children begin to react independently to these standards; they feel pride or shame as they develop the ability to reflect on and compare their behaviors to standards they set for themselves. Three-year-olds still depend on others' reactions for these feelings; they beam with pride because mom is proud of them. It is not until about 8 years of age that children say they feel proud or ashamed of themselves independently of others' approval or disapproval (Stipek, Recchia, & McClintic, 1992).

From toddlerhood on, girls are more likely than boys to show shame when they fail at a task (Lewis, Alessandri, & Sullivan, 1992). What is particularly interesting about this finding is that girls often show more shame than boys do even though they perform as well as the boys; that is, girls show more shame than boys do despite a lack of difference in their abilities. Research indicates that the same is true in adulthood: women express more shame than men do (Tangney, 1990).

These findings suggest that gender differences in the expression of shame appear early and persist throughout life. One reason is that girls and women are more likely than boys and men to be taught to assume personal responsibility for failure (Dweck & Leggett, 1988). Additionally, girls are more likely than boys to receive negative feedback from caregivers and teachers (Lewis, 1987). Thus, there is good reason to believe that early socialization experiences account for the gender differences in the expression of shame and other self-conscious emotions (Fredrickson, 1998).

manipulative tantrums
tantrums children throw to manipulate others into giving them what they want

temperamental tantrums
anger response when some aspect of a child's style of interacting has been violated

self-conscious emotions
those emotions that involve injury to or enhancement of one's sense of self (such as pride and shame)

PLAY AND EMOTIONAL DEVELOPMENT

Fifteen-month-old Ben tries to get his 4-year-old sister's attention by taking one of her dolls and offering it to her. When his sister fails to respond, he drops the doll and laughs. When his sister again fails to respond, he does this a second and third time. Soon his sister tells him to stop bothering her, and Ben becomes upset and takes the doll to the kitchen, where his mother is. He shows the doll to his mother, and she asks, "Is the doll hungry?" Ben first looks sad, then smiles and says "yes." His mother gives him a piece of carrot, which Ben tries to feed to the doll. When he cannot get the carrot in the doll's mouth, he gets upset until his mother suggests that he put the baby to sleep. Ben then puts the baby on the chair and puts a napkin over it.

Ben's story provides vivid evidence that many of children's early emotional responses occur in the context of play. Even before the toddler years, infants smile and laugh when mother plays with them while they are being bathed or diapered. Play provides young children with the opportunity to experiment with emotions in a relatively stress-free environment (Sutton-Smith, 1998).

Play also provides young children with an opportunity to learn about their world. Ben, for example, learned that he can use play to attract others' interest and attention. It may not always work and sometimes produces feelings of frustration and sadness, but Ben's understanding of the world is enhanced by these playful interactions (Sutton-Smith, 1994).

Infants' and toddlers' play often is repetitive and ritualistic. Initially, it revolves around the child's body and physical actions, such as when 6-month-old Teri repeatedly splashes water in the bath and laughs each time. By 12 months, children begin to use objects and involve others in their play (Goncu, 1993). These playful interactions can be emotionally intense, and they can quickly lead to anger and aggression because of the egocentric and impulsive nature of toddlers. But even these negative interactions help children learn about their emotional worlds—they provide children with opportunities to gain self-control and cope with negative social interactions and feelings (Eisenberg, Fabes, & Guthrie, 1997).

HOW DOES TEMPERAMENT INFLUENCE DEVELOPMENT DURING INFANCY AND TODDLERHOOD?

From the moment of birth, infants differ in their responses to their environment. Some babies cry frequently and intensely; others rarely cry, and when they do their cries are relatively quiet. Some newborns get on a schedule very quickly and adapt easily to changes in their environment; others are unpredictable and do not easily adjust to change. These differences in infants' responses to their environment often are considered to be linked to biological and genetic processes that predispose them to respond in certain ways. This predisposition to respond in certain enduring and characteristic ways to one's environment is known as **temperament** (Wachs & King, 1994).

An important aspect of temperament is its consistency. Temperament sometimes shows stability from infancy to adolescence and even adulthood (Caspi & Silva, 1995; Caspi et al., 1995). Research suggests that temperamental differences are present prenatally: Very active fetuses are more unpredictable and unadapatable as infants (DiPietro, Hodgson, Costigan, & Johnson, 1996). The heritability of temperament distinguishes it from the closely related concept of personality, which refers to a person's unique behavioral, motivational, and temperamental ways of responding. Personality therefore is a broader term, and a person's personality is more likely to be a product of diverse influences (Rothbart & Bates, 1998; Strelau, 1994).

THE STRUCTURE OF TEMPERAMENT

What qualities make up a person's temperament? This question has received the attention of many researchers, who have yet to come up with a single, agreed-upon set of qualities that

temperament the predisposition to respond in certain enduring and characteristic ways to one's environment

represent the structure of temperament. Instead, a variety of components of temperament have been identified (Buss & Plomin, 1984; Rothbart, 1989), with the most well-known being the nine components identified by Thomas and Chess (1970, 1977):

- **Rhythmicity.** The regularity of basic functions, such as sleep, wakefulness, excretion, and hunger.
- **Activity level.** The intensity and frequency of motor movements.
- **Approach-withdrawal.** The degree to which a child accepts or rejects new people, objects, or situations.
- **Persistence.** The amount of time a child devotes to an activity.
- **Adaptability.** How quickly and easily a child adjusts to change.
- **Quality of mood.** The extent to which a child expresses positive or negative emotions.
- **Distractibility.** The degree to which stimuli in the environment can alter a child's behavior.
- **Threshold of responsiveness.** The intensity of stimulation needed to elicit a response.
- **Intensity of reaction.** The energy level of a child's response.

More recent research on temperament suggested that this original list needed to be revised to include a smaller number of characteristics. Researchers found that many of the items and constructs in Thomas and Chess's components overlapped considerably, suggesting that some of the components measure close to the same, if not the same, construct (Rothbart & Bates, 1998). Thus, today's temperament researchers have sought to give a cleaner and more precise structure to temperament. Mary Rothbart and her colleagues identified a shorter list of six reliable and nonoverlapping temperamental constructs (Rothbart & Mauro, 1990). Generally speaking, these include the following:

- **Fearful distress,** reflecting a child's tendency to withdraw and become distressed in new situations or circumstances.
- **Anger/frustration,** reflecting the degree to which a child becomes angry or frustrated when his or her needs or desires are not met.
- **Positive affect,** reflecting the amount of positive emotion, pleasure, and excitement shown by a child.
- **Activity level,** reflecting a child's level of gross motor activity and energy.
- **Attention span/persistence,** reflecting a child's ability to maintain focus and interest.
- **Regularity,** reflecting the predictability of a child's behavior.

As you can see, some of Thomas and Chess's original nine dimensions are not included in these new constructs. For example, the newer view separates positive and negative emotions as distinct components of temperament. Intensity of responding is now included within many of the constructs and does not stand on its own. Suppose an infant who experienced a bath for the first time became intensely upset but lay in the bath water placidly while crying. How would "intensity of responding" be coded? In this case, the infant responded with intense emotions but did not show intensity in gross motor activity. The old system would not differentiate between these two reactions; Rothbart's new dimensions do a better job of capturing the different responses.

Temperamental traits are thought to be stable and enduring throughout the life span. To the extent that this is true, children who are active and angry as infants can be expected to be active and angry as older children, adolescents, and adults. For example, an infant who is high in positive affect and low in fearful distress will enjoy his or her first bath. As a preschooler, this child likely will play happily with new peers, and as a school-aged child she or he likely will look forward to beginning a new school year.

Although there is considerable evidence that temperament is consistent across development (Braungart-Rieker & Stifter, 1996; Caspi & Silva, 1995), temperament does not always follow a predictable course. Thomas and Chess (1985) found that some children in their study showed consistency in temperamental traits, whereas other children were consistent in certain aspects of temperament but inconsistent in others. Some children changed completely in a number of temperamental qualities. These findings suggest that the expression of one's temperament may be modifiable and that socialization and other environmental influences affect what we observe in others (Wachs & King, 1994).

CONTRIBUTIONS OF TEMPERAMENT TO INFANT DEVELOPMENT

Temperament theorists believe that temperament has a profound influence on the course of an individual's development (Molfese & Molfese, 2000). For example, a child's temperament has an impact on how he or she learns about his or her environment. A child who responds with fear and distress to new situations is more likely to avoid new situations and people than is a child who is less fearful. A child low in fearfulness not only does not experience fear when exposed to new situations and people, but may experience pleasure in interactions with strangers. If this is so, the child may develop a conditioned approach to future interactions with strangers. You can see how positive reinforcement in these situations can magnify initial temperamental differences and how this might influence future adjustment (Rothbart & Bates, 1998). Similarly, children who are high in fearful distress might actively avoid situations in which they are tested and evaluated (such as school). This may lead to feelings of inadequacy and to future avoidance of these situations (Posner & Rothbart, 2000). Thus, temperamental qualities can be related to both positive and negative adjustment and outcomes.

Children's development of conscience and morality also may be related to temperament. Kochanska (1995; Kochanska, Murray, & Harlan, 1999) has found that these qualities are related to children's ability to control their behavior and attention. Temperament also influences how children respond to their parents' efforts to socialize them (Kochanska, 1997). For fearful toddlers, gentle discipline appears to promote later conscience development. For fearless toddlers, who are often unaroused by gentle discipline, alternative socialization practices—perhaps capitalizing on positive mother-child relationships—are more likely to promote conscience and morality development. Thus, temperament and socialization practices interact in a transactional way to influence the development of children's conscience and morality.

Some temperament theorists have tried to identify different patterns of temperamental responding that can be used to classify types of children and their development. For example, by identifying different combinations of temperamental traits, Thomas and Chess (1985) tried to classify infants into one of three temperamental groups: (1) *easy*—infants who behave predictably and respond positively to new situations, (2) *difficult*—infants who are irregular in their schedules and bodily functions, are slow to adapt to change, cry longer and louder than other infants, and generally are wary of new people or situations, and (3) *slow-to-warm-up*—infants who tend to be active but initially do not respond well to new situations or people.

Although these categories of temperament have some appeal, research has not supported their usefulness. For example, about one-third of all children cannot be classified into any of the three temperamental groups. In addition, most children display a wide range of responses to their environment and do not fit neatly into a particular category. Easy children are not always easy, and difficult children are not difficult in all situations (Thomas & Chess, 1985). Because of issues like these, the concept of "difficult" temperament has been questioned (Bates, 1987). Is difficult temperament a pattern of traits in the child or a social perception of the caregiver? What is considered difficult by one caregiver may not be considered difficult by another, although difficult temperament at 18 months is predictive of behavior problems ten years later (Guerin, Gottfried, & Thomas, 1997).

In addition, the perception of temperamental qualities in an infant is influenced by cultural factors. For example, caregivers in areas of Brazil where infant mortality is very high because of impoverished conditions show a preference for difficult infants (Scheper-Hughes, 1987). This preference is based on the perception that difficult infants are "stronger" than placid, easy infants and are more likely to survive the harsh conditions.

THE SCIENTIFIC IMPACT: INTERPRETING RESEARCH

What Are the Early Roots of Shyness?

My daughter and I have never been close. . . . I gave up my career to do special things with her and we often times clash. She prefers doing things alone instead of playing with me. . . . She now is very passive at school, does not want group attention, prefers to play alone but likes to watch others play. . . . I feel that Julie was born this way.

—*Rubin & Asendorpf*, 1993, pp. 3–4

In this excerpt from a letter, a mother comes to the conclusion that her daughter's shyness and social withdrawal have a genetic basis, were present from birth, and are part of her temperament. This mother's conclusion is consistent with research findings on the early roots of shyness. For example, Kagan and colleagues (Kagan, 1989; Kagan, Snidman, & Arcus, 1993) found that about 15 to 20 percent of healthy 1- to 2-year-old Caucasian children are extremely and consistently shy, timid, and fearful when they encounter unfamiliar situations. These children hesitate in their approach to objects, remain quiet with new people, and stay close to their mother. Longitudinal studies indicate that over 75 percent of these children retain this shyness through the eighth year of life (Kagan et al., 1993). By contrast, approximately 30 percent of Caucasian children are fearless, uninhibited, and outgoing. They approach objects without hesitation, talk sponta-

neously to unfamiliar persons, and spend little time close to their mothers.

In comparing shy children with those who are not, Kagan found that a combination of temperamental traits, including high motor activity and frequent crying upon novel stimulation, predicts early shyness. These qualities are thought to reflect differences in inherited physiological processes. Using these predictors, Kagan and colleagues identified two groups of infants, who were seen at 4 and 14 months of age. At 4 months, one group of infants showed frequent and vigorous motor activity, such as flexing and extending their limbs, arching the back, and crying frequently. The second group of infants showed low levels of motor activity and rarely cried (Kagan et al., 1993). At 14 months, the two groups of infants were observed in situations likely to produce fearful reactions, such as being presented with a noisy metal robot. Over 60 percent of the infants who were active and cried a lot at 4 months were fearful at 14 months. In contrast, only 12 percent of the infants who were low in temperamental reactivity at 4 months were fearful at 14 months.

These findings suggest that some children have a biological predisposition to respond with fear and withdrawal to new or strange environ-

ments. The relationship between the 4-month profile of motor activity and crying and later signs of shyness was not due to differences in gestational age at birth, health, or stressful conditions. Instead, it appears that the children's nervous systems made them vulnerable to anxiety and distress. This does not mean, however, that children cannot learn to control these feelings and the urge to withdraw. The environment appears to play a more substantial role in helping children overcome their tendencies toward shyness than in making them shy in the first place (Kagan et al., 1993).

Thinking It Through:

1. Were you or one of your siblings shy as a young child? (Offer evidence for your answer.) If so, what were some consequences of shyness for your (or your sibling's) development?

2. What learning principles might explain how shyness develops in children? How might shyness be overcome?

3. Why was it important for Kagan to control for gestational age, health, and stress? What roles might these factors play in the development of shyness?

Similarly, difficult infants born into the Masai tribe in Kenya are preferred over easy infants because they are viewed as potential "warriors" for the tribe, a role that is highly valued (DeVries, 1984). Thus, the links between infant temperament and caregivers' perceptions and beliefs are influenced by the context in which they live (Wachs & Kohnstamm, 2001).

HOW DO PARENT-INFANT ATTACHMENTS INFLUENCE DEVELOPMENT?

During infancy and toddlerhood, more than at any other time in their development, children are dependent on their parents to meet their basic needs for healthy growth and development. Although the influence of parents is just one of many, most people believe that different child-rearing experiences early in development relate to differences in the way children turn out. These early parental influences primarily relate to **attachment**—an enduring emotional tie characterized by a tendency to seek and maintain closeness to a specific figure (the attachment figure), particularly under conditions of stress. Children's patterns of attachment to their caregivers help explain individual differences.

attachment an enduring emotional tie characterized by a tendency to seek and maintain closeness to a specific figure (the attachment figure), particularly under conditions of stress

Why are some children shy and others not? How can caregivers help children overcome their tendencies toward shyness?

As you have learned, young children perceive and respond to their environments differently. Some infants appear to have a strong sense of security that enables them to explore and be curious about their world, even in situations that are new and potentially stressful. Other infants appear anxious and uncertain about their world, and this anxiety and uncertainty inhibit their ability to cope successfully with new and demanding situations.

Temperament theorists explain these differences primarily as a product of differences in children's biological dispositions. Another explanation focuses on the quality of the relationships they have with their caregivers. Based on the work of John Bowlby (1969) and Mary Ainsworth (1973), attachment theory was developed to account for individual differences in personality, social development, and interpersonal relationships. Unlike temperament theory, attachment theory places great emphasis on the caregiver-child relationship as the foundation for individual differences. In contemporary Western societies, attachment theory is widely regarded as one of the most promising theories of personality and social development (Colin, 1996).

ATTACHMENT THEORY

Attachment refers to a long-lasting relationship; it is not a product of transient enjoyment or comfort. For most people, the best example of attachment is the tie that usually develops between an infant and his or her primary caregiver (most often the mother). Evidence of this attachment is seen in a child's attempts to seek out and maintain contact with his or her primary caregiver and in the child's distress when separated from that person.

Attachment is distinct from bonding (see Chapter 4), which generally refers to the caregiver's tie to the infant. Some scientists believe that there is a sensitive period in the first hours or days after birth during which bonding must occur (Klaus & Kennell, 1982). Evidence for this sensitive bonding period in humans is scarce. Human parents have the ability to bond with their child even if they do not have contact with the child early in life. Adopting parents, for example, form deep and meaningful emotional ties to their adopted children (Edens & Cavell, 1999; Juffer & Rosenboom, 1997), even when the adoption occurs years after the child is born (Brodzinsky, Lang, & Smith, 1995).

When not stressed, infants are curious and naturally seek interaction with their environments. They explore their world contentedly if an attachment figure is present, but become distressed and stop exploring when separated from the attachment figure (Posada et al., 1995). Infants do not have to be in physical contact with the attachment figure for exploration and curiosity to occur—just knowing that the attachment figure is near seems sufficient to support play and exploration. Thus, infants use the attachment figure as a base from which they attend to, learn about, and explore their world. When a threat arises, the attachment figure serves as a base of security and safety.

As Bowlby (1969) noted, attachments also give rise to the views that individuals develop about themselves and others. Through their attachments, children develop an "internal working model" that consists of general expectations of their own worthiness and the availability of others. This internal working model serves as a basis for future relationships (Griffin & Bartholomew, 1994). Infants whose needs are neglected or ignored come to expect that their needs will be neglected or ignored in the future. In turn, this expectation may lead these children to avoid intimate personal relationships because they believe they cannot rely on others to be available. Attachments therefore not only represent the past experiences of children, but also relate to how children construct their own representations of relationships. This internal working model subsequently affects their interactions with others (Thompson, 1998).

Not all infants form the same kind of attachment or internal working model of relationships. For example, infants differ in their ability to use an attachment figure as a secure base and in the intensity and quality of emotions they feel toward the attachment figure. Caregivers also differ considerably in how they respond to their infants and in the feelings they hold toward their infants.

THE DEVELOPMENT OF ATTACHMENT

Based on Bowlby's theory (1969) and on Mary Ainsworth's (1973) observations of infants in Uganda (Africa) and Baltimore, the development of early attachment relationships has been broken down into four phases (see Table 6.3). The first three phases take place during infancy and toddlerhood. Despite the large cultural differences between African and US infants, the sequence of the development of attachment was found to be very similar, and subsequent research on infants raised in other cultures confirmed these basic findings (Colin, 1996).

The Preattachment Phase

During the first eight weeks of life, infants are sometimes referred to as "asocial" because both social and nonsocial stimuli produce positive responses. Infants at this age rarely protest when caregivers leave and do not distinguish among the various caregivers who attend to them (Thompson, 1998).

This first phase is called the *preattachment phase,* in reference to the fact that young infants do not discriminate in their responses to caregivers. There is little evidence that infants consistently prefer the primary caregiver to any other person. Recall from Chapters 4 and 5 that infants are drawn to human faces and to the human voice but at first do not associate these with any particular person. Although infants' responses to caregivers generally are reflexive rather than voluntary, their reflexive behaviors strengthen the emotional tie with caregivers and draw caregivers to them.

The Attachment-in-the-Making Phase

After a period of indiscriminate responding, infants around 2 to 6 months of age gradually begin to direct their responses to familiar rather than unfamiliar people. This shift characterizes the second phase. In this *attachment-in-the-making phase,* infants more often smile at, look at, reach for, and are soothed by familiar rather than unfamiliar people.

Despite increased preference for familiar caregivers, infants at this phase do not have full-fledged attachments. By definition, attachments cannot occur until the child understands that people and objects have an independent existence—that is, when the infant develops object permanence. As you read in Chapter 5, for a young infant, when a parent is "out of sight" the parent is "out of mind." Thus, in the second phase of attachment, infants may recognize caregivers and respond with a delight and pleasure that they do not show to strangers, but attachment has not yet fully developed.

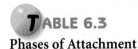

TABLE 6.3

Phases of Attachment

PHASE	AGE (IN MONTHS)	CHARACTERISTICS OF PHASE
1. Preattachment	0–2	Nondiscriminate responses to caregivers; reflexive rather than voluntary behaviors; positive response to both social and nonsocial stimuli
2. Attachment-in-the-making	2–6	Clear preference for social stimuli; positive response to familiar caregivers but not to unfamiliar ones; no single attachment preference observable
3. Clear-cut attachment	7–12	Clear preference for a single attachment figure; evidence of stranger and separation anxiety
4. Goal-corrected partnership	48	Recognition that caregivers have feelings or goals that may be different from the child's; attempts to change caregivers' plans and goals and become a partner in planning how the relationship proceeds (discussed in Chapter 8)

The Clear-Cut Attachment Phase

Important changes that take place around 7 months of age enable infants to develop clear-cut attachments with their primary caregivers. Evidence of these changes comes from studies of infants who are placed in foster care. If infants are placed prior to 7 months of age, they usually adapt to a new caregiver quite easily. In contrast, infants placed in foster care after 7 months of age do not adjust quickly or easily (Colin, 1996). These findings provide us with evidence of the developing attachment; disruption of this attachment elicits specific and adverse responses.

In addition to developing object permanence around this age, infants become able to develop goals (see Chapter 5)—they make planned efforts to achieve contact with the attachment figure, such as protesting when separated or lifting their arms to be picked up. These early efforts at making contact and influencing caregivers are primitive, however. An infant may pull a book out of mother's hand if she is reading or may pull the telephone cord while father is talking. As children mature, they develop more sophisticated and acceptable forms of achieving contact. Nevertheless, in both cases, children are developing ways of satisfying their own needs for help and comfort (Maccoby, 1980).

STRANGER ANXIETY   **Stranger anxiety,** a characteristic of the clear-cut attachment phase, is a wary and fearful reaction to strangers, which appears at about 7 months. Until that time, infants often respond positively to strangers, but after forming attachments they soon become fearful of them. The intensity of their responses peaks between 8 and 10 months and gradually declines during the second year of life (Thompson, 1998). Stranger anxiety may not completely subside; even some 4-year-old children show signs of wariness when encountering a stranger, particularly in an unfamiliar setting.

Although most children show some stranger anxiety, this wariness of strangers is not universal or consistent. For example, an infant is less likely to respond negatively to a stranger if the caregiver is holding the child, if the caregiver greets the stranger in a warm and pleasant tone of voice, or if the caregiver talks to the child about the stranger in a soothing voice (Gunnar, 1980). Additionally, infants who are exposed regularly to large numbers of adults show less stranger anxiety than others (Colin, 1996). Infants with little experience with strangers, on the other hand, may associate them with negative experiences, such as going to the doctor for a vaccination.

SEPARATION ANXIETY   Another response that characterizes the clear-cut attachment phase is **separation anxiety,** in which negative protests accompany separation from the attachment figure. Protests over the attachment figure's leaving usually peak in frequency and strength between 12 and 18 months of age, but commonly remain strong through the second year of life (Colin, 1996). Studies of infants in diverse cultures reveal similar patterns: Before 7 or 8 months of age, infants rarely protest when separated from their caregivers. Separation anxiety then increases during the second year of life and declines thereafter (Kagan, 1976). Infants protest and show distress when attachment figures depart and express joy and relief when reunited with them. These responses are not shown when strangers depart or reappear. Thus, separation from attachment figures represents a significant source of stress for infants—and their caregivers (Deater-Deckard, Scarr, McCartney, & Eisenberg, 1994).

The final phase of attachment shown in Table 6.3, the goal-corrected partnership, is not reached until 4 years of age, when children begin to negotiate relationships more directly. This phase is discussed in Chapter 8.

ASSESSING PATTERNS OF ATTACHMENT IN THE STRANGE SITUATION

Ainsworth developed the most common method of assessing attachment; it is based on the characteristic responses of infants to the presence or absence of caregivers and strangers. Ainsworth's purpose was to create a situation that would activate infant attachment behav-

stranger anxiety a wary and fearful reaction to strangers

separation anxiety a response in which negative protests accompany separation from attachment figures

Strange Situation a procedure used to assess infants' attachment behavior under conditions of increasing stress due to separations from caregivers and strangers

TABLE 6.4
Ainsworth's Strange Situation Procedure

EPISODE	PEOPLE PRESENT*	PROCEDURE
Setup	E	Appropriate for infants 11–18 months old, the procedure requires an unfamiliar room with two chairs, an attractive collection of toys, and space for the infant to move about. Two chairs and the toys are on the three points of a triangle, far enough apart so that the observer can determine whether the infant is nearer the caregiver, the toys, or the other adult.
Episode 1	I, C, E	E shows C where to put I and where to sit, then leaves. If necessary, C gets I to start playing with the toys.
Episode 2	I, C	C does not initiate interaction with I but may respond if necessary.
Episode 3	I, C, S	S enters, sits quietly for 1 minute, talks with C for 1 minute, and engages I in interaction or play for 1 minute.
Episode 4	I, S	C exits. S lets I play. If I needs comfort, S tries to provide it. If I cries hard, the episode is terminated early.
Episode 5	I, C	C calls to I from outside the door; C enters, greets I, and pauses. If I needs comfort, C may provide it. When I is ready to play with the toys, C sits in a chair. If I is very upset and needs extra time, the episode can be extended.
Episode 6	I	C exits. I is left alone. If I cries hard, the episode is terminated early.
Episode 7	I, S	S enters, greets I, and pauses. If I is OK, S sits. If I needs comfort, S tries to provide it. If I cries hard, the episode is terminated early.
Episode 8	I, C	C calls to I from outside the door; C enters, greets I, and pauses. If I needs comfort, C may provide it. C lets I return to play when ready.

*I = Infant, C = Caregiver, E = Experimenter, S = Stranger
SOURCE: Adapted from Colin, 1996.

ior that is not routinely observed in the home. The **Strange Situation** is a procedure used with infants between 11 and 18 months of age (Ainsworth, Blehar, Waters, & Wall, 1978). Carried out in an environment that is unfamiliar to the infant, this procedure consists of eight 3-minute episodes involving exploration, separation, and reunion sequences with a caregiver (usually the mother) and an adult stranger. Table 6.4 describes the eight episodes of the Strange Situation.

Episode 1 involves establishing rapport. During Episode 2, observers assess the extent to which the infant uses his or her mother as a secure base for exploring the new room and toys. Reactions to a stranger are assessed in Episode 3. Separation anxiety is assessed in Episode 4, when the mother leaves the infant with the stranger. In Episode 6, separation responses are observed in a more stressful context, when the infant is left alone. If the infant becomes highly upset, these episodes are terminated early. The infant's responses to being reunited with the mother are observed in Episodes 5 and 8, and the infant's ability to be soothed by the stranger is assessed in Episode 7. Thus, Ainsworth devised a series of episodes that allow researchers to compare and contrast infants' responses to the presence and absence of their mother (or other caregiver) and to the presence and absence of a stranger. Based on the responses observed over the eight episodes of the Strange Situation, four patterns of attachment were identified. These four patterns are outlined in Table 6.5 on page 190.

Toddlers are more willing to explore when they have a safe base. How do parents act as a safe base for children?

TABLE 6.5

Patterns of Attachment

PATTERN	CHARACTERISTICS
Secure	Uses caregiver as secure base for exploration Seeks and maintains contact with caregiver at reunion Shows little or no resistance to contact with caregiver Shows clear distress during separation If distressed, seeks caregiver and is soothed by contact
Avoidant	Does not seek or maintain contact with caregiver Responds positively to stranger Shows little distress at separation from caregiver Often shows some avoidance of caregiver at reunion
Ambivalent	Appears nervous and timid in exploration episodes Seeks contact with and resists release from caregiver but also is openly resistant to interaction with caregiver Is distressed during separations but has difficulty settling down during reunion episodes Often shows angry behavior—hits, kicks, or squirms while being held by caregiver Sometimes appears passive, unhappy, or helpless
Disorganized/ Disoriented	Often shows avoidance and resistance Sometimes freezes in place in odd postures Shows bizarre repetitions of behavior Lacks a coherent strategy for handling separations and reunions Responds inconsistently in Strange Situation May exhibit behaviors reflecting child abuse and neglect

SOURCE: Colin, 1996; Thompson, 1998.

Secure Attachment

The first type of attachment, a relatively common one, is referred to as **secure attachment.** When securely attached infants and their mothers go through the Strange Situation, the children tend to explore the new room and the new toys right away (Episode 2). They often vocalize and show the toys to their mother. When the stranger comes in during Episode 3, they look intensely at her, move closer to their mother, and resume their play. When their mother leaves, secure infants stop playing and become upset. When the stranger tries to comfort them, they accept the contact and stop crying but show little interest in playing. Upon their mother's return, they smile, rush to meet her, and eagerly accept her comfort. Afterwards, they return to playing with the toys.

When left alone during Episode 6, secure infants stop playing and begin to cry. When the stranger enters during Episode 7, they resist attempts to be comforted. Their mother's final return is met with clear signals to be picked up, and their distress is soothed right away. Secure infants then resume playing with the toys until the end of the final episode.

Based on these qualities of response, secure infants appear to use their mother as a secure base from which they can separate to some degree and explore their environment. Securely attached infants seek out their attachment figures, obtain much pleasure and comfort from their presence, and are distressed and bothered by their absence. Approximately 68 percent of middle-class American infants are classified as securely attached infants.

secure attachment pattern in which infants use their attachment figures as a secure base, obtaining comfort from their presence and becoming distressed by their absence

Avoidant Attachment

The second pattern of attachment is referred to as **avoidant attachment.** Infants who fall into this pattern show conspicuous avoidance of contact or interaction with their caregiver. These infants readily separate from their mother and explore the toys during Episode 2. The entrance of the stranger during Episode 3 often is met with a smile. When their mother leaves, avoidant infants continue to play contentedly during her absence. During Episode 5, they react neutrally to their mother's return and quickly turn back to the toys. In contrast to secure infants, avoidant infants do not seek physical contact with their mother when she returns. When left alone during Episode 6, they become unhappy and fussy. This negative response disappears when the stranger enters. When their mother returns in the final episode, avoidant infants barely take notice of her.

On first glance, avoidant infants appear to be very independent. They do not respond to the presence or absence of their mother. They clearly dislike being left alone, but are as easily calmed by the stranger as they are by their mother. Does this mean that avoidant infants are indifferent to their attachment figures? After much consideration, Ainsworth and colleagues concluded that avoidant infants might be masking the insecure distress they feel and suppressing their impulses to seek comfort from their mother. Studies that examine the physiological responses of these infants show that they are aroused—their heart rates rise during the stressful segments of the Strange Situation (Sroufe & Waters, 1977). Their behaviors may suggest that these infants are unresponsive, but their internal responses reveal the discomfort they feel (Colin, 1996). Approximately 20 percent of infants are classified as exhibiting avoidant attachment.

Ambivalent Attachment

The third attachment pattern is called **ambivalent attachment.** During Episode 2, ambivalent infants are reluctant to leave their mother's side and explore the new room and toys very little. They are noticeably anxious when the stranger enters. When their mother first leaves, these infants cry angrily and reject the stranger's attempts to comfort them. When their mother returns, she is greeted with a cry and clear signals that they want to be picked up. When their mother picks them up, the infants wrap their arms around her but also push, kick, and cry. The second departure of the mother during Episode 6 elicits immediate and strong protests. When the stranger comes in, ambivalent infants scream and struggle against being held by her. When their mother is sent back in, ambivalent infants cry to her with their arms held up, indicating that they want to be picked up. But again, when their mother picks them up, these infants scream even louder, cling to her skirt, and thrash out at her. When picked up again, they continue to be upset and are stiff and uncomfortable in her arms. After a period of time, they begin to relax in her arms and eventually resume playing with the toys.

Ambivalent infants' behavior toward their mother is inconsistent. They appear to want to be comforted by their mother but also seem to receive little comfort once in her arms. These infants' responses are ambivalent—simultaneously desiring and resisting their mother's contact and comfort. About 12 percent of infants are classified as ambivalently attached.

Disorganized/Disoriented Attachment

A fourth pattern of attachment was later added to Ainsworth's original classification system (Main & Solomon, 1990). The **disorganized/disoriented attachment** classification was developed in response to the concern that a high percentage of infants who had been abused and/or neglected were classified as securely attached (Crittenden, 1988). Many researchers doubted that maltreated infants could have secure attachments, and closer examination of their behaviors in the Strange Situation revealed some abnormalities (van IJzendoorn, Schnuengel, & Bakermans, 1999).

Infants classified as disorganized/disoriented in their attachments have no coherent strategy for handling separations from and reunions with their mother. Consequently, their behavior is inconsistent, disorganized, and disoriented. For example, when Brooks was

avoidant attachment
pattern characterized by conspicuous avoidance of contact or interaction with the caregiver

ambivalent attachment
pattern characterized by inconsistent behavior toward a caregiver

disorganized/disoriented attachment pattern characterized by lack of a coherent strategy for handling separations from and reunions with the caregiver

Notice this mother's attentiveness to her child. In what other ways do caregivers demonstrate their sensitivity to children? How do children signal their needs to caregivers?

assessed in the Strange Situation, she first approached her mother after reunion and then froze and became dazed, avoiding her completely. When her mother returned, she began to cry. During the exploration phase (Episode 2), Brooks approached her mother with a toy but then became apprehensive toward her.

Why infants like Brooks, who have been abused and neglected, might react to the Strange Situation with this type of behavior is clear: They have the same need for contact and warmth from the caregiver that other children have, but their prior experiences of maltreatment have taught them that the caregiver may ignore or punish their bids for contact (Crittenden & Ainsworth, 1989). Thus, Brooks's inconsistent and disorganized responses reflect both her need for closeness and her expectations of her mother's aversive responses. About 15 percent of infants from normal middle-class families develop disorganized attachment behavior (van IJzendoorn et al., 1999), and these children are at risk for future adjustment problems (Moss, St. Laurent, & Parent, 1999).

CAREGIVER AND CHILD FACTORS AFFECTING ATTACHMENT

What determines the type of attachment formed? Researchers have found that two influences are particularly important: (1) the sensitivity of the caregiver and (2) characteristics of the child.

Caregiver Sensitivity

Based on her research, Ainsworth concluded that what matters the most to the development of attachment is the caregiver's sensitive responsiveness to the infant (De Wolff & van IJzendoorn, 1997). Sensitive responsiveness includes the ability to notice signals from the infant, interpret these signals accurately, and then respond appropriately. So it is not surprising that sensitive parenting is an important predictor of a child's development of a secure attachment (Braungart-Rieker, Garwood, Powers, & Wang, 2001; Atkinson et al., 2000). Securely attached infants come to believe that their signals will elicit the help they need and that their needs will be met (Isabella, 1993). Insensitive caregiving does not necessarily mean coldness or hostility; it refers to caregivers who fail to respond accurately and supportively to their infants' needs. For example, infants whose mothers are depressed are unlikely to have their needs met and will therefore be more likely to develop insecure attachments (Cicchetti, Rogosch, & Toth, 1998; Martins & Gaffan, 2000). Insensitive caregivers teach infants that their signals are ineffective (Susman-Stilman, Kalkose, Egeland, & Waldman, 1996).

Infant Characteristics

Ainsworth and her colleagues believe that the quality of attachment depends solely on the caregiver's behavior. Other researchers, however, believe that characteristics of the infant play a role in influencing the caregiver's behavior (Belsky, 1999). Remember that theories of temperament suggest that infants react very differently; for example, some infants are more responsive to their environments, and some are more resistant to being held and cuddled than others (Seifer et al., 1996). Such characteristics may shape the behaviors of their caregivers. Infants who like to be held, cuddled, and looked at foster caregiver sensitivity, whereas those who are difficult to soothe or easily overstimulated may discourage it (Bridges, Connell, & Belsky, 1988; Seifer & Schiller, 1995).

Additional evidence of the role that infant characteristics may play in the formation of attachment comes from studies of children with disabilities or who are at risk. For example, deaf or blind infants often are slow to develop secure attachments to their mothers (Meadow-Orlans & Spencer, 1999). Compared with nondisabled children, these infants may respond in ways that are less likely to promote sensitive caregiving. Blind infants, for instance, cannot use their gaze to attract their caregivers the way sighted infants can. Similarly, very-low-birthweight preterm infants are more likely to be insecurely attached because they are less socially responsive and more difficult to soothe than are full-term infants (Mangelsdorf et al., 1996). Although disabled and at-risk infants can form healthy attachments, their behaviors do not encourage caregiver responsiveness to the same extent as other infants' behaviors do.

THE ROLE OF CULTURE IN ATTACHMENT

Attachment theory was proposed as a universal theory of human development. However, because child-rearing goals, values, and behaviors vary from culture to culture, attachments may not have the same meaning in different cultures (Crittenden & Claussen, 2000). For example, infants who rarely experience separation from their mothers may react differently to the Strange Situation than do infants who experience separation more frequently. Japanese infants, who are encouraged to be dependent on their mothers, are more likely than US infants to cry and become passive when left alone. Correspondingly, Japanese mothers are more likely than US mothers to hold and maintain contact with their infants (Rothbaum, Weisz, Pott, Miyake, & Kazuo, 2000; Takahashi, 1990). Because of the increased stress experienced by Japanese infants in the Strange Situation, a higher percentage of Japanese infants than US infants are classified as ambivalently attached (32 percent and 16 percent, respectively).

Research has confirmed different patterns of attachment in infants from different cultures (Miyake, Chen, & Campos, 1985). Figure 6.2 shows how the percentages of infants

IGURE 6.2

Cultural Differences in Patterns of Attachment in Children

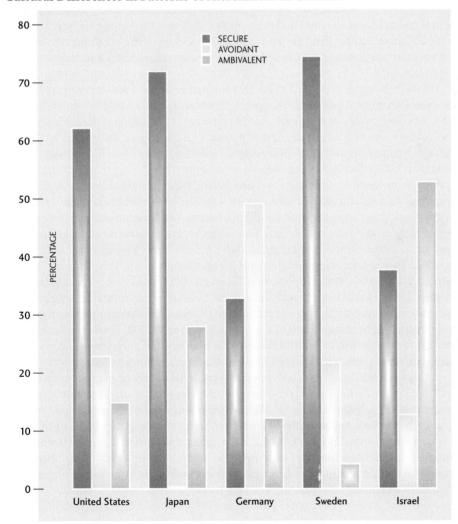

SOURCE: Miyake, Chen, and Campos, 1985.

Notice how the patterns of attachment vary from one culture to the next. What child-rearing and cultural factors contribute to these differences?

classified as secure, avoidant, and ambivalent vary from one culture to the next. In Germany, for example, where parents press infants to behave independently and rebuff their bids for contact, a sizable percentage of children are classified as avoidant. In contrast, in Japan, where mothers value contact and dependence, almost no children are classified as avoidant. In Israel, where children have only infrequent contact with unfamiliar people, almost half of the infants are classified as ambivalent. Compare this to the patterns of attachment found in Sweden, where children are exposed to large numbers of unfamiliar people.

American cultural diversity also leads to differences in attachment behaviors and patterns. European-American mothers place a great deal of emphasis on self-confidence and self-reliance. These values reflect the individualism of the traditional European-American culture. In contrast, Puerto Rican mothers place more emphasis on respect, obedience, and remaining connected with others (Harwood, Miller, & Irizarry, 1995). As a result, Puerto Rican infants are more likely to be classified as ambivalently attached than are European-American infants.

CONSEQUENCES OF ATTACHMENT

How much does the nature of early attachment matter to children's later development? The answer to this question is the subject of debate. Kohlberg and Kramer (1969) questioned the impact of early relationships on later development unless these relationships are extreme and traumatic. They maintained that the quality of early relationships is greatly transformed by the cognitive changes that take place later in life and it is therefore difficult to imagine how an infant's attachment early in life can have a strong effect on his or her development later in life.

Other researchers, however, believe that the nature of early attachment plays an important role in influencing later development (Thompson, 1998). Children who have secure attachments see themselves as lovable and feel their needs will be met. They act in ways that are consistent with this benevolent view of the world (Belsky, Spritz, & Crnic, 1996). In contrast, children with insecure attachments tend to develop a dramatically different internal working model of themselves and their environments. They believe that the world is unsupportive, inconsistent, and rejecting. These beliefs, feelings, and behaviors link their past experiences and attachments with the present (Cassidy, Kirsh, Scolton, & Parke, 1996).

Some support has been found for a link between early attachment and later development. For example, some studies have found that securely attached children have better social skills, tolerate frustration more successfully, and express a wider range of emotions than children who are not securely attached (Arend, Gove, & Sroufe, 1979; Bohlin, Hagekull, & Rydell, 2000; Sroufe, 1996). Children with secure attachments as infants have been found to approach their environments with interest and pleasure, are comfortable in seeking help from others, follow directions easily, and seldom cry, fuss, or become angry when encountering frustrating circumstances (Elicker, Englund, & Sroufe, 1992). Securely attached children also tend to remember positive events better than negative ones, whereas the reverse is true for insecurely attached children (Belsky et al., 1996).

Although these studies appear to provide support for the effects of attachment on later development, the findings are inconsistent and relatively weak when the scientific evidence is examined as a whole (Belsky & Cassidy, 1994). In some cases, researchers have failed to replicate the findings; and when the findings have been replicated, the effects have tended to be small (Booth, Rose-Krasnor, & Rubin, 1991; Easterbrooks & Goldberg, 1990; Frankel & Bates, 1992). The inconsistency of these findings suggests that, although the nature of early attachment may be an important factor in children's lives, other factors also influence later adjustment and functioning (Thompson, 1999).

ATTACHMENT TO FATHERS

In the United States, fathers spend considerably less time interacting with their infants than do mothers (Bailey, 1994), and this difference has been found across a wide range

What roles do fathers take in caregiving and how do these roles differ from the ones mothers often take? Do differences in roles influence infants' tendencies to become attached to their fathers?

of culturally diverse populations (Fracasso, Lamb, Schoelmerich, & Leyendecker, 1997). There are, however, large individual differences among fathers, with some being very involved in caregiving and others almost completely disengaged (Jain, Belsky, & Crnic, 1996). As children get older, father involvement increases (Coltrane, 1995; Cooksey & Fondell, 1996).

Not only do fathers and mothers spend different amounts of time with their infants, but they also interact differently. Fathers typically interact as playmates, rather than as protectors, comforters, or care providers (Bornstein & Tamis-LeMonda, 1997). When infants need caring for, many fathers let mothers take over (Parke, 1995). But despite these differences in the nature of the interactions of US mothers and fathers with their young children, infants do develop secure attachments with fathers (Belsky, 1996).

Research comparing infants' responses to mothers and fathers in the Strange Situation suggests that infants cry when both mothers and fathers leave the room, but do not cry when strangers leave the room. When reunited with either parent, most infants show relief and comfort. Exploration of the room generally is greater when either mothers or fathers are present than when they are gone (Colin, 1996). Although infants' reactions tend to be less intense with their fathers, they nonetheless treat fathers as attachment figures who serve as secure bases (Doherty, 1997; Parke, 1995). When given the opportunity, fathers have as much capacity as mothers do to form intimate ties with their infants, to be sensitive to their needs, and to be competent in nurturing them (Beitel & Parke, 1998).

Do infants who are securely attached to their mother also develop a secure attachment to their father? According to a meta-analysis of studies that examined the relationship between infant-mother and infant-father attachment, there is some consistency (Fox, Kimmerly, & Schafer, 1991). Infants who are securely attached to one parent generally are securely attached to the other parent, and infants who are insecurely attached to one parent are insecurely attached to the other. Thus, mothers and fathers generally provide caregiving behaviors that mutually support the development of attachment. This consistency also suggests that one sensitive parent may buffer the infant from deficiencies in the other parent's behavior, thereby promoting secure attachments to both parents (Colin, 1996).

HOW DOES DAY CARE INFLUENCE INFANTS' AND TODDLERS' DEVELOPMENT?

In the United States, there are almost 20 million children under the age of 6, and the parents of about 12 million of these children work outside the home (US Census Bureau, 2001b). This situation is radically different from that in the 1950s, when only 12 percent of married women with preschool children worked outside the home. Until 1975, the Census Bureau did not even collect labor force data on mothers with infants or toddlers because it was assumed that few mothers worked (National Issues Forum, 1989). Now, about 60 percent do so, largely for economic reasons. The increase in the number of working mothers with children less than 3 years of age is especially dramatic. More than half of all mothers with children under age 1 are in the work force, either full or part time (US Department of Labor, 2001a). The rapid entry of women into the labor force over the past few decades has altered the way very young children are raised, and the demands for—and concerns about—day care have soared.

PATTERNS OF DAY CARE USE

Although it is popularly believed that most infants and toddlers with working mothers are cared for in group day care centers, the fact is that the majority are cared for in homes by relatives, such as fathers, mothers, siblings, grandparents, uncles, aunts, or cousins (Ehrle, Adams, & Tout, 2001; US Department of Commerce, 1996). As Figure 6.3 indicates, children under 3 are more likely to be cared for by relatives than are older children. Young children are more likely to be cared for by relatives, particularly the father, if the mother works part

FIGURE 6.3

Day Care Arrangements for Children of Employed Mothers, by Children's Age

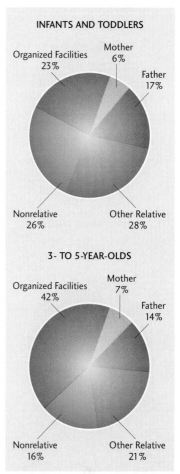

INFANTS AND TODDLERS

Organized Facilities 23%
Mother 6%
Father 17%
Nonrelative 26%
Other Relative 28%

3- TO 5-YEAR-OLDS

Organized Facilities 42%
Mother 7%
Father 14%
Nonrelative 16%
Other Relative 21%

NOTE: Care by mothers includes that of mothers working at home and away from home. Other relatives include siblings, grandparents, uncles, aunts, and cousins.

SOURCE: US Department of Commerce, 1996.

Compare the figures for infants and toddlers to those for preschool children. Notice especially the increase in the percentage of older children who receive care from someone other than a relative. What factors contribute to these differences?

FIGURE 6.4

Day Care Arrangements, by Family Structure

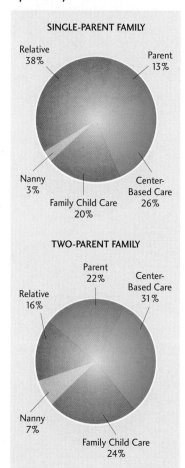

SINGLE-PARENT FAMILY

Relative 38%
Parent 13%
Nanny 3%
Family Child Care 20%
Center-Based Care 26%

TWO-PARENT FAMILY

Parent 22%
Center-Based Care 31%
Relative 16%
Nanny 7%
Family Child Care 24%

SOURCE: Ehrle, Adams, and Tout, 2001.

What differences do you see when you compare the arrangements made by single-parent and two-parent families? What aspects of family structure may account for these differences?

time rather than full time. Mothers who work full time are more likely to rely on organized day care centers or nonrelatives to care for their children (US Department of Commerce, 1996). As shown in Figure 6.4, day care arrangements for infants and toddlers vary by whether or not there are two parents in the household. Children in single-parent families are more likely to be taken care of by relatives, whereas children in two-parent families are more likely to receive care from a parent or a nanny or in family or center-based care facilities.

Child care arrangements for infants and toddlers also differ for different ethnic groups. As depicted in Figure 6.5, African American children are most likely to be cared for in center-based programs, whereas Hispanic children are likely to be cared for by family members (either parents or relatives). Caucasian children are more likely than either minority group to be cared for by nannies. These differences reflect differences in income, access to child care arrangements, and the values and standards held by each ethnic group.

With the exception of government-sponsored programs for children from poor families, child care (particularly infant care) in the United States is privately owned and operated (Lamb, Sternberg, & Ketterlinus, 1992). Nationwide regulations have never been mandated by the federal government, and existing state and local regulations generally establish only minimal levels to ensure that children are protected from harm (Phillips, Lande, &

FIGURE 6.5

Day Care Arrangements, by Ethnicity

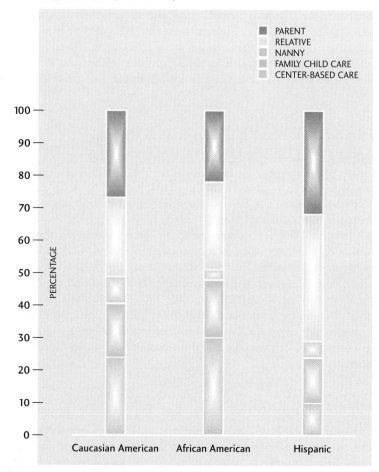

- PARENT
- RELATIVE
- NANNY
- FAMILY CHILD CARE
- CENTER-BASED CARE

PERCENTAGE

Caucasian American   African American   Hispanic

SOURCE: Ehrle, Adams, and Tout, 2001.

What are the most noticeable differences in the graphs? How might ethnic differences contribute to differences in day care use?

Goldberg, 1990; Scarr, 1998). According to some estimates (Whitebook, Howes, & Phillips, 1989), 67 percent of child care centers are "barely adequate" in quality, and about 60 percent lack positive caregiving (NICHD, 2000a). Infants from high-income families, as well as those from low-income families that receive subsidies, are more likely to receive high-quality day care than are infants from middle-income families (NICHD, 1997; Vandell & Wolfe, 2000).

EFFECTS OF DAY CARE

With so many infants and toddlers spending so much time away from their parents, particularly their mothers, how might children's development in general and their attachments in particular be affected? As you might expect, this question is not easily answered.

Attempts to examine the effects of early child care have led to contradictory conclusions. The results from several studies show that day care may benefit low-income children and have benign, sometimes even beneficial, effects on middle-class children (Clarke-Stewart, Allhusen, & Clements, 1995; Hausfather, Toharia, LaRoche, & Engelsmann, 1997). Day care generally enhances the intellectual performance of low-income children, increases their curiosity and concentration, and fosters independence, social competence, and cooperativeness (Lamb et al., 1992; NICHD, 1996; Phillips, McCartney, & Scarr, 1987). But the results from other studies have not been as positive. For example, some studies report that day care increases children's aggression and decreases their compliance (Vandell & Corasaniti, 1990).

Beginning in the late 1980s, the accumulation of evidence regarding the impact of infant day care on mother-infant attachment led some researchers to conclude that day care has adverse effects on attachment. Specifically, Belsky (1988, 1990) concluded that infants may be at risk for insecure attachments if they spend more than 20 hours per week in nonmaternal care during their first year of life. When observed in the Strange Situation, infants with early extended day care experiences were more likely to avoid and ignore their mothers.

Belsky's conclusions have drawn intense criticism (Clarke-Stewart, 1992). One criticism is that Belsky's conclusions are too strong: the majority of infants with early extended day care experiences are securely attached to their mothers (Thompson, 1991). Other researchers note that it is not day care itself that leads to insecure attachments but rather the comparatively greater stress that parents who rely on early extended infant care may be experiencing. Families under stress report that they spend less time researching day care options, need longer hours of day care for their infants, and accept poorer quality day care (Lamb, 1998; Phillips & Howes, 1987).

More young children than ever before are being cared for by someone other than their parents. What social changes contribute to this increase in nonparental care? How do you feel about this? What factors should parents consider when looking for high-quality care for their young children?

THE PRACTICAL IMPACT: NURTURING CHILDREN

What Day Care Teachers Earn

As you have learned, high-quality child care is related to positive outcomes for many children. But what factors contribute to high-quality child care? In several studies (Howes, Phillips, & Whitebook, 1992; Phillipsen, Burchinal, Howes, & Cryer, 1997; Scarr, Eisenberg, & Deater-Deckard, 1994), caregiver wages often were the single best predictor of day care quality. But what do we as a society pay for this extremely important job of caring for our youngest members? The answer is not very encouraging.

In 1999, child care teachers averaged $8.57 per hour. Child care assistants averaged even less—only $7.28 per hour (US Department of Labor, 2001b). Averaged across a 35-hour workweek for fifty weeks, the salaries for those who care for young children were about $15,000 and $12,700 (day care teachers and assistants, respectively). As you can see in the table, these wages were lower than those for most other jobs (US Department of Labor, 2001b). In fact, they were some of the lowest wages listed and were about half of what the average US worker earned.

Given these wages, it is no wonder that turnover rates for day care

JOB	AVERAGE FULL-TIME HOURLY WAGE
National US	
Average Wage	$15.36
Receptionist	$10.07
Hairdresser	$9.83
Janitor	$9.77
Taxi Driver	$8.85
Day Care Teacher	**$8.57**
Fast Food	
Service Worker	$7.44
Day Care Assistant	**$7.28**
Baggage Porter	$6.79

workers are so high. In 1997, 27 percent of teachers and 39 percent of assistants left their jobs (Whitebook, Howes, & Phillips, 1998). Not surprisingly, those who left their jobs tended to be the ones who were making less money (Vandell & Wolfe, 2000). Moreover, the low wages make it difficult to hire well-educated and highly trained day care staff.

If the wages we pay reflect the value we place on a particular job, what does the table above say about the value we place on providing out-of-home care for our youngest children? Because caring for young children is a critically important job, we need to be able to attract talented and committed people to this profession. Of course, raising day care workers' salaries would mean that the cost of day care would increase. But until we raise the wages and working conditions of those who care for our youngest children, raising the overall quality of day care may be a difficult task.

Howes (1990) found that the quality of care was a better predictor of later functioning than was the age at which children entered day care. Secure relationships with day care teachers have been found to enhance children's play, competence, and social relationships (Howes, Hamilton, & Matheson, 1994). A more recent large-scale study, involving 1300 families in ten different states over five years, found that early child care itself did not harm mother-infant attachment (NICHD, 1996). Additionally, sensitive and responsive mothering is more strongly predictive of positive outcomes for young children in day care than are child care factors (NICHD, 1998). Thus, what transpires in a young child's family appears to be more important than the day care itself in determining how children are affected by day care.

This debate highlights the need for affordable, high-quality day care (Scarr, 1998). Even Belsky (1990) notes that affordable, high-quality day care is not as available as it needs to be and that it is inappropriate to conclude that only mothers can care for their infants or that day care is bad for infants. High-quality day care clearly has positive effects on children's intellectual and verbal development, especially when children come from impoverished and unstimulating environments. Poor-quality day care may have negative effects (Burchinal & Caskie, 2001; Lamb, 1998; NICHD, 2000b). Evidence from countries like Sweden, where high-quality infant day care is readily available, also shows that infants with high-quality day care experience have more positive developmental outcomes (such as greater social skills and intellectual competence) than infants without such experience (Broberg, Hwang, Lamb, & Ketterlinus, 1989; Field, 1991). In the United States, where most child care is a for-profit enterprise, parental decisions regarding day care are more often determined by cost and availability than by quality (Griffin & Fein, 1996).

Given the importance of high-quality care, it is critical that parents be able to judge the quality of day care programs. The following guidelines, based on the research (Child Care Action Campaign, 1996; NAEYC, 1995), can be used to judge a program's quality:

◆ **Safety.** Child care settings should be safe. Look for fences around the outdoor playground and well-constructed play equipment. Dangerous and toxic substances should be locked out of the children's reach. Electrical outlets and radiators should be covered. The child care workers should wash their hands before feeding, handling food, diapering, and washing surfaces. A system for identifying the parent or guardian responsible for picking up the child should be well established and adhered to.

◆ **Adult/child ratios and group size.** The more adults present, the more individual attention children receive. Younger children need more adults present than do older children. The total size of the group also is important. There should be no more than eight in a group for infants and no more than twenty in a group for 5-year-olds. For each adult, there should be no more than the following number of children:

> 3–4 infants or toddlers
> 4–6 2-year-olds
> 7–8 3-year-olds
> 8–9 4-year-olds
> 8–10 5-year-olds

◆ **Staff training and program.** Licensing and training requirements vary from state to state. Although compliance does not guarantee quality, the program should be in compliance with state requirements. Some professional organizations (such as the National Association for the Education of Young Children) accredit programs that meet high standards of quality. Ask for evidence of such accreditation. Qualified staff should have some direct education in early childhood education or child development.

◆ **Curriculum.** The materials provided to children should be appropriate for their age and level of development. For infants and toddlers, there should be soft, washable, colorful toys that can be looked at or sucked. There should be no small parts that could come off and be swallowed. Preschoolers should have access to books as well as toys, blocks, and equipment that emphasizes gross motor development.

These are just a few of the factors parents need to consider when determining the quality of a day care program. Finding high-quality day care takes time and effort. Parents should look at many programs and talk to relatives, friends, neighbors, and parents familiar with the programs. They should visit programs at various times; if a program discourages such visits, they probably should look elsewhere. It is essential for parents to remember that this critical decision requires considerable attention and thought.

CULTURE AND DAY CARE

Variations in caregiving and day care for infants and children in different countries reflect different political, cultural, and social values (Rosenthal, 1999). In the People's Republic of China, many day care policies reflect the collectivist values mandated by the central government as well as traditional values emphasizing obedience and respect. Because of China's overpopulation problems and one-child policy, most contemporary families are made up of six adults (four grandparents and two parents) and one child. The child therefore becomes the center of adult attention and care. To cultivate the correct socialistic spirit, day care is designed to train children in developing self-control, good habits, and obedience (Lee, 1992). By 2 or 3 years of age, children are learning how to satisfy others and behave according to formal and rigid standards, which mandate behaviors rarely expected of toddlers from Western cultures (such as sharing).

Very different child care conditions exist for children and families in Brazil, where three-quarters of the people live in impoverished urban areas. Intense urbanization has not been matched by corresponding increases in job, educational, health, or housing opportunities.

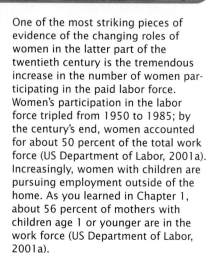

THE SOCIAL IMPACT: DEBATING THE ISSUE

How Does Mom's Working Affect Children's Development?

One of the most striking pieces of evidence of the changing roles of women in the latter part of the twentieth century is the tremendous increase in the number of women participating in the paid labor force. Women's participation in the labor force tripled from 1950 to 1985; by the century's end, women accounted for about 50 percent of the total work force (US Department of Labor, 2001a). Increasingly, women with children are pursuing employment outside of the home. As you learned in Chapter 1, about 56 percent of mothers with children age 1 or younger are in the work force (US Department of Labor, 2001a).

But what impact does mothers' employment have on their young children? A large body of research has focused on comparing children whose mothers are employed with those whose mothers are at home full time. This research generally has found no consistent differences in cognitive, social, or emotional development between these two groups of children (Hoffman & Youngblade, 1999).

Although some researchers have raised concerns about the impact of maternal employment on infants' and toddlers' attachment (Belsky, 1990), this concern has been debated and challenged (Clarke-Stewart, 1989). In fact, there is some evidence that maternal employment may be beneficial for certain groups of children. For example, daughters of employed women have been found to have higher academic achievement, to have greater independence, and to be more assertive than those of unemployed women (Aube, Fleury, & Smetana, 2000). Studies of children from low-income households have consistently found that maternal employment is associated with better socioemotional and cognitive functioning, for both boys and girls (Hoffman & Youngblade, 1999).

In general, these findings suggest that, in itself, maternal employment is not a cause for alarm and does not harm young children's physical or psychological well-being. One set of factors that seems to be particularly important concerns the quality of women's experiences on the job.

Although women have made important strides in the work force, in many ways the work of women tends to be characterized by less status, less pay, and less power than the work of men, even for women with higher levels of education. Moreover, women are more likely to be victims of sexual harassment and discrimination than are men (Aube et al., 2000). Social and economic policies that promote women's greater job equity and satisfaction likely will facilitate positive outcomes associated with maternal employment. For example, in 1993, the Family and Medical Leave Act was passed. This act provides unpaid leave for a limited period of time at key moments in a family's life—such as when a baby is born or a family member becomes ill. Such policies enhance women's (and men's) abilities to meet the needs of their family without prejudice to their job. Greater satisfaction with their ability to meet the demands of home and work is likely to result, improving the chances of positive outcomes for children and families (Aube et al., 2000).

Often, small children are confined in cramped spaces with little food, while adults and older siblings work long hours. Thus, there is great need for *creches* (day care), but only about 23 percent of preschool-aged children attend such programs. For the very young, such care is even less available; only about 10 percent of infants and toddlers attend *creches* (Campos, 1992). As you might imagine, in most of the *creches,* particularly those serving low-income families, children are placed in large groups supervised by relatively untrained staff. Although some improvements have been made, the unfavorable economic conditions and overcrowding lead to rigid routines in the *creches,* with little tolerance for child initiative and autonomy (Goncalves, 1990).

In the Kenyan community of Morongo, where infant mortality is very high, infants and toddlers are never left alone. An infant is carried by his or her mother until about 6 months of age, at which time the child is taken care of by others in the family or community. This "dense caretaking environment" in early childhood reflects the Morongon child care strategy, which seeks to maximize survival in a high-mortality context during the most vulnerable period of the child's life (LeVine et al., 1994). The differences among child care in China, Brazil, and Kenya demonstrate how child care and its impact on children are influenced by the broader cultural, social, political, economic, and physical environments in which children and families find themselves (Morelli & Verhoef, 1999).

WHY ARE CHILDREN ABUSED AND NEGLECTED?

Katy was shaken so hard as a baby that her brain was smashed inside her skull. The damaged areas eventually had to be cut out, leaving her with half a brain. . . . A stroke at age 4 left her

partially paralyzed. Tests revealed problems with Katy's pituitary gland and thyroid. . . . She goes to the hospital twice a week for 2 hours of occupational and speech therapy. Her sister, Micki, escaped the wrath of their angry father . . . while Micki was getting taller and slimmer, Katy was squat. Micki stands as testimony to what Katy's life might have been.
—*Adapted from K. Bland* (1997)

Katy's story illustrates the horror and tragedy of the abuse and neglect of a child. The media have flooded us with stories of infants and children who have been abandoned, beaten, or killed by their caregivers; deprived of essential emotional and physical comfort; or sexually molested and abused. Such reports have increased the public's awareness of the incidence and severity of child abuse. In 1976, only 10 percent of Americans surveyed considered child abuse to be a problem; less than 20 years later, that figure had risen to over 90 percent (Finkelman, 1995). Although the stories attract tremendous attention and outrage, they fail to reveal the complex interplay of factors that make up the causes and consequences of child abuse and neglect.

DEFINITIONS OF CHILD ABUSE AND NEGLECT

Four categories of child maltreatment generally are distinguished: (1) **physical abuse,** in which caregivers cause death, serious physical harm, or imminent risk of serious harm to children; (2) **sexual abuse,** in which caregivers engage in sexual activity with children; (3) **neglect,** in which children's physical or emotional well-being is jeopardized by the failure to provide shelter, clothing, or protection; and (4) **psychological maltreatment,** in which caregivers emotionally abuse children by threatening them or conveying that they are worthless, unloved, or unwanted (Berliner & Elliot, 1996; Kolko, 1996; Lutzker, 2000). According to the scientific evidence, psychological maltreatment often is the strongest predictor of harmful developmental outcomes for a child (Hart, Brassard, & Karlson, 1996).

Caregivers who maltreat children often abuse or neglect them in more than one way (Belsky, 1993). In one study (Kaufman & Cicchetti, 1995), not one of the seventy physically abused children had experienced physical abuse alone. Each type of maltreatment has its own rates of occurrence, factors that influence it, and potential consequences. Because researchers and therapists tend to focus on one type of abuse or another, we know little about the extent to which different types of child abuse and neglect share common factors or respond to different types of treatment (Widom, 2001).

INCIDENCE OF CHILD ABUSE AND NEGLECT

The findings of the Third National Incidence Study of Child Abuse and Neglect (Sedlak & Broadhurst, 1996) indicated a sharp increase in the scope of the child maltreatment problem. Using a broad definition of maltreatment, this study estimated that the total number of US children who were reported as abused or neglected in 1994 was 2,815,600. By 1999, over 3 million children were reported abused or neglected (National Clearinghouse on Child Abuse and Neglect, 1999). This total reflected a 98 percent increase since 1986. The incidences for the various categories of abuse had increased as follows:

> ✦ The number of sexually abused children had risen from 133,600 to 300,200 (a 125 percent increase).
> ✦ The number of neglected children had increased from 917,200 to 1,961,300 (a 114 percent increase).
> ✦ The number of physically abused children had increased from 311,500 to 614,100 (a 92 percent increase).

Although rates of child victimization have decreased somewhat since the mid-1990s, the rates are still considerably higher than they were a quarter of a century ago (National Child Abuse and Neglect Data System, 2001). Sadly, not all cases of alleged child abuse and neglect are investigated: In only 28 percent of the cases where children were harmed by abuse and neglect did an investigation take place.

physical abuse abuse that causes death, serious physical harm, or imminent risk of serious harm

sexual abuse abuse that involves engaging in sexual activity

neglect failure to provide shelter, clothing, or protection for a child

psychological maltreatment emotional abuse caused by threatening harm or conveying to an individual that she or he is worthless, unloved, or unwanted

CHARACTERISTICS OF VICTIMS OF CHILD ABUSE AND NEGLECT

Certain children face greater risk of experiencing abuse than others. Of course these children are not responsible for their abusive conditions; however, they possess characteristics known to increase the chance that abuse will occur. Following are some findings about how child and family characteristics are related to child abuse and neglect (Goodman, Emery, & Haugaard, 1998; Kapitanoff, Lutzker, & Bigelow, 2000; Widom, 2001; Wiese & Daro, 1996):

✦ **Gender.**   Girls are sexually abused more often than boys. This gender difference in the incidence of sexual abuse leads to higher rates of abuse in general for girls.

✦ **Age.**   Young children are more at risk for maltreatment than older children. The lower rates as children get older reflect the reality that older children have more opportunities to escape, defend themselves, or retaliate.

✦ **Temperament.**   Children with difficult temperamental qualities (such as negative moods or intense crying) may tax parental tolerance, increasing the risk of abuse.

✦ **Income.**   Children living in families that earn less than $15,000 annually are 25 times more likely to experience some form of maltreatment than children in families earning $30,000 or more. (This statistic may be due to reporting bias.)

✦ **Ethnicity.**   Rates of child abuse and neglect vary by ethnicity. As depicted in Figure 6.6, Asian American children have the lowest rates and American Indian and African American children have the highest rates; rates for Caucasian and Hispanic children fall in between. These variations probably are due to differences in income and/or cultural beliefs and behaviors.

✦ **Family size.**   Children from large families are more likely to be abused and neglected than children from small families.

✦ **Disabilities.**   Children with disabilities are 4 to 10 times more likely to experience abuse or neglect than their nondisabled peers. Similarly, children with medical or health problems (such as birth complications, prematurity, or asthma) are more likely to experience abuse or neglect.

These findings tell us that some children are more at risk than others for maltreatment, often because they place more stress or demands on parents. Although they may not do so evenly, child abuse and neglect cross all social class, racial, religious, and educational boundaries (Sidebotham, 2000; Wolfner & Gelles, 1993).

CHARACTERISTICS OF CHILD ABUSERS

The image most people have of a child abuser is a person with a serious psychological disturbance, but the research evidence does not support this conclusion. In fact, less than 10 percent of child abusers evidence extremely disturbed symptoms (Murphy & Smith, 1996). What, then, are the characteristics of those who commit child abuse and neglect? From the existing research (Kolko, 1996; Lutzker, 1998; Reder & Duncan, 2000; Sedlak & Broadhurst, 1996), the following conclusions can be drawn:

✦ Parents are more likely than any other group to abuse children (see Figure 6.7). Although the popular press highlights cases where nonparental caregivers and foster parents perpetrate abuse, they are the adults least likely to do so.

FIGURE 6.6

Rates of Child Abuse Victimization, by Ethnicity

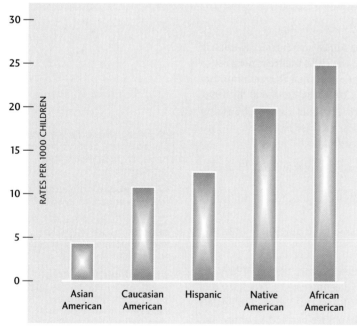

SOURCE: US Department of Health and Human Services, 2001.

◆ Because mothers carry the major responsibility for child care, they tend to abuse more often than fathers, as indicated in Figure 6.7 (although fathers are more often involved in sexual abuse). However, the severity of the injury or impairment that a child experiences as a result of maltreatment is not related to the sex of the perpetrator.

◆ Probably because children most often live with their biological parents, biological parents are responsible for the majority of the cases of child abuse and neglect. Sixty-two percent of abuse cases and 91 percent of neglect cases are perpetrated by biological parents.

◆ Single parents have a particularly high rate of committing abuse and neglect.

◆ Children are more likely to be abused by younger than by older caretakers.

◆ Adults who commit child abuse tend to be isolated, lack family and peer support networks, and not be involved in community activities.

◆ Abusive adults have limited knowledge of caregiving, have unrealistic expectations for children's behavior, find child rearing difficult, have a low tolerance for infant behaviors (such as crying), and tend to use harsh disciplinary practices.

Perpetrators of Child Abuse

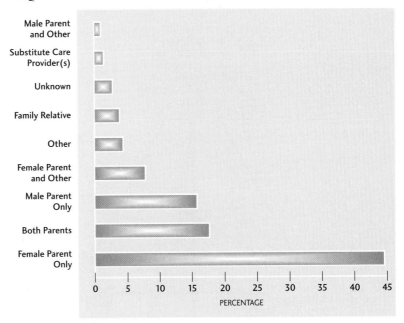

SOURCE: US Department of Health and Human Services, 1999.

There is a dramatic difference between the rates at which child abuse is perpetrated by parents—especially mothers—and all others. What impact might such findings have for intervention and prevention programs?

◆ Although committing child abuse is not consistently associated with alcohol use, it is associated with drug use. The rate of child maltreatment is about 46 percent higher for drug users than for those who do not use drugs.

One of the most consistently reported findings regarding characteristics of child abusers is that they are likely to have experienced abuse themselves when they were children. Approximately 30 percent of abused children grow up to be abusive, compared with 4 percent of the general population (Gelles, 1987; Maxfield & Widom, 1996). Additionally, child abuse often occurs in a general context of family violence. When a child is abused, it is likely that a spouse is also abused (Appel & Holden, 1998; McCloskey, Figueredo, & Koss, 1995). Domestic violence appears to promote negative views of children and of being a parent, increasing the risk of child abuse (McGuigan, Vuchinich, & Pratt, 2000). Child abuse thus frequently reflects an atmosphere of violent and abusive family relationships.

Together, these findings present a complex picture of the person who commits child abuse and neglect. Although they suggest that some individuals are more at risk than others for committing child abuse, the potential for acting abusively is present in varying degrees in many individuals (Reder & Duncan, 2000; Wolfner & Gelles, 1993). No single profile fits all child abusers.

To address the complex causes of child abuse, Belsky (1980, 1993) developed an ecological model showing different pathways leading to child maltreatment (see Figure 6.8 on page 204). According to Belsky, child maltreatment is most likely to occur when the stressors outweigh the supportive conditions in a person's environment. These stressors and supports take many forms and include a variety of parent factors (personality, attitudes), child factors (temperament, age, health condition), family and community factors (stress, family structure, social support), cultural norms (attitudes toward parenting and toward violence), historical developments (children's rights), and evolutionary factors (fitness).

IGURE 6.8

Ecological Model of Child Abuse and Neglect

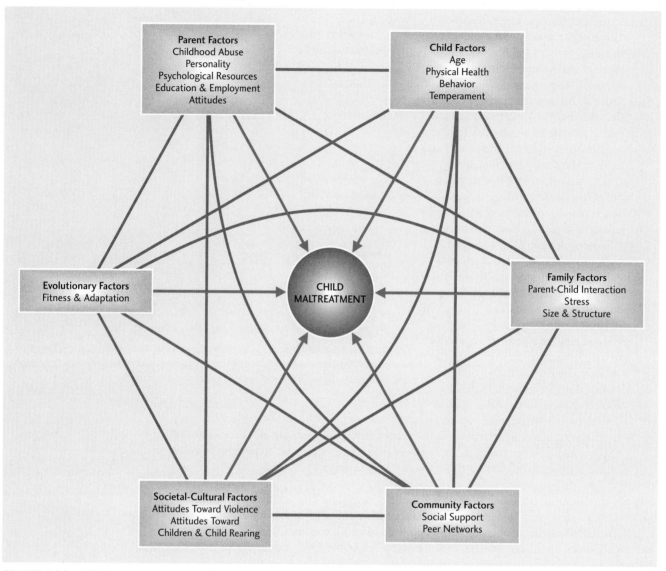

SOURCE: Belsky, 1993.

This model illustrates how different contextual factors might interact to increase children's risk for abuse and neglect. How does this model help us understand the dynamics of child maltreatment? How might this model be used to design effective intervention and prevention programs?

As an illustration of the broad array of factors that influence child abuse and neglect, consider the case of Amos. Amos was born to parents who were fundamentalist in their religious beliefs and who approached parenting with a traditional and physical style of parenting (Melzak, 1992). At the time of Amos's birth, his mother was preoccupied with her new relationship with Amos's father and with a custody battle she was having over her eldest son from a prior marriage. Amos's mother was an insecure, intelligent, anxious woman, and his father was a gentle, quiet man who often was humiliated by his wife. Amos was described as an active, difficult-to-manage child who did not sleep regularly and did not live up to his elder brother's model of maturity, obedience, and self-control. Beginning sometime after his first birthday, Amos was beaten at home by both parents and sometimes by his grandparents. When Amos began preschool, he often got in trouble and was severely beaten with a belt by his parents for doing so. The parents reported that this was how they were punished when they were children.

The case of Amos reveals the complex factors that contribute to abuse. Amos's parents came from a background where physical punishment and physical control of children were acceptable. The facts that Amos also was beaten by his grandparents and that intense physical punishment was used by the grandparents on Amos's parents when they were children reflect an intergenerational history of abuse. Additionally, because of the stress associated with the new marriage and the custody battle, Amos's parents had limited abilities to cope with the stress of child rearing. Faced with a sensitive, impulsive, and out-of-control little boy, Amos's parents were overwhelmed.

Amos's case supports Belsky's (1993) proposal that child abuse and neglect are multiply determined by the interaction of processes associated with various individual, familial, cultural, and historical factors. There is no one cause of child maltreatment, and no single determining factor or profile of a child abuser or a victim has emerged from the literature. The most consistent conclusion seems to be that child abuse, its causes, and its consequences result from the transaction of risk and protective factors that exist at multiple levels (Korbin, Coulton, Chard, Platt-Houston, & Su, 1998; Stockhammer, Salzinger, Feldman, & Mojica, 2001). The exact conditions that contribute to child abuse, however, vary from family to family, from situation to situation, and from culture to culture.

EFFECTS OF CHILD ABUSE AND NEGLECT

In the United States in 1999, 1082 children died from maltreatment, almost 3 children every day, and the rate is up 27 percent since 1985 (US Department of Health and Human Services, 2001; Wiese & Daro, 1996). Younger children are more at risk of loss of life from maltreatment than are older children—86 percent of the fatalities from maltreatment occurred in children under 5 years of age, and 43 percent occurred in children under 1 year of age. As Katy's story at the beginning of this section reveals, even if young children survive maltreatment, it can have irreparable effects on their development (Emery & Laumann-Billings, 1998).

Even when there is no evidence of neurological or physical impairment, the consequences of child abuse can be devastating. Abused and neglected children sometimes show delayed intellectual development, particularly in the area of verbal intelligence (Augoustinos, 1987); poor school performance (Kendall-Tackett & Eckenrode, 1997; Leiter & Johnsen, 1997); and deficits in attention and information processing (Dodge, Bates, & Pettit, 1990).

Child abuse and neglect also have strong effects on children's psychological and social development, and these consequences are extremely powerful in the early stages of development (Lutzker, 2000; National Research Council, 1993). Early child abuse and neglect may harm the development of children's attachments, sense of security, self-esteem, and emotional stability (Trickett & McBride-Chang, 1995). Children who have been abused or neglected also may have negative mental health outcomes, such as depression, anxiety disorders, and aggressiveness (Cuffe & Shugart, 2001; McCloskey et al., 1995). A consistent finding is that sexually abused young children exhibit inappropriate sexual behavior (Trickett & McBride-Chang, 1995).

PREVENTING CHILD ABUSE AND NEGLECT

As the number of victims increases, there is a growing awareness of the need to prevent child abuse and neglect. Unfortunately, most efforts are devoted to helping children only after a major incident of maltreatment has been identified (Wolfe, 1993). Yet, because of the high financial and human costs associated with child maltreatment, preventing it is critical (Daro, 2000).

Prevention is commonly categorized as primary, secondary, or tertiary. **Primary prevention** is directed at the population as a whole. Educational programs that sensitize society to basic issues of maltreatment or that provide essential parenting skills to all individuals before they become parents are examples of primary prevention programs (Daro, 1996, 2000). **Secondary prevention** targets a specific segment of the population thought to be at high risk for child maltreatment. Generally, these programs are designed to provide support for poor single mothers and fathers, helping them cope with the demands of child rearing. **Tertiary prevention** is directed at situations in which child maltreatment already

primary prevention efforts targeted at the population as a whole, to sensitize people to basic issues or to provide particular skills

secondary prevention efforts targeted at a specific segment of the population thought to be at high risk

tertiary prevention efforts directed at preventing or decreasing the reoccurrence of an event that has already occurred

has occurred. The goal is to prevent or decrease its reoccurrence. Providing parenting skills training programs to individuals who have committed child abuse is an example of tertiary prevention (Dubowitz, 1989).

Most prevention efforts focus on parent training (Edgeworth & Carr, 2000; National Research Council, 1993). Training parents in child management (such as discipline techniques), child care, and self-control skills (such as managing frustration and anger) has been effective in promoting positive parent-child interactions (Britner & Reppucci, 1997). There also is some evidence that parent training reduces parental distress, thereby reducing the chances of abuse and neglect (Shifflett & Cummings, 1999). When parenting programs are combined with efforts to provide families with services that address critical family needs—such as for child care, mental health counseling, social support, and home improvements—the effectiveness of the intervention is improved (Reuter, Conger, & Ramisetty-Mikler, 1999; Striefel, Robinson, & Truhn, 1998).

Unfortunately, given that reports of child abuse and neglect are increasing, it seems that prevention efforts have been relatively ineffective (Emery & Laumann-Billings, 1998). In fact, there is some evidence that one-third or more of the abusive parents served by prevention programs maltreated their children while in these programs (Cohn & Daro, 1987). To date, most interventions have been designed to address child abuse and neglect using secondary or tertiary prevention rather than primary prevention. In Scandinavian countries such as Sweden and Denmark, nationwide primary prevention programs provide support and services to all families. In these countries, rates of child abuse and neglect are about eight times lower than those in the United States (Pransky, 1991). Thus, it appears we can do something about the rates of child abuse and neglect in the United States, but it will take broader interventions and policies to make a difference.

TRY IT OUT

Activities Relating to Infants and Toddlers

1. How would you describe your temperament? What were some socioemotional and behavioral expressions of your temperament when you were a baby or young child? How would you characterize your pattern of attachment with your primary caregiver? How do you think your attachment pattern might have influenced your social and emotional development?

2. At a playground, observe infants and toddlers interacting with their parents. Using qualities associated with different types of attachments, try to determine what kind of attachment each child has. What behaviors do you focus on? What factors affect your judgments?

3. Arrange to observe infants and toddlers in a day care program, especially at the beginning and the end of the day, when they are being dropped off and picked up. Observe and record the behavior and social and emotional responses of parents, children, and day care workers. Before you observe, however, you should develop a research design. What will be your research question? What, exactly, will you observe, when, and for how long? How will you systematize and interpret your observations to answer your research question?

SUM IT UP

How do emotions develop during infancy and toddlerhood?

✦ Many of the basic emotions are present at birth or shortly thereafter.

✦ Smiling is an important emotional behavior because it is a powerful social reinforcer. By about 6 to 8 weeks, infants move from reflexive smiling to social smiling. Laughter appears about a month later.

✦ Crying is an infant's most effective way of communicating. Several different types of cries have been identified, based on their characteristics—basic, anger, pain, and hunger cries.

✦ Infants increasingly respond to the limits of their abilities and their environments with anger and temper tantrums. Tantrums are brought about in part by important developmental changes, such as increased ability to express anger and strivings toward independence, coupled with limited social understanding.

✦ The self-conscious emotions of shame, embarrassment, and pride, which appear at about age 2, reflect young children's increased self-awareness and cognitive development.

✦ Play provides infants and toddlers with opportunities to explore emotional development, and many early emotions occur in the context of play.

How does temperament influence development during infancy and toddlerhood?

✦ Temperament refers to individual differences in how people respond to their environments. A variety of components of temperament are thought to be present at birth and are constant over time and situations.

✦ The expression of temperament can be modified by social and cultural environments.

How do parent-infant attachments influence development?

✦ Attachments are enduring emotional ties characterized by the tendency to seek closeness to a specific attachment figure. The mother usually is the first attachment figure.

✦ Attachment theory suggests that attachment is a long-lasting relationship. Evidence of attachment is seen in children's attempts to seek out and maintain contact with attachment figures and in children's distress when separated from attachment figures.

✦ Attachment develops in phases. The preattachment phase is the first eight weeks of life, when infants do not discriminate in their responses to caregivers. The attachment-in-the-making phase lasts until about 7 months and is a period in which infants discriminate familiar from unfamiliar caregivers. The clear-cut attachment phase is next and reflects a clear preference for a particular caregiver.

✦ Two characteristics of the clear-cut attachment phase are stranger anxiety and separation anxiety.

✦ Attachment is assessed using the Strange Situation—a series of separations from and reunions with a caregiver and a stranger. Securely attached infants use the attachment figure as a secure base, respond with distress when separated from that person, and are relieved and joyful at reunion.

✦ Avoidant attachments are characterized by a lack of contact or interaction with the caregiver.

✦ Ambivalent attachments are characterized by both a desire for comfort and a resistance to contact.

✦ Disorganized/disoriented attachments are characterized by avoidance, resistance, and bizarre repetitions of behavior.

✦ Caregiver sensitivity, infant characteristics, and cultural factors influence the quality of parent-child attachment.

✦ Attachment affects later development. Infants with secure attachments generally are more socially and emotionally competent.

✦ Infants become attached to their fathers, despite having less contact with them than with their mothers. Given the opportunity, fathers can be as sensitive and nurturing as mothers.

How does day care influence infants' and toddlers' development?

✦ There has been a dramatic increase in the number of infants and toddlers cared for by individuals other than their parents. The rapid entry of women into the work force is primarily responsible for this change.

✦ The majority of infants and toddlers with working mothers are cared for by relatives. As children get older and as women work longer hours, children are more likely to be placed in organized group day care.

✦ Concerns have been raised about the possibility that day care could have an adverse effect on infants' attachments, especially for infants who have caregivers other than parents for more than 20 hours per week.

✦ Caregiving arrangements for very young children vary considerably across cultures. The types of care provided to infants and toddlers are influenced by the values of a culture and by economic, political, and health conditions.

Why are children abused and neglected?

✦ Four categories of child maltreatment are physical abuse, sexual abuse, neglect, and psychological maltreatment. Recent statistics reveal increases in the rates of reported child maltreatment.

✦ Certain children face greater chances of experiencing maltreatment than others. Girls generally are maltreated more often than boys are; in particular, they are more likely to be sexually abused. Younger children are more at risk for maltreatment than are older children.

✦ Child abuse and neglect cross all social class, racial, religious, and educational boundaries. Most child abusers are not psychologically disturbed. Because they carry out the majority of child rearing, biological parents, particularly mothers, are the adults most likely to abuse and neglect children. Only a very small percentage of abuse occurs in day care or foster care.

✦ Adults who commit abuse are low in child-rearing knowledge, have unrealistic expectations and low tolerance for children's behavior, and rely on physical punishment for discipline. They also tend to be socially isolated and to have been abused themselves as children.

✦ The effects of child maltreatment can be devastating, and sometimes fatal. Even when there is no evidence of physical impairment, social, psychological, and intellectual damage may occur. These consequences are particularly powerful early in development.

✦ Three types of prevention models have been identified: primary, secondary, and tertiary. Most prevention efforts focus on parent training, but these have been relatively ineffective.

KEY TERMS and CONCEPTS

ambivalent attachment (*191*)
attachment (*185*)
avoidant attachment (*191*)
disorganized/disoriented attachment (*191*)
endogenous smile (*176*)
exogenous smile (*177*)
manipulative tantrums (*181*)
neglect (*201*)

physical abuse (*201*)
primary prevention (*205*)
psychological maltreatment (*201*)
secondary prevention (*205*)
secure attachment (*190*)
self-conscious emotions (*181*)
separation anxiety (*188*)
sexual abuse (*201*)

social smile (*177*)
Strange Situation (*189*)
stranger anxiety (*188*)
temperament (*182*)
temperamental tantrums (*181*)
tertiary prevention (*205*)

PART **3** _____   **SEE the IMPACT**

BENCHMARKS in
Infant and Toddler Development

PHYSICAL/MOTOR DEVELOPMENT	COGNITIVE DEVELOPMENT	SOCIAL/EMOTIONAL DEVELOPMENT
Rapid growth, particularly in lower portions of body	Coordination and integration of reflex actions into more complex schemas	Evidence of early individual differences in temperamental and emotional characteristics
Increased voluntary control of muscles and movements	Evidence of color, pattern, face, motion, and depth perception and preferences	Increasing evidence of attachments to significant caregivers
Improved control of trunk; ability to roll over	First evidence of problem solving	Socialization through experience, primarily with family members
Reaching of motor milestones—creeping, crawling, sitting, standing, cruising, walking, and running	Development of the concept of object permanence	Enhanced experience with peers and nonfamilial caregivers
	Development of prelanguage skills—cooing, babbling	Greater probability of being a victim of abuse and neglect
	Acquisition of true language—one-word stage (holophrase)	

NATIONAL HOTLINES FOR INFANTS AND TODDLERS

Child Abuse Hotline: 800-422-4453

La Leche League: 800-525-3243

Women, Infants, and Children (WIC): 703-305-2746

impact Report on Infants and Toddlers

Child maltreatment is greatest at the youngest ages and decreases as children get older. Can you suggest some reasons why?

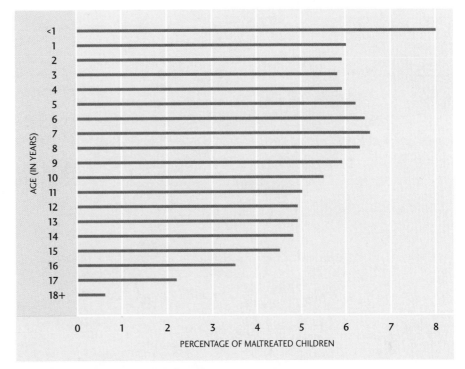

Child Maltreatment, by Age of Child

SOURCE: US Department of Health and Human Services, 1999.

RECOMMENDED WEBSITES

Attachment Theory and Research Center: Maintained by the State University of New York at Stony Brook, this site contains information about infant-mother attachment. It includes comments, bibliographies, measures, and artifacts from John Bowlby and Mary Ainsworth.
http://www.psy.sunysb.edu/attachment/

Child Abuse Prevention Network: Maintained by Cornell University, this network is dedicated to providing comprehensive Internet resources for the prevention of child abuse and neglect and to reducing the negative conditions in the family and community that lead to child maltreatment.
http://child-abuse.com/

International Society on Infant Studies: This site is devoted to the scientific study of infant development. It provides information about infant journals, conferences, and newsletters.
http://www.isisweb.org/

KidsHealth: Created by medical experts at the Nemours Foundation, this rich Website is devoted to the health of children. It has accurate, up-to-date information about growth, food, and fitness; childhood infections; immunizations; lab tests; medical and surgical conditions; and the latest treatments.
http://KidsHealth.org/

La Leche League: This site is dedicated to providing education, information, support, and encouragement to women who want to breast-feed.
http://www.lalecheleague.org/

National Association for the Education of Young Children: This site is devoted to providing information on issues surrounding early childhood care and promoting excellence in early childhood education.
http://www.naeyc.org/

Temperament.com: This site is a clearinghouse for research and practical information about temperamental characteristics.
http://www.temperament.com/

Zero to Three: This site provides expansive information on topics related to healthy infant and toddler development.
http://www.zerotothree.org/

Early Childhood Development

During early childhood, children experience an increase in the complexity with which they think about and participate in their worlds. Although family members, particularly parents, remain important, children begin to experience life outside the family. They are increasingly exposed to non–family members and influences such as school and television. Most of these experiences involve peers, and most peer interactions take place in the context of play.

Children make significant advances in their cognitive development in early childhood. Their reasoning becomes more abstract and less bound by motor actions. Their language and communication skills increase, and they can ask and answer many rich and complex questions. Their reasoning, however, remains limited compared to that of older children and adults. Young children's thinking is dominated by their own perceptions, feelings, and perspectives. They have difficulty understanding that others have views different from their own. These new ways of thinking set the stage for even more advanced forms of reasoning and understanding.

DID YOU KNOW THAT

Over half a million children in the United States currently reside in some form of foster care. Since the passage of the Adoption and Safe Families Act in 1997, increasing attention has been paid to the performance of the foster care system and how well the system is meeting the needs of children. Foster care most often is employed in situations of abuse and neglect. Other reasons for foster placement include severe behavioral problems in the child and a variety of parental problems, such as abandonment, neglect, illness, alcohol/substance abuse, and death.

- Currently, there are almost 600,000 children in foster care.

- The number of children placed in foster care has more than doubled since 1982. The numbers of boys and girls are almost equal.

- The average age of children in foster care is 9.9 years.

- Thirty-nine percent of children in foster care are African American, 34 percent are Caucasian, 17 percent are Hispanic, 2 percent are Native American, and 1 percent are Asian.

- In 88 percent of the foster care cases, parents have not had their parental rights terminated.

- The average stay in foster care is thirty-two months, and 17 percent of the children spend more than five years in foster care.

- Thirty percent of children in foster care have severe emotional, behavioral, or physical health problems.

- Currently, there are 127,000 children who are waiting to be adopted. Each year, about 46,000 children are adopted.

SOURCE: Adoption and Foster Care Analysis and Reporting System, 2001.

Cognitive, Language, and Physical Development in Early Childhood

CHAPTER OUTLINE

✦ How Do Children's Bodies and Motor Skills Develop During Early Childhood?

✦ What Are the Nutritional and Health Issues for Young Children?

✦ How Do Young Children Think and Solve Problems?

✦ What Changes Occur in Young Children's Language Development During Early Childhood?

The world of the young child is different from the world of older children and adults: A child may think that a moving plastic duck is alive, that a broken cookie doesn't taste as good as an unbroken one, or that the stars shine so that he or she can see at night. Children view the world through their own perspective, and they tend to be easily fooled by what things look like—they fail to recognize which are the more stable features of objects. Children's physical development is not as dramatic as it is during infancy, but the changes are still very apparent—they no longer have their "babyish" appearance. Unlike infants, preschoolers can dress themselves, draw pictures, throw a ball, and run forward and backward. Language development occurs rapidly during this time, as children master many complexities of grammar and the use of language. As you will see in this chapter, cognitive, language, and motor skills develop best in the context of social interactions with caregivers and other adults in the community.

HOW DO CHILDREN'S BODIES AND MOTOR SKILLS DEVELOP DURING EARLY CHILDHOOD?

Consider the following scene. Tracy, age 4, throws a large red ball to her 15-month-old sister, Kim. Kim reaches for it, but is unable to catch it. Kim leans forward to retrieve the ball and toddles unsteadily. Tracy runs toward her, picks up the ball, hands it to Kim, and says, "Now you throw it to me." Kim tries to throw the ball, but it falls out of her hand and rolls away. Leaner and taller preschoolers like Tracy move more quickly and steadily than toddlers like Kim and can run, jump, and throw a ball with good accuracy.

CHANGING BODY SIZE AND APPEARANCE

Remember the general physical characteristics of infants, which we discussed in Chapter 5—protruding stomach, short bowed legs, and a large head relative to body size. Compared to infants, the most notable physical feature of preschool children is that they lose their babyish appearance. Body fat decreases to approximately 12 percent of body weight, the stomach flattens as muscles strengthen, arms and legs grow longer and slimmer, and the body grows in size relative to the head.

During the preschool years, growth is not as rapid as it is during the infant years, but most children grow approximately 3 inches a year and gain 4 pounds a year. Girls and boys are very similar in their patterns of physical growth and development during the preschool years. The average 3-year-old boy is 38 inches tall and weighs 33 pounds, and the average 3-year-old girl is slightly smaller and lighter (Tanner, 1975).

Some children grow taller and develop more quickly than other children. What factors account for these differences? As you learned in Chapter 5, children's genetic endowment influences growth and development, with taller children being born to taller parents. In the United States, African American children tend to be taller than Caucasian American children, and both groups tend to be taller than Asian American children. However, children born in the United States, regardless of ethnic and racial background, tend to be taller than almost all other children around the world (Cratty, 1986). In addition to genetic endowment, good nutritional habits and better health care tend to foster taller children.

BRAIN DEVELOPMENT

During the preschool years, a child's brain develops quickly, reaching 75 to 90 percent of adult size by age 5. The brain grows larger during this time because the neurons grow more interconnections, increasing the number and size of nerve endings (Nosphitz & King, 1991). Another change is an increase in myelination, which allows information to move more quickly between the cells in the brain (see Chapter 4). The rate of development of many children's skills and abilities may depend on myelination. For instance, the areas of the brain involved in hand-eye coordination are not completely myelinated until around the age of 4 or 5 (Konner, 1991; Tanner, 1978).

Remember from your reading in Chapter 5 that the two hemispheres of the brain develop at different times. The left hemisphere develops rapidly around the age of 2; the right hemisphere, with its visual recognition systems, does not develop at the same rate. The growth spurt for the right hemisphere occurs around the age of 4 or 5 (Borsting, 1994; Fischer & Rose, 1994). Also around age 5, the connections between the two hemispheres increase in number and become more efficient, allowing children to better coordinate functions involving both sides of the brain and body (Huttenlocher, 1990; 1994).

GROSS MOTOR SKILLS

After a year of coordinating all the systems required for standing and walking, toddlers take another year to perfect walking. Soon after, children begin trying many variations in their movements, including walking sideways, walking backward, and walking on their toes. New skills are emerging rapidly in the third year. With little training, children learn to run, throw balls, and jump. How do they acquire these skills?

One key factor in the development of motor skills is the development of children's visual systems. Areas of the brain associated with the ability to focus the eyes and with eye movements continue to develop through early childhood. The development of visual pathways, combined with improving communication between the hemispheres, results in advances in eye-hand coordination and allows preschoolers to become better at left-right directions.

Another important factor for motor development is balance, which contributes greatly to the proliferation of skills children exhibit during the preschool years. Children with visual or inner-ear problems may have difficulty integrating the sensory information necessary for good balance (Hatton, Bailey, Burchinal, & Ferrell, 1997). A lack of balance interferes with the stability they need to perform more complex skills like kicking and throwing. Practice, imitating others, and others' expectations and encouragement also play important roles in motor development. For example, children with older siblings develop motor skills more rapidly than other children (Samuels, 1980).

Although some children take longer to develop motor skills than others, a small group of children are clumsy—they are unable to coordinate parts of their bodies for activities such as throwing a ball, hopping, or drawing. Because clumsy children may be improperly labeled as learning disabled or may suffer from teasing, early identification of motor development problems and referral to treatment programs can benefit children (Bertenthal & Clifton, 1998).

Running and Jumping

Young children sometimes appear to be running; however, it is not until they are 2 to 3 years of age that they show true running, during which both feet leave the ground. Even then, they are not well-controlled runners, because they are unable to stop or start quickly. By the time children are 4 to 5 years old, their running ability has greatly improved, and most can run twice as fast as they did when they were 2 (Cratty, 1986).

Children's first attempts at jumping are one-footed steps off an object, usually occurring at around 18 months of age. By 2, most children can use a two-footed take-off to propel themselves off an object, but they are not very efficient in using their arms to help their motion. By 4, most children can jump on level ground, using their arms appropriately to help propel them. And by 5, most children can jump a distance of 3 feet (Cratty, 1986).

Throwing and Catching

Throwing and catching a ball are complex motor skills that develop in stages over the early childhood period (Marques-Bruna & Grinshaw, 1997). Throwing gradually comes to involve more of the body and greater body rotation. Mature throwers rotate around the central axis of their body and shift their weight forward. In contrast, 2- to 3-year-olds often use a rigid underhand toss with no body movement. By 3½ years, children can throw overhand

FIGURE 7.1

Developmental Changes in Throwing

(a)   (b)   (c)   (d)

SOURCE: Cratty, 1999. © 1999 by Allyn & Bacon. Adapted by permission.

Throwing proceeds from (a) a toddler's accidental letting go of an object to (b and c) 2- to 4-year-olds' variable throws to (d) a mature throw accompanied by a step with the foot opposite the throwing arm. Throughout late childhood, girls are less likely than boys to involve their whole body in throwing.

with some body rotation, but they keep their feet firmly on the ground. By 5 or 6, most children step with the opposite foot and shift their weight when throwing, and their speed and accuracy improve with age (see Figure 7.1).

Children's ability to catch a ball also develops during childhood, with better visual tracking of the ball, more flexible positioning of their arms during the "catch," and faster reaction times. Very young children tend to hold their arms stiffly in front of them to catch a ball and sometimes close their eyes or turn their head away to avoid the ball. By 4, most children watch the ball coming and hold their hands open to receive it. By 5 to 5½ years of age, most children hold their arms and elbows flexibly to absorb the force of the ball.

FINE MOTOR SKILLS

To be able to cut with a pair of scissors or fold pieces of paper, children must be able to organize the coordination of their hands and eyes, using the small muscles in their hands precisely. These fine motor skills develop markedly during the early childhood period.

Tadpole People

SOURCE: From ARTFUL SCRIBBLES by HOWARD GARDNER. Copyright © 1980 by Howard Gardner. Reprinted by permission of Basic Books, a member of Perseus Books Group, L.L.C.

About how old were the children who drew these "tadpole" people? What physical characteristics do these children represent in their drawings? What aspects of the physical development of young children do the drawings represent?

Although infants can grasp small objects between their forefinger and thumb, precise movements of individual fingers take several more years to achieve (Geraldson & Hopkins, 1997). Biological factors play a role in finger differentiation: Children with brain damage often cannot use each finger individually and instead use their hands as though they were encased in a fingerless mitt (Cratty, 1986).

The developmental progression in fine motor skills from less to more differentiation, coordination, and control is apparent during the preschool years. For instance, 2-year-olds can scribble, put on some articles of clothing, turn pages in a book, and construct towers consisting of six to eight blocks. Three-year-olds have better developed fine motor skills: they can eat with a spoon, copy a circle, and pour from a pitcher. By 4, children can dress themselves, draw tadpolelike human figures (see Figure 7.2), and cut on a line with scissors. Most 5-year-olds can fasten buttons, draw letters, unzip a zipper, and string beads.

Parents often wonder whether their children will be right or left handed. Handedness is influenced more by genetics than environment (McManus & Bryden, 1992), and most children and adults (92 percent) are right handed (Coren & Porac, 1977). Infants do not show strong hand preferences; instead, they vary their use of hands. Stable preferences emerge for most children around 3 to 4 years of age. Some evidence suggests that an early (4 to 6 months of age) and strong hand preference may indicate that the infant has a neurological problem (Harris, 1992). To test a preschooler's hand preference, it is best to use a task that is somewhat challenging, because either hand may be used for a simple task such as reaching for an object. For children, the tasks commonly used to assess handedness include writing, drawing, eating, pointing, and throwing. However, an indeterminate number of children and adults are ambidextrous—they switch preferred hands depending on the task they need to do. Even for the same task, they will sometimes prefer the right hand and other times the left hand (Porac, Coren, & Searleman, 1986). For many generations, left-handedness was actively discouraged in schools. Even today, our environment is structured to favor right-handers, but parents are encouraged to let children's natural handedness prevail (Coren, 1993).

CULTURAL AND RACIAL INFLUENCES ON MOTOR DEVELOPMENT

Children with African origins typically are more advanced in motor development than children with European origins: They throw farther, balance better, and are better able to run (Cratty, 1986). The reasons for these differences are varied and complex. Genetic factors may play a role, specifically in influencing the length and proportions of arms, legs, and the overall body size. Cultural factors—including parenting practices, nutrition, and the perceived importance of motor skill development—also play a role, however. Mothers in Nigeria, Uganda, Sierra Leone, India, and Pakistan encourage their children to walk and stand up more quickly and train them in motor development. For instance, Nigerian and West Indian mothers use passive stretching movements, massage, and active encouragement in the first year of a child's life to promote motor development (Hopkins, 1991). Interestingly, in two African groups that do not encourage early motor development (the Baganda and the Somia), the infants and children show slower development of motor skills than Caucasian children in the United States (Kilbride, 1980).

Cultural and biological factors likely interact to influence children's motor development. For instance, African American infants show early motor precocity and are especially reactive, which may, in turn, contribute in a transactional way to caregivers' encouragement of their motor skills (Rosser & Randolph, 1989).

WHAT ARE THE NUTRITIONAL AND HEALTH ISSUES FOR YOUNG CHILDREN?

Children's physical, motor, and cognitive development depends on good health and nutrition (Georgieff & Rao, 2001). As children grow older, their nutritional requirements change to meet their different growth and activity needs. Whereas the infant and toddler spend much of their active time standing and learning to walk, young children may be running, jumping, and climbing. However, because the rate of growth slows in childhood, their appetite may not be as strong as it was when they were infants and toddlers. Caregivers often worry that children are not eating enough to obtain adequate nutrition. However, the nutritional requirements of young children can be met with small, healthy meals. An average preschooler requires about 1700 calories per day, with less than 35 percent of the calories coming from fat.

Children over the age of 2 need a varied diet that includes whole grains, vegetables, fruits, milk and high protein foods, and moderate fat. Compared with infants and toddlers, young children need more energy and protein because of their greater body size. The fat content of young children's diets should be gradually reduced; much of the needed reduction in fat can be achieved by using reduced-fat dairy products (Smolin & Grosnevor, 2000). Exposure to others in the family who are eating healthy foods is useful for encouraging children to adopt a healthy diet. However, caregivers often find it challenging to deal with young children's strong food preferences—for instance, a desire to eat only peanut-butter-and-jelly sandwiches every day. Offering other foods in addition to the desired foods can help to maintain healthy nutrition in children. Creativity in food preparation also helps: Making foods into interesting shapes, giving foods special names to encourage eating, and letting children help prepare foods may be useful strategies for encouraging healthy nutrition.

UNDERNOURISHMENT AND MALNOURISHMENT

Inadequate nutrition is implicated in more than half the child deaths worldwide (UNICEF, 2001). Almost 200 million of the world's children below 5 years of age are underweight and likely to be suffering from undernourishment. Undernourishment is more common in parts of Africa and Asia than elsewhere in the world (UNICEF, 2001; Pollitt et al., 1996). Undernourishment is closely associated with economic impoverishment, limited health care and educational opportunities, and poor living conditions. When food is scarce, children's diets consist largely of cereals and legumes, and they eat few fruits, vegetables, and animal products. Thus, undernourished children often are malnourished as well—they do not receive adequate proteins, vitamins, and minerals.

Children in developing nations are more likely than children in the United States to have inadequate diets. Children in Africa, South and Central America, the Near East, and the Far East are at risk for protein-energy malnutrition (PEM), which ranges from pure protein deficiency, called **kwashiorkor,** to energy deficiency, called **marasmus.** In the language of the Ga tribe of the African Gold Coast, kwashiorkor means "the disease that the first child gets when a second child is born." With the birth of a new sibling, children who have been fed protein-rich breast milk are switched to a watered-down version of the diet the adults eat. This diet is low in protein and high in fiber, so it is difficult to digest. Because children grow more quickly than adults, their protein requirements are higher and the effects of protein deficiency are more evident. Children with kwashiorkor have stunted growth, susceptibility to infection, and bloated stomachs. Bloating is due to fluids that accumulate in the stomach because there is not enough protein to maintain the fluids in the blood.

Marasmus, which means "to waste away," is due to a deficiency of energy. Children with marasmus are emaciated because their body fat has been used to provide energy. Marasmus has devastating effects on development: Early energy deficiencies cause decreases in intelligence and learning ability that persist throughout life. Children may develop marasmus because of limited access to food; for instance, marasmus can result from being fed diluted infant formula by caregivers trying to stretch limited supplies. Protein-energy malnutrition is a major public health problem. Approximately one-third of children under the age of 5 in developing countries are underweight, and about 10 percent have wasting (WHO, 1997). Nutritional supplements can be given to counteract the cognitive and other developmental problems associated with nutritional deficiencies (Grantham-McGregor, Ani, & Fernald, 2001).

Approximately 13 million children in the United States are malnourished—about 1 in 4—and most of these children are from low-income families (UNICEF, 2001). A common

kwashiorkor a form of protein-energy malnutrition in which only protein is deficient

marasmus a form of protein-energy malnutrition involving severe body wasting

FIGURE 7.3

Bidirectional Model of Outcomes for Children with Nutritional Developmental Problems

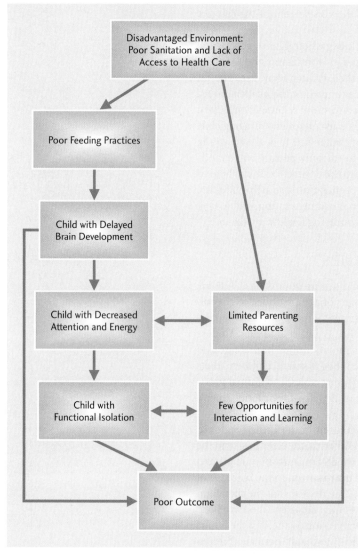

SOURCE: Lozoff et al., 1998.

Notice that a disadvantaged environment has multiple effects, both direct and indirect, on children's development. The bidirectional effects can be seen in the interplay between children's having less energy and paying less attention and caregivers' having limited resources and lowered expectations. Each factor is an action as well as a reaction to the other factors.

iron-deficiency anemia a nutrient deficiency common in infants and toddlers

functional isolation the increased disengagement from one's social and physical environments that may result from a poor environment and inadequate nutrition

problem for young children who do not eat enough meats and green vegetables is lack of iron, which results in chronic fatigue. Serious iron deficiencies lead to **iron-deficiency anemia,** a common nutrient deficiency. Some children may be malnourished even though they consume enough calories. These children fill up on "empty" nonnutritional calories (such as those found in cookies and potato chips) and fail to eat enough healthy foods.

Undernutrition among preschoolers and school-aged children is a serious health concern because of the many adverse consequences associated with it. Undernourished children tend to have stunted growth and delayed motor development (Simeon & Grantham-McGregor, 1990). They also are at risk for cognitive disabilities such as low levels of attention, learning impairments, and poor academic and school-related performance (Hurtado et al., 1999; Wachs, 1995).

Why do undernourishment and malnourishment have such pervasive and negative effects on children? One idea that may explain these effects is **functional isolation**—malnourished children become increasingly disengaged from their social and physical environments (Brown & Pollitt, 1996). Functional isolation results from direct and indirect effects of poor environments and inadequate nutrition. If children's diets lack iron, for example, their brain development is impaired and delayed (Georgieff & Rao, 2001). Diminished brain development—accompanied by attempts to reduce energy expenditures by withdrawing from stimulation—influences children's behavior. The children may become more wary, easily tired, less attentive, and less playful, and they rarely show delight and pleasure (Lozoff et al., 1998; Lozoff et al., 2000). Because these children are not very responsive, caregivers do not interact with them much. Caregivers expect less from these children, so the children receive even less stimulation. Over time, they withdraw from their physical and social environments, increasing the likelihood that outcomes will be poor (see Figure 7.3).

Some children with inadequate nutrition live in families that cannot afford the food they need. However, many children lack nutritious diets even when food is abundant. Because of increased demands on family time, families often stop for fast food meals or prepare high-fat convenience foods at home, thereby including high levels of fat and sodium in the diet. Caregivers can limit children's fat and sodium intake by screening convenience foods based on their labels, curtailing fast food consumption, and carefully selecting the fast foods that are offered.

ACCIDENTS AND DISEASES

Children today are generally healthier than children of twenty years ago. Death rates from diseases such as influenza and pneumonia have decreased. Many dangerous and contagious childhood diseases (measles and polio, for instance) were virtually eliminated in the United States by the 1980s because of routine vaccinations given during childhood. However, some caregivers, especially those from low-income families, have not ensured that their children receive these vaccinations, with the result that 1 in 5 children is not protected against rubella, polio, mumps, and measles (Centers for Disease Control, 1999). Diseases reemerge in the population if children do not receive their sequence of vaccinations (Kassianos, 1998).

The leading cause of death in the preschool years is accidents, often automobile accidents. In the United States, children are required to wear seat belts. Until they are 5, children should travel in special car safety seats that protect them from injuries (American Academy of Pediatrics, 1999b). Automobile manufacturers offer airbags and side-impact protection. Because the force of an opening airbag can harm children, young children should always be in the back seat of the car. Disarming airbags is not recommended. Restraint laws have been quite effective in protecting children: children who are not restrained are much more likely to die in automobile accidents than are children who are properly restrained (American Academy of Pediatrics, 1999b; Decker, Dewey, Hutcheson, & Schaffner, 1984).

Many accidents occur in homes. Children fall into swimming pools, drink poisonous substances, are burned in fires, are cut by broken glass, fall into bathtubs, injure themselves on sharp corners of furniture, and fall down stairs. Accidental poisonings have decreased markedly in the last twenty years; nevertheless, 500,000 children ingest some type of poison every year, and 2000 die from the poison. And children get injured on playgrounds, often from falling off equipment (Sacks et al., 1989).

Lead poisoning is a common health problem for young children in the United States. Although the incidence of lead poisoning has decreased, it continues to be a significant health issue. About 5 percent of young children (approximately 900,000) have a toxic level of lead in their blood (American Academy of Pediatrics, 1999a). Lead can be found everywhere—in paints, gasoline, foods, water, dust, and soil. The most common route of exposure for children is through lead-based paint in older homes. Children with high levels of lead are at risk for many behavioral problems. They may be hyperactive, impulsive, easily frustrated, or withdrawn. Even low levels of exposure increase the risk for social withdrawal and disinterest (Mendelsohn et al., 1998). Children who live in older neighborhoods and homes or who play on old playground equipment may be exposed to lead. Not surprisingly, children who live in the inner city are more likely to suffer elevated lead levels and anemia than other children (Adams, Geva, Coffman, Palfrey, & Bauchner, 1998).

Using seatbelts is one way of increasing children's safety in cars. Why should children traveling in car safety seats be placed in the back seat of the car rather than the front?

What health and safety risks do these children face? What is the most common kind of playground injury? How can it be prevented?

HOW DO YOUNG CHILDREN THINK AND SOLVE PROBLEMS?

Four-year-old Ginny, like other children her age, can identify many kinds of dinosaurs. She knows that some dinosaurs eat only plants and others only meat. She is more knowledgeable about dinosaurs than many adults. She also can easily be fooled by appearances: she thinks that a tall, thin glass holds more grape juice than a small, wide glass of the same volume. Ginny thinks differently than infants, older children, and adults. When it comes to dinosaurs, she is an expert; but when it comes to understanding physical laws of nature, she is a novice with little understanding of the world. To fully understand young children's thinking, we must consider the physical, social, and cultural contexts they experience, as well as how they interpret problem-solving situations.

The major theoretical approaches used to understand children's thinking are Piaget's theory of cognitive development, which concentrates on children's different view of the world; Vygotsky's sociocultural perspective, in which children's thinking is thought to be guided by their social interactions with others; and the information processing approach, which considers the constraints and limitations on children's thinking and on their memories.

PIAGET'S VIEW OF PREOPERATIONAL THINKING

According to Jean Piaget, young children have made tremendous strides in their understanding of the world, and their thinking is qualitatively different from that of infants. As you learned in Chapter 5, infants do not fully understand that objects continue to exist when they are not directly experiencing them, but young children have no difficulty comprehending object permanence. Infants experience the world in the here and now, with little comprehension of the past or future, but preschoolers can think about the future and discuss the past.

Young children have moved into the *preoperational stage* of cognitive development (2 to 7 years of age). At this stage, they use **symbolic representations**—they can mentally represent objects and people and manipulate these representations. Children first show this ability at the end of the sensorimotor period (Chapter 5). Because of their ability to use symbolic representations, young children are not confined, as infants are, to thinking in the present. Young children's symbolic capacities are illustrated in how they play, what they remember, and their increasingly sophisticated use of language. For instance, children in the preoperational stage often imitate behaviors they have seen in the past. Four-year-old Lynna provides an example of deferred imitation. Days after she saw her friend Maria trying a ballet pose, Lynna tried the same pose for the first time. Lynna remembered Maria's actions from days earlier and reproduced these actions.

Children at this stage show remarkable ability to communicate with language, which requires the use of symbols. Young children's thinking is no longer dominated by motor actions; they can use symbols to manipulate information mentally, allowing for faster and more flexible thinking. Before an action occurs, children can anticipate the outcome. Unlike infants, preschoolers have better memories for past events such as a family trip, and they can plan for the future, thinking about whom they will invite to a birthday party that is still weeks away.

According to Piaget, young children, unlike older children, adolescents, and adults, are preoperational thinkers because they are unable to apply **operations**—actions internalized as symbols that can be reversed and coordinated. The ability to use operations is based on the ability to apply basic logic to problem solving. Preoperational children are able to internalize actions in symbols, but cannot yet reverse and coordinate these symbols.

Conservation Tasks

To illustrate the difference between operational and preoperational thinking, Piaget used **conservation tasks.** These are tasks in which children are shown an object, watch a transformation of that object, and then decide whether the transformed object is the same as or

symbolic representations mental representations of objects and people that can be manipulated in the mind

operations actions internalized as symbols that can be reversed and coordinated

conservation tasks tasks used to assess children's use of operations, in which children must decide whether a transformed object is the same as or different from what it was before

different from what it was before it was transformed. For instance, 4-year-old Jason is shown two balls of clay, both of which are exactly the same size and shape. One ball is then rolled out into a long thin snake shape, and Jason is asked to decide if one piece has more clay in it than the other or if they have the same amount. His answer may come as a surprise to many adults: He is likely to say that the long skinny shape has more clay in it than the ball.

In recognizing that the snake and the ball have the same amount of clay, adults apply basic logical principles regarding the conservation of matter. In contrast to Jason, older children understand that an object transformed into a new form contains the same amount of matter so long as nothing is added or taken away. Older children and adults understand the **identity concept,** which involves recognizing the essential "sameness" of an object despite physical changes to it.

Jason, like other preschool children, does not consistently apply the idea of identity to problem-solving experiences. Because young children do not use logical operations, their reasoning often seems flawed to us. Young children's thinking exhibits **centration**—the tendency to focus attention on the most obvious and striking characteristic of an object while ignoring others. They see the snake as having more clay than the ball, for example, because it is longer. Young children centrate on the length of the snake while ignoring its comparative thinness. Their thinking is guided by appearances—what things look like—rather than by logic. Eight-year-old Carol used to take advantage of her 4-year-old sister's tendency to centrate on size (and lack of knowledge of money) by trading big nickels for her sister's small dimes. To her younger sister, bigger meant more.

Why will this 4-year-old say that the snake has more clay in it than the ball? What property of physical objects is not being observed? According to Piaget, what is this child's stage of cognitive development?

Static Thinking

The focus on one dimension also is obvious in children's **static thinking**—their tendency to attend to the outcome rather than to the changes that produced the outcome. For example, a preschool child may watch her friend dress in a monster costume at Halloween and then focus only on the final state; that is, she may become scared of the monster who has magically replaced her friend. Children may even make up unbelievable stories about what happened during a transition. When asked what had happened to her friend, the child might say that her friend had gone home. Young children often exhibit static thinking when they tell stories: They focus only on the beginning of the story and its end. Three-year-old Erin's favorite story is "Once upon a time there was a princess. The end."

Precausal Reasoning

Young children's reasoning about the causes of events does not match adults'. Adults reason *inductively*, from particular examples to the general principle, or *deductively*, from the general principle to the specific example. For instance, inductive reasoning would suggest that if every swan you've ever seen is white, then all swans are white. Deductive reasoning would be used to determine that if all swans are white, and this bird is a swan, then this bird must be white. Piaget argued that young children are more likely than adults to use a different form of reasoning, called **transductive reasoning.** Transductive reasoning suggests that if two particular examples or events occur together, they must be causally related. For example, when Joshua sees his mother pick up her bagged lunch and leave for work, he may believe that the bagged lunch caused her to leave the house. Because the events occurred at the same time, he believes that one caused the other. Also, young children seem to infer that all things happen for a reason, so they search to find a cause, even when events are unrelated or arise by chance.

Understanding Concepts and Categories

Preschoolers' simple classifications of objects and people are based on partial concepts (sometimes called preconcepts) that allow them to make distinctions among global categories, such as animals, food, and people (Mandler, Bauer, & McDonough, 1991). In simple situations, young children can categorize on the basis of a single attribute, but their ability to vary strategies when necessary is limited (Freund, Baker, & Sonnenschein, 1990). Young children's ability to understand differences within a category also is limited. They may dis-

identity concept the essential "sameness" of an object despite physical changes to it

centration the tendency to focus attention on the most obvious and striking characteristic of an object while ignoring others

static thinking the tendency to attend more to the outcome than to the changes that produced the outcome

transductive reasoning the inference that if two particular examples or events occur together, they must be causally related

tinguish between dogs and elephants, for example, but have difficulty distinguishing different kinds of dogs.

Young children have difficulty understanding some of the more complex aspects of categorization. They have trouble with multiple classification; that is, they fail to understand that one person or object may belong to multiple categories simultaneously (Winer, 1980). For instance, they may not understand how their mother can also be a daughter. Young children also have difficulty with categorization problems involving **class inclusion,** or part-whole relations of categories. When 4-year-old Elsie is shown ten brown dogs and five white dogs and is asked whether there are more brown dogs or more white dogs, she is likely to answer the question correctly. However, when asked whether there are more brown dogs (a subclass) or more dogs (the whole class), she is likely to say there are more brown dogs. Elsie's answers show that she can make comparisons within a classification level (brown versus white dogs), but she cannot make comparisons across different levels of classification (brown dogs versus all dogs combined). A number of factors influence how well young children perform on class inclusion problems, which suggests that they have an understanding of part-whole relationships but may have difficulty activating that knowledge to solve problems until they are older (Bjorklund, 1995).

Although Piaget described some of the changes that occur in children's classification abilities, other researchers have provided additional insights about children's classification abilities. Whereas very young children often group objects based on perceptual characteristics (e.g., size), slightly older children also form groups based on themes (e.g., saying that a horse and apple go together because horses eat apples). Children continue to use perceptual and thematic groupings as they grow older, but they also gain the ability to use conceptual or taxonomic groupings, which are based on category membership. For instance, a 7-year-old may classify a horse and a dog together as animals and an apple and a banana together as foods. Even with these changes, young children continue to use a variety of methods of classifying information (Bjorklund, 1995).

Egocentrism

One of the most interesting aspects of preschoolers' thought is their tendency toward **egocentrism;** they assume that their own perspective is shared by other people. Preschoolers rely on their own perception of events rather than recognizing that other people may have a different perception. The result is that they fail to take another person's point of view into account (Piaget & Inhelder, 1958). Egocentrism is evident in many aspects of preschoolers' thinking. When 3-year-old Kirra pulled a blanket over her head and announced that we should try to find her, she exhibited egocentric thinking. She reasoned that if she could not see us, we could not see her.

Piaget and Inhelder (1958) designed a special task, called the *three-mountain task,* to assess whether children can adopt another's point of view. In this task, a child and a doll sit at opposite sides of a table with a view of a scene of three mountains varying in size and appearance. From the child's perspective, the tallest mountain has a different location in the scene than it does from the doll's perspective. The child examines the scene from each position around the table, including the doll's, and then is shown pictures representing all views. When asked which view the doll sees, preschoolers are likely to select the scene that best matches the view from their seat, not the doll's seat. Their egocentric thinking leads them to believe that others see things the way they do.

Children's lack of ability to recognize another's point of view influences their social interactions. Young children often have difficulty communicating effectively, especially on the telephone, because they do not understand that the other person does not see what they see or know what they know. Also, they may have difficulties dealing with others' emotions because they do not understand that others feel differently than they do.

Another feature of egocentric thought is **animism**—attributing lifelike qualities to objects that are not alive. By the preoperational stage, children recognize that most inanimate objects are not alive but have difficulty with inanimate objects that move freely. A 4-year-old girl, asked whether a river is alive, may assert that the river is alive because the water moves.

class inclusion part-whole relations of categories

egocentrism the assumption, characteristic of most preschoolers, that their own perspective is shared by other people

animism attributing lifelike qualities to objects that are not alive

When children talk about the moon being happy or the sun going to sleep, their comments suggest that they believe that the moon or sun is alive. According to Piaget, preoperational children's egocentric thinking inhibits their ability to distinguish between things that are alive and those that are not. Children focus on their own view of the object and their perception of it, and this distracts them from attending to the features that determine whether or not something is alive. A child may consider a wind-up plastic duck to be alive because the child pays attention to the movement—how it looks from his or her view—rather than assessing whether the duck is breathing or whether it moves because it propels itself.

EVALUATING PIAGET'S THEORY OF PREOPERATIONAL DEVELOPMENT

Piaget's ideas about development were unlike those of his predecessors; they were so unusual and surprising that many studies were designed to replicate his findings. Even with children from other countries, Piaget's ideas have been confirmed when the same procedures have been used. Children go through the stages described by Piaget, in the order he outlined. Nonetheless, Piaget may have underestimated children's abilities in some ways. Many of Piaget's tasks may have been too demanding or confusing for preschool children. Developmental researchers have simplified Piaget's tasks to explore whether children will perform the simpler tasks the same way they do the more difficult versions (Gelman & Baillargeon, 1983). The implication is that if children show higher levels of problem solving on simplified tasks, we must reconsider the meaning of Piaget's earlier research.

Children's egocentric thinking has been examined using tasks simpler than the three-mountain task. In one set of studies conducted by Hughes (cited in Donaldson, 1978), children were shown a four-room house without a roof. Two police officer dolls were placed in different locations in the house, and the children were asked to hide a boy doll from the officers' sight. Piaget's theory would predict that preschool children could not succeed at this task, just as they do not succeed at the three-mountain task. Surprisingly, most of the 3-year-olds and almost all of the 4-year-olds were successful in placing the boy doll in a position that neither adult doll could see. Making the task more understandable and providing some practice may improve children's ability to adopt another's perspective. Even 3-year-old children are able to imagine others' perspectives on tasks that involve familiar scenes (such as a pond or farmhouse with animals) and familiar characters (such as Grover from *Sesame Street*) (Borke, 1975).

Young children also are more likely to demonstrate an understanding of conservation when tasks are simplified. When children do not witness the transformation (making the snake from clay), they sometimes respond as though they have conserved (Rose & Blank, 1974). Some children can be trained to conserve, especially when simpler tasks are used, but younger children respond less to training than older children (Case, 1998).

Animistic thinking is less evident when children are asked about familiar concrete objects (such as dolls and rocks) rather than the less familiar objects Piaget used (such as the sun or moon). In tasks with familiar objects, young children recognize the qualities associated with being alive earlier than Piaget expected. For instance, young children realize that movement, growth, and emotions are associated with people but not with rocks or dolls (Massey & Gelman, 1988; Rakison & Poulin-Dubois, 2001).

FIGURE 7.4
Three-Mountain Egocentrism Task

Why will this 3-year-old assume that the stuffed animal sees exactly what he sees? What term did Piaget give to this kind of thinking? Does this experimental result mean that a young child is not capable of taking the perspective of another person? Why or why not?

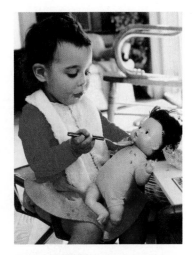

Can this child imagine what the world would look like for her doll? Why does using familiar objects improve children's abilities to demonstrate their understanding of conservation and perspective-taking?

When familiar and comfortable situations are used for testing, children's understanding of causality also is more sophisticated than Piaget believed (Bullock, 1984). For instance, most preschool children know that causes precede outcomes, or effects. When shown an apparatus in which a Snoopy doll pops up if a marble is dropped into the left side but not the right side, 3-year-old children understand that the cause (dropping the marble) must occur prior to the effect (Snoopy's appearance) and select the correct side in which to drop the marble (Bullock & Gelman, 1979; Bullock, Gelman, & Baillargeon, 1982).

Children exhibit higher levels of categorization skills under simplified conditions. They can solve some kinds of class inclusion problems when the wording is changed or when simpler versions of the task are used. For instance, young children recognize that a person would have more to color in a picture if he or she colored the whole bird rather than just its wings (Siegler, 1998).

These studies show that Piaget underestimated young children's capabilities to solve problems using logical principles. Nevertheless, his theory still provides us with a good description of many of the ways in which young children's thinking differs from that of older children and adults. Piaget's ideas about preoperational development are a good starting point for understanding children's problem solving, and they guide us in the right direction for conducting new studies on how young children think about the problems they face every day.

YOUNG CHILDREN'S MEMORY

Four-year-old Abe and 8-year-old Sophie just visited the zoo with their parents. On the car ride home, Abe says he saw a bear and some snakes. Sophie recites a much longer list; she reports that they also saw elephants, birds, monkeys, zebras, kangaroos, and lions. The children's parents remember even more of the animals than either of the children. This example illustrates a typical pattern: young children remember less than older children. Information processing approaches to understanding children's thinking have focused attention on what children forget and what they remember. For instance, they consider whether young children simply fail to pay attention or whether older children have special capabilities for remembering.

Have you ever noticed that as soon as you read a phone number out of the telephone book and dial it, you forget it? Conversely, are you surprised at how vividly you remember some things? Many people say they can remember exactly what they were doing when they heard that Princess Diana of Great Britain was killed in an automobile crash in Paris. Most people have vivid memories of what they were doing when they heard about horrific events of September 11, 2001. However, these same people may not remember what they ate for lunch the day before. Why are some memories so vivid, whereas others are so fleeting?

People have different ways to store memories, which determine the likelihood that the memories will be remembered later. In Chapter 2, you learned that the memory system has three components: sensory storage, short-term memory, and long-term memory. A phone number you want to dial immediately after looking it up would be held briefly in short-term memory; it would never be transferred to long-term memory, because you have no need to remember it for a longer time period. In contrast, an event such as your wedding or an automobile accident you witnessed is likely to be moved into long-term memory, because it is reviewed, involves visual imagery, evokes emotions, and may be important to

How much will these children remember about their trip to an aquatic park? What contributes to young children's lack of memory?

remember. Like older children and adults, young children have a three-component memory system that allows them to store information in their memories. Why, then, do they remember less than older children and adults?

All humans have limits on their capacities to process information. When people are distracted or tired or are presented with too much information, they will not remember it as well as when they are attentive and alert and are presented with less information. However, young children's capacities are more limited than older children's and adults' for three basic reasons:

+ **Tendency to be easily distracted.** Young children are more easily distracted than older children. Children who are distracted by loud noises or colorful scenes will not pay as much attention as children who can focus their attention more systematically. Attention to relevant information increases between 3 and 8 years of age (DeMarie-Dreblow & Miller, 1988).

+ **Failure to use memory strategies.** Memory strategies are techniques used to improve memory, such as **rehearsal** (reviewing information), **organization** (clustering information into groups of similar objects or into meaningful categories), and **elaboration** (thinking of associations among objects). These strategies help move information into long-term memory. Consider how you study for an exam. To increase the likelihood of doing well on an exam, you might rehearse new terms and try to think of ways to relate them to meaningful concepts. For instance, you might study terms concerning prenatal development in the order in which developments occur month to month. The use of strategies develops during childhood. Toddlers show evidence of using very simple precursors to memory strategies (DeLoache, Cassidy & Brown, 1985). Preschoolers begin to develop memory strategies, but use rehearsal, organization, or elaboration only rarely to help them remember information.

+ **Lack of awareness of memory.** Young children are unlikely to use **metacognition;** that is, they are less likely than older children to be aware of memory and to monitor their memory performance. Around age 5, children begin to be aware of their learning processes, probably because of their school experiences, and this awareness grows throughout childhood. The better children monitor their memory and learning processes, the more likely they are to store and retrieve information effectively (Siegler, 1998).

YOUNG CHILDREN'S UNDERSTANDING OF EVERYDAY EVENTS

By the time a child is 5, she or he may have taken hundreds of baths, eaten at fast food restaurants many times, and helped bake cookies a dozen times. What do children remember from these kinds of events? Do they understand that the actions involved in everyday interactions take place in some order? Do they understand which pieces of information are essential and which are not? For instance, in a fast food restaurant, a child can order a hamburger one day and chicken pieces the next, but in both cases, she or he must place the order and pay before picking up the food. The causal sequence of events is crucial, although the type of food is not (Schlottmann, 1999).

The concepts that people form about routines involved in everyday interactions and events may be thought of as **scripts.** As children experience these activities, they have opportunities to learn the sequencing of events (Nelson, 1986). By the age of 3, children begin to develop rudimentary scripts. For example, 3-year-old Jenny may describe the script for grocery shopping as "First, we go to the store, and then we pick out food we like." This basic script has little detail, but reveals Jenny's understanding that going to the store happens before picking out food. As children mature, they develop more elaborate scripts with more details and more sequencing of events (Farrar & Goodman, 1992; Mandler, 1993). For instance, a 5-year-old may remember the script for going to the store as driving to the store, parking the car, getting a cart for the food, picking out food, paying, going to the car, going

rehearsal memory strategy involving the reviewing of information

organization memory strategy involving the clustering of information into groups of similar objects or into meaningful categories

elaboration memory strategy involving the forming of associations among objects

metacognition awareness of memory and monitoring of memory performance

scripts concepts that people form about routines involved in everyday interactions and events

Over time, as children experience the same events repeatedly, they begin to learn the scripts involved in those events. What kind of script does this child likely have?

home, and putting the groceries away (Hudson, Shapiro, & Sosa, 1995). Children's first successes at planning future events are based on their script-based knowledge of events (Hudson & Fivush, 1991).

Children's memory for everyday routines and activities influences how they remember specific information. Young children may inaccurately remember an uncommon event by distorting their memories in the direction of a familiar script. For instance, children who have eaten at a nice restaurant may inaccurately report that the food was paid for before they ate, because this is what they experienced in fast food restaurants. Familiarity with the fast food restaurant script colors their memory (Siegler, 1998). As children grow older, they become better able to distinguish between actual and script memories.

Parents help children develop and remember scripts by asking them to recall past events and by asking questions about the activities that occurred (Hudson, 1990). In this way, parents provide children with hints about what kinds of information are important to remember and give them cues about the ordering of events (Nelson, 1993; Price & Goodman, 1990).

YOUNG CHILDREN AS EXPERTS

Despite their limitations in remembering information, young children are able to learn a large amount of information on topics that interest them. Some children learn enough information in an area to become experts, developing a vast store of knowledge about dinosaurs or becoming a chess whiz. One study focused on a 4½-year-old dinosaur expert who had been exposed to information about dinosaurs for a little over a year. This child could name and recognize over forty types of dinosaurs and describe where they lived, their diets, and their forms of locomotion (Chi & Koeske, 1983).

Children and adults who are experts on a specific topic retain more details about that topic and think about that topic both more extensively and differently than other people (Chase & Simon, 1973). Most importantly, an expert organizes information differently. For instance, chess experts are better than nonexperts at remembering the positions of chess pieces in real games, but they do not have an advantage when the pieces are randomly arranged on the board (Chi, 1978). This suggests that a chess expert's better memory for chess is due not to better memory abilities overall but to a better understanding of chess.

Just as experts remember information relevant to their area of expertise better than novices, children remember familiar information better than unfamiliar information (Harris, Durso, Mergler, & Jones, 1990). When information is familiar, children can apply new strategies more efficiently. With practice, these strategies become more automatic and require fewer processing demands. Because processing demands are minimal, children develop the capacity to apply memory strategies to unfamiliar content (Siegler, 1998).

THEORY OF MIND: YOUNG CHILDREN'S UNDERSTANDING OF MENTAL EVENTS

Tammy, age 3, played a trick one day with the help of her father. She called for her uncle to come into the room, knowing that as soon as he opened the door wide enough to enter, he would be hit by the pillow that she and her father had balanced on the top of the door. For Tammy to enjoy this trick, she had to recognize that her uncle did not know what was about to happen and would be surprised when the pillow dropped on him. Which he was.

Tammy's behavior indicates that she has some understanding of mental states—what people know, think, and feel. Preschoolers often use the words

Why do some children become experts on dinosaurs? How does their knowledge of dinosaurs differ from that of someone who is not an expert?

THE SOCIAL IMPACT: DEBATING THE ISSUE

Can Young Children's Eyewitness Testimony Be Believed?

In 1988, Margaret Michaels was convicted of sexually abusing preschool children at the school where she worked in New Jersey (*State v. Michaels*, 1988). She was accused of molesting children during regular school hours over a period of seven months. None of the alleged acts had been noticed by staff or parents, and none of the children had reported any instances to their parents. The first suspicion occurred when a 4-year-old former student told a nurse who was taking his temperature rectally, "That's what my teacher does to me." This started a series of investigations, and many other children began to disclose similar stories, but only after they had been repeatedly interviewed by case workers. On the basis of testimony provided by nineteen child witnesses, Michaels was convicted of 115 counts of sexual abuse and sentenced to serve forty-seven years in prison. An Appeals Court reversed her conviction, and the New Jersey State Supreme Court upheld this reversal (*State v. Michaels*, 1994), ruling that in order to retry the case, the prosecution would first have to convince the court that the child witnesses could provide reliable testimony. The prosecution then dropped all charges against Michaels (Ceci & Bruck, 1995).

The Michaels case is not an isolated case. There have been many similar cases, some of which you may remember because of the extensive media coverage they received. Often the sole witnesses are preschool-aged children who disclosed the abuse only after a long delay and after intensive interviewing. Usually, no corroborative evidence is found and the defendants maintain their innocence (Ceci & Bruck, 1995). Can the testimony of young children be believed?

Children can be reliable witnesses, but many conditions influence the accuracy of their testimony:

- **Suggestibility and vulnerability to leading questions.** Existing research indicates that preschoolers are more vulnerable than older children to leading questions and are more suggestible. This is not to say that young children cannot provide accurate and reliable testimony, but they are more susceptible to a variety of factors that contribute to unreliable testimony (Ceci & Bruck, 1998). A child who is repeatedly asked about how her teacher touched her in a "bad" place may be led into believing that this happened, even if it did not.
- **Desire for approval from adults.** Young children are very reliant on adults for approval and are eager to please them. It is common for a preschooler to provide a desired answer to an adult's question just to win the adult's approval (Garbarino & Stott, 1992). For example, when an adult asks young children to select a suspect from a series of photographs that does not contain a picture of the actual suspect, children rarely acknowledge that they do not recognize any of the photographs. They are likely to make a false identification because they want to please the adult. This is true even when children are warned that the lineup may not contain a picture of the suspect (King & Yuille, 1987).
- **Repeated questioning.** Young children's testimony is less likely to be distorted after one interview than after several interviews (Ceci & Bruck, 1995). The constant questioning, and sometimes leading questions, may cause children to think that they are supposed to answer questions in certain ways. Repeating questions to young children may make them feel that their previous answers were wrong. A child who initially answered that the teacher didn't do anything "bad" may eventually say that the teacher *did* do something bad, simply because an adult asked repeatedly. The child may think that if his or her initial answer had been OK, then the adult would not have asked the question again and again. Children's desire to please adults may lead them to change their answers to what they believe the adult wants rather than what is accurate.

Of course, older children and adults also are suggestible and vulnerable to leading questions. However, because of their limited memory skills, dependence on adults, and limited experiences, young children are more easily influenced by the suggestions and leading questions. The impact of persistent and suggestive questioning is likely to be especially powerful on children (Ceci & Bruck, 1998).

Thinking It Through:

1. Why did prosecutors drop their appeal in the Margaret Michaels case?
2. What are the three main factors that can lead to inaccuracy in children's testimony, and why do they decrease accuracy?
3. How can young children's reports of sexual abuse be obtained with the fewest inaccuracies?

---

think, pretend, and *imagine,* providing clues that they have ideas about the inner mental events that people experience (Bartsch & Wellman, 1995). An understanding of inner mental events means that children have developed a **theory of mind;** that is, they understand that people think, imagine, pretend, and wonder about the world around them.

Developing a theory of mind represents a tremendous accomplishment in which children learn to separate the external world from the inner workings of the mind (Wellman & Gelman, 1998). This achievement influences many aspects of children's lives, including how they distinguish pretend and real events, understand deception and lies, interpret other people's behavior, and distinguish between beliefs and desires. For instance, children who

theory of mind the understanding of inner mental events—that people think, imagine, pretend, and wonder about the world around them

have a theory of mind are likely to understand how to anger or entertain a younger sibling (Dunn, 1988) and how to ensure that their communications have been understood (Shwe & Markman, 1997). The extent to which children all over the world develop a theory of mind is unclear. Cultural factors such as schooling, emphasis on science, and group cohesiveness may influence how and whether members of a culture develop and use beliefs about others' minds and behaviors (Gauvain, 1998; Lillard, 1998).

For North American children, whose understanding of theory of mind has been studied the most extensively, understanding of inner mental states increases in sophistication during early childhood. Three- and 4-year-old children realize that people, but not objects, can "think" and that thinking is an internal process. By 5 years of age, children tend to believe that people think using their brains and realize that one can think about things that are not present (Flavell, Green, & Flavell, 1987). In addition, young children's theory of mind gives rise to fantasy play, as they now can pretend and imagine what others feel or think (Taylor & Carlson, 1997).

The method most commonly used to assess children's understanding of others' minds is the false-belief task (Wimmer & Perner, 1983). In the "Maxi" task, candy is hidden in a box while the child and another person, Maxi, watch. Maxi then leaves the room. While Maxi is gone, the treat is moved to another container. The question for the child is "When Maxi returns, will he know where the treat is hidden?" Usually, 4-year-olds recognize that Maxi will look where the candy was originally hidden, since that is the situation as Maxi experienced it. However, 3-year-olds usually cannot solve the problem, instead stating that Maxi will look in the new hiding place. This shortcoming in thinking suggests that younger children do not understand others' beliefs. Many studies have confirmed this developmental trend, including studies of children of Baka pygmies living in the rain forests of Cameroon (Avis & Harris, 1991). Young children appear to be unable to "read the minds" of others (Wellman, 1990).

Children are capable of misleading someone intentionally using their theory of mind. To mislead someone, children must understand that the other person does not know what they know. When simple and concrete situations are used, even 3-year-olds can intentionally mislead someone (Chandler, Fritz, & Hala, 1989). However, young children's understanding of mental states is not sophisticated nor is it applied consistently. They may be poor at inferring from a situation what others are thinking (Flavell, Green, & Flavell, 1995). For example, Tammy continued to try to fool her uncle, not recognizing that he now knew the pillow trick. Preschool children also fail to realize that people tend to focus their thinking on one topic at a time rather than on many.

YOUNG CHILDREN'S UNDERSTANDING OF PRETEND AND REAL

Given that children spend much of their time playing "make believe" and watch many hours of fantasy situations on television, it is important to determine how well they can distinguish between pretend and real situations. The answer depends on the type of fantasy-reality comparison that is made. Children often are quite capable of making these distinctions. When 2½-year-old children are involved in fantasy play using make-believe substances such as "tea" in a cup, they recognize the fantasy nature of the play and respond appropriately—maybe even wiping up imaginary spilled tea after they watch another "spill" it (Harris & Kavanaugh, 1993; Leslie, 1987). Similarly, by age 3, young children understand the difference between a real object and a "play" toy (Woolley & Wellman, 1990).

Children do, however, have difficulty identifying an object when its appearance conflicts with its true identity. When children are shown a deceptive object, such as a sponge that looks like a rock, they are confused by the object's appearance and do not pay attention to its true nature (Flavell, 1988). At age 3, most children do not distinguish the appearance of deceptive objects from their reality, even after training (Taylor & Hort, 1990). However, in simplified situations, even 3-year-olds may recognize these distinctions (Rice, Koinis, Sullivan, Tager-Flusberg, & Winner, 1997). Children's ability to make more difficult discriminations increases with age (Flavell, Green, & Flavell, 1987). By age 5, children generally make these distinctions, even in cognitively demanding situations (Martin & Halverson, 1983).

These children have dressed up to play store. At this age, what do they understand about what is real and what is pretend?

The boundaries children draw between fantasy play and reality also become more differentiated between 2 and 6 years of age: Whereas younger children might scare themselves playing monster, older children will not (DiLalla & Watson, 1988).

THE SOCIAL CONTEXT OF COGNITIVE DEVELOPMENT

As you learned in Chapter 5, infants gain knowledge through interactions with other people. The social context continues to play an important role in young children's cognitive development. In Piaget's view, children are explorers who discover many interesting and valuable ideas through their interactions with people and objects. According to the Russian psychologist Lev Vygotsky, children and caregivers discover ideas together (Martin, 2000).

Just as parents of infants and toddlers can scaffold their learning of language, parents of preschoolers can promote their cognitive development through the use of a scaffolding system. This cognitive scaffolding provides a continually evolving, moderately challenging learning environment, which changes in response to the child's developing cognitive competencies.

Scaffolding involves many different strategies, including engaging the child's attention, reducing the number of steps in a task, motivating the child, and demonstrating the skill to be performed (Berk & Winsler, 1999; Karpov & Haywood, 1998). To see how caregivers' scaffolding strategies work, consider the way Anita helps her 4-year-old daughter Rachel with a challenging animal puzzle. To make the task easier, Anita breaks it into more manageable units. After turning all the pieces right side up, Anita suggests that Rachel select the pieces that have straight edges, because these pieces make up the border of the puzzle. Then Anita gives Rachel strategies for putting the pieces together. As Rachel selects each piece, Anita describes the color and the animal on the piece, giving Rachel clues to help her decide where the piece might fit. At each step, Anita provides subgoals for finishing the puzzle, which help Rachel avoid frustration. She also suggests ways to think about the puzzle pieces, providing Rachel with keys to the thinking process.

Anita is extending Rachel's problem-solving abilities and understanding about puzzles by working within Rachel's zone of proximal development (Chapter 5). The next time they get a puzzle out, Anita waits to see whether Rachel turns the pieces right side up before suggesting this strategy. Anita also is less likely to discuss the colors of each piece, and Rachel is more likely to mention these qualities herself as she tries to fit pieces together. Anita and Rachel continually renegotiate strategies, with Anita tuning in to Rachel's skills each time they play.

If Anita tried the same strategies with a much more challenging game, Rachel probably would not complete the game. Both probably would feel frustrated in their efforts because they would be working outside of Rachel's zone of proximal development. If Anita tried the same strategies with a simple game that Rachel had already mastered, Rachel's cognitive skills would not be facilitated. By working within the frame of Rachel's abilities and providing a nurturing context, Anita gives Rachel a challenging experience, and Rachel's problem-solving abilities improve (Tappan, 1998).

When Rachel works on the puzzles, an interesting thing takes place: Rachel talks out loud to herself. Her tendency to talk about the puzzle aloud when she is alone demonstrates Vygotsky's idea of **private speech,** which individuals speak to themselves when solving problems. Piaget assumed that children's tendency to talk to themselves simply indicated egocentrism, and so he labeled this **egocentric speech.** Vygotsky, however, believed that private speech is an internalized voice that helps guide thinking. In solving the puzzle, Anita suggested strategies ("Let's put the straight-edged pieces together first"), which Rachel used to put the puzzle together. Later, when Rachel worked on the puzzle alone, she repeated out loud the strategies that her mom had proposed. Over time, these conversations become internalized and children can, on their own, use them to help direct their behavior (Winsler, Diaz, & Montero, 1997).

Recent research has confirmed and expanded upon the idea of private speech (Duncan & Pratt, 1997). Children use private speech more often to direct their actions than to

private speech Vygotsky's term for speech directed toward the self, used when solving problems

egocentric speech Piaget's term for speech directed toward the self

make egocentric remarks. As children grow older, their private speech becomes quieter (Berk, 1994).

CULTURAL INFLUENCES ON YOUNG CHILDREN'S THINKING

Just as caregivers provide learning environments for children's cognitive development, so too do the communities or cultures in which children are raised (DiMaggio, 1997). Children's learning takes place through active participation with others. One can think of children as apprentices who are actively involved in organizing and supporting their own learning experiences by working with other people in everyday cultural activities (Rogoff, Mistry, Goncu, & Mosier, 1993). Through apprenticeships with adults, children essentially become experts on their own culture; they learn the skills, the background knowledge, and the values and norms of their community.

Given the great diversity of cultures and communities, it is not surprising that children's exposure to their own culture results in specific experiences and scripts that differ from those of children raised in different cultures. How do children learn the specific cognitive skills and values associated with their own culture?

◆ **Through exposure.**   To learn cultural scripts, children need exposure to the situations associated with the scripts. In their day-to-day experiences and interactions with others, children are exposed to their culture's values regarding particular skills (Jacobs, 1997). For instance, the Inuits, who live near the Arctic Circle, often demonstrate the value of knowing one's whereabouts as a survival skill, and so their children learn to use spatial skills to navigate their environment.

◆ **Through practice.**   Children also learn cultural scripts through practice (DiMaggio, 1997). A young child raised in a rural environment, for example, is more likely than a city child to learn about the care of farm animals. Similarly, children who are raised with the cultural expectation that they will learn certain skills, such as weaving, receive many opportunities to practice such skills.

◆ **Through regulation.**   Cultural differences in child-rearing practices include variations in the extent to which adults control and regulate children's roles in everyday activities. Children may be allowed or required to observe a valued activity before practicing it. As children become more accomplished and skilled, adults may increase children's involvement in the activity. Providing graded levels of exposure to valued activities helps children learn the details needed to perform them (Rogoff et al., 1993).

◆ **Through encouragement.**   Adults provide different learning experiences for children by encouraging them to become involved in certain activities (Cole, 1997). Encouragement may be indirect and social or direct and material. In Zimbabwe, many parents encourage their children to learn about marketing, because trading is an important part of daily life. In contrast, young children in the United States receive little parental encouragement to become involved in trading. Thus, children from Zimbabwe develop sophisticated cognitive scripts for and knowledge of trading more readily than children from the United States do.

◆ **Through assignment of responsibility.**   Cultures vary in the extent to which parents and adults structure the learning environment. In some cultures, adults provide structure by guiding children's attention, motivation, and involvement and by providing lessons in important activities. This greater level of parental involvement is typical in societies in which children's participation in adult life is delayed until they are much older. Children learn skills that are assumed to help them later, when they take on adult roles (Rogoff et al., 1993).

In other cultures, children direct their own attention and motivation and determine for themselves their level of involvement in adult activities. The role of adults is to provide feedback in response to children's requests but not to try to direct the children. For instance, in a Mayan Indian town in Guatemala, children routinely observe their mothers' involvement

In what way is this child taking primary responsibility for learning to weave? By what means do children learn the scripts associated with their culture? How would cultural differences change this scene if you were learning to weave?

in adult economic activities—for example, weaving and sewing. Children are responsible for watching the activities and deciding whether and when to enter into them. While the mothers respond to children's questions and requests, typically they do not give direct instruction (Rogoff et al., 1993). Children raised in traditional Native American cultures learn through quiet observation. A Navajo girl may decide she is ready to weave after spending time watching her mother, but without receiving direct instruction in weaving (Collier, 1988).

EDUCATING YOUNG CHILDREN

Young children's cognitive development is influenced by the stimulation and interactions that caregivers provide for them. Some of these interactions are very direct, such as those discussed earlier in which caregivers provide scaffolding for their children. Caregivers also act as teachers and facilitators of learning by providing stimulating environments for their children. Outside the home, children experience opportunities to learn in preschool and kindergarten settings.

How can trips to the library promote cognitive development? What else can parents do to help their children become talented and gifted?

Parents as Teachers

How do children grow up to become gifted or talented in a particular cognitive area? Do their parents treat them in any special ways to help encourage their talents? Not surprisingly, parents play a very important role in encouraging the cognitive abilities of their children. In a fascinating study of twenty-five famous mathematicians, it was discovered that twenty-one of these talented individuals had experienced early intellectual stimulation (Fowler, 1986). For example, the father of René Descartes (1596–1650; credited with unifying algebra and geometry) began René's intensive intellectual stimulation when he was only 14 months of age. Blaise Pascal (1632–1662; credited with developing the first calculating machine and famous for his work on probability theory) and Karl Gauss (1777–1855; considered to be the father of modern mathematics) had parents who intensively schooled them to calculate, read, and write early and engaged them in many intellectual discussions. Almost all of these great mathematicians were, as children, exposed to highly intellectual adults who stimulated their cognitive development.

Parents promote cognitive development by constructing an optimal learning environment in the home—they provide materials, experiences, and encouragement that help children to become curious explorers of their worlds. An instrument designed to measure these aspects of a stimulating environment is called the Home Observation for Measurement of the Environment (HOME) Scale (see Table 7.1). Studies using the HOME Scale have investigated the roles in children's cognitive development of parental encouragement of learn-

TABLE 7.1

Assessing the Home Environment

SUBSCALE	SAMPLE ITEMS
Stimulation of academic behavior	Child is encouraged to learn colors
Variety in daily stimulation	Child is frequently taken on outings with other family members
Access to toys and games for stimulation	Home has toys and games
Encouragement of maturity	Child is encouraged to be responsible and sociable
Language stimulation	Parent teaches child about language through the use of games, books, puzzles
Punishment methods	Parent does not spank or slap child during visit
Physical environment	Rooms are clean and uncluttered
Pride and acceptance	Parent is proud of child

SOURCE: Elardo and Bradley, 1981.

TABLE 7.2

Stimulating Young Children's Intellectual Development

Read to children and let them see you read.
Visit the library and allow children to select their own books.
Set limits on television viewing to encourage more conversational skills and reading.
Provide pencils, crayons, and markers for children to practice drawing and writing.
Ask children questions and listen to their answers.
Take children to museums, art galleries, and historical sites.
Encourage children to think critically and solve problems.
Explore and play with children.

SOURCE: National Association for the Education of Young Children, 1995.

ing and the physical environment to which the child is exposed (Bradley, 1999). Higher scores on the HOME Scale relate to better outcomes for children. When children are exposed to a large variety of learning materials in a safe environment and when they receive encouragement for learning, they score higher on tests of language development and cognitive development than do children with less stimulating environments (Bradley, Burchinal, & Casey, 2001). African American, Caucasian American, and Hispanic children show similar relationships between HOME features and cognitive development (Bradley et al., 1989).

During the early years, parents can encourage children's cognitive development in many ways. Probably the most important is spending time with children (see Table 7.2). Although most parents are aware of the importance of reading to their children, not all parents routinely provide this type of experience. Many children are read to very little or not at all during the early years, and how often children are read to varies by income level and race-ethnicity of the family (see Figure 7.5).

FIGURE 7.5

Percent of Young Children Who Were Read to Three or More Times per Week, by Race-Ethnicity

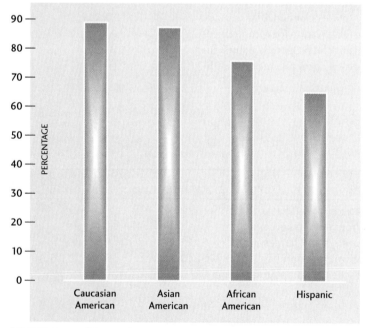

SOURCE: National Center for Education Statistics, 1999.

What generalizations can you draw from this figure? What factors may contribute to the differences found among the racial-ethnic groups?

Young Children's Educational Experiences

Since the first public nursery schools for children were opened in the United States in the early 1900s, the idea of an education-oriented setting for young children has become increasingly popular. Even with fewer children being born today in the United States than in past decades, enrollment in preschools has risen dramatically, from about 20 percent in the 1970s to about 50 percent today.

A good preschool uses developmentally appropriate practices. This means that the activities are based on knowledge about the developmental level of children within a particular age range. At the same time, a good preschool encourages and recognizes the unique qualities that each child brings to the educational experience. Activities in the preschool curriculum foster children's physical, social, cognitive, and emotional development.

A good preschool does not mimic older children's elementary education classes. Instead, a good preschool is geared specifically for the active young child. Rather than sitting at desks and being guided by a teacher, children should be encouraged to actively explore their environments. Some children might play with water containers, others listen to a story, and still others build a block fortress. Teachers can facilitate children's involvement by asking questions or offering suggestions. A good preschool focuses on the individual needs of each child and on enhancing children's self-esteem and self-control.

The effectiveness of preschool programs has been studied extensively. High-quality preschool programs have low student-teacher ratios, a well-educated staff, and developmentally appropriate activities. Children in such programs show advances in cognitive and social skills compared with children from the same kind of backgrounds who do not attend preschools (Clarke-Stewart, 1984). This is especially true for disadvantaged children (Burchinal, Lee, & Ramey, 1989). In one study, the cognitive and social advantages of preschool were still apparent after three years of elementary school (Howes, 1988b). Children who attended high-quality preschools had fewer behavior problems and better academic skills in first grade than did children who did not attend high-quality preschools.

Notice that the children in this class are not sitting at desks studying. How do children learn in preschool? What are some developmentally appropriate methods for encouraging cognitive development in preschool children?

Clearly, a major issue for parents must be the quality of care that their children receive. Given the importance of a good preschool, it is essential that parents learn how to assess the quality of preschools so that children have the optimal early childhood education experience. Table 7.3 outlines some of the features that parents should look for in preschools.

Children's first experience with formal schooling usually occurs in kindergarten. The first kindergartens, opened in the mid-nineteenth century, were designed to nurture young children. Today in the United States, kindergarten has become another tier of the public education system. Many people believe that children's cognitive development needs to be accelerated, and one means of doing so is to increase the academic emphasis in kindergarten.

ABLE 7.3
Indicators of a High-Quality Preschool

Licensing/Accreditation	The program is licensed by the state. If the program is accredited by the National Association for the Education of Young Children, it is a top-notch program.
Setting	There is a safe, fenced, outdoor play area, well equipped for many activities. The indoor area has space for many different activities and a wide variety of toys, books, puzzles, and games.
Teacher-Child Ratio	The number of children supervised by a team of two teachers is not greater than 18 to 20. Each teacher is responsible for no more than 8 to 10 children.
Teacher Qualifications	Teachers have college-level training in child development or early childhood education.
Parent Involvement	Parents are encouraged to drop in to observe the children and to participate in activities with them. Teachers frequently review and discuss children's development with parents.

SOURCE: National Association for the Education of Young Children, 1997.

THE SCIENTIFIC IMPACT: INTERPRETING RESEARCH

When Are Young Children Prepared to Start School?

"By the year 2000, all children in America will start school ready to learn." These words were uttered in 1989 by then President George H. Bush and the state governors, who established this as the top goal for American education. Few argued with this goal, but how *readiness* was to be defined and how this goal was to be reached were hotly debated (Gredler, 1997; Shepard, 1997).

Readiness to learn has been conceptualized as the level of development at which a child is prepared to undertake the learning of specific material and content. For most preschoolers, learning is an active and enjoyable process. Most enter kindergarten ready to learn, but this readiness does not always guarantee success in school (Lewit & Baker, 1995).

Historically, chronological age has served as the major criterion for school entry. In the United States, although some children enter kindergarten at age 4, the majority enter at between 5 and 6 years of age, with about 6 percent held back each year to begin school after they are 6 (National Center for Education Statistics, 2001a). The tendency to hold children back has been increasing; in recent years, almost 16 percent of first-grade

children were held back for one year (Brent, May, & Kundert, 1996). Because some aspects of development, such as language skills, are strongly correlated with age, older children, particularly boys, do better in school during the early grades than do younger class-mates. However, these differences tend to disappear by third grade (Stipek & Byler, 2001). Age generally is not a good predictor of academic success (Morrison, Alberts, & Griffith, 1997).

Although there is no agreement as to what constitutes readiness for school, being physically healthy, having adequate communication skills, having an interest in learning, being able to sit still, and controlling one's impulses have been identified as key components (Lewit & Baker, 1995). According to a large-scale study of kindergartners and their parents (US Department of Education, 1993), only 63 percent of kindergartners had all of these school readiness qualities. These findings are in line with an earlier study in which kindergarten teachers said that 65 percent of their students were not ready to participate successfully in school (US Department of Education, 1993). In addition, when teachers were asked to compare the readiness of their current students

with that of their students five years ago, only 25 percent said that today's kindergartners were more ready; 42 percent said fewer students were ready now than before.

School readiness does not reside solely with children. Families, schools, and communities have the responsibility to ensure children's school readiness (Carlton & Winsler, 1999). Supportive environments that promote healthy, concerned, developmentally appropriate interactions with young children are likely to produce the most active and eager learners in kindergarten and beyond (May & Kundert, 1997).

Thinking It Through:

1. What kinds of things can parents and teachers do to promote young children's school readiness?
2. What individual characteristics of young children enhance their readiness to enter school?
3. In your opinion, what are the most important qualities that determine a young child's readiness to enter kindergarten? What factors put children at risk for not being ready to enter school?

These people see preschools and kindergartens as obvious places to begin academic training and promote readiness for school. Many experts in child development, however, oppose an emphasis on early academic training in reading, writing, and arithmetic (Charlesworth, 1989; Elkind, 1987, 1988), primarily for two reasons. One reason relates to the belief that children learn best when they are actively involved in learning. Good kindergarten and preschool programs lay the foundation for later cognitive skills by encouraging developmentally appropriate play and supplying hands-on experiences. Another reason is that children who are pushed academically at a young age may lose interest in learning, which has serious long-term consequences for children's education.

EARLY INTERVENTION AND YOUNG CHILDREN'S COGNITIVE DEVELOPMENT

Young children's cognitive development is stimulated and nurtured when they are exposed to intellectually challenging environments and have positive role models to emulate. For instance, children are more likely to be interested in reading if they observe their parents routinely reading for pleasure in the home. Unfortunately, not all children have such ideal conditions for cognitive development. Many young children are in stressful, distracting environments that lack intellectual stimulation. These children do not have the kinds of early experiences that foster the development of competent intellectual performance and achievement. For instance, they may not be taken to libraries or read to often because the parents are overworked or in poor health. Can these unstimulating environments be overcome or supplemented?

Head Start

Project Head Start originated in 1965, during America's "War on Poverty," and was designed to serve preschool-age children from economically disadvantaged backgrounds. In 1998, there were over 40,000 Head Start classrooms serving 793,809 children. The program has serviced almost 17 million children since 1965. In 1994, approximately 61 percent of Head Start families had an annual income of less than $9,000. Of the children enrolled in Head Start, 36 percent were African American, 31 percent were Caucasian American, 26 percent were Hispanic, 4 percent were Native American, and 3 percent were Asian American. Head Start serves about 30 percent of all eligible children (Administration on Children, Youth, and Families, 1998).

Children living in low-income families are at risk for failure in school because these families may not give priority to academic values or encourage children to think critically. The families simply may not have the resources to promote cognitive development. Head Start programs were developed to overcome these problems. Children begin Head Start classes at age 3 and can continue for two years. Although Head Start is more than an educational program, one of its stated goals is to provide environmental interventions that stimulate children's cognitive growth. For this reason, much of the research on the effectiveness of Head Start has focused on the intellectual performance of the young children enrolled in the program (Raver & Zigler, 1997).

Studies of the immediate effects of Head Start showed that young children's IQ scores rose by at least 10 points and that their achievement levels sometimes rose after just a few weeks of attending Head Start (Datta, 1985). Unfortunately, findings on later effects were not as optimistic. Research found that young children attending Head Start did not continue to do better on cognitive tests or in school (Nieman & Gaithright, 1981). These reports dashed the hopes of those who believed that early intervention in the form of intellectually stimulating preschools could improve children's success in school permanently. In fact, plans were drawn up to discontinue Head Start (Lubeck, DeVries, Nicholson, & Post, 1997).

Fortunately, parents of the preschoolers enrolled in Head Start protested, and their actions saved the program. Soon afterward, new research was undertaken using more sophisticated designs and techniques. These studies found that young children who attend Head Start show an initial boost in intellectual performance that sometimes lasts for years, but that this initial boost often fades over time (Barnett, 1998).

Why might children's intellectual performance fade over time? One answer may be the formal education these children receive after the preschool years. Low-income families often live in communities where schools do not receive adequate funding. These children thus may find themselves in inferior educational settings and less than stimulating environments. The drop in performance may therefore be a by-product of the relatively poor school environments disadvantaged children encounter (Zigler & Styfco, 1998).

The research also showed, however, that important lasting effects of Head Start exist in other areas. Specifically, participants of Head Start were found to compare favorably in the following ways with low-income children who did not attend Head Start (Consortium for Longitudinal Studies, 1983; Gamble & Zigler, 1989):

- They were less likely to be assigned to special education classes.
- They were less likely to be held back a grade in school.
- They had fewer school absences.

The focus on the intellectual benefits of Head Start for disadvantaged young children obscures the benefits of Head Start in other areas. Preschoolers who attend Head Start show improved physical health, nutritional status, family interactions, and social-emotional behaviors (Raver & Zigler, 1997). Thus, there are considerable benefits to the early interventions provided by Head Start (Fantuzzo & Mohr, 2000).

Head Start is expanding its services to include children younger than 3 years of age. The rationale for this extension is clear: Waiting until a child is 3 or 4 years old is too late (Kagan &

Why has Sesame Street *been successful in promoting the intellectual growth of preschool children all around the world?*

Neuman, 1998). With children beginning Head Start earlier, it may be possible to provide preventive services that are more effective than the remedial services provided after problems arise. Children who are healthy, who have positive relationships with caregivers, and who receive adequate stimulation have the foundations for learning in preschool and beyond (Zigler, 1999).

SESAME STREET

Television reaches many eligible children that Head Start does not reach. Because of its wide acceptance and use, television is viewed by educators as a "teacher" in every home. Between 1960 and 1970, Congress passed legislation funding the construction of public educational television stations and the development of educational programming. Today, public television provides a wide range of educational programming, and almost every US family has access to these programs.

Most children know and recognize the characters Grover and Big Bird, attesting to the popularity of the highly successful educational program *Sesame Street*. *Sesame Street* is watched by almost half of all preschoolers on a weekly basis. In the United States, 77 percent of preschool children watch the show at least once a week (Public Broadcasting Service, 1999). *Sesame Street* was the first educational program that combined the attention-holding qualities of commercial television with developmentally appropriate educational material designed to help prepare children for school. The goal of *Sesame Street* is to promote the intellectual growth of preschoolers, particularly disadvantaged preschoolers.

Sesame Street is successful in teaching children many skills; regular viewing increases young children's understanding of numbers, letters, and vocabulary and boosts their reasoning skills. Children from varied racial, social, geographic, and educational backgrounds all seem to learn from watching *Sesame Street* (Children's TV Workshop, 1991; Rice, Huston, Truglio, & Wright, 1990). Measurable effects have been found 10 to 12 years later, and many effects have been found to be consistent across different cultures and countries (Fisch, Truglio, & Cole, 1999). In addition, mothers of preschoolers are pleased with the educational benefits provided by it (Yankelovich & White, 1989).

The influence of *Sesame Street* is stronger on 3-year-old children than on 5-year-olds, suggesting that the effects of *Sesame Street* may be greatest when children first begin to watch it. The effects of *Sesame Street* also are stronger the more often children watch it (Sell, Ray, & Lovelace, 1995). Early on, some critics of *Sesame Street* argued that its apparent effectiveness was due to children's watching the show with parents who used the television show as a means to teach their children (Cook et al., 1975). However, in later research (Rice et al., 1990), parents reported that they watched *Sesame Street* with their preschoolers only 25 percent of the time that the preschoolers watched the program. Thus, 75 percent of the time preschoolers spent watching *Sesame Street* was without their parents. *Sesame Street* provides young children with valuable educational experiences that they can profit from on their own, as well as when they watch with their caregivers (Comstock & Paik, 1991).

Sesame Street is not just an American phenomenon. The show has been adapted for use all over the world and is recognized as beneficial in many countries. In its various adaptations, *Sesame Street* plays in over eighty countries around the world. In each country, *Sesame Street* has been tailored to meet educational goals specific to children in that cultural setting:

✦ The Arabic version of *Sesame Street, Iftah Ya Simsim,* focuses on bridging the gap between the informal language that Arabic-speaking children are exposed to in their homes and the classic Arabic language used in the schools. *Iftah Ya Simsim* makes learning formal Arabic fun as well as interesting (Ezzaki, 1990).

✦ In Portugal, *Sesame Street* is called *Rua Sesamo.* Because only 30 percent of children in Portugal go to preschool, *Rua Sesamo* plays an even greater role in early education than *Sesame Street* does in the United States (Brederode, 1990).

✦ The Turkish version of *Sesame Street* is called *Susam Sokagi.* In Turkey, concern about illiteracy—particularly among women and people who live in rural areas—

is great. One goal of *Susam Sokagi* is to get mothers to watch with their children, so that both the mothers and the children will learn to read and write (Sahin, 1990).

The variations in *Sesame Street* reflect cultural differences in values, education, and economic conditions. Regardless of the culture, research evidence shows that *Sesame Street,* in its different versions, successfully meets the wide variety of educational needs of children in various countries (Children's Television Workshop, 1991).

WHAT CHANGES OCCUR IN YOUNG CHILDREN'S LANGUAGE DEVELOPMENT DURING EARLY CHILDHOOD

Most children are competent speakers of their native language by the age of 5. They have learned many of the subtleties of language; for example, they can distinguish between two similarly worded sentences that have quite different meanings, such as "The bird is in the tree" and "The bird is in the dark." They learn the meanings of thousands of words during the early preschool years. Language development is a primary focus of socialization in a culture. **Social communicative competence** is the ability to effectively convey an intended message to others (Wilcox & Terrell, 1985). Children whose social communicative competence is low are at risk for problem behaviors and poor social relationships (Rice, Hadley, & Alexander, 1993).

VOCABULARY

Children's vocabularies expand rapidly during the preschool years and even faster during the school years. Researchers estimate that before first grade, children learn about five words a day, but in first grade to third grade, they learn about twelve words a day. Using a large sample of words from an English dictionary and asking children about the meaning of these words, researchers have estimated the numbers of words children recognize and how their vocabularies change with age. Children average about 10,000 words in their vocabulary by first grade and about 20,000 words by third grade (Anglin, 1993).

Although young children have a much larger vocabulary than toddlers, they still experience the frustration of not being able to get adults to understand their meaning. There are some words that children want to say but cannot. Some sounds are difficult for them to produce, and children around the world will avoid words that they find difficult to say (Ingram, 1989). Often children create words to better express themselves. For instance, a 4-year-old said, "Try to be more remberful, mom" when disappointed by his mother's forgetfulness (Clark, 1993).

Even with their larger vocabularies, young children continue to be faced with the problem of not knowing as many words as the adults around them know. Just as they did when they were younger, these children find ways to express themselves, using general-purpose nouns such as *thing* or general-purpose verbs such as *do* to describe objects and actions. They also create new words, as noted above. One method of word creation is to add *-er* to the end of a term to indicate an agent taking a particular action. For instance, one child added *-er* to the end of *hang* to refer to a person who hangs pictures as "a hanger." Another method is to coin terms by making nouns into verbs: When trying to pick food up from his plate, one child said, "I'm gonna fork this" (Clark, 1993).

Much of the research on children's word learning focuses on how children learn about words for concrete objects that they can see and touch. But how do children solve the mystery of word meaning for verbs? Think about how much more difficult it is to figure out the meaning of a word such as *push* than that of a word such as *cat.* Verbs are more difficult to learn than nouns are; hence children's early vocabularies have many more nouns than verbs. To learn verbs, children appear to employ a process called **syntactic bootstrapping,** in which they use the structure of a sentence to provide cues about the meaning of the novel

social communicative competence the ability to effectively convey an intended message to others

syntactic bootstrapping children's use of the structure of sentences to provide cues about word meaning

verb (Gleitman & Gillette, 1995). (The word *bootstrapping* refers to "pulling yourself up by the bootstraps.") Suppose a parent says, "Look! The dog is gorping the cat." The child is likely to assume that *gorping* is something that one agent does to another. If the parent says instead, "Look! The dog and cat are gorping," the child is more likely to assume that gorping involved a mutual action (Naigles, 1990).

YOUNG CHILDREN'S LANGUAGE STYLES

Two types of language styles have been identified in middle-class US families. Children with a **referential language style** develop a vocabulary that includes many object names and use these labels to name the things in their environments. Children with an **expressive language style,** however, use words to regulate social interactions with adults and have fewer object names in their vocabulary (Nelson, 1973). The vocabulary explosion is likely to occur at the end of the second year for children with a referential style, who quickly add many names of things to their vocabulary at this time (Goldfield & Reznick, 1990).

   All children use both referential and expressive styles of language on occasion, but some children emphasize one style over the other. Mothers of expressive children direct and control their children's actions through the use of language. For instance, a mother might say, "Say 'good-bye' to your grandmother." In contrast, mothers of referential children comment on aspects of the environment and name activities and objects their children interact with— for example, naming the different toys a child picks up during play (Goldfield, 1987). A child's interests may contribute to the mother's use of language. The mother of a child who shows special interest in a certain toy may encourage that interest by providing names more freely than does the mother of a child who shows less interest (Bridges, 1986).

BEYOND TWO-WORD SENTENCES

As children grow older, their understanding and use of language become increasingly sophisticated. Sentences grow longer than two words, allowing children much more flexibility in communicating their ideas and desires. Between 2 and 3 years of age, many children form sentences of three words or more, using an agent-action-recipient word order to convey meaning. For instance, they might say, "I hugged the cat." Three-year-olds can use negatives such as *no, not, can't,* and *don't.* They may ask questions using *what* and *where,* but they are unlikely to form questions using *why* or *how.*

   During the preschool years, children show evidence of trying to discover and apply grammatical regularities to their speech (Owens, 1996). It appears that children use many language cues to develop increasingly sophisticated knowledge about syntax. For instance, children pay close attention to the ends of words; this helps them understand past tense and plurals. They also pay close attention to word order, and they attempt to preserve the word order they hear in the adult speech directed to them. Children's vocabularies provide a way for them to use what they already know to learn the rules of language. In **semantic bootstrapping,** children use what they know about the meaning of words to help them decipher the syntactic structure of language (Pinker, 1984). For instance, actions indicate verbs, and persons and objects form categories indicated by nouns. These bootstrapping techniques are imperfect; nonetheless, they provide children with a way of using previous knowledge to inform their language development.

   During young childhood, children gain mastery over many rules of grammar, indicating past tense by adding -*ed* to the end of a verb and forming the plural by adding -*s* to the end of a noun. Their application of these rules becomes obvious when they use them in situations in which the rules do *not* apply, in a process called **overregularization.** At around 3 to 4 years of age, English-speaking children may begin to apply the rules for regular forms to irregular cases. Children overregularize infrequently, and when they do, it tends to be with words that parents do not use often (Fenson et al., 1994; Marcus et al., 1992). A child might say, "My teeths hurt" or "I breaked my toy." Caregivers' attempts to correct overregularizations are often ineffective. For example, when 3-year-old Brenda said, "I goed to school

referential language style language style focused on developing a vocabulary that includes many object names

expressive language style language style focused on using words to regulate social interactions with adults

semantic bootstrapping children's use of word meaning to provide cues about syntax

overregularization application of language rules when they do not apply

today," her mother tried to correct her by saying "You mean you went to school today." Without missing a beat, Brenda replied, "Yeah, I goed to school today."

Even in completely unfamiliar situations, children assume that rules for regular plural forms apply. In one study, children were first shown a picture of a birdlike creature called a *wug* and then shown a picture depicting two of the creatures. The children were asked to finish the sentence "There are two _____." Most children said, "There are two *wugs*" (Berko, 1958). They assumed that the plural of *wug* would follow the regular form and be *wugs*.

An interesting twist on children's application of grammatical rules is that younger children correctly use the appropriate plurals and past tenses for even the irregular forms. It appears that very young children memorize the irregular forms and reproduce them accurately. Later, when they learn the rules for the regular forms, they assume that these apply to the irregular forms. Even later, they learn to distinguish between the regular forms and the irregular forms and produce both correctly.

Around 4 years of age, children begin to use connectives to conjoin two events in a complex sentence, such as "You watch television and I'll play with my doll." Use of the connective word *and* is one of the first ways children combine simple sentences. As they mature, children learn to form complex sentences in which two events occur sequentially in time, such as "Let's go to the store and buy some cookies." Even later, children form complex sentences expressing causality. Children use *and* as an all-purpose connective word, but they begin to add others, such as *then* and *when* to represent temporal orderings of events and *because* and *so* to represent causal events (Bloom, 1998).

Five-year-old children have an amazing mastery of language and can use language to entertain and tell stories. Nonetheless, subtle aspects of syntax elude them, and they struggle with some forms of grammar such as the past tense of *to be* (*was* and *were*), possessive pronouns (*his, her, your*), and infinitives ("I want *to go* now") (Owens, 1996). Children gain mastery over the more complex and subtle aspects of grammar and vocabulary during the school years.

UNDERSTANDING CONVERSATIONAL RULES

Six-year-old Robbie sat at the dinner table with a group of adults, patiently trying to find a time when he could break into the conversation to make a point. By the time he found an opening in the conversation, he had forgotten what he wanted to say. For adults, most of the rules of conversation are so ingrained that they do not think about them. They know when they can take a turn in the conversation. But young children face the challenge of learning to follow conversational rules while at the same time applying the rules for forming sentences. This is one aspect of the pragmatics of language development.

Young children are surprisingly good at following basic conversational rules. Even at the age of 2, most children realize they should begin speaking once someone has spoken to them, and they recognize that certain statements require specific answers (yes or no) (Bloom, Rocissano, & Hood, 1976). By the age of 4, many children are aware that they must adjust their speech to fit the speaker; in other words, they must be mindful of whether the person they are speaking to can understand them. For instance, young children shorten their sentences, simplify their vocabulary, and speak more slowly when talking to even younger children (Tomasello & Mannie, 1985). The ability to adjust to the level of the listener continues to develop during childhood. It is important to remember, though, that these skills are not used all the time by all speakers: even adults are not always mindful of the capabilities of their listeners.

THE SOCIAL CONTEXT OF LANGUAGE DEVELOPMENT

Social experiences continue to play an important role in children's language acquisition after infancy (Huttenlocher, 1998; Wilcox, Hadley, & Ashland, 1996). Parents direct children's language exposure when they read to children and engage in a scripted activity like a tea party. They provide opportunities for children to be involved in conversations by asking

THE PRACTICAL IMPACT: NURTURING CHILDREN

Helping Children to Learn Language

Caregivers find many ways to provide an optimal learning environment for preschool children's language acquisition (Owens, 1996). Following are some important strategies for helping children learn language.

- **Recast and expand children's own sentences into longer and more correct forms.** If a child says, "The dinosaur walked in the woods," a caregiver might expand and recast the sentence by saying "That dinosaur walked a long time in the woods, didn't it?" Or a parent might expand a child's statement "I breaked my new doll" into "I'm sorry that you broke your new doll." These variant forms of sentences maintain the basic meaning but display it in a new sentence structure, as well as in correct grammatical form. Children

learn more rapidly about language when parents use these methods (Farrar, 1990). Caregivers use more complex expansions with preschoolers than with toddlers (Hoff-Ginsberg, 1985).

- **Maintain the child's attention to verbal tasks.** Children learn about conversations when caregivers provide topic continuity and reintroduce topics.
- **Build language activities into everyday routines.** For example, while baking cookies, a caregiver might describe every step in the process. By using language skills for everyday activities, children develop scripts for these events that include the use of language.
- **Provide a moderately challenging language environment for the child.** Caregivers should not adjust their language level down to

the child's at all times, but instead should regularly expose the child to a combination of moderately challenging and highly challenging language environments.

- **Encourage the child to experience many language partners.** Children who are encouraged to speak to a wide range of social partners are more likely to hear varied types of input at different levels than are children who speak with fewer partners.
- **Encourage the child's own style of language learning.** Some children are likely to imitate others, and some children tend to avoid imitation. Some children like to make a game out of naming objects. Try to determine the methods the child uses and then incorporate them into everyday language experiences.

them to comment on activities and experiences. For instance, to prompt Sarah to begin a conversation with her father, Sarah's mother asks her at the dinner table, "Can you tell Daddy about the toy we bought for Erin?" Both parents are likely to continue to focus her attention on this topic by asking questions about the shopping trip. Caregivers use more sophisticated and complex forms of expansion as a way of encouraging children to pay attention to the grammatically challenging aspects of their speech (Bloom, 1998). Caregivers also socialize politeness in children's language. A father might say to his child, "Say, 'Please may I have a cookie'" to encourage appropriate manners (Gleason, Ely, Perlmann, & Narasimhan, 1996).

Beyond parent-directed language activities is the larger social context of language use, which involves both the child and the caregiver as active agents who negotiate the activities of daily living (Ninio & Snow, 1996; Tomasello, 1992; Tomasello & Akhtar, 1995). Children play a more active role in directing speech than early research suggested. In fact, children may be the primary force in directing language interactions and often take the lead in their everyday conversations with adults and caregivers (Bloom, Margulis, Tinker, & Fujita, 1996). Caregivers are more likely to respond to children than to initiate conversations with them.

As children grow older, they spend more time with their siblings, and this new, expanded social context influences language development. Siblings' speech among themselves is different from caregivers' speech to children—it is more playful and includes more reciprocal verbal interchanges (Brown & Dunn, 1992). Having a variety of language partners, each with a particular language style and vocabulary, encourages and supports children's language development.

Thus, language learning occurs in a social context, driven by children's need to communicate and share meaning with others. Caregivers, siblings, peers, and teachers all contribute to learning by responding to the meanings children communicate, providing scripted language experiences, and being responsive partners in communication. Children's desire to communicate, opportunities to connect with others through language, and changes in cognitive development converge to facilitate language development (Bloom, 1998).

code switching the alternate use of two or more languages

LANGUAGE DEVELOPMENT IN BILINGUAL CHILDREN

A boy named Christian was born in Germany to an American-Estonian father and an American mother. The mother generally spoke to Christian in English, the father mainly spoke to him in Estonian, and the nanny and other children in the neighborhood spoke to him in German. Christian's parents spoke to each other in English. Whereas most children hear one name or label associated with each noun early in their development, Christian often heard two or three different labels. Do you think this situation would be confusing for Christian?

For many years researchers have been intrigued by bilingual (two-language) and trilingual (three-language) language learning. As you can imagine, researchers have been interested in how children keep the languages straight and whether the children fall behind in learning. Although many researchers concluded that bilingual children (who have been studied more than trilingual ones) tend to develop language skills comparable to those of other children, at first they believed that the best strategy in the home was relatively unmixed language exposure, in which one language was associated with one person and the other with another person. The assumption was that the association between the language and its source (a particular person) would provide cues to the child about which language was appropriate to use. However, more recent work on this topic suggests a different conclusion: that most bilingual children receive both mixed and unmixed language input and that children are able to use these rich input sources in combination with their cognitive and language skills to make sense of the two languages (Bhatia & Ritchie, 1999). Overall, bilingual children develop language skills in the same order and the same time frame as do children exposed to only one language. Christian followed this pattern: Within a few years, he was speaking German, English, and Estonian.

For bilingual speakers, the pragmatics of using language are complex. They have to learn the circumstances under which they should use each language. In Christian's case, he could use the predominant language spoken by each of his parents as a cue in deciding which language to speak to them. With people he did not know, he used appearance to help him decide which language to speak. For instance, while living in the United States, he spoke German to an unfamiliar blond woman because, he said, she looked German. Both children and adult bilinguals frequently engage in **code switching**—alternating use of two or more languages to communicate their ideas. Just as most children are sensitive to the perceived language capabilities of the people they talk to, bilingual children use social cues and information about the target's language preferences—for instance, whether the other person uses one or two languages—to help them select a method of communication. The language they employ depends on the setting, the person they are talking to, and the nature of the idea to be expressed. Bilingual children learn to code switch at an early age, and these skills come in part from observing the use of language by others around them (Bhatia & Richie, 1999; de Houwer, 1995).

TRY IT OUT
Activities Relating to Young Children

1. Go to a playground and observe children of different ages playing. Are the preschool children able to throw, jump, and catch with greater maturity than the younger children? How can you tell that their behavior is more highly developed? Do you notice some children who seem less skilled for their age than others?
2. Watch Saturday morning television for children and notice the kinds of food advertisements that are shown. Then go to the grocery store and read the nutritional information on these foods. Are children being encouraged to eat and drink nutritious foods? How might you remedy this situation if you were a parent?
3. Try some Piagetian tasks with a 4- or 5-year-old child. Ask the child about why the stars shine at night. Does the child give an

egocentric response? Try a conservation task with the child. Does the child think a piece of clay that is long like a snake has more clay in it than one shaped like a ball? Give the child a choice between a broken and an unbroken cookie and see if he or she thinks the unbroken one would taste better.
4. Listen to a parent and young child in a problem-solving situation. Does the parent or the child seem to be directing the conversation topics? Does the parent encourage politeness, expand the child's sentences to make them more complex, or repeat the child's ideas back to her or him? In what ways does the parent help in the child's problem solving and in the child's use of language?

SUM IT UP

How do children's bodies and motor skills develop during early childhood?

✦ Physical growth is fairly rapid during early childhood and is affected by many factors, including genetic inheritance, nutrition, family income, and ethnic group.

✦ A child's brain develops in structure and function during the preschool years. New neural connections form, and the increase in myelination of the axons allows for more efficient communication across different areas of the brain.

✦ The left hemisphere of the brain, which is specialized for language processing, develops rapidly in the first two years. The right hemisphere, which is specialized for spatial information, develops rapidly around the age of 5.

✦ Preschool children make tremendous advances in their gross and fine motor skills. The improvement in skills is due to brain development, a better sense of balance, and increased eye-hand coordination.

✦ Motor development is influenced by practice, parental expectations, imitation, genetic inheritance, brain development, and ethnicity.

What are the nutritional and health issues for young children?

✦ Many children are undernourished and/or malnourished because they do not receive adequate nutrition. Undernourishment is associated with economic impoverishment, limited health care and educational opportunities, and poor living conditions.

✦ Undernourished and malnourished children have stunted growth and motor development, learning impairments, and poor school performance. These effects may be due to functional isolation, whereby children become disengaged from their social environments because of impaired brain development and lack of responsiveness.

✦ Children in developing countries are at risk for protein-energy deficiencies, which can cause long-lasting and serious problems in development.

✦ Lead poisoning is a common health problem for young children. It occurs most often in children living in older neighborhoods where lead-based paints have been used.

How do young children think and solve problems?

✦ In the preoperational stage of cognitive development, children think using symbols. This greatly increases their abilities to consider the past and the future, anticipate actions, and think flexibly.

✦ Preoperational thinking is best illustrated using conservation tasks. These tasks show that young children tend to be fooled by the appearance of an object, rather than recognizing that transformations may not change the identity of the object.

✦ Preschoolers tend to think egocentrically, assuming that other people's perspectives are the same as theirs.

✦ Although Piaget's ideas have been confirmed in many studies that used the same tasks, later studies with simpler tasks indicate that young children may be more advanced in their problem solving than Piaget believed.

✦ Young children tend to have shorter memories than older children because they are easily distracted, do not consistently use memory strategies, and are less likely to monitor their memory performance.

✦ Children tend to have good memories for scripted events, especially those they experience frequently. Children's ability to remember scripts increases with age, especially as reflected in better memory for details and sequencing.

✦ Young children have some understanding of pretend versus real situations. They are more likely to confuse pretense and reality when an object's appearance conflicts with its true identity.

✦ Children's cognitive development is influenced by their caregivers, who transmit cultural information and direct their learning experiences. Children eventually direct their own actions through the use of private speech, which is similar to the speech that caregivers used with them earlier.

✦ Children can be encouraged to develop their cognitive skills through exposure to preschool and kindergarten programs as well as educational television.

✦ Head Start programs have played a very important role in the education of young children from economically disadvantaged backgrounds.

What changes occur in young children's language development during early childhood?

✦ By the age of 5, most children are competent speakers of a language and have mastered the basics of semantics, syntax, and pragmatics.

✦ A child's vocabulary expands rapidly during the preschool years.

✦ Children use a variety of cues, including bootstrapping from their previous knowledge of language, to help them analyze the language they hear around them and develop a more sophisticated use of language.

✦ Preschool children master more complexities of grammar, such as the ability to negate a sentence, use plurals, and use past tense markers.

✦ Children guide and direct many interactions with their caregivers. They learn best from experiences that are relevant to them.

✦ Bilingual children develop language skills in the same order and the same time frame as children exposed to only one language.

KEY TERMS and CONCEPTS

animism (*222*)
centration (*221*)
class inclusion (*222*)
code switching (*241*)
conservation tasks (*220*)
egocentric speech (*229*)
egocentrism (*222*)
elaboration (*225*)
expressive language style (*238*)
functional isolation (*218*)

identity concept (*221*)
iron-deficiency anemia (*218*)
kwashiorkor (*217*)
marasmus (*217*)
metacognition (*225*)
operations (*220*)
organization (*225*)
overregularization (*238*)
private speech (*229*)
referential language style (*238*)

rehearsal (*225*)
scripts (*225*)
semantic bootstrapping (*238*)
social communicative competence (*237*)
static thinking (*221*)
symbolic representations (*220*)
syntactic bootstrapping (*237*)
theory of mind (*227*)
transductive reasoning (*221*)

Social and Emotional Development in Early Childhood

CHAPTER OUTLINE

- ✦ How Does Self-Awareness Change During Early Childhood?
- ✦ How Do Young Children Develop a Concept of Gender?
- ✦ What Are the Contemporary Theories of Gender Development?
- ✦ How Do Emotions Develop During Early Childhood?
- ✦ How Do Parenting Behaviors Influence Young Children's Development?
- ✦ How Does Divorce Affect Young Children's Development?
- ✦ How Do Peer and Sibling Relationships Develop During Early Childhood?
- ✦ How Does Television Influence Young Children's Emotional and Social Development?

uring early childhood, children's social and emotional lives become increasingly complex as they encounter a broader range of people, situations, and environments. This rich array of interactive partners and contexts provides many opportunities to learn about social interactions, about their own and others' emotions, and about their capabilities and characteristics. Preschoolers' social and emotional lives are often playful and positive, but they can also be tumultuous and uncertain.

HOW DOES SELF-AWARENESS CHANGE DURING EARLY CHILDHOOD?

During early childhood, dramatic changes occur in children's awareness and image of themselves and in their feelings of self-worth. For some children, these changes lead to a positive view of self: They see themselves as active, independent, and persistent. For other children, these changes lead to a negative view of self, filled with uncertainty, helplessness, and failure.

Some young children have difficulty coping with challenging and possibly frustrating events. This may lead to negative views of themselves that then contribute to feelings of inadequacy and defeat. In contrast, positive self-images help young children face challenges without becoming upset and frustrated. They have images of themselves as being able to solve problems, so they do not fear failure. Importantly, how young children perceive and feel about themselves has significant long-term effects (Verschueren, Buyck, & Marcoen, 2001).

DEVELOPING SELF-CONCEPT

Self-concept refers to an individual's beliefs about the attributes and capacities she or he possesses (Coopersmith, 1967; Lynch, 1981). The fundamental requirement for a concept of self is the recognition that you are distinguishable from others. By age 2, most toddlers recognize themselves as individuals—they can state their own name, identify themselves in a mirror, and distinguish and label themselves in pictures that include other children of the same age and same sex (Snow, 1990; Wolf, 1990).

Important advances in self-concept are made during early childhood as children develop an awareness of their own characteristics. Three-year-old children first describe themselves in global terms, based on external qualities ("I'm fast") rather than psychological qualities ("I'm kind"). This global tendency leads young children to think that if they are good at drawing they also are good at puzzles, running, or singing; that is, self-definitions are generalized to other contexts. By 4 years of age, children's judgments are more specific and differentiated (Measelle, Ablow, Cowan, & Cowan, 1998). They acknowledge that they are good at one skill, but not so good at others. Or they may acknowledge that they are good at doing something in one situation but not in other situations (Harter, 1998). For instance, older preschoolers may believe that they are good at puzzles but not at drawing or that they are good at playing basketball with other preschoolers but not with older children.

Young children have a more difficult time developing an understanding of their internal psychological qualities. They often describe themselves in an all-or-none fashion, failing to recognize that traits can co-occur. Thus, children ages 3 to 5 view themselves as either good or bad, but not *both* good and bad. Likewise, young children believe that they cannot feel both happy and sad at the same time (Ruble & Dweck, 1995). Between 6 and 8 years of age, children begin to acknowledge that two traits or feelings can co-occur, but only sequentially; that is, one quality is initially experienced, followed by the other.

By about age 8, children acknowledge that two opposing qualities of the self can exist simultaneously. However, at this age, children typically attach one quality to one situation and another quality to a different situation (such as "I'm smart in reading but dumb in math"). It is not until age 10 or later that children recognize simultaneous positive and negative qualities in the same situation—for instance, one can be both nice and mean to the same person or in the same situation (Harter, 1998).

self-concept an individual's beliefs about the attributes and capacities she or he possesses

Notice how this young child's smile reveals the pride she feels in her accomplishment. How does this pride contribute to her self-concept and self-esteem?

Older children and adults recognize that their characteristics and traits are fairly stable over time and situations. Preschoolers, however, rarely describe themselves in terms of stable traits, and when they do, they use very global terms (Harter, 1999). Instead, their descriptions are likely to be based on characteristics and behaviors that change from time to time ("I'm clean" or "I'm happy").

Based on our discussion of cognitive development in Chapter 7, we could say that preschoolers lack "conservation of self." Just as young children do not recognize that a ball of clay retains its identity (contains the same amount of clay) when it is transformed from a ball to a snake, they do not recognize that their identity can be consistent in different situations and at different times (Bales & Sera, 1995). One consequence of this lack of recognition is that young children often overestimate their abilities, remaining confident even in the face of negative feedback (Pomerantz & Ruble, 1997; Stipek, Recchia, & McClintic, 1992). Given young children's tendencies to inaccurately estimate their abilities, caregivers should be skeptical when young children claim that they can do something that seems too advanced for them. By late childhood, a child's self-concept reflects an understanding of enduring qualities and traits and is more accurate and realistic in its representations of the child and the child's characteristics (Schuster, Ruble, & Weinert, 1998).

DEVELOPING SELF-ESTEEM

Self-concept and self-esteem are closely related. Self-concept refers to the mental picture we develop about ourselves. **Self-esteem** refers to the value we attach to the mental pictures of ourselves (Coopersmith, 1967). Children with high self-esteem have positive feelings about themselves—they see themselves as confident, worthy, and effective. Children with low self-esteem have negative feelings about themselves—they feel uncertain, timid, and sad.

As children enter early childhood, they are increasingly capable of making judgments about themselves, but these judgments are global and vary depending on the situation. Young children's self-esteem revolves around feelings of good and bad—feeling "good" when they succeed in a task and feeling "bad" when they fail (Ruble & Dweck, 1995). For example, 5-year-olds Hector and Barry show clear signs of making evaluative judgments. Hector persists at a challenging computer game, is elated when he succeeds, and is motivated to play the game again. Barry feels bad when he begins to fail, becoming frustrated and helpless. Their evaluations of themselves are based on meeting a single standard, such as completing or failing at a task. As children get older (around age 7 or 8), they move away from this global good-bad evaluation of themselves and begin to make more complex assessments, evaluating themselves in comparison to others or in relation to the difficulty of the task (Pomerantz, Ruble, Frey, & Greulich, 1995). With age, children become more focused on distinguishing unique aspects of themselves (Daniels, 1998; Mintz, 1995).

Research suggests that self-esteem can be understood as a combination of two qualities: worthiness (feelings of being valued) and competence (feelings of being effective). Mruk (1999) put these two qualities on a matrix and used the various combinations of high and low worthiness and competence to identify four types of self-esteem. The matrix is presented in Figure 8.1.

For the first two types of self-esteem, high self-esteem and low self-esteem, there is a match between feelings of competence and worthiness. A combination of high competence and high worthiness results in high self-esteem. Children with high self-esteem are better prepared to face challenges because they have acquired feelings about themselves that are associated with success and positive worth. In contrast, children with low self-esteem feel unworthy and have ineffective interactions, producing feelings of unhappiness and anxiety.

In Mruk's two other types of self-esteem, there is a discrepancy between feelings of worthiness and competence. These types of self-esteem demand that children "defend" their sense of self against others' view of them. Defensive self-esteem I combines high worthiness and low competence. Children with this pattern feel valued despite the fact that they lack the accomplishments or abilities to be successful. Thus, worthiness is not deserved. Children

self-esteem the value an individual attaches to the mental picture of himself or herself

who possess this pattern of self-esteem often behave in ways that might be labeled spoiled, stuck-up, or self-centered.

The other discrepant type of self-esteem, defensive self-esteem II, combines high competence and low worthiness. In this case, children may be quite skilled, but their feelings of unworthiness distort their view of themselves. They tend to worry about performance and failure (performance anxiety), and they have difficulty experiencing satisfaction in their achievements. These children feel they must constantly prove their worth (Mruk, 1999).

Young children derive their feelings of competence and worthiness primarily from significant others, especially parents and other caregivers. Statements and expressions that affirm (or disaffirm) a child's accomplishments and value are rooted in how significant others regard the child and his or her particular behaviors and achievements. In a sense, competence is a measure of how effectively the child responds to the world, and worthiness is a measure of how the world responds to the child. In both cases, the values and judgments of children's social environments influence their self-esteem.

FIGURE 8.1
Matrix of Self Esteem

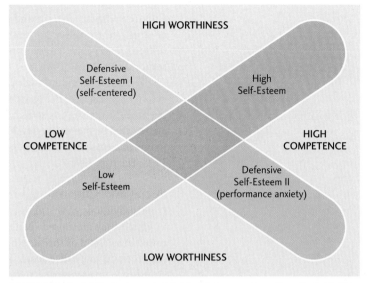

SOURCE: Mruk, 1999. Springer Publishing Company, Inc., New York 10012. Used with permission.

According to this model, patterns of self-esteem are made up of combinations of competence and worthiness. Can you explain the different combinations? Can you assign combinations to yourself and people you know?

INFLUENCES ON YOUNG CHILDREN'S PERCEPTION OF SELF

How do children develop positive concepts and feelings about themselves? What factors contribute to the differences observed in children's reactions? According to research, young children's self-concept and self-esteem are influenced by their own characteristics, their family and peer relationships, and the environments in which they live (Frome & Eccles, 1998).

Physical Appearance

Even at a young age, a person's physical appearance predicts self-esteem (Feingold, 1992). Individuals who are more physically attractive have higher levels of self-esteem than those who are less physically attractive, and this relationship is consistent throughout the life span (Harter, 1998). This correlation is just as high in special populations such as the intellectually gifted and the learning disabled (Harter, 1993; Serketich & Dumas, 1997). Thus, from an early age, those who are judged to be attractive by societal standards receive more positive attention than those judged to be less physically attractive. Young children are well aware of societal standards and incorporate them into their sense of self early in life.

The importance of physical appearance is first evident in infancy. Parents react to the physical appearance of their infants and toddlers, responding more positively to children who are more physically attractive (Langlois, 1981). During early childhood, girls and boys are equally satisfied with their appearance. Boys continue to evaluate their appearance positively as they move through the school years, but girls' evaluations begin to decline during elementary school (Harter, 1993). Girls' self-esteem also declines with age, and it becomes particularly low for those girls whose self-esteem hinges on their looks.

Society and the media place great importance on physical appearance at every age and for both sexes (Kilbourne, 1994; Wheeler & Kim, 1997). The standards are particularly narrow and rigid for women—emphasizing unrealistic ideals of thinness and desirable body characteristics (Henderson-King & Henderson-King, 1997). These standards are difficult for women and girls, even young girls, to live up to, and they create a situation in which females are likely to become dissatisfied with their physical appearance. In turn, their self-esteem may suffer.

Relationships with Caregivers and Peers

Children who have warm and secure relationships with their parents and other caregivers generally have positive concepts and feelings about themselves. In contrast, children who are rejected, overprotected, dominated, or neglected develop a negative self-concept and low self-esteem (Kernis, Brown, & Brody, 2000; Mruk, 1999).

In addition, children with good peer relationships develop a positive self-concept and positive self-esteem. Being accepted by peers affirms a sense of being liked. Having positive peer relations also provides children with support and affection. In contrast, children who are rejected by peers may develop doubts about being able to relate to others, which can lead to low self-esteem, withdrawal, victimization, and aggression (Cordell, 1999; Egan & Perry, 1998; Hartup, 1996).

Social and Cultural Conditions

How individuals view and feel about themselves is tied to the social and cultural conditions in which they are raised (Miller, 2000; Watkins & Regmi, 1999). Young children who are raised in stressful or threatening environments are at greater risk for developing a poor self-concept and low self-esteem. For example, children who live in poverty face a variety of stressors, such as violence, overcrowding, and inadequate nutrition, that more affluent children do not. These stressful conditions undermine individuals' sense of dignity, value, and self-worth. As discussed in Chapter 6, conditions of abuse or neglect also damage children's self-esteem (Stern, Lynch, Oates, O'Toole, & Cooney, 1995).

People in different cultures are strikingly different in how they see themselves (Raeff, 1997). For example, the North American representation of self is based on an appreciation of how one is different from others and on the importance of asserting oneself. In contrast, the Japanese representation of self is based on fitting in with others and the importance of being connected with them (Markus & Kitayama, 1991). The factors that contribute to a positive self-concept and high self-esteem for North American children and Japanese children differ in accord with the cultural values and practices to which they are exposed. Japanese culture, for instance, values *suano*—a term used to describe the development of cooperation and the yielding of personal autonomy (White & LeVine, 1986). Unlike North Americans, the Japanese do not view *suano* as a sign of weakness; it is thought to reflect maturity, self-control, and healthy adaptation. For Japanese children, therefore, *suano* forms an important basis for self-concept and self-esteem. In Western cultures, however, independence and autonomy are highly valued. Consequently, the self-concepts and self-esteem of children in North America are determined in part by the degree to which the children reflect these characteristics (Markus & Kitayama, 1991).

Within North American cultures, there are important differences among the values and practices of different subcultures (Frable, 1997). Various religious groups (such as the Quakers) and ethnic groups (such as Native Americans) explicitly value and promote interdependence to a greater extent than does the larger culture. In addition, children who live in small, rural communities are more likely to be exposed to values and practices that emphasize connectedness than are children growing up in larger metropolitan communities (Sampson, 1989).

How Do Young Children Develop a Concept of Gender

During the preschool years, children come to understand which gender group they belong to and that this is a stable part of one's self-concept (Frable, 1997). Learning this fundamental aspect of the self is only the beginning. Children also learn about the roles and expectations associated with their own and the other sex. These beliefs, roles, and expectations

THE SCIENTIFIC IMPACT: INTERPRETING RESEARCH

Is Self-Esteem Lower in African American and Hispanic Children?

Because self-esteem is influenced by what other people think, it is sometimes assumed that minority children have lower levels of self-esteem than Caucasian American children. What is not considered, however, is that many minorities do not compare themselves to the larger society. Their self-esteem may be based less on what the general society thinks of them than on the perceptions of their family and friends and other important people in the minority community (van-Laar, 2001). Some of the current research has identified the factors that account for the healthy development of self-esteem in African American and Hispanic children.

African American Children. African American children are likely to live in close proximity to their relatives. These relatives often are an important source of affection, care, and support for African American children. The additional caregiving also serves as a source of comfort and help in times of stress (Brodsky & DeVet, 2000). The increased support and nurturance provided by this extended family network promotes positive self-esteem.

The presence of a father plays an especially important role in the development of self-esteem among African American children—particularly African American boys. An African American child who lives in a home where the father is absent is likely to exhibit low self-esteem (Espinoza & Ehrlich, 1989).

African American children with a poor sense of ethnic identity—recognition and acceptance of membership in

an ethnic group—suffer from low self-esteem (Ogbu, 1991). Some people believe that young children are "color blind," but as early as 4 years of age, children are capable of distinguishing different ethnic groups (Aries & Moorehead, 1989). Children whose parents teach them about being African American and instill in them a sense of pride show healthy and positive self-esteem (Bowman & Howard, 1985). These parents help their children cope with the negative stereotypes and harassment they encounter (Walker, Taylor, McElroy, & Phillip, 1995).

Hispanic Children.   Like African American families, Hispanic families provide supportive and nurturing environments that often buffer children against the assaults that occur in the broader society (Solis, 1995; Valdez, 1996). Hispanics place a high value on family support (McDermott, 2001; Sabogal, Marín, & Otero-Sabogal, 1987), and this support is provided not only by parents but also by grandparents, uncles, aunts, and cousins. Often, no sharp distinction is made between relatives and friends, with friends being considered family if a close relationship has been formed (Chilman, 1993). The term *compadrazo* is often used to describe this relationship. Children living in these relatively large families have extensive networks of support and nurturance that protect and enhance their self-esteem.

Another important characteristic of Hispanic families that helps their children develop positive relationships

and self-esteem is their traditional preference for smooth and pleasant social relationships. The term *simpatía* refers to the high regard the Hispanic culture has for feelings and actions geared to safeguarding the dignity of individuals by showing respect and striving for harmony. This does not mean that Hispanic families and children do not express anger, aggression, or frustration. However, when situations have the potential for conflict, particularly among family members or friends, solutions are sought that avoid confrontation, hurt feelings, and loss of self-respect. *Simpatía* and supportive extended families foster the development of positive self-esteem among Hispanic children (Marín, 1994).

Although minority children generally have positive and healthy self-esteem, they face greater threats to their self-esteem than do Caucasian American children. These threats appear to be due to economic and social conditions rather than minority status *per se*.

Thinking It Through:

1. How does being a member of a minority group influence self-esteem differently than being a member of a majority group?
2. Why is it important to understand the development of self-esteem among minority children? What implications does this understanding have for social policy?
3. How do parents and other family members influence minority children's self-esteem?

are shared cultural constructs, but each child develops her or his own set of individual beliefs about the sexes.

An important part of young children's self-concept is **gender identity**—the understanding and acceptance that one is a boy or a girl. Gender identity is based on the understanding that there are different sexes and that a person's gender group is stable over time and situations (Kohlberg, 1966). For most children, understanding of gender progresses through three stages:

1. By about 30 months of age, children engage in **gender labeling**—they label themselves and others according to their gender group. At this time, children call themselves *boys* and *girls* and use pronouns that correctly match the gender group.
2. By 3 to 4 years of age, children understand **gender stability**—they know that gender is stable over time. A boy who has achieved gender stability knows that he will always be a boy and will grow up to be a man, not a woman.

gender identity understanding and acceptance that one is a boy or a girl

gender labeling labeling oneself and others on the basis of gender group

gender stability understanding that gender is stable over time

3. By 4 to 5 years of age, children understand **gender consistency**—they know that gender does not change despite changes in appearance or activities. For instance, a child who has achieved gender consistency understands that a boy who dresses as a girl remains a boy despite his appearance.

Not all children develop gender identity easily. Because of certain genetic disorders, a small number of children are born with ambiguous-looking genitals. Early research found that children with ambiguous-looking genitals have problems developing gender identity if their gender group is assigned late in childhood (Money & Ehrhardt, 1972). However, some of these children have fewer problems if they are assigned to a gender group early in life (by 18–36 months), are raised consistently with their gender group assignment by their parents, and are given surgical or hormonal support for their assigned gender group. Surprisingly, even children who are raised to be one sex but are genetically the other sex can develop a stable gender identity. This is not always the case, however, and research has been undertaken to decide how best to determine gender group assignments (Bradley, Gillian, Avinoam, & Zucker, 1998; Diamond & Sigmundson, 1997).

Questions regarding the relative contributions of biological and social influences to gender identity development are being raised because of a rare genetic disorder first found in children in the Dominican Republic. In this disorder, boys are born with female-looking genitals and are usually raised as girls. At puberty, the male hormone testosterone is released and these children develop masculine features and attributes. Thus, these children, who were raised as girls, suddenly look like boys. Surprisingly, many of these children adjust to a male gender identity with little difficulty, probably because in their culture being a male is more highly valued than being a female. These cases suggest that a stable gender identity may not be fully developed until adolescence and that raising a child to be one sex does not always offset the biological influence of genes (Imperato-McGinley, Peterson, Gautier, & Sturla, 1979).

YOUNG CHILDREN'S GENDER STEREOTYPES

Gender stereotypes are the beliefs people share about the typical characteristics of males and females. As early as age 2½, children have learned basic stereotypes about the sexes, including information about appearance and activities. For instance, young children think that girls have long and curly hair and that they cry a lot (Intons-Peterson, 1988). They think that boys are taller and stronger than girls and hit people more (Kuhn, Nash, & Brucken, 1978). Young children even believe that softness is associated with being female and hardness with being male (Leinbach, Hort, & Fagot, 1997). Young children do not, however, think that males and females differ in personality, except in very concrete terms such as being strong or being nice.

Gender stereotypes influence children in many ways. First, children (and adults) use them to make judgments about other people, especially when their information about the other people is limited (Martin, 1989; Martin, Woods, & Little, 1990). These judgments often have to do with familiar activities and roles. For instance, 4-year-old Claudia decides that her new neighbor, Polly, might be fun to play with because she is a girl and therefore will probably like the kinds of things that Claudia likes.

Second, young children's stereotypes influence what they remember. Generally, children remember information that fits their stereotypic beliefs (Stangor & McMillan, 1992). After being shown pictures of girls and boys engaged in many activities, children better remember the pictures of children engaged in stereotypic activities (such as a boy playing with a car) than those of children engaged in counter-stereotypic activities (such as a boy playing with a doll). Young children also remember more about people of the same sex than about people of the other sex (Signorella, Bigler, & Liben, 1998).

Several studies have shown that children experience memory distortions; that is, they misremember information with a bias toward their stereotypes (Martin & Halverson, 1983; Signorella & Liben, 1984). For example, when 5- to 9-year-old children of both sexes saw

gender consistency understanding that gender does not change despite changes in appearance or activities

gender stereotypes beliefs people share about the typical characteristics of males and females

television commercials of a boy playing with a doll and a girl playing with a truck, over half the children distorted the sex of the actor in one of the commercials and 25 percent distorted the sex of the actor in both commercials (Stangor & Ruble, 1989).

Many caregivers hope that their children will not learn gender stereotypes if they see many examples of people who break from gender stereotypic expectations. The fact that children distort information to fit their gender stereotypes, however, makes it difficult to change stereotypes. Rather than breaking stereotypes, their memories respond in ways that confirm gender stereotypes. It seems unlikely that caregivers can change young children's stereotypes merely by exposing them to examples of people engaging in counter-stereotypic behaviors and activities. Instead, parents and caregivers may need to take more active measures, such as teaching children that not all people believe gender stereotypes or act on the basis of them (Bem, 1983).

Children often prefer toys and activities that reinforce their own gender identity. What factors contribute to this preference? How might children be encouraged to play with more cross-sex toys?

YOUNG CHILDREN'S GENDER-TYPED PLAY PREFERENCES

By 2 years of age, girls and boys show preferences for different toys (Ruble & Martin, 1998). By the age of 3 or 4, girls play more often than boys with dolls, tea sets, art materials, and domestic toys (ironing boards, kitchen sets). One reason children prefer stereotypic toys and activities is because they have a history of playing with them and are familiar with them. Parents give children toys that are gender-stereotyped and encourage them to play with these toys (Ruble & Martin, 1998). Children also prefer toys and activities that reinforce their own gender identity. For example, when a toy that children have never seen before is described as a toy that is liked by others of their own sex, both girls and boys prefer that toy. If the new toy is described as being liked by members of the other sex, the toy often is avoided (Bradbard, Martin, Endsley, & Halverson, 1986).

Children are particularly likely to avoid toys gender-stereotyped for the other sex if they are discouraged from or punished for playing with them (Langlois & Downs, 1980). This avoidance reaction is so strong that children will stay away from even very attractive toys if they think the toys are intended for the other sex (Martin, Eisenbud, & Rose, 1995). For instance, Joe chose to play with a deflated football rather than a new kitchen set. Ian happily played with a race car until the helmet of the driver fell off, revealing a woman with long blonde hair. Ian immediately dropped the car like a "hot potato." Such findings suggest that children use stereotypic expectations to decide whether or not they like specific toys. These expectations prevent children from learning about the toys and activities used by the other sex (Boston & Levy, 1991).

SIMILARITIES AND DIFFERENCES BETWEEN YOUNG GIRLS AND BOYS

Gender stereotypes are based on beliefs about differences between the sexes in behavior, appearance, and personality. But to what extent do boys and girls really differ? Observable differences between the behaviors of boys and girls generally have not been found before age 2 (Huston, 1983). Thus, if you were brought into a room full of young infants and could not tell by their appearance which were boys and girls, you would not consistently be able to distinguish girls from boys based on their behavior. Interestingly, although there are no noticeable differences between very young boys and girls, parents often say that their young sons and daughters *are* different. Based on these perceptions, parents may interact with their sons and daughters differently, thereby setting the stage for sex differences to emerge.

In a classic review, Maccoby and Jacklin (1974) concluded that there are four sex differences found consistently in children and adolescents. On average, males have better visual-spatial skills (such as map-reading skills), have better mathematical reasoning abilities, and are more physically aggressive, whereas females have better verbal skills. Maccoby and Jacklin (1974) also noted that these differences tend to be small and highly variable within each sex—girls, for example, are as different from one another as they are from boys.

The results of recent research suggest that sex differences occur in more areas than Maccoby and Jacklin originally identified (Ruble & Martin, 1998). For instance, boys tend to be more active than girls (Eaton & Enns, 1986), although the level of activity varies considerably depending on the situation and age. Boys also are more likely to take risks (Ginsburg & Miller, 1982) and engage in rough play, such as wrestling (Braza, Braza, Carreras, & Munoz, 1997; Pellegrini & Smith, 1998). Gender differences in forms of play increase with age, are observed in cultures all around the world (Whiting & Edwards, 1988), and are even found in monkeys, apes, and rats (Meaney, 1988).

Boys throw a ball with considerably more accuracy and velocity than girls, whereas girls have better fine eye-motor skills and flexibility (Thomas & French, 1985). Girls and boys also exhibit different types of nonverbal communication (Hall, 1984). Girls are more likely than boys to smile, and boys are more likely than girls to stare at others.

Gender differences also are found in social behavior and personality. Girls generally are more socially oriented, are more easily influenced, and are seen by teachers as more dependent than boys (Ruble & Martin, 1998). Boys tend to show more aggression and anger, and girls show more fear (Eisenberg, Martin, & Fabes, 1996).

The reasons for these differences are complex. As you will soon learn, many different theories have been proposed to explain why males and females differ. Some of these theories focus on the effects of biological and physiological differences (Kimura, 1993; Levy & Heller, 1992), whereas others focus on environmental and social factors (Bussey & Bandura, 1992) or cognitive processes (Martin, 1991).

WHAT ARE THE CONTEMPORARY THEORIES OF GENDER DEVELOPMENT?

During early childhood, critical changes take place affecting children's gender development. Several contemporary theoretical approaches have been developed in an attempt to explain these changes. Each theory provides insight into why boys and girls behave differently and the ways they use their knowledge of gender. Although the theories differ in the aspects of gender they emphasize, all the theories consider gender to be an important part of development.

BIOLOGICAL THEORIES

Biological theories focus on specific physiological or biochemical processes that affect gender development. The biological influences that have been studied most extensively concern the actions of hormones, and the most commonly studied hormones are androgens, especially testosterone. These hormones often are referred to as "male hormones" because they occur at higher levels in males than in females. When animals are exposed to androgens during prenatal development, they show more male-typical behaviors, such as aggression, and fewer female-typical behaviors, such as nurturance (Collaer & Hines, 1995). Prenatal androgens are thought to masculinize the brain as it develops, making it more sensitive to some types of environmental stimulation and less sensitive to others. As a result, males and females may be predisposed to develop different skills, abilities, and personalities.

Levels of hormones vary in humans, and some children are exposed to higher than normal prenatal levels of androgens, usually because of genetic disorders. An example is girls who have congenital adrenal hyperplasia (CAH). These girls may be born with somewhat masculinized genitals, but they usually are raised as girls and receive treatment and sometimes surgery to offset the masculine hormones. Parents report that their CAH daughters behave as tomboys and prefer to play with boys' toys (Berenbaum & Snyder, 1995). Many researchers believe that the behavior of CAH girls is the result of their exposure to high prenatal levels of androgens.

Biological theories suggest that children's abilities, behaviors, and personality may all be influenced by levels of hormones, especially those that are present during prenatal development. Some people worry that if biological factors influence gender development, then there is no way to change girls' or boys' behavior. However, this is not the case—some biological influences can easily be changed. Furthermore, most researchers believe that even if gender development is influenced by biological factors, environmental factors such as socialization and reinforcement can influence the course of a child's development (Hoyenga & Hoyenga, 1993).

SOCIAL LEARNING THEORIES

The basis of social learning theories is that children learn gender roles through two processes: direct learning and observation. In direct learning, children learn gender roles from the rewards and punishments they receive (Mischel, 1966). Children may be rewarded for exhibiting stereotypic traits and engaging in stereotypic activities and be punished for behaving in ways deemed gender inappropriate. Thus, their gender-related behavior is conditioned. For instance, when Jason is teased for playing with a baby doll, he discovers that this behavior is regarded as inappropriate for him and quickly learns to avoid baby dolls in favor of trucks or blocks.

Many research studies have shown that boys and girls receive different rewards and punishments for gender-related behaviors. Parents and peers reward girls and boys for different activities, but in both cases, stereotypic activities are encouraged more than counter-stereotypic ones (Trice & Rush, 1995). Interestingly, boys are more likely than girls to be punished for engaging in cross-sex behaviors and activities, suggesting that boys are held to more rigid standards than are girls (Burnett, Anderson, & Heppner, 1995). Parents treat their sons and daughters differently by presenting gender-stereotypic toys and assigning gender-stereotypic chores (Lytton & Romney, 1991; Ruble & Martin, 1998). Girls are more likely to be assigned kitchen and cleaning chores, and boys are more likely to be assigned yard work. Surprisingly, there is little evidence that parents treat boys and girls differently in other ways, such as encouraging daughters to be dependent or encouraging sons to be aggressive and dominant.

Children also learn gender roles by observing others (Bandura, 1976). When Lucas observes children tease Jason for playing with a doll, he too learns that boys should avoid dolls. By observing the consequences that befell Jason, Lucas learns without directly experiencing the same consequences. As children experience consequences, they develop expectations that can then guide their future behavior (Bussey & Bandura, 1999).

Children do not pay equal attention to, and learn equally from, everyone. A reasonable supposition would be that children observe and imitate the behavior of others of the same sex, which would explain why girls act differently than boys. It is not so simple, though. Children imitate same-sex models if the models are familiar but not if they are unfamiliar. However, they also imitate behaviors if they view many same-sex models, even if they do not know the people (Bussey & Bandura, 1984; Bussey & Perry, 1982). Because children pay attention to people who are prestigious and nurturant—such as sports and movie stars, teachers, and family members—they are likely to imitate these individuals (Lockwood & Kunda, 1997). Sometimes children imitate the behaviors of other-sex people; girls are more likely to do this than boys. Boys will imitate girls only if they are shown to be powerful (Bussey & Bandura, 1984).

COGNITIVE THEORIES

Cognitive theories contribute to our understanding of gender development by considering children to be actively involved in learning gender roles and motivated to adhere to them (Ruble & Martin, 1998). The earliest cognitive theory was proposed by Kohlberg (1966) and is based on the idea that children's understanding of gender emerges as part of their general

FIGURE 8.2
Model of Gender Schematic Processing

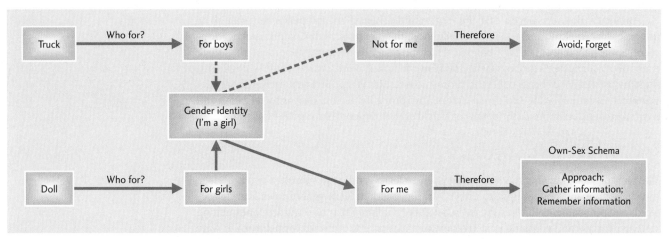

SOURCE: Martin and Halverson, 1981. Reprinted by permission.

This model illustrates how children's gender schemas influence their memory, attention, and behavior. In this example, a girl decides to play with a doll because she believes it is a toy appropriate for girls. How does this model help in understanding the influence of gender schemas and stereotypes?

cognitive development. Kohlberg argued that children's understanding of gender provides the key to the development of gender-stereotypic behavior. As children learn about their gender, they are motivated to behave in ways that are consistent with their gender group. Kohlberg believed that once children develop the idea that gender is a stable attribute, they will show stronger stereotypic behavior, pay more attention to same-sex models, and have better memory for stereotypic information than do children who lack basic gender knowledge (Stangor & Ruble, 1987).

A recent extension of cognitive-developmental theory is gender schema theory. People use **gender schemas,** which are mental representations about the sexes, to guide their behavior and thinking (Bem, 1981; Martin, 1991; Martin & Halverson, 1981). As children interact with their world, their experiences are filtered through gender schemas. Over time, many events come to be interpreted through these male-female schemas. Children then behave according to their interpretation of what it means to be male or female.

Most children have extensive gender schemas, which become more elaborate as they grow older. For instance, as part of her gender schema, 4-year-old Shawntel has information that girls like to make cookies and paint their toenails and boys like to play with trucks and spaceships. With this information, she can form ideas about what is appropriate for her to do.

Gender schemas influence what children pay attention to, what they remember, and how they behave (Martin, 1991). The influence of gender schemas is best summarized by the principle of **schematic consistency,** referring to the tendency of children's behavior and thinking to match their schemas (see Figure 8.2). For instance, children pay more attention to and better remember information if it is relevant to their own gender group (Signorella, Bigler, & Liben, 1998).

gender schemas mental representations about the sexes

schematic consistency the tendency of children's behavior and thinking to match their schemas

HOW DO EMOTIONS DEVELOP DURING EARLY CHILDHOOD

As you saw in Chapter 6, even newborns express a variety of emotions. During early childhood, children's emotional lives become increasingly differentiated and rich. Young children become better at communicating their emotions, more emotionally responsive to others, and more aware of emotions in themselves and others.

DEALING WITH CONFLICT, ANGER, AND AGGRESSION

As young children become actively involved in social relationships, it is not surprising that they encounter more situations that elicit conflict, anger, frustration, and aggression. During the second year of life, young children begin to confront their parents and siblings with increasing frequency. For example, conflicts between children and their mothers double in frequency between 18 and 24 months of age (Dunn & Munn, 1987). Children's aggressive acts also increase during the first three years of life, although the patterns vary depending on the type of aggression studied.

Young Children's Angry Conflicts

Most expressions of anger and aggression occur in the context of interactions with others. For young children, conflicts involve struggles over objects and possessions (Fabes & Eisenberg, 1992; O'Brien et al., 1999). As children mature, their conflicts increasingly have social causes, such as being rejected, ignored, or challenged (Ross & Conant, 1992). Angry tantrums and outbursts peak at about 2 years of age and are relatively uncommon after age 4. For 2-year-olds, the most common cause of anger is parents' attempts to establish household routines (such as for eating or sleeping). Among older preschoolers, anger is likely to be caused by difficulties with playmates (Laursen, Hartup, & Koplas, 1996), and how children respond influences how much they are liked by their peers (Murphy & Eisenberg, 1996).

Changes in the frequency of conflicts reflect changes in children's cognitive and social competencies. As children grasp social rules and order, they respond to violations of these with anger and frustration. Children's developing sense of autonomy during the second and third years also intensifies their negative reactions to others' attempts to control them. During this time, children begin to understand that rules can be questioned (Dunn & Slomkowski, 1992). In addition, their enhanced understanding of intentions makes it more likely that children will hold others responsible for their actions when there is no indication that the behavior was accidental. Holding others responsible increases the chance that a child will become angry when someone acts in a way that she or he does not like. These factors combine to increase the significance of others' behaviors in relation to young children's goals and desires.

Children respond to conflict in a variety of ways that change over the course of early childhood (Sandy & Cochran, 2000). When a conflict occurs, young children might become physically aggressive, try to reason out a solution, stand around, cry or throw a tantrum, go for help, or try to assert themselves (such as by taking back a toy that was taken from them). Interestingly, physical aggression in response to conflict is rare among young children; less than 20 percent of conflicts include acts of aggression such as hitting or kicking. As language develops, children increasingly rely on verbal strategies, such as negotiating, to resolve conflicts (Ross & Conant, 1992). In addition, as children gain a better understanding of social relationships, they begin to look for ways to resolve conflicts that do not damage their ongoing interactions—that is, they try to find a cooperative solution (Ashley & Tomasello, 1998; Verbeek, Hartup, & Collins, 2000).

Young Children's Aggression

Aggression is commonly defined as a behavior intended to harm or injure another (Grusec & Lytton, 1988). Although infants get angry and sometimes strike people and objects, it is difficult to say they are aggressive. Consider the following excerpt from Piaget (1952), describing what happened when he offered a matchbox to his 7-month-old son Laurent, but held his other hand in front of the matchbox so that Laurent could not reach it:

> I present a box of matches above my hand, but behind it, so that he cannot reach it
> without setting the obstacle aside. But Laurent, after trying to remove or lower

Children's conflicts at this age revolve primarily around possession of objects and space. The frequency of conflicts increases during the preschool years. What factors account for this increase?

it, . . . suddenly tries to hit my hand as though to remove or lower it. . . . Laurent tries to reach the box, and bothered by the obstacle, he at once strikes it, definitely lowering it until the way is clear.

—*Jean Piaget,* 1952 (p. 217)

Laurent's behavior looks very much like aggression, but is it? It is unlikely that Laurent intended to harm his father; rather, it is more likely that he treated his father's hand as an obstruction that needed to be removed. Laurent's goal seems to have been focused more on possessing the interesting object than on inflicting harm or pain.

Near the end of the second year, things begin to change. Maccoby (1980) identified at least five kinds of information a child must master before the child's behavior can be judged as aggressive:

* that other people experience distress and feel pain
* that the child's own actions can cause distress
* which actions cause distress in other people
* how to carry out distress-producing actions
* that distress can cause other people to act the way the child wants them to

These types of information are learned during early childhood, some earlier than others (Loeber & Hay, 1997). As children master these types of information, their ability to act aggressively increases. By the end of early childhood, most children have learned alternatives to aggressive behaviors, and those who have not are at increased risk of becoming aggressive teens or adults (Tremblay, 2001).

Different kinds of aggression have been identified. Physical aggression, such as hitting, kicking, and pushing, decreases between 2 and 4 years of age, while verbal aggression, such as threatening and name calling, increases (Coie & Dodge, 1998). The aggressive behavior of children 4 to 6 years of age often is aimed at the retrieval of objects or territory (Fabes & Eisenberg, 1992). This type of aggression is referred to as **instrumental aggression**— aggression used for a specific purpose. Kindergarten children (6 to 7 years of age) show less overall aggression, but they are more likely to aggress in ways that are designed to harm another person. This type of aggression is sometimes called **hostile aggression,** referring to the fact that it is directed against another person and is often used in retaliation for another's actions. Because hostile aggression requires that a child understand others' intentions, this type of aggression occurs less often in younger children (Atkins et al., 2001).

Gender Differences in Aggression

The issue of gender differences in aggression has been of interest for decades (for an early example, see Green, 1933). In several reviews (Hyde, 1984; Knight, Fabes, & Higgins, 1996; Maccoby & Jacklin, 1980), boys were found to be both more physically and more verbally aggressive than girls. These findings are not restricted to studies conducted in the United States. Boys have been found to be more aggressive than girls in Switzerland, Ethiopia, Kenya, India, the Philippines, Mexico, and Japan (Smith & Green, 1974; Whiting & Whiting, 1975). Thus, there is considerable evidence that boys are more aggressive than girls. The cross-cultural consistency of these findings suggests that there may be biological contributions to aggressive behavior.

Is it possible that girls express aggression differently than boys do? Crick and Rose (Crick & Rose, 2000) suggest that girls may exhibit unique forms of aggression that have been overlooked in past research. Crick agrees that boys may be more physically and verbally aggressive than girls. She argues, however, that because girls are more likely than boys to focus on establishing close relationships with others, they are more likely than boys to harm others through relational aggression. **Relational aggression** is defined as aggression that is designed to damage someone's relationships with others by withdrawing friendship, excluding someone from a group, and so on. Several studies have found that girls use relational aggression more than boys do (Crick & Grotpeter, 1995; Fabes, Eisenberg, Smith, & Murphy, 1996). Findings have been consistent across a wide range of ages and across a variety of cultures (Rys & Bear, 1997; Tomada & Schneider, 1997), suggesting that *both* young boys and young girls are aggressive but they display distinct forms of aggression.

instrumental aggression aggression used for a specific purpose

hostile aggression aggression directed against another person, generally in retaliation for his or her actions

relational aggression aggression designed to damage someone's relationships with others, by withdrawing friendship, excluding someone from a group, and so on

DEVELOPING CARING FEELINGS AND ACTIONS

A recently divorced father drops off his 3- and 4-year-old daughters, Aimee and Erin, at his former wife's house. Aimee and Erin burst out of the car and run into the waiting arms of their mother. The father clearly is sad, and Erin, the older daughter, notices her father's sad expression, becomes sad herself, and goes to tell her dad that she will miss him. She hugs him and says, "Things will be OK."

Erin feels sorry for her father and attempts to comfort him, an example of prosocial emotions and actions. **Prosocial behavior** refers to voluntary actions intended to benefit another person. Prosocial emotions motivate prosocial behavior (Eisenberg & Fabes, 1998). As you will see, it is during early childhood that prosocial emotions and actions increasingly become a part of the ways children relate to others.

Prosocial Emotions: Empathy and Sympathy

Empathy refers to an emotional state that matches another person's emotional state—for instance, feeling bad because someone else feels bad (Eisenberg & Strayer, 1987). In contrast, **sympathy** involves feeling sorry or concerned for other people because of their emotional states or conditions (Eisenberg & Fabes, 1999). When Erin felt sad at the sight of her father's sadness, she was displaying empathy. When she felt sorry for him, she was displaying sympathy. Sympathy frequently, but not always, results from empathy.

Empathy and sympathy are important to study because they often motivate prosocial behaviors and actions (Roberts & Strayer, 1996). Because of Erin's feelings of empathy and sympathy for her father, she felt compelled to help her father feel better. The link between sympathy or empathy and prosocial behavior has been confirmed by research in the United States (Eisenberg & Fabes, 1998; Miller, Kozu, & Davis, 2001) and in countries as diverse as Germany (Trommsdorff, 1995), Brazil (Eisenberg, Zhou, & Koller, 2001), and Japan (Ando, 1987).

Empathy appears fairly early and increases across childhood (Hoffman, 2000). Although infants cannot distinguish their own feelings and needs from those of others, they occasionally respond to others' emotions. For example, they often cry when they hear the cry of another infant (Sagi & Hoffman, 1976), although this tendency is not consistent or universal (Zahn-Waxler, Radke-Yarrow, Wagner, & Chapman, 1992).

Early in childhood, children tend to act and think in an egocentric manner. Thus, they are likely to respond to another's distress in ways that they themselves might find comforting. When 3-year-old Thomas saw his mother crying, he became sad and brought her his favorite stuffed animal to cheer her up. In this situation, Thomas projected his own needs onto his mother. Thomas's response is not purely egocentric, however, because his attempt to cheer up his mother is based on empathy for his mother's emotional state.

As children develop the capacity to take the perspective of others, they become increasingly aware that other people's feelings are independent of, and sometimes different from, their own. Four-year-old Erin's response to her father's sadness reflected her understanding of her father's needs, and she responded appropriately. Until later childhood, however, children's empathic and sympathetic responses are limited to the feelings of familiar persons in familiar or directly observed situations. Preschoolers, for example, are most likely to be emotionally responsive to everyday events (such as getting scratched or being made fun of) that cause distress to familiar people or animals (Szagun, 1992). During later childhood, the scope of children's concerns widens to include the conditions of unknown others who are less fortunate than they are (Damon, 1988; Hoffman, 2000).

Helping, Sharing, and Acting Responsibly

Prosocial actions appear early in development (Dunn, 2001; Hay et al., 1999). Two-year-olds share toys and food with others, often without prompting. They also begin to help take care of their younger siblings and spontaneously help with some household chores (Garner, Jones, & Palmer, 1994; Rheingold, 1982). For example, 2-year-old Maggie responds to the cries of her younger sister by saying "Sister is crying; let's go to her. Let me hold her. You'd better nurse her, Mommy. Does she have to burp?" Maggie is trying to comfort and care for her younger sister. Maggie's ability to meet the needs of her baby sister is limited, but her

prosocial behavior voluntary actions intended to benefit another person

empathy an emotional state that matches another person's emotional state—for instance, feeling bad because someone else is feeling bad

sympathy feeling sorry or concerned for other people because of their emotional states or conditions

During the preschool years, children's prosocial emotions and behaviors become more advanced and appropriate. Children become genuinely concerned about the well-being of others. What can be done to foster and promote such feelings and behaviors?

responses show genuine concern for her sister's well-being and a desire to help. Across the preschool years, these acts of caring become more common. Preschoolers also act in more responsible ways; they are more likely to comply with parents' requests and are less likely to ignore or defy parental demands (Power, McGrath, Hughes, & Manire, 1994). Evidence suggests that individual differences in prosocial behavior have their origins in early childhood (Eisenberg, Guthrie et al., 1999).

Reasons and motives for helpful and responsible behaviors also change during early childhood. When asked why they share or help, young preschoolers often explain their behavior by referring to the other person's needs ("I gave him some crackers because he's hungry") or practical reasons ("I helped clean up because the table was dirty"). Thus, they appear to be motivated by an understanding of another's situation or needs. At other times, children focus on the task at hand or other practical aspects of the situation (Eisenberg, 1992). Older preschoolers occasionally justify prosocial behaviors by referring to their relationship with the person who needs help ("I helped her carry the toys because she's my friend") or their desire for others' approval ("I gave him some of my blocks so he'll like me"). Four- and 5-year-olds also justify prosocial behavior on the basis of selfish reasons ("If I share with him, the teacher will let me play outside"). With maturity, children recognize the social nature of helping relationships. It is not until later childhood that children's reasons for helping become altruistic, reflecting the desire to help others without any apparent personal gain or benefit (Damon, 1988).

Socialization of Prosocial Emotions and Behavior

Caregivers have considerable influence on young children's prosocial responses (Carlo, Fabes, Laible, & Kupanoff, 1999). Children who have warm and secure relationships with their caregivers are more likely to show prosocial feelings and behaviors (Kestenbaum, Farber, & Sroufe, 1989). In contrast, if the parents express anger and hostility and use physical punishment, the children are less empathic and less prosocial (Denham, Renwick-DeBardi, & Hughes, 1994; Denham, Zoller, & Couchoud, 1994).

When caregivers frequently talk to and reason with children about prosocial activities and the importance of feeling concern for and helping others, the children are more empathic and prosocial (Buchanan & Hudson, 2000). Children also learn about acting prosocially by watching the actions of their caregivers. But parents' talk must be backed by action; parents or caregivers who preach prosocial behavior but do not model it have little effect on children's prosocial development (Bryan & Walbek, 1970). It is important to note that children also can learn to be uncaring by imitating the selfish or uncaring behaviors modeled by adults (Eisenberg, 1992).

HOW DO PARENTING BEHAVIORS INFLUENCE YOUNG CHILDREN'S DEVELOPMENT?

During early childhood, children's attachments change significantly. Preschoolers come to understand that caregivers have feelings and plans that often differ from their own. This understanding enables preschoolers to attempt to change caregivers' plans and goals.

Ainsworth (1973) referred to this new type of attachment relationship as a **goal-corrected partnership.** In this new, emerging relationship, the child becomes a partner in planning how the relationship develops. This change in attachment places greater emphasis on how caregivers respond to children's more active behaviors. Caregivers' behaviors influence children's development in many other ways (Parke & Buriel, 1998). For example, through parents or their substitutes, young children learn the ways and values of their society (Bugental & Goodnow, 1998).

DISCIPLINING YOUNG CHILDREN

When you think of the term *discipline,* punishment may be the first thing that comes to mind. However, punishment is only one type of discipline. In the context of child rearing, **discipline** refers to any attempt by parents to alter children's behaviors or attitudes. The goal of discipline is to help children develop self-control and act in ways that society deems acceptable and appropriate. Before the age of 2, children are rarely disciplined. After children reach the age of 2, however, disciplinary encounters dominate parent-child interactions, and parents increasingly expect children to be able to obey their rules. According to one estimate (Minton, Kagan, & Levine, 1971), almost half of all parent-child interactions after the age of 2 center around discipline, and disciplinary encounters between parent and child occur an average of 9 times per hour.

Children may behave appropriately for different reasons. **Compliance** occurs when children obey and act appropriately because they know that they are being watched or that they will be rewarded or punished for their actions. **Internalization** occurs when children's obedience is based on internal controls and standards that they have incorporated into their own expectations of themselves. That is, they act appropriately because they want to (internalization), not because they have to (compliance).

How discipline is used influences whether or not children internalize standards. Discipline is more effective if it is *consistent* (Deal, Halverson, & Wampler, 1989), is not threatening to the child's well-being (Weiss & Dodge, 1992), and occurs as soon as possible after the child's misbehavior (Grusec, 1988). Supportive discipline does not create anxiety, helps children see the consequences of their actions, and aids internalization and adaptation (Pettit, Bates, & Dodge, 1997).

Although there are many ways to discipline children, the most common methods fall into three general categories:

   ◆ **Power assertion** encompasses attempts by parents to use physical force or threats of physical force to control children's behavior. It includes physical punishment, taking away of privileges or possessions, and threatening such acts. About 90 percent of parents report using some type of power assertion technique at some time over the course of their children's lives (Simons, Johnson, & Conger, 1994). Boys are spanked more often than girls, mothers do more spanking than fathers, children under the age of 7 are spanked more often than older children, and African American mothers (but not fathers) spank more often than Caucasian American mothers (Day, Peterson, & McCracken, 1998). Excessive use of power assertive discipline—particularly harsh or frequent use—puts children at risk for a variety of psychological and behavioral problems, including aggression, delinquency, and peer rejection (Peterson & Haan, 1999; Pettit et al., 2001).

       The effects of power assertive discipline vary for children of different ethnic and racial backgrounds. For example, African American parents report using harsh and punitive parenting more often than do Caucasian American parents, but the use of such parenting practices does not appear to have the same detrimental consequences for African American children that it does for Caucasian American children (Kelley, Power, & Wimbush, 1992; McLoyd, Cauce, Takeuchi, & Wilson, 2000). These differences likely result from differences in attitudes about the use of punishment—African American parents are more accepting of its use than are

goal-corrected partnership an attachment relationship in which the child becomes a partner in planning how the relationship develops

discipline attempts by parents to alter children's behaviors or attitudes

compliance obedience brought about by external pressures (such as the knowledge that one will be rewarded or punished for actions)

internalization obedience based on internal controls and standards that children have incorporated into their own expectations of themselves

power assertion disciplinary techniques in which parents use physical force or threats of physical force to control children's behavior

Caregivers vary considerably in their attitudes toward and choices about discipline. Even within a family, mothers and fathers may have very different approaches to discipline. Can you identify some of the factors that contribute to such differences?

Caucasian American parents (Heffer & Kelly, 1987). Attitude differences are due in part to differences in socioeconomic status and hence in stress levels; they may also relate to the belief of many African American parents that such parenting practices will help prepare their children for the harsh treatment they are likely to receive from society as they grow older (Snyder, 1996). These findings reflect the fact that parenting and its effects on children vary according to cultural values and the conditions in which parents and children find themselves.

Reinforcing good behavior also is a type of power assertive discipline because it is based on a difference in power between parents and their children. Just like the overuse of punishment, the overuse of rewards can have detrimental effects on children. In one study, children whose parents relied on rewards to get them to act appropriately were less helpful and generous when rewards were no longer offered (Fabes, Fultz, Eisenberg, Plumlee, & Christopher, 1989). Children may see rewards as "bribes" and comply only to get the rewards rather than because of their internal motivation (Kohn, 1993).

◆ **Love withdrawal** refers to attempts by a parent to gain obedience by ignoring or isolating the child, withholding affection, or expressing lack of love for the child. Love withdrawal can be effective in the short term because of the threat of losing the caregiver's love. In the long term, however, the constant anxiety about being rejected or abandoned has negative consequences for children's internalization (Grusec & Goodnow, 1994; Magai, Hunziker, Mesias, & Culver, 2000).

◆ **Inductive reasoning** is a disciplinary technique in which parents use reasoning and verbal communication for the purpose of changing children's behavior (McGrath, Wilson, & Franssetto, 1995). Parents' use of inductive reasoning may include the following: explanations of rules and standards expected of children ("You need to stay close to me because you might get lost"), moral persuasion ("It's nice to help others"), personal appeals ("It will make Mommy happy if you help your brother"), explanations of the hurtful consequences of children's actions for others ("It hurt your sister's feelings when you wouldn't let her play with you"), and character attributions ("A kind boy like you helps his friend"). During early childhood, as children develop the cognitive ability to understand their parents' reasoning, parents begin to favor the use of inductive reasoning (Kuczynski, Kochanska, Radke-Yarrow, & Girnius-Brown, 1987). Children whose parents use inductive reasoning tend to be more prosocial and popular and have more internalized values and acceptable behavior (Eisenberg & Murphy, 1995; Hart, DeWolf, Wozniak, & Burts, 1992).

INFLUENCES ON PARENTS' USE OF DISCIPLINE

The reasons a parent chooses one disciplinary technique over another are not entirely clear. Parents have different beliefs and values about how to discipline children and what is or is not effective. Additionally, parents' use of discipline depends on a variety of factors—such as the characteristics of the child and the situation (Grusec, Goodnow, & Kuczynski, 2000).

Characteristics of the Child

Parents use different disciplinary techniques with different children. They are more likely to use power assertion with their sons than with their daughters because they often expect their sons to be harder to control (Leve & Fagot, 1997). Similarly, parents are more likely to use power assertion with children who are difficult to manage than with children who are easy to manage (Greenwald, Bank, Reid, & Knutson, 1997). Parents are more likely to reason with older children, who can recognize and respond to parents' intentions. Moreover, as children mature, they are less tolerant of parental demands in areas they regard as outside the legitimate control of parents, such as the types of clothes they wear and the appearance of their rooms. Thus, parental discipline changes in response to children's increasing autonomy and cognitive development (Smetana, 1988).

love withdrawal disciplinary techniques in which parents ignore, withhold affection from, or express lack of love for the child

inductive reasoning disciplinary techniques in which parents use reasoning and verbal communication for the purpose of changing children's behavior

A similar trend is found in other cultures. For example, in mainland China, early childhood is divided into two periods: *budongshi,* the age of innocence (the first 6 years), when children lack cognitive understanding, and *dongshi,* the age of understanding (after age 6). Chinese parents rely on power assertive techniques during *budongshi* but use them less often once children reach *dongshi* (Stevenson, Chen, & Lee, 1992).

Nature of the Misbehavior

The discipline parents use varies depending on the nature of the child's misbehavior. For example, parents might use a combination of power assertion and inductive reasoning in response to lying and stealing, whereas they might use inductive reasoning alone when children fail to show concern for others (Grusec, Dix, & Mills, 1982; Trickett & Kuczynski, 1986). Parents also are more likely to use spanking and removal for dangerous misbehaviors than for behaviors that are merely annoying (Socolar & Stein, 1996).

Cultural, Ethnic, and Social Values

Disciplinary methods vary across cultures and among ethnic groups, in part because of different parenting goals and values. For example, many Hispanics and Asian Americans believe that children should be obedient, so they use power assertive discipline more than other groups of parents (Carter & Middlemiss, 1992). In contrast, Japanese mothers tend to indulge their children, with the intention of promoting a strong sense of dependency on the family—an outcome that is valued more in Japanese than in American culture (Azuma, 1986).

Among Aka pygmies, a hunter-gatherer tribe in the tropical rain forests of central Africa, parents seldom use power assertion. They are accepting of and responsive to their children but do not firmly or consistently enforce standards for behavior. Because of the demands of their environment, Aka children must be able to care for themselves at an early age. Aka parents value the development of autonomy more than obedience and respect for elders, and their disciplinary practices reflect these values (Hewlett, 1992).

Contextual and social factors also influence parents' choice of discipline. One factor that is associated with power assertive parenting, as noted earlier, is socioeconomic status. In general, poor parents, regardless of their ethnic background, are likely to stress obedience and to use power assertion (Fox & Solis-Camera, 1997; Kelley, Sanchez-Hucles, & Walker, 1993). Parents' ability to rear competent children may be undermined by the stress and strain of the undesirable conditions associated with poverty (McLoyd, 1998b). Poverty diminishes parents' psychological well-being and their capacity for supportive parenting as well (McLoyd, 1998b). Adults who are poor are more likely to experience physical and mental health problems than are their economically advantaged counterparts. In addition, parents who are poor face a variety of negative life conditions—the threat of eviction, criminal assault, poor nutrition, inadequate housing, and so on—that increase their frustration and stress (Hashima & Amato, 1994). Poverty also is associated with single-parenting, and those who have to care for children alone face additional stress (Chase-Linsdale et al., 1999; Huston, 1991).

As a family's economic situation worsens, the parent or parents exhibit less nurturance and more negative discipline toward the children (Elder, Conger, Foster, & Ardelt, 1992; Lamb, 1999). Poor parents are more likely to issue commands without explanation, less likely to consult children about their wishes, and less likely to reward children for behaving in desirable ways (Conger et al., 1994; McLoyd, 1998a). This is especially true if poor parents do not have a network of social support—friends or relatives they can rely on (Hashima & Amato, 1994). Not surprisingly, these parenting practices can have negative consequences for the well-being of their children.

Importantly, however, not all parents who are poor are depressed or disengaged parents. Many poor parents effectively buffer their children from the potentially detrimental effects of poverty (McLoyd, 1998b). When poor parents have the psychological strength to manage the demands of being a parent, they can and do provide their children with supportive and responsive parenting behaviors (Jack, 2000). It is important to remember that stress in any family, regardless of how much money the family might have, can undermine the quality of parenting. Unfortunately, it is the nature of poverty to cause increased stress

How are parents' abilities to rear competent children challenged when the family lives in poverty?

IGURE 8.3

Classification of Baumrind's Parenting Styles

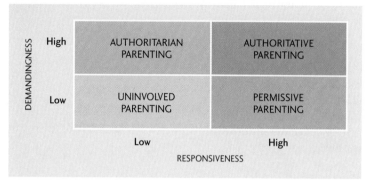

Baumrind's parenting styles were based on differences in demandingness and responsiveness. Can you describe the qualities of parents within each classification and the impact the different styles have on children?

in parents and thus potentially influence their parenting negatively.

PARENTING STYLES

Although parents' disciplinary methods vary, there are consistencies in their use of discipline. One of the most prominent studies of parents' styles of discipline was carried out by Diana Baumrind. In a long-term study of how parents influence children's development, Baumrind identified two important parenting characteristics (Baumrind, 1967, 1971, 1989). One is **demandingness**—the tendency to exert firm control over children, requiring them to act in mature and appropriate ways. The other is **responsiveness**—the tendency to be warm, accepting, and willing to take into account the wishes and feelings of the child. On the basis of these two characteristics, Baumrind identified four main parenting styles (see Figure 8.3).

Authoritarian Parenting

Authoritarian parenting is characterized by efforts by parents to shape, control, and judge the behaviors and attitudes of their children according to rigid standards of conduct. These parents usually value obedience and favor harsh, forceful measures, including physical punishment, to ensure that children comply with their rules. These parents discourage verbal give-and-take, believing that children should accept their word for what is right. Thus, authoritarian parents are high in demandingness and low in responsiveness. They set the rules, and children are to obey these rules because the parents say so. Preschoolers from authoritarian homes have low levels of self-control and independence, and they tend to be aggressive, anxious, and resistant to correction (Baumrind, 1971; Kochanska & Askan, 1995).

Permissive Parenting

Parents who practice **permissive parenting** make few demands on their children—they are accepting and tolerant of their children's impulses and desires. These parents view themselves as resources to be used as their children wish rather than as agents responsible for shaping or altering their children's behavior. Permissive parents avoid the use of force to accomplish their goals and thus are low in demandingness and high in responsiveness. Because permissive parents fail to set limits on their children's behavior, preschoolers raised by permissive parents resemble those from authoritarian homes. They tend to be relatively immature, demanding, rebellious, impulsive, aggressive, and less socially competent (Baumrind, 1971).

Uninvolved Parenting

Uninvolved parenting describes the style of parents who make few demands on their children but are unresponsive or rejecting as well. Uninvolved parents do whatever they can to minimize the costs of being a parent and put little time and effort into interactions with their children (Maccoby & Martin, 1983). Parents' efforts relate more to their own immediate comfort and convenience than to the long-term development of the child. For example, these parents are unlikely to establish and enforce rules about bedtime or children's diets. At the extreme, uninvolved parents may be neglectful. Parental depression is sometimes related to uninvolved parenting; depressed parents tend to be withdrawn, disengaged, and unresponsive to their children (Lee & Gotlib, 1995). As you might expect, children from homes where the parents are uninvolved, neglectful, or depressed do not fare very well. These children tend to be noncompliant, aggressive, withdrawn, and insecure in their at-

demandingness the tendency of parents to exert firm control over children, requiring them to act in mature and appropriate ways

responsiveness the tendency of parents to be warm, accepting, and willing to take into account the wishes and feelings of the child

authoritarian parenting a style of parenting in which parents try to shape, control, and judge the behaviors and attitudes of their children according to rigid standards of conduct

permissive parenting a style of parenting in which parents make few demands on their children—they are accepting and tolerant of their children's impulses and desires

uninvolved parenting a style of parenting in which parents make few demands on their children and are unresponsive or rejecting

tachments to others (Egeland & Sroufe, 1983; Miller, Cowan, Cowan, Hetherington, & Clingempeel, 1993).

Authoritative Parenting

Authoritative parenting is exhibited by parents who encourage verbal give-and-take and share with their children the reasons behind discipline and household rules. These parents value conformity to their rules and exert consistent and firm—but not excessive—control to bring it about. Authoritative parents are loving and supportive, and they recognize the importance of children's individual interests and needs. Authoritative parents can be classified as high in demandingness and high in responsiveness (Baumrind, 1996). Preschool children raised in authoritative homes tend to be friendly, cooperative, socially competent, confident, and self-reliant (Dekovic & Janssens, 1992; Hinshaw et al., 1997).

Thus, authoritative parenting produces the best outcomes for children. But why is that the case? Baumrind (1989) argues that the optimal parent-child relationship at any stage of development is characterized by reciprocity—the tendency to engage in mutual give-and-take. Authoritative parenting is associated with a pattern of family functioning in which children are required to be responsive to parental demands and parents accept a reciprocal responsibility to be as responsive as possible to the reasonable demands of their children. Authoritative parents maintain a balance between structure and control on the one hand and warmth and respect on the other, and they encourage the same balance in their children. In Western cultures, this balance represents competent parenting, and parents who cannot provide the necessary control and guidance have children who are difficult to manage (Belsky, Woodworth, & Crnic, 1996a; Gray & Steinberg, 1999).

Because different cultures hold different values, it is not surprising that the degree to which parents are authoritative or authoritarian differs across cultures and subcultures. Authoritative parenting is more prevalent in two-parent nondivorced families than in single-parent families or stepfamilies (Hetherington & Clingempeel, 1992). Authoritarian parenting is more common among families experiencing financial difficulties and among ethnic minorities (Steinberg, Mounts, Lamborn, & Dornbusch, 1991). Moreover, parents who adhere to conservative religious beliefs tend to adhere to an authoritarian parenting style more often than do parents who are less conservative in their religious beliefs (Day, Peterson, & McCracken, 1998). Authoritarian parenting also is more common in cultures emphasizing collectivist, rather than individualist, values (Rudy & Grusec, 2001). These findings indicate that parenting styles and their impact on children are influenced by family circumstances and cultural beliefs and attitudes.

How DOES DIVORCE AFFECT YOUNG CHILDREN'S DEVELOPMENT?

Divorce is more commonplace today than at any time in the past. Although marriage is still viewed as a lifelong commitment, many people believe that couples who are unhappy should not be forced to stay together, not even for the sake of the children. When a sample of young mothers was interviewed in 1962, half of them said that couples with children should stay together, even if they did not get along. By 1989, fewer than 1 in 5 women gave that answer when asked the same question (Arland, 1989).

Divorce rates in the United States generally increased from 1960 to 1988 and then stabilized between 1988 and 1998. Approximately 1,135,000 divorces were granted in 1998 (Centers for Disease Control, 2001a). This trend is not unique to the United States. Table 8.1 on page 264 presents divorce rates in selected countries for 1960, 1970, 1988, and 1998. As you can see, before stabilizing or even declining recently, the divorce rates increased over time in all countries listed, in some cases more than tripling. Although similar trends are seen in all countries, divorce rates in the United States continue to be among the highest in the world.

authoritative parenting a style of parenting in which parents encourage verbal give-and-take and share with their children the reasons behind discipline and household rules

TABLE 8.1

Divorce Rates in Selected Countries (divorces per 1000 married women)

COUNTRY	1960	1970	1988	1998
United States	9.2	14.9	20.7	20.1
France	2.9	3.3	8.4	8.9
Canada	1.8	6.3	12.9	10.0
Denmark	5.9	7.6	13.1	11.4
Japan	3.6	2.9	5.4	7.9
Netherlands	2.2	3.3	8.1	7.5
Sweden	5.0	6.8	11.7	11.4
United Kingdom	2.0	4.7	12.3	12.5

SOURCE: National Center for Health Statistics, 1990; *Miami Herald,* 1998.

In the United States, about half of divorcing couples had children who were under 18 years of age at the time of their divorce (Centers for Disease Control, 2001a). By some estimates (Amato, 2000), nearly half of all children will experience the divorce of their parents and will live some of their life in a single-parent household, in most cases with their mother. Divorce has both short- and long-term consequences for an individual's development and adjustment (Simons et al., 1999). For example, a 70-year longitudinal study showed that children from divorced families grew up to have a higher risk of premature mortality (Tucker et al., 1997).

YOUNG CHILDREN'S UNDERSTANDING OF DIVORCE

Divorce and separation are difficult concepts for children to grasp. Divorce is an abstract concept, and children's understanding of divorce is influenced by their ability to understand abstract ideas (Hetherington & Clingempeel, 1992).

Preschoolers have difficulty distinguishing between inner motives and outward appearances. They see divorce as one parent's moving away—they do not understand the complex motivations underlying the behaviors of both parents (Johnston, Breunig, Garrity, & Baris, 1997). Preschoolers view parents as possessions that belong to them and have only vague notions as to how parents relate to each other. They do not understand why their parents have to live apart, and they do not comprehend that divorce is usually permanent. School-age children, however, are more likely to understand the motives of their parents and that divorce is a permanent state in which parents grow apart from each other (Kurdek, 1988).

Young children's conception of *family* is concrete and is limited to those people who live together (Wedemeyer, Bickhard, & Cooper, 1989). The idea of blood relations is often too abstract for them to understand. When Dad leaves home because of a divorce or separation, it is not uncommon for young children to consider him no longer a family member. This reasoning reflects their tendency to focus on the observable qualities of a situation rather than the underlying and unseen qualities. Older children come to define families and family transitions such as divorce in psychological rather than physical terms (Mazur, 1993).

Divorce can be emotionally upsetting and frightening to young children. Because young children are more dependent on the people they live with than are older children, the possibility of abandonment poses a more serious threat to them. The egocentric nature of young children's thinking leads them to see themselves as at least partly to blame for their parents' separation. Children who feel this way may try to undo the situation by making amends. Similarly, when a parent stops visiting, the young child may think that it is because of something he or she did and feel unloved or rejected. Older children are more likely to recognize that the reasons for the divorce have little to do with them and that the divorce reflects the incompatibility of their parents (Kurdek, 1988).

In families that have experienced divorce, parents often have to adopt roles and responsibilities that they did not have before. What roles do divorced mothers adopt?

EFFECTS OF DIVORCE ON YOUNG CHILDREN'S BEHAVIOR AND ADJUSTMENT

Over the past decade or so, researchers have come to understand that divorce is not a single event—rather, it is a complex process that does not begin with the dissolution of the marriage. Often, divorce is a lengthy sequence of events, involving "predivorce" experiences that may be as important for determining children's welfare as is the separation itself. Additionally, children do not react uniformly to divorce; their reactions depend on their age and developmental stage, their temperament, the way the process is managed by their parents, and the conditions associated with the breakup (such as the economic impact and the amount of lingering conflict) (Furstenberg & Kiernan, 2001).

Divorce can generate painful emotions, uncertainty, and confusion (Guidubaldi, 1988; Maccoby & Mnookin, 1992). Divorce forces mothers, fathers, and children to adapt to changes that can affect nearly every aspect of their lives. Two households must be established where there was only one before. Family finances and schedules are radically altered. Family loyalties are divided. Parental roles and responsibilities change dramatically.

Nearly all children react with shock and are extremely upset when they learn of their parents' breakup. Even when parents are openly fighting, young children often do not grasp the significance of these behaviors and cannot envision a separation. Most parents do not inform their young children of an impending separation until shortly before it occurs (Furstenberg & Cherlin, 1991).

In a series of longitudinal studies, Wallerstein and colleagues (Wallerstein & Kelly, 1975, 1976, 1980; Wallerstein & Lewis, 1998) found that children respond to divorce differently, according to age. Young preschoolers (2½ to 3½ years) are likely to show increased aggression; middle preschoolers (3½ to 4½ years) are likely to show increased irritability, aggression, self-blame, and confusion; and older preschoolers (5 to 6 years) are likely to show increased anxiety and aggressive behavior. Many of these negative behaviors ended within a year or two for children who experienced stable caregiving environments. However, 44 percent of the preschoolers continued to show emotional distress and poor psychological adjustment a year or two following the divorce.

Because of findings such as these, some researchers have labeled the first two years following a divorce as a "crisis period" for children and adults (Chase-Linsdale & Hetherington, 1990; Hetherington & Stanley-Hagan, 1999a). Young children have special needs during this crisis period. First, they need additional emotional support as they try to adapt to the new and frightening challenges brought about by their parents' divorce. Second, they need the predictable daily structure they had previously in their pre-divorce home life. Many single parents, however hard they may try, cannot meet these needs. Parents often lack the emotional energy to comfort children as they try to sort out their own anger, depression, and anxiety. The increased demands of single-parenthood often cause schedules to change from day to day. As a result, young children lose some of the support and structure they need, which may increase their aggression, fear, and uncertainty. In young children, the increased stress and confusion can result in regressed behavior, such as bed-wetting or sleep problems, that did not exist before the divorce (Benedek & Brown, 1995).

The adverse consequences of divorce appear to be greater for young boys than for young girls (Chase-Linsdale & Hetherington, 1990). It is possible that boys fare worse because they typically live with their mother, and there is some evidence that children adjust better after a divorce if they reside with the same-sex parent (Emery, 1988). Girls may be no less affected by divorce, though. Their responses (depression and withdrawal) may simply be less noticeable than boys' responses (aggression and hostility), and problems stemming from divorce may not appear until years after the breakup (Furstenberg & Cherlin, 1991).

For the sake of the children, should parents stay together in an unhappy marriage? This question has been asked repeatedly by parents, researchers, clinicians, and policy makers. The answer is complex. It is clear that high levels of parental conflict put children at greater risk for developing psychological and behavioral problems (Hetherington, 1999a). It is also clear, however, that divorce puts children at risk for a variety of poor developmental outcomes. If the stresses on family processes associated with an unhappy marriage can be reduced by a divorce, then the divorce may be advantageous. But the diminished resources that result from a divorce, coupled with inept parenting, may cause children to be better off if their parents stay in an unhappy marriage (Hetherington, 1999b). Most of the scientific research shows that, although growing up in a divorced family elevates the risk for certain kinds of problems, divorce by no means dooms children to having a terrible life. Additionally, research suggests that many of the problems in children that have been attributed to divorce were actually present prior to the divorce (Amato, 2000).

FACTORS THAT AFFECT YOUNG CHILDREN'S ADJUSTMENT TO DIVORCE

Several factors influence how well children adapt to a divorce. Some of the important research findings can be summarized in terms of several main factors (Hetherington, Bridges, & Insabella, 1998):

- **Amount of conflict between the parents.**   Children who are exposed to overt parental conflict (both before and after a divorce) have more adjustment problems (Cummings & Davies, 1996; Davis, Hops, Alpert, & Sheeber, 1998). When parents have hostile battles in front of young children, children's stress and anxiety increase. In fact, there is some indication that moving from a household with two parents who always are fighting in front of the children to a stable one-parent household can lead to better adjustment for children (Peterson & Zill, 1986). When divorced parents maintain civil and cordial relationships, children's adaptation to divorce is enhanced (Walsh & Stolberg, 1989).

- **Effectiveness of the parents.**   A critical factor in children's short- and long-term adjustment to divorce is how effectively the ex-spouses (particularly the custodial parent) function as parents. Divorced parents experience more stress because of the increased demands and more limited resources they face, and as a result, the relationships between parents and their children can deteriorate. In divorced families, parent-child relationships generally are more negative (especially between mothers and their sons) and parenting is less authoritative than in nondivorced families (Parke & Buriel, 1998). Mothers tend to become more authoritarian after a divorce, whereas fathers become more permissive. The better able parents are to cope with the disruptions brought about by a divorce, the less likely they are to dramatically alter their parenting styles and the more capable they are of providing their children with the structure, consistent discipline, and love they need (Katz & Gottman, 1997).

- **Characteristics of the child.**   Some children react more negatively to divorce than others. As discussed earlier, age and sex are important determinants of children's responses. Recall from our discussions in Chapter 6 that children's reactivity to and resiliency in stressful environments vary. Children who are sensitive to changes in their environment and do not readily adapt may be more affected by divorce than are children whose temperaments are more adaptive to change. Similarly, children who are moody and irritable may react to divorce more negatively than children who are less emotionally sensitive and less easily upset (Monahan, Buchanan, Maccoby, & Dornbusch, 1993). Children's perception of the quality of the relationship between their parents also influences their response to marital conflict and divorce (Fincham, 1998).

- **Relationship of the child with the noncustodial parent.**   Young children's adjustment to divorce is enhanced when both parents are able to maintain relationships with them. In many cases, the father, who often is the noncustodial parent, may break off the relationship with his children, or the mother may actively try to undermine this relationship. Loss of the father's relationship generally has a greater impact on boys than on girls. Also, the younger the child is when separated from a parent, the more affected the child is by the loss (Stanley, Weikel, & Wilson, 1986). When a noncustodial parent is able to maintain an active and supportive parenting relationship, children are better off. Part of the reason for this is that noncustodial parents who maintain regular contact with their children also are likely to keep paying child support (Peters, Argys, Maccoby, & Mnookin, 1993). Additionally, the more often a father sees his children, the better he feels about the visits and the less likely problems are to occur (Arditti & Keith, 1993). Despite visitation and custody arrangements, contact with noncustodial parents drops off sharply over time. According to some estimates, by the end of the second year after a divorce, only 1 child in 6 sees his or her father as often as once a week, and close to half have not seen their father at all over the course of the preceding year (Furstenberg & Cherlin, 1991).

CHILD CUSTODY ARRANGEMENTS

Until recently, the dominant legal standard for awarding custody of children, particularly young children, favored mothers. This practice was based on the "tender years" doctrine, which assumed that child rearing during the early years should be undertaken by women (Maccoby & Mnookin, 1992). Today, however, the "best interests of the child" standard has replaced the tender years doctrine in most states (Krauss & Sales, 2001). This doctrine is based on the notion that the custody arrangement should be the one that best suits the child. The increased recognition that fathers' involvement with their children is beneficial to them is a reason many states have adopted joint-custody statutes (Wallerstein & Corbin, 1999).

Several different types of custody arrangements are available (see Table 8.2). These arrangements vary in the degree to which both parents are involved in physical care of and decision making for the children. As you can see from the charts in Figure 8.4 on page 268, the majority of children are placed in sole custody of the mother (National Center for Health Statistics, 1995). Joint custody is awarded in a small number of cases; the percentage of arrangements in which sole custody is given to the father is even smaller. These charts also show that African American children are more likely than Caucasian American children to be placed in sole custody of their mother.

YOUNG CHILDREN'S ADJUSTMENT TO REMARRIAGE

When parents remarry, children must share them with a widening circle of other people—stepparents and stepsiblings. After a divorce, between 70 and 80 percent of parents remarry (Coleman, Ganons, & Fine, 2000).

*T*ABLE 8.2

Types of Custody Arrangements

TYPE OF CUSTODY	DESCRIPTION
Sole legal custody	Custodial parent is assigned all legal rights, duties, and powers and is responsible for all decisions regarding child's welfare. Noncustodial parent has limited rights and powers.
Sole physical custody	Custodial parent has primary physical custody of child. Noncustodial parent is usually awarded visitation rights.
Joint legal custody	Both parents retain rights to make decisions regarding child's health and welfare.
Joint physical custody	Both parents retain rights to share in day-to-day physical care of child. Child spends substantial amount of time with each parent.
Divided custody	Each parent has child for a portion of the year or in alternating years. Each parent has legal rights and makes decisions when child is with that parent.
Split custody	Each parent has sole legal and physical custody of one or more children. Noncustodial parent has visitation rights.

SOURCE: Kelly, 1994.

IGURE 8.4

Custody Arrangements for African American and Caucasian American Children

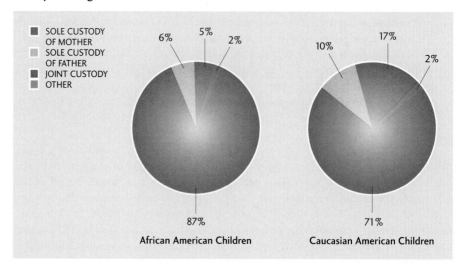

Compare the figures for African American and Caucasian American children. Notice that joint custody and father custody are more common among Caucasian American children than among African American children. What factors contribute to these differences?

More than half of all Americans alive today have been, are now, or eventually will be in one or more stepfamily situations during their lives. One-third of all children are expected to become stepchildren before they reach the age of 18, and about 1 of every 3 Americans is a stepparent, stepchild, stepsibling, or some other member of a stepfamily. African American children are most likely to live in stepfamilies—32 percent of African American children live in stepfamilies, versus 16 percent of Hispanic children and 15 percent of Caucasian children (Arnold, 1998).

Currently, the vast majority of stepfamilies (86 percent) are composed of a biological mother and a stepfather (Hetherington & Stanley-Hagan, 1999b). The dramatic increase in the number of people living in stepfamilies is largely due to America's increasing divorce rate. Two-thirds of the people who are divorced and widowed choose to remarry, and the number of stepfamilies has grown proportionately. The other major reason for the increasing number of people living in stepfamilies is the fact that more children are being born out of wedlock. One-third of children entering stepfamilies do so after birth to an unmarried mother, a situation that is four times more common in African American stepfamilies than in Caucasian stepfamilies. The mode of entry into stepfamilies varies with the age of the child. A majority of preschoolers who enter stepfamilies do so after nonmarital birth; 16 percent become members of a stepfamily through parental remarriage following divorce. About half of the stepfamilies into which children over the age of 10 enter are formed when a parent remarries following a divorce (Arnold, 1998).

The changes brought about by remarriage are dramatic (Mason, 1998). Newly remarried parents report experiencing twice the stress of nondivorced parents. The changing dynamics of family life after remarriage lead to changes in parenting behaviors. For example, mothers report that they are less emotionally responsive to their children and more punitive in their discipline than they were before remarrying (Hetherington, Hagan, & Anderson, 1989). The changes associated with stepfamily life may put some children at risk for poor outcomes. In one study (Nicholson, Fergusson, & Horwood, 1999), children entering a stepfamily for the first time between the ages of 6 and 16 years had had higher rates of juvenile delinquency, tobacco dependence, illicit substance abuse or dependence, truancy, and early onset of sexual activity by the time they were 18 years of age. These risks, however, appear to be associated with factors related to previous family life (such as low income, family conflict, preexisting

THE SOCIAL IMPACT: DEBATING THE ISSUE

Does Custody Make a Difference?

Proponents of joint custody argue that it gives both parents legal rights with regard to their children and reduces the chances that one parent will abduct the children. Each year, over 394,000 children are abducted by the noncustodial parent (US Department of Justice, 1999). Joint custody also eliminates the "winner takes all" mentality of sole custody. In contrast, opponents of joint custody argue that it disrupts the continuity of care that children receive, increases children's sense of loss of control, and increases interparent conflict.

The few studies that have been conducted show modest benefits at best for children who are in joint custody arrangements. For example, joint legal custody does not necessarily increase the father's decision-making authority or involvement in child rearing (Furstenberg & Cherlin, 1991), although fathers with joint custody

generally are more satisfied with their arrangement than noncustodial fathers (Arditti, 1992). Similarly, joint physical custody has not necessarily been found to be better for children's overall adjustment (Lye, 1999; Maccoby, Depner, & Mnookin, 1990). Former spouses often have difficulty co-parenting and end up avoiding each other. In addition, conflict among joint custody couples is as high as it is among sole custody couples (Maccoby & Mnookin, 1992). What seems to matter for children's well-being is not the custody arrangement, but how much conflict there is between parents and how well the parents function as parents (Buchanan, Maccoby, & Dornbusch, 1996).

Using this information, Furstenberg and Cherlin (1991) concluded that joint custody, particularly joint physical custody, should be encouraged only in cases where both parents voluntarily

agree to it. Joint physical custody may be especially difficult for young children who, because of their limited cognitive and perspective-taking skills, find the different living arrangements and changing schedules confusing. Joint custody usually does little harm, however, and a legal preference for it may send a message to fathers that our society respects and encourages their roles and responsibilities in the care of their children.

Thinking It Through:

1. What factors would you use to decide which type of custody was best for a child?
2. What are the advantages and disadvantages of each type of custody arrangement?
3. How are young children likely to respond to each type of custody?

---

mental health problems) rather than the new stepfamily itself. Once these other factors were taken into account, the risks associated with stepfamily life were reduced substantially.

In contrast to the findings on divorce, girls have more problems than boys in making the transition to the new family. Young girls, who are likely to have enjoyed a good relationship with their single mother, may become angry and resentful of the new husband. Competition for the mother's time and attention increases the daughter's rivalry with the stepfather, regardless of how supportive the new father is (Hetherington & Stanely-Hagan, 2000).

Young children seem to adapt more readily to their parents' remarriages than do older children and adolescents (Hetherington & Stanely-Hagan, 2000). Because young children define a family as the people who live together under the same roof, they are more accepting of new parents, brothers, and sisters than older children are. Also, because young children are more dependent on adults than older children and adolescents are, issues related to independence and resistance to authority are less likely to erupt.

At the same time, young children lack the abilities and resources of older children to adapt to the many transitions and stressors brought about by divorce and remarriage. If the parent's response to remarriage is to invest heavily in the new marriage at the expense of the child, a young child's ability to cope may be overtaxed. Thus, the quality of young children's relationships with their parents and stepparents may be crucial to their adjustment to remarriage and stepfamily life (Hetherington & Stanley-Hagan, 1999b).

HOW DO PEER AND SIBLING RELATIONSHIPS DEVELOP DURING EARLY CHILDHOOD?

As children develop, their social relationships widen to include people other than family members. There is a gradual shift in the importance of peers and friends after infancy. By the end of childhood, nearly 50 percent of children's social activities involve peers (Grusec & Lytton, 1988).

A child's peer group typically consists of other children who are about the same age, are the same sex, and have similar interests and activities. Relationships with peers differ in important ways from family relationships (Hartup, 1996):

✦ Peer relationships are voluntary relationships chosen by the child.
✦ Peer relationships are based on equality and mutual give-and-take, whereas family relationships, particularly parent-child relationships, are based more on the authority of parents or older siblings.
✦ Children learn things from peers that they are less likely to learn from adults, such as cooperation and reciprocity, as well as competition, lying, cheating, and fighting.
✦ Families tend to love and care for children no matter what they do; peers are not so accepting.

The quality of peer relationships affects children's development. Children who have poor peer relationships are more likely than others to drop out of school, become delinquent, and suffer many kinds of psychological and behavioral problems (Parker & Asher, 1987). Young children enjoy the companionship provided by peers, and those who lack friends and companions report being lonely (Cohn, Lohrmann, & Patterson, 1985).

YOUNG CHILDREN'S FRIENDSHIPS

Friendships consist of mutual emotional bonds expressed through interactions that have qualities different from those of interactions with nonfriends (Hartup & Stevens, 1999). For example, friends express more positive and negative emotions to one another than they do to nonfriends, and they are likely to continue to interact even after a disagreement (Newcomb & Bagwell, 1995).

Friendships provide children with opportunities to learn effective interpersonal skills such as sharing, cooperating, and resolving conflicts, which then serve as the basis for other relationships (Hartup, 1996). Friendships also provide opportunities to gain experience in displaying and controlling emotions and in responding to others' emotions (Rose & Asher, 2000). In addition, friends share information and ideas and engage in social problem solving (Azmitia & Montgomery, 1993).

During toddlerhood, children begin to seek out specific children and develop with them special relationships that are mutually satisfying. They may have one to two friendships, however, that are fragile and dependent on the context. For example, toddlers who are friends may engage in a give-and-take encounter where one toddler plays with a toy while the other watches, and then they change places. If this pattern of play breaks down, so does the interaction and the friendship. After age 2, children have expanded capabilities to communicate and interact. As a result, their friendships are more flexible, and the number and stability increase. By age 3, children differentiate friends from playmates, and friendships become a basis for many of their decisions about their social interactions (Howes, 1989; Rose & Asher, 2000).

The major developmental advances during early childhood that lead to these changes in friendship patterns include the abilities to manipulate symbols, use language, and engage in pretend play. These cognitive advances allow older preschoolers to share understandings about relationships with a wider range of children (Roffey, Majors, & Tarrant, 1997). Children's ability to control their emotions also increases during early childhood, and they become better able to respond appropriately and effectively to both positive and negative social interactions (Fabes et al., 1996).

During early childhood, friendship is based on the exchange of common interests and activities.

Children tend to develop friendships with same-sex peers. Why do you think girls prefer to play with girls and boys prefer to play with boys?

Friends are children who are readily accessible, pleasurable, and entertaining and who have nice toys (Furman, 1996; Gottman, 1983). Young children usually make friends with children who are of the same sex and race, are of similar age, and have similar interests and values (Poulin et al., 1997). When they make friends with a child who is dissimilar (such as someone of the other sex), the friendship tends to be short-lived (Maccoby, 1990).

Young children's friendships are fluid and changeable (Rose & Asher, 2000). Friends are those you are sharing a game with at the moment. Consider the following exchange among three 5-year-old girls:

Bethany: [talking to Maria, who is playing in the block area with Claudia] What are you playing, Maria?

Maria: Claudia and I are playing Pocahontas. You can't play with us.

Bethany: Why can't I play?

Maria: Cause we're friends and we're playing.

Bethany: Well, Maria, . . . do you remember when we were playing together yesterday? You said I was your friend.

Maria: [initially looks confused and then brightens] I know; we can all be friends and you can play!

In this example, Maria and Bethany negotiate the status of their relationship. Maria at first resists Bethany's attempt to play with her and Claudia, because she and Claudia are friends. When Bethany reminds Maria that they played together the day before, Maria resolves the dilemma by acknowledging that one can have more than one friend at a time and invites Bethany to join them. A younger child might not have been as flexible in her view of friendships.

Although young children are more likely than older children to define friendships according to the situation, their friendships can be quite intense and involving. Young children express distress at being separated from or losing a friend (Howes, 1988a). It is not until mid–elementary school, however, that children recognize that friendships are based on mutual sympathy and loyalty and that the relationship between friends is stable and enduring even if they do not see each other for some time (Newcomb & Bagwell, 1998; Youniss, 1980).

YOUNG CHILDREN AT PLAY

Play among young children is observed in virtually every human culture. Play is an optimal experience for young children. It is intrinsically motivating—children play for no obvious tangible external reward. The primary reward is the satisfaction that is inherent in the play. When young children play, they usually become fully absorbed in their play activities, losing their sense of time and having feelings of great fulfillment (Csikszentmihalyi, 1991). Through play, children learn about themselves and the people and world around them. Young children's play experiences generally are rewarding in and of themselves, and attempts by adults to structure children's play or to make it more rewarding by adding external rewards often undermine intrinsic motivation (Lepper & Henderlong, 2000).

Even in societies where there is little time for play, children somehow manage to integrate it into their work routines. For example, in the Kipsigis community in Kenya, children have many chores that take up considerable amounts of their time. Yet, Kipsigis children incorporate play into their chores by playing tag while they watch cows or climb trees (Harkness & Super, 1983).

Although play is universal among children, there are differences in the amounts and kinds of play observed across and within cultures (Roopnarine, Lasker, Sacks, & Stores, 1998). Families in various cultures encourage different types of play and attach different meanings to play activities. For instance, differences were apparent in a study that compared how Japanese and American mothers interacted with their young children in a free-play situation (Tamis-LeMonda, Bornstein, Cyphers, Toda, & Ogino, 1992). Japanese mothers encouraged their young children to engage in pretend play—suggesting, for example, that the child kiss a doll or offer the doll some food. American mothers emphasized the functional uses of the toys— "Push the bus"—and spoke more about the toys as objects than did Japanese mothers. Japanese mothers viewed the play situation as an opportunity to teach their children how to interact with others, whereas American mothers used play to teach their children about the world and

IGURE 8.5

Percentages of Time Marquesan and American Children Spend in Different Types of Play

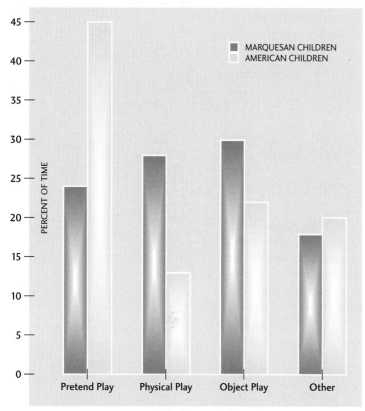

SOURCE: Martini, 1994. Reprinted by permission from *Children's Play in Diverse Cultures* by Jaipaul L. Roopnarine, James E. Johnson, and Frank H. Hooper (Eds.), the State University of New York Press © 1994, State University of New York. All rights reserved.

What differences do you see when you compare the figures for Marquesan and American children? What accounts for the high rate of pretend play among American children?

how to explore it on their own (Tamis-LeMonda et al., 1992).

The amount of time children spend in various play activities also is influenced by their cultural environments. For example, American children and young children growing up in the Marquesas Islands in the South Pacific allocate different amounts of time to various play activities. Figure 8.5 presents a breakdown of these differences. As you can see in this figure, Marquesan children spend considerably less time in pretend play and more time in physical and object play than do American children. This difference is due in part to cultural differences in their views of social status. Because Marquesan children are taught to be cautious about forming status hierarchies, they avoid play that requires distinct leaders, preferring activities that do not require much individual competition (Martini, 1994). Pretend play requires cooperation and structure; Marquesan children are more likely to engage in types of play that do not include these elements. They prefer play that is object oriented (pounding rocks to make noise) or physical (searching for insects or eels, chasing waves). Their preferences reflect the cultural values of the society in which they are reared.

Development of Social Play

The amount of time spent in play depends on the age of the individual—it begins to increase in early infancy, peaks during childhood, declines during adolescence, and all but disappears by adulthood (Pellegrini & Smith, 1998). The form of play also changes with age. In a classic study, Parten (1933) identified five forms of play relating to the level of involvement with other children. Her observations were so keen that her categories of play are still used as measures of children's social maturity.

solitary play play in which a child is alone, even if surrounded by other children

onlooker play play in which one child watches another child or children but does not directly participate

parallel play play in which two or more children engage in the same activity at the same time and place, but each child still plays separately

associative play play in which various children engage, but with different goals

cooperative play play in which two or more children engage, with a common goal that requires social interaction

✦ In **solitary play,** the lowest level of social play, the child plays alone, even if surrounded by other children. This type of play is typical of 2-year-olds; Parten found that approximately half of 2-year-olds' play was solitary.

✦ In **onlooker play,** the child watches another child or children playing but does not directly participate. Two-year-olds engage in a considerable amount of onlooker play, sometimes even asking questions or offering suggestions to the children playing.

✦ In **parallel play,** the child engages in an activity that another is engaged in at the same time and place, but each child is still playing separately. The children play side by side but not *with* each other. Parallel play is commonly observed in preschoolers.

✦ In **associative play,** the child engages in play that involves other children, but each child has a different goal. Associative play involves a considerable amount of social interaction, turn-taking, and expressive communication. Associative play is occurring when two children draw pictures at the same table, sharing crayons and commenting on each other's picture. Each child has his or her own design and goal in mind, but they share and socialize with each other as they draw. Associative play is common among 3- and 4-year-olds.

✦ In **cooperative play,** two or more children engage in a play activity with a common goal that requires social interaction. For instance, two children might dig through sand with their bare hands, opposite each other, with the goal of meeting in the middle to form a tunnel. Cooperative play represents the highest level of social play.

It is best not to think of these categories as discrete developmental stages of play. Although their play becomes increasingly social and interactive as children develop, even toddlers engage in cooperative play, and most children display a blend of all varieties of play (Howes & Matheson, 1992). Also, the kind of play children engage in is not always a measure of social maturity. For example, the meaning of solitary play depends on what the child is doing (Coplan & Rubin, 1998; Coplan, Rubin, Fox, Calkins, & Stewart, 1994) and on the physical environment (Frost, Shin, & Jacobs, 1998). Solitary play may be appropriate for a 4-year-old child when cutting and pasting paper but not when engaging in pretend play. Thus, if a child is engaged alone in an activity that is best done as a group, then solitary play may be detrimental to the child's development.

The culture children grow up in influences the amount of time they spend immersed in the different forms of play. Marquesan children almost never play alone, whereas American children spend about 35 percent of their time engaged in solitary play (Martini, 1994). Because the play of American preschoolers is almost always supervised by adults who set limits, they are not exposed to the dangers Marquesan children face. Large play groups are necessary for the protection and safety of Marquesan children.

In this example of parallel play, notice how these children are playing the same thing but are not taking notice of each other. What factors contribute to the development of more advanced forms of social play?

Young Children's Pretend Play

Much of children's play is **pretend play**—play based on make-believe situations and fantasies. In pretend play, children let objects or persons symbolize things or people they are not. Pretend play appears by age 3 and peaks around age 6 or 7. Because of its infinite themes and variety, pretend play may be the most important type of play for children's development (Slade & Wolf, 1994).

Pretend play undergoes several changes during the early childhood years (Lyytinen, Poikkeus, & Laasko, 1997). Initially, the pretend play of 2- to 3-year-olds centers on their solitary actions (such as pretending to go to sleep). As children become less egocentric, they are increasingly able to pretend that other people or objects (such as Mom or stuffed animals) are sleeping or eating. After age 3, children's pretend play becomes less self-focused and more social (Hughes, 1995). Because of their concrete and literal way of thinking, young children have trouble letting an object serve as a symbolic representation of something else. For example, 2- or 3-year-old children have difficulty pretending that a paper cup is a hat—to them, a cup is for drinking.

The roles children take in pretend play also change during the preschool years. At first, 2- and 3-year-olds play roles that are very familiar to them, such as mother or baby. Older preschoolers, because of their increased experience and ability to think abstractly, are able to incorporate roles that are less familiar or that they have never directly experienced, such as doctor or police officer. These new play patterns help children develop important new cognitive and social skills (Curran, 1999). For example, the communication that takes place during young children's pretend play is positively related to literacy skills when they reach kindergarten (Katz, 2001).

YOUNG CHILDREN'S SIBLING RELATIONSHIPS

Almost 80 percent of children in the United States have siblings (Dunn, 1992). But the arrival of a new brother or sister is not an easy adjustment for children, and it sometimes leads to increased withdrawal, aggression, or dependency (Teti, 1992). There is evidence that mother-child attachment security decreases following the birth of a sibling (Teti, Sakin, Kucera, Corns, & Eiden, 1996). These negative reactions are especially likely among preschool-age children who have a limited understanding of their relationship to the new

pretend play play in which children let objects or persons symbolize things or people they are not

This child is looking at her baby brother. In what ways do siblings influence child development?

baby. Young children may react strongly to the stress brought about by the new demands. Furthermore, because parents often pay a lot of attention to the newborn, at the expense of the preschooler, the preschooler may feel neglected.

When siblings are similar in age, marked changes in the nature of their relationship begin to appear during early childhood. Between 3 and 4 years of age, children become more interested in their siblings (Brown & Dunn, 1992)—they collaborate, cooperate, and play together with increasing frequency. They also fight and struggle more than they did before, and they get along better with friends than with each other (Volling, Youngblade, & Belsky, 1997).

Dynamics of Sibling Relationships

Siblings spend considerable time interacting with one another and therefore influence one another in a variety of ways. Siblings are a source of comfort and support, as well as conflict and antagonism, and they serve as role models, helping children learn new behaviors. Positive sibling relationships foster healthy adaptation in a variety of settings (Richman, Stevenson, & Graham, 1982). Negative sibling relationships also have pervasive effects. For example, children who are aggressive with their siblings are likely to have poor peer relationships (Dishion, 1990).

Sibling relationships change as children move through different developmental periods. When siblings are more than a few years apart in age, the older sibling assumes roles that are more parentlike than peerlike, often acting as teacher and caregiver for the younger brothers and sisters (Brody, Stoneman, MacKinnon, & MacKinnon, 1985; Dunn, 1988). During early childhood, children begin to share intimate feelings and thoughts with their siblings and are quite dependent on each other for companionship and support. Older siblings often become particularly important to young children in families that have recently immigrated to the United States, especially when the parents have less understanding of the new culture than the older siblings do (Perez-Granados & Callanan, 1997). During later childhood and adolescence, friends and peers take on more of these roles, and siblings are less important sources of intimacy and support. This is not to say that siblings are not important after early childhood, but their relative importance compared to peers decreases somewhat (Buhrmester, 1992).

Differences in the Quality of Sibling Relationships

As early as young childhood, striking differences in sibling relationships appear. Some siblings are very close, others extremely antagonistic. There are at least three factors influencing the quality of sibling relationships (Dunn, 1992):

1. **Temperaments of the siblings.**   The temperamental qualities of the siblings influence the level of conflict between them. Children who are active, intense, or unadaptable in temperament are likely to have antagonistic sibling relationships (Miller, Volling, & McElwain, 2000). The temperament match between siblings also is important: siblings who are temperamentally similar are more likely to have positive relationships (Boer, 1990; Munn & Dunn, 1988).
2. **Parental treatment.**   Negative relationships between siblings often are attributed to the parents' favoritism toward one of the siblings (Brody, Stoneman, & McCoy, 1992; McHale, Crouter, McGuire, & Updegraff, 1995). Often it is difficult to avoid treating children differently, especially if siblings are of different ages. If 4-year-old Erin is sent to bed earlier than her 9-year-old sister Sarah, for example, she may accuse her parents of favoring her sister. But if they are both sent to bed at the same time, Sarah may find this unfair because she was not allowed to stay up so late when she was 4. Although the ages and sexes of the siblings significantly affect the degree to which differential treatment disrupts sibling relationships (McHale et al., 2000), the effects become more profound if one sibling is treated with less warmth and affection or with more punishment. That child is more likely to behave in an aggressive, rivalrous, and unaffectionate manner toward his or her sibling (Boer, Goedhart, & Treffers, 1992; Volling & Elins, 1998). Children are less likely to respond negatively if they perceive that the differential treatment was justified (Kowal & Kramer, 1997).
3. **Family life events.**   Sibling relationships can be influenced by stressful events affecting the family, such as divorce, job loss, or death (Erel, Margolin, & John, 1998).

For example, sibling relationships often deteriorate in families that experience a divorce. Because of changes in caregiving following a divorce, older siblings are likely to engage in more caretaking behavior with their younger siblings; younger siblings may reject this caregiving, thereby setting the stage for conflict (MacKinnon, 1989). Sibling relationships also may become more hostile as siblings compete for the limited time and attention of their parents (Beaudry, Simard, Drapeau, & Charbonneau, 2000). The stress and new demands of making the transition to school also are likely to negatively affect siblings' relationships (Dunn, 1992). Stress also exacerbates parents' tendencies to treat siblings differently, thereby increasing the possibility of conflicted sibling relationships (Crouter, McHale, & Tucker, 1999).

HOW DOES TELEVISION INFLUENCE YOUNG CHILDREN'S EMOTIONAL AND SOCIAL DEVELOPMENT

You learned in Chapter 7 that television viewing affects young children's cognitive development. As you might expect, children's social development also is influenced by television. Television plays a central role in the life of most contemporary families and often provides people with common points of reference for relating to others. Many of the themes in young children's play revolve around what they see on television.

During early childhood, many children begin to spend a large amount of time watching television, and long-term relations have been found between early television viewing and later adjustment (Anderson et al., 2001). The amount of time children spend watching television and the content of many television programs have generated concerns and questions about the impact of television on family life and children's emotional and social development.

EFFECTS OF TELEVISION ON FAMILY LIFE

The acceptance and popularity of television began slowly and then exploded. In 1950, only 5 percent of US households owned a television set, but within ten years, almost 90 percent of households owned one (Van-Evra, 1998). Today, only 2 percent of households do not own a television set, and about two-thirds of households own two or more sets.

Time spent watching television has steadily increased. The television set is now on for an average of almost 7 hours per day (A. C. Nielsen Media Research, 2000). Although almost everyone watches some television, low-income families watch more television than middle- or upper-income families; television is relatively cheap entertainment, and low-income families may not have the money to spend on other sources of entertainment (Huston et al., 1992).

Most children are exposed to television from the time they are born. As you can see in Figure 8.6, children's television viewing time increases during the preschool years to an average of 2.5 hours each day and continues to increase through the elementary-school years. Viewing time peaks at about 4 hours per day just before the start of adolescence, when competing activities reduce the number of hours adolescents spend in front of the television set (Condry, 1989). When computers, VCRs, and video games are taken into account, children today spend an average of 5 hours a day in front of "video screens" (Woodward & Gridina, 2001). Similar patterns have been found in other countries (Liebert & Sprafkin, 1988).

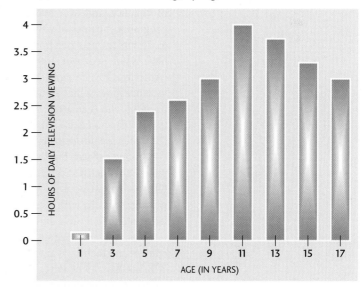

FIGURE 8.6

Hours of Television Viewing, by Age

SOURCE: Figure from TELEVISION AND THE AMERICAN CHILD by G. Comstock and H. Paik, copyright © 1991 by Academic Press, reproduced by permission of the publisher.

Notice the increase in rates of viewing early in development. What factors contribute to this increase? Why does television play such a large role in everyday family life?

Television viewing, which increases during the preschool years, has important effects on children's development and family life. Can you identify these effects? How are they produced?

The dramatic rise in the popularity of television and the time devoted to watching it has had a significant effect on family life (Kotler, Wright, & Huston, 2001). Compared with families that do not own television sets, families that watch television spend less time sleeping, visiting others outside the home, having conversations, cleaning the house, participating in community or school activities, and pursuing hobbies or sports, and they have poorer dietary habits (Coon, Goldberg, Rogers, & Tucker, 2001; Robinson, 1981; Williams, 1986). More than half of all elementary school children watch television while eating meals, and an even larger percentage watch while doing their homework. Children's television viewing is inversely related to parental instruction, the number of books in the home, and school readiness; children who watch more television spend less time reading and do not value reading as much as those who watch less (Clarke & Kutz-Costes, 1997; Koolstra, van-der-Voort, & van-der-Kamp, 1997). By the time children graduate from high school, they have spent more time watching television than in any other waking activity (Josephson, 1995).

Although parents express concern about the time their children spend watching television and the effects it may have on them, only about half of parents control their children's viewing (Federman, 1998). About 40 percent of parents in one survey said that they restricted the amount of their children's television viewing, and 50 percent said that they restricted what their children could watch (Woodward & Gridina, 2001). Moreover, over 50 percent of US children have a television set in their bedroom, making it difficult for parents to monitor what their children watch (Woodward & Gridina, 2001).

EFFECTS OF TELEVISION VIOLENCE ON CHILDREN'S AGGRESSION

Despite efforts at regulation, children's television still contains a good deal of violent content (Federman, 1998). Violent acts typically are defined as any deliberate acts of physical or verbal force to achieve a goal. In 1997, 61 percent of all television programs had some form of violence, and over half of all violent acts were lethal (Federman, 1998). For children's programs, the rates of violence also are high. By some estimates, children's shows contain 20 to 25 violent acts per hour (Murray, 1995). By the time they reach adolescence, children have witnessed over 100,000 acts of televised violence, including over 20,000 murders (American Psychological Association, 1993). In addition, children's programs tend to depict violence in ways that glamorize and reward it. These depictions frequently involve (1) a perpetrator who is an attractive role model (such as a super hero), (2) violence that seems justified, (3) violence that goes unpunished, (4) minimal consequences to victims, and (5) violence that seems realistic to the viewer (Federman, 1998).

Young children hold mixed views about the violence in television programs. Some find the violence attractive. Some do not view a program as being violent unless there is bloodshed. Others disapprove of the violent behaviors portrayed and realize that the violent themes and messages conflict with what is good. Thus, young children interpret and define television violence in different ways, and these differences affect their responses to it (Wilson & Smith, 1998).

Scientific evidence supports a relationship between children's exposure to violent television content and their own aggressive and risky behaviors and attitudes (Jason, Kennedy-Hanaway, & Brackshaw, 1999; Potts, Doppler, & Hernandez, 1994). This relationship has been demonstrated in studies of thousands of children of different ages and backgrounds, using a variety of procedures and methods (Hearold, 1986; Paik & Comstock, 1994). The link between television violence and children's aggression has been found worldwide (Huesmann & Eron, 1986).

With literally thousands of studies showing a relation between television violence and children's aggressive behaviors and attitudes, what conclusions can be drawn? Several important themes are highlighted in the research (Huston & Wright, 1998; Jason et al., 1999):

THE PRACTICAL IMPACT: NURTURING CHILDREN

Supervising Children's Television Viewing

Given the attractiveness of television and its dominant role in American family life, what guidelines can caregivers follow to establish positive viewing habits in children? Here are some practical ideas (Davis, 1990/1991; Fabes, Wilson, and Christopher, 1989; and Murray, 1995):

- **Start early.** The younger children are, the easier it is to establish positive television viewing habits.
- **Set daily limits.** Most professionals suggest that children be limited to a maximum of 2 hours of television per day.

- **Encourage planned viewing.** Have children select programs you approve of from television schedules.
- **Don't locate a television set in a child's room.** It encourages isolated television viewing.
- **Remember that children learn from their caregivers and other role models.** If caregivers watch a lot of television, children are likely to watch a lot of television.
- **Watch television with children.** Encourage children to discuss what they see on television and how they

feel about it. Let them know what you think about it.
- **Talk to children about television advertising.** Tell children that the purpose of advertising is to sell as many products as possible to as many viewers as possible.
- **Read to children rather than watching television.** Reading to children fosters more intimate interactions and enhances children's appreciation of books and reading.
- **Use V-chip technology.** This technology allows caregivers to block out shows that are offensive or inappropriate for children.

◆ Children's aggressive tendencies are likely to be increased by violence on television when it is portrayed realistically (Atkin, 1983), when it is portrayed by human rather than cartoon characters (Hayes & Casey, 1992), when it is not subject to critical commentary (Peracchio, 1993), and when the aggressive behavior is seen as justified or rewarded (Perry, Perry, & Rasmussen, 1986).

◆ Increased arousal after viewing violent television disposes children to behave more impulsively (Zillmann, 1982), and implied violence elicits as much arousal as does actual violence (Kalamas & Gruber, 1998).

◆ Children who are abused, emotionally disturbed, or predisposed to act aggressively are more influenced by television violence than others (Sprafkin et al., 1992).

◆ Television violence can have long-term consequences. Children with high levels of exposure to television violence were likely to be aggressive ten years later and were more likely to be arrested or convicted for violent crime or abuse twenty-two years later than children with less exposure to television violence (Eron, 1982; Eron, Huesmann, Lefkowitz, & Walder, 1996).

Although exposure to television violence relates to children's aggressive behaviors and attitudes, many factors influence this relationship. Debate continues about the extent to which we can conclusively say that television violence *causes* increased aggression in children (Josephson, 1995).

EFFECTS OF TELEVISION ON CHILDREN'S PROSOCIAL BEHAVIOR

Not all behavior on television is violent or aggressive; acts of kindness and cooperation are common. Rates of prosocial behaviors generally are comparable to rates of aggressive and violent behaviors (Greenberg, Edison, Korzenny, Fernandez-Collado, & Atkin, 1980).

Some of the programs designed for young children (such as *Sesame Street, Barney,* and *Mr. Rogers' Neighborhood*) specifically focus on teaching prosocial behavior. Soon after these shows were introduced, scientists became interested in determining their effectiveness in increasing children's prosocial behavior. They found that preschoolers who watched characters on *Sesame Street* or *Mr. Rogers' Neighborhood* cooperated with and helped each other more than those who did not (Friedrich-Cofer, Huston, Kipnis, Susman, & Clewett, 1979; Singer & Singer, 1998). However, simply exposing young children to prosocial television characters is not enough to strongly influence their prosocial behavior (Singer & Singer, 2001). The extent to which young children learn prosocial lessons and behaviors from television depends on two factors related to presentation:

◆ **Environmental cues and supports.**   A parent or teacher may need to supplement prosocial television programming with related materials (puppets, costumes) that promote role playing. Verbal discussions and labeling of prosocial behavior also are effective, but role playing is most effective in helping young children apply television content to their own behavior (Friedrich & Stein, 1975).

◆ **Competing messages in the program.**   In many television programs, characters display both prosocial and aggressive behaviors. Story lines often continue over several programs, with characters displaying conflicts and maladaptive behaviors as well as helpful and sympathetic responses. Young children learn best when the prosocial message clearly replaces aggressive behavior. Combined prosocial and aggressive messages sometimes lead to increased aggressive behavior in children, perhaps because children find the aggressive action more interesting and memorable than the prosocial lessons contained in the program (Lovelace & Huston, 1983).

Without environmental cues and clearly contrasting depictions of prosocial behavior, young children may not be able to apply the prosocial lessons they watch on television to their own lives.

TRY IT OUT

Activities Relating to Young Children

1. In light of what you have learned, think about two children you know well. How might the different aspects of social development (parenting behavior, peer relationships, divorce, television, and siblings) exert an influence on these children's self-concept and self-esteem?

2. Using Baumrind's definitions, describe the parenting styles of your parents. Identify the specific parenting behaviors that you used to classify your parents in one of the four categories. Discuss the difficulties you had in classifying them. What effects do you think your parents had on your development? What style of parenting will you use with your own children?

3. Arrange to observe preschool children playing on a playground. What kinds of play can you identify? Who do the children play with? What kinds of activities do they engage in with their peers? Why are some children more likely than others to play with peers?

4. Watch some children's television shows and record the numbers of aggressive and prosocial acts. How did you define these behaviors? What kinds of characters displayed these behaviors? What impact might these televised acts have on young children's development?

SUM IT UP

How does self-awareness change during early childhood?

◆ Although their self-concepts become increasingly complex and differentiated, young children rarely see themselves in terms of stable traits and qualities.

◆ As children enter early childhood, they become better able to make evaluative judgments about themselves.

◆ Self-esteem can be understood as a combination of worthiness and competence. Different combinations produce four types of self-esteem: high self-esteem (high in both), low self-esteem (low in both), defensive self-esteem I (high in worthiness, low in competence), and defensive self-esteem II (high in competence, low in worthiness).

◆ Important influences on young children's self-concept and self-esteem include their physical appearance, their relationships with parents and peers, and the social and cultural conditions, values, and practices they experience.

How do young children develop a concept of gender?

◆ Children label themselves as boys or girls by 2½ years of age. By the end of the preschool years, children understand that gender is stable and constant.

◆ Young children learn gender stereotypes as early as age 2½, and these stereotypes become increasingly complex with age.

◆ Boys and girls have different abilities, skills, and interests, but the magnitude of these differences often is small and the variation within each sex is large.

What are the contemporary theories of gender development?

◆ Biological theories focus on how physiological and biochemical processes (such as hormones) affect characteristics and abilities.

◆ Social learning theories attempt to explain how direct learning and observation mold and shape gender development.

✦ Cognitive theories view gender development as an outcome of normal cognitive development. Gender schema theory suggests that children actively construct their concept of gender by building schemas—networks of associated information—and then use these schemas to guide their behavior and thinking.

How do emotions develop during early childhood?

✦ As young children become socially active, they are likely to get into more conflicts with others and become angry as a result.

✦ Young children respond to conflicts in a variety of ways depending on the type of conflict. As they get older, they are likely to resolve conflicts in ways that are less harmful to others.

✦ Aggression changes in frequency and form across early childhood, with physical and instrumental aggression decreasing and verbal and hostile aggression increasing.

✦ Increased social interactions foster prosocial emotions and actions.

✦ Children's motivations for helping others change from pragmatic and approval-based reasons during the preschool years to altruistic reasons in later childhood.

✦ Children develop prosocial emotions and actions in the context of secure relationships with caregivers.

How do parenting behaviors influence young children's development?

✦ As preschoolers become more independent and active, parental disciplinary efforts increase. Disciplinary methods used include power assertion, love withdrawal, and inductive reasoning.

✦ Three factors influence caregivers' choice of disciplinary practices: the nature of the misbehavior, characteristics of the child, and cultural and ethnic values.

✦ Baumrind identified four parenting styles that differ in the degree of parental responsiveness and demandingness. Authoritarian parents are high in demandingness but low in responsiveness; permissive parents are the reverse; uninvolved parents are low in both; and authoritative parents are high in both. In contemporary western cultures, authoritative parenting is associated with optimal outcomes for children.

How does divorce affect young children's development?

✦ Young children's understanding of divorce is limited; they respond emotionally and fail to understand the permanence of the situation. Because of their egocentric thinking, young children are likely to believe that they somehow caused the divorce.

✦ The quality of a young child's adjustment to divorce depends on the amount of conflict between parents, characteristics of the child, and the ability of the child to maintain a relationship with the noncustodial parent.

✦ When parents remarry, children often experience a difficult adjustment period. The quality of the relationships children have with their caregivers influences their adjustment to stepfamily life.

How do peer and sibling relationships develop during early childhood?

✦ As young children widen their social relationships, peers become increasingly important influences in their lives.

✦ Children's conceptions of friendship change over early childhood. The basis of friendships changes from mutual interests to mutual sympathy and loyalty, with an understanding of the stability and intimacy between friends.

✦ Most peer interactions take place in the context of play. Play takes many forms, including solitary, onlooker, parallel, associative, cooperative, and pretend play.

✦ Young children become more responsive to their siblings during early childhood. This responsiveness can lead to enhanced caring and prosocial interactions, as well as more conflict and fighting.

✦ Sibling relationships are influenced by the temperaments of the siblings, parental treatment, and family life events.

✦ Positive relationships with peers and siblings are beneficial for children, whereas poor peer and sibling relationships are associated with negative outcomes.

How does television influence young children's emotional and social development?

✦ By high school graduation, children have spent more time in front of the television than in any other waking activity.

✦ Most parents do little to control children's television viewing.

✦ Children who watch more television have lower reading comprehension and interest in reading and decreased readiness for school.

✦ Television contains a lot of violent content that can increase children's aggressive behavior and attitudes. Television also contains considerable prosocial content that can positively affect young children's behavior.

KEY TERMS and CONCEPTS

associative play (*272*)
authoritarian parenting (*262*)
authoritative parenting (*263*)
compliance (*259*)
cooperative play (*272*)
demandingness (*262*)
discipline (*259*)
empathy (*257*)
gender consistency (*250*)
gender identity (*249*)
gender labeling (*249*)
gender schemas (*254*)

gender stability (*249*)
gender stereotypes (*250*)
goal-corrected partnership (*259*)
hostile aggression (*256*)
inductive reasoning (*260*)
instrumental aggression (*256*)
internalization (*259*)
love withdrawal (*260*)
onlooker play (*272*)
parallel play (*272*)
permissive parenting (*262*)
power assertion (*259*)

pretend play (*273*)
prosocial behavior (*257*)
relational aggression (*256*)
responsiveness (*262*)
schematic consistency (*254*)
self-concept (*245*)
self-esteem (*246*)
solitary play (*272*)
sympathy (*257*)
uninvolved parenting (*262*)

PART 4

SEE the IMPACT

BENCHMARKS in Early Childhood Development

PHYSICAL/MOTOR DEVELOPMENT	COGNITIVE DEVELOPMENT	SOCIAL/EMOTIONAL DEVELOPMENT
More adultlike physical appearance and body proportions	Increased symbolic representation; development of preoperational thinking and problem solving; egocentrism; perception-based reasoning; lack of conservation	Concept of self based on external qualities, situational changes, and others' feedback
Growth rapid but not as rapid as in earlier years		Maturing concept of gender
Increased myelination in brain and development of neural pathways	Improved memory but easily distracted and misled in recall; limited ability to use memory strategies for better recall	Increased social interactions and resulting angry conflicts; prosocial emotions and caring actions
Improved coordination and development of advanced gross and fine motor skills	Enhanced understanding of mental events; development of theory of mind	Changing attachments and parental disciplinary efforts; increased responsiveness to changing family relationships (such as divorce or remarriage)
Increased risk for accidents, injuries, and poor nutrition	Increased responsiveness to social context of learning; preparedness for school	Development of friendships and peer and sibling relationships, particularly during play
		Greater experience with mass media, particularly television

NATIONAL HOTLINES FOR PRESCHOOL CHILDREN

American Society for Deaf Children: 800-942-2733

Child Support Hotline: 800-256-4650

National Association for the Education of Young Children: 800-424-2460

National Association of Working Women: 800-522-0925

Impact Report on Early Childhood

You have seen that amount of television viewing differs for younger and older children. In this figure, you can see that other types of media use also vary by the age of the child. Many factors contribute to these differences. Compare and contrast the patterns of media use for children of different ages. What trends do you see? Can you identify some of the factors that may contribute to these changes?

Parents' Reports of Children's Media Usage, by Age and Type of Media

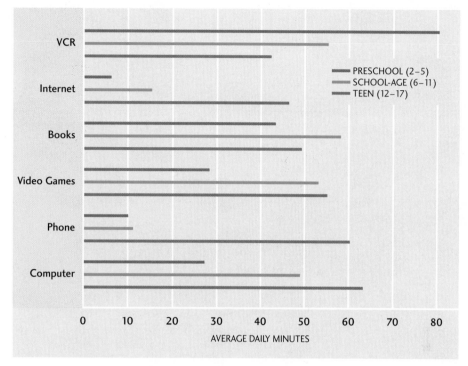

SOURCE: Woodward & Gridina, 2001.

RECOMMENDED WEBSITES

Action Alliance for Children: This site provides information about current trends and policy issues affecting children and their families.
http://www.4children.org/

Center for Media Education: Organization dedicated to improving the quality of electronic media. Its site presents summaries of research on children's use of interactive technologies.
http://www.cme.org/

Children's Defense Fund: An advocate for the children of America, paying particular attention to the needs of poor and minority children and those with disabilities. Its site contains key facts about the welfare of children in the United States and information about how to improve their lives.
http://www.childrensdefense.org/

Children's Health Environmental Coalition Network: This site is dedicated to protecting children and preventing childhood cancers and other illnesses. It provides information on the risks children face from environmental toxins and how to prevent them from being exposed.
http://www.checnet.org/

Culturally and Linguistically Appropriate Services (CLAS): The Early Childhood Research Institute, at the University of Illinois at Urbana-Champaign, identifies, evaluates, and promotes early intervention and preschool practices that are sensitive to culturally and linguistically diverse young children and their families.
http://clas.uiuc.edu/

National Institute of Child Health and Human Development (NICHD): Part of the National Institutes of Health, US Department of Health and Human Services. Its site provides useful information on the biological, developmental, and behavioral processes that determine and maintain the health of children, adults, families, and populations.
http://www.nichd.nih.gov/

National Parenting Center: One of America's foremost parenting information services, dedicated to giving parents guidance from some of the world's most renowned child-rearing authorities. Its site provides information, chat rooms, and materials to expand parenting skills and strengths.
http://www.tnpc.com/

Late Childhood Development

During the school-age years, children undergo pervasive changes, affecting their physical and psychological well-being. New contexts provide additional impetus for change. When children enter school, they are exposed to a wide variety of new intellectual and social demands. Teachers, other students, principals, classes, homework, and extracurricular activities take on added significance. Family members remain important, but the amount of time children spend with family members drops and the amount of time they spend in school and with peers increases. Thus, children experience important changes in the nature of the environmental influences and social transactions that they face.

School-age children often find their performance compared to that of others. They are evaluated by teachers, and their parents receive reports about their performance and behavior in school. Tests, homework, and assignments take up more of children's time and provide additional sources of comparisons with others. New acquaintances, friends, and enemies develop. Many of these challenges and stressors were not present before children entered school. Thus, during late childhood, children have to develop new coping strategies to deal with the stress and demands placed on them by their changing environment. Many children cope easily and adjust well. But some children are overwhelmed by their environment and lack the skills and support to cope effectively. Children's cultural backgrounds affect how they cope with the demands of their environments, as well as influencing the types of challenges they face.

The number of children in kindergarten through grade eight in the United States rose from 29.9 million in fall 1990 to 33.5 million in fall 2000. The increase was most rapid in the elementary grades, but this pattern is expected to change. During the next decade, the growing numbers of young pupils who have been filling the elementary schools will cause significant increases at the secondary school level. Public school enrollment is projected to set new records every year until 2005. However, the status of our schools has been questioned.

- About 25 percent of US schools have at least one building in "less than adequate" condition; about 50 percent have at least one building feature in "less than adequate" condition, and about 40 percent have at least one building feature in "unsatisfactory" condition. The total amount needed to correct these problems is estimated to be approximately $127 billion.

- The estimated cost of repairs, renovations, and modernization to put schools in good overall condition is about $2.2 million per school or about $3,800 per student.

- Researchers have documented that the optimal class size for elementary school classrooms is 13 to 17. In 1999, the average class size was 23 and almost half of all classrooms had 25 or more children in them.

- Current estimates indicate that over 600,000 children between the ages of 6 and 17 years are schooled at home.

- Although many educators and policy analysts consider technology a vehicle for transforming education, relatively few teachers (20 percent) report feeling very well prepared to integrate educational technology into classroom instruction.

SOURCES: National Center for Education Statistics, 2001a.

CHAPTER

9

Cognitive, Language, and Physical Development in Late Childhood

CHAPTER OUTLINE

✦ How Do Children Develop Physically During Late Childhood?

✦ How Do School-Age Children Think and Solve Problems?

✦ What Characteristics Define Children's Intelligence and Creativity?

✦ How Do Language and Literacy Develop During the School Years?

✦ How Do School-Age Children Understand the Social World?

✦ How Does Schooling Influence Children's Cognitive Development?

✦ How Do Schools Address Students' Special Needs?

✦ How Do Family and Culture Influence Children's Intellectual Development?

The hallmarks of cognitive development in late childhood include learning to read, write, think, create, and solve problems. The formal process of acquiring such skills in school is hard work. When children enter school, their lives are changed by the many new demands placed on them. Exams, reports, homework, and grades become important and take up a good bit of their time. Additionally, extracurricular activities such as playing sports and practicing creative arts become a part of their daily routines. Children's lives are significantly influenced by the physical and cognitive changes that take place when they enter late childhood.

How do children develop physically during late childhood?

During late childhood, physical changes are not as obvious as they were during early childhood. Although growth is slower during this period, motor and physical abilities improve significantly. This period of the life span is one of the healthiest; older children are less likely than younger children, adolescents, or adults to get sick or injured.

BRAIN DEVELOPMENT

In children from 6 to 8 years of age, the brain continues to develop. During the school years, the functioning of a child's brain improves (Black, 1998). Information is processed more efficiently because of increased myelination of the nerve fibers of the brain and increased lateralization of the two hemispheres of the brain (see Chapter 4). Redundant synaptic connections between neurons continue to be pruned, especially in the areas involved in higher cognitive functioning, increasing the organization of the brain (Case, 1992). These changes may relate to the development of problem solving, memory, and understanding of language that occurs during childhood (Byrnes & Fox, 1998; Diamond, 2000).

BODY SIZE AND APPEARANCE

Children grow more slowly during the school years than they did as younger children—usually about 2 to 3 inches and 3 to 6 pounds a year—and this slower rate of growth continues until preadolescence. During the elementary school years, boys and girls develop very similarly: the arms and legs grow longer relative to the trunk of the body, and the body lengthens and fills out. One effect of this slower growth rate is that children have time to become accustomed to their bodies. This brings about gains in motor control and coordination (Gallahue & Ozmun, 1995).

At this age, individual differences among children's bodies are striking, and these differences tend to remain relatively constant over time. Research shows that, generally, children's body builds remain about the same through childhood and into adolescence. Height is usually more constant than weight and musculature, which are more influenced by exercise and diet.

Few studies have examined the relation of body build to athletic ability. Observations of Olympic athletes suggest that certain sports require particular body builds. For instance, most gymnasts are short and small-boned, whereas most volleyball players are tall. Although in many countries trainers try to select the "perfect" body build for each type of athletic performance (especially for early identification of possible Olympic athletes), predicting the performance of an average-looking child based only on his or her body shape and size is very difficult (DiGirolamo, Geis, & Walker, 1998). How muscular a child is, however, does relate to physical performance: children who are more muscular usually perform physical tasks somewhat better than children who are less muscular.

MOTOR DEVELOPMENT

During the early school years, children show remarkable improvements in their motor skills. Basic motor skills become fine-tuned and coordinated (Cowden, Sayers, & Torrey, 1998).

Whereas young children have difficulty jumping, older children can jump without losing their balance. A 6-year-old might throw a ball 10 feet, but an 11-year-old can throw one 30 feet (Cratty, 1986). Older children have more strength, agility, and balance than younger ones. In each of these areas, improvements can be seen every year until preadolescence, when improvement slows down. Despite children's improved coordination and agility, though, not all activities are easily learned. Children need considerable practice to master tasks that require high levels of hand-eye coordination, such as striking a ball with a bat. During the school years, children also gain better control of their fine motor movements. Their writing becomes neater, and their ability to master difficult and intricate tasks, such as knitting or playing a musical instrument, increases.

School-aged girls and boys perform similarly in almost all motor activities, although there are some differences. Boys generally have somewhat more upper body strength than girls and throw faster and more accurately than girls (Thomas & French, 1985). Girls are more flexible in their hip joints and so may be more agile than boys (Plimpton & Regimbal, 1992). Biological factors and different experiences of boys and girls may account for some performance differences. Boys' leisure activities involve more sports than do girls', giving them more time to practice motor skills (Cratty, 1986).

PHYSICAL FITNESS AND SPORTS

Since the 1950s, when fitness comparisons showed that 55 percent of American children were unfit versus only 15 percent of European youth, much attention has been paid to assessing children's fitness in the United States. Concerns about children's fitness are still warranted today—more than one-half of children and adolescents are not vigorously active on a regular basis (Surgeon General, 1996).

Why are so many children physically unfit? One reason is that many children prefer sedentary activities, such as watching television or playing video games. Another is that a significant number of children live in urban settings that limit opportunities for exercise. Although many children are sedentary, the rise in popularity of sports participation over the last twenty years has been phenomenal. Approximately 46 million children and adolescents in the United States participate in some type of sport (Griffin, 1998). Besides simply enjoying themselves, children who participate in sports benefit from regular activity and establish habits and skills that help them enjoy physical activities throughout their lives (Telama, Yang, Laakso, & Viikari, 1997). In team sports, children also learn how to cooperate with other children.

Children's involvement in sports can also have a downside: they can sustain acute injuries, from sprained ankles to spinal cord injuries. There is no clear evidence, however, that these injuries occur more often in organized sports than in free play (Bijur et al., 1995). For

How does involvement in organized sports such as baseball have both positive and negative influences on children's development? How can baseball-related injuries be prevented?

example, children playing on trampolines or in-line skating are particularly at risk of injury (American Academy of Pediatrics, 1998; Smith & Shields, 1998). Some organized sports are riskier than others. Children who are involved in gymnastics, baseball, or basketball, for instance, are more likely to be injured than children who play other sports (O'Neill & Micheli, 1988).

Another downside is that sports injuries may damage the growth of children's long bones, which can result in permanent joint deformities or delay in growth. However, these injuries are relatively infrequent and rarely are associated with involvement in organized sports. Children's sports injuries are more likely to be due to overuse, in which repetitive action causes stress and strain to the joints and muscles. Most of these injuries can be successfully treated, and few result in permanent damage (Watkins & Peabody, 1996).

Because of fear of injuries, pediatricians used to urge parents not to let their children participate in organized sports too early. Today, the focus is on improving sports safety. For example, the Consumer Product Safety Commission (1996) recommends that softer balls and new kinds of batting helmets be used to reduce the number of baseball-related injuries.

NUTRITION

Because children continue to grow in size and weight throughout the elementary-school years, a healthy diet continues to be important for optimal growth. During the school years, children need approximately double the calories and protein (per pound) that adults need. Children also need to obtain adequate zinc, calcium, and iron because these minerals are crucial for facilitating growth (Lifshitz, Finch, & Lifshitz, 1991).

Adult standards of healthy eating may not be appropriate for children. For instance, nutritional guidelines for adults recommend avoiding fats and cholesterol, but these are essential for the healthy development of children, especially for optimal brain development. Children on reduced-fat diets may develop nutritional deficiencies. Red meat and eggs, often avoided by health-conscious adults, are excellent sources of minerals such as iron and zinc, essential for children's growth. Avoidance of red meats may contribute to the prevalence of iron deficiencies in children, who need more iron for their weight than adults do.

Children who fail to receive the nutrients they need are adversely affected in academic and social domains. In a national US study, children who reported that their families did not have enough food to eat were more likely to repeat a grade, had lower arithmetic scores, were more likely to have seen a psychologist, were more likely to have been suspended from school, and had more difficulty getting along with other children (Alaimo, Olson, & Frongillo, 2001). In the United States, approximately one-third of children experience either short-term or chronic hunger (Kleinman et al., 1998). Because of the importance of good nutrition for improving children's educational opportunities, free lunch and breakfast programs have been instituted in schools in many developing countries, and food supplementation in schools began in the United States as early as the 1890s (Levinger, 1986). Children in the United States who have been given school breakfasts are more likely to attend school and show improvements in language, mathematics, and reading (Myers, Sampson, Weitzman, Rogers, & Kayne, 1989). Overall, it appears that supplemental food programs help children have more positive attitudes toward school, perform better in school, increase time on tasks, and improve attendance (Grantham-McGregor, Ani, & Fernald, 2001).

OBESITY

According to a national report on nutrition in the United States, children from 6 to 9 years of age are heavier and fatter today than they were twenty years ago (Life Sciences Research Office, 1995). Those children (and adults) who weigh more than 20 percent over their ideal weight (based on height, sex, and body composition) are defined as **obese** (Wisniewski & Marcus, 1998). National surveys show that about 13 percent of children are overweight, and that the number of overweight children and adults is markedly higher today than it was in the 1970s and 1980s (Centers for Disease Control [CDC], 2001d). Hispanic and African-American children are particularly at risk for being overweight (Strauss & Pollack, 2001).

obese weighing more than 20 percent over one's ideal weight (based on height, sex, and body composition)

What causes childhood obesity? How is it treated? What are some consequences of obesity for children's physical development? for children's social and emotional development?

Obese children are at risk for serious health problems that result in shorter life spans, including heart disease, diabetes mellitus, cancer, and respiratory diseases (Gunnell, Frankel, Nanchahal, Peters, & Davey, 1998; Rossner, 1998).

Why do children become obese? Genetics plays a role—children inherit a predisposition for obesity from their parents. Sedentary lifestyles are another major contributor. Studies show that active children have less body fat than sedentary children and that obese children are less active than those who are lean (CDC, 2001d; Rowland, 1991). Family distress also contributes to obesity. Children in families experiencing chronic stress are more at risk for obesity because of the tendency to eat and low activity levels that accompany stress (Dietz & Gortmaker, 1985; Lifshitz et al., 1991). Programs that are successful in dealing with children's obesity are multicomponent ones. They often involve parents, teachers, and health workers, and they include education about nutrition, counseling, and opportunities for physical activity (Golan, Weizman, Apter, & Fainaru, 1998).

HOW DO SCHOOL-AGE CHILDREN THINK AND SOLVE PROBLEMS

At roughly age 6 or 7, most children move to the next stage of thinking identified by Piaget—called *concrete operations*—and continue to function at this level until they are around 11 or 12 years of age. In the concrete operational stage of cognitive development, children show remarkable advances in their thinking and problem-solving strategies. For the first time, they can apply logic to solve problems in an adultlike manner. School-age children's thinking is more flexible and reversible and less egocentric than preschoolers'. The older child considers multiple dimensions of a problem rather than focusing on only one dimension, as preoperational children do. These advances allow for more sophisticated and systematic methods of solving problems. Older children's problem solving is somewhat more constrained than the problem solving of adolescents and adults, though, because older children can apply logic only to concrete or familiar situations.

CHILDREN'S LOGICAL PROBLEM SOLVING

For Piaget, the best indicator of concrete operational thinking is a child's use of logical principles. These principles are most vividly demonstrated when children solve conservation problems. As you learned in Chapter 7, understanding of conservation of mass is assessed by showing children two identical balls of clay and then rolling one ball into a snake. To demonstrate an understanding of conservation of mass, children must infer that the two shapes still contain the same amount of clay even though they look different. Preschool children do not draw this conclusion. Centrating on one dimension (such as length), they assume that the snake must have more clay in it than the ball because it is longer. Between 6 and 7 years of age, children begin to solve conservation problems. To do so, they must be able to do the following (Siegler, 1998):

✦ **Mentally represent the action.**   Concrete operational children can mentally visualize the changes that occur in conservation tasks. In the clay example, they recall how the clay was transformed from a ball into a snake.

✦ **Focus on more than one dimension.**   The concrete operational child has the ability to think about both the length and the height of the clay, rather than focusing on only one dimension.

✦ **Recognize that appearances can be deceiving.**   Unlike preschoolers, who are easily deceived by the appearances of objects, concrete operational children recognize that what they see can sometimes be misleading. They can use logic to override misleading appearances.

According to Piaget, an older child draws the same conclusion as an adult about the clay by applying operations. Most children who correctly answer conservation questions

FIGURE 9.1

Examples of Different Types of Conservation Tasks

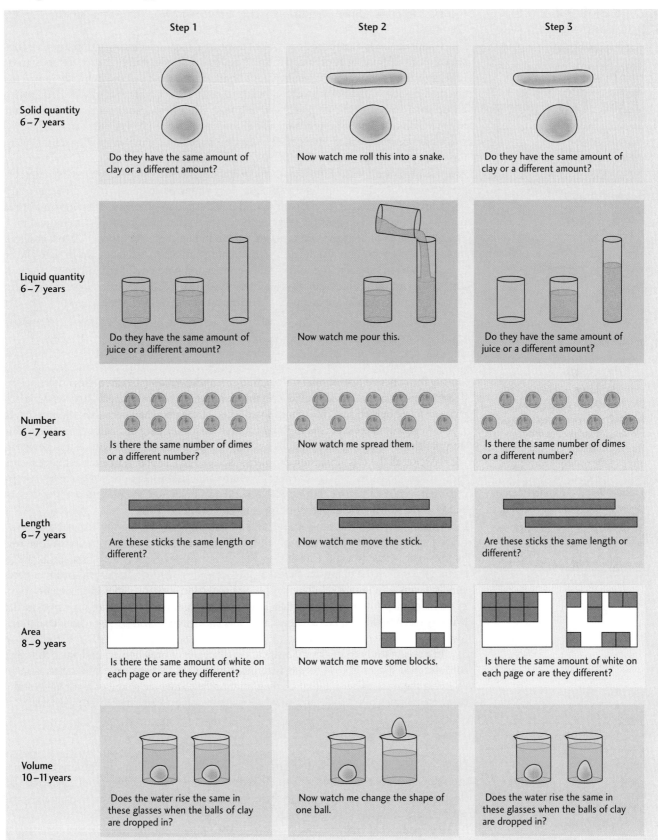

	Step 1	Step 2	Step 3
Solid quantity 6–7 years	Do they have the same amount of clay or a different amount?	Now watch me roll this into a snake.	Do they have the same amount of clay or a different amount?
Liquid quantity 6–7 years	Do they have the same amount of juice or a different amount?	Now watch me pour this.	Do they have the same amount of juice or a different amount?
Number 6–7 years	Is there the same number of dimes or a different number?	Now watch me spread them.	Is there the same number of dimes or a different number?
Length 6–7 years	Are these sticks the same length or different?	Now watch me move the stick.	Are these sticks the same length or different?
Area 8–9 years	Is there the same amount of white on each page or are they different?	Now watch me move some blocks.	Is there the same amount of white on each page or are they different?
Volume 10–11 years	Does the water rise the same in these glasses when the balls of clay are dropped in?	Now watch me change the shape of one ball.	Does the water rise the same in these glasses when the balls of clay are dropped in?

What cognitive advances must children make to solve conservation problems? At what stage of cognitive development are most children when they start first grade?

289

IGURE 9.2

Example of a Multiple Classification Task

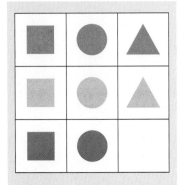

Pick the picture that fits in the blank.

SOURCE: Inhelder and Piaget, 1964.

In this task, children are asked to classify objects on two dimensions. Why might young children classify objects in this task differently than older children? What stage of cognitive development does mastery of the task indicate? Consider how mastery of the multiple classification task may relate to concept development and the understanding of categories.

reversible thinking the understanding that actions can be undone or reversed

compensation the understanding that one change can offset another

use the concept of identity; that is, they reason that because no clay was added or removed, there has to be the same amount, regardless of any apparent changes in appearance (see Chapter 7).

Children also use other concepts, such as reversibility and compensation, to solve conservation problems. **Reversible thinking** reflects an understanding that actions can be undone or reversed. For instance, in a conservation task, the child can mentally return the changed object to its original form (the snake can be made back into the ball). Through **compensation,** the child decides whether one change offsets another—that is, is a change in the height of a piece of clay compensated for by a change in its width?

Children master many kinds of conservation during the school years (Goswami, 1998), including conservation of number. In one conservation of number task, a child is shown two rows of five dimes, placed 1 inch apart, and watches as an adult spreads the dimes in the second row 2 inches apart. Which row contains more dimes, or do they contain the same number? Children who conserve number respond that the two rows contain the same number of dimes. Children who do not conserve number respond that the longer row has more dimes.

Other types of conservation tasks are shown in Figure 9.1 on page 289. Most children understand conservation of solid and liquid quantity, number, and length by the age of 6 or 7 years. Children can solve area and weight conservation problems at around 8 or 9, and volume conservation problems at around 10 or 11. The exposure children have to different types of conservation may explain why they learn them at different rates.

CHILDREN'S UNDERSTANDING OF CATEGORIES AND CONCEPTS

During the concrete operational stage, children's understanding of categories and concepts becomes more sophisticated. Unlike preschool children, who are inflexible in classifying objects, concrete operational children can vary their strategies when necessary (Freund et al., 1990). In addition, concrete operational children no longer have difficulty with class inclusion problems—making comparisons between a whole class of objects and subsets within the class. Recall the class inclusion problem discussed in Chapter 7, in which children were asked to compare the whole class "dogs" with the subclass "brown dogs." Unlike his preoperational 4-year-old sister Tammy, 8-year-old Jonathan understands that the category "dogs" is more inclusive than the subset based on the dogs' color.

Older children's ability to consider several dimensions at once is illustrated by their solutions to multiple classification problems. Children are shown an array of objects that differ in two or more ways and are asked to select the missing object that best fits the array. To accurately answer the question, children must consider the two dimensions of the objects simultaneously. In Figure 9.2, for example, the objects in a matrix differ in shape and color. After examining the objects and their layout, children are asked to place an object in the blank space. A child who has mastered multiple classification will choose a blue triangle as the solution.

In a classic study comparing classification strategies of preschoolers and older children, Inhelder and Piaget (1964) found that most preschoolers used only one dimension in selecting the missing object; that is, they might select any blue shape or a triangle of any color. In contrast, older children tended to select the object that satisfied both criteria.

CHILDREN'S UNDERSTANDING OF SERIATION

Older children understand the logic of serial position. When 4-year-old Tammy is shown a group of sticks that vary in length and asked to arrange them in order from the longest to the shortest, she is likely to arrange them slowly in a discontinuous way, usually by comparing pairs of sticks (see Figure 9.3).

Preoperational children like Tammy do not understand the comparative length of a number of objects and are likely to be distracted by other dimensions, such as visual alignment. As a result, they cannot accurately place all the sticks in sequence by height. But con-

THE SCIENTIFIC IMPACT: INTERPRETING RESEARCH

Are There Cultural Differences in Children's Reasoning?

Do children all around the world reason in the same way? Attempts to answer this question have sent researchers to many different countries to ask children about how they think and solve problems. One of Piaget's students, Pierre Dasen (1994), conducted a study of Australian Aboriginal children. The Aborigines were the first inhabitants of Australia. Today, many Aborigines still live in harsh environments, covering a very large territory as they move from place to place in search of water and food. Because they are continually on the move, they own few objects. They have an active and complex spiritual life, which includes elaborate rituals, myths, and symbolic art forms. For instance, they draw and paint map-like scenes that they call "dreamtime stories," containing symbols for important physical features in the environment and for movements between locations. These scenes bear no obvious resemblance to landscape scenes drawn by European artists.

Given the many differences between Aboriginal life and the lives of most European children, Dasen set out to determine whether there were differences in the ways they reason about the world. For the study, Dasen tested Aboriginal children from 8 to 14 years of age who had been in school. Several of Piaget's tasks were used. The tasks assessed conservation skills, spatial understanding, and the ability to view a scene from another person's perspective. In one spatial task, the child was shown a landscape scene with an ani-

mal in it. The child then had to find where the animal would be in a second scene, which was the original scene shifted 180 degrees. The second spatial task involved a bottle half filled with water, which was tilted (with the water level hidden behind a screen). The child had to match the water level to a series of pictures.

For European children, the ability to understand the liquid conservation task appeared around the age of 6 or 7. Aboriginal children showed the same changes as the European children in moving from preoperational thinking to concrete operational thinking, but the shift to understanding liquid conservation did not occur until they were between 10 and 13 years of age. Even some Aboriginal adolescents and adults failed the liquid conservation task. Similar results were found for the other conservation tasks.

Although the Aboriginal children were "behind" European children in their level of understanding of conservation, their understanding of the spatial task was quite advanced. Aboriginal children moved through the stages of understanding of this task more quickly than European children did.

To try to understand these results, Dasen considered the different cultures of the two groups of children. In European countries, quantification of amounts is important. Children may learn these skills more quickly because they are of value in the culture. Children in European countries count many things, and they begin doing so

when they are young. In contrast, Aboriginal culture places less value on quantification. Counting things beyond five is unusual. Because of this difference in the cultural emphasis on quantification, it is not surprising that European children can solve conservation problems earlier than Aboriginal children can.

The differences in spatial tasks also may be due to cultural variations in lifestyles. European children tend to be more sedentary and certainly are not nomadic like the Aboriginal children. Aboriginal children travel through difficult landscapes, often separately, and meet up again at the end of the day. Finding water is crucial for survival. Without good spatial skills, they would be unable to roam as freely in search of food or to find water as easily. Their spatial abilities are also fostered and reinforced by their "dreamtime stories," in which they attach meaning to physical features of the landscape.

Thinking It Through:

1. How did Dasen's study reveal the impact of culture on children's development of cognitive skills?
2. Why do European children learn conservation of quantities at an earlier age than Australian Aboriginal children do? Why is the reverse true for spatial skills?
3. How do you think Aboriginal and European children would compare on other tests of reasoning?

crete operational children like 8-year-old Jonathan can control for apparent height by aligning the bases of the sticks and focusing on their actual length.

CULTURE AS A CONTEXT FOR CHILDREN'S COGNITIVE DEVELOPMENT

Culture and community influence children's cognitive development in a number of ways (see Chapter 7). Children are exposed to scripts of daily activities and events valued in their culture, and they have opportunities to practice and learn how to carry out activities valued by their community. To what extent do cultural variations influence children's performance on cognitive tasks?

Children from nonindustrial cultures often fall behind children from industrialized cultures in their abilities to conserve, to take others' perspectives, and to understand causal relationships (Segall, Dansen, Berry, & Poortinga, 1990). Based on these findings, some

FIGURE 9.3

Example of a Seriation Task

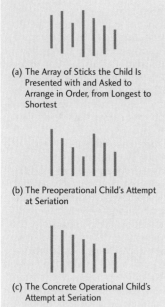

(a) The Array of Sticks the Child Is
    Presented with and Asked to
    Arrange in Order, from Longest to
    Shortest

(b) The Preoperational Child's Attempt
    at Seriation

(c) The Concrete Operational Child's
    Attempt at Seriation

What skills enable concrete operational children to seriate correctly? How do those skills transfer to academic tasks in the school years?

Peruvian child vendors are business whizzes compared to most European children of the same age. What accounts for their better understanding of commerce and business practices?

researchers wondered whether concrete operational thinking may be characteristic only of children in industrialized countries.

To understand why children from nonindustrialized cultures perform differently on these cognitive tasks, two issues need to be considered. The first has to do with communication. Not surprisingly, children who are interviewed in their native language show better performance than children interviewed in a language they use but do not know as well (Nyiti, 1982).

The second issue has to do with experience. Children's cognitive abilities relate to their culture and the types of experiences they have in their culture. If the ability does not match experience well, its development may be slower. If the cognitive ability matches well with experience, its development may be advanced. Children in nonindustrialized societies may display more advanced development than children in industrialized societies if the cognitive tasks selected tap into specialized experiences of their own culture. For instance, when 9- to 12-year-old children from Zimbabwe were evaluated on their understanding of profit, over three-quarters of the children understood the need to sell a product for more than one paid for it. In comparison, only about half of the same-age Scottish children understood the concept. This difference is likely due to the Zimbabwe children's greater experience in helping their families buy and sell things in the public market (Jahoda, 1983).

When children are tested in appropriate situations and when their own cultural "specialties" are assessed, the results support the notion that people in every culture reach concrete operational levels of understanding. The differing patterns that have been found are related to communication difficulties and to the types of tasks that are used to assess cognitive development.

INFORMATION PROCESSING IN SCHOOL-AGED CHILDREN

Information processing theorists consider the human mind to be a complex, symbol-manipulating system that processes many kinds of information (Chen & Siegler, 2000). The changes that occur in children's thinking and problem solving are believed to be due to increased capacities, use of different strategies, and a stronger knowledge base. Furthermore, information processing theorists assume that developmental transitions from one level of thinking to another reflect improvements in the synchronization of processing in different regions of the brain (Chen & Siegler, 2000).

Strategies for Remembering

Recall from Chapter 7 that one reason very young children have poor memories is that they fail to use the memory strategies of rehearsal, organization, and elaboration to help them remember information. During the school-age years, children become more likely to use two of these strategies—rehearsal and organization (elaboration is not typically used until adolescence).

Given the task of remembering a group of objects they have been shown, older children are apt to repeat a whole list of words in their minds to help them remember the names of the objects; younger children tend to repeat the name of only one object at a time (Ornstein, Naus, & Liberty, 1975). When children have been trained to use rehearsal strategies, they can improve their memory (Cox, Ornstein, Naus, Maxfield, & Zimler, 1989).

Similarly, whereas older children will organize information into conceptual categories to help their memory, younger children fail to do so. Though younger children can be encouraged to use organization strategies on specific tasks, they seldom generalize their use to new situations. And when they do, often they do not gain much advantage from the strategies, suggesting that the effectiveness of an organizational strategy depends on becoming familiar with it (Bjorklund, Miller, Coyle, & Slawinski, 1997). Thus, although younger children are able to employ organizational strategies, they tend not to use them.

Learning How to Learn

Children's own thinking and problem solving produces information that then leads to changes in their thinking. That is, the outcomes of their thinking contribute information that helps them modify their strategies for future problem solving. For example, children use many different types of strategies to solve mathematics problems, and through their attempts, they learn which strategies are more effective for particular types of problems (Siegler & Shipley, 1995). Furthermore, the knowledge base that children have acquired through prior learning influences how new information is stored and integrated into their previous knowledge, as well as the speed with which information is processed (Bjorklund, 2000). Children who are "experts" in a certain domain, such as dinosaurs or chess or tennis, are better able to chunk information related to that domain into meaningful units, thereby increasing their memory for the information (McPherson & Thomas, 1989). They are then able to engage in faster and more efficient processing of domain-related information.

As children move through the school years, their metacognition improves—that is, their awareness and knowledge about how to learn. They become more knowledgeable about how to learn information and how to apply useful strategies that increase learning. For instance, after having been given information about solving a difficult problem, children given different but similar problems showed a learning-to-learn effect. They were much more likely to solve the new problems than were children who had not received any hints (Brown & Kane, 1988; Brown, Kane, & Long, 1989). Children develop the ability to use the knowledge they gain in one context in another situation.

WHAT CHARACTERISTICS DEFINE CHILDREN'S INTELLIGENCE AND CREATIVITY?

A pair of twins is given a date in the future—say, August 17, 3040. Almost instantly, they announce the day of the week on which the date falls. Or, give them a thirty-digit number to remember and they can report it back as accurately as if it had only three digits (Sacks, 1970). In another case, a young boy sets up a laboratory in his basement in which he invents burglar alarms and fixes radios. As an adult, he deciphers a Mayan Indian code and solves physics problems (Feynman, 1985). These people seem to be extraordinarily gifted, and we might assume they have high levels of intelligence. But, to what extent do these capabilities actually relate to intelligence? In the cases just discussed, not very well: although the young inventor, Richard Feynman, grew up to win the Nobel prize in physics, the twins had low IQ scores (around 60) and were institutionalized.

If you ask people on the street what makes someone intelligent, they are likely to suggest that there are three facets to intelligence: practical problem-solving abilities (reasoning logically), verbal abilities (reading comprehension, being a good conversationalist), and social abilities (being sensitive to social cues). Many scientists, but not all, agree that there are several different types of intelligence.

MEASURING INTELLIGENCE

Few children graduate from high school without having taken at least one intelligence test. Intelligence tests were first developed at the beginning of the twentieth century by Alfred Binet and Theodore Simon. These tests were designed for pragmatic reasons, especially to differentiate between those children who would benefit from standard schooling and those who might need special types of instruction.

Today, many types of intelligence tests exist, but the most popular individual test for school children is the Wechsler Intelligence Scale for Children–Third Edition, or WISC–III (Sattler, 2001). The WISC has two major components. The first component is verbal intelligence, which is measured by assessing general world knowledge ("How many pennies make a dime?"), vocabulary, comprehension of written passages, digit span memory (how many numbers the child can remember), and arithmetic. The second component is performance intelligence. To assess performance intelligence, many different tasks are used, including finding what is missing in a picture, arranging pictures in order so that they tell a sensible story, arranging blocks to reproduce a particular design, and unscrambling pieces

As a child, Richard Feynman invented burglar alarms and fixed radios. Are early achievements like these necessarily related to having a very high IQ?

IGURE 9.4

Distribution of IQ Scores

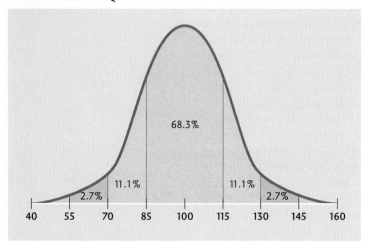

Intelligence is assumed to be normally distributed in the population. Explain what this means. What percentage of children have an IQ greater than 130?

of objects. The child receives scores on the two major components. The WISC also provides a profile of skills that the child possesses.

Intelligence quotient (IQ) was originally used to express the relationship between the number of items passed and the child's age. The method used today compares a child to other children of the same age. This method assumes that intelligence is normally distributed across the population (see Figure 9.4), with most people falling in average ranges and fewer people falling in the upper and lower ends of the scale. Children who score 100 have an IQ equal to or greater than that of 50 percent of children of the same age. Children with a score of 70 have an IQ equal to or greater than that of about 3 percent of children of the same age (Bjorklund, 1995).

UNDERSTANDING THE LIMITS OF IQ SCORES

For many children, especially highly verbal children, IQ scores predict school achievement and success (Sattler, 2001). IQ tests also accurately identify children who need special help in school and those who are especially bright. Despite these encouraging results, the usefulness of IQ tests has been questioned. For example, IQ scores do not predict life outcomes for many individuals. People who score high on IQ tests tend to complete more years of school and have more prestigious occupations (Morris & Levinson, 1995), but within normal ranges, IQ does not relate to success in a career (McClelland, 1993). Career success is due to many factors such as motivation and social skills (Sternberg & Wagner, 1993).

Because IQ scores do not always predict life success, IQ testing has come under scrutiny in federal courts and several state legislatures. Furthermore, IQ tests may not be used similarly for all children. In California, for example, because disproportionate numbers of African American children were placed in special education classes on the basis of IQ scores, the court has banned the use of these scores for student placement. The irony here is that tests designed to help decide a child's placement are now banned from the use for which they were designed (Weinberg, 1989).

The reasons IQ tests are questioned are many, but one of the most common reasons is that they are culturally biased—that is, they test material that is more important or familiar to people from one culture than people from another (Ogbu, 1994). For many years, researchers have attempted to develop culture-free tests in which general abilities are assessed rather than the knowledge that has been acquired through one's specific culture. One example is the Raven Progressive Matrices Test, which presents material in pictorial form. Although this test eliminates many of the problems of culture-bound tests, such as heavy reliance on language skills, it still relies on some culturally relevant material. For instance, it requires children to recognize that three-dimensional objects can be represented in two dimensions, which is not a typical skill for children in nonliterate societies (Deregowski, 1980). Another alternative has been to try to devise tests that are culture-fair—that is, they assess aspects of functioning that are common to all cultures. These tests, however, still favor the skills of some cultures over the skills of other cultures (Anastasi, 1988).

Today, many educators and researchers believe that the assumptions underlying IQ tests are flawed and that the best approach is to use an IQ test as only one part of a comprehensive assessment of an individual's functioning (Howe, 1997). Instead of using an IQ test as the sole indicator of a child's abilities, an educator should carry out a full assessment of each child, taking into consideration her or his everyday behavior outside of school, opportunities for schooling, and classroom performance (Weinberg, 1989). In fact, some scientists suggest that a better indicator of children's developmental status is social or emotional IQ (Salovey & Sluyter, 1997).

IDENTIFYING THE COMPONENTS OF INTELLIGENCE

> When Steven was growing up, I didn't know he was a genius. Frankly, I didn't know what the hell he was. I'm really ashamed, but I didn't recognize the symptoms of talent. For one thing—and he'll probably take away my charge accounts for saying this—Steven was never a good student. Once, his teacher told me he was "special"—and I wondered how she meant it.
> —*Leah Adler* (mother of Steven Spielberg, who has made some of the most famous movies of all time—*ET, Jaws, Raiders of the Lost Ark, Amistad, Schindler's List,* and *Saving Private Ryan*)

Whether an individual succeeds in life may depend on aspects of functioning that are not captured in the typical IQ test. For that reason, several theorists have proposed that people differ in various components of intelligence. For instance, in his *triarchic theory of intelligence,* Robert Sternberg (1985) proposes that people differ in three components that relate to how they process information:

- **Performance.**   This component involves encoding and interpreting information and retrieving information from memory. Consider the following problem: Cake is to ice cream as eggs are to (a) bacon or (b) pie. Solving this analogy first requires encoding the words and their meanings. Next, the relation between cake and ice cream has to be inferred (often eaten together). Then, the relation between cake and eggs has to be determined (both foods) and then related to the choices. For this analogy, the reasoning might be that eggs and bacon are often eaten together just as cake and ice cream are.
- **Knowledge-acquisition.**   This component involves strategies for gaining and acting on information. Successful problem solving requires that relevant information be distinguished from irrelevant information. Consider the following problem: A person spends $20 buying 5 grocery items. The oranges cost $.50 each, and each box of cereal costs $4.00. How much did the person pay for 3 oranges? To solve this problem most effectively, children should attend only to the price of the oranges and ignore the irrelevant information about the numbers of items on the shopping list and the cost of cereal. Gifted children tend to be more selective in attending to information than nongifted children (Davidson & Sternberg, 1984).
- **Metacomponents.**   Metacomponents are abilities that allow for monitoring of task performance and constructing of strategies to solve problems. Metacomponents permit the transfer of information from one context to another. Older children, children with higher IQs, and children with greater expertise are better able to apply information from one situation to another (Siegler, 1998).

Intelligence involves all of these components working together to help solve problems. Research has demonstrated that individuals differ in these three components and that the triarchic theory provides a useful way to think about changes in intelligence as children grow older.

In contrast to Sternberg's focus on processing strategies, Gardner (1983) emphasizes *multiple intelligences*—that is, intellectual domains in which individuals may have different strengths. As you can see in Table 9.1, Gardner proposed seven "frames of mind," or distinct areas of skill that are relatively independent of one another. In any of these, a person can display talent or genius. Only three of these frames of mind are assessed in standard IQ tests (Simonton, 1994). The frames-of-mind approach is useful for thinking about intelligence across cultures and throughout time. In some cultures, it may be adaptive to have good spatial skills so that one can be a successful hunter. In most western cultures, linguistic and logical-mathematical skills are especially valued.

TABLE 9.1

Gardner's Seven Frames of Mind: Examples of Abilities and People Who Exemplify Them

FRAME OF MIND	ABILITIES	PEOPLE
Linguistic	Good conversationalist; has learned several languages; writes well	T. S. Eliot
Logical-Mathematical	Able to solve logical and mathematical problems; analytical	Marie Curie, Albert Einstein
Musical	Plays several instruments; understands music theory; composes music	Wolfgang Mozart, John Lennon
Spatial	Good at visualizing, solving visual problems, and negotiating directions; artistic	Pierre Renoir
Bodily-Kinesthetic	Good athlete or dancer; has good motor skills	Jackie Joyner-Kersey, Alvin Ailey
Interpersonal	Socially competent; understands others' feelings	Sigmund Freud
Intrapersonal	Knows himself or herself	Mahatma Gandhi

SOURCE: Adapted from H. Gardner, 1983.

FIGURE 9.5

Christene's Puzzle: Is It Creative?

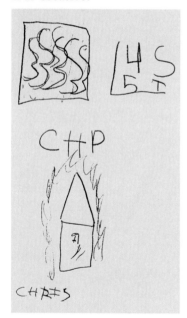

SOURCE: T. M. Amabile, 1993.

"The answer to the puzzle is me! These lines stand for my wavy hair, the numbers show that I'm four going on five, and the rest doesn't stand for anything at all!" Do you think this puzzle depicts creativity? How might this puzzle fit the definition of creativity?

The seven frames of mind were identified from research on brain-damaged individuals and from studies of exceptional children. Individuals who have particular forms of brain damage due to strokes or injury will exhibit normal skills in some areas but have extremely limited skills in other areas. For instance, a person with damage to the frontal lobes of the neocortex may have very limited interpersonal skills but intact logical-mathematical functioning. Similarly, some children—like the twins who could associate days with dates—are known as **savants** because they show exceptional abilities in one domain of intelligence but are incompetent in some other domains. One popular example of a savant is the autistic man played by Dustin Hoffman in the movie *Rainman*. He could memorize the cards perfectly during a game of blackjack but could not carry on a conversation with his brother. Children called **prodigies** show exceptional abilities at a very young age in one domain but not necessarily in others. Wolfgang Amadeus Mozart was a musical prodigy who composed keyboard pieces at age 5, published a composition by age 7, and wrote symphonies and operas by age 15. Otherwise, he was a typical, playful child and teenager (Simonton, 1994).

The concept of multiple intelligences has inspired many educational innovations in North America, including the ideas that it is important to match instruction to learning styles, to provide instruction in more than one way, and to encourage student specialization (Krechevsky & Seidel, 1998). The theory has been criticized, however, for its static view of student competence (Klein, 1997).

CREATIVITY IN CHILDREN

Four-year-old Christene and her mother were waiting for their dinner at a restaurant. Using the pad and pen they brought along, Christene drew a puzzle for her mother to solve. After her mother tried but could not solve the puzzle, Christene explained, "The answer to the puzzle is me! These lines stand for my wavy hair, the numbers show that I'm four going on five, and the rest doesn't stand for anything at all!"

—*T. M. Amabile* (1993, p. 18)

Creativity is novel and appropriate behavior, different from what the person has done before or seen before (Amabile, 1992). According to this definition, Christene's actions would be considered creative, because the puzzle includes a novel and appropriate representation of herself (see Figure 9.5).

Because the creativity of a work of art or a solution to a problem is defined by the culture in which it occurs (Csikszentmihalyi, 1996), it is difficult to assess creativity (Runco

What skills do these children need to be creative? Are all children creative? How should creativity be defined?

& Pritzker, 1999). The most commonly used assessments, designed by E. P. Torrance (1966), involve verbal and graphic tests. In the verbal section, the student is asked to think of as many uses as possible for objects like a tin can or paperclip. In the graphic section, the student is presented with a page covered with thirty lines and asked to create different drawings from these lines. Responses are scored for three aspects: how many answers are given (which measures fluency), unusualness of answers (which assesses originality), and number of categories of responses (which assesses flexibility) (Sattler, 2001). Research shows that children who score well on these tests are more likely to have creative achievements later in life, although the relationship is not strong (Torrance, 1988).

Some researchers who have studied creativity think that anyone can be creative in the right situation (Amabile, 2001; Hennessey & Amabile, 1988; Mellou, 1996). Four components appear to be needed for creativity:

- ◆ **Domain skills.** Creativity requires a solid background and ability in the particular domain of interest. For example, a scientist is unlikely to make a creative breakthrough in understanding cellular functioning without an extensive knowledge of biology.
- ◆ **Creative working style.** A creative working style is characterized by a dedication to working well, ability to concentrate, willingness to work hard, and persistence when roadblocks occur in thinking.
- ◆ **Creative thinking style.** Creative thinking includes "breaking set"—that is, being willing to drop old ways of thinking to try new ways. Creative thinking also involves perceiving things freshly, or taking a different perspective on the problem than most people would take (Feldman, 1999; Runco, 1999; Russ, 1996).
- ◆ **Intrinsic motivation.** Creativity is facilitated when people are internally interested in and challenged by the problem (Amabile, 2001; Hennessey & Amabile, 1988; Martindale, 2001).

HOW DO LANGUAGE AND LITERACY DEVELOP DURING THE SCHOOL YEARS

By the time children enter school, they have mastered many of the basic building blocks of language. They have a large vocabulary, use many grammatical rules in their speech, adjust

savants people who show exceptional abilities in one domain of intelligence but have retarded mental development in some other domains

prodigies children who show exceptional abilities at a very young age in one domain of intelligence but not necessarily in others

creativity novel and appropriate behavior that is different from what the person has done or seen before

their speech to fit their listeners, and understand how to communicate many of their needs to others. During the school years, children's language skills continue to develop, but the changes are more subtle than those that occurred during the preschool years. Compared to the preschool child, the school-age child is able to communicate more effectively over a broader range of contexts, use and understand more complex grammatical forms, and think about better ways to communicate using language. Additionally, a dramatic advance occurs during these years—children learn to read.

DEVELOPMENT OF SYNTAX

During the school years, children's understanding and use of grammar expand to include more complex forms of sentences, such as passive sentences. If preschool children overhear, "Big Bird was followed by the children," they are likely to picture in their mind Big Bird following behind children, rather than the accurate scenario. Preschool children often are confused by a passive sentence, probably because young children rely heavily on word order and interpret the sentence as being in the active voice. That is, they expect the object of the action to follow the verb in a sentence. By the age of 5, children understand passive sentences with action verbs ("was bitten"), but only during the school years do they come to understand passive sentences with non-action-oriented verbs ("was followed by"). Children's understanding of passive sentences continues to develop through the school years, but the full range of understanding is not usually acquired until adolescence (Bloom, 1998).

Some children learn to understand passive sentences earlier. Children who speak Sesotho (an African dialect) understand passive sentences by age 3. Compared to English-speakers, Sesotho-speakers use passive constructions for sentences much more frequently. For instance, there is no way to ask a question except in a passive form. Instead of asking, "Who asked you?" a Sesotho child must say, "Whom were you asked by?" (de Villiers & de Villiers, 1992). This cultural difference suggests that children learn more quickly those forms of language to which they are exposed (Demuth, 1990).

Young children use a variety of strategies for understanding spoken language. One example is the **minimal distance principle (MDP),** in which children assume that the noun most closely preceding the verb is the subject of the sentence. For instance, using the MDP, children would correctly interpret the sentence "Aladdin told Jasmine to eat the bread" to mean that Jasmine will be the person eating the bread. However, some verbs are exceptions to the rule, and when children use the MDP to help them understand a sentence with such a verb, they incorrectly interpret it. For example, if the MDP is applied to the sentence "Jasmine promised Aladdin to feed the dog," it will be misinterpreted to mean that Aladdin will feed the dog—when, in fact, the intended meaning is that Jasmine will feed the dog. It isn't until around 8 or 9 years of age that most children learn that *promise* sentences are exceptions to the MDP.

DEVELOPMENT OF SEMANTICS

Children's understanding of word meanings continues to develop during the school years (Hoff-Ginsberg, 1997). They add new words to their vocabulary, and their understanding of these new words often is acquired by listening to the context in which the words are used. By the time they enter first grade, children know about 10,000 words, and by fifth grade, they know about 40,000 words. Between first and third grade, children learn approximately eight to ten new words a day (Anglin, 1993).

Not all children learn that many words a day or have 40,000 words in their vocabulary by fifth grade. The variation among children is great, and the differences become larger with age. The variation is likely due in part to the relationship between reading and vocabulary size. Children who like to read when they are young develop larger vocabularies than other children (Nagy, Anderson, & Herman, 1987), and then, because these children continue to read more than other children, they continue to learn more words (Robbins & Ehri, 1994).

School-age children become increasingly sophisticated in their ability to understand subtle aspects of meaning, such as the double meanings some words carry. Terms such as

minimal distance principle (MDP) the assumption that the noun most closely preceding the verb is the subject of the sentence

cold, bright, and *sweet* have a physical meaning ("The pie is *sweet*") and also a psychological meaning ("She is a *sweet* person"). Not until children are 7 or 8 years old do they use these terms to refer to people, and complete mastery of these terms may not be achieved until a child reaches 12 years of age (Bloom, 1998).

Children also learn to understand the meanings expressed by idioms, which cannot be interpreted literally. If 4-year-old Tara heard her mother say "It's raining cats and dogs," she might run to the door and look to the sky to witness this amazing sight of dogs and cats falling from the sky. Or, overhearing her father say, in a conversation about someone at work, "She hit the ceiling," Tara might imagine a woman pounding her fist on the ceiling. These and other English idioms are difficult for young children—and people learning English as a second language—to understand. Children misinterpret these sentences because they interpret them literally. For instance, when a third-grade child participating in a study of word meanings was asked the meaning of *moneybags,* the child said, "It means that money goes into bags, and they have like dollar signs on them, and usually people bring moneybags to rob banks and stuff . . ." (Anglin, 1993, p. 110). To understand idioms, children must ignore the literal meaning of the words and instead rely solely on the context to infer the meaning of the phrase. They gradually develop an understanding of idioms, but full understanding does not occur until adolescence.

Is this how a 6-year-old would understand the sentence "Big Bird was followed by the children"? Why would a young child make this mistake while an older child would not?

DEVELOPMENT OF PRAGMATICS

The basic knowledge that children acquired as preschoolers about the pragmatics of language is refined and expanded during the school years. Children become more skilled in these aspects of communication because they come to recognize more of the unwritten "rules" of conversations (Holzman, 1996).

During the school years, two changes in children's understanding of the pragmatics of language are particularly noteworthy. The first change is the school-age child's increased ability to maintain a conversation (Bloom, 1998). Older children will continue to converse on one topic longer than young children will. Also, unlike preschoolers, who maintain the flow of a topic by repeating information, older children introduce new and relevant information into a conversation to maintain the topic.

The second change is school-age children's growing ability to be sensitive and "repair" conversations when listeners do not understand what they are saying. Although preschool children have some ability to clarify messages to help listeners understand, they do not deal well with repeated requests to clarify messages. Older children, on the other hand, continue to add information to make their message clear to the listener. By 9 years of age, children also provide definitions or background information as cues to help listeners understand their statements (Ninio & Snow, 1996).

CHILDREN'S LITERACY

One of the most dramatic changes that occurs in many cultures during the school years is that children learn to read and write. Unlike speech, which is universal and is quickly and easily acquired by most children all over the world, reading and writing are not common to all cultures and usually require extensive training before they are learned (Liberman, 1996). Both reading and writing require that children develop many complex skills involving attention, perception, memory, and background knowledge.

Cracking the Code: Learning to Read

Reading depends on a complex set of skills that children learn gradually as they grow older (Adams, Treiman, & Pressley, 1998). These skills help children to crack the code of written words and their meanings.

Children move through phases in learning to read (Chall, Jacobs, & Baldwin, 1990). The first phase occurs during the preschool years. During this time, children master many of the skills required for reading, such as learning the letters of the alphabet, recognizing some

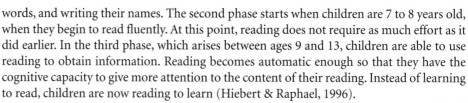

What phases do children move through in learning to read? Why is reading so challenging?

words, and writing their names. The second phase starts when children are 7 to 8 years old, when they begin to read fluently. At this point, reading does not require as much effort as it did earlier. In the third phase, which arises between ages 9 and 13, children are able to use reading to obtain information. Reading becomes automatic enough so that they have the cognitive capacity to give more attention to the content of their reading. Instead of learning to read, children are now reading to learn (Hiebert & Raphael, 1996).

What skills do children need to learn to become successful readers? One important skill that children need to understand is that the written words they *see* are related to the language they *hear*. Just because a caregiver holds a book while conveying a story to a child does not mean the child understands that the book has in it the words to tell the story. Caregivers can help children understand this connection by showing children that they are reading words from the book and that the words provide the story to be told (Foorman, Francis, Fletcher, Schatschneider, & Mehta, 1998).

Some of the skills involved in reading come easily to children. English-speaking children readily acquire the following specific prerequisite knowledge about reading:

- Words are read from left to right across the page.
- Words continue from the extreme right of one line to the extreme left of the next line down.
- Spaces between chunks of letters indicate words.

Other skills do not come so easily. Many children, for instance, have difficulty discriminating letters. To discriminate letters, children must be able to recognize the unique form of each letter and its orientation on the page. Mastering the orientation of letters can be quite taxing for young children because few things in their world depend on orientation to define them. A child looks around and sees a cat; a cat is a cat, regardless of its position—lying down, sitting, or standing facing to the right or the left. The same cannot be said about letters. A *b* is not a *b* when it faces in the other direction; it becomes a *d*. Children's lack of attention to orientation can be seen in their earliest attempts at "writing" where the letters they draw are scattered on the page, slanted, and even placed on their sides. It is not surprising, then, that over 50 percent of 5- and 6-year-old children reverse letters and numbers. Only about 10 percent of 7-year-olds do so (Kaufman, 1980). Even after they learn letters, many children confuse those that differ only in orientation, such as *b* and *d* (Adams et al., 1998).

Another challenge for children is mastering phonemic awareness (see Chapter 5). To read a word, children must recognize the sounds associated with the letters and be able to blend these sounds together to form a word. The ability to recognize the correspondence between sounds and letters relates to reading achievement in the early grades (Bruck, 1992). Preschool children are not very aware of these correspondences, but school-age children become more skilled at recognizing them.

How can children's awareness of phonemes be improved? Exposure to nursery rhymes or other rhyming activities promotes phonemic awareness, as children hear the subtle variations in the sounds of similar words. Rhyming games also increase children's general awareness that words consist of various sounds (McBride-Chang, 1995). Phoneme deletion exercises, such as asking a child to say *cat* without the *c* sound, can also improve children's understanding of phonemes. Training preschool and kindergarten children in phonemic awareness leads to improved reading skills up to four years later (Byrne & Fielding-Barnsely, 1995).

Children's Reading Readiness

Pushing children to read before they are ready may cause them to become discouraged. Instead, caregivers should be on the lookout for general cues that their children are ready to read. Following are some of the cues that indicate readiness to read (National Association for the Education of Young Children [NAEYC], 1998):

- Attempting to tell stories while scanning and turning pages in a book
- Understanding that stories start at the front of the book and move to the back in order, page by page

How will this activity help the child develop an awareness of phonemes? Why is phonemic awareness a prerequisite for learning to read? What other activities contribute to children's reading readiness?

◆ Recognizing written labels or signs
◆ Pointing out individual letters
◆ Showing interest in seeing his or her name in print

Once children have shown that they are ready to read, caregivers can arrange many activities to encourage reading. The complex skills involved in reading are best practiced and learned in the social context of interactions with caregivers, peers, and siblings. Competence in reading is fostered by practice and experience in all language domains. Reading to children certainly encourages reading skills, but so do other language-related activities such as carrying on conversations with them.

Controversies About Teaching Children to Read

Reading has been taught in many different ways, but controversy today surrounds the relative merits of two methods (Freppon & Dahl, 1998). In the **phonics approach,** children are trained to translate letters and groups of letters into sounds. For instance, children practice sounding out words that they cannot initially pronounce. Only simple and basic materials are used to study individual words. In the **whole language approach,** learning to read is assumed to be a natural process that occurs most effectively in a print-rich environment. Children become readers by guessing the meanings of words based on each word's context within the passage and their prior knowledge (Smith, 1992). Associated with this approach is the idea of **emergent literacy,** which assumes that children naturally develop the skills involved in written and oral language over the years and gradually improve these skills as they grow older (Teale & Sulzby, 1985). Although many educators have adopted the whole language approach, research provides little support that this method facilitates children's reading (Vellutino, 1991).

Rather than focusing on one approach to the exclusion of the other, some researchers argue that the best method is to incorporate aspects of both approaches (Pressley, 1998). For instance, the developmental approach to reading proposed by Spear-Swerling and Sternberg (1994) allows for changes in the method as children grow older and as their reading competencies change. In the earliest phase, children use visual cues to learn words. In the next phase, they make limited use of phonetic features of words. In the final phase, which begins around 6 or 7 years of age and continues through adulthood, children achieve automatic word recognition. At this point, the most important skills to stress are those involving comprehension of the material (Adams et al., 1998).

The whole language and phonics approaches appear to help different kinds of children. The whole language approach particularly benefits children with low initial reading scores, whereas those with high initial reading scores benefit more from a phonics approach (Sacks & Mergendoller, 1997).

How Do School-Age Children Understand the Social World?

Children use their cognitive skills to solve a wide array of problems, ranging from conservation tasks to arithmetic problems, but they also use cognitive skills to help them understand people and their actions. As children progress through later childhood, their knowledge about people and social situations becomes increasingly sophisticated. This increased understanding of the social world contributes to their more mature and responsible behavior and improved interactions with others.

SOCIAL PERSPECTIVE TAKING: COMMUNICATING WITH OTHERS

Imagine 3-year-old Shannon trying to communicate to 3-year-old Michael that he should pick a particular stuffed toy rabbit out of a group of toys. Shannon might say, "Pick up the one I like the most," not considering that Michael would not know which one was her

---

phonics approach technique used to teach children to read, in which children are trained to translate letters and groups of letters into sounds

whole language approach technique used to teach children to read, in which learning to read is assumed to be a natural process that occurs most effectively in a print-rich environment

emergent literacy educational approach in which it is assumed that children will naturally develop the skills involved in written and oral language and gradually improve these skills as they grow older

On what basis are these girls likely to describe each other? How do their descriptions differ from those of preschool children?

favorite. To be able to effectively communicate with others, children (and adults) must be skilled in **social perspective taking**—the ability to move away from one's own perspective and recognize what others perceive.

In contrast to the preoperational child, concrete operational children are better able to view a wide variety of problems from another person's perspective. Concrete operational children are less egocentric because they have the ability to both consider their own view and recognize that others see things from different vantage points. Children's understanding of others' perspectives extends into many domains; they now can communicate effectively with others because they can better imagine what others are thinking and seeing.

Similar to how they think about themselves (see Chapter 8), preschool children tend to think about others by focusing on external characteristics and temporary situations. School-age children show a more sophisticated understanding of people (Hala, 1997; Yuille, 1997). Preschoolers tend to refer to other people in very concrete terms (focusing on age, appearance, and possessions), seldom using abstract characteristics to describe others (Miller & Aloise, 1989). Around the age of 8, children's thinking about others becomes more refined, and they are more likely to think about others in abstract and internal psychological terms. For instance, an 8-year-old child will describe her friend as shy rather than simply saying that she is a girl.

Because of their focus on external characteristics and behavior, preschoolers tend to think that people change frequently; they do not observe the stability in personality that older children notice. A 10-year-old child is likely to believe that a girl in his class who shared her lunch with another child would probably help someone who was hurt, inferring from this one behavior that the girl is helpful in many situations (Rholes & Ruble, 1984).

Just as preschoolers cannot easily view a scene from another person's perspective, they generally cannot view social events from any perspective but their own. By late childhood, children come to recognize that two different people involved in a social interaction may have differing views and attitudes about the event. They still, however, may not use both points of view to understand the event the way an adolescent or adult might (Flavell & Miller, 1998).

CHILDREN'S UNDERSTANDING OF OTHERS' BELIEFS AND FEELINGS

As you learned in Chapter 7, a key feature of developing social skills is coming to understand that others have thoughts, feelings, and beliefs of their own. By school age, children have learned to "read minds"—that is, they are aware of others' thoughts, beliefs, knowledge, desires, and intentions (Hala & Carpendale, 1997).

Imagine a situation in which 9-year-old Iris watches her friend Lisa walk into the room and then turn around and walk out of the room. Iris, like most older children, can consider the existence of mental events, so she might guess that Lisa was looking for something she thought was in the room or that Lisa heard a noise in the room and was looking for the source. In either case, Iris is considering mentalistic explanations for the actions that Lisa took. Mentalistic explanations are those that involve consideration of other people's mental states—their beliefs and thoughts. Not all children have the ability to consider mentalistic explanations. Some children, such as autistic children, are *mindblind*—they have no mentalistic explanations to help them understand others' actions. A mindblind person would have no explanation for Lisa's actions other than the suggestion that Lisa might carry out this action every day, and this explanation is likely to be proven wrong. Imagine how difficult it would be for a mindblind person to interpret other social events, especially a complex interaction involving several people. Most children, however, develop more sophisticated mentalistic concepts as they grow older and can readily understand that others experience feelings, emotions, and beliefs.

CHILDREN'S UNDERSTANDING OF RACE AND PREJUDICE

The images that come to mind when we think of prejudice tend to be of adults or adolescents. For instance, we might visualize neo-Nazi groups or members of the Ku Klux Klan. When people encounter prejudicial or racist attitudes in children, they are quick to attribute them to children's imitation of adults rather than to the children's own personal preferences. This attribution, however, has been questioned by research on race and prejudice, which indicates that the level of prejudice in children has not declined since the middle of the twentieth century, as it has in adults (Aboud, 1988).

At what age do children use ethnicity to group people? Is ethnic awareness the same as prejudice?

Prejudice refers to having preconceived ideas about a person or group of people, often having to do with physical characteristics, ethnicity, or race. Some people respond to their prejudices with **discrimination**—acting in an unfavorable manner toward people because of their affiliation with a group. Awareness of ethnic and racial groups is considered to be a prerequisite for some types of prejudice and discrimination (Carter & Rice, 1997). When do children consciously recognize ethnicity in individuals?

By 6 months of age, many infants can perceptually categorize people on the basis of physical appearance (Walsh, Katz, & Downey, 1991). Simply recognizing that some people look different does not indicate that a child understands ethnicity, however. But children show strong same-race peer preferences by 2 years of age, and these preferences become more clearly established in early grade school (Katz, 1992). By 4 years of age, children have considerable knowledge about racial stereotypes of African Americans and Caucasians (Levy & Katz, 1993). Although children distinguish between Caucasian and African American people by age 4, their recognition of other ethnic groups, such as Native Americans, Chinese Americans, or Mexican Americans, is delayed for a few years, probably because the distinctive physical features of members of these groups can be less obvious (Aboud, 1988).

Perception of differences among other ethnic groups arises between the ages of 6 and 8 years. At this time, children begin to use ethnicity to group people together and to understand and make guesses about what people are like. For instance, they assume that people of the same race are similar in many ways despite the fact that they have different facial features or different shades of color, and they assume that people of different races are different in many ways even when they have many features in common (Ramsey, 1987). By age 11, children have incorporated more flexibility into their beliefs. No longer do children always perceive people to be different because they are of different races; children often find similarities based on individual features such as emotional expressions or abilities.

Awareness that different ethnic groups exist plays a role in the development of prejudice, but ethnic awareness does not determine prejudice (Carter & Rice, 1997). Children may hold stereotypes about and be prejudiced against groups that they cannot identify. Also, most people are aware of stereotypes, yet not all people apply this knowledge or act in prejudicial ways.

The most widely held theory about the formation of prejudice is that children adopt their parents' prejudicial attitudes and behaviors. According to this theory, children learn prejudice from their parents either by direct instruction, as when a parent tells a child not to play with children of another race because they are not "good," or by observation of the

social perspective taking the ability to move away from one's own perspective and recognize what others perceive

prejudice preconceived ideas about a person or group of people, often based on physical characteristics, ethnicity, or race

discrimination acting in an unfavorable manner toward people because of their affiliation with a group

THE PRACTICAL IMPACT: NURTURING CHILDREN

Reducing Prejudice in Children

What can be done to reduce prejudice in children? The answer to this question depends upon the age of the child. For children 4 to 7 years of age, the following suggestions may be helpful (Aboud, 1988; Katz, 1992):

- Help children develop perspective-taking skills. Prejudice at this age is based on the egocentric belief that there is only one way of experiencing the world.
- Help children develop a concern and compassion for others. Foster an ethic of caring rather than prejudice.

- Increase children's exposure to people of other races. Children's preferences for people of their own race and their negative attitudes toward people of other races will decrease. These effects generally are stronger for Caucasian American children than for minority children, although interracial exposure has been found to decrease African American children's lack of trust in and suspicion of Caucasians.

For children 7 to 12 years of age, a different set of principles should be followed to reduce prejudice:

- Encourage children to judge others on the basis of internal qualities rather than external attributes.
- Help children attend to similarities in different groups. Pointing out the ways that children are similar, even though they may look or act different, helps children identify qualities they can relate to and should reduce prejudice.
- Help children recognize that their perspective may differ from those of others and that two different perspectives can both be valid. Children's acceptance of ethnic differences will be enhanced.

---

parents' words or actions toward people of different races. The scientific evidence, however, suggests that children do not always adopt the prejudicial attitudes of their parents, and if they do, it is usually after 7 years of age (Branch & Newcombe, 1986). In addition, cases have been found in which children held prejudicial attitudes when their parents did not (Davey, 1983). For these reasons, it is unlikely that children's prejudice can be explained solely on the basis of learning from parents, other adults, or peers (Aboud & Doyle, 1996).

Theories of the development of prejudice also must account for the age-related changes observed in the development of children's prejudice (Black-Gutman & Hickson, 1996). There is an important shift in prejudice at about 7 years of age. After 7 years of age, Caucasian American children often show a decline in prejudice (Augoustinos & Rosewarne, 2001) and minority children show a more widespread preference for their own group (Bigler & Liben, 1993).

A social-cognitive theory has been proposed to account for the development of prejudice. According to this theory, the ways in which children think about the social world around them are influenced by the level of cognitive development they have attained (Aboud, 1988). Early on, children's thinking is dominated by their emotions and preferences. Later, children begin to consider how similar or dissimilar other people are to themselves. Prejudice is related to the perceived degree of dissimilarity. People with different skin color, language, and/or clothing are noticeably different, and these perceptions dominate children's reactions. Finally, children begin to understand the difference between categories and individual qualities and learn to attend to more than one quality of a person at the same time (they realize that a person can have a different skin color but similar interests). Then, they can use categories as the basis for determining ethnicity and individual qualities as the basis for forming preferences.

Thus, as children acquire more advanced modes of thinking, their views of others become less extreme and polarized. They become aware of individuals' internal qualities, understand that ethnicity is permanent and unchangeable, and realize that ethnic differences are reconcilable. In other words, because of changes in cognitive development, older children's prejudice is reduced (Aboud, 1988; Black-Gutman & Hickson, 1996).

How does schooling influence children's cognitive development

As children enter late childhood, schooling becomes a more and more important aspect of their intellectual (and social) life. Literally thousands of hours of a child's life are spent in the

constructivist theories of learning educational approach in which students are encouraged to actively participate in their education

cooperative learning educational approach in which students work together in groups to solve problems

discovery learning educational approach in which students are encouraged to discover principles for themselves

generative learning educational approach in which students are taught how to use specific methods of problem solving to integrate new information with pre-existing information

multicultural education educational practices and curricula that present non-European perspectives or improve educational outcomes for students from a wide spectrum of backgrounds

classroom. In addition to being influenced by what they do in the classroom, children are influenced by their schools' philosophies of education. Beliefs about the goals of education have varied; a strong emphasis on the basics in the early 1950s gave way to open classrooms, in which children explored and learned independently, in the 1960s. Although the debate over teaching the basics versus encouraging thinking skills continues, some broad patterns can be identified. Trends in education today include an emphasis on making the child an active participant in the learning process and using child-relevant situations to teach thinking skills.

OPPORTUNITIES FOR ACTIVE LEARNING

Some teachers today, trained in the cognitive developmental theories of Piaget and Vygotsky, have adopted **constructivist theories of learning,** in which students are encouraged to actively participate in their own education. These teachers think of themselves as mentors for their students, encouraging them to discover and transform complex information for themselves (Paris, 2001; Steffe & Gale, 1995). Classroom environments that support children's autonomy improve academic performance, as well as increasing children's sense of competence and self-esteem (Fry & Addington, 1984; Ryan & Grolnick, 1986). Research shows that constructivist approaches have been used effectively for teaching many different topics, including science (Neale, Smith, & Johnson, 1990) and reading (Rosenshine & Meister, 1997). The variety of techniques teachers use to encourage students to become actively involved with the material include the following (Slavin, 1997):

- In **cooperative learning,** students work together in groups to solve problems.
- In **discovery learning,** students are encouraged to discover principles for themselves.
- In **generative learning,** students are taught how to use specific methods of problem solving to integrate new information with pre-existing information.

MULTICULTURAL AND MULTILINGUAL EDUCATION

Schools are facing new challenges as they try to provide optimal educational experiences for the increasingly diverse students who are entering schools today. Educating children from various backgrounds will become an even more central issue in the future.

What is the best way to balance the educational issues of minority cultures with those of the larger culture? Some people believe that a focus on diversity may cause divisions among groups at a national level, whereas others assert that an emphasis on minority cultures will strengthen the national culture. The practices of educators mirror these different beliefs. Educational practices in the schools range from emphasizing minority cultures to focusing on human relationship skills.

The many definitions of **multicultural education** reflect the lack of agreement about how best to deal with a diverse population of students. Some definitions describe multicultural education as a curriculum that includes non-European perspectives—for instance, discussions of Hispanic authors and their works in an English class. Other, broader definitions suggest that multicultural education refers to policies and practices that improve educational outcomes for students from a wide spectrum of ethnic, religious, gender, and disability backgrounds (Banks, 1995; Banks & Banks, 1993). The types of programs using multicultural curricula vary considerably, and research efforts have been focused on assessing their effectiveness (Aboud & Levy, 2000; Bigler, 1999).

This teacher is demonstrating a science experiment. Describe some of the other ways in which teachers influence children's cognitive development.

THE SOCIAL IMPACT: DEBATING THE ISSUE

How Successful Is Bilingual Education?

Bilingual education consists of programs designed to teach English-language skills to children who have only limited proficiency in English. Educators agree about the need for bilingual education but do not agree on how to best accomplish it (Brisk, 1998). One group of educators recommends that children be given training in English at an early age, usually by removing them from the classroom for special instruction (Lampert, 1984). These children then spend the reminder of their school day in regular classrooms, learning math and science in their non-native language (English). The advantage of this approach is that children receive early exposure to English, but the disadvantage is that children spend hours a day in classes in which they have difficulty understanding the language being used.

Another group of educators advocates conducting children's primary education in their native language—teaching them to read, write, and communicate effectively in that language before introducing them to English (Willig, 1985). These educators believe that the skills children develop for thinking critically in their own language will easily translate into their new language (English). The advantage of this approach is that children do not fall behind in school, because they receive instruction in all topics in their native language. The disadvantage is that

these children are separated from other children for their schooling.

Research has demonstrated that high-quality bilingual education programs are effective (Brisk, 1998) and enhance self-esteem in children (Wright & Taylor, 1995). Canadian studies suggest that bilingualism increases students' achievement in areas other than language (Bain & Yu, 1980). The type of program that is most beneficial to students remains unclear, however (Hakuta & McLaughlin, 1996). Some evidence suggests that children show good short-term gains from being trained early in English, but longer-term gains in academic ability seem to be promoted more by providing children with education in their native language (Willig, 1985). Furthermore, it is clear that it takes children five to seven years to become competent English speakers, but most programs involve only two to three years of training (Hakuta & McLaughlin, 1996).

A complicating factor in bilingual education is the many different native languages that are represented in some school districts. For instance, 58 percent of California's school-age children are non-native English speakers. The large majority of these children are Spanish speaking, but more than thirty-five other languages also are represented, including (in order of their occurrence) Vietnamese, Filipino, Cantonese, Korean, Cambodian,

Hmong, Mandarin, Lao, Armenian, Japanese, and Farsi. There are not enough teachers available to teach this variety of languages in the California school system. Only in school districts with a large concentration of students from one or two language backgrounds is it possible to develop high-quality bilingual educational programs.

Bilingual education recently has come under attack. Critics contend that children are damaged by bilingual education because of their inability to learn English well enough (Rothstein, 1998). In response to these attacks, California passed a proposition that practically bans bilingual education in state schools, scrapping bilingual programs and replacing them with intensive one-year immersion courses (Cornwell, 1998). Whether or not other states follow California's lead depends in part on how much current bilingual programs are improved.

Thinking It Through:

1. What are the advantages and disadvantages to children of being educated in their native language? What difficulties do schools face in trying to accomplish this?
2. Do you think that, as the US population becomes more diverse, concerns about the effectiveness of bilingual education will increase?
3. Should all children in the United States learn to speak more than one language, as children in Europe do?

Some children have limited English proficiency (Hakuta & McLaughlin, 1996). By 2026, about 25 percent of children will come from families in which the primary language is not English (National Center for Education Statistics, 1998). What is the best way to help these children succeed in school? The issue of how to best educate students from diverse backgrounds with various language skills is especially a concern in the large US cities of Los Angeles, New York, Miami, and Atlanta. Consider, for instance, the question of whether immigrant children should take their classes in English or in their native language (see the Social Impact box).

TEACHERS' BIAS IN ACHIEVEMENT EXPECTATIONS

Children differ from one another in many ways—in their sex, ethnicity, abilities, social class, and religion. Although in the ideal situation each child would receive equal attention and opportunities in school, this is not always the case.

Children's classroom performance is influenced by the expectations teachers hold about their capabilities. Many studies have demonstrated that teachers have different expectations for and act differently toward students whom they believe to be high and low achievers. For example, children who are expected to be high achievers are given more opportunities to participate in class and more time to respond. They also receive more praise for giving right answers and less criticism for giving wrong answers. Children who are not expected to perform well are given less opportunity to participate (Jussim, Madon, & Chatman, 1994; Kolb & Jussim, 1994).

Many teachers are not even aware of the preferential treatment they give to some children. This lack of awareness makes training in diversity and multicultural issues particularly important, to ensure that all children have equal opportunities for education. Unfortunately, few educators have become sensitized to the unequal treatment that children receive in the classroom (American Association of University Women [AAUW], 1994).

HOW DO SCHOOLS ADDRESS STUDENTS' SPECIAL NEEDS?

About 10 percent of the children in the educational system have special needs due to physical disabilities, emotional disturbances, or mental retardation (see Table 9.2). Most children with special needs are between the ages of 6 and 11 (46 percent) or 12 and 17 (41 percent) (US Department of Education, 2000). Another 5 percent have special needs because they are gifted or particularly talented. The educational needs of children vary depending on their abilities.

Dramatic changes have occurred in the education of special needs children over the last twenty-five years. These changes are largely due to the passage of Public Law 94-142, the Education for All Handicapped Children Act of 1975, and its extension, the Individuals with Disabilities Education Acts of 1990 and 1994. These bills state that every disabled child is entitled to a public education appropriate to the child's needs, at public expense.

One feature of these bills that has had particular impact on educational practices is the mandate that children be educated in the least restrictive environment possible. Efforts to ensure that children spend as much time as possible in the "normal" academic environment

TABLE 9.2
The Numbers and Percentages of 0- to 21-Year-Olds with Disabilities: 2000

DISABILITY	INCIDENCE AMONG 0- TO 21-YEAR-OLDS	PERCENTAGE OF ALL DISABLED 0- TO 21-YEAR-OLDS	PERCENT INCREASE/DECREASE IN INCIDENCE FROM 1990
Specific learning disabilities	2,789,000	46.1	3.1
Speech or language impairment	1,068,000	17.6	−14.2
Mental retardation	597,000	9.9	−11.6
Serious emotional disturbance	462,000	7.6	−7.3
Multiple disabilities	106,000	1.8	−1.1
Hearing impairments	70,000	1.2	0
Orthopedic impairments	69,000	1.1	10
Other health impairments	221,000	3.6	200
Visual impairments	26,000	.4	−20
Autism and brain injury*	67,000	1.1	1000
All disabilities	4,915,168	100	27.2

*Data from 1990 and 1991 were unavailable; data from 1992 were used instead.

SOURCE: Adapted from US Department of Education, 2000b.

have led to **mainstreaming**—including children with all sorts of disabilities in regular classrooms. For instance, a disabled student might spend most of the day in a special class but attend one or two regular classes. Most schools do not integrate severely disabled students into regular classrooms, although there is a debate about the advantages and disadvantages of full inclusion of these students in regular classes. The advantages of full inclusion are that it provides a less restrictive learning environment for disabled children and that it allows all children to have opportunities to interact and become friends with children of varied abilities (Marks, 1997). The disadvantages are that the special needs of the disabled child may not receive adequate attention in the general education classroom, that these children may become socially isolated, and that teachers may not be prepared to work with these students (Kelly, 1992; Keogh & MacMillan, 1996).

CHILDREN WITH PHYSICAL DISABILITIES

Education for the physically disabled child must be tailored to meet the specific needs of the child. Some children require spaces accessible to wheelchairs but need no other assistance. Other children, such as those with cerebral palsy, may need someone to guide their fingers over a computer keyboard so that they can communicate, because they have difficulties speaking.

Children who are blind or deaf also have specific educational requirements. Until the 1970s, most blind and deaf children were educated in residential centers, but today, most are educated in regular classrooms. Most commonly, blind children are provided with Braille reading materials. However, many blind children can read print if it is enlarged sufficiently, in which case they can be educated more flexibly in regular classrooms than when only Braille books can be used.

CHILDREN WITH ATTENTION-DEFICIT HYPERACTIVITY DISORDERS

Eight-year-old Reese lives in a fast-moving world where sounds, images, and thoughts are constantly changing. He is easily bored and has difficulty keeping his mind on the tasks he needs to complete. He often is unable to sit still, plan ahead, or finish a task he has started, and sometimes he does not seem fully aware of what is going on around him. He tends to overreact, sometimes fighting with others who accidentally bump into him, and this has gotten him into trouble several times. Reese often loses things, and he seems to be careless and sloppy in his work and play.

The world that Reese lives in is shared by many other children. Reese has been diagnosed as having **attention-deficit hyperactivity disorder (ADHD),** which is the most common mental disorder among children, affecting as many as 2 million American children. ADHD is marked by an inappropriately low level of attention and inappropriately high levels of impulsivity and activity. On the average, at least one child in every US classroom needs help for ADHD (Taylor, 1995). ADHD is diagnosed six times more often in boys than in girls (Arcia & Conners, 1998; Safer & Krager, 1994). Some children have attention deficit disorder without hyperactivity (ADD). These disorders can continue into adolescence and adulthood, causing a lifetime of frustration and pain.

In approximately half of the cases, onset of ADHD appears before age 4. During the preschool years, caregivers notice that the child is very active and energetic (Taylor, 1995). Caregivers' complaints about a child's hyperactivity at age 3 are predictive of later childhood problems (Biederman et al., 1998).

In late childhood, the demands of school make prolonged attention more important. Some children cope with the transition well and meet the demands of school, even if they are still highly active and uncontrolled at home (Taylor, 1995). Other children, like Reese, who are inattentive and highly active, are at risk for failing to learn and for developing poor peer relationships (Greene et al., 2001). Because ADHD children are likely to have problems in school, the disorder is frequently recognized when the child enters school.

mainstreaming including children with all sorts of disabilities in regular classrooms

attention-deficit hyperactivity disorder (ADHD) a disorder marked by an inappropriately low level of attention and inappropriately high levels of impulsivity and activity

As Reese's case shows, children with ADHD have difficulty staying on task and organizing and completing work. Written work is often sloppy and is characterized by impulsive, careless errors that are a result of not following directions or of guessing without considering all the alternatives. ADHD children frequently do not seem to be listening to adults' instructions. Group situations and those that require sustained attention are the most difficult for ADHD children (Jacobs, 1998).

Many children outgrow their hyperactivity after adolescence and escape later adjustment problems, but about one-third continue to show attention problems into adulthood (Klein & Mannuzza, 1991). Those who continue to have problems with ADHD are also likely to have an explosive or immature personality (Barkley, Fischer, Edelbrock, & Smallish, 1990; Hechtman & Weiss, 1986).

ADHD can be difficult to accurately diagnose. Even pediatricians who treat ADHD children find the diagnosis problematic (Kwasman, Tinsley, & Lepper, 1995). For ADHD to be diagnosed, a disturbance of at least six months' duration must occur prior to the age of 7 and at least eight of the following symptoms must be present (American Psychiatric Association [APA], 1994):

- ✦ Often fidgets with hands or feet or squirms in seat
- ✦ Has difficulty remaining seated when required to do so
- ✦ Is easily distracted by extraneous stimuli
- ✦ Has difficulty awaiting a turn in game or group situations
- ✦ Often blurts out answers to questions before they have been completed
- ✦ Has difficulty following through on instructions from others
- ✦ Has difficulty sustaining attention in tasks or play activities
- ✦ Often shifts from one uncompleted activity to another
- ✦ Has difficulty playing quietly
- ✦ Often talks excessively
- ✦ Often interrupts or intrudes on others
- ✦ Often does not seem to listen to what is being said to him or her
- ✦ Often loses things necessary for tasks or activities at school or home (toys, books, assignments, etc.)
- ✦ Often engages in physically dangerous activities without considering the possible consequences

The challenge for pediatricians is to distinguish these characteristics from normal, age-appropriate attentional and active behaviors.

Scientists believe that biological factors influence ADHD. For example, brain imaging studies show that parts of the frontal lobe of the brain function at lower levels in children with ADHD, which in turn decreases their ability to inhibit their behavior and focus their attention (Castellanos, 1997). As a result, ADHD children are less able to regulate their activity in response to the demands of the situation (Barkley, 1997).

Evidence from several studies suggests a genetically inherited component to ADHD (Hewett et al., 1997; Quist & Kennedy, 2001). Consistent with the pattern expected in genetic disorders, if one monozygotic twin has ADHD, the other is likely to be hyperactive too; the same is not true of dizygotic twins (Nadder, Silberg, Eaves, Maes, & Meyer, 1998). Children who have ADHD usually have at least one close relative who also has ADHD. At least one-third of all fathers who had ADHD as a child have children who have ADHD (Taylor, 1995).

Environmental factors involved in ADHD include poor maternal health during pregnancy, postmaturity (but *not* prematurity), long duration of labor, maternal use of alcohol and cigarettes, malnutrition during the first year of life, and chronic lead poisoning (Dulcan, 1989). These organic environmental factors affect the child's nervous system directly. Researchers also have identified various nonorganic environmental factors. For example, ADHD children are more common in families in which there is a considerable amount of hostility, either between parents or between parents and children (DuPaul, McGoey, Eckert, & VanBrakle, 2001; Lorys et al., 1993). ADHD is associated with overstimulating, anxious, and intrusive styles of mothering, as well as with single-parent families (Carlson, Jacobvitz,

& Sroufe, 1995; Jacobvitz & Sroufe, 1987). Furthermore, ADHD children are more likely to come from families with low socioeconomic status (Pellegrini & Landers-Pott, 1996).

The most common way to treat many of the symptoms of ADHD is to use stimulant medications such as Ritalin. Parents naturally are concerned when their young children take such strong medication. Many children begin treatment with Ritalin very early in life (Bowen, Fenton, & Rappaport, 1991), and parents often complain about the side effects (Pelham et al., 1999): insomnia, headaches, decreased appetite, nervousness, and sadness (Kwasman et al., 1995). Critics argue that many children who do not have true ADHD are medicated with Ritalin as a way to control their disruptive or simply active behavior (Taylor, 1995). Given these concerns, it becomes particularly important to consider what the research evidence shows about the effectiveness and the drawbacks of treating ADHD children with medication.

High-quality medication treatment offers substantial benefits to those children who receive it (Jensen et al., 2001). When taking medication, ADHD children become less negative and more responsive to parents; they also are less disruptive and impulsive in the classroom and when interacting with peers (Pelham, Bender, Caddell, Booth, & Moorer, 1985; Whalen & Henker, 1991; Whalen et al., 1989). Medication also helps school performance; the children show improved attentional, writing, and learning skills (Dulcan, 1986; Pelham, Milich, & Walker, 1986).

These drugs, when properly supervised, are generally considered to be safe. Although they can be addictive to adolescents and adults if misused, these medications are not addictive to children and do not lead to later addiction. In fact, by preventing the negative experiences ADHD children have with others in their environments, these drugs may actually help prevent later addictions (Taylor, 1995). These drugs do not make children "high," nor do they sedate children. Rather, they appear to help children control their hyperactivity, impulsiveness, and inattention.

There are drawbacks to these medications, however. It is difficult to predict how an individual child will respond to stimulants, so careful monitoring is required (Dulcan, 1989). Additionally, these medications appear to produce undesirable negative emotions such as sadness, depression, nervousness, and withdrawal in some children (Buhrmester, Whalen, Henker, MacDonald, & Hinshaw, 1992). Because the medication alleviates the symptoms but does not cure ADHD, it is likely to be needed for a long time; about 80 percent of those who need medication as children also need it as adolescents, and about 50 percent continue to need it as adults (Taylor, 1995).

Like children on any medication, children on stimulants need to be monitored by a physician, and parents need to be informed about possible side effects. Generally speaking, the benefits of medication appear to outweigh the drawbacks (Greenhill, 2001).

Behavior management strategies, such as rewarding appropriate behavior and ignoring inappropriate behavior, also are effective strategies for dealing with ADHD, and they require the cooperation of parents and teachers (Dulcan, 1989). Diet therapies, such as restricting children's intake of food additives, have become popular, although the scientific evidence for their effectiveness is limited and complex (Breakey, 1997). Dietary treatments are most effective if there is direct evidence of an allergic disorder and changes in behavior associated with specific foods (Scahill & deGraft, 1997). For most ADHD children, neither medication nor behavioral strategies alone are sufficient to normalize behavior and improve academic performance. Most professionals therefore use a combination of treatments for children with ADHD (Greene & Ablon, 2001).

CHILDREN WITH MENTAL RETARDATION

Even prior to the advent of IQ testing, many children were identified by their parents or teachers as having low levels of intellectual functioning, often because they did not adapt well to life's circumstances. IQ tests provide a means of classifying people according to degree of intellectual functioning. Used alone, however, IQ scores are not always highly predictive of adult functioning. For instance, some children with very low IQ scores have been quite successful in their daily living, usually because they have "street smarts" and a sup-

TABLE 9.3

Characteristics of Individuals with Various Degrees of Mental Retardation

DEGREE OF MENTAL RETARDATION	APPROXIMATE PERCENTAGE OF THE MENTALLY RETARDED	IQ SCORE	CHARACTERISTICS
Mild	85%	50–70	Acquire academic skills up to approximately sixth-grade level May become self-sufficient Can live successfully in the community
Moderate	10%	35–55	Acquire academic skills up to approximately second-grade level May be able to perform jobs, under supervision Adapt well to life in the community, but usually in supervised group homes
Severe	3–4%	20–40	Have limited academic skills May perform simple tasks, with close supervision Adapt well to life in the community, usually in group homes or with families
Profound	1–2%	Below 20 or 25	Require a highly structured environment with constant aid for optimal development Can perform simple tasks under close supervision May live in the community, in group homes, or with families

SOURCE: American Psychiatric Association, 1994.

portive environment (Kasari & Bauminger, 1998). Today, **mental retardation** is defined broadly to include subaverage general intellectual functioning and impaired adaptive functioning, with onset during childhood (APA, 1994).

Four degrees of severity of intellectual impairment have been identified (see Table 9.3). A total of about 1 percent of the population falls into these categories, with more males than females being labeled as mentally retarded (APA, 1994). Mental retardation should not be considered a permanent feature of a person. Research has shown that many children labeled as mildly retarded "lose" their mental retardation as adults (Koegel & Edgerton, 1984). Some research suggests that even profoundly and severely retarded individuals can learn to live semi-independently, can maintain employment, and are able to develop social relationships (Mest, 1988).

A leading known cause of mental retardation is very early prenatal events (30 percent), including exposure to teratogens (as through maternal alcohol consumption). Environmental influences (such as lack of nurturance or cognitive stimulation) and other mental disorders (such as the onset of schizophrenia) account for many of the milder cases of mental retardation. About 10 percent of cases are due to genetic factors, such as Down syndrome, and health problems of childhood, such as lead poisoning and infections (Burack, Hodapp, & Zigler, 1998). The causes are unknown in about one-third of the cases of mental retardation.

Today, mentally retarded children are often integrated into general education classrooms, where they may receive specific step-by-step skill training, but these practices may not be the most effective. Research shows that it is more effective to teach these children cognitive skills, such as general problem-solving strategies and self-monitoring skills. Mentally retarded children have been taught, for instance, to use a specific strategy, to apply it appropriately, and to recognize the effort necessary to apply it. From these experiences, children learn how to behave in certain situations, as well as learning the importance of

mental retardation
condition characterized by subaverage general intellectual functioning and impaired adaptive functioning, with onset in childhood

TABLE 9.4

Students Enrolled in Regular Educational Programs and Gifted Programs

GROUP	PERCENTAGE OF GENERAL ENROLLMENT	PERCENTAGE OF ENROLLMENT IN GIFTED PROGRAMS
Caucasian Americans	71.2%	81.4 %
African Americans	16.2%	8.4 %
Hispanics	9.1%	4.7 %
Asian Americans	2.5%	5.0 %

SOURCE: L. M. Cohen, 1996.

This girl is considered a child prodigy. Why is it difficult for teachers to identify gifted children, and what kinds of programs should they receive in school to promote their skills?

acceleration programs
educational programs that encourage children to move rapidly through the usual coursework, compressing the time usually spent in each course

enrichment programs
educational programs that encourage problem solving and creative activities through independent study or individualized instruction and mentoring

planning (Gordon, Saklofske, & Hildebrand, 1998). Other successful approaches are prevention-directed, helping younger children who are at risk for being labeled mentally retarded. If these children learn adaptive strategies early, they may adapt more easily to school.

GIFTED AND TALENTED CHILDREN

Just as it is difficult to define *intelligence,* it is difficult to define *giftedness* (Gardner, 2000; Runco, 1997). The federal guidelines defining *giftedness* suggest that gifted children have outstanding abilities and need to have special programs and services beyond those that most children receive. Gifted children may have a single ability or many, including general intellectual ability, specific academic aptitude, creative thinking, leadership ability, talents in the visual and performing arts, and motor skills (Keogh & MacMillan, 1996). For instance, Picasso possessed remarkable artistic talents even as a young child, but he was not a good student (Gardner, 1983).

Because teachers often identify children as gifted based on their school performance, they miss children who do not perform well in school or who are gifted in athletics, music, or performing arts. Some indication of these problems can be seen in Table 9.4, which compares the percentages of children from diverse backgrounds who are enrolled in gifted programs. Minority children are not included in gifted programs as often as Caucasian American children because of their tendency to come from disadvantaged backgrounds.

Gifted children are often bored and unchallenged by their school experiences. In some school districts, 60 percent of elementary school children scored above 80 percent on a test of the content of their math textbook *before* they had begun to use the book (Reis, 1989). If books present little or no challenge to the majority of students, it is clear that they will pose no challenge at all to gifted students.

Some gifted children attend special schools that focus on math and science or on the arts. Other gifted children attend special classes in regular schools. Whether in special classes or in special schools, the question is, What kind of program should gifted children receive? **Acceleration programs** encourage children to move rapidly through the usual coursework, compressing the time usually spent in each course. For instance, the Study of Mathematically Precocious Youth program speeds up the pace at which children learn mathematics so that they are taking advanced college-level math courses before they complete eighth grade (Stanley & Benbow, 1983). Acceleration programs have been very successful in increasing students' achievement and academic abilities.

In contrast, **enrichment programs** encourage problem solving and creative activities, often through independent study or programs with individualized instruction and mentoring (Renzulli, 1999). Children might be asked to conduct an extensive science project or to write a newspaper. The effects of these programs are less clear because the skills that children develop are difficult to assess (Keogh & MacMillan, 1996).

HOW DO FAMILY AND CULTURE INFLUENCE CHILDREN'S INTELLECTUAL DEVELOPMENT

Children's intelligence and achievement are influenced by the kind of family and community in which they grow up. Some children grow up in a home with many disadvantages. These children may have a difficult time developing their full intellectual potential. Other children have the advantages of good housing, health care, and nutrition and supportive caregivers, which increase their chances for optimal intellectual development.

IMPACT OF POVERTY ON CHILDREN'S INTELLECTUAL DEVELOPMENT

The incidence of mental retardation is about six times higher among children who are raised in chronic poverty than among children who are raised in middle- and upper-income families (Baumeister & Baumeister, 1989). Children raised in poverty also are likely to be undernourished, have substandard housing, be ill more often, receive less health care, and come from more disorganized families than children from wealthier backgrounds (Aber, Jones, & Cohen, 2000; Huston, 1999). Thus, poverty has the potential to adversely affect children's intellectual development and performance in school. Racial and ethnic differences in IQ and school achievement all but disappear once adjustments are made for economic and social differences (Brooks-Gunn, Klebanov, & Duncan, 1996).

The problems of poverty are intergenerational, complex, and enduring. For example, women living in poverty receive less prenatal care and have more difficulties with their pregnancies. Not surprisingly, they are more likely to give birth to premature and unhealthy babies, who then face high rates of illness and all the other debilitating conditions associated with poverty (McLoyd, 1998a). The cumulative effects of poverty on many aspects of development make it all the more important to find ways to keep families out of the poverty cycle.

ROLE OF THE FAMILY IN CHILDREN'S GIFTEDNESS

Families and communities play a role in the development of gifted children. Studies of the early lives of remarkably accomplished young adults showed that these young people shared many family characteristics, even though they had diverse talents, as they ranged from concert pianists and neurologists to Olympic swimmers. In most cases, the family was intact and parents went to enormous lengths to help their children succeed at whatever task they undertook. Below are some of the characteristics that are commonly found in families of successful and talented children (Feldman, 1999; Howe, 1999):

✦ Parents value success and encourage children to do their best.
✦ Parents supervise practice sessions and training.
✦ Parents encourage active pursuits; they do not encourage television viewing or other passive pursuits.
✦ Parents devote time and energy to their children by reading to them, playing games with them, teaching them, checking homework, and supervising practice sessions.
✦ Family life is firmly structured, and children are required to share in responsibilities at home.

It is the parents who first introduce many children to the area in which they eventually excel, and often the parent is talented in this area as well. With parental encouragement and informal teaching, children can develop a high level of skill at home. The parents of gifted children realize the importance of practice and are sensitive to the need to support and encourage their children's practice (Strom, Strom, Strom, & Collinsworth, 1994). Although the families involved in these studies differed from one another in many ways, the one constant factor was the encouragement and support the parents gave their children.

In a longitudinal study, information was obtained about the lives of children from 1 to 8 years of age. At age 8, some of the children were identified as being gifted. When the early lives of the gifted children were compared with those of the other children, surprisingly few differences were found. Gifted and nongifted children had similar personalities, similar rates of behavioral and emotional problems, and similar social relationships. However, gifted and nongifted children's families differed. Gifted children's parents were more highly educated, and their families showed healthier functioning. Gifted children had more learning opportunities, more educational stimulation, more exposure to books, and more trips to libraries than children who were not gifted (Gottfried, Gottfried, Bathurst, & Guerin, 1994).

Hispanic parents have high expectations for their children's school performance. How do parents provide support and encouragement for their children in school?

ROLES OF PARENTAL INVOLVEMENT AND CULTURAL BELIEFS IN ACADEMIC ACHIEVEMENT

For many years, American children have not performed as well as Chinese and Japanese children in most academic areas. Several factors, including classroom strategies and cultural beliefs and ceremonies, contribute to these differences (DeCorte, Greer, & Verschaffel, 1996; Stevenson, 1998a). Families also contribute to the differences found in the performance levels of children in different cultures. In an extensive research program, Harold Stevenson and his colleagues investigated mathematics achievement among first- and third-grade children in three large cities—Sendai, Japan; Minneapolis, Minnesota; and Taipei, Taiwan (Stevenson & Lee, 1990).

Although the children's performance did not differ much in the first grade, by the third grade, the Asian children were far outperforming the American children. The researchers found dramatic differences between the Asian and the American families. Parents in Japan and Taiwan mobilized their resources to help their children as soon as the children entered school. For instance, the percentage of parents who bought their children mathematics workbooks varied from 58 percent in Japan and 56 percent in Taiwan to only 28 percent in the United States. Almost all of the Japanese (98 percent) and Taiwanese (95 percent) children had their own desk and work space at home, compared to only 28 percent of the American children. The Asian parents monitored their children's homework more than the American parents did. And, although the Asian children were performing quite well overall, their parents expressed more concerns with the school system than American parents did. Another clue to the success of the Asian students may be the interpretation parents placed on good mathematics performance. Asian parents were likely to attribute good mathematics skills to hard work, whereas American parents were more likely to attribute these skills to natural ability (Stevenson, 1998b; Stevenson, Lee, & Mu, 2000).

Parents' involvement, especially in holding high aspirations and expectations for their children, plays a significant role in children's academic achievement (Fan & Chen, 2001). Research suggests that families' attitudes toward and encouragement of education are important factors in the lives of children from diverse ethnic groups within the United States (Stevenson, Chen, & Lee, 1993). In a large-scale study of African American, Caucasian American, and Hispanic children in Chicago schools, mothers' and children's attitudes toward school were investigated, as well as children's school achievement in reading and mathematics (Stevenson, Chen, & Uttal, 1990). In early elementary grades, African American and Hispanic children had lower school achievement scores than Caucasian American children did; by fifth grade, these differences had disappeared for mathematics but not for reading. Differences in children's mathematics achievement in fifth grade related to the mother's educational level, rather than the child's ethnicity. Children whose mothers had lower levels of education did not perform as well in mathematics as children whose mothers had higher levels of education. Overall, minority children were more positive in some of their attitudes about school. For instance, African American children tended to like homework more than

FIGURE 9.6

African American, Hispanic, and Caucasian American Mothers' Attitudes About Improving Children's Educational Performance

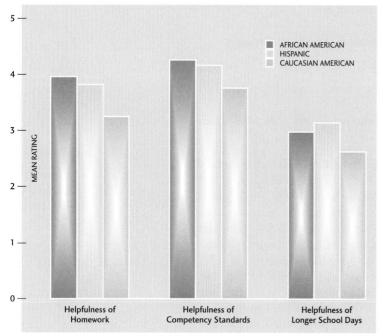

SOURCE: Stevenson, Chen, and Uttal, 1990 (p. 517).

Notice how the data contradict the stereotyped belief that minority parents do not emphasize academic achievement and hold high standards. How do parents' attitudes influence children's school performance?

Caucasian American children did, and in fifth grade, Hispanic children liked school more than Caucasian American children did.

Hispanic and African American children and their mothers were very positive about education, and the mothers held high expectations about their children's future prospects for education (Stevenson et al., 1990). Compared to Caucasian American mothers and teachers, minority mothers and teachers were more positive about the value of homework, competency testing, and lengthening school days to improve educational opportunities for children (see Figure 9.6).

Given the positive attitudes that children and their mothers have about schooling in the elementary grades, it seems surprising that so many minority children experience school failure during junior high and high school. An important goal for future research is to discover what factors have a destructive effect on older minority children's school achievement.

TRY IT OUT

Activities Relating to School-Age Children

1. Watch children play an organized sport such as soccer or softball. What benefits do you think the children are deriving from their participation in the sport? What kinds of cognitive and social skills are encouraged by participation in this sport? Is it likely that different sports encourage different sorts of cognitive and social skills in children?

2. Try some of the Piagetian tasks in Figure 9.1 with an elementary-school child. Does the child exhibit an understanding of conservation of liquid quantities but not more difficult types of conservation? Does the child show evidence of understanding seriation (see Figure 9.3)?

3. Visit an elementary school during an art or music class. By simply watching or listening, can you identify children who appear to be particularly talented or creative? Ask the teacher for his or her definition of *creativity* in children, and find out what cues he or she uses to determine whether a child is particularly creative.

4. Talk to a child in elementary school about what she or he does in school, and try to determine the extent to which the child's teachers are using active thinking strategies. Does the child engage in projects that encompass several domains of learning (such as mathematics, language skills, and musical instruction)? What kind of reading instruction is stressed?

SUM IT UP

How do children develop physically during late childhood?

✦ Compared to preschoolers, older children have slower growth rates, which enable their coordination abilities to "catch up" to their body size.

✦ During the school years, children show marked improvements in motor development. Older children are stronger and more agile and have better balance than young children.

✦ Children who participate in sports benefit from regular exercise and may learn to cooperate with others.

✦ Although children generally are healthy during the school years, health issues include poor physical fitness, sports injuries, and obesity.

How do school-age children think and solve problems?

✦ During the school years, for the first time, children's thinking and problem solving show the same type of logic—the use of operations—that is evident in adult thinking.

✦ Children's understanding of seriation and number becomes increasingly sophisticated during these years.

✦ Children's thinking is influenced by their family, their culture, and their everyday life experiences.

What characteristics define children's intelligence and creativity?

✦ The defining and measuring of intelligence are complex and controversial issues. The most common IQ test for children is the Wechsler Intelligence Scale for Children–Third Edition (WISC–III), which measures verbal and performance intelligence.

✦ Among the many controversial issues surrounding intelligence testing is the possibility that cultural biases may decrease IQ scores for some ethnic groups.

✦ Sternberg's triarchic theory describes three components involved in information processing that influence intelligence. Gardner's view of multiple intelligences suggests that there are many domains in which people may be intelligent.

✦ Creativity is difficult to assess. The most common tests use verbal and graphic components to measure fluency, flexibility, and originality.

How do language and literacy develop during the school years?

◆ Children's vocabulary continues to expand at a rapid rate, and children begin to master idiomatic expressions, which cannot be interpreted literally.

◆ School-age children come to understand the pragmatics of language better, developing the ability to maintain a topic in a conversation and the ability to "repair" a conversation so that others understand what they are saying.

◆ Major accomplishments for most children during the school years include learning to read and write.

How do school-age children understand the social world?

◆ Older children are more likely than young children to think of other people as having internal and stable personalities. As they grow older, children focus less on external appearances and more on other sources of information when making predictions about other people's actions.

◆ As children progress through the school years, they experience changes in their understanding of ethnic groups.

◆ Prejudice and discrimination may decrease as children apply more advanced cognitive skills to their understanding of people.

How does schooling influence children's cognitive development?

◆ Many educators use student-centered activities to encourage children to think and solve problems rationally and creatively.

◆ Because teachers may not be aware of their biases, workshops and training programs have been developed to provide methods for recognizing and overcoming biases.

How do schools address students' special needs?

◆ Children with special needs are guaranteed a free public education that is suitable to their needs. Schools are obliged to place these children in the least restrictive environment possible, which provides a broad range of opportunities for them.

◆ The most common mental disorder among children is attention-deficit hyperactivity disorder, affecting approximately 2 million American children. Children with ADHD have an inappropriately low level of attention and are hyperactive and impulsive.

◆ Children who are mentally retarded have subaverage intellectual functioning and impaired adaptive functioning. Four levels of retardation have been identified, but these labels do not always predict later functioning.

◆ Early prenatal events are the leading known cause of mental retardation, but environmental events may cause many cases of milder retardation.

◆ Children who are mentally retarded are less likely to be placed in special education classes today than previously. They are likely to be integrated into general classrooms.

◆ Gifted children may be difficult to identify, especially if they are underachievers or minority students. Gifted children may be bored and unchallenged in the typical classroom.

◆ Gifted children may be encouraged to enter special schools or classes that focus on their areas of talent.

How do family and culture influence children's intellectual development?

◆ Children raised in poverty are less likely to achieve their full potential for intellectual development because of inadequate nutrition, health care, and housing.

◆ Families can provide important support for their children's intellectual and talent development through encouragement, supervision of practice sessions, and educational and intellectual stimulation.

◆ Cross-cultural studies illustrate the importance of families and their cultural values to children's achievements.

KEY TERMS and CONCEPTS

acceleration programs (*312*)
attention-deficit hyperactivity disorder (ADHD) (*308*)
compensation (*290*)
constructivist theories of learning (*305*)
cooperative learning (*305*)
creativity (*296*)
discovery learning (*305*)

discrimination (*303*)
emergent literacy (*301*)
enrichment programs (*312*)
generative learning (*305*)
mainstreaming (*308*)
mental retardation (*311*)
minimal distance principle (MDP) (*298*)
multicultural education (*305*)

obese (*287*)
phonics approach (*301*)
prejudice (*303*)
prodigies (*296*)
reversible thinking (*290*)
savants (*296*)
social perspective taking (*302*)
whole language approach (*301*)

Social and Emotional Development in Late Childhood

CHAPTER 10

CHAPTER OUTLINE

✦ How Do Emotions Develop During Late Childhood?

✦ What Emotional and Psychological Disturbances Affect Children in Late Childhood?

✦ How Do Children's Family Relationships Change During Late Childhood?

✦ What Factors Influence School-Age Children's Peer Relationships?

✦ How Does School Affect Social and Emotional Development in Late Childhood?

✦ What Changes Take Place in Moral Development During Late Childhood?

Late childhood marks a distinctive period of development. Children assume new roles and acquire new capabilities that launch them into more complex and diverse environments, with increased expectations from adults. Many of these expectations revolve around children's behavior and adherence to social and moral standards.

Late childhood also is the time when most children enter school, making new contacts with both older and younger children and a widening array of adults. The new environments and expanded interactions have major effects on children's social and emotional development. Most children meet these challenges with excitement and success. But some children become overwhelmed by these demands and changes.

HOW DO EMOTIONS DEVELOP DURING LATE CHILDHOOD?

During late childhood, children's emotional lives, as well as the environments that affect their emotional responses, become more complex and demanding. School-age children have enhanced competencies and resources that they can call on to help them respond to these increased demands. Unfortunately, some children find themselves overwhelmed by their emotions and the demands made on them, which leads to behavior problems, depression, fear, and anxiety.

STRESS AND COPING

As children grow and change, their vulnerability to stress and the situations that produce it also changes. Events that cause stress in young children often appear innocuous to older children, and the situations that create stress in older children often leave young children unaffected. For example, young children may find being left alone overwhelmingly stressful, whereas older children generally do not. Older children, however, may become stressed about an upcoming exam at school, whereas young children usually do not confront this kind of situation.

The ways that older and younger children cope with stress also differ. Infants who are distressed by a loud noise may cope by crying out to elicit comfort and assistance from caregivers. Toddlers may cope with the fear of a stranger by clinging to their mother's skirt. Preschoolers may cope with a frightening scene on television by covering their eyes. And elementary school children may cope with the fear of performing in front of others during a recital by distracting themselves with thoughts of something pleasant.

Changes in Contexts That Cause Stress

Developmental changes in children's relations to their environments contribute to changes in the contexts that cause stress. Because infants rely on caregivers, it is not surprising that early forms of stress relate to issues of caregiver presence or absence (Gunnar & Brodersen, 1992). During the early preschool years, stress is more likely to be caused by caregivers' efforts to exercise discipline in order to get their children to obey and comply. During the late preschool years, children are more likely to come into contact with stressors that involve other children (Eisenberg, Fabes, & Guthrie, 1997).

During late childhood, school increasingly becomes a source of stress (Skinner & Wellborn, 1997). Children in different countries perceive school as a source of trying and stressful experiences (Torsheim & Wold, 2001; Yamamoto, Soliman, Parsons, & Davies, 1987). The increased focus on intellectual skills, evaluation, and achievement elicits stressors—in the form of homework, tests, grades, and comparisons with classmates—that do not face younger children. School also is associated with increased stress related to peer relationships. Thus, the school context brings about changes in children's conceptions of themselves, in their relationships with peers and adults, and in the social situations in which they find themselves. Sometimes these changes disrupt the child's sense of well-being and consequently cause stress (Bryant, 1998).

Stress also may be produced when people change the culture in which they live (Gonzales & Kim, 1997). The type of stress that is associated with making a transition from one culture to another is referred to as **acculturative stress** (Roysircar-Sodowsky & Maestas, 2000). When families immigrate to the United States, they often must learn a new language, as well as adapt to new foods, traditions, and laws. Acculturation is a complex process of cultural adjustment that changes the conditions of one's life (Ager & Young, 2001). Because children have spent less time in their original culture, they acculturate faster than do their parents (Szapocznik & Kurtines, 1993). Although highly acculturated parents are likely to follow the parenting practices of their new culture (Dumka, Roosa, & Jackson, 1997), differences in rates of acculturation can lead to conflict within immigrant families, as parents and children develop conflicting cultural values and behaviors. Highly acculturated children may be critical of their less acculturated parents, seeing them as old fashioned, traditional, and embarrassing (Gil, Vega, & Dimas, 1994). Thus, in addition to the demands placed on families and children when adapting to a new culture, familial differences in the degree of acculturation may represent a source of stress and conflict (Gil & Vega, 1996; Hovey, 2000).

Changes in Coping Skills

Older children's responses to stress are different from those of young children. For example, older children are more likely to use **emotion-focused coping strategies**—efforts to manage or reduce the emotional distress (frustration, fear) that is aroused in stressful situations—than are younger children (Band & Weisz, 1988; Compas et al., 2001). Thinking of happy things and telling oneself that good things will come from the situation are examples of the emotion-focused coping strategies that increase over the elementary-school years. Because of their more advanced cognitive development, older children have a better understanding of stressful situations than young children do and can better use cognitive strategies (such as thinking of something pleasant) to cope with emotional distress (Eisenberg et al., 1997).

During late childhood, children also become more skilled in using **problem-focused coping strategies**—efforts to manage or modify the source of the stressful situation, such as finding a solution to the problem. As children develop better motor, communication, cognitive, and social skills, they are better able to effectively address and solve problems (Compas et al., 1999).

To cope effectively in situations involving other people, children need to understand the intentions of those involved. Understanding others' intentions is critical for developing a plan of action and interacting successfully with others (Kliewer, Fearnow, & Walton, 1998). Children who do not accurately interpret the intentions of others may cope ineffectively or inappropriately.

Research on aggressive children supports the importance of accurate interpretations of others' intentions. A child who interprets another's behavior as threatening and hostile is likely to respond aggressively, even when the other person's intentions are unclear (Dodge, 1991; Dodge & Coie, 1987). Suppose 9-year-olds Ian and Mason are playing on the school playground. Ian bumps into Mason, but Ian's intentions are unclear. Mason must decide whether or not Ian meant to hurt him. Mason concludes that Ian bumped into him on purpose, so he responds by pushing and hitting Ian. If Mason consistently makes this kind of interpretation, he will continue to respond to others in harmful ways. Some children are more likely than other children to make inaccurate or inappropriate interpretations (Coleman & Kardash, 1999). Children who have a tendency to interpret ambiguous behaviors as benign tend to be more prosocial than those who do not (Nelson & Crick, 1999). Generally, however, their advanced cognitive development and social experience permit school-age children to more accurately interpret the intentions and behaviors of other people.

Older children also cope better because they are more likely than young children to understand which situations they have some control over and which they do not (Harris, 1989). As discussed in Chapter 8, young children overestimate their capabilities, including

acculturative stress stress associated with making a transition from one culture to another

emotion-focused coping strategies efforts to manage or reduce the emotional distress that is aroused in a stressful situation

problem-focused coping strategies efforts to manage or modify the source of a stressful situation

THE PRACTICAL IMPACT: NURTURING CHILDREN

Helping Children Cope with Disaster

On September 11, 2001, terrorists hijacked four US commercial aircraft and used three of them as missiles to attack the World Trade Center in New York and the Pentagon in Washington, DC. Thanks to the heroic efforts of passengers, the fourth aircraft was crashed in a rural area of Pennsylvania as terrorists prepared to target another Washington, DC, site. About 3,000 people lost their lives in the worst terrorist attack in history, and many more were affected by the aftermath of the ruin, destruction, and loss associated with these attacks. The media played the events of this day over and over, and many children were exposed to the intense emotions and reactions related to this attack.

Not surprisingly, children sense the anxiety and tension in adults around them. And, like adults, children experience the feelings of helplessness and lack of control that disaster-related stress can bring about. Unlike adults, however, children have little experience to help them place their current situation in perspective. How can parents and other concerned adults help children cope with such disasters? The following suggestions are adapted from the National Mental Health Association (2001).

Each child responds differently to a disaster, depending on his or her understanding and maturity. It is easy to see how an event like that of September 11 can create a great deal of anxiety in children of all ages, because they will interpret the disaster as a personal danger to themselves and those they care about. Whatever the child's age or relationship to the damage caused by the disaster, it's important that you be open about the consequences for your family and that you encourage him or her to talk about it.

Preschool children may show signs of anxiety in their behaviors. Behaviors such as bed wetting, thumb sucking, baby talk, or a fear of sleeping alone may intensify or reappear in children who had previously outgrown them. Children may complain of stomachaches or headaches and be reluctant to go to school. It is important to remember that these children are not "being bad"—they are afraid. Children of this age need extra comfort and contact.

School-age children may ask many questions about the disaster. Be careful about providing false assurances—children of this age will know they are not true. Instead, remind children that they are safe now or that adults are working hard to make things safe. Remind children that disasters are very rare. Images of a disaster and the resulting damage are extremely frightening to children, so consider limiting the amount of media coverage they see. Do not be afraid to say "I don't know" to some of the questions children will have.

Adolescents can be encouraged to work out their concerns about a disaster. It is generally a good idea to talk about these issues, keeping the lines of communication open and remaining honest about the financial, physical, and emotional impact of the disaster on your family or on the community or nation. When adolescents are frightened, they may express their fear by acting out or regressing to younger habits. Adolescents may turn to their friends for support. Encourage friends and families to get together and discuss the event to allay fears.

It is important for children to feel as safe and secure as possible in the face of upsetting events. Concrete supportive actions, such as collecting money or designing cards for victims, may be helpful. These activities focus children's attention and help teach them how to offer support in times of crisis. Caring and attentive adults can help children return to a normal routine that psychologically stabilizes the situation for them.

---

their ability to control situations. They often use problem-focused strategies in situations where these are not going to have much effect. These attempts can cause frustration; it is difficult to address the source of the problem when the source is uncontrollable. Older children are more likely to use coping strategies that accurately reflect the actual control they have in the situation.

Resilience: Stress-Resistant Children

In any stressful situation, some children will come out relatively unscathed, whereas other children will be adversely affected. Several studies (Masten, Morrison, Pellegrini, & Tellegen, 1990; Nuechterlein, Phipps-Yonas, Driscoll, & Garmezy, 1990) have shown that children whose mothers had mental disorders (schizophrenia or depression) were at risk for problems with cognitive and social functioning. But equally important were the large numbers of children who showed little, if any, signs of problem behavior. These children were resistant to stress despite their mothers' mental disorders (Tebes, Kaufman, Adnopoz, & Racusin, 2001).

Findings such as these tell us that some children are more stress resistant than others. Stress-resistant children seem to have **resilience**—the capacity to bounce back or recover

resilience the capacity to bounce back or recover from stressful situations

from stressful situations. Resilience reflects healthy functioning despite exposure to stressful events (Masten & Coatsworth, 1998; Reynolds, 1998).

Marian Radke-Yarrow and her colleagues (Radke-Yarrow & Sherman, 1990) studied children who cope well despite having been reared in chaotic and threatening conditions by a parent who was emotionally ill. Let's consider one of these resilient children.

Dominique is the second daughter in a family of four daughters. Her mother, who suffers from severe depression, supports her family through prostitution and welfare. Dominique's father is intermittently in her life. He too suffers from depression and serious drug abuse. Dominique's mother, when not ill, is tough with her children. She yells at them much of the time and gets what she wants, even if she has to resort to physical violence. Dominique is healthy and sturdy and has been since birth. Her mother is proud of Dominique's health and appearance, spending hours keeping Dominique's hair stylishly braided.

Life in Dominique's family is very disorganized, with frequent moves, changes in caregivers, and limited opportunities to attend school. Despite these conditions, Dominique is curious, creative, outgoing, and charming. She also is doing well in school, and reports being happy and unafraid. In essence, Dominique is surviving despite the chaotic environment in which she finds herself.

In Dominique's case, there are several factors that protect her from the stressful and risky conditions in which she lives. Despite her mother's illness, Dominique has a warm relationship with her. Dominique's health and attractiveness are qualities that her mother values. Her mother prides herself on taking good care of her. Dominique also feels proud of her appearance and the fact that she can take care of herself when she needs to. Thus, Dominique has developed a positive self-concept and feelings of positive self-esteem. Dominique is popular with other children, and her teachers view her as independent and competent. This positive regard feeds back to her family life. It is a source of great joy to her mother, and Dominique receives praise for bringing home good school reports.

Resilient children like Dominique possess certain qualities that protect them and help them adapt to their stressful and demanding environments. These qualities also are valued by others. Other children possess qualities that lower their resilience. Recall from Chapter 6 that children who react more intensely and who are more temperamentally difficult, unpredictable, and moody also are less adaptable to stress than other children (Carson & Bittner, 1994). In addition to being more vulnerable to stress, these children are viewed less positively by others than are children like Dominique.

Based on case studies like the one of Dominique, researchers have identified common characteristics of resilient children. Such children have above-average intelligence, possess attractive qualities that elicit positive responses in others, and have a positive place in the family (Masten & Coatsworth, 1998; Radke-Yarrow & Sherman, 1990).

CHILDREN'S RESPONSES TO COMMUNITY VIOLENCE

Community violence is a major source of stress for many children (Gorman-Smith & Tolan, 1998; Margolin & Gordis, 2000). In his book *There Are No Children Here*, Alex Kotlowitz (1991) tells the story of two boys growing up in an inner-city low-income housing project in Chicago. Lafeyette and Pharoah were 7 and 10 years of age when Kotlowitz began documenting their lives in a community filled with crime and violence. Kotlowitz describes how Lafeyette and Pharoah often had to huddle on the floor of their tiny apartment as gun shots rang out nearby:

What kinds of stress are associated with poverty? How do children cope with these stressors? What factors make some children more resilient than others?

> Pharoah shook with each gun pop, his eyes darting nervously from one end of the long
> hallway to the other. He clutched a garbage bag filled with aluminum cans he'd collected;
> his small body was curled up against the security of the cool concrete wall.
> —*A. Kotlowitz* (1991, p. 6)

Children like Lafeyette and Pharoah face constant violence and danger in their neighborhoods. By some estimates (Berman, Silverman, & Kurtines, 2000), about 40 percent of the children in high-crime neighborhoods in US cities witness a homicide and more than two-thirds witness a serious assault. Mothers in a housing project in Chicago identified shootings as their major safety concern for their children (Dubrow & Garbarino, 1989).

In war-torn countries like Bosnia and Lebanon, children face traumatizing violence on a regular basis (Kocijan-Hercigonja, Rijavec, Marusic, & Hercigonja, 1998). For example, in Sarajevo, where almost 25 percent of all children were wounded in the war, 97 percent of the children interviewed said they had experienced being shelled with bombs, 55 percent said they had been shot at by snipers, and 66 percent said they had been in situations where they thought they would die (UNICEF, 1993). In response to these conditions, 29 percent of the children in Sarajevo said they felt "unbearable sorrow" and 20 percent said they had constant terrifying dreams. In addition to the physical dangers, these children were confronted with other extremely adverse conditions—schools were destroyed, teachers were attacked and killed, food and water became scarce, and families were torn apart. Because of the violence, these children face both physical and psychological risks.

How children respond to community violence depends on their developmental level (Straussner & Straussner, 1997). Because children's ability to control their environment is limited, safety is especially important to them (Garbarino, Dubrow, Kostelny, & Pardo, 1992). The younger the child, the more likely it is that safety issues are critical to her or his well-being (Garbarino, 1999). Children who experience traumatic violence prior to age 11 are three times more likely to have psychological problems (such as depression) than are children who experience such events after age 12 (Davidson & Smith, 1990). Children who experience traumatic violence and have been separated from their families (as is often the case for children in war-torn countries) are particularly susceptible to psychological impairment (Macksoud & Aber, 1996).

Young children often respond to violence with passivity, displaying behaviors typical of younger children. For example, they may become clingy, wet their bed, and show little desire to talk to or be with others. Young children's responses to community violence also may include increased aggression. In one study (Farver & Frosch, 1996), the play behavior of 4-year-old children who lived in the neighborhoods of south-central Los Angeles where the 1992 riots occurred was compared to the behavior of another group of 4-year-olds who were not exposed to the riots. The play behavior of the children exposed to the riots contained more aggressive and unfriendly themes, words, and outcomes than did the play behavior of those children who were not exposed to the riots.

Older children also are vulnerable to community violence, but they respond to it differently than do younger children. Because of their increased ability to understand the dangerous situations they encounter, older children are more likely to recognize the significance of the events that take place around them. School-age children may become aggressive, as well as depressed, and may develop physical complaints, distortions in thought, and learning difficulties as a result of the violence they are exposed to (Garbarino et al., 1992). They also may become increasingly distrustful of others. In Kotlowitz's (1991) description of Lafeyette's response to the violent death of his friend, nicknamed Bird Leg, we see evidence of these kinds of responses:

> Bird Leg's funeral haunted him. He believed he had seen Bird Leg's spirit at a friend's
> apartment. "He was trying to tell us something," he told his mother. . . . His face
> masked his troubles. It was a face without affect, without emotion . . . in Lafeyette
> it conveyed wariness. . . . "I don't have friends," he told his mother. "Just associates.
> Friends you trust."
> —*A. Kotlowitz* (1991, p. 55)

This picture depicts a funeral for a child. How does community violence undermine a child's sense of well-being? How might the responses of children exposed to urban violence relate to those of children in countries at war?

In the United States, exposure to community violence is greater for low-income children, who include a disproportionate number of minority children. According to one estimate (Gladstein, Slater-Rusonis, & Heald, 1992), 42 percent of inner-city African American children had seen someone shot, 25 percent had seen someone stabbed, and 23 percent had seen someone murdered. Hispanic and Native American children in the United States also are exposed to high rates of violence (Soriano, 1994; Yung & Hammond, 1994). For nonminority children, the percentages were half of those above.

One way to feel safe in a violent community is to identify with those who behave violently (Garbarino, 1999). Children growing up in violent communities often model themselves and their behavior on those individuals who cause the violence. In these communities, guns and knives are symbols of status, and their use often is positively reinforced (Bell, 1991). Exposure to violence puts children at risk of becoming violent themselves (Gorman-Smith & Tolan, 1998), feeding back into the cycle of community violence, victimization, and fear.

As discussed earlier, children can be quite resilient in the face of what appears to be overwhelming stress. But children's resilience is not unlimited. For many children, community violence may be "the last straw." Community violence can undermine children's development by providing constant reminders of their vulnerability and of the inability of their families and communities to protect them (Milgram, 1998).

WHAT EMOTIONAL AND PSYCHOLOGICAL DISTURBANCES AFFECT CHILDREN IN LATE CHILDHOOD

Late childhood is a time when emotional and psychological problems often surface, especially in children who lack the skills necessary to cope with their increasingly demanding environments. For example, referrals for mental health services rise rapidly after the age of 5 (Verhulst & Koot, 1995). School-age children's emotional and psychological problems become closely intertwined with their functioning in school, often interfering with their general educational development. Many of the emotional and psychological problems of adolescents and adults are direct outgrowths of disorders that appear during late childhood (Violato & LeRoy, 1995). Some of these problems may be self-correcting and need little intervention beyond that provided by parents or teachers. Others require professional help. Although a wide variety of emotional and psychological disturbances may occur, our discussion will focus on some of the more common problems: antisocial behavior, depression, and fear and anxiety.

ANTISOCIAL BEHAVIOR

A pattern of behavior that is aggressive, defiant, uncooperative, irresponsible, and/or dishonest defines **antisocial behavior** (American Psychiatric Association [APA], 1994). This pattern of behavior is disruptive to the individual, to his or her relationships, and to the community at large. Antisocial children often fail at school and are disliked by peers, teachers, and sometimes even their parents (Frick, 1998). Nearly half of all children referred to clinics for treatment are referred for antisocial behavior (Kazdin, 1989). A history of antisocial behavior as a child is related to a wide array of adult mental health problems, including troubled marriages, failure at work, and crime (Dishion, French, & Patterson, 1995). Antisocial adults tend to rear antisocial children, thus perpetuating the cycle across generations (Patterson & Dishion, 1988; Steinhausen, Meier, & Angst, 1998).

Boys are much more likely than girls to be referred for treatment for antisocial behavior (Dishion et al., 1995; Patterson, Reid, & Dishion, 1998). This phenomenon may be due to higher rates of antisocial behavior in boys, or it may be due to biased perceptions—that is, these kinds of behaviors are expected to occur more often in boys than in girls and therefore may be noticed more often in boys. Gender differences in antisocial behavior become even more apparent during late childhood, in settings that involve peer and school interactions (Sprague, Sugai, & Walker, 1998). For example, teachers generally find boys to be more antisocial than girls, although parents seldom report similar gender differences (Dishion & Andrews, 1996).

Children who are antisocial at early ages are likely to be so in later years (Derzon, 2001; Patterson & Yoerger, 1993). For instance, boys who were identified as aggressive and hostile at age 8 were more likely to be antisocial at age 30 (Huesmann, Eron, Lefkowitz, & Walder, 1984). The evidence of stability for girls is more limited but still considerable (Silverthorn & Frick, 1999).

Antisocial children show a progression of coercive and aversive behaviors across childhood. As toddlers, antisocial children tend to be noncompliant, have frequent temper tantrums, and use physical aggression. As preschoolers, they continue to use these behaviors to coerce parents into letting them have their own way (Patterson, 1982). When children use coercive behaviors to get their way and are successful, the antisocial behavior pattern is reinforced and maintained. School-age children extend their antisocial behavior into the school setting. Teachers report that these children often fight and steal and are disobedient (Patterson et al., 1998). Thus, over the course of a lifetime, antisocial behavior begins in the form of noncompliance with parental requests and frequent temper tantrums; progresses to fighting, stealing, and lying in late childhood; and culminates in noncompliance with authority and law in adolescence and adulthood (Dishion et al., 1995).

Factors Affecting the Development of Antisocial Behavior

Diverse factors influence the development of antisocial behavior. The important influences can be grouped into four categories:

✦ **Biological factors.** Antisocial behavior is partially influenced by biological factors. Studies of identical twins reveal similar life-course patterns of antisocial behavior (Moffitt, 1993). However, the genetic component of antisocial behavior is demonstrated more clearly in adolescents and adults than in children (Plomin, Nitz, & Rowe, 1990). Studies also show that ADHD (see Chapter 9) and certain traits associated with a difficult temperament, such as impulsivity and irritability (see Chapter 6), are related to antisocial behavior patterns (Barkley, 1989;

antisocial behavior a pattern of behavior that is aggressive, defiant, uncooperative, irresponsible, and/or dishonest

Schwartz, Snidman, & Kagan, 1996). Underlying these characteristics may be biochemical factors such as enzymes or neurotransmitters. Some researchers have proposed that antisocial children have an overactive reward system and an underactive inhibition system, resulting in impulsive and reward-seeking behavior (Fowles, 2000). Overactive reward systems and underactive inhibitory systems have been linked to the production of certain biochemicals, such as dopamine (Quay, 1988). However, in almost all of these studies, environmental factors such as the family have been identified as significant influences too (Dishion et al., 1995).

✦ **Family factors.**   Families contribute to children's antisocial behavior (Patterson, 1982; Stern & Smith, 1999). Children who receive little parental supervision are more prone to antisocial behavior than are more closely supervised children, especially in high-risk urban neighborhoods (Shaw & Winslow, 1997). Antisocial behavior also is likely to be found in children who have few opportunities to engage in positive social interactions with parents (Snyder, Schrepferman, & St. Peter, 1997) and in children who observe physical spouse abuse (Jouriles et al., 1998). Having a parent who suffers from a mental illness is related to antisocial behavior too (Patterson et al., 1998); parents who are stressed, depressed, or antisocial generally use ineffective or inappropriate parenting practices, which contribute to antisocial behavior in their children (Belsky, Woodworth, & Crnic, 1996b; Brenner & Fox, 1998). Finally, children identified as insecurely attached (see Chapter 6) are more prone to be antisocial if they come from high-risk backgrounds (Greenberg, Speltz, & DeKlyen, 1993).

✦ **Peer relationships.**   Experiences with peers promote antisocial behavior in three ways. First, children who have poor peer relationships are at risk for antisocial behavior because they lack positive experiences that help them learn how to control their antisocial impulses. Second, peers act as models and reinforcers for antisocial behavior (Laird, Pettit, Dodge, & Bates, 1999). Third, antisocial children sometimes attract one another and form their own groups that then promote antisocial behavior (Dishion et al., 1995).

✦ **Social milieu.**   The degree to which children engage in antisocial behavior depends on their social environment. For example, antisocial behavior is more prevalent in urban than suburban areas and in low-income than middle-class neighborhoods (Crane, 1991). Moreover, the relationship between antisocial behavior and living in a stressful neighborhood increases over time because the stressful effects of such neighborhoods accumulate (Aber, Jones, Brown, Chaudry, & Samples, 1998). Elevated rates of antisocial behavior are found among minority children in the United States (Yung & Hammond, 1997), probably because they most often live in low-income urban areas (McLoyd, 1998b).

Treatments for Antisocial Behavior

Several forms of treatment have been developed for antisocial behavior. Some treatments focus solely on the antisocial children, others on the family, and still others focus on the community. This diversity in emphasis reflects the fact that the treatment of antisocial children often requires the involvement of many people, including parents, peers, teachers, social workers, law enforcement officers, and judges. At present, no single treatment has been found to effectively address antisocial behavior problems (Lane, Beebe, Lambros, & Pierson, 2001). The difficulty of identifying a single effective treatment is due to the multiple causes of antisocial behaviors, representing a complex interplay of individual, family, peer, and societal factors (Reid & Eddy, 1997).

Treatment may include counseling and psychotherapy, behavior modification, family therapy, and, sometimes, medication. Treatment is more successful with children and families who are motivated to receive help. In many cases, however, the motivation is not there. The long-term treatment outcome for children with antisocial behavior problems also depends on the severity of the antisocial behavior. Children whose antisocial behavior is lim-

The child in this picture suffers from depression. Notice the sad and blank look on his face. What are some of the other signs of childhood depression? Can you identify some of the factors that contribute to the development of childhood depression?

ited to minor or isolated antisocial acts respond reasonably well to treatment. In contrast, children with severe and chronic antisocial problems do not respond positively to treatment (Graham, 1986). These findings highlight the importance of identifying ways to prevent antisocial behavior problems from developing (Olds et al., 1998).

CHILDHOOD DEPRESSION

Childhood depression is a serious mental health problem; about 1 in 6 children experiences a depressive disorder at some time during childhood (NIMH, 2000). Among young children, roughly equal numbers of boys and girls are classified as depressed. By the end of late childhood, however, girls outnumber boys 2 to 1 (NIMH, 2000). In the last thirty years, more children than ever before have been identified as depressed, and it is likely that there will be even more in the future as our ability to identify such children increases. To make matters worse, most depressed children do not receive treatment (Mufson & Moreau, 1997).

Childhood depressive disorders are conditions in which children display persistent negative moods and lack of pleasure in life. To be identified as clinically depressed, a child must exhibit four of the following eight symptoms on an almost daily basis (APA, 1994):

- significant weight loss or weight gain
- insomnia (inability to sleep) or hypersomnia (oversleeping)
- motor agitation or retardation
- loss of interest or pleasure in usual activities
- fatigue or loss of energy
- feelings of worthlessness or excessive guilt
- impairment in thinking or concentrating
- reoccurring thoughts of suicide

Symptoms of depression vary with age. Because young children have difficulty verbally expressing their feelings of depression, depression is more often inferred from their behavior. Depressed infants and preschoolers may spend much of their time crying or rocking. They may refuse food and sleep poorly. Although no physical abnormalities can be found, these young children may fail to thrive and are fretful, insecure, and clearly unhappy (Kaslow, Morris, & Rehm, 1998). Before age 6, children express their depression almost entirely through sadness without the guilt or loss of self-esteem that typically accompanies older children's depression (Bemporad, 1994).

By the age of 6 or 7 years, children begin to describe their emotional state somewhat as adults do—they refer to themselves as being sad or miserable. By 7 or 8 years, depressed children experience a devalued view of themselves. Additionally, they may believe that their future holds little to be positive about—something young children have difficulty doing because of their focus on the here-and-now.

Although older children describe feelings of depression better than young children do, they may not admit to such feelings readily. Instead, they may display psychosomatic symptoms, especially headaches or stomachaches that result from emotional distress. They may complain of being bored or uninterested in activities. All children complain sometimes about being bored, but nondepressed children do so only when they have nothing to do. In contrast, depressed children are likely to say they are bored most of the time. Additionally, depressed children generally are not well engaged with school or with learning and thus have lower grades and academic achievement (Barrett & Waterfield, 1997). Depressed children may be irritable, withdrawn, and unable to cope with even minor frustrations. As a result, depression tends to be more prolonged and enduring in older children than in young children (Kashani, Rosenberg, & Reid, 1989).

Factors Affecting the Development of Childhood Depression

The causes of depression in children are not well understood, partly because childhood depression is not well defined and partly because we are just beginning to grasp its complexity. Despite these problems, the causes of depression can be grouped into three categories relating to biology, temperament, and social relationships.

✦ **Genetic and biological factors.**   Several kinds of scientific evidence suggest that there is a genetic component to depression (Goodyear, 2001). Depressive symptoms are more common in children who have a history of depression in the family (Grabill, Griffith, & Kaslow, 2001; Puig-Antich et al., 1989). Additionally, the chance that a depressive disorder diagnosed in one twin is shared by the other was found to be about 50 percent for identical twins, compared to only about 25 percent for fraternal twins (Nurcombe, 1994). Other evidence points to the role of neurochemistry—the chemistry of the brain. Neurochemicals such as serotonin and norepinephrine have powerful effects on emotional states in adults and adolescents and are implicated in some types of childhood depression (Emslie, Weinberg, Kennard, & Kowatch, 1994).

✦ **Temperament.**   In the discussion of temperament in Chapter 6, you learned that some children are predisposed to react more intensely and with greater negative moods than others. Thus, some children possess temperamental qualities that may predispose them to depression (Merikangas, Swendsen, Preisig, & Chazan, 1998). Children who are quiet and avoidant, slow to adapt to new situations, and prone to negative moods are likely to become depressed if they are stressed (Lengua, West, & Sandler, 1998; Thomas, Chess, & Birch, 1968). Children with difficult temperaments also are prone to feelings of hopelessness and low self-esteem (Bemporad, 1994).

✦ **Family and social factors.**   Children who are depressed often live in circumstances where they are undervalued or rejected. Parents who are emotionally unavailable to their children (perhaps because they themselves are depressed) or are critical and rejecting put their children at risk for depression (Nilzon & Palmerus, 1997). Children who are suffering abuse also are at risk for depression; however, children with a history of past abuse are no more likely to be depressed than are nonabused children (Kazdin, Moser, Colbus, & Bell, 1985). Children who have poor social skills and difficulty establishing meaningful relationships with others are prone to depression (Parker & Asher, 1987). Childhood depression also is associated with stressful life events, such as the loss of a parent (Goodyear, Kolvin, & Gatzanis, 1985). These findings suggest that depression in children is often dependent on the social situations in which they find themselves (Beardslee & Gladstone, 2001; Boyce et al., 1998).

Treatments for Childhood Depression

Most children with depression (about two-thirds) improve substantially following treatment (Stark, Rouse, & Kurowski, 1994). Unfortunately, a significant number remain depressed for a considerable period of time. Treatment of childhood depression takes many forms, depending on the specific symptoms, the age of the child, and the cause of the depression. Reducing stressors that affect children can relieve their depression. Children who are depressed because of repeated failure at school may benefit from individualized instruction, tutoring, positive feedback, activities that promote peer acceptance and self-esteem, and counseling. Although these measures may not be sufficient on their own, they are worth pursuing (Graham, 1986).

Intervention provided by counselors or therapists can help children and their families cope with depression (Schwartz, Kaslow, Racusin, & Carton, 1998). For children who have little prior experience with or knowledge of events that cause depression (such as the loss of a family member), facilitating communication within the family can help. Once children understand that other family members too are affected by the loss, they can identify with them and share the burden of the loss. Also, helping children develop a better self-concept and more self-esteem can be useful in treating depression (Stark et al., 1994).

Antidepressant medications generally are used only for seriously depressed children and are only modestly effective (Wagner & Ambrosini, 2001). These medications were not developed for children, and there are few studies on their safe use with children. Many of these drugs have negative side effects such as nausea, dizziness, headache, or insomnia (Johnston & Fruehling, 1994). Children's use of antidepressants should be closely monitored by doctors and caregivers.

Young children are afraid of animals, imaginary creatures, the dark, and robbers. What kinds of things most often scare school-age children? What accounts for these changes?

CHILDREN'S FEARS

The emotions of fear and anxiety evolved as warning signals and a way of mobilizing thought and action in response to psychological or physical dangers. Some causes of fear and anxiety are common to us all. Gray (1971) classified these as **innate fears**—fears that are inborn and reflexive. Innate fears are caused by intense stimuli (loud noises or severe pain), novelty (strange places and people), signals of danger (high places or darkness), and threatening or aggressive social interactions. People also instinctually fear being alone and being approached suddenly (Bowlby, 1973). Many day-to-day fears are extensions of these innate fears. Children's fear of ghosts or monsters, for example, may be an extension of the natural fear of darkness. Some fears are learned from others. For instance, children may come to fear snakes if their parents react fearfully toward snakes.

In early childhood, fears that were common in infancy—such as fear of strangers or separation—decrease, while other fears increase. Classic studies of children's fears have shown that fear of animals, imaginary creatures, the dark, being left alone, death, and robbers all increase during the preschool years (Jersild & Holmes, 1935; Macfarlane, Allen, & Honzik, 1954). School-age children are less likely to fear imaginary things that look scary, but they are more likely to fear real-life events such as being attacked, being injured in an airplane crash, or going on a roller coaster (Bauer, 1976). Early experience with diminished control fosters a vulnerability to fear (Chorpita & Barlow, 1998).

Between 7 and 8 years of age, as children master the concept of causality, they begin to fear things that might harm them. In addition, as children realize the importance of achievement and begin comparing themselves to others, they come to fear or worry about performing poorly or failing. Because school-age children tend to internalize negative experiences and information, their self-concept is more easily threatened than that of a younger child, leading to increased fear that their abilities are inadequate (Thompson, 1990).

Young children express fear by crying or looking sad or uncomfortable. During later childhood, children resist crying when they are scared (Izard, 1977). Throughout childhood, girls are more likely to express fear than boys are (Silverman, La Greca, & Wasserstein, 1995).

Children's Phobias

Although most children fear something specific, some children develop extreme fears, or **phobias**—persistent and irrational fears that significantly affect their social functioning (APA, 1994; Muris & Merckelbach, 2001). Only about 3 to 5 percent of children have phobias, although girls consistently report more extreme fears than boys do (Strauss & Francis, 1989). It is not clear, however, if the higher rate of fear and phobic reactions for girls reflects greater fearfulness among girls or simply a greater willingness of girls and their parents to express such fears.

One of the most common phobias of late childhood is **school phobia,** an extreme fear associated with school environments (Elliott, 1999). Because children with this extreme fear typically refuse to attend school, school phobias cause considerable disruption to their academic and social functioning (Jenni, 1997). The frequent absenteeism of children with school phobia can cause them to fall behind in their coursework and then to lose contact with their peers if they have to repeat a grade. Thus, such fears can have long-term consequences. Compared to their nonphobic peers, children with school phobias have poorer psychological functioning as adults (Flakierska-Praquin, Lindstroem, & Gillberg, 1997).

Children with school phobias need to be distinguished from nonphobic children who simply do not like school and want to avoid it for that reason. School-age children often express a lack of interest in school or a dislike for school, but they do not have the extreme and dysfunctional anxiety that children with school phobias have. Children with temporary fear or anxiety because of a change or transition in schooling, such as going to a new school for the first time, are not considered school phobic. Refusal to go to school because of separa-

innate fears fears that are inborn and reflexive

phobias persistent and irrational fears that significantly affect social functioning

school phobia an extreme fear associated with school environments

tion anxiety is not considered a part of school phobia. In separation anxiety responses, children avoid school out of fear of being separated from a caregiver or from home rather than fear of the school environment itself. Children who refuse to go to school because of separation anxiety also usually show distress in other situations where they must be separated from the caregiver, such as visiting a friend's house without the caregiver (Strauss & Francis, 1989).

Treatments for Children's Phobias

Several effective techniques have been developed to treat children's phobic responses. The most widely used treatment method is modeling, in which the fearful child first observes someone else approaching a feared object or situation and then attempts that same approach. Modeling is particularly effective if the approach to the feared object or situation is gradual (Morris & Kratcochwill, 1998).

For school-age children, who have more advanced cognitive skills, cognitive techniques for treating childhood phobias may be effective (Last, Hansen, & Franco, 1998). Enhancing children's perceptions of control and competence—for example, training them to tell themselves "I am a brave boy" or "I am a brave girl"—helps them cope with fear-inducing events (Cortez & Bugental, 1995; Kanfer, Karoly, & Newman, 1975).

The age of the child when the phobia began is important both in selecting treatment and in predicting outcomes. For young children who experience an abrupt onset of school phobia, the most effective treatment approach is to get the child to return to school as quickly as possible. In contrast, for older children with a lengthy history of school phobia, the most effective treatment approach is a gradual one (Strauss & Francis, 1989).

HOW DO CHILDREN'S FAMILY RELATIONSHIPS CHANGE DURING LATE CHILDHOOD?

Although the family continues to play a significant role in school-age children's development, important changes take place that modify the nature of that role. The new abilities and competencies that develop during late childhood affect how children respond to their parents and how their parents respond to them. When 7- and 10-year-old children were asked to identify the ten most important individuals in their lives, 80 percent included their mother and 79 percent included their father (Bryant, 1985). Siblings and other relatives also were important. Nonrelated peers appeared in the top 10 list 72 percent of the time, and 23 percent of the children identified at least one nonrelated adult in their top 10 list.

REDUCED PARENT-CHILD INTERACTION

As children enter late childhood, there is a decline in the amount of time they spend with their parents and in the amount of time their parents devote to them. Compared with parents of preschool-aged children, parents of school-age children spend less than half as much time caring for, teaching, reading to, talking with, and playing with their children (Hill & Stafford, 1980). The drop in amount of interaction is greater among parents with less education (Maccoby, 1984).

Children's social interactions also change over the course of late childhood, becoming centered on activities that are beyond the context of the family. Figure 10.1 on page 330 displays the percentages of their time that school-age children devote to different activities. As you can see in this figure, children spend a considerable amount of time (44 percent) involved in activities outside of the family—school, job/school activities, and socializing. Direct family interaction accounts for only 6 percent of their daily activities (Larson & Richards, 1994). How the time is spent at home also changes. Older children spend more time studying, watching television, and performing chores or housework, whereas young children spend more time playing (Bryant, 1985).

FIGURE 10.1

How School-Age Children Spend Their Time: Average Daily Percentages of Waking Hours

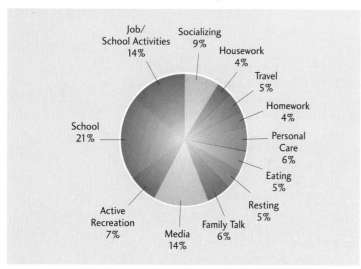

SOURCE: From DIVERGENT REALITIES by REED LARSON and MARYSE H. RICHARDS. Copyright © 1994 by Reed Larson and Maryse Richards. Reprinted by permission of Basic Books, a member of Perseus Books Group, L.L.C.

According to this figure, school, jobs, media, and socializing account for a large part of school-age children's daily activities. How do the ways children spend their time change as they grow older? What factors account for these trends?

FIGURE 10.2

Labor Force Participation of Women: 1950–1998

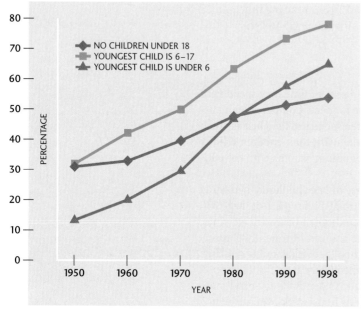

SOURCE: Hayghe, 1997; US Census Bureau, 2001b.

These changes reflect issues relevant to American and other Western cultures. In many non-Western societies, the period of late childhood is when children enter the work force and begin contributing to the necessary functions of the family by assuming tasks such as caring for younger children or tending animals or crops. For example, in Kumasi, one of the leading market cities in central Ghana, it is common for 8- or 9-year-old children to participate in the local trade, selling goods on their own and contributing the proceeds to family needs (Clark, 1994). In societies like that of Kumasi, most of the issues that occupy Western parents and children are of little relevance.

REDUCED PARENTAL SUPERVISION

Today's parents supervise their children less than parents did in the past. The decreased amount of supervision provided by parents comes at a cost. School-age children who are not well supervised by their parents are more likely to engage in antisocial and delinquent behaviors than are children who are well supervised (Dishion et al., 1995). Adequate parental supervision deters such behaviors.

Economic conditions have contributed to the change in parental roles. Parental supervision has been reduced in part because of the increased participation of mothers in the paid work force. Figure 10.2 illustrates how the number of women in the work force grew between 1950 and 1998. As you can see in this figure, labor force participation by women is greatest among mothers of school-age children and has risen steadily since 1950. Although many families prefer to have a parent available to supervise children, few families can afford to forgo the additional income brought in when both parents work outside the home. Also, more women are now single mothers who must earn an income to provide for their children. And fewer families than in the past have access to extended family members who can provide after-school supervision. For these reasons, school-age children are increasingly likely to come home from school to a household where the mother and father are still at work. According to one estimate (Hafer, 1995), nearly 5 million school-age children spend time after school without adult supervision during a typical week.

The phrase **latchkey children** is used to describe children who are left unsupervised during the day or return home to an empty house after school. Each day, about 1.6 million school-age children in the United States are latchkey children (Casper, Hawkins, & O'Connell, 1994). About 20 percent of 6- to 12-year-olds spend at least some time caring for themselves (Urban Institute, 2000).

Age is an important predictor of whether children are left to care for themselves. As you can see in Figure 10.3, as children get older, they are more likely to come home to an empty house. By the time a child reaches the teenage years, he or she is two to three times more likely to be a latchkey child than is a younger child (US Census Bureau, 1996). Suburban children are about twice as likely to be latchkey children as are children living either in a city or in a rural area. This may be because suburban parents feel safer in their neighborhoods or because they can rely on their neighbors to a greater extent than can people who live in cities or rural areas (Casper et al., 1994).

Latchkey children are more likely than well-supervised children to be truant from school, feel stressed, receive poor grades, engage in risky behaviors, and use alcohol or tobacco (Dwyer et al., 1990). Such problems are particularly likely to arise when children are unsupervised and their parents do not know their whereabouts (Shulman, Kedem, Kaplan, Sever, & Braja, 1998; Steinberg, 1986). In contrast, enrollment in after-school care programs is associated with good grades and good peer relationships (Posner & Vandell, 1994). Thus, formal after-school care and supervision for children whose parents are not at home when they get out of school has the potential to protect children from possibly detrimental environments (Garbarino et al., 1992), particularly if the program is of high quality (Rosenthal & Vandell, 1996).

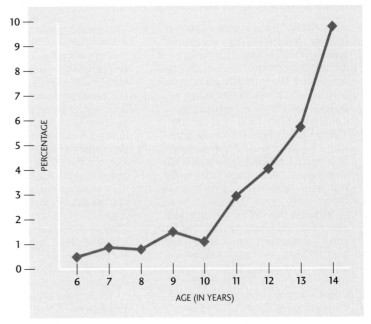

FIGURE 10.3

Percentage of Children Who Are Latchkey Children, by Age

SOURCE: US Census Bureau, 1996.

Notice the dramatic increase in the number of children older than 10 who are left alone after school. What developmental changes might contribute to parents' willingness to allow older children to take care of themselves after school? How does lack of supervision relate to children's behavior problems?

INCREASED IMPORTANCE OF SIBLING RELATIONSHIPS

Sibling relationships change during late childhood. By the time children enter school, those who have siblings spend considerably more time with them than they spend with their parents (Brody, 1998). According to one estimate, one-third of siblings share a room, 25 percent share chores, and 50 percent report that playing with their siblings is a central activity (Bryant, 1982). During late childhood, siblings increasingly compare themselves to one another, and it is through these comparisons that siblings learn how they are different from one another. An age gap of 2 to 4 years heightens the differences between siblings (Dunn, 1983). Thus, sibling relationships provide children with opportunities to learn about themselves (Updegraff & Obeidallah, 1999).

Older siblings often take on some of the functions that parents serve, sometimes providing caretaking, comforting, and support. But does sibling caretaking substitute for parental caretaking? At least in the United States, the answer appears to be no. Sibling caretaking lacks the richness and complexity of the care provided by parents (Bryant, 1992). For instance, when children go to parents and to siblings to discuss emotionally stressful experiences, parents suggest more coping strategies than do siblings. Siblings may provide support or comfort, but it is not comparable to that provided by parents or other adult caregivers.

Many children return from school to an empty home. What do these children do while they wait for their parents to return home? In what ways do parents try to overcome the problems associated with lack of supervision and stimulation for these children?

latchkey children children who are left unsupervised during the day or return home to an empty house after school

ONLY CHILDREN

Early in the twentieth century, the famous developmental psychologist G. Stanley Hall (see Chapter 1) was quoted as saying, "Being an only child is a disease in itself" (Fenton, 1928, p. 547). At that time, not having siblings was thought to be a type of social deprivation for children and was considered to have detrimental effects on their social development. The

THE SCIENTIFIC IMPACT: INTERPRETING RESEARCH

How Can Public Policy Affect Children and Families?

In mainland China, overpopulation is a concern. In 1998, China's population was over 1.25 billion, making up almost 21 percent of the world's population. As a result, family planning was proclaimed a fundamental state policy—one that was necessary if China was to progress in social and economic development. China established a goal of reducing its population to under 1.2 billion by the year 2000 and made plans to reach this goal by restricting families to having only one child.

Begun in the 1970s, the one-child policy has had mixed results. The birth rate dropped from a high of 40.6 births per 1000 people in 1964 to less than 20 (van der Heijden, 1996). In addition, the average number of births to Chinese women of child-bearing age dropped from four in 1970 to two (Heinemann, 1995). One-child couples account for about 70 percent of the total married populations of the larger cities and provinces. The policy has been less successful, however, in the rural areas. The reality for the Chinese people is that the average yearly increase in population must remain under 1 percent (Jiao, Ji, & Jing, 1986). As of 1998, population growth in

China was right at this critical rate (United Nations, 1998).

The policy has led to an increase in female infanticide and adoptions (as many rural couples still prefer boys) and between 5 and 10 million unregistered births per year. In addition, the policy may be contributing to a change in the culture's attitudes about children and childbearing (Heinemann, 1995).

Since the 1970s, urban Chinese couples who have become parents have known from the beginning of their child's life that she or he will be their only child. Knowing this, do Chinese parents treat their only child differently than American parents do? For example, do they indulge or protect their only child more than American parents do?

The limited evidence from China is inconsistent. There is some evidence that Chinese children with siblings are more cooperative and popular than are only children (Jiao et al., 1986) and have fewer behavior problems (Wang, Oakland, & Liu, 1992). Still other evidence fails to find any differences between Chinese only children and those who have siblings (Falbo & Poston, 1993). Findings also vary across provinces and for urban and

rural children (Falbo, 1992). Even when differences are found, it is difficult to know exactly what the reasons for the differences are. For example, in one study, only children were physically larger than those with siblings (Polit & Falbo, 1987). This finding may suggest that only children in China have better diets than children with siblings, who may have to share and who do not enjoy the rewards parents receive for having only one child. Additionally, findings reveal that the value Chinese parents place on the only-child policy influences their adherence to it and the possible effects it may have on their children (Jing & Wan, 1997).

Thinking It Through:

1. What are the demographic and cultural contexts that encouraged the adoption of China's one-child policy?
2. What are some consequences of this policy for Chinese children's development?
3. Based on your own or another's personal experiences, what do you think are some disadvantages and advantages of being an only child?

popular stereotype calls for an only child to be spoiled, insensitive, socially awkward, and egocentric. The research evidence, however, suggests that this belief is more popular myth than scientific fact (Richards & Goodman, 1996).

When findings from many studies were summarized, only children and children with siblings differed in just two out of sixteen ways (Polit & Falbo, 1987). Only children scored higher than children with siblings on motivation to achieve and on self-esteem. Only children were just as likely as children with siblings to be resourceful, popular, self-reliant, and successful in their relationships as children and adults (Blake, 1989; Dawson, 1991). Despite G. Stanley Hall's concern about the detrimental effects of being an only child, there appear to be few differences between only children and those who have siblings (Falbo, 1992).

WHAT FACTORS INFLUENCE SCHOOL-AGE CHILDREN'S PEER RELATIONSHIPS?

With the increase in recent years in the numbers of working mothers and single-parent families, children today enter into peer groups earlier and for longer periods of time than their predecessors did. Peer relationships may therefore play a more important role today than they did in earlier times (Asher, 1990). The period of late childhood is a critical time for the development of these peer relationships. As you learned in Chapter 8, friendships become more stable and significant during late childhood, and children spend more time with their peers and friends. Most of this time is spent playing or socializing with peers. As school-age children develop more advanced social, emotional, and cognitive skills, they become more adept at communicating with peers, understanding peers' behaviors and intentions, and coordinating their actions with those of others. Peer relationships also are important for children with disabilities, because peer relationships offer a context in which these children become valued members of a social circle (Salisbury & Palombaro, 1998). Thus, peer relationships represent important resources for children's successful adjustment (Ladd & Kochenderfer, 1998).

During late childhood, stable social groups emerge. By age 10 or 11, children report that most of their peer interactions take place in the context of these groups (Parker, Rubin, Price, & De Rosier, 1995). Although most children report being a member of a group, some do not, and those children who do not have good peer relationships are at risk for a variety of problem behaviors (Bagwell, Newcomb, & Bukowski, 1998; Rubin, Bukowski, & Parker, 1998).

PEER REJECTION

Most children find interacting with peers rewarding and satisfying. Unfortunately, though, for some children, peer relationships are difficult, painful, and unsatisfying.

The number of children who have serious peer relationship problems during the school years varies depending on the group that is assessed. In general, however, among average-achieving elementary school children, about 10 to 15 percent do not have any friends (Parker et al., 1995). But not all children who lack friends are the same. Two types of unpopular children have been identified. The first type is referred to as **rejected children**—those who are overtly disliked by their peers. The second type is referred to as **neglected children**—those who are reasonably well liked even though they lack friends. When children are asked to rate how much they like to play with other children, they like neglected children as much as they like most other children but do not like or want to play with rejected children (Asher, Rose, & Gabriel, 2001; Rubin et al., 1998). Rejected children are unpopular for long periods of time, and their status rarely changes. In contrast, neglected children's popularity and status may change from time to time or from situation to situation (Asher, 1990). Thus, rejected children have enduring difficulties in their peer relationships, whereas neglected children usually do not.

Additionally, rejected and neglected children have different emotional experiences with peers. Rejected children are more likely than neglected children to be lonely and feel victimized (McDougall, Hymel, Vaillancourt, & Mercer, 2001). When rejected and neglected children were asked if they would like to learn how to get along better with their peers, 48 percent of the rejected children said they would but only 16 percent of the neglected said they would (Asher, Zelis, Parker, & Bruene, 1991). Rejected children are more isolated than neglected children and therefore more emotionally distressed by poor peer relationships.

The research evidence suggests that certain behavioral, personality, and cognitive tendencies contribute to children's being rejected or neglected (Parker et al., 1995). For instance, rejected children are likely to be aggressive (Coie, Dodge, Terry, & Wright, 1991) or depressed (Little & Garber, 1995). Neglected children have poor social skills and may be shy or withdrawn.

These findings suggest that different strategies are needed to improve rejected and neglected children's peer relationships. For rejected children, an important aim of intervention is to reduce the aggressive and disruptive nature of their peer interactions (Waas & Graczyk, 1998). Roughly half of all rejected children are characterized as behaving in ways that interfere with the smooth functioning of the peer group (French, 1988). Altering the consequences for aggressive and disruptive behavior (such as removing any reinforcement received for such behaviors) and teaching self-control strategies (such as recognizing anger cues) can help rejected children generate more adaptive solutions to anger-arousing sit-

rejected children children who are overtly disliked by their peers

neglected children children who are reasonably well liked by their peers but lack friends

uations (Coie & Koeppl, 1990). For neglected children, helping them develop social skills that enhance the initiation and maintenance of peer interactions (such as teaching them effective skills for communicating) can improve their status among their peers (Mize & Ladd, 1990).

DEVELOPMENT OF SOCIAL COMPETENCE

The discussion of rejected and neglected children points out that some children are more skilled at making friends than others are. Popular children find it easy to make friends and influence playmates, manage conflicts, and make peers want to be with them. Other children lack these skills and, as a result, are isolated or excluded from peer relationships.

The term **social competence** refers to a child's ability to use age-appropriate social behaviors to enhance peer relationships without harming anyone (Schneider, 1993). Notice that this definition emphasizes that social competence is a developmental concept; what is socially competent at one stage of development may not be socially competent at another. Social competence is measured by the degree to which a child is accepted by his or her peers and the degree to which this acceptance is based on social behaviors that do not harm anyone. Teasing another child to gain the admiration of peers, for example, would not be considered a socially competent behavior because of the harm that is done to the child who is teased.

Social competence requires skills that foster smooth and satisfying interactions. Existing research demonstrates that socially competent children are skilled in at least four areas in which their less competent peers are not:

◆ **Initiating social interactions.**   Socially competent children initiate new relationships more gracefully than less competent children. For example, socially competent children are adept at gaining entry into an existing peer group without being rejected (Rydell, Hagekull, & Bohlin, 1997). They integrate themselves into a group in ways that do not disrupt the ongoing activity (Dodge, Pettit, McClaskey, & Brown, 1986). Socially competent children also are more confident of their social skills and keep trying to make friends, even if they do not always succeed (Putallaz & Wasserman, 1990).

◆ **Maintaining social interactions.**   Once they form relationships, socially competent children are successful at maintaining them (Creasey, Jarvis, & Berk, 1998). They smile at, attend to, and comply with others more than do children who have less social competence. They also are more helpful and less aggressive than children with less social competence (Denham et al., 2001; Parker et al., 1995).

◆ **Managing conflicts.**   Socially competent children settle disputes effectively, without damaging their relationships. They are assertive but also recognize the importance of sharing and taking turns. In contrast, children low in social competence attempt to resolve conflicts with behaviors such as fighting, throwing a temper tantrum, or sulking and are less likely to suggest alternative ways of dealing with conflicts (Murphy & Eisenberg, 1996).

◆ **Communicating for social purposes.**   Socially competent children have well-developed communication skills (Farmer, 1997). They express themselves effectively and are good listeners. Because speech and language are important prerequisites of social competence, children with speech or language deficiencies or impairments often have low social competence (Rice, Hadley, & Alexander, 1993) and poor peer relations (Guralnick, Connor, Hammond, Gottman, & Kinnish, 1996). Basic conversation and communication skills are necessary for initiating and maintaining positive social interactions with peers (Black & Hazen, 1990; Hadley & Schuele, 1995).

social competence the ability to use age-appropriate social behaviors to enhance peer relationships without harming anyone

Children's social competence is influenced by a variety of factors. Children who are adaptable and positive and have well-regulated temperaments are more socially skilled than are children who are more temperamentally difficult (Eisenberg & Fabes, 1992; Eisenberg et al., 2001). Children who have secure attachments with caregivers are more likely to form friendships and be popular with other children (Elicker, Englund, & Sroufe, 1992). In contrast, children whose parents are uninvolved and use harsh and inconsistent discipline tend to be low in social competence (Travillion & Snyder, 1993).

Children who violate common expectations may be at risk for low popularity and low social competence. As you learned in Chapter 8, children generally play with same-sex peers, and violations of this pattern may have serious consequences for children. During late childhood, elaborate rules and rituals surround other-sex interaction. In general, contact with members of the other sex in public settings evokes negative reactions (Thorne & Luria, 1986). Children often claim to be infected by the "germs" of the opposite sex (sometimes called *cooties*) and are teased for playing with someone of the other sex. Research shows that children who frequently cross gender boundaries in inappropriate ways have relatively low levels of social competence and are unpopular with peers (Sroufe, Bennett, Englund, & Urban, 1993).

The living conditions children experience influence their level of social competence. Children who are low in social competence are likely to experience adverse living conditions or to have experienced a negative life event recently (Patterson, Griesler, Vaden, & Kupersmidt, 1992). Rejected children are likely to come from single-parent, low-income, unstimulating homes and are likely to have experienced stressful events in their families and schools. The more of these factors children experienced, the greater the chances that their social competence was adversely affected. For example, in one study (Patterson, Vaden, & Kupersmidt, 1991), the percentage of children who were rejected rose from 18 percent of children who had no risk factors to almost 75 percent of those who experienced at least five risk factors. These findings point out that the stress of certain conditions and events can undermine children's social competence and their ability to form positive peer relationships.

During late childhood, peers play an increasingly important role in social and emotional development. Notice the exuberance of emotions displayed by the child in this picture. What factors contribute to positive peer relationships at this stage?

HOW DOES SCHOOL AFFECT SOCIAL AND EMOTIONAL DEVELOPMENT IN LATE CHILDHOOD?

The most widely recognized function of school is to provide children with basic intellectual skills such as the abilities to read, write, and do arithmetic. A less frequently discussed, but equally important, function is to further children's social and emotional development. Children must learn to cooperate with teachers and other children and to deal with a diverse population of peers (Ryan, Adams, Gullotta, Weissberg, & Hampton, 1995).

INFLUENCE OF THE SCHOOL ENVIRONMENT

About 98 percent of children between the ages of 5 and 17 are enrolled in school, and this rate has held steady since the 1960s (National Center for Education Statistics, 1998). Classes generally are organized with a single teacher, usually female, in charge of 20 to 30 same-aged students. The total enrollment for many schools often exceeds several hundred children.

As indicated in Figure 10.4 on page 336, the proportion of the school enrollment made up of ethnic minority students has increased. Thus, when children enter school today, they face an ethnically diverse environment, which provides both opportunities and challenges. Exposure to other children's personalities, values, behaviors, and customs requires new coping and interactional skills (Eisenberg et al., 1997). Because classmates tend to stay together from year to year, acceptance into the peer group becomes important, and not being accepted by one's schoolmates has negative consequences that can last for years (Parker et al., 1995).

The functioning and structure of the classroom affect children's emotional and social development. The classroom generally is task-oriented—daily classroom activities revolve around specific objectives. Preset performance standards are in place, and children's abilities to meet these standards vary. This structure focuses the attention of both the teacher and the students on differences in abilities and motivation, making competition and comparisons more likely than they were before children began school (Carlo, Fabes, Laible, & Kupanoff,

IGURE 10.4

School Enrollments of Children 5 to 17 Years Old, by Ethnicity: 1979–1999

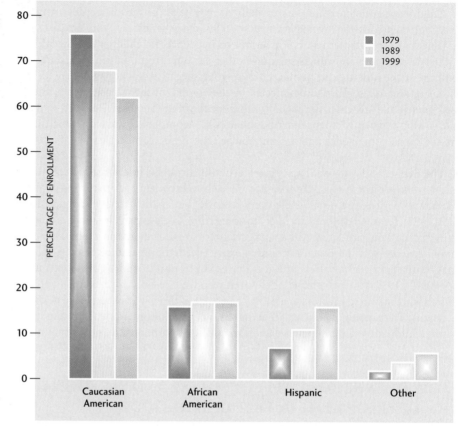

SOURCE: Adapted from US Census Bureau, 2001e.

Notice the increase in the school enrollments of ethnic minorities. What changes account for these increases? What impact might these increases have on schools?

1999). As you learned earlier in this chapter, the increased competition and focus on school performance sometimes cause fear and anxiety in children. But these pressures also produce feelings of pride and satisfaction when a school task is done well.

Children's responses to the increased demands of the school environment vary. Some children underestimate their school abilities, and they may undermine their own achievement by limiting their efforts in school, avoiding schoolwork, and spending extra time in other activities (such as music or sports). Focusing on nonacademic activities helps some children maintain a positive sense of self-worth (Paris & Cunningham, 1996). Other students, however, generalize their low perceptions of competence to other areas of achievement and may drop out or engage in antisocial behavior. Parents and teachers can unwittingly contribute to children's low perceptions of competence by overemphasizing grades, achievement, and social comparisons as a basis for self-worth (Covington, 1992).

Other children form a different kind of school-related misperception about themselves: despite low or merely average school achievement, they have an extremely positive view of their school competence. This pattern appears in some inner-city minority students who have positive views of their competence and achievement even though they make low test grades (Stevenson, Chen, & Uttal, 1990). Such "illusions of competence" may result from unchallenging curricula or inflated praise by teachers and parents. Children with optimistic illusions may reduce their efforts and thereby lower their future achievement. Students who have an excessively pessimistic or optimistic view of their own competence, as a result of

THE SOCIAL IMPACT: DEBATING THE ISSUE

Are Schools Safe?

Most Americans agree that schools should provide a safe environment for students. Feeling secure and safe enhances children's social and academic competence and increases their motivation to go to school. After the tragic events in 1999 at Columbine High School in Littleton, Colorado, it is clear that crime and victimization in the schools pose serious threats to students' and teachers' well-being. In the United States, an estimated 2.7 million violent crimes take place annually at or near schools (National Center for Education Statistics, 2001b). A large majority (71 percent) of students report having knowledge of someone's being bullied, physically attacked, or robbed at school, and more than half (56 percent) indicate that they witnessed such victimization (National Center for Education Statistics, 1995). In addition, most students (approximately 70 percent) report that drugs are easy to obtain at school (National Center for Education Statistics, 1998). In response to these kinds of statistics, most adults favor a zero-tolerance weapon and

drug policy in schools (Gallup Organization, 1997), and such policies have reduced violence at schools. Importantly, children are twice as likely to be victims of violent crime away from school as at school (National Center for Education Statistics, 2001b).

Attending school in an environment where disturbing and fearful events happen has an impact on students' sense of security. In one survey (National Center for Education Statistics, 2001b), worries about becoming a victim at school were found to be more common among middle and junior high school students (23 percent) than among senior high school students (16 percent). Threats of victimization and crime had motivated many students to develop strategies for avoiding harm. Students indicated that they took special routes to school, avoided certain parts of the school building or school grounds, stayed away from school-related events, stayed in groups while at school, or skipped school because they worried that someone might hurt or bother them. Minority

children were more likely than non-minority children to indicate that they would stay away from school or school events to avoid being victimized. Although students develop coping strategies for dealing with victimization in school, this diverts energy that they could be using to play and learn.

Thinking It Through:

1. How do children's concerns about their personal safety affect their motivation to attend school? What coping strategies do children develop to feel safe?
2. Did you feel safe in elementary school and junior high school? Recall events in which you were threatened or victimized by peers. How did these experiences affect you and your relationships with others? How did the experiences interfere with your schooling?
3. What do you think can be done to improve school safety?

their experiences in school, may not invest appropriate effort in academic work and may have difficulty dealing with feedback that is not consistent with their perceptions of themselves (Paris & Cunningham, 1996).

With age, children's understanding of school becomes more complex and complete (Buchanan-Barrow & Barrett, 1998). As they acquire a better understanding of school and its demands, they also learn a great deal about self-control. To become effective students, children must plan, evaluate, monitor, and revise their actions as they adapt to the demands of the school environment. Children who cannot or do not make these adjustments are at risk for poor school outcomes (Nicholls, 1992).

INFLUENCE OF TEACHER-CHILD RELATIONSHIPS

Teachers act as role models, caregivers, and mentors for children. Relationships between teachers and children have important effects on children's social and emotional development and their adaptation to the school environment. For example, children who have warm, secure, and positive relationships with teachers are more cognitively and socially competent (Howes, Matheson, & Hamilton, 1994; Pianta & Nimetz, 1991). Sometimes, the quality of teacher-child relationships is more predictive of a child's behavior than is the quality of the child's relationships with his or her parents (Howes et al., 1994).

Teachers can have a significant influence on children's social development. This influence can be quite positive, encouraging feelings of competence and well-being. For example, teachers have been found to enhance positive outcomes for students if they (1) reduce the tendency of students to compare themselves with one another, (2) use cooperative interaction strategies in the classroom, (3) promote beliefs about students' competencies rather

In addition to helping students with their coursework, how can teachers promote children's learning? What factors influence how teachers respond to different children?

than their deficiencies, (4) increase chances for students to be successful, and (5) are warm, encouraging, and supportive (Shuell, 1996; Stipek, 1997). How teachers respond to and influence their students depends on many factors:

✦ **Children's behaviors.**   Teachers generally respond more positively to students who achieve, conform, and are agreeable and compliant. They give attention to students who make demands that are appropriate to classroom activities, but they are indifferent to students who are silent or withdrawn. Teachers also may reject children who make many demands they consider illegitimate or who present behavior problems (Minuchin & Shapiro, 1983; Zimmerman, 1998).

✦ **Children's racial, ethnic, and socioeconomic backgrounds.**   Teachers sometimes stereotype children on the basis of race, culture, and social class. For example, teachers may attribute failure in school to a child's class or ethnic background (Persell, 1993; Weinstein, 1998). Some teachers expect less from lower-class and minority children, even when these children have abilities similar to those of other children. Teachers act more positively toward students they hold in high esteem, and they spend more time interacting with students whom they expect to work hard and achieve more (Demaray & Elliot, 1998). Because teachers' expectations are influenced more by negative than by positive information about their students (Persell, 1993) and because stereotypes about children from lower-class and/or ethnic families are more likely to be negative than positive, children from these socially vulnerable backgrounds are more susceptible than other children to teachers' expectations and behaviors (Ferguson, 1998; Tom & Cooper, 1986).

✦ **Children's gender.**   The available research supports the view that teachers treat boys and girls differently. Teachers generally give boys more attention than they give girls and more freedom (Sadker & Sadker, 1994). Teachers believe that boys possess greater school-related skills than girls do (Shepardson & Pizzini, 1992), so boys receive more approval, instruction, and time from their teachers (Bailey, 1993). Teachers believe that being nice and obedient is related to intellectual skills in girls but not in boys, although no research supports this argument (Gold, Crombie, & Noble, 1987). Thus, teacher-child relationships differ for boys and girls and are based on different qualities (Ruble & Martin, 1998).

WHAT CHANGES TAKE PLACE IN MORAL DEVELOPMENT DURING LATE CHILDHOOD

A critical aspect of social and emotional development is the acquisition of moral values, intentions, and behaviors (Turiel, 1998). **Morality** is a set of principles or values that helps individuals distinguish right from wrong (Damon, 1988). Morality becomes a fundamental and important part of children's lives as soon as they start to develop relationships with others. Very early in life, children are aware of moral issues. As you learned in Chapter 8, young children and infants sometimes express concern about others' well-being and sometimes act prosocially. Young children also respond intensely when they feel their rights have been violated. Older children have an even more advanced understanding of fairness and justice, and they know that they are supposed to be responsible, honest, fair, kind, and cooperative to parents, siblings, teachers, friends, and strangers.

PIAGET'S THEORY OF MORAL DEVELOPMENT

Although many theories address the issue of moral development (such as Freud's psychoanalytic concept of the superego; see Chapter 2), in recent years the cognitive developmental theories of Piaget and Kohlberg have been perhaps the most influential. Moral development provides an important example of the interconnectedness of developmental domains; advances in cognitive development and reasoning bring about important changes in how children interact with others and engage in moral behavior.

morality a set of principles or values that helps individuals distinguish right from wrong

premoral period Piagetian stage of moral development in which young children do not yet understand cooperative rules and goals

heteronomous morality stage Piagetian stage of moral development in which children adhere strictly to rules and base moral decisions on the authority of others

moral realism the belief that morality is based on conforming to established rules set by powerful adults

Piaget (1932/1965) based much of his theory of moral development on his observation and questioning of children playing marbles. He believed that the essence of morality lies in respect for rules. While playing marbles, children must deal with issues of fairness, turn taking, reciprocity, and justice. By studying how children thought about and followed the rules of the marble game, Piaget believed he could discover the principles of moral development.

Piaget's Stages of Moral Development

When preschoolers play a game, the point of the game is to have fun. They do not play systematically and do not have the intention to win. They make up their own rules and play the game according to whatever rules they like at the moment. Piaget labeled this stage of moral development the **premoral period**—the stage of moral development in which young children do not yet understand cooperative rules and goals associated with playing a game. Table 10.1 summarizes Piaget's stages of moral development and shows how children in these stages differ in terms of how they view rules, intentions, and punishment.

After age 5, children become concerned about playing by the rules and playing to win. During the period of concrete operations (between 6 and 10 years of age), children strictly adhere to rules—a stage of moral development that Piaget referred to as the **heteronomous morality stage.** Their moral decisions are based on the authority of others. Rules must be obeyed because they are sacred and unalterable. Any act that conforms to a rule is "good"; any act that does not conform is "bad." At this age, children have a sense of **moral realism**—judgments about morality are based on conforming to established rules set by powerful adults. Children between the ages of 6 and 10 react strongly to rule violations. Have you ever broken a rule in front of a child this age, perhaps by jaywalking or

Piaget believed he could study the development of morality by observing children play games. How does children's game playing reflect their level of moral development?

TABLE 10.1

Outline of Piaget's Stages of Moral Development

CONCEPT	PREMORAL PERIOD (BEFORE AGE 6)	HETERONOMOUS MORALITY STAGE (AGES 6 TO 10)	AUTONOMOUS MORALITY STAGE (AFTER AGE 10)
Adherence to rules	Have little concern for or awareness of rules. Do not understand that rules are a cooperative agreement about how a game should be played	Obey rules because they are sacred and unchangeable. Believe that being "right" means always following the rules. Believe that rules are made by those who have absolute authority	Understand that rules are arbitrary social agreements that can be challenged or changed. Understand that rules can be violated in the service of human needs
Intentionality	Are too egocentric to take others' intentions into account	Judge acts of goodness or badness in terms of the physical consequences and not the motivation behind them	Believe that morality is determined by one's intentions rather than the consequences of an act
Punishment	Act to avoid punishment and maximize rewards	Favor severe punishment regardless of the misdeed—punishment does not fit the crime. Base judgments of good or bad on whether the act elicits punishment and how much punishment it elicits. Think that misdeeds inevitably lead to punishment—immanent justice	Favor milder punishment if it helps the person see that her or his action was wrong. Believe that punishment should fit the crime

SOURCE: Adapted from Hoffman, 1970.

parking in a no-parking zone? Even if you have a good reason for doing so, children in this stage often consider these actions to be wrong and react strongly.

In contrast to adolescents and adults, children between the ages of 6 and 10 years believe that right and wrong are determined by the consequences associated with an action. When an action results in positive consequences, it is "good"; when an action results in negative consequences, it is "bad," regardless of the intentions behind the action. Consider the following exchange between a kindergarten child and her teacher:

Katie: I told my dad the truth. I was fighting with my brother, and my dad came and said, "Who started this?" I said it happened by accident.
Teacher: Did your father believe you?
Katie: He really did.
Teacher: Was it an accident?
Katie: Kind of.
Teacher: Did you do it on purpose?
Katie: Yeah, but I didn't get yelled at. See, I told you it was an accident.

Because her father believed her and because she did not get yelled at, Katie defines her actions and intentions as truthful and moral. This is not the case for older children.

In his work with children, Piaget (1932/1965) relied on children's reasoning for information about the development of morality. For example, he asked children of different ages questions about the following two stories:

(1) A little boy who is called John is in his room. He is called to dinner. He goes into the dining room. But behind the door there is a chair and on this chair there is a tray with 15 cups on it. John couldn't have known that all this was behind the door. He goes in, the door knocks against the tray, and the 15 cups fall to the floor and break!

(2) Once there was a little boy named Henry. One day when his mother was out he tried to get some jam out of the cupboard. He climbed up on a chair and stretched out his arm. But the jam was too high up and he couldn't reach it. While he was trying to get it he knocked over a cup. The cup fell and broke on the floor!

In the first story, the child accidentally breaks 15 cups; in the second, the child breaks one cup in an attempt to sneak some jam while his mother is out. Who is naughtier?

Children in the heteronomous morality stage of moral development (between 6 and 10 years of age) answer that John is naughtier because he broke more cups. Their beliefs about morality are based on the consequences of the act—John broke more cups than Henry did. They do not take intentions into account. They believe that because John broke more cups than Henry did, he is likely to be punished more severely than Henry. Piaget referred to this belief of children in the stage of moral realism—that breaking a rule always leads to punishment—as **immanent justice.**

From the age of 11 years on, coinciding with the end of the concrete operational period (see Chapter 9), children's ideas about rules are no longer as rigid and constrained as they had been. Older children's understanding of morality is based on the knowledge that rules can be changed if everybody agrees on the changes. Piaget refers to this stage of moral development, in which rules can be changed by the will of those involved in the game, as the **autonomous morality stage.**

Older children are likely to consider Henry to be the naughtier child because he was trying to sneak the jam. They take into account one's intentions and do not focus solely on the consequences of one's actions. Piaget argued that older children are more likely to believe that punishment should "fit the crime," whereas young children believe that punishment should always be severe no matter what the misdeed might be. This more realistic view reflects children's increased flexibility and perspective taking as they move beyond concrete operational thinking and into formal operational thinking.

Evaluation of Piaget's Theory of Moral Development

The findings of several studies suggest that Piaget may have exaggerated young children's tendency to focus on *consequences* and overlook the *intentions* behind another's actions

immanent justice the belief that breaking a rule always leads to punishment

autonomous morality stage Piagetian stage of moral development in which one believes that rules can be changed by the will of those involved

(Nelson-Le Gall, 1985; Schultz, Wright, & Schleifer, 1986). For example, even preschoolers evaluate a child who lied about a misdeed and got away with it more negatively than they do a child who told the truth and was punished for the misdeed (Bussey, 1992). Preschool children also judge a child who lied about a misdeed more negatively than they do a child who merely committed the misdeed. These findings are inconsistent with Piaget's belief that young children are moral realists. Because Piaget presented children with stories in which the information about the consequences of the actions was more obvious than the information about the children's intentions, young children tended to focus their attention on the information that was most obvious (Nelson, 1980). Young children have difficulty using subtle information about others' intentions, but when the intentions of another are made clear, they can and do use such information. By age 5, children understand that intentions and consequences are different kinds of information (Suber, 1982).

Although Piaget may have underestimated young children's ability to take into account the intentions of others, there is some support for his theory. For example, younger children's moral judgments depend on whether or not the misbehavior led to punishment. Children who were punished, regardless of whether they lied or told the truth, are more likely to be judged as bad than are children who behaved similarly but were not punished. In contrast, older children's judgments of goodness or badness are not influenced by whether the child was punished (Bussey, 1992).

KOHLBERG'S THEORY OF MORAL DEVELOPMENT

One theorist who was greatly influenced by Piaget and who contributed many new and important insights into the development of morality was Lawrence Kohlberg (1969, 1984). Kohlberg identified six stages of moral development, based on his interviews with children, adolescents, and adults. In these interviews, he presented moral dilemmas in which the respondent was required to choose between obeying a rule or law and taking some action that conflicted with the rule or law but served a need. Consider the following moral dilemma:

> Judy was a 12-year-old girl. Her mother promised her that she could go to a special concert coming to their town if she saved up from baby-sitting and lunch money for a long time so she would have enough money to buy a ticket to the concert. She managed to save up the $5 the ticket cost plus another $3. But then her mother changed her mind and told Judy that she had to spend the money on new clothes for school. Judy was disappointed and decided to go to the concert anyway. She bought a ticket and told her mother that she had only been able to save $3. That Saturday she went to the performance and told her mother that she was spending the day with a friend. A week passed without her mother finding out. Judy then told her older sister, Louise, that she had gone to the performance and had lied to her mother about it. Louise wonders whether to tell their mother what Judy did. Should Louise, the older sister, tell her mother that Judy had lied about the money or should she keep quiet?
>
> —*Kohlberg, Colby, Gibbs, and Speicher-Dubin*
> (1978, p. 9)

Kohlberg was not interested in the specific answers respondents gave to the question—should Louise tell or not—but instead focused on the reasons they gave to justify their answers. From his analysis of the reasons they provided for their responses to this moral dilemma, Kohlberg identified three broad levels of moral development, with two stages at each level. These six stages are listed in Table 10.2 on page 342, along with qualities that characterize each stage.

Kohlberg's Stages of Moral Development

At the first broad level of moral development, the **Preconventional Level,** morality is based on external forces. Children conform to rules to avoid punishment or to obtain personal rewards, and their reasoning reflects a belief that goodness or badness is determined by consequences. At the first stage within this level, *Punishment-and-Obedience Orientation,* obedience is valued for its own sake and the motivation for acting morally is to avoid punishment. Children have difficulty considering others' points of view. Actions are evaluated

Preconventional Level first level of Kohlberg's theory of moral development, in which morality is based on external forces

TABLE 10.2

Kohlberg's Levels and Stages of Moral Development

STAGE	CONTENT OF STAGE		SOCIAL PERSPECTIVE OF STAGE
	WHAT IS RIGHT	REASONS FOR DOING RIGHT	
Preconventional Level			
Stage 1: Punishment-and-Obedience Orientation	Definitions of right and wrong are based on consequences. Rules should not be broken. Obedience is important for its own sake. Physical damage to persons and property should be avoided.	To avoid punishment Belief in the superiority of authority figures	Fails to consider others' points of view Cannot consider two points of view Considers actions in terms of their physical consequences
Stage 2: Instrumental-Purpose Orientation	Rules should be followed only when it is in one's immediate interest. Pragmatic reciprocity is the underlying principle: "You scratch my back; I'll scratch yours."	To serve one's own needs or interests	Is aware that others have interests they pursue and that these conflict Believes that being right is relative to one's needs
Conventional Level			
Stage 3: Interpersonal Orientation ("Good boy–Good girl" orientation)	Doing right is what pleases others. Being good means having good motives and showing concern about others. Being loyal, trustworthy, and respectful to others is important.	To be seen as a nice person by others To maintain rules and authority Belief in the Golden Rule	Is aware of shared feelings and expectations, which are more important than individual interests
Stage 4: Social-Order-Maintenance Orientation	One should conform to social rules in order to avoid disapproval by authorities. Doing good is fulfilling what one has agreed to do.	Belief that rules and law maintain the social order and are worth following To avoid breakdown in the system if rules are not followed	Takes the point of view of the larger social system Considers individual relations in terms of their place in the larger social system
Postconventional Level			
Stage 5: Social-Contract Orientation	Moral actions are usually those that reflect the will of the majority. Rules must be determined by democratic procedures and must be impartial. Some values must be upheld in any society, regardless of the majority opinion.	A sense of obligation to laws To uphold the social contract that protects all people's rights To do the greatest good for the greatest number of people	Is aware of values and rights prior to social contracts Recognizes that moral and legal points of view may conflict
Stage 6: Universal-Ethical-Principle Orientation*	Right and wrong are based on self-chosen ethical principles. Laws and social agreements are valid because they rest on such principles. When laws violate these principles, one should act in accordance with the principles rather than the laws. Principles are universal principles of justice: the equality of human rights and respect for others as individuals.	Belief in the validity of universal moral principles and a sense of personal commitment to them	Gives equal consideration to the rights of all human beings Has respect for the value and dignity of all people

*In later work, Kohlberg (1984) proposed that stage 6 is not distinguishable from stage 5 and suggested that the two be combined.
SOURCE: Kohlberg, 1969; Rest, 1983.

in terms of their physical consequences, such as the amount of damage done. Here is an example of a stage 1 answer to the moral dilemma:

> Louise should tell her mother about Judy's lie because if she doesn't, Louise is a liar.

At this stage, Louise's telling her mother is justified based on the simple, or absolute, standard that not telling her mother would be a lie and Louise would be a liar if she did not tell. No reason is needed beyond the fact that it would be considered wrong not to do so. Children under 10 typically are at this stage of moral development.

In stage 2 of this first level of moral development, *Instrumental-Purpose Orientation,* children believe that rules should be followed when it is in one's best interest to do so. Morality is based on serving one's own needs or interests. Children in stage 2 have some awareness of others' interests, but being right is considered only in relation to one's own needs. Here is a typical stage 2 answer to the moral dilemma:

> Louise should keep quiet because if she does then Judy may keep quiet for Louise in the future.

Louise's not telling is justified based on her self-interest and on an appreciation of the value of not telling their mom. Typically, stage 2 of moral development appears at age 10.

The next broad level of moral development is the **Conventional Level.** At this level, individuals strive to win praise and recognition for good conduct and for maintaining social order. Within this level, stage 3 morality—*Interpersonal Orientation*—reflects the belief that doing right is what pleases other people. Individuals are motivated to be seen by others as being nice and good. At this stage, individuals show more awareness of, and concern for, others' feelings and expectations than at earlier stages. Here is an example of stage 3 reasoning:

> Louise should not tell her mother about Judy's lie because telling would destroy Judy's trust and betray her confidence in Louise.

According to this stage of moral development, Louise should not tell her mother because it is important that she maintain her relationship with her sister. The desire to be seen as being loyal and trustworthy is imperative. Stage 3 of moral development begins to appear in early adolescence (ages 13–14).

Stage 4 of moral development, *Social-Order-Maintenance Orientation,* reflects a belief that rules maintain the social order and that the social system will break down if people do not follow rules. At this stage, doing good involves following through on what you have agreed to do, for the good of the larger social system. Here is an example of stage 4 reasoning:

> Louise should not tell her mother because her mom promised Judy that she could use the money to go to the concert and her mom should keep her word. A promise should be sacred.

This answer reflects concern about the promise that Judy's mother made to her. The mother is seen to have a duty, or obligation, to carry out her promise because society depends upon reliability and maintaining social contracts.

The third and highest broad level of moral development is the **Postconventional Level.** At this level, the individual is personally committed to a set of principles that are shared with others but go beyond particular authority figures. Moral standards are internalized and become part of the individual. In stage 5, *Social-Contract Orientation,* moral actions are defined as those that reflect the will of the majority. Morality reflects a sense of obligation to uphold social laws and contracts that protect all people's rights. At this stage, individuals have an awareness of many points of view and have a desire to do the greatest good for the greatest number of people. Here is an example of stage 5 reasoning:

> Before you can say that Louise should tell her mother, you've got to consider the whole situation. Louise should respect her mother's point of view but parents' expectations and rules should not violate what one believes to be right.

Judgments about morality are no longer seen as black or white. Moral judgments focus on the obligation of each person and the recognition that everyone involved has rights.

The final stage of Kohlberg's theory of moral development is stage 6, *Universal-Ethical-Principle Orientation.* At this stage, right and wrong are based on self-chosen ethical principles.

Conventional Level second level of Kohlberg's theory of moral development, in which moral reasoning is based on winning praise and recognition for good conduct and maintaining the social order

Postconventional Level third level of Kohlberg's theory of moral development, in which judgments about morality are based on principles that the individual is personally committed to and that are shared by others

These are not concrete rules such as the Golden Rule, but rather are abstract moral principles of universal justice and respect for all individuals. When laws violate these moral principles, individuals should act in accordance with their principles rather than the law. At this stage, individuals consider the rights of all human beings. Here is an example of this level of reasoning:

> One must always do what he or she thinks is right. If that means disobeying your parents, then so be it. Louise ought to do what she thinks a just person would do in this case, not do it just because of emotion or obligation.

In this answer, the person recognizes that laws and social agreements are valid only because they rest on ethical principles. If a law violates these principles, one may disobey the law. Reasoning at this stage is based on universal principles and one's personal sense of commitment to these principles. Interestingly, none of Kohlberg's participants ever reached stage 6 (Kohlberg, 1981). Kohlberg described this stage as a "potential" stage and suggested that moral leaders such as Jesus, Gandhi, and Martin Luther King, Jr., exemplify this level of moral reasoning. In later work, Kohlberg (1984) proposed that stage 6 is not distinguishable from stage 5 and suggested that the two be combined.

Evaluation of Kohlberg's Theory of Moral Development

Several longitudinal studies provide support for Kohlberg's stages (Colby, Kohlberg, Gibbs, & Lieberman, 1983; Walker, 1989). As children grow older, their level of moral development becomes more abstract and advanced. Figure 10.5 illustrates some of these findings. This figure depicts the percentages of children and adults who display lower levels of moral development (focus on consequences) and higher levels of moral development (emphasis on dignity and autonomy). As you can see, the percentage of individuals using lower-level reasoning decreases with age, whereas the percentage of individuals using higher-level reasoning increases with age (Walker, 1989).

Kohlberg argued that higher moral reasoning is based on a decline in egocentrism and an increase in perspective taking and abstract reasoning. As indicated in Table 10.2, children at the Preconventional Level show only a limited awareness of others' thoughts, needs, and intentions. Morality at the Conventional Level is characterized by an increased recognition of others' points of view, and moral reasoning at the Postconventional Level is based on abstract principles and consideration of the rights of others. If Kohlberg was correct, there should be a correspondence between level of moral reasoning and cognitive development.

Formal tests of the relationship between level of moral reasoning and cognitive development generally support Kohlberg's theory—higher levels of cognitive development and role taking are related to higher levels of moral reasoning (Rest, 1983; Walker, 1988). But people with higher levels of cognitive development do not necessarily act more morally than those with lower levels of cognitive development (Blasi, 1983; Walker & Henning, 1997). Although a person in stage 5 will often act differently in moral situations than a person in stage 3 or 2, it is difficult to predict how that person will act based simply on knowledge of his or her level of moral reasoning, because other factors influence actual moral behavior. Moreover, at each stage there is considerable variability within an individual in the use of moral reasoning—individuals use moral concepts differently as they cycle through developmental and personal changes (Thoma & Rest, 1999).

F IGURE 10.5

Percentages of Individuals at Lower and Higher Levels of Moral Reasoning Across Age Groups

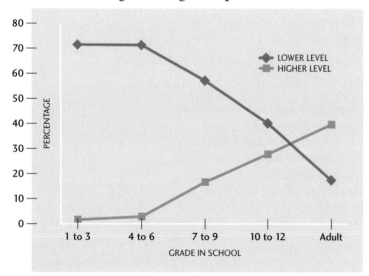

SOURCE: Walker, 1989.

This figure shows that lower levels of moral reasoning decrease with age, whereas higher levels of moral reasoning increase with age. What factors might account for these changes? How do these data support Kohlberg's theory of moral development?

CULTURE AND MORALITY

According to Kohlberg, moral development was not learned by imitation or reinforcement. Nor did he believe that moral development was influenced by the specific content of the rules and laws of a culture. Rather, Kohlberg believed that morality was based on universal principles that developed in an invariant sequence, regardless of the culture in which a person was raised (Kohlberg, 1981).

Cross-cultural research provides evidence in support of Kohlberg's stages. Although stages 1 and 5 occur infrequently, stages 2, 3, and 4 can be found in many cultures (Eckensberger, 1994). Additionally, the sequence of stages is similar across different cultures (Snarey, 1985).

Moral themes, however, vary from culture to culture (Kahn, 1997). People in India, like people in many non-Western cultures, treat moral rules as part of the natural world. For example, Indian children consider violations of food customs more important than uncharitable behavior or stealing (Schweder et al., 1987). Violations of customs are serious moral offenses because they are considered to be as much a breach of natural moral principles as is an intentional act that harms someone. In contrast, American children view morality as a contract between people (Damon, 1988). Thus, Indian and American children have very different views of morality, and these cultural differences serve as a basis for differences in judgments about what is right and wrong.

Within American culture, there are differences in the moral values and orientations of different groups. For example, Mexican American children have a group orientation in which sharing, affiliation, and cooperation are highly valued moral qualities (Kagan, Knight, Martinez, & Santa, 1981). African American children generally focus on finding solutions to moral problems.

These differences in orientation influence how children respond to situations calling for moral judgements. In one study (Rotheram-Borus & Phinney, 1990), Mexican American and African American children were asked to identify what a person should do in certain moral situations, such as when someone asks for a loan, when someone is scolded by a teacher who is disappointed in that person, or when others are fighting. As you can see in Table 10.3, Mexican American children favored sharing money more often than African American children did. African American children were more inclined to stop a fight than were Mexican American children, who tended to feel bad or not want to get involved. After being scolded by a

*T*ABLE 10.3

Children's Ideas of What Should Be Done in Different Moral Scenarios, by Ethnicity and Age

MORAL SCENARIO	THIRD-GRADERS		SIXTH-GRADERS	
	AFRICAN AMERICAN	MEXICAN AMERICAN	AFRICAN AMERICAN	MEXICAN AMERICAN
Asked to share money				
Share	24%	50%	76%	100%
Do not share	76%	50%	24%	0%
Scolded by teacher				
Apologize	28%	9%	62%	10%
Do something to change things	28%	18%	24%	14%
Feel bad	28%	36%	14%	67%
Get angry	16%	36%	0%	10%
Peers fighting				
Stop fight	48%	18%	62%	38%
Encourage fight	20%	23%	24%	10%
Feel bad	24%	45%	5%	24%
Do not get involved	8%	14%	10%	29%

SOURCE: Rotheram-Borus and Phinney, 1990.

teacher, African American children favored apologizing more frequently than did Mexican American children, who were inclined to feel bad or angry. The differences generally are greater with age, perhaps reflecting the increased exposure older children have to the norms of their ethnic group (Rotheram-Borus & Phinney, 1990). Thus, moral development occurs as the result of the joint, reciprocal, and simultaneous influences of individual development and cultural socialization (Navaez, Getz, Rest, & Thoma, 1999).

GENDER AND MORALITY

Carol Gilligan (1982, 1994) argued that, just as people from different cultures vary in their ideas about morality, females and males differ in their moral judgments. According to Gilligan, females rely on a morality of *caring* rather than of justice. The ethic of care is based on the assumption that people are not separate units with conflicting needs that require arbitration; rather, people are connected to one another. Based on an ethic of care, females place more emphasis on the maintenance of relationships, whereas males place more emphasis on law and order (Haste & Baddeley, 1991). These differences come from the sex-typed cultures in which males and females grow up (Skoe et al., 1999). In Gilligan's (1982) words, the sexes speak "in a different voice." Neither voice is louder or better; they are just different.

Generally, however, the scientific evidence does not support Gilligan's belief that males and females have different moral voices (Turiel, 1998). Although there are a few studies that show gender differences in moral reasoning, the majority of studies do not find such differences (Walker, 1984, 1991). Both genders report more care reasoning when relationship issues are being discussed and more justice reasoning when nonrelationship issues (e.g., legal matters) are being discussed. Because women tend to report more relationship issues than do men, the greater care ethic used by women may be a result of the dilemmas they tend to face (Turiel, 1998). Thus, it appears that the ethics of justice and care are not in opposition to each other and that moral problems do not force a choice between them (Walker, 1995).

TRY IT OUT

Activities Relating to School-Age Children

1. Interview school-age children about their experiences in school. Have them discuss their relationships with classmates and teachers. Ask them if they have ever experienced any safety issues while at school (such as being threatened or seeing someone with a knife). Use the material in the chapter to draw some conclusions about the impact of these experiences and relationships on the children's development.

2. Describe how individual, familial, and social factors contribute to the problems of rejected children. What kinds of interventions and treatments might be effective in helping these children cope with their problems?

3. Look through newspapers, magazines, or the Internet for a story on heroism or extreme courage displayed by a school-age child. How do such actions relate to moral development? What factors lead to heroism and courage? Draw some conclusions about the relationship between these types of behaviors and moral reasoning.

SUM IT UP

How do emotions develop during late childhood?

◆ As children develop, their vulnerability to stress changes. The situations that produce stress and the ways they cope with stress also change.

◆ Older children are more likely to become stressed because of increased expectations and pressures to achieve at school, whereas young children's stress revolves primarily around parent-child relationships.

◆ Stress also may be experienced when people change cultural environments.

◆ Older children's ways of coping with stress are more abstract and cognitive than those of younger children.

◆ Some children are resilient, or stress-resistant, and adapt well even in situations that seem overwhelmingly stressful. Having above-average intelligence, possessing attractive qualities, and having a positive place in the family are common characteristics of resilient children.

◆ Community violence can undermine children's sense of well-being and place them at risk. Because of their increased ability to understand dangerous situations, older children respond to community violence in more diverse ways than younger children do.

What emotional and psychological disturbances affect children in late childhood?

◆ Late childhood is a time when emotional and psychological disturbances often surface. These problems are relatively rare, but when they do occur, they often are serious and have powerful effects on both the children who experience these problems and those who interact with them.

◆ Antisocial behavior is a pattern of behavior that is aggressive, defiant, uncooperative, and disruptive to the individual, to his or her relationships, and to the community.

◆ Biological, familial, peer, and social factors all contribute to antisocial behavior. At present, no single treatment has been found to effectively address antisocial problems. Instead, the best outcomes involve multiple interventions addressing the diverse factors that contribute to antisocial behavior.

◆ Children can experience symptoms of depression similar to those suffered by adults—sadness, disengagement, and self-deprecation.

◆ Genetic, biological, temperamental, familial, and social factors contribute to depressive disorders in children. Effective treatment begins with helping children communicate depressed feelings.

◆ Fears that are common in infancy and early childhood usually disappear during late childhood. During late childhood, children are no longer afraid of things simply because of the way they look but now are fearful of threats to their physical and psychological well-being.

◆ Phobias are extreme, persistent, and irrational fears that significantly affect a child's functioning. One of the most common phobias of late childhood is school phobia—an extreme fear associated with school environments.

How do children's family relationships change during late childhood?

◆ During late childhood, children spend less time with their families and more time with peers and in school activities. In recent years, parental supervision of school-age children has decreased. Many school-age children are latchkey children, left to care for themselves when they come home from school.

◆ Those children who have siblings near their own age spend more time with them than they spend with their parents. Children with younger siblings spend time caring for them.

◆ Children who have no siblings tend to grow up much like children with brothers and sisters.

What factors influence school-age children's peer relationships?

◆ During late childhood, peer relationships take on greater importance.

◆ Children who have poor peer relationships are not all the same. Rejected children are actively disliked, whereas neglected children are not disliked but overlooked and ignored by peers.

◆ Children's levels of social competence—how well they initiate, maintain, manage, and communicate in social relationships—determine their ability to form meaningful and positive peer relationships. Many factors influence children's social competence, including individual, familial, and social factors.

How does school affect social and emotional development in late childhood?

◆ Entry into school exposes children to a wide variety of personalities, values, behaviors, and customs.

◆ The increased focus on academic performance and achievement leads children to compare themselves to one another. These pressures produce feelings of fear and anxiety, as well as feelings of pride and satisfaction.

◆ Teachers enhance outcomes for students when they minimize competition and promote cooperation and supportive relationships.

◆ Teachers' responses to children are influenced by children's behaviors; their racial, ethnic, and socioeconomic backgrounds; and their gender.

What changes take place in moral development during late childhood?

◆ Piaget based his theory of morality on his observations of children's understanding of rules and how it changes with age.

◆ Based on his interviews with children, Kohlberg identified six stages of moral development.

◆ Longitudinal evidence generally supports Kohlberg's stage theory, and higher levels of cognitive development are related to higher levels of moral reasoning.

◆ Some aspects of moral development are similar across different cultures. Variation in other aspects is associated with cultural norms. Scientific evidence generally does not support the contention that males and females differ in their moral reasoning.

KEY TERMS and CONCEPTS

acculturative stress (*319*)
antisocial behavior (*324*)
autonomous morality stage (*340*)
Conventional Level (*343*)
emotion-focused coping strategies (*319*)
heteronomous morality stage (*339*)
immanent justice (*340*)

innate fears (*328*)
latchkey children (*330*)
moral realism (*339*)
morality (*338*)
neglected children (*333*)
phobias (*328*)
Postconventional Level (*343*)

Preconventional Level (*341*)
premoral period (*339*)
problem-focused coping strategies (*319*)
rejected children (*333*)
resilience (*320*)
school phobia (*328*)
social competence (*334*)

BENCHMARKS in Late Childhood Development

PHYSICAL/MOTOR DEVELOPMENT	COGNITIVE DEVELOPMENT	SOCIAL/EMOTIONAL DEVELOPMENT
Slower growth than in previous years	Development of concrete operational thinking; decreased egocentrism and increased ability to mentally represent actions and objects; increased understanding of multiple classification and seriation	Change in contexts and types of stressors, increased use of emotion-focused and cognitive coping responses
Continuing myelination of brain and development of neural pathways		Increased evidence of antisocial behavior, depression, and fears, phobias, and anxieties
Increasing coordination and physical strength and improved motor skills	Increasingly complex understanding of syntax and use of language; increasing vocabulary and understanding of idioms	Reduced interactions with parents and increased interest in siblings and peers
Increased participation in sports and athletics	Development of reading and writing	Increased emphasis on peer relationships and problems related to them
Increased risk for accidents, injuries, and obesity	Increased emphasis on IQ and creativity because of the focus on school performance and achievement	Increased emphasis on the social aspects of school
	Enhanced ability to think of other people in abstract and differentiated ways; increased understanding of others' perspectives	Change in moral development from a focus on the consequences of one's actions (heteronomous morality) to a focus on one's intentions (autonomous morality)
	Changing views of race and ethnic groups	Change in moral reasoning from the preconventional to the conventional level

NATIONAL HOTLINES FOR SCHOOL-AGE CHILDREN

Education Reform Hotline: 800-521-2118

Mental Health Information Center: 800-336-4797

National PTA Headquarters: 800-307-4782

Safe School Hotline: 800-419-6423, ext. 359

Large differences exist in the amount of money countries spend on primary education. Large differences also exist in students' performance on math tests. What factors contribute to these differences? Can you detect a relationship between the amount of money a country spends on its students and student performance on math tests? What are the implications of your conclusions?

International Comparisons of Expenditures and Math Performance in Primary Education

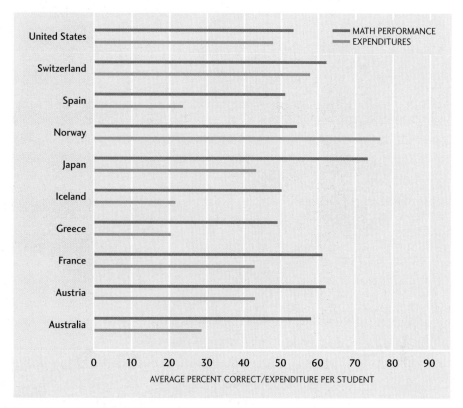

Expenditures represent funds expended per student (in hundreds of dollars). Math performance represents average percent correct on overall math testing.

SOURCE: US Department of Education, 2000a.

RECOMMENDED WEBSITES

KidsHealth: This site is devoted to the health of children and teens. Created by the Nemours Foundation, KidsHealth has information about growth, food and fitness, childhood physical and mental health, and the latest treatments for medical and surgical conditions.
http://kidshealth.org/

National Center for Education Statistics (NCES): An organization that collects and reports statistics and information on the condition and progress of education in the United States and other nations.
http://nces.ed.gov/

National Parents and Teachers Association: This site is designed to help governmental bodies and other organizations make decisions affecting children and to assist parents in developing the skills they need to raise and protect their children.
http://www.pta.org/

Research Network on Successful Pathways Through Middle Childhood: An organization established to study the influences and experiences that contribute to successful outcomes for children during the school years. Its site focuses on children from the time they enter school until early adolescence.
http://midchild.soe.umich.edu/

Studies in Moral Development and Education: This site links educators, scholars, and citizens who want to share their work and learn more about research, practices, and activities in the area of moral development and education. It is hosted by the College of Education at the University of Illinois, Chicago.
http://www.uic.edu/~lnucci/MoralEd/

Early Adolescent Development

arly adolescence is a time when the complex inter-actions of biology and environment are particularly dramatic. Biological influences are apparent in many of the physical changes that take place, including growing taller, gaining weight, and developing to sexual maturity. Environmental influences come into play as the adolescent's family, friends, and significant others react to the changing adolescent. Adolescents undergo dramatic changes in virtually every aspect of their development—their bodies, relationships, thinking skills, and emotional understanding. As development occurs in each of these areas, it brings about changes in the others. Young adolescents may not always understand or be prepared for the changes this development fosters, but with time and support, most learn to adapt.

The timing of puberty makes some adolescents seem older, and some younger, than their peers. Thus, the timing of puberty has an impact on adolescents' adjustment and social lives. Additionally, girls and boys reach puberty at different times, and the timing of these events has different outcomes for boys and girls, probably because of the different expectations for men and women in American culture.

11

Cognitive and Physical Development in Early Adolescence

CHAPTER OUTLINE

✦ What Is Early Adolescence?

✦ How Do Physical Growth and Sexual Maturation Occur During Early Adolescence?

✦ What Are the Health Concerns for Young Adolescents?

✦ How Do Young Adolescents Think and Solve Problems?

✦ How Does School Influence Early Adolescent Development?

Adolescence is a time of great change. For many people, adolescence conjures up only negative images—a time of storm and stress when young people take drugs, become rebellious and disrespectful, and are the victims of raging hormones. These images are accurate for only a small minority of adolescents. Most adolescents make the necessary adjustments to cope with the changes in positive ways. Early in adolescence, these adjustments involve physical changes in the body and changing expectations. Later in adolescence, these adjustments involve changing relationships and responsibilities.

WHAT IS EARLY ADOLESCENCE?

A 13-year-old and a 17-year-old are both adolescents, but they experience very different worlds. Until recently, however, little distinction was made among adolescents of different ages because the period of adolescence was comparatively brief. In the early twentieth century, it was common for people to be married and have children by the age of 15 or 16. Consider the following personal account, told by 71-year-old David:

> My teen years were pretty typical. I went to school until I was 15 and then quit to help my dad in his store. Shortly after that, I met Elizabeth and we were married within a year. I had my first child when I was 17 and I remember having all our friends over for his first birthday. By that time, they were all married too and many had children of their own. My adolescence didn't last too long. I was too busy working and taking care of my children. But I didn't mind; it was the thing to do in those days.
>
> —*Interview with Author's Grandparent*

Compared to David's experience, adolescence today is a much longer period of time. Adolescents reach physical maturity earlier and delay adult responsibilities longer than they did in the past.

Adolescence often is defined as covering the period from about 11 years of age to about 19, although some psychologists maintain that adolescence extends into the adult years (Sheehy, 1995). Distinguishing between early adolescence (ages 11 to 14 years) and late adolescence (ages 15 to 19 years) is important because they represent different transitional periods. During early adolescence, the individual is making the transition from a child to an adolescent. During late adolescence, the transition is from an adolescent to an adult (Sherrod, Haggerty, & Featherman, 1993). Thus, younger and older adolescents must deal with different developmental issues and tasks.

Physical changes occur more rapidly during early adolescence than at any other point in the life span except infancy. Family members, friends, and teachers notice these changes and respond to adolescents based partly on how "grown up" they appear. In turn, young adolescents' views of themselves are affected by the physical changes and how they are treated by others.

The early adolescent period is a unique and significant stage of human development, marking the end of childhood. No longer a child but not yet an adult, the young adolescent is somewhere in between. Young adolescents are one of the least studied and least understood age groups. Before we focus specifically on early adolescent development, it is important to understand how the concept of adolescence, and its study, came about.

HISTORICAL PERSPECTIVES ON ADOLESCENCE

The term **adolescence** generally refers to the developmental period between childhood and adulthood. Although this transitional period was recognized by ancient Romans, Greeks, and Egyptians (Offer, Ostrov, Howard, & Atkinson, 1988), the concept of adolescence as we know it did not exist until the mid–nineteenth century. At that time, increased urbanization led to social and legal reforms that contributed to the social acceptance of adolescence as a stage of development. These reforms included the following:

adolescence the developmental period between childhood and adulthood

◆ Child labor laws removed children and adolescents from factories and workplaces.

◆ Changes in criminal laws allowed courts to treat juveniles differently from adults. Children and adolescents are not subject to the same legal procedures and punishments as adults.

◆ Mandatory public education placed large numbers of young people into schools and formally separated them from adults. Additionally, the age-graded school system separated children from adolescents.

In the twentieth century, as technology advanced, increasingly specialized skills were demanded from workers. More extensive and finely tuned education and training were needed to produce highly skilled workers, and these pressures continued to expand the time period of adolescence.

Postponing adult responsibilities gives young people increased opportunities to explore different roles and values and to greatly extend their education. Not all youths take advantage of the time available for educational training and experimentation with different roles, though. Some adolescents, such as those who plan to work in jobs involving manual labor, resent being forced to continue studying "irrelevant" course materials in school and want the opportunity to begin their adult roles. And extending adolescence has some negative consequences. For instance, it makes career choices more difficult for many adolescents, as the link between work and school becomes less obvious, and it increases the length of time young people are dependent on their parents, which may contribute to family conflict.

Today, adolescents represent a smaller proportion of the US population than they did in the past. This trend reflects the declining birth rate and increased life expectancy of the US population. Although adolescents represent a relatively small and declining proportion of the United States population, issues related to them—such as juvenile crime, substance abuse, and education—demand considerable time, attention, and resources.

CULTURAL PERSPECTIVES ON ADOLESCENCE

As a developmental period, adolescence varies from one culture to the next (Dusek, 1996). In less industrialized cultures, the period of adolescence may be very brief and adulthood may begin early. For instance, in some groups of African hunter-gatherers, adulthood is considered to begin once girls menstruate and boys participate successfully in a hunt (Abbott, 1997). Similarly, among the Punan Bah, a tiny ethnic group in the rainforest in Borneo, boys and girls are supposed to understand and participate in adult life from the age of 9 or 10. By age 13 or 14, Punan Bah members are expected to work on their own and take on the morals and responsibilities of the adult society (Nicolaisen, 1988). Like adolescence early in the twentieth century in the United States, the period of adolescence in Punan Bah society is considerably shorter (four to five years) than it is in present-day US society.

Many adolescents undergo initiations, or **rites of passage,** that mark their new status and roles within their community. The nature of these rites varies across cultures. In some African cultures, 13-year-old boys receive months of training in the basic skills needed for adulthood and then undergo circumcision to mark their new status (Dacey & Kenny, 1997). Young Australian aboriginal adolescents do a walkabout, in which they leave their village and must survive on their own for six months. These rites of passage soften the blow of making an abrupt change to a new status. They inform the individuals of their new duties and roles, announce their status to the community, and provide a sense of belongingness (Sebald, 1992).

Modern US society has nothing that corresponds in scope to the rites of passage experienced in other cultures; however, there are transition rituals that mark changes in some domains. For instance, the *bar mitzvah* (or *bat mitzvah,* for girls) in Judaism marks the end of a boy's childhood within the religion, although it does not influence how the boy is treated by the rest of society.

rites of passage initiations that mark an adolescent's new status and roles within the community

In the United States, there are some markers of the transition into adult roles, but these occur later than, say, an aboriginal walkabout, since adolescence in the United States extends for a longer time period. Also, these markers, such as the legal age for driving or voting, do not carry with them the same cultural significance as the rites of passage experienced by youth in other cultures.

In the Jewish religion, boys and girls go through a religious ceremony at the age of 13 that signifies the end of childhood. This rite of passage marks their new status and roles within the community.

Even in those cultures that have an expanded period of adolescence, the experience of adolescence is colored by variability in the societal expectations for youth. For example, as you will see, individual autonomy and independence are important goals of adolescent development in the United States. In contrast, because individual autonomy is valued less than group cooperation in Chinese cultures, Chinese adolescents are not expected, and do not expect themselves, to act independently as early as Western adolescents do (Feldman & Rosenthal, 1994). Thus, Chinese and Western adolescents hold different concepts of themselves—concepts that reflect cultural variations in perceptions and beliefs about adolescence.

In some cultures, the notion of adolescence as a period of development separate from childhood and adulthood does not exist. The following comments are from a Samoan-born young woman:

> As a Samoan born, I had never heard of it [adolescence] until I came to New Zealand. I don't think it was part of my life because it is a western concept, and from a non-western society all those developmental stages didn't relate to me. All I know is that my aiga [family] and my community and my culture are important. They determine the way I behave, think, and feel. . . . So adolescence as a developmental stage is foreign to our culture.
>
> —*J. Kroger* (1996, p. 3)

Even subcultures within a country have different expectations for adolescents. For example, Amish and Hutterite children step from childhood expectations directly into adult roles and are less affected than other US youth by elements of the larger society that promote an extended period of adolescence (Sebald, 1992).

TERMINOLOGY USED IN DEFINING ADOLESCENCE

The term most commonly associated with adolescent development is **puberty,** the developmental milestone reached when a person becomes sexually mature and capable of having children. Because sexual maturation actually takes place over several years, the term **pubescence** is used to refer to the time during which sexual maturation is taking place.

Youth is a broad, nonspecific term for the younger generation—children, adolescents, and young adults. All societies have a younger generation, but not all societies have adolescents. Thus, the term *youth* is practically universal, but it is not always interchangeable with the term *adolescents* (Sebald, 1992).

The term **teenager,** applied to anyone who is 13 to 19 years of age, is widely used to refer to adolescents. This term is imprecise, however, as it measures time rather than the experiences that mark this stage of development. Another age-defined term is **juvenile.** This legal term is used to refer to an individual who is not an adult in the eyes of the law. In most states, anyone under the age of 18 is a juvenile. Although age-related definitions are commonly used, age is not a good marker for adolescence because of the large variability in the timing of physical changes, experiences individuals are exposed to, and cultural expectations held for adolescents.

puberty developmental milestone reached when a person becomes sexually mature and capable of having children

pubescence the period of time during which sexual maturation takes place

youth a broad, nonspecific term for the younger generation—children, adolescents, and young adults

teenager a youth between 13 and 19 years of age

juvenile an individual who is not yet an adult in the eyes of the law

HOW DO PHYSICAL GROWTH AND SEXUAL MATURATION OCCUR DURING EARLY ADOLESCENCE?

Eleven-year-old Karen anxiously waits for her aunt to take off her shoes so that they can stand back to back to compare heights. Karen's feet have surpassed her aunt's in size over the past year, and now she wonders if she has grown taller. Karen is surprised that she and her aunt are the same height.

Karen is excited about the changes in her body. She is growing in height and weight, and her body is changing from its earlier childlike proportions to a more mature shape. Unlike the boys in her class, Karen is "growing like a weed"—she is undergoing the growth spurt of early adolescence. Later, the boys in her class will experience a similar growth spurt, and many will eventually become taller, heavier, and stronger than Karen.

BRAIN DEVELOPMENT IN EARLY ADOLESCENCE

You may be surprised to learn that, during adolescence, the brain continues to undergo physical changes and these changes may be linked to adolescents' behavior. Dramatic transformations take place during adolescence in the prefrontal cortex and limbic brain regions. The amygdala, a part of the limbic system, grows quickly in response to testosterone during adolescence and is involved with feelings of fear and anger. Not surprisingly, boys change more than girls in this area of the brain (Giedd, 1997). This change may account for the increased aggressiveness and irritability often associated with adolescence. The prefrontal cortex is involved in organization and planning of behavior and is involved in anticipating future events. People with damage to the prefrontal areas of the brain often have little concern for the past and future and are not good at sequencing events in time (Knight & Grabowecky, 2000). The limbic system plays a central role in the regulation of emotional behaviors and sexuality and is involved in the regulation of memory. These systems continue to develop during adolescence and early adulthood, and their development may contribute to changes in cognitive functioning (Benes, 2001; Casey, Giedd, & Thomas, 2000; Goldman-Rakic, Bourgeois, & Rakic, 1997). There is some speculation that the development of these areas and the systems associated with them may play a role in drug use, the lack of foresight some adolescents show, and the failure of some adolescents to recognize the consequences of their behavior (Spear, 2000).

THE ADOLESCENT GROWTH SPURT

Girls and boys are approximately the same height until early adolescence, when girls begin their growth spurt (see Figure 11.1). The average age at which girls begin their growth spurt is around 10½ years. Peak rates of growth are reached between ages 11 and 12, and growth tapers off by 13 (Marshall & Tanner, 1986). During their spurt, girls grow about 3 inches per year, about twice as fast as they did before puberty. Growth slows down when girls reach **menarche,** the onset of their menstrual cycle. Most girls reach their adult height and weight by about age 15 or 16, but a few continue growing until they are 18 or 19 (Tanner, 1991).

On average, boys begin their growth spurt about two years later than girls—around 12½ years—and reach their peak rate of growth between 13 and 15. Boys grow about 4 inches a year during their spurt, but during the peak growth time they may grow 6 to 8 inches in one year (Malina & Bouchard, 1991; Marshall & Tanner, 1986). Most boys reach their adult height at about 17 or 18 years of age, but some continue growing for several more years.

Weight changes also occur during the growth spurt. Early in adolescence, both sexes gain body fat; later, boys stop gaining fat while girls continue to gain it (Forbes, 1986). Although girls have somewhat more fat on their body even as children, during early adolescence the differences between the sexes become more pronounced. Boys and girls differ in

menarche the onset of the menstrual cycle

FIGURE 11.1

Pattern of Growth in Height for Boys and for Girls

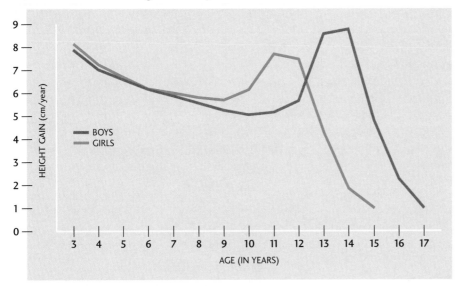

SOURCE: Adapted from Tanner and Davies, 1985.

Notice how the graphs for boys and girls diverge at about 7 years of age. Girls' growth peaks at ages 11 and 12, whereas boys' growth peaks at 13 or 14. What factors account for these differences? How do these physical changes influence adolescents' interactions with others?

the amounts of fat versus muscle they gain during the growth spurt, with boys gaining more muscle mass and girls gaining more body fat (Holliday, 1986; Malina, 1986). The fat that girls gain during adolescence is related to reproduction—their bodies gain enough stored energy to support pregnancy and nursing.

The growth spurt affects all parts of an adolescent's body, but different parts of the body grow at different rates. An adolescent's hands, feet, head, and nose grow more quickly than the rest of the body. Only later do the arms, legs, and trunk reach adult size. Body proportions change from the narrow hips and shoulders of childhood to more sexually defined shapes, with girls developing broader hips and boys broader shoulders. Internal organs such as the lungs and heart also grow in size during adolescence.

Large and noticeable individual differences characterize the timing and extent of growth during early adolescence. For instance, some girls begin their growth spurt as early as age 9, whereas others do not begin until 13 or 14. Boys may enter the growth spurt at age 10 or as late as 15. Many adolescents have some variation in their growth, with later or earlier than usual development of height or weight or sexual maturation.

THE PROCESS OF PUBERTY

Puberty is not a single event but a progression of physical changes that usually begin in late childhood and culminate in early adolescence (see Table 11.1). These events include the development of the

The young teens in this picture are the same age. Notice the dramatic differences in their heights and body shapes. The girls tend to be taller and more physically mature than the boys. What factors account for such differences?

TABLE 11.1

The Progression of Pubertal Events in Girls and Boys

AGE (IN YEARS)	GIRLS	BOYS
8 to 10	Breast buds appear	
10 to 12	Pubic hair begins to grow Vagina, ovaries, uterus, and labia grow rapidly Breasts enlarge Growth spurt occurs	
12 to 13	Menarche occurs Underarm hair grows	Testes and scrotum grow Pubic hair begins to grow
13 to 16	Breasts fill out Ova mature and girl becomes capable of conception (about one year after menarche) Voice deepens	Penis enlarges Voice changes begin First ejaculation of semen occurs Underarm hair and hair on upper lip begin to grow Growth spurt occurs
16 to 18		Hair grows on cheeks, chin, and body Marked changes occur in voice

primary sexual characteristics—physical features directly related to reproduction, such as the ovaries, penis, and testes—and the development of **secondary sexual characteristics**—features that are outward manifestations of sexual development but are not directly involved in reproduction, such as breasts, facial and body hair, and an adult body shape.

Biological Influences on Pubertal Development

The physical changes that accompany puberty are influenced by biological factors; however, scientists have not identified one specific biological trigger for puberty. Instead, a complex interplay of the endocrine system, the nervous system, and the gonads leads to puberty, largely through the influence of hormones.

Hormones are released from the master gland of the endocrine system, called the pituitary gland. The hypothalamus, a part of the brain that sends signals to the pituitary gland and to the gonads, responds to levels of hormones in the body. The interplay among these components acts as a feedback loop, in which each part influences and reacts to each other part. For instance, the brain provides instructions to the endocrine system to maintain a certain level of hormones in the body. Depending on the levels of hormones in the bloodstream, the endocrine system will then increase or decrease the release of hormones.

The endocrine system, which circulates and regulates hormones within the body, develops before birth but stays relatively inactive until about the age of 7. At that time, the system gradually begins to secrete hormones into the bloodstream during sleep (Nottelmann et al., 1987). These hormones, called **gonadotropins,** travel to the brain carrying messages about changes to the body. When they reach the brain, they stimulate the production of hormones by the sex glands, or gonads. Gradually, over about a 4- or 5-year span, the influence of these hormones becomes apparent in adolescents' bodies (Connolly, Paikoff, & Buchanan, 1996).

The hormonal changes during adolescence include increased levels of both sex hormones (testosterone and estrogen) and growth hormones. Boys and girls have approximately the same amounts of these sex hormones in their bodies throughout most of child-

primary sexual characteristics physical features directly related to reproduction, such as the ovaries, penis, and testes

secondary sexual characteristics features that are outward manifestations of sexual development but are not directly involved in reproduction, such as breasts, facial and body hair, and an adult body shape

gonadotropins chemical messengers that stimulate the production of hormones by the glands

precocious puberty extremely early puberty, often caused by a genetic disorder

hood, but during early adolescence this balance changes. In girls, the key hormone is estrogen, which is secreted in higher amounts through the stimulation of the ovaries. In boys, the key hormone is the androgen testosterone, which is secreted in higher amounts through stimulation of the testes. The relative amounts of these hormones in the body account for the physical changes associated with puberty. For instance, hair growth is related to androgens, and the onset of menstruation involves estrogen (Petersen, 1987).

Although the general sequence of events associated with puberty is predictable, the timing of these events varies considerably from one person to another (see Figure 11.2). Genetics plays a dominant role in the timing of puberty, as is evident in research showing that the events of puberty are more closely linked in time for monozygotic twins than for dizygotic twins or siblings (Tanner, 1989). It is unlikely, however, that genetic factors set a particular age for puberty to begin in an individual. Instead, each individual appears to have a genetically influenced predisposition to begin puberty within a certain age range and to move through the physical changes of puberty at a certain rate. Thus, genetic factors set upper and lower limits on the timing of puberty and on the rate of pubertal development. A very small number of girls and boys experience unusually early puberty, called **precocious puberty,** often because of genetic disorders.

Puberty is considered precocious when it begins before the age of 8 in a girl or before the age of 9 in a boy (Cutler, 1988). About 1 child in every 10,000 in the United States experiences precocious puberty, and the disorder is nine times more common in girls than in boys (Root, 2000). Like normal puberty, precocious puberty is associated with a growth spurt and an increase in the rate of bone maturation.

Sexual characteristics also develop early in children who experience precocious puberty. Girls develop breasts and grow pubic hair. They often menstruate and can even ovulate. An extreme case of precocious puberty comes from Peru, where a 5-year-old girl, who was initially suspected by her mother of being possessed by a demon, became pregnant and eventually gave birth to a healthy baby boy. She was the youngest mother in the world and still holds that dubious honor today (Rose, 1988). Precocious boys experience spontaneous erections and may produce sperm. Although these children are advanced in sexual maturation, their mental development is normal. Thus, they

FIGURE 11.2
Variations in Sexual Maturation

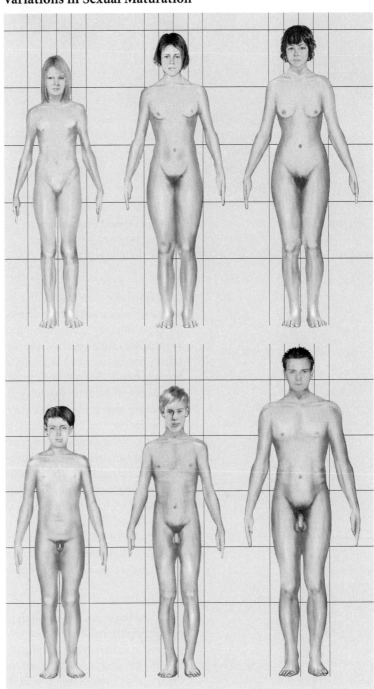

SOURCE: Tanner, 1975.

Notice how different the boys look and how different the girls look, even though they are of the same age (the females are about 13 years old, and the males are about 15 years old). Such comparisons reveal the large individual differences in the rates with which teens achieve sexual maturation.

possess the physical characteristics of adolescents but do not possess the higher level of abstract thinking that adolescents do. Because these children mature so far ahead of their peers,

Girls raised in harmonious families tend to mature somewhat later than girls raised in stressful families. What evolutionary argument has been proposed to explain the early maturation of girls in stressful families?

they often suffer teasing and rejection, leading to feelings of loneliness and isolation. (Sonis et al., 1985).

Treatment of precocious puberty includes dealing with any obvious condition that caused the accelerated rate of puberty (such as removing a tumor or cyst) and changing the hormonal balance of the body. Drugs that block the production of hormones associated with puberty have been effective in arresting and regressing sexual development and growth. (Cutler, 1993).

Environmental Influences on Pubertal Development

Environmental influences determine whether puberty occurs earlier or later within the genetically influenced age range for the onset of puberty—again illustrating the complex interplay of biological and environmental factors in human development (Connolly et al., 1996). Two powerful environmental influences are general health and nutrition. Adolescents who are healthy and who have received adequate nutrition throughout their early years are likely to enter puberty earlier. Adolescents who have been chronically ill may have delayed puberty (Brooks-Gunn, 1988). Children who are malnourished have delayed growth spurts and onset of puberty, possibly because of lower gonadotropin secretions (Hopwood et al., 1990). Girls who exercise strenuously (such as gymnasts, runners, and ballet dancers) and who have low levels of body fat often have delayed puberty (Bancroft & Reinisch, 1990). From an evolutionary perspective, girls appear to begin pubertal changes when their bodies have adequate fat to maintain pregnancy.

Although both biological and environmental factors are known to influence the timing of puberty, new evidence has given rise to speculation about how family experiences influence puberty. One controversial idea is that stressful family experiences trigger puberty. Based on evolutionary theories of development (Chapter 2), some researchers have speculated that early maturation may be an evolutionary mechanism that increases the chances of survival for girls who have a stressful family environment: By maturing early, they are able to leave their birth families and establish their own families earlier than other girls (Belsky, Steinberg, & Draper, 1991). Research supports the link between timing of maturation and family stress. Young girls raised in families that experience high levels of conflict reach puberty about six months earlier than girls from more harmonious homes (Belsky et al., 1991; Wierson, Long, & Forehand, 1993). However, the precise reasons for this effect and how it occurs are not yet fully understood (Graber, Brooks-Gunn, & Warren, 1995).

Sex and Race Differences in Puberty

Girls and boys progress through puberty differently and at different times. Girls begin and complete puberty about two years earlier than boys. Although it is commonly believed that menarche signals the beginning of puberty for girls, menarche actually occurs relatively late in pubertal development. The typical progression of pubertal changes in girls begins with breast growth and development. Between 8 and 10 years of age, enlarged breast buds develop, and the breasts continue to grow in size during adolescence. Growth of pubic hair is the second marker of puberty in girls, typically beginning at 10 to 12 years of age and continuing until the hair has formed the adultlike triangular pattern, usually by age 14. The third marker of puberty is the development of the female genitalia. The external sex organs—the labia, vulva, and clitoris—all increase in size and in sensitivity. The internal sex organs—the ovaries and uterus—also grow rapidly. Menarche usually occurs about two years after the beginning of breast development. Typically, girls do not ovulate until about a year after menarche. The final pubertal changes for females include deepening of the voice and the tendency to have acne.

The age at which girls achieve puberty varies by race. According to the results of a large-scale study of over 18,000 children 3 to 12 years old, about 38 percent of African American girls and 11 percent of Caucasian American girls showed breast development by age 8 (Herman-Giddens et al., 1997). Thus, it appears that girls today are undergoing puberty about a year earlier than has been reported before, with African American girls beginning puberty from 1 to 2 years earlier than their Caucasian American peers. Why these recent trends are occurring is not yet understood.

The pattern of pubertal development for boys is more variable than that for girls, and events occur in a different order (Marshall & Tanner, 1986). In the most typical pattern for boys, the growth of the testes is the first marker, usually beginning at 11½ to 12 years of age. Growth of pubic hair may be next, although boys vary widely in the age at which this begins (10 to 15 years). About a year later, growth of the penis and scrotum usually occurs. Between ages 12 and 16, boys typically have their first ejaculation of seminal fluid, although mature sperm may not be produced until about age 15 (Caissy, 1994). About two years after the appearance of pubic hair, underarm and facial hair begin to appear. Facial hair first appears on the upper lip, then on the upper cheeks, and last on the chin and lower jaw. In males, body hair continues to develop well after puberty (Marshall & Tanner, 1986). A sometimes embarrassing aspect of adolescent male development is the change in voice that occurs as the larynx increases in size. Comparative studies show that, in contrast to girls, African American and Caucasian American boys exhibit no differences in pubertal development (Marshall & Tanner, 1986).

FIGURE 11.3

Cross-Cultural Comparisons of Changes in Age at Menarche

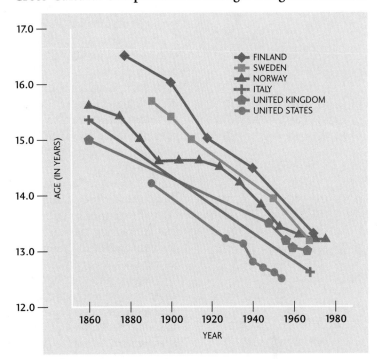

SOURCE: Marshall and Tanner, 1986.

Notice that the age at which girls achieve menarche has been dropping consistently over the past century. How are these findings explained? What factors contribute to these patterns?

Generational Differences in Puberty

Children today achieve puberty, start the growth spurt, and reach adult height about three years earlier than children did 100 years ago. This generational trend is more apparent in girls than in boys (Papadimitriou, 2001). For instance, in the United States, the age at menarche has dropped about two to three years over the last century (Wyshak, 1983), with girls today reaching menarche at about 12½ years (Herman-Giddens et al., 1997). This pattern is seen all over the world (see Figure 11.3).

One explanation for earlier maturation is improved nutrition and health care. These improvements may have reduced the time it takes for girls to reach a critical weight, which is regarded by some as the signal to the body to begin the adolescent growth spurt (Frisch, 1991). The trend toward earlier puberty and growth began with groups that had better nutrition, such as economically well-off adolescents. However, in many countries, such as the United States and Denmark, the differences among groups is now small, and the trend toward earlier puberty and growth spurts has ceased (Helm & Grolund, 1998; Eveleth & Tanner, 1990).

YOUNG ADOLESCENTS' RESPONSES TO PHYSICAL AND SEXUAL MATURATION

Two elderly men watch as a young adolescent boy and girl hug and kiss each other in a movie theater. "Those kids' hormones are out of control," says one of the men.

Like the men at the movie theater, many people tend to blame hormones for adolescents' interest in the other sex, their moods swings, and their tendency to argue. This view, however, is inaccurate. Although the hormonal changes that trigger puberty are associated with changes in young adolescents' behavior, they are not direct causes of this behavior. Surprisingly little evidence suggests that hormones directly affect behavior. More support has been found for an indirect influence—hormonally triggered maturation brings about changes in an individual's self-concept and social interactions (Connolly et al., 1996). The indirect effects begin when hormones cause physical changes in the secondary sexual characteristics, which are visible signs of physical maturity. These signs then influence how others treat the adolescent. For instance, their parents' and peers' expectations for them change once adolescents undergo growth spurts because they seem older than other children. These changes influence the way they are treated. In turn, changes in how adolescents are treated influence how they feel about themselves (see Figure 11.4).

If a girl matures early and her father withdraws from her because he is uncomfortable with her emerging sexuality, she may feel rejected and begin to lose confidence in herself. On the other hand, a boy who matures early may be treated more like an adult by his teachers, thereby becoming more confident. In each case, it is not the biological changes at puberty that are causing the young adolescent's behavior. Instead, it is the meaning attributed to these changes by the young adolescent or by significant others that is influencing the adolescent's behavior (Brooks-Gunn & Warren, 1989).

Parents and their adolescent children can have different culture-based expectations about development. Hopi Indian girls know, for instance, that once they start to menstruate, they begin a new phase of life in which they may no longer roam at will but must instead stay at home. People in traditional Hopi society believe that running free is inappropriate after menarche because girls should guard their chastity and reputation and devote their

FIGURE 11.4

Direct and Indirect Effects of Hormones on Adolescents' Psychological Adjustment and Behavior

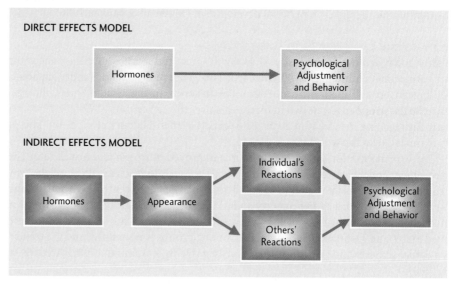

This figure depicts the influence of hormones on adolescents' adjustment and behavior. In the top model, hormones directly influence adjustment and behavior without any variables intervening. In the lower model, the effects of hormones on adjustment and behavior are mediated by the effects they have on the adolescent's appearance, which then influences how others behave, which then influences the adolescent's behavior and adjustment. Which model do you feel better depicts the ways hormones influence adolescents' adjustment and behavior?

time to preparing family meals. Girls also are expected to marry, which presents a dilemma: they must find a spouse while remaining secluded. Hopi girls are encouraged by their families to bring a new worker into the family in the form of a spouse, and yet they are not allowed the freedom to find that spouse. Although restrictions on freedom and pressure to marry make adolescence a trying time for Hopi girls, most learn to balance the expectations of their new status and adapt accordingly. Such responses to puberty, which vary across cultures, have important implications for interpersonal and personal adjustment.

Effects of Timing of Puberty in Boys and Girls

In early adolescence, early maturing boys are taller, heavier, and stronger than their peers, whereas late maturing boys are shorter, thinner, and weaker. Because the traditional culture values strength and athleticism in men, early maturing boys have an advantage. In light of their strength, these boys are likely to be better athletes than their peers and may feel more confident and competent, which can lead to increased self-esteem and elevated social status (Petersen, 1988; Simmons & Blyth, 1987). Late maturing boys tend to be treated as though they were younger than their peers and may come to feel insecure about their own abilities (Caissy, 1994). They also are at risk for adjustment problems (Graber, Lewinsohn, Seeley, & Brooks-Gunn, 1997). Late maturing boys also tend to be more dissatisfied with their body because they may weigh 25 to 30 pounds less and be 6 to 8 inches shorter than their peers (Alsaker, 1992).

Girls who mature early face different challenges than girls who mature later. What risks do these girls encounter?

Early maturing boys are more likely than their peers to have problems at school and to use drugs and alcohol (Andersson & Magnusson, 1990; Duncan, Ritter, Dornbusch, Gross, & Carlsmith, 1985). One reason for these behaviors may be that early maturing boys tend to make friends with older adolescents before they have had time to develop the strong coping skills they need to adjust to the physical changes of puberty (Alsaker, 1996). In contrast, late maturing boys have the advantage of sufficient time in which to develop coping skills and values before they face the challenges of puberty (Susman, Koch, Maney, & Finkelstein, 1993).

Girls who mature early face a very different set of circumstances. Not only are they developing two or three years earlier than other girls; they also are four to six years ahead of the boys in their class. Being one of the first to enter puberty can be difficult, for there are no peers with whom to share the experience. Also, as early maturing girls develop from slender preadolescents into fuller-breasted, wider-hipped adolescents, they may become concerned about the weight gain and increase in body fat that are normal to puberty. Some early maturing girls perceive these changes as unattractive. The slim, long-legged body represents a standard of beauty that many young girls believe they must match in order to be accepted and considered attractive (Alsaker, 1996; Martin, 1996).

Because of dissatisfaction with the changes their body undergoes at puberty, early maturing girls are at risk for eating disorders and disturbances (Koff & Rierdan, 1993). An exception to the poorer body image of early maturers is breast development: girls who develop breasts earlier tend to have a better body image, possibly because of the value placed on well-developed breasts in American society (Tobin-Richards, Boxer, & Petersen, 1983).

Early maturing girls are more popular, have more older friends, gain more attention from older boys, and begin dating earlier than later maturing girls. Like early maturing boys, early maturing girls tend to associate with older girls and boys, which may lead to use of alcohol and drugs (Tschann et al., 1994) and delinquency (Petersen, 1988). They also are more likely than their peers to be depressed, and they may do less well in school (Alsaker, 1992). Early onset of puberty seems to magnify preexisting behavior problems, so girls with earlier problems have the most difficulty adjusting (Ge, Conger, & Elder, 1996; Hayward, Killen, Wilson, & Hammer, 1997).

Late maturing girls may have the best situation of all adolescents—they are not the first to enter a new stage and probably enter puberty at about the same time as many early maturing boys. They are not the last to mature, since that position is held by late maturing boys. Although these girls may have some initial doubts about their status, they have longer to learn to cope with the changes and more opportunities to share the experience with peers than do early maturing girls.

Thus, early maturers of both sexes may be unprepared for the changes they experience; late maturers are less surprised by these changes and better informed. Late maturers have many mature role models, as well as family members who are prepared for the changes the adolescents undergo (Alsaker, 1996).

Individual characteristics—personality factors, attitudes, values, and prior experiences—play an important role in how adolescents respond to the physical changes that occur at puberty, the early or late timing of these changes, and the cultural expectations associated with them. For instance, one early maturing girl may gravitate toward friends who are older and resemble her more, as they may make her feel more comfortable with her bodily changes. Through her older friends, she will be exposed to the norms and expectations for behavior among older adolescents (Alsaker, 1996). Another early maturing girl, however, may continue to interact with same-age peers and thus respond quite differently to pubertal changes.

Outcomes for Early and Later Maturers

Several classic longitudinal studies have examined the characteristics of early and late maturers as they grow older and reach adulthood. These studies reveal that the early maturing boys who enjoyed advantages over their peers take on more leadership roles later in life. They rate themselves as more responsible and warmer, but also as more rigid and conforming, than do other males (Jones & Mussen, 1958). Late maturing boys, who are the last of their peers to mature, rate themselves as more rebellious, impulsive, and childish, but also as more creative. As adults, they hold fewer executive jobs, but they report being happier and having more successful marriages than do early maturing males (Jones, 1965; Mussen & Jones, 1957).

Early maturing girls, who face many challenges from adults and peers while dealing with puberty, continue to experience difficulties as they grow older. Although this certainly is not true of all early maturing girls, early maturing girls as a group complete fewer years of education and are more likely to develop negative attitudes about school (Alsaker, 1995). As young adults, they have more children than later developing girls, especially if they developed relationships with older friends during adolescence (Magnusson, 1988). In middle age, they rate themselves as more self-directed and self-assured than later developing girls do (Peskin, 1973).

PSYCHOLOGICAL REACTIONS TO PUBERTAL EVENTS

Puberty brings with it dramatic physical changes. Adolescents grow taller and gain weight, and their body proportions change. Girls begin to menstruate, and boys begin having wet dreams. How do young adolescents react to the changes in the appearance and functioning of their bodies?

Reactions to Changes in Appearance

Adolescents expend considerable time and energy thinking about their appearance. One reason for this preoccupation is that adolescents are experiencing sudden changes in the way they look. Another source of adolescents' concern with their bodies is changes in their cognitive abilities, which cause them to focus more of their attention on themselves. This concern about appearance also is due in part to the positive characteristics attributed to attractive individuals. For example, research has demonstrated that people believe that attractive adolescents are successful, friendly, and intelligent (Lerner, Delaney, Hess, Jovanovic, & von Eye, 1990). Adolescents' body images also become more important as they become interested in the other sex; they want to be desirable to the other sex so that they will be able to get dates and be popular (Martin, 1996).

Adolescents' body images are shaped by societal expectations conveyed through magazines, television, and movies, as well as by people's responses to their appearance. For instance, hours of television viewing exposes adolescents to actors and actresses who tend to be young, attractive, and slim. The ideals concerning attractiveness for females are highly ingrained in our culture (Phelps et al., 1993). Girls know these standards by age 6 and believe that they relate to popularity. Being slim is a central feature of what it means to be attractive. At an early age, children develop negative stereotypes about overweight people (Counts, Jones, Frame, & Jarvie, 1986). Girls are more worried about being slim than boys are, and they are more critical of their own appearance. As you learned in reading about early and late maturing adolescents, early maturing girls, in particular, have difficulty as they gain weight during puberty because they perceive this change as moving them away from the ideal of beauty in our culture (La-Porte, 1997). Despite all the societal pressures, though, many young girls develop a good body image, causing them to be less preoccupied than other girls with weight and with comparing themselves to others (Rosenbaum, 1993).

In the United States, the cultural expectation of long legs and a slim body, especially for girls and women, is a relatively recent notion. Even twenty-five years ago, the US ideal for women was more voluptuous and curvaceous. The pressure to be slim is related to socioeconomic class in the United States, with women of higher socioeconomic status being thinner than women of middle and lower socioeconomic status. Historically, however, being thin has been associated with a poor diet and with disease.

These girls have different ideas about what it means to be attractive. What standards of beauty do Caucasian girls use? African-American girls?

Within the United States, different ethnic groups hold varying standards for attractiveness. Some African American females report more flexible concepts of attractiveness, including "making what you've got work for you" (Parker, Rubin, Price, & De Rosier, 1995). Caucasian American girls express a need to be "perfect" in their appearance, meaning they must have a flat stomach, little waist, and slim thighs to be attractive. In contrast, African American girls are less likely to focus on physical attributes, instead considering attitude, confidence, and grooming to be important to attractiveness. These more flexible and attainable standards for attractiveness may contribute to the better body images and lower risk of eating disorders among African American girls than among Caucasian American girls (Parker et al., 1995).

Reactions to Markers of Sexual Maturity

All I could think of was what I would feel if someone saw me buying sanitary napkins at the drugstore.

I was scared and embarrassed. I felt like everyone who looked at me could tell I was wearing one of those awful Kotex pads!

My mother and my school had prepared me for it, and although it was a surprise, it was kind of exciting to feel like I was a woman.

—*Adolescent girls responding to menarche*
(Dacey & Kenny, 1997, p. 83)

A milestone of puberty for girls is menarche. Most women vividly recall their first period (Gallant & Derry, 1995). But as the comments of the girls above indicate, responses to menarche are mixed. On the positive side, adolescent girls believe that menarche is a sign of maturity, signals their ability to have children, is a part of being a woman, and makes them more similar to other females. On the negative side, they find that it is a hassle because of the need to carry pads or tampons with them, the physical discomfort, and the limitations it places on their activities (McGrory, 1990; Ryan, Millstein, & Irwin, 1996).

Girls' adjustment to menarche is influenced by how prepared they are. Compared to girls who are prepared for menarche, unprepared girls report feeling more negative symptoms and have a more negative self-image (McGrory, 1990). Girls' prior expectations about menstruation also influence their feelings. Girls who expect pain and discomfort are more likely to report pain and discomfort once they begin menstruating (Brooks-Gunn & Ruble, 1982).

Two health problems related to menstruation may become issues for young girls. **Dysmenorrhea** is the name for menstrual cramps and discomfort, and **premenstrual syndrome (PMS)** refers to a whole constellation of emotional and physical symptoms, such

dysmenorrhea menstrual cramps and discomfort

premenstrual syndrome (PMS) a whole constellation of emotional and physical symptoms, such as backaches, headaches, moodiness, and water retention, that occur before menstruation

THE SOCIAL IMPACT: DEBATING THE ISSUE

Do Gender Roles Intensify When Adolescents Reach Puberty?

As a young adolescent's body matures and interest in dating increases, it may become more important to act in ways that are consistent with gender-role expectations. Boys who do not act masculine enough or girls who do not act feminine enough may not be accepted by their peers (Steinberg, 1996). Because of the noticeable physical changes that occur during early adolescence, and others' reactions to these, boys and girls may feel compelled to fit into traditional gender roles (Huston & Alvarez, 1990). The idea that adolescents' sex-role behaviors and attitudes become more traditional in early adolescence is referred to as *gender intensification* (Hill & Lynch, 1983). Whether or not this pattern actually occurs is not clear.

Some support has been found for gender intensification. For example, gender differences increase over the course of early adolescence (Galambos, Almeida, & Petersen, 1991), and girls have been found to spend more time engaging in interpersonal activities and

household chores and less time playing sports than they did before reaching puberty (Ruble & Martin, 1998). Additionally, the relationship between school achievement and self-image strengthens during early adolescence for boys but weakens for girls (Roberts, Sarigiani, Petersen, & Newman, 1993). This sex difference is thought to occur because boys are pressured to excel in school, whereas girls are pressured to excel socially. Because boys and girls experience increasingly different socialization pressures and expectations during early adolescence, their behavior may come to reflect these differences.

Other studies, however, do *not* support gender intensification—especially in gender-role attitudes—during early adolescence (Antill, Russell, Goodnow, & Cotton, 1993). In some cases, gender intensification occurs only for certain groups of children. For instance, in a study of tomboys and nontomboys, only the nontomboys showed an increase in feminine preferences and

activities during early adolescence (Plumb & Cowan, 1984).

Given all the changes occurring during adolescence, it is not surprising that there is considerable fluctuation in gender-role attitudes and behaviors throughout the adolescent years (Ruble & Martin, 1998). Because puberty is a social as well as a physical event, the changes it brings in gender roles are determined by the context in which puberty take place, its timing and course, and the characteristics possessed by the individuals when they enter early adolescence.

Thinking It Through:

1. What role may parents play in intensifying gender behaviors and attitudes during early adolescence?
2. Is gender intensification desirable? How might it be avoided?
3. What factors might make some young adolescents more susceptible to gender intensification than others?

---

as backaches, headaches, moodiness, and water retention, that occur before menstruation. Dysmenorrhea is caused by the uterus's release of a hormone called prostaglandin during menstruation. The resulting pain can be treated by taking antiprostaglandin medications. Many adolescent girls experience dysmenorrhea; over 90 percent report having cramps with their periods, and 64 percent say that cramps are moderate or severe (Wilson & Keye, 1989). Adolescent girls also report having the symptoms of PMS (Fisher, Trieller, & Napolitano, 1989). Although social expectancies influence girls' reporting of symptoms of PMS, this does not imply that the symptoms of PMS are not real. Instead, it may be that knowledge of impending menstruation sensitizes adolescent girls and women to certain physical and emotional symptoms associated with it.

Little research is available about boys' responses to puberty. An important marker of puberty for boys is their first ejaculation. Generally, boys are not well informed about ejaculation, and the little information they have is gained from peers or the media. Probably because ejaculation is associated with masturbation, boys are often secretive about their first ejaculation, seldom talking with others about it (Gaddis & Brooks-Gunn, 1985). In addition, boys' anxiety about puberty may be heightened by erections that occur frequently and without warning, sometimes causing guilt and embarrassment.

WHAT ARE THE HEALTH CONCERNS FOR YOUNG ADOLESCENTS?

Adolescence is a period of enhanced awareness of and attention to well-being. For most adolescents, this is a time of optimal health, with young adolescents as a group showing low levels of chronic disease and low death rates. Adolescents describe themselves as being healthy overall. In a large-scale study of adolescents from Europe, Canada, and the United States, over 90 percent of adolescents described themselves as feeling healthy, although adolescents in the United States reported somewhat lower rates (Health Behavior in School-Aged Children, 2000). However, developing into adolescents brings children into contact with more diverse, and sometimes more dangerous, environments. Accidents and injuries are the most likely cause of death during adolescence, especially for boys and for older rather than younger adolescents (CDC, 1998). Nonetheless, death rates remain low during this period of development—about 53 deaths per 100,000 (CDC, 1998).

Many of the major health issues for young adolescents center on their rapid growth and the changes associated with puberty. Because they may grow 4 to 8 inches a year, young adolescents need good nutrition, yet they often have inadequate diets. Societal norms make some adolescents, especially young girls, overly concerned about the normal changes associated with puberty (such as weight gain). This combination of societal expectations and normal developmental changes may lead to eating disturbances or, in rare cases, full-blown eating disorders.

NUTRITION

The rapid physical growth experienced by adolescents requires a high-quality diet. But the reality is that many adolescents' diets are far from adequate. Many adolescents skip meals, eat high-fat snacks, avoid eating fruits and vegetables, and have inadequate knowledge about nutrition (Hertzler & Frary, 1989). In a study of 120,000 young adolescents from twenty-six European countries, Canada, and the United States, adolescents living in the United States were found to be less likely to have a good diet than adolescents in other countries. US adolescents were less likely to eat fruits and vegetables each day and more likely to eat potato chips and French fries than students from other countries. The United States ranked among the top three countries for adolescent consumption of sweets and soft drinks each day (Health Behaviors of School-Aged Children, 2000).

Nutritional needs during early adolescence vary widely depending on rate of growth and amount of physical activity. For instance, a very active adolescent girl in the peak of her growth spurt may need 20 percent more calories than a younger girl (Ensminger, Ensminger, Konlande, & Robson, 1986). Not surprisingly, the most calories are needed during the peak of the growth spurt (Schebendach & Shenker, 1992). Adolescents who have inadequate food intake are at risk for a variety of psychological problems, school suspension, and peer relationship difficulties (Alaimo et al., 2000).

Because of the increased growth of muscles, young adolescent girls and boys need more protein than children do. Dramatic bone growth increases calcium requirements, but many adolescents consume less than the recommended amounts. Girls in particular fall far short in calcium consumption, consuming only about 60 to 78 percent of the required amount. Lack of adequate calcium may increase the likelihood of osteoporosis—a loss of density and weakening of the bones—in later life (Schebendach & Shenker, 1992; Life Sciences Research Office [LSRO], 1995). Young adolescents also require additional iron but often fail to eat foods that are rich in iron. Lack of iron can lead to anemia and influence the ability to think, work, and adequately function (Beard, 1995).

EXERCISE AND SPORTS PARTICIPATION

The majority of young adolescents get vigorous physical activity at least twice a week, and boys are more likely than girls to exercise (Crocker, Eklund, & Kowalski, 2000). For girls more than for boys, the proportion of adolescents who exercise decreases with age over the adolescent years. Regular exercise is strongly associated with feeling healthy and confident, making friends, and spending time with friends (Health Policy for Children and Adolescents, 2000).

The late childhood and early adolescent period is the peak time for involvement in sports. In addition to the benefits of exercising, sports participation may provide a wide

Boys are more likely than girls to engage in vigorous physical activity. How does exercise enhance health and development? What can be done to increase fitness in young adolescents?

range of other benefits to adolescents. Every so often, newspapers print stories in which involvement in sports leads to a turning point in adolescents' lives. For instance, the *New York Times* printed a story about a girls' basketball team on a Navaho reservation. All of a sudden, after getting a new coach, the team started winning. This experience greatly improved the girls' opportunities and revitalized the community, whose members turned out in droves to support the team (Starsen, 1991).

Only a few studies have been done to assess the effects of sports participation on adolescents, but these studies suggest that involvement in sports can serve many functions. One function is developing social ties with others. Sports and other extracurricular activities integrate adolescents into the social world by connecting them with peers and adults in the community. Adolescents also are exposed to positive role models and have opportunities to engage in ethical behavior with other people. Young athletes derive support not only from connections with adults outside their family, such as coaches, but also from connections within their family. Athletic competitions provide a social setting in which family connections can be reaffirmed; parents often attend events to watch their sons and daughters compete and help their children cope with the pressures (Weiss & Hayashi, 1995). Parents and peers can provide support and encouragement for young athletes by having realistic expectations for them and avoiding negative evaluations of their performance (President's Council, 1997).

Sports participation, like other forms of exercise, may improve adolescents' mental health and psychological well-being (Biddle, 1995; Morgan, 1994; Steiner, McQuivey, Pavelski, Pitts, & Kraemer, 2000). Teens who exercise regularly are less likely to be depressed and anxious than those who are sedentary (Landers & Petruzzello, 1994; Morgan, 1994). Exercise may be a protective factor, helping adolescents cope with stress. For instance, girls who exercise regularly are able to deal with high levels of stress better than girls who do not exercise regularly (Brown & Lawton, 1986). Moderate levels of exercise are best for increasing mental health. Adolescents who exercise strenuously for long periods or who are in highly competitive sports contexts may suffer negative moods, lose their ability to concentrate, and become depressed and anxious (Singer, 1992).

Additionally, sports serve as a vehicle for personal integration. Participation may improve adolescents' self-esteem and self-concept by helping them realize their particular strengths and improve their sense of mastery, concentration, and planning (Larson, 1994; Williams & McGee, 1991). Individual benefits depend on the type of sports involvement, attitudes about winning, and qualities of the coaches or adult leaders involved in the activity (Larson, 1994). For instance, athletes who use sports to measure their self-worth, especially boys, experience negative effects on their self-evaluation when they do poorly or when they lose. In contrast, athletes who use their sports performance to gain a sense of mastery are more likely to experience positive effects on their self-evaluation (Danish, Kleiber, & Hall, 1987; Duda, 1988).

Body image, which influences self-esteem, can be improved or denigrated because of sports. Coaches sometimes discourage overweight adolescents from involvement in sports, which can negatively affect these adolescents' self-esteem. A young gymnast whose coach tells her she is too fat will feel worse rather than better about her body image. In contrast, when parents and coaches have a positive attitude toward adolescents' participation and appearance, adolescents feel better about their body as well as their accomplishments (President's Council, 1997).

EATING DISTURBANCES AND DISORDERS

The full spectrum of eating problems can be seen during adolescence. One of the most common problems, occurring in about 1 in 5 adolescents, is being overweight. Additionally, many adolescents have eating disturbances in which they eat too little or have unhealthy eating habits. A small group of adolescents—girls in particular—develop serious and life-threatening eating disorders such as anorexia and bulimia.

Obesity

About 14 percent of adolescents in the United States are seriously overweight, and this figure has doubled since the 1970s (CDC, 2001d), especially for adolescents who immigrated to the United States (Popkin & Udry, 1998). The reasons for the increase are unclear, although lack of exercise and poor eating habits contribute to the problem, as they do for younger children (see Chapter 9). Like overweight children, overweight adolescents watch more television and are less active than their normal-weight peers (Jelalian & Lloyd, 1997). Obesity in adolescence is related to a variety of serious health risks in later life (Vogt, 1999). For instance, overweight adolescents are more likely than their normal-weight peers to suffer heart disease, colon cancer, and arthritis and have generally poorer health as adults. About 75 percent of overweight adolescents become overweight adults (CDC, 2001d).

Many adolescents are concerned about their weight but attempt to control it in ineffective ways. Many adopt dieting as a strategy for weight control when increased physical activity is more likely to be beneficial. According to one health study, about one-half of girls and one-third of boys ages 11 to 13 feel they should be dieting (Health Behavior in School-Aged Children, 2000).

Anorexia Nervosa

Sylvia is a 14-year-old adolescent who is 5 feet 6 inches tall but weighs only 85 pounds. She is not pleased with her appearance. Despite others' views that she is too skinny, Sylvia worries she is too fat. Because of this, she exercises frequently and eats little. Her diet is very restricted; she consumes only about 1000 calories a day, mainly eating lettuce, carrots, and fruit. She has stopped having menstrual periods and often is sick. She has no idea that she is undernourished. Instead, Sylvia feels that she has a healthy fear of being fat and shows strong self-discipline because of her strict adherence to her low-calorie diet. Nonetheless, she is moody, depressed, and exhausted all the time. Sylvia is anorexic and has had to be hospitalized to prevent starvation.

Anorexia nervosa is an eating disorder, occurring most often in young women, in which individuals eat very little but believe that they are fat. Food and weight become obsessions. Many anorexics eat less than 800 calories a day and only three or four different foods. A core symptom of this disorder is an unrelenting pursuit of thinness, usually beginning during adolescence (Bon-De-Matte, 1998). This illness is marked by psychological disturbances as well as physical symptoms. The essential symptoms include a dramatic loss of weight or failure to gain expected weight, an intense fear of gaining weight or becoming fat, a negative body image, and, for females, an absence of menstrual cycles (American Psychiatric Association, 1994).

Although it is commonly believed that anorexic individuals have a distorted body image, research does not clearly support this belief. That is, anorexics perceive their body fairly accurately; nonetheless, they have a negative body image since their ideal shape (what they *want* to look like) is much thinner than their actual shape. Furthermore, the particular focus of concern varies from girl to girl—some worry about the size of their abdomen or waist; others worry about having their inner thighs touch when they walk (Hsu & Sobkiewicz, 1991). People prone to anorexia are described as being overly perfectionistic, highly controlled, and "model children." Anorexia occurs nine times more often in females than in males and is more common in girls from middle-class and upwardly mobile families (Coupey, 1992; Silber, 1986).

Many factors relate to anorexia, but the extent to which they may cause the disorder is unclear. Also, wide individual differences exist in the causes of anorexia. Genetic predisposition plays a small role, but family relationships may play a larger role. Families of anorexics often have disturbed functioning (Rastam & Gillberg, 1991). For example, there is some evidence that parents of anorexic adolescents tend toward intense and intrusive involvement in their children's lives, as a result of frustration and disappointment in their own lives. This parental overinvolvement leaves the children ill-equipped to cope with the

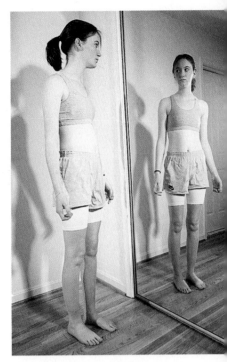

The young teenager in this picture is thin but still feels that she is overweight. She is concerned with being thin, which is a common characteristic in people with eating disorders and disturbances. What factors contribute to dramatically higher rates of eating disorders and disturbances among girls?

anorexia nervosa an eating disorder, occurring most often in young women, in which individuals eat very little but believe that they are overweight

challenges experienced during early adolescence (Fisher & Brone, 1991). Additionally, victims of anorexia tend to have certain psychological characteristics, including the following:

+ Personality traits such as shyness, social anxiety and fearfulness, overcontrol, passivity, and perfectionism
+ Loss of a family member early in life (Coupey, 1992)
+ Depression (Fombonne, 1995)

Anorexia poses serious health hazards. Inadequate intake of calories may lead to poor growth, delayed sexual development, osteoporosis, and infertility (Lifshitz, Finch, & Lifshitz, 1991). Anorexia can last for long periods of time, and death may result from starvation and its complications (National Institute of Mental Health [NIMH], 1994).

Cultural beliefs concerning ideal weight and body shape appear to be important factors in the development of eating disorders. In industrialized cultures, where thinness is the societal ideal for women, anorexia and other eating disorders are more prevalent. In Argentina, for example, almost 1 in 10 girls suffers from a serious eating disorder—many more than in the United States. Health experts blame this "epidemic" on an obsession with thinness. In some parts of the world, the ideal body is heavier than it is in the United States (Booth, 1994). Being large and having body fat are emblems of wealth and fertility in many cultures. Among Africans, African Americans, Filipinos, Middle Easterners, and Native Americans, the ideal of attractiveness includes a higher level of body fat than it does among Caucasians. Being overweight in these cultures is a protective factor in overall health (Kittler & Sucher, 1998; Williamson, 1998).

In the United States, 1 percent of adolescents are diagnosed with anorexia (Katzman, 1996). This figure is higher for certain subcultures in the United States. For example, athletic women and men such as dancers and gymnasts are at a higher risk for this disorder (Fombonne, 1995). An extreme example is the case of Heidi Guenther, a young dancer who was told by one of the directors of the Boston Ballet Company that she needed to lose weight. After a few months of intense dieting, Heidi collapsed and died, probably from complications of poor nutrition caused by anorexia. At the time of her death, she was 5 feet 5 inches tall but weighed only 100 pounds.

Treatment for anorexia must include consideration of both physical and psychological aspects of the disorder. Treatments that deal only with the weight loss, such as medication or surgery, are rarely effective (Bowers, Evans, & Van-Cleve, 1996). The most effective treatments involve structured programs with positive reinforcement for weight gain, as well as nutritional supplements, therapy to help the individual overcome the fear of getting fat, and family and group therapy, all of which are likely to be needed for several years (Coupey, 1992).

Bulimia Nervosa

Like Sylvia's, Lisa's strange eating behavior began during adolescence. Lisa diets and exercises to lose weight, but, unlike Sylvia, she regularly eats huge amounts of food; she maintains her normal weight by forcing herself to vomit. She feels lonely and isolated, and when things do not go well, she is overcome with an uncontrollable desire for sweets. She eats pounds of cake or cookies at a time and often does not stop until she is exhausted or in severe pain. Then, overwhelmed by guilt and disgust, she makes herself vomit (NIMH, 1994). Lisa is bulimic.

Bulimia nervosa, an eating disorder characterized by secret eating binges and purges, often begins later in adolescence than anorexia does. During eating binges, bulimics consume a large quantity of food over a short period of time and feel no control over their food consumption. Bulimics have been known to eat over 7 pounds of food in a single binge (Lifshitz, Finch, & Lifshitz, 1991). Like Lisa, bulimics feel guilty and uncomfortable after bingeing. To avoid gaining weight, and to reduce their anxiety and guilt, they purge themselves by vomiting, using laxatives, or exercising excessively. Table 11.2 compares the major symptoms of bulimia and anorexia.

bulimia nervosa an eating disorder characterized by secret eating binges and purges

TABLE 11.2

Comparison of Common Symptoms of Anorexia and Bulimia

SYMPTOMS	ANOREXIA	BULIMIA
Excessive weight loss	X	
Continuation of dieting although bone-thin	X	
Dissatisfaction with appearance	X	
Loss of monthly menstrual periods	X	X
Unusual interest in food	X	X
Development of strange eating rituals	X	X
Eating in secret	X	X
Obsession with exercise	X	X
Serious depression	X	X
Consumption of large amounts of food		X
Vomiting or use of drugs to stimulate defecation		X
Disappearance into bathroom for long periods of time		X
Abuse of drugs or alcohol		X

NOTE: Some individuals suffer from both anorexia and bulimia and have symptoms of both disorders.
SOURCE: NIMH, 1994.

Like anorexics, bulimics are persistently overconcerned with body shape and weight (American Psychiatric Association, 1994). Bulimia typically continues intermittently over many years, during which periods of normal eating are interspersed with binges and purges. Although prevalence estimates vary widely, about 2 to 5 percent of females and about 1 percent of males are diagnosed with bulimia (Boeck, 1992).

Personality, social, and cultural factors relate to bulimia. Individuals with bulimia often have family members who are obese and suffer from depression (Rastam & Gillberg, 1991). Bulimic individuals tend to be depressed and have poor self-esteem (Fombonne, 1995). Like anorexia, bulimia is more likely to occur in adolescents from middle- and upper-class families and is more common in societies where thinness is the ideal (Furnham & Alibhai, 1983).

Successful therapy for bulimia targets the physical and psychological aspects of the disorder. Bulimia is treated through behavior modification programs, nutrition education, medications for depression, and counseling (Beock, 1992a). Bulimia is most successfully treated when it is diagnosed early, but because bulimics maintain a normal body weight, they often are able to hide their illness from others for years.

Eating Disturbances

Although anorexia and bulimia are relatively rare, milder versions of these eating patterns, referred to as **eating disturbances,** are quite common in adolescents. For instance, some adolescents skip meals, avoid certain foods, or take in an inadequate number of calories (Lifshitz et al., 1991). Binge eating, but usually without purging, also is common. Eating disturbances are more common in adolescent girls than in any other group of people (Moore & Gullone, 1995; Page & Allen, 1995).

Why are eating disturbances so common? Even before puberty, US children have excessive concern with weight. In a study of 8- to 13-year-old children, over one-third of the youngest children reported that they wanted to be thinner. By age 13, about 75 percent of the girls and 40 percent of the boys desired to be thinner (Maloney, McGuire, Daniels, & Specker, 1989). These weight-conscious children enter puberty already aware of the cultural belief that being thin is beautiful and healthy. Parental concerns and the media—especially

eating disturbances mild versions of eating disorders

television and fashion magazines—contribute to adolescents' weight concerns (Field et al., 2001). The weight concerns of adolescents may be magnified by newly emerging cognitive abilities, which increase their attention and focus on themselves and their concerns about what others think of them, as will be discussed later in the chapter.

As you can see in Figure 11.5, by adolescence, eating and weight concerns are more pronounced among girls than among boys (CDC, 2001d), and this difference gets larger as young adolescents get older (Richards, Casper, & Larson, 1990). Young girls, in particular, skip meals and avoid snacks or favorite foods to try to lose weight (CDC, 2001d; Stein & Reichert, 1990). Although taking laxatives, vomiting, and taking diet pills are uncommon and extreme dieting behaviors, girls are more likely to use these forms of dieting than boys (CDC, 2001d).

Eating disturbances also may be common because adolescents in the United States weigh more now than in the past. This increase in body weight, coupled with the increased emphasis on thinness, may add to the dissatisfaction that many adolescents feel as they enter puberty and begin to gain weight. A longitudinal study of eating disturbances found that young adolescent girls with negative feelings about their body were more likely than their peers to develop eating problems when they gained weight (Attie & Brooks-Gunn, 1989). Thus, societal and developmental factors combine to increase the pressure for adolescents,

FIGURE 11.5

Sex Difference in Young Adolescents' Concerns About Weight and Eating, by Grade

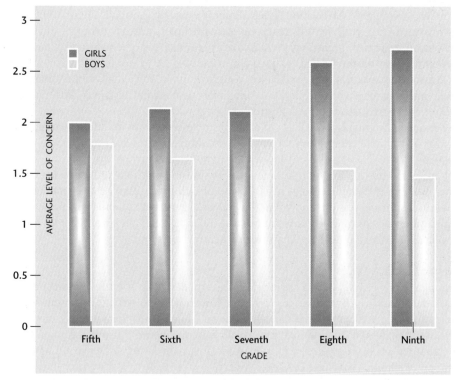

NOTE: A higher average score reflects a greater concern about weight gain and eating.

SOURCE: Richards, Casper, and Larson, 1990. Reprinted by permission of Elsevier Science. Copyright 1990 by The Society for Adolescent Medicine.

Notice that concerns about weight and eating are greater for girls than for boys at every age. Notice also how these concerns increase for girls and decrease for boys beginning in eighth grade. Can you explain the reasons for these differences and why these differences would be magnified around eighth grade?

particularly girls, to maintain a below-average body weight (Fombonne, 1995; Levine, Smolak, Moodey, Shuman, & Hessen, 1994).

Changing relationships with others may influence the risk that an adolescent will develop eating disturbances. Dating increases concerns about one's popularity, appearance, and body image. For instance, young adolescent girls who have achieved menarche and begun dating are more likely to develop eating disturbances than girls who are not dating (Cauffman & Steinberg, 1996). Interactions with mothers and fathers may buffer some girls from the stresses of puberty: girls who had better relationships with their parents, especially their fathers, had fewer weight and eating concerns and healthier eating habits than girls with strained relationships. Relationships with fathers are particularly important in conveying messages to daughters about whether their pubertal changes are acceptable (Field et al., 2001; Swarr & Richards, 1996).

As you learned in the discussion of adolescents' body images, ideals for attractiveness vary across ethnic groups. These differences may account for the research findings that Hispanic and Caucasian American students are more likely to think of themselves as being overweight than African American students are (CDC, 2001d).

How do young adolescents think and solve problems

The inward focus that many adolescents have with respect to their body and the physical changes they are undergoing is prompted in part by changes that occur in their cognitive abilities. Young adolescents have a new perspective on themselves and on their worlds. For instance, 14-year-old Justin devours science fiction books, enjoys movies, and spends hours playing video and computer games. He also belongs to the Sierra Club and worries about recycling, pollution, and the depletion of the ozone layer. He ponders deep questions about why we exist and the meaning of life while also worrying about his looks and girls. When he has a small blemish, he believes that everyone at school notices it and stares at him.

Justin's thinking reflects an interesting mix of abilities that accounts for some of his behavior. Like many young adolescents, Justin has entered the last of Piaget's stages of cognitive development, the *formal operational stage,* and is now able to think logically about a wider range of situations than he could before. Broad social issues, such as what will happen to the world if we run out of natural resources or whether assisted suicide should be made legal, become interesting to him because he can imagine many alternatives and perspectives. Justin also can use these new-found cognitive abilities to examine his own life. For most adolescents, the result is an intense inward focus and self-centeredness in their thinking.

REACHING COGNITIVE MATURITY: FORMAL OPERATIONAL THINKING

Justin's 9-year-old brother Gene recognizes that the amount of water stays the same when water is poured from a short, wide glass into a tall, narrow one, because he can apply basic logic to solve problems involving concrete objects. As a concrete operational thinker, Gene understands the principle of conservation of volume as it relates to liquids in containers. Justin, however, can apply logical operations more broadly to encompass hypothetical and abstract problems. As a formal operational thinker, Justin can imagine what it would be like to live on Mars, what would happen if the temperature on Earth got warmer, and how the universe began (Mueller, Overton, & Reene, 2001; Overton & Byrnes, 1991). Because formal operational thinkers can consider many alternatives and possibilities, they can be effective planners. Formal operational thinking appears between ages 11 and 15, although it may not be completely developed until late adolescence (Niaz, 1997; Piaget, 1977).

Justin is considered to have reached cognitive maturity, or formal operational thinking, because he can use **hypothetico-deductive reasoning,** which is the type of reasoning

To solve many problems in science classes, students need to systemically vary and test factors. Young children have difficulty systematically testing factors, but teens like the ones in this picture are able to formulate hypotheses and test them. What changes bring about this improved ability to think scientifically?

hypothetico-deductive reasoning the type of reasoning used in science

THE SCIENTIFIC IMPACT: INTERPRETING RESEARCH

What Do Boys Do When They Find a Real Gun?

Every day we see tragic headlines about accidental gun deaths involving children. A young boy shot his cousin accidentally after finding a loaded gun. Two 10-year-old boys were playing "police," and one boy died from an accidental gun shot. Gun control advocates suggest that child safety locks would prevent these accidents; gun advocates suggest that training in firearms and education would be enough to prevent them. Do children who know about guns avoid them? Do children recognize a real gun when they see one?

A recent study assessed what young boys, from 8 to 12 years old, actually do when they find a gun. First, parents of sixty-four boys completed a survey on firearm ownership, storage practices, and parental perceptions. Then, small groups of these boys and their friends went into an observation room that contained a one-way mirror. Within the room, several water pistols and an actual .380 handgun were concealed in separate drawers. The handgun had been modified so that a radio transmitter activated a light whenever the trigger was depressed with enough force to fire the gun. After playing in the room for 15 minutes, the boys were asked whether they thought the gun was real or a toy, and each child was counseled about gun safety. The results of the study are as follows:

- 72 percent of the boys discovered the handgun.
- Of those, 76 percent handled the gun and 48 percent pulled the trigger.
- About 50 percent were not sure whether or not the gun was real.

Parents were not very accurate in predicting what their sons would do. Boys whose parents said their sons had little interest in guns were as likely to handle the gun and pull the trigger as boys whose parents said they had high interest in guns. More than 90 percent of the boys reported that they had received prior gun safety instructions.

The lesson from this study is that many 8- to 12-year-old boys will handle a handgun if they find one, even if they have had safety instructions. Guns kept in homes should be stored so that they are inaccessible to children (Jackman, Farah, Kellermann, & Simon, 2001).

Thinking It Through:

1. Why might guns be so appealing to children? What can be done to decrease their appeal?
2. Can you think of ways in which parents and schools could provide more effective methods of educating children to avoid handling guns?
3. Would gun safety locks be enough to protect children from accidental gun injuries? What other protections might be needed?

---

employed in science. This type of reasoning encompasses three phases of thinking (Small, 1990):

1. An inductive phase, which involves thinking about and generating possible hypotheses based on prior knowledge
2. A deductive phase, which involves deriving conclusions from these hypotheses
3. A testing phase, which involves assessing the accuracy of the hypotheses

Piaget used a pendulum problem to assess thinking in children and adolescents (Inhelder & Piaget, 1958). Suppose Justin and Gene are given a pendulum; the length of the string by which it hangs can be varied, and the weights that attach to the string can be changed. After being shown how the pendulum works, they are told that their goal is to discover the factor or factors that influence the rate at which the pendulum swings. Besides the weight and the length of the string, factors might include how high they hold a weight before dropping it and how much force they use to push the weight.

Recall from the description of scientific thinking in Chapter 2 how a scientist would solve this problem. A scientist would begin by generating a hypothesis—say, that a heavier weight will make the pendulum swing faster—and then systematically test the hypothesis. Although Gene and other concrete operational children can generate hypotheses (Ruffman, Perner, Olson, & Doherty, 1993), they have difficulty testing them, especially if the situation is complex (Kuhn, 1989). For instance, Gene is likely to change more than one factor at a time, making it hard to see which factor influences the swing of the pendulum. In contrast, Justin considers the whole structure of a problem and knows that he must systematically vary one factor while holding the others constant. Justin might try the heavier weight and then the lighter weight while maintaining the same string length, height from which the weight is dropped, and force of push. Gene and Justin will also differ in how they keep track of their tests. Gene is less likely than Justin to keep track of the factors (Byrnes, 1988;

Schauble, 1990) and more apt to forget the instances when testing disconfirms his hypotheses (Dunbar & Klahr, 1989; Foltz, Overton, & Ricco, 1995). Also, Gene may not change his hypothesis in light of new evidence, whereas Justin will probably do so (Kuhn et al., 1988; Strauss, 1998). For these reasons, Gene is less likely than Justin to determine the relevant factor or factors. Because Justin will try all variations of the factors, he will probably conclude that it is only the length of the string that matters (Small, 1990).

Formal operational thinkers also can think about their thinking. Piaget called this ability **reflective abstraction**—the ability to rearrange and rethink information already acquired (Piaget, 1971). According to Piaget, the ability to reflect upon the content of their thinking allows adolescents to draw new conclusions and insights through contemplation. Reflective abstraction provides more flexibility in thinking; formal operational thinkers can consider alternative solutions to problems based on their prior knowledge (Bjorklund, 1995).

Applying hypothetico-deductive reasoning consistently to all sorts of problems is difficult. Careful analyses of adolescents' reasoning on different tasks often reveal that their reasoning varies from one problem to another and depends on the type of problem to be solved. Using many of the same tasks that Piaget and Inhelder had used, Martorano (1977) assessed formal operational thinking among sixth-, eighth-, tenth-, and twelfth-grade students. She found that, although formal operational thinking emerges between 12 and 15 years of age, even the oldest students failed to use formal operational thinking consistently across all the tasks. Only 50 percent of tenth-graders succeeded in using formal operational thinking on the pendulum problem. Similarly, adolescents rely on different forms of reasoning depending on their beliefs. When presented with information that is inconsistent with their beliefs, adolescents tend to use higher-order reasoning to reject the information; when presented with information that is consistent with their beliefs, they use quick processing and cognitive "shortcuts" to evaluate the information (Klaczynski, 2000).

Many studies confirm that adolescents and even adults do not always apply formal operational thinking. Even when tasks are made simple and the information is easy to obtain, not all adolescents ask for information to help them solve problems. Rather than applying formal operational thinking, adolescents often make decisions based on limited amounts of information (Linn, de Benedictis, & Delucchi, 1982). Adults also fail to use formal operational thinking consistently, especially in everyday problem solving. For instance, when adult grocery shoppers were asked to decide whether a 67-gram bottle of garlic powder at 77 cents was a better buy than a 35-gram bottle at 41 cents, only 20 percent of the shoppers used formal operational thinking to determine the price per gram for each, even when they had paper and pencil to calculate the difference. Most of the shoppers simply applied the informal rule that bigger amounts tend to be better values (Capon & Kuhn, 1979). They used a **heuristic**—that is, a shortcut for thinking.

Does the use of formal operational thinking vary across cultures? When Piagetian tests are given to individuals from non-Western cultures, evidence of formal operational thinking sometimes is not found. For example, when the pendulum problem was given to students in New Guinea, not a single student showed evidence of formal operational thinking (Kelly, 1977). These findings do not suggest that students in New Guinea are less intelligent. Instead, such differences may be due to cultural variations in formal schooling, how knowledge is represented, language processing, and beliefs about intellectual and cognitive processes. These differences suggest that formal operational thinking may not be universal (Altarriba, 1993; van de Vijver & Willemsen, 1993).

Another reason formal operational thinking may appear to be lacking in some cultures is researchers' failure to use problems indigenous to the culture. That is, the problems may be unfamiliar and not relevant to the culture. Thus, research on formal operational thinking must take into account cultural differences in how best to test for it.

ADOLESCENT EGOCENTRISM

In Chapter 7, you learned about the egocentric 3-year-old who hid her head under a blanket and thought no one could see her. She believed that everyone else saw the world exactly

reflective abstraction the ability to rearrange and rethink information already acquired

heuristic a shortcut or rule of thumb used to help solve a problem

Many adolescents daydream about their lives. What changes in cognitive abilities contribute to the development of personal fables?

as she did. Young adolescents show a different form of egocentrism called **adolescent egocentrism,** which reflects their belief that their thoughts and ideas are unique to them and are not understood by parents, teachers, or other adults. Adolescent egocentrism may account, in part, for some of the conflicts that arise between adolescents and their parents. As adolescents grow older, their self-centered beliefs about what they know evolve to become more realistic.

The Imaginary Audience

Because of their egocentric perspective, adolescents develop the mistaken idea that other people are as concerned with their feelings and behavior as they themselves are. Adolescents' self-consciousness translates into the feeling that they are on stage with an **imaginary audience** watching their every move (Buis & Thompson, 1989; Vartanian, 1997). For example, when Michael feels uncomfortable at a party, he believes that all the other people know it; when he is proud of his athletic ability, he believes that everyone admires him. The influence of the imaginary audience peaks in early adolescence for girls and a bit later for boys (Vartanian & Powlishta, 1996).

The Personal Fable

Egocentrism is also expressed by creating a **personal fable**—a story adolescents tell themselves that is not quite true. This story usually emphasizes the uniqueness and invulnerability of the young adolescent (Elkind, 1967; Lapsley, 1993). Because of their central role in playing to an imaginary audience, young adolescents may come to believe that their feelings and experiences are unique in the history of humankind. As many adolescents' diaries can attest, only the teen writing the diary suffers with such agonizing intensity or experiences such exquisite pleasure. Adolescents also tend to see themselves as invincible, which may account for their tendency toward risk taking, such as drinking and driving or failing to use birth control. As adolescents gain more experience, especially once an intimate relationship has been formed, they see themselves in a more realistic light and the personal fable gradually fades. Nonetheless, the risk-taking behavior that emerges because of personal fables may have some long-term adaptive value in that it encourages adolescents to experiment with new ideas and behave more independently (Farber, 1994; Greene, Rubin, Hale, & Walters, 1996).

HOW DOES SCHOOL INFLUENCE EARLY ADOLESCENT DEVELOPMENT?

While adolescents are changing in appearance and thinking, they are also experiencing changes in their schools and academic environments. This is a time when many young adolescents enter new schools—going from elementary to middle or junior high school. Although most young adolescents adjust to their new environment without excessive problems, some do not make the transition smoothly and instead experience difficulty with school (Dryfoos, 1990). A substantial portion of adolescents do not succeed in school, and between 15 and 30 percent of adolescents drop out before completing high school. Many school-related problems begin to appear during the early adolescent years, leading researchers to wonder whether there is something unique about early adolescence that puts individuals at risk for school failure, dropping out, and similar problems (Wigfield, Eccles, & Pintrich, 1996).

Although most young adolescents experience some stress as they change school environments, they do not all experience the same degree of stress. For example, adolescents who have close friends before and during the transition adapt more successfully to a new school environment than their friendless peers do (Berndt & Perry, 1990). Students whose parents have a good understanding of adolescent development and parenting also tend to make a favorable transition to secondary school (Bronstein et al., 1996). Parents' perceptions

adolescent egocentrism an adolescent's belief that his or her thoughts and ideas are unique and are not understood by others

imaginary audience a characteristic of adolescents' self-consciousness, involving the feeling that they are on stage with people watching their every move

personal fable a story adolescents tell themselves that emphasizes their uniqueness and invulnerability

influence how adolescents feel about their abilities in academic domains (Frome & Eccles, 1998). Once again, the importance of social support is apparent: Young adolescents who have social and personal support when changes in schools occur tend to cope successfully with the changes.

ADAPTATION TO A CHANGE IN SCHOOLS

For some adolescents, the early adolescent years are the beginning of a downward spiral that eventually leads to academic failure and dropping out of school. The spiral may begin with a marked decline in grades, common when students move out of elementary school. The greater the decline in grades, the greater the likelihood that the adolescent will fail and drop out of school (Simmons & Blyth, 1987). During this time, adolescents report feeling anxiety, frustration, helplessness, and a lack of confidence in school (Eccles & Midgley, 1989; Wigfield & Eccles, 1989). Teachers in post-elementary schools commonly complain that young adolescent students are unmotivated, put little effort into their schoolwork, and seem generally disinterested in learning (Midgley, 1993). Although the changes associated with moving to middle or junior high school are not extreme for most young adolescents, evidence suggests that students who experience declines in school performance and motivation are at risk for later school and social adjustment problems (Wigfield et al., 1996). One study found that young adolescent girls who moved to a junior high school experienced losses in self-esteem, while those who stayed in the same school through eighth grade did not (Simmons & Blyth, 1987). These effects persisted: Academically, the girls who moved to a junior high school during puberty were still behind the girls who did not, even after both groups made the transition to high school.

Puberty and School Transitions

One explanation for young adolescents' school adjustment problems is that the transition from elementary school often occurs while they are adjusting to the physical changes of puberty (Simmons, Burgeson, Carlton-Ford, & Blyth, 1987). As you learned earlier in this chapter, hormonal adjustments associated with puberty bring on physical changes and powerful feelings that influence how young adolescents see themselves and their relationships with others (Ames & Miller, 1994). These changes and feelings influence motivation and performance in school. This is particularly true for girls because the school transition coincides with the onset of puberty—and possibly the initiation of dating. Although the effects for boys are not as severe, there is evidence that delaying the change of schools is beneficial for them, too (Simmons et al., 1987).

Changes in School and Classroom Environment

Declines in young adolescents' school performance and interest also may be due to the failure of traditional junior high schools to provide developmentally appropriate educational environments for young adolescents (Anderman et al., 2001; Eccles et al., 1993; Eccles & Midgley, 1989; Roeser & Eccles, 2000). For instance, most junior high schools are larger, more impersonal, and more formal than elementary schools. Usually, each junior high school teacher specializes in one subject area and teaches many more students than does an elementary school teacher—making it difficult for the teacher to get to know and trust students (Wigfield, 1993). As a result, junior high school teachers emphasize control and discipline more, have less positive relationships with students, and provide young adolescent students with fewer opportunities for independence (Midgley, Feldlaufer, & Eccles, 1988; Miller et al., 1990).

Because junior high school teachers must interact with a large number of students, they are not likely to notice individual declines in school interest and motivation. Thus, students can gradually slip onto less than optimal developmental pathways (Eccles et al., 1993). Also, teachers' expectations continue to influence students' achievement, particularly for low-achieving students (Madon, Jussim, & Eccles, 1997). A poor fit between the developmental needs of young adolescents and the experiences provided to them by the junior high school

The large and impersonal nature of most junior high schools can have a detrimental effect on young teens. To address this problem, many educators advocate developmentally appropriate middle schools. What qualities need to be taken into account to help young teens when they leave elementary school?

THE PRACTICAL IMPACT: NURTURING CHILDREN

Developmentally Appropriate Middle Schools

Concern over the impact that junior high schools have on young adolescents has led to increased attention to developing middle schools that better meet the needs of these students. Many teachers and school administrators believe that middle schools have great potential to influence a wide range of choices and decisions about issues (such as gang membership, drug and alcohol use, and occupations) that confront students more often during this period of development than at any other time (US Department of Education, 1995). What can parents and educators do to improve the ability of middle schools to meet the developmental needs of young adolescents? To address this question, researchers identified the following key components, or characteristics, of a developmentally appropriate middle school (Lounsbury,

1996; National Middle School Association, 1995):

1. **Educators trained to understand the developmental qualities of young adolescents.** Educators must know how the developmental needs of young adolescents are distinct from those of children and older adolescents.
2. **An atmosphere of high expectations for all.** Teachers, parents, and students have to have high expectations that empower students to learn, to become intellectually engaged, and to behave in keeping with responsible citizenship.
3. **Encouragement of family and community partnerships.** The need for open communication between schools and parent/community organizations and joint involvement in decisions

about curriculum and instruction must be recognized.
4. **A positive school climate.** Teachers and administrators must recognize that the school environment plays a role in young adolescents' ability to learn.
5. **Varied teaching approaches within the curriculum.** Teachers have to address the diverse needs of students with different learning styles, mental and physical maturation levels, and interests.
6. **Comprehensive guidance and support services.** Schools are responsible for providing young adolescents with more than instruction. Young adolescents, especially, need programs that provide for peer discussion, personal attention by professionals, and referral to specialists when needed.

environment may partly explain the declines in school performance and motivation associated with the transition from elementary to junior high school.

To address the issues related to the transition to junior high, middle schools (serving children in grades six to eight) have been developed. Middle schools, designed to better meet the unique developmental needs of young adolescents (see the Practical Impact box) are now the predominant form of school organization for young adolescents. About 12,000 middle schools in the United States enroll more than 8 million students (Morrison, 1997). These schools feature guidance and transition programs, team teaching, cooperative learning, career exploration, and athletics programs. Children who have more positive middle school experiences generally continue to have better attitudes and achievement for several years (Roeser, Eccles, & Sameroff, 1998). Although middle schools are more responsive to the needs of young adolescents, the problems associated with leaving elementary school persist—particularly for girls, who are likely to be undergoing the physical changes of puberty (Wigfield et al., 1996).

PERCEPTIONS OF ACADEMIC COMPETENCE

Students' performance in school is determined in part by the perceptions they have of their own academic abilities. During early adolescence, these perceptions undergo important changes. Before entering early adolescence, children are optimistic about their school-related abilities. In one study (Stipek, 1981), more than 80 percent of first-grade children thought they were the best student in the class! As students move beyond the elementary school years, their perceptions of their abilities become more realistic—and pessimistic (Paris & Cunningham, 1996). Furthermore, very young children are more confident about the extent to which they can improve their abilities than are older children. By fourth grade, children begin to doubt that they can become the best at their current worst activity (Freedman-Doan, Wigfield, Eccles, Blumenfeld, Arbreton, & Harold, 2000).

One reason is the increased emphasis on grades. Junior high school teachers tend to apply higher standards in judging students' competence and in grading their performance than do elementary school teachers (Eccles & Midgley, 1989). Additionally, students and teachers make more social comparisons concerning grades during junior high than they did during elementary school. Students therefore become more aware of how others do in school and more aware of their own level of performance (Wigfield et al., 1996). Interestingly, the drop in grades associated with the transition to middle-level schooling is not matched by a decline in young adolescents' performance on standardized achievement tests (Kavrell & Petersen, 1984). This finding suggests that grades are lower because of changes in grading practices and standards rather than a change in the rate of students' learning (Simmons & Blyth, 1987).

ACADEMIC ACHIEVEMENT AND CULTURAL DIVERSITY

When Huang Liu moved from China to the United States, he was surprised at how easy the math classes were. He also was surprised at how short the school year was. Huang Liu's reactions reveal important cultural differences in academic expectations and environments. Several decades of research have documented consistent differences in academic performance and motivation among students from various countries and different racial and ethnic groups. For example, students in the United States typically perform at lower levels than students from China, Hong Kong, Japan, and Korea (Stevenson, Chen, & Lee, 1993). Within the United States, Caucasian American students score higher than minority students, with the exception of Asian American students (Chen & Stevenson, 1995; Children's Defense Fund, 1992; R. D. Taylor, 1995). The reasons for these differences are complex, but such findings suggest that the beliefs, values, and experiences of different racial and ethnic groups influence the impact that schools have on students.

Cross-Cultural Studies

In a series of studies, Stevenson and colleagues (Chen & Stevenson, 1995; Stevenson & Lee, 1990) compared the academic performance of US, Chinese, and Japanese students at age 7 and age 11. As you can see in Figure 11.6, Asian children outperformed US students in math, and these differences were magnified for young adolescents. Of the top 100 students at age 7, only 14 were American. By age 11, only 1 was American.

One reason for these differences is found in the cultural values of the groups of students. In many Asian countries, the connection between educational attainment and occupational success is stronger than in the United States. In Asian cultures, the centuries-old examination system is the means by which most governments select civil officials. To attend school beyond junior high, Chinese students must pass examinations; only a third of junior high students continue to high school (Chen & Stevenson, 1995). In Japan, acceptance to a prestigious university is considered a virtual guarantee of favorable employment. In contrast, in the United States, education is thought of as only one of many avenues to success. What ultimately is valued is occupational and financial success, regardless of how it is accomplished. When asked about their wishes for the future, 70 percent of students in

FIGURE 11.6

Cross-Cultural Comparison of Math Achievement

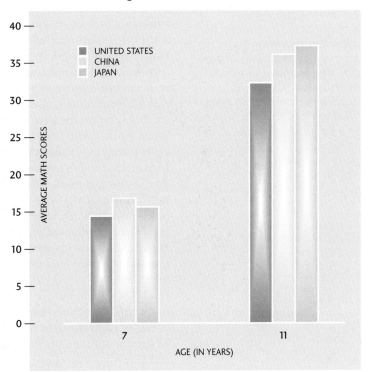

SOURCE: Reprinted from *Advances in Motivation and Achievement*, Vol. 9, C. Chen and H. W. Stevenson, "Culture and Academic Achievement," pp. 119–151, Copyright 1995, with permission from Elsevier Science.

Notice that differences in math achievement among US, Chinese, and Japanese children are relatively small at age 7. But US children have noticeably lower average scores four years later. What factors contribute to these differences? What role does culture play in influencing these patterns?

**IGURE 11.7**

Comparison of Math Achievement of US Students from Different Ethnic Groups

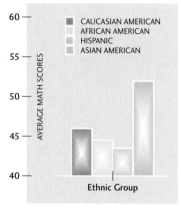

SOURCE: Reprinted from *Advances in Motivation and Achievement,* Vol. 9, C. Chen and H. W. Stevenson, "Culture and Academic Achievement," pp. 119–151, Copyright 1995, with permission from Elsevier Science.

This figure depicts the math achievement of US students from different ethnic groups. Asian American students clearly outperform their peers, and Caucasian American students outperform children of other US ethnic groups. What implications do these findings have for our schools and for social policy?

China expressed wishes related to education, such as attending college or doing well in school, whereas only 10 percent of US students expressed a comparable wish (Stevenson & Stigler, 1992).

A second reason is found in differences in educational policies. The length of the school year is one reflection of a nation's values and commitment to education. In the United States, students attend school for 1044 hours a year, compared to 1655 hours for Chinese students and 1466 hours for Japanese students (Stevenson & Lee, 1990). As each year passes, the accumulated difference in the amount of time students have spent in school translates into higher achievement. For instance, after ten years of schooling, Chinese children have received over 6000 more hours of instruction than US children, which amounts to an additional *six years* of schooling.

Cultural differences also exist in students' lives at home. School children from the United States, China, and Japan allocate their time in different ways. The higher academic performance of Asian students may relate to the fact that they work longer and harder on their schoolwork. In Japan and China, students spend more time outside of school on academic activities and homework than do their counterparts in the United States. US children spend more of their out-of-school time engaged in social interactions with friends and family. US parents are tolerant of their children's spending large amounts of time on nonschool activities and believe that these activities help make them well-rounded individuals. Chinese and Japanese parents believe more strongly in education as the route to future happiness (Stevenson & Lee, 1990).

US Racial and Ethnic Differences

Within the United States, academic performance varies for different racial and ethnic groups. Figure 11.7 reveals that the math performance of 11-year-old Asian American students far outstripped that of any other ethnic group and that African American and Hispanic students had the lowest levels of performance (Chen & Stevenson, 1995). Whereas Caucasian American families value education less than Asian American families do, the same cannot be said of African American and Hispanic families. Like Asian American families, African American and Hispanic families place a high value on education. Despite this emphasis, the academic achievement of African American and Hispanic students is lower than that of either Asian American or Caucasian American students (Chen & Stevenson, 1995).

Many factors interfere with the translation of African Americans' and Hispanics' high values for education into high levels of academic achievement (Graham, 1994). The parents of these students do not put as much pressure on their children to achieve academically, relying more strongly on punishment as a disciplinary method than parents in the other groups do (Chen & Stevenson, 1995). Parents who do not forcefully emphasize academic achievement and who routinely use punishment may undermine their children's motivation to learn independently (R. D. Taylor, 1995). Additionally, African American and Hispanic students enroll in fewer advanced courses, have more part-time jobs, watch more television, and have higher rates of absenteeism than other students do (Stevenson & Lee, 1990). Racial discrimination and limited English proficiency also play roles in the lower school performance of US minorities.

School conditions contribute to racial and ethnic group differences. Thirty-seven percent of African American and 32 percent of Hispanic adolescents are enrolled in the largest city school districts in the United States, compared to 5 percent of Caucasian American and 22 percent of Asian American adolescents (Wigfield et al., 1996). More African American and Hispanic students live in impoverished neighborhoods, and the schools in these areas are less likely than schools serving advantaged populations to offer high-quality remedial services or advanced courses (MacIver & Epstein, 1991). Even children who are extremely motivated may find it difficult to perform well under these adverse conditions. Such findings suggest that economic conditions are important in explaining the differences in academic achievement and performance found between Caucasian American and Asian American students on the one hand and African American and Hispanic students on the other. Many African American and Hispanic students perform poorly in school not because they lack basic intellectual capacities or do not value education, but because of the economic and social conditions they grow up in (R. D. Taylor, 1995).

TRY IT OUT

Activities Relating to Young Adolescents

1. Review David's account of adolescence as a stage of development (page 353). In general, what considerations do you think led to efforts to differentiate stages of development? What historical trends contributed to defining adolescence in the United States? What considerations have led to differentiating early and late adolescence? How would you define adolescence as a stage of development?

2. Reflect on your own experiences with adolescent growth spurts, puberty, and the timing of onset of puberty. How did you, your parents, and your peers respond to your physical and sexual maturation? How did your maturation and others' responses to it affect your self-concept and self-esteem?

3. Collaborate with classmates to develop an interview protocol you could use as part of a clinical study on eating disturbances and eating disorders among young adolescents. Assume you want to discover how and when and in what social contexts these behaviors first began in your respondents. How could responses to your interview be used to develop an effective eating disorders prevention program? What do you think should be the first three steps in any such program?

4. Formal operational thinking is a benchmark in cognitive development during adolescence. However, some cognitive researchers believe that this level of thinking is rare, even among adults. Describe or illustrate an experiment other than the pendulum problem that you think could help resolve questions about adolescents' and adults' use of formal operational thinking.

SUM IT UP

What is early adolescence?

+ Early adolescence covers the period from 11 to 14 years of age and represents a time when the individual is making the transition from a child to an adolescent.
+ The concept of adolescence as a period of development was brought about by urbanization and changes in laws related to children. The period of adolescence is longer now than it was in the past.
+ Many terms are used to refer to adolescence. Some of these relate to biological changes (puberty, pubescence); others relate to legal and age-related definitions (juvenile, teenager).

How do physical growth and sexual maturation occur during early adolescence?

+ Young adolescents grow rapidly in size and weight, and their bodies develop more mature shapes. On average, these changes occur about two years earlier in girls than in boys.
+ The growth spurt of early adolescence affects all parts of the adolescent's body, but the hands, feet, and head grow more quickly than other parts.
+ Puberty refers to the onset of sexual maturity, and the changes that bring it about take place over several years. During this time, adolescents develop primary sexual characteristics (features related directly to reproduction) and secondary sexual characteristics (the outward manifestations of sexual development).
+ The specific trigger for puberty is unknown, but the changes that result occur largely because of the actions of hormones.

+ Boys and girls react differently to the timing of puberty. Boys who mature early have increased social status. Girls who mature early feel uncomfortable and may not fit in.
+ In general, adolescents who are considerably "off time" relative to their peers have a more difficult time adjusting to the changes that occur during early adolescence.

What are the health concerns for young adolescents?

+ Most of the major health issues for young adolescents center on their rapid physical growth and the changes associated with puberty.
+ Obesity is a serious health concern during this period. About 14 percent of adolescents are overweight, putting them at risk for a variety of serious health problems.
+ Anorexia nervosa is an eating disorder that occurs most often in young women, in which individuals eat very little and yet believe they are fat. Many factors relate to this disorder, and it poses a very serious health risk. Treatment for anorexia should focus on both physical and psychological aspects of the disorder.
+ Bulimia nervosa is an eating disorder characterized by secret eating binges followed by purges. Bulimia is difficult to detect because normal body weight is not dramatically altered.
+ Eating disturbances are quite common in adolescents, occurring more often in adolescent girls than boys. One of the major reasons for the rise in eating disturbances is the concern US children have about weight gain.

How do young adolescents think and solve problems?

✦ During early adolescence, the ability to use formal operational thinking develops. This advanced ability to think abstractly allows young adolescents to think logically about a wider range of situations and social issues.

✦ Young adolescents show a form of egocentrism in the belief that their thoughts and ideas are unique to them.

✦ The egocentric perspective of young adolescents leads them to feel as if they were the central focus of an imaginary audience. Egocentrism also results in the creation of personal fables that emphasize young adolescents' unique and invulnerable nature.

How does school influence early adolescent development?

✦ The transition from elementary school to middle or junior high school presents young adolescents with many challenges. Most meet these challenges successfully, but a sizable proportion do not.

✦ The transition to middle-level school often coincides with puberty; the multiple changes that occur during this period put some young adolescents at risk for negative outcomes.

✦ Declines in young adolescents' school performance and interest also may be due to the fact that traditional junior high schools do not meet the developmental needs of young adolescents. Middle schools were developed to better meet these needs.

✦ During early adolescence, students' perceptions of their academic skills change in important ways. Their perceptions of their abilities become more realistic and sometimes more pessimistic.

✦ Adolescents in the United States do not perform in school as well as adolescents in China, Hong Kong, and Japan. Within the United States, Caucasian American and Asian American students outperform other minority students. These findings highlight the important influence of cultural values and social conditions on school performance.

KEY TERMS and CONCEPTS

adolescence (*353*)
adolescent egocentrism (*376*)
anorexia nervosa (*369*)
bulimia nervosa (*370*)
dysmenorrhea (*365*)
eating disturbances (*371*)
gonadotropins (*358*)
heuristic (*375*)

hypothetico-deductive reasoning (*373*)
imaginary audience (*376*)
juvenile (*355*)
menarche (*356*)
personal fable (*376*)
precocious puberty (*359*)
premenstrual syndrome (PMS) (*365*)
primary sexual characteristics (*358*)

puberty (*355*)
pubescence (*355*)
reflective abstraction (*375*)
rites of passage (*354*)
secondary sexual characteristics (*358*)
teenager (*355*)
youth (*355*)

Social and Emotional Development in Early Adolescence

CHAPTER 12

CHAPTER OUTLINE

- ✦ How Do Young Adolescents View Themselves?
- ✦ How Do Adolescents Form an Identity?
- ✦ How Do Family Relationships Change During Early Adolescence?
- ✦ What Are the Characteristics of Early Adolescent Peer Relationships?
- ✦ How Do Mass Media Influence Young Adolescents' Development?

As children begin adolescence, they find themselves cast into many new roles and environments that are sometimes conflicting and confusing. Complicating the challenge of dealing with a changing social reality are the physical changes associated with puberty. As a result, early adolescence is a period when relationships within and outside the family change dramatically. Adolescents begin to focus more attention on establishing intimate and meaningful relationships with peers, and these relationships are an important source of support and pleasure. For some adolescents, peer relationships can be frustrating, scary, and risky, and these feelings are reflected in their developing identity. The world of young adolescents also includes more time spent with new technologies that entertain, educate, and communicate. Early adolescence is a time in life during which adolescents and their families must balance these changing dynamics.

HOW DO YOUNG ADOLESCENTS VIEW THEMSELVES

Compared to children, young adolescents have a more complex sense of themselves, in part because of their advanced abilities to understand and imagine how others perceive and evaluate them (Harter, 1998). Their growing self-awareness results from interacting with, and receiving feedback from, a wider circle of significant others (peers, siblings, and teachers). They develop a more complete picture of themselves because of the many changes that occur during early adolescence.

SELF-CONCEPT DURING EARLY ADOLESCENCE

The most fundamental change in young adolescents' self-concepts is their development of a more differentiated view of themselves. Adolescents tend to describe themselves in terms of eight domains—scholastic performance, athletic competence, behavioral conduct, social acceptance, physical appearance, job competence, close friendships, and romantic appeal. In contrast, young children see themselves in terms of only the first five of these domains (Harter, 1998). The increased complexity of adolescents' view of self reflects their more advanced thinking skills and more diverse social environments, which encourage them to think about themselves in more complex ways as they take on new roles within their families, peer groups, schools, workplaces, and communities (Harter, 1999).

Fourteen-year-old Dylan's diary entry illustrates young adolescents' enhanced ability to understand that the way they view themselves changes to fit situations and individuals.

> When I'm in math class, I feel smart and creative. Nothing bothers me. But when I have to write an English essay, I feel like an airhead. It's hard and I just don't think I've got what it takes.

Like Dylan, young adolescents view themselves in conflicting ways—as both "smart" and "an airhead"—depending on the situation. Because of their increased cognitive skills, young adolescents can now make distinctions in their self-concept by considering different circumstances (Harter, 1998).

Young adolescents also distinguish between the **actual self**—how they see themselves now—and the **possible self**—how they wish to be in the future. Adolescents with a small or moderate difference between actual and possible selves are likely to feel good about themselves and be motivated to improve. In contrast, adolescents with a large discrepancy between actual and possible selves are likely to feel frustrated, dissatisfied, and depressed. These individuals may experience a sense of hopelessness because they cannot imagine becoming how they want to be (Harter, 1990).

At the beginning of adolescence, the awareness of opposites within oneself can cause distress and confusion (Harter & Monsour, 1992). Adolescents at this very early stage frequently demonstrate all-or-none thinking and vacillate from one extreme to the other (Harter, 1998). Like Dylan, they may view themselves as brilliant at one point and a total

actual self how adolescents see themselves

possible self how adolescents wish themselves to be in the future

airhead at another. But eventually, young adolescents begin to understand that their core self, or personality, remains fairly consistent across time and situations. They can better integrate qualities of the self that seem inconsistent or that change from one setting to another. As you learned in Chapter 8, young children describe themselves in disconnected ways ("I'm quiet"; "I'm friendly"). In contrast, adolescents are much more likely to organize incongruent or even conflicting traits into a logically connected whole (Harter, 1999). Young adolescents are able to recognize that there is an underlying consistency or coherence to themselves and their actions. They are able to see how their seemingly contradictory qualities work together to reflect their true selves.

SELF-ESTEEM DURING EARLY ADOLESCENCE

Recall from Chapter 8 that self-esteem is the good or bad feelings one has about oneself. High self-esteem is thought to promote many positive outcomes, including academic achievement, popularity, and happiness. Most people believe that positive self-esteem is a protective factor that shelters adolescents from delinquency, academic failure, early sexual involvement, alcohol use, and depression (Hewitt, 1998; Scheir, Botvin, Griffin, & Diaz, 2000). But research has not consistently supported these expectations (Deci & Ryan, 1995; Liu, Kaplan, & Risser, 1992). Some studies have actually found the reverse—that adolescents who drop out, are delinquent, or become sexually active are the ones who have high self-esteem (Strouse & Fabes, 1988). High self-esteem prevents some teens from developing realistic perceptions of the risks of their behaviors. In fact, some adolescents *enhance* their self-esteem by winning peer approval for involvement in high-risk behaviors (Damon, 1995). High self-esteem also leads some adolescents to feel entitled to status that has not been earned, as is seen sometimes among members of gangs (Baumeister, 1993; Kernis, 1993).

Despite the inconsistencies in the research, self-esteem provides an important way of understanding young adolescents' feelings of personal well-being. Young adolescents' self-esteem is not entirely stable; it fluctuates considerably because they experience so many physical, cognitive, and social changes (Killeen & Forehand, 1998). But as with their self-concept, there is a component of adolescent self-esteem that gradually becomes less subject to immediate experiences and events (Zimmerman, Copeland, Shope, & Dielman, 1997).

GENDER AND THE SELF DURING EARLY ADOLESCENCE

When Polly was a girl, she was energy in motion. She danced, did cartwheels and splits, played football, basketball, and baseball with the neighborhood boys. She yelled out orders and advice, shrieked for joy when she won a bet or heard a good joke, laughed with her mouth wide open. . . . Then Polly had her first period and started junior high. She tried to keep up her old ways, but she was called a tomboy and chided for not acting more ladylike. She was excluded by her boy pals and by the girls, who were moving into makeup and romances. This left Polly confused and shaky. She had temper tantrums and withdrew from both boys' and girls' groups.

—*M. Pipher* (1994, p. 17)

Because of their increased cognitive abilities, young adolescents are now more capable of engaging in self-reflection and self-evaluation (Alfieri, Ruble, & Higgins, 1996). They spend a good deal of time imagining what others are thinking about them and feeling self-conscious. Girls often wear loose shirts and walk around with their notebook hugged to their chest to hide their developing breasts. Boys worry about erections that develop at inconvenient times (Beal, 1994).

One way to cope with these feelings of self-consciousness is to blend in by doing what everyone else is doing. Although both boys and girls become more self-conscious during early adolescence, the increase is greater for girls (Richards, Crowe, Larson, & Swarr, 1998).

Erik Erikson believed that adolescence is a period of the life cycle during which identity development is the critical psychosocial crisis. If the challenges of this crisis are met successfully, adolescents form a secure sense of themselves.

Thus, for many girls like Polly, the beginning of early adolescence is marked by a decrease in self-esteem and confusion about roles and self-concept (Quatman & Watson, 2001).

Young adolescent girls may suffer difficulties with their self-concept and self-esteem because of the important roles played by physical appearance and body image in peer acceptance (Polce, Myers, Kliewer, & Kilmartin, 2001). For example, the strongest predictor of a girl's popularity is being thin and pretty and wearing the "right" clothes (Adler, Kless, & Adler, 1992). A drop in self-esteem is particularly likely for girls who acknowledge that they base their self-esteem on their appearance (Harter, 1993). And few girls are so confident that they are unaffected by others' evaluations. Consider the case of Diane Sawyer, the television announcer. As a young teenager, Diane won a national beauty pageant. But when she overheard a boy at a dance say, "Is that her? She's not so great," she ran back to her room and avoided dating for several years afterward (Bosworth, 1985).

In contrast, young adolescent boys place more value on what they do than what they look like. Adolescent boys generally have a stronger sense of self-confidence and competence about their appearance and physical abilities than do girls; girls place more value on their social selves than do boys (Eccles, Wigfield, Flanagan, & Miller, 1989). These deeply ingrained cultural beliefs put adolescent girls at a disadvantage in learning how to develop positive feelings about themselves and their bodies.

Adolescent girls' self-esteem also can be undermined by their experiences in school. Researchers have found that teachers may treat boys and girls differently. When boys and girls are engaged in academic tasks, teachers give more positive attention to the boys (Eisenberg, Martin, & Fabes, 1996). In addition, teachers praise boys more often, provide more feedback to them, and call on them more often to answer questions. Girls sit patiently with their hands raised, while boys grab teachers' attention—they are eight times more likely than girls to call out answers to questions. Girls who try these tactics may be ignored or admonished (Windass, 1989). Over time, girls come to feel less confident and begin to question how they feel about themselves.

HOW DO ADOLESCENTS FORM AN IDENTITY

One of the most important developmental tasks for adolescents is the formation of a sense of **identity,** defined as a sense of who one is, where one has been, and where one is going in life. Developing a sense of personal identity prepares people to deal with the challenges that arise later in development (Grotevant, 1998).

Identity formation does not begin or end during adolescence, but adolescents' increased ability to think abstractly about personal qualities and about future possibilities heightens the importance of identity issues. Adolescents' expanding social world—a world of peers, school, work, leisure, and community involvements—provides motivation for developing a sense of identity (Erikson, 1968).

ERIKSON'S THEORY OF ADOLESCENT IDENTITY DEVELOPMENT

As you learned in Chapter 2, Erikson believed that development involves psychosocial crises. During adolescence, the crisis revolves around identity issues. Adolescents begin making choices about who they are and want to be. If the challenges of this crisis are met successfully, adolescents form a secure sense of identity. To do so, adolescents must evaluate their personal assets and liabilities (Wallerstein & Goldberger, 1998).

If the challenges of the psychosocial identity crisis are not dealt with successfully, adolescents may develop an incomplete sense of self, called **identity diffusion.** Identity diffused adolescents experience self-doubt, are preoccupied with their own concerns, and may be either too dependent on or excessively isolated from others (Erikson, 1980). Having a diffused identity is like wandering aimlessly in search of oneself, without roots and lacking a vision for the future. Extreme forms of identity diffusion leave individuals vulnerable to

identity one's sense of who one is, where one has been, and where one is going in life

identity diffusion an incomplete sense of self

psychosocial moratorium a period during which youths are reasonably free of adult responsibilities that might prevent them from adequately addressing identity issues

crisis/exploration the process of making choices about life directions by considering options, values, and goals

commitment the making of voluntary choices about life directions from among the many available options

personality and behavioral disorders such as depression, delinquency, and substance abuse and to suicide (Erikson, 1968).

Forming an identity is a process and product of individual and social factors (Bosma & Kunnen, 2001). Adolescents use abstract thinking to assess their options and speculate about the future. In addition, they use their relationships with others as a kind of "mirror" that reflects back information about what they are like (Kerpelman, Pittman, & Lamke, 1997). Forming an identity provides adolescents with information about themselves, their direction in life, and their place in relationships that matter (Meeus, Iedema, Helsen, & Vollebergh, 1999).

Erikson argued that adolescence should be a time of **psychosocial moratorium**—a period during which youths are reasonably free of adult responsibilities that might prevent them from adequately addressing identity issues. According to Erikson, adolescents in present-day Western societies should use this moratorium period to consider who they are and their direction in life. An important part of this process is experimenting with a variety of roles, lifestyles, relationships, and value choices (Wallerstein & Goldberger, 1998).

Adolescents who experience a moratorium and are able to experiment with roles have an important advantage in identity formation (Erikson, 1968). When a period of experimentation does not occur, adolescents are at risk for identity diffusion and may not realize their capabilities. As a result, they may be unprepared to enter adulthood. For example, identity-diffused adolescents may not be ready for intimate adult relationships. According to Erikson, individuals must first develop a healthy sense of who they are before they are ready to engage in mature and intimate relationships with others.

Erikson (1959) believed that a sense of identity continuously develops throughout one's life. Identity issues may reemerge at any time and are subject to change later in life. For adolescents, however, identity formation is particularly important because it gets them "on track" and moves them in a meaningful direction toward adulthood.

MARCIA'S THEORY OF ADOLESCENT IDENTITY DEVELOPMENT

James Marcia (1987, 1993) expanded Erikson's theory, describing the basic processes involved in adolescent identity formation. Marcia proposed that there are two essential aspects of an adolescent's search for identity:

◆ **Crisis/exploration** refers to the process of considering options, values, and goals. Making choices about life directions is an active process of searching among alternatives in religious beliefs, political views, sexuality, roles, and relationships. Because the term *crisis* implies that identity development is an unpleasant and disruptive experience, the term *exploration* often is used to provide a more neutral or even positive tone.

◆ **Commitment** refers to the making of voluntary choices about life directions from the many available options. By making voluntary choices, adolescents become invested in their identity decisions.

The concepts of exploration and commitment are used to classify adolescents into four categories with respect to identity status (see Figure 12.1). These status categories provide a way to recognize adolescents who are in the different phases of identity development (Marcia, 1999):

FIGURE 12.1

Marcia's Identity Status Categories

	Experienced Crisis/Exploration	Did Not Experience Crisis/Exploration
Made a Commitment	Identity Achieved	Foreclosure
Did Not Make a Commitment	Moratorium	Identity Confused

SOURCE: Marcia, 1993.

Marcia's theory of identity development involved different combinations of crisis/exploration and commitment. Can you describe the identity outcomes for the various combinations depicted in this figure?

◆ Adolescents who have not explored choices or committed themselves to a specific identity are considered **identity confused.** These adolescents may appear aimless and preoccupied.

◆ Adolescents who have not explored alternatives but nonetheless have made a definite commitment to a specific identity are in **foreclosure.** In this case, the commitment has been made prematurely, without adequate searching or questioning.

◆ Adolescents who are actively exploring identity issues but have not yet made any firm commitment are in **moratorium.** Adolescents must experience moratorium before developing a mature identity. This status may be uncomfortable, but it allows adolescents to consider a variety of ideas and behaviors.

◆ Adolescents who have experienced a period of exploration and crisis and have made a personal commitment to their choice are considered **identity achieved.** Identity-achieved adolescents experience greater self-acceptance and have a better sense of their own strengths and weaknesses.

Marcia believed that identity development is a process of moving or progressing from one status to another as issues related to who one is and what one wants to become are explored (Muuss, 1998). These categories do not follow each other in a definite order; regressions are common. For example, both foreclosed and identity achieved adolescents may at some point return to the less advanced status of identity confusion (Kroger, 1993; Waterman, 1988). Identity issues reemerge at various times, and individuals may move back and forth among the various statuses as they experience different roles, environments, relationships, and challenges (Cote, 1996; Kroger, 2000).

Identity issues are not completely resolved during adolescence. Many of these issues continue into early adulthood and come up again during later periods of the life span (Hoover, Marcia, & Parris, 1997; Magdola, 1999). The important factor, however, is that adolescents start making constructive progress on identity formation. Identity-achieved adolescents are psychologically healthier than those classified in the other categories. Identity-achieved adolescents, for example, attain greater levels of achievement, morality, and intimacy than others (Archer, 1993). Adolescents experiencing moratorium are likely to have problems with authority issues, whereas adolescents in foreclosure have a great need for social approval and a low level of autonomy. Those adolescents classified as identity-confused are likely to be withdrawn, less intimate with peers, more neurotic, and less explorative in their interests and activities (Schmitt & Vondracek, 1999; Wallace-Broscious, Serafica, & Osipow, 1994). Thus, adolescent identity status has important consequences for the quality of adolescents' adjustment and their relationships with others.

ETHNIC IDENTITY

Because minority adolescents are raised in cultures whose values and beliefs differ from those of the mainstream culture, they often find the process of forming an identity to be particularly complicated (Spencer & Dornbusch, 1990). As a result, minority adolescents must work to integrate a sense of their own ethnicity into the identity they define.

An important issue in ethnic identity development is how much the dominant culture is viewed as either valuing or devaluing the adolescent's ethnic heritage (Phinney & Rosenthal, 1992; Tomlinson-Clarke, 2001). Contributing to this view are the experiences minority youths have with prejudice, discrimination, and barriers to their educational, occupational, and economic progress (Martinez & Dukes, 1997).

Together, these issues are reflected in one's **ethnic identity**—one's sense of belonging to an ethnic group. Ethnic identity involves thoughts, perceptions, feelings, and behavior that reflect ethnic group membership (Bernal & Knight, 1997; Rotheram-Borus & Phinney, 1990). The components of ethnic identity include the following (Phinney & Rosenthal, 1992; Spencer & Markstrom-Adams, 1990):

◆ Identifying oneself as a member of an ethnic group
◆ Developing a sense of belonging to an ethnic group

identity confused identity status of those adolescents who have not explored or committed themselves to a specific identity choice

foreclosure identity status of those adolescents who have not explored alternatives but nonetheless have made a definite commitment to a specific identity

moratorium identity status of those adolescents who are actively exploring identity issues but have not yet made any firm commitment

identity achieved identity status of those adolescents who have experienced a period of exploration and crisis and have made a commitment

ethnic identity the sense of belonging to an ethnic group

◆ Forming attitudes (either positive or negative) toward one's ethnic group
◆ Having a sense of shared attitudes and values with an ethnic group
◆ Following the specific traditions and practices of an ethnic group (language, customs, and behavior)

Although members of different ethnic groups have different identity experiences, they share a common pathway (Phinney, Ong, & Madden, 2000). The first step along this pathway involves being either unidentified or prematurely identified with one's ethnic culture (ethnic identity diffusion). Next is a period of exploration of one's ethnicity (ethnic identity moratorium), followed by a period of commitment to a particular way of being an ethnic group member (ethnic identity achieved). As with general identity development, ethnic identity issues may reappear at any time (Phinney, 1996).

The sense of belonging to an ethnic group reflects one's ethnic identity. The young Hispanic teens congregating together in this picture share common values, rituals, and interests. Can you identify the different components of ethnic identity?

Ethnic identity development is further complicated by the way in which ethnic identity issues are resolved. Four different ways of resolving identity issues have been identified (Phinney, 1996):

1. An individual who identifies with the majority culture and rejects his or her ethnic culture is define as **assimilated.**
2. An individual who lives within the majority culture but feels alienated or outcast is considered to be **marginal.**
3. An individual who identifies only with his or her ethnic culture and rejects the majority culture is said to be **separated.**
4. An individual who identifies with both the majority and the minority culture is defined as **bicultural.**

Adolescents from different ethnic minorities report distinct outcomes with respect to ethnic identity. European American adolescents most frequently define themselves as assimilated, African American and Puerto Rican adolescents more frequently choose the separated category, and Mexican American adolescents and their Asian American peers more frequently define themselves as bicultural (Phinney, DuPont, Espinosa, Revell, & Sanders, 1994). Once a secure ethnic identity is formed, adolescents in these different outcome groups are similar in mental health, self-esteem, grades, and social competence (Phinney, Cantu, & Kurtz, 1997; Roberts et al., 1999).

Parents represent one of the most important influences on the formation of ethnic identity. Secure ethnic identities are fostered in families in which parents do the following (Thornton, Chatters, Taylor, & Allen, 1990):

◆ Teach adolescents to be proud of their heritage
◆ Model participation in the ethnic community
◆ Discuss ethnic issues with their adolescents

Like many of the general identity issues faced by adolescents, ethnic identity issues are likely to give rise to competing and ambivalent feelings. For example, a person can develop a preference for her or his own culture but also recognize the advantages of accepting the majority culture. Additionally, contextual factors influence ethnic identity development. For example, ethnic identity commitment was found to be greater for Native American teens enrolled in schools with a predominantly Native American student body than for those in schools with predominantly Caucasian American students (Lysne & Levy, 1997). In general, a central task for minority teenagers is to integrate their contrasting viewpoints into a unified sense of self.

assimilated identifying with the majority culture and rejecting one's ethnic culture

marginal living within the majority culture but feeling alienated or outcast

separated identifying only with one's ethnic culture and rejecting the majority culture

bicultural identifying with both the majority and the minority culture

In this picture, the young teenager and her mother are disagreeing about how the teen is dressed. Parent-adolescent conflict most often focuses on everyday lifestyle choices and rarely is destructive or abusive.

Ηow do family relationships change during early adolescence

If you were like most young teenagers, then, contrary to the stereotype, your family life was not marked by constant struggle and emotional distance. Instead, your family continued to be your primary source of influence and security. Although some adolescents do experience troubled family relationships, a large majority feel close to their parents, value their parents' opinions, believe that their parents love and care for them, and respect their parents as authority figures (Holmbeck, Paikoff, & Brooks-Gunn, 1995; Steinberg, 1990). Adolescents tend to agree with their parents on attitudes toward work, education, religion, and politics. In fact, differences of opinion are greater among adolescents than they are between adolescents and their parents (Gecas & Seff, 1990; Holmbeck, Paikoff, & Brooks-Gunn, 1995). If there are serious problems between parents and teens, these usually have their roots earlier in childhood (Patterson, Reid, & Dishion, 1998).

Nonetheless, an important period of family change and adjustment occurs when children enter adolescence. This is a time when parents and young adolescents undergo challenging shifts in the established ways of dealing with each other (Steinberg, 2001). Families face the task of altering existing relationships to allow adolescents more involvement in social relationships beyond the family (such as with peers) and more independent decision making about lifestyle preferences. At the same time, parents must continue to supervise, protect, and provide guidance to reduce the chances that young teens will develop problem behaviors (Deslandes & Royer, 1997; Small, Eastman, & Cornelius, 1988).

Families must therefore strike a balance between allowing changes that foster greater individual competence and maintaining stable connections that prevent adolescents from drifting into risky and problem behaviors (such as delinquency and drug use). As adolescence progresses, the relationship between parents and their teens must gradually evolve from one in which parents are clearly in charge to one in which greater equality and independence are granted to the teens (Avenevoli, Sessa, & Steinberg, 1999).

PARENTING AND EARLY ADOLESCENT DEVELOPMENT

Adolescence can be disruptive for both adolescents and their families, as various tensions and dilemmas surface in new and sometimes unexpected ways. For example, young teenagers have a greater need for privacy than they did when they were children. Thus, they are less likely to share their personal lives and more likely to become embarrassed or angry when their privacy is invaded. Another example is that adolescents begin to look for (and find) faults in their parents. Small children idealize their parents, but adolescents have a more realistic and critical view of them (Steinberg & Levine, 1990).

When adolescents and their parents handle these potentially disruptive situations successfully, teens become clearer about themselves, their goals, and their direction in life (Hauser, Borman, Bowlds, Powers, Jacobson, Noam, & Knoebber, 1991). When teens do not cope successfully, serious problems can arise. Thus, how parents respond to the changes in the family that occur as their children enter adolescence plays an important role in helping their adolescents cope.

The physical changes, new cognitive abilities, and expanded social world of young adolescents serve as stimulants for parents to adjust how they relate to, discipline, and seek to guide them (Henricson & Roker, 2000; Steinberg, 1990). Children often enter adolescence quite dependent on their parents, but they exit this period in a more equal relationship with them.

Parents and adolescents must renegotiate their relationships during early adolescence (Collins & Repinski, 1994). For example, teens' and parents' influence within the family shifts. Mothers generally lose status in the family, whereas sons gain influence (Papini & Sebby, 1987). In the first few months after menarche, daughters are treated more harshly than they were before they reached menarche and participate less in family activities (Steinberg, 1989). Most young teens and their families eventually make the necessary adjustments and adapt positively.

Support, Warmth, and Acceptance

Warm, supportive, and accepting parental behavior is associated with the development of social competence by adolescents and children of all ages (Carlo, Fabes, Laible, & Kupanoff, 1999; Stafford & Bayer, 1993). Parents who hug, kiss, praise, and spend positive time with their adolescents foster close ties and communicate confidence in their adolescents' abilities (Fuligni & Eccles, 1993; Rohner, 1986). Adolescents who receive support and nurturance from their parents have high self-esteem and a well-developed identity and are less anxious, depressed, and aggressive than those who do not (Peterson & Haan, 1999; Scaramella, Conger, & Simons, 1999). Warm, supportive parenting also prepares adolescents for intimate peer relationships (Laursen & Williams, 1997; Peterson & Leigh, 1990). Teens who have warm and close relationships with their parents select peers who reinforce rather than contradict parental values.

Induction

As you learned in Chapter 8, an important way many parents influence their sons and daughters is by using logical reasoning, or induction, to persuade them to accept the parental viewpoint (Stafford & Bayer, 1993). This moderate form of control legitimizes parental authority but does not produce hostile feelings. Parents may use induction to appeal to adolescents' concern for others, their desire to be mature, or their ability to understand and accept parents' points of view. Induction helps teens understand many things (Peterson & Haan, 1999):

- ✦ Why rules are necessary
- ✦ Why their misbehavior is unacceptable
- ✦ How their behavior affects others
- ✦ How their behavior might become more acceptable
- ✦ How they might make amends for any harm they caused

Parents who use induction do not impose their authority; they communicate confidence in adolescents' abilities to make good decisions and voluntarily comply. This parenting technique is more effective with young adolescents than with younger children because of adolescents' increased ability to think abstractly and consider several possibilities (Hill, 1987). Parents who rely on induction have teens with positive social values, high self-esteem, and good school performance (Aunola, Stattin, & Nurmi, 2000; Hoffman, 1994).

Monitoring and Supervision

"Where are you going?" "When will you be home?" "Who will you be with?" These questions are commonly overheard in households with teenagers. Questions like these provide a way for parents to monitor and supervise their adolescents' schedules, peer associations, activities, and physical whereabouts. Effective monitoring requires that parents be involved in the lives of adolescents and maintain clear expectations about curfews, appropriate activities, acceptable peers, and places where they can and cannot go (Barber, Olson, & Shagle, 1994; Fuligni & Eccles, 1993). Although some adolescents resist such monitoring and supervision, most adolescents affirm parents' legitimate authority to set rules and monitor their whereabouts (Smetana, 2000). Adolescents whose parents fail to monitor their activities are more

In what ways do parents monitor their children's activities? Does monitoring decrease the risk of dangerous behaviors in adolescents?

likely to become involved in delinquency, antisocial behavior, early sexuality, and drug use (Ambert, 1997; Miller, Benson, & Galbraith, 2001).

Punitiveness

Parental punitiveness refers to the use of force to influence children's behavior and qualities—either through spanking, slapping, or other forms of physical force or through nagging, name-calling, or yelling (Strauss & Donnelly, 1994; Turner & Finkelhor, 1996). Although parents are more likely to use physical punishment with younger children, over 40 percent of parents continue to use physical punishment frequently with their adolescents (Strauss & Donnelly, 1994). When parents rely on physical or verbal punitiveness, their children may develop hostility toward them and may resist or reject their authority (Stafford & Bayer, 1993; Turner & Finkelhor, 1996). Adolescents may respond to parents' punitive behavior with their own punitive behaviors (such as yelling or insulting parents), thereby creating a cycle of punitive responses in the family (Patterson, Reid, & Dishion, 1998).

Adolescents whose parents use harsh punishment are likely to develop lower self-esteem and less advanced moral values than their peers. They also are more likely to have problems in school, use drugs, and develop behavior problems (Palmer & Hollin, 2001; Pettit et al., 2001).

THE BIDIRECTIONALITY OF PARENT-ADOLESCENT RELATIONSHIPS

The emphasis on parental influence often leaves the impression that parent-adolescent relationships are a one-way street, with mothers and fathers dictating the flow of traffic that shapes who adolescents are. However, adolescents also influence their parents in many ways (Collins et al., 2000; Henry, Peterson, & Wilson, 1997). One example of the influence of teens is that parents adapt their parenting practices to adolescents' behaviors and personalities (Ambert, 1997; O'Connor & Dvorak, 2001). For instance, adolescents who defy, talk back to, communicate disrespect for, and even physically assault parents tend to stimulate parents to "crack down" on them with more forceful monitoring and punitiveness. If the result is better compliance and more peace, parents are likely to continue this coercive strategy, which appears on the surface to work (Ambert, 1997; Patterson, 1982). This bidirectional relationship is illustrated in Figure 12.2.

In contrast, parents who view their adolescents as capable and trustworthy are more likely to use nonpunitive parenting practices. These parents tend to exercise more moderate monitoring and elicit more positive responses from their teens. Parents also may feel more positive about themselves when they view their adolescents as competent and as responding to rational and supportive approaches to parenting (Henry & Peterson, 1995; Henry et al., 1997). These behaviors mutually reinforce the positive qualities of both parents and adolescents.

FIGURE 12.2

Model of a Bidirectional Parent-Adolescent Relationship

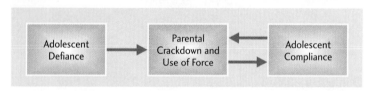

This model depicts the mutual influence that parents and adolescents have on each other. When adolescents are defiant, they may stimulate parents to "crack down" on them. If the result is more compliance on the part of the adolescent, parents are likely to continue this coercive strategy.

PARENT-ADOLESCENT CONFLICT

Despite the widespread notion that parents and adolescents spend much of their time battling each other in an endless power struggle, most research suggests that a more tranquil atmosphere is the norm in most homes. Thus, there is little support for the existence of a **generation gap**—a conflict of basic interests, beliefs, and values between youths and their parents. When differences do exist, they are more likely to revolve around personal lifestyle choices, such as styles of dress, hairstyles, tastes in music, and selection of leisure activities (Smetana, 2000; Steinberg, 1990). Although overt conflict between parents and adoles-

THE SCIENTIFIC IMPACT: INTERPRETING RESEARCH

What Roles Do Mothers and Fathers Play in Teens' Peer Relationships?

Parents can play an important role in influencing the type and quality of their children's peer relationships. However, the nature of parental involvement in their children's social relationships differs across developmental periods. For example, during early childhood, parents directly intervene in and supervise children's peer interactions, whereas parents of older children and teens may use a less direct approach, such as encouraging friendships and monitoring social activities. Although parents have considerable influence on children's peer relationships, little is known about the ways in which mothers and fathers involve themselves in their teenagers' peer relationships and the degree to which this involvement is related to the qualities of teens' friendships and peer experiences.

To address these issues, Kimberly Updegraff and her colleagues (Updegraff, McHale, Crouter, & Kupanoff, 2001) collected information from 197 mothers, fathers, and first-born teens (average age 15 years). Family members participated in a home interview regarding parental involvement in adolescents' peer relationships (with questions such as "How much time do you spend talking with

your son/daughter about his/her friends?" " . . . talking to the parents of his/her friends?") and on the quality of the teens' peer relationships. In addition, each family participated in seven evening phone calls designed to provide information about daily home and personal activities. During these phone calls, information was obtained on the activities and events that took place in the home and with friends.

The results showed that mothers and fathers differed in their involvement in their teenagers' peer relationships. Specifically, mothers reported being more involved in and were more knowledgeable about adolescents' peer interactions than were fathers. No differences were found, however, in the amount of time mothers and fathers spent with adolescents and their friends. Closer examination of the phone call information showed that the time parents spent with teens and their friends most commonly involved chauffeuring adolescents and their friends, attending sports events, and eating meals together. Although mothers may be more involved in traditional caregiving activities with their teens, which may contribute to their greater involvement

in and knowledge of peer interactions, fathers appear to share equally in leisure time with their teens and the teens' friends.

Importantly, Updegraff and colleagues found that direct parental involvement was related to positive peer relationships. This finding, however, was stronger for boys than for girls. Thus, parents' direct peer involvement was more central to boys' than to girls' peer experiences. The authors concluded that because boys' socialization experiences tend to encourage individuality and achievement, perhaps at the expense of intimate relationships with other teens, mothers' and fathers' efforts to facilitate their sons' peer relationships may be particularly beneficial to their social development.

Thinking It Through:

1. How do societal expectations influence the ways in which mothers and fathers interact and involve themselves in their teens' peer relationships?
2. What are the implications of these findings for the development of parenting programs for mothers and fathers of young teenagers?

cents is less frequent in Hispanic, Native American, and Asian American families than in Caucasian families, those conflicts that do occur center on the same lifestyle issues (Fuligni, 1998).

Adolescents and parents have their most intense conflicts during early adolescence, when adolescents try to become more independent before parents are ready to accept this independence. These conflicts may be due in part to the changes brought on by puberty (Sagrestano, McCormick, Paikoff, & Holmbeck, 1999). Several studies indicate that conflicts intensify as adolescents reach the midpoint of puberty and try to distance themselves from parents (Laursen, Coy, & Collins, 1998; Paikoff & Brooks-Gunn, 1991). Conflicts also result from the different perceptions that parents and adolescents hold about day-to-day events (Larson & Richards, 1994). For example, a father may view his use of induction as a sensible way to persuade his 14-year-old daughter not to date an older boy. His daughter, however, may view his reasoning as an unfair intrusion into an area that she believes is none of his business. The daughter may define her father's stance as a violation of her privacy or an insult to her ability to make mature decisions. Most parent-adolescent conflicts are resolved by adolescents' giving in to parents. However, the number of unresolved conflicts and parents' use of punishment during a conflict generally increase as adolescents get older, because adolescents become less likely to give in (Smetana & Gaines, 1999).

Some developmental researchers view conflict as a process that fosters adaptive changes in parent-adolescent relationships (Collins, 1990). In early adolescence, teens often begin to

generation gap a conflict of basic interests, beliefs, and values between youth and their parents

"talk back" to their parents. They verbally question adult authority and may treat their parents with less respect. They may tell parents that "you can't tell me what to do" and may even use an occasional obscenity. These disrespectful behaviors are often disturbing and can be sources of conflict between parents and their young teens. But these parent-adolescent conflicts reflect the teen's attempt to assert his or her individuality (Lerner & Olson, 1994). Conflict encourages parents and adolescents to revise their expectations and renegotiate their relationship without fundamentally changing their feelings of being connected to each other (Laursen & Collins, 1994). Parent-adolescent conflict may have greater consequences for parents than for teens, as parents' well-being may be more dependent on how they relate to their teens (Dekovic, 1999). Thus, conflict *per se* is not considered to be a critical factor in influencing outcomes for adolescents and their families. What appears to be more influential is how conflict is managed and resolved. For example, high rates of *intense* conflict characterize troubled parent-adolescent relationships and contribute to adolescents' greater involvement in deviant and antisocial behavior (Ambert, 1997; Patterson, Griesler, Vaden, & Kupersmidt, 1992).

WHAT ARE THE CHARACTERISTICS OF EARLY ADOLESCENT PEER RELATIONSHIPS?

Adults and parents often worry that adolescents will be led astray by their peers or by peer pressure. Underlying this concern is the idea that adolescent peer groups are at odds with the desires and goals of parents and other adults (Fuligni & Eccles, 1993). In almost a seductive fashion, peers are believed to lure young adolescents away from social norms and parental wisdom toward behavior and activities that defy parental standards—bizarre dress, alcohol and drug use, promiscuous sex, and truancy. But in reality, although some adolescents are pressured by their peers to use drugs, skip school, and engage in delinquent activities, most are not. In fact, peers influence the development of important social, cognitive, and educational skills (Ambert, 1997; Brendgen, Bowen, Rondeau, & Vitaro, 1999). Thus, adolescent peer influences represent a combination of diverse and interrelated processes, most of which are constructive—though some are not.

THE ADOLESCENT PEER CULTURE

Since World War II, adolescents have been spending more time with each other and less time with adults (Freeman, Csikszentmihalyi, & Larson, 1986). The emergence of an adolescent peer culture is the product of several social developments of the twentieth century (Greenberger & Steinberg, 1986; Modell & Goodman, 1990):

◆ Adolescence became a lengthy period of preparing for, but not participating in, the adult world. The absence of adult roles and responsibilities gave rise to the growth of youth cultures that give meaning and organization to the social world of adolescence.

◆ The development of low-wage jobs designed specifically for adolescents (such as those in the fast food industry) reinforced age segregation by creating work environments populated largely by teens.

◆ The growth of industries devoted to adolescents as consumers further contributed to adolescent culture by providing consumer items (clothing, pop music) designed specifically for this age group.

Adolescent peer culture is characterized by two kinds of peer groups. **Cliques** are small groups of peers, usually of the same sex and age, who interact with one another on a regular basis. Common activities, shared interests, proximity, and familiarity are the foundations for the development of cliques. Cliques provide a stable social atmosphere in which

cliques small groups of peers, usually of the same sex and age, who interact with one another on a regular basis

crowds peer groups defined by members' activities and social standing

THE SOCIAL IMPACT: DEBATING THE ISSUE

Do Friends Lead Adolescents into Trouble?

As you have learned, adolescents are strongly influenced by their friends. One common-sense conclusion is that those adolescents who get involved with undesirable friends are more likely to get into trouble. But do friends actually "lead" one another into trouble?

Two theoretical models have been proposed to account for friends' apparent detrimental influences. The first model, the Peer Influence Model, suggests that association with undesirable friends is the critical factor in influencing later behavior problems. The second model, the Individual Characteristics Model, suggests that problem behavior during childhood leads to both later problem behavior and association with undesirable friends. The first model proposes that undesirable peers cause later problem behavior, whereas the second model proposes that having undesirable friends or having no friends at all is a by-product of earlier behavior problems.

To test these models, a longitudinal study of 868 Canadian boys was conducted (Vitaro, Tremblay, Kerr, Pagant, & Bukowski, 1997). The friendships of the boys were assessed at ages 10 and 11 by asking the boys to identify their friends. Classmates then rated the aggressiveness and disruptiveness of these friends. Based on the

ratings of their friends, the boys were categorized into four groups— aggressive-disruptive friends, average friends, nonaggressive-nondisruptive friends, and no friends. In addition, the boys rated themselves at ages 11, 12, and 13 for their involvement in problem behavior. The relationship between type of friends and problem behavior was then examined.

One of the key comparisons in this study focused on the group of boys who had no friends. According to the Peer Influence Model, boys who have no friends should not develop behavior problems. According to the Individual Characteristics Model, children with no friends should be at highest risk for behavior problems because their disruptive behavior contributes to a lack of friends.

The results provide partial support for both models. In support of the Peer Influence Model, boys who were moderately disruptive at ages 11 and 12 and had aggressive-disruptive friends had more behavior problems at age 13. However, data supporting the Individual Characteristics Model were found in the fact that boys who were highly disruptive at ages 11 and 12 had the most behavior problems at age 13, regardless of how they were categorized on the basis of friends. Highly disruptive boys who had nonaggressive-nondisruptive friends were just as

likely to develop behavior problems as those who had aggressive-disruptive friends. Boys who were not disruptive were not influenced by their friends.

These findings suggest that there may be multiple pathways to problem behaviors. Boys who are highly disruptive before they enter adolescence do not need to be influenced by undesirable peers to develop later behavior problems. Boys who are more moderately disruptive before adolescence are more likely to engage in problem behavior if they associate with undesirable friends. Thus, friends' characteristics may influence some boys' developmental pathways to problem behavior, but this influence depends on the boys' own characteristics.

Thinking It Through:

1. Can you describe the basic difference between the Peer Influence Model and the Individual Characteristics Model? Draw a diagram that shows how these models relate to problem behavior.
2. Why was the "no friends" group so important in testing the two models?
3. How do you think the results would change if the study were done with girls rather than boys?

members know each other well and engage in intimate friendships (Degirmencioglu, Urberg, Tolson, & Richard, 1998; Montemayor, Adams, & Gullotta, 1990).

When a teen defines himself as a "nerd," he is telling everyone of his membership in a particular peer culture. He may be part of a clique, but he also is a member of a larger group that is characterized by stereotypes. **Crowds** are peer groups defined by members' activities and social standing. Crowds have larger and more diverse memberships than cliques do and are based on perceptions of social reputation (Ennett & Bauman, 1996). Members of crowds may or may not spend time in direct interaction with each other. Crowds are distinguished from one another by lifestyle characteristics, such as members' clothing, activities, and traits (Brown, Mory, & Kinney, 1994).

Describe the two types of peer groups. What kind of group is pictured here? In what ways do peers develop their own culture?

How do peer cliques differ from peer groups? How does being a member of a peer group influence an adolescent's development?

Adolescents who become part of a particular crowd through clothing style, language, or choice of hangout engage in social experimentation that temporarily defines how they view themselves and how they are viewed by others. The typical American school is a major social arena for a great diversity of crowds (such as "populars," "jocks," and "nerds"). In Table 12.1, you can see that adolescents use highly stereotyped images and descriptors to identify crowd members. Additionally, you can see that more adolescents think of themselves as normal or popular than as loners or toughs (Youniss, McLellan, & Strouse, 1994).

Being a member of a particular crowd has consequences for adolescents' self-esteem and popularity. Members of more prestigious crowds, such as "jocks," often have higher self-esteem than those in lower-status crowds, such as "toughs" and "brains" (Brown & Lohr, 1987). Youths who are members of the high-status groups of "populars" and "jocks" spend more time with peers and friends than do those who are members of the low-status groups of "loners" and "brains" (Brown et al., 1994). These differences are not simply a function of crowd norms; they are the consequence of many factors—level of social skills, family experiences, personality, and so on (LaGreca, Prinstein,

TABLE 12.1
Descriptors of Various Adolescent Crowds

TYPE OF CROWD	PERCENTAGE OF ADOLESCENTS IN CROWD	DESCRIPTORS
Populars	23%	Have many friends Are well known Are invited to and attend social events Look good Are cool Have positive social principles
Jocks	10%	Like sports Participate in physical activities
Brains	9%	Have high academic skills and make good grades Are smart
Normals	45%	Are average Go to social events and have fun Don't have problems
Loners	6%	Belong to tiny groups Feel alone Do not conform Are not accepted by others
Toughs	7%	Use drugs/alcohol Are aggressive

SOURCE: Youniss, McLellan, and Strouse, 1994. Copyright © 1994 by Sage Publications. Reprinted by permission of Sage Publication, Inc.

& Fetter, 2001). It is clear, however, that crowd affiliation is an important factor in influencing the patterns of identity and social relationships among members (Stone & Brown, 1999).

Adolescent peer cultures vary widely from one region, community, or school to another (Gecas & Seff, 1990). Whatever the lifestyle characteristics, though, all adolescent peer cultures do the following (Hartup, 1993; Rice, 1996):

◆ Provide ways of experimenting with different self-concepts
◆ Provide symbols of group membership
◆ Serve as symbols of independence from the adult world
◆ Serve as symbols of prestige or status within the peer world
◆ Allow for the expression of personal beliefs, feelings, and values on topics that are important to adolescents (such as love, sexuality, dating relationships, substance use, and rebellion against adults)

Adolescent peer groups change as youths become more capable of intimacy. At the start of adolescence, peer activities revolve primarily around cliques or crowds composed of either males or females. One of the first changes begins during early adolescence when separate boy and girl cliques come together for shared activities. Soon after, couples begin to form within the cliques. Clique leaders often initiate this transition to relationships with peers of the other sex, and they are followed by other members. Thus, same-sex cliques transform into mixed-sex cliques, but the activities of these mixed-sex cliques remain linked to the group as a whole.

Further change in peer relationships occurs during later adolescence when the cliques and crowds begin to dissolve and couples go their separate ways. Attention becomes focused on specific friendships or dating relationships rather than larger group interests. The safety and security of larger numbers is no longer a top priority, and the structure of adolescent peer groups becomes increasingly fragmented (Shrum, Cheek, & Hunter, 1988).

FRIENDSHIPS DURING EARLY ADOLESCENCE

Close friendships during early adolescence provide a means for developing trust, security, and intimacy (Fischer, Munsch, & Greene, 1996). These issues are prominent throughout most of the life span, and adolescent friendships are important for making progress toward many of the psychological and social competencies that define mature intimacy and trust (Erikson, 1968).

During early adolescence, important changes take place in the qualities that define friendship. Friends become defined as those who share intimate thoughts, feelings, and expressions of support (Phillipsen, 1999). As you learned in Chapter 8, younger children define friends as those with whom they spend time and share activities. For example, a 9-year-old might describe a friend as someone who "plays games with me a lot." In contrast, a 14-year-old might describe a friend as someone who "listens to me and is someone I can talk to about my private feelings" (Epstein, 1986).

Adolescents are more likely than younger children to share secrets, empathize, and cooperate with friends rather than compete with them (Buhrmeister, Goldfarb, & Cantrell, 1992). Knowledge of one's own and others' personal qualities increases, and this understanding fosters the ability to develop friendships based on mutual generosity, support, and helpfulness (Berndt & Perry, 1990).

Adolescents demand loyalty from friends and express anxiety over the possibility of being rejected. Because of this emphasis on having trustworthy, loyal, and supportive friends, adolescents often become angry and upset when friends talk behind their back and share their secrets with others (Berndt & Perry, 1990). Friendships can be "double-edged swords," providing joy, security, and support when they work, but also heartache and despair when they do not.

Although both boys and girls make progress toward more mature intimacy during adolescence, girls do so earlier and more thoroughly (Fischer et al., 1996). Compared to boys, adolescent girls express more interest in close friendships, have more intimate conversations

During adolescence, friendships become more intense and intimate, based on sharing personal thoughts, feelings, and expressions of support. What factors account for this change in how friendships are defined?

with friends, are more concerned about receiving loyalty from friends, and express more anxiety about rejection (Bukowski, Gauze, Hoza, & Newcomb, 1993). Teen girls prefer more exclusive friendships, are more sensitive, and express greater empathy with friends than teen boys do (Brendgen, Markiewicz, Doyle, & Bukowski, 2001; Fischer et al., 1996). Adolescent girls also have higher expectations for intimacy in relationships with friends, but these expectations can be unrealistically high, leading to frustration and disappointment. In contrast, boys' friendships remain more focused on shared activities (Clark & Ayers, 1993).

Many of the gender differences in friendships are consistent with the ways girls and boys are socialized. Girls generally are socialized to be focused on interpersonal qualities and communication, whereas boys are encouraged to become autonomous and goal-oriented in their social lives (Ruble & Martin, 1998). For girls, intimacy is often expressed overtly through conversation and self-disclosure. Girls' activities with their friends focus primarily on sharing personal lifestyle qualities (clothing, makeup, and so forth) and aspects of heterosexual relationships (talking about boys) (Seiffge-Krenke, 1993). For boys, the expression of support is often nonverbal (Black, 2000)—as one boy said, when he and his friends were down, they would get together and listen to heavy metal music (Arnett, 1991). This is due in part to the concern that boys have about being too intimate with other boys, fearing that close friendships might be mistaken for homosexual interest. Thus, differences in the expectations and interactions of adolescent girl and boy friendships reflect their socialization contexts and experiences.

PEER POPULARITY AND REJECTION

As you learned in Chapter 10, not all children are accepted by their peers. The same is true for adolescents. What makes some teens popular whereas others are outcasts? One answer focuses on adolescents' social skills. Popular adolescents have skills such as the following, which foster smooth and comfortable relationships (Wentzel & Erdley, 1993):

- The ability to act appropriately in a variety of social situations
- The ability to perceive and meet the needs of others
- Being agreeable and cheerful and having a sense of humor
- The ability to communicate effectively

Adolescents who are unpopular and are rejected by their peers often lack these skills and have difficulty making others feel comfortable. But not all unpopular and rejected adolescents have the same problems. Aggressive adolescents may be unpopular because they are hostile and bully or badger others. Withdrawn adolescents may be unpopular because they are shy and timid (Hymel, Bowker, & Woody, 1993). Adolescents who are both aggressive and shy have problems controlling their hostility and aggression but also are hesitant or shy about making friends (Olweus, 1995; Pope & Bierman, 1999).

Unpopular and rejected adolescents are at risk for a variety of adverse consequences, such as depression, behavior problems, and academic difficulties (Olweus, 1995; Vitaro, Tremblay, & Bukowski, 2001), and these problems may have long-term effects (Giordano, Cernkovich, Groat, Pugh, & Swinford, 1998). But the problems vary for each type of rejected adolescent. Aggressive adolescents tend to make friends with one another, and their associations may foster even more aggressive behavior, placing them at risk for behavior problems and delinquency. Withdrawn adolescents tend to experience loneliness, low self-esteem, and diminished social competence. Adolescents who are classified as both aggressive and withdrawn are at greatest risk, because they are vulnerable to the problems faced by both aggressive and withdrawn adolescents (Parkhurst & Asher, 1992; Rubin, LeMare, & Lollis, 1990).

DATING AND ROMANTIC RELATIONSHIPS

One of the biggest changes and challenges in early adolescence is the development of dating and romantic relationships (Gray & Steinberg, 1999). Other-sex peers who previously seemed like aliens from another planet now become attractive. The boundaries between boys' and girls' worlds that were so vigorously defended early in development start to crumble in early adolescence. Today, dating plays a different role in the lives of adolescents than it did in earlier historic periods (Furman & Wehner, 1997). Several social changes have redefined dating relationships:

+ Dating during adolescence is an end in itself, not a practice that frequently leads to marriage.
+ Parents are less available to control and monitor adolescents' dating.
+ Dating is less structured, more informal, and more focused on leisure-time activities.
+ Dating is a means for sexual experimentation, especially when dating relationships last for a while and become exclusive.

In early adolescence, dating and sexuality come to play a more prominent role in adolescents' daily lives. What changes occur during this period that increase the importance of intimate heterosexual relationships?

On average, girls begin dating between 12 and 13 years of age, and boys begin a year or so later. Young adolescents usually date in small groups of couples, often meeting at the mall or movies. At this age, "going with" someone enhances an adolescent's status, but the relationship is often more form than content: the two may not talk to each other directly at school but pass along messages through intermediaries or over the phone (Beal, 1994). As adolescents mature and begin to drive cars and as their curfews become less confining, dating involves spending more time together as separate couples. During early adolescence, dating partners generally are chosen on the basis of membership in specific peer groups (Connolly, Furman, & Konarski, 2000). With age, partners are selected more on the basis of physical attraction, personal preferences, and personality qualities (Connolly & Johnson, 1996; Furman & Wehner, 1997). Dating becomes more intimate as adolescents mature.

Despite the fact that only a few dating relationships last beyond adolescence, these relationships can be critically important to adolescents and their development (Davies & Windle, 2000; Shulman, Collins, & Knafo, 1997). Young adolescents learn about love, life, and emotions through dating, and they report that problems with boyfriends or girlfriends create more stress than family-related events (Dornbusch, Mont-Reynaud, Ritter, Chen, & Steinberg, 1991). Adolescents who frequently date have been found to perform more poorly at school and to be at risk for depression (Quatman, Sampson, Robinson, & Watson, 2001). However, adolescents who never date are at risk for depression, excessive dependency on parents, and deficient social skills (Seiffge-Krenke, 1997). Thus, extremes in dating are related to problem behaviors in young teens.

There is evidence that adolescent boys and girls experience dating and romantic relationships differently (Leaper & Anderson, 1997). Boys emphasize the sexual aspects of dating and the physical attractiveness of the partner. Girls focus on the opportunities that dating relationships provide for closeness, self-disclosure, and communication (Furman & Wehner, 1997; Shulman & Seiffge-Krenke, 2001).

EMERGING SEXUALITY DURING EARLY ADOLESCENCE

Before puberty, sexual activity consists primarily of self-exploration, masturbation, and interactions between boys and girls that entail holding hands, hugging, and playing games with sexual overtones (such as playing married partners). Once children reach puberty, however, sexual behavior becomes more explicit, ceases to be play, and becomes an increasingly important part of their relationships (Graber & Archibald, 2001).

During early adolescence, sexuality continues to revolve around the adolescent's own body, and particularly masturbation. Masturbation is the most common source of orgasm for young teens of both sexes, and it is the first source of ejaculation among 75 percent of adolescent boys. Most girls who masturbate do so around age 12, and most boys have their first experience at age 14 (Reinisch, 1990). Although masturbation persists into adulthood, it is more frequent among young adolescents.

Another source of orgasm for young adolescents is nocturnal emissions ("wet dreams"). Erections during sleep (usually during REM sleep) can be observed in prepubescent boys, but nocturnal orgasms with ejaculation occur after puberty. A similar response occurs in girls. These orgasms are relatively rare, accounting for about 2 to 3 percent of the total sexual outlet for girls and 5 to 8 percent for boys, although most adolescents experience these at one time or another. Like menarche for girls who are unprepared, nocturnal emissions can be disconcerting for unprepared boys, and the telltale evidence of the ejaculate often is a source of embarrassment (Katchadourian, 1990).

Sexual interactions between boys and girls also begin during early adolescence. These early interactions often begin as curiosity and sex play. Over the course of early adolescence, sexual behaviors become more and more a part of intimate relationships. This represents a significant advance in sexual behavior because it requires the ability to negotiate and share sexual experiences. Kissing, hugging, and fondling represent increasingly important and frequent behaviors between young adolescent boys and girls. By the time they get to high school, most adolescents change from sexual behavior focused on themselves to more interpersonal sexual behaviors, such as petting.

The most important sexual milestone that heterosexual adolescents achieve is the initiation of sexual intercourse. Teens who engage in sexual intercourse cross a line that irrevocably alters themselves and the nature of their relationships. Sexual intercourse for young adolescents generally is, however, a sporadic and rare experience. Fewer than 1 in 10 adolescents (8.3 percent) of both sexes engages in sexual intercourse before age 13, with a larger percentage of boys (12.2 percent) than girls (4.5 percent) doing so (CDC, 2000a). Ethnic differences exist in early sexual activities—African American adolescents are more likely (20.5 percent) than Caucasian American (5.5 percent) or Hispanic (9.5 percent) adolescents to begin having sexual intercourse before age 13 (CDC, 2000a).

The age at which adolescents begin to have sex is important for many reasons. Early sexual intercourse exposes one for a longer period to the risk of becoming pregnant. Another problem arises from the fact that development in the cognitive, emotional, and physical domains does not necessarily occur at the same rate. The earlier the onset of sexual intercourse, the greater the discrepancy between physical development and cognitive and emotional development. This discrepancy makes it more difficult for young adolescents to understand the consequences of their sexual behavior, and they are therefore less likely to use contraception to avoid an unintended pregnancy (Paikoff, McCormick, & Sagrestano, 2000). In addition, sexual activity that begins in early adolescence is likely to be part of a larger pattern of high-risk behavior, often including experimentation with drugs and alcohol (Miller, 1998; Miller et al., 1997). Initiation of intercourse at age 15 or earlier is associated with an increased incidence of both early pregnancy and sexually transmitted diseases. It is important to note that many adolescent girls (70 percent) who had sex before they were 14 report that the sexual experience was unwanted or involuntary (Moore, 1998); that is, most girls who engage in sex very early are victims of exploitation and do not do so because of their own wishes and desires (Elo, King, & Furstenberg, 1999).

Many factors influence adolescents' decisions to have sex. Although most teens will have sex before they leave high school, when asked when first intercourse should occur, most believe it is better to wait until they are at least 16 or older. This holds true for both boys and girls (National Center for Health Statistics, 1994).

Adolescents' reasons for waiting to have sex are listed in Table 12.2. As you can see, most of the reasons focus on either avoiding negative outcomes (such as pregnancy) or waiting until the right person comes along. Religious beliefs were identified by only a minority of adolescents. But remaining a virgin is difficult, and the likelihood of retaining their virginity decreases as adolescents get older. For example, 91 percent of 12-year-olds are virgins and 70 percent of 15-year-olds are, but only 18 percent of 19-year-olds are (Singh & Darroch, 1999). Thus, at least during early adolescence, most teens experiment with their sexuality but do not yet engage in sexual intercourse of their own choice.

DEVIANT PEER GROUPS: ADOLESCENT GANGS

I was a member of an organization called the Spanish Cobras. I got into street gangs because of the environment. The people around me were mostly gang members and it was

TABLE 12.2

Adolescents' Reasons for Waiting to Have Sex

REASON	PERCENTAGE CITING REASON
1. Want to wait until I'm in a committed relationship	87%
2. Worry about sexually transmitted diseases	85%
3. Worry about pregnancy	84%
4. Not old enough	84%
5. Worry about AIDS	83%
6. Haven't met the right person yet	80%
7. Just not ready for sex	79%
8. Want to wait until I'm married	71%
9. Against my religion	40%

SOURCE: National Center for Health Statistics, 1994.

a way of life in the neighborhood I was brought up in. . . . The gang gave me a sense of belonging. . . . It started out as a social thing, then got off into a drug thing because there was money involved, and then it got into organized crime stuff. . . . Being a gang member meant doing whatever the gang saw as necessary.

—*Jackie, a former youth gang member* (Spergel, 1990)

Some peer involvements do not contribute to positive outcomes. Deviant peer activities range from becoming preoccupied with drug use to engaging in delinquent activities. A prominent deviant youth peer group is the street gang. As Jackie's comments suggest, a gang represents many different things to its members: a source of status and belonging, a means to money, and a source of power through crime and violence (Branch, 1998).

Contrary to popular belief, gangs are not a recent invention: they emerged in nineteenth-century America and continued to develop in many US cities throughout the twentieth century (Quamina, 1999). Popular stereotypes of adolescent gangs fail to capture their diversity. Gang members may be Caucasian Americans, Asian Americans, African Americans, Mexican Americans, Puerto Ricans, or a mixture of ethnic minorities; they may be skinheads; and they may be all males, all females, or of both sexes (Flannery, Huff, & Manos, 1998; Wang, 2000). Despite great variations in structure, membership, and meaning, most adolescent gangs share the following characteristics (Branch, 1998; Vigil, 1988):

- ✦ They are groups of adolescents who hang out or interact with one another on a frequent basis.
- ✦ Members share a common identity that usually is expressed through a gang name such as Crips, Bloods, or Latin Kings.
- ✦ Members adopt various status symbols such as styles of dress, colors, hand signals, language, initiation rituals, and graffiti.
- ✦ They exercise control over and defense of specific "turf" as an expression of territoriality.

Gangs share many of the qualities of other cliques or crowds. What functions do gangs serve for adolescents? What factors influence a teen's involvement in gang activities?

THE PRACTICAL IMPACT: NURTURING CHILDREN

Gang Prevention

What factors contribute to effective gang prevention programs for youths? According to the research, successful gang prevention programs include five elements (Chance, 1992; Esbensen, 2000; Soriano, 1993):

1. **Mobilizing the community.** Effective programs must involve the community in detecting, suppressing, and finding solutions to gang-related problems. This includes eliciting the cooperation of families, schools, and neighborhood organizations in targeting high-risk youths, identifying current gang members, cleansing graffiti, fostering an intolerance for gangs and gang activities, and assisting law enforcement efforts.
2. **Providing alternatives to gangs.** Providing adolescents with education, training, and employment opportunities is important in the long-term reduction and prevention of youth gang problems, particularly in low-income urban neighborhoods. A key objective of these programs is to help youths develop skills and interests that decrease their reliance on participation in criminal gang activities.
3. **Targeting at-risk youths.** To effectively deal with youth gang problems, it is important to target youths who are most at risk. For example, programs should target core gang members and establish ways to reintegrate them into legitimate pursuits. Also, programs should identify young "wanna be's" who give clear signs of early involvement in criminal gang activities.
4. **Suppressing gang activities.** Effective gang control includes procedures that suppress gang activities. Such suppression involves not only law enforcement but also a variety of other agencies and community groups that monitor, supervise, and restrain gang offenders. Law enforcement alone cannot suppress gang activity without the collaboration of community members, who assist in surveillance and information gathering.
5. **Developing trusting relationships in the community.** Effective gang prevention programs are culturally sensitive and establish rapport with members of the community. Incorporating ethnic minorities into the staffing of gang prevention programs is crucial. This increases the programs' ability to communicate with targeted ethnic groups and establishes a degree of familiarity and trust among ethnic groups that are represented in gangs.

Gang membership often starts off as social involvement, to cope with difficult social and economic conditions (Flannery et al., 1998). Although gang activity is found most frequently in low-income areas of inner-city neighborhoods in which there is poor community integration and little meaningful employment, it has been spreading into suburban, middle-class neighborhoods (Flannery et al., 1998). This development suggests that adolescent gangs have become part of American culture, assisted in part by stereotyped media images.

Estimates of the extent of gang activity vary widely. In one study, 4881 gangs with 249,324 members were identified in the United States (Spergel & Curry, 1993). In another report, at least 840,500 youngsters were identified as members of some 26,000 youth gangs (Egley, 2000). Despite disagreement about the number of gangs and gang members, most studies suggest that a relatively small percentage of adolescents actually become members of gangs (Flannery et al., 1998). Even in high-risk areas, no more than 10 percent of adolescents actually join gangs, and gang-related activities account for only 2 percent of juvenile crimes (Huff, 1996). Regardless of the precise numbers, all states and almost all large cities report youth gang problems (Howell, 1997). Concern is growing about gang activities because of several recent developments:

- A higher incidence of what is believed to be gang-related violence (such as drive-by shootings)
- Greater access to lethal weapons (such as automatic weapons) by gang members
- Greater emphasis on organized criminal activity (such as car theft rings and trafficking in drugs and weapons)
- A trend for members to remain active in gangs well into adulthood
- The spread of gang culture beyond inner city areas into suburban areas
- A more diverse membership in youth gangs, including growing participation by females

The violent and illegal activities of some gangs aside, many youth gangs are simply variations of adolescent crowds and cliques (Baba, 2001; Cairns, Cadwallader, Estell, &

Neckerman, 1997). For example, in Brooklyn, New York, members of the Neck Road Boys tend to be nonviolent and are known for their participation in raves—events where they gather to listen to music and use drugs. Individuals join through a social process of hanging out with the group (Goldstein, Glick, Carthan, & Blancero, 1994). Adolescents are drawn to gangs for many of the same reasons they adopt the lifestyles of cliques or crowds in the larger world of peer associations.

HOW DO MASS MEDIA INFLUENCE YOUNG ADOLESCENTS' DEVELOPMENT?

Notice the enjoyment that the girls in this photo display as they listen to their music. During early adolescence, music and other media play increasingly important roles. Can you identify the changes that bring about this interest in media other than television?

Adolescents spend a significant portion of their time with mass media. According to some estimates, they spend about 8 hours a day with one or more of the mass media, sometimes as a primary activity, often as a secondary activity—for instance, listening to music while doing their homework (Fine, Mortimer, & Roberts, 1990). Although television remains an important source of entertainment and information for adolescents, television viewing drops during adolescence by about 10 percent; the teen years is the only period of development in which television viewing declines (Liebert & Sprafkin, 1988). As they enter adolescence, youths spend more time with other media such as music, computers, and video games.

POPULAR MUSIC

Music is a pervasive phenomenon in the lives of many adolescents (Zillmann & Gan, 1997). From the time they enter junior high school until they graduate from high school, teens spend over 10,000 hours listening to pop music (Thompson, 1993). Whereas television in many ways reflects adult society, music is more often associated with the values of youth. Thus, adolescents spend less time exposed to the mainstream adult messages presented on television and more time tuned to the teen-focused messages of popular music. (Chapin, 2000). Many teens use music to shape their identity and to help define their social group. Some social groups are identified primarily by their choice of music.

Young teenagers listen to slightly over 3 hours of music daily and girls tend to listen to music more than boys (Roberts & Christenson, 2001). African American youths listen to more music than Caucasian American youths, with African American teenage girls the most avid listeners, averaging about 7 hours a day (Hakanen, 1995).

Music represents a significant topic of discussion among adolescents, and almost 80 percent consider music to be very important in their lives (Larson, Kubey, & Colletti, 1989; Thompson, 1993). In fact, teens cite musicians more frequently than athletes as their heroes, and they rate the influence of music higher than that of religion or books (Knight-Ridder/ Tribune News Service, 1999). Liking and being able to talk about music are crucial to adolescents' peer relationships, and the heaviest music listeners spend more time with friends and less time with their families and schoolwork (Larson et al., 1989; Tarrant, North, & Hargreaves, 2000). Music affects emotions, and teens use music to enhance or intensify their mood or to change mood directions (Christenson & Roberts, 1998).

Much concern has been expressed over the time adolescents spend listening to music and its messages (Villani, 2001). As a result of the potentially negative influence of music containing violent, satanic, sexually explicit, and drug-related lyrics, warning labels are now found on many releases. But there is little evidence that popular music and its lyrics influence adolescents' behavior. Most adolescents do not attend to music lyrics—many do not even know the lyrics to their favorite songs (Thompson, 1993). In addition, teenagers do not agree on the meanings of messages in popular songs (Pettegrew et al., 1995). Although popular music is a central part of adolescent culture, it is not necessarily a powerful influence on their values and behaviors. Studies that examine the relation between adolescents' music and aggressive, sexual, or suicidal behavior fail to find significant relationships (Gardstrom, 1999; Scheel & Westfeld, 1999).

FIGURE 12.3

Percentage of Children Who Use Computers at Home or School, by Age

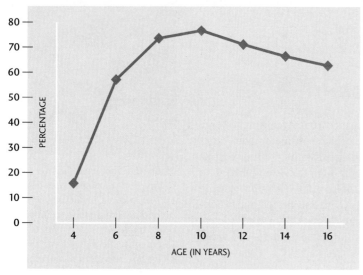

SOURCE: National Center for Education Statistics, 1996.

This figure shows how computer use increases through childhood and peaks during early adolescence. After that time, computer use drops off. Can you identify the factors that produce these changes?

FIGURE 12.4

How Adolescents Spend Time on a Computer

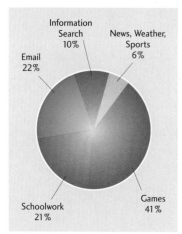

SOURCE: Adapted from US Census Bureau, 2001a.

Notice that adolescents spend most of their computer time playing computer games. What reasons can you think of to explain this tendency? What does this say about the importance of computers in young adolescents' lives?

COMPUTERS

Computers offer enormous opportunities to young people. They entertain and educate and are now a vital part of daily living. With advances in computer networking, people have enhanced abilities to communicate and access information about an infinite variety of topics and ideas (Bremer & Rauch, 1998). Computer technology is now an integral part of education. In 1984, only 31 percent of all public schools provided access to computers. Now, almost all schools (98 percent) have some computers in classrooms. Unfortunately, because of lack of funding, public schools that serve low-income and minority students provide less access to computers—increasing the gap in education and technology training between these students and those from higher-income school districts (Market Data Retrieval, 2001). Perceiving the benefits, many parents have bought computers for their children. Between 1984 and 2000, the number of American households with a computer increased over fourfold, from 8.2 percent to 51 percent (National Telecommunications and Information Administration [NTIA], 1998; US Census Bureau, 2001a).

Use of Computers

Use of computers varies with age. As indicated in Figure 12.3, computer use increases dramatically between the ages of 4 and 10 years, when it peaks and begins to level off. For children, computers represent primarily a source of entertainment and basic learning. Although they continue to take advantage of these important functions, adolescents use the computer in more advanced ways—solving problems, doing homework, and communicating with others. Figure 12.4 presents the favorite computer activities of adolescents.

Adolescents' use of computers is determined in part by their access to them. Over 82 percent of US households with incomes over $50,000 have access to a computer, whereas only about 23 percent of those with incomes under $15,000 do (US Census Bureau, 2001a). Access to computers also varies according to race and ethnicity, reflecting differences in socioeconomic status. Figure 12.5 illustrates this lack of equity: The rate of access of African American and Hispanic children is about half that of Caucasian American children. With computers playing an increasingly prominent role in everyday life, low-income minority children and adolescents are at a disadvantage because of their limited access to them.

Young Adolescents' Reactions to Computers

Young adolescents generally believe that computers can be fun and are an important part of their lives. They also believe that computers can be used for harmful purposes and that they sometimes are intimidating.

Boys and girls react differently to computers (Wright et al., 2001). Put a computer in a classroom and the boys will approach and use it. In contrast, the girls will often back away from it (Griffiths, 1991; Yelland & Lloyd, 2001). Boys tend to view computers as games and toys, whereas girls tend to view them as tools. Thus, boys will sit down at a computer and play with it, exploring it with no particular purpose; girls will respond to its usefulness but are not particularly taken with the technology itself. When games were the main reason to use a computer, boys spent much more time with computers than girls did. Now that the array of nongame applications has widened, girls report using home computers as often, and with as much confidence, as boys do. Both boys and girls surf the Web for music and

FIGURE 12.5

Percentage of US Households with Access to a Computer, by Ethnicity: 1984–2000

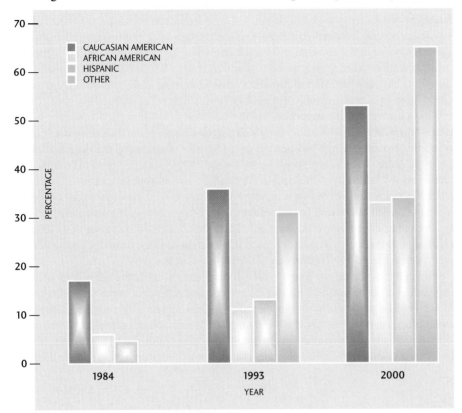

NOTE: Data were not available for the "Other" ethnic category in 1984.

SOURCE: Adapted from National Telecommunications and Information Administration, 1998; US Census Bureau, 2001a.

This figure illustrates how the percentage of US households with a computer has increased since 1984. Notice that this increase is greatest for Caucasian American and "other" households and lowest for African American and Hispanic households. What factors account for these differences among ethnic groups? What might the impact be of this lack of access for African American and Hispanic children?

photos of movie stars, use email to exchange messages with friends, and (especially in the case of teens) visit chat rooms (Shields & Behrman, 2000).

It is clear that computer software products for home use generally are designed with boys in mind (Levin & Barry, 1997). Many computer games involve blasting alien invaders or fighting tough foes—contexts that demand aggression and dominance (Kirsh, 1998). Even female characters tend to be violent, and almost half of the top-selling video games contain negative messages about or images of females (Children Now, 2000). The aggressive nature of computer games has been linked to increased aggressiveness in the children and adolescents who play them (Schutte, Malouff, Post-Gordon, & Rodasta, 1988). Although this is a matter of concern, the results of a recent study show that the effect of violent video games on aggression is less significant than the effect of viewed television violence (Sherry, 2001).

Computer games sometimes are a source of concern for parents because of the amount of time adolescents spend playing them, their seemingly addictive qualities, and the violent themes that characterize many of them. On average, American children who have home video games play with them about 1½ hours a day. Next to television, video games are the second most popular form of entertainment among children (Mediascope, 1999). The most popular video games are those that involve either fantasy, sport, or violent competition (Dietz, 1998). Educational games make up only 2 percent of the sales of video games (Mediascope, 1996).

For some adolescents, computer games become all-consuming. There have been reports of adolescents who spend their lunch money at video arcades or steal to get money to feed their computer game habit (Klein, 1984). Currently, research on the effects of computer games on children and adolescents is limited. However, the research that does exist suggests that most of the children and adolescents who play computer games frequently are no more maladjusted than those who play infrequently (Emes, 1997). Additionally, computer games have the potential to provide a sense of control and accomplishment and can improve hand-eye coordination (Anderson & Ford, 1986; Yi & Lee, 1997).

With the advent of the **Internet,** a global network of computers, people now have access to worldwide information 24 hours a day. According to some estimates, over 500 million people across the world (8.5 percent of the world's population) use the Internet (Nua Ltd., 2001). About 166 million people in the United States (about 60 percent) use the Internet, and about 10 percent of these users are children and adolescents. Currently, the number of households that are online is almost 70 million, and the percentage of children and adolescents using the Internet has increased to over 30 percent (US Census Bureau, 2001a). Internet use has increased particularly among teenagers. According to one 1998 report, 65 percent of all teens surveyed said they used the Internet at some time during the year, a 50 percent increase from 1996 (Simmons Marketing Research, 1998).

Although the Internet has much to offer, the online world, like the rest of society, is made up of a broad array of people. Most are decent and respectful, but some are obnoxious and even exploitative, particularly of young people (Federal Bureau of Investigation, 1998). The Internet is not governed by any entity—there are almost no limits or checks on the kind of information that is available and who provides it. Because children and adolescents often are trusting and curious, they can be easy targets of online exploitation (Bremer & Rauch, 1998).

Internet a global network of computers

TRY IT OUT

Activities Relating to Young Adolescents

1. Describe your crowd and/or clique in middle school or junior high school. By what names or labels were crowds and cliques known in your school? What were the "rules" for membership or acceptance in a group? How were members of a group expected to cultivate the group image and identity? To what extent did your self-concept and self-esteem rest on being a member in good standing?
2. What is different about being a young teen today? Think back over your own teen years and compare your life with what young teens today experience. Think about internal and psychological issues, as well as the changes in society that have an impact on young teens today.
3. Design a research project with the goal of discovering links among age, amount of recreational use of computer-based technologies, and the hypothesized outcomes of antisocial thinking and behavior. How will you define and measure these variables and outcomes? What do you expect to find, and how might you explain your data? How will you know if your data predict the outcomes on the basis of the variables?

SUM IT UP

How do young adolescents view themselves?

✦ Compared to children, young adolescents have a more complex sense of themselves. This is due in part to their increased cognitive ability to understand themselves and the more diverse environments in which they find themselves.

✦ Young adolescents are able to make important distinctions in the ways they view themselves—recognizing differences between actual and possible selves.

✦ During early adolescence, youths become capable of recognizing not only that their behaviors vary according to the situation but also that there is a part of them that is consistent across time and context. They begin to integrate qualities of themselves that seem inconsistent into an organized sense of self.

✦ High self-esteem during early adolescence is thought to protect teens from negative outcomes, but some research suggests that high self-esteem may contribute to risky behaviors and unrealistic perceptions.

◆ Young adolescents are at risk for low self-esteem because they experience many physical and social changes. Young adolescent girls are more at risk than boys are.

How do adolescents form an identity?

◆ Identity is a sense of who one is. Identity issues come to the forefront during early adolescence because of the physical, cognitive, and social changes that take place during this time.

◆ Erikson believed that the formation of identity involves a psychosocial crisis. Failure to address identity issues leads to an incomplete sense of self (identity diffusion).

◆ Marcia's theory of identity development focuses on two essential aspects: crisis/exploration and commitment. The possible combinations of these aspects are used to identify different phases of adolescent identity development—identity confused, foreclosure, moratorium, and identity achieved.

◆ Ethnic identity reflects a sense of belonging to one's ethnic group. Four types of resolutions of ethnic identity were identified: assimilated, marginal, separated, and bicultural.

How do family relationships change during early adolescence?

◆ Family relationships remain a primary source of influence and support for young adolescents. These relationships change in response to the physical and social changes that young adolescents experience.

◆ Adolescents are more likely to have positive outcomes if their parents are warm, supportive, and reasonable and provide supervision. In contrast, the use of harsh punitive parenting techniques is associated with negative outcomes.

◆ Although parents influence their young adolescents, young adolescents also influence how their parents respond to them. Thus, parent-adolescent relationships are bidirectional.

◆ In general, parent-adolescent conflict is relatively infrequent, occurring most often over lifestyle choices.

What are the characteristics of early adolescent peer relationships?

◆ Although the common stereotype of peer relationships during early adolescence is one of undue negative influence, most adolescent peer relationships are constructive and beneficial.

◆ Cliques are often based on common interests and values and are important for identity development.

◆ Adolescent peer groups vary widely but change in predictable ways as adolescents grow older. Initially, these groups consist of either boys or girls, but they become mixed as dating becomes more prominent.

◆ During early adolescence, friendships provide an important means for the development of intimacy. Girls develop intimate friendships earlier than boys.

◆ Popular adolescents make people around them feel comfortable. Other adolescents may be rejected because they are aggressive, withdrawn, or both.

◆ Dating relationships become more prominent during early adolescence, with girls dating earlier than boys.

◆ Sexuality for young adolescents is initially focused on their own bodies but increasingly becomes more intimate and focused in the context of relationships.

◆ Sexual intercourse is rare and sporadic during early adolescence—it may be involuntary or part of a broad array of behavior problems.

◆ Some adolescents become involved in deviant peer groups, particularly gangs. Gangs provide status and give a sense of belonging, but they are also a source of crime and violence.

How do mass media influence young adolescents' development?

◆ Popular music is an important feature of young adolescents' lives. During early adolescence, television viewing decreases whereas music listening increases.

◆ Concerns have arisen about the influence of popular music and its messages, but there is little evidence to justify these concerns.

◆ Computer technology is now an integral part of many adolescents' and children's lives, but computer use depends on age and economic status.

◆ The Internet can be educational and entertaining, but through it children and adolescents are at risk for exploitation.

KEY TERMS and CONCEPTS

actual self (384)
assimilated (389)
bicultural (389)
cliques (394)
commitment (387)
crisis/exploration (387)
crowds (395)

ethnic identity (388)
foreclosure (388)
generation gap (392)
identity (386)
identity achieved (388)
identity confused (388)
identity diffusion (386)

Internet (406)
marginal (389)
moratorium (388)
possible self (384)
psychosocial moratorium (387)
separated (389)

PART **6**

SEE the IMPACT

BENCHMARKS in Early Adolescence

PHYSICAL/MOTOR DEVELOPMENT	COGNITIVE DEVELOPMENT	SOCIAL/EMOTIONAL DEVELOPMENT
Growth spurt	Formal operational thinking and problem solving	More complex self-concept and identity
Onset of puberty; development of primary and secondary sexual characteristics	Adolescent egocentrism, imaginary audience, and personal fable	Changes in family relationships
Risk factors for obesity, eating disorders, and eating disturbances	Increased self-evaluation of academic competence	Entry into middle or junior high school
Development of body image		Emerging sexuality; others' responses to changes in sexual development
		Development of close friendships, group relationships, and dating relationships
		Greater attention to mass media

NATIONAL HOTLINES FOR YOUNG TEENS

Covenant House (for troubled teens and families): 800-999-9999

National Association of Anorexia Nervosa: 847-831-3438

National Runaway Hotline: 800-231-6946

Youth Crisis Hotline: 800-448-4663

*I*mpact Report on Young Adolescents

Approximately 1 out of 5 children/adolescents in the United States lives in poverty. This graph depicts some of the differences in well-being between those children/ adolescents who live in poverty and those who do not. As you can see, poverty has wide-ranging detrimental effects on the health, education, and general quality of life of children and adolescents. How do you feel about this information? What do you believe should be done to remedy this situation?

Indicators of Well-Being for Poor and Nonpoor Children and Adolescents

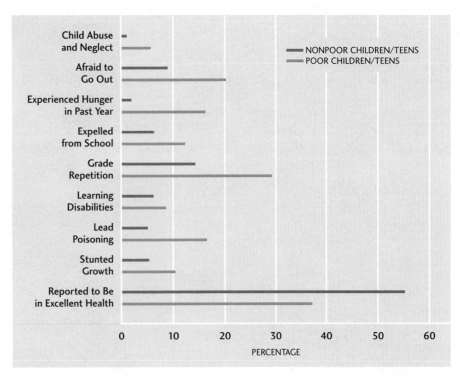

SOURCE: Brooks-Gunn and Duncan, 1997.

RECOMMENDED WEBSITES

American Academy of Child and Adolescent Psychiatry: Information at this site aids parents and caregivers in understanding developmental, behavioral, and mental disorders in children and adolescents.
http://www.aacap.org/

Center for Adolescent Studies: This site, hosted by Indiana University, provides information on adolescent issues.
http://education.indiana.edu/cas/

Children, Youth and Family Consortium: Sponsored by the University of Minnesota, this site serves as an electronic bridge to information and resources on children, youth, and families.
http://www.cyfc.umn.edu/

Family and Youth Services Bureau: This site contains information about effective, comprehensive services for at-risk youths and their families.
http://www.acf.dhhs.gov/programs/fysb/

Gang Crime Prevention Center: This site is dedicated to raising public awareness of the effects of gangs. A wide variety of information is provided on gang prevention, intervention, and research.
http://www.gcpc.state.il.us/

Girls Incorporated: National youth organization dedicated to helping girls achieve and become strong, smart, and bold.
http://www.girlsinc.org/

National Network for Youth: In addition to providing links to other resources, this site gives information about the challenges facing America's young people and their families.
http://www.nn4youth.org/

SafeSurfer: Information and materials for making the Internet safe for children can be found at this site.
http://www.safesurf.com/

PART 7

Late Adolescent Development

No longer children but still not adults, older adolescents struggle with issues of identity and independence. Older adolescents face a new series of health and safety risks and school-related adjustments. They also confront many temptations to indulge in risky behaviors that can interfere with healthy development. Many teens experiment with alcohol, tobacco, drugs, sex, and crime; however, most do not go on to abuse drugs or become promiscuous or delinquent. In fact, most older teens lead happy and productive lives and enter adulthood as well-adapted individuals.

● Most teens (78 percent) agree that they can turn to their parents in times of need. Boys are more likely than girls to say that they turn to their parents for advice (84 percent vs. 72 percent).

● Not having enough time with their parents is the top concern among teenagers today.

● Parents are far more concerned about outside threats such as drugs and alcohol (24 percent) than about family time. Family time comes in as parents' fourth most important priority (at 8 percent).

● Eighty-four percent of teens say that religion is important in their lives. More than half of teens (51 percent) say that they attend religious services weekly.

● Almost half of all teens (47 percent) report that getting good grades is of great or very great importance.

● Eight out of ten teens report that they are likely to get married.

● A little over one-third of all teens (36.5 percent) agree that it is usually a good idea for a couple to live together before getting married in order to find out whether they really get along.

● Seventy-seven percent of teens report that having a good marriage and family is extremely important to them.

● Almost 70 percent of teens believe that a working mother can establish just as warm and secure a relationship with her children as a mother who does not work.

● About half (48.7 percent) of all teens agree that being a father and raising children is one of the most fulfilling experiences a man can have.

● Sixty-three percent of teens report that being successful in their line of work is extremely important.

SOURCES: Monitoring the Future, 1999; National Campaign to Prevent Teen Pregnancy, 2001; Public Agenda, 2000; YMCA, 2000.

13

Cognitive and Physical Development in Late Adolescence

CHAPTER OUTLINE

✦ How Does Physical Development Occur During Late Adolescence?

✦ What Are the Health and Safety Issues in Late Adolescence?

✦ What Changes Occur in Older Adolescents' Thinking and Reasoning?

✦ What Gender Differences Are Found in Adolescents' Cognitive Abilities and Achievement?

✦ What Factors Contribute to Dropping Out of School?

Finding a common theme to describe the physical development and health concerns of older adolescents is difficult because there is such a wide range of differences within this age group. Many older adolescents are physically fit and healthy, but some adolescents face serious and sometimes deadly health problems because they engage in risky behaviors. As a group, older adolescents—especially boys and minority youths—have a number of health problems, many of which are preventable.

There is also wide variation in the cognitive abilities of older adolescents. Compared with children and younger adolescents, older adolescents are more likely to apply high-level abstract reasoning to a fuller range of the activities that are part of their daily lives, especially their social, political, and moral lives.

HOW DOES PHYSICAL DEVELOPMENT OCCUR DURING LATE ADOLESCENCE?

The early adolescent years are marked by rapid physical growth and dramatic changes in appearance. In later adolescence, physical growth slows down. Recent research suggests that some of the most significant changes that take place during late adolescence are unseen changes occurring in the brain. Physical changes in brain development during adolescence may influence some of the behaviors associated with the teen years.

PHYSICAL GROWTH AND DEVELOPMENT DURING LATE ADOLESCENCE

During the early years of adolescence, girls and boys grow taller, they gain muscle and fat, their body shapes change, and their reproductive organs reach maturity. Later in adolescence, the physical changes are much less pronounced. Both sexes continue to grow taller, but the rate of growth is slower than it was during the growth spurt of early adolescence. Both boys and girls may continue to gain muscle and fat on their bodies, but the changes associated with later adolescence are somewhat more evident in boys than in girls, who began their growth spurt earlier. Boys' voices deepen, and they continue to develop hair on their chins, cheeks, and bodies. Girls may show continued breast development. The exceptions to these patterns are the late-developing boys, who may be just beginning to show the physical changes associated with the adolescent growth spurt (see Chapter 11).

BRAIN DEVELOPMENT AND BEHAVIOR IN LATE ADOLESCENCE

Suppose you heard someone make insulting comments about a good friend. Your limbic system, which is involved in emotional responses, might respond by becoming angry, but other parts of the brain, particularly in the prefrontal cortex, would also become activated, to sort out why someone might think these things (even if they are wrong) and to provide brakes for the emotional system. The brain of the adolescent reacts differently. The limbic system responds, but the prefrontal cortex is less likely to do so. This pattern of response was demonstrated by researchers who showed photographs of faces expressing fear to both adults and adolescents. The adults could identify the expressions with much less difficulty than the adolescents. Also, the adults showed activation of the brain in both the limbic and the prefrontal areas, whereas the adolescents showed activation only in the limbic region (Baird et al., 1999). Interestingly, adolescents with conduct disorders have a particularly difficult time identifying expressions of sadness and fearfulness in others (Blair, James, & Cole, 2001).

Remember that one aspect of brain development is the increasing organization of the brain as neuronal connections are pruned, apparently strengthening the connections that remain. Research on developmental changes in brain structure and functions provides additional evidence of the importance of pruning. Studies of the prefrontal cortex illustrate that children and adolescents show more diffuse brain activity than adults do (Casey, Giedd, & Thomas, 2000; Giedd, 1997) (see Chapter 11). As the areas of activation become more specialized, presumably they are able to direct attention and memory more effectively, and thus cognitive functioning improves.

Imaging studies of the brains of adolescents and children have examined the degree of myelination of the neuronal connections. Remember from earlier chapters that myelination improves the speed of information transmission in the brain. Magnetic imaging studies done with children and adolescents aged 4 to 17 found age-related increases in certain brain regions, suggesting a gradual development of the brain that continues through adolescence (Paus et al., 1999). Boys and girls undergo myelination in several regions at different rates, with girls showing more myelination in relay areas between the hippocampus (involved in emotions) and the frontal cortex (involved in higher functioning). These gender differences in brain development may be one of the reasons that girls show more reasoned and mature judgment than boys do (Benes, Turles, Khan, & Farol, 1994).

Although it is exciting to consider the effects of brain development on behavior, it is important to remember that the effects go both ways: The experiences that adolescents have also influence how the brain develops. Practice and experience help to lay a solid foundation for brain development. Sports, computer games, reading, music, and learning a new language all set the stage for positive brain development; drinking and taking drugs may set the stage for less positive brain development.

WHAT ARE THE HEALTH AND SAFETY ISSUES IN LATE ADOLESCENCE?

Most people assume that adolescence is a healthy and carefree time of life. In reality, although adolescents are seldom sick, they are much more likely to die than are children. Death rates for all age groups have decreased, but death rates for older adolescents and young adults have declined the least. In fact, the death rates for African American males and Hispanic males and females have not decreased at all. Adolescents die at twice the rate of infants and toddlers (from 1 to 4 years old) and four times the rate of children ages 5 to 14 (Friedman, Fisher, & Schonberg, 1992).

The newspapers are full of stories about adolescents who die violent deaths. Most deaths during late adolescence stem from events that are preventable—accidents, homicides, and suicides. In 1998 in the United States, almost 11,000 older adolescents died; 75 percent of these deaths were due to accidents, homicides, and suicides (Federal Interagency Forum on Child and Family Statistics, 2001).

ACCIDENTS

Driving is one of the riskiest activities for adolescents, killing over 5000 adolescents a year. Auto-related deaths increase almost sixfold during adolescence, from about 5 per 100,000 for children under 15 to about 28 per 100,000 for older adolescents and young adults (National Center for Health Statistics [NCHS], 2001c).

As you can see in Figure 13.1, the death rate from car accidents is highest for Caucasian American males. Across each racial/ethnic group, more boys than girls

FIGURE 13.1

Car Accident Death Rates, by Race/Ethnicity and Sex

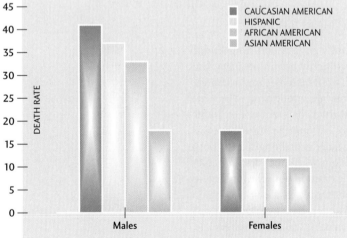

NOTE: Rates are per 100,000 population for 15- to 24-year-olds.
SOURCE: National Center for Health Statistics, 2001c.

Notice the striking differences between males and females in death rates from car accidents. What factors account for these differences?

TABLE 13.1

Risky Behaviors of Adolescents: Grades Nine Through Twelve

BEHAVIOR	STATISTIC
Failure to use safety belts	16 percent of students rarely or never used a safety belt (seat belt) when riding with others.
Failure to wear motorcycle helmets	36 percent of students who had ridden motorcycles in the preceding twelve months rarely or never wore a helmet.
Failure to wear bicycle helmets	85 percent of students who had ridden bicycles during the preceding twelve months rarely or never wore a helmet.
Riding with a driver who has been drinking alcohol	33 percent of students had, during the preceding month, ridden with a driver who had been drinking alcohol.
Driving after drinking alcohol	13 percent of students had, during the preceding month, driven a vehicle after drinking alcohol.
Fighting at school	14 percent of students had, during the preceding twelve months, been involved in a fight at school.
Illegal steroid use	3 percent of teens said that they had, sometime in their lives, used illegal steroids to improve performance.
Taking laxatives or vomiting to lose weight	5 percent of teens said they had either taken laxatives or made themselves vomit to lose weight or control weight gain.

SOURCE: Centers for Disease Control, 2001c.

die in car accidents. Adolescents who are 16 are more likely than any other age group to die in car accidents (Cerrelli, 1998), showing that inexperience contributes to car accidents. Research shows that teenagers are more likely than older drivers to speed, run red lights, make illegal turns, ride with an intoxicated driver, and drive after using alcohol and drugs, all of which contribute to their high accident rates (CDC, 2001c). In addition, adolescents engage in other activities that increase their risk of being hurt or killed. National surveys (CDC, 2001c) report high rates of risky behaviors among adolescents in high school (see Table 13.1).

HOMICIDES

It began as a typical dispute—two Texas teenagers talking trash over broken car windows. "And then I pulled out the gun," says Victor, 15, whose 1984 Cutlass had been damaged. "And he said, 'You ain't going to shoot me,' and I just started shooting, because he didn't think I would. It would have looked stupid if I pulled the gun and then didn't shoot him. I would have looked dumb."

—*G. Witkin* (1991, p. 29)

Victor's story is not that unusual. With children and adolescents having easy access to guns, even minor disputes can become lethal. US adolescents are particularly at risk for death by homicide. The United States has the highest homicide rate in the industrialized world: about 9 homicides per 100,000 people. Japan has the lowest rate: only about 1 homicide per 100,000 people.

As in Victor's story, most adolescent victims and murderers are males. Arrests of teenagers for murder rose dramatically during the 1980s and into the early 1990s. Although the number of arrests dropped in the late 1990s, homicides continue to occur at a high rate among young people. Males are much more likely to be murdered than females, and certain groups of males, such as young African American males, are much more likely than other groups to die from homicide. For instance, African American males between 15 and 24 years of age are about nine times more likely to die from homicide than are Caucasian American males. Typically, the murderer and the victim are of the same race (NCHS, 2001c).

The most common murder weapon is a gun—90 percent of homicides in the United States involve guns (National Center for Injury Prevention and Control, 1996). Although rates have leveled off recently, the number of adolescent killings involving a gun quadrupled in ten years (CDC, 2000b). Homicides are about twice as likely to occur in big cities as in rural or suburban areas, although most of the violence is concentrated only in small pockets of urban areas. The number of teen homicides over the last fifteen years has contributed to the rising fear of crime, as adolescents are more likely than adults to kill or assault strangers.

In the past, children found a refuge from violent neighborhoods in their schools. Sadly, school is no longer a safe haven for children. Some schools have become violent places where murders occur (Kachur et al., 1996). In a recent survey, 7 percent of students said they had carried a weapon to school in the month before the survey and 18 percent said they had carried a weapon somewhere (CDC, 2000b).

Because youth violence is so widespread, the US government has taken a key role in co-ordinating programs to deter violence (Dodge, 2001). Large-scale projects are under way in many cities to determine which interventions are effective in preventing and reducing aggressive and violent behavior (Cunningham & Henggeler, 2001). Most of the projects emphasize cooperative efforts among schools, health departments, and community partners.

SUICIDE

Suicide is a major cause of death among adolescents. In 1999, 12 out of every 100,000 adolescents between 15 and 24 died from suicide (NCHS, 2001c). The suicide rate among adolescents has almost tripled since 1960, especially for Caucasian American males, but has been relatively unchanged since the 1990s (CDC, 1998; Setterberg, 1992).

Nationally, about one-fifth of high school students in grades nine to twelve think seriously about suicide during the year. Of even more concern is the fact that about 15 percent of these adolescents make specific suicide plans, and about 3 percent are injured in a suicide attempt (CDC, 1998). These rates are higher for girls than for boys (see Figure 13.2). Adolescent boys commit suicide about four times more often than girls, but girls attempt suicide about twice as often as boys. A disturbing trend is that students in ninth grade were more likely to have made a suicide attempt than those in twelfth grade (CDC, 1998). Fortunately, only a fraction of adolescents who attempt suicide are successful, with only 1 in 50 attempts resulting in death (Jellinek & Snyder, 1998). Those who complete suicide are more likely to have had severe psychological problems (Setterberg, 1992). For instance, when teens become so depressed that they lose interest in outside activities and friends, this downward spiral can culminate in suicide.

A number of studies reveal ethnic differences in the tendencies both to have suicidal thoughts and to make suicide attempts. Specifically, suicide risks tend

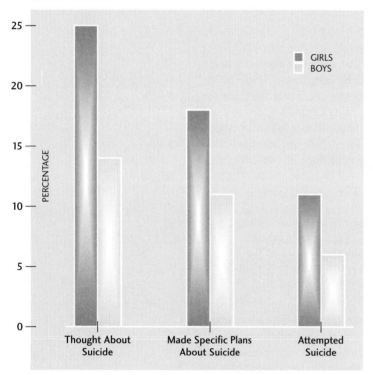

FIGURE 13.2

Suicidal Thoughts, Plans, and Attempts Among High School Students in 1999

SOURCE: Centers for Disease Control, 1998.

Notice that girls have more suicidal thoughts, plans, and attempts than boys. Why might girls have more suicidal thoughts and make more attempts than boys? Why do boys end up completing suicide more often than girls?

to be higher for Native American and Hispanic teens and lower for Caucasian American and African American youths (CDC, 1998; Sells & Blum, 1996).

Numerous explanations have been suggested for the high suicide rates among American adolescents, including pressures to grow up fast, high rates of family instability, frequent residential mobility, and insecure economic futures (Cohen, Spirito, & Brown, 1996). The most prominent risk factors for attempting suicide during adolescence include the following (Cohen et al., 1996; Jellinek & Snyder, 1998):

- A psychiatric problem (such as depression), antisocial behavior, and substance abuse
- Belonging to a family that has a history of suicide
- Experiencing high levels of stress
- Experiencing family problems (such as parental rejection) or high levels of family conflict

SEXUALLY TRANSMITTED DISEASES

Adolescents face many serious challenges to their health because of the physical and cognitive changes they experience as they develop. Their emerging sexuality puts adolescents at particular risk for a wide variety of **sexually transmitted diseases (STDs),** which are diseases that may be transmitted from one person to another through sexual contact. Gonorrhea, syphilis, and chlamydia are all STDs. Sexual contact is not the only method for transmitting STDs. Some STDs can be transmitted through such means as contaminated needles used in drug injections and contaminated blood used in transfusions. These diseases have serious long-term consequences, including decreased fertility later in life and death. One of the major concerns is that, although the symptoms for STDs are often not obvious, the disease seriously damages the reproductive system nonetheless.

STDs are an epidemic in the United States and around the world. Young people are particularly at risk for contracting STDs. Every year, 3 million teens—about 25 percent of sexually active teens—acquire an STD (Alan Guttmacher Institute, 1999). Rates for some STDs, such as gonorrhea, have decreased in the United States, but older adolescents continue to be one of the age groups most likely to have the disease (CDC, 2000a). In a single act of unprotected sex with an infected partner, a teenage woman has a 1 percent risk of acquiring HIV, a 30 percent risk of getting genital herpes, and a 50 percent risk of contracting gonorrhea (Alan Guttmacher Institute, 1999). Teens' higher risk for these diseases may be due to the following (Public Health Service, 1996b):

- Multiple sexual partners rather than a single long-term relationship
- Unprotected intercourse
- High-risk partners

Some ethnic groups are more at risk than others for STDs. In the United States, African Americans are ten to thirty times more likely than Caucasian Americans to contract STDs. There are no known biological reasons for the disparity; the risk factors likely to lead to these patterns are poverty, lack of access to health care, illicit drug use, negative attitudes toward condom use, and living in communities with high numbers of STD-infected people (PHS, 1996b).

AIDS

The same behaviors that put adolescents at risk for nondeadly STDs also increase their risk for Acquired Immunodeficiency Syndrome (AIDS). In 1999, AIDS became the sixth leading killer of adolescents and young adults. Although the rates have been declining over the last few years, the number of HIV infection cases in adolescents is not declining (CDC, 2000a). Because of the long latency (up to ten years) for HIV, the virus responsible for AIDS, many adolescents become infected but do not exhibit obvious symptoms of the disease until they are young adults. The higher rate of AIDS infections among young adults likely results from exposure to HIV during adolescence.

sexually transmitted diseases (STDs) diseases that may be transmitted from one person to another through sexual contact

AIDS is a major cause of death for young adults, many of whom were infected with the HIV virus during their teen years. What can people do to avoid exposure to HIV?

Certain groups of adolescents are more likely to test positive for HIV than other groups. At highest risk are homosexuals, drug users, homeless or runaway adolescents, African American and Hispanic adolescents (CDC, 2001b; Futterman & Hein, 1992), hemophiliacs, and inner-city youth. Additional risk factors for adolescents include having STDs, being sexually abused, selling sex for survival (to make money for food, drugs, or shelter), being sexually active without using condoms, and abusing alcohol (Millstein, 1990).

Figure 13.3 presents the major causes of AIDS in adolescents. As you can see, the causes vary for boys and girls. For boys, homosexual contact and having hemophilia are the two most likely sources of AIDS. In contrast, girls are much more likely to acquire AIDS through heterosexual contact (CDC, 2001b). Adolescent girls' immature reproductive systems may not produce progesterone consistently, and the lack of this hormone makes the mucus in the vagina a less effective barrier against all types of infections (Futterman & Hein, 1992).

DISEASES AND CHRONIC ILLNESSES

Adolescents typically miss only about five days of school a year because of illness, and girls typically miss one more day of school than boys. About 14 percent of all adolescents are chronically ill. Not surprisingly, adolescents who have chronic illnesses are more likely to miss school and are more limited in their activities than other adolescents (Coupey, 1992).

FIGURE 13.3

Causes of AIDS in Adolescent Boys and Girls

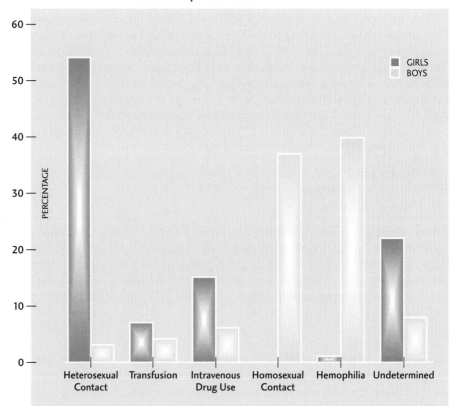

SOURCE: CDC, 1996.

This figure shows that girls and boys acquire AIDS in very different ways. What factors account for girls' higher risk of contracting HIV infection through heterosexual transmission? Why are boys more likely to be exposed to HIV through hemophilia?

Patrick wears braces, is anxious to begin driving, and dreams of becoming a rock star. Like many other teens, Patrick struggles against his parents' protectiveness as he develops his own sense of self. He sometimes ignores his parents' advice. His parents say he is rebellious. The struggles that Patrick has with his parents could be deadly. Patrick has cystic fibrosis, a chronic disease that requires daily treatments and a strict regimen of pill taking—up to 30 pills a day. If Patrick ignores reminders about taking his pills or doing his treatments, he could die. "I hate bringing my pills to school 'cause I feel embarrassed," Patrick said. "No one else takes medicine. I'm the only one."

Chronically ill adolescents like Patrick face many challenges. Patrick knows that he has to deal with these challenges every day for the rest of his life. He has to learn to cope with a life-threatening disease that requires constant attention. His health can deteriorate quickly if he forgets to take treatments or pills, and his mental health can be negatively affected by the continual struggle to manage his disease (Costa & VandenBos, 1996).

The number of adolescents with chronic illnesses has increased, not because more children are identified as having these illnesses but because diseases that would have killed children twenty years ago now do not. Improved treatments have extended the lifespan of these children into adolescence and beyond. For instance, childhood cancer has been transformed from being almost uniformly fatal to being chronic and potentially curable.

Adolescents who test limits during their teens may engage in behaviors that are dangerous to their health. A diabetic teen may eat forbidden foods or take the wrong amount of insulin. Even adolescents who take responsibility for their own care and treatment may lack the knowledge to do so. Errors in self-treatment are common among adolescents (Palardy, Greening, Ott, Holderby, & Atchinson, 1998).

THE PRACTICAL IMPACT: NURTURING CHILDREN

Adolescent AIDS: The Legacy of Ryan White

Ryan White was born in December, 1971. When he was 3 days old, doctors found he was a severe hemophiliac—his blood would not clot. As treatment for his condition, Ryan received many injections and transfusions, and it was from a transfusion of infected blood that Ryan contracted HIV. At age 13, he was diagnosed with AIDS and told he had 6 months to live. Because he had AIDS, Ryan and his family became victims of discrimination: bullets were fired into their home, children called Ryan names, adults refused to shake hands with him and his family, and many people shunned them. School officials refused to allow Ryan to attend classes because of the public fear of the disease.

Ryan and his family did not give in to this discrimination. His desire to continue his education led to a series of court battles that lasted nine months. During that time, Ryan attended classes by telephone. Eventually, he won the right to attend school

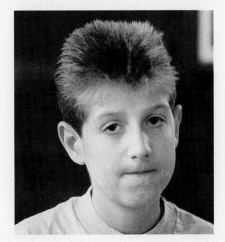

on the condition that he use a separate bathroom and drinking fountain, use disposable eating utensils and trays, and not attend gym class.

Ryan's fight to continue his schooling gained widespread media attention and support from entertainers and athletes such as Elton John, Charlie Sheen, and Greg Louganis. As Ryan's health deteriorated, his family faced severe financial hardships from his medical bills. Relief came in the form of a movie about his life, *The Ryan White Story*. Ryan and his family then moved to a new town where they were welcomed by a supportive school and community.

In his testimony before a presidential commission on AIDS, Ryan noted, "I'm a normal happy teenager again. I have a learner's permit. I attend sports functions and dances. My studies are important to me. I made the honor role . . . and I look forward to graduating in 1991." Sadly, Ryan did not live to fulfill his dream of graduating—he died in April, 1990. But his legacy lives on. Although discrimination and fear of people with AIDS may never completely disappear, Ryan played a major role in teaching adults and youths the realities of AIDS and the importance of AIDS education (Channiah, 1997).

This gymnast is demonstrating strength and flexibility. How do boys and girls differ in strength and flexibility during late adolescence?

Adolescents with chronic illnesses are at increased risk for psychological difficulties, especially depression. Nonetheless, the vast majority of these adolescents, even those with very serious diseases, are mentally healthy and well adjusted. The longer adolescents have a disease, the more likely it is that they will learn to cope with it (Thompson, Sobowlew-Shubin, Graham, & Janigan, 1989).

The entire family is affected by an adolescent's chronic disease. In addition to the time spent on medical treatments and the costs incurred, the family has to deal with dramatic changes in family functioning. The added stress may cause marital difficulties between parents and feelings of neglect and resentment among siblings (Wysocki & Green, 1997). However, families play a crucial role in helping adolescents adjust to a chronic disease. For instance, social support from family members has been found to help diabetic adolescents control their disease (Garrison & McQuiston, 1989).

FITNESS AND EXERCISE

Physical activity is an important part of a healthy lifestyle. Despite Americans' preoccupation with fitness and health, many adolescents today weigh more than they should and do not exercise enough to be physically fit. US teens are less physically fit than adolescents in many other countries (Health Behaviors in School-Aged Children, 2000). **Physical fitness** refers to a state of physical well-being that allows one to function effectively without undue fatigue. Four assessments are used to measure fitness, and boys' and girls' ratings in these categories change in different ways during adolescence:

 ✦ **Aerobic endurance.**   During early adolescence, untrained boys and girls improve in aerobic endurance, which relates to the functioning of the heart and lungs. Girls then taper off, but boys continue to improve throughout adolescence (Gallahue & Ozmun, 1995). Training improves aerobic endurance and narrows the gap between girls and boys (Krahenbuhl, Skinner, & Korht, 1985).
 ✦ **Muscle strength and endurance.**   Girls and boys are indistinguishable in muscle strength until adolescence, at which time boys' strength improves more rapidly than girls', probably because of boys' increased muscle growth. Girls and boys differ more on measures of upper-body strength (such as pull-ups) than they do on other measures of strength (such as sit-ups).
 ✦ **Muscle flexibility.**   Beginning at age 10, girls are more flexible than boys, and they show more improvement than boys throughout adolescence (Gallahue & Ozmun, 1995). Flexibility peaks at age 17 but can be maintained through training.
 ✦ **Body fat.**   Girls' percentage of body fat increases during adolescence while boys' decreases (see Chapter 11). Despite the emphasis on fitness, a lack of activity and the popularity of fast foods have contributed to the fact that the average teen today carries more body fat than teens in 1960 did (Galluhue & Ozum, 1995).

Adolescents who are active have a lower percentage of body fat, greater muscle strength and endurance, and greater aerobic capacity (President's Council on Physical Fitness and Sports, 2001). With exercise, the heart becomes more efficient and pumps more blood with each beat, thus decreasing the rate at which it beats. Exercise also raises the level of "good" cholesterol and lowers blood pressure, thereby reducing the risk of heart disease. Obesity can be prevented through regular exercise. Exercise also steps up the effectiveness of the immune system, heightening people's resistance to disease (Harris, 1991).

Adolescents who exercise are more likely to be healthy adults. In a longitudinal study, female athletes had lower levels of breast cancer and reproductive system cancers than did nonathletes. Most of these athletes began their training before or during high school (Frisch et al., 1985). Long-term exercise reduces the risk of serious diseases later in life (Kelder, Perry, Klepp, & Lytle, 1994). For instance, professional ballet dancers and weight lifters have stronger bones than nonathletes, and strong bones lower the risk for osteoporosis later (Loucks, 1988).

In large-scale national studies of high school students' behavior, only 44 percent of senior boys and 27 percent of senior girls exercised either every day or almost every day, but

physical fitness a state of physical well-being that allows a person to function effectively without undue fatigue

THE SOCIAL IMPACT: DEBATING THE ISSUE

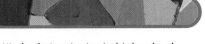

Should Schools Start Later for Teens?

Kimberly is a junior in high school. She sets her alarm clock to go off at 6:30 AM, the latest possible time that allows her to shower and get to school, usually without eating breakfast. Her school day starts at 7:20 AM, a common opening time for high schools in the United States. She often feels as if she is in a daze during her first few classes and has a hard time staying awake.

A growing body of research now suggests that Kimberly's fatigue is the result of a school schedule that is insensitive to her biological clock. During late adolescence, teens have a physiological need for extra sleep that younger teenagers do not need (Carskadon, 1990). In other words, as teenagers move through adolescence, they need increasing amounts of sleep. Yet, adolescents typically get less sleep as they mature (Wolfson & Carskadon, 1998), in part because most high schools start an hour of so earlier than junior high schools.

Conventional wisdom suggests that the older you get, the less sleep you need. But new research contradicts this belief. Studies of teenagers who are allowed to get as much sleep as they need show no decline in sleep requirements with age. In fact, the reverse is true: Older adolescents need more sleep than they did when they were younger. Late in adolescence, a

hormonal shift pushes their preprogrammed period of wakefulness about an hour later than it was earlier in their teens. This shift is caused by a delay in the release of the hormone melatonin, which induces sleepiness and helps set the body's biological clock. As a result, teenagers need nine hours of sleep nightly, but few get this much (Maas, 1995).

Risks for adolescents who do not get enough sleep include daytime sleepiness, susceptibility to accidents, mood and behavior problems, vulnerability to drug and alcohol use, and development of major sleep disorders (Carskadon, 1990; Wolfson et al., 1995). According to recent research, 20 percent of high school students fall asleep in school (Maas, 1995). Students with poor grades report that they get less sleep and go to sleep later on school nights than students with higher grades (Wolfson & Carskadon, 1996, 1998).

Sleep loss also results in grogginess, lack of attention in class, poor performance on exams, and disciplinary problems. These findings led school officials in Edina, Minnesota, to change the start time for high school from 7:20 AM to 8:30 AM. Teens now report sleeping more, and the extra rest has resulted in greater classroom participation and attentiveness, fewer absences due to illness, and fewer dis-

cipline problems (Center for Applied Research and Educational Improvement, 1997).

This time change also caused concerns, though. Many students were involved in extracurricular activities that began after school. Starting school later caused these students to work later into the night during the school week and lowered after-school participation in student activities, particularly among those who held after-school jobs. Additionally, certain meetings, practices, and events ended after dark, especially during the winter months, again lowering participation. Parents also faced difficulties adapting schedules when there were younger children in the family. Thus, despite the advantages, there are important disadvantages to consider.

Thinking It Through:

1. What social and family factors might influence the amount of sleep an adolescent gets?
2. How can parents make certain that their high school–age teenagers get the sleep they need?
3. What other effects (both positive and negative) might result from changing the start time of high school to later in the day?

---

nearly two-thirds of all high school boys and about half of the girls exercised two or more times a week (CDC, 1998; Health Behaviors in School-Aged Children, 2000). Overall, compared to younger children and adults, 12- to 17-year-olds are more likely to participate in organized sports (such as football, softball, or soccer), bicycling, and swimming and are less likely to participate in aerobics, walking, and exercise with equipment. A dramatic increase has occurred over the last three decades in the number of girls participating in high school sports. In 1971, 4 percent of girls were active in high school athletics; recently the number has increased to 42 percent (CDC, 1998; President's Council, 1997).

SPORTS AND DEVELOPMENT IN LATE ADOLESCENCE

In later adolescence, many teens, especially girls, drop out of sports. The factors that influence adolescents' involvement in sports include physical development, conflicts of interest, perceived skills, maturity, gender role expectations, and encouragement from family members and peers. Teens who continue to be involved in sports tend to be labeled "athletes" and often differ from their peers both in their physical development and in their confidence in their athletic abilities (President's Council, 1997). The most popular sports among high school boys are basketball, track and field, baseball, and football; among girls, the most popular

THE SCIENTIFIC IMPACT: INTERPRETING RESEARCH

How Does Athletic Performance Influence Girls' Development?

The success of the Women's National Basketball Association is one sign of changing patterns of participation of girls in sports over the last two decades. More and more girls are joining sports teams—42 percent of high school athletes are now girls (President's Council on Physical Fitness and Sports, 1997). The effects of girls' participation have not been extensively studied. How do female athletes fare in their social and academic lives?

In a large-scale comparison of female athletes and nonathletes (Melnick, Vanfossen, & Sabo, 1988), over 5000 students were surveyed and tested over a two-year period during their sophomore and senior years in high school. Girls who participated in sports as sophomores were much more likely to participate as seniors (50 percent) than were those who did not participate earlier (7 percent). However, about half the girls involved in sports during their sophomore year stopped

participating in sports within two years. The strongest relationship was found between athletic participation and popularity: girls who participated in sports were more popular than nonathletes. Athletes were more involved in other sorts of extracurricular activities as well. Athletes also had somewhat higher educational aspirations, even when social class was taken into account, and they were somewhat less likely to become delinquents. However, female athletes did not have higher self-esteem or sociability than nonathletes.

Another large-scale study examined the impact of sports on teenage girls' likelihood of becoming pregnant (Women's Sports Foundation, 1998). Female athletes in the nationwide survey were less than half as likely as female nonathletes to get pregnant (5 percent and 11 percent, respectively). Female athletes also were more likely to be virgins, had their first intercourse

later, and had sex less often than their nonathlete peers. These results add to the growing consensus that sports programs promote girls' development by helping to ward off peer pressures.

Thinking It Through:

1. In these studies, the researchers did not investigate whether different sports have different effects. Do you think that different sports may encourage different qualities in young girls and boys? Do you think team sports differ from individual sports in their effects on adolescents?
2. How would you design a study to discover whether it is sports participation or personality factors that account for differences in popularity between athletes and nonathletes?
3. Might boys and girls be affected differently by sports participation?

---

sports are basketball, track and field, volleyball, and softball (National Federation of State High School Associations, 2001). Male athletes who play football and basketball tend to be stronger and more physically developed than nonathletes. Adolescents of both sexes who are involved in gymnastics and track often are delayed in maturity; for instance, female gymnasts and figure skaters tend to enter puberty later than other girls (Malina & Bouchard, 1991).

Like younger adolescents, older adolescents who continue to be involved in sports benefit from these experiences in a wide variety of ways, including having better mental and physical health than non-athletes, although they are more at risk for injuries (Steiner, McQuivey, Pavelski, Pitts, & Kraemer, 2000). Not surprisingly, 15- and 16-year-old boys involved in contact sports have more injuries than adolescents involved in other sports (Backx, Erich, Kemper, & Verbeek, 1989). Although team sport involvement has been linked to positive educational paths, it has also been linked to involvement in one type of risky behavior—drinking alcohol (Eccles & Barber, 1999). Furthermore, additional research is needed about the effects of intense training during adolescence and of pressures from coaches and parents to succeed in sports (Marsh & Daigneault, 1999).

WHAT CHANGES OCCUR IN OLDER ADOLESCENTS' THINKING AND REASONING

What influence does involvement in sports have on adolescents' physical, social, and emotional development? How might different sports contribute differently to development?

Because of their increased independence, older adolescents face a wide variety of demanding situations, which allow them many opportunities to apply formal operational thinking (see Chapter 11). As dating and social interactions occupy more of adolescents' time, the ways they apply cognitive abilities to their social interactions become more sophisticated. Thus, the changes that occur during later adolescence provide opportunities for teens to think abstractly about a variety of issues.

SOCIAL COGNITION: THINKING ABOUT PEOPLE AND RELATIONSHIPS

Tom, a 17-year-old employee at a music store, is asked at the last moment to work late on a Friday night. He already has made plans and does not want to work that night, but he needs the money and does not want to make his boss angry. Jelia, a 17-year-old girl, decides that she wants to start going out with other boys, but she is not sure how to tell the boy she is currently going out with. To solve these problems, Tom and Jelia must apply their cognitive decision-making skills to social situations. **Social cognition**—thinking about people and interpersonal relationships—involves trying to make sense of people's actions in terms of how they think, feel, and react (Hala, 1997). Will Tom's employer understand that Tom cannot put in extra hours on Friday night? Will Jelia's boyfriend understand why Jelia does not want to go out with him exclusively? Social cognition involves thinking about other people's feelings and views, trying to understand other people's behavior, and recognizing the social rules that guide everyday interpersonal behavior.

As children grow older, their social cognitive abilities change. What kinds of characteristics do these older adolescent boys focus on when thinking about others?

One aspect of understanding other people's behavior is forming impressions about them and then using these impressions to interpret their behavior. The ways in which children develop impressions and interpret other people's behavior change during adolescence. For example, when asked in a classic study to "describe what sort of person" someone is, children and adolescents focused on different characteristics (Livesley & Bromley, 1973, pp. 217–221):

> He is always fighting and he is cruel. He does silly things and is very stupid. He has brown hair and cruel eyes. . . . He has a croaky voice and always chews on his pencil.
> —*9-year-old boy*

> Andy is very modest. He is even shyer than I am when near strangers and yet is very talkative with people he knows and likes.
> —*15-year-old boy*

As these examples show, children and adolescents observe different qualities when forming impressions of others. The 9-year-old makes more superficial and globally negative statements than does the adolescent, who considers Andy's behavior as it changes in different situations.

As adolescents gain more experience in social situations, their views on other people change in several ways (Flavell & Miller, 1998; Yuille, 1997):

- ✦ Their impressions become more differentiated. They use more focused evaluative descriptors rather than relying on global attributes. Younger children are likely to describe people in terms of global evaluations such as "nice."
- ✦ Their impressions become more abstract. They consider subtle psychological aspects of other people rather than concentrating on obvious physical characteristics, as younger children do.
- ✦ Their impressions are based more on indirect evidence and information supplied by others.
- ✦ Justifications for impressions are more likely to be provided because they realize that there can be many different interpretations of behavior.

The demands of children's and adolescents' environments also influence the ways people are described (Newman, 1991). Very young children interact with relatively few people—members of their immediate family and a few friends—and this limited group of people can

social cognition thinking about people and interpersonal relationships

be easily distinguished on the basis of a few superficial characteristics, such as sex, age, and size. When children enter school, however, more detailed differentiations become necessary (Yuille, 1997).

As children grow older, cultural influences come more into play. People in different cultures value different qualities in others and thus tend to use different descriptors. For instance, traditional Hindus in India emphasize relationship descriptors to distinguish individuals ("he is Jaya's son") and explain behaviors in terms of the social context ("she is excited because her brother is coming home"); in the United States, however, adults tend to attribute behavior to internal, personal dispositions ("she's friendly because she is a warm and caring person") (Miller, 1986). Adolescents' descriptions of others reflect cultural influences to a greater extent than do those of children.

UNDERSTANDING OTHER PEOPLE'S PERSPECTIVES

Effective social problem solving requires understanding other people's viewpoints, and to do that one must be able to consider more than one's own point of view. Recall how young children's egocentric thinking limits their ability to understand others' motivations and behavior. For instance, a young child asked to help select a birthday present for her dad may decide that the perfect gift would be a toy *she* wants. In contrast, adolescents' improved cognitive abilities allow them to view a situation from the other person's perspective. This valuable skill, called social perspective taking, emerges in stages, brought about through biological influences, cognitive development, and experiences with people (Selman, 1980).

Between the ages of 10 and 15, adolescents begin to develop the ability to view a situation from the perspective of a neutral outsider (Fabes, Carlo, Kupanoff, & Laible, 1999). Later in adolescence, they reach an even more abstract level of reflection in which they develop the ability to coordinate perspectives of all the other people involved. Adolescents' social perspective taking leads to more accurate communication, negotiation, and problem solving (see Table 13.2).

Teens do not use social perspective taking skills consistently; they may apply a high level of skill in one situation and then only a low level in another (Selman, Lavin, & Brion-Meisels, 1982). They tend to apply high-level skills to situations that are relevant to them, such as peer relations or personal problems, and lower-level skills to less relevant situations, such as work-related ones or those involving adults. For example, adolescents are more likely to apply high-level social reasoning to resolve Jelia's dating dilemma than to settle Tom's staying-late-at-work situation (Selman, Beardslee, Schultz, Krupa, & Podorefsky, 1986). Furthermore, social problems are not automatically resolved simply by understanding others'

TABLE 13.2

Developmental Changes in Perspective Taking During Adolescence

STAGE	AGES (IN YEARS)	DESCRIPTION
Self-reflective and reciprocal perspective taking	7 to 12	Children can reflect on their own thoughts from another person's viewpoint, but cannot hold both their own and the outside position simultaneously
Third-person, or mutual, perspective taking	10 to 15	Adolescents can step outside their own viewpoint and those of others and assume the perspective of a neutral third person
In-depth and symbolic perspective taking	12 to adult	Individuals are able to recognize multiple and more abstract levels of perspectives, including a societal perspective

SOURCE: Selman, 1980.

perspectives. Problems require solutions. An adolescent who has the ability to understand another person's feelings still may not know how to solve the problem.

Adolescents vary in their ability to apply cognitive skills in social situations. Some adolescents use their cognitive skills effectively to develop new and better ways to interact with others. When 16-year-old Jerry wants to have a phone installed in his room, he realizes that he can make a better and stronger case if he considers the situation from his parents' perspective. He therefore develops a plan to help cover the expense of a new phone. Other adolescents do not use sophisticated cognitive skills—a more egocentric adolescent might simply argue that he needs a phone and that everyone else he knows has one.

MORAL REASONING AND MORAL EDUCATION IN LATE ADOLESCENCE

As you learned in Chapter 10, important changes take place in moral development after early childhood; individual conscience can become a stronger force than societal rules in guiding moral judgments and decisions. Adolescents can see many sides of a moral dilemma, and deciding what is right can be a very difficult struggle. Kohlberg used the term *postconventional moral reasoning* to refer to the use of general principles that underlie rules and the recognition that rules can be broken to serve a higher purpose (see Chapter 10). Young children believe that rules are absolute and should never be broken. It is during adolescence, particularly late adolescence, that moral reasoning becomes rooted in the basic principles of fairness and regard for life and human welfare (Power, Higgins, & Kohlberg, 1989).

Because of adolescents' risk-taking behaviors, there is a public outcry about an American youth culture that is in moral crisis (Bennett, 1993; Ryan, 1996; Wynne, 1997). Increases in violent juvenile crime, teen pregnancy, suicide, and drug use are seen as evidence of a moral crisis and the cultural degeneration of youth. In response to public concern, more attention is being paid to educational practices that contribute to moral development and the development of character.

But how does one go about developing a model for educating a complete moral person? One way to begin is to ask people to identify the characteristics of a moral person. In one study, Canadians identified moral characteristics embedded in emotional, cognitive, behavioral, and personality factors (Walker & Pitts, 1998; Walker, Pitts, Henning, & Matsuba, 1995); some of these characteristics are listed in Table 13.3. Similar results have been found in the United States, Scotland, Switzerland, and the Netherlands (Berkowitz, 1997). These findings suggest that morality is perceived as consisting of diverse factors and encompassing many domains (Damon, 2000).

Domains Relevant to Social Responsibility

Another approach to developing morality is to consider the domains most relevant to the development of responsibility and character. Elliot Turiel (1983) distinguished three types of social knowledge: moral, social-conventional, and personal. The **moral domain** is characterized by consideration of universal principles reflecting the concepts of harm, welfare, and fairness. For example, killing is a moral issue because it robs victims of their mortal existence. Additionally, the moral issue of killing is applicable to all humans regardless of nationality, race, gender, or ethnicity.

In contrast, the **social-conventional domain** consists of actions that have no inherent moral nature, but are defined as right or wrong because of a social agreement that they are so. For example, in North America and Northern Europe, people line up to buy movie tickets. This is largely a matter of social convention. If you travel outside of these areas, you will find that there is no shared social agreement on lining up, and people generally do not do so. Although this is a social convention, it has moral consequences. In the United States, "butting in line" in front of people who have been waiting violates a basic sense of fairness.

The **personal domain** concerns issues that are not socially regulated. One's favorite colors and favorite foods reflect personal preference and taste rather than social-conventional

TABLE 13.3

Exemplary Moral Characteristics Cited by Canadians

1. Honest
2. Ethical
3. Truthful
4. Faithful
5. Respectful
6. Consistent
7. Sincere
8. Just
9. Caring
10. Thoughtful
11. Self-sacrificing
12. Empathic

SOURCE: Walker and Pitts, 1998.

moral domain issues that concern universal principles reflecting concepts of harm, welfare, and fairness

social-conventional domain issues and actions that are defined as right or wrong because of a social agreement that they are so

personal domain issues that reflect personal preference and taste and are not socially regulated or moral issues. Turiel's work suggests that effective moral education should distinguish among these different domains and should focus particularly on moral and social-conventional, rather than personal, domains.

Many scientists believe that adolescence, particularly late adolescence, is the optimal time for moral education because abstract reasoning gives moral education its greatest impact. It is at this time that youths have a larger capacity to examine moral issues (Lind, 1997).

Approaches to Moral Education

On the basis of Kohlberg's work, moral educators have developed programs designed to encourage individuals to achieve a higher level of moral reasoning, particularly postconventional reasoning. To accomplish this, educators apply the basic Piagetian assumption of cognitive development: development occurs when learners encounter information that does not fit easily into their existing view. A common approach of educators is to present students with a "moral dilemma" (see Chapter 10) that requires them to determine what course of action the actor in the dilemma should take and justify their decision. Through discussion, students are forced to face the contradictions present in any course of action that is not based on principles of justice or fairness.

But Kohlberg believed that moral education requires more than individual moral reasoning—it also needs to include experiences in which students operate as "moral agents" in their community. To provide students with these experiences, Kohlberg and his colleagues developed the **just community schools** (Power et al., 1989). In a just community school, students become part of a democratic community in which decisions are made through consensus rather than by majority rule. The school community is small in size (often called a school within a school) and provides a sense of belonging to a group that is responsive to individual needs. In community meetings, students establish norms of fairness for all members of the community. Teachers play a crucial leadership role in these discussions, promoting norms that reflect concern for justice and community and ultimately enforcing the rules (Power & Makogon, 1995). The just community approach therefore affects students' actions, not just their reasoning. Students are expected to practice what they preach.

Consider how teachers at one school applied the just community approach to the issue of cheating on homework assignments that were to be completed alone (Power & Power, 1992). The teachers were concerned because the students felt free to lend each other their homework assignments. The teachers helped the students see the benefits of doing certain assignments on their own—such as the skills and confidence they would gain. As a result, the students and teachers agreed on an honor code policy that was rarely violated. Through discussion and the sharing of ideas, most of the students came to accept the argument that real caring and respect for others usually means encouraging them to do their own homework (Power & Makogon, 1995).

Critics of the moral reasoning approach point out its emphasis on reflection rather than on day-to-day good behavior (Bennett, 1993). Alternative approaches include **character education,** in which the curriculum and instruction focus on students' conduct and models of traditional core values and behaviors such as honesty, respect for others, and promptness (DeRoche & Williams, 2001; Wynne, 1997). Character education is designed to help students understand, commit to, and act on these shared core moral values. Effective character education requires that a school do the following (Lickona, Schaps, & Lewis, 1997):

◆ Be a caring community that promotes core values in all phases of school life
◆ Provide students with opportunities to act morally
◆ Develop a meaningful and challenging academic curriculum that respects all learners and helps them succeed
◆ Have staff and faculty that adhere to the same core values that guide the education of students
◆ Recruit parents and community members as full partners in character building

just community schools schools in which students participate in a democratic community and decisions are made through consensus rather than by majority rule

character education curriculum and instruction focused on students' conduct and models of traditional values and behaviors

Do character education and just community schools influence adolescents' moral development? Programs that systematically engage students in moral discussions result in significant advances in the students' moral reasoning skills. Evidence in support of character education is more limited (Damon, 1988). A combination of the two may be best—students need to develop the ability to think morally and make their own moral decisions, but they also need to develop morally responsible habits.

The role that schools should play in moral education is itself controversial, particularly given the diversity of views on morality within contemporary societies like that of the United States. Additionally, in a time of limited resources, some argue that schools in a democracy should concentrate on the "three R's" and leave questions of morality to the family and church. However, schools are important training grounds and provide many opportunities for learning and mastering moral values and behaviors. Given the amount of time children spend in school, it seems likely that schools will be asked to do more in the future to foster the moral development of youth.

POLITICAL AND RELIGIOUS THINKING

Late adolescence is a time when youths often begin to question authority figures and institutions of social control, such as government, the law, and religion. Part of the reason for these changes lies in teens' increased abilities to think about abstract concepts and consider new and different ways of viewing these social institutions (Benson, Donahue, & Erickson, 1989; Torney-Purta, 1992). As their thinking becomes more abstract and less absolute, adolescents become more capable of considering alternative viewpoints and more tolerant of those who hold beliefs different from theirs.

Consider the differences between the ways 8-year-old Kally and her 17-year-old brother Justin interpret acts of civil disobedience. Like other children her age, Kally thinks that a person who illegally blocks an entrance to a government building to protest racial discrimination should be arrested. Kally feels this way because she believes that laws are absolute and cannot be changed. However, Justin and other adolescents are more inclined to understand civil disobedience because they view laws as abstract social agreements that are subject to interpretation and change at the will of the people. They may also recognize that civil disobedience is a way to bring issues to public attention and promote new legislation.

Justin's political thinking differs from his sister's in another crucial way: He is less likely to obey authority figures (such as parents and other adults) without question. Adolescents like Justin have gained the ability to think for themselves about rules, laws, governments, and institutions. Justin also is capable of thinking about abstract political concepts such as democracy and justice. In contrast, Kally and other younger children are likely to view the government in a personal way, realizing that their government consists of a person like the President, but not understanding the principles behind the political institutions (Torney-Purta, 1992, 1994).

What cognitive factors influence adolescents' ability to think about abstract political concepts such as democracy and justice? Would younger children be able to understand why these adolescents are marching for human rights? Why or why not?

How do the qualities of girls' interactions provide practice in using verbal skills?

Religious thinking also becomes more abstract, spiritual, and ideological during adolescence. Although adolescents attend church less frequently than children and say that religion is less important to them, they place greater emphasis on their personal beliefs and experiences (Donahue, 1995). Cognitive abilities influence the understanding of religious ideas. For example, whereas most young children in Judeo-Christian cultures tend to envision God in very concrete terms as an actual person who exists somewhere in physical space (such as heaven), adolescents are capable of grasping a concept of God as a spiritual guide having no observable or physical form (Coles, 1990).

Developmental changes in deference to authority figures are mirrored in religious thinking. When asked about their religious beliefs, young children often identify authority figures as justification for their beliefs. For example, many young children raised as Christians say they believe in God because "the Bible tells me so." In contrast, a Christian adolescent considers religious issues in a more personal, abstract, and thoughtful way. He or she might provide the following rationale: "My religious beliefs help me to make choices in life. It seems like the Bible has more than one answer about many things, with some of the answers not being very clear. I make choices for myself." Because of changes in their thinking, older teens begin to question the religious and political ideas they were taught during childhood, instead of simply relying on authority figures.

WHAT GENDER DIFFERENCES ARE FOUND IN ADOLESCENTS' COGNITIVE ABILITIES AND ACHIEVEMENT?

During childhood, boys and girls show few differences in their specific cognitive abilities or achievement levels. But as they grow older, differences in these areas become apparent. Also, during adolescence, levels of girls' and boys' confidence in their academic skills change. For boys, confidence increases; for girls, confidence in their academic abilities drops (Halpern, 1992).

It is important to remember that, compared with the very high variability from person to person within each sex, gender differences in cognitive abilities are very small. They account for only 1 to 5 percent of the variation in abilities. Furthermore, it is important to identify the origins of these gender differences—which may include family influences, cultural practices, and differing hormone levels in girls and boys—and how both sexes can be encouraged to develop a wide range of skills.

GENDER DIFFERENCES IN VERBAL SKILLS

Girls excel on a variety of verbal tasks, even in early childhood. Girls talk earlier and have larger vocabularies than boys and are less likely to have speech problems (Shucard, Shucard, & Thomas, 1987). Gender differences in reading comprehension appear during adolescence, with girls showing higher levels of comprehension than boys (Hedges & Nowell, 1995). Overall, girls show somewhat higher scores in reading, writing, and spelling, and these differences persist into high school (Gleason & Ely, 2002). Although the gender differences in verbal skills are generally small, a few verbal skills show relatively large gender differences.

associational fluency ability to produce synonyms for a given word

spatial-visual skills the cognitive abilities involved in orienting oneself in the environment

spatial perception the ability to locate the horizontal or vertical while ignoring distracting information

mental rotation the ability to imagine how objects would appear if their positions were rotated

spatial visualization the ability to find figures and shapes hidden within other figures

In particular, females are much better than males at **associational fluency,** or producing synonyms for words (Hines, 1990). For example, given the word *vivacious,* girls and women can generate more words with similar meaning than boys and men can.

GENDER DIFFERENCES IN SPATIAL-VISUAL SKILLS

Spatial-visual skills are the abilities involved in orienting oneself in the environment—for example, finding one's way or imagining how an object may be changed or rotated in space. For many years, researchers have reported that males outperform females in spatial-visual tasks (Maccoby & Jacklin, 1974), but in fact the sexes differ on only some of the spatial-visual tasks. The types of tasks shown in Figure 13.4 are used to measure the three categories of spatial/visual skills (Halpern, 1992):

1. **Spatial perception** is the ability to locate the horizontal or vertical while ignoring distracting visual information.
2. **Mental rotation** is the ability to imagine how objects would appear if they were rotated or changed positionally.
3. **Spatial visualization** is the ability to find figures hidden within other figures.

Boys and girls differ least in spatial visualization. The greatest difference, favoring boys, is in mental rotation skills; it first appears around the age of 10 or 11 (Linn & Petersen, 1986). It is important to realize that both girls and boys can mentally rotate objects; the gender difference is in the speed with which they do this (Newcombe, Mathason, & Terlecki, 2002). Boys' advantage in spatial perception is evident in their performance on the water-level task. In this task, a person is shown a drawing of a glass tilted at an angle and is asked to draw in the water line where it would be if the glass were half full. Based on the principle that the water level remains horizontal, we would expect that everyone would accurately draw a line parallel to the ground. But this is not so. In studies conducted in different countries, girls and women were more likely than boys and men to place the water line inaccurately (Halpern, 1992). The gender difference in the water-level task is moderately large, but training in this task can improve performance for both sexes and can eliminate the performance difference between girls and boys (Vasta, Nott, & Gaze, 1996).

Although large gender differences are found in some forms of spatial-visual skills, the few studies that have examined real-world applications of these skills find negligible differences. For instance, boys and men do not appear to be better at reading maps or finding their way in real environments than girls or women are (Pearson & Ferguson, 1989). It is interesting, however, that females and males use different strategies for way-finding and for giving directions. Females often rely on "route" strategies, attending to how to get from place to place and using landmarks as guides. Males tend to apply "orientation" strategies, using

FIGURE 13.4

Tests of Spatial Ability

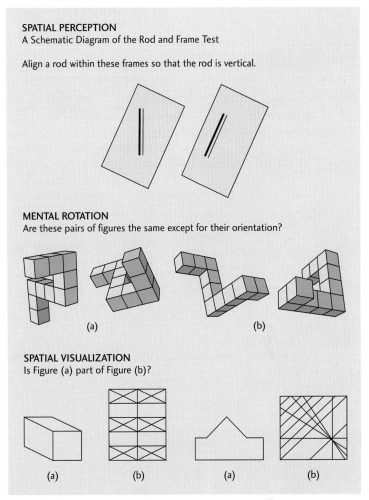

SOURCE: Adapted from Halpern, 1992.

This figure illustrates the three major forms of spatial abilities. In the spatial perception task, individuals are asked to put the rod in a vertical position within a tilted rectangular frame (as shown in the left frame). In the mental rotation task, individuals are asked to identify the pairs that are alike except for orientation. In the spatial visualization task, individuals are asked whether Figure (a) is part of Figure (b). How do these abilities differ from one another?

directional markers of north, south, and so forth (Lawton, 1994; Ward, Newcombe, & Overton, 1986).

GENDER DIFFERENCES IN MATH AND SCIENCE SKILLS

Amy is one of those girls who have little faith in her math skills, although her performance is well above average. "School is important to me," she says during lunch one day when struggling with a homework assignment. . . . "I want to do good in school. . . . And I'll need math when I'm older. There's math in everything. . . . So I know I should have a better attitude, but I just want to give up. It's not that I don't try, it's just that I don't believe in myself and I don't get it." She glares down at her paper.

—P. Orenstein (1994, pp. 18–19)

As ninth-grade Amy's comments reveal, many girls lose confidence in their math and science abilities as they move through adolescence. This drop in confidence often precedes a drop in performance. Like visual-spatial skills, mathematical skills have many different components, and the extent to which boys and girls differ in math skills depends on the type of math ability considered (De Lisi & McGillicuddy-De Lisi, 2002; Hyde, Fennema, & Lamon, 1990). In the elementary school years, girls outperform boys in math. For example, in third grade, girls outperform boys in almost every type of math problem. The stronger performance of girls declines by sixth grade, however, and they start to lose pace compared with boys (Hyde et al., 1990; Marshall & Smith, 1987). Boys begin to outperform girls on standardized tests during early adolescence, and the differences increase during the adolescent years (Hyde et al., 1990; Ruble & Martin, 1998). Differences are particularly pronounced in students with high math ability (Stanley & Benbow, 1982).

When girls' and boys' test-taking performance and grades in mathematics (as well as in other academic areas) are examined, an interesting difference emerges: For many boys the pattern is tests higher than grades, whereas for many girls the pattern is grades higher than tests (De Lisi & McGillicuddy-De Lisi, 2002; Dwyer & Johnson, 1997). These findings suggest that both sexes are competent in math but that they exhibit their skills differently.

As with math, girls and boys have similar scores on science proficiency tests at age 9 but boys outperform girls through adolescence (US Department of Education, 1996). This trend is not limited to the United States. As you can see in Figure 13.5, by eighth grade, boys outperformed girls in science in each country tested (International Association for the Evaluation of Educational Achievement [IAEEA], 1996), although girls in some countries outperformed boys in others.

Differences between boys' and girls' math and science performance have long been a source of concern. More boys than girls take advanced math and science, such as calculus and physics, and the number of girls studying math and science drops during high school (Status of Women Council, 1994). Additionally, many girls feel that they are not good at math and science and say that they do not like these subjects (American Association of University Women, 1994). Girls' lack of confidence in their math and sci-

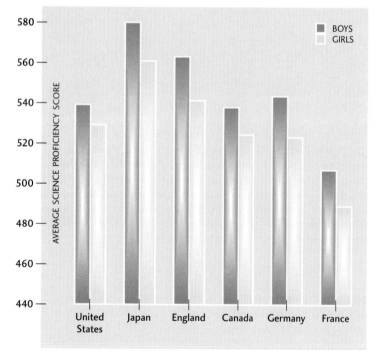

FIGURE 13.5

Average Science Proficiency of Eighth-Grade Boys and Girls, by Country

SOURCE: Adapted from IAEEA, 1996.

Notice that the gender difference in science proficiency exists in many countries. However, the absolute level of proficiency for girls in some countries, such as Japan, is higher than that of boys in other countries, such as Canada and the United States. What do these patterns indicate about the nature of this gender difference?

ence abilities contributes to their lower performance (Casey, Nuttal, & Pezaris, 1997). What is most troubling about these attitudes is that girls' grades in math and science are often equal to or better than those of their male peers (Jovanovic & Dreves, 1995). Girls can do math and science, but they are more likely than boys to opt out of advanced training in these areas and are thus less prepared for the many careers that involve math and science.

Female participation in math and science careers remains low—about 20 percent (National Science Foundation, 1996). By the time they enter high school, boys are more than twice as likely as girls to aspire to be scientists or engineers (Bae & Smith, 1996). Because overall cognitive differences between adolescent boys and girls are small or limited to very specific skills, other factors must account for the discrepancies between the numbers of men and women in math and science careers.

EXPLAINING GENDER DIFFERENCES IN COGNITIVE ABILITIES AND ACHIEVEMENT

When Mattel Toy Company decided in 1992 to market the first talking Barbie doll, the doll's first words were "Math class is tough," "I love dressing up," and "Do you want to braid my hair?" The toy makers thought they were expressing the feelings of many school-age girls. They did not foresee the negative response of many parents and teachers to these first words. As a result, this talking Barbie never made it to store shelves (Jovanovic & Dreves, 1995).

The controversy surrounding talking Barbie and her comment about math highlights the issue of gender differences in academic performance and achievement. Why do boys and girls perform differently on some cognitive tasks?

Biological Influences on Boys' and Girls' Academic Achievement

Sex hormones may be involved in some gender differences because males and females differ in the relative concentrations of sex hormones. In prenatal development, differing levels of sex hormones affect the development of the brain—particularly how it is organized. Because brain organization can determine how information is received and processed and can sensitize the brain to circulating hormones later in development, early hormonal effects could influence intellectual abilities. Later in development, especially during adolescence, boys and girls have different levels of sex hormones circulating freely through their bloodstream, stimulating and regulating many biological functions. But do these hormones explain differences in boys' and girls' academic performance and interests?

Understanding the effects of hormones is complicated by the interrelationship of biological and environmental factors, which makes it difficult to separate out the effects due only to hormones (Halpern, 1997). For example, women with Turner's syndrome (see Chapter 3) have extremely low levels of androgens. These women possess normal intelligence but show specific problems in spatial-visual functioning. But these women also have certain behavioral and physical characteristics that might contribute to these findings. For example, they tend to have poor social skills (Halpern, 1992), which may decrease their social interactions so that they do not get as much attention or encouragement to develop their cognitive abilities. What appears to be a physiological response in Turner's women to low levels of hormones may be due in part to a social response to their behavior.

Although untangling the effects of hormones from environmental effects is difficult, some causal links between hormones and cognitive abilities have been suggested (Fitch & Bimonte, 2002). Individuals with disorders that influence the production of prenatal sex hormones often show patterns of cognitive abilities that differ from those of other members of their sex (Collaer & Hines, 1995; Halpern, 1992). For instance, girls with a disorder that causes increased prenatal production of male hormones show male-typical patterns of cognitive abilities (Berenbaum, Korman, & Leveroni, 1995). Sex hormones also affect cognitive performance when they are given later in life. For instance, elderly men given male hormones to enhance their sexual functioning show improved scores on visual-spatial tests (Janowksy, Oviatt, & Orwoll, 1994).

How do boys and girls differ in mathematical abilities? What factors related to the learning environment of the classroom contribute to these differences? What other factors contribute to these differences? How can teachers help make mathematics more accessible to all adolescents?

Influence of Strategies and Stereotypes on Gender Differences in Academic Achievement

Two new lines of research provide some insights into gender differences in mathematics achievement. These findings may also relate to other areas of cognitive differences, which have yet to be investigated. The first line of research focuses on the strategies that girls and boys use to answer questions on standardized tests (De Lisi & McGillicuddy-De Lisi, 2002). It appears that girls perform better on conventional problems that involve applying computational approaches taught in school and assigning values to find the solutions. Boys, on the other hand, perform better on unconventional problems whose solutions require the use of insight, logic, or estimation. These findings may explain gender differences in grades and test performance. Classroom tests are more likely to involve solution methods that have been taught, and thus girls are likely to do well on them; standardized tests include these items but also include nonconventional items likely to favor boys' strategies (Gallagher & De Lisi, 1994; Gallager et al., 2000).

To improve performance in mathematics for both sexes, it might be ideal for teachers to train students to adopt both types of strategies, depending on the kind of problem they face. Also, these findings illustrate how important it is to go beyond the basic information about a gender difference to explore the specific aspects of the difference.

The second line of research on gender differences in mathematics performance involves stereotypes. Although older adolescents hold more flexible beliefs than younger children do, adolescents have some stereotypic ideas about academic and occupational domains, and these may influence the courses they choose to take in school (Gleason & Ely, 2002). Students' ideas about their own competence in academic domains also are influenced by their beliefs about whether these domains are relevant and important for their future careers (Wigfield, Battle, Keller, & Eccles, 2002). Furthermore, stereotypes can exert a negative influence on performance indirectly. When stereotypes about their own groups are made salient, students may become anxious about or distracted by what others think about them, and this attitude can undermine their test-taking performance. Specifically, researchers have demonstrated—under controlled conditions—that when students are concerned about the stereotypes that other people have about their skills (when they are under a "stereotype threat") they perform more poorly than when stereotypes are not salient (Steele, 1997). The negative influence of stereotype threat has been found for intelligence testing and race (Steele & Aronson, 1995) and for mathematics performance and gender (Brown & Josephs, 1999).

Family Influences on Boys' and Girls' Academic Achievement

Parents' beliefs have important influences on their children's academic achievement and performance (Fan & Chen, 2001; Jacobs, 1991). In fact, parents' beliefs about children's abilities in math and science have a greater impact on achievement and attitudes than do the children's earlier performance in those subjects (Eisenberg et al., 1996).

Some parents convey stereotypic beliefs about cognitive abilities, varying their message depending on the sex of their child. Parents who believe that girls are less able than boys to do math or science are more likely to have daughters who believe that they will not do very well in these subjects (Eccles, Freedman-Doan, Frome, Jacobs, & Yoon, 2000; Yee & Eccles, 1988). When parents hold such beliefs, daughters are less likely to take math courses (Jacobs & Eccles, 1985). Conversely, sons are more likely to receive messages that they are supposed to do well in math and science because they have "natural talent" in these areas. Thus, parents' expectations influence their adolescents' expectations about their academic abilities, which then affect the adolescents' academic performance—those with higher expectations perform better (Jacobs, 1991).

Parents' influence on children's academic performance and attitudes can be traced to the activities parents provide and encourage. Opportunities to learn math and science principles are more likely to be provided to sons than to daughters. For example, parents provide more science-related equipment such as microscopes and chemistry sets to boys than to girls (Halpern, 1992). Parents also encourage their sons and daughters to participate in

This boy is building a model. What other activities are boys encouraged to do, and how do these activities potentially contribute to interest in math and science?

This girl is sewing. What other activities are girls encouraged to do? Do you think girls' activities provide skills that will help them in math and science?

different activities and hobbies. Boys are encouraged more often than girls are to do math- or science-related activities at home (Eccles et al., 2000). Boys are encouraged to select leisure activities that involve science and math skills, such as making models, taking things apart, and helping with repairs around the house. In contrast, girls are likely to be encouraged to show interest in activities that involve domestic skills (Burns & Homel, 1989; Johnson, 1987). Additionally, boys spend more time involved with computers and computer video games than girls do, and some studies suggest that video games contribute to abstract problem-solving abilities, particularly those that involve spatial skills (McClurg & Chaille, 1987).

Gender Bias in School

As you learned previously, when students are engaged in academic tasks, many teachers give more positive attention, praise, and feedback to boys than to girls (Kimball, 1989). When teachers are asked if they treat boys and girls differently, most teachers say they do not (Sadker & Sadker, 1985). Thus, most teachers do not realize how their behavior may be affecting the behavior of male and female students.

The different expectations teachers hold for boys and girls also influence students' academic performance and achievement. For example, teachers' standards for "good" students differ for girls and boys. Girls who conform to traditional gender stereotypes and are compliant and well-behaved are viewed by teachers as more capable than other girls (Gold, Crombie, & Noble, 1987). Yet teachers' evaluations of boys are not influenced by whether the boy is compliant. Thus, teachers' judgments of what constitutes a good student are based less on how well students do in school and more on gender-stereotyped attitudes and expectations (Eisenberg et al., 1996).

The guidance that students receive at school also is affected by gender stereotypes. School counselors tend to give conventional, gender-typed advice to students and do not encourage them to explore new fields (Eccles & Jacobs, 1986). The potential for peer ridicule adds to the pressure to avoid courses that do not fit gender stereotypes. Girls interested in math and science, for example, may be viewed as weird or unfeminine. Although in recent decades great strides have been made in attempting to remedy sexism and stereotyping, schools and communities still have a long way to go to overcome gender bias.

What factors contribute to whether students continue in school or drop out?

WHAT FACTORS CONTRIBUTE TO DROPPING OUT OF SCHOOL?

During late adolescence, most boys and girls transfer from a junior high or middle school to senior high. For many students, this transition is exciting and motivating and represents the next big step toward developing advanced academic skills and preparing for college. But this transition also is a difficult one. High schools typically are larger and more impersonal than junior high or middle schools. The large size and bureaucratic structure of high schools undermine the development of close relationships, particularly between teachers and students (Bryk & Driscoll, 1988; Bryk, Lee, & Smith, 1990). These qualities weaken the motivation and involvement of many students, especially those not enrolled in the favored courses and those not expected to do well (Wigfield, Eccles, & Pintrich, 1996). Important differences among students begin to emerge during high school, and these differences can lead to lowered performance and school dropout.

CHARACTERISTICS OF HIGH SCHOOL DROPOUTS

> At 16 years of age, Quanese moved from North Carolina to Connecticut. She felt out of place, had few friends, and was lonely and isolated. That summer she got pregnant and had to combine motherhood with school. During her junior year, her mother, with whom Quanese was very close, died. Quanese had to take on many of the household responsibilities that her mother had done. Six months before finishing her senior year, Quanese found the circumstances of her life too demanding to finish school and dropped out. The traumas she had experienced left her feeling as if she couldn't achieve anything.
>
> —*Adapted from L. Royce* (1996)

Quanese is just one of almost half a million older adolescents who drop out of high school each year (US Census Bureau, 2001e). As many as 30 percent of the youths in school in the 1990s dropped out prior to graduating, and even higher rates are predicted in the future. One of the major differences between younger and older adolescents is that older adolescents can choose to leave school. In most states, students can make the decision to leave school at age 16. For many, like Quanese, the decision to drop out is related to life circumstances. For others, like Robert in the following story, dropping out is less a conscious decision than a consequence of personal behavior.

> Robert was an OK student in junior high school. In his sophomore year, he began drinking and smoking pot. His drug use escalated, and he started hanging out with an older group. He'd rather be partying than in class, and his attendance became erratic. During his junior year, he found school to be less and less important. Ultimately, he gave up on it and dropped out.
>
> —*Adapted from C. Kramer* (1995)

As the examples of Robert and Quanese show, adolescents drop out of school for a variety of reasons. Table 13.4 lists some of the reasons given for leaving school before graduation; attitudes about school and academic performance are the most common reasons for both boys and girls. Studies show that low achievement, low ability, and low interest in school are characteristics of students who are likely to drop out (Entwisle, 1990; Rosenthal, 1998). These characteristics can be traced back to elementary school—elementary school children who do poorly, who are absent frequently, and who have attitude and behavior problems are more likely than their peers to drop out of high school (Finn, 1989; Roeser, Eccles, & Freedman-Doan, 1999). As children and young adolescents, they cannot leave school voluntarily, but they may disengage from school by not trying, acting out, or being truant. As older adolescents, they can decide for themselves, and many of these low-achieving students choose to leave school.

Table 13.4 also reveals that the reasons for dropping out differ for boys and girls. Like Quanese, girls are more likely to drop out because of social factors that influence or limit their choices, such as getting pregnant, getting married, or having to take care of the family.

TABLE 13.4
Students' Reasons for Dropping Out of High School

REASON	PERCENTAGE OF BOYS CITING	PERCENTAGE OF GIRLS CITING
Did not like school	58	44
Did not get along with teachers	52	17
Was failing school	46	33
Could not keep up with school work	38	25
Did not feel safe at school	19	12
Expelled	18	9
Friends dropped out	17	11
Had to get a job	15	16
Got married	5	23
Had to care for family	5	12
Was pregnant	—	31

SOURCE: US Department of Education, 1997.

In contrast, as Robert's case suggests, boys are more likely to drop out because of behavior problems or getting expelled.

Race, ethnicity, and social class are all related to dropout rates. A worrisome number of minority students leave school before graduating. In some low-income, minority school districts in urban areas, as many as 50 percent or more of students leave school before obtaining a high school diploma (Bryk, Lee, & Smith, 1990). Examination of Figure 13.6 shows that the high school dropout rates for African American and Hispanic students, while not dramatically higher than that for Caucasian Americans, are nonetheless disproportionately high.

Adolescents living in poverty are five times more likely than those from affluent families to drop out of school. Students from families in the bottom 20 percent of the population's income levels represent over 30 percent of all dropouts (US Census Bureau, 2001e). Because racial and ethnic minority students are more likely to come from families with low incomes, their increased dropout rates are due in part to income level.

Cultural factors also are significant. For example, dropout rates for Hispanic youths are consistently high regardless of family income, but the dropout rate for Hispanic immigrants is two and a half times the dropout rate for Hispanic youths born in the United States (US Department of Education, 1997). Proficiency in English is clearly a factor. The dropout rate for Hispanic students with limited English proficiency is over three times higher than that for Hispanic students who speak English well (US Census Bureau, 2001e). Bilingual education and English as a Second Language (ESL) programs improve the likelihood that these Hispanic students will stay in school. For students in these programs, the dropout rate is reduced (US Department of Education, 1997), but drop-out rates are still considerably higher than those for other groups of high school students.

FIGURE 13.6

Percentage of Students in 8th to 12th Grade Who Drop Out of High School, by Race/Ethnicity

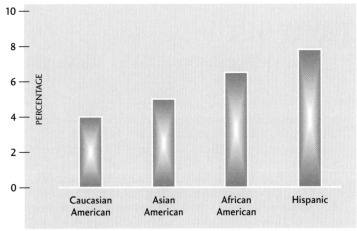

SOURCE: US Census Bureau, 2001e.

Notice that the dropout rates differ by race/ethnicity. What are the consequences of dropping out of high school? How many dropouts eventually finish their high school education?

PREVENTING HIGH SCHOOL DROPOUT

The consequences of dropping out can be profound. Leaving school before graduation seriously reduces an adolescent's chances of obtaining a well-paying job. In 1998, male dropouts earned about $21,000 a year and female dropouts earned about $11,000 a year—about one-third less than high school graduates (National Center for Education Statistics, 2001a). The economic and social costs of dropping out, both to the individual and to society, run into the billions of dollars (Cohen, 1998). Not only do individuals who drop out lose potential earnings, but society often must pay for extensive social services because dropouts are likely to need assistance or have behavior problems. High school dropouts make up nearly half of the heads of households on welfare and half of the prison population (Schwartz, 1995).

Many different programs have been developed to keep students in school. Effective dropout prevention programs have the following characteristics (Burt, Resnick, & Novick, 1998; National Diffusion Network, 1993; Woods, 1995):

- High expectations and standards for all students and programs to help at-risk youths meet these expectations
- Identification of potential dropouts as early as possible and early intervention to ensure school success
- Effective and flexible classroom instruction—a mix of academic instruction and experiential learning appears to be most effective
- Caring teachers with interest in and concern for at-risk youths
- Skills training and counseling necessary for success after graduation (such as occupational training and job counseling)
- Inclusion of families, peers, and the community in the program—the use of peer tutors, parents, and local business and government agencies provides a broad support system for at-risk youths

Dropping out of school is not an irrevocable action. Nearly half of all dropouts eventually earn a high school diploma (US Department of Education, 1997). Some return to school, whereas others obtain some sort of equivalency credential. For example, both Quanese and Robert obtained their high school diplomas. After the birth of her second child, Quanese returned to school at age 22. She became a mentor in an adult education program, to help inspire others to complete their education (Royce, 1996). Robert quit using drugs and passed the equivalency exam six years after he left school. Impressively, he applied to Yale University and was accepted (Kramer, 1995).

Try It Out

Activities Relating to Older Adolescents

1. Reflect on your experiences in late adolescence. What stressors and challenges placed (or place) you at risk? In what ways did you (or do you) place yourself at risk? What three risky behaviors would you place highest on your personal list of behaviors to avoid?

2. Arrange to interview older adolescents about their perceptions of gender differences in academic abilities and their experiences with gender bias in school. Begin by designing specific questions. Then note what you think you will learn or what views you think you will hear most often, based on your own high school experiences. Compare respondents' perceptions and experiences with your predictions. How do you account for the similarities or differences you find in gender expectations?

3. Investigate dropout prevention and intervention programs and services in your state or in a school district near you. What makes these programs effective? What personal or professional role might you take in a dropout prevention program in your community?

SUM IT UP

How does physical development occur during late adolescence?

✦ Physical growth is slower during late adolescence than it was during the early adolescent growth spurt, although some changes continue to occur, especially for boys.

✦ Physical changes in brain development during adolescence are significant and may account for some adolescent behavior.

What are the health and safety issues in late adolescence?

✦ Adolescents are generally healthy, but they are more likely than those in other age groups to die from violent causes such as accidents, homicides, and suicides. Males and minority youth are more at risk for violent death than other adolescents.

✦ The diseases most common during adolescence are sexually transmitted diseases. The incidence of HIV and STDs is high for this age group because of risky sexual practices.

✦ Many adolescents do not engage in sufficient exercise to encourage fitness.

✦ Adolescents who are involved in sports may develop stronger social ties with others and improve their social status. Sports participation also can improve adolescents' self-esteem and their sense of mastery and concentration.

What changes occur in older adolescents' thinking and reasoning?

✦ Adolescents form impressions of other people differently than younger children do—they are more likely to develop abstract impressions based on psychological factors and to provide focused evaluative descriptions of others.

✦ Adolescents are more effective social problem solvers than younger children are because they have learned to consider other people's perspectives. This higher level of perspective taking allows adolescents to be more accurate in communicating and negotiating with other people.

✦ During adolescence, moral reasoning becomes more abstract and focuses on general ethical principles like fairness and integrity rather than on strict obedience to authority.

✦ Turiel described three domains of social knowledge relevant to the development of responsibility and character: the moral domain, referring to universal principles of fairness and human well-being; the social-conventional domain, referring to matters that are defined as right and wrong by social agreement; and the personal domain, referring to matters of personal preference.

✦ Two approaches to moral education are the just community approach of Kohlberg, which focuses on moral discussions that involve students in decision making, and character education, which emphasizes students' conduct and the learning of traditional core moral values.

✦ Adolescents' improved cognitive abilities influence their religious thinking—they consider religious issues in more personal, abstract, and thoughtful ways.

What gender differences are found in adolescents' cognitive abilities and achievement?

✦ Differences between girls' and boys' cognitive abilities emerge during late adolescence. However, most differences are small and are confined to only a few areas.

✦ Girls tend to perform better than boys on verbal tasks, with the largest differences seen on tests of associational fluency.

✦ Boys tend to perform better than girls on some spatial-visual tasks—most notably the speed with which they can mentally rotate objects.

✦ Boys tend to perform better than girls on some math and science skills such as problem solving. Differences favoring boys become more pronounced over time and are more evident in the highest ability groups.

✦ Gender differences in cognitive abilities may be influenced by exposure to prenatal hormones, which affect the structure and development of the brain, and by circulating hormones later in life. However, these effects are difficult to disentangle from social and cultural factors.

✦ Stereotypes, stereotype threat, and the strategies that girls and boys use influence their performance in academic domains.

✦ Families influence adolescents' performance in school through the kinds of expectations they have about achievement for girls and boys and the kinds of activities they encourage.

✦ Teachers influence adolescents' academic performance by responding differently to girls and boys, holding different expectations for the sexes, and providing guidance based on traditional gender roles.

What factors contribute to dropping out of school?

✦ Entering high school, which tends to be a larger and less personal environment than junior high or middle school, weakens the academic motivation and involvement of some students.

✦ Almost one-third of adolescents drop out of high school before graduation. Girls may drop out because of family issues or pregnancy; boys may drop out because of their involvement in deviant activities. Minority and poor adolescents are particularly at risk for dropping out.

✦ Many programs have been developed that attempt to decrease dropout rates by helping at-risk students meet high expectations for academic success, providing flexible instruction, and providing skills training for job success.

KEY TERMS and CONCEPTS

associational fluency (*429*)
character education (*426*)
just community schools (*426*)
mental rotation (*429*)
moral domain (*425*)

personal domain (*425*)
physical fitness (*420*)
sexually transmitted diseases (STDs) (*417*)
social cognition (*423*)
social-conventional domain (*425*)

spatial perception (*429*)
spatial-visual skills (*429*)
spatial visualization (*429*)

Social and Emotional Development in Late Adolescence

CHAPTER 14

CHAPTER OUTLINE

◆ How Do Older Adolescents Develop Autonomy?

◆ How Does Sexuality Change During Late Adolescence?

◆ What Types of Behavior Problems Occur During Late Adolescence?

◆ How Does Employment Affect Older Adolescents?

◆ What Factors Influence Adolescents' Vulnerability and Resiliency?

n Western societies, the ability to function independently becomes increasingly important as children grow older (Fuligni, 1998). Because the United States is a society preoccupied with self-reliance, personal freedom, and individual success (Peterson, 1995), most adolescents receive a lot of encouragement to follow principles like "look out for yourself," "make up your own mind," and "do your own thing." For most adolescents, the increased independence and responsibilities promote new strengths and competencies. But for some adolescents, this period is fraught with risk.

How do older adolescents develop autonomy

As you learned in Chapter 11, adolescence often is a time when children separate themselves from their parents. Adolescents are encouraged to develop **autonomy**—the ability to govern oneself, make independent decisions, control one's feelings, and choose one's values. The desire for autonomy becomes especially prominent during late adolescence, as youths prepare to leave home and enter adulthood (Borman & Schneider, 1998; Silverberg & Gondoli, 1996).

Historically, this distancing process was thought to lead to conflict and turbulence in parent-adolescent relationships. According to contemporary interpretations, however, adolescent autonomy generally is not achieved through rebellion or rejection of parents. Adolescents assume their individuality while remaining connected to their parents (Silverberg & Gondoli, 1996). This interpretation provides a *constructive model* of the development of autonomy—one that emphasizes a balance between adolescents' needs to assert their individuality and to remain close and connected to others.

FORMS OF AUTONOMY

The development of autonomy is a complex process through which an individual becomes independent in three major areas:

- ✦ **Emotional autonomy** is the ability to understand oneself as a person who is emotionally distinct from one's parents. As adolescents become more autonomous, what they feel depends less on their parents and more on their own individual experiences and concerns (Peterson, 1986).
- ✦ **Behavioral autonomy** is the capacity to make and follow through with decisions regulating one's behavior (Sessa & Steinberg, 1991). This form of autonomy is the one that adolescents are most often aware of and is the source of many parent-adolescent conflicts (Collins, 1990).
- ✦ **Values autonomy** is the capacity to make judgments and choices with respect to personal beliefs and principles. This form of autonomy means that adolescents do not merely adopt the opinions and values of others but become committed to belief systems they choose voluntarily (Sessa & Steinberg, 1991).

As each form of autonomy develops, adolescents move toward constructive autonomy, in which they question many of the ideas they were taught during childhood. During this time of exploration, adolescents identify their own choices apart from those imposed by authority figures (Chen & Dornbusch, 1998; Peterson, 1995).

FACTORS THAT CONTRIBUTE TO ADOLESCENT AUTONOMY

Autonomy issues occur throughout life; they are not restricted to the period of adolescence (Baltes & Silverberg, 1994). During adulthood, for example, husbands and wives may struggle over how much time they spend together or how much they invest in their individual careers versus the marriage. However, the period of adolescence is somewhat unique because the physiological changes of puberty bring autonomy issues to the forefront. As adolescents

autonomy the ability to govern oneself and make independent decisions

emotional autonomy the ability to understand oneself as a person who is emotionally distinct from one's parents

behavioral autonomy the capacity to make and follow through with decisions on regulating one's behavior

values autonomy the capacity to make judgments and choices about personal beliefs and principles

acquire the physical characteristics of adults, parents and others are likely to view them as more mature, respond to them more as adults, and grant them more freedom (Connolly, Paikoff, & Buchanan, 1996). Perceiving these changes in how they are treated by others, adolescents feel they are mature enough for greater autonomy and responsibility.

Changes in the ways adolescents think about problems and issues also contribute to their greater autonomy. For example, the development of metacognitive and critical thinking skills promotes autonomy by enhancing adolescents' abilities to analyze their own thought processes, examine several aspects of a situation at the same time, consider more than one viewpoint, and question what they and others believe in (Keating & Sasse, 1996; Smetana, 1988). These abilities permit greater flexibility in thought and independent decision-making. Thus, changes in abstract thinking abilities pave the way for adolescents to define themselves as individuals.

What roles do peers play in helping adolescents become more autonomous? How do diverse environments facilitate the development of autonomy?

Greater autonomy results when parents are supportive and nurturing (Thompson & Zuroff, 1998) and when they allow their teens to be involved in peer groups, work, and school activities (Silverberg & Gondoli, 1996). Becoming involved in diverse activities exposes adolescents to different viewpoints, values, and lifestyles. Adolescents may take this opportunity to evaluate their own beliefs and values and to assert or negotiate greater autonomy with authority figures.

HOW DOES SEXUALITY CHANGE DURING LATE ADOLESCENCE?

Sexual maturation is one of the most distinctive transitions of adolescence, and the common perception is that this transition brings about unbridled passions that dominate adolescents' lives. How true is this? Sexuality is a key component of our lives and identities, and it seems to be everywhere. The variety of emotions evoked by sexuality—feelings of love, excitement, arousal, embarrassment, guilt, and anxiety—and the experiences associated with them often are among the most memorable of one's life.

SEXUAL ATTITUDES AND BEHAVIORS OF OLDER ADOLESCENTS

Compared to their counterparts in decades past, adolescents today generally are more accepting of sexual involvement before marriage (Christopher, 2001). The same is true for adults. Especially during the late 1960s and the 1970s, the sexual revolution led to more liberal attitudes toward sex (Gershman, 1997). This trend persists despite the rise of conservatism in the 1990s (Herold & Marshall, 1996).

Most adolescents begin having sex during their late teens, and the likelihood of being sexually active increases steadily with age. By the age of 20, more than 80 percent of both males and females have had sex (Sonenstein, Ku, Lindberg, Turner, & Kleck, 1998). As noted in Chapter 12, ethnic differences exist in the percentages of sexually active teens (Upchurch, Levy-Storms, Sucoff, & Aneshensel, 1998). For example, African American high school students (71 percent) are substantially more likely to have had sexual intercourse than are either Caucasian (45 percent) or Hispanic (54 percent) peers (CDC, 2000a).

Traditionally, boys were much more likely than girls to experience sexual intercourse during adolescence. Today, however, that pattern is disappearing (Miller, Forehand, & Kotchick, 1999; Moreau, Ferron, Jeannin, & Dubois, 1996). Although boys begin having sexual

What are the characteristics of the typical adolescent relationship? How likely is it that older adolescents will be sexually active in their intimate relationships?

intercourse earlier, girls close the gap and catch up with boys by late adolescence. Recent evidence indicates that among high school students, 41 percent of boys and 40 percent of girls are sexually active (CDC, 2000a).

The pattern of sexuality for teenagers often begins with embraces and kisses, moves on to fondling, and culminates in sexual intercourse and other forms of reaching orgasm (Martin, 1996). In the case of African American teenagers, there is a tendency to proceed more rapidly to intercourse. Ethnic differences reflect different cultural beliefs and expectations about sexuality and the role it plays in relationships (Upchurch et al., 1998).

A common misconception is that most adolescents are promiscuous. But this is not so. Only about 16 percent of high school students have had four or more sexual partners since becoming sexually active (CDC, 2000a). Teenage boys (19 percent) are more likely than girls (13 percent) to have four or more partners. Ethnic differences again are apparent, with 34 percent of African American, 16 percent of Hispanic, and 12 percent of Caucasian adolescents reporting four or more partners. The majority of youngsters, therefore, have few sexual partners during adolescence.

CORRELATES OF ADOLESCENT SEXUAL ATTITUDES AND BEHAVIORS

A large body of research has identified the factors associated with adolescent sexual activity. Teens are more likely to have early and frequent sex if they live in disadvantaged communities, have low occupational and educational aspirations, and perform poorly in school (Allen & Mitchell, 1996; Brooks-Gunn, Duncan, Klebanov, & Sealand, 1993). Adolescents appear to have few incentives for delaying sexual intercourse when they have limited opportunities for upward mobility and reduced hopes for success.

Family relationships also play a role in teenage sexual activity (Herold & Marshall, 1996). Although parents and adolescents rarely talk about sex, discussions that do occur are most often between mothers and daughters (Miller, 1998). Fathers generally are less involved in these discussions and report feeling uncomfortable talking about sex with their children. Thus, both boys and girls direct their questions about sex (usually about pregnancy and childbirth) to their mothers. When parents answer these questions, they usually do so on a one-time basis rather than as part of an ongoing dialogue (Raffaelli, Bogenschneider, & Flood, 1998).

The impact of discussions about sex depends on the messages conveyed. Parents who communicate permissive attitudes about sex may encourage early sexual activity. In contrast, parents who convey more strictly traditional or conservative attitudes often discourage this behavior in their teens (Casper, 1990). Parents who monitor and supervise their adolescents reduce the opportunities for early sexual activity (Paikoff, Luster, Villarruel, & Small, 1998). Teens whose parents are overly controlling and authoritarian, however, are more likely to rebel by engaging in early sexual activity. Thus, extreme levels of parental control (either high or low) often lead to earlier and higher rates of teenage sexual activity, particularly among teenage girls (Rodgers, 1999). Teenagers who enjoy close relationships with their parents and whose parents use moderate levels of control often postpone becoming sexually active (Davis & Friel, 2001; Raffaelli et al., 1998).

Peers may have more influence than the family on a teen's initial sexual experience and rate of sexual activity (DuBois-Reymond & Ravesloot, 1996). Teenagers' sexual attitudes are influenced by values and information conveyed by their peers. These values differ from adults', whose perceptions of adolescent sexuality are stereotypical. Adults tend to view teen sex as impulsive, irresponsible, shallow, impetuous, and transient (such as "puppy love"). Adolescents have a more positive view; they see their sexual and romantic involvements as spontaneous, honest, and meaningful (Katchadourian, 1990).

When peers become sexually active, social norms are created that legitimize sex and make it more acceptable. Peer encouragement may occur when the best friends of teenagers either are believed to be—or actually are—sexually active (Brooks-Gunn & Furstenberg, 1989; Rodgers, Rowe, & Buster, 1998). For instance, when teens who were sexually active were asked why they had not waited until they were older to have sex, the top reason given by both boys and girls was peer pressure (Keller, Duerst, & Zimmerman, 1996).

Pressure from one's partner also influences sexual behavior. Generally, adolescent females have sex with older males. According to one study, among girls who had their first voluntary intercourse before age 16, over half said that their first partner was older, with 34 percent saying that their first partner was at least 18 years old (CDC, 1997). Another study found that 65 percent of teen mothers had partners who were older than they were (Landry & Forrest, 1995), and the younger the mother, the greater the age difference between her and the father (Lindberg, Sonenstein, Ku, & Martinez, 1997). Additionally, teens who are younger than their partners are less likely to use contraception (Moore & Driscoll, 1997). Thus, teens who are involved with older boys or men may experience pressure to have sex so as to continue the relationship and may engage in risky sexual behaviors (Elo et al., 1999).

The influence of undesirable friends on a teen's sexual behavior has long been a concern of parents. It is difficult, however, to separate the influence of friends from the choice of friends. The sexual behavior and expectations of a teenager are a factor in determining the teen's choice of a crowd or clique with which to associate. Conversely, the sexual norms of the crowd or clique influence the behavior and expectations of its members (Katchadourian, 1990).

What roles do peers and social expectations play in adolescent sexuality? What types of social scripts do girls and boys have concerning sexuality?

THE SOCIAL-PSYCHOLOGICAL CONTEXT OF ADOLESCENT SEXUALITY

Sexuality during adolescence involves more than physiological responses and erotic sensations (Brooks-Gunn & Graber, 1999). For most teenagers, sexuality is governed more by the social meanings and expectations that shape their behavior than by the biological urges associated with puberty (Christopher, 2001). Adolescent sexual activity is learned and maintained within everyday social relationships. Thus, an accurate view of teen sexuality recognizes complex social meanings, complicated feelings, difficult decision making, and elaborate behaviors shaped in part by the teenager's culture (Ruusuvaara, 1997). A major challenge for adolescents is integrating this complex sexuality with the broader issue of establishing intimacy with another person (Erikson, 1968).

Some theorists suggest that sexual activity is socially scripted (Gagnon, 1990; Simon & Gagnon, 1986). Social scripting is evident in the different ways male and female adolescents are socialized for sexuality. Male sexual behavior tends to be more independent of intimate relationships and focused on physical gratification. Many boys first express themselves sexually through masturbation. Boys also tend to view early sexual experiences in terms of sexual conquest, peer status, and recreation rather than intimate relationships (Hendrick & Hendrick, 1995). The most common responses of teenage boys to their first sexual intercourse are feelings of excitement, satisfaction, happiness, and achieved status. Only later do they engage in sexual activity that involves close emotional ties (Martin, 1996).

For girls, however, the experiences and feelings associated with sexual behavior are quite different (Haka-Ikse, 1997). Teenage girls are less likely than boys to begin with masturbation (Martin, 1996), and social expectations and pressures are directed toward intimacy and relationship issues rather than sexual gratification. As a result, girls are more likely to experience their first sexual activity within the context of an emotional relationship. Teenage girls also are more likely than boys to report conflicted feelings about sex—often feeling guilty and anxious, as well as happy and excited (Brooks-Gunn & Paikoff, 1997).

Another example of social scripting is the **double standard**—social expectations for sexual attitudes and behavior that differ for males and females. Although the impact of the double standard has been declining (Sprecher, 1989), it continues to govern how teenagers express themselves sexually. Boys, for example, are supposed to value sex, pursue sex when opportunities arise, and be the sexual aggressors. In contrast, girls are expected to be more cautious, experience less enjoyment, and remain virgins as long as possible (Gagnon, 1990).

double standard the imposition of different social expectations for males' and females' sexual attitudes and behavior

ADOLESCENT CONTRACEPTIVE USE

A troubling finding is that American teenagers are less likely than their peers from other countries to regularly and effectively use contraception (Arnett & Balle-Jensen, 1993). Today, however, American teenagers use contraception more often than their counterparts in previous decades did. Between the late 1970s and the 1990s, for example, adolescents' condom use more than doubled (Herold & Marshall, 1996). Increased condom use also reflects concerns about "safe sex" and protection from AIDS. Recent evidence indicates that about 60 percent of sexually active adolescents use some type of contraception during intercourse. But the percentage of teens who use contraception varies according to age. The older girls are when they have sex for the first time, the greater the likelihood that they or their partners will use contraception. Additionally, the type of contraception used during intercourse varies with age. Younger adolescents are more likely to use condoms, whereas older adolescents tend to prefer birth control pills (CDC, 2000a). Ethnic differences also exist in adolescent contraception use. For example, according to recent estimates, 70 percent of African American, 55 percent of Caucasian, and 55 percent of Hispanic adolescents reported that either they or their partner used condoms the last time they had sex (CDC, 2000a).

Although adolescents give various reasons for not using contraception (see Table 14.1), the most common reason is that they do not believe they—or their partner—will get pregnant (Treboux & Bush-Rossnagel, 1991). This belief may reflect a personal fable that one is invulnerable to the consequences of sexual activity. Thus, adolescents' decision making about sexuality and contraception is influenced by their level of cognitive development and the egocentrism characteristic of adolescent thought (see Chapter 11).

The use of drugs and alcohol sometimes contributes to failure to use contraceptives. About one-quarter of sexually active adolescents report that they used alcohol or drugs during their last sexual experience (CDC, 2000a). Boys were considerably more likely than girls to have used alcohol or drugs during their last sexual experience (31 versus 19 percent).

Contraceptive use involves complex decision making and planning. Available research indicates that successful use of contraception evolves out of a five-stage process (Byrne, 1983; Kelley, 1991):

✦ Acquiring, processing, and retaining contraceptive information
✦ Acknowledging the likelihood of sexual intercourse
✦ Obtaining the chosen contraception

TABLE 14.1

Reported Reasons Teenagers Do Not Use Contraception Regularly

- Lack of availability of contraceptives
- Inadequate knowledge about contraceptives, how to get them, and how to use them
- Failure to identify pregnancy as a serious problem or one that should be prevented
- False thinking that "pregnancy can't happen to me"
- Reluctance to admit loss of virginity or sexual activity
- Fear that parents will find out
- Fear and embarrassment associated with the physical examination that may be required
- Embarrassment associated with buying contraceptives
- Cost of contraception

SOURCE: Coles and Stokes, 1985; Moore and Rosenthal, 1993.

◆ Communicating about contraceptive issues with one's partner
◆ Using the chosen method of contraception correctly

In recent years, increased emphasis on adolescent abstinence as a form of contraception has been advocated. However, once an adolescent becomes sexually active, it is unlikely that he or she will remain inactive for any length of time. For example, only about 27 percent of adolescents who are sexually active go without sex for three months (CDC, 2000a). Boys are more likely than girls to be abstinent (31 versus 24 percent), and younger adolescents are more likely than older adolescents to be abstinent (31 versus 22 percent). These sex and age differences in abstinence are likely due to the comparative lack of available sexual partners for boys and younger adolescents relative to girls and older adolescents.

TEEN PREGNANCY

One of the potential outcomes of sexual activity is unintentional pregnancy. Pregnancy during adolescence brings dramatic emotions and dilemmas—how to tell parents, partners, and friends; how to support a child; how to continue an education; and how to deal with being a parent. Adolescents must deal with these issues at a time when they are changing and may not be ready for such responsibilities (Martin, Hill, & Welsh, 1998).

In the United States, every 26 seconds an adolescent becomes pregnant and every 56 seconds an adolescent gives birth (Campaign for Our Children, 1997). These rates are the highest among developed nations, although the rate of US teen pregnancy has dropped since 1990 (CDC, 2000a). As you can see in Figure 14.1, the US teen birth rate is five times the rate in France, fourteen times the rate in Japan, and twice the rate in England (Singh & Darroch, 2000).

Of the approximately 11 million teenage girls who are sexually active, about 1 million become pregnant each year (Henshaw, 2001). Eighty-five percent of these pregnancies are unintentional, and 76 percent occur outside of marriage (CDC, 2000a). Ethnic-racial differences are apparent in teen pregnancy rates, with African American and Hispanic teens

---

THE SOCIAL IMPACT: DEBATING THE ISSUE

Is Childhood Sexual Abuse Related to Teen Pregnancy?

Several studies found that pregnant teenagers were more likely than the general population to have experienced sexual abuse in childhood. As a result, many researchers hypothesized that childhood sexual abuse was a major contributor to teen pregnancy (Boyer & Fine, 1992; Fiscella, Kitzman, Cole, Sidora, & Olds, 1998). According to some estimates, between 51 and 75 percent of teens reported childhood sexual abuse (Boyer & Fine, 1992; Gershenson et al., 1989). However, because none of the studies compared the incidence of sexual abuse among pregnant teens to the incidence among their nonpregnant peers, it was impossible to determine whether sexual abuse contributed to a greater risk for teen pregnancy.

To address this problem, researchers collected data on the sexual histories of approximately 2000

young women (Roosa, Tein, Reinholtz, & Angelini, 1997). The women provided information on their age at menarche, age at first sexual experience, use of birth control, and whether they had ever been pregnant. Sexual precocity was defined as voluntarily having sexual intercourse before age 16. In addition, the respondents answered questions about whether they had experienced childhood sexual abuse perpetrated by males.

Being a victim of childhood sexual abuse did not in itself predict teen pregnancy. The rate of teen pregnancy for victims of sexual abuse was similar to the rate for those who were neither victims nor precocious (11 versus 12 percent). Rates were higher when precocious sexual activity was present (43 percent). The highest rate occurred among those who were victimized in childhood and later were precocious

(more than 50 percent). Thus, early sexual activity was strongly related to teen pregnancy, independent of the presence or absence of a history of sexual abuse. In contrast, a history of sexual abuse was related to teen pregnancy only when combined with precocity.

Thinking It Through:

1. Why might researchers expect a relationship between childhood sexual abuse and teen pregnancy? What do the findings of this study have to say about this relationship?
2. Why is sexual precocity related to teen pregnancy? What roles do cognitive, biological, and social factors play?
3. Based on these findings, what approach to reducing teen pregnancy would you advocate?

IGURE 14.1

Adolescent Birth Rates Worldwide

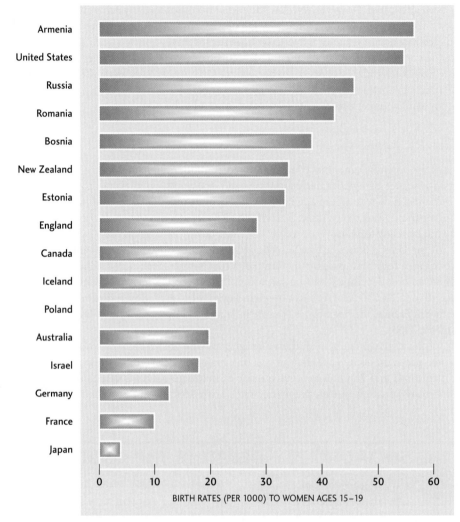

SOURCE: Singh & Darroch, 2000.

As you can see in this graph, the percentage of births to adolescents varies dramatically among the different parts of the world. What cultural and social factors likely contribute to these differences? Why is the US rate so high compared to those of other countries?

having over three times the rate of Caucasian teenagers. Additionally, African American and Hispanic teens are more likely than their Caucasian peers to say they want to become parents early in life (Trent & Crowder, 1997). Thus, ethnic differences in teen pregnancy may be due in part to differences in the cultural norms, attitudes, and expectations about early pregnancy and parenthood (Miller, Benson, & Galbraith, 2001).

Teenagers who become pregnant rarely place their child for adoption. Instead, they either have an abortion or give birth and raise the child themselves. Only about 56 percent of all teen pregnancies result in the actual birth of a child. Of the total number of pregnancies, approximately 30 percent end in abortion and another 14 percent are miscarried or end in a stillbirth (Henshaw, 1999). Since the late 1980s, the proportion of teens giving birth has risen (Alan Guttmacher Institute, 1997). This may be due in part to a greater acceptance of out-of-wedlock births, as well as the federal government's policy of providing medical coverage for prenatal care and delivery services but not for abortion.

Repeat pregnancies are common during adolescence. Research (Gilmore, Lewis, Lohr, Spence, & White, 1997) has shown that about half of the teenagers who become pregnant have a repeat pregnancy within eighteen months of their first pregnancy, and 8 percent have more than one repeat pregnancy during that time. Younger adolescents and those with a history of behavior problems are more at risk for repeat pregnancies. Race, ethnicity, and social class are not associated with repeat pregnancies.

Pregnancy during adolescence can have negative consequences for the mother, the father, and their children (Corcoran, 1998; Martin et al., 1998). Women who bear children during adolescence are likely to have fewer educational and job opportunities than their peers and to remain in poverty longer. Although it is illegal to exclude pregnant teenagers from public school, as many as 80 percent drop out and do not return (Manlove, 1998; White & DeBlassie, 1992). An important social consequence of teen pregnancy is long-term dependency on public assistance (Jorgensen, 1993).

Pregnant teens also are more vulnerable to health problems, such as toxemia, hemorrhaging, miscarriage, and even maternal death (Dell, 2001; Stevens-Simon & McAnarney, 1996). Infants born to adolescent mothers are more likely to be premature and to have low birthweight, birth defects, cognitive deficiencies, and impaired social-emotional development. A major contributor to these problems is lack of prenatal care—at least a third of pregnant teens receive inadequate prenatal care (Alan Guttmacher Institute, 2001). According to recent research, long-term consequences for children born to adolescent mothers include lower educational levels and less financial independence. In addition, children born to adolescent mothers are more likely to become teenage parents themselves (Hardy et al., 1997).

The life course for pregnant teens is not very optimistic. Can you identify the problems associated with teen pregnancy? What solutions can you think of to adequately address this issue?

ADOLESCENT PARENTING

> I haven't had a full night's sleep in a long time. I really miss that. . . . I can't get her down when I need to do my homework . . . I'll sit there and play with her to make her happy. But I'll stay up till 2 or 3 o'clock in the morning doing homework. . . . I have to support her and I'm proud of what I have done for her. I'm her mother, but I don't know what our future will be like. I do know that it's time for me to grow up. . . . I want her to have a good life and not make the mistakes that me and her father have.
>
> *—Interview with 16-year-old Amber, mother of a 2-month-old daughter* (adapted from Valdez, 1994)

In Amber's words you can hear the conflicting feelings that teen mothers often have about being a young parent. Hope, fatigue, pride, determination, and uncertainty mark her life. Amber's determination to "grow up" reflects the fact that teen parents have to take on adult responsibilities, often before they have the psychological, social, and economic abilities to do so. Compared to adults, adolescent parents are more likely to exhibit the following characteristics (Coley & Chase-Linsdale, 1998; Jorgensen, 1993):

✦ Lack of knowledge about child development
✦ Anxiousness and frustration about parenting
✦ Little interaction with their infants
✦ Negative exchanges with their children
✦ Negative attitudes toward parenting

Although teenage girls generally have difficulties taking on the responsibilities of being a parent, it also is true that they vary widely in their abilities to cope with child rearing. Given adequate support and access to resources, many teenage girls are capable of assuming these demanding responsibilities and of becoming effective mothers (Flanagan, 1998).

Less is known about teen dads, however. According to some estimates, about 28 percent of males become a father by the age of 19. The rate is substantially higher among minority teens (Thornberry, Smith, & Howard, 1997). Boys who come from impoverished neighborhoods and are involved in problem behaviors are more apt to become teen fathers than

What are the consequences—for themselves, their partners, their parents, and their children—of adolescents' keeping their babies? What factors increase the likelihood that the father will continue to be involved in parenting?

other boys are. In addition, the parents of teen fathers are likely to have become parents at an early age and to have little formal education (Thornberry et al., 1997).

Teenage fathers suffer many of the same adverse psychological, educational, and occupational circumstances as teen mothers do. Teenage fathers are more likely than their peers to drop out of school, have an unstable work record, become depressed, engage in criminal behavior, and use drugs and alcohol. Many young fathers are cognitively and emotionally immature, have inaccurate expectations for their children, are ambivalent about being a father, and fail to become involved with their children (Marsiglio & Cohan, 1997).

A key element in how likely teen fathers are to remain involved with teen mothers and their children is whether the young males can secure stable employment and fulfill the breadwinner role. But this is no easy task.

The economic support and personal involvement of the father can have positive consequences for teen mothers and their children (Hawkins, Christiansen, Sargent, & Hill, 1995). However, many young fathers are psychologically unprepared for fatherhood, and their continued involvement with the mother often results in additional pregnancies (Marsiglio & Cohan, 1997). Both circumstances decrease the long-term stability and economic prospects of these families.

An alternative point of view is that the major disadvantages experienced by teenage mothers and fathers and their children—inadequate health care, poor nutrition, limited educational and career opportunities, troubled neighborhoods, and high family instability—result from poverty (Marsiglio & Cohan, 1997; Ross-Leadbeater & Way, 2001). Adolescents living in poverty are more likely to become parents during their teenage years and to develop long-term dependency on public assistance. Findings like these suggest that at least some of the problems associated with teenage parenting may be products of socioeconomic issues rather than a lack of maturity or competence on the part of adolescents.

ADOLESCENT SEX EDUCATION

Most American teenagers know little about effective birth control. Certain myths about sexuality abound, such as the naive belief that a teenage girl cannot get pregnant during her first experience with sexual intercourse (Levinson, 1995). To debunk these myths and provide basic information, many parents and professionals advocate school-based sex education (Herold & Marshall, 1996). One roadblock to the effective implementation of sex education has been the stormy political debate over whether the primary focus of these programs should be the encouragement of abstinence or a comprehensive strategy that includes discussion of protection against pregnancy and sexually transmitted diseases. Abstinence-based programs seek to discourage teenage sexual activity and do not provide information about contraception. Assessments of these programs show that they do not have long-term effects on adolescent sexual behavior (Kirby, 1997; Roosa & Christopher, 1990; Thomas, 2000).

The primary goals of comprehensive sex education programs are to assist young people in developing a positive view of sexuality, provide them with information about taking care of their sexual health, and help them acquire the skills needed to make satisfying and healthy sexual decisions (Sex Information and Education Council of the United States [SIECUS], 1997). Effective comprehensive sex education programs for adolescents do the following (Kirby, 1997; SIECUS, 1997):

- Provide practice in communication, negotiation, and refusal skills
- Focus on reducing sexual behaviors that lead to unintended pregnancies or STDs
- Provide basic, accurate information about methods of avoiding unprotected intercourse
- Use a variety of teaching methods to personalize information
- Are taught by trained teachers
- Include activities that address social and media pressures related to sex

Sex education programs have the best outcomes when they are introduced before teens become sexually active and when information is included about both abstinence and contraception, as well as STD prevention. Importantly, research shows that sex education programs do not encourage sexual experimentation or increase sexual activity and that comprehensive approaches to sex education have been successful in helping young people postpone intercourse or use contraception (Grunseit, Kippax, Aggleton, Baldo, & Slutkin, 1997).

GAY AND LESBIAN YOUTH

> I remember my first crush, this girl with dark hair. I was 15 and I felt terribly guilty about my feelings for her. I never felt like I fit in with the other girls. I don't know why for sure. I felt different. I knew at that time that I wasn't normal, and I wanted nothing more in the world than to be normal. So, I ignored my true feelings. I did everything I could to convince myself that I wasn't a lesbian and that my feelings were just a phase.
> —*Holly*, age 17

Holly's story describes the feelings and thoughts of a teenager questioning her **sexual orientation,** determined by the sex of the sexual partners one is attracted to. A person with a sexual attraction to members of the other sex is **heterosexual** in orientation, whereas a person who is sexually attracted to members of the same sex is **homosexual** (gay or lesbian). Although figures vary, 5 to 10 percent of the population classify themselves as lesbian or gay (Savin-Williams, 2001). These figures may not be accurate because many homosexuals hide their sexual orientation out of fear of prejudice and discrimination (Rhode, 1997).

Few teens, whether heterosexual or homosexual, recall when they first became aware of their sexual orientation. Thus, development of sexual orientation appears to be more a process than an event. Sexual orientation may be present before one has the ability to reflect upon and label sexual feelings and attractions. Studies of twins and gender-atypical children show that sexual orientation is determined early in life (Remafedi, 1991). Both hereditary and environmental factors have been implicated, but there is no consensus as to which is more influential.

During adolescence, sexual orientation and sexual behavior may be quite independent of each other. Adolescents engage in many forms of sexual activities, regardless of sexual orientation. For example, some lesbian and gay youths have extensive heterosexual experiences, whereas some heterosexual youths engage in prolonged homosexual behaviors (Savin-Williams & Diamond, 1999). Although "pre-gay" youths are more likely than others to engage in homosexual behaviors, they also frequently participate in heterosexual behaviors (Blumenfeld & Raymond, 1993).

As in Holly's case, awareness of same-sex attraction usually begins during adolescence. Because of their attraction to same-sex people, many gay and lesbian youths, like Holly, often feel different from the majority of their peers and come to believe that they are weird or abnormal. Homosexual experiences may occur prior to this awareness or may be delayed until years later. Labeling oneself as "homosexual" almost always occurs in late adolescence or early adulthood.

Many gay and lesbian youths struggle because they are ostracized, rejected, teased, and abused by their peers (Savin-Williams & Cohen, 1996). For example, over half of the gay men in one study said they were victimized in junior and senior high school (Gross, Aurand, & Adessa, 1988). In another study (Hunter, 1990), over 40 percent of lesbian and gay youths said they had been physically attacked. In extreme cases, homosexual youths are the victims of terrible hate crimes. Recall the story of Matthew Shepard of Laramie, Wyoming, who was brutally attacked and killed in October of 1998 because he chose not to hide his homosexuality. The verbal and physical abuses gays and lesbians endure cause great stress, are detrimental to their mental health, and often lead to school-related problems, substance abuse, prostitution, and even suicide (Savin-Williams, 1994).

New findings show gay and lesbian youths reporting an array of risk factors linked to suicidal thoughts and suicide attempts. In a study using nationally representative data, researchers found that youths with same-sex sexual orientations were twice as likely as their peers to attempt suicide and have suicidal thoughts (Russell & Joyner, 2001). The elevated

sexual orientation characteristic determined by the sex of the sexual partners one is attracted to

heterosexual having a sexual attraction to members of the other sex

homosexual having a sexual attraction to members of the same sex

Describe the mixed messages adolescents are exposed to in their homes and in the media about drinking. How many adolescents try drinking and drugs?

risk of suicide among gay teens can be explained partly by risk factors that could affect any adolescent: depression, hopelessness, substance abuse, the recent suicide or attempted suicide of a family member or close friend, and experiences of victimization. However, the study showed that adolescent gays and lesbians reported experiencing significantly more of these factors. These findings provide strong evidence that sexual minority youths are more likely than their peers to think about and attempt suicide. The problems faced by gay and lesbian adolescents relate to the social and cultural contexts of sexuality and gender. Having supportive and accepting families and being comfortable with their sexual orientation help buffer gay and lesbian youths from the stress they face (Hershberger & D'Augelli, 1995).

In many important ways, lesbian and gay teens are similar to other adolescents. Levels of cognitive, physical, and self-concept development are not different for gay and straight youths (Boxer, Cohler, Herdt, & Irvin, 1993). In response to these facts, homosexuality was dropped as a mental disorder from the official diagnostic manual of the American Psychiatric Association in 1973. Furthermore, the belief that homosexual youths are promiscuous is not supported by scientific evidence—one-quarter of gay and lesbian youths are virgins when they graduate from high school (Savin-Williams, 1995). Although lesbian and gay youths have their difficulties (such as keeping their sexual orientation hidden from others for fear of retribution), most apparently adapt well and emerge from adolescence with positive views of themselves, their lives, and their futures (Savin-Williams, 1994).

WHAT TYPES OF BEHAVIOR PROBLEMS OCCUR DURING LATE ADOLESCENCE?

Although many adolescents experiment with some risky activities such as alcohol use and minor forms of deviant behavior (for example, curfew violations or vandalism), few of these are lasting or serious. Only a small percentage of adolescents are responsible for the more serious and dangerous activities (Gottfredson, Sealock, & Koper, 1996; Loeber, Farrington, Stouthamer-Loeber, & Van-Kammen, 1998). Many youths become involved in deviant activities during adolescence; however, those with serious problem behaviors often show signs of problems earlier in their development (Maughan & Rutter, 1998).

Behavior problems may be thought of in terms of two general categories. **Externalizing problems** are psychological difficulties in which individuals "act out" against society through behavior such as truancy or substance abuse. **Internalizing problems** are psychological difficulties, such as anxiety or depressive disorders, in which individuals focus on or within themselves (Achenbach & Edelbrock, 1989).

Adolescents often have multiple behavior problems. **Risk-taking behavior** is a syndrome associated with the co-occurrence of various acts, such as experimenting with drugs, having sex very early in adolescence, having sex without contraception, and engaging in delinquent and accident-inducing activities like reckless driving (Jessor, 1992). There is a general tendency for adolescents to behave defiantly and unconventionally in their risk taking (Ketterlinus, Lamb, & Nitz, 1995). Defiant behavior may relate to underlying personality traits, such as sensation seeking; biologically inherited factors that predispose one to develop problem behaviors (Rowe, 1995); social conditions, such as impoverished neighborhoods; or a combination of these (Udry, 1995). Needless to say, the precise factors that lead to behavior problems vary from adolescent to adolescent.

Explanations of behavior problems need to consider a wide array of factors. One model is presented in Figure 14.2. This model includes societal and cultural factors, such as neighborhood disorganization and extreme economic deprivation; individual factors, such as poor impulse control; familial factors, such as incompetent parenting and family conflict; and peer and school factors, such as deviant peers, academic failure, and dropping out

externalizing problems psychological difficulties that involve acting out against society

internalizing problems psychological difficulties, such as anxiety or depression, that involve a focus on or within the self

risk-taking behavior a syndrome of multiple behavior problems

FIGURE 14.2

Contextual Model of Adolescent Problem Behaviors

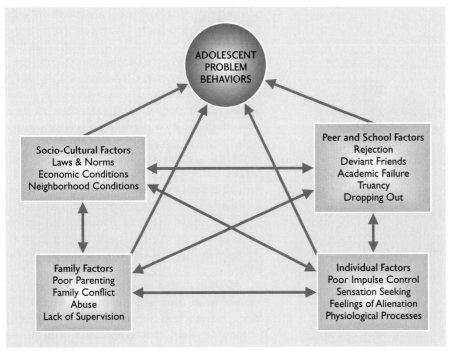

SOURCE: Hawkins, Catalano, and Miller, 1992. Copyright © 1992 by the American Psychological Association. Adapted with permission.

This contextual model emphasizes the idea that a wide variety of factors may influence an adolescent's behavior problems. Can you think of other factors that should be included in this model?

(Hawkins, Catalano, & Miller, 1992). Such models illustrate how problem behaviors have their origins in a complex array of influences.

ANTISOCIAL BEHAVIOR

As you learned in Chapter 10, one large category of risk-taking behavior is antisocial behavior—behavior that conflicts with the norms of society. Antisocial behavior includes **delinquency,** a term widely used to refer to a variety of legally defined antisocial acts committed by juveniles. Although many delinquent acts, such as homicide or robbery, are illegal for both adults and juveniles, others, such as underage drinking, skipping school, and running away from home, are **status offenses**—acts that are illegal for juveniles but not for adults (Gottfredson, Sealock, & Koper, 1996).

Adolescents and young adults violate the law more often than any other age group. Even if we ignore status offenses, violent crimes (such as assault, rape, and homicide) and property crimes (such as robbery, theft, and arson) increase during adolescence, peak during the high school years, and begin to decline in early adulthood. As Figure 14.3 shows, the rate of violent crime among juveniles increased until 1995 and then dropped (Federal Bureau of Investigation [FBI], 2000).

Individuals under the age of 24 account for well over half of all violent crimes in the United States (FBI, 2000). A distressing trend is the growing tendency of adolescents to use weapons. A recent national survey of youth indicated that 17 percent of high school students had carried a weapon such as a gun, knife, or club at some time during the preceding thirty days (CDC, 2000b). Boys were almost five times more likely to do so than girls (29 versus 6 percent).

delinquency the legal term for antisocial acts committed by juveniles

status offenses acts that are illegal for juveniles but not for adults, such as running away from home

FIGURE 14.3

Changes in Juvenile Violent Crime

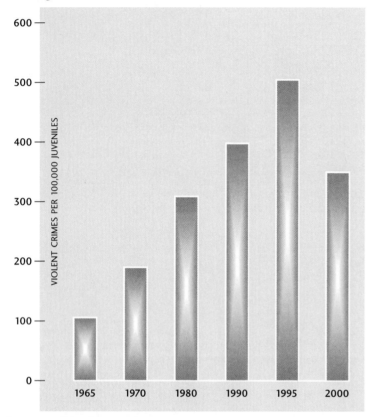

SOURCE: Federal Bureau of Investigation, 2000.

As you can see in this graph, juvenile violent crimes increased at a relatively steady rate between 1965 and 1995. What social, cultural, and family factors likely influenced the increased rates? Between 1995 and 2000, the rate dropped significantly. What changed over the past few years to decrease the rate?

DEPRESSION

In the last 35 years, the age of onset of depression has dropped. Depression is an internalizing disorder that now commonly begins during adolescence (Cicchetti & Toth, 1998; Kazdin & Marciano, 1998). Estimates of the prevalence of clinical depression range from 4 percent to 12 percent of adolescents (Kazdin & Marciano, 1998; Schwartz, Gladstone, & Kaslow, 1998) with older adolescents having higher rates (Strober, McCracken, & Hanna, 1991). Depressed adolescents have symptoms such as dysphoria (sad mood), social withdrawal, fatigue, apathy, impaired school performance, feelings of hopelessness, sleep disturbances, eating disorders, concentration difficulties, and self-destructive impulses (American Psychiatric Association, 1994; Kazdin & Marciano, 1998). Before puberty, rates of depression are low and are equal for boys and girls. After puberty, girls report increased rates of depression (Ge, Conger, & Elder, 2001).

Although only a small percentage of teens are diagnosed with depression, a sizable percent report feeling extremely sad or hopeless. For example, in a nationwide study, about 28 percent of high school students said that they felt so sad or hopeless almost every day for over two weeks in a row that they stopped participating in some usual activities (CDC, 2000a). Overall, girls (36 percent) were significantly more likely than boys (21 percent) to feel this way, and this sex difference held for all racial/ethnic groups.

Evidence is growing that problems with hormonal activity in the brain and nervous system often result in depression (Susman, Dorn, & Chrousos, 1991). The onset of puberty and associated hormonal changes may influence adolescents' emotional states (Paikoff, Brooks-Gunn, & Warren, 1991). Also, some teens seem prone to depression because they have cognitive mind sets that cause them to define their circumstances in terms of hopelessness, pessimism, and self-blame (Garber, Weiss, & Shanley, 1993).

Depression is more common when adolescents are experiencing stressful transitions—changing schools, beginning to date, or facing disruptions in family relationships (such as parental divorce). Moreover, having a depressed parent increases the chances that an adolescent will suffer from depression (Harrington, 1996). In addition, parental behaviors and parenting styles affect adolescent depression (Ge, Lorenz, Conger, Elder, & Simon, 1994; Steinberg, Lamborn, Darling, Mounts, & Dornbusch, 1994). For example, adolescent depression occurs more frequently in families that are low in warmth and high in conflict (Ge et al., 1994; Greenberger & Chen, 1996).

Although suicide is a serious health risk during adolescence (see Chapter 13), the relationship between suicide and depression is not straightforward (Metha, Chen, Mulvenon, & Dode, 1998). Some depressed youngsters are not suicidal, whereas other teenagers who are not depressed become suicidal (Aoki & Turk, 1997; Kazdin & Marciano, 1998). These findings indicate that depression and suicide are two related, but distinct, forms of internalizing disorders.

THE SCIENTIFIC IMPACT: INTERPRETING RESEARCH

What Family Factors Relate to Violence Among Minority Youths?

The increasing incidence of adolescent violence in the 1990s intensified the search for ways to reduce it. According to a transactional model, delinquent and violent behavior among adolescents is dependent on the interaction of individual and contextual characteristics. One important contextual characteristic is the family. Family relationships and parenting behaviors are consistently strong predictors of risk for antisocial behavior (Neher & Short, 1998; Tolan & Loeber, 1993). Ethnic groups have distinctly different beliefs and values with respect to family relationships that may have important effects on the risk for antisocial behavior (MacKune-Karrer, 1992). Studies suggest that minority adolescents, particularly minority boys, are at the highest risk for committing violent offenses (Elliott, 1994; Farrington, 1998).

To examine ethnic differences in family functioning and their relationship to youth violence, a longitudinal study was conducted of African American and Hispanic teenage boys at risk for delinquency (Gorman-Smith, Tolan, Zelli, & Huesmann, 1996). The results supported an important role for families in influencing risk for participation in serious delinquent behaviors. Poor parental supervision, poor discipline, and lack of family cohesiveness increase youths' risk for serious delinquency, regardless of ethnic or socioeconomic group.

There were some noticeable differences between African American and Hispanic families relating to beliefs about the importance of family relationships. African American adolescents whose families accorded the least importance to family relationships were the most violent. For Hispanic teens, however, the opposite was found: Teens from the families with the strongest beliefs about the need for close family relationships were more likely to be violent. Thus, strong emphasis on family duty and loyalty affects the risk for adolescent violent behavior differently depending on ethnic background.

One explanation of how family beliefs affect the risk of violent behavior has to do with how deeply ingrained in US culture the family is. Most of the Hispanic families in this study were first- or second-generation Mexican Americans. Researchers hypothesize that generational differences arise within Mexican American families as native values and beliefs come into conflict with the beliefs of the larger culture. When the traditional beliefs that organize and guide the family are threatened, family cohesiveness also is threatened, increasing the likelihood that teens will stay away from home. The more they stay away from home, the more susceptible these youths are to involvement in violent behavior. Any proposed method of preventing the development of violent behavior must therefore take into consideration the cultural and ethnic backgrounds of the youths and their families.

Thinking It Through:

1. On what aspects of family functioning did this study focus? What other aspects of family functioning might influence violent behavior among minority teens?
2. How did cultural beliefs and values about family roles and responsibilities influence your development during adolescence?

SUBSTANCE USE AND ABUSE

Most teens try alcohol and other drugs. The majority of these teens will experiment and stop or will continue to use casually without significant problems. Some will use regularly, with varying degrees of physical, emotional, and social problems. Some will develop a dependency and will become destructive to themselves and others. Some will die, and some will cause others to die.

American adolescents grow up in a society that has contradictory attitudes about the use of drugs and alcohol. Governmental and law enforcement agencies seek to discourage adolescents from using illegal drugs, yet the media commonly associate dangerous and addictive substances, such as alcohol and tobacco, with images of prestige, style, and glamour. Although advertisements may not target adolescents, they present attractive and positive images of alcohol to those who see them, including adolescents.

Alcohol

Alcohol is the most commonly used and abused substance. The vast majority of high school students (about 80 percent) have had at least one alcoholic drink during their lifetime, and virtually all high school seniors have had some experience with alcohol (CDC, 2000a). More than half of all high school students have had at least one drink of alcohol in the preceding month, with boys and girls showing similar patterns of use. New evidence suggests that the younger a teen is when he or she starts drinking, the greater the chance that he or she will develop problems with alcohol abuse and dependence at some point in life (Grant

IGURE 14.4

High School Students' Experiences with Alcohol

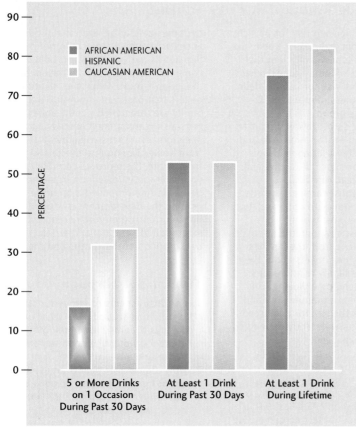

SOURCE: Centers for Disease Control, 2000a.

This graph shows that most adolescents have had some experience with alcohol and about one-third have engaged in heavy consumption in the last month. Notice that African American youth drink less than the other groups of adolescents. What might account for these differences?

& Dawson, 1998). There are ethnic differences in alcohol consumption, though, with generally higher levels of alcohol consumption for Hispanic and Caucasian American adolescents than for African American youngsters (see Figure 14.4). An especially troubling pattern is the high percentage (33 percent) of students in grades 8 through 12 who engage in heavy or binge drinking—consuming five or more drinks of alcohol on at least one occasion during the preceding month. Parents do little to dissuade adolescents from drinking. Fewer than one-third of parents of tenth-graders give their children a clear "no use" message about alcohol (Johnson Institute, 1993).

At present, there is no known "safe dose" of alcohol for adolescents. Very little is known about the biological impact of alcohol on teens. However, pubertal changes, hormonal fluctuations, and incomplete muscle and body mass development may make adolescents more vulnerable to alcohol than are adults. Because personal identity and social skills are still developing, "social drinking" may have more serious consequences for adolescents than it does for adults. Teens may learn to use alcohol to handle interpersonal relationships, deal with peer pressure, and control sexual impulses. Any use of intoxicants—even one beer—can have serious and unpredictable consequences for adolescents because of their low impulse control, emotional volatility, lack of a sense of limits, and feelings of invulnerability.

Often there is a dangerous tendency toward risky and unruly behavior among teens who drink. Automobile accidents are the major cause of death among teenagers (see Chapter 13), with alcohol playing a significant role in about 40 percent of these fatalities. In 1998, over 2200 high school students died in alcohol-related crashes (National Highway Traffic Safety Administration, 1999). Adolescent drivers are still developing driving skills and are easily disoriented by alcohol or distracted by passengers who are drinking.

Tobacco

A large majority (70 percent) of high school students in the United States try tobacco during their teenage years (CDC, 2000a). According to some estimates, as many as 3000 teens start smoking each day, and ultimately 1000 of these teens will die from smoking (American Academy of Pediatrics, 1996). Most teens begin using tobacco before graduation from high school and soon after start to use it regularly (CDC, 2000a). Thus, most people who are going to smoke are hooked by the time they are 20. Additionally, early cigarette use is associated with heavier use; those who begin to use tobacco as young adolescents are among the heaviest users in late adolescence and adulthood (CDC, 2000a).

Although smoking has been linked to lung cancer, heart disease, and various other diseases, many teenagers do not believe they are at risk for diseases associated with tobacco use. Studies reveal that less than half of high school students believe smoking is a great risk to one's health (Monitoring the Future, 2001). This is especially true for younger teens. Fewer than 40 percent of eighth-graders think there is "great risk" to smoking a pack or more a day. By twelfth grade, over 45 percent of students believe there is "great risk" in smoking.

Most people who smoke began during adolescence. What cognitive and social factors increase the likelihood that adolescents will engage in activities, such as smoking, that put their health at risk?

During the 1990s, the number of young adolescents using tobacco rose, and rates among older adolescents remained high (Monitoring the Future, 2001). Overall, over one-third of high school–age adolescents in the United States currently smoke or use smokeless tobacco. As shown in Figure 14.5, Caucasian American teenagers use tobacco more often than either African American or Hispanic youngsters (CDC, 2000a).

The development of tobacco use among adolescents progresses through five stages: forming positive attitudes and beliefs about tobacco, trying tobacco, experimenting with it, beginning to use it regularly, and ending up addicted to it. This process, which begins during early adolescence, generally takes place over a three-year period. Factors associated with tobacco use during adolescence include the following (CDC, 2000a):

✦ Low socioeconomic status
✦ Easy access to tobacco
✦ Peers' and siblings' use of tobacco
✦ Parental indifference
✦ Low academic achievement
✦ Low self-esteem
✦ Lack of knowledge of the health consequences of tobacco use

Young people face enormous pressures to use tobacco, and it is readily available to teens. By tenth grade, over 90 percent say they can get cigarettes easily if they want to. Despite efforts to limit access to cigarettes, the percentage of underage minors who buy their own cigarettes has actually increased since 1989 (from 58 to 68 percent). Each year, nearly 1 billion packs of cigarettes are sold to children under the age of 18 (CDC, 2000a). Despite the widespread notion that there is little parents can do to prevent their

High School Students' Tobacco Use

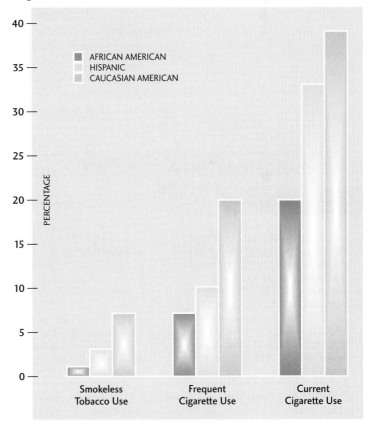

SOURCE: Centers for Disease Control, 2000a.

As you can see in this graph, Caucasian American adolescents use tobacco more frequently than either Hispanic or African American adolescents. What factors may influence adolescents' use of tobacco products? What is the danger of early smoking for long-term health?

What factors have contributed to the rise in the numbers of adolescents who have tried marijuana? What reasons do adolescents give for drug use?

teens from smoking, adolescents who perceive that both parents would respond negatively to, and be upset by, their smoking are less likely to smoke (Sargent & Dalton, 2001).

Illicit Drugs

Other than marijuana, illegal drugs are seldom used regularly by adolescents (National Institute on Drug Abuse [NIDA], 2000). Less than 2 percent of teenagers inject drugs (NIDA, 1995). Daily use of stimulants, hallucinogens, LSD, PCP, inhalants, barbiturates, tranquilizers, cocaine, crack, steroids, and heroin also is relatively rare (less than 5 percent), although use of these drugs has increased since 1990 (NIDA, 2000). In particular, the use of the drug "ecstasy" has risen sharply among teens and is growing in popularity even among seventh- and eighth-grade students (NIDA, 2000). Use of illicit drugs is greatest among minority youths.

Marijuana use among adolescents has increased since 1990. The number of adolescents who say they used marijuana in the preceding month has increased by more than 250 percent for eighth-graders since 1991 and by more than 150 percent for tenth-graders since 1992. In one year alone (1995 to 1996), marijuana use went from 9 percent to 11 percent among eighth-graders and from 17 percent to 20 percent among tenth-graders (NIDA, 2000). One reason for rising marijuana use may be a belief among teens that marijuana is not harmful to their health; only 43 percent of seniors say that marijuana is "very harmful" to their health. Adolescents can also obtain marijuana easily, with almost three-quarters saying it is easy to get (National Parents Resource Institute for Drug Education [NPRIDE], 1996).

Despite the increased attention to drug abuse, the percentage of students who say their parents talk to them about drugs has decreased. For example, the percentage of students who said their parents talked to them often or a lot about the problems of drugs dropped from about 40 percent in 1991 to about 31 percent in 1997 (NPRIDE, 1997). Yet parents'

THE PRACTICAL IMPACT: NURTURING CHILDREN

Preventing Teenage Drug Use

In 1937, the classic movie *Reefer Madness* told a horrifying story of the downfall of a youth who had a promising future—until he tried marijuana. But the film's message backfired, and today it is a cult favorite among young users of marijuana. Like many early efforts to scare teens away from drugs, *Reefer Madness* failed to have a positive impact.

Drug prevention has changed dramatically since then. Today, thousands of schools, community organizations, congregations, and government agencies across the country are designing programs aimed at preventing alcohol, tobacco, and drug use among teens. The question is, Which

programs are most effective? According to the research (Bukoski, 1997; NIDA, 1997; Roche, 1998), effective teen drug prevention programs do the following:

- Target all forms of drug abuse, including the use of tobacco, alcohol, marijuana, and inhalants
- Teach the skills youths need to resist drugs when they are offered and to strengthen a personal commitment against their use
- Employ interactive methods that make use of peer discussion groups rather than just lectures
- Include a parent or caregiver component designed to help parents reinforce the programs'

messages regarding drugs and their harmful effects
- Are long-term, lasting throughout the school career, with repeated interventions that reinforce the original prevention goals
- Strengthen norms against drug use in all settings, including the family, school, and community
- Address the specific nature of the drug abuse problem in a local community
- Are age-specific, developmentally appropriate, and culturally sensitive
- Become more intensive as the level of risk of the target population increases

warnings can be effective, leading to less drug use among adolescents. About 37 percent of teens who say their parents never talked to them about drugs used an illicit drug during the preceding year, compared to 26 percent of those whose parents spoke to them a lot about drugs.

Adolescents' reasons for using and not using drugs are complex and diverse. Figure 14.6 presents some of these reasons. As you can see, teens rarely say that they use drugs because they are stressed, rebellious, or have family or personal problems. Instead, they say they use drugs because it is "in" to do so and because it makes them feel good. Figure 14.6 also reveals that teens' main reasons for not using drugs are fear of getting caught, the damage drugs might do to them, and because it is wrong to do so. Although teen drug use is influenced by peers, abstinence may have more to do with teens' relationships with parents and the degree

IGURE 14.6

Teens' Reasons for Using and Not Using Drugs

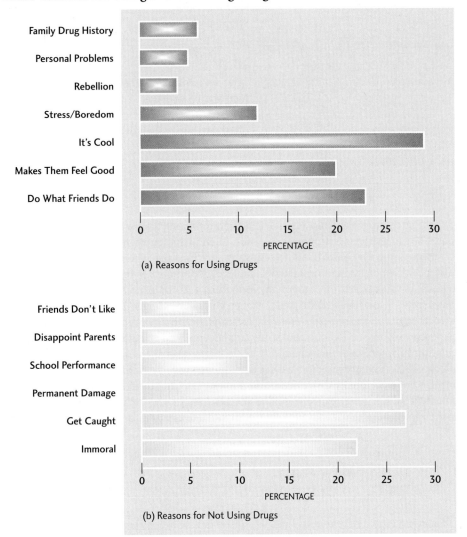

(a) Reasons for Using Drugs

(b) Reasons for Not Using Drugs

SOURCE: National Center on Addiction and Substance Abuse, 1996.

Many adults believe that adolescents use drugs because of personal problems and to rebel against their families. Adolescents report that they use drugs because it is cool and because their friends do. How might adolescents' reasons for using and not using drugs be helpful in planning prevention programs?

TABLE 14.2
Factors Related to Adolescent Drug Use

TYPE OF FACTOR	EXAMPLES
Individual	Physiological characteristics Aggression Hyperactivity Difficult temperament Early initiation into drug use
Family	Family history of alcoholism Parental use of illegal drugs Poor family management practices Family conflict
Peer group	Early peer rejection Peer modeling Friends who use drugs
School	Academic failure Lack of commitment to school
Culture	Laws and norms favorable to drug use Availability of drugs Poverty Alienation and rebelliousness

SOURCE: CDC, 2000a; Fitzgerald et al., 1994.

to which parents monitor and provide information about the physical and moral consequences of using drugs (National Center on Addiction and Substance Abuse, 1996).

Research into the causes of adolescent substance use must take into account individual, family, peer, school, and cultural factors. Table 14.2 summarizes the risk factors related to drug use. As you can see, there are many individual and contextual factors that contribute to adolescents' use of drugs (Fitzgerald, Davies, Zucker, & Klinger, 1994).

Most drug use during adolescence is experimental and is not related to long-term problems. According to one longitudinal study, adolescents who engaged in some drug experimentation (primarily with marijuana) were the best adjusted teens in the sample (Shedler & Block, 1990). Adolescents who used drugs frequently were maladjusted (had poor impulse control, were emotionally distressed), and adolescents who, by age 18, had never experimented with drugs were relatively anxious and lacking in social skills. These findings suggest that problem drug use may be a symptom, not a cause, of maladjustment.

HOW DOES EMPLOYMENT AFFECT OLDER ADOLESCENTS?

Eighteen-year-old Dave wakes up at dawn, slurps some strawberry jam for a sugar rush, goes to high school until 2:30 PM, hurries home to change and go off to his job at a clothing store where he works almost 30 hours a week. He gets home around 10:30, does maybe an hour of homework . . . and goes to bed around midnight. . . . He's sacrificed some of his school life for his job, misses playing soccer and baseball . . . and he had to give up a challenging class because he had so little time for studying.

—*S. Waldman and K. Springen* (1992, p. 80)

For many adolescents like Dave, working is a major part of life. More than 5 million adolescents now work—twice the rate of working adolescents in the 1950s. Nearly half of all high school senior boys work more than 20 hours a week, and about one-third of senior girls do so (Crispell, 1995).

The jobs teens hold generally are low paying and involve retail sales, fast food, or unskilled labor. Most teens, like Dave, find their work intellectually dull, unchallenging, and monotonous. They rarely are allowed to act independently or make their own decisions while they work. The skills involved in most of these jobs are not very demanding; less than 6 percent of teens' time on the job requires activities such as reading, writing, or math. About 25 percent of their time is spent either cleaning or carrying things (Greenberger & Steinberg, 1986).

Many adults believe that work is a good way to keep adolescents out of trouble. It is assumed that getting a job helps teens accept responsibility, teaches them about the value of work and money, and prepares them for future adult roles. However, only 10 percent of high school seniors save most of their earnings for college, and only about 6 percent use most of their earnings to help pay for family living expenses (Waldman & Springen, 1992). Most teens use their earnings to buy clothing, music, or other items they desire.

Jobs can teach adolescents to be accepting and tolerant of others by forcing them to meet and interact with people of different social, racial, and cultural backgrounds (Waldman & Springen, 1992). Family economic conditions force some teens into the job market. Working can bring about positive outcomes if the adolescent contributes to the well-being of the family or is closely supervised by parents (Hansen & Jarvis, 2000; Mortimer & Finch, 1996). Also, students who are on the verge of dropping out or who are at risk for delinquency can be kept on track through a good job.

The critical number appears to be 20. Working less than 20 hours a week can give a teen higher self-esteem and a sense of responsibility, along with a paycheck. This teen can find the time needed to work by cutting the amount of time she or he spends watching television. Working more than 20 hours puts work too much at the center of a teen's life. Simple arithmetic explains why more than 20 hours of work is harmful. A teenager typically spends 35 hours a week in school and 10 hours a week doing homework; adding a 20-hour job results in a 65-hour work week (Resnick, 1997).

As in Dave's case, adolescents who work have less time available for homework and often struggle to keep up with their coursework. Thus, students who work the most hours perform the most poorly in school (Markel & Frone, 1998; Steinberg & Dornbusch, 1991). Additionally, students who work cut more classes, spend less time on homework, and have lower educational aspirations than those who do not work (Steinberg, Fegley, & Dornbusch, 1993).

Compared to adolescents in other industrialized countries such as Japan, more US adolescents work. They also work longer hours and have more spending money than their counterparts in Japan. Given the impact that work has on teens' school performance, one reason for the lower achievement of US teens may be that they spend so much more of their time working than do their peers in comparable cultures.

School is not the only aspect of an adolescent's life that is affected by work. Adolescents who work also are more likely to have behavior problems and use alcohol or drugs (Steinberg et al., 1993), to get into arguments with their parents, to get inadequate sleep and exercise, and to fail to eat breakfast (Bachman & Schulenberg, 1993).

What is not clear is whether working more than 20 hours itself causes problematic outcomes or whether the adolescents who work these longer hours are, for example, less interested in school than their peers and more inclined to use drugs and alcohol before they enter the work force. Longitudinal research that followed teens as they entered and dropped out of the work force suggests that working directly contributes to these problems (Steinberg et al., 1993). Even after controlling for differences among teenagers before they became employed, research suggests that taking on a job, particularly for more than 20 hours a week, diminishes teens' investment in school, increases rates of delinquency and drug use, and decreases feelings of self-reliance. When adolescents quit working,

Consider the typical jobs held by adolescents and the kinds of activities and skills they are likely to use in these jobs. What mistaken beliefs do many adults hold about the advantages of adolescents' working? What are the disadvantages of adolescents' working?

improvements in schooling and achievement were found. Thus, for too many teenagers, too much work may squander their future (Schoenhals, Tienda, & Schneider, 1998).

WHAT FACTORS INFLUENCE ADOLESCENTS' VULNERABILITY AND RESILIENCY

Although teenagers today face increasing risks associated with drugs, unprotected sexual intercourse, violence, crime, and depression, no more than 20 percent of US adolescents have behavior or adjustment problems (Ebata, Petersen, & Conger, 1990). In addition, as you have already learned, many problems that arise during adolescence have their roots in earlier development. This fact is important because behavior problems that persist from childhood tend to be more severe and have different causes than behavior problems that develop during adolescence (Price & Lento, 2001).

It also is important to recognize that large individual differences exist in adolescents' abilities to cope with the stressors and temptations they face, and these abilities play a key role in whether outcomes are healthy or problematic. Individual qualities such as perseverance, intelligence, determination, and having good health act as protective factors for adolescents who overcome adversity (Smokowski, Reynolds, & Bezruczko, 1999). From a transactional perspective, optimal coping results from a good balance between the characteristics of the individual and the demands of the situation. This balance changes across development. For example, according to a classic longitudinal study of coping, personal qualities (such as temperament) strongly influence outcomes early in development; school and cognitive factors are keys to adjustment during middle childhood; and during adolescence, the ability to develop interpersonal relationships is central to adjustment because the peer group and other aspects of the social context become more crucial (Werner & Smith, 1982).

The challenges and demands of adolescence create stresses that overwhelm some adolescents' abilities to cope and adapt. A 16-year-old who finds the demands of cliques and dating increasingly stressful may begin to drink alcohol as a way of coping with these social situations. Drinking alcohol may enable this teen to continue to go to parties and

Late adolescence is a period of time in which many new responsibilities and challenges must be met. Most adolescents find these exciting and are resilient in the face of the increased demands of late adolescence. Can you identify the factors that contribute to resilience in older adolescents?

TABLE 14.3

Qualities That Enhance Adolescents' Resiliency and Ability to Cope

QUALITY	DEFINITION
Support	• Family support provides high levels of love and acceptance • Parental involvement provides help and advice when needed • Nonfamilial adult support provides advice and mentoring • School climate is positive
Control	• Parents have standards for appropriate conduct • Parents discipline teen when rules are violated • Teen is at home at least four nights a week • Best friends model responsible behavior
Structured time use	• Teen is involved in extra-curricular school activities • Teen is involved in organizations or clubs outside of school • Teen is involved in religious programs or services
Educational commitment	• Teen is motivated to do well in school • Teen aspires to post–high school education • Teen's school performance is above average • Teen spends at least 6 hours per week doing homework
Positive values	• Teen places high personal value on helping other people • Teen is concerned about the conditions of others and their feelings • Teen values postponing sexual activity
Social competence	• Teen has the ability to stand up for what he or she believes in • Teen is good at making friends • Teen is good at making decisions and planning ahead • Teen has high self-esteem • Teen is optimistic about the future

SOURCE: Benson, 1993.

interact socially, but it is unlikely to promote optimal social development. In addition, it is likely to make subsequent development more difficult (Bloom, 1998; Ebata et al., 1990).

For most teens, the demands of adolescence bring opportunities that promote growth. Having a new peer group from which to select friends, experiencing more challenging learning environments in school, and taking on new responsibilities in the family and community are beneficial to most adolescents. Learning to drive and being able to accomplish more physically and intellectually demanding tasks also can be exciting. In fact, a certain amount of challenge and stress may be necessary for healthy development (Garbarino et al., 1992).

Adolescents' abilities to face these challenges and stressors are influenced greatly by their relationships. Warm and supportive relationships with parents serve as protective factors, even in the face of serious stress (Kiser, Ostoja, & Pruitt, 1998). Being liked and accepted by one's peers also serves a protective function. Having someone to talk to, confide in, and share with helps adolescents deal with the stressors of everyday life (Haveman & Wolfe, 1994). Positive relationships are particularly important for adolescents who are most at risk for developing behavior problems. Table 14.3 lists some of the qualities that enhance adolescents' resiliency and ability to cope.

Late adolescence is a period in which teens prepare to enter adulthood. Physically, cognitively, socially, and emotionally, older adolescents reach peak or near-peak levels. Because of these advances, they feel the need to function more independently, and parents and other adults give them more independence and responsibility.

Late adolescence also is a period in which teens experiment and try out a wider variety of adultlike behaviors. Some of these behaviors promote and enhance development, and some impair it. Older teens explore more educational and occupational opportunities, but they also experiment with drugs, alcohol, sexuality, and crime to a greater extent than they did as younger teens.

Older teens' lives also become more complex as they experience more varied environments and people with different interests, skills, and backgrounds. In a classic study (Csikszentmihalyi & Larson, 1984), teens kept daily diaries about their lives. Seventeen-year-old Greg's diary entries for one week, shown in Figure 14.7, illustrate the complexity and variation in the individual and contextual issues older teens face. As you can see from his diary, Greg's week was filled with thoughts and activities related to his education, job, friends, girlfriend, and family, as well as recreational drug use, entertainment, and sex. The issues Greg dealt with ranged from taking care of himself (getting himself fed) to social issues (equal rights) to anxiety about dating and relationships (calling his girlfriend). His emotional states varied dramatically from day to day, ranging from relatively positive when he was with his friends at the mall to relatively negative when he was alone daydreaming or at work engaged in menial labor.

Today's adolescents have significant assets and strengths. Many of these strengths are the result of cumulative experiences acquired over the course of their lives. Because older adolescents are on the verge of becoming adults but are not quite there yet, it is easy to discount their skills and their potential contributions (Grotevant, 1998). The dynamic interplay of individual and contextual changes brings about greater adaptability and resourcefulness, as well as greater stress and demands for adjustment (Mitchell, 1996). Fortunately, most adolescents are able to meet these challenges and become contributing, responsible, and competent adults.

TRY IT OUT

Activities Relating to Older Adolescents

1. Go to a local mall and observe older teens. Notice their dress, conduct, and actions. What characteristics of and concerns about late adolescent social and emotional development can you identify? How do these fit with the stereotypes we hold about older teens?
2. Find some magazines, such as *Teen* or *Seventeen,* or some "webzines," such as *Teens-Online* (at http://www.teens-online.com) or *TechnoTeen* (at http://www.technoteen.com), that are read primarily by teens. What insights do the features in these magazines provide about teens' development? Do teen boys and girls face different issues? What kinds of advertisements appear in these publications, and what do these tell you about issues related to adolescence?
3. Choose three television programs of interest to teenagers and analyze the sexual content in each and its advertising. How did you identify and classify sexual content? How pervasive was this content in the programs you targeted? Do you think the programs and ads influence teens' attitudes and behaviors regarding sex?

FIGURE 14.7

17-Year-Old Greg's Weekly Diary Entries

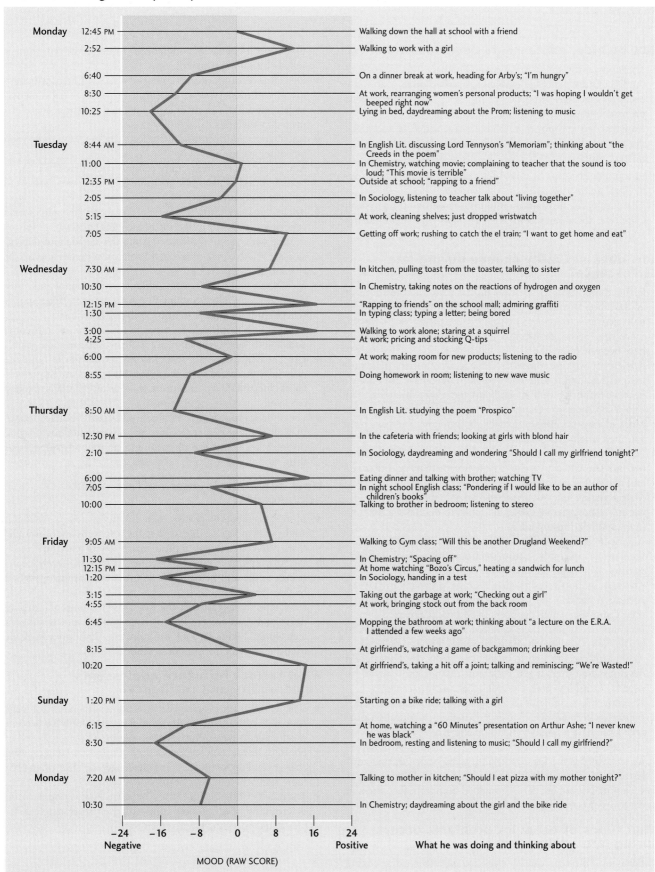

SOURCE: From BEING ADOLESCENT: CONFLICT AND GROWTH IN THE TEENAGE YEARS by MIHALY CSIKSZENTMIHALYI and REED LARSON. Copyright © 1984 by Basic Books, Inc. Reprinted by permission of Basic Books, a member of Perseus Books, L.L.C.

SUM IT UP

How do older adolescents develop autonomy?

✦ Autonomy is the ability to govern and manage oneself. Because the US culture generally emphasizes self-reliance, autonomy becomes especially important during late adolescence as teens prepare to leave home and enter adulthood.

✦ Constructive autonomy emphasizes a balance between the need to assert individuality and the need to remain close to significant others.

✦ Autonomy develops in three areas: emotional autonomy, behavioral autonomy, and values autonomy.

✦ The development of autonomy is influenced by the physical, cognitive, social, and contextual changes that occur during adolescence.

How does sexuality change during late adolescence?

✦ Sexual maturation is one of the most distinctive transitions of adolescence. During late adolescence, most teens become sexually active.

✦ Since the 1960s, adolescents' sexual attitudes and behaviors have become more liberal.

✦ Adolescent boys are somewhat more likely than girls to be sexually active, but the differences between them have been disappearing. Minority teens generally are more sexually active than Caucasian American teens.

✦ Most adolescents are not sexually promiscuous and have only a limited number of sexual partners.

✦ Peer influences on sexual activity are significant. When peers become sexually active, they create norms that legitimize sex and make it more acceptable.

✦ Male sexuality tends to be focused on gaining physical gratification, whereas female sexuality tends to be focused on intimacy and relationship issues.

✦ American teenagers are less likely to use contraception than are their peers from other countries. Cognitive, social, and relationship factors influence whether contraception is used.

✦ About 1 million teenage girls become pregnant each year. African American and Hispanic teens are more likely than their Caucasian American peers to become pregnant.

✦ Pregnant teens and their children are more vulnerable to health complications during pregnancy, birth, and delivery.

✦ Adolescent parents tend to be less knowledgeable about child development, interact less with their infants, and have more negative attitudes about parenting than older parents.

✦ To reduce the number of teen pregnancies, adolescent sex education has been advocated. Comprehensive sex education programs can have a positive impact on adolescent sexual behavior and reduce the number of unintentional adolescent pregnancies.

✦ Awareness of same-sex attraction usually begins during adolescence. Most gay and lesbian teens do not label themselves as such until late adolescence. Gay and lesbian teens face stress in the form of peer rejection and victimization.

What types of behavior problems occur during late adolescence?

✦ Behavior problems can be classified as either externalizing (acting out) or internalizing (focused on oneself). When mul-

tiple problem behaviors often occur together, the syndrome is called risk-taking behavior.

✦ One large category of risk-taking activities is antisocial behavior. A common type of antisocial behavior is delinquency, which refers to a variety of legally defined antisocial acts committed by juveniles.

✦ Adolescents and young adults violate the law more often than any other age group.

✦ Adolescent depression is more common now than it was thirty years ago, and teenage girls are more likely than teenage boys to suffer from depression.

✦ Adolescent depression is especially common when adolescents experience stressful transitions (such as changing schools or dealing with parental divorce). Although suicide and depression are related, most depressed adolescents do not attempt or commit suicide.

✦ Most teens will have some experience with alcohol and other drugs. An especially troubling finding is that one-third of high school students engage in heavy or binge drinking.

✦ A large majority of teens try tobacco. Most people who become addicted to tobacco begin using it during their teenage years.

✦ Use of illicit drugs is a relatively uncommon event, but the rates have increased since the 1980s. Marijuana use in particular has increased, in part because teens believe that it is not very harmful.

✦ Use of drugs appears to be influenced by peers, but abstinence may relate to the degree to which parents monitor and provide information about the physical and moral consequences of drug use.

How does employment affect older adolescents?

✦ More adolescents work now than did fifty years ago. Although adults tend to believe that work helps keep teens out of trouble, work often contributes to problems at school and home.

✦ Working can have positive outcomes when adolescents contribute to the well-being of the family or are closely supervised by their parents.

✦ Most studies suggest that the negative outcomes of working during adolescence are linked to how much, not whether, a teen works. Taking on a job for more than 20 hours a week diminishes a teen's investment in school.

What factors influence adolescents' vulnerability and resiliency?

✦ Despite the images portrayed by the popular media, most teens cope well with the demands of adolescence—only 20 percent of adolescents have adjustment problems.

✦ For most teens, adolescence is a time of important and exciting changes and opportunities. The challenges they face often promote rather than hinder healthy development.

✦ The quality of the relationships that teens have is important in determining how well they cope with their increasingly complex and demanding environments.

KEY TERMS and CONCEPTS

autonomy (*440*)
behavioral autonomy (*440*)
delinquency (*451*)
double standard (*443*)
emotional autonomy (*440*)

externalizing problems (*450*)
heterosexual (*449*)
homosexual (*449*)
internalizing problems (*450*)
risk-taking behavior (*450*)

sexual orientation (*449*)
status offenses (*451*)
values autonomy (*440*)

BENCHMARKS in
Late Adolescence

PHYSICAL/MOTOR DEVELOPMENT	COGNITIVE DEVELOPMENT	SOCIAL/EMOTIONAL DEVELOPMENT
Final stages of sexual maturity	Advances in social cognition and perspective taking	Development of autonomy
Athletic maturity	Postconventional moral reasoning	Increased involvement in sexual activity
Need for fitness		Development of sexual orientation
Vulnerability to STDs, AIDS, accidents, homicide, and suicide	Development of advanced moral reasoning, responsibility, and character	Exploration of interpersonal intimacy
	Development of advanced religious and political thinking	Risk for substance abuse, delinquency, and depression
		Transition to high school, preparation for college, and possible termination of schooling
		Experience in the community and world of work

NATIONAL HOTLINES FOR LATE ADOLESCENT DEVELOPMENT

AIDS Hotline: 800-342-2437 (Spanish: 800-344-7432)

ALATEEN: 800-344-2666

National Drug Abuse Hotline: 800-662-4357

Youth Crisis Hotline: 800-448-4663

*i*mpact Report on Older Adolescents

This figure depicts the goals of high school boys and girls. Notice the importance of work, friendships, and leisure time. In these areas, few differences are found between boys and girls. Note, however, the differences between boys and girls in other life goals, particularly those relating to money and children. What factors account for these differences? How do these goals compare to yours?

Percentage of High School Seniors Who Feel That Specified Life Goals Are "Very Important," by Sex

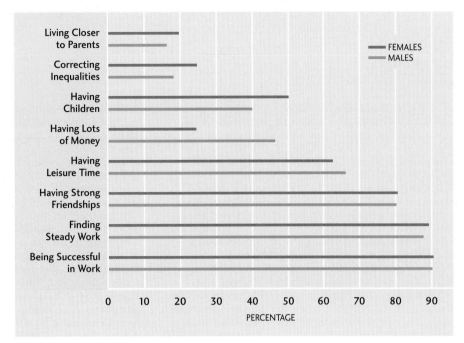

SOURCE: National Center for Education Statistics, 1996.

RECOMMENDED WEBSITES

Alan Guttmacher Institute: This site gives resources and information on adolescent sexuality and pregnancy.
http://www.agi-usa.org

National Clearinghouse for Alcohol and Drug Information: This site is an information service of the Substance Abuse and Mental Health Services Administration of the US Department of Health and Human Services. It is the world's largest resource for current information and materials concerning substance abuse.
http://www.health.org/

National Dropout Prevention Center: This is a clearinghouse for information on issues related to school reform and dropout prevention.
http://www.dropoutprevention.org/

National Prevention Information Network: Resources and information about education on and prevention of AIDS, STDs, and TB are provided by the Centers for Disease Control and Prevention.
http://www.cdcnpin.org/

Office of Juvenile Justice and Delinquency Prevention: Facts on violence by and against juveniles are accompanied by information on intervention efforts for at-risk youth.
http://virlib.ncjrs.org/JuvenileJustice.asp/

Sexuality Information and Education Council of the United States (SIECUS): An organization that develops, collects, and disseminates information that should be included in any comprehensive education about sexuality.
http://www.siecus.org/

YouthInfo: This Website was developed by the US Department of Health and Human Services to provide the latest information about America's adolescents.
http://www.acf.dhhs.gov/programs/fysb/youthinfo/

Youth Resource: A project of Advocates for Youth, this Website provides information for gay and lesbian youths.
http://www.youthresource.com/

Photo Credits

Facing p. 1, © Julie Fisher/Stone/GettyImages; p. 2, © Daniel Pangbourne/ FPG International/GettyImages; p. 5, Kevin Higley/AP/Wide World Photos; p. 6, PhotoFest/© 1970, United Artists Corporation, all rights reserved; p. 8, © Paul Avis/Stone/GettyImages; p. 10, © Photo Researchers Inc./Science Photo Library; p. 12, Eric Lessing/Art Resource, NY; p. 14 (*left to right*), Courtesy of the Library of Congress, Corbis-Bettmann, Corbis-Bettmann, Courtesy of the National Library of Medicine; p. 17, © Deborah Davis/PhotoEdit; p. 21, Louisa Buller/AP/Wide World Photos; p. 25, © David Young-Wolff/Stone/GettyImages; p. 29, Doug Plummer/Photo Researchers; p. 31, National Library of Medicine/Photo Researchers/Mark Marten; p. 33, Courtesy of the National Library of Medicine; p. 35, Elizabeth Crews/The Image Works; p. 37 (*top to bottom*), Dion Ogust/The Image Works, Elizabeth Crews, Bob Daemmrich/The Image Works, Bob Daemmrich/The Image Works; p. 38, © David Young-Wolff/PhotoEdit; p. 42, © Bob Daemmrich/Stone/GettyImages; p. 45, Will Faller; p. 47, Anderson/Photo Researchers; p. 52, McLaughlin/The Image Works; p. 58, © Nancy Sheehan/PhotoEdit; p. 60, © Ken Eward/Science Source/Photo Researchers; p. 64, CNRI/SPL/ Science Source, Photo Researchers; p. 65, Simon Fraser/RVI, Newcastle-upon-Tyne/Science Photo Library/Photo Researchers; p. 70, Gary Parker/ Science Photo Library/Photo Researchers; p. 71 (*top*), Med. Illus., (*bottom*), SBHS/Stone/GettyImages; p. 78, Petit Format/ Nestle/Science Source/ Photo Researchers; p. 81, John Giannicchi/Science Source/Photo Researchers; p. 83, Petit Format/Nestle/Science Source/Photo Researchers; p. 87, © 1997 George Steinmetz; p. 90, Rob Crandall/The Image Works; p. 93, © Paul Chesley/Stone/GettyImages; p. 96, © Mel Yates/FPG International; p. 98, Cliff Moore/Photo Researchers; p. 99, © Bob Daemmrich/ The Image Works; p. 100, S.I.U./Science Source/Photo Researchers; p. 101, Hattie Young/Photo Researchers; p. 102, © David J. Sams/Stone/ GettyImages; p. 104, © David Young-Wolff/Stone/GettyImages; p. 105, © Elizabeth Crews/The Image Works; p. 107, H. Dratch/The Image Works; p. 110 (*top to bottom*), J. Da Cunha/Petit Format/Science Source/Photo Researchers, Petit Format/J. M. Steinlein/Photo Researchers, Petit Format/ J. M. Steinlein/Photo Researchers, Diana Rasche/Stone/GettyImages, Petit Format/J. M. Steinlein/Photo Researchers; p. 111, Taeke Henstra/ Petit Format/Science Source; p. 112, Ellen Senisi/The Image Works; p. 113, Elizabeth Crews; p. 114 (*left, top and bottom*), E. Crews/The Image Works, (*right, top and bottom*), Elizabeth Crews, Sondra Dawes/The Image Works; p. 119, Barbara Peacock/FPG International; p. 121, © SuperStock; p. 125 (*top*), Doug Martin/Photo Researchers, (*bottom*) Susan Leavines/Photo Researchers; p. 132, Myrleen Ferguson Cate/ PhotoEdit; p. 134, SuperStock; p. 138, J. Sulley/The Image Works; p. 139, Ken Cavanagh/Photo Researchers; p. 140, © David Young-Wolff/Stone/ GettyImages; p. 141, © Michael Newman/PhotoEdit; p. 143, Richard Lord/The Image Works; p. 144, Bob Daemmrich/The Image Works; p. 146, Rosanne Kermoian; p. 148 (*top*), Photo courtesy of Dr. Carolyn Rovee-Collier, Director, Rutgers Early Learning Project, Rutgers University, (*bottom*) © Myrleen Ferguson Cate/PhotoEdit; p. 150, © Tony Freeman/PhotoEdit; p. 152, Cary/The Image Works; p. 158, © Dave Bartruff/Stock Boston; p. 161, © D. Greco/The Image Works; p. 165, A. Chaumat/Petit Format/Photo Researchers; p. 169, © Michael Wickes/ PhotoEdit; p. 171, © David Young-Wolff/PhotoEdit; p. 175, EyeWire/ GettyImages; p. 177, Network Prod./The Image Works; p. 178, Alan Carey/The Image Works; p. 179, David M. Grossman/Photo Researchers; p. 180, Greenlar/The Image Works; p. 181, Elizabeth Crews; p. 186,

© Dennis MacDonald/PhotoEdit; p. 189, © Myrleen F. Cate/PhotoEdit; p. 192, © Esbin-Anerson/The Image Works; p. 194, © D. Greco/The Image Works; p. 197, Eliazbeth Crews/The Image Works; p. 210, Alan Levanson/Stone/GettyImages; p. 212, The Image Bank/GettyImages; p. 219 (*top*) © SuperStock, (*bottom*) Will Faller; p. 221, Will Hart; p. 223, © SuperStock; p. 224, © Mark Richards/PhotoEdit; p. 226 (*top*) © Tony Freeman/PhotoEdit, (*bottom*) © Andy Sacks/Stone/GettyImages; p. 228, © Laura Dwight/PhotoEdit; p. 230, © Phil Schermeister/Stone/ GettyImages; p. 231, © Chuck Keeler/Stone/GettyImages; p. 233, Will Faller; p. 236, PhotoFest/Sesame Street, 1993; © Rosanne Olson/Stone/ GettyImages; p. 244, © Roseanne Olson/Stone/GettyImages; p. 246, Mary Kate Denny/Stone/GettyImages; p. 251, © Erika Stone/ Photo Researchers; p. 255, Townsend P. Dickinson; p. 258, B. Daemmrich/The Image Works; p. 260, Elizabeth Crews; p. 261, © Leonard Freed/Magnum Photos; p. 264, © Jose Carrillo/PhotoEdit; p. 270, © Tom Prettyman/ PhotoEdit; p. 273, E. Crews/The Image Works; p. 274, © Jonathan Morgan/ Stone/GettyImages; p. 276, E. Crews/The Image Works; p. 282, Will Faller; p. 284, Bob Daemmrich/Stone/GettyImages; p. 286, © Don Spiro/ Stone/GettyImages; p. 288, Will Hart; p. 292, Bill Cardoni/Liaison International; p. 293, Cern/Science Photo Library/Photo Researchers, Inc.; p. 297, Brian Smith; p. 299, PhotoFest, Courtesy of Warner Brothers; p. 300, (*top*) © Ellen Senisi/Photo Researchers, (*bottom*) Will Faller; p. 302, © Myrleen Ferguson/PhotoEdit; p. 303, © David Young-Wolff/PhotoEdit; p. 305, © Will Hart/PhotoEdit; p. 312, Ed Wray/AP/Wide World Photos; p. 314, © Laura Dwight/PhotoEdit; p. 317, © David Young-Wolff/ PhotoEdit; p. 321, © 1988 Paul Fusco/Magnum Photos, Inc.; p. 323, Paul Sakuma/AP/Wide World Photos; p. 326, © Martin Rogers/Stone/ GettyImages; p. 328, © Tom McCarthy/PhotoEdit; p. 331, B. Daemmrich/ The Image Works; p. 335, © Mark Lewis/Stone/GettyImages; p. 338, © Mary Kate Denny/PhotoEdit; p. 339, B. Bachman/The Image Works; p. 350, © Hunter Freeman/Stone/GettyImages; p. 352, © Marc Dolphin/ Stone/GettyImages; p. 355, © Bill Aron/Stone/GettyImages; p. 357, Suzanne Arm/The Image Works; p. 360, © Dwayne Newton/PhotoEdit; p. 363, © Jose Carillo/PhotoEdit; p. 365, Gary Walts/The Image Works; pg. 368, © Michelle Bridwell/PhotoEdit; p. 369, Richard T. Nowitz/Photo Researchers; p. 373, Will Hart; p. 376, D. Wray/The Image Works; p. 377, Will Faller; p. 383, © Neil Ricklen/PhotoEdit; p. 386, Courtesy of the Library of Congress; p. 389, © Don Smetzer/Stone/GettyImages; p. 390, Robert Clay/Monkmeyer; p. 391, © Michael Newman/PhotoEdit; p. 395, © David Young-Wolff/PhotoEdit; p. 396, © Journal Courier/The Image Works; p. 397, © Myrleen Cate/Stone/GettyImages; p. 399, Esbin/Anderson/The Image Works; p. 401, Douglas Burrows/Gamma Liaison; p. 403, © Mary Kate Denny/Stone/GettyImages; p. 410, © David Young-Wolff/Stone/ GettyImages; p. 412, © Richard Hutchings/PhotoEdit; p. 418, Vanessa Vick/ Photo Researchers; p. 419, AP/Wide World Photos; p. 420, © David Young-Wolff/PhotoEdit; p. 422, Robert Harbison; p. 423, © Michael Newman/ PhotoEdit; p. 427, Mark Reinstein/The Image Works; p. 428, © Robert Brenner/PhotoEdit; p. 431, Will Hart; p. 433 (*left*), © Tony Freeman/ PhotoEdit, (*right*) © David Young-Wolff/PhotoEdit; p. 434, © Myrleen F. Kate/PhotoEdit; p. 439, © David Young-Wolff/Stone/GettyImages; p. 441, Will Hart; p. 442, Paul Harris; p. 443, © Clea Photography/ PhotoEdit; p. 447, © David Young-Wolff/Stone/GettyImages; p. 448, © Mike Siluk/The Image Works; p. 450, © Bob Daemmrich/The Image Works; p. 455, Richard T. Nowitz; p. 456, © Richard Hutchings/PhotoEdit; p. 459, © Diane Graham-Henry/Stone/GettyImages; p. 460, Will Faller.

Glossary

acceleration programs educational programs that encourage children to move rapidly through the usual coursework, compressing the time usually spent in each course

accommodation changing a scheme to fit new information from the environment

acculturative stress stress associated with making a transition from one culture to another

active G-E interaction a situation in which the child seeks out environments compatible with his or her genotype

actual self how adolescents see themselves

adolescence the developmental period between childhood and adulthood

adolescent egocentrism an adolescent's belief that his or her thoughts and ideas are unique and are not understood by others

age of viability the point at which postnatal survival is likely

ambivalent attachment pattern characterized by inconsistent behavior toward a caregiver

amniocentesis a procedure used to determine whether genetic defects are present, in which amniotic fluid is collected

amnion a membrane that grows over the embryo and becomes filled with amniotic fluid, which protects the embryo

animism attributing lifelike qualities to objects that are not alive

anorexia nervosa an eating disorder, occurring most often in young women, in which individuals eat very little but believe that they are overweight

A-not-B error infants' tendency to search in the first hiding spot (A) while ignoring the second (B)

antisocial behavior a pattern of behavior that is aggressive, defiant, uncooperative, irresponsible, and/or dishonest

Apgar Scale a method of diagnosing potential problems in newborns, in which five vital signs are examined: respiration, reflex responsiveness, muscle tone, color, and heart rate

assimilated identifying with the majority culture and rejecting one's ethnic culture

assimilation directly processing information that fits a scheme

associational fluency ability to produce synonyms for a given word

associative play play in which various children engage, but with different goals

attachment theory explanation of development that focuses on the quality of the early emotional relationships developed between children and their caregivers

attachment an enduring emotional tie characterized by a tendency to seek and maintain closeness to a specific figure (the attachment figure), particularly under conditions of stress

attention-deficit hyperactivity disorder (ADHD) a disorder marked by an inappropriately low level of attention and inappropriately high levels of impulsivity and activity

authoritarian parenting a style of parenting in which parents try to shape, control, and judge the behaviors and attitudes of their children according to rigid standards of conduct

authoritative parenting a style of parenting in which parents encourage verbal give-and-take and share with their children the reasons behind discipline and household rules

autonomous morality stage Piagetian stage of moral development in which one believes that rules can be changed by the will of those involved

autonomy the ability to govern oneself and make independent decisions

autosomes the first twenty-two pairs of chromosomes, which account for most of the body cells

avoidant attachment pattern characterized by conspicuous avoidance of contact or interaction with the caregiver

axon long part of a neuron that is located at the cell base and sends messages to other neurons

babbling repeating consonant-vowel combinations, such as "mama" or "dada," two or more times

balanced polymorphism a kind of genetic diversity in which the genes that cause diseases provide certain genetic advantages as well as disadvantages

behavioral autonomy the capacity to make and follow through with decisions on regulating one's behavior

bicultural identifying with both the majority and the minority culture

blended family family structure formed when a widowed or divorced person remarries

Braxton-Hicks contractions mild, irregular contractions of the uterus experienced throughout pregnancy, especially during the last month or two

breech presentation fetal position in which the buttocks or feet lead the way

bulimia nervosa an eating disorder characterized by secret eating binges and purges

carriers people who are heterozygous for a recessive disorder

case study method in which the researcher collects information about aspects of a person's life

centration the tendency to focus attention on the most obvious and striking characteristic of an object while ignoring others

cephalocaudal development the principle that growth occurs from the head downwards

cesarean section procedure by which the fetus is delivered through an incision in the mother's abdomen

character education curriculum and instruction focused on students' conduct and models of traditional values and behaviors

child development changes in physical, social, emotional, and intellectual functioning over time, from conception through adolescence

child-directed speech a special version of language that caregivers use with their children; also called motherese

chorion a membrane that grows to surround the embryo after about one month of development and helps form the placenta

chorionic villus sampling (CVS) a procedure used to assess genetic material in fetal cells, in which cells are removed from the projections on the chorionic membrane

chromosomes the structures on which genes reside

class inclusion part-whole relations of categories

classical conditioning Pavlov's theory of how responses to neutral stimuli become conditioned

clinical interview method in which the researcher asks detailed questions while interacting with the participant

cliques small groups of peers, usually of the same sex and age, who interact with one another on a regular basis

code switching the alternate use of two or more languages

codons the parts of exons that provide coding information for amino acids in DNA

cognitive development involves development of mental processes used to process information, become aware, solve problems, and gain knowledge

cohort a group of individuals who are the same age or who experience similar events at the same time

cohort-sequential research design a cross-sectional study expanded so that data are collected from the same cohorts at different points in time

colostrum a pre-milk substance containing antibodies from the mother that protect the baby from infections

commitment the making of voluntary choices about life directions from among the many available options

compensation the understanding that one change can offset another

compliance obedience brought about by external pressures (such as the knowledge that one will be rewarded or punished for actions)

concrete operational stage Piaget's third stage of cognitive development (7 to 11 years), in which children begin to use logic to solve problems

conservation tasks tasks used to assess children's use of operations, in which children must decide whether a transformed object is the same as or different from what it was before

constructivist theories of learning educational approach in which students are encouraged to actively participate in their education

control group comparison group that is treated in the same way as the experimental group but does not receive the independent variable

control parameters the individual parts of a dynamic system

Conventional Level second level of Kohlberg's theory of moral development, in which moral reasoning is based on winning praise and recognition for good conduct and maintaining the social order

cooing making soft, repetitive vowel sounds such as "aah" and "ooh"

cooperative learning educational approach in which students work together in groups to solve problems

cooperative play play in which two or more children engage, with a common goal that requires social interaction

correlation coefficients calculated measures of the relations between variables

correlational study method in which researchers compare participants on two variables to determine whether the variables relate to each other

creativity novel and appropriate behavior that is different from what the person has done or seen before

crisis/exploration the process of making choices about life directions by considering options, values, and goals

critical periods periods during which specific biological or environmental events must occur if development is to proceed normally

cross-sectional study method in which individuals of different ages are tested at the same point in time and the results from each age group are compared

crowds peer groups defined by members' activities and social standing

crowning when the top of the baby's head becomes visible

cruise in infant development, to move around while holding onto things for support

deferred imitation imitation of behaviors that occurred in the past

delinquency the legal term for antisocial acts committed by juveniles

demandingness the tendency of parents to exert firm control over children, requiring them to act in mature and appropriate ways

dendrites parts of a neuron that are located on the cell body and receive messages from other neurons

dependent variable the behavior thought to be affected by the independent variable

developmental domains the three categories established to provide a basis for focusing on the specific areas of physical, cognitive, and social-emotional development

discipline attempts by parents to alter children's behaviors or attitudes

discovery learning educational approach in which students are encouraged to discover principles for themselves

discrimination acting in an unfavorable manner toward people because of their affiliation with a group

dishabituation an increase in attention to a new stimulus after an infant has habituated to a previous stimulus

disorganized/disoriented attachment pattern characterized by lack of a coherent strategy for handling separations from and reunions with the caregiver

dizygotic (DZ) twins twins who develop from two separate eggs fertilized by two separate sperm cells; fraternal twins

dominant gene a gene whose code is expressed when only one copy of the gene is present

double standard the imposition of different social expectations for males' and females' sexual attitudes and behavior

dynamic systems theory a theory based on the idea that complex systems form from basic and simple conditions without requiring a master plan for development

dysmenorrhea menstrual cramps and discomfort

eating disturbances mild versions of eating disorders

ecological model Bronfenbrenner's model of the different spheres of influence

ectopic pregnancy a pregnancy that occurs outside the uterus

ego the part of the psyche that is the source of reason and operates within the conditions and demands of the real world

egocentric speech Piaget's term for speech directed toward the self

egocentrism the assumption, characteristic of most preschoolers, that their own perspective is shared by other people

elaboration memory strategy involving the forming of associations among objects

embryonic stage the second stage of prenatal development, which begins at implantation and lasts until about eight weeks

emergent literacy educational approach in which it is assumed that children will naturally develop the skills involved in written and oral language and gradually improve these skills as they grow older

emotional autonomy the ability to understand oneself as a person who is emotionally distinct from one's parents

emotion-focused coping strategies efforts to manage or reduce the emotional distress that is aroused in a stressful situation

empathy an emotional state that matches another person's emotional state—for instance, feeling bad because someone else is feeling bad

empirically based based on observation and experimentation

endogenous smile smile that is triggered by changes in nervous system activity and involves only the lower face muscles

enrichment programs educational programs that encourage problem solving and creative activities through independent study or individualized instruction and mentoring

epidural block a common method for controlling the pain of labor, in which a local anesthetic is delivered to block pain in the region from the waist to the feet

episiotomy a small incision made in the skin below the vagina to prevent tearing of the vaginal tissues as the baby emerges

ethnic identity the sense of belonging to an ethnic group

ethnicity a group whose members share a common cultural heritage and a sense of belonging

ethological theory explanation of development that focuses on the causes and adaptive value of behavior, considering both the evolutionary history of the species and the social context

evocative G-E interaction a situation in which the child's genotype draws responses from others

evolutionary theories explanations of development that focus on how behaviors promote the survival of the individual and the species

exogenous smile smile that is triggered by external stimuli

exons the parts of DNA providing protein-coding information

exosystem the part of the ecological model that represents the linkages among settings, one of which does not include the child, and how these influence development

expansion taking young children's simplified language and adding complexity and completeness to it

experimental group group that receives the independent variable

experimental study method in which scientists bring people into a laboratory where the situation is manipulated and the effects of the manipulation are noted

expressive language style language style focused on using words to regulate social interactions with adults

expressive language children's ability to produce language

extended family family structure consisting of one or more parents, one or more of the parents' children, and one or more other relatives living together in one household

externalizing problems psychological difficulties that involve acting out against society

extinction reducing unwanted behavior by withholding all positive consequences

fact a statement, based on observation, with which many people would agree

failure to thrive (FTT) a term used to describe infants and children who do not grow at the expected rates

false labor moderately intense, rhythmic contractions late in the pregnancy

fast mapping associating the sound of a word with the concept the word stands for, sometimes in a single exposure

fetal alcohol effects (FAE) the effects, including mildly retarded physical development and learning disabilities, that may occur if a mother drinks moderately during pregnancy

fetal alcohol syndrome (FAS) a constellation of problems, including physical deformities and intellectual deficits, that may occur if a mother drinks heavily during pregnancy

fetal stage the third and final stage of prenatal development, which begins at about eight weeks and lasts until birth

foreclosure identity status of those adolescents who have not explored alternatives but nonetheless have made a definite commitment to a specific identity

formal operational stage Piaget's fourth stage of cognitive development (begins around the age of 11), in which individuals are capable of applying logical principles to hypothetical and abstract situations

fragile X syndrome a condition passed on by sex-linked transmission and characterized by protruding ears, prominent jaw, unusual speech, poor eye contact, and mild to moderate retardation

functional isolation the increased disengagement from one's social and physical environments that may result from a poor environment and inadequate nutrition

gender consistency understanding that gender does not change despite changes in appearance or activities

gender identity understanding and acceptance that one is a boy or a girl

gender labeling labeling oneself and others on the basis of gender group

gender schemas mental representations about the sexes

gender stability understanding that gender is stable over time

gender stereotypes beliefs people share about the typical characteristics of males and females

gene-environment (G-E) interaction a situation in which the influence of a gene varies depending on its environment

generation gap a conflict of basic interests, beliefs, and values between youth and their parents

generative learning educational approach in which students are taught how to use specific methods of problem solving to integrate new information with pre-existing information

genes the structures containing the code that provides the blueprint for development

genotype a person's genetic code

germinal stage the first stage of prenatal development, which begins at conception and lasts until the fertilized egg implants itself in the uterine wall

goal-corrected partnership an attachment relationship in which the child becomes a partner in planning how the relationship develops

gonadotropins chemical messengers that stimulate the production of hormones by the glands

habituation a decrease in attention to a stimulus that has been presented repeatedly

heritability an estimate of the degree to which variation of a characteristic in a population is influenced by genetic factors

heteronomous morality stage Piagetian stage of moral development in which children adhere strictly to rules and base moral decisions on the authority of others

heterosexual having a sexual attraction to members of the other sex

heterozygous describes a child's condition with respect to a trait when each parent has contributed a different copy of the gene for that trait to their child

heuristic a shortcut or rule of thumb used to help solve a problem

holophrases individual words that convey as much meaning as whole sentences

homosexual having a sexual attraction to members of the same sex

homozygous describes a child's condition with respect to a trait when both parents have contributed identical copies of the gene for that trait to their child

hostile aggression aggression directed against another person, generally in retaliation for his or her actions

hypothetico-deductive reasoning the type of reasoning used in science

id the part of the psyche that is primitive and instinctual

identity achieved identity status of those adolescents who have experienced a period of exploration and crisis and have made a commitment

identity concept the essential "sameness" of an object despite physical changes to it

identity confused identity status of those adolescents who have not explored or committed themselves to a specific identity choice

identity diffusion an incomplete sense of self

identity one's sense of who one is, where one has been, and where one is going in life

image schemas primitive notions, based on the visual appearance of objects, that lay a foundation for thinking about them

imaginary audience a characteristic of adolescents' self-consciousness, involving the feeling that they are on stage with people watching their every move

immanent justice the belief that breaking a rule always leads to punishment

independent variable condition that is assumed to be the cause of the behavior and is manipulated by the scientist

inductive reasoning disciplinary techniques in which parents use reasoning and verbal communication for the purpose of changing children's behavior

infantile amnesia inability to recall events that occurred very early in life

information processing theory explanations for development that are based on a model in which people have limited capacities for learning but can flexibly apply strategies to find ways around those limitations

innate fears fears that are inborn and reflexive

instrumental aggression aggression used for a specific purpose

internalization obedience based on internal controls and standards that children have incorporated into their own expectations of themselves

internalizing problems psychological difficulties, such as anxiety or depression, that involve a focus on or within the self

Internet a global network of computers

introns the noncoding parts of DNA

iron-deficiency anemia a nutrient deficiency common in infants and toddlers

just community schools schools in which students participate in a democratic community and decisions are made through consensus rather than by majority rule

juvenile an individual who is not yet an adult in the eyes of the law

karyotype a photograph of chromosomes, used by geneticists to align each chromosome with the other member of its pair

kwashiorkor a form of protein-energy malnutrition in which only protein is deficient

language acquisition device (LAD) in biological theory, a part of the brain that allows children to understand the properties of all human languages

latchkey children children who are left unsupervised during the day or return home to an empty house after school

learning changes that occur as the result of observation, experience, instruction, or practice

libido the source of action and sexual desire

lightening when the fetus drops into the pelvic cavity, decreasing pressure on the mother's diaphragm

longitudinal study method in which the same group of individuals is tested at different points in time

long-term memory the part of the information processing system that has an unlimited capacity for storing information over long periods of time

love withdrawal disciplinary techniques in which parents ignore, withhold affection from, or express lack of love for the child

low birthweight term describing infants born after 37 weeks' gestation but weighing less than 5½ pounds

macrosystem the outermost sphere of the ecological model, which represents societal values and attitudes

mainstreaming including children with all sorts of disabilities in regular classrooms

manipulative tantrums tantrums children throw to manipulate others into giving them what they want

marasmus a form of protein-energy malnutrition involving severe body wasting

marginal living within the majority culture but feeling alienated or outcast

maturation changes brought about largely as a result of the unfolding of one's genetic code

meiosis the process of cell replication undergone by ova and sperm, involving one duplication of chromosomes and two cell divisions, resulting in twenty-three chromosomes

menarche the onset of the menstrual cycle

mental retardation condition characterized by subaverage general intellectual functioning and impaired adaptive functioning, with onset in childhood

mental rotation the ability to imagine how objects would appear if their positions were rotated

mesosystem the middle sphere of the ecological model, which encompasses the connections among settings including the child and how these connections influence the child

metacognition awareness of memory and monitoring of memory performance

microsystem the inner sphere of the ecological model, which represents the immediate environment and includes influences such as physical objects, the structure of the environment, and the roles of and relationships among family members

minimal distance principle (MDP) the assumption that the noun most closely preceding the verb is the subject of the sentence

mitosis the process of cell replication involving one duplication of chromosomes and one cell division, resulting in twenty-three pairs of chromosomes (forty-six total)

molding when the bones of the baby's skull, which are not yet fused, press together and even overlap to accommodate passage through the birth canal

monozygotic (MZ) twins twins who share the same genetic code because they developed from one fertilized egg, which divided into two separate individuals; identical twins

moral domain issues that concern universal principles reflecting concepts of harm, welfare, and fairness

moral realism the belief that morality is based on conforming to established rules set by powerful adults

morality a set of principles or values that helps individuals distinguish right from wrong

moratorium identity status of those adolescents who are actively exploring identity issues but have not yet made any firm commitment

multicultural education educational practices and curricula that present non-European perspectives or improve educational outcomes for students from a wide spectrum of backgrounds

multiparous women women who have previously given birth

multiracial a term used to describe people who are of two or more races

myelination the process in which a neuron is sheathed in a smooth layer of fatty proteins (myelin)

natural selection the process, in nature, whereby individuals who are best adapted to their surroundings survive and reproduce, and the adaptive characteristics of those individuals are passed on to the next generation

naturalistic study method in which researchers observe the behavior of people in their natural environments

nature versus nurture debate controversy over the extent to which biological/genetic and environmental factors influence development

negative reinforcement removal of a negative or aversive stimulus, which increases the likelihood that a behavior will recur

neglect failure to provide shelter, clothing, or protection for a child

neglected children children who are reasonably well liked by their peers but lack friends

Neonatal Behavioral Assessment Scale a measure commonly used to assess a newborn's responses to the environment

neonate an infant who is in the first one to two months of life

neurodevelopmental approaches explanations of development that focus on the relationship of brain development to behavior and thinking

neurons the nerve cells that make up the communication system of the brain

nuclear family family structure in which the biological mother and father and their children live together

obese weighing more than 20 percent over one's ideal weight (based on height, sex, and body composition)

object permanence the concept that people and objects have an independent existence beyond one's own perception of them

onlooker play play in which one child watches another child or children but does not directly participate

operant conditioning learning based on the principle that the consequences of a behavior affect the likelihood that the behavior will be repeated

operations actions internalized as symbols that can be reversed and coordinated

organization memory strategy involving the clustering of information into groups of similar objects or into meaningful categories

overextension the use of words to refer to objects or things that are outside the bounds of the category named by the word

overregularization application of language rules when they do not apply

ovum a human egg

parallel play play in which two or more children engage in the same activity at the same time and place, but each child still plays separately

parity the number and spacing of children a woman bears

passive G-E interaction a situation in which parents provide a rearing environment that matches the child's own genotype

permissive parenting a style of parenting in which parents make few demands on their children—they are accepting and tolerant of their children's impulses and desires

personal domain issues that reflect personal preference and taste and are not socially regulated

personal fable a story adolescents tell themselves that emphasizes their uniqueness and invulnerability

personality a person's unique behavioral, motivational, and mental styles of responding

phenotype the outward expression of the genotype

phobias persistent and irrational fears that significantly affect social functioning

phonemes the sounds of a language that are the basis for word construction

phonemic awareness knowledge of permissible and nonpermissible strings of sounds in one's native language

phonics approach technique used to teach children to read, in which children are trained to translate letters and groups of letters into sounds

physical abuse abuse that causes death, serious physical harm, or imminent risk of serious harm

physical development involves growth and change in a person's body and bodily functions

physical fitness a state of physical well-being that allows a person to function effectively without undue fatigue

placenta the structure through which nutrients and waste products are exchanged between the mother and the developing embryo

placental barrier a line of protection for the unborn child, created by blood vessel walls that separate the maternal and fetal circulatory systems

positive reinforcement presentation of stimuli that increase the likelihood that a behavior will recur

possible self how adolescents wish themselves to be in the future

Postconventional Level third level of Kohlberg's theory of moral development, in which judgments about morality are based on principles that the individual is personally committed to and that are shared by others

postpartum depression intense feelings of sadness, anxiety, or despair experienced by a mother after the birth of a child

power assertion disciplinary techniques in which parents use physical force or threats of physical force to control children's behavior

pragmatics the practical rules guiding the use of verbal and nonverbal communication in differing situations

precocious puberty extremely early puberty, often caused by a genetic disorder

Preconventional Level first level of Kohlberg's theory of moral development, in which morality is based on external forces

prejudice preconceived ideas about a person or group of people, often based on physical characteristics, ethnicity, or race

premenstrual syndrome (PMS) a whole constellation of emotional and physical symptoms, such as backaches, headaches, moodiness, and water retention, that occur before menstruation

premoral period Piagetian stage of moral development in which young children do not yet understand cooperative rules and goals

preoperational stage Piaget's second stage of cognitive development (2 to 7 years), in which children begin to think in symbols but are egocentric and perceptually bound in their thinking

pretend play play in which children let objects or persons symbolize things or people they are not

preterm or **premature** term describing infants born prior to 37 weeks' gestation

primary circular reactions repetitive actions that are centered on an infant's own body and motions

primary prevention efforts targeted at the population as a whole, to sensitize people to basic issues or to provide particular skills

primary sexual characteristics physical features directly related to reproduction, such as the ovaries, penis, and testes

primiparous women women who are having their first child

private speech Vygotsky's term for speech directed toward the self, used when solving problems

problem-focused coping strategies efforts to manage or modify the source of a stressful situation

prodigies children who show exceptional abilities at a very young age in one domain of intelligence but not necessarily in others

prosocial behavior voluntary actions intended to benefit another person

proximodistal development the principle that body parts closer to the central axis of the body develop first, while those farther away from the center of the body develop later

psychoanalytic theories explanations of development that focus on the unconscious drives and forces that develop within the mind

psychological maltreatment emotional abuse caused by threatening harm or conveying to an individual that she or he is worthless, unloved, or unwanted

psychosexual development Freud's stage theory of development, based on how the libido is transformed into different structures and modes of expression

psychosocial crises in Erikson's lifespan theory, the struggles that occur at the various stages of development between two conflicting personality characteristics

psychosocial moratorium a period during which youths are reasonably free of adult responsibilities that might prevent them from adequately addressing identity issues

puberty developmental milestone reached when a person becomes sexually mature and capable of having children

pubescence the period of time during which sexual maturation takes place

punishment application of unpleasant consequences to decrease the likelihood that a behavior will be repeated

quickening fetal movements during pregnancy

race a group whose members share a genetic heritage

random assignment randomly assigning people to groups in a study so that the effects of uncontrolled variables will be the same for all groups in the study

random sampling selecting participants for a study at random

rate-limiting component the slowest, or last-developing, part of a dynamic system

receptive language children's understanding of language

recessive gene a gene whose code is not expressed in the presence of a dominant gene

referential language style language style focused on developing a vocabulary that includes many object names

reflective abstraction the ability to rearrange and rethink information already acquired

reflexes simple, coordinated, unlearned responses

rehearsal memory strategy involving the reviewing of information

rejected children children who are overtly disliked by their peers

relational aggression aggression designed to damage someone's relationships with others, by withdrawing friendship, excluding someone from a group, and so on

relational play actions demonstrating an understanding of the relationship between two objects

resilience the capacity to bounce back or recover from stressful situations

responsiveness the tendency of parents to be warm, accepting, and willing to take into account the wishes and feelings of the child

reversible thinking the understanding that actions can be undone or reversed

risk-taking behavior a syndrome of multiple behavior problems

rites of passage initiations that mark an adolescent's new status and roles within the community

savants people who show exceptional abilities in one domain of intelligence but have retarded mental development in some other domains

scaffolding informal teaching methods that guide children's participation in daily events

schematic consistency the tendency of children's behavior and thinking to match their schemas

schemes cognitive guides, or blueprints, for processing information about the world

school phobia an extreme fear associated with school environments

scripts concepts that people form about routines involved in everyday interactions and events

secondary circular reactions repetitive actions focused on the qualities of objects, such as the noises they make or their shapes and colors

secondary prevention efforts targeted at a specific segment of the population thought to be at high risk

secondary sexual characteristics features that are outward manifestations of sexual development but are not directly involved in reproduction, such as breasts, facial and body hair, and an adult body shape

secure attachment pattern in which infants use their attachment figures as a secure base, obtaining comfort from their presence and becoming distressed by their absence

self-concept an individual's beliefs about the attributes and capacities she or he possesses

self-conscious emotions those emotions that involve injury to or enhancement of one's sense of self (such as pride and shame)

self-esteem the value an individual attaches to the mental picture of himself or herself

semantic bootstrapping children's use of word meaning to provide cues about syntax

semantics the meanings associated with words

sensitive periods periods of time that are optimal for the development of certain behaviors or functions

sensorimotor stage Piaget's first stage of cognitive development (0 to 2 years), in which the child relates to objects and people through his or her senses and motor skills

sensory register the part of the information processing system that allows people to very briefly retain information taken in through the senses

separated identifying only with one's ethnic culture and rejecting the majority culture

separation anxiety a response in which negative protests accompany separation from attachment figures

sex chromosomes the twenty-third pair of chromosomes, which accounts for a person's sex

sexual abuse abuse that involves engaging in sexual activity

sexual orientation characteristic determined by the sex of the sexual partners one is attracted to

sexually transmitted diseases (STDs) diseases that may be transmitted from one person to another through sexual contact

shaping the process of rewarding behaviors that approximate the desired behavior

short-term memory the part of the information processing system that holds information long enough for the person to evaluate and selectively act on the input

single-parent family family structure in which children live with only their mother or their father

social cognition thinking about people and interpersonal relationships

social communicative competence the ability to effectively convey an intended message to others

social competence the ability to use age-appropriate social behaviors to enhance peer relationships without harming anyone

social learning theory Bandura's theory that individuals are greatly influenced by observing and imitating other people

social perspective taking the ability to move away from one's own perspective and recognize what others perceive

social smile smile that is triggered by social stimuli (such as the mother's face)

social-conventional domain issues and actions that are defined as right or wrong because of a social agreement that they are so

social-emotional development involves development of processes related to one's interactions with others

socialization the process by which children learn social roles and become members of groups

solitary play play in which a child is alone, even if surrounded by other children

spatial perception the ability to locate the horizontal or vertical while ignoring distracting information

spatial visualization the ability to find figures and shapes hidden within other figures

spatial-visual skills the cognitive abilities involved in orienting oneself in the environment

spermatids the result of the division of spermatocytes, each one containing twenty-three chromosomes and including either an X or a Y sex chromosome

spermatocytes sperm in the early stages of development, at which time each one contains forty-six chromosomes, including one X and one Y sex chromosome

spermatogenesis the process by which sperm develop

spermatozoa mature spermatids, which are fully functional and capable of fertilizing a human ovum

state of arousal the degree to which an infant is alert, attentive, and awake

static thinking the tendency to attend more to the outcome than to the changes that produced the outcome

status offenses acts that are illegal for juveniles but not for adults, such as running away from home

stepfamily family structure formed when a person who has children from a former marriage remarries

Strange Situation a procedure used to assess infants' attachment behavior under conditions of increasing stress due to separations from caregivers and strangers

stranger anxiety a wary and fearful reaction to strangers

superego the part of the psyche that represents one's conscience and morals and social conventions

survey study method in which a number of people respond to a set of structured questions

symbolic representation the use of mental symbols to represent objects

symbolic representations mental representations of objects and people that can be manipulated in the mind

sympathy feeling sorry or concerned for other people because of their emotional states or conditions

synapses small gaps, or spaces, between the cells through which information is transmitted from one neuron to the next

syntactic bootstrapping children's use of the structure of sentences to provide cues about word meaning

syntax the grammar, or rules, of a language

teenager a youth between 13 and 19 years of age

telegraphic speech early language in which only highly informative words are used and less informative words are neglected

temperament the predisposition to respond in certain enduring and characteristic ways to one's environment

temperamental tantrums anger response when some aspect of a child's style of interacting has been violated

teratogens agents that cross the placental barrier and cause or increase the incidence of physical malformations and behavioral and cognitive deficits

tertiary circular reactions subtle modifications infants make in their behavior so as to explore the effects of those modifications

tertiary prevention efforts directed at preventing or decreasing the reoccurrence of an event that has already occurred

theory of mind the understanding of inner mental events—that people think, imagine, pretend, and wonder about the world around them

theory a structured set of ideas that attempts to organize and explain facts

transactional perspective the view that development occurs as the result of the interplay between the diversity of qualities individuals bring to their environments and the diversity of environments individuals experience

transductive reasoning the inference that if two particular examples or events occur together, they must be causally related

transverse presentation fetal position in which the shoulders and arms lead the way

ultrasound a procedure used to identify some developmental problems, in which video images of the fetus and the fetus's internal organs are produced from the echoes of sound waves

umbilical cord the lifeline of the embryo, consisting of two arteries and one vein

underextension the use of words to refer to a smaller group than the word actually names

uninvolved parenting a style of parenting in which parents make few demands on their children and are unresponsive or rejecting

values autonomy the capacity to make judgments and choices about personal beliefs and principles

vernix caseosa a white, waxy covering that provides the infant with protection from bacteria

vicarious reinforcement learning by watching the consequences to others of their behaviors

visual cliff apparatus a checkerboard pattern covered with Plexiglas, used to create an illusion of depth

whole language approach technique used to teach children to read, in which learning to read is assumed to be a natural process that occurs most effectively in a print-rich environment

youth a broad, nonspecific term for the younger generation—children, adolescents, and young adults

zone of proximal development Vygotsky's term for the distance between what a child can do unaided and what a child can do through interaction with skilled helpers

zygote the fertilized ovum

References

Abbott, S. (1997). Gender, status, and values among Kikuyu and Appalachian adolescents. In T. S. Weisner & C. Bradley (Eds.), *African families and the crisis of social change* (pp. 86–105). Westport, CT: Bergin & Garvey/Greenwood Publishing Group.

Abel, E. L. (1996). Introduction. In E. Abel (Ed.), *Fetal alcohol syndrome.* Boca Raton, FL: CRC Press.

Aber, J. L., Jones, S. M., Brown, J. L., Chaudry, N., & Samples, F. (1998). Resolving conflict creatively: Evaluating the developmental effects of a school-based violence prevention program in neighborhood and classroom context. *Development and Psychopathology, 10,* 187–213.

Aber, J. L., Jones, S. M., & Cohen, J. (2000). The impact of poverty on the mental health and development of very young children. In C. H. Zeanah (Ed.), *Handbook of infant mental health* (pp. 113–128). New York: Guilford.

Aboud, F. E. (1988). *Children and prejudice.* New York: Blackwell.

Aboud, F. E., & Doyle, A. B. (1996). Parental and peer influences on children's racial attitudes. *International Journal of Intercultural Relations, 20,* 371–383.

Aboud, F. E., & Levy, S. R. (2000). Interventions to reduce prejudice and discrimination in children and adolescents. In S. Oskamp (Ed.), *Reducing prejudice and discrimination: The Claremont symposium on applied social psychology* (pp. 269–293). Mahwah, NJ: Erlbaum.

Abrams, S. M., Field, T., Scafidi, F., & Prodromidis, M. (1995). Newborns of depressed mothers. *Infants Mental Health Journal, 16,* 233–239.

Achenbach, T. M., & Edelbrock, C. (1989). Diagnostic, taxonomic, and assessment issues. In T. H. Ollendick & M. Hersen (Eds.), *Handbook of child psychopathology* (pp. 53–69). New York: Plenum.

Acredolo, L., & Goodwyn, S. (1988). Symbolic gesturing in normal infants. *Child Development, 59,* 450–466.

Acredolo, L., & Goodwyn, S. (1996). *Baby signs.* New York: Contemporary Books.

Adams, M. J., Treiman, R., & Pressley, M. (1998). Reading, writing, and literacy. In W. Damon (Ed.), *Handbook of child psychology* (Vol. 4, pp. 275–356). New York: Wiley.

Adams, R. J. (1989). Newborn's discrimination among mid- and long-wave length stimuli. *Journal of Experimental Child Psychology, 47,* 130–141.

Adams, W. G., Geva, J., Coffman, J., Palfrey, S., & Bauchner, H. (1998). Anemia and elevated lead levels in underimmunized inner-city children. *Pediatrics, 101,* 1–7.

Adler, P. A., Kless, S. J., & Adler, P. (1992). Socialization to gender roles: Popularity among elementary school boys and girls. *Sociology of Education, 65,* 169–187.

Adolph, K. E. (1997). Learning in the development of infant locomotion. *Monographs of the Society for Research in Child Development 3,* Serial No. 251.

Adoption and Foster Care Analysis and Reporting System. (2001). *The AFCARS Report.* Washington, DC: Children's Bureau.

Agency for Healthcare Research and Quality. (2001). *Healthcare cost and utilization project.* Rockville, MD: Agency for Healthcare Research and Quality.

Ager, A., & Young, M. (2001). Cultivating the psychosocial health of refugees. In M. MacLachlan (Ed.), *Cultivating health: Cultural perspectives on promoting health* (pp. 177–197). New York: Wiley.

Aharoni, A., Keizer, L. C., Bouwmeester, H. J., Sun, Z., Alvarez-Huerta, M., Verhoeven, H. A., Blaas, J., van Houwelingen, A. M., De Vos, R. C., van der Voet, H., Jansen, R. C., Guis, M., Mol, J., Davis, R. W., Schena, M., van Tunen, A. J., & O'Connell, A. P. (2000). Identification of the SAAT gene involved in strawberry flavor biogenesis by use of DNA microarrays. *Plant Cell, 12,* 647–662.

Ainsworth, M. D. (1973). The development of infant-mother attachment. In B. M. Caldwell & H. N Ricciuti (Eds.), *Review of child development research* (Vol. 3, pp. 1–94). Chicago: University of Chicago Press.

Ainsworth, M. D., Blehar, M. C., Waters, E., & Wall, S. (1978). *Patterns of attachment: A psychological study of the strange situation.* Hillsdale, NJ: Erlbaum.

Akbas, S. H., Ozben, T., Alper, O., Ugar, A., Yucel, G., & Luleci, G. (2001). Maternal serum screening for Down's syndrome. *Clinical Chemisty and Laboratory Medicine, 39,* 487–490.

Akhtar, N., Carpenter, M., & Tomasello, M. (1996). The role of discourse novelty in early word learning. *Child Development, 67,* 635–645.

Alaimo, K., Olson, C. M., & Frongillo, E. A. (2001). Food insufficiency and American school-aged children's cognitive, academic, and psychosocial development. *Pediatrics, 108,* 44–53.

Alan Guttmacher Institute. (1997). *The risk and realities of early childbearing worldwide, facts in brief.* New York: Alan Guttmacher Institute.

Alan Guttmacher Institute. (1999). *Teen sex and pregnancy.* New York: Alan Guttmacher Institute.

Alan Guttmacher Institute. (2001). *Teenagers' sexual and reproductive health.* New York: Alan Guttmacher Institute.

Alessandri, S. M., Sullivan, M. W., Imaizumi, S., & Lewis, M. (1993). Learning and emotional responsivity in cocaine-exposed infants. *Developmental Psychology, 29,* 989–997.

Alexander, J. M., Bloom, S. L., McIntire, D. D., & Leveno, K. J. (1999). Severe preeclampsia and the very low birth weight infant: Is induction of labor harmful? *Obstetrics and Gynecology, 93,* 485–488.

Alfieri, T., Ruble, D. N., & Higgins, E. T. (1996). Gender stereotypes during adolescence: Developmental changes and the transition to junior high school. *Developmental Psychology, 32,* 1129–1137.

Allen, L., & Mitchell, C. M. (1996). Poverty and adolescent health. In M. Kagawa-Singer & P. A. Katz (Eds.), *Health issues for minority adolescents* (pp. 1–35). Lincoln, NE: University of Nebraska Press.

Allen, M. C. (1993). The high-risk infant. *Pediatric Clinics of North America, 40,* 479–490.

Allen, M. C. (1996). The neonatal neurodevelopmental examination. In A. J. Capute and P. J. Accardo (Eds.), *Developmental disabilities in infancy and childhood* (pp. 293–310). Baltimore: Paul H. Brookes.

Allen, M. C., Donohue, P. K., & Dusman, A. E. (1993). The limit of viability—neonatal outcome of infants born at 22 to 25 weeks' gestation. *New England Journal of Medicine, 329,* 1597–1601.

Alsaker, F. D. (1992). Pubertal timing, overweight, and psychological adjustment. *Journal of Early Adolescence, 12,* 396–412.

Alsaker, F. D. (1995). Timing of puberty and reactions to pubertal changes. In M. Rutter (Ed.), *Psychosocial disturbances in young people: Challenges for prevention* (pp. 37–82). New York: Cambridge University Press.

Alsaker, F. D. (1996). Annotation: The impact of puberty. *Journal of Child Psychology and Psychiatry, 37,* 249–258.

Altarriba, J. (1993). The influence of culture on cognitive processes. In J. Altarriba (Ed.), *Cognition and culture* (pp. 379–385). Amsterdam: North-Holland.

Amabile, T. M. (1993). What does a theory of creativity require? *Psychological Inquiry, 4,* 179–181.

Amabile, T. M. (2001). Beyond talent: John Irving and the passionate craft of creativity. *American Psychologist, 56,* 333–336.

Amato, M. (1997, April). Can this baby be soothed? *Child, 12,* 32–34.

Amato, P. R. (2000). The consequences of divorce for adults and children. *Journal of Marriage and the Family, 62,* 1269–1287.

Ambert, A. M. (1997). *Parents, children, and adolescents: Interactive relationships and development in context.* New York: Haworth Press.

American Academy of Pediatrics. (1991). *Recommendations for preventive pediatric health care.* Elk Grove, IL: American Academy of Pediatrics.

American Academy of Pediatrics. (1996). *Smoking: Straight talk for teens.* Elk Grove, IL: American Academy of Pediatrics.

American Academy of Pediatrics. (1998). In-line skating injuries in children and adolescents. *Pediatrics, 101,* 720–722.

American Academy of Pediatrics. (1999a). *Lead screening for children.* Elk Grove, IL: American Academy of Pediatrics.

American Academy of Pediatrics. (1999b). *2 to 4 years: Safety for your child.* Elk Grove, IL: American Academy of Pediatrics.

American Academy of Pediatrics. (2001). *Reduce the risk of SIDS.* Elk Grove, IL: American Academy of Pediatrics.

American Association of University Women. (1994). *Shortchanging girls, shortchanging America.* Washington, DC: Greenberg-Lake Analysis Group.

American College of Obstetricians and Gynecologists. (2000). *Planning your pregnancy and birth.* Chicago: American College of Obstetricians and Gynecologists.

American Heart Association. (2001). *Targeting the facts.* Dallas, TX: American Heart Association.

American Medical Association. (1996). *Physicians' guide to media violence.* Washington, DC: American Medical Association.

American Psychiatric Association. (1994). *Diagnostic and Statistical Manual of Mental Disorders* (Fourth Edition). Washington, DC: American Psychiatric Association.

American Psychological Association. (1993). *Violence and youth: Psychology's response. Volume I: Summary report of the American Psychological Association Commission on Violence and Youth.* Washington, DC: American Psychological Association.

Ames, N. L., & Miller, E. (1994). *Changing middle schools.* San Francisco: Jossey-Bass.

Anand, K. J. S., & Hickey, P. R. (1987). Pain and its effects in the human neonate and fetus. *New England Journal of Medicine, 137,* 1321–1329.

Anastasi, A. (1988). *Psychological testing.* New York: Macmillan.

Anderman, E. M., Eccles, J. S., Yoon, K. S., Roeser, R., Wigfield, A., & Blemnfeld, P. (2001). Learning to value mathematics and reading: Relations to mastery and performance-oriented instructional practices. *Contemporary Educational Psychology, 26,* 76–95.

Anderson, C. A., & Ford, C. M. (1986). Affect of the game player: Short-term effects of highly and mildly aggressive video games. *Personality and Social Psychology Bulletin, 12,* 390–402.

Anderson, D. R., Huston, A. C., Schmitt, K. L., Linebarger, D. L., & Wright, J. C. (2001). Early childhood television viewing and adolescent behavior: The recontact study. *Monographs of the Society for Research in Child Development, 66* (Whole No. 264).

Andersson, T., & Magnusson, D. (1990). Biological maturation in adolescence and the development of drinking habits and alcohol abuse among young males: A prospective longitudinal study. *Journal of Youth and Adolescence, 19,* 33–41.

Ando, K. (1987, July). *The development of empathy in prosocial behavior.* Paper presented to the International Society for the Study of Behavioral Development, Tokyo.

Andres, R. L., & Jones, K. L. (1994). Social and illicit drug use in pregnancy. In R. K. Creasy & R. Resnik (Eds.), *Maternal-fetal medicine: Principles and practice* (pp. 237–287). Philadelphia: Saunders.

Anglin, J. M. (1985). The child's expressible knowledge of word concepts. In K. E. Nelson (Ed.), *Children's language* (pp. 77–127). Hillsdale, NJ: Erlbaum.

Anglin, J. M. (1993). Vocabulary development. *Monographs of the Society for Research in Child Development, 58* (Whole No. 165).

Antill, J. K., Russell, G., Goodnow, J. J., & Cotton, S. (1993). Measures of children's sex typing in middle childhood. *Australian Journal of Psychology, 45,* 25–33.

Antonucci, T. C., & Mikus, K. (1988). The power of parenthood: Personality and attitudinal changes during the transition to parenthood. In G. Y. Michaels & W. A. Goldberg (Eds.), *The transition to parenthood: Current theory and research* (pp. 62–84). New York: Cambridge University Press.

Aoki, W. T., & Turk, A. A. (1997). Adolescent suicide: A review of risk factors and implications for practice. *Journal of Psychology and Christianity, 16,* 273–279.

Apgar, V. A. (1953). Proposal for a new method of evaluation of the newborn infant. *Anesthesia and Analgesia, Current Research, 22,* 260.

Appel, A. E., & Holden, G. W. (1998). The co-occurrence of spouse and physical child abuse: A review and appraisal. *Journal of Family Psychology, 12,* 578–599.

Archer, S. L. (1993). Identity in relational contexts. In J. Kroger (Ed.), *Discussions on ego identity* (pp. 75–99). Hillsdale, NJ: Erlbaum.

Arcia, E., & Conners, C. K. (1998). Gender differences in ADHD? *Journal of Developmental and Behavioral Pediatrics, 19,* 77–83.

Arditti, J. A. (1992). Investigating differences between joint custody and noncustodial fathers. *American Journal of Orthopsychiatry, 62,* 186–195.

Arditti, J. A., & Keith, T. Z. (1993). Visitation frequency, child support payment, and the father-child relationship postdivorce. *Journal of Marriage and the Family, 55,* 699–712.

Arend, R., Gove, F. L., & Sroufe, L. A. (1979). Continuity of individual adaptation from infancy to kindergarten: A predictive study of ego-resiliency and curiosity in preschoolers. *Child Development, 50,* 950–959.

Aries, E., & Moorehead, K. (1989). The importance of ethnicity in the development of identity in Black adolescents. *Psychological Reports, 65,* 75–82.

Aries, P. (1962). *Centuries of childhood.* New York: Vintage.

Arland, T. (1989). Changing attitudes towards family issues in the United States. *Journal of Marriage and the Family, 51,* 873–893.

Arms, K. G., Davidson, J. K., & Moore, N. B. (1992). *Cultural diversity and families.* Dubuque, IA: Brown.

Arnett, J. (1991). Adolescents and heavy metal music: From the mouths of metalheads. *Youth and Society, 23,* 76–98.

Arnett, J., & Balle-Jensen, L. (1993). Cultural bases of risk behavior: Danish adolescents. *Child Development, 64,* 1842–1855.

Arnold, C. (1998). *Children and stepfamilies.* Washington, DC: Center for Law and Social Policy.

Asher, S. R. (1990). Recent advances in the study of peer rejection. In S. R. Asher & J. D. Coie (Eds.), *Peer rejection in childhood* (pp. 3–16). Cambridge, England: Cambridge University Press.

Asher, S. R., Rose, A. J., & Gabriel, S. W. (2001). Peer rejection in everyday life. In M. R. Leary (Ed.), *Interpersonal rejection* (pp. 105–142). New York: Oxford University Press.

Asher, S. R., Zelis, K. M., Parker, J. G., & Bruene, C. M. (1991, April). *Self-referral for peer relationship problems among aggressive and withdrawn low-accepted children.* Paper presented at the biennial meeting of the Society for Research in Child Development, Seattle.

Ashley, J., & Tomasello, M. (1998). Cooperative problem-solving and teaching in preschoolers. *Social Development, 7,* 143–163.

Aslin, R. N. (1987). Visual and auditory development in infancy. In J. D. Osofsky (Ed.), *Handbook of infant development* (pp. 5–97). New York: Wiley.

Aslin, R. N., & Hunt, R. H. (2001). Development, plasticity, and learning in the auditory system. In C. A. Nelson & M. Luciana (Eds.), *Handbook of developmental cognitive neuroscience* (pp. 205–220). Cambridge, MA: MIT Press.

Aslin, R. N., Jusczyk, P. W., & Pisoni, D. B. (1998). Speech and auditory processing during infancy: Constraints on and precursors to language. In D. Kuhn & R. S. Siegler (Eds.), *Handbook of child psychology* (Vol. 2, pp. 147–198). New York: Wiley.

Association of SIDS and Infant Mortality Program. (1998). *Sudden infant death syndrome.* Minneapolis: Association of SIDS and Infant Mortality Program.

Astolfi, P., & Zonta, L. A. (1999). Risks of preterm delivery and association with maternal age, birth order, and fetal gender. *Human Reproduction, 14,* 2891–2894.

Atkin, C. (1983). Effects of realistic TV violence vs. fictional violence on aggression. *Journalism Quarterly, 60,* 615–621.

Atkin, L. C., Olvera, M. C., Givaudan, M., & Landeros, G. (1989). Neonatal and maternal perceptions of urban Mexican infants. In J. K. Nugent, B. M. Lester, & T. B. Brazelton (Eds.), *The cultural context of the infant* (Vol. 2, pp. 201–238). Norwood, NJ: Ablex.

Atkins, M. S., Osborne, M. L., Bennett, D. S., Hess, L., & Halperin, J. M. (2001). Children's competitive peer aggression during reward and punishment. *Aggressive Behavior, 27,* 1–13.

Atkinson, L., Niccols, A., Paglia, A., Coolbear, J., Parker, K. C. H., Poulton, L., Guger, S., & Sitarenios, G. (2000). A meta-analysis of time between maternal sensitivity and attachment assessments: Implications for internal working models in infancy/toddlerhood. *Journal of Social and Personal Relationships, 17,* 791–810.

Attie, I., & Brooks-Gunn, J. (1989). Development of eating problems in adolescent girls: A longitudinal study. *Developmental Psychology, 25,* 70–79.

Aube, J., Fleury, J., & Smetana, J. (2000). Changes in women's roles: Impact on and social policy implications for the mental health of women and children. *Development and Psychopathology, 12,* 633–657.

Augoustinos, M. (1987). Developmental effects of child abuse. *Child Abuse and Neglect, 11,* 15–27.

Augoustinos, M., & Rosewarne, D. L. (2001). Stereotype knowledge and prejudice in children. *British Journal of Developmental Psychology, 19,* 143–156.

Aunola, K., Stattin, H., & Nurmi, J. E. (2000). Parenting styles and adolescents' achievement strategies. *Journal of Adolescence, 23,* 205–222.

Avenevoli, S., Sessa, F. M., & Steinberg, L. (1999). Family structure, parenting practices, and adolescent adjustment: An ecological examination. In E. M. Hetherington (Ed.), *Coping with divorce, single parenting, and remarriage: A risk and resiliency perspective* (pp. 65–90). Mahwah, NJ: Erlbaum.

Avis, J., & Harris, P. L. (1991). Beliefs-desire reasoning among Baka children: Evidence for a universal conception of mind. *Child Development, 62,* 460–467.

Aylward, G. P. (1997). Conceptual issues in developmental screening and assessment. *Journal of Developmental and Behavioral Pediatrics, 18,* 340–349.

Azmitia, M., & Montgomery, R. (1993). Friendship, transactive dialogues, and the development of scientific reasoning. *Social Development, 2,* 202–221.

Azuma, H. (1986). Why study child development in Japan? In H. Sherman, H. Azuma, & K. Hakuta (Eds.), *Child development and education in Japan* (pp. 213–249). New York: Freeman.

Azuma, S. D., & Chasnoff, I. J. (1993). Outcome of children prenatally exposed to cocaine and other drugs; A path analysis of three-year data. *Pediatrics, 92,* 396–402.

Baba, Y. (2001). Vietnamese gangs, cliques and delinquents. *Journal of Gang Research, 9,* 51–62.

Bachman, J. G., & Schulenberg, J. (1993). How part-time work intensity relates to drug use, problem behavior, time use, and satisfaction among high school seniors: Are these consequences or merely correlates? *Developmental Psychology, 29,* 220–235.

Backx, F. J., Erich, W. B., Kemper, A. B., & Verbeek, A. L. (1989). Sports injuries in school-aged children. An epidemiologic study. *American Journal of Sports Medicine, 17,* 234–240.

Bae, Y., & Smith, T. M. (1996). *Women in mathematics and science.* Washington, DC: US Department of Education.

Bagwell, C. L., Newcomb, A. F., & Bukowski, W. M. (1998). Preadolescent friendship and peer rejection as predictors of adult adjustment. *Child Development, 69,* 140–153.

Bailey, S. M. (1993). The current status of gender equality research in American schools. *Educational Psychologist, 28,* 321–339.

Bailey, W. T. (1994). A longitudinal study of fathers' involvement with young children: Infancy to age 5 years. *Journal of Genetic Psychology, 155,* 331–339.

Baillargeon, R., & Graber, M. (1988). Evidence of location memory in 8-month-old infants in a nonsearch AB task. *Developmental Psychology, 24,* 502–511.

Baillargeon, R., Spelke, E. S., & Wasserman, S. (1985). Object permanence in five-month-old infants. *Cognition, 20,* 191–208.

Bain, B., & Yu, A. (1980). Cognitive consequences of raising children bilingually. *Canadian Journal of Psychology, 34,* 304–313.

Baird, A. A., Gruber, S. A., Fein, D. A., Maas, L. C., Steingard, R. J., Renshaw, P. F., Cohen, B. M., & Yurgelun-Todd, D. A. (1999). Functional magnetic resonance imaging of facial affect recognition in children and adolescents. *Journal of the American Academy of Child and Adolescent Psychiatry, 38,* 195–199.

Baird, S. M., Campbell, D., Ingram, R., & Gomez, C. (2001). Young children with cri-du-chat: Genetic, developmental and behavioral profiles. *Infant Toddler Intervention, 11,* 1–14.

Balcazar, H., Peterson, G. W., & Krull, J. L. (1997). Acculturation and family cohesiveness in Mexican American pregnant women: Social and health implications. *Family Community Health, 20,* 16–31.

Bales, D. W., & Sera, M. D. (1995). Preschoolers' understanding of stable and changeable characteristics. *Cognitive Development, 10,* 69–107.

Baltes, M. M., & Silverberg, S. B. (1994). The dynamics between dependency and autonomy: Illustrations across the life span. In D. L. Featherman & R. M. Lerner (Eds.), *Life-span development and behavior* (Vol. 12, pp. 41–90). Hillsdale, NJ: Erlbaum.

Baltimore, D. (2001). Our genome unveiled. *Nature, 409,* 814–816.

Bancroft, J., & Reinisch, J. (1990). *Adolescence and puberty.* New York: Oxford University Press.

Band, E. B., & Weisz, J. R. (1988). How to feel better when it feels bad: Children's perspectives on coping with everyday stress. *Developmental Psychology, 24,* 247–253.

Bandura, A. (1977). *Social learning theory.* Englewood Cliffs, NJ: Prentice-Hall.

Banks, J. A. (1995). Multicultural education and the modification of students' racial attitudes. In W. D. Hawley & A. W. Jackson (Eds.), *Toward a common destiny: Improving race and ethnic relations in America* (pp. 315–339). San Francisco: Jossey-Bass.

Banks, J. A., & Banks, C. A. M. (1993). *Multicultural education.* Boston: Allyn & Bacon.

Banks, M. S. (1988). Visual recalibration and the development of contrast and optical flow. In A. Yonas (Ed.), *Perceptual development in infancy* (Vol. 20, pp. 145–196). Hillsdale, NJ: Erlbaum.

Barbarin, O. A. (1993). Emotional and social development of African American children. *Journal of Black Psychology, 19,* 381–390.

Barber, B. K., Olsen, J. E., & Shagle, S. C. (1994). Associations between parental psychological and behavioral control and youth internalized and externalized behaviors. *Child Development, 65,* 1120–1136.

Bard, K. A. (1994). Evolutionary roots of intuitive parenting: Maternal competence in chimpanzees. *Early Development and Parenting, 3,* 19–28.

Bardin, C., Zelkowitz, P., & Papageorgious, A. (1997). Outcome for small-for-gestational-age and appropriate-for-gestational-age infants born before 27 weeks of gestation. *Pediatrics, 100,* 1–5.

Barkley, R. A. (1989). Attention deficit-hyperactivity disorder. In E. J. Mash & R. A. Barkley (Eds.), *Treatment of childhood disorders* (pp. 39–72). New York: Guilford.

Barkley, R. A. (1997). Attention-deficit/hyperactivity disorder, self-regulation, and time. *Journal of Developmental and Behavioral Pediatrics, 18,* 271–279.

Barkley, R. A., Fischer, M., Edelbrock, C. S., & Smallish, L. (1990). The adolescent outcome of hyperactive children diagnosed by research criteria: I. An 8-year prospective follow-up study. *Journal of the American Academy of Child and Adolescent Psychiatry, 29,* 546–557.

Barness, L. A., & Gilbert-Barness, E. (1992). Cause of death: SIDS or something else? *Contemporary Pediatrics, 9,* 13–31.

Barnett, S. W. (1998). Long-term cognitive and academic effects of early childhood education of children in poverty. *Preventive Medicine, 27,* 204–207.

Barr, H. M., Streissguth, A. P., Darby, B. L., & Sampson, P. D. (1990). Prenatal exposure to alcohol, caffeine, tobacco, and aspirin: Effects on fine and gross motor performance in 4-year-old children. *Developmental Psychology, 26,* 339–348.

Barr, R. G., Hopkins, B., & Green, J. A. (2000). *Crying as a sign, a symptom, and a signal: Clinical emotional and developmental aspects of infant and toddler crying.* New York: Cambridge University Press.

Barrett, M., & Waterfield, J. (1997). The hidden factor: An educational perspective on depression in learning. In K. N. Dwivedi & V. P. Varma (Eds.), *Depression in children and adolescents* (pp. 106–123). London: Whurr Publishers.

Bartsch, K., & Wellman, H. M. (1995). *Children talk about the mind.* New York: Oxford University Press.

Bates, E., Carlson-Luden, V., & Bretherton, I. (1980). Perceptual aspects of tool using in infancy. *Infant Behavior and Development, 3,* 127–140.

Bates, E., Dale, P. S., & Thal, D. (1995). Individual differences and their implications for theories of language development (pp. 96–151). In P. Fletcher & B. MacWhinney (Eds.), *The handbook of child language.* Oxford, England: Blackwell.

Bates, E., O'Connell, B., & Shore, C. (1987). Language and communication in infancy. In J. D. Osofsky (Ed.), *Handbook of infant development* (pp. 149–203). New York: Wiley.

Bates, J. E. (1987). Temperament in infancy. In J. D. Osofsky (Ed.), *Handbook of infant development* (pp. 1101–1149). New York: Wiley.

Bauer, D. H. (1976). An exploratory study of developmental changes in children's fears. *Journal of Child Psychology and Psychiatry, 17,* 69–74.

Baumeister, A. A., & Baumeister, R. F. (1989). Mental retardation. In C. G. Last & M. Hersen (Eds.), *Handbook of child psychiatric diagnosis* (pp. 61–94). New York: Wiley.

Baumeister, R. F. (1993). *Self-esteem: The puzzle of low self-regard.* New York: Plenum.

Baumrind, D. (1967). Child care practices anteceding three patterns of preschool behavior. *Genetic Psychology Monographs, 75,* 43–88.

Baumrind, D. (1971). Current patterns of parental authority. *Developmental Psychology Monographs, 4* (1, Part 2).

Baumrind, D. (1989). Rearing competent children. In W. Damon (Ed.), *Child development today and tomorrow* (pp. 349–378). San Francisco: Jossey-Bass.

Baumrind, D. (1996). The discipline controversy revisited. *Family Relations, 45,* 405–414.

Beal, C. R. (1994). *Boys and girls: The development of gender roles.* New York: McGraw-Hill.

Beard, J. (1995). One person's view of iron deficiency, development, and cognitive function. *American Journal of Clinical Nutrition, 62,* 709–710.

Beardslee, W. R., & Gladstone, T. R. G. (2001). Prevention of childhood depression: Recent findings and future prospects. *Biological Psychiatry, 49,* 1101–1110.

Beaudry, M., Simard, M., Drapeau, S., & Charbonneau, C. (2000). What happens to the sibling subsystem following parental divorce? In C. Violato & E. Oddone-Paolucci (Eds.), *The changing family and child development* (pp. 105–116). Aldershot, England: Ashgate Publishing.

Beckman, D. A., & Brent, R. L. (1986). Mechanisms of known environmental teratogens: Drugs and chemicals. *Clinical Perinatalogy, 13,* 649–689.

Begley, S. (1996, February 19). Your child's brain. *Newsweek.*

Beitel, A. H., & Parke, R. D. (1998). Parental involvement in infancy: The role of maternal and paternal attitudes. *Journal of Family Psychology, 12,* 268–288.

Bell, C. (1991). Traumatic stress and child in danger. *Journal of Health Care for the Poor and Underserved, 2,* 175–188.

Bellinger, D. C., & Adams, H. F. (2001). Environmental pollutant exposures and children's cognitive abilities. In R. Sternberg & E. Grigorenko (Eds.), *Environmental effects on cognitive abilities* (pp. 157–188). Mahwah, NJ: Erlbaum.

Belsky, J. (1980). Child maltreatment: An ecological integration. *American Psychologist, 35,* 320–335.

Belsky, J. (1990). Parental and nonparental child care and children's socioemotional development: A decade in review. *Journal of Marriage and the Family, 52,* 885–903.

Belsky, J. (1993). Etiology of child maltreatment: A developmental-ecological analysis. *Psychological Bulletin, 114,* 413–434.

Belsky, J. (1996). Parent, infant, and social-contextual antecedents of father-son attachment security. *Developmental Psychology, 32,* 905–913.

Belsky, J. (1999). Infant-parent attachment. In L. Balter & C. S. Tamis-LeMonda (Eds.), *Child psychology: A handbook of contemporary issues* (pp. 45–63). Philadelphia: Psychology Press.

Belsky, J., & Cassidy, J. (1994). Attachment: Theory and evidence. In M. Rutter & D. Hay (Eds.), *Development through life* (pp. 373–402). Oxford, England: Blackwell.

Belsky, J., Spritz, B., & Crnic, K. (1996). Infant attachment security and affective-cognitive information processing at age 3. *Psychological Science, 7,* 111–114.

Belsky, J., Steinberg, L., & Draper, P. (1991). Childhood experience, interpersonal development, and reproductive strategy: An evolutionary theory of socialization. *Child Development, 62,* 647–670.

Belsky, J., Woodworth, S., & Crnic, K. (1996a). Trouble in the second year: Three questions about family interactions. *Child Development, 67,* 556–578.

Belsky, J., Woodworth, S., & Crnic, K. (1996b). Troubled family interaction during toddlerhood. *Development and Psychopathology, 8,* 477–495.

Bem, S. L. (1981). Gender schema theory: A cognitive account of sex typing. *Psychological Review, 88,* 354–364.

Bem, S. L. (1983). Gender schema theory and its implications for child development: Raising gender-aschematic children in a gender-schematic society. *Signs, 8,* 598–616.

Bemporad, J. R. (1994). Dynamic and interpersonal theories of depression. In W. M. Reynolds & H. F. Johnston (Eds.), *Handbook of depression in children and adolescents* (pp. 81–95). New York: Plenum.

Benedek, E. P., & Brown, C. F. (1995). *How to help your child overcome your divorce.* Washington, DC: American Psychiatric Press.

Benes, F. (2001). The development of prefrontal cortex: The maturation of neurotransmitter systems and their interactions. In C. Nelson & M. Luciana (Eds.), *Handbook of developmental cognitive neuroscience* (pp. 79–92). Cambridge, MA: MIT Press.

Benes, F., Turtle, M., Khan, Y., & Farol, P. (1994). Myelination of a key relay zone in the hippocampal formation occurs in the human brain during childhood, adolescence, and adulthood. *Archives of General Psychiatry, 51,* 477–484.

Bennett, V. R., & Brown, L. K. (1993). The fetus. In V. R. Bennett & L. K. Brown (Eds.), *Myles textbook for midwives* (pp. 365–376). London: Churchill Livingstone.

Bennett, W. (1993, April 7). Is our culture in decline? *Education Week, 12,* 32.

Benson, P. (1993). *The troubled journal: A portrait of 6th–12th grade youth.* Minneapolis: The Search Institute.

Benson, P. L., Donahue, M. J., & Erickson, J. A. (1989). Adolescence and religion. In M. L. Lynn & D. O. Moberg (Eds.), *Research in the social scientific study of religion* (pp. 153–181). Greenwich, CT: JAI Press.

Berenbaum, S. A., & Snyder, E. (1995). Early hormonal influences on childhood sex-typed activity and playmate preferences: Implications for the development of sexual orientation. *Developmental Psychology, 31,* 31–42.

Berg, W. K., & Berg, K. M. (1987). Psychophysiological development in infancy: State, startle, and attention. In J. D. Osofsky (Ed.), *Handbook of infant development* (pp. 238–317). New York: Wiley.

Berk, L. E. (1994). Why children talk to themselves. *Scientific American, 272,* 78–83.

Berk, L. E., & Winsler, A. (1999). *Scaffolding children's learning: Vygotsky and early childhood education.* Washington: National Association for the Education of Young Children.

Berko, J. (1958). The child's learning of English morphology. *Word, 14,* 150–177.

Berkowitz, M. W. (1997). *The education of the complete moral person.* Champaign: University of Illinois Press.

Berliner, L., & Elliot, D. M. (1996). Sexual abuse of children. In J. Briere, L. Berliner, J. A. Bulkley, C. Jenny, & T. Reid (Eds.), *The APSAC handbook on child maltreatment* (pp. 51–71). Thousand Oaks, CA: Sage.

Berman, C. M., Rasmussen, K. L. R., & Suomi, S. J. (1994). Responses of free-ranging rhesus monkeys to a natural form of social separation. I. Parallels with mother-infant separation in captivity. *Child Development, 65,* 1028–1041.

Berman, S. L., Silverman, W. K., & Kurtines, W. M. (2000). Children's and adolescents' exposure to community violence, post-traumatic stress reactions, and treatment implications. *Journal of Disaster and Trauma Studies, 2000–1,* 1–11.

Bernal, M. E., & Knight, G. P. (1997). Ethnic identity of Latino children. In J. G. Garcia & M. C. Zea (Eds.), *Psychological interventions and research with Latino populations* (pp. 15–38). Boston: Allyn & Bacon.

Berndt, T. J., & Perry, T. B. (1990). Distinctive features and effects of early adolescent friendships. In R. Montemayor, G. R. Adams, & T. Gullotta (Eds.), *From childhood to adolescence* (pp. 269–287). Newbury Park, CA: Sage.

Bertenthal, B. I. (1996). Origins and early development of perception, action, and representation. *Annual Review of Psychology, 47,* 431–459.

Bertenthal, B. I., & Campos, J. J. (1984). A reexamination of fear and its determinants on the visual cliff. *Psychophysiology, 21,* 413–417.

Bertenthal, B. I., & Clifton, R. K. (1998). Perception and action. In W. Damon (Ed.), *Handbook of child psychology* (Vol. 2, pp. 51–102). New York: Wiley.

Bertenthal, B. I., Proffitt, D. R., Kramer, S. J., & Spetner, N. B. (1987). Infants' encoding of kinetic displays varying in relative coherence. *Developmental Psychology, 23,* 171–178.

Best, C. T. (1995). Learning to perceive the sound patterns of English. In C. Rovee-Collier & L. P. Lipsitt (Eds.), *Advances in infancy research* (pp. 122–156). Norwood, NJ: ABLEX.

Bettes, B. A. (1988). Maternal depression and motherese: Temporal and intonational features. *Child Development, 59,* 1089–1096.

Bhatia, T. K., & Ritchie, W. C. (1999). The bilingual child: Some issues and perspectives. In W. Ritchie & T. Bhatia, (Eds.), *Handbook of child language acquisition* (pp. 569–643). San Diego: Academic Press.

Biddle, S. (1995). Exercise and psychosocial health. *Research Quarterly for Exercise and Sport, 66,* 292–297.

Biederman, J., Faraone, S. V., Taylor, A., Sienna, M., Williamson, S., & Fine, C. (1998). Diagnostic continuity between child and adolescent ADHD: Findings from a longitudinal clinical sample. *Journal of the American Academy of Child and Adolescent Psychiatry, 37,* 305–313.

Bier, J. A. B., Ferguson, A. E., Morales, Y., Liebling, J. A., Oh, W., & Vohr, B. R. (1997). Breastfeeding infants who were extremely low birth weight. *Pediatrics, 100,* 1–4.

Bigler, R. S. (1999). The use of multicultural curricula and materials to counter racism in children. *Journal of Social Issues, 55,* 687–705.

Bigler, R. S., & Liben, L. S. (1993). A cognitive-developmental approach to racial stereotyping and reconstructive memory in Euro-American children. *Child Development, 64,* 1507–1518.

Bijur, P. E., Trumble, A., Harel, Y., Overpeck, M. D., Jones, D., & Scheidt, P. C. (1995). Sports and recreation injuries in U.S. children and adolescents. *Archives of Pediatric and Adolescent Medicine, 149,* 1009–1016.

Biller, H. B. (1993). *Fathers and families.* Westport, CT: Greenwood Publishing.

Bingol, N., Fuchs, M., Diaz, V., Stone, R. K., & Gromisch, D. S. (1987). Teratogenicity of cocaine in humans. *Journal of Pediatrics, 110,* 93–96.

Bithoney, W. G., & Newberger, E. H. (1987). Child and family attributes of failure to thrive. *Journal of Developmental and Behavioral Pediatrics, 8,* 32.

Bjorklund, D. F. (1995). *Children's thinking.* Pacific Grove, CA: Brooks/Cole.

Bjorklund, D. F. (2000). *Children's thinking: Developmental function and individual differences.* Belmont, CA: Wadsworth/Thomson.

Bjorklund, D. F., Miller, P. H., Coyle, T. R., & Slawinski, J. L. (1997). Instructing children to use memory strategies: Evidence of utilization deficiencies in memory training studies. *Developmental Review, 17,* 411–442.

Bjorklund, D. F., & Pellegrini, A. D. (2000). Child development and evolutionary psychology. *Child Development, 71,* 1687–1708.

Black, B., & Hazen, N. L. (1990). Social status and patterns of communication in acquainted and unacquainted preschool children. *Developmental Psychology, 26,* 379–387.

Black, J. E. (1998). How a child builds its brain: Some lessons from animal studies of neural plasticity. *Preventative Medicine, 27,* 168–171.

Black, K. A. (2000). Gender differences in adolescents' behavior during conflict resolution tasks with best friends. *Adolescence, 35,* 499–512.

Black, M. M., Nair, P., Kight, C., Wachtel, R., Roby, P., & Schuler, M. (1994). Parenting and early development among children of drug-abusing women. *Pediatrics, 94,* 440–448.

Black-Gutman, D., & Hickson, F. (1996). The relationship between racial attitudes and social-cognitive development in children. *Developmental Psychology, 32,* 448–456.

Blair, R., James, R., & Coles, M. (2001). Expression recognition and behavioural problems in early adolescence. *Cognitive Development, 15,* 421–434.

Blake, J. (1989). *Family size and achievement.* Berkeley: University of California Press.

Bland, K. (1997, March 9). Infant abuse leaves lasting repercussions. *Arizona Republic,* pp. B1, B4.

Blasi, A. (1983). Moral cognition and moral action: A theoretical perspective. *Developmental Review, 3,* 178–210.

Blass, E. M., Ganchrow, J. R., & Steiner, J. E. (1984). Classical conditioning in newborn humans 2–48 hours of age. *Infant Behavior and Development, 7,* 223–235.

Bloom, L. (1994). Meaning and expression. In W. Overton & D. Palermo (Eds.), *The ontogenesis of meaning* (pp. 215–235). Hillsdale, NJ: Erlbaum.

Bloom, L. (1998). Language acquisition in its developmental context. In W. Damon (Ed.), *Handbook of child psychology* (Vol. 2, pp. 309–370). New York: Wiley.

Bloom, L., Margulis, C., Tinker, E., & Fujita, N. (1996). Early conversations and word learning: Contributions from child and adult. *Child Development, 67,* 3154–3175.

Bloom, L., Rocissano, L., & Hood, L. (1976). Adult-child discourse. *Cognitive Psychology, 8,* 521–552.

Blum, N. J., Taubman, B., & Osborne, M. L. (1997). Behavioral characteristics of children with stool toileting refusal. *Pediatrics, 99,* 50–53.

Blumenfeld, W. J., & Raymond, D. (1993). *Looking at gay and lesbian life.* Boston: Beacon Press.

Boeck, M. A. (1992). Bulimia nervosa. In S. B. Friedman, M. Fisher, & S. K. Schonberg (Eds.), *Comprehensive adolescent health care* (pp. 232–237). St. Louis, MO: Quality Medical Publishing.

Boer, F. (1990). *Sibling relationships in middle childhood.* Leiden, Germany: DSWO University of Leiden Press.

Boer, F., Goedhart, T., & Treffers, P. D. A. (1992). Siblings and their parents. In F. Boer & J. Dunn (Eds.), *Children's sibling relationships* (pp. 41–54). Hillsdale, NJ: Erlbaum.

Bohannon, J. N., & Warren-Leubecker, A. (1989). Theoretical approaches to language acquisition. In J. Berko-Gleason (Ed.), *The development of language* (pp. 167–223). Columbus, OH: Merrill.

Bohlin, G., Hagekull, B., & Rydell, A. M. (2000). Attachment and social functioning: A longitudinal study from infancy to middle childhood. *Social Development, 9,* 24–39.

Bon-De-Matte, L. (1998). Anorexic syndrome in adolescence and anorexia. In P. Bria & A. Ciocca (Eds.), *Psychotherapeutic issues in eating disorders* (pp. 41–48). Rome: Abramowicz.

Booth, C. L., Rose-Krasnor, L., & Rubin, K. H. (1991). Relating preschoolers' social competence and their mothers' parenting behaviors to early attachment security and high-risk status. *Journal of Social and Personal Relationships, 8,* 363–382.

Booth, D. A. (1994). *Psychology of nutrition.* London: Taylor and Francis.

Borke, H. (1975). Piaget's mountains revisited: Changes in the egocentric landscape. *Developmental Psychology, 11,* 240–243.

Borman, K., & Schneider, B. (1998). *The adolescent years.* Chicago: The National Society for the Study of Education.

Bornstein, M. H. (1985). Habituation of attention as a measure of visual information processing in human infants: Summary, systematization, and synthesis. In G. Gottlieb & N. A. Krasnegor (Eds.), *Measurement of audition and vision in the first year of postnatal life: A methodological overview* (pp. 253–300). Norwood, NJ: Ablex.

Bornstein, M. H. (1989). Sensitive periods in development. *Psychological Bulletin, 105,* 179–197.

Bornstein, M. H., & Lamb, M. E. (1992). *Development in infancy,* 3rd ed. New York: McGraw-Hill.

Bornstein, M. H., & Ludemann, P. M. (1989). Habituation at home. *Infant Behavior and Development, 12,* 525–529.

Bornstein, M. H., Tal, J., & Tamis-LeMonda, C. S. (1991). Parenting in cross-cultural perspective: The United States, France, and Japan. In M. H. Bornstein (Ed.), *Cultural approaches to parenting* (pp. 69–90). Hillsdale, NJ: Erlbaum.

Bornstein, M. H., & Tamis-LeMonda, C. S. (1990). Activities and interactions of mothers and their firstborn infants in the first six months of life: Covariation, stability, continuity, correspondence, and prediction. *Child Development, 61,* 1206–1217.

Bornstein, M. H., & Tamis-LeMonda, C. S. (1997). Maternal responsiveness and infant mental abilities. *Infant Behavior and Development, 20,* 283–296.

Borstelmann, L. J. (1983). Children before psychology: Ideas about children from antiquity to the late 1800s. In P. H. Mussen (Ed.), *Handbook of child psychology* (Vol. 1, pp. 1–40). New York: Wiley.

Borsting, E. (1994). Overview of vision and visual processing development. In M. Scheiman & M. Rouse (Eds.), *Optimetric measure of learning-related vision problems* (pp. 131–145). St. Louis, MO: Mosby.

Bosma, H. A., & Kunnen, E. S. (2001). Determinants and mechanisms in ego identity development: A review and synthesis. *Developmental Review, 21,* 39–66.

Boston, M. B., & Levy, G. D. (1991). Changes and differences in preschoolers' understanding of gender scripts. *Cognitive Development, 6,* 412–417.

Bosworth, P. (1985, February). Diane Sawyer. *Ladies' Home Journal,* 28–34.

Bowen, J., Fenton, T., & Rappaport, L. (1991). Stimulant medication and attention deficit–hyperactivity disorder: The child's perspective. *AJDC, 145,* 291–295.

Bower, J. (1982). *Development in infancy.* San Francisco: Freeman.

Bower, M. (1995). *Thalidomide.* San Francisco: Project Inform.

Bowers, W. A., Evans, K., & Van-Cleve, L. (1996). Treatment of adolescent eating disorders. In M. A. Reinecke & F. M. Daggilio (Eds.), *Cognitive therapy with children and adolescents* (pp. 227–250). New York: Guilford.

Bowlby, J. (1969). *Attachment and loss, Vol. 1.* New York: Basic Books.

Bowlby, J. (1973). *Attachment and loss, Vol. 2.* New York: Basic Books.

Bowman, P. J., & Howard, C. (1985). Race-related socialization, motivation, and academic achievement: A study of Black youths in three-generation families. *Journal of the American Academy of Child Psychiatry, 24,* 134–141.

Boxer, A. M., Cohler, J. J., Herdt, G., & Irvin, F. (1993). Gay and lesbian youth. In P. H. Tolan & J. J. Cohler (Eds.), *Handbook of clinical research and practice with adolescents* (pp. 249–280). New York: Wiley.

Boyce, W. T., Frank, E., Jensen, P. S., Kessler, R. C., Nelson, C. A., Steinberg, L., & The MacArthur Foundation Research Network on Psychopathology and Development. (1998). Social context in developmental psychopathology. *Development and Psychopathology, 10,* 143–164.

Boyer, D., & Fine, D. (1992). Sexual abuse as a factor in adolescent pregnancy and maltreatment. *Family Planning Perspectives, 24,* 4–11, 19.

Brackbill, Y., McManus, K., & Woodward, L. (1985). *Medication in maternity: Infant exposure and maternal information.* Ann Arbor: University of Michigan Press.

Bradbard, M. R., Martin, C. L., Endsley, R. C., & Halverson, C. F. (1986). Influence of sex stereotypes on children's exploration and memory: A competence versus performance distinction. *Developmental Psychology, 22,* 481–486.

Bradley, R. H. (1999). The home environment. In S. L. Friedman & T. D. Wachs (Eds.), *Measuring environment across the life span: Emerging methods and concepts* (pp. 31–58). Washington, DC: American Psychological Association.

Bradley, R. H., Burchinal, M. R., & Casey, P. H. (2001). Early intervention: The moderating role of the home environment. *Applied Developmental Science, 5,* 2–8.

Bradley, R. H., & Caldwell, B. M. (1976). The relation of infants' home environments to mental test performance at fifty-four months: A follow-up study. *Child Development, 47,* 1172–1174.

Bradley, R. H., Caldwell, B. M., Rock, S. L., Ramey, C. T., Barnard, K. E., Gray, C., Hammond, M. A., Mitchell, S., Gottfried, A. W., Siegel, L., & Johnson, D. L. (1989). Home environment and cognitive development in the first three years of life: A collaborative study involving six sites and three ethnic groups in North America. *Developmental Psychology, 25,* 217–235.

Bradley, S. J., Gillian, D. O., Avinoam, B. C., & Zucker, K. J. (1998). Experiment of nuture: Abolatio penis at 2 months, sex reassignment at 7 months, and a psychosexual follow-up in young adulthood. *Pediatrics, 102,* 1–5.

Bradley, R. H., Whiteside, L., Mundfrom, D. J., Casey, P. H., Kelleher, K. J., & Pope, S. K. (1994). Early indications of resilience and their relation to experiences in the home environments of low birthweight, premature children living in poverty. *Child Development, 65,* 346–360.

Braine, M. (1963). On learning the grammatical order of words. *Psychological Review, 70,* 323–348.

Branch, C. (1998). *Adolescent gangs: Old issues, new approaches.* Philadelphia: Brunner/Mazel.

Branch, C. W., & Newcombe, N. (1986). Racial attitude development among young Black children as a function of parental attitudes: A longitudinal and cross-sectional study. *Child Development, 57,* 712–721.

Braungart-Rieker, J. M., Garwood, M. M., Powers, B. P., & Wang, X. (2001). Parental sensitivity, infant affect, and affect regulation: Predictors of later attachment. *Child Development, 72,* 252–270.

Braungart-Rieker, J. M., & Stifter, C. A. (1996). Infants' responses to frustrating situations: Continuity and change in reactivity and regulation. *Child Development, 67,* 1767–1779.

Braza, F., Braza, P., Carreras, M. R., & Munoz, J. M. (1997). Development of sex difference in preschool children: Social behavior during an academic year. *Psychological Reports, 80,* 179–188.

Brazelton, T. B. (1991). *Touchpoints: Your child's emotional and behavioral development.* Reading, MA: Addison-Wesley.

Brazelton, T. B., Nugent, K. J., & Lester, B. M. (1987). Neonatal behavioral assessment scale. In J. D. Osofsky (Ed.), *Handbook of infant development* (pp. 780–817). New York: Wiley.

Breakey, J. (1997). The role of diet and behavior in childhood. *Journal of Pediatric Child Health, 33,* 190–194.

Brederode, M. E. (1990). Research on Rua Sesamo, the Portuese coproduction. In Children's Television Workshop (Ed.), *Sesame Street Research* (pp. 63–67). New York: Children's Television Workshop.

Bremer, J., & Rauch, P. K. (1998). Children and computers: Risks and benefits. *Journal of the American Academy of Child and Adolescent Psychiatry, 37,* 559–560.

Brendgen, M., Bowen, F., Rondeau, N., & Vitaro, F. (1999). Effect of friends' characteristics on children's social cognitions. *Social Development, 8,* 41–51.

Brendgen, M., Markiewicz, D., Doyle, A. B., & Bukowski, W. M. (2001). The relations between friendship quality, ranked-friendship preference, and adolescents' behavior with their friends. *Merrill-Palmer Quarterly, 47,* 395–415.

Brendgen, M., Vitaro, M., Bukowski, W. M., Doyle, A. B., & Markiewicz, D. (2001). Developmental profiles of peer social preference over the course of elementary school: Associations with trajectories of externalizing and internalizing behavior. *Developmental Psychology, 37,* 308–320.

Brenner, R. A., Overpeck, M. D., Trumble, A. C., DerSimonian, R., & Berendes, H. (2001). Deaths attributable to injuries in infants, United States, 1983–1991. *Pediatrics, 103,* 968–974.

Brenner, V., & Fox, R. A. (1998). Parental discipline and behavior problems in young children. *Journal of Genetic Psychology, 159,* 251–256.

Brent, D., May, D. C., & Kundert, D. K. (1996). The incidence of delayed school entry. *Early Education & Development, 7,* 121–135.

Bridges, A. (1986). Actions and things: What adults talk about to 1-year-olds. In S. Kuczaj & M. Barrett (Eds.), *The development of word meaning* (pp. 225–255). New York: Springer.

Bridges, K. (1932). Emotional development in early infancy. *Child Development, 3,* 324–341.

Bridges, L. J., Connell, J. P., & Belsky, J. (1988). Similarities and differences in mother-infant and father-infant interaction in the strange situation. *Developmental Psychology, 24,* 92–100.

Brisk, M. E. (1998). *Bilingual education.* Mahwah, NJ: Erlbaum.

Britner, P., & Reppucci, N. D. (1997). Prevention of child maltreatment: Evaluation of a parent education program for teen mothers. *Journal of Child and Family Studies, 6,* 165–175.

Broberg, A., Hwang, C., Lamb, M., & Ketterlinus, R. D. (1989). Child care effects on socioemotional and intellectual competence in Swedish preschoolers. In J. S. Lande, S. Scarr, & N. Gunzenhauser (Eds.), *Caring for children: Challenge to America* (pp. 49–76). Hillsdale, NJ: Erlbaum.

Brodsky, A. E., & DeVet, K. A. (2000). "You have to be real strong": Parenting goals and strategies of resilient, urban, African American, single mothers. *Journal of Prevention and Intervention in the Community, 20,* 159–178.

Brody, G. H. (1998). Sibling relationship quality: Its causes and consequences. *Annual Review of Psychology, 49,* 1–24.

Brody, G. H., Stoneman, Z., MacKinnon, C. E., & MacKinnon, R. (1985). Role relationships and behavior between preschool-aged and school-aged sibling pairs. *Developmental Psychology, 21,* 124–129.

Brody, G. H., Stoneman, Z., & McCoy, J. K. (1992). Associations of maternal and paternal direct and differential behavior with sibling relationships: Contemporaneous and longitudinal analyses. *Child Development, 63,* 82–92.

Brodzinsky, D. M., Lang, R., & Smith, D. W. (1995). Parenting adopted children. Fathers and families. In M. H. Bornstein (Ed.), *Handbook of parenting* (Vol. 3, pp. 233–254). Mahwah, NJ: Erlbaum.

Bronfenbrenner, U. (1979). *The ecology of human development: Experiments by nature and design.* Cambridge, MA: Harvard University Press.

Bronfenbrenner, U. (1986). Ecology of the family as a context for human development: Research perspectives. *Developmental Psychology, 22,* 723–742.

Bronfenbrenner, U., & Ceci, S. J. (1994). Nature-nurture reconceptualized in developmental perspective: A bioecological model. *Psychological Review, 101,* 568–586.

Bronfenbrenner, U., & Evans, G. W. (2000). Developmental science in the 21st century: Emerging questions, theoretical models, research designs and empirical findings. *Social Development, 9,* 115–125.

Bronfenbrenner, U., & Morris, P. A. (1998). The ecology of developmental processes. In W. Damon (Ed.), *Handbook of child psychology* (Vol. 1, pp. 993–1029). New York: Wiley.

Bronstein, P., Duncan, P., D'Air, A., Pieniadz, J., Fitzgerald, M., Abrams, C. L., Frankowski, B., Franco, O., Hunt, C., & Oh-Cha, S. Y. (1996). Family and parenting behaviors predicting middle school adjustment: A longitudinal study. *Family Relations, 45,* 415–426.

Brook, J. S., Brook, D. W., & Whiteman, M. (2000). The influence of maternal smoking during pregnancy on the toddler's negativity. *Archives of Pediatric and Adolescent Medicine, 154,* 381–385.

Brooks, J. B. (1998). *Parenting.* Mountain View, CA: Mayfield Publishing.

Brooks-Gunn, J. (1988). Antecedents and consequences of variations in girls' maturational timing. *Journal of Adolescent Health Care, 9,* 365–373.

Brooks-Gunn, J. (1995). Children in families in communities: Risk and intervention in the Bronfenbrenner tradition. In P. Moen, G. H. Elder, & K. Luscher (Eds.), *Examining lives in context: Perspectives on the ecology of human development* (pp. 467–519). Washington, DC: American Psychological Association.

Brooks-Gunn, J., & Duncan, G. J. (1997). The effects of poverty on children. *The Future of Children, 7,* 55–71.

Brooks-Gunn, J., Duncan, G. J., Klebanov, P. K., & Sealand, N. (1993). Do neighborhoods influence child and adolescent development? *American Journal of Sociology, 99,* 353–395.

Brooks-Gunn, J., & Furstenberg, F. F. (1989). Adolescent sexual behavior. *American Psychologist, 44,* 249–257.

Brooks-Gunn, J., & Graber, J. A. (1999). What's sex got to do with it? The development of sexual identities during adolescence. In R. J. Contrada & R. D. Ashmore (Eds.), *Self, social identity, and physical health: Interdisciplinary explorations* (Vol. 2., pp. 155–182). New York: Oxford University Press.

Brooks-Gunn, J., Klebanov, P. K., & Duncan, G. J. (1996). Ethnic differences in children's intelligence test scores: Role of economic deprivation, home environment, and maternal characteristics. *Child Development, 67,* 396–408.

Brooks-Gunn, J., & Paikoff, R. (1997). Sexuality and developmental transitions during adolescence. In J. Schulenberg & J. Maggs (Eds.), *Health risks and developmental transitions during adolescence* (pp. 190–219). New York: Cambridge University Press.

Brooks-Gunn, J., & Ruble, D. (1982). The development of menstrual-related beliefs and behaviors during early adolescence. *Child Development, 53,* 1567–1577.

Brooks-Gunn, J., & Warren, M. P. (1989). Biological and social contributions to negative affect in young adolescent girls. *Child Development, 60,* 40–55.

Brown, A. L., & Kane, M. J. (1988). Preschool children can learn to transfer: Learning to learn and learning by example. *Cognitive Psychology, 20,* 493–523.

Brown, A. L., Kane, M. J., & Long, C. (1989). Analogical transfer in young children: Analogies as tools for communication and exposition. *Applied Cognitive Psychology, 3,* 275–293.

Brown, B. B., & Lohr, M. J. (1987). Peer-group affiliation and adolescent self-esteem: An integration of ego-identity and symbolic-interaction theories. *Journal of Personality and Social Psychology, 52,* 47–55.

Brown, B. B., Mory, M. S., & Kinney, D. (1994). Casting adolescent crowds in a relational perspective. In R. Montemayor & G. R. Adams (Eds.), *Personal relationships during adolescence* (pp. 123–167). Thousand Oaks, CA: Sage.

Brown, J., & Pollitt, E., (1996). Malnutrition, poverty and intellectual development. *Scientific American, 274,* 38–43.

Brown, J. D., & Lawton, M. (1986). Stress and well-being in adolescence: The moderating role of physical exercise. *Journal of Human Stress, 12,* 125–131.

Brown, J. R., & Dunn, J. (1992). Talk with your mother or your sibling? Developmental changes in early family conversations about feelings. *Child Development, 63,* 336–349.

Brown, K. H., Robertson, A. D., & Akhtar, N. A. (1986). Lactational capacity of marginally nourished mothers: Infants' milk nutrient consumption and patterns of growth. *Pediatrics, 78,* 920–927.

Brown, R. P., & Josephs, R. A. (1999). A burden of proof. Stereotype relevance and gender differences in math performance. *Journal of Personality and Social Psychology, 76,* 246–257.

Browne, J. V. (2000). Developmental care—considerations for touch and massage in the neonatal intensive care unit. *Neonatal Network, 19,* 1–10.

Bruck, M., (1992). Persistence of dyslexics' phonological deficits. *Developmental Psychology, 28,* 874–886.

Bruner, J. S. (1983). *Child's talk: Learning to use language.* New York: Norton.

Bryan, J. H., & Walbek, N. H. (1970). The impact of words and deeds concerning altruism upon children. *Child Development, 41,* 747–757.

Bryant, B. K. (1982). Sibling relationships in middle childhood. In M. E. Lamb & B. Sutton-Smith (Eds.), *Sibling relationships* (pp. 87–122). Hillsdale, NJ: Erlbaum.

Bryant, B. K. (1985). The neighborhood walk. *Monographs of the Society for Research in Child Development, 3* (Whole No. 210). Chicago: Society for Research in Child Development.

Bryant, B. K. (1992). Sibling caretaking: Providing emotional support during middle childhood. In F. Boer & J. Dunn (Eds.), *Children's sibling relationships: Developmental and clinical issues* (pp. 55–70). Hillsdale, NJ: Erlbaum.

Bryant, B. K. (1998). Children's coping at school. In L. H. Meyer & H. Park (Eds.), *Making friends: The influence of culture and development* (Vol. 3, pp. 353–367). Baltimore: Brookes Publishing.

Bryk, A. S., & Driscoll, M. E. (1988). *The school as community.* Madison: University of Wisconsin Press.

Bryk, A. S., Lee, V. E., & Smith, J. B. (1990). High school organization and its effects on teachers and students: An interpretive summary of the research. In J. Witte & W. Clure (Eds.), *Choice and control in American education* (pp. 135–226). London: Falmer Press.

Buchanan, A., & Hudson, B. (2000). *Promoting children's emotional wellbeing.* New York: Oxford University Press.

Buchanan, C. M., Maccoby, E. E., & Dornbusch, S. M. (1996). *Adolescents after divorce.* Cambridge, MA: Harvard University Press.

Buchanan-Barrow, B., & Barrett, M. (1998). Individual differences in children's understanding of the school. *Social Development, 7,* 250–268.

Bugental, D. B., & Goodnow, J. J. (1998). Socialization processes. In W. Damon (Ed.), *Handbook of child psychology* (Vol. 3, 389–462). New York: Wiley.

Buhrmester, D. (1992). The developmental courses of sibling and peer relationships. In F. Boer & J. Dunn (Eds.), *Children's sibling relationships* (pp. 19–40). Hillsdale, NJ: Erlbaum.

Buhrmester, D., Goldfarb, J., & Cantrell, D. (1992). Self-presentation when sharing with friends and nonfriends. *Journal of Early Adolescence, 12,* 61–79.

Buhrmester, D., Whalen, C. K., Henker, B., MacDonald, V., & Hinshaw, S. P. (1992). Prosocial behavior in hyperactive boys: Effects of stimulant medication and comparison with normal boys. *Journal of Abnormal Child Psychology, 20,* 103–121.

Buis, J. M., & Thompson, D. N. (1989). Imaginary audience and personal fable: A brief review. *Adolescence, 24,* 773–781.

Bukoski, W. J. (1997). *Meta-analysis of drug abuse prevention programs.* Washington, DC: U.S. Department of Health and Human Services.

Bukowski, W. M., Gauze, C., Horz, B., & Newcomb, A. F. (1993). Differences and consistency between same-sex and other-sex peer relationships during early adolescence. *Developmental Psychology, 29,* 255–263.

Bullock, M. (1984). Preschool children's understanding of causal connections. *British Journal of Developmental Psychology, 2,* 139–142.

Bullock, M., & Gelman, R. (1979). Preschool children's assumptions about cause and effect: Temporal ordering. *Child Development, 50,* 89–96.

Bullock, M., Gelman, R., & Baillargeon, R. (1982). The development of causal reasoning. In W. F. Friedman (Ed.), *The developmental psychology of time* (pp. 209–253). New York: Academic Press.

Burack, J. A., Hodapp, R. M., & Zigler, E. (1998). *Handbook of mental retardation and development.* New York: Cambridge University Press.

Burchinal M., Lee, M., & Ramey, C. (1989). Type of day-care and preschool intellectual development in disadvantaged children. *Child Development, 60,* 128–137.

Burchinal, M. R., & Caskie, G. I. L. (2001). Maternal employment, child care, and cognitive outcomes. In E. L. Grigorenko & R. J. Sternberg (Eds.), *Family environment and intellectual functioning* (pp. 119–139). Mahwah, NJ: Erlbaum.

Burd, B. (1986). Infant swimming classes: Immersed in controversy. *The Physician and Sports Medicine, 14*(3), 239–244.

Bureau of Labor Statistics. (1999). *Current employment statistics.* Washington, DC: Bureau of Labor Statistics.

Burnett, J. W., Anderson, W. P., & Heppner, P. P. (1995). Gender roles and self-esteem: A consideration of environmental factors. *Journal of Counseling and Development, 73,* 323–326.

Burns, A., & Homel, R. (1989). Gender division of tasks by parents and their children. *Psychology of Women Quarterly, 13,* 113–125.

Burt, M. R., Resnick, G., & Novick, E. R. (1998). *Building supportive communitites for at-risk adolescents.* Washington, DC: American Psychological Association.

Buss, A., & Plomin, R. (1984). *Temperament: Early developing personality traits.* Hillsdale, NJ: Erlbaum.

Buss, D. (1998). *Evolutionary psychology.* Boston: Allyn & Bacon.

Buss, K., & Goldsmith, H. H. (1998). Fear and anger regulation in infancy: Effects on the temporary dynamics of affective expression. *Child Development, 69,* 359–374.

Bussey, K. (1992). Lying and truthfulness: Children's definitions, standards, and evaluative reactions. *Child Development, 63,* 129–137.

Bussey, K., & Bandura, A. (1984). Influence of gender constancy and social power on sex-linked modeling. *Journal of Personality and Social Psychology, 47,* 1292–1302.

Bussey, K., & Bandura, A. (1992). Self-regulatory mechanisms governing gender development. *Child Development, 63,* 1236–1250.

Bussey, K., & Bandura, A. (1999). Social cognitive theory of gender development and differentiation. *Psychological Review, 106,* 676–713.

Bussey, K., & Perry, D. G. (1982). Same-sex imitation: The avoidance of cross-sex models or the acceptance of same-sex models? *Sex Roles, 8,* 773–785.

Butler, J., & Rovee-Collier, C. (1989). Contextual gating of memory retrieval. *Developmental Psychobiology, 22,* 533–552.

Byers, J. (1989). AIDS in children. Effects of neurological development and implications for the future. *Journal of Special Education, 23,* 5–16.

Byrne, D. (1983). Sex without contraception. In D. Byrne & W. A. Fisher (Eds.), *Adolescents, sex, and contraception* (pp. 3–31). Hillsdale, NJ: Erlbaum.

Byrnes, J. P. (1988). Formal operations: A systematic reformulation. *Developmental Review, 8,* 66–87.

Byrnes, J. P., & Fox, N. A. (1998). The educational relevance of research in cognitive neuroscience. *Educational Psychology Review, 10,* 297–342.

Cairns, R. B. (1998). The making of developmental psychology. In W. Damon (Ed.), *Handbook of child psychology* (Vol. 1, pp. 25–107). New York: Wiley.

Cairns, R. B., Cadwallader, T. W., Estell, D., & Neckerman, H. J. (1997). Groups to gangs: Developmental and criminological perspectives and relevance for prevention. In D. M. Stoff & J. Breiling (Eds.), *Handbook of antisocial behavior* (pp. 194–204). New York: Wiley.

Caissy, G. A. (1994). *Early adolescence.* New York: Insight Books.

Callanan, M. A. (1989). Development of object categories and inclusion relations: Preschoolers' hypotheses about word meanings. *Developmental Psychology, 25,* 207–216.

Camarota, A. (2001). *Immigrants in the United States 2000.* Washington, DC: Center for Immigration Studies.

Campaign for Our Children (1997). *National teen pregnancy clock.* Baltimore: Campaign for Our Children.

Campos, F. (1996). *Latino, Hispanic, both, neither?* Austin: University of Texas Press.

Campos, J. J., Kermoian, R., & Zumbahlen, M. R. (1992). Socioemotional transformations in the family system following infant crawling onset. In N. Eisenberg & R. A. Fabes (Eds.), *Emotion and its regulation in early development* (pp. 25–40). San Francisco: Jossey-Bass.

Campos, M. M. (1992). Child care in Brazil. In M. E. Lamb, K. J. Sternberg, C. Hwang, & A. G. Broberg (Eds.), *Child care in context* (pp. 479–508). Hillsdale, NJ: Erlbaum.

Caplovitz, A. G., Lee, J. H., Hofferth, S., & Finkelstein, J. (2001). American children's use of electronic media in 1997: A national survey. *Journal of Applied Developmental Psychology, 22,* 31–47.

Capon, N., & Kuhn, D. (1979). Logical reasoning in the supermarket: Adult females' use of proportional reasoning strategy in an everyday context. *Developmental Psychology, 15,* 450–452.

Carlo, G., Fabes, R. A., Laible, D., & Kupanoff, K. (1999). Early adolescence and prosocial/moral behavior II: The role of social and contextual influences. *Journal of Early Adolescence, 19,* 133–147.

Carlson, E. A., Jacobvitz, D., & Sroufe, L. A. (1995). A developmental investigation of inattentiveness and hyperactivity. *Child Development, 66,* 37–54.

Carlton, M. P., & Winsler, A. (1999). School readiness: The need for a paradigm shift. *School Psychology Review, 28,* 338–352.

Carskadon, M. A. (1990). Patterns of sleep and sleepiness in adolescents. *Pediatrician, 17,* 5–12.

Carson, D. K., & Bittner, M. T. (1994). Temperament and school-aged children's coping abilities and responses to stress. *Journal of Genetic Psychology, 155,* 289–302.

Carter, C., & Rice, C. L. (1997). Acquisition and manifestation of prejudice in children. *Journal of Multicultural Counseling and Development, 25,* 185–194.

Carter, D. B., & Middlemiss, W. A. (1992). The socialization of instrumental competence in families in the United States. In J. L. Roopnarine & D. B. Carter (Eds.), *Parent-child socialization in diverse cultures* (pp. 107–120). Norwood, NJ: Ablex.

Cartwright, T., & Brent, M. R. (1997). Syntactic categorization in early language acquisition: Formalizing the role of distributional analysis. *Cognition, 63,* 121–170.

Case, R. (1992). Neo-Piagetian theories of child development. In R. Sternberg & C. Berg (Eds.), *Intellectual development* (pp. 161–196). New York: Cambridge University Press.

Case, R. (1998). The development of conceptual structures. In W. Damon (Ed.), *Handbook of child psychology* (Vol. 2, pp. 851–898). New York: Wiley.

Case, R., & Edelstein, W. (1993). The new structuralism in cognitive development. *Contributions to Human Development, 23.*

Case, R., & Okamoto, Y. (1996). Modeling the process of conceptual change in a continuously evolving hierarchical system. *Monographs of the Society for Research in Child Development, 61,* 283–295.

Casey, B. J., Giedd, J. N., & Thomas, K. M. (2000). Structural and functional brain development and its relation to cognitive development. *Biological Psychology, 54,* 241–257.

Casey, M. B., Nuttall, R. L., & Pezaris, E. (1997). Mediators of gender differences in mathematics college entrance test scores: A comparison of spatial skills with internalized beliefs and anxiety. *Developmental Psychology, 33,* 669–680.

Casey, P. H. (1992). Failure to thrive. In M. D. Levine, W. B. Carey, & A. C. Crocker (Eds.), *Developmental-behavioral pediatrics* (pp. 375–383). Philadelphia: Saunders.

Casper, L. B. (1990). Does family interaction prevent adolescent pregnancy? *Family Planning Perspectives, 30,* 54–61.

Casper, L. M., Hawkins, M., & O'Connell, M. (1994). *Who's minding the kids?* Washington, DC: US Census.

Caspi, A., Henry, B., McGee, R. O., Moffitt, T. E., & Silva, P. A. (1995). Temperamental origins of child and adolescent behavior problems: From age three to age fifteen. *Child Development, 66,* 55–68.

Caspi, A., & Silva, P. A. (1995). Temperamental qualities at age three predict personality traits in young adulthood: Longitudinal evidence from a birth cohort. *Child Development, 66,* 486–498.

Cassidy, J., Kirsh, S. J., Scolton, K. L., & Parke, R. D. (1996). Attachment and representations of peer relationships. *Developmental Psychology, 32,* 892–904.

Cassidy, J., & Shaver, P. (1999). *Handbook of attachment.* New York: Guilford.

Cassidy, P. (1993). The first stage of labor: Physiology and early care. In V. R. Bennett & L. K. Brown (Eds.), *Myles textbook for midwives* (pp. 149–167). London: Churchill Livingstone.

Castellanos, F. X. (1997). Neuroimaging of attention-deficit hyperactivity disorder. *Child and Adolescent Psychiatric Clinics of North America, 6,* 383–411.

Castex, G. M. (1997). Immigrant children in the United States. In N. K. Phillips & S. L. A. Straussner (Eds.), *Children in the urban environment* (pp. 43–60). Springfield, IL: Thomas Publishing.

Cauffman, E., & Steinberg, L. (1996). Interactive effects of menarcheal status and dating on dieting and disordered eating among adolescent girls. *Developmental Psychology, 32,* 631–635.

Ceci, S. J., & Bruck, M. (1995). *Jeopardy in the courtroom.* Washington, DC: American Psychological Association.

Ceci, S. J., & Bruck, M. (1998). Children's testimony: Applied and basic issues. In W. Damon (Ed.), *Handbook of child psychology* (Vol. 4, pp. 713–774). New York: Wiley.

Center for Applied Research and Educational Improvement. (1997). *School start time study.* Minneapolis: University of Minnesota Press.

Center for the Evaluation of Risks to Human Reproduction (1999a, March 19). *Folic acid.* Washington, DC: Center for the Evaluation of Risks to Human Reproduction.

Center for the Evaluation of Risks to Human Reproduction (1999b, March 19). *Thalidomide.* Washington, DC: Center for the Evaluation of Risks to Human Reproduction.

Centers for Disease Control. (1996). *HIV/AIDS Surveillance Report* (Vol. 8). Atlanta: Centers for Disease Control.

Centers for Disease Control. (1997). *Fertility, family planning, and women's health.* Washington, DC: Centers for Disease Control.

Centers for Disease Control. (1998). *Youth risk behavior surveillance—United States, 1997.* Washington, DC: Centers for Disease Control.

Centers for Disease Control. (1999). *Immunization and infectious disease.* Washington, DC: Centers for Disease Control.

Centers for Disease Control (2000a). *Adolescent and school health.* Washington, DC: Centers for Disease Control.

Centers for Disease Control (2000b). *Gun deaths among children and teens drop sharply.* Washington, DC: Centers for Disease Control.

Centers for Disease Control. (2001a). *Births, marriages, divorces, and deaths for 1999–2001.* Washington, DC: Centers for Disease Control.

Centers for Disease Control. (2001b). *HIV/AIDS Surveillance Report.* Washington, DC: Centers for Disease Control.

Centers for Disease Control (2001c). *Motor vehicle–related crashes among teenagers.* Washington, DC: Centers for Disease Control.

Centers for Disease Control (2001d). *Prevalence of overweight among children and adolescents: US, 1999.* Washington, DC: National Center for Health Statistics.

Cernoch, J. M., & Porter, R. H. (1985). Recognition of maternal axillary odors by infants. *Child Development, 56,* 1593–1598.

Cerrelli, E. C. (1998). Crash data and rates for age-sex groups of drivers, 1996. *National Highway Traffic Safety Administration Research Note.* Washington, DC: US DOT.

Chall, J. S., Jacobs, V. A., & Baldwin, L. E. (1990). *The reading crisis.* Cambridge, MA: Harvard University Press.

Chan, R. W., Raboy, B., & Patterson, C. J. (1998). Psychosocial adjustment among children conceived via insemination by lesbian and heterosexual mothers. *Child Development, 69,* 443–457.

Chance, R. (1992). *Probation: Technical assistance manual.* Rockville, MD: Juvenile Justice Clearinghouse.

Chandler, M., Fritz, A. S., & Hala, S. (1989). Small-scale deceit: Deception as a marker of two-, three-, and four-year-olds' early theories of mind. *Child Development, 60,* 1263–1277.

Channiah, D. (1997). *The Ryan White story.* Charlottesville: University of Virgina Press.

Chapin, J. R. (2000). Adolescent sex and mass media: A developmental approach. *Adolescence, 35,* 799–811.

Charlesworth, R. (1989). "Behind" before they start? *Young Children, 44,* 5–13.

Chase, W. G., & Simon, H. A. (1973). Perception in chess. *Cognitive Psychology, 4,* 55–81.

Chase-Linsdale, P. L., Gordon, R. A., Coley, R. L., Wakschlag, L. S., & Brooks-Gunn, J. (1999). Young African American multigenerational families in poverty: The contexts, exchanges, and processes of their lives. In E. M. Hetherington (Ed.), *Coping with divorce, single parenting, and remarriage: A risk and resiliency perspective* (pp. 165–191). Mahwah, NJ: Erlbaum.

Chase-Linsdale, P. L., & Hetherington, E. M. (1990). The impact of divorce on life-span development: Short- and long-term effects. In D. L. Featherman & R. M. Lerner (Eds.), *Life span development and behavior* (Vol. 10, pp. 105–151). Hillsdale, NJ: Erlbaum.

Chasnoff, I. J., Burns, W. J., Schnoll, S. H., & Burns, K. A. (1985). Cocaine use in pregnancy. *New England Journal of Medicine, 313,* 666–669.

Chasnoff, I. J., Chisum, G. M., & Kaplan, W. E. (1988). Maternal cocaine use and genitourinary tract malformations. *Teratology, 37,* 201–204.

Chen, C., & Stevenson, H. W. (1995). Culture and academic achievement. In M. L. Maher & P. R. Pintrich (Eds.), *Advances in motivation and achievement* (Vol. 9, pp. 119–151). Greenwich, CT: JAI Press.

Chen, Z. Y., & Dornbusch, S. M. (1998). Relating aspects of adolescent emotional autonomy to academic achievement and deviant behavior. *Journal of Adolescent Research, 13,* 293–319.

Chen, Z., & Siegler, R. S. (2000). Intellectual development in childhood. In R. J. Sternberg (Ed.), *Handbook of intelligence* (pp. 92–116). Cambridge, England: Cambridge University Press.

Chi, M. T. H. (1978). Knowledge structures and memory development. In R. S. Siegler (Ed.), *Children's thinking: What develops?* (pp. 73–96). Hillsdale, NJ: Erlbaum.

Chi, M. T. H., & Koeske, R. D. (1983). Network representation of a child's dinosaur knowledge. *Developmental Psychology, 19,* 29–39.

Child Care Action Campaign. (1996). *A child care primer for parents.* New York: Child Care Action Campaign.

Children Now. (2000). *Girls and gaming.* Oakland, CA: Children Now.

Children's Defense Fund. (1992). *The state of America's children.* Washington, DC: Children's Defense Fund.

Children's Television Workshop. (1991). *What research indicates about the educational effects of Sesame Street.* New York: Children's Television Workshop.

Chilman, C. S. (1993). Hispanic families in the United States. In H. P. McAdoo (Ed.), *Family ethnicity* (pp. 141–163). Newbury Park, CA: Sage.

Chisholm, J. S. (1989). Biology, culture, and the development of temperament: A Navajo example. In J. K. Nugent, B. M. Lester, & T. B. Brazelton (Eds.), *The cultural context of the infant* (Vol. 1, pp. 341–366). Norwood, NJ: Ablex.

Choi, S., & Gopnik, A. (1995). Early acquisition of verbs in Korean: A cross-linguistic study. *Journal of Child Language, 22,* 497–529.

Chomsky, N. (1965). *Aspects of the theory of syntax.* Cambridge, MA: MIT Press.

Chomsky, N. (1986). *Knowledge of language: Its nature, origin and use.* New York: Praeger.

Chorpita, B. F., & Barlow, D. H. (1998). The development of anxiety: The role of control in the early environment. *Psychological Bulletin, 124,* 3–21.

Christenson, P. G., & Roberts, D. F. (1998). *It's not only rock & roll: Popular music in the lives of adolescents.* Cresskill, NJ: Hampton Press.

Christopher, F. S. (2001). *To dance the dance: A symbolic interactional exploration of premarital sexuality.* Mahwah, NJ: Erlbaum.

Cicchetti, D., Rogosch, F. A., & Toth, S. L. (1998). Maternal depressive disorder and contextual risk: Contributions to the development of attachment insecurity and behavior problems in toddlerhood. *Development and Psychopathology, 10,* 283–300.

Cicchetti, D., & Toth, S. L. (1998). The development of depression in children and adolescents. *American Psychologist, 53,* 221–241.

Clark, E. V. (1981). Lexical innovations: How children learn to create new words. In W. Deutsch (Ed.), *The child's construction of language* (pp. 299–328). London: Academic Press.

Clark, E. V. (1993). *The lexicon in acquisition.* Cambridge, England: Cambridge University Press.

Clark, E. V. (1997). Conceptual perspective and lexical choice in acquisition. *Cognition, 64,* 1–37.

Clark, G. (1994). *Onions are my husband: Survival and accumulation by West African market women.* Chicago: University of Chicago Press.

Clark, M. L., & Ayers, M. (1993). Friendship expectations and friendship evaluations. *Youth and Society, 24,* 299–313.

Clarke, A. T., & Kutz-Costes, B. (1997). Television viewing, educational quality of the home, and school readiness. *Journal of Educational Research, 90,* 279–285.

Clarke-Stewart, K. A. (1984). Day care: A new context for research and development. In M. Perlmutter (Ed.), *Parent-child interactions and parent-child relations in children's development* (Vol. 17, pp. 61–100). Hillsdale, NJ: Erlbaum.

Clarke-Stewart, K. A. (1989). Infant day care: Maligned or malignant? *American Psychologist, 44,* 266–273.

Clarke-Stewart, K. A. (1992). Consequences of child care for children's development. In A. Booth (Ed.), *Child care in the 1990s: Trends and consequences* (pp. 63–82). Hillsdale, NJ: Erlbaum.

Clarke-Stewart, K. A., Allhusen, V. D., & Clements, D. C. (1995). Nonparental caregiving. Fathers and families. In M. H. Bornstein (Ed.), *Handbook of parenting* (Vol. 3, pp. 151–176). Mahwah, NJ: Erlbaum.

Clinton, J. F. (1986). Expectant fathers at risk for couvade. *Nursing Research, 35,* 290–295.

Clubb, R. (1991). Chronic sorrow: Adaptation of parents with chronically ill children. *Pediatric Nursing, 17,* 461–466.

Cnattingius, S., Bergstrom, R., Lipworth, L., & Kramer, M. S. (1998). Prepregnancy weight and the risk of adverse pregnancy outcomes. *New England Journal of Medicine, 388,* 147–152.

Cohen, L. M. (1996). Meeting the needs of gifted and talented minority language students. *ERIC Digest* (No. E480).

Cohen, M. A. (1998). The monetary value of saving a high-risk youth. *Journal of Quantitative Criminology, 14,* 5–53.

Cohen, Y., Spirito, A., & Brown, L. K. (1996). Suicide and suicidal behavior. In R. DiClemente & W. B. Hansen (Eds.), *Handbook of adolescent health risk behavior* (pp. 193–224). New York: Plenum.

Cohn, A. H., & Daro, D. (1987). Is treatment too late: What ten years of evaluative research tells us. *Child Abuse and Neglect, 11,* 433–442.

Cohn, D. A., Lohrmann, B. C., & Patterson, C. (1985, April). *Loneliness and peer relations in young children.* Paper presented at the biennial meeting of the Society for Research in Child Development, Kansas City.

Coie, J. D., & Dodge, K. A. (1998). Aggression and antisocial behavior. In W. Damon (Ed.), *Handbook of child psychology* (Vol. 3, 778–862). New York: Wiley.

Coie, J. D., Dodge, K., Terry, R., & Wright, V. (1991). The role of aggression in peer relations: An analysis of aggression episodes in boys' play groups. *Child Development, 62,* 812–826.

Coie, J. D., & Koeppl, G. K. (1990). Adapting intervention to the problems of aggressive and disruptive rejected children. In S. R. Asher & J. D. Coie (Eds.), *Peer rejection in childhood* (pp. 309–337). Cambridge, England: Cambridge University Press.

Colby, A., Kohlberg, L., Gibbs, J., & Lieberman, M. (1983). A longitudinal study of moral judgment. *Monographs of the Society for Research in Child Development, 48* (Whole No. 200).

Cole, E. B. (1992). *Learning and talking: A guide to promoting spoken language in hearing-impaired children.* Washington, DC: Alexander Graham Bell Association for the Deaf.

Cole, M. (1997). Cultural mechanisms of cognitive development. In E. Amsel & K. A. Renninger (Eds.), *Change and development* (pp. 245–263). Hillsdale, NJ: Erlbaum.

Coleman, J. M., & Kardash, C. M. (1999). Encoding and retrieval of ambiguous and unambiguous information by aggressive and nonaggressive elementary boys. *Child Study Journal, 29,* 133–151.

Coleman, M., Ganong, L., & Fine, M. (2000). Reinvestigating remarriage: Another decade of progress. *Journal of Marriage and the Family, 62,* 1288–1307.

Coles, C. (1994). Critical periods for prenatal alcohol exposure. *Alcohol Health and Research World, 18,* 22–29.

Coles, R. (1990). *The spiritual life of children.* Boston: Houghton Mifflin.

Coles, R., & Stokes, G. (1985). *Sex and the American teenager.* New York: Harper & Row.

Coley, R. L., & Chase-Linsdale, P. L. (1998). Adolescent pregnancy and parenthood. *American Psychologist, 53,* 152–166.

Colin, V. L. (1996). *Human attachment.* New York: McGraw-Hill.

Collaer, M. L., & Hines, M. (1995). Human behavioral sex differences: A role for gonadal hormone during early development? *Psychological Bulletin, 118*(1), 55–107.

Collier, J., Jr. (1988). Survival at Rough Rock: A historical overview of Rough Rock demonstration school. *Anthropology and Education Quarterly, 19,* 253–269.

Collins, W. A. (1990). Parent-child relationships in the transition to adolescence. In R. Montemayor, G. R. Adams, & T. Gullotta (Eds.), *From childhood to adolescence* (Vol. 2, pp. 85–106). Newbury Park, CA: Sage.

Collins, W. A., Maccoby, E. E., Steinberg, L., Hetherington, E. M., & Bornstein, M. H. (2000). Contemporary research on parenting: The case for nature and nurture. *American Psychologist, 55,* 218–232.

Collins, W. A., & Repinski, D. J. (1994). Relationships during adolescence: Continuity and change in interpersonal perspective. In R. Montemayor & G. R. Adams (Eds.), *Personal relationships during adolescence* (pp. 7–36). Thousand Oaks, CA: Sage.

Coltrane, S. (1995). *Family man.* New York: Oxford University Press.

Committee on Pediatric AIDS. (1998). Surveillance of pediatric HIV infection. *Pediatrics, 101,* 315–319.

Compas, B. E., Connor-Smith, J. K., Saltzman, H., Thomsen, A. H., & Wadsworth, M. E. (1999). Getting specific about coping: Effortful and involuntary responses to stress in development. In M. Lewis & D. Ramsay (Eds.), *Soothing and stress* (pp. 229–256). Mahwah, NJ: Erlbaum.

Compas, B. E., Connor-Smith, J. K., Saltzman, H., Thomsen, A. H., & Wadsworth, M. E. (2001). Coping with stress during childhood and adolescence: Problems, progress, and potential in theory and research. *Psychological Bulletin, 127,* 87–127.

Comstock, G., & Paik, H. (1991). *Television and the American child.* New York: Academic Press.

Condry, J. (1989). *The psychology of television.* Hillsdale, NJ: Erlbaum.

Conger, R. D., Ge, X., Elder, G. H., Lorenz, F. O., & Simons, R. L. (1994). Economic stress, coercive family process, and developmental problems of adolescents. *Child Development, 65,* 541–561.

Connolly, J., Furman, W., & Konarski, R. (2000). The role of peers in the emergence of heterosexual romantic relationships in adolescence. *Child Development, 71,* 1395–1408.

Connolly, J. A., & Johnson, A. M. (1996). Adolescents' romantic relationships and the structure and quality of their close interpersonal ties. *Personal Relationships, 3,* 185–195.

Connolly, S. D., Paikoff, R. L., & Buchanan, C. M. (1996). Puberty: The interplay of biological and psychosocial processes in adolescence. In G. R. Adams & R. Montemayor (Eds.), *Psychosocial development during adolescence* (Vol. 8, pp. 259–299). Thousand Oaks, CA: Sage.

Connor, D. B., Knight, D. K., & Cross, D. R. (1997). Mothers' and fathers' scaffolding of their 2-year-olds during problem-solving and literacy interactions. *British Journal of Developmental Psychology, 15,* 323–338.

Consortium for Longitudinal Studies. (1983). *As the twig is bent . . . Lasting effects of preschool programs.* Hillsdale, NJ: Erlbaum.

Consumer Product Safety Commission. (1996). *Baseball safety.* Washington, DC: Consumer Product Safety Commission.

Consumer Product Safety Commission. (2001). *Nursery products report for 2000.* Washington, DC: Consumer Product Safety Commission.

Cook, T. D., Appleton, H., Conner, R. F., Shaffer, A., Tamkin, G., & Weber, S. (1975). *Sesame Street revisited.* New York: Russell Sage Foundation.

Cooksey, E. C., & Fondell, M. M. (1996). Spending time with his kids: Effects of family structure on fathers' and children's lives. *Journal of Marriage and the Family, 58,* 693–707.

Coon, K. A., Goldberg, J., Rogers, B. L., & Tucker, K. L. (2001). Relationships between use of television during meals and children's food consumption patterns. *Pediatrics, 107,* 1–7.

Coopersmith, S. (1967). *The antecedents of self-esteem.* San Francisco: Freeman.

Coplan, R. J., & Rubin, K. H. (1998). Exploring and assessing nonsocial play in the preschool. *Social Development, 7,* 72–91.

Coplan, R. J., Rubin, K. H., Fox, N. A., Calkins, S. D., & Stewart, S. L. (1994). Being alone, playing alone, and acting alone: Distinguishing among reticence and passive and active solitude in young children. *Child Development, 65,* 129–137.

Copstick, S. M., Taylor, K. E., Hayes, R., & Morris, N. (1986). Partner support and the use of coping technique in labour. *Journal of Psychosomatic Research, 30,* 497–503.

Corcoran, J. (1998). Consequences of adolescent pregnancy/parents: A review of the literature. *Social Work and Health Care, 27,* 49–67.

Cordell, A. S. (1999). Self-esteem in children. In Carlock, C. J. (Ed), *Enhancing self-esteem* (pp. 287–376). Philadelphia: Accelerated Development, Inc.

Coren, S. (1993). *The left-hander syndrome.* New York: Vintage Books.

Coren, S., & Porac, C. (1977). Fifty centuries of right-handedness. *Science, 198,* 631–632.

Corkum, V., & Moore, C. (1998). The origins of joint visual attention in infants. *Developmental Psychology, 34,* 28–38.

Cornwell, T. (1998, June 12). California votes for English alone. *Times Educational Supplement,* 25.

Cortez, V. L., & Bugental, D. B. (1995). Priming of perceived control in young children as a buffer against fear-inducing events. *Child Development, 66,* 687–696.

Cote, J. F. (1996). Sociological perspectives on identity formation. *Journal of Adolescence, 19,* 417–428.

Counts, C. R., Jones, C., Frame, C. L., & Jarvie, G. J. (1986). The perception of obesity by normal-weight versus obese school-age children. *Child Psychiatry and Human Development, 17,* 113–120.

Coupey, S. M. (1992). Anorexia nervosa. In S. B. Friedman & M. Fisher (Eds.), *Nutrition and eating disorders* (pp. 206–249). St. Louis, MO: Quality Medical Publishing.

Covington, M. C. (1992). *Making the grade.* Cambridge, England: Cambridge University Press.

Cowden, J. E., Sayers, L. K., & Torrey, C. C. (1998). *Pediatric adapted motor development and exercise: An innovative, multisystem approach for professionals and families.* Springfield, IL: Charles C. Thomas.

Cozby, P. C., Worden, P. E., & Kee, D. W. (1989). *Research methods in human development.* Mountain View, CA: Mayfield.

Crain, W. (1992). *Theories of development: Concepts and applications.* Englewood Cliffs, NJ: Prentice-Hall.

Crane, J. (1991). The epidemic theory of ghettos and neighborhood effects on dropping out and teenage childbearing. *American Journal of Sociology, 100,* 1226–1259.

Crane, J. P., LeFevre, M. L., Winborn, R. C., Evans, J. K., Ewigman, B. G., Bain, R. P., Frigoletto, F. D., & McNellis, D. (1994). A randomized trial of prenatal ultrasonographic screening: Impact on the detection, management, and outcome of anomalous fetuses. *American Journal of Obstetrics and Gynecology, 171,* 392–399.

Cratty, B. J. (1986). *Perceptual and motor development in infants and children.* Englewood Cliffs, NJ: Prentice-Hall.

Cratty, B. J. (1999). *Movement behavior and motor learning.* Ann Arbor, MI: Books on Demand.

Creasey, G. L., Jarvis, P. A., & Berk, L. E. (1998). Play and social competence. In O. N. Saracho & B. Spodek (Eds.), *Multiple perspectives on play in early childhood education* (pp. 116–143). Albany: State University of New York Press.

Crick, N. R., & Grotpeter, J. K. (1995). Relational aggression, gender, and social-psychological adjustment, *Child Development, 66,* 710–722.

Crick, N. R., & Rose, A. J. (2000). Toward a gender-balanced approach to the study of social-emotional development: A look at relational aggression. In P. H. Miller & E. K. Scholnick (Eds.), *Toward a feminist developmental psychology* (pp. 153–168). Florence, KY: Taylor & Francis.

Crispell, D. (1995). Why working teens get into trouble. *American Demographics,* 19–20.

Crittenden, P. M. (1988). Distorted patterns of relationship in maltreating families. *Journal of Reproductive and Infant Psychology, 6,* 183–199.

Crittenden, P. M., & Ainsworth, M. D. (1989). Child maltreatment and attachment theory. In D. Cicchetti & V. Carlson (Eds.), *Child maltreatment* (pp. 432–463). Cambridge, England: Cambridge University Press.

Crittenden, P. M., & Claussen, A. H. (2000). *The organization of attachment relationships: Maturation, culture, and context.* New York: Cambridge University Press.

Crocker, P. R., Eklund, R. C., & Kowalski, K. C. (2000). Children's physical activity and physical self-perceptions. *Journal of Sports Sciences, 18,* 383–394.

Crouter, A. C., McHale, S. M., & Tucker, C. J. (1999). Does stress exacerbate parental differential treatment of siblings? A pattern-analytic approach. *Journal of Family Psychology, 13,* 286–299.

Crowell, J., & Treboux, D. (2001). Attachment security in adult partnerships. In C. Clulow (Ed.), *Adult attachment and couple psychotherapy* (pp. 28–42). Philadelphia: Brunner-Routledge.

Csikszentmihalyi, M. (1996). *Creativity: Flow and the psychology of discovery and invention.* New York: HarperCollins.

Csikszentmihalyi, M. (1991). An investment theory of creativity and its development. *Human Development, 34,* 32–34.

Csikszentmihalyi, M., & Larson, R. (1984). *Being adolescent.* New York: Basic Books.

Cuffe, S. P., & Shugart, M. (2001). Child abuse and psychic trauma in children. In V. H. Booney & A. Pumariega (Eds.), *Clinical assessment of child and adolescent behavior* (pp. 328–357). New York: Wiley.

Culp, A. M., Osofsky, J. D., & O'Brien, M. (1996). Language patterns of adolescent and older mothers and their one-year-old children: A comparison study. *First Language, 16,* 61–75.

Cummings, E. M., & Davies, P. (1996). Emotional security as a regulatory process in normal development and the development of psychopathology. *Development and Psychopathology, 8,* 123–139.

Cunningham, F. G., MacDonald, P. C., & Gant, N. F. (1993). *Williams obstetrics.* Norwalk, CT: Appleton & Lange.

Cunningham, P. B., & Henggeler, S. W. (2001). Implementation of an empirically based drug and violence prevention and intervention program in public school settings. *Journal of Clinical Child Psychology, 30,* 221–232.

Curran, D. J., & Renzetti, C. M. (1996). *Social problems.* Boston: Allyn & Bacon.

Curran, J. M. (1999). Constraints of pretend play: Explicit and implicit rules. *Journal of Research in Childhood Education, 14,* 47–55.

Curtiss, S. (1977). *Genie: A psycholinguistic study of a modern-day "wild child."* New York: Academic Press.

Curtiss, S. (1989). The independence and task-specificity of language. In A Bornstein & J. Bruner (Eds.), *Interaction in human development* (pp. 105–137). Hillsdale, NJ: Erlbaum.

Cutler, G. B., Jr. (1988). Precocious puberty. In J. W. Hurst (Ed.), *Medicine for the practicing physician* (pp. 526–530). Boston: Butterworths.

Cutler, G. B., Jr. (1993). Treatment of precocious puberty. In R. M. Lerner, A. C. Petersen, & J. Brooks-Gunn (Eds.), Encyclopedia of adolescence (Vol. 2, pp. 903–907). New York: Garland.

Dacey, J., & Kenny, M. (1997). *Adolescent development.* Dubuque, IA: Brown and Benchmark.

Dainton, M. (1993). The myths and misperceptions of the stepmother identity: Descriptions and prescriptions for identity management. *Family Relations, 42,* 93–98.

Daly, K. (1993). Reshaping fatherhood: Finding the models. *Journal of Family Issues, 14,* 510–530.

Damasio, A. R., & Damasio, H. (1992). Brain and language. *Scientific American, 14,* 597–611.

Damon, W. (1988). *The moral child.* New York: Free Press.

Damon, W. (1995). *Greater expectations: Overcoming the culture of indulgence in America's homes and schools.* New York: Free Press.

Damon, W. (2000). Setting the stage for the development of wisdom: Self-understanding and moral identity during adolescence. In W. S. Brown (Ed.), *Understanding wisdom: Sources, science, & society* (Vol. 3, pp. 339–360). Philadelphia: Templeton Foundation Press.

Daniels, D. H. (1998). Age differences in concepts of self-esteem. *Merrill-Palmer Quarterly, 44,* 234–258.

Danish, S., Kleiber, D., & Hall, H. (1987). Enhancing motivation in the context of sport. In M. Maehr & D. Kleiber (Eds.), *Enhancing motivation* (pp. 211–238).Greenwich, CT: JAI Press.

Dannemiller, J. L. (2001). Brain-behavior relationships in early visual development. In C. A. Nelson & M. Luciana (Eds.), *Handbook of developmental cognitive neuroscience* (pp. 221–235). Cambridge, MA: MIT Press.

Dannemiller, J. L., & Stephens, B. R. (1988). A critical test of infant pattern preference models. *Child Development, 59,* 210–216.

D'Apolito, K. (1998). Substance abuse: Infant and childhood outcomes. *Journal of Pediatric Nursing, 13,* 307–316.

Daro, D. (1996). Preventing child abuse and neglect. In J. Briere, L. Berliner, J. A. Bulkley, C. Jenny, & T. Reid (Eds.), *The APSAC handbook on child maltreatment* (pp. 343–358). Thousand Oaks, CA: Sage.

Daro, D. (2000). Child abuse prevention: New directions and challenges. In D. J. Hansen (Ed.), *Motivation and child maltreatment* (pp. 161–219). Lincoln: University of Nebraska Press.

Darwin, C. (1859). *On the origin of species.* London: J. Murray.

Darwin, C. (1877). Biographical sketch of an infant. *Mind, 2,* 285–294.

Datta, L. E. (1985). Benefits without gains: The paradox of the cognitive effects of early childhood programs and implications for policy. *Special Services in the Schools, 3,* 103–126.

Davey, A. G. (1983). *Learning to be prejudiced.* London: Edward Arnold.

Davidson, J., & Smith, R. (1990). Traumatic experiences in psychiatric outpatients. *Journal of Traumatic Stress Studies, 3,* 459–475.

Davidson, J. E., & Sternberg, R. J. (1984). The role of insight in intellectual giftedness. *Gifted Child Quarterly, 28,* 58–64.

Davies, P. T., & Windle, M. (2000). Middle adolescents' dating pathways and psychosocial adjustment. *Merrill-Palmer Quarterly, 46,* 90–118.

Davis, B. E., Moon, R. Y., Sachs, H. C., & Ottolini, M. C. (1998). Effects of sleep position on infant motor development. *Pediatrics, 102,* 1135–1140.

Davis, B. T., Hops, H., Alpert, A., & Sheeber, L. (1998). Child responses to parental conflict and their effect on adjustment. *Journal of Family Psychology, 12,* 163–177.

Davis, E. C., & Friel, L. V. (2001). Adolescent sexuality: Disentangling the effects of family structure and family context. *Journal of Marriage and the Family, 63,* 669–681.

Davis, J. F. (1990/1991). Five important ideas to teach your kids about television. *Media & Values, 52/53,* 16–19.

Dawson, D. A. (1991). Family structure and children's mental health and well-being. *Journal of Marriage and the Family, 53,* 573–584.

Day, R. D., Peterson, G. W., & McCracken, C. (1998). Predicting spanking of younger and older children by mothers and fathers. *Journal of Marriage and the Family, 60,* 79–94.

De Houwer, A. (1995). Bilingual language acquisition. In P. Fletcher & B. MacWhinney (Eds.), *The handbook of child language* (pp. 219–250). Oxford, England: Blackwell.

De Lisi, R., & McGillicuddy-De Lisi, A. V. (2002). Sex differences in mathematical abilities and achievement. In A. McGillicuddy-De Lisi & R. De Lisi (Eds.), *Biology, society, and behavior: The development of sex differences in cognition.* (pp. 155–182). Westport, CT: Ablex.

de Villiers, P., & de Villiers, J. (1992). Language development. In M. H. Bornstein & M. E. Lamb (Eds.), *Developmental psychology: An advanced textbook* (pp. 255–290). Hillsdale, NJ: Erlbaum.

De Wolff, M. S., & van IJzendoorn, M. H. (1997). Sensitivity and attachment: A meta-analysis of parental antecedents of infant attachment. *Child Development, 68,* 571–591.

Deak, G. O., & Maratsos, M. (1998). On having complex representations of things: Preschoolers use multiple words for objects and people. *Developmental Psychology, 34,* 224–240.

Deal, J. E., Halverson, C. F., & Wampler, K. S. (1989). Parental agreement on child-rearing orientations: Relations to parental, marital, and child characteristics. *Child Development, 60,* 1025–1034.

Deater-Deckard, K., Scarr, S., McCartney, K., & Eisenberg, M. (1994). Paternal separation anxiety: Relationships with parenting stress, child-rearing attitudes, and maternal anxieties. *Psychological Science, 6,* 341–346.

DeCasper, A. J., & Fifer, W. P. (1987). Of human bonding: Newborns prefer their mothers' voices. In J. Oates & S. Sheldon (Eds.), *Cognitive development in infancy* (pp. 111–118). Hove, England: Erlbaum.

DeCasper, A. J., & Spence, M. J. (1986). Prenatal maternal speech influences newborn's perception of speech sounds. *Infant Behavior and Development, 9,* 133–150.

Deci, E. L., & Ryan, R. M. (1995). Human autonomy: The basis for true self-esteem. In M. H. Kernis (Ed.), *Efficacy, agency, and self-esteem* (pp. 31–46). New York: Plenum.

Decker, M. D., Dewey, M. J., Hutcheson, R. H., & Schaffner, W. (1984). The use and efficacy of child restraint devices. *Journal of the American Medical Association, 252,* 2571–2575.

DeCorte, E., Greer, B., & Verschaffel, L. (1996). Mathematics teaching and learning. In D. C. Berliner & R. C. Calfee (Eds.), *Handbook of educational psychology* (pp. 491–549). New York: Macmillan.

Deford, F. (1986). *Alex: The life of a child.* New York: Signet/New American Library.

Degirmencioflu, S. M., Urberg, K. A., Tolson, J. M., & Richard, P. (1998). Adolescent friendship networks: Continuity and change over the school year. *Merrill-Palmer Quarterly, 44,* 313–337.

deHass, I., Harlow, B. L., & Cramer, D. W. (1991). Spontaneous preterm birth: A case-control study. *American Journal of Obstetrics and Gynecology, 165,* 1290–1296.

Dekovic, M. (1999). Parent-adolescent conflict: Possible determinants and consequences. *International Journal of Behavioral Development, 23,* 977–1000.

Dekovic, M., & Janssens, J. M. (1992). Parents' child-rearing style and child's sociometric status. *Developmental Psychology, 28,* 925–932.

Dell, D. L. (2001). Adolescent pregnancy. In N. L. Stotland & D. E. Stewart (Eds.), *Psychological aspects of women's health care: The interface between psychiatry and obstetrics and gynecology* (pp. 95–116). Washington, DC: American Psychiatric Press.

DeLoache, J. S., Cassidy, D. J., & Brown, A. L. (1985). Precursors of mnemonic strategies in very young children's memory. *Child Development, 56,* 125–137.

DeLongis, A., & Preece, A. (2002). Emotional and relational consequences of coping in stepfamilies. *Marriage & Family Review.*

Demaray, M. K., & Elliot, S. N. (1998). Teachers' judgments of students' academic functioning: A comparison of actual and predicted performance. *School Psychology Quarterly, 13,* 8–24.

DeMarie-Dreblow, D., & Miller, P. H. (1988). The development of children's strategies for selective attention: Evidence for a transitional period. *Child Development, 59,* 1504–1513.

DeMier, R. L., Hunan, M. T., Hatfield, R. F., Varner, M. W., Harris, H. B., & Maniello, R. L. (2000). A measurement model of perinatal stressors: Identifying risk for postnatal emotional distress in mothers of high-risk infants. *Journal of Clinical Psychology, 56,* 89–100.

Demuth, K. (1990). Maturation and the acquisition of the Sesotho passive. *Language, 65,* 56–81.

Denham, S. A., Mason, T., Caverly, S., Schmidt, M., Hackney, R., Caswell, C., & DeMulder, E. (2001). Preschoolers at play: Co-socializers of emotional and social competence. *International Journal of Behavioral Development, 25,* 290–301.

Denham, S. A., Renwick-DeBardi, S., & Hughes, S. (1994). Emotional communication between mothers and preschoolers: Relations with emotional competence. *Merrill-Palmer Quarterly, 40,* 488–508.

Denham, S. A., Zoller, D., & Couchoud, E. A. (1994). Socialization of preschoolers' emotion understanding. *Developmental Psychology, 30,* 928–936.

Deregowski, J. B. (1980). *Illusions, patterns, and pictures: A cross-cultural perspective.* London: Academic Press.

DeRoche, E. F., & Williams, M. M. (2001). *Educating hearts and minds: A comprehensive character education framework.* Thousand Oaks, CA: Corwin Press.

Derzon, J. H. (2001). Antisocial behavior and the prediction of violence: A meta-analysis. *Psychology and the Schools, 38,* 93–106.

Deslandes, R., & Royer, E. (1997). Family-related variables and school disciplinary events at the secondary level. *Behavioral Disorders, 23,* 18–28.

Devlin, B., Daniels, M., & Roeder, K. (1997). The heritability of IQ. *Nature, 338,* 468–471.

DeVries, M. (1984). Temperament and infant mortality among the Masai of East Africa. *American Journal of Psychiatry, 141,* 1189–1994.

DeVries, M., & Sameroff, A. J. (1984). Culture and temperament: Influences on temperament in three East African societies. *American Journal of Orthopsychiatry, 54,* 83–96.

Diamond, A. (1991). Frontal lobe involvement in cognitive changes during the first year of life. In K. R. Gibson & A. C. Petersen (Eds.), *Brain maturation and cognitive development: Comparative and cross-cultural perspectives* (pp. 127–180). New York: Aldine de Gruyter.

Diamond, A. (2000). Close interrelation of motor development and cognitive development and of the cerebellum and prefrontal cortex. *Child Development, 71,* 44–56.

Diamond, M., & Sigmundson, K. (1997). Sex reassignment at birth: Long-term review and clinical implications. *Archives of Pediatric Adolescent Medicine, 151,* 298–304.

Diehl, S. F., Moffitt, K. A., & Wade, S. M. (1991). Focus group interview with parents of children with medically complex needs: An intimate look at their perceptions and feelings. *Children's Health Care, 20,* 170–178.

Dietz, T. L. (1998). An examination of violence and gender role portrayals in video games. *Sex Roles, 38,* 423–444.

Dietz, W. H., & Gortmaker, S. L. (1985). Do we fatten our children at the television set? Obesity and television viewing in children and adolescents. *Pediatrics, 75,* 807–812.

DiGirolamo, A. M., Geis, H. K., & Walker, C. E. (1998). Developmental issues. In R. T. Ammerman & J. V. Campo (Eds.), *Handbook of pediatric psychology and psychiatry* (pp. 1–22). Boston: Allyn & Bacon.

DiLalla, L. F., & Watson, M. W. (1988). Differentiation of fantasy and reality: Preschoolers' reactions to interruptions in their play. *Developmental Psychology, 24,* 286–291.

DiMaggio, P. (1997). Culture and cognition. *Annual Review of Sociology, 23,* 263–267.

DiPietro, J. A., Hodgson, D. M., Costigan, K. A., & Johnson, T. R. B. (1996). Fetal antecedents of infant temperament. *Child Development, 67,* 2568–2583.

DiPietro, J. A., Larson, S. K., & Porges, S. W. (1987). Behavioral and heartrate pattern differences between breast-fed and bottle-fed neonates. *Developmental Psychology, 23,* 467–474.

Dishion, T. J. (1990). The peer context of troublesome child and adolescent behavior. In P. E. Leone (Ed.), *Understanding troubled and troubling youth* (pp. 128–153). Newbury Park, CA: Sage.

Dishion, T. J., & Andrews, D. W. (1996). A multicomponent intervention for families of young adolescents at risk: An analysis of short-term outcomes. *Journal of Consulting and Clinical Psychology, 63,* 538–548.

Dishion, T. J., French, D. C., & Patterson, G. R. (1995). The development and ecology of antisocial behavior. In D. Cicchetti & D. J. Cohen (Eds.), *Developmental psychopathology* (Vol. 2, pp. 421–471). New York: Wiley.

Dodge, K. A. (1991). Emotion and social information processing. In J. Garber & K. A. Dodge (Eds.), *The development of emotion: Regulation and dysregulation* (pp. 159–181). Cambridge, England: Cambridge University Press.

Dodge, K. A. (2001). The science of youth violence prevention: Progressing from developmental epidemiology to efficacy to effectiveness to public policy. *American Journal of Preventive Medicine, 20,* 63–70.

Dodge, K. A., Bates, J. E., & Pettit, G. S. (1990). Mechanisms in the cycle of violence. *Science, 250,* 1678–1683.

Dodge, K. A., & Coie, J. D. (1987). Social-information-processing factors in reactive and proactive aggression in children's peer groups. *Journal of Personality and Social Psychology, 53,* 1146–1158.

Dodge, K. A., Pettit, G. S., McClaskey, C. L., & Brown, M. M. (1986). Social competence in children. *Monographs of the Society for Research in Child Development* (Vol. 51, No. 2). Chicago: University of Chicago Press.

Doherty, W. J. (1997). The best of times and the worst of times: Fathering as a contested arena of academic discourse. In A. J. Hawkins & D. C. Dollahite (Eds.), *Generative fathering: Beyond deficit perspectives* (pp. 217–227). Newbury Park, CA: Sage.

Dollaghan, C. (1985). Child meet word: "Fast mapping" in preschool children. *Journal of Speech and Hearing Research, 28,* 449–454.

Dollberg, S., Fainaru, O., Mimouni, F. B., Shenhav, M., Lessing, J. B., & Kupferminc, M. (2000). Effect of passive smoking on neonatal nucleated red blood cells. *Pediatrics, 106*, 1–3.

Donahue, M. J. (1995). Religion and the well-being of adolescents. *Journal of Social Issues, 51*, 145—160.

Donaldson, M. (1978). *Children's minds*. New York: W. W. Norton.

Dornbusch, S. M., Mont-Reynaud, R., Ritter, P. L., Chen, Z. Y., & Steinberg, L. (1991). Stressful events and their correlates among adolescents of diverse backgrounds. In M. E. Colten & S. Gore (Eds.), *Adolescent stress: Causes and consequences* (pp. 111–130). New York: Aldine de Gruyter.

Doussard-Roosevelt, J. A., Porges, S. W., Scanlon, J. W., Alemmi, B., & Scanlon, K. B. (1997). Vagal regulation of heart rate in the prediction of development outcome for very low birth weight preterm infants. *Child Development, 68*, 173–186.

Doyle, L. W., Rickards, A. L., Kelly, E. A., Ford, G. W., & Callanan, C. (1992). Breastfeeding and intelligence. *Lancet, 339*, 744–745.

Drewett, R. F. (1993). The infant's regulation of nutritional intake. In I. St. James-Roberts, G. Harris, & D. Messer (Eds.), *Infant crying, feeding, and sleeping: Development, problems, and treatments* (pp. 83–98). New York: Harvester Wheatsheaf.

Dryfoos, J. G. (1990). *Adolescents at risk: Prevalence and prevention.* New York: Oxford University Press.

DuBois-Reymond, M., & Ravesloot, J. (1996). The roles of parents and peers in the sexual and relational development of adolescents. In K. Hurrelmann & S. F. Hamilton (Eds.), *Social problems and social contexts in adolescence* (pp. 175–197). New York: Aldine de Gruyter.

Dubowitz, H. (1989). Prevention of child maltreatment: What is known. *Pediatrics, 83*, 570–577.

Dubrow, N. F., & Garbarino, J. (1989). Living in the war zone: Mothers and young children in a public housing development. *Child Welfare, 68*, 3–20.

Duda, J. (1988). The relationship between goal perspectives, persistence and behavioral intensity among male and female recreational sport participants. *Leisure Sciences, 10*, 95–106.

Dulcan, M. K. (1986). Comprehensive treatment of children and adolescents with attention deficit disorders: The state of the art. *Clinical Psychology Review, 6*, 539–569.

Dulcan, M. K. (1989). Attention deficit disorders. In C. G. Last & M. Hersen (Eds.), *Handbook of child psychiatric diagnosis* (pp. 95–128). New York: Wiley.

Dumka, L. E., Roosa, M. W., & Jackson, K. M. (1997). Risk, conflict, mothers' parenting, and children's adjustment in low-income, Mexican immigrant and Mexican American families. *Journal of Marriage and the Family, 59*, 309–323.

Dunbar, K., & Klahr, D. (1989). Developmental differences in scientific discovery processes. In D. Klahr & K. Kotovsky (Eds.), *Complex information processing: The impact of Herbert A. Simon* (pp. 109–143). Hillsdale, NJ: Erlbaum.

Duncan, P., Ritter, P., Dornbusch, S., Gross, R., & Carlsmith, J. (1985). The effects of pubertal timing on body image, school behavior, and deviance. *Journal of Youth and Adolescence, 14*, 227–236.

Duncan, R. M., & Pratt, M. W. (1997). Microgenetic change in the quantity and quality of preschoolers' private speech. *International Journal of Behavioral Development, 20*, 367–383.

Dunn, J. (1983). Sibling relationships in early childhood. *Child Development, 54*, 787–811.

Dunn, J. (1988). *The beginnings of social understanding.* Cambridge, MA: Harvard University Press.

Dunn, J. (1992). Sisters and brothers: Current issues in developmental research. In F. Boer & J. Dunn (Eds.), *Children's sibling relationships* (pp. 1–18). Hillsdale, NJ: Erlbaum.

Dunn, J. (2001). The development of children's conflict and prosocial behavior: Lessons from research on social understanding and gender. In J. Hill & B. Maughan (Eds.), *Conduct disorders in childhood and adolescence* (pp. 49–66). New York: Cambridge University Press.

Dunn, J., & Munn, P. (1987). The development of justification in disputes. *Developmental Psychology, 23*, 791–798.

Dunn, J., & Slomkowski, C. (1992). Conflict and the development of social understanding. In C. U. Shantz & W. W. Hartup (Eds.), *Conflict in child and adolescent development* (pp. 70–92). Cambridge, England: Cambridge University Press.

DuPaul, G. J., McGoey, K. E., Eckert, T. L., & VanBrakle, J. (2001). Preschool children with attention-deficit/hyperactivity disorder: Impairments in behavioral, social, and school functioning. *Journal of the American Academy of Child and Adolescent Psychiatry, 40*, 508–515.

Dusek, J. B. (1996). *Adolescent development and behavior.* Saddle River, NJ: Prentice-Hall.

Dweck, C. S., & Leggett, E. L. (1988). A social-cognitive approach to motivation and personality. *Psychological Review, 95*, 256–273.

Dwyer, C. A., & Johnson, L. M. (1997). Grades, accomplishments, and correlates. In W. Willingham & N. Cole (Eds.), *Gender and fair assessment* (pp. 127–156). Mahwah, NJ: Erlbaum.

Dwyer, K. M., Richardson, J. L., Danley, K. L., Hansen, W. B., Sussman, S. Y., Brannon, B., Dent, C. W., Johnson, C. A., & Flay, B. R. (1990). Characteristics of eighth-grade students who initiate self-care in elementary and junior high school. *Pediatrics, 86*, 448–454.

Eason, E., & Feldman, P. (2000). Much ado about a little cut: Is episiotomy worthwhile? *Obstetrics and Gynecology, 95*, 616–618.

Easterbrooks, M. A., & Goldberg, W. A. (1990). Security of toddler-parent attachment. In M. T. Greenberg, D. Cicchetti, & E. M. Cummings (Eds.), *Attachment in the preschool years* (pp. 221–244). Chicago: University of Chicago Press.

Eaton, W. O, & Enns, L. R. (1986). Sex differences in human motor activity level. *Psychological Bulletin, 100*, 19–28.

Ebata, A. T., Petersen, A. C., & Conger, J. (1990). The development of psychopathology in adolescence. In J. Rolf, A. S. Masten, D. Cicchetti, K. H. Nuechterlein, & S. Weintraub (Eds.), *Risk and protective factors in the development of psychopathology* (pp. 308–333). Cambridge, England: Cambridge University Press.

Eccles, J. S., & Barber, B. L. (1999). Student council, volunteering, basketball, or marching band: What kinds of extracurricular involvement matters? *Journal of Adolescent Research, 14*, 10–43.

Eccles, J. S., Freedman-Doan, C., Frome, P., Jacobs, J., & Yoon, K. S. (2000). Gender-role socialization in the family: A longitudinal approach. In T. Eckes & H. Trautner (Eds.), *The developmental social psychology of gender* (pp. 333–360). Mahwah, NJ: Erlbaum.

Eccles, J. S., & Jacobs, J. E. (1986). Social forces shape math attitudes and performance. *Signs, 11*, 367–380.

Eccles, J. S., & Midgley, C. (1989). Stage-environment fit: Developmentally appropriate classrooms for young adolescents. In C. Ames & R. Ames (Eds.), *Research on motivation in education* (Vol. 3, pp. 139–186). Greenwich, CT: JAI Press.

Eccles, J. S., Wigfield, A., Flanagan, C. A., & Miller, C. (1989). Self-concepts, domain values, and self-esteem: Relations and changes at early adolescence. *Journal of Personality, 57*, 282–310.

Eccles, J. S., Wigfield, A., Midgley, C. H., Reuman, D., MacIver, D., & Feldlaufer, H. (1993). Negative effects of traditional middle schools on students' motivation. *Elementary School Journal, 93*, 553–574.

Eckensberger, L. H. (1994). Moral development and its measurement across cultures. In W. J. Lonner & R. S. Malpass (Eds.), *Psychology and culture* (pp. 75–79). Boston: Allyn & Bacon.

Edens, J. F., & Cavell, T. A. (1999). A review and reformulation of adoptive relationships from an attachment perspective. *Adoption Quarterly, 3*, 43–70.

Edgeworth, J., & Carr, A. (2000). Child abuse. In A. Carr (Ed.), *What works with children and adolescents?: A critical review of psychological interventions with children, adolescents and their families* (pp. 17–48). Florence, KY: Taylor & Francis/Routledge.

Egeland, B., & Sroufe, L. A. (1983). Developmental sequelae of maltreatment in infancy. In R. Rizley & D. Cicchetti (Eds.), *New directions for child development* (Vol. 11, pp. 77–72). San Francisco: Jossey-Bass.

Egley, A. (2000). *Highlights of the National Youth Gang Survey.* Washington, DC: Office of Juvenile Justice and Delinquency Prevention.

Ehrle, J., Adams, G., & Tout, K. (2001). *Who's caring for our youngest children?* Washington, DC: The Urban Institute.

Eiberg, H., & Mohr, J. (1987). Major genes of eye color and hair color linked to LU and SE. *Clinical Genetics, 31,* 186–191.

Eisenberg, A., Murkoff, H. E., & Hathaway, S. E. (1999). *What to expect when you're expecting.* New York: Workman.

Eisenberg, N. (1992). *The caring child.* Cambridge, MA: Harvard University Press.

Eisenberg, N., & Fabes, R. A. (1992). Emotion regulation and the development of social competence. In P. Clark (Ed.), *Emotion and social behavior* (Vol. 14, pp. 119–150). Newbury Park, CA: Sage.

Eisenberg, N., & Fabes, R. A. (1998). Prosocial development. In W. Damon (Ed.), *Handbook of child psychology* (Vol. 3, pp. 701–778). New York: Wiley.

Eisenberg, N., & Fabes, R. A. (1999). Emotion, emotion-related regulation, and quality of socioemotional functioning. In L. Balter & C. S. Tamis-LeMonda (Eds.), *Child psychology: A handbook of contemporary issues* (pp. 318–335). Philadelphia: Psychology Press.

Eisenberg, N., Fabes, R. A., & Guthrie, I. K. (1997). Coping with stress: The roles of regulation and development. In S. A. Wolchik & I. N. Sandler (Eds.), *Handbook of children's coping* (pp. 41–72). New York: Plenum.

Eisenberg, N., Gershoff, E. T., Fabes, R. A., Shepard, S. A., Cumberland, A. J., Losoya, S. H., Guthrie, I. K., & Murphy, B. C. (2001). Mother's emotional expressivity and children's behavior problems and social competence: Mediation through children's regulation. *Developmental Psychology, 37,* 475–490.

Eisenberg, N., Guthrie, I. K., Fabes, R. A., Shepard, S., Losoya, S., Murphy, B. C., Jones, S., Poulin, R., & Reiser, M. (2000). Prediction of elementary school children's externalizing problem behaviors from attentional and behavioral regulation and negative emotionality. *Child Development, 71,* 1367–1382.

Eisenberg, N., Guthrie, I. K., Murphy, B. C., Shepard, S. A., Cumberland, A., & Carlo, G. (1999). Consistency and development of prosocial dispositions: A longitudinal study. *Child Development, 70,* 1360–1372.

Eisenberg, N., Martin, C. L., & Fabes, R. A. (1996). Gender development and gender effects. In D. Berliner & R. Calfee (Eds.), *Handbook of educational psychology* (pp. 358–398). New York: Macmillan.

Eisenberg, N., & Murphy, B. (1995). Parenting and children's moral development. In M. C. Bornstein (Ed.), *Handbook of parenting* (Vol. 4, pp. 227–257). Hillsdale, NJ: Erlbaum.

Eisenberg, N., & Strayer, J. (Eds.) (1987). *Empathy and its development.* Cambridge, England: Cambridge University Press.

Eisenberg, N., Zhou, Q., & Koller, S. (2001). Brazilian adolescents' prosocial moral judgment and behavior: Relations to sympathy, perspective taking, gender-role orientation, and demographic characteristics. *Child Development, 72,* 518–534.

Elardo, R., & Bradley, R. H. (1981). The Home Observation for Measurement of the Environment (HOME) Scale: A review of research. *Developmental Review, 1,* 113–145.

Elardo, R., Bradley, R. H., & Caldwell, B. M. (1975). The relation of infants' home environments to mental test performance from six to thirty-six months: A longitudinal analysis. *Child Development, 46,* 71–76.

Elbert, T., Heim, S., & Rockstroh, B. (2001). Neural plasticity and development. In C. Nelson & M. Luciana (Eds.), *Handbook of developmental cognitive neuroscience* (pp. 191–202). Cambridge, MA: MIT Press.

Elder, G. H., Conger, R. D., Foster, E. M., & Ardelt, M. (1992). Families under economic pressure. *Journal of Family Issues, 13,* 5–37.

Elicker, J., Englund, M., & Sroufe, L. A. (1992). Predicting peer competence and peer relationships in childhood from early parent-child relationships. In R. D. Parke & G. W. Ladd (Eds.), *Family-peer relationships: Modes of linkage* (pp. 77–106). Hillsdale, NJ: Erlbaum.

Elkind, D. (1967). Egocentrism in adolescence. *Child Development, 38,* 1025–1033.

Elkind, D. (1986). *The miseducation of children: Superkids at risk.* New York: Knopf.

Elkind, D. (1987). *Miseducation: Preschoolers at risk.* New York: Knopf.

Elkind, D. (1988, January). Educating the very young: A call for clear thinking. *NEA Today,* 22–27.

Elliott, D. S. (1994). Serious violent offenders: Onset, developmental course, and termination. *Criminology, 32,* 1–21.

Elliott, J. G. (1999). School refusal: Issues of conceptualization, assessment, and treatment. *Journal of Child Psychology and Psychiatry and Allied Disciplines, 40,* 1001–1012.

Elo, I. T., King, R. B., & Furstenberg, F. F. (1999). Adolescent females: Their sexual partners and the fathers of their children. *Journal of Marriage and the Family, 61,* 74–84.

Emery, R. E. (1988). *Marriage, divorce, and children's adjustment.* Beverly Hills, CA: Sage.

Emery, R. E., & Laumann-Billings, L. (1998). An overview of the nature, causes, and consequences of abusive family relationships. *American Psychologist, 53,* 121–135.

Emes, C. E. (1997). Is Mr. Pac Man eating our children? *Canadian Journal of Psychiatry, 42,* 409–414.

Emslie, G. J., Weinberg, W. A., Kennard, B. D., & Kowatch, R. A. (1994). Neurobiological aspects of depression in children and adolescents. In W. M. Reynolds & H. F. Johnston (Eds.), *Handbook of depression in children and adolescents* (pp. 143–165). New York: Plenum.

Ennett, S. T., & Bauman, K. E. (1996). Adolescent social networks: School, demographic and longitudinal considerations. *Journal of Adolescent Research, 11,* 194–215.

Ensminger, A. H., Ensminger, M. E., Konlande, J. E., & Robson, J. R. K. (1986). *Food for health: A nutritional encyclopedia.* Clovis, CA: Peguis Press.

Entwisle, D. R. (1990). Schooling and the adolescent. In S. S. Feldman & G. R. Elliott (Eds.), *At the threshold: The developing adolescent* (pp. 197–224). Cambridge, MA: Harvard University Press.

Epperson, C. N. (1999). Postpartum major depression: Detection and treatment. *American Family Physician,* 2247–2258.

Epstein, J. L. (1986). Friend selection: Developmental and environmental influences. In E. Mueller & C. Cooper (Eds.), *Process and outcome in peer relationships* (pp. 171–192). New York: Academic Press.

Epstein, L. G., Sharer, L. R., Oleske, J. M., Connor, E. M., Goudsmit, J., Bagdon, L., Robert-Guroff, M., & Koenigsberger, M. R. (1986). Neurologic manifestations of human immunodeficiency virus infection in children. *Pediatrics, 78,* 678–687.

Erel, O., Margolin, G., & John, R. S. (1998). Observed sibling interaction: Links with marital and the mother-child relationship. *Developmental Psychology, 34,* 288–298.

Ericsson, R. J., & Beernink, F. (1987). Sex chromosome ratios in human sperm. *Fertility and Sterility, 47,* 531–532.

Erikson, E. H. (1959). *Identity and the life cycle in psychological issues* (Vol. 1). New York: International Universities Press.

Erikson, E. H. (1963). *Childhood and society.* New York: Norton.

Erikson, E. H. (1968). *Identity: Youth and crisis.* New York: Norton.

Erikson, E. H. (1969). *Gandhi's truth on the origins of militant nonviolence.* New York: Norton.

Erikson, E. H. (1980). *Identity and the life cycle.* New York: Norton.

Eron, L. D. (1982). Parent-child interaction, television violence, and aggression of children. *American Psychologist, 37,* 197–211.

Eron, L. D., Huesmann, L. R., Lefkowitz, M. M., & Walder, L. O. (1996). Does television violence cause aggression? In D. F. Greenberg (Ed.), *Criminal careers* (Vol. 2, pp. 311–321). Aldershot, England: Dartmouth Publishing.

Esbensen, F. (2000). *Preventing adolescent gang involvement.* Washington, DC: Office of Juvenile Justice and Delinquency Prevention.

Escarce, M. E. W. (1989). A cross-cultural study of Nepalese neonatal behavior. In J. K. Nugent, B. M. Lester, & T. B. Brazelton (Eds.), *The cultural context of infancy* (Vol. 1, pp. 65–86). Norwood, NJ: Ablex Publishing.

Espinoza, R. L., & Ehrlich, A. (1989). Personality, family relationships, and moral development in Chicano and Black adolescent gang members. *Adolescent Psychiatry, 16,* 216–227.

Eveleth, P. B., & Tanner, J. M. (1990). *Worldwide variation in human growth.* Cambridge, England: Cambridge University Press.

Eyler, F. D., & Behnke, M. (1999). Early development of infants exposed to drugs prenatally. *Clinical Perinatology, 26,* 107–150.

Ezzaki, A. (1990). Research on Iftah Ya Simsim, the Arabic coproduction. In Children's Television Workshop (Ed.), *Sesame Street research* (pp. 60–62). New York: Children's Television Workshop.

Fabes, R. A., Carlo, G., Kupanoff, K., & Laible, D. (1999). Transition to adolescence and prosocial/moral development I: Individual processes. *Journal of Early Adolescence, 14,* 1–14.

Fabes, R. A., & Eisenberg, N. (1992). Young children's coping with interpersonal anger. *Child Development, 63,* 116–128.

Fabes, R. A., Eisenberg, N., Smith, M. C., & Murphy, B. C. (1996). Getting angry at peers: Associations with liking of the provocateur. *Child Development, 67,* 942–956.

Fabes, R. A., & Filsinger, E. E. (1988). Odor communication and parent-child interaction. In E. E. Filsinger (Ed.), *Biosocial perspectives on the family* (pp. 93–118). Newbury Park, CA: Sage.

Fabes, R. A., Fultz, J., Eisenberg, N., Plumlee, T. M., & Christopher, F. S. (1989). The effects of rewards on children's prosocial motivation: A socialization study. *Developmental Psychology, 25,* 509–515.

Fabes, R. A., Martin, C. L., Hanish, L., & Updegraff, K. (2000). New criteria for evaluating child development research. *Child Development, 71,* 212–221.

Fabes, R. A., Martin, C. L., & Smith, M. (1994). Further perspectives on child development research: A reconsideration and a recall; Invited response to McKinney and Lerner's paper. *Family Sciences Research Journal, 23,* 43–56.

Fabes, R. A., Wilson, P., & Christopher, F. S. (1989). A time to reexamine the role of television in family life. *Family Relations, 38,* 337–341.

Fabris, C., Prandi, G., Perathoner, C., & Soldi, A. (1998). Neonatal drug addiction. *Panminerva Medicine, 40,* 239–243.

Falbo, T. (1992). Social norms and the one-child family: Clinical and policy implications. In F. Boer & J. Dunn (Eds.), *Children's sibling relationships: Developmental and clinical issues* (pp. 71–82). Hillsdale, NJ: Erlbaum.

Falbo, T., & Poston, D. L. (1993). The academic, personality, and physical outcomes of only children in China. *Child Development, 64,* 18–35.

Falk, P. J. (1989). Lesbian mothers: Psychosocial assumptions in family law. *American Psychologist, 44,* 941–947.

Fan, X., & Chen, M. (2001). Parental involvement and students' academic achievement: A meta-analysis. *Educational Psychology Review, 13,* 1–22.

Fanaroff, A. A., Martin, R. J., & Miller, M. J. (1994). Identification and management of high-risk problems in the neonate. In R. K. Creasy & R. Resnik (Eds.), *Maternal-fetal medicine: Principles and practice* (pp. 390–443). Philadelphia: W. B. Saunders.

Fang, J., Madhavan, S., & Alderman, M. H. (1999). Low birth weight: Race and maternal nativity—impact of community income. *Pediatrics, 103,* 1–6.

Fantuzzo, J., & Mohr, W. K. (2000). Pursuit of wellness in Head Start: Making beneficial connections for children and families. In D. Cicchetti & J. Rappaport (Eds.), *The promotion of wellness in children and adolescents* (pp. 341–369). Washington, DC: Child Welfare League of America.

Fantz, R. L., Ordy, J. M., & Udelf, M. S. (1962). Maturation of pattern vision in infants during the first six months. *Journal of Comparative and Physiological Psychology, 55,* 907–917.

Farber, N. (1994). Perceptions of pregnancy risk: A comparison by class and race. *American Journal of Orthopsychiatry, 64,* 479–484.

Farmer, M. (1997). Exploring the links between communication skills and social competence. *Educational and Child Psychology, 14,* 38–44.

Farrar, M. J. (1990). Discourse and the acquisition of grammatical morphemes. *Journal of Child Language, 17,* 607–624.

Farrar, M. J., & Goodman, G. S. (1992). Developmental changes in event memory. *Child Development, 63,* 173–187.

Farrington, D. P. (1998). Youth crime and antisocial behavior. In A. Campbell & S. Muncer (Eds.), *The social child* (pp. 353–392). Hove, England: Psychology Press.

Farver, J. A. M., & Frosch, D. L. (1996). L. A. stories: Aggression in preschoolers' spontaneous narratives after the riots of 1992. *Child Development, 67,* 19–32.

Federal Bureau of Investigation. (1998). *A parent's guide to Internet safety.* Washington, DC: Federal Bureau of Investigation.

Federal Bureau of Investigation. (2000). *Uniform crime reports: 2000.* Washington, DC: Federal Bureau of Investigation.

Federal Interagency Forum on Child and Family Statistics. *America's children.* Washington, DC: Federal Interagency Forum on Child and Family Statistics.

Federman, J. (1998). *National television violence study* (Vol. 3). Santa Barbara, CA: Center for Communication and Social Policy.

Feingold, A. (1992). Good-looking people are not what we think. *Psychological Bulletin, 111,* 304–341.

Feldman, D. H. (1999). The development of creativity. In R. J. Sternberg (Ed.), *Handbook of creativity* (pp. 169–186). Cambridge, England: Cambridge University Press.

Feldman, R., Weller, A., Leckman, J. F., Kuint, J., & Eidelman, A. I. (1999). The nature of the mother's tie to her infant: Maternal bonding under conditions of proximity, separation, and potential loss. *Journal of Child Psychology and Psychiatry and Allied Disciplines, 40,* 929–939.

Feldman, S. S., & Rosenthal, D. A. (1994). Culture makes a difference . . . or does it? A comparison of adolescents in Hong Kong, Australia, and the United States. In R. K. Silbereisen & T. Eberhard (Eds.), *Adolescence in context* (pp. 99–124). New York: Springer-Verlag.

Fenson, C., Kagan, J., Kearsley, R. B., & Zelazo, P. R. (1976). The developmental progression of manipulative play in the first two years. *Child Development, 47,* 232–236.

Fenson, L., Dale, P. S., Reznick, J. S., Bates, E., Thal, D. J., & Pethick, S. J. (1994). Variability in early communicative development. *Monographs of the Society for Research in Child Development, 59* (Whole No. 242). Chicago: Chicago University Press.

Fenton, N. (1928). The only child. *Journal of Genetic Psychology, 35,* 546–556.

Ferguson, R. E. (1998). Teachers' perceptions and expectations and the Black-White test score gap. In C. Jenks & M. Phillips (Eds.), *The Black-White test score gap* (pp. 273–317). Washington, DC: Brookings Institution.

Fergusson, D. M., Beautrais, A. L., & Silva, P. A. (1982). Breast-feeding and cognitive development in the first seven years of life. *Social Science Medicine, 16,* 1705–1708.

Fergusson, D. M., Horwood, L. J., & Lynskey, M. T. (1993). Maternal smoking before and after pregnancy: Effects on behavioral outcomes in middle childhood. *Pediatrics, 92,* 815–822.

Fernald, A. (1985). Four-month-old infants prefer to listen to motherese. *Infant Behavior and Development, 8,* 181–195.

Fernald, A. (1989). Intonation and communicative intent in mothers' speech to infants: Is the melody the message? *Child Development, 60,* 1497–1510.

Feynman, R. P. (1985). *"Surely you're joking, Mr. Feynman!"* Toronto: Bantam Books.

Field, A. E., Camargo, C. A., Taylor, C. B., Berkey, C. S., Roberts, S. B., & Colditz, G. A. (2001). Peer, parent, and media influences on the development of weight concerns and frequent dieting among preadolescent and adolescent girls and boys. *Pediatrics, 107,* 54–60.

Field, T. M. (1991). Quality of infant day-care and grade school behavior and performance. *Child Development, 62,* 863–870.

Fincham, F. D. (1998). Child development and marital relationships. *Child Development, 69,* 543–574.

Fine, G. A., Mortimer, J. T., & Roberts, D. F. (1990). Leisure, work, and the mass media. In S. S. Feldman & G. R. Elliot (Eds.), *At the threshold: The developing adolescent* (pp. 225–252). Cambridge, MA: Harvard University Press.

Finkelman, B. (1995). *Physical and emotional abuse and neglect.* New York: Garland.

Finn, J. D. (1989). Withdrawing from school. *Harvard Educational Research, 59,* 117–142.

Fiscella, K., Kitzman, H. J., Cole, R. E., Sidora, K. J., & Olds, D. (1998). Does child abuse predict adolescent pregnancy? *Pediatrics, 101,* 620–624.

Fisch, S., Truglio, R. T., & Cole, C. F. (1999). The impact of *Sesame Street* on preschool children: A review and synthesis of 30 years' research. *Media Psychology, 1,* 165–190.

Fischer, J. L., Munsch, J., & Greene, S. M. (1996). Adolescence and intimacy. In G. R. Adams & R. Montemayor (Eds.), *Psychosocial development during adolescence* (Vol. 8, pp. 95–129). Thousand Oaks, CA: Sage.

Fischer, K. W., & Bidell, T. K. (1998). Dynamic relationship of psychological structures in action and thought. In W. Damon (Ed.), *Handbook of child psychology* (Vol. 1, pp. 467–562). New York: Wiley.

Fischer, K. W., & Rose, S. P. (1994). Dynamic development of coordination components in brain and behavior: A framework for theory and research. In G. Dawson & K. W. Fischer (Eds.), *Human behavior and the developing brain* (pp. 3–66). New York: Guilford.

Fisher, C. B., & Brone, R. J. (1991). Eating disorders in adolescence. In R. M. Lerner, A. C. Petersen, & J. Brooks-Gunn (Eds.), *Encyclopedia of adolescence* (Vol. 1, pp. 272–277). New York: Garland.

Fisher, M., Trieller, K., & Napolitano, B. (1989). Premenstrual symptoms in adolescents. *Journal of Adolescent Health Care, 10,* 369–375.

Fitch, R. H., & Bimonte, H. A. (2002). Hormone, brain, and behavior: Putative biological contributions to cognitive sex differences. In A. McGillicuddy-De Lisi & R. De Lisi (Eds.), *Biology, society, and behavior: The development of sex differences in cognition* (pp. 55–92). Westport, CT: Ablex.

Fitzgerald, B. (1999). Children of lesbian and gay parents: A review of the literature. *Marriage & Family Review, 29,* 57–75.

Fitzgerald, H. E., Davies, W. H., Zucker, R. A., & Klinger, M. (1994). Developmental systems theory and substance abuse. In L. L'Abate (Ed.), *Handbook of developmental family psychology and psychopathology* (pp. 350–372). New York: Wiley.

Fix, M., & Passell, J. S. (1994). *Immigration and immigrants: Setting the record straight.* Washington, DC: Urban Institute.

Flake, A. W., Roncarolo, M., Puck, J. M., Almeida-Porada, G., Evans, M. I., Johnson, M. P., Abella, E. M., Harrison, D. D., & Zanjani, E. D. (1996). Treatment of X-linked severe combined immunodeficiency by in utero transplantation of paternal bone marrow. *New England Journal of Medicine, 335,* 1806–1810.

Flanagan, P. (1998). Teen mothers: Countering the myths of dysfunction and developmental disruption. In C. G. Coll & J. L Surrey (Eds.), *Mothering against odds* (pp. 238–254). New York: Guilford Press.

Flannery, D. J., Huff, C. R., & Manos, M. (1998). Youth gangs: A developmental perspective. In T. P. Gullotta & G. R. Adams (Eds.), *Delinquent violent youth* (pp. 175–204). Thousand Oaks, CA: Sage.

Flavell, J. H. (1982). On cognitive development. *Child Development, 53,* 1–10.

Flavell, J. H. (1988). From cognitive connections to mental representations. In J. Astington, P. Harris, & D. Olson (Eds.), *Developing theories of mind* (pp. 244–267). New York: Cambridge University Press.

Flavell, J. H., Green, F. L., & Flavell, E. R. (1987). Development of knowledge about the appearance-reality distinction. *Monographs of the Society for Research in Child Development, 51* (Whole No. 212). Chicago: University of Chicago Press.

Flavell, J. H., Green, F. L., & Flavell, E. R. (1995). The development of children's knowledge about attentional focus. *Developmental Psychology, 31,* 706–712.

Flavell, J. H., & Miller, P. H. (1998). Social cognition. In W. Damon (Ed.), *Handbook of child psychology* (pp. 851–898). New York: Wiley.

Fleming, J., Challela, M., Eland, J., Hornick, R., Johnson, P., Martinson, I., Nativio, D., Nokes, K., Riddle, I., Steele, N., Sudela, K., Thomas, R., Turner, Q., Wheeler, B., & Young, A. (1994). Impact on the family of children who are technology dependent and cared for in the home. *Pediatric Nursing, 20,* 379–388.

Fletcher, J. L., & Gordon, R. C. (1990). Perinatal transmission of bacterial sexually transmitted diseases: Part I. Syphilis and gonorrhea. *Journal of Family Practice, 30,* 448–456.

Focus on the Family. (1992). Oppressed minority or counterfeits? *Focus on the Family Citizen, 6,* 1–5.

Fogel, A. (1997). *Infancy.* Minneapolis: West.

Fogel, A., & Thelen, E. (1987). Development of early expressive and communicative action: Reinterpreting the evidence from a dynamic systems perspective. *Developmental Psychology, 23,* 747–761.

Foltz, C., Overton, W. F., & Ricco, R. B. (1995). Proof construction: Adolescent development from inductive to deductive problem-solving strategies. *Journal of Experimental Child Psychology, 59,* 179–195.

Fombonne, E. (1995). Eating disorders: Time trends and possible explanatory mechanisms. In M. Rutter & D. J. Smith (Eds.), *Psychosocial disorders in young people: Time trends and their causes* (pp. 616–685). New York: Wiley.

Foorman, B. R., Francis, D. J., Fletcher, J. M., Schatschneider, C., & Mehta, P. (1998). The role of instruction in learning to read: Preventing reading failure in at-risk children. *Journal of Educational Psychology, 90,* 37–55.

Forbes, G. B. (1986). Body composition in adolescence. In F. Faulkner & J. M. Tanner (Eds.), *Human growth: A comprehensive treatise* (Vol. 2, pp. 119–145). New York: Plenum.

Fowler, A. E., Gelman, R., & Gleitman, L. R. (1994). The course of language learning in children with disabilities. In H. Tager-Flusberg (Ed.), *Constraints on language acquisition: Studies of atypical children* (pp. 91–140). Hillsdale, NJ: Erlbaum.

Fowler, F. J. (1993). *Survey research methods.* Thousand Oaks, CA: Sage.

Fowler, W. (1986). Early experiences of great men and women mathematicians. *New Directions in Child Development, 32,* 87–109.

Fowles, D. C. (2000). Electrodermal hyporeactivity and antisocial behavior: Does anxiety mediate the relationship? *Journal of Affective Disorders, 61,* 177–189.

Fox, G. L., Bruce, C., & Combs-Orne, T. (2000). Parenting expectations and concerns of fathers and mothers of newborn infants. *Family Relations, 49,* 123–131.

Fox, N. A., Kimmerly, N. L., & Schafer, W. D. (1991). Attachment to mother/attachment to father: A meta-analysis. *Child Development, 62,* 210–225.

Fox, R. A., & Solis-Camera, P. (1997). Parenting of young children by fathers in Mexico and the United States. *Journal of Social Psychology, 137,* 489–495.

Frable, D. S. (1997). Gender, racial, sexual, and class identities. *Annual Review of Psychology, 48,* 139–162.

Fracasso, M. P., Lamb, M. E., Schoelmerich, A., & Leyendecker, B. (1997). The ecology of mother-infant interaction in Euro-American and immigrant Central American families living in the United States. *International Journal of Behavioral Development, 20,* 207–217.

Frankel, K. A., & Bates, J. E. (1990). Mother-toddler problem solving: Antecedents in attachment, home behavior, and temperament. *Child Development, 61,* 810–819.

Fredrickson, B. L. (1998). Cultivated emotions: Parental socialization of positive emotions and self-conscious emotions. *Psychological Inquiry, 9,* 279–281.

Freedman-Doan, C., Wigfield, A., Eccles, J. S., Blumenfeld, P., Arbreton, A., & Harold, R. D. (2001). What am I best at? Grade and gender differences in children's beliefs about ability improvement. *Journal of Applied Developmental Psychology, 21,* 379–402.

Freeman, M., Csikszentmihalyi, M., & Larson, R. (1986). Adolescence and its recollection. *Merrill Palmer Quarterly, 32,* 167–185.

French, D. C. (1988). Heterogeneity of peer rejected boys: Aggressive and non-aggressive subtypes. *Child Development, 59,* 976–985.

Freppon, P. A., & Dahl, K. L. (1998). Balanced instruction: Insights and considerations. *Reading Research Quarterly, 33,* 240–251.

Freud, S. (1960). *The ego and the id* (J. Riviere, Trans.). New York: W. W. Norton. (Original work published 1923)

Freud, S. (1965). *A general introduction to psychoanalysis* (J. Riviere, Trans.). New York: Washington Square Books. (Original work published 1920)

Freund, L. S., Baker, L., & Sonnenschein, S. (1990). Developmental changes in strategic approaches to classification. *Journal of Experimental Child Psychology, 49,* 343–362.

Frick, P. J. (1998). *Conduct disorders and severe antisocial behavior.* New York: Plenum.

Friedman, S. B., Fisher, M., & Schonberg, S. K. (Eds.). (1992). *Comprehensive adolescent care.* St. Louis, MO: Quality Medical Publishing.

Friedrich, L. K., & Stein, A. H. (1975). Prosocial television and young children: The effects of verbal labeling and role playing on learning and behavior. *Child Development, 46,* 27–38.

Friedrich-Cofer, L. K., Huston, A., Kipnis, D. M., Susman, E. J., & Clewett, A. S. (1979). Environmental enhancement of prosocial television content: Effects on interpersonal behavior, imaginative play, and self-regulation in a natural setting. *Developmental Psychology, 15,* 637–646.

Frisch, R. E. (1991). Puberty and body fat. In R. M. Lerner, A. C. Petersen, & J. Brooks-Gunn (Eds.), *Encyclopedia of adolescence* (Vol. 2). New York: Garland.

Frisch, R. E., Wyshak, G., Albright, N. L., Albright, T. E., Schiff, I., Jones, K. P., Witschi, J., Shiang, E., Koff, E., & Marguglio, M. (1985). Lower prevalence of breast cancer and cancers of the reproductive system among former college athletes compared to non-athletes. *British Journal of Cancer, 52,* 885–891.

Frith, U. (1989). *Autism.* Oxford, England: Oxford University Press.

Frolund, L. (1997). Early shame and mirroring. *Scandinavian Psychoanalytic Review, 20,* 35–57.

Frome, P. M., & Eccles, J. S. (1998). Parents' influence on children's achievement-related perceptions. *Journal of Personality and Social Psychology, 74,* 435–452.

Frost, J. L., Shin, D., & Jacobs, P. J. (1998). Physical environments and children's play. In O. N. Saracho & B. Spodek (Eds.), *Multiple perspectives on play in early childhood education* (pp. 255–294). Albany: State University of New York Press.

Fry, P. S., & Addington, J. (1984). Comparison of social problem solving of children from open and traditional classrooms: A two-year longitudinal study. *Journal of Educational Psychology, 76,* 318–329.

Fuligni, A. J. (1998). Authority, autonomy, and parent-adolescent conflict and cohesion: A study of adolescents from Mexican, Chinese, Filipino, and European backgrounds. *Developmental Psychology, 34,* 782–792.

Fuligni, A. J., & Eccles, J. S. (1993). Perceived parent-child relationships and early adolescents' orientation toward peers. *Developmental Psychology, 29,* 622–632.

Furman, W. (1996). The measurement of friendship perceptions: Conceptual and methodological issues. In W. M. Bukowski, A. F. Newcomb, & W. W. Hartup (Eds.), *The company they keep: Friendships in childhood and adolescence* (pp. 41–65). Cambridge, England: Cambridge University Press.

Furman, W., & Wehner, E. A. (1997). Adolescent romantic relationships: A developmental perspective. In S. Shulman & W. A. Collins (Eds.), *Romantic relationships in adolescence* (pp. 21–36). San Francisco: Jossey-Bass.

Furnham, A., & Alibhai, M. (1983). Cross-cultural differences in the perception of female body shape. *Psychological Medicine, 13,* 829–837.

Furstenberg, F. F., & Cherlin, A. J. (1991). *Divided families.* Cambridge, MA: Harvard University Press.

Furstenberg, F. F., & Kiernan, K. E. (2001). Delayed parental divorce: How much do children benefit? *Journal of Marriage and the Family, 63,* 446–457.

Futterman, D., & Hein, K. (1992). AIDS and HIV infection. In S. B. Friedman, M. Fisher, & S. K. Schonberg (Eds.), *Comprehensive adolescent health care* (pp. 521–531). St. Louis, MO: Quality Medical Publishing.

Future of Children. (1995). *Critical issues for children and youths.* Los Altos, CA: Packard Foundation.

Gaddis, A., & Brooks-Gunn, J. (1985). The male experience of pubertal change. *Journal of Youth and Adolescence, 14,* 61–70.

Gagnon, J. H. (1990). The explicit and implicit use of the scripting perspective in sex research. *Annual Review of Sex Research, 1,* 1–43.

Galambos, N. L., Almeida, D. M., & Petersen, A. C. (1991). Masculinity, femininity, and sex role attitudes in early adolescence. *Annual Progress in Child Psychiatry and Child Development, 5,* 77–91.

Gallagher, A. M., & De Lisi, R. (1994). Gender differences in scholastic aptitude test—mathematics problem solving among high ability students. *Journal of Educational Psychology, 86,* 204–211.

Gallagher, A. M., De Lisi, R., Host, P. C., McGillicuddy-De Lisi, A. V., Morely, M., & Cahalan, C. (2000). Gender differences in advanced mathematical problem solving. *Journal of Experimental Child Psychology, 75,* 165–190.

Gallahue, D. L., & Ozmun, J. C. (1995). *Understanding motor development.* Madison, WI: Brown & Benchmark.

Gallant, S. J., & Derry, P. S. (1995). Menarche, menstruation, and menopause: Psychosocial research and future directions. In A. L. Stanton & S. J. Gallant (Eds.), *The psychology of women's health* (pp. 199–259). Washington, DC: American Psychological Association.

Gallup Organization. (1997). *Public attitudes toward the public schools.* New York: Gallup Organization.

Galotti, K. M., Pierce, B., Reimer, R. L., & Luckner, A. E. (2000). Midwife or doctor: A study of pregnant women making delivery decisions. *Journal of Midwifery and Women's Health, 45,* 320–329.

Gamble, T. J., & Zigler, E. (1989). The Head Start Synthesis Project. *Journal of Applied Developmental Psychology, 10,* 267–274.

Garbarino, J. (1999). The effects of community violence on children. In L. Balter & C. S. Tamis-LeMonda (Eds.), *Child psychology: A handbook of contemporary issues* (pp. 412–425). Philadelphia: Psychology Press.

Garbarino, J., Dubrow, N., Kostelny, K., & Pardo, C. (1992). *Children in danger.* San Francisco: Jossey-Bass.

Garbarino, J., & Stott, F. M. (1992). *What children can tell us.* San Francisco: Jossey-Bass.

Garber, J., Weiss, B., & Shanley, N. (1993). Cognitions, depressive symptoms, and development in adolescence. *Journal of Abnormal Psychology, 102,* 47–57.

Garcia Coll, C. T. (1990). Developmental outcome of minority infants: A process-oriented look into our beginnings. *Child Development, 61,* 270–289.

Garcia Coll, C. T., Lamberty, G., Jenkins, R., McAdoo, H. P., Crnic, K., Wasik, B. H., & Garcia, H. V. (1996). An integrative model for the study of developmental competencies in minority children. *Child Development, 67,* 1891–1914.

Gardner, H. (1980). *Artful scribbles.* New York: Basic Books.

Gardner, H. (1983). *Frames of mind.* London: Heinemann.

Gardner, H. (2000). The giftedness matrix: A developmental perspective. In R. Friedman & B. Shore (Eds.), *Talents unfolding: Cognition and development* (pp. 77–88). Washington, DC: American Psychological Association.

Gardstrom, S. C. (1999). Music exposure and criminal behavior: Perceptions of juvenile offenders. *Journal of Music Therapy, 36,* 207–221.

Garner, P. W., Jones, D. C., & Palmer, D. (1994). Social cognitive correlates of preschool children's sibling caregiving behavior. *Developmental Psychology, 30,* 905–911.

Garrison, W. T., & McQuiston, S. (1989). *Chronic illness during childhood and adolescence.* Newbury Park, CA: Sage.

Gauvain, M. (1998). Culture, development, and theory of mind: Comment on Lillard (1998). *Psychological Bulletin, 123,* 37–42.

Ge, X., Conger, R. D., & Elder, G. H. (1996). Coming of age too early: Pubertal influences on girls' vulnerability to psychological distress. *Child Development, 67,* 3386–3400.

Ge, X., Conger, R. D., & Elder, G. H. (2001). Pubertal transition, stressful life events, and the emergence of gender differences in adolescent depressive symptoms. *Developmental Psychology, 37,* 404–417.

Ge, X., Lorenz, F. O, Conger, R. D., Elder, G. H., & Simon, R. L. (1994). Trajectories of stressful life events and depressive symptoms during adolescence. *Developmental Psychology, 30,* 467–483.

Geary, D. C., & Bjorklund, D. F. (2000). Evolutionary developmental psychology. *Child Development, 71,* 57–65.

Gecas, V., & Seff, M. A. (1990). Social class and self-esteem. *Social Psychological Quarterly, 53,* 165–173.

Gelles, R. J. (1987). The family and its role in the abuse of children. *Psychiatric Annals, 17,* 229–232.

Gelman, R., & Baillargeon, R. (1983). A review of some Piagetian concepts. In P. Mussen (Ed.), *Handbook of child psychology* (Vol. 3, pp. 167–230). New York: Wiley.

Gelman, S. A., & Taylor, M. (1984). How two-year-old children interpret proper and common names for unfamiliar objects. *Child Development, 55,* 1535–1540.

Georgieff, M. K., & Rao, R. (2001). The role of nutrition in cognitive development. In C. Nelson & M. Luciana (Eds.), *Handbook of developmental cognitive neuroscience* (pp. 491–504). Cambridge, MA: MIT Press.

Geraldson, B., & Hopkins, W. D. (1997). Children's lateralization on a finger-localization task. *Perceptual and Motor Skills, 84,* 1259–1264.

Gershenson, H. P., Musick, J. S., Ruch-Ross, H. S., Magee, V., Rubino, K. K., & Rosenberg, D. (1989). The prevalence of coercive sexual experience among teenage mothers. *Journal of Interpersonal Violence, 4,* 204–219.

Gershman, H. (1997). Sexual permissiveness and its consequences. In L. B. Schlesinger & E. Revitch (Eds.), *Sexual dynamics of anti-social behavior* (pp. 76–87). Springfield, IL: Charles C Thomas.

Gibbs, R. S., & Sweet, R. L. (1994). Clinical disorders. In R. K. Creasy & R. Resnik (Eds.), *Maternal-fetal medicine: Principles and practice* (pp. 355–411). Philadelphia: Saunders.

Giedd, J. N. (1997). Normal development. *Child and Adolescent Psychiatric Clinics of North America, 6,* 265–282.

Gil, A. G., & Vega, W. A. (1996). Two different worlds: Acculturation stress and adaptation among Cuban and Nicaraguan families. *Journal of Social and Personal Relationships, 13,* 435–456.

Gil, A. G., Vega, W. A., & Dimas, J. M. (1994). Acculturative stress and personal adjustment among Hispanic adolescent boys. *Journal of Community Psychology, 22,* 43–54.

Gillman, M. W., Rifas-Shiman, S. L., Camargo, C. A., Berkey, C. S., Frazier, A. L., Rockett, H. R., Field, A. E., & Colditz, G. A. (2001). Risk of overweight among adolescents who were breastfed as infants. *Journal of the American Medical Association, 285,* 2461–2467.

Gilmore, M. R., Lewis, S. M., Lohr, M. J., Spencer, M. S., & White, R. D. (1997). Repeat pregnancies among adolescent mothers. *Journal of Marriage and the Family, 59,* 536–550.

Ginsburg, H. J., & Miller, S. M. (1982). Sex differences in children's risk-taking behavior. *Child Development, 53,* 426–428.

Giordano, P. C., Cernkovich, S. A., Groat, H. T., Pugh, M. D., & Swinford, S. P. (1998). The quality of adolescent friendships: Long-term effects. *Journal of Health and Social Behavior, 39,* 55–71.

Gladstein, J., Slater-Rusonis, E., & Heald, F. (1992). A comparison of inner-city and upper-middle-class youths' exposure to violence. *Journal of Adolescent Health, 13,* 275–280.

Glass, R. H. (1994). Gamete transport, fertilization, and implantation. In R. K. Creasy & R. Resnik (Eds.), *Maternal-fetal medicine* (pp. 89–95). Philadelphia: Saunders.

Glastris, P. (1997, May 26). The alien payoff. *U.S. News & World Report,* 20–22.

Gleason, J. B. (1993). *The development of language.* New York: Macmillan.

Gleason, J. B., & Ely, R. (2002). Gender differences in language development. In A. McGillicuddy-De Lisi & R. De Lisi (Eds.), *Biology, society, and behavior: The development of sex differences in cognition* (pp. 127–154). Westport, CT: Ablex.

Gleason, J. B., Ely, R., Perlmann, R. Y., & Narasimhan, B. (1996). Patterns of prohibition in parent-child discourse. In D. I. Slobin & J. Gerhardt (Eds.), *Social interaction, social context, and language* (pp. 205–217). Mahwah, NJ: Erlbaum.

Gleitman, L. R., & Gillette, J. (1995). The role of syntax in verb learning. In P. Fletcher & B. MacWhinney (Eds.), *The handbook of child language* (pp. 413–427). Oxford, England: Blackwell.

Gleitman, L. R., Newport, E. L., & Gleitman, H. (1984). The current status of the motherese hypothesis. *Journal of Child Language, 11,* 43–79.

Glover, V. (1997). Maternal stress or anxiety in pregnancy and emotional development of the child. *British Journal of Psychiatry, 171,* 105–106.

Golan, M., Weizman, A., Apter, A., & Fainaru, M. (1998). Parents as exclusive agents of change in the treatment of childhood obesity. *American Journal of Clinical Nutrition, 67,* 1130–1135.

Gold, D., Crombie, G., & Noble, S. (1987). Relations between teachers' judgments of girls' and boys' compliance and intellectual competence. *Sex Roles, 16,* 351–358.

Goldberg, S. (1983). Parent-to-infant bonding: Another look. *Child Development, 54,* 1355–1382.

Goldberg, S., & DiVitto, B. (1995). Parenting children born preterm. In M. Bornstein (Ed.), *Handbook of parenting* (Vol. 1, pp. 209–231). Mahwah, NJ: Erlbaum.

Goldfield, B. (1987). The contributions of child and caregiver to referential and expressive language. *Applied Psycholinguistics, 8,* 267–280.

Goldfield, B., & Reznick, J. S. (1990). Early lexical acquisition: Rate, content, and the vocabulary spurt. *Journal of Child Language, 17,* 171–183.

Goldin-Meadow, S. (1997). When gestures and words speak differently. *Current Directions in Psychological Science, 6,* 138–143.

Goldin-Meadow, S., & Mylander, C. (1998). Spontaneous sign systems created by deaf children in two cultures. *Nature, 391,* 279–281.

Goldman-Rakic, P. S., Bourgeois, J. P., & Rakic, P. (1997). Synaptic substrate of cognitive development. Life span analysis of synaptogenesis in the prefrontal cortex of nonhuman primate. In *Development of prefrontal cortex. Evolution, neurobiology and behavior.* Baltimore: Brookes.

Goldstein, A. P., Glick, B., Carthan, W., & Blancero, D. A. (1994). *The prosocial gang.* Thousand Oaks, CA: Sage.

Golombok, S., & Tasker, F. L. (1996). Do parents influence the sexual orientation of their children? Findings from a longitudinal study of lesbian families. *Developmental Psychology, 32,* 3–11.

Goncalves, M. (1990). *A representaca da escola feita pela crianca de baixa renda em sua primeira experància discente.* Paper presented at the 13th annual congress of ANPED, Belo Horizonte, Brazil.

Goncu, A. (1993). Development of intersubjectivity in social pretend play. *Human Development, 36,* 185–198.

Gonzales, N. A., & Kim, L. A. (1997). Stress and coping in an ethnic minority context. In S. A. Wolchik & I. N. Sandler (Eds.), *Handbook of children's coping* (pp. 481–514). New York: Plenum.

Goodman, G. S., Emery, R. E., & Haugaard, J. J. (1998). Developmental psychology and law: Divorce, child maltreatment, foster care, and adoption. In W. Damon (Ed.), *Handbook of child psychology* (Vol. 4, pp. 775–874). New York: Wiley.

Goodman, R. A., & Whitaker, H. A. (1985). Hemispherectomy: A review (1928–1981) with special reference to the linguistic abilities and disabilities of the residual right hemisphere. In C. T. Best (Ed.), *Hemispheric function and collaboration in the child* (pp. 121–156). Orlando, FL: Harcourt Brace Jovanovich.

Goodyear, I. M. (2001). *The depressed child and adolescent.* New York: Cambridge University Press.

Goodyear, I., Kolvin, I., & Gatzanis, S. (1985). Recent undesirable life events and psychiatric disorders in childhood and adolescence. *British Journal of Psychiatry, 147,* 517–533.

Gopnik, A. (1988). Three types of early words. *First Language, 8,* 49–70.

Gopnik, A., & Meltzoff, A. (1986). Relations between semantic and cognitive developments in the one-word stage: The specificity hypothesis. *Child Development, 57,* 1040–1053.

Gordon, B., Saklofske, D. H., & Hildebrand, D. K. (1998). Assessing children with mental retardation. In V. H. Booney (Ed.), *Psychological assessment of children* (pp. 454–481). New York: Wiley.

Gorman-Smith, D., & Tolan, P. H. (1998). The role of exposure to community violence and developmental problems among inner-city youth. *Development and Psychopathology, 10,* 101–116.

Gorman-Smith, D., Tolan, P. H., Zelli, A., & Huesmann, L. R. (1996). The relation of family functioning to violence among inner-city minority youths. *Journal of Family Psychology, 10,* 115–129.

Goswami, U. (1998). *Cognition in children.* Hove, England: Psychology Press.

Gottesman, I. I. (1991). *Schizophrenia genesis: The origins of madness.* New York: Freeman.

Gottfredson, D. C., Sealock, M. D., & Koper, C. S. (1996). Delinquency. In R. J. DiClemente & W. B. Hansen (Eds.), *Handbook of adolescent health risk behavior* (pp. 259–288). New York: Plenum.

Gottfried, A. W. (1985). Environment of newborns in special care units. In A. W. Gottfried & J. L. Gaiter (Eds.), *Infant stress under intensive care:*

Environmental neonatology (pp. 251–257). Baltimore: University Park Press.

Gottfried, A. W., Gottfried, A. E., Bathurst, K., & Guerin, D. W. (1994). *Gifted IQ: Early developmental perspectives.* New York: Plenum Press.

Gottlieb, G. (1997). *Synthesizing nature-nurture: Prenatal roots of instinctive behavior.* Mahwah, NJ: Erlbaum.

Gottman, J. M. (1983). How children become friends. *Monographs of the Society for Research in Child Development, 48* (Whole No. 201). Chicago: University of Chicago Press.

Gottwald, S. R., & Thurman, S. K. (1990). Parent-infant interaction in neonatal intensive care units: Implications for research and service delivery. *Infants and Young Children, 2,* 1–10.

Goubet, N., & Clifton, R. K. (1998). Object and event representation in 6½-month-old infants. *Developmental Psychology, 34,* 63–76.

Gould, E. (1999). Neurogenesis in adulthood: A possible role in learning. *Trends in Cognitive Sciences, 3,* 186–192.

Graber, J. A., & Archibald, A. B. (2001). Psychosocial change at puberty and beyond: Understanding adolescent sexuality and sexual orientation. In A. R. D'Augelli & C. J. Patterson (Eds.), *Lesbian, gay, and bisexual identities and youth: Psychological perspectives* (pp. 3–26). New York: Oxford University Press.

Graber, J. A., Brooks-Gunn, J., & Warren, M. P. (1995). The antecedents of menarcheal age: Heredity, family environment, and stressful life events. *Child Development, 66,* 346–359.

Graber, J. A., Lewinsohn, P. M., Seeley, J. R., & Brooks-Gunn, J. (1997). Is psychopathology associated with the timing of puberty? *Journal of the American Academy of Child and Adolescent Psychiatry, 36,* 1768–1776.

Grabill, C. M., Griffith, J. R., & Kaslow, N. J. (2001). Depression. In M. Hersen & V. B. Van Hasselt (Eds.), *Advanced abnormal psychology* (pp. 243–260). New York: Kluwer Academic.

Graham, P. (1986). *Child psychiatry: A developmental approach.* Oxford, England: Oxford University Press.

Graham, S. (1994). Motivation in African Americans. *Review of Educational Research, 64,* 55–117.

Grant, B. (1993). Multiple pregnancy. In V. R. Bennett & L. K. Brown (Eds.), *Myles textbook for midwives* (pp. 365–376). London: Churchill Livingstone.

Grant, B. F., & Dawson, D. A. (1998). *Age of drinking onset predicts future alcohol abuse and dependence.* Washington, DC: National Institute on Alcohol Abuse and Alcoholism.

Grantham-McGregor, S., Ani, C., & Fernald, L. (2001). The role of nutrition in intellectual development. In R. Sternberg (Ed.), *Environmental effects on cognitive abilities* (pp. 119–155). Mahwah, NJ: Erlbaum.

Gray, J. A. (1971). *The psychology of fear and stress.* New York: McGraw-Hill.

Gray, M. R., & Steinberg, L. (1999). Unpacking authoritative parenting: Reassessing a multidimensional construct. *Journal of Marriage and the Family, 61,* 574–587.

Gredler, G. R. (1997). Issues in early childhood screening and assessment. *Psychology in the Schools, 34,* 98–106.

Green, E. H. (1933). Friendships and quarrels among preschool children. *Child Development, 4,* 236–252.

Green, M. (1989). *Theories of human development.* New York: Prentice-Hall.

Greenberg, B. D., Li, Q., Lucas, F. R., Hu, S., Sirota, L. A., Benjamin, J., Lesch, K. P., Hamer, D., & Murphy, D. L. (2000). Association between the serotonin transporter promoter polymorphism and personality traits in a primarily female population sample. *American Journal of Medical Genetics, 96,* 202–216.

Greenberg, B. S., Edison, N., Korzenny, F., Fernandez-Collado, C., & Atkin, C. K. (1980). Antisocial and prosocial behaviors on television. In B. S. Greenberg (Ed.), *Life on television: Content analysis of U.S. television drama* (pp. 99–128). Norwood, NJ: Ablex Publishing.

Greenberg, M. T., Speltz, M. L., & DeKlyen, M. (1993). The role of attachment in early development of disruptive behavior problems. *Development and Psychopathology, 5,* 191–213.

Greenberger, E., & Chen, C. (1996). Perceived family relationships and depressed mood in early and late adolescence: A comparison of European and Asian Americans. *Developmental Psychology, 32,* 707–716.

Greenberger, E., & Steinberg, L. (1986). *When teenagers work: The psychological and social costs of adolescent employment.* New York: Basic Books.

Greene, B. (1984). *Good morning, merry sunshine.* New York: Penguin Books.

Greene, K., Rubin, D. L., Hale, J. L., & Walters, L. H. (1996). The utility of understanding adolescent egocentrism in designing health promotion messages. *Health Communication, 8,* 131–152.

Greene, R. W., & Ablon, J. S. (2001). What does the MTA study tell us about effective psychosocial treatment for ADHD? *Journal of Clinical Child Psychology, 30,* 114–212.

Greene, R. W., Biederman, J., Faraone, S. V., Monuteaux, M. C., Mick, E., DuPre, E. P., Fine, C. S., & Goring, J. G. (2001). Social impairment in girls with ADHD: Patterns, gender comparisons, and correlates. *Journal of the American Academy of Child and Adolescent Psychiatry, 40,* 704–710.

Greenhill, L. L. (2001). Clinical effects of stimulant medication in ADHD. In M. V. Solanto & A. F. T. Arnsten (Eds.), *Stimulant drugs and ADHD: Basic and clinical neuroscience* (pp. 31–71). New York: Oxford University Press.

Greenough, W. T., & Alcantara, A. A. (1993). The roles of experience in different developmental information stage processes. In B. de Boysson-Bardies, S. de Schonen, P. Jusczyk, P. McNeilage, & J. Morton (Eds.), *Developmental neurocognition* (pp. 3–16). Dordrecht: Kluwer.

Greenough, W. T., & Black, J. E. (1992). Induction of brain structure by experience: Substrates for cognitive development. In M. R. Gunnar & C. A. Nelson (Eds.), *Developmental behavioral neuroscience* (pp. 155–200). Hillsdale, NJ: Erlbaum.

Greenough, W. T., Black, J. E., & Wallace, C. S. (1987). Experience and brain development. *Science, 58,* 539–560.

Greenspan, S. I., & Greenspan, N. T. (1985). *First feelings: Milestones in the emotional development of your baby and child.* New York: Viking.

Greenwald, R. L., Bank, L., Reid, J. B., & Knutson, J. F. (1997). A discipline-mediated model of excessively punitive parenting. *Aggressive Behavior, 23,* 259–280.

Griffin, A., & Fein, G. (1996). *Infant day care: The critical issues.* Urbana, IL: ERIC Clearinghouse.

Griffin, D. W., & Bartholomew, K. (1994). Models of the self and other: Fundamental dimensions underlying measures of adult attachment. *Journal of Personality and Social Psychology, 67,* 430–445.

Griffin, R. S. (1998). *Sports in the lives of children and adolescents.* Westport, CT: Praeger.

Griffith, D. R., Azuma, S. D., & Chasnoff, I. J. (1994). Three-year outcome of children exposed prenatally to drugs. *Journal of the American Academy of Child and Adolescent Psychiatry, 33,* 20–27.

Griffiths, M. D. (1991). Amusement machine playing in childhood and adolescence: A comparative analysis of video games and fruit machines. *Journal of Adolescence, 14,* 53–73.

Groome, L. J., Swiber, M. J., Atterbury, J. L., Bentz, L. S., & Holland, S. B. (1997). Similarities and differences in behavioral state organization during sleep periods in the infant before and after birth. *Child Development, 68,* 1–11.

Gross, L., Aurand, S., & Adessa, R. (1988). *Violence and discrimination against lesbian and gay people in Philadelphia and the Commonwealth of Pennsylvania.* Philadelphia: Philadelphia Lesbian and Gay Task Force.

Grotevant, H. D. (1998). Adolescent development in family contexts. In W. Damon (Ed.), *Handbook of child psychology* (Vol. 3, pp. 1097–1150). New York: Wiley.

Grunseit, A., Kippax, S., Aggleton, P., Baldo, M., & Slutkin, G. (1997). Sexuality education and young people's sexual behavior: A review of studies. *Journal of Adolescent Research, 12,* 421–453.

Grusec, J. (1988). *Social development.* New York: Springer-Verlag.

Grusec, J. E., Dix, T., & Mills, R. (1982). The effects of type, severity, and victim of children's transgressions on maternal discipline. *Canadian Journal of Behavioural Sciences, 14,* 276–289.

Grusec, J. E., & Goodnow, J. J. (1994). Impact of parental discipline methods on the child's internalization of values: A reconceptualization of current points of view. *Developmental Psychology, 30,* 4–19.

Grusec, J. E., Goodnow, J. J., & Kuczynski, L. (2000). New directions in analyses of parenting contributions to children's acquisition of values. *Child Development, 71,* 205–211.

Grusec, J. E., & Lytton, H. (1988). *Social development: History, theory, and research*. New York: Springer-Verlag.

Guerin, D. W., Gottfried, A. W., & Thomas, C. W. (1997). Difficult temperament and behavior problems: A longitudinal study from 1.5 to 12 years. *International Journal of Behavioral Development, 21,* 71–90.

Guidubaldi, J. (1988). Differences in children's divorce adjustment across grade level and gender: A report from the NASP–Kent State Nationwide Project. In S. A. Wolchik & P. Karoly (Eds.), *Children of divorce* (pp. 185–232). New York: Gardner Press.

Gunnar, M. R. (1980). Contingent stimulation: A review of its role in early development. In S. Levine & H. Ursin (Eds.), *Coping and health* (pp. 316–345). New York: Plenum.

Gunnar, M. R. (1989). Studies of the human infant's adrenocortical response to potentially stressful events. *New Directions for Child Development, 45,* 3–18.

Gunnar, M. R., & Brodersen, L. (1992). Infant stress reactions to brief maternal separations in human and nonhuman primates. In T. M. Field, P. M. McCabe, & N. Schneiderman (Eds.), *Stress and coping in infancy and childhood* (pp. 1–18). Hillsdale, NJ: Erlbaum.

Gunnar, M. R., Bruce, J., & Grotevant, H. D. (2000). International adoption and institutionally reared children: Research and policy. *Development and Psychopathology, 12,* 677–694.

Gunnar, M. R., Fisch, R., Korsvik, S., & Donhowe, J. (1981). The effects of circumcision on serum cortisol and behavior. *Psychoneuroendocrinology, 6,* 269–275.

Gunnell, D. J., Frankel, S. J., Nanchahal, K., Peters, T. J., & Davey, S. G. (1998). Childhood obesity and adult cardiovascular mortality. *American Journal of Clinical Nutrition, 67,* 1111–1118.

Guralnick, M. J., Connor, R. T., Hammond, M. A., Gottman, J. M., & Kinnish, K. (1996). The peer relations of preschool children with communication disorders. *Child Development, 67,* 471–489.

Gustafson, G. W., Wood, R. M., & Green, J. A. (2000). Can we hear the causes of infants' crying? In R. G. Barr, B. Hopkins, & J. A. Green (Eds.), *Crying as a sign, a symptom, and a signal: Clinical emotional and developmental aspects of infant and toddler crying* (pp. 8–22). New York: Cambridge University Press.

Hack, M., Klein, N. K., & Taylor, H. G. (1995). Long-term developmental outcomes of low birth weight infants. *The Future of Children, 5,* 176–196.

Hack, M., Taylor, H. G., Klein, N., & Eiben, R. (1994). Outcome of < 750 gm birthweight children at school age. *New England Journal of Medicine, 331,* 753–759.

Hadley, P. A., & Schuele, C. M. (1995). Verbal interactions with peers in a preschool language intervention classroom. In M. Rice & K. Wilcox (Eds.), *Building a language-focused curriculum for the preschool classroom* (pp. 105–125). Baltimore: Brookes.

Hafer, S. (1995). *Facts on school-age children.* Boston: Wellesley College Press.

Hagen, E. H. (1999). The functions of postpartum depression. *Evolution and Human Behavior, 20,* 325–359.

Haith, M. M., & Benson, J. B. (1998). Infant cognition. In W. Damon (Ed.), *Handbook of child psychology* (Vol. 2, pp. 199–254). New York: Wiley.

Haka-Ikse, K. (1997). Female adolescent sexuality: The risks and management. In G. Creatsas & G. Mastorakos (Eds.), *Adolescent gynecology and endocrinology* (Vol. 816, pp. 446–470). New York: Academy of Sciences.

Hakanen, E. A. (1995). Emotional use of music by African American adolescents. *Howard Journal of Communication, 5,* 214–222.

Hakuta, K., & McLaughlin, B. (1996). Bilingualism and second language learning. In D. C. Berliner & R. C. Calfee (Eds.), *Handbook of educational psychology* (pp. 603–621). New York: Macmillan.

Hala, S. (1997). Theoretical and conceptual issues. In S. Hala (Ed.), *The development of social cognition* (pp. 3–34). East Sussex, England: Psychology Press.

Hala, S., & Carpendale, J. (1997). All in the mind: Children's understanding of mental life. In S. Hala (Ed.), *The development of social cognition* (pp. 189–240). East Sussex, England: Psychology Press.

Hall, D. G., & Graham, S. A. (1998). Beyond mutual exclusivity: Children use lexical form class information to constrain word-referent mapping. In E. V. Clark (Ed.), *Proceedings of the 29th Annual Child Language Research Forum* (pp. 181–190). Stanford, CA: Center for the Study of Language and Information.

Hall, J. A. (1984). *Nonverbal sex differences: Communication accuracy and expressive style.* Hillsdale, NJ: Erlbaum.

Halpern, D. F. (1992). *Sex differences in cognitive abilities.* Mahwah, NJ: Erlbaum.

Halpern, D. F. (1997). Sex differences in intelligence: Implications for education. *American Psychologist, 52,* 1091–1102.

Hamer, D., & Copeland, P. (1998). *Living with our genes.* New York: Doubleday.

Hansen, D. M., & Jarvis, P. A. (2000). Adolescent employment and psychosocial outcomes: A comparison of two employment contexts. *Youth and Society, 31,* 417–436.

Hardy, J. B., Shapiro, S., Astone, N. M., Miller, T. L., Brooks-Gunn, J., & Hilton, S. C. (1997). Adolescent childbearing revisited: The age of inner-city mothers at delivery is a determinant of their children's self-sufficiency at age 27 to 33. *Pediatrics, 100,* 802–809.

Harkness, S., & Super, C. M. (1983). *The cultural structuring of children's play in a rural African community.* Paper presented at the annual meeting of the Association for the Anthropological Study of Play, Baton Rouge, LA.

Harpin, V., Chellappah, G., & Rutter, N. (1983). Responses of the newborn infant to overheating. *Biology and the Neonate, 44,* 65–75.

Harrington, R. (1996). Family-genetic findings in child and adolescent depressive disorders. *International Review of Psychiatry, 8,* 355–368.

Harris, D. V. (1991). Exercise and fitness during adolescence. In R. M. Lerner, A. C. Petersen, & J. Brooks-Gunn (Eds.), *Encyclopedia of adolescence* (pp. 324–327). New York: Garland.

Harris, J. F., Durso, F. T., Mergler, N. L., & Jones, S. K. (1990). Knowledge base influences on judgments of frequency of occurrence. *Cognitive Development, 5,* 223–233.

Harris, J. R. (1995). Where is the child's environment? A group socialization theory of development. *Psychological Review, 102,* 458–489.

Harris, L. J. (1992). Left-handedness. In I. Rapid & S. J. Segalowitz (Eds.), *Handbook of neuropsychology* (Vol. 6, pp. 145–208). Amsterdam: Elsvier.

Harris, P. L. (1989). *Children and emotion.* Cambridge, MA: Blackwell.

Harris, P. L., & Kavanaugh, R. D. (1993). Young children's understanding of pretense. *Monographs of the Society for Research in Child Development, 58* (Whole No. 231). Chicago: University of Chicago Press.

Hart, B., & Risely, T. R. (1995). *Meaningful differences in the everyday experiences of young American children.* Baltimore: Brookes.

Hart, C. H., DeWolf, D. M., Wozniak, P., & Burts, D. C. (1992). Maternal and paternal disciplinary styles: Relations with preschoolers' playgroup behavior orientations and peer status. *Child Development, 63,* 879–892.

Hart, S. N., Brassard, M. R., & Karlson, H. C. (1996). Psychological maltreatment. In J. Briere, L. Berliner, J. A. Bulkley, C. Jenny, & T. Reid (Eds.), *The APSAC handbook on child maltreatment* (pp. 72–89). Thousand Oaks, CA: Sage.

Harter, S. (1990). Self and identity development. In S. S. Feldman & G. R. Elliot (Eds.), *At the threshold* (pp. 352–387). Cambridge, MA: Harvard University Press.

Harter, S. (1993). Causes and consequences of low self-esteem in children and adolescents. In R. F. Baumeister (Ed.), *Self-esteem: The puzzle of low self-regard* (pp. 87–116). New York: Plenum.

Harter, S. (1998). The development of self-representations. In W. Damon (Ed.), *Handbook of child psychology* (Vol. 3, pp. 553–618). New York: Wiley.

Harter, S. (1999). *The construction of the self: A developmental perspective.* New York: Guilford.

Harter, S., & Monsour, A. (1992). Developmental analysis of conflict caused by opposing attributes in the adolescent self-portrait. *Developmental Psychology, 28,* 251–260.

Hartup, W. W. (1993). Adolescents and their friends. In B. Laursen (Ed.), *Close friendships in adolescence* (Vol. 60, pp. 3–22). San Francisco: Jossey-Bass.

Hartup, W. W. (1996). The company they keep: Friendships and their developmental significance. *Child Development, 67,* 1–13.

Hartup, W. W., & Stevens, N. (1999). Friendships and adaptation across the life span. *Current Directions in Psychological Science, 8,* 76–79.

Harwood, R. L., Miller, J. G., & Irizarry, N. L. (1995). *Culture and attachment.* New York: Guilford Press.

Harwood, R. L., Schoelmerich, A., Ventura-Cook, E., Schulze, P. A., & Wilson, S. A. (1996). Culture and class influences on Anglo and Puerto Rican mothers' beliefs regarding long-term socialization goals and child behavior. *Child Development, 67,* 2446–2461.

Hashima, P. Y., & Amato, P. R. (1994). Poverty, social support, and parental behavior. *Child Development, 65,* 394–403.

Hassold, T. J., & Patterson, D. (1998). *Down syndrome.* New York: Wiley.

Haste, H., & Baddeley, J. (1991). Moral theory and culture: The case of gender. In W. Kurtines & J. L. Gewirtz (Eds.), *Handbook of moral behavior and development* (Vol. 1, pp. 223–250). Hillsdale, NJ: Erlbaum.

Hatton, D. D., Bailey, D. B., Jr., Burchinal, M. R., & Ferrell, K. A. (1997). Development growth curves of preschool children with vision impairments. *Child Development, 68,* 788–806.

Hauser, S. T., Borman, E. H., Bowlds, M. K., Powers, S. L., Jacobson, A. M., Noam, G. I., & Knoebber, K. (1991). Understanding coping within adolescence. In E. M. Cummings & A. Greene (Eds.), *Life-span developmental psychology: Perspectives on stress and coping* (pp. 177–194). Hillsdale, NJ: Erlbaum.

Hausfather, A., Toharia, A., LaRoche, C., & Engelsmann, F. (1997). Effects of age of entry, day-care quality, and family characteristics on preschool behavior. *Journal of Child Psychology and Psychiatry, 38,* 441–448.

Haveman, R., & Wolfe, B. (1994). *Succeeding generations.* New York: Russell Sage Foundation.

Hawkins, A. J., Christiansen, S. L., Sargent, K. P., & Hill, E. J. (1995). Rethinking fathers' involvement in child care: A developmental perspective. In W. Marsiglio (Ed.), *Fatherhood: Contemporary theory, research, and social policy* (pp. 41–56). Thousand Oaks, CA: Sage.

Hawkins, J. D., Catalano, R. F., & Miller, J. Y. (1992). Risk and protective factors for alcohol and other drug problems in adolescence and early adulthood: Implications for substance abuse prevention. *Psychological Bulletin, 112,* 64–105.

Hay, D. F., Castle, J., Davies, L., Demetriou, H., & Stimson, C. A. (1999). Prosocial action in very early childhood. *Journal of Child Psychology and Psychiatry and Allied Disciplines, 40,* 905–916.

Hayes, D. S., & Casey, D. M. (1992). Young children and television: The retention of emotional reactions. *Child Development, 63,* 1423–1436.

Hayghe, H. V. (1997, September). Developments in women's labor force participation. *Monthly Labor Review,* 41–47.

Hayne, H., & Rovee-Collier, C. (1995). The organization of reactivated memory in infancy. *Child Development, 66,* 893–906.

Hayne, H., Rovee-Collier, C., & Perris, E. E. (1987). Categorization and memory retrieval by three-month-olds. *Child Development, 58,* 750–767.

Haynes de Reght, H. L., Minkoff, H. L., Feldman, J., & Schwartz, R. H. (1986). Relation of private or clinic care to cesarean birth rate. *New England Journal of Medicine, 315,* 619–624.

Hayward, C., Killen, J. D., Wilson, D. M., & Hammer, L. D. (1997). Psychiatric risk associated with early puberty in adolescent girls. *Journal of the American Academy of Child and Adolescent Psychiatry, 36,* 255–262.

Health Behavior in School-Aged Children (2000). *Health policy for children and adolescents.* Geneva: World Health Organization.

Hearold, S. (1986). A synthesis of 1043 effects of television on social behavior. In G. Comstock (Ed.), *Public communications and behavior* (Vol. 1, pp. 65–133). New York: Academic Press.

Hechtman, L., & Weiss, G. (1986). Controlled prospective fifteen-year follow-up of hyperactives as adults. *Canadian Journal of Psychiatry, 31,* 557–567.

Hedges, L. V., & Nowell, A. (1995). Sex differences in mental test scores, variability, and numbers of high scoring individuals. *Science, 269,* 41–45.

Hediger, M. L., Overpeck, M. D., Kuczmarski, R. J., & Ruan, W. J. (2001). Association between infant breastfeeding and overweight in young children. *Journal of the American Medical Association, 285,* 2453–2460.

Heffer, R. W., & Kelley, M. L. (1987). Mothers' acceptance of behavioral interactions for children. *Behavior Therapy, 2,* 153–163.

Hegyi, T., Carbone, T., Anwar, M., Ostfeld, B., Hiatt, M., Koons, A., Pinto-Martin, J., & Paneth, N. (1998). The Apgar score and its components in the preterm infant. *Pediatrics, 101,* 77–81.

Heimann, M. (2001). Neonatal imitation—a "fuzzy" phenomenon? In F. Lacerda & C. von Hofsten (Eds.), *Emerging cognitive abilities in early infancy* (pp. 231–246). Mahwah, NJ: Erlbaum.

Heinemann, R. (1995). [Population tables]. Unpublished data.

Helm, P., & Grolund, J. (1998). A halt in the secular trend toward earlier menarche in Denmark. *Acta Obstetrics and Gynecology Scandanavia, 77,* 198–200.

Henderson-King, E., & Henderson-King, D. (1997). Media effects on women's body esteem: Social and individual difference factors. *Journal of Applied Social Psychology, 27,* 399–417.

Hendrick, S. S., & Hendrick, C. (1995). Gender differences and similarities in sex and love. *Personal Relationships, 2,* 55–65.

Hennessey, B. A., & Amabile, T. M. (1988). The conditions of creativity. In R. Sternberg (Ed.), *The nature of creativity: Contemporary psychological perspectives* (pp. 11–38). New York: Cambridge University Press.

Henricson, C., & Roker, D. (2000). Support for the parents of adolescents: A review. *Journal of Adolescence, 23,* 763–783.

Henry, C. S., & Peterson, G. W. (1995). Adolescent social competence, parental qualities, and parental satisfaction. *American Journal of Orthopsychiatry, 65,* 249–262.

Henry, C. S., Peterson, G. W., & Wilson, S. M. (1997). Adolescent social competence and parental satisfaction. *Journal of Adolescent Research, 12,* 389–409.

Henshaw, S. (1999). *Teenage pregnancy: overall trends and state-by-state information.* New York: The Alan Guttmacher Institute.

Henshaw, S. (2001). *U.S. teenage pregnancy statistics with comparative statistics for women aged 20–24.* New York: The Alan Guttmacher Institute.

Herman-Giddens, M. E., Slora, E. J., Wasserman, R. C., Bourdony, C. J., Bhapkar, M. V., Koch, G. G., & Hasemeier, C. M. (1997). Secondary sexual characteristics and menses in young girls seen in office practice: A study from the Pediatric Research in Office Settings Network. *Pediatrics, 99,* 505–512.

Herold, E. S., & Marshall, S. K. (1996). Adolescent sexual development. In G. R. Adams & R. Montemayor (Eds.), *Psychosocial development during adolescence* (Vol. 8, pp. 62–94). Thousand Oaks, CA: Sage.

Herrmann, D. J. (1998). The relationship between basic research and applied research in memory and cognition. In C. P. Thompson & D. J. Herrmann (Eds.), *Autobiographical memory* (pp. 13–27). Mahwah, NJ: Erlbaum.

Hershberger, S. L., & D'Augelli, A. R. (1995). The impact of victimization on the mental health and suicidality of lesbian, gay, and bisexual youths. *Developmental Psychology, 31,* 65–74.

Hertzler, A. A., & Frary, R. B. (1989). Food behavior of college students. *Adolescence, 24,* 349–356.

Hetherington, E. M. (1999a). Should we stay together for the sake of the children? In E. M. Hetherington (Ed.), *Coping with divorce, single parenting, and remarriage: A risk and resiliency perspective* (pp. 93–116). Mahwah, NJ: Erlbaum.

Hetherington, E. M. (1999b). Social capital and the development of youth from nondivorced, divorced and remarried families. In W. A. Collins & B. Laursen (Eds.), *Relationships as developmental contexts* (pp. 177–209). Mahwah, NJ: Erlbaum.

Hetherington, E. M., Bridges, M., & Insabella, G. M. (1998). What matters? What does not? Five perspectives on the association between marital transitions and children's adjustment. *American Psychologist, 53,* 167–184.

Hetherington, E. M., & Clingempeel, W. G. (1992). Coping with marital transitions. *Monographs of the Society for Research in Child Development, 57* (Whole No. 227).

Hetherington, E. M., Hagan, M. S., & Anderson, E. R. (1989). Marital transitions: A child's perspective. *American Psychologist, 44,* 303–312.

Hetherington, E. M., & Stanley-Hagan, M. (1999a). The adjustment of children with divorced parents: A risk and resiliency perspective. *Journal of Child Psychology and Psychiatry and Allied Disciplines, 40,* 129–140.

Hetherington, E. M., & Stanley-Hagan, M. (1999b). Stepfamilies. In M. E. Lamb (Ed.), *Parenting and child development in "nontraditional" families* (pp. 137–159). Mahwah, NJ: Erlbaum.

Hetherington, E. M., & Stanley-Hagan, M. (2000). Diversity among stepfamilies. In D. H. Demo & K. R. Allen (Eds.), *Handbook of family diversity* (pp. 173–196). New York: Oxford University Press.

Hewett, J. K., Silberg, J. L., Rutter, M., Simonoff, E., Meyer, J. M., Maes, H., Pickles, A., Neale, M. C., Loeber, R., Erickson, M. T., Kendler, K. S., Heath, A. C., Turett, K. R., Reynolds, C. A., & Eaves, L. J. (1997). Genetics and developmental psychopathology. *Journal of Child Psychology and Psychiatry and Allied Disciplines, 38,* 943–963.

Hewitt, M. P. (1998). *The myth of self-esteem.* New York: St. Martin's Press.

Hewlett, B. S. (1992). The parent-infant relationship and social-emotional development among Aka Pygmies. In J. L. Roopnarine & D. B. Carter (Eds.), *Parent-child socialization in diverse cultures* (pp. 223–244). Norwood, NJ: Ablex.

Hiebert, E. H., & Raphael, T. E. (1996). Psychological perspectives on literacy and extensions to educational practice. In D. C. Berliner & R. C. Calfee (Eds.), *Handbook of educational psychology* (pp. 550–562). New York: Macmillan.

Hill, C. R., & Stafford, F. P. (1980). Parental care of children: Time diary estimates of quantity, predictability, and variety. *Journal of Human Resources, 15,* 219–239.

Hill, J. P. (1987). Research on adolescents and their families. In C. E. Irwin (Ed.), *Adolescent social behavior and health* (Vol. 13, pp. 13–31). San Francisco: Jossey-Bass.

Hill, J. P., & Lynch, M. E. (1983). The intensification of gender-related role expectations during early adolescence. In J. Brooks-Gunn & A. C. Petersen (Eds.), *Girls at puberty* (pp. 201–228). New York: Plenum.

Hines, M. (1990). Gonadal hormones and human cognitive development. In J. Balthazart (Ed.), *Hormones, brain and behavior in vertebrates. 1. Sexual differentiation, neuroanatomical aspects, neurotransmitters and neuropeptides* (pp. 51–63). Basel, Switzerland: Barger.

Hinshaw, S. P., Zupan, B. A., Simmel, C., Nigg, J. T., & Melnick, S. (1997). Peer status in boys with and without attention-deficit hyperactivity disorder. *Child Development, 68,* 880–896.

Hiscock, H., & Wake, M. (2001). Infant sleep problems and postnatal depression: A community-based study. *Pediatrics, 107,* 1317–1322.

Hobar, J. D., & Lucey, J. F. (1995). Evaluation of neonatal intensive care technologies. *The Future of Children, 5,* 139–161.

Hochschild, A. R. (1997). *The time bind.* New York: Metropolitan Press.

Hodnett, E. D., & Osborn, R. W. (1989). Effects of continuous intrapartum professional support on childbirth outcomes. *Research in Nursing and Health, 12,* 289–297.

Hoff-Ginsberg, E. (1985). Some contributions of mothers' speech to their children's syntactic growth. *Journal of Child Language, 12,* 367–385.

Hoff-Ginsberg, E. (1986). Function and structure in maternal speech: Their relation to the child's development of syntax. *Developmental Psychology, 22,* 155–163.

Hoff-Ginsberg, E. (1997). *Language development.* Pacific Grove, CA: Brooks/Cole.

Hoffman, L. W., & Youngblade, L. M. (1999). *Mothers at work: Effects on children's well-being.* Cambridge, England: Cambridge University Press.

Hoffman, M. L. (1970). Conscience, personality, and socialization techniques. *Human Development, 13,* 90–126.

Hoffman, M. L. (1994). Discipline and internalization. *Developmental Psychology, 30,* 26–28.

Hoffman, M. L. (2000). *Empathy and moral development: Implications for caring and justice.* New York: Cambridge University Press.

Holditch-Davis, B. P., Harris, B. G., Sandelowski, M., & Edwards, L. (1994). Beyond couvade: Pregnancy symptoms in couples with a history of infertility. *Health Care Women International, 15,* 537–548.

Holliday, M. A. (1986). Body composition and energy needs during growth. In F. Faulkner & J. M. Tanner (Eds.), *Human growth: A comprehensive treatise* (Vol. 2, pp. 101–117). New York: Plenum.

Holmbeck, G. N., Paikoff, R. L., & Brooks-Gunn, J. (1995). Parenting adolescents. In M. H. Bornstein (Ed.), *Handbook of parenting* (Vol. 1, pp. 91–118). Mahwah, NJ: Erlbaum.

Holzman, C., & Paneth, N. (1994). Maternal cocaine use during pregnancy and perinatal outcomes. *Epidemiology Review, 16,* 215–334.

Holzman, L. H. (1996). Pragmatism and dialectical materialism in language development. In H. Daniels (Ed.), *An introduction to Vygotsky* (pp. 75–98). London: Routledge.

Hoover, K. R., Marcia, J. E., & Parris, K. D. (1997). *The power of identity.* Chatham, NJ: Chatham House.

Hopkins, B. (1991). Facilitating early motor development: An intracultural study of West Indian mothers and their infants living in Britain. In J. Nugent, B. Lester, & T. Brazelton (Eds.), *The cultural context of infancy: Multicultural and interdisciplinary approaches to parent-infant relations* (pp. 93–143). Norwood, NJ: Ablex.

Hoppenbrouwers, T., Hodgman, J. E., Arawaka, K., Geidel, S. A., & Sterman, M. B. (1988). Sleep and waking states in infancy: Normative studies. *Sleep, 11,* 387–402.

Hopwood, N. J., Kelch, R. P., Hale, P. M., Mendes, T. M., Foster, C. M., & Beitins, I. Z. (1990). The onset of human puberty: biological and environmental factors. In J. Bancroft & J. Reinisch (Eds.), *Adolescence and puberty* (pp. 29–49). New York: Oxford University Press.

Horn, J. L., & Trickett, P. K. (1998). Community violence and child development: A review of research. In P. K. Trickett & C. J. Schellenbach (Eds.), *Violence against children in the family and the community* (pp. 103–138). Washington, DC: American Psychological Association.

Horney, K. (1967). *Feminine psychology.* New York: Norton.

Horowitz, F. D. (2000). Child development and the PITS: Simple questions, complex answers, and developmental theory. *Child Development, 71,* 1–10.

Horwood, L. J., & Fergusson, D. M. (1998, January). Breastfeeding and later cognitive and academic outcome. *Pediatrics, 101,* 1–7.

Hovey, J. D. (2000). Psychosocial predictors of acculturative stress in Mexican immigrants. *Journal of Personality, 134,* 490–502.

Howe, M. J. A. (1997). *IQ in question: The truth about intelligence.* London: Sage.

Howe, M. J. A. (1999). Prodigies and creativity. In R. J. Sternberg (Ed.), *Handbook of creativity* (pp. 431–446). Cambridge, England: Cambridge University Press.

Howell, J. C. (1997). *Youth gangs.* Washington, DC: Office of Juvenile Justice and Delinquency Prevention.

Howes, C. (1988a). Peer interaction in young children. *Monographs of the Society for Research in Child Development, 53* (Whole No. 217). Chicago: University of Chicago Press.

Howes, C. (1988b). Relations between early child care and schooling. *Developmental Psychology, 24,* 53–57.

Howes, C. (1989). Friendships in very young children: Definition and functions. In B. H. Schneider, G. Attili, J. Nadel, & R. P. Weissberg (Eds.), *Social competence in developmental perspective* (pp. 127–130). Boston: Kluwer.

Howes, C. (1990). Can the age of entry into child care and the quality of child care predict adjustment in kindergarten? *Developmental Psychology, 26,* 292–303.

Howes, C., Hamilton, C. E., & Matheson, C. C. (1994). Children's relationships with peers: Differential associations with aspects of the teacher/child relationship. *Child Development, 65,* 253–263.

Howes, C., & Matheson, C. C. (1992). Sequences in the development of competent play with peers: Social and pretend play. *Developmental Psychology, 28,* 961–974.

Howes, C., Matheson, C. C., & Hamilton, C. E. (1994). Maternal, teacher, and child care history correlates of children's relationships with peers. *Child Development, 65,* 264–273.

Howes, C., Phillips, D., & Whitebook, M. (1992). Thresholds of quality: Implications for the social development of children in center-based child care. *Child Development, 63,* 449–460.

Hoyenga, K. B., & Hoyenga, K. T. (1993). *Gender related differences: Origins and outcomes.* Needham Heights, MA: Allyn & Bacon.

Hoyt, C. (1996, April). Debunking the myth of the terrible toddler. *Child,* 50–52.

Hsu, L. K. G., & Sobkiewicz, T. A. (1991). Body image disturbance: Time to abandon the concept of eating disorders? *International Journal of Eating Disorders, 10,* 15–30.

Hudson, J. A. (1990). The emergence of autobiographical memory in mother-child conversation. In R. Fivush & J. A. Hudson (Eds.), *Knowing and remembering in young children* (pp. 166–196). Cambridge, England: Cambridge University Press.

Hudson, J. A., & Fivush, R. (1991). Planning in the preschool years: The emergence of plans from general event knowledge. *Cognitive Development, 6,* 393–415.

Hudson, J. A., Shapiro, L. R., & Sosa, B. B. (1995). Planning in the real world: Preschool children's scripts and plans for familiar events. *Child Development, 66,* 984–998.

Hudson, J. A., & Sheffield, E. G. (1998). Deja vu all over again: Effects of reenactment on toddlers' event memory. *Child Development, 69,* 51–67.

Huesmann, L. R., & Eron, L. D. (Eds.). (1986). *Television and the aggressive child: A cross national comparison.* Hillsdale, NJ: Erlbaum.

Huesmann, L. R., Eron, L. D., Lefkowitz, M. M., & Walder, L. O. (1984). Stability of aggression over time and generations. *Developmental Psychology, 20,* 1120–1134.

Huff, C. R. (1996). The criminal behavior of gang members and nongang at-risk youth. In C. R. Huff (Ed.), *Gangs in America* (pp. 75–102). Thousand Oaks, CA: Sage.

Hughes, F. P. (1995). *Children, play, and development.* Boston: Allyn & Bacon.

Hunter, F. T., McCarthy, M. E., MacTurk, R. H., & Vietze, P. M. (1987). Infants' social-constructive interactions with mothers and fathers. *Developmental Psychology, 23,* 249–254.

Hunter, J. (1990). Violence against lesbian and gay youths. *Journal of Interpersonal Violence, 5,* 295–300.

Hurt, H., Malmud, E., Betancourt, L. M., Brodsky, N. L., & Giannetta, J. M. (2001). A prospective comparison of developmental outcome of children with in utero cocaine exposure and controls using the Battelle Developmental Inventory. *Journal of Developmental and Behavioral Pediatrics, 22,* 27–34.

Hurtado, A. (1995). Variations, combinations, and evolutions. In R. E. Zambrana (Ed.), *Understanding Latino families* (pp. 40–61). Thousand Oaks, CA: Sage.

Hurtado, E. K., Claussen, A. H., & Scott, K. G. (1999). Early childhood anemia and mild/moderate mental retardation. *American Journal of Clinical Nutrition, 69,* 115–119.

Huston, A. C. (1983). Sex-typing. In E. M. Hetherington (Ed.), *Handbook of child psychology: Socialization, personality, and social development* (Vol. 4, pp. 388–467). New York: Wiley.

Huston, A. C. (1991). Children in poverty: Developmental and policy issues. In A. C. Huston (Ed.), *Children in poverty* (pp. 1–22). Cambridge, England: Cambridge University Press.

Huston, A. C. (1999). Effects of poverty on children. In L. Balter & C. S. Tamis-LeMonda (Eds.), *Child psychology: A handbook of contemporary issues* (pp. 391–411). Philadelphia: Psychology Press.

Huston, A. C., & Alvarez, M. M. (1990). The socialization context of gender role development in early adolescence. In R. Montemayor & G. R. Adams (Eds.), *From childhood to adolescence* (pp. 156–179). Newbury Park, CA: Sage.

Huston, A. C., Donnerstein, E., Fairchild, H., Feshbach, N. D., Katz, P. A., Murray, J. P., Rubinstein, E. A., Wilcox, B., & Zuckerman, D. (1992). *Big world, small screen: The role of television in American society.* Lincoln: University of Nebraska Press.

Huston, A. C., & Wright, J. C. (1998). Mass media and children's development. In W. Damon (Ed.), *Handbook of child psychology* (Vol. 4, pp. 999–1058). New York: Wiley.

Huttenlocher, J. (1998). Language input and language growth. *Preventive Medicine, 27,* 195–199.

Huttenlocher, P. R. (1979). Synaptic density in human prefrontal cortex: Developmental changes and effects of aging. *Brain Research, 163,* 195–205.

Huttenlocher, P. R. (1990). Morphometric study of human cerebral cortex development. *Neuropsychologia, 28,* 517–527.

Huttenlocher, P. R. (1994). Synaptogenesis in human cerebral cortex. In G. Dawson & K. W. Fischer (Eds.), *Human behavior and the developing brain* (pp. 35–54). New York: Guilford.

Huttenlocher, P. R., & Dabholkar, A. S. (1997). Regional differences in synaptogenesis in human cerebral cortex. *Journal of Comparative Neurology, 387,* 167–178.

Hyde, J. S. (1984). How large are gender differences in aggression? A developmental meta-analysis. *Developmental Psychology, 20,* 722–736.

Hyde, J. S., Fennema, E., & Lamon, S. J. (1990). Gender differences in mathematics performance. *Psychological Bulletin, 107,* 139–155.

Hymel, S., Bowker, A., & Woody, E. (1993). Aggressive versus withdrawn unpopular children. *Child Development, 64,* 879–896.

Imperato-McGinley, J., Peterson, R. E., Gautier, T., & Sturla, E. (1979). Androgens and the evolution of male gender identity among male pseudohermaphrodites with 5-alpha-reductase deficiency. *New England Journal of Medicine, 300,* 123–127.

Ingram, D. (1989). *First language acquisition.* New York: Cambridge University Press.

Inhelder, B., & Piaget, J. (1958). *The growth of logical thinking from childhood to adolescence.* New York: Basic Books.

Inhelder, B., & Piaget, J. (1964). *The growth of logical thinking in the child.* New York: Harper & Row.

Institute of Medicine. (1990). *Science and babies: Private decisions, public dilemmas.* Washington, DC: National Academy Press.

International Association for the Evaluation of Educational Achievement. (1996). *IEA's third international mathematics and science study.* Washington, DC: US Department of Education.

Intons-Peterson, M. J. (1988). *Children's concepts of gender.* Norwood, NJ: Ablex.

Isabella, R. A. (1993). Origins of attachment: Maternal interactive behavior across the first year. *Child Development, 64,* 605–621.

Itard, J. (1972a). *Of the first developments of the young savage of Aveyron.* New York: Monthly Review Press. (Original work published 1801)

Itard, J. (1972b). *Report of the progress of Victor of Aveyron.* New York: Monthly Review Press. (Original work published 1806)

Izard, C. E. (1977). *Human emotions.* New York: Plenum.

Izard, C. E., & Malatesta, C. Z. (1987). Perspective on emotional development I: Differential emotions theory of early emotional development. In J. D. Osofsky (Ed.), *Handbook of infant development* (pp. 419–494). New York: Wiley.

Jack, G. (2000). Ecological influences on parenting and child development. *British Journal of Social Work, 30,* 703–720.

Jackman, G. A., Farah, M. M., Kellermann, A. L., & Simon, H. K. (2001). Seeing is believing: What do boys do when they find a real gun? *Pediatrics, 107,* pp. 1247–1250.

Jacobs, E. H. (1998). *Fathering the ADHD child.* Northvale, NJ: Jason Aronson, Inc.

Jacobs, J. E. (1991). Influence of gender stereotypes on parent and child mathematics attitudes. *Journal of Educational Psychology, 83,* 518–527.

Jacobs, J. E., & Eccles, J. S. (1985). Gender differences in math ability: The impact of media reports on parents. *Educational Researcher, 14,* 20–25.

Jacobs, R. A. (1997). Nature, nurture, and the development of functional specializations. *Psychonomic Bulletin and Review, 4,* 299–309.

Jacobson, S. W., Chiodo, L. M., & Jacobson, J. L. (1999). Breastfeeding effects on intelligence quotient in 4- and 11-year-old children. *Pediatrics, 103,* e71.

Jacobvitz, D., & Sroufe, L. A. (1987). The early caregiver-child relationship and attention-deficit disorder with hyperactivity in kindergarten: A prospective study. *Child Development, 58,* 1496–1504.

Jaffe, M. L. (1997). *Understanding parenting.* Boston: Allyn & Bacon.

Jahoda, G. (1983). European "lag" in the development of an economic concept: A study in Zimbabwe. *British Journal of Developmental Psychology, 1,* 113–120.

Jain, A., Belsky, J., & Crnic, K. (1996). Beyond father behaviors: Types of dads. *Journal of Family Psychology, 10,* 432–442.

Janowsky, J. S., Oviatt, S. K., & Orwoll, E. S. (1994). Testosterone influences spatial cognition in older men. *Behavioral Neuroscience, 108,* 325–332.

Jason, L. A., Kennedy, C. L., Hanaway, L., & Brackshaw, E. (1999). Television violence and children: Problems and solutions. In T. P. Gullotta & S. J. McElhaney (Eds.), *Violence in homes and communities: Prevention, intervention, and treatment. Issues in children's and families' lives* (Vol. 11, pp. 133–156). Thousand Oaks, CA: Sage.

Jelalian, E., & Lloyd, E. E (1997). Adolescent obesity: Assessment and treatment. *Medical Health, 80,* 367–369.

Jellinek, M. B., & Snyder J. B. (1998). Depression and suicide in children and adolescents. *Pediatric Review, 19,* 255–264.

Jenni, C. B. (1997). School phobia: How home-school collaborations can tame this frightful dragon. *School Counselor, 44,* 206–217.

Jensen, P. S., Hinshaw, S. P., Swanson, J. M., Greenhill, L. L., Conners, C. K., Arnold, L. E., Abikoff, H. B., Elliott, G., Hechtman, L., Hoza, B., March, J. S., Newcorn, J. H., Severe, J. B., Vitiello, B., Wells, K., & Wigal, T. (2001). Findings from the NIMH Multimodal Treatment Study of ADHD (MTA): Implications and applications for primary care providers. *Journal of Developmental and Behavioral Pediatrics, 22,* 60–73.

Jersild, A., & Holmes, F. (1935). Children's fears. *Child Development Monographs* (Vol. 20). Chicago: University of Chicago Press.

Jessor, R. (1992). Risk behavior in adolescence: A psychosocial framework for understanding and action. In D. E. Rogers & E. Ginzberg (Eds.), *Adolescents at risk: Medical and social perspectives* (pp. 19–34). Boulder, CO: Westview Press.

Jiao, S., Ji, G., & Jing, Q. (1986). Comparative study of behavioral qualities of only children and sibling children. *Child Development, 57,* 357–361.

Jing, Q., & Wan, C. (1997). Socialization of Chinese children. In H. S. R. Kao & D. Sinha (Eds.), *Asian perspectives on psychology* (pp. 59–73). New Delhi: Sage.

Johnson, D. E. (2001). The impact of orphanage rearing on growth and development. In C. A. Nelson (Ed.), *Minnesota Symposia on Child Psychology* (Vol. 27, pp. 23–57). New York: Erlbaum.

Johnson, J. S., & Newport, E. L. (1989). Critical period effects in second language learning: The influence of maturational state on the acquisition of English as a second language. *Cognitive Psychology, 21,* 60–99.

Johnson, S. (1987). Early-developed sex differences in science and mathematics in the United Kingdom. *Journal of Early Adolescence, 7,* 21–33.

Johnson Institute. (1993). *Drugs mean alcohol too.* Minneapolis,: Johnson Institute.

Johnston, H. F., & Fruehling, J. J. (1994). Pharmacotherapy for depression in children and adolescents. In W. M. Reynolds & H. F. Johnston (Eds.), *Handbook of depression in children and adolescents* (pp. 365–397). New York: Plenum.

Johnston, J. R., Breunig, K., Garrity, C., & Baris, M. A. (1997). *Through the eyes of children.* New York: Free Press.

Jones, C. P., & Adamson, L. B. (1987). Language use in mother-child and mother-child-sibling interactions. *Child Development, 58,* 356–366.

Jones, M. C. (1965). Psychological correlates of somatic development. *Child Development, 36,* 899–911.

Jones, M. C., & Mussen, P. H. (1958). Self-conceptions, motivations and interpersonal attitudes of early and late maturing girls. *Child Development, 29,* 491–501.

Jones, O. W., & Cahill, T. C. (1994). Basic genetics and patterns of inheritance. In R. K. Creasy & R. Resnik (Eds.), *Maternal-fetal medicine: Principles and practice* (pp. 103–189). Philadelphia: Saunders.

Jones, R. E. (1997). *Human reproductive biology.* New York: Academic Press.

Jones, S. S., Collins, K., & Hong, H. (1991). An audience effect on smile production in 10-month-old infants. *Psychological Science, 2,* 45–49.

Jorgensen, S. R. (1993). Adolescent pregnancy and parenting. In T. P. Gullotta & G. R. Adams (Eds.), *Adolescent sexuality* (Vol. 5, pp. 103–140). Newbury Park, CA: Sage.

Joseph, R. (2000). Fetal brain behavior and cognitive development. *Developmental Review, 20,* 81–98.

Josephson, W. L. (1995). *Television violence: A review of the effects on children of different ages.* Montreal: Department of Canadian Heritage.

Jouriles, E. N., McDonald, R., Norwood, W. D., Ware, H. S., Spiller, L. C., & Swank, P. R. (1998). Knives, guns, and interparent violence: Relations with child behavior problems. *Journal of Family Psychology, 12,* 178–194.

Jovanovic, J., & Dreves, C. (1995). *Math, science, and girls: Can we close the gender gap?* Urbana: University of Illinois Cooperative Extension Service.

Juffer, F., & Rosenboom, L. G. (1997). Infant-mother attachment of internationally adopted children in the Netherlands. *International Journal of Behavioral Development, 20,* 93–107.

Jusczyk, P. W. (1997). *The discovery of spoken language.* Cambridge, MA: Bradford.

Jussim, L., Madon, S., & Chatman, C. (1994). Teacher expectations and student achievement. In L. Heath & T. R. Scott (Eds.), Applications of heuristics and biases to social issues (Vol. 3, pp. 303–334). New York: Plenum.

Kachur, S. P., Stennies, G. M., Powell, K. E., Modzeleski, W., Stephens, R., Murphy, R., Kresnow, M., Sleet, D., & Lowry, R. (1996). School-associated violent deaths in the United States, 1992 to 1994. *Journal of the American Medical Association, 275*(22), 1729–1733.

Kagan, J. (1976). Emergent themes in human development. *American Scientist, 64,* 196.

Kagan, J. (1989). Temperamental contributions to social behavior. *American Psychologist, 44,* 668–674.

Kagan, J., Snidman, N., & Arcus, D. (1993). On the temperamental categories of inhibited and uninhibited children. In K. H. Rubin & J. B. Asendorpf (Eds.), *Social withdrawal, inhibition, and shyness in childhood* (pp. 19–30). Hillsdale, NJ: Erlbaum.

Kagan, S., Knight, G., Martinez, S., & Santa, P. (1981). Conflict resolution style among Mexican children. *Journal of Cross-Cultural Psychology, 12,* 222–232.

Kagan, S. L., & Neuman, M. J. (1998). Lessons from three decades of transition research. *Elementary School Journal, 87,* 365–379.

Kahn, P. H. (1997). Bayous and jungle rivers: Cross-cultural perspectives on children's environmental moral reasoning. In H. D. Saltzstein (Ed.), *Culture as a context for moral development* (pp. 23–37). San Francisco: Jossey-Bass.

Kalamas, A. D., & Gruber, M. L. (1998). Electrodermal responses to implied versus actual violence on television. *Journal of General Psychology, 125,* 31–37.

Kallen, K. (2000). Maternal smoking during pregnancy and infant head circumference at birth. *Early Human Development, 58,* 197–204.

Kanfer, F., Karoly, P., & Newman, A. (1975). Reduction of children's fear of the dark by competence-related and situational threat-related verbal cries. *Journal of Consulting and Clinical Psychology, 43,* 251–258.

Kapitanoff, S. H., Lutzker, J. R., & Bigelow, K. M. (2000). Cultural issues in the relation between child disabilities and child abuse. *Aggression and Violent Behavior, 5,* 227–244.

Karpov, Y. V., & Haywood, H. C. (1998). Two ways to elaborate Vygotsky's concept of mediation. *American Psychologist, 53,* 27–36.

Kasari, C., & Bauminger, N. (1998). Social and emotional development in children with mental retardation. In J. A. Burack & R. M. Hodapp (Eds.), *Handbook of mental retardation and development* (pp. 411–433). New York: Cambridge University Press.

Kashani, J. H., Rosenberg, T. K., & Reid, J. C. (1989). Developmental perspectives in child and adolescent depressive symptoms in a community sample. *American Journal of Psychiatry, 146,* 871–876.

Kaslow, N. J., Morris, M. K., & Rehm, L. P. (1998). Childhood depression. In R. J. Morris & T. R. Kratochwill (Eds.), *The practice of child therapy* (pp. 48–90). Boston: Allyn & Bacon.

Kassianos, G. C. (1998). *Immunization: Childhood and travel health.* Malden, MA: Blackwell.

Katchadourian, H. (1990). Sexuality. In S. S. Feldman & G. R. Elliot (Eds.), *At the threshold: The developing adolescent* (pp. 330–351). Cambridge, MA: Harvard University Press.

Katz, J. R. (2001). Playing at home: The talk of pretend play. In D. K Dickinson & P. O. Tabors (Eds.), *Beginning literacy with language: Young children learning at home and school* (pp. 53–73). Baltimore: Brookes.

Katz, L., & Gottman, J. M. (1997). Buffering children from marital conflict and dissolution. *Journal of Child Clinical Psychology, 26,* 157–171.

Katz, P. (1992). *Progress report to NIMH.* Unpublished manuscript.

Katzman, D. K. (1996). Adolescent eating disorders. In R. H. A. Haslam & P. J. Valletutti (Eds.), *Medical problems in the classroom* (pp. 491–513). Austin, TX: Pro-Ed.

Kaufman, J., & Cicchetti, D. (1995). The effect of maltreatment on school age children's socioemotional development. *Developmental Psychology, 25,* 516–524.

Kaufman, N. L. (1980). Review of reversal errors. *Perceptual and Motor Skills, 51,* 55–79.

Kavrell, S. M., & Petersen, A. C. (1984). Patterns of achievement in early adolescence. In M. L. Maehr (Ed.), *Advances in motivation and achievement* (Vol. 4, pp. 1–35). Greenwich, CT: JAI Press.

Kazdin, A. E. (1989). Conduct and oppositional disorders. In C. G. Last & M. Hersen (Eds.), *Handbook of child psychiatric diagnosis* (pp. 129–155). New York: Wiley.

Kazdin, A. E., & Marciano, P. L. (1998). Childhood and adolescent depression. In E. J. Mash & R. A. Barkley (Eds.), *Treatment of childhood disorders* (pp. 211–248). New York: Guilford Press.

Kazdin, A. E., Moser, J., Colbus, D., & Bell, R. (1985). Depressive symptoms among physically abused and psychiatrically disturbed children. *Journal of Abnormal Psychology, 94,* 298–307.

Keating, D. P., & Sasse, D. K. (1996). Cognitive socialization in adolescence: Critical period for a critical habit of mind. In G. R. Adams & R. Montemayor (Eds.), *Psychosocial development during adolescence* (Vol. 8, pp. 232–258). Thousand Oaks, CA: Sage.

Keel, B. A., May, J. V., & DeJonge, C. J. (2000). *Handbook of assisted reproduction.* Boca Raton, FL: CRC Press.

Kehoe, E. J., & Macrae, M. (1998). Classical conditioning. In W. T. O'Donohue (Ed.), *Learning and behavior therapy* (pp. 36–58). Boston: Allyn & Bacon.

Keil, F. C. (1998). Cognitive science and the origins of thought and knowledge. In W. Damon (Ed.), *Handbook of child psychology* (Vol. 1, pp. 341–414). New York: Wiley.

Kelder, S. H., Perry, C. L., Klepp, K. I., & Lytle, L. L. (1994). Longitudinal tracking of adolescent smoking, physical activity, and food choice behaviors. *American Journal of Public Health, 84,* 1121–1126.

Keller, M. L., Duerst, B. L., & Zimmerman, J. (1996). Adolescents' views of sexual decision-making. *Journal of Nursing Scholarship, 28,* 125–130.

Keller, R. W., & Snyder-Keller, A. (2000). Prenatal cocaine exposure. *Annals of the New York Academy of Science, 909,* 217–232.

Kelley, K. (1991). Contraceptive behavior as a process. In R. M. Lerner, A. C. Petersen, & J. Brooks-Gunn (Eds.), *Encyclopedia of adolescence* (pp. 175–180). New York: Garland.

Kelley, M. L., Power, T. G., & Wimbush, D. D. (1992). Determinants of disciplinary practices in low-income Black mothers. *Child Development, 63,* 573–582.

Kelley, M. L., Sanchez-Hucles, J., & Walker, R. R. (1993). Correlates of disciplinary practices in working- to middle-class African-American mothers. *Merrill-Palmer Quarterly, 39,* 252–264.

Kellman, P. J., & Banks, M. S. (1998). Infant visual perception. In W. Damon (Ed.), *Handbook of child psychology* (Vol. 2, 103–146). New York: Wiley.

Kelly, D. P. (1992). Hearing impairment. In M. D. Levine, W. B. Carey, & A. C. Crocker (Eds.), *Developmental-behavioral pediatrics* (pp. 510–518). Philadelphia: Saunders.

Kelly, J. B. (1994). The determination of child custody. *The Future of Children, 4,* 121–142.

Kelly, M. (1977). Papua New Guinea and Piaget: An eight-year study. In P. R. Dasen (Ed.), *Piagetian psychology: Cross-cultural contributions.* New York: Gardner.

Kendall-Tackett, K. A., & Eckenrode, J. (1997). The effects of neglect on academic achievement and disciplinary problems. In G. K. Kantor & J. L. Jasinski (Eds.), *Out of darkness: Contemporary perspectives on family violence* (pp. 105–112). Thousand Oaks, CA: Sage.

Keogh, B. K., & MacMillan, D. L. (1996). Exceptionality. In D. C. Berliner & R. C. Calfee (Eds.), *Handbook of educational psychology* (pp. 311–330). New York: Macmillan.

Kernis, M. H. (1993). The role of stability and level of self-esteem in psychological functioning. In R. F. Baumeister (Ed.), *Self-esteem: The puzzle of low self-regard* (pp. 167–180). New York: Plenum.

Kernis, M. H., Brown, A., & Brody, G. H. (2000). Fragile self-esteem in children and its associations with perceived patterns of parent-child communication. *Journal of Personality, 68,* 225–252.

Kerns, K., Don, A., Mateer, C. A., & Streissguth, A. P. (1997). Cognitive deficits in nonretarded adults with fetal alcohol syndrome. *Journal of Learning Disabilities, 30,* 685–693.

Kerpelman, J. L., Pittman, J. F., & Lamke, L. K. (1997). Revisiting the identity control theory. *Journal of Adolescence Research, 12,* 363–371.

Kestenbaum, R., Farber, E. A., & Sroufe, L. A. (1989). Individual differences in empathy among preschoolers: Relation to attachment history. In N. Eisenberg (Ed.), *New directions for child development: Empathy and related emotional responses* (Vol. 44, pp. 51–64). San Francisco: Jossey-Bass.

Ketterlinus, R. D., Lamb, M. E., & Nitz, K. A. (1995). Adolescent nonsexual and sex-related problem behaviors: Their prevalence, consequences, and co-occurence. In R. D. Ketterlinus & M. E. Lamb (Eds.), *Adolescent problem behaviors* (pp. 17–40). Hillsdale, NJ: Erlbaum.

Kilbourne, J. (1994). Still killing us softly: Advertising and the obsession with thinness. In P. Fallon, M. Katzman, & S. Wooley (Eds.), *Feminist perspectives on eating disorders* (pp. 395–418). New York: Guilford.

Kilbride, P. L. (1980). Sensorimotor behavior of Baganda and Somia infants: A controlled comparison. *Journal of Cross-Cultural Psychology, 11,* 131–149.

Killeen, M. R., & Forehand, R. (1998). A transactional model of adolescent self-esteem. *Journal of Family Psychology 12,* 132–148.

Kimball, M. M. (1989). A new perspective on women's math achievement. *Psychological Bulletin, 105,* 198–214.

Kimura, D. (1993). Sex differences in the brain. *Mind and brain: Readings from Scientific American* (pp. 79–89). New York: Freeman.

King, M., & Yuille, J. (1987). Suggestibility and the child witness. In S. J. Ceci, D. Ross, & M. Toglia (Eds.), *Children's eyewitness memory* (pp. 24–35). New York: Springer-Verlag.

Kirby, D. (1997). *No easy answers: Research findings on programs to reduce teen pregnancy.* Washington, DC: The National Campaign to Prevent Teen Pregnancy.

Kirsh, S. J. (1998). Seeing the world through Mortal Kombat–colored glasses. *Childhood, 5,* 177–184.

Kiser, L. J., Ostoja, E., & Pruitt, D. B. (1998). Dealing with stress and trauma in families. *Child and Adolescent Psychiatric Clinics of North America, 7,* 87–103.

Kittler, P. G., & Sucher, K. P. (1998). *Food and culture in America: A nutrition handbook.* Belmont, CA: West/Wadsworth.

Klaczynski, P. A. (2000). Motivated scientific reasoning biases, epistemological beliefs, and theory polarization: A two-process approach to adolescent cognition. *Child Development, 71,* 1347–1366.

Klaus, M. H., & Kennell, J. H. (1982). *Parent-infant bonding.* St. Louis, MO: Mosby.

Klaus, M. H., Kennell, J. H., Plumb, N., & Zeuhlke, S. (1970). Human maternal behavior at the first contact with her young. *Pediatrics, 46,* 187–192.

Klebanoff, M. A., Levine, R. J., DerSimonian, R., Clemens, J. D., & Wilkins, D. G. (1999). Maternal serum paraxanthine, a caffeine metabolite, and the risk of spontaneous abortion. *New England Journal of Medicine, 341,* 1639–1644.

Klein, H. (1991). Couvade syndrome: Male counterpart to pregnancy. *International Journal of Psychiatry and Medicine, 21,* 57–69.

Klein, M. H. (1984). The bite of Pac-Man. *Journal of Psychohistory, 11,* 395–401.

Klein, P. D. (1997). Multiplying the problems of intelligence by eight: A critique of Gardner's theory. *Canadian Journal of Education, 22,* 377–394.

Klein, R. G., & Mannuzza, S. (1991). Long-term outcome of hyperactive children: A review. *Journal of the American Academy of Child and Adolescent Psychiatry, 30,* 383–387.

Kleinman, R. W., Murphy, J. M., Little, M., Pagano, M., Wehler, C. A., Regal, K., & Jellinek, M. S. (1998). Hunger in children in the United States: Potential behavioral and emotional correlates. *Pediatrics, 101,* e3.

Klinefelter Syndrome and Associates. (2001). *Sex chromosomes variations.* Roseville, CA: Klinefelter Syndrome and Associates.

Kliewer, W., Fearnow, M. D., & Walton, M. N. (1998). Dispositional, environmental, and context-specific predictors of children's threat perceptions in everyday stressful situations. *Journal of Youth and Adolescence, 27,* 83–100.

Knight, G., Fabes, R. A., & Higgins, D. (1996). Concerns about drawing causal inferences from meta-analyses of gender differences: An example in the study of aggression. *Psychological Bulletin, 119,* 410–421.

Knight, R. T., & Grabowecky, M. (2000). Prefrontal cortex, time, and consciousness. In M. S. Gazzaniga (Ed.), *The new cognitive neurosciences* (pp. 1319–1339). Cambridge, MA: MIT Press.

Knight-Ridder/Tribune News Service (1999, July 9). *Popular music's influence on teens is undeniable and sometimes negative.* New York: Knight-Ridder/Tribune News Service.

Kochanska, G. (1995). Children's temperament, mothers' discipline, and security of attachment: Multiple pathways to emerging internalization. *Child Development, 66,* 597–615.

Kochanska, G. (1997). Multiple pathways to conscience for children with different temperaments: From toddlerhood to age 5. *Developmental Psychology, 33,* 228–240.

Kochanska, G., & Askan, N. (1995). Mother-child mutually positive affect, the quality of child compliance to requests and prohibitions, and maternal control as correlates of early internalization. *Child Development, 66,* 236–254.

Kochanska, G., Coy, K. C., Tjebkes, T. L., & Husarek, S. J. (1998). Individual differences in emotionality in infancy. *Child Development, 69,* 375–390.

Kochanska, G., Murray, K. T., & Harlan, E. T. (2000). Effortful control in early childhood: Continuity and change, antecedents, and implications for social development. *Developmental Psychology, 36,* 220–232.

Kocijan-Hercigonja, D., Rijavec, M., Marusic, A., & Hercigonja, V. (1998). Coping strategies of refugee, displaced, and non-displaced children in a war area. *Nordic Journal of Psychiatry, 52,* 45–50.

Koegel, P., & Edgerton, R. B. (1984). Black "six-hour retarded children" as young adults. In R. B. Edgerton (Ed.), *Lives in process: Mildly retarded adults in a large city* (pp. 145–171). Washington, DC: American Association on Mental Deficiency.

Koff, E., & Rierdan, J. (1993). Advanced pubertal development and eating disturbance in early adolescent girls. *Journal of Adolescent Health, 14,* 433–439.

Kohlberg, L. (1966). A cognitive-developmental analysis of children's sex role concepts and attitudes. In E. E. Maccoby (Ed.), *The development of sex differences* (pp. 82–173). Stanford, CA: Stanford University Press.

Kohlberg, L. (1969). Stage and sequence: The cognitive-developmental approach to socialization. In D. A. Goslin (Ed.), *Handbook of socialization theory and research* (pp. 347–480). Chicago: Rand McNally.

Kohlberg, L. (1981). *Essays on moral development: Volume 1.* New York: Harper & Row.

Kohlberg, L. (1984). *Essays on moral development: Volume 2.* New York: Harper & Row.

Kohlberg, L., Colby, A., Gibbs, J., & Speicher-Dubin, B. (1978). *Standard form scoring manual.* Cambridge, MA: Harvard University Center for Moral Education.

Kohlberg, L., & Kramer, R. (1969). Continuities and discontinuities in childhood and adult moral development. *Human Development, 12,* 3–120.

Kohn, A. (1993). *Punished by rewards.* Boston: Houghton Mifflin.

Kolb, K. J., & Jussim, L. (1994). Teacher expectations and underachieving gifted children. *Roeper Review, 17,* 26–30.

Kolko, D. J. (1996). Child physical abuse. In J. Briere, L. Berliner, J. A. Bulkley, C. Jenny, & T. Reid (Eds.), *The APSAC handbook on child maltreatment* (pp. 21–50). Thousand Oaks, CA: Sage.

Koller, H., Lawson, K., Rose, S. A., Wallace, I., & McCarton, C. (1997). Patterns of cognitive development in very low birth weight children during the first six years of life. *Pediatrics, 99,* 383–389.

Konner, M. (1991). Universals of behavioral development in relation to brain myelination. In K. R. Gibson & A. C. Petersen (Eds.), *Brain maturation and cognitive development: Comparative and cross-cultural perspectives* (pp. 181–224). New York: Aldine de Gruyter.

Koolstra, C. M., van der Voort, T. H. A., & van der Kamp, L. J. T. (1997). Television's impact on children's reading comprehension and decoding skills: A 3-year panel study. *Reading Research Quarterly, 32,* 128–152.

Kopp, C. B. (1992). Emotional distress and control in young children. In N. Eisenberg & R. A. Fabes (Eds.), *Emotion and its regulation in early development* (Vol. 55, pp. 41–57). San Francisco: Jossey-Bass.

Korbin, J. E., Coulton, C. J., Chard, S., Platt-Houston, C., & Su, M. (1998). Impoverishment and child maltreatment in African American and European American neighborhoods. *Development and Psychopathology, 10,* 215–233.

Korkman, M., Liikanen, A., & Fellman, V. (1996). Neurophysiological consequences of very low birth weight and asphyxia at term: Follow-up until school-age. *Journal of Clinical and Experimental Neuropsychology, 18,* 220–233.

Korte, D., & Scaer, R. (1992). *A good birth, a safe birth.* Boston: Harvard Common Press.

Kotler, J. A., Wright, J. C., & Huston, A. C. (2001). Television use in families with children. In J. Bryant & J. A. Bryant (Eds.), *Television and the American family* (pp. 33–48). Mahwah, NJ: Erlbaum.

Kotlowitz, A. (1991). *There are no children here.* New York: Doubleday.

Kowal, A., & Kramer, L. (1997). Children's understanding of parental differential treatment. *Child Development, 68,* 113–126.

Krahenbuhl, G. S., Skinner, J. S., & Korht, W. M. (1985). Developmental aspects of maximal aerobic power in children. *Exercise and Sport Science Review, 13,* 503.

Kramer, C. (1995, September 19). Former dropout makes new life at Yale. *Yale Daily News.*

Krauss, D. A., & Sales, B. D. (2001). The child custody standard: What do twenty years of research teach us? In S. O. White (Ed.), *Handbook of youth and justice* (pp. 411–435). New York: Kluwer.

Kroger, J. (1993). On the nature of structural transition in the identity formation process. In J. Kroger (Ed.), *Discussions on ego identity* (pp. 205–234). Hillsdale, NJ: Erlbaum.

Kroger, J. (2000). Ego identity status research in the new millennium. *International Journal of Behavioral Development, 24,* 145–148.

Kuchuk, A., Vibbert, M., & Bornstein, M. H. (1986). The perception of smiling and its experiential correlates in three-month-old infants. *Child Development, 57,* 1054–1061.

Kuczynski, L., Kochanska, G., Radke-Yarrow, M., & Girnius-Brown, O. (1987). A developmental interpretation of young children's noncompliance. *Developmental Psychology, 23,* 799–806.

Kuhn, D. (1989). Children and adults as intuitive scientists. *Psychological Review, 96,* 674–689.

Kuhn, D., Amsel, E., O'Loughlin, M., Schauble, L., Leadbeater, B., & Yotive, W. (1988). *The development of scientific reasoning skills.* San Diego, CA: Academic Press.

Kuhn, D., Nash, S. C., & Brucken, L. (1978). Sex role concepts of two- and three-year-old children. *Child Development, 49,* 445–451.

Kuhn, L., Kline, J., Ng, S., Levin, B., & Susser, M. (2000). Cocaine use during pregnancy and intrauterine growth retardation: New insights based on maternal hair tests. *American Journal of Epidemiology, 152,* 112–119.

Kumra, S., Wiggins, E., Krasnewich, D., Meck, J., Smith, A. C. M., Bedwell, J., Fernandez, T., Jacobsen, L. K., Lenane, M., & Rapoport, J. L. (1998). Association of sex chromosome anomalies with childhood-onset psychotic disorders. *Journal of the American Academy of Child and Adolescent Psychiatry, 37,* 292–296.

Kurdek, L. A. (1988). Cognitive mediators of children's adjustment to divorce. In S. A. Wolchik & P. Karoly (Eds.), *Children of divorce* (pp. 233–266). New York: Gardner.

Kwasman, A., Tinsley, B. J., & Lepper, H. S. (1995). Pediatricians' knowledge and attitudes concerning diagnosis and treatment of attention deficit and hyperactivity disorders. *Archives of Pediatric and Adolescent Medicine, 149,* 1211–1216.

Ladd, G. W., & Kochenderfer, B. J. (1998). Linkages between friendship and adjustment during early school transition. In W. M. Bukowski & A. F. Newcomb (Eds.), *The company they keep: Friendship in childhood and adolescence* (pp. 322–345). New York: Cambridge University Press.

Lagercrantz, H., & Slotkin, T. A. (1986). The "stress" of being born. *Scientific American, 254,* 100–107.

LaGreca, A. M., Prinstein, M. J., & Fetter, M. D. (2001). Adolescent peer crowd affiliation: Linkages with health-risk behaviors and close friendships. *Journal of Pediatric Psychology, 26,* 131–143.

Laird, R. D., Pettit, G. S., Dodge, K. A., & Bates, J. E. (1999). Best friendships, group relationships, and antisocial behavior in early adolescence. *Journal of Early Adolescence, 19,* 413–437.

Lamb, M. E. (1982a). The bonding phenomenon: Misinterpretations and their implications. *Journal of Pediatrics, 101,* 555–557.

Lamb, M. E. (1982b). Early contact and mother-infant bonding: One decade later. *Pediatrics, 70,* 763–768.

Lamb, M. E. (1998). Nonparental child care: Context, quality, correlates, and consequences. In W. Damon (Ed.), *Handbook of child psychology* (Vol. 4, pp. 73–134). New York: Wiley.

Lamb, M. E., Sternberg, K. J., & Ketterlinus, R. D. (1992). Child care in the United States: The modern era. In M. E. Lamb, K. J. Sternberg, C. Hwang, & A. G. Broberg (Eds.), *Child care in context* (pp. 207–222). Hillsdale, NJ: Erlbaum.

Lampert, W. E. (1984). An overview of issues in immersion education. In Office of Bilingual and Bicultural Education (Ed.), *Studies in immersion education* (pp. 8–30). Sacramento: California Department of Education.

Landers, D. M., & Petruzzello, S. J. (1994). Physical activity, fitness and anxiety. In C. Bouchard, R. J. Shephard, & T. Stephens (Eds.), *Physical activity, fitness and health* (pp. 868–882). Champaign, IL: Human Kinetics Publishers.

Landry, D. J., & Forrest, J. D. (1995). How much older are U.S. fathers? *Family Planning Perspectives, 27,* 159–165.

Lane, K. L., Beebe, M. E., Lambros, K. M., & Pierson, M. (2001). Designing effective interventions for children at-risk for antisocial behavior: An integrated model of components necessary for making valid inferences. *Psychology in the Schools, 38,* 365–379.

Langendorfer, S. (1987). Separating fact from fiction in preschool aquatics. *National Aquatics Journal, 3,* 2–4.

Langer, J., & Killen, M. (1998). *Piaget, evolution, and development.* Mahwah, NJ: Erlbaum.

Langlois, J. H. (1981). Beauty and the beast: The role of physical attractiveness in the development of peer relations and social behavior. In S. S. Brehm, S. S. Kassin, & F. X. Gibbons (Eds.), *Developmental social psychology* (pp. 47–63). New York: Oxford University Press.

Langlois, J. H., & Downs, A. C. (1980). Mothers, fathers and peers as socialization agents of sex-typed play behaviors in young children. *Child Development, 51,* 1237–1247.

Langlois, J. H., Ritter, J. M., Roggman, L. A., & Vaughn, L. S. (1991). Facial diversity and infant preferences for attractive faces. *Developmental Psychology, 27,* 79–84.

Langlois, J. H., Roggman, L. A., Casey, R. J., Ritter, J. M., Rieser-Danner, L. A., & Jenkins, V. Y. (1987). Infant preferences for attractive faces: Rudiments of a stereotype? *Developmental Psychology, 23,* 363–369.

LaPorte, D. J. (1997). Gender differences in perceptions and consequences of an eating binge. *Sex Roles, 36,* 479–489.

Lapsley, D. K. (1993). Toward an integrated theory of adolescent ego development. *American Journal of Orthopsychiatry, 63,* 562–571.

Larson, R. (1994). Youth organizations, hobbies, and sports as developmental contexts. In R. Silbereisen & E. Todt (Eds.), *Adolescence in context: The interplay of family, school, peers, and work in adjustment* (pp. 46–65). New York: Springer-Verlag.

Larson, R., Kubey, R., & Colletti, J. (1989). Changing channels: Early adolescent media choices and shifting investments in family and friends. *Journal of Youth and Adolescence, 18,* 583–599.

Larson, R., & Richards, M. H. (1994). *Divergent realities: The emotional lives of mothers, fathers, and adolescents.* New York: Basic Books.

Lassen, K., & Oei, T. P. (1998). Effects of maternal cigarette smoking during pregnancy on long-term physical and cognitive parameters of child development. *Addictive Behavior, 23,* 635–653.

Last, C. G., Hansen, C., & Franco, N. (1998). Cognitive-behavioral treatment of school phobia. *Journal of the American Academy of Child and Adolescent Psychiatry, 37,* 404–411.

Laursen, B., & Collins, W. A. (1994). Interpersonal conflict during adolescence. *Psychological Bulletin, 115,* 197–209.

Laursen, B., Coy, K. C., & Collins, W. A. (1998). Reconsidering changes in parent-child conflict across adolescence. *Child Development, 69,* 817–832.

Laursen, B., Hartup, W. W., & Koplas, A. L. (1996). Towards understanding peer conflict. *Merrill-Palmer Quarterly, 42,* 76–102.

Laursen, B., & Williams, V. A. (1997). Perceptions of interdependence and closeness in family and peer relationships among adolescents with and without romantic partners. In S. Shulman & W. A. Collins (Eds.), *Romantic relationships in adolescence* (pp. 3–20). San Francisco: Jossey-Bass.

Lawton, C. (1994). Gender differences in way-finding strategies: Relationship to spatial ability and spatial anxiety. *Sex Roles, 30,* 765–779.

Leach, P. (1997). *Your baby and child.* New York: Knopf.

Leaper, C., & Anderson, K. J. (1997). Gender development and heterosexual romantic relationships during adolescence. In S. Shulman & W. A. Collins (Eds.), *Romantic relationships in adolescence* (pp. 85–104). San Francisco: Jossey-Bass.

Lee, C. M., & Gotlib, I. H. (1995). Mental illness and the family. In L. L'Abate (Ed.), *Handbook of developmental family psychology and psychopathology* (pp. 243–264). New York: Wiley.

Lee, L. C. (1992). Day care in the People's Republic of China. In M. E. Lamb, K. J. Sternberg, C. Hwang, & A. G. Broberg (Eds.), *Child care in context* (pp. 355–392). Hillsdale, NJ: Erlbaum.

Leger, D. W., Thompson, R. A., Merritt, J. A., & Benz, J. J. (1996). Adult perception of emotion intensity in human infant cries: Effects of infant age and cry acoustics. *Child Development, 67,* 3238–3249.

Legerstee, M., Anderson, D., & Schaffer, A. (1998). Five- and eight-month-old infants recognize their faces and voices as familiar and social stimuli. *Child Development, 69,* 37–50.

Leinbach, M. D., & Fagot, B. I. (1993). Categorical habituation to male and female faces: Gender schematic processing in infancy. *Infant Behavior and Development, 16,* 317–332.

Leinbach, M. D., Hort, B. E., & Fagot, B. I. (1997). Bears are for boys: Metaphorical associations in young children's gender stereotypes. *Cognitive Development, 12,* 107–130.

Leiter, J., & Johnsen, M. C. (1997). Child maltreatment and school performance declines: An event-history analysis. *American Educational Research Journal, 34,* 563–589.

Lemons, J. A., Bauer, C. R., Oh, W., Korones, S. B., Papile, L., Stoll, B. J., Verter, J., Temprosa, M., Wright, L. L., Ehrenkranz, R. A., Fanaroff, A. A., Stark, A., Carlo, W., Tyson, J. E., Donovan, E. F., Shankaran, S., & Stevenson, D. K. (2001). Very low birth outcomes of the National Institute of Child Health and Development Neonatal Research Network, January 1995 through December 1996. *Pediatrics, 107,* 1–14.

Lengua, L. J., & West, S. G. (1998). Temperament as a predictor of symptomatology in children. *Child Development, 69,* 164–181.

Lengua, L. J., West, S. G., & Sandler, I. (1998). Temperament as a predictor of symptomatology in children. *Child Development, 69,* 164–181.

Lenneberg, E. (1967). *Biological foundations of language.* New York: Wiley.

Lepper, M. R., & Henderlong, J. (2000). Turning "play" into "work" and "work" into "play": 25 years of research on intrinsic versus extrinsic motivation. In C. Sansone & J. M. Harackiewicz (Eds.), *Intrinsic and extrinsic motivation: The search for optimal motivation and performance* (pp. 257–307). San Diego: Academic Press.

Lerner, R. M., Delaney, M., Hess, L. I., Jovanovic, J., & von Eye, A. (1990). Early adolescent physical attractiveness and academic competence. *Journal of Early Adolescence, 10*, 4–20.

Lerner, R. M., Fisher, C. B., & Weinberg, R. A. (2000). Toward a science for and of the people: Promoting civil society through the application of developmental science. *Child Development, 71*, 11–20.

Lerner, R. M., & Olson, C. K. (1994, February). "Don't talk back!" *Parents*, 97–98.

Leslie, A. M. (1987). Pretense and representation: The origins of "theory of mind." *Psychological Review, 94*, 412–426.

Lester, B. M. (1985). There's more to crying than meets the ear. In B. M. Lester & C. F. Z. Boukydis (Eds.), *Infant crying* (pp. 1–28). New York: Plenum.

Lester, B. M., ElSohly, M., Wright, L. L., Smeriglio, V. L., Verber, J., Bauer, C. R., Shankaran, S., Bada, H. S., Walls, H. S., Walls, H. C., Huestis, M. A., Finnegan, L. P., & Maza, P. L. (2001). The maternal lifestyle study: Drug use by meconium toxicology and maternal self report. *Pediatrics, 107*, 309–317.

Lester, B. M., Freier, K., & LaGasse, L. (1995). Prenatal cocaine exposure and child outcome: What do we really know? In M. Lewis and M. Bendersky (Eds.), *Mothers, babies, and cocaine: The role of toxins in development* (pp. 19–39). Hillsdale, NJ: Erlbaum.

Leve, L. D., & Fagot, B. I. (1997). Gender-role socialization and discipline processes in one- and two-parent families. *Sex Roles, 36*, 1–21.

Leventhal, E. A., Leventhal, H., Shacham, S., & Easterling, D. V. (1989). Active coping reduces reports of pain from childbirth. *Journal of Consulting and Clinical Psychology, 57*, 365–371.

Leventhal, J. M., Forsyth, B. W. C., Qi, K., Johnson, L., Schroeder, D., & Votto, N. (1997). Maltreatment of children born to women who used cocaine during pregnancy. *Pediatrics, 100*, 1–6.

Levin, B. B., & Barry, S. M. (1997). Children's views of technology: The role of age, gender, and school setting. *Journal of Computing in Childhood Education, 8*, 267–290.

Levine, M. P., Smolak, L., Moodey, A. F., Shuman, M. D., & Hessen, L. D. (1994). Normative developmental challenges and dieting and eating disturbances in middle school girls. *International Journal of Eating Disorders, 15*, 11–20.

LeVine, R. A., Dixon, S., LeVine, S., Richman, A., Leiderman, P. H., Keefer, C. H., & Brazelton, T. B. (1994). *Child care and culture: Lessons from Africa.* Cambridge, England: Cambridge University Press.

Levinger, B. (1986). *Schoolfeeding programs in developing countries: An analysis of actual and potential impact.* Washington, DC: USAID.

Levinson, R. A. (1995). Reproductive and contraceptive knowledge, contraceptive self-efficacy, and contraceptive behavior among teenage women. *Adolescence, 30*, 65–85.

Levy, G. D. (1999). Gender-typed and non-gender-typed category awareness in toddlers. *Sex Roles, 41*, 851–873.

Levy, G. D., & Katz, P. A. (1993, March). *Differences in preschoolers' race schemas.* Paper presented at the biennial meeting of the Society for Research in Child Development, New Orleans, LA.

Levy, J., & Heller, W. (1992). Gender differences in human neuropsychological function. In A. A. Gerall & H. Moltz (Ed.), *Sexual differentiation* (Vol. 11, pp. 245–274). New York: Plenum.

Lewis, H. B. (1987). The role of shame in depression in women. In R. Formanek & A. Gurian (Eds.), *Women and depression* (pp. 182–199). New York: Springer.

Lewis, M. (1993). Self-conscious emotions: Embarrassment, pride, shame, and guilt. In M. Lewis & J. M. Haviland (Eds.), *Handbook of emotions* (pp. 563–573). New York: Guilford.

Lewis, M., Alessandri, S. M., & Sullivan, M. W. (1992). Differences in shame and pride as a function of children's gender and task difficulty. *Child Development, 63*, 630–638.

Lewit, E. M., & Baker, L. S. (1995). School readiness. *Future of Children, 5*, 128–139.

Liberman, A. M. (1996). *Speech: A special code.* Cambridge, MA: MIT Press.

Lickona, T., Schaps, E., & Lewis, C. (1997). *Eleven principles of effective character education.* Washington, DC: The Character Education Partnership.

Lieberman, P. (1984). *The biology and evolution of language.* Cambridge, MA: Harvard University Press.

Liebert, R. M., & Sprafkin, J. (1988). *The early window: Effects of television on children and youth.* New York: Pergamon Press.

Life Sciences Research Office. (1995). *Third report on nutrition monitoring in the United States.* Washington, DC: U.S. Government Printing Office.

Lifshitz, F., Finch, N. M., & Lifshitz, J. Z. (1991). *Children's nutrition.* Boston: Jones and Bartlett.

Lillard, A. (1998). Ethnopsychologies: Cultural variations in theories of mind. *Psychological Bulletin, 123*, 3–32.

Lillo-Martin, D. (1999). Modality effects and modularity in language acquisition: The acquisition of American Sign Language. In W. Ritche & T. Bhatia (Eds.), *Handbook of child language acquisition.* (pp. 531–567). San Diego: Academic Press.

Lind, G. (1997). *The optimal age of moral education.* Constance, Germany: Unversity of Constance.

Lindberg, L. D., Sonenstein, F. L., Ku, L., & Martinez, G. (1997). Age differences between minors who give birth and their adult partners. *Family Planning Perspectives, 29*, 61–66.

Lindley, A. A., Becker, S., Gray, R. H., & Herman, A. A. (2000). Effect of continuing or stopping smoking during pregnancy on infant birth weight, crown-heel length, head circumference, ponderal index, and brain : body weight ratio. *American Journal of Epidemiology, 152*, 219–225.

Lingenfelter, S. G. (1993). Courtship and marriage on Yap. In R. A. Marksbury (Ed.), *The business of marriage* (pp. 149–174). Pittsburgh: University of Pittsburgh Press.

Linn, M. C., de Benedictis, T., & Delucchi, K. (1982). Adolescent reasoning about advertisements: Preliminary investigations. *Child Development, 53*, 1599–1613.

Linn, M. C., & Petersen, A. C. (1986). A meta-analysis of gender differences in spatial ability: Implications for mathematics and science achievement. In J. S. Hyde & M. C. Linn, (Eds.), *The psychology of gender: Advances through meta-analysis* (pp. 67–101). Baltimore: The Johns Hopkins University Press.

Lipsitt, L. P., Engen, T., & Kaye, H. (1963). Developmental changes in the olfactory threshold of the neonate. *Child Development, 34*, 371–376.

Little, S., & Garber, J. (1995). Aggression, depression, and stressful life events predicting peer rejection in children. *Development and Psychopathology, 7*, 845–856.

Liu, X., Kaplan, H. B., & Risser, W. (1992). Decomposing the reciprocal relationships between academic achievement and general self-esteem. *Youth and Society, 24*, 123–148.

Livesley, W. J., & Bromley, D. B. (1973). *Person perception in childhood and adolescence.* London: John Wiley.

Locke, J. (1964). *Some thoughts concerning education.* Woodbury, NH: Barron's Educational Series. (Original work published 1690)

Lockwood, P., & Kunda, Z. (1997). Superstars and me: Predicting the impact of role models on the self. *Journal of Personality and Social Psychology, 73*, 91–103.

Loeber, R., Farrington, D. P., Stouthamer-Loeber, M., & Van-Kammen, W. B. (1998). *Antisocial behavior and mental health problems.* Mahwah, NJ: Erlbaum.

Loeber, R., & Hay, D. (1997). Key issues in the development of aggression and violence from childhood to early adulthood. *Annual Review of Psychology, 48*, 371–410.

Logsdon, M. C., McBride, A. B., & Birkimer, J. C. (1994). Social support and postpartum depression. *Research in Nursing & Health, 17*, 449–457.

Lorys, V. A. R., Hynd, G. W., Lyytinen, H., & Hern, K. (1993). Etiology of attention deficit hyperactivity disorder. In J. L. Matson (Ed.), *Handbook of hyperactivity in children* (pp. 47–65). Boston: Allyn & Bacon.

Loucks, A. B. (1988). Osteoporosis prevention begins in childhood. In E. W. Brown & C. F. Branta (Eds.), *Competitive sports for children and youth* (pp. 213–223). Champaign, IL: Human Kinetics Books.

Lounsbury, J. H. (1996). Characteristics of middle level schools. *ERIC Digest* (No. ED 401 050).

Lovelace, V. O., & Huston, A. C. (1983). Can television teach prosocial behavior? *Prevention in Human Services, 2*, 93–106.

Lozoff, B., Jimenez, E., Hagen, J., Mollen, E., & Wolf, A. W. (2000). Poorer behavioral and developmental outcomes more than 10 years after treatment for iron deficiency in infancy. *Pediatrics, 105,* 51.

Lozoff, B., Klein, N. K., Nelson, E. C., McClish, D. K., Manuel, M., & Chacon, M. E. (1998). Behavior of infants with iron-deficiency anemia. *Child Development, 69,* 24–36.

Lubeck, S., DeVries, M., Nicholson, J., & Post, J. (1997). Head Start in transition. *Early Education and Development, 8,* 219–244.

Lucas, A., Morely, R., Cole, T. J., Lister, G., & Leeson-Payne, C. (1992). Breast milk and subsequent intelligence quotient in children born before preterm. *Lancet, 339,* 261–264.

Lutzker, J. R. (1998). *Handbook of child abuse research and treatment.* New York: Plenum.

Lutzker, J. R. (2000). Child abuse. In V. B. Van Hasselt & M. Hersen (Eds.), *Aggression and violence* (pp. 54–66). Needham Heights, MA: Allyn & Bacon.

Lye, D. N. (1999). *Scholarly research on post-divorce parenting and child well-being.* Seattle, WA: Washington State Domestic Relations Commission.

Lynch, M. D. (1981). Self-concept development in childhood. In M. D. Lynch, A. A. Norem-Hebeisen, & K. Gergen (Eds.), *Self-concept: Advances in theory and research* (pp. 110–143). Cambridge, MA: Ballinger.

Lysne, M., & Levy, G. D. (1997). Differences in ethnic identity in Native American adolescents as a function of school context. *Journal of Adolescent Research, 12,* 372–388.

Lytton, H., & Romney, D. M. (1991). Parents' differential socialization of boys and girls: A meta-analysis. *Psychological Bulletin, 109,* 267–296.

Lyytinen, P., Poikkeus, A. M., & Laakso, M. L. (1997). Language and symbolic play in toddlers. *International Journal of Behavioral Development, 21,* 289–302.

Maas, J. (1995, November). *Asleep in the fast lane.* Paper presented at the Master's Forum, Minneapolis, MN.

Maccoby, E. E. (1980). *Social development.* San Diego, CA: Harcourt Brace Jovanovich.

Maccoby, E. E. (1984). Middle childhood in the context of the family. In W. A. Collins (Ed.), *Development during middle childhood* (pp. 184–239). Washington, DC: National Academy Press.

Maccoby, E. E. (1990). Gender and relationships. *American Psychologist, 45,* 513–520.

Maccoby, E. E. (1998). *The two sexes: Growing up apart, coming together.* Cambridge, MA: Belknap Press.

Maccoby, E. E., Depner, C. E., & Mnookin, R. H. (1990). Coparenting in the second year after divorce. *Journal of Marriage and the Family, 52,* 141–155.

Maccoby, E. E., & Jacklin, C. N. (1974). *The psychology of sex differences.* Stanford, CA: Stanford University Press.

Maccoby, E. E., & Jacklin, C. N. (1980). Sex differences in aggression: A rejoinder and reprise. *Child Development, 51,* 964–980.

Maccoby, E. E., & Martin, J. A. (1983). Socialization in the context of the family. In E. M. Hetherington (Ed.), *Handbook of child psychology: Vol. 4. Socialization, personality, and social development* (pp. 1–101). New York: Wiley.

Maccoby, E. E., & Mnookin, R. H. (1992). *Dividing the child: Social and legal dilemmas of custody.* Cambridge, MA: Harvard University Press.

MacFarlane, A. (1975). Olfaction in the development of social preferences in the human neonate. *Ciba Foundation Symposium, 33,* 103–117.

Macfarlane, J. W., Allen, L., & Honzik, M. P. (1954). *A developmental study of the behavior problems of normal children between twenty-one months and fourteen years.* Berkeley: University of California Press.

MacIver, D. J., & Epstein, J. L. (1991). *How equal are opportunities for learning in disadvantaged and advantaged middle grade schools?* Baltimore: Johns Hopkins University.

Mackey, M. C. (1990). Women's preparation for the childbirth experience. *Maternal and Child Nursing Journal, 19,* 143–173.

Mackey, W. C. (2001). Support for the existence of an independent man-to-child affiliative bond: Fatherhood as a biocultural invention. *Psychology of Men and Masculinity, 2,* 51–66.

MacKinnon, C. E. (1989). Sibling interactions in married and divorced families: Influence of ordinal position, socioeconomic status, and play context. In C. A. Everett (Ed.), *Children of divorce* (pp. 221–234). New York: Haworth Press.

Macksoud, M. S., & Aber, J. L. (1996). The war experiences and psychosocial development of children in Lebanon. *Child Development, 67,* 70–88.

MacKune-Karrer, B. (1992). Unifying diverse parameters: The multicultural framework. In D. Breunlin, R. C. Schwartz, & B. MacKune-Karrer (Eds.), *Metaframeworks* (pp. 193–236). San Francisco: Jossey-Bass.

MacLean, P. D. (1985). Brain evolution relating to family, play, and the separation call. *Archives of General Psychiatry, 42,* 405–417.

MacWhinney, B. (1989). Competition and lexical categorization. In R. Corrigan, F. Eckman, & M. Noonam (Eds.), *Linguistic categorization* (pp. 195–241). Amsterdam: John Benjamin.

Madon, S., Jussim, L., & Eccles, J. (1997). In search of the powerful self-fulfilling prophecy. *Journal of Personality and Social Psychology, 72,* 791–809.

Magai, C., Hunziker, J., Mesias, W., & Culver, L. C. (2000). Adult attachment styles and emotional biases. *International Journal of Behavioral Development, 24,* 301–309.

Magnusson, D. (1988). *Individual development from an interactional perspective: A longitudinal study.* Hillsdale, NJ: Erlbaum.

Magnusson, D. (1995). Individual development: A holistic, integrated model. In P. Moen, G. H. Elder, & K. Luscher (Eds.), *Examining lives in context* (pp. 19–60). Washington, DC: American Psychological Association.

Magolda, M. B. B. (1999). Constructing adult identities. *Journal of College Student Development, 40,* 629–644.

Maier, S. E., Chen, W. A., & West, J. R. (1996). The effects of timing and duration of alcohol exposure on development of the fetal brain. In E. Abel (Ed.), *Fetal alcohol syndrome* (pp. 27–50). Boca Raton, FL: CRC Press.

Main, M., & Solomon, J. (1990). Procedures for identifying infants as disorganized/disoriented during the Ainsworth Strange Situation. In M. Greenberg, D. Cicchetti, & M. Cummings (Eds.), *Attachment in the preschool years* (pp. 121–160). Chicago: University of Chicago Press.

Malatesta, C. Z. (1990). The role of emotions in the development and organization of personality. In R. A. Thompson (Ed.), *Socioemotional development* (Vol. 36, pp. 1–56). Lincoln: University of Nebraska Press.

Malina, R. M. (1986). Growth of muscle tissue and muscle mass. In F. Faulkner & J. M. Tanner (Eds.), *Human growth: A comprehensive treatise* (Vol. 2, pp. 77–99). New York: Plenum.

Malina, R. M., & Bouchard, C. (1991). *Growth, maturation, and physical activity.* Champaign, IL: Human Kinetics.

Maloney, M. J., McGuire, J., Daniels, S. R., & Specker, B. (1989). Dieting behavior and eating attitudes in children. *Pediatrics, 84,* 482–489.

Malson, L. (1972). *Wolf children and the problem of human nature.* New York: Monthly Review Press.

Mander, R. (2000). The meanings of labour pain or the layers of an onion? A woman-oriented view. *Journal of Reproductive and Infant Psychology, 18,* 133–141.

Mandler, J. M. (1990). A new perspective on cognitive development in infancy. *American Scientist, 78,* 236–243.

Mandler, J. M. (1992). The foundations of conceptual thought in infancy. *Cognitive Development, 7,* 273–285.

Mandler, J. M. (1993). On concepts. *Cognitive Development, 8,* 141–148.

Mandler, J. M., & Bauer, P. (1988). The cradle of categorization: Is the basic level basic? *Cognitive Development, 3,* 247–264.

Mandler, J. M., Bauer, P. J., & McDonough, L. (1991). Separating the sheep from the goats: Differentiating global categories. *Cognitive Psychology, 23,* 263–298.

Mange, E. J., & Mange, A. P. (1994). *Basic human genetics.* Sunderland, MA: Sinauer.

Mangelsdorf, S. C., Plunkett, J. W., Dedrick, C. F., Berlin, M., Meisels, S. J., McHale, J. L., & Dichtellmiller, M. (1996). Attachment security in very low birth weight infants. *Developmental Psychology, 32,* 914–920.

Manlove, J. (1998). The influence of high school dropout and school disengagement on the risk of school-age pregnancy. *Journal of Research on Adolescence, 8,* 187–220.

Maratsos, M. (1998). The acquisition of grammar. In W. Damon (Ed.), *Handbook of child psychology* (Vol. 2, pp. 421–467). New York: Wiley.

March of Dimes. (2000). *Birth defects.* White Plains, NY: March of Dimes.

March of Dimes. (2001). *Prenatal care.* White Plains, NY: March of Dimes.

Marcia, J. E. (1993). The relational roots of identity. In J. Kroger (Ed.), *Discussions on ego identity* (pp. 101–120). Hillsdale, NJ: Erlbaum.

Marcia, J. E. (1999). Representational thought in ego identity, psychotherapy, and psychosocial developmental theory. In I. Sigel (Ed.), *Development of mental representation: Theories and applications* (pp. 391–414). Mahwah, NJ: Erlbaum.

Marcus, G. F., Pinker, S., Ullman, M., Hollander, M., Rosen, T. J., & Xu, F. (1992). Overregularization in language acquisition. *Monographs of the Society for Research in Child Development, 57* (Whole No. 228). Chicago: University of Chicago Press.

Margolin, G., & Gordis, E. B. (2000). The effects of family and community violence on children. *Annual Review of Psychology, 51,* 445–479.

Marin, G. (1994). The experience of being a Hispanic in the United States. In W. J. Lonner & R. S. Malpas (Eds.), *Psychology and culture* (pp. 23–28). Boston: Allyn & Bacon.

Markel, K. S., & Frone, M. R. (1998). Job characteristics, work-school conflict, and school outcomes among adolescents. *Journal of Applied Psychology, 83,* 277–287.

Market Data Retrieval. (2001). *Technology in education 2001.* Shelton, CT: Market Data Retrieval.

Marks, S. B. (1997). Reducing prejudice against children with disabilities in inclusive settings. *International Journal of Disability, Development, and Education, 44,* 117–131.

Markson, L., & Bloom, P. (1997). Evidence against a dedicated system for word learning in children. *Nature, 385,* 813–815.

Markus, H. R., & Kitayama, S. (1991). Culture and the self: Implications for cognition, emotion, and motivation. *Psychological Review, 98,* 224–253.

Marques-Bruna, P., & Grimshaw, P. N. (1997). 3-dimensional kinematics of overarm throwing action of children age 15 to 30 months. *Perceptual and Motor Skills, 84,* 1267–1283.

Marsh, J. S., & Daigneault, J. P. (1999). The young athlete. *Current Opinions in Pediatrics, 11,* 84–88.

Marshall, S. P., & Smith, J. D. (1987). Sex differences in learning mathematics: A longitudinal study with item and error analyses. *Journal of Educational Psychology, 79,* 372–383.

Marshall, W. A., & Tanner, J. M. (1986). Puberty. In F. Faulkner & J. M. Tanner (Eds.), *Human growth: A comprehensive treatise* (pp. 171–210). New York: Plenum.

Marsiglio, W., & Cohan, M. (1997). Young fathers and child development. In M. E. Lamb (Ed.), *The role of the father in child development* (pp. 227–244). New York: Wiley.

Marsiglio, W., Hutchinson, S., & Cohan, M. (2000). Envisioning fatherhood: A social psychological perspective on young men without kids. *Family Relations, 49,* 133–142.

Martin, C. A., Hill, K. K., & Welsh, R. (1998). Adolescent pregnancy, a stressful life event. In T. W. Miller (Ed.), *Children of trauma* (pp. 141–160). Madison, CT: International Universities Press.

Martin, C. L. (1989). Children's use of gender-related information in making social judgments. *Developmental Psychology, 25,* 80–88.

Martin, C. L. (1991). The role of cognition in understanding gender effects. In H. Reese (Ed.), *Advances in child development and behavior* (Vol. 23, pp. 113–149). San Diego, CA: Academic Press.

Martin, C. L. (1994). Cognitive influences on the development and maintenance of gender segregation. In C. Leaper (Ed.), *Childhood gender segregation* (pp. 35–52). San Francisco: Jossey-Bass.

Martin, C. L., Eisenbud, L., & Rose, H. (1995). Children's gender-based reasoning about toys. *Child Development, 66,* 1453–1471.

Martin, C. L., & Fabes, R. A. (2001). The stability and consequences of young children's same-sex peer interactions. *Developmental Psychology, 37,* 431–446.

Martin, C. L., & Halverson, C. F. (1981). A schematic processing model of sex typing and stereotyping in children. *Child Development, 52,* 1119–1134.

Martin, C. L., & Halverson, C. F. (1983). Gender constancy: A methodological and theoretical analysis. *Sex Roles, 9,* 775–790.

Martin, C. L., Woods, C. H., & Little, J. K. (1990). The development of gender stereotype components. *Child Development, 61,* 1891–1904.

Martin, K. (1996). *Puberty, sexuality, and the self: Boys and girls at adolescence.* New York: Routledge.

Martin, L. M. (2000). The compatibility of Vygotsky's theoretical framework with the developmental-interaction approach. In N. Nager & E. Shapiro (Eds.), *Revisiting a progressive pedagogy: The developmental-interaction approach. Early childhood education.* (pp. 73–93). Albany: State University of New York Press.

Martindale, C. (2001). Oscillations and analogies: Thomas Young, MD, FRS, genius. *American Psychologist, 56,* 342–345.

Martinez, R. O., & Dukes, R. L. (1997). The effects of ethnic identity, ethnicity, and gender on adolescent well-being. *Journal of Youth and Adolescence, 26,* 503–516.

Martini, M. (1994). Peer interaction in Polynesia: A view from the Marquesas. In J. L. Roopnarine, J. E. Johnson, & F. H. Hooper (Eds.), *Children's play in diverse cultures* (pp. 73–103). New York: State University of New York Press.

Martins, C., & Gaffan, E. A. (2000). Effects of early maternal depression on patterns of infant-mother attachment: A meta-analytic investigation. *Journal of Child Psychology and Psychiatry and Allied Disciplines, 41,* 737–746.

Martorano, S. C. (1977). A developmental analysis of performance on Piaget's formal operations task. *Developmental Psychology, 13,* 666–672.

Masataka, N. (1996). Perception of motherese in a signed language by 6-month-old deaf infants. *Developmental Psychology, 32,* 874–879.

Mason, M. A. (1998). The modern American stepfamily: Problems and possibilities. In M. A. Mason (Ed.), *All our families: New policies for a new century* (pp. 95–116). New York: Oxford University Press.

Massey, C. M., & Gelman, R. (1988). Preschoolers' ability to decide whether a photographed unfamiliar object can move itself. *Developmental Psychology, 24,* 307–317.

Masten, A. S., & Coatsworth, J. D. (1998). The development of competence in favorable and unfavorable environments. *American Psychologist, 53,* 205–220.

Masten, A. S., & Curtis, W. J. (2000). Integrating competence and psychopathology: Pathways toward a comprehensive science of adaptation in development. *Development and Psychopathology, 12,* 529–550.

Masten, A. S., Morrison, P., Pellegrini, D., & Tellegen, A. (1990). Competence under stress. In J. E. Role & A. S. Masten (Eds.), *Risk and protective factors in the development of psychopathology* (pp. 236–256). New York: Cambridge University Press.

Mastrogiannis, D. S., Decavalas, G. O., Verma, U., & Tejani, N. (1990). Perinatal outcome after recent cocaine usage. *Obstetrics and Gynecology, 76,* 8–11.

Maughan, B., & Rutter, M. (1998). Continuities and discontinuities in social behavior from childhood to adult life. *Advances in Child Clinical Psychology, 20,* 1–47.

Maurer, D., & Barrerra, M. E. (1981). Infants' perception of natural and distorted arrangements of a schematic face. *Child Development, 52,* 196–202.

Maurer, D., & Lewis, T. L. (2001). Visual acuity and spatial contrast sensitivity: Normal development and underlying mechanisms. In C. A. Nelson & M. Luciana (Eds.), *Handbook of developmental cognitive neuroscience* (pp. 237–252). Cambridge, MA: MIT Press.

Maxfield, M., & Widom, C. (1996). The cycle of violence: Revisited 6 years later. *Archives of Pediatric Adolescent Medicine, 150,* 390–395.

May, D. C., & Kundert, D. K. (1997). School readiness practices and children at-risk. *Psychology in the Schools, 34,* 73–84.

Mayes, L. C., Granger, R. H., Bornstein, M. H., & Zuckerman, B. (1992). The problem of prenatal cocaine exposure: A rush to judgment. *Journal of the American Medical Association, 267,* 406–408.

Mazur, E. (1993). Developmental differences in children's understanding of marriage, divorce, and remarriage. *Journal of Applied Developmental Psychology, 14,* 191–212.

McAdoo, H. P. (1993). *Family ethnicity.* Newbury Park, CA: Sage.

McBride-Chang, C. (1995). What is phonological awareness? *Journal of Educational Psychology, 87,* 179–192.

McCall, R. B., & Groark, C. J. (2000). The future of applied child development research and public policy. *Child Development, 71,* 197–204.

McCauley, E., Kay, T., Ito, J., & Treder, R. (1987). The Turner syndrome: Cognitive deficits, affective discrimination, and behavior problems. *Child Development, 58,* 464–473.

McClelland, D. C. (1993). Intelligence is not the best predictor of job performance. *Current Directions in Psychological Science, 2,* 5–6.

McCloskey, L. A., Figueredo, A. J., & Koss, M. P. (1995). The effects of systemic family violence on children's mental health. *Child Development, 66,* 1239–1261.

McClurg, P. A., & Chaille, C. (1987). Computer games: Environments for developing spatial cognition? *Journal of Educational Computing Research, 3,* 95–111.

McCormick, M. C., Gortmaker, S. L., & Sobol, A. M. (1990). Very low birth weight children: Behavior problems and school difficulty in a national sample. *Journal of Pediatrics, 117,* 687–693.

McDermott, D. (2001). Parenting and ethnicity. In M. J. Fine & S. W. Lee (Eds.), *Handbook of diversity in parent education: The changing faces of parenting and parent education* (pp. 73–96). San Diego, CA: Academic Press.

McDonnell, L. M., & Hill, P. T. (1993). *Newcomers in American schools: Meeting the educational needs of immigrant youth.* Santa Monica, CA: Rand.

McDougall, P., Hymel, S., Vallancourt, T., & Mercer, L. (2001). The consequences of childhood peer rejection. In M. R. Leary (Ed.), *Interpersonal rejection* (pp. 213–247). New York: Oxford University Press.

McGlaughlin, A., & Grayson, A. (2001). Crying in the first year of infancy: Patterns and prevalence. *Journal of Reproductive and Infant Psychology, 19,* 47–59.

McGrath, M. P., Wilson, S. R., & Franssetto, S. (1995). Why some forms of induction are better than others at encouraging prosocial behavior. *Merrill-Palmer Quarterly, 41,* 347–360.

McGrory, A. (1990). Menarche: Responses of early adolescent females. *Adolescence, 25,* 265–270.

McGuigan, W. M., Vuchinich, S., & Pratt, C. C. (2000). Domestic violence, parents' view of their infant, and risk for child abuse. *Journal of Family Psychology, 14,* 613–624.

McHale, S. M., Crouter, A. C., McGuire, S., & Updegraff, K. A. (1995). Congruence between mothers' and fathers' differential treatment of siblings: Links with family relations and children's well-being. *Child Development, 66,* 116–128.

McHale, S. M., Updegraff, K. A., Jackson-Newsom, J., Tucker, C. J., & Crouter, A. C. (2000). When does parents' differential treatment have negative implications for siblings? *Social Development, 9,* 149–172.

McLoyd, V. C. (1998a). Children in poverty. In W. Damon (Ed.), *Handbook of child psychology* (Vol. 4, pp. 135–208). New York: Wiley.

McLoyd, V. C. (1998b). Socioeconomic disadvantage and child development. *American Psychologist, 53,* 185–204.

McLoyd, V. C., Cauce, A. M., Takeuchi, D., & Wilson, L. (2000). Marital processes and parental socialization in families of color: A decade review of research. *Journal of Marriage and the Family, 62,* 1070–1093.

McManus, I. C., & Bryden, M. P. (1992). The genetics of handedness, cerebral dominance, and lateralization. In I. Rapin & S. J. Segalowitz (Eds.), *Handbook of neuropsychology* (Vol. 6., pp. 115–144). Amsterdam: Elsevier.

McPherson, S. L., & Thomas, J. R. (1989). Relation of knowledge and performance in boys' tennis: Age and expertise. *Journal of Experimental Child Psychology, 48,* 190–211.

Meadow-Orlans, K. P., & Spencer, P. E. (1999). Maternal sensitivity and the visual attentiveness of children who are deaf. *Early Development and Parenting, 5,* 213–223.

Meaney, M. J. (1988). The sexual differentiation of social play. *Trends in Neuroscience, 7,* 54–58.

Measelle, J. R., Ablow, J. C., Cowan, P. A., & Cowan, C. P. (1998). Assessing young children's views of their academic, social, and emotional lives. *Child Development, 69,* 1556–1576.

Mediascope. (1996, June). *Interactive video games.* Los Angeles: EBS International.

Meeus, W., Iedema, J., Helsen, M., & Vollebergh, W. (1999). Patterns of adolescent identity development: Review of literature and longitudinal analysis. *Developmental Review, 19,* 419–461.

Mellou, E. (1996). Can creativity be nurtured in young children? *Early Child Development and Care, 119,* 119–130.

Melnick, M. J., Vanfossen, B. E., & Sabo, D. F. (1988). Developmental effects of athletic participation among high school girls. *Sociology of Sport Journal, 5,* 22–36.

Meltzer, D. (1981). *Birth: An anthology of ancient texts, songs, prayers, and stories.* San Francisco: North Point Press.

Meltzoff, A. N. (1995). What infant memory tells us about infantile amnesia: Long-term recall and deferred imitation. *Journal of Experimental Child Psychology, 59,* 497–515.

Meltzoff, A. N., & Moore, M. K. (1994). Imitation, memory, and the representation of persons. *Infant Behavior and Development, 17,* 83–99.

Melzak, S. (1992). The secret life of children who have experienced physical aggression and violence. In V. P. Varma (Ed.), *The secret life of vulnerable children* (pp. 101–129). New York: Routledge.

Mendelsohn, A. L., Dreyer, B. P., Fierman, A. H., Rosen, C. M., Legano, L. A., Kruger, H. A., Lim, S. W., & Courtlandt, C. D. (1998). Low-level lead exposure and behavior in early childhood. *Pediatrics, 101,* 1–6.

Mennella, J. A., Jagnow, C. P., & Beauchamp, G. K. (2001). Prenatal and postnatal flavor learning by human infants. *Pediatrics, 107,* 1–12.

Menyuk, P. (1988). *Language development: Knowledge and use.* New York: Harper Collins.

Menyuk, P., Liebergott, J. W., & Schultz, M. C. (1995). *Early language development in full-term and premature infants.* Hillsdale, NJ: Erlbaum.

Mercer, R. T., Ferketich, S., May, K., DeJoseph, J., & Sollid, D. (1988). Further exploration of maternal and paternal fetal attachment. *Research in Nursing and Health, 11,* 83–95.

Merikangas, K. R., Swendsen, J. D., Preisig, M. A., & Chazan, R. Z. (1998). Psychopathology and temperament in parents and offspring: Results of a family study. *Journal of Affective Disorders, 51,* 63–74.

Merriman, W. E., & Bowman, L. L. (1989). The mutual exclusivity bias in children's word learning. *Monographs of the Society for Research in Child Development, 54* (Whole No. 130).

Mest, G. M. (1988). With a little help from their friends: Use of social support by persons with retardation. *Journal of Social Issues, 44,* 117–125.

Metha, A., Chen, E., Mulvenon, S., & Dode, I. (1998). A theoretical model of adolescent suicide risk. *Archives of Suicide Research, 4,* 115–133.

Midgley, C. M. (1993). Motivation and middle level schools. In M. L. Maehr & P. R. Pintrich (Eds.), *Advances in motivation and achievement* (Vol. 8, pp. 217–274). Greenwich, CT: JAI Press.

Midgley, C. M., Feldlaufer, H., & Eccles, J. S. (1988). The transition to junior high school. *Journal of Youth and Adolescence, 17,* 543–562.

Milgram, N. A. (1998). Children under stress. In T. H. Ollendick & M. Hersen (Eds.), *Handbook of child psychopathology* (pp. 505–553). New York: Plenum.

Miller, A. L., Volling, B. L., & McElwain, N. L. (2000). Sibling jealousy in a triadic context with mothers and fathers. *Social Development, 9,* 433–457.

Miller, B. C. (1998). *Family matters: A research synthesis of family influences on adolescent pregnancy.* Washington, DC: The National Campaign to Prevent Teen Pregnancy.

Miller, B. C., Benson, B., & Galbraith, K. A. (2001). Family relationships and adolescent pregnancy risk: A research synthesis. *Developmental Review, 21,* 1–38.

Miller, B. C., Norton, M. C., Curtis, T., Hill, E. J., Schvaneveldt, P., & Young, M. H. (1997). The timing of sexual intercourse among adolescents: Family, peer, and other antecedents. *Youth and Society, 29,* 54–83.

Miller, C. L., Eccles, J. S., Flanagan, C., Midgley, C. M., Feldlaufer, H., & Goldsmith, R. (1990). Parents' and teachers' beliefs about adolescence: Effects of sex and experience. *Journal of Youth and Adolescence, 19,* 363–394.

Miller, H. M. (2000). Cross-cultural validity of a model of self-worth: Application to Finnish children. *Social Behavior and Personality, 28,* 105–118.

Miller, J. G. (1986). Early cross-cultural commonalities in social explanation. *Developmental Psychology, 22,* 514–520.

Miller, K. S., Forehand, R., & Kotchick, B. A. (1999). Adolescent sexual behavior in two ethnic minority samples. *Journal of Marriage and the Family, 61,* 85–98.

Miller, N. B., Cowan, P. A., Cowan, C. P., Hetherington, E. M., & Clingempeel, W. G. (1993). Externalizing in preschoolers and early adolescents: A cross-study replication of a family model. *Developmental Psychology, 29,* 4–18.

Miller, P. A., Kozu, J., & Davis, A. C. (2001). Social influence, empathy, and prosocial behavior in cross-cultural perspective. In W. Wosinska & R. B. Cialdini (Eds.), *The practice of social influence in multiple cultures. Applied social research* (pp. 63–77). Mahwah, NJ: Erlbaum.

Miller, P. H. (1993). *Theories of developmental psychology.* New York: Freeman.

Miller, P. H., & Aloise, P. A. (1989). Young children's understanding of the psychological causes of behavior: A review. *Child Development, 60,* 257–285.

Millstein, S. G. (1990). Risk factors for AIDS among adolescents. In W. Gardner, S. G. Millstein, & B. L. Wilcox (Eds.), *Adolescents in the AIDS epidemic: New directions for child development* (pp. 3–15). San Francisco: Jossey-Bass.

Minton, C., Kagan, J., & Levine, J. A. (1971). Maternal control and obedience in the two-year-old. *Child Development, 42,* 1873–1894.

Mintz, J. (1995). Self in relation to other: Preschoolers' verbal social comparisons within narrative discourse. In L. L. Sperry & P. A. Smiley (Eds.), *Exploring young children's concepts of self and other through conversation* (pp. 61–74). San Francisco: Jossey-Bass.

Minuchin, P. P., & Shapiro, E. K. (1983). The school as a context for social development. In P. Mussen (Ed.), *Handbook of child psychology* (Vol. 4, pp. 197–274). New York: Wiley.

Mischel, W. (1966). A social-learning view of sex differences in behavior. In E. E. Maccoby (Ed.), *The development of sex differences* (pp. 57–81). Stanford, CA: Stanford University Press.

Mitchell, J. J. (1996). *Adolescent vulnerability: A sympathetic look at the frailties and limitations of youth.* Calgary: Detselig Enterprises Ltd.

Miyake, K., Chen, S., & Campos, J. J. (1985). Infant temperament, mother's mode of interaction, and attachment in Japan: An interim report. In I. Bretherton & E. Waters (Eds.), *Growing points of attachment theory and research* (pp. 276–297). Chicago: Society for Research in Child Development.

Mize, J., & Ladd, G. W. (1990). Toward the development of successful social skills training for preschool children. In S. R. Asher & J. D. Coie (Eds.), *Peer rejection in childhood* (pp. 338–364). Cambridge, England: Cambridge University Press.

Moerk, E. L. (1989). The LAD was a lady and the tasks were ill-defined. *Developmental Review, 9,* 21–57.

Moffitt, T. E. (1993). Adolescence-limited and life course persistent antisocial behavior: Developmental taxonomy. *Psychological Review, 100,* 674–701.

Molfese, V. J., & Molfese, D. L. (2000). *Temperament and personality development across the lifespan.* Mahwah, NJ: Erlbaum.

Monahan, S. C., Buchanan, C. N., Maccoby, E. E., & Dornbusch, S. M. (1993). Sibling differences in divorced families. *Child Development, 63,* 152–168.

Money, J., & Ehrhardt, A. A. (1972). *Man and woman. Boy and girl.* Baltimore: Johns Hopkins University Press.

Monitoring the Future. (1999). *Youth attitudes on family, work, and community service: implications for welfare reform.* Ann Arbor: University of Michigan.

Monitoring the Future. (2001). *Monitoring the Future national survey results on drug use, 1975–2000.* Bethesda, MD: National Institute on Drug Abuse.

Monk, C., Fifer, W. P., Myers, M. M., Sloan, R. P., Trien, L., & Hurtado, A. (2000). Maternal stress responses and anxiety during pregnancy: Effects on fetal heart rate. *Developmental Psychobiology, 36,* 67–77.

Montemayor, R., Adams, G. R., & Gullotta, T. P. (1990). *From childhood to adolescence: A transitional period?* Newbury Park, CA: Sage.

Montour, K. (1977). William James Sidis, the broken twig. *American Psychologist, 32,* 265–279.

Moon, C., Cooper, R. P., & Fifer, W. P. (1993). Two-day-olds prefer their native language. *Infant Behavior and Development, 16,* 495–500.

Moore, K. A., & Driscoll, A. (1997). *Partners, predators, peers, protectors: Males and teen pregnancy.* Washington, DC: Child Trends Inc.

Moore, K. L. (1998). *The developing human: Clinically oriented embryology,* 6th ed. Philadelphia: Saunders.

Moore, S. M., & Gullone, E. (1995). Fear of weight gain: Its correlates among school-aged adolescents. *Psychological Reports, 76,* 1305–1306.

Moore, S., & Rosenthal, D. (1993). *Sexuality in adolescence.* London: Routledge.

Moreau, G. F., Ferron, C., Jeannin, A., & Dubois, A. F. (1996). Adolescent sexuality: The gender gap. *AIDS Care, 8,* 641–653.

Morelli, G. A., & Verhoef, H. (1999). Who should help me raise my child? A cultural approach to understanding nonmaternal child care decisions. In L. Balter & C. S. Tamis-LeMonda (Eds.), *Child psychology: A handbook of contemporary issues* (pp. 491–509). Philadelphia: Psychology Press.

Morgan, W. P. (1994). Physical activity, fitness and depression. In C. Bouchard, R. J. Shephard, & T. Stephens (Eds.), *Physical activity, fitness and health* (pp. 851–867). Champaign, IL: Human Kinetics Publishers.

Morris, K. (1998). Short course of AZT halves HIV-1 perinatal transmission. *Lancet, 351,* 651.

Morris, R. J., & Kratochwill, T. R. (1998). Childhood fears and phobias. In R. J. Morris & T. R. Kratochwill (Eds.), *The practice of child therapy* (pp. 91–131). Boston: Allyn & Bacon.

Morris, T. W., & Levinson, E. M. (1995). Relationship between intelligence and occupational adjustment and functioning. *Journal of Counseling and Development, 73,* 503–514.

Morrison, F. J., Alberts, D. M., & Griffith, E. M. (1997). Nature-nurture in the classroom: Entrance age, school readiness, and learning in children. *Developmental Psychology, 33,* 254–262.

Morrison, G. S. (1997). *Teaching in America.* Needham Heights, MA: Allyn & Bacon.

Mortimer, J. T., & Finch, M. D. (1996). *Adolescents, work, and family.* Thousand Oaks, CA: Sage.

Moss, E., St. Laurent, D., & Parent, S. (1999). Disorganized attachment and developmental risk at school age. In J. Solomon & C. George (Eds.), *Attachment disorganization* (pp. 160–186). New York: Guilford.

Mruk, C. (1999). *Self-esteem research, theory, and practice.* New York: Springer Publishing.

Mueller, U., Overton, W. F., & Reene, K. (2001). Development of conditional reasoning: A longitudinal study. *Journal of Cognition and Development, 2,* 27–49.

Mufson, L., & Moreau, D. (1997). Depressive disorders. In R. T. Ammerman & M. Hersen (Eds.), *Handbook of prevention and treatment with children and adolescents* (pp. 403–430). New York: Wiley.

Muller, T., & Espenshade, T. J. (1985). *The fourth wave: California's newest immigrants.* Washington, DC: Urban Institute Press.

Munakata, Y. (1998). Infant perseveration and implications for object permanence theories: A PDP model of the AB task. *Developmental Science, 1,* 161–184.

Munakata, Y., McClelland, J. L., Johnson, M. H., & Siegler, R. S. (1997). Rethinking infant knowledge: Toward an adaptive process account of successes and failures in object permanence tasks. *Psychological Review, 104,* 686–713.

Munn, P., & Dunn, J. (1988). Temperament and the developing relationship between siblings. *International Journal of Behavioral Development, 12,* 433–451.

Muret-Wagstaff, S., & Moore, S. G. (1989). The Hmong in America: Infant behavior and rearing practices. In J. K. Nugent, B. M. Lester, & T. B. Brazelton (Eds.), *The cultural context of infancy* (Vol. 1, pp. 319–340). Norwood, NJ: Ablex.

Muris, P., & Merckelbach, H. (2001). The etiology of childhood specific phobia: A multifactorial model. In M. W. Vasey & M. R. Dadds (Eds.), *The developmental psychopathology of anxiety* (pp. 355–385). New York: Oxford University Press.

Murphy, B. C., & Eisenberg, N. (1996). Provoked by a peer: Children's anger-related responses and their relations to social functioning. *Merrill-Palmer Quarterly, 42*, 103–124.

Murphy, W. D., & Smith, T. A. (1996). Sex offenders against children. In J. Briere, L. Berliner, J. A. Bulkley, C. Jenny, & T. Reid (Eds.), *The APSAC handbook on child maltreatment* (pp. 175–191). Thousand Oaks, CA: Sage.

Murray, J. P. (1995). Children and television violence. *Kansas Journal of Law & Public Policy, 4*, 7–14.

Murray, L., & Trevarthen, C. (1986). The infant's role in mother-infant communication. *Journal of Child Language, 13*, 15–29.

Mussen, P. H., & Jones, M. C. (1957). Self-concepts, motivations, and interpersonal attitudes of late and early maturing boys. *Child Development, 28*, 243–256.

Muuss, R. E. (1998). Marcia's expansion of Erikson's theory of identity formation. In R. E. Muuss & H. D. Porton (Eds.), *Adolescent behavior and society* (pp. 260–270). New York: McGraw-Hill.

Myers, A., Sampson, A., Weitzman, M., Rogers, B., & Kayne, H. (1989). School breakfast program and school performance. *American Journal of Diseases of Childhood, 143*, 1234–1239.

Myers, B. J. (1984). Mother-infant bonding: The status of this critical-period hypothesis. *Developmental Review, 4*, 240–274.

Nadder, T. S., Silberg, J. L., Eaves, L. J., Maes, L. J., & Meyer, J. M. (1998). Genetic effects on ADHD symptomatology in 7- to 13-year-old twins. *Behavioral Genetics, 28*, 83–99.

Nagy, W. E., Anderson, R. C., & Herman, P. A. (1987). Learning word meanings from context during normal reading. *American Educational Research Journal, 24*, 237–270.

Naigles, L. R. (1990). Children use syntax to learn verb meanings. *Journal of Child Language, 17*, 357–374.

Nash, J. M. (1997, February 3). Fertile minds. *Time*, 49–62.

Nathanieisz, P. W. (1995). The role of basic science in preventing low birth weight. *The Future of Children, 5*, 57–70.

National Association for the Education of Young Children. (1995). *How to choose a good early childhood program.* Washington, DC: NAEYC.

National Association for the Education of Young Children. (1997). *Developmentally appropriate practice in early childhood programs.* Washington, DC: NAEYC.

National Association for the Education of Young Children. (1998). Learning to read and write. *Young Children, 53*, 30–46.

National Campaign to Prevent Teen Pregnancy. (2001). *Faithful nation: What American adults and teens think about faith, morals, religion, and teen pregnancy.* Washington, DC: National Campaign to Prevent Teen Pregnancy.

National Center for Education Statistics. (1995). *Student victimization at school.* Washington, DC: US Department of Education.

National Center for Education Statistics. (1996). *Youth indicators, 1996.* Washington, DC: US Department of Education.

National Center for Education Statistics. (1998). *Condition of education.* Washington, DC: US Department of Education.

National Center for Education Statistics. (1999). *Parent and family involvement in education.* Washington, DC: US Department of Education.

National Center for Education Statistics. (2001a). *Digest of education statistics, 2000.* Washington, DC: US Department of Education.

National Center for Education Statistics. (2001b). *Indicators of school crime and safety.* Washington, DC: US Department of Education.

National Center for Health Statistics. (1976). *Growth charts.* Washington, DC: National Center for Health Statistics.

National Center for Health Statistics. (1990). *International divorce rates.* Washington, DC: National Center for Health Statistics.

National Center for Health Statistics. (1994). *Health, United States, 1993.* Washington, DC: National Center for Health Statistics.

National Center for Health Statistics. (1995). Advance report of final divorce statistics. *Monthly Vital Statistics Report, 43*, 1–32.

National Center for Health Statistics. (1996). *Health, United States, 1995.* Hyattsville, MD: Public Health Service.

National Center for Health Statistics. (2001a). *Births 2000.* Washington, DC: National Center for Health Statistics.

National Center for Health Statistics. (2001b). *Entering kindergarten.* Washington, DC: National Center for Health Statistics.

National Center for Health Statistics. (2001c). *Healthy people, 2000.* Washington, DC: National Center for Health Statistics.

National Center for Injury Prevention and Control. (1996). *Ten leading causes of death, 1994.* Atlanta, GA: NCIPC.

National Center on Addiction and Substance Abuse. (1996). *National survey of American attitudes and substance abuse II.* New York: Columbia University Press.

National Child Abuse and Neglect Data System. (2001). *Child maltreatment 1999: Reports from the states to the National Child Abuse and Neglect Data System.* Washington, DC: US Government Printing Office.

National Clearinghouse on Child Abuse and Neglect. (1999). *Child abuse and neglect fact sheet.* Washington, DC: NCCAN.

National Diffusion Network. (1993). *Educational programs that work.* Longmont, CO: Sopris West.

National Down Syndrome Society. (2000). *About Down syndrome.* New York: National Down Syndrome Society.

National Federation of State High School Associations. (2001). *Athletics participation summary: 1999–2000.* Indianapolis: National Federation of State High School Associations.

National Highway Traffic Safety Administration. (1999). *Youth fatal crash and alcohol facts.* Washington, DC: National Highway Traffic Safety Administration.

National Institute of Mental Health. (1994). *Eating disorders.* Washington, DC: National Institute of Mental Health.

National Institute of Mental Health. (2000). *Depression in children and adolescents.* Bethesda, MD: NIMH.

National Institute on Drug Abuse. (1999). Cocaine, marijuana, and heroin abuse up, methamphetamine abuse down. *NIDA Notes, 15*, 1.

National Institute on Drug Abuse. (2000). *Monitoring the future.* Washington, DC: National Institute on Drug Abuse.

National Issues Forum. (1989). *The day care dilemma.* Dubuque, IA: Kendall/Hunt Publishing.

National Mental Health Association. (2001). *Helping children handle disaster-related anxiety.* Alexandria, VA: National Mental Health Association.

National Middle School Association. (1995). *Developmentally responsive middle level schools.* Columbus, OH: National Middle School Association.

National Research Council. (1993). *Understanding child abuse and neglect.* Washington, DC: National Academy Press.

National Research Council. (1998). *The new Americans: Economic, demographic, and fiscal effects of immigration.* Washington, DC: National Research Council.

National Research Council. (2000). *Eager to learn.* Washington, DC: National Academy Press.

National Research Council. (2001). *Getting to positive outcomes for children in child care.* Washington, DC: National Academy Press.

National Research Council and Institute of Medicine. (2000). *From neurons to neighborhoods: The science of early childhood development.* Washington, DC: National Academy Press.

National Science Foundation. (1996). *Women, minorities, and persons with disabilities in the sciences and engineering.* Washington, DC: National Science Foundation.

National Telecommunications and Information Administration. (1998). *Falling through the Net II.* Washington, DC: National Telecommunications and Information Administration

Navaez, D., Getz, I., Rest, J. R., & Thoma, S. J. (1999). Individual moral judgment and cultural ideologies. *Developmental Psychology, 35,* 478–488.

Neale, D. C., Smith, D., & Johnson, V. G. (1990). Implementing conceptual change teaching in primary science. *Elementary School Journal, 91,* 109–131.

Neher, L. S., & Short, J. L. (1998). Risk and protective factors for children's substance use and antisocial behavior following parental divorce. *American Journal of Orthopsychiatry, 68,* 154–161.

Nelson, C. A., & Bloom, F. E. (1997). Child development and neuroscience. *Child Development, 68,* 970–987.

Nelson, D. A., & Crick, N. R. (1999). Rose-colored glasses: Examining the social information processes of prosocial young adolescents. *Journal of Early Adolescence, 19,* 17–38.

Nelson, K. (1973). Structure and strategy in learning to talk. *Monographs of the Society for Research in Child Development, 38* (Whole No. 149).

Nelson, K. (1986). *Event knowledge: Structure and function in development.* Hillsdale, NJ: Erlbaum.

Nelson, K. (1993). The psychological and social origins of autobiographical memory. *Psychological Science, 4,* 1–8.

Nelson, K. E. (1981). Individual differences in language development. *Developmental Psychology, 17,* 170–187.

Nelson, S. A. (1980). Factors influencing young children's use of motives and outcomes as moral criteria. *Child Development, 51,* 823–829.

Nelson-Le Gall, S. A. (1985). Motive-outcome matching and outcome foreseeability: Effects on attribution of intentionality and moral judgments. *Developmental Psychology, 21,* 332–337.

Newcomb, A. F., & Bagwell, C. L. (1995). Children's friendship relations: A meta-analytic review. *Psychological Bulletin, 117,* 306–347.

Newcomb, A. F., & Bagwell, C. L. (1998). The developmental significance of children's friendship relations. In W. M. Bukowski, A. F. Newcomb, & W. W. Hartup (Eds.), *The company they keep: Friendships in childhood and adolescence* (pp. 289–312). New York: Cambridge University Press.

Newcombe, N., Mathason, L., & Terlecki, M. (2002). Maximization of spatial competence: More important than finding the cause of sex differences. In A. McGillicuddy-De Lisi & R. De Lisi (Eds.), *Biology, society, and behavior: The development of sex differences in cognition* (pp. 155–182). Westport, CT: Ablex.

Newman, L. F., & Buka, S. L. (1991). Every child a learner. *American Educator, 42,* 27–33.

Newman, L. S. (1991). Why are traits inferred spontaneously? A developmental approach. *Social Cognition, 9,* 221–253.

Newport, E. L. (1990). Maturational constraints on language learning. *Cognitive Science, 14,* 11–28.

Newport, E. L. (1991). Contrasting concepts of the critical period for language. In S. Carey & R. Gelman (Eds.), *The epigenesis of mind: Essays on biology and cognition* (pp. 111–130).

Newport, E. L., & Meier, R. P. (1985). The acquisition of American Sign Language. In D. I. Slobin (Ed.), *The cross-linguistic study of language acquisition.* (Vol. 1, pp. 881–938). Hillsdale, NJ: Erlbaum.

Niaz, M. (1997). How early can children understand some form of "scientific reasoning"? *Perceptual and Motor Skills, 85,* 1272–1274.

NICHD Early Child Care Research Network. (1996, April). *Infant child care and attachment security.* Symposium presented at the NICHD Early Child Care Research Network meeting, Providence, RI.

NICHD Early Child Care Research Network. (1997). Familial factors associated with the characteristics of nonmaternal care for infants. *Journal of Marriage and the Family, 59,* 389–408.

NICHD Early Child Care Research Network. (1998). Early child care and self-control, compliance, and problem behavior at twenty-four and thirty-six months. *Child Development, 69,* 1145–1170.

NICHD. (2000a). Characteristics and quality of child care for toddlers and preschoolers. *Applied Developmental Science, 4,* 116–135.

NICHD. (2000b). The relation of child care to cognitive and language development. *Child Development, 71,* 960–980.

Nicholls, J. G. (1992). Students as educational theorists. In D. Schunk & J. Meece (Eds.), *Student perceptions in the classroom* (pp. 267–286). Hillsdale, NJ: Erlbaum.

Nicholson, J. M., Fergusson, D. M., & Horwood. L. J. (1999). Effects on later adjustment of living in a stepfamily during childhood and adolescence. *Journal of Child Psychology and Psychiatry and Allied Disciplines, 40,* 405–416.

Nicolaisen, I. (1988). Concepts and learning among the Punan Bah of Sarawak. In G. Johoda (Ed.), *Acquiring culture: Cross cultural studies of child development* (pp. 193–222). London: Croom Helm.

Nieman, R. H., & Gaithright, J. F. (1981). *The long-term effects of ESEA Title I preschool and all-day kindergarten.* Cincinnati, OH: Cincinnati Public Schools.

Nilzon, K. R., & Palmerus, K. (1997). The influence of familial factors on anxiety and depression in childhood and early adolescence. *Adolescence, 32,* 935–943.

Ninio, A., & Snow, C. E. (1996). *Pragmatic development.* Boulder, CO: Westview Press.

Nosphitz, J. D., & King, R. A. (1991). *Pathways of growth: Essentials of child psychiatry.* New York: Wiley.

Nottelmann, E. D., Susman, E. J., Blue, J. H., Inoff-Germain, G. D., Dorn, L. D., Loriaux, D. B., Cutler, G. P., & Chrousos, G. P. (1987). Gonadal and adrenal hormone correlates of adjustment in early adolescence. In R. Lerner & T. Foch (Eds.), *Biological-psychological interactions in early adolescence* (pp. 303–321). Hillsdale, NJ: Erlbaum.

Nozza, R. J. (1995). Estimating the contribution of nonsensory factors to infant-adult differences in behavioral thresholds. *Hearing Research, 91,* 72–77.

Nsamenang, A. B. (1987). A West African perspective. In M. E. Lamb (Ed.), *The father's role: Cross-cultural perspectives* (pp. 273–293). Hillsdale, NJ: Erlbaum.

Nsamenang, A. B. (1992). *Human development in cultural context: A third world perspective.* Newbury Park, CA: Sage.

Nsamenang, A. B., & Laosebikan, S. (1981, April). *Father-child relationship and the development of psychopathology.* Paper presented to the Nigerian Psychological Society Conference, Jos, Nigeria.

Nua Ltd. (2001). *Internet statistics.* Dublin, Ireland: Nua Ltd.

Nuechterlein, K. H., Phipps-Yonas, S., Driscoll, R., & Garmezy, N. (1990). Vulnerability factors in children at risk: Anomalies in attentional functioning and social behavior. In J. E. Role & A. S. Masten (Eds.), *Risk and protective factors in the development of psychopathology* (pp. 445–479). New York: Cambridge University Press.

Nurcombe, B. (1994). The validity of the diagnosis of major depression in childhood and adolescence. In W. M. Reynolds & H. F. Johnston (Eds.), *Handbook of depression in children and adolescents* (pp. 61–77). New York: Plenum.

Nyiti, R. M. (1982). The validity of "cultural differences" explanations for cross-cultural variation in the rate of Piagetian cognitive development. In D. Wagner & H. Stevenson (Eds.), *Cultural perspectives on child development* (pp. 167–202). New York: Freeman.

Oakes, L. M., Plumert, J. M., Lansink, J. M., & Merryman, J. D. (1996). Evidence for task-dependent categorization in infancy. *Infant Behavior and Development, 19,* 425–440.

Oates, R. K., Peacock, A., & Forrest, D. (1985). Long-term effects of nonorganic failure to thrive. *Pediatrics, 75,* 36–40.

O'Brien, M., Roy, C., Jacobs, A., Macaluso, M., & Peyton, V. (1999). Conflict in the dyadic play of 3-year-old children. *Early Education and Development, 10,* 289–313.

O'Connor, B. P., & Dvorak, T. (2001). Conditional associations between parental behavior and adolescent problems: A search for personality-environment interactions. *Journal of Research in Personality, 35,* 1–26.

Offer, D., Ostrov, E., Howard, K. I., & Atkinson, R. (1988). *The teenage world: Adolescents' self image in ten countries.* New York: Plenum.

Office of Management and Budget. (1995). Standards for the classification of federal data on race and ethnicity. *Federal Register, 60,* 44673–44693.

Office of Minority Health. (1998). *Ethnic disparities in health.* Washington, DC: Office of Minority Health.

Ogbu, J. U. (1991). Immigrant and involuntary minorities in comparative perspective. In M. G. Gibson & J. U. Ogbu (Eds.), *Minority status and schooling* (pp. 131–156). New York: Garland.

Ogbu, J. U. (1994). From cultural differences to differences in cultural frame of reference. In P. Greenfield & R. Cocking (Eds.), *Cross-cultural roots of minority child development* (p. 365–391). Hillsdale, NJ: Erlbaum.

Olds, D., Pettitt, L. M., Robinson, J., Henderson, C., Eckenrode, J., Kitzman, H., Cole, B., & Powers, J. (1998). Reducing risks for antisocial behavior with a program of prenatal and early childhood home visitation. *Journal of Community Psychology, 26,* 65–83.

Olweus, D. (1995). Bullying or peer abuse in school: Intervention and prevention. In G. Davies, S. Lloyd-Bostock, M. McMurran, & C. Wilson (Eds.), *Psychology, law, and criminal justice.* Berlin, Germany: Walter De Gruyter.

O'Neill, D. B., & Micheli, L. J. (1988). Overuse injuries in the young athlete. *Clinical Sports Medicine, 7,* 591–610.

Orenstein, P. (1994). *School girls.* New York: Anchor Books.

Ornstein, P. A., Naus, M. J., & Liberty, C. (1975). Rehearsal and organizational processes in children's memory. *Child Development, 46,* 818–830.

Ortiz, V. (1995). The diversity of Latino families. In R. E. Zambrana (Ed.), *Understanding Latino families* (pp. 18–29). Thousand Oaks, CA: Sage.

Osher, Y., Hamer, D., & Benjamin, J. (2000). Association and linkage of anxiety-related traits with a functional polymorphism of the serotonin transporter gene regulatory region in Israeli sibling pairs. *Molecular Psychiatry, 5,* 216–219.

Otake, M., & Schull, W. J. (1984). In utero exposure to A-bomb radiation and mental retardation. *British Journal of Radiology, 57,* 409–414.

Overton, W. F. (1998). Developmental psychology: Philosophy, concepts, and methodology. In W. Damon (Ed.), *Handbook of child psychology* (Vol. 1, pp. 107–188). New York: Wiley.

Overton, W. F., & Byrnes, J. P. (1991). Cognitive development. In R. M. Lerner, A. C. Petersen, & J. Brooks-Gunn (Eds.), *Encyclopedia of adolescence* (Vol. 1, pp. 151–156). New York: Garland.

Owens, R. E. (1996). *Language development: An introduction.* Boston: Allyn & Bacon.

Padilla, M. T. (1997, May 14). Tiger Woods helps bring multiracial issue to fore. *Arizona Republic,* pp. 1, 2.

Page, R. M., & Allen, O. (1995). Adolescent perceptions of body weight and weight satisfaction. *Perceptual and Motor Skills, 81,* 81–82.

Paik, H., & Comstock, G. (1994). The effects of television violence on antisocial behavior: A meta-analysis. *Communication Research, 21,* 516–546.

Paikoff, D. F., Luster, T., Villarruel, F. A., & Small, S. (1998). An ecological risk-factor examination of adolescents' sexual activity in three ethnic groups. *Journal of Marriage and the Family, 60,* 660–673.

Paikoff, R. L., & Brooks-Gunn, J. (1991). Do parent-child relationships change during puberty? *Psychological Bulletin, 110,* 47–66.

Paikoff, R. L., Brooks-Gunn, J., & Warren, M. P. (1991). Effects of girls' hormonal status on depressive and aggressive symptoms over the course of one year. *Journal of Youth and Adolescence, 20,* 191–215.

Palardy, N., Greening, L., Ott, J., Holderby, A., & Atchinson, J. (1998). Adolescents' health attitudes and adherence to treatment for insulin-dependent diabetes mellitus. *Journal of Developmental and Behavioral Pediatrics, 19,* 31–37.

Palmer, E. J., & Hollin, C. R. (2001). Sociomoral reasoning, perceptions of parenting and self-reported delinquency in adolescents. *Applied Cognitive Psychology, 15,* 85–100.

Papadimitrious, A. (2001). Sex differences in the secular changes in pubertal maturation. *Pediatrics, 108,* 65.

Papini, D. R., & Sebby, R. A. (1987). Adolescent pubertal status and affective family relationships: A multivariate assessment. *Journal of Youth and Adolescence, 16,* 1–15.

Paris, S. G. (2001). Classroom applications of research on self-regulated learning. *Educational Psychologist, 36,* 89–101.

Paris, S. G., & Cunningham, A. E. (1996). Children becoming students. In D. C. Berliner & R. C. Calfee (Eds.), *Handbook of educational psychology* (pp. 117–147). New York: Macmillan.

Parke, R. D. (1995). Fathers and families. In M. H. Bornstein (Ed.), *Handbook of parenting* (Vol. 3, pp. 27–64). Mahwah, NJ: Erlbaum.

Parke, R. D., & Buriel, R. (1998). Socialization in the family. In W. Damon (Ed.), *Handbook of child psychology* (Vol. 3, pp. 463–552). New York: Wiley.

Parker, B., McFarlane, J., & Socken, K. (1994). Abuse during pregnancy: Effects on maternal complications and birth weight in adult and teenage women. *Obstetrics and Gynecology, 84,* 323–328.

Parker, J. G., & Asher, S. R. (1987). Peer relations and later personal adjustment: Are low-accepted children at risk? *Psychological Bulletin, 102,* 357–389.

Parker, J. G., Rubin, K. H., Price, J., & De Rosier, M. E. (1995). Peer relationships, child development, and adjustment: A developmental psychopathology perspective. In D. Cicchetti & D. J. Cohen (Eds.), *Developmental psychopathology* (Vol. 2, pp. 96–161). New York: Wiley.

Parkhurst, J. T., & Asher, S. R. (1992). Peer rejection in middle school. *Developmental Psychology, 28,* 231–241.

Parten, M. (1933). Social play among preschool children. *Journal of Abnormal and Social Psychology, 28,* 136–147.

Pasupathi, M., Staudinger, U. M., & Baltes, P. B. (2001). Seeds of wisdom: Adolescents' knowledge and judgment about difficult life problems. *Developmental Psychology, 37,* 351–361

Patterson, C. J. (1992). Children of lesbian and gay parents. *Child Development, 63,* 1025–1042.

Patterson, C. J. (1995). Lesbian mothers, gay fathers, and their children. In A. R. D'Augelli & C. J. Patterson (Eds.), *Lesbian, gay, and bisexual identities over the lifespan* (pp. 262–290). New York: Oxford University Press.

Patterson, C. J., & Chan, R. W. (1999). Families headed by lesbian and gay parents. In M. E. Lamb (Ed.), *Parenting and child development in "nontraditional" families* (pp. 191–219). Mahwah, NJ: Erlbaum.

Patterson, C. J., Griesler, P. C., Vaden, N. A., & Kupersmidt, J. B. (1992). Family economic circumstances, life transitions, and children's peer relations. In R. D. Parke & G. W. Ladd (Eds.), *Family-peer relationships: Modes of linkage* (pp. 385–424). Hillsdale, NJ: Erlbaum.

Patterson, C. J., Vaden, N. A., & Kupersmidt, J. B. (1991). Family background, recent life events, and peer rejection during childhood. *Journal of Social and Personal Relationships, 8,* 347–361.

Patterson, G. R. (1982). *Coercive family process.* Eugene, OR: Castalia.

Patterson, G. R., & Dishion, T. J. (1988). Multilevel modes of family process: Traits, interactions, and relationships. In R. Hinde & J. Stevenson-Hinde (Eds.), *Relationships and families: Mutual influences* (pp. 283–310). Oxford, England: Clarendon Press.

Patterson, G. R., Reid, J. B., & Dishion, T. J. (1998). *Antisocial boys.* Eugene, OR: Castalia.

Patterson, G. R., & Yoerger, K. (1993). Developmental models for delinquent behavior. In S. Hodgins (Ed.), *Crime and mental disorder* (pp. 140–172). Newbury Park, CA: Sage.

Paul, R. (1991). Profiles of toddlers with slow expressive language development. *Topics in Language Disorders, 11,* 1–13.

Paul, R., Spangle-Looney, S., & Dahm, P. S. (1991). Communication and socialization skills in ages 2 and 3 in late-talking young children. *Journal of Speech and Hearing Research, 4,* 858–865.

Paus, T., Zijdenbos, A., Worsley, K., Collins, D. L., Blumenthal, J., Giedd, J. N., Rapoport, J. L., & Evans, A. C. (1999). Structural maturation of neural pathways in children and adolescents: In vivo study. *Science, 283,* 1908–1911.

Pearson, J. L., & Ferguson, L. R. (1989). Gender differences in patterns of spatial ability, environmental cognition, and math and English achievement in late adolescence. *Adolescence, 24,* 421–431.

Pelham, W. E., Aronoff, H. R., Midlam, J. K., Shapiro, C. J., Gnagy, E. M., Chronis, A. M., Onyango, A. N., Forehand, G., Nguyen, A., & Waxmonsky, J. (1999). A comparison of Ritalin and Aderall: Efficacy and timecourse in children with ADHD. *Pediatrics, 103,* 1–14.

Pelham, W. E., Bender, M. E., Caddell, J., Booth, S., & Moorer, S. H. (1985). Methylphenidate and children with attention deficit disorder: Dose effects on classroom academic and social behavior. *Archives of General Psychiatry, 42,* 948–952.

Pelham, W. E., Milich, R., & Walker, J. L. (1986). Effects of continuous and partial reinforcement and methylphenidate on learning in children with attention deficit disorder. *Journal of Abnormal Psychology, 95,* 319–325.

Pellegrini, A. D., & Landers-Pott, M. (1996). Children, classroom context and activity and attention to tasks. *Emotional and Behavioral Difficulties, 1,* 29–35.

Pellegrini, A. D., & Smith, P. K. (1998). Physical activity play: The nature and function of a neglected aspect of play. *Child Development, 69,* 577–598.

Peracchio, L. A. (1993). Young children's processing of a televised narrative: Is a picture really worth a thousand words? *Journal of Consumer Research, 20,* 281–293.

Perez-Granados, D. R., & Callanan, M. A. (1997). Parents and siblings as early resources for young children's learning in Mexican-descent families. *Hispanic Journal of Behavioral Sciences, 19,* 3–33.

Perris, E. E., Myers, N. A., & Clifton, R. K. (1990). Long-term memory for a single infancy experience. *Child Development, 61,* 1796–1807.

Perry, D. G., Perry, L. C., & Rasmussen, P. (1986). Cognitive social learning mediators of aggression. *Child Development, 57,* 700–711.

Persell, C. H. (1993). Social class and educational equality. In J. A. Banks & C. A. M. Banks (Eds.), *Multiculture education: Issues and perspectives* (pp. 71–89). Boston: Allyn & Bacon.

Perusse, D., Neale, M. C., Heath, A. C., & Eaves, L. J. (1994). Human parental behavior: Evidence for genetic influence and potential implication for gene-culture transmission. *Behavioral Genetics, 24,* 327–335.

Peskin, H. (1973). Influence of the developmental schedule of puberty on learning and ego development. *Journal of Youth and Adolescence, 2,* 273–290.

Peters, H. E., Argys, L. M., Maccoby, E. E., & Mnookin, R. H. (1993). Enforcing divorce settlements: Evidence from child support compliance and award modifications. *Demography, 30,* 719–735.

Petersen, A. C. (1987). The nature of biological-psychosocial interactions: The sample case of early adolescence. In R. M. Lerner & T. T. Foch (Eds.), *Biological-psychological interactions in early adolescence* (pp. 35–61). Hillsdale, NJ: Erlbaum.

Petersen, A. C. (1988). Adolescent development. *Annual Review of Psychology, 39,* 583–607.

Peterson, G. W. (1986). Parent-youth power dimensions and the behavior autonomy of adolescents. *Journal of Adolescent Research, 1,* 231–249.

Peterson, G. W. (1995). The need for common principles in prevention programs for children, adolescents, and families. *Journal of Adolescent Research, 10,* 470–485.

Peterson, G. W., & Haan, D. (1999). Socializing children and parents in families. In M. Sussman, S. Steinmetz, & G. W. Peterson (Eds.), *Handbook of marriage and the family* (pp. 455–501). New York: Plenum.

Peterson, G. W., & Leigh, G. K. (1990). The family and social competence in adolescence. In T. P. Gullotta & G. R. Adams (Eds.), *Developing social competency in adolescence* (Vol. 3, pp. 97–138). Newbury Park, CA: Sage.

Peterson, J. L., & Zill, N. (1986). Parent-child relationships and behavior problems in children. *Journal of Marriage and the Family, 48,* 295–307.

Pettegrew, J., Lewis, L. A., Brown, J. D., Schulze, L., Zook, K. B., Perry, I., Rose, T., & Ledbetter, J. (1995). Music videos and rap music: Cultural conflict and control in the age of the image. In G. Dines & J. M. Humez (Eds.), *Gender, race, and class in media* (pp. 479–544). Thousand Oaks, CA: Sage.

Pettit, G. S., Bates, J. E., & Dodge, K. A. (1997). Supportive parenting, ecological context, and children's adjustment. *Child Development, 68,* 908–923.

Pettit, G. S., Laird, R. D., Dodge, K. A., Bates, J. E., & Criss, M. M. (2001). Antecedents and behavior-problem outcomes of parental monitoring and psychological control in early adolescence. *Child Development, 72,* 583–598.

Phelps, L. A., Johnston, L. S., Jimenesez, D. P., Wilczenski, F. L., Andrea, R. K., & Healy, R. W. (1993). Figure preference, body dissatisfaction, and body distortion in adolescence. *Journal of Adolescent Research, 8,* 297–310.

Phillips, D., & Howes, C. (1987). Indicators of quality in child care. In D. Phillips (Ed.), *Quality in child care: What does research tell us?* (pp. 1–20). Washington, DC: NAEYC.

Phillips, D., Lande, J., & Goldberg, M. (1990). The state of childcare regulation: A comparative analysis. *Early Childhood Research Quarterly, 5,* 151–179.

Phillips, D., McCartney, K., & Scarr, S. (1987). Child-care quality and children's social development. *Developmental Psychology, 23,* 537–543.

Phillipsen, L. C. (1999). Associations between age, gender, and group acceptance and three components of friendship quality. *Journal of Early Adolescence, 19,* 438–464.

Phillipsen, L. C., Burchinal, M. R., Howes, C., & Cryer, D. (1997). The prediction of process quality from structural features of child care. *Early Childhood Research Quarterly, 12,* 281–303.

Phinney, J. S. (1996). Understanding ethnic diversity: The role of ethnic identity. *American Behavioral Scientist, 40,* 143–152.

Phinney, J. S., Cantu, C. L., & Kurtz, D. A. (1997). Ethnic and American identity as predictors of self esteem among African American, Latino, and White adolescents. *Journal of Youth and Adolescence, 26,* 165–185.

Phinney, J. S., DuPont, S., Espinosa, C., Revill, J., & Sanders, K. (1994). Ethnic identity and American identification among ethnic minority youths. In A. M. Bouvy & F. J. R. van de Vijver (Eds.), *Journeys into cross-cultural psychology* (pp. 167–183). Amsterdam: Swets & Zeitlinger.

Phinney, J. S., Ong, A., & Madden, T. (2000). Cultural values and intergenerational value discrepancies in immigrant and non-immigrant families. *Child Development, 71,* 528–539.

Phinney, J. S., & Rosenthal, D. A. (1992). Ethnic identity in adolescence. In G. R. Adams & T. P. Gullotta (Eds.), *Adolescent identity formation* (Vol. 4, pp. 145–172). Newbury Park, CA: Sage.

Piaget, J. (1952). *The origins of intelligence in children.* New York: Norton.

Piaget, J. (1963). *The origins of intelligence in children* (M. Cook, Trans.). New York: W. W. Norton. (Original work published 1936)

Piaget, J. (1969). *The child's conception of time* (A. J. Pomerans, Trans.). London: Routledge. (Original work published 1946)

Piaget, J. (1971). *Biology and knowledge.* Chicago: University of Chicago Press.

Piaget, J. (1977). *The development of thought.* New York: Viking.

Piaget, J., & Inhelder, B. (1958). *The growth of logical thinking from childhood to adolescence.* New York: Basic Books.

Pianta, R. C., & Nimetz, S. L. (1991). Relationships between children and teachers: Associations with classroom and home behavior. *Journal of Applied Developmental Psychology, 12,* 379–393.

Pinker, S. (1984). *Language learnability and language development.* Cambridge, MA: Harvard University Press.

Pipher, M. (1994). *Reviving Ophelia.* New York: Grosset/Putnam.

Plimpton, C. E., & Regimbal, C. (1992). Differences in motor proficiency according to gender and race. *Perceptual and Motor Skills, 74,* 399–402.

Plomin, R. (1994). *Genetics and experience: The interplay between nature and nurture.* Thousand Oaks, CA: Sage.

Plomin, R., DeFries, J. C., & McClearn, G. E. (1990). *Behavioral genetics: A primer.* New York: Freeman.

Plomin, R., DeFries, J. C., McClearn, G. E., & Rutter, M. (1997). *Behavioral genetics.* New York: Freeman.

Plomin, R., Fulker, D. W., Corley, R., & DeFries, J. C. (1997). Nature, nurture, and cognitive development from 1 to 16 years: A parent-offspring adoption study. *Psychological Science, 8,* 442–447.

Plomin, R., Nitz, K., & Rowe, D. C. (1990). Behavior genetics and aggressive behavior in childhood. In M. Lewis & S. Miller (Eds.), *Handbook of development psychology* (pp. 119–133). New York: Plenum.

Plumb, P., & Cowan, G. (1984). A developmental study of stereotyping and androgynous activity preference of tomboys, nontomboys, and males. *Sex Roles, 10,* 703–712.

Plunkett, J. W., Meisels, S. J., Stiefel, G. S., Pasick, P. L., & Roloff, D. W. (1986). Patterns of attachment among preterm infants of varying biological risk. *Journal of the American Academy of Child Psychiatry, 25,* 794–800.

Polce, L. M., Myers, B. J., Kliewer, W., & Kilmartin, C. (2001). Adolescent self-esteem and gender: Exploring relations to sexual harassment, body image, media influence, and emotional expression. *Journal of Youth and Adolescence 30,* 225–244.

Polit, D. F., & Falbo, T. (1987). Only children and personality development: A quantitative review. *Journal of Marriage and the Family, 49,* 309–325.

Pollitt, E., Golub, M., Gorman, K., Grantham-McGregor, S., Levitsky, D., Schurch, B., Strupp, B., & Wachs, T. (1996). A recommendation of the effects of undernutrition on children's biological, psychosocial, and behavioral development. *Society for Research in Child Development Social Policy Report, 10,* 1–23.

Pollock, L. A. (1983). *Forgotten children.* Cambridge, England: Cambridge University Press.

Pomerantz, E. M., & Ruble, D. N. (1997). Distinguishing multiple dimensions of conceptions of ability: Implications for self-evaluation. *Child Development, 68,* 1165–1180.

Pomerantz, E. M., Ruble, D. N., Frey, K. S., & Greulich, F. (1995). Meeting goals and confronting conflict: Children's changing perceptions of social comparison. *Child Development, 66,* 723–738.

Pooler, W. S. (1991). Sex of child preferences among college students. *Sex Roles, 25,* 569–576.

Pope, A. W., & Bierman, K. L. (1999). Predicting adolescent peer problems and antisocial activities: The relative roles of aggression and dysregulation. *Developmental Psychology, 35,* 335–346.

Popkin, B. M., & Udry, J. R. (1998). Adolescent obesity increases significantly in second and third generation U.S. immigrants. *Journal of Nutrition, 128,* 701–706.

Porac, C., Coren, S., & Searleman, A. (1986). Environmental factors in hand preference formation. *Behavior Genetics, 16,* 251–261.

Porter, R. H., Cernoch, J. M., & McLaughlin, F. J. (1983). Maternal recognition of neonates through olfactory cues. *Physiology and Behavior, 30,* 151–154.

Porter, R. H., Makin, J. W., Davis, L. B., & Christensen, K. M. (1992). Breast-fed infants respond to olfactory cues from their own mother and unfamiliar lactating females. *Infant Behavior and Development, 15,* 85–93.

Posada, G., Gao, Y., Wu, F., Posada, R., Tascon, M., Schoelmerich, A., Sagi, A., Kondo-Ikemura, K., Haaland, W., & Synnevaag, B. (1995). The secure-base phenomenon across cultures: Children's behavior, mothers' preferences, and experts' concepts. In E. Waters, B. Vaughan, G. Posada, & K. Kondo-Ikemura (Eds.), *Caregiving, cultural, and cognitive perspectives on secure-base behavior and working models* (pp. 27–48). Chicago: Society for Research in Child Development.

Posner, J. K., & Vandell, D. L. (1994). Low-income children's after-school care: Are there beneficial effects of after-school programs? *Child Development, 65,* 440–456.

Posner, M. J., & Rothbart, M. K. (2000). Developing mechanisms of self-regulation. *Development and Psychopathology, 12,* 427–441.

Potegal, M., Kosorok, M. R., & Davidson, R. J. (1996). The time course of angry behavior in the temper tantrums of young children. *Annals of the New York Academy of Sciences, 794,* 31–45.

Potts, R., Doppler, M., & Hernandez, M. (1994). Effects of television content on physical risk-taking in children. *Journal of Experimental Child Psychology, 58,* 321–331.

Poulin, F., Cillessen, A. H. N., Hubbard, J. A., Coie, J. D., Dodge, K. A., & Schwartz, D. (1997). Children's friends and behavioral similarity in two social contexts. *Social Development, 6,* 224–236.

Powell, G. F., Low, J. F., & Speers, M. A. (1987). Behavior as a diagnostic aid in failure to thrive. *Journal of Developmental Behavioral Pediatrics, 8,* 18–24.

Power, A. R., & Power, F. C. (1992). A raft of hope: Democratic education and the challenge of pluralism. *Journal of Moral Education, 21,* 193–205.

Power, F. C., Higgins, A., & Kohlberg, L. (1989). *Lawrence Kohlberg's approach to moral education.* New York: Columbia University Press.

Power, F. C., & Makogon, T. A. (1995). *The just community approach to care.* South Bend, IN: Notre Dame University Press.

Power, T. G., McGrath, M. P., Hughes, S. O., & Manire, S. H. (1994). Compliance and self-assertion: Young children's responses to mothers versus fathers. *Developmental Psychology, 30,* 980–989.

Pransky, J. (1991). *Prevention: The critical need.* Springfield, MO: Burrell Foundation.

Prectl, H. F. R., & Beintema, D. (1965). *The neurological examination of the full-term newborn infant.* London: William Heinemann Medical Books.

President's Council on Physical Fitness and Sports. (2001, March). Healthy people 2010: Physical activity and fitness. *Research Digest,* Series 3, No. 13.

Price, D. W. W., & Goodman, G. S. (1990). Visiting the wizard: Children's memory for a recurring event. *Child Development, 61,* 664–680.

Price, J. M., & Lento, J. (2001). The nature of child and adolescent vulnerability: History and definitions. In R. E. Ingram & J. M. Price (Eds.), *Vulnerability to psychopathology: Risk across the lifespan* (pp. 20–38). New York: Guilford.

Prugh, D. G., Staub, E. M., Sands, H. H., Kirschbaum, R. M., & Lenihan, E. A. (1953). A study of the emotional reactions of children in families to hospitalization and illness. *American Journal of Orthopsychiatry, 23,* 70–106.

Prysak, M., & Castronova, F. C. (1998). Elective induction versus spontaneous labor. *Obstetrics and Gynecology, 92,* 47–52.

Public Agenda. (2000). *About kids these days, 1999.* New York: Public Agenda.

Puig-Antich, J., Geotz, D., Davies, M., Kaplan, T., Davies, S., Ostrow, L., Asnis, L., Toomey, J., Iyengar, S., & Ryan, N. (1989). A controlled family history study of prepubertal major depressive disorder. *Archives of General Psychiatry, 46,* 406–418.

Putallaz, M., & Wasserman, A. (1990). Children's entry behavior. In S. R. Asher & J. D. Coie (Eds.), *Peer rejection in childhood* (pp. 60–89). Cambridge, England: Cambridge University Press.

Quamina, A. (1999). Adolescent gangs: A practitioner's perspective. In C. W. Branch (Ed.), *Adolescent gangs: Old issues, new approaches* (pp. 39–56). Philadelphia: Brunner/Mazel.

Quatman, T., Sampson, K., Robinson, C., & Watson, C. M. (2001). Academic, motivational, and emotional correlates of adolescent dating. *Genetic, Social, and General Psychology Monographs, 127,* 211–234.

Quatman, T., & Watson, C. M. (2001). Gender differences in adolescent self-esteem: An exploration of domains. *Journal of Genetic Psychology, 16,* 93–117.

Quist, J. F., & Kennedy, J. L. (2001). Genetics of childhood disorders: ADHD. Part 7: The serotonin system. *Journal of the American Academy of Child and Adolescent Psychiatry, 40,* 253–256.

Radke-Yarrow, M., & Sherman, T. (1990). Hard growing: Children who survive. In J. Rolf, A. S. Masten, D. Cicchetti, K. H. Nuechterlein, & S. Weintraub (Eds.), *Risk and protective factors in the development of psychopathology* (pp. 97–119). Cambridge, England: Cambridge University Press.

Raeff, C. (1997). Cultural values, children's social interactions, and the development of an American individualistic self. *Developmental Review, 17,* 205–238.

Raffaelli, M., Bogenschneider, K., & Flood, M. F. (1998). Parent-teen communication about sexual topics. *Journal of Family Issues, 19,* 315–333.

Rakison, D. H., & Poulin-Dubois, D. (2001). Developmental origin of the animate-inanimate distinction. *Psychological Bulletin, 127,* 209–228.

Ramsey, P. G. (1987). Young children's thinking about ethnic differences. In J. S. Phinney & M. J. Rotheram (Eds.), *Children's ethnic socialization* (pp. 56–72). Beverly Hills, CA: Sage.

Rastam, M., & Gillberg, C. (1991). The family background in anorexia nervosa: A population-based study. *Journal of the American Academy of Child and Adolescent Psychiatry, 30,* 283–289.

Rathus, S. A., Nevid, J. S., & Fichner-Rathus, L. (1993). *Human sexuality in a world of diversity.* Boston: Allyn & Bacon.

Raver, C. C., & Zigler, E. F. (1997). New perspectives on Head Start. *Early Childhood Research Quarterly, 12,* 363–385.

Reder, P., & Duncan, S. (2000). Child abuse and parental mental health. In P. Reder & M. McClure (Eds.), *Family matters: Interfaces between child and adult mental health* (pp. 166–179). London: Routledge.

Reichman, N. E., & Pagnini, D. L. (1997). Maternal age and birth outcomes. *Family Planning Perspectives, 29,* 268–272.

Reid, J. B., & Eddy, J. M. (1997). The prevention of antisocial behavior: Some considerations in the search for effective interventions. In D. M. Stoff &

J. Breiling (Eds.), *Handbook of antisocial behavior* (pp. 343–356). New York: Wiley.

Reinisch, J. M. (1990). *The Kinsey Institute new report on sex: What you must know to be sexually literate.* New York: St. Martin's Press.

Reis, S. M. (1989). Reflections on policy affecting the education of gifted and talented students. *American Psychologist, 44,* 399–408.

Reisman, J. E. (1987). Touch, motion, and proprioception. In P. Salapatek & L. Cohen (Eds.), *Handbook of infant perception* (Vol. 1, pp. 265–303). New York: Academic Press.

Reissland, N. (1988). Neonatal imitation in the first hour of life: Observations in rural Nepal. *Developmental Psychology, 24,* 464–469.

Remafedi, G. (1991). Adolescent homosexuality. In R. M. Lerner, A. C. Petersen, & J. Brooks-Gunn (Eds.), *Encyclopedia of adolescence* (pp. 504–507). New York: Garland.

Renzulli, J. S. (1999). What is this thing called giftedness, and how do we develop it? A twenty-five year perspective. *Journal for the Education of the Gifted, 23,* 3–54.

Repacholi, B. M., & Gopnik, A. (1997). Early reasoning about desires: Evidence from 14- and 18-month-olds. *Developmental Psychology, 33,* 12–21.

Rescorla, L., & Schwartz, E. (1990). Outcome of toddlers with specific expressive language impairment. *Applied Psycholinguistics, 11,* 393–408.

Resnick, M. D. (1997). *Adolescents and work.* Unpublished data, University of Minnesota.

Rest, J. R. (1983). Morality. In J. H. Flavell & E. M. Markman (Eds.), *Handbook of child psychology* (Vol. 3, pp. 556–629). New York: Wiley.

Reuter, M. A., Conger, R. D., & Ramisetty-Mikler, S. (1999). Assessing the benefits of a parenting skills training program: A theoretical approach to predicting direct and moderating effects. *Family Relations, 48,* 67–77.

Rheingold, H. L. (1982). Little children's participation in the work of adults: A nascent prosocial behavior. *Child Development, 53,* 114–125.

Rhode, M. (1997). *Sexual orientation.* Seattle: Friends Project.

Rholes, W. S., & Ruble, D. N. (1984). Children's understanding of dispositional characteristics of others. *Child Development, 33,* 550–560.

Rice, C., Koinis, D., Sullivan, K., Tagar-Flusberg, H., & Winner, E. (1997). When 3-year olds pass the appearance-reality test. *Developmental Psychology, 33,* 54–61.

Rice, E. P. (1996). *The adolescent: Development, relationships, and culture.* Boston: Allyn & Bacon.

Rice, M. L. (1990). Preschoolers QUIL: Quick incidental learning of words. In G. ContiRamsden & C. Snow (Eds.), *Children's language* (Vol. 7, pp. 171–195). Hillsdale, NJ: Erlbaum.

Rice, M. L., Hadley, P. A., & Alexander, A. (1993). Social biases toward children with specific language impairment: A correlative causal model of language limitations. *Applied Psycholinguistics, 14,* 445–471.

Rice, M. L., Huston, A. C., Truglio, R. T., & Wright, J. C. (1990). Words from Sesame Street: Learning vocabulary while viewing. *Developmental Psychology, 26,* 421–428.

Richards, H., & Goodman, R. (1996). Are only children different? A study of psychiatric referrals. *Journal of Child Psychology and Psychiatry, 37,* 753–757.

Richards, M. H., Casper, R. C., & Larson, R. (1990). Weight and eating concerns among pre- and young adolescent boys and girls. *Journal of Adolescent Health, 11,* 203–209.

Richards, M. H., Crowe, P. A., Larson, R., & Swarr, A. (1998). Developmental patterns and gender differences in the experience of peer companionship during adolescence. *Child Development, 69,* 154–163.

Richardson, G. A., Hamel, S. C., Goldschmidt, L., & Day, N. L. (1999). Growth of infants prenatally exposed to cocaine/crack: Comparison of a prenatal care and a no prenatal care sample. *Pediatrics, 104,* 18–22.

Richman, N., Stevenson, J. E., & Graham, P. (1982). *Preschool to school: A behavioral study.* London: Academic Press.

Ridley, M. (1999). *Genome: The autobiography of a species in 23 chapters.* New York: Harper Collins.

Rieber, R. W., & Hall, M. J. (1998). *The collected works of L. S. Vygotsky.* New York: Plenum.

Robbins, C., & Ehri, L. C. (1994). Reading storybooks to kindergartners helps them learn new vocabulary words. *Journal of Educational Psychology, 86,* 54–64.

Roberts, D. F., & Christenson, P. G. (2001). Popular music in childhood and adolescence. In D. G. Singer & J. L. Singer (Eds.), *Handbook of children and the media* (pp. 395–414). Thousand Oaks, CA: Sage.

Roberts, L. R., Sarigiani, P. A., Petersen, A. C., & Newman, J. L. (1993). Gender differences in the relationship between achievement and self-image during early adolescence. In R. A. Pierce & M. A. Black (Eds.), *Life span development* (pp. 126–139). Dubuque, IA: Kendall/Hunt.

Roberts, R. E., Phinney, J. S., Masse, L. C., Chen, Y. R., Roberts, C. R., & Romero, A. (1999). The structure of ethnic identity of young adolescents from diverse ethnocultural groups. *Journal of Early Adolescence, 19,* 301–322.

Roberts, W., & Strayer, J. (1996). Empathy, emotional expressiveness, and prosocial behavior. *Child Development, 67,* 449–470.

Robertson, J. A. (1996). Legal uncertainties in human egg donation. In C. B. Cohen (Ed.), *New ways of making babies* (pp. 175–187). Bloomington: Indiana University Press.

Robinson, A., Goodman, S., & O'Brien, D. (1984). Genetic and chromosomal disorders, including inborn errors of metabolism. In C. H. Kempe, H. K. Silver, & D. O'Brien (Eds.), *Current pediatric diagnosis and treatment* (pp. 322–367). Los Altos, CA: Lange Medical.

Robinson, D. L. (1996). *Brain, mind, and behavior: A new perspective on human nature.* Westport, CT: Praeger.

Robinson, J. P. (1981). Television and leisure time. *Journal of Communication, 31,* 120–130.

Roche, A. F. (1979). Secular trends in human growth, malnutrition, and development. *Monographs of the Society for Research in Child Development, 44* (Whole No. 179).

Roche, A. M. (1998). Alcohol and drug education: A review of key issues. *Drugs: Education, Prevention, and Policy, 5,* 85–99.

Rodgers, B. R. (1999). Parenting processes related to sexual risk-taking behaviors of adolescent males and females. *Journal of Marriage and the Family, 61,* 99–109.

Rodgers, J. L., Rowe, D. C., & Buster, M. (1998). Social contagion, adolescent sexual behavior, and pregnancy. *Developmental Psychology, 34,* 1096–1113.

Roeser, R. W., & Eccles, J. S. (2000). Schooling and mental health. In A. Sameroff & M. Lewis (Eds.), *Handbook of developmental psychopathology* (pp. 135–156). New York: Kluwer/Plenum.

Roeser, R. W., Eccles, J. S., & Freedman-Doan, C. (1999). Academic functioning and mental health in adolescence: Patterns, progressions, and routes from childhood. *Journal of Adolescent Research, 14,* 135–174.

Roeser, R. W., Eccles, J. S., & Sameroff, A. J. (1998). Academic and emotional functioning in early adolescence: Longitudinal relations, patterns, and prediction by experience in middle school. *Development and Psychopathology, 10,* 321–352.

Roffey, S., Majors, K., & Tarrant, T. (1997). Friends—who needs them? *Educational and Child Psychology, 14,* 51–56.

Rogoff, B. (1990). *Apprenticeship in thinking: Cognitive development in social context.* New York: Oxford University Press.

Rogoff, B. (1998). Cognition as a collaborative process. In D. Kuhn & R. S. Siegler (Eds.), *Handbook of child psychology* (Vol. 2, pp. 679–744). New York: Wiley.

Rogoff, B., Mistry, J., Goncu, A., & Mosier, C. (1993). Guided participation in cultural activity by toddlers and caregivers. *Monographs of the Society for Research in Child Development, 58* (Whole No. 179).

Rohner, R. P. (1986). *The warmth dimension: Foundations of parental acceptance-rejection theory.* Beverly Hills, CA: Sage.

Roopnarine, J. L., Lasker, J., Sacks, M., & Stores, M. (1998). The cultural contexts of children's play. In O. N. Saracho & B. Spodek (Eds.), *Multiple perspectives on play in early childhood education* (pp. 194–219). Albany: State University of New York Press.

Roosa, M. W., & Christopher, F. S. (1990). Evaluation of an abstinence-only adolescent pregnancy prevention program. *Family Relations, 39,* 363–367.

Roosa, M. W., Tein, J., Reinholtz, C., & Angelini, P. J. (1997). The relationship of sexual abuse to teenage pregnancy. *Journal of Marriage and the Family, 59,* 119–130.

Roper Organization. (1993). Survey of March 13–27, 1993. *Roper Reports, 93.*

Rose, A. J., & Asher, S. R. (2000). Children's friendships. In C. Hendrick & S. Hendrick (Eds.), *Close relationships: A sourcebook* (pp. 47–57). Thousand Oaks, CA: Sage.

Rose, K. J. (1988). *The body in time.* New York: Wiley.

Rose, S. A., & Blank, M. (1974). The potency of context in children's cognition. *Child Development, 45,* 499–502.

Rosenbaum, M. B. (1993). The changing image of the adolescent girl. In M. Sugar (Ed.), *Female adolescent development* (pp. 62–80). New York: Brunner/Mazel.

Rosenblith, J. F. (1992). *In the beginning: Development from conception to age two.* Newbury Park, CA: Sage.

Rosenshine, B., & Meister, C. (1997). Cognitive strategy instruction in reading. In S. A. Stahl & D. A. Hayes (Eds.), *Instructional models in reading* (pp. 85–107). Mahwah, NJ: Erlbaum.

Rosenstein, D., & Oster, H. (1988). Differential facial responses to four basic tastes in newborns. *Child Development, 59,* 1555–1568.

Rosenthal, B. S. (1998). Non-school correlates of dropout: An integrative review of the literature. *Child and Youth Services Review, 20,* 413–433.

Rosenthal, M. K. (1999). Out-of-home child care research: A cultural perspective. *International Journal of Behavioral Development, 23,* 477–518.

Rosenthal, R., & Vandell, D. L. (1996). Quality of care at school-aged child-care programs: Regulatable features, observed experiences, child perspectives, and parent perspectives. *Child Development, 67,* 2434–2445.

Ross, H. S., & Conant, C. L. (1992). The social structure of early conflict: Interaction, relationships, and alliances. In C. U. Shantz & W. W. Hartup (Eds.), *Conflict in child and adolescent development* (pp. 153–186). Cambridge, England: Cambridge University Press.

Ross-Leadbeater, B. J., & Way, N. (2001). *Growing up fast: Transitions to early adulthood of inner-city adolescent mothers.* Mahwah, NJ: Erlbaum.

Rosser, P. L., & Randolph, S. M. (1989). Black American infants: The Howard University normative study. In J. K. Nugent, B. M. Lester, & T. B. Brazelton (Eds.), *The cultural context of infancy* (Vol. 1, pp. 133–165). Norwood, NJ: Ablex.

Rossner, S. (1998). Childhood obesity and adulthood consequences. *Acta Pediatrics, 87,* 1–5.

Rothbart, M. K. (1989). Temperament and development. In G. Kohnstamm, J. Bates, & M. K. Rothbart (Eds.), *Temperament in childhood* (pp. 187–247). Chichester, England: Wiley.

Rothbart, M. K., & Bates, J. E. (1998). Temperament. In W. Damon (Ed.), *Handbook of child development* (Vol. 3, pp. 105–176). New York: Wiley.

Rothbart, M. K., & Mauro, J. A. (1990). Questionnaire approaches to the study of infant temperament. In J. W. Fagen & J. Colombo (Eds.), *Individual differences in infancy: reliability, stability, and prediction* (pp. 411–429). Hillsdale, NJ: Erlbaum.

Rothbaum, F., Weisz, J., Pott, M., Miyake, K., & Kazuo, G. (2000). Attachment and culture: Security in the United States and Japan. *American Psychologist, 55,* 1093–1104.

Rothenberg, S. J., Manalo, M., Kiang, J., Khan, F., Cuellar, R., Reyes, S., Sanchez, M., Reynoso, B., Aguilar, A., Diaz, M., Acosta, S., Jauregui, M., & Johnson, C. (1999). Maternal blood lead level during pregnancy in South Central Los Angeles. *Archives of Environmental Health, 54,* 151–157.

Rotheram-Borus, M. J., & Phinney, J. S. (1990). Patterns of social expectations among Black and Mexican-American children. *Child Development, 61,* 542–556.

Rothstein, R. (1998). Bilingual education: The controversy. *Phi Delta Kappan, 79,* 672.

Rousseau, J. J. (1911). *Emile* (B. Foxley, Trans.). London: Dent. (Original work published 1762)

Rovee-Collier, C. K., Enright, M., Lucas, D., Fagan, J., & Gekoski, M. J. (1981). The forgetting of newly acquired and reactivated memories of 3-month-old infants. *Infant Behavior and Development, 4,* 317–331.

Rovee-Collier, C. K., & Fagen, J. W. (1981). The retrieval of memory in early infancy. *Advances in Infancy Research, 1,* 225–254.

Rovee-Collier, C. K., & Shyi, C. W. G. (1992). A functional and cognitive analysis of infant long-term retention. In M. L. Howe, C. J. Brainerd, & V. F. Reyna (Eds.), *Development of long-term retention* (pp. 456–494). New York: Springer-Verlag.

Rovet, J., Netley, C., Keenan, M., Bailey, J., & Stewart, D. (1996). The psychoeducational profile of boys with Klinefelter syndrome. *Journal of Learning Disabilities, 29,* 180–196.

Rowe, D. C. (1995). Genetic and cultural explanations of adolescent risk taking and problem behavior. In R. D. Ketterlinus & M. E. Lamb (Eds.), *Adolescent problem behaviors* (pp. 109–126). Hillsdale, NJ: Erlbaum.

Rowland, T. W. (1991). Effects of obesity on aerobic fitness in adolescent females. *American Journal of Diseases of Children, 145,* 764–768.

Royce, L. (1996, June 19). Grad's degree late, but sweet. *Danbury News-Times.*

Roysircar-Sodowsky, G., & Maestas, M. V. (2000). Acculturation, ethnic identity, and acculturative stress: Evidence and measurement. In R. H. Dana (Ed.), *Handbook of cross-cultural and multicultural personality assessment* (pp. 131–172). Mahwah, NJ, Erlbaum.

Rubin, K. H., & Asendorpf, J. B. (1993). Social withdrawal, inhibition, and shyness in childhood: Conceptual and definitional issues. In K. H. Rubin & J. B. Asendorpf (Eds.), *Social withdrawal, inhibition, and shyness in childhood* (pp. 3–18). Hillsdale, NJ: Erlbaum.

Rubin, K. H., Bukowski, W., & Parker, J. G. (1998). Peer interactions, relationships, and groups. In W. Damon (Ed.), *Handbook of child psychology* (Vol. 3, pp. 619–700). New York: Wiley.

Rubin, K. H., LeMare, L. J., & Lollis, S. (1990). Social withdrawal in childhood: Developmental pathways to peer rejection. In S. R. Asher & J. D. Coie (Eds.), *Peer rejection in childhood* (pp. 217–249). New York: Cambridge University Press.

Ruble, D. N., & Dweck, C. S. (1995). Self-perceptions, person conceptions, and their development. In N. Eisenberg (Ed.), *Social development* (Vol. 15, pp. 109–139). Thousand Oaks, CA: Sage.

Ruble, D. N., & Martin, C. L. (1998). Gender development. In W. Damon (Ed.), *Handbook of child psychology* (Vol. 3, pp. 933–1016). New York: Wiley.

Rudy, D., & Grusec, J. E. (2001). Correlates of authoritarian parenting in individualist and collectivist cultures and implications for understanding the transmission of values. *Journal of Cross-Cultural Psychology, 32,* 202–212.

Ruff, H. A. (1986). Components of attention during infants' manipulative exploration. *Child Development, 57,* 105–114.

Ruffman, T., Perner, J., Olson, D. R., & Doherty, M. (1993). Reflecting on scientific thinking: Children's understanding of the hypothesis-evidence relation. *Child Development, 64,* 1617–1636.

Runco, M. A. (1997). Is every child gifted? *The Roeper School, 19,* 220–224.

Runco, M. A. (1999). A longitudinal study of exceptional giftedness and creativity. *Creativity Research Journal, 12,* 161–164.

Runco, M. A., & Pritzker, S. R. (1999). *The encyclopedia of creativity.* San Diego, CA: Academic Press.

Russ, S. W. (1996). Development of creative process in children. In M. Runco (Ed.), *Creativity from childhood through adulthood: The developmental issues. New directions for child development* (pp. 31–42). San Francisco: Jossey-Bass.

Root, A. W. (2000). Precocious puberty. *Pediatric Review, 21,* 10–19.

Russell, M., Czarnecki, D. M., Cowan, R., & McPherson, E. (1991). Measures of maternal alcohol use as predictors of development in early childhood. *Alcoholism, 15,* 991–1000.

Russell, S. T., & Joyner, K. (2001). Adolescent sexual orientation and suicide risk: Evidence from a national study. *American Journal of Public Health, 91,* 1276–1281.

Rutter, M., Dunn, J., Plomin, R., Simonoff, E., Pickles, A., Maughan, B., Ormel, J., Meyer, J., & Eaves, L. (1997). Integrating nature and nurture: Implications of person-environment correlations and interactions for developmental psychopathology. *Development and Psychopathology, 9,* 335–364.

Ruusuvaara, L. (1997). Adolescent sexuality. In G. Creatsas & G. Mastorakos (Eds.), *Adolescent gynecology and endocrinology* (Vol. 816, pp. 411–413). New York: Academy of Sciences Press.

Ryan, A. S. (1997). The resurgence of breastfeeding in the United States. *Pediatrics, 99,* 1–6.

Ryan, B. A., Adams, G. R., Gullotta, T. P., Weissberg, R. P., & Hampton, R. L. (1995). *The family–school connection.* Thousand Oaks, CA: Sage.

Ryan, K. (1996). Character education in the United States. *Journal for a Just and Caring Education, 2,* 75–84.

Ryan, R. M., & Grolnick, W. S. (1986). Origins and pawns in the classroom: Self-report and projective assessments of individual differences in children's perceptions. *Journal of Personality and Social Psychology, 50,* 550–558.

Ryan, S. A., Millstein, S. G., & Irwin, C. E. (1996). Puberty questions asked by early adolescents. *Journal of Adolescent Health, 19,* 145–152.

Rydell, A. M., Hagekull, B., & Bohlin, G. (1997). Measurement of two social competence aspects in middle childhood. *Developmental Psychology, 33,* 824–833.

Rymer, R. (1993). *Genie.* New York: HarperPerennial.

Rys, G. S., & Bear, G. G. (1997). Relational aggression and peer relations: Gender and developmental issues. *Merrill-Palmer Quarterly, 43,* 87–106.

Saarni, C., Mumme, D. L., & Campos, J. J. (1998). Emotional development: Action, communication, and understanding. In W. Damon (Ed.), *Handbook of child psychology* (Vol. 3, 237–310). New York: Wiley.

Sabogal, F., Marin, G., & Otero-Sabogal, R. (1987). Hispanic familism and acculturation: What changes and what doesn't? *Hispanic Journal of Behavioral Sciences, 9,* 397–412.

Sacks, C. H., & Mergendoller, J. R. (1997). The relationship between teachers' theoretical orientation toward reading and student outcomes in kindergarten children with different initial reading abilities. *American Educational Research Journal, 34,* 721–739.

Sacks, J. J., Smith, J. D., Kaplan, K. M., Lambert, D. A., Sattin, W., & Sikes, K. (1989). The epidemiology of injuries in Atlanta day-care centers. *Journal of the American Medical Association, 262,* 1641–1645.

Sacks, O. (1970). *The man who mistook his wife for a hat.* New York: Harper & Row.

Sadker, M., & Sadker, D. (1994). *Failing at fairness: How America's schools cheat girls.* New York: Charles Scribner's Sons.

Sadler, T. W. (2000). *Langman's medical embryology.* Philadelphia: Lippincott Williams & Wilkins.

Safer, D. J., & Krager, J. M. (1994). The increased rate of stimulant treatment for hyperactive/inattentive students in secondary schools. *Pediatrics, 94,* 462–464.

Saffran, J. R., Aslin, R. N., & Newport, E. L. (1996). Statistical learning by 8-month-old infants. *Science, 274,* 1926–1928.

Saffron, L. (1996). *What about the children?* New York: Wellington House.

Sagi, A., & Hoffman, H. L. (1976). Empathic distress in the newborn. *Developmental Psychology, 12,* 15–176.

Sagrestano, L. M., McCormick, S. H., Paikoff, R. L., & Holmbeck, G. N. (1999). Pubertal development and parent–child conflict in low-income, urban, African American adolescents. *Journal of Research on Adolescence, 9,* 85–107.

Sahin, N. (1990). Research on Susam Sokagi, the Turkish coproduction. In Children's Television Workshop (Ed.), *Sesame Street research* (pp. 68–72). New York: Children's Television Workshop.

Salihu, H. M., Boos, R., & Schmidt, W. (1997). A report on 158 cases of transcervical chorionic villus sampling. *Archives of Gynecology and Obstetrics, 259,* 91–95.

Salisbury, C. L., & Palombaro, M. M. (1998). Friends and acquaintances: Evolving relationships in an inclusive elementary school. In L. H. Meyer & H. Park (Eds.), *Making friends: The influence of culture and development* (Vol. 3, pp. 81–104). Baltimore: Brookes.

Salovey, P., & Sluyter, D. J. (1997). *Emotional development and emotional intelligence.* New York: Basic Books.

Sameroff, A. J. (1987). The social context of development. In N. Eisenberg (Ed.), *Contemporary topics in developmental psychology* (pp. 273–291). New York: Wiley.

Sameroff, A. J. (1989). Principles of development and psychopathology. In A. J. Sameroff & R. N. Emde (Eds.), *Relationship disturbances in early childhood* (pp. 17–32). New York: Basic Books.

Sampaio, R. C., & Truwit, C. L. (2001). Myelination in the developing human brain. In C. A. Nelson & M. Luciana (Eds.), *Handbook of developmental cognitive neuroscience* (pp. 35–44). Cambridge, MA: MIT Press.

Sampson, E. E. (1989). The challenge of social change for psychology. Globalization and psychology's theory of the person. *American Psychologist, 44,* 914–921.

Samuels, C. A., & Ewy, R. (1985). Aesthetic perception of faces during infancy. *British Journal of Developmental Psychology, 3,* 221–228.

Samuels, H. R. (1980). The effect of an older sibling on infant locomotor exploration of a new environment. *Child Development, 51,* 607–609.

Samuelson, L. K., & Smith, L. B. (1998). Memory and attention make smart word learning. *Child Development, 69,* 94–104.

Sandy, S. V., & Cochran, K. M. (2000). The development of conflict resolution skills in children: Preschool to adolescence. In M. Deutsch & P. T. Coleman (Eds.), *The handbook of conflict resolution: Theory and practice* (pp. 316–342). San Francisco: Jossey-Bass.

Sargent, J. D., & Dalton, M. (2001). Does parental disapproval of smoking prevent adolescents from becoming established smokers? *Pediatrics, 108,* 1256–1262.

Sattler, J. M. (2001). *Assessment of children: Cognitive applications.* San Diego: Sattler.

Savin-Williams, R. C. (1994). Verbal and physical abuse as stressors in the lives of lesbian, gay male, and bisexual youths: Associations with school problems, running away, substance abuse, prostitution, and suicide. *Journal of Consulting and Clinical Psychology, 62,* 261–269.

Savin-Williams, R. C. (1995). An exploratory study of pubertal maturation timing and self-esteem among gay and bisexual male youths. *Developmental Psychology, 31,* 56–64.

Savin-Williams, R. C. (2001). *Mom, dad. I'm gay. How families negotiate coming out.* Washington, DC: American Psychological Association.

Savin-Williams, R. C., & Cohen, K. M. (1996). Psychosocial outcomes of verbal and physical abuse among lesbian, gay, and bisexual youths. In R. C. Savin-Williams & K. M. Cohen (Eds.), *The lives of lesbians, gays, and bisexuals: Children to adults* (pp. 181–200). Fort Worth, TX: Harcourt Brace.

Savin-Williams, R. C., & Diamond, L. M. (1999). Sexual orientation. In W. K. Silverman & T. H. Ollendick (Eds.), *Developmental issues in the clinical treatment of children* (pp. 241–258). Needham Heights, MA: Allyn & Bacon.

Savin-Williams, R. C., & Esterberg, K. G. (2000). Lesbian, gay, and bisexual families. In D. H. Demo & K. R. Allen (Eds.), *Handbook of family diversity* (pp. 197–215). New York: Oxford University Press.

Scahill, L., & deGraft, J. A. (1997). Food allergies, asthma, and attention deficit hyperactivity disorder. *Journal of Child and Adolescent Psychiatric Nursing, 10,* 36–42.

Scaramella, L. V., Conger, R. D., & Simons, R. L. (1999). Parental protective influences and gender-specific increases in adolescent internalizing and externalizing problems. *Journal of Research on Adolescence, 9,* 111–141.

Scarr, S. (1998). American child care today. *American Psychologist, 53,* 95–109.

Scarr, S., Eisenberg, M., & Deater-Deckard, K. (1994). Measure quality in child care centers. *Early Childhood Research Quarterly, 9,* 131–151.

Scarr, S., & McCartney, K. (1984). How people make their own environment: A theory of genotype-environment effects. *Child Development, 54,* 424–435.

Schaefer, C. E., & DiGeronimo, T. F. (1995, September). Understanding anger. *Child,* 48–55.

Schauble, L. (1990). Belief revision in children: The role of prior knowledge and strategies for generating evidence. *Journal of Experimental Child Psychology, 49,* 31–57.

Schebendach, J., & Shenker, I. R. (1992). Nutrition. In S. B. Friedman, M. Fisher, & S. K. Schonberg (Eds.), *Comprehensive adolescent health care* (pp. 206–212). St. Louis, MO: Quality Medical Publishing.

Scheel, K. R., & Westefeld, J. S. (1999). Heavy metal music and adolescent suicidality: An empirical investigation. *Adolescence, 34,* 253–273.

Scheier, L. M., Botvin, G. J., Griffin, K. W., & Diaz, T. (2000). Dynamic growth models of self-esteem and adolescent alcohol use. *Journal of Early Adolescence, 20,* 178–209.

Schepher-Hughes, N. (1987). Basic strangeness: Maternal estrangement and infant death. In C. Super (Ed.), *The role of culture in developmental disorders* (pp. 131–153). San Diego, CA: Academic Press.

Scher, M. S., Richardson, G. A., & Day, N. L. (2000). Effects of prenatal cocaine/crack and other drug exposure on electroencephalographic sleep studies at birth and one year. *Pediatrics, 105,* 39–48.

Schiff-Myers, N. (1988). Hearing children of deaf parents. In D. Bishop & K. Mogford (Eds.), *Language development in exceptional circumstances* (pp. 47–61). New York: Churchill Livingstone.

Schlottmann, A. (1999). Seeing it happen and knowing how it works: How children understand the relation between perceptual causality and underlying mechanisms. *Developmental Psychology, 35,* 303–317.

Schmitt, R. E., & Vondracek, F. W. (1999). Breadth of interests, exploration, and identity development in adolescence. *Journal of Vocational Behavior, 55,* 298–317.

Schneider, B. (1993). *Children's social competence in context.* New York: Pergamon Press.

Schneider, K. (1997). Development of emotions and their expression in task-oriented situations in infants and preschool children. In U. C. Segerstrale & P. Molnar (Eds.), *Nonverbal communication: Where nature meets culture* (pp. 109–130). Hillsdale, NJ: Erlbaum.

Schneider, W., & Bjorklund, D. F. (1998). Memory. In W. Damon (Ed.), *Handbook of child psychology* (Vol. 2, pp. 467–521). New York: Wiley.

Schoenhals, M., Tienda, M., & Schneider, B. (1998). The educational and personal consequences of adolescent employment. *Social Forces, 77,* 723–762.

Schothorst, P. F., & van Engeland, H. (1996). Long-term behavioral sequelae of prematurity. *Journal of the American Academy of Child and Adolescent Psychiatry, 35,* 175–183.

Schultz, R. T., Wright, K., & Schleifer, M. (1986). Assignment of moral responsibility and punishment. *Child Development, 57,* 177–184.

Schuster, B., Ruble, D. N., & Weinert, F. E. (1998). Causal inferences and the positivity bias in children: The role of the covariation principle. *Child Development, 69,* 1577–1596.

Schutte, N. S., Malouff, J. M., Post-Gordon, J. C., & Rodasta, A. L. (1988). Effects of playing video games on children's aggressive and other behaviors. *Journal of Applied Social Psychology, 18,* 103–109.

Schwartz, C. E., Snidman, N., & Kagan, J. (1996). Early childhood temperament as a determinant of externalizing behavior in adolescence. *Development and Psychology, 8,* 527–537.

Schwartz, J. A., Gladstone, T. R. G., & Kaslow, N. J. (1998). Depressive disorders. In T. H. Ollendick & M. Hersen (Eds.), *Handbook of child psychopathology* (pp. 269–289). New York: Plenum.

Schwartz, J. A., Kaslow, N. J., Racusin, G. R., & Carton, E. R. (1998). Interpersonal family therapy for childhood depression. In V. B. Van Hasselt & M. Hersen (Eds.), *Handbook of psychological treatment protocols for children and adolescents* (pp. 109–151). Mahwah, NJ: Erlbaum.

Schwartz, W. (1995). School dropouts: New information about an old problem. *ERIC Digest* (No. ED 386 515).

Schwebel, D. C., Plumert, J. M., & Pick, H. L. (2000). Integrating basic and applied developmental research: A new model for the twenty-first century. *Child Development, 71,* 222–230.

Scopesi, A., Zanobini, M., & Carossino, P. (1997). Childbirth in different cultures: Psychophysical reactions of women delivering in US, German, French, and Italian hospitals. *Journal of Reproductive and Infant Psychology, 15,* 9–30.

Sebald, H. (1992). *Adolescence: A social psychological analysis.* Englewood Cliffs, NJ: Prentice-Hall.

Sedlak, A. J., & Broadhurst, D. D. (1996). *Executive summary of the Third National Incidence Study of Child Abuse and Neglect.* Washington, DC: US Department of Health and Human Services.

Segall, M. H., Dasen, P. R., Berry, J. W., & Poortinga, Y. H. (1990). *Human behavior in global perspective: An introduction to cross-cultural psychology.* New York: Pergamon Press.

Seidenberg, M. S. (1997). Language acquisition and use: Learning and applying probabilistic constraints. *Science, 275,* 1599–1603.

Seifer, R., & Schiller, M. (1995). The role of parenting sensitivity, infant temperament, and dyadic interaction in attachment theory and assessment. *Monographs of the Society for Research in Child Development, 60,* 146–174.

Seifer, R., Schiller, M., Sameroff, A. J., Resnick, S., & Riordan, K. (1996). Attachment, maternal sensitivity, and infant temperament during the first year of life. *Developmental Psychology, 32,* 12–25.

Seiffge-Krenke, I. (1993). Close friendship and imaginary companions in adolescence. *New Directions in Child Development, 60,* 73–87.

Seiffge-Krenke, I. (1997). The capacity to balance intimacy and conflict: Differences in romantic relationships between healthy and diabetic adolescents. In S. Shulman & W. A. Collins (Eds.), *Romantic relationships in adolescence* (pp. 53–68). San Francisco: Jossey-Bass.

Sell, M. A., Ray, G. E., & Lovelace, L. (1995). Preschool children's comprehension of a *Sesame Street* video tape: The effects of repeated viewing and previewing instructions. *Educational Technology Research and Development, 43,* 49–60.

Sells, C. W., & Blum, R. W. (1996). Morbidity and mortality among U.S. adolescents: An overview of data and trends. *American Journal of Public Health, 86,* 513–519.

Selman, R. L. (1980). *The growth of interpersonal understanding.* New York: Academic Press.

Selman, R. L., Beardslee, W., Schultz, L. H., Krupa, M., & Podorefsky, D. (1986). Assessing adolescent interpersonal negotiation strategies: Toward the integration of structural and functional models. *Developmental Psychology, 22,* 450–459.

Selman, R. L., Lavin, D. R., & Brion-Meisels, S. (1982). Troubled children's use of self-reflection. In F. C. Serafica (Ed.), *Social-cognitive development in context.* London: Methuen.

Serketich, W. J., & Dumas, J. E. (1997). Adults' perceptions of the behavior of competent and dysfunctional children based on the children's physical appearance. *Behavior Modification, 21,* 457–469.

Sessa, F. M., & Steinberg, L. (1991). Family structure and the development of autonomy during adolescence. *Journal of Early Adolescence, 11,* 38–55.

Setterberg, S. R. (1992). Suicidal behavior and suicide. In S. B. Friedman, M. Fisher, & S. K. Schonberg (Eds.), *Comprehensive adolescent health care* (pp. 862–867). St. Louis, MO: Quality Medical Publishing.

Shavinina, L. (1997). Extremely early high abilities, sensitive periods, and development of giftedness. *High Ability Studies, 8,* 247–258.

Shaw, D., & Winslow, E. B. (1997). Precursors and correlates of antisocial behavior from infancy to preschool. In D. M. Stoff & J. Breiling (Eds.), *Handbook of antisocial behavior* (pp. 148–158). New York: Wiley.

Shedler, J., & Block, J. (1990). Adolescent drug use and psychological health: A longitudinal inquiry. *American Psychologist, 45,* 612–630.

Sheehy, G. (1995). *New passages: Mapping your life across time.* New York: Random House.

Shepard, L. A. (1997). Children are not ready to learn? The invalidity of school readiness testing. *Psychology in the Schools, 34,* 85–97.

Shepardson, D. P., & Pizzini, E. L. (1992). Gender bias in female elementary teachers' perceptions of the scientific ability of students. *Science Education, 76,* 147–163.

Sherrod, L. R., Haggerty, R. J., & Featherman, D. L. (1993). Introduction: Late adolescence and the transition to adulthood. *Journal of Research on Adolescence, 3,* 216–226.

Sherry, J. L. (2001). The effects of violent video games on aggression: A meta-analysis. *Human Communication Research, 27,* 409–431.

Shettles, L., & Rorvik, D. M. (1984). *How to choose the sex of your baby.* New York: Doubleday.

Shields, M. K., & Behrman, R. E. (2000). Children and computer technology: Analysis and recommendations. *Future of Children, 10,* 191–196.

Shifflett, K., & Cummings, E. M. (1999). A program for educating parents about the effects of divorce and conflict on children. *Family Relations, 48,* 79–89.

Shrum, W., Cheek, N. H., & Hunter, S. M. (1988). Friendship in school: Gender and racial homophily. *Sociology of Education, 61,* 227–239.

Shucard, D. W., Shucard, L. L., & Thomas, D. G. (1987). Sex differences in electrophysiological activity in infancy: Possible implications for language development. In S. U. Philips, S. Steele, & C. Tanz (Eds.), *Language, gender, and sex in a comparative perspective* (pp. 278–295). Cambridge, England: Cambridge University Press.

Shulman, S., Collins, W. A., & Knafo, D. (1997). Romantic relationships in adolescence—more than casual dating. In S. Shulman & W. A. Collins (Eds.), *Romantic relationships in adolescence* (pp. 105–110). San Francisco: Jossey-Bass.

Shulman, S., Kedem, P., Kaplan, K. J., Sever, I., & Braja, M. (1998). Latchkey children: Potential sources of support. *Journal of Community Psychology, 26*, 185–197.

Shulman, S., & Seiffge-Krenke, I. (2001). Adolescent romance: Between experience and relationships. *Journal of Adolescence, 24*, 417–428.

Shurkin, J. N. (1992). *Terman's kids.* Boston: Little, Brown.

Shute, N. (1997, November 10). No more hard labor. *U.S. News & World Report*, 92–95.

Shwe, H., & Markman, E. M. (1997). Young children's appreciation of the mental impact of their communicative signals. *Developmental Psychology, 33*, 630–636.

Sidebotham, P. (2000). Patterns of child abuse in early childhood: A cohort study of the "children of the nineties." *Child Abuse Review, 9*, 311–320.

Siegler, R. S. (1996). *Emerging minds: The process of change in children's thinking.* New York: Oxford University Press.

Siegler, R. S. (1998). *Children's thinking.* New York: Prentice-Hall.

Siegler, R. S., & Shipley, C. (1995). Variation, selection, and cognitive change. In T. Simon and G. Halford (Eds.), *Developing cognitive competence: New approaches to process modeling.* Hillsdale, NJ: Erlbaum.

Sigal, J. J., & Weinfeld, M. (2001). Do children cope better than adults with potentially traumatic stress? A 40-year follow-up of Holocaust survivors. *Psychiatry: Interpersonal and Biological Processes, 64*, 69–80.

Sigman, M., Beckwith, L., Cohen, S. E., & Parmelee, A. H. (1989). Stability in the biosocial development of the child born preterm. In M. H. Bornstein & N. A. Krasnegor (Eds.), *Stability and continuity in mental development* (pp. 29–42). Hillsdale, NJ: Erlbaum.

Signorella, M. L., Bigler, R. S., & Liben, L. S. (1993). Developmental differences in children's gender schemata about others: A meta-analytic review. *Developmental Review, 13*, 147–183.

Signorella, M. L., Bigler, R. S., & Liben, L. S. (1998). A meta-analysis of children's memories for own-sex and other-sex information. *Journal of Applied Developmental Psychology, 18*, 429–445.

Signorella, M. L., & Liben, L. S. (1984). Recall and reconstruction of gender-related pictures: Effects of attitudes, task difficulty, and age. *Child Development, 55*, 393–405.

Silber, T. J. (1986). Anorexia nervosa in blacks and Hispanics. *International Journal of Eating Disorders, 5*, 121–128.

Silver, L. (1999). *Human cloning.* Alexandria, VA: PBS.

Silverberg, S. B., & Gondoli, D. M. (1996). Autonomy in adolescence: A contextual perspective. In G. R. Adams & R. Montemayor (Eds.), *Psychosocial development during adolescence* (Vol. 8, pp. 12–61). Thousand Oaks, CA: Sage.

Silverman, W. K., La Greca, A. M., & Wasserstein, S. (1995). What do children worry about? Worries and their relation to anxiety. *Child Development, 66*, 671–686.

Silverthorn, P., & Frick, P. J. (1999). Developmental pathways to antisocial behavior: The delayed-onset pathway in girls. *Development and Psychopathology, 11*, 101–126.

Simeon, D. T., & Grantham-McGregor, S. (1990). Nutritional deficiencies and children's behavior and mental development. *Nutrition Research Reviews, 3*, 1–24.

Simmons, R. G., & Blyth D. A. (1987). *Moving into adolescence: The impact of pubertal change and school context.* New York: Aldine de Gruyter.

Simmons, R. G., Burgeson, R., Carlton-Ford, S., & Blyth, D. (1987). The impact of cumulative change in early adolescence. *Child Development, 58*, 1220–1234.

Simmons Marketing Research. (1998). *Simmons teen age research study.* New York: Simmons Marketing Research.

Simon, W., & Gagnon, J. H. (1986). Sexual scripts: Permanence and change. *Archives of Sexual Behavior, 15*, 97–120.

Simons, R. L., Johnson, C., & Conger, R. D. (1994). Harsh corporal punishment versus quality of parental involvement as an explanation of adolescent maladjustment. *Journal of Marriage and the Family, 56*, 591–607.

Simons, R. L., Lin, K. H., Gordon, L. C., Conger, R. D., & Lorenz, F. O. (1999). Explaining the higher incidence of adjustment problems among children of divorce compared with those in two-parent families. *Journal of Marriage and the Family, 61*, 1020–1033.

Simonton, D. K. (1994). *Greatness: Who makes history and why.* New York: Guilford.

Simpson, J. L., & Elias, S. (1994). Fetal cells in maternal blood: Overview and historical perspective. *Annals of the New York Academy of Sciences, 731*, 1–8.

Singer, D. G., & Singer, J. L. (2001). *Handbook of children and the media.* Thousand Oaks, CA: Sage.

Singer, L. T., Salvator, A., Guo, S., Colling, M., Lilen, L., & Baley, J. (1999). Maternal psychological distress and parenting stress after the birth of a very low-birth-weight infant. *Journal of the American Medical Association, 28*, 799–805.

Singer, R. S. (1992). Physical activity and psychological benefits: A position statement of the International Society of Sport Psychology (ISSP). *The Sports Psychologist, 6*, 199–203.

Singh, S., & Darroch, J. E. (1999). Trends in sexual activity among adolescent American women: 1982–1995. *Family Planning Perspectives, 31*, 211–219.

Sizer, F., & Whitney, E. (1997). *Nutrition: Concepts and controversies.* Belmont, CA: West.

Skinner, B. F. (1957). *Verbal behavior.* New York: Appleton-Century-Crofts.

Skinner, E. A., & Wellborn, J. G. (1997). Children's coping in the academic domain. In S. A. Wolchik & I. N. Sandler (Eds.), *Handbook of children's coping* (pp. 387–422). New York: Plenum.

Skoe, E. E. A., Hansen, K. L., Morch, W., Bakke, I., Hoffmann, T., Larsen, B., & Aasheim, M. (1999). Care-based moral reasoning in Norwegian and Canadian early adolescents. *Journal of Early Adolescence, 19*, 280–291.

Skuse, D., Wolke, D., & Reilly, S. (1992). Failure to thrive: Clinical and developmental aspects. In H. Remschmidt & M. H. Schmidt (Eds.), *Developmental psychopathology* (pp. 46–71). Goettingen, Germany: Hogrefe & Huber.

Slade, A., & Wolf, D. P. (1994). *Children at play: Clinical and developmental approaches to meaning and representation.* New York: Oxford University Press.

Slater, A., Mattock, A., Brown, E., & Bremner, G. J. (1991). Form perception at birth: Cohen and Younger revisited. *Journal of Experimental Child Psychology, 51*, 395–406.

Slavin, R. E. (1997). When does cooperative learning increase student achievement? In E. Dubinsky & D. Mathews (Eds.), *Readings in cooperative learning for undergraduate mathematics* (pp. 71–84). Washington, DC: The Mathematical Association of America.

Sleep, J. (1993). Physiology and management of the second stage of labor. In V. R. Bennett & L. K. Brown (Eds.), *Myles textbook for midwives* (pp. 199–215). London: Churchill Livingstone.

Slotkin, T. A., Kudlacz, E. M., Hou, Q. C., & Seidler, F. J. (1990). Maturation of the sympathetic nervous system: Role in neonatal physiological adaptations and in cellular development of peripheral tissues. In J. M. Cuezva, A. M. Pascual-Leone, & M. S. Patel (Eds.), *Endocrine and biochemical development of the fetus and neonate* (pp. 67–75). New York: Plenum.

Slotkin, T. A., & Seidler, F. J. (1989). Catecholamines and stress in the newborn. In O. Zinder & S. Berznitz (Eds.), *Molecular biology of stress* (pp. 133–142). New York: A. R. Liss.

Small, M. Y. (1990). *Cognitive development.* San Diego, CA: Harcourt Brace Jovanovich.

Small, S. S., Eastman, G., & Cornelius, S. (1988). Adolescent autonomy and parental stress. *Journal of Personality and Social Psychology, 17*, 377–391.

Smetana, J. G. (1988). Adolescents' and parents' conceptions of parental authority. *Child Development, 59*, 321–335.

Smetana, J. G. (2000). Middle-class African American adolescents' and parents' conceptions of parental authority and parenting practices: A longitudinal investigation. *Child Development, 71,* 1672–1686.

Smetana, J. G., & Gaines, C. (1999). Adolescent-parent conflict in middle-class African American families. *Child Development, 70,* 1447–1463.

Smith, B. A., & Blass, E. M. (1996). Taste-mediated calming in premature, preterm, and full-term human infants. *Developmental Psychology, 32,* 1084–1089.

Smith, F. (1992). Learning to read: The never-ending debate. *Phi Delta Kappan, 74,* 432–441.

Smith, G. A., Bowman, M. J., Luria, J. W., & Shields, B. J. (1997). Babywalker-related injuries continue despite warning labels and public education. *Pediatrics, 100,* 1–7.

Smith, G. A., & Shields, B. J. (1998). Trampoline-related injuries to children. *Archives of Pediatric and Adolescent Medicine, 152,* 694–699.

Smith, P. K., & Green, M. (1974). Aggressive behavior in English nurseries and playgroups. Sex differences and response of adults. *Child Development, 45,* 211–214.

Smokowski, P. R., Reynolds, A. J., & Bezruczko, N. (1999). Resilience and protective factors in adolescence: An autobiographical perspective from disadvantaged youth. *Journal of School Psychology, 37,* 425–448.

Smolin, L. A., & Grosvenor, M. B. (2000). *Nutrition: Science and applications.* Fort Worth: Saunders.

Smulders, B. (1999). *The Dutch midwivery system.* Camperdown, Australia: Birth International.

Snarey, J. R. (1985). Cross-cultural universality of social-moral development: A critical review of Kohlbergian research. *Psychological Bulletin, 92,* 202–232.

Snow, C. E. (1990). Building memories: The ontogeny of autobiography. In D. Cicchetti & M. Beeghly (Eds.), *The self in transition* (pp. 213–242). Chicago: University of Chicago Press.

Snow, C. W. (1989). *Infant development.* Englewood Cliffs, NJ: Prentice-Hall.

Snyder, H. N. (1996). The juvenile court and delinquency cases. *The Future of Children, 6,* 53–63.

Snyder, J., Schrepferman, L., & St. Peter, C. (1997). Origins of antisocial behavior: Negative reinforcement and affect dysregulation of behavior as socialization mechanisms in family interaction. *Behavior Modification, 21,* 187–215.

Soberon, H. (1996). *Latino, Hispanic, both, neither?* Gainesville: University of Florida.

Socolar, R. R. S., & Stein, R. E. K. (1996). Maternal discipline of young children: Context, belief, and practice. *Journal of Developmental and Behavioral Pediatrics, 17,* 1–8.

Solis, J. (1995). The status of Latino children and youth: Challenges and prospects. In R. E. Zambrama (Ed.), *Understanding Latino families* (pp. 62–84). Thousand Oaks, CA: Sage.

Sonenstein, F. L., Ku, L., Lindberg, L. D., Turner, C. F., & Pleck, J. H. (1998). Changes in sexual behavior and condom use among teenaged males. *American Journal of Public Health, 88,* 956–959.

Sonis, W. A., Comite, F., Blue, J., Pescovitz, O. H., Rahn, C. W., Hench, K. D., Cutler, G. B., Jr., Loriaux, D. L., & Klein, R. P. (1985). Behavior problems and social competence in girls with precocious puberty. *Journal of Pediatrics, 106,* 156–160.

Soriano, F. I. (1993). Cultural sensitivity and gang intervention. In A. P. Goldstein & C. R. Huff (Eds.), *The gang intervention handbook* (pp. 421–462). Champaign, IL: Research Press.

Soriano, F. I. (1994). U.S. Latinos. In L. D. Eron, J. H. Gentry, & P. Schlegel (Eds.), *Reason to hope: A psychosocial perspective on violence and youth* (pp. 119–132). Washington, DC: American Psychological Association.

Sotos, J. F. (1997). Genetic-disorder with overgrowth. *Clinical Pediatrics, 36,* 37–49.

Spear, L. (2000). Modeling adolescent development and alcohol use in animals. *Alcohol Research and Health, 24,* 115–123.

Spelke, E. S., Breinlinger, K., Macomber, J., & Jacobson, K. (1992). Origins of knowledge. *Psychological Review, 99,* 605–632.

Spencer, M. B. (1990). Development of minority children: An introduction. *Child Development, 61,* 267–269.

Spencer, M. B., & Dornbusch, S. M. (1990). Challenges in studying minority youth. In S. S. Feldman & G. R. Elliott (Eds.), *At the threshold* (pp. 123–146). Cambridge, MA: Harvard University Press.

Spencer, M. B., & Markstrom-Adams, C. (1990). Identity processes among racial and ethnic minority children in America. *Child Development, 61,* 290–310.

Spergel, I. A. (1990). *Perceptions of former youth gang influentials.* Rockville, MD: Juvenile Justice Clearinghouse.

Spergel, I. A., & Curry, G. D. (1993). The National Youth Gang Survey. In A. P. Goldstein & C. R. Huff (Eds.), *The gang intervention handbook* (pp. 359–400). Champaign, IL: Research Press.

Sprafkin, J., Gadow, K. D., & Abelman, R. (1992). *Television and the exceptional child: A forgotten audience.* Hillsdale, NJ: Erlbaum.

Sprague, J., Sugai, G., & Walker, H. (1998). Antisocial behavior in schools. In T. S. Watson & F. M. Gresham (Eds.), *Handbook of child behavior therapy* (pp. 451–474). New York: Plenum.

Sprecher, S. (1989). Premarital sexual standards for different categories of individuals. *Journal of Sex Research, 26,* 232–248.

Sroufe, L. A. (1977). *Knowing and enjoying your baby.* Englewood Cliffs, NJ: Prentice-Hall.

Sroufe, L. A. (1996). *Emotional development.* Cambridge, England: Cambridge University Press.

Sroufe, L. A., Bennett, C., Englund, M., & Urban, J. (1993). The significance of gender boundaries in preadolescence: Contemporary correlates and antecedents of boundary violation and maintenance. *Child Development, 64,* 455–466.

Sroufe, L. A., & Waters, E. (1976). The ontogenesis of smiling and laughing: A perspective on the organization of development in infancy. *Psychological Review, 83,* 173–189.

Sroufe, L. A., & Waters, E. (1977). Attachment as an organizational construct. *Child Development, 48,* 1184–1199.

St. James-Roberts, I. (1993). Infant crying: Normal development and persistent crying. In I. St. James-Roberts, G. Harris, & D. Messer (Eds.), *Infant crying, feeding, and sleeping* (pp. 7–25). London: Harvester Wheatsheaf.

St. James-Roberts, I., & Halil, T. (1991). Infant crying patterns in the first year: Normative and clinical findings. *Journal of Child Psychology and Psychiatry, 32,* 951–968.

St. James-Roberts, I., & Plewis, I. (1996). Individual differences, daily fluctuations, and developmental changes in amounts of infant waking, fussing, crying, feeding, and sleeping. *Child Development, 67,* 2527–2540.

Stack, D. M., & LePage, D. E. (1996). Infants' sensitivity to manipulations of maternal touch during face-to-face interactions. *Social Development, 5,* 41–55.

Stafford, L., & Bayer, C. L. (1993). *Interaction between parents and children.* Newbury Park, CA: Sage.

Stang, H. J., Snellman, L. W., Condon, L. M., Conroy, M. M., Liebo, R., Brodersen, L., & Gunnar, M. R. (1997). Beyond dorsal penile nerve block: A more humane circumcision. *Pediatrics, 100,* 1–6.

Stangor, C., & McMillan, D. (1992). Memory for expectancy-congruent and expectancy-incongruent information. *Psychological Bulletin, 111,* 42–61.

Stangor, C., & Ruble, D. N. (1987). Development of gender role knowledge and gender constancy. In L. S. Liben and M. L. Signorella (Eds.), *Children's gender schemata* (pp. 5–22). San Francisco: Jossey-Bass.

Stangor, C., & Ruble, D. N. (1989). Differential influences on gender schemata and gender constancy on children's information processing and behavior. *Social Cognition, 7,* 353–372.

Stanley, B. K., Weikel, W. J., & Wilson, J. (1986). The effects of father absence on interpersonal problem-solving skills of nursery school children. *Journal of Counseling and Development, 64,* 383–385.

Stanley, J. C., & Benbow, C. P. (1982). Huge sex ratios at upper end. *American Psychologist, 37,* 972.

Stanley, J. C., & Benbow, C. P. (1983). SMPY's first decade: Ten years of posing problems and solving them. *Journal of Special Education, 17,* 11–25.

Stark, K. D., Rouse, L. W., & Kurowski, C. (1994). Psychological treatment approaches for depression in children. In W. M. Reynolds & H. F. Johnston (Eds.), *Handbook of depression in children and adolescents* (pp. 275–307). New York: Plenum.

Starsen, M. (1991, February 25). A team spawns pride in a land of despair. *The New York Times,* A1, A16.

State vs. Michaels, Superior Court, Essex County (New Jersey, 1988).

State v. Michaels, 136 N.J. 299, 642 A.2d 489 (New Jersey, 1994).

Status of Women Council. (1994). *Girls and science.* Yellowknife, NWF: Status of Women Council.

Steele, C. M. (1997). A threat in the air: How stereotypes shape intellectual identity and performance. *American Psychologist, 52,* 613–629.

Steele, C. M., & Aronson, J. A. (1995). Stereotype threat and the intellectual test performance of African Americans. *Journal of Personality and Social Psychology, 69,* 797–811.

Steffe, L. P., & Gale, J. E. (1995). *Constructivism in education.* Hillsdale, NJ: Erlbaum.

Stein, D. M., & Reichert, P. (1990). Extreme dieting behaviors in early adolescence. *Journal of Early Adolescence, 10,* 108–121.

Stein, N. L., & Trabasso, T. (1989). Children's understanding of changing emotional states. In C. Saarni & P. L. Harris (Eds.), *Children's understanding of emotion* (pp. 50–77). New York: Cambridge University Press.

Steinberg, L. (1987). Impact of puberty on family relations: Effects of pubertal status and pubertal timing. *Developmental Psychology, 23,* 451–460.

Steinberg, L. (1989). Pubertal maturation and parent-adolescent distance. In G. R. Adams & R. Montemayor (Eds.), *Biology of adolescent behavior and development* (pp. 71–97). Newbury Park, CA: Sage.

Steinberg, L. (1990). Autonomy, conflict, and harmony in the family relationship. In S. S. Feldman & G. R. Elliot (Eds.), *At the threshold* (pp. 255–276). Cambridge, MA: Harvard University Press.

Steinberg, L. (1996). *Adolescence.* New York: McGraw-Hill.

Steinberg, L. (2001). We know some things: Parent-adolescent relationships in retrospect and prospect. *Journal of Research on Adolescence, 11,* 1–19.

Steinberg, L., & Dornbusch, S. (1991). Negative correlates of part-time work in adolescence: Replication and elaboration. *Developmental Psychology, 17,* 304–313.

Steinberg, L., Fegley, S., & Dornbusch, S. M. (1993). Negative impact of part-time work on adolescent adjustment: Evidence from a longitudinal study. *Developmental Psychology, 29,* 171–180.

Steinberg, L., Lamborn, S. D., Darling, N., Mounts, N., & Dornbusch, S. M. (1994). Over-time change in adjustment and competence among adolescents from authoritative, authoritarian, indulgent, and neglectful families. *Child Development, 65,* 754–766.

Steinberg, L., & Levine, A. (1990). Enjoying your child's teenage years. *Temple Review,* 20–23.

Steinberg, L., Mounts, N. S., Lamborn, S. D., & Dornbusch, S. M. (1991). Authoritative parenting and adolescent adjustment across varied ecological niches. *Journal of Research on Adolescence, 1,* 19–36.

Steiner, H., McQuivey, R. W., Pavelski, R., Pitts, T., & Kraemer, H. (2000). Adolescents and sports: risk or benefit? *Clinical Pediatrics, 39,* 161–166.

Steinhausen, H. C., Meier, M., & Angst, J. (1998). The Zurich long-term outcome study of child and adolescent psychiatric disorders in males. *Psychological Medicine, 28,* 275–383.

Steissguth, A. P., Sampson, P. D., & Barr, H. M. (1989). Neurobehavioral dose-response effects of prenatal alcohol exposure in humans from infancy to adulthood. *Annals of the New York Academy of Sciences, 562,* 145–158.

Stephens, M. B., Montefalcon, R., & Lane, D. A. (2000). The maternal perspective on prenatal ultrasound. *Journal of Family Practice, 49,* 601–604.

Stern, A. E., Lynch, D. L., Oates, R. K., O'Toole, B. I., & Cooney, G. (1995). Self esteem, depression, behaviour and family functioning in sexually abused children. *Journal of Child Psychology and Psychiatry, 36,* 1077–1089.

Stern, D. (1992). *Diary of a baby.* New York: Basic Books.

Stern, S. B., & Smith, C. A. (1999). Reciprocal relationships between antisocial behavior and parenting: Implications for delinquency intervention. *Families in Society, 80,* 169–181.

Sternberg, R. J., & Wagner, R. K. (1993). The g-ocentric view of intelligence and job performance is wrong. *Current Directions in Psychological Science, 2,* 1–5.

Stevens-Simon, C., & McAnarney, E. R. (1996). Adolescent pregnancy. In R. J. DiClemente & W. B. Hansen (Eds.), *Handbook of adolescent health risk behavior* (pp. 313–332). New York: Plenum.

Stevenson, H. W. (1998a). Cultural interpretations of giftedness: The case of East Asia. In R. C. Friedman & K. B. Rogers (Eds.), *Talent in context* (pp. 61–77). Washington, DC: American Psychological Association.

Stevenson, H. W. (1998b). A study of three cultures: Germany, Japan, and the United States. *Phi Delta Kappan, 79,* 524–529.

Stevenson, H. W., Chen, C., & Lee, S. (1992). Chinese families. In J. L. Roopnarine & D. B. Carter (Eds.), *Parent-child socialization in diverse cultures* (pp. 17–34). Norwood, NJ: Ablex.

Stevenson, H. W., Chen, C., & Lee, S. (1993). Mathematics achievement in Chinese, Japanese, and American children. *Science, 259,* 53–58.

Stevenson, H. W., Chen, C., & Uttal, D. (1990). Beliefs and achievement: A study of black, white, and Hispanic children. *Child Development, 61,* 508–523.

Stevenson, H. W., & Lee, S. (1990). Contexts of achievement. *Monographs of the Society for Research in Child Development, 55* (Whole No. 221). Chicago: University of Chicago Press.

Stevenson, H. W., Lee, S., & Mu, X. (2000). Successful achievement in mathematics: China and the United States. In C. F. M. van Lieshout & P. G. Heymans (Eds.), *Developing talent across the life span* (pp. 167–183). Philadelphia: Psychology Press.

Stevenson, H. W., & Stigler, J. W. (1992). *The learning gap.* New York: Summit Books.

Stipek, D. J. (1981). Children's perceptions of their own and their classmates' ability. *Journal of Educational Psychology, 73,* 404–410.

Stipek, D. J., & Byler, P. (2001). Academic achievement and social behaviors associated with age of entry into kindergarten. *Journal of Applied Developmental Psychology, 22,* 175–189.

Stipek, D. J., Recchia, S., & McClintic, S. (1992). Self-evaluation in young children. *Monographs of the Society for Research in Child Development, 57* (Whole No. 226). Chicago: University of Chicago Press.

Stockhammer, T. F., Salzinger, S., Feldman, R. S., & Mojica, E. (2001). Assessment of the effect of physical child abuse within an ecological framework: Measurement issues. *Journal of Community Psychology, 29,* 319–344.

Stone, M. R., & Brown, B. B. (1999). Identity claims and projections: Descriptions of self and crowds in secondary school. In J. A. McLellan & M. J. V. Pugh (Eds.), *The role of peer groups in adolescent social identity: Exploring the importance of stability and change* (pp. 7–20). San Francisco: Jossey-Bass.

Straus, M. A., & Donnelly, D. A. (1994). *Beating the devil out of them: Corporal punishment in American families.* New York: Lexington Books.

Strauss, C. C., & Francis, G. (1989). Phobic disorders. In C. G. Last & M. Hersen (Eds.), *Handbook of child psychiatric diagnosis* (pp. 170–190). New York: Wiley.

Strauss, R., & Goldberg, W. A. (1999). Self and possible selves during the transition to fatherhood. *Family Psychology, 13,* 244–259.

Strauss, R. S., & Pollack, H. A. (2001). Epidemic increase in childhood overweight, 1986–1998. *JAMA, 286,* 2845–2848.

Strauss, S. (1998). Cognitive development and science education: Toward a middle level model. In W. Damon (Ed.), *Handbook of child psychology* (Vol. 4, pp. 357–399). New York: Wiley.

Straussner, J. H., & Straussner, S. L. A. (1997). Impact of community and school violence on children. In N. K. Phillips & S. L. A. Straussner (Eds.), *Children in the urban environment* (pp. 61–77). Springfield, IL: Charles C Thomas.

Streissguth, A. P. (1997). *Fetal alcohol syndrome.* Baltimore: Brookes.

Streissguth, A. P., Barr, H. M., Sampson, P. D., Darby, B. L., & Martin, D. C. (1989). IQ at age 4 in relation to maternal alcohol use and smoking during pregnancy. *Developmental Psychology, 25,* 3–11.

Strelau, J. (1994). The concepts of arousal and arousability as used in temperament studies. In J. E. Bates & T. D. Wachs (Eds.), *Temperament: In-*

dividual differences at the interface of biology and behavior (pp. 117–143). Washington, DC: American Psychological Association.

Striefel, S., Robinson, M. A., & Truhn, P. (1998). Dealing with child abuse and neglect within a comprehensive family-support program. In J. R. Lutzker (Ed.), *Handbook of child abuse and treatment* (pp. 267–289). New York: Plenum.

Stringer, P. (1998). One night Vygotsky had a dream: Implications for educational psychologists. *Educational and Child Psychology, 15,* 14–20.

Strober, M., McCracken, J., & Hanna, G. (1991). Affective disorders. In R. M. Lerner, A. C. Petersen, & J. Brooks-Gunn (Eds.), *Encyclopedia of adolescence* (pp. 18–25). New York: Garland.

Strom, R., Strom, S., Strom, P., & Collinsworth, P. (1994). Parent competence in families with gifted children. *Journal for the Education of the Gifted, 18,* 39–54.

Stromswold, K. (2000). The cognitive neuroscience of language acquisition. In M. Gazzaniga (Ed.), *The new cognitive neurosciences,* 2nd ed., (pp. 897–932). Cambridge, MA: MIT Press.

Strouse, J. S., & Fabes, R. A. (1987). A conceptualization of transition to non-virginity in adolescent females. *Journal of Adolescent Research, 2,* 331–348.

Suber, C. F. (1982). Separable effects of motives, consequences, and presentation order on children's moral judgments. *Developmental Psychology, 18,* 257–266.

Super, C. M., & Harkness, S. (1991). The development of affect in infancy and childhood. In M. Woodhead & R. Carr (Eds.), *Becoming a person: Child development in social context* (Vol. 1, pp. 56–73). London: Routledge.

Surgeon General. (1996). *Physical activity and health.* Washington, DC: US Department of Health.

Susman, E. J., Dorn, L. D., & Chrousos, G. P. (1991). Negative affect and hormone levels in young adolescents. *Journal of Youth and Adolescence, 20,* 167–190.

Susman, E. J., Koch, P. B., Maney, D. W., & Finkelstein, J. W. (1993). Health promotion in adolescence: Developmental and theoretical considerations. In R. M. Lerner (Ed.), *Early adolescence: Perspectives on research, policy, and intervention* (pp. 247–260). Hillsdale, NJ: Erlbaum.

Susman-Stillman, A., Kalkose, M., Egeland, B., & Waldman, I. (1996). Infant temperament and maternal sensitivity as predictors of attachment security. *Infant Behavior and Development, 19,* 33–47.

Sutton, H. E. (1988). *An introduction to human genetics.* San Diego: Harcourt Brace Jovanovich.

Sutton-Smith, B. (1994). Does play prepare the future? In J. H. Goldstein (Ed.), *Toys, play, and child development* (pp. 130–146). Cambridge, England: Cambridge University Press

Sutton-Smith, B. (1998). *The ambiguity of play.* Cambridge, MA: Harvard University Press.

Swarr, A. E., & Richards, M. H. (1996). Longitudinal effects of adolescent girls' pubertal development, perceptions of pubertal timing, and parental relations on eating patterns. *Developmental Psychology, 32,* 636–646.

Synnott, A. (1988). Little angels, little devils: A sociology of children. In G. Handel (Ed.), *Childhood socialization* (pp. 25–43). Hawthorne, NY: Aldine de Gruyter.

Szagun, G. (1992). Children's understanding of the feeling experience and causes of sympathy. *Journal of Child Psychology and Psychiatry, 33,* 1183–1191.

Szapocznik, J., & Kurtines, W. (1993). Family psychology and cultural diversity: Opportunities for theory, research, and application. *American Psychologist, 48,* 400–407.

Taffel, S. M., Placek, P. J., & Moien, M. (1989). Cesarean section rate levels off in 1987. *Family Planning Perspective, 21,* 227–228.

Tager-Flusberg, H. (1994). *Constraints on language acquisition: Studies of atypical children.* Mahwah, NJ: Erlbaum.

Takahashi, K. (1990). Are the key assumptions of the "Strange Situation" procedure universal? A view from Japanese research. *Human Development, 30,* 23–30.

Tamis-LeMonda, C. S., Bornstein, M. H., Cyphers, L., Toda, S., & Ogino, M. (1992). Language and play at one year: A comparison of toddlers and mothers in the United States and Japan. *International Journal of Behavioral Development, 15,* 33–45.

Tangney, J. P. (1990). Sharing shame and guilt. *Contemporary Social Psychology, 14,* 83–88.

Tangney, J. P. (1999). The self-conscious emotions: Shame, guilt, embarrassment and pride. In T. Dalgleish & M. J. Power (Eds.), *Handbook of cognition and emotion* (pp. 541–568). New York: Wiley.

Tanner, J. M. (1975). Growth and endocrinology of the adolescent. In L. Gardner (Ed.), *Endocrine and genetic diseases of childhood* (pp. 77–121). Philadelphia: Saunders.

Tanner, J. M. (1989). *Fetus into man.* Cambridge, MA: Harvard University Press.

Tanner, J. M. (1991). Growth spurt, adolescent I. In R. M. Lerner, A. C. Petersen, & J. Brooks-Gunn (Eds.) *Encyclopedia of adolescence* (Vol. 1, pp. 277–303). New York: Garland.

Tanner, J. M., & Davies, P. S. (1985). Clinical longitudinal standards for height and height velocity for North American children. *Journal of Pediatrics, 107,* 317–329.

Tappan, M. B. (1998). Sociocultural psychology and caring pedagogy: Exploring Vygotsky's "hidden curriculum." *Educational Psychologist, 33,* 23–33.

Tarrant, M., North, A. C., & Hargreaves, D. J. (2000). English and American adolescents' reasons for listening to music. *Psychology of Music, 28,* 166–173.

Tasker, F. L., & Golombok, S. (1997). *Growing up in a lesbian family.* New York: Guilford.

Tatzer, E., Schubert, M. T., Timischl, W., & Simbruner, G. (1985). Discrimination of taste and preference for sweet in premature babies. *Early Human Development, 12,* 23–30.

Taubman, B. (1997). Toilet training and toileting refusal for stool only: A prospective study. *Pediatrics, 99,* 54–58.

Taylor, E. (1995). Dysfunctions of attention. In D. Cicchetti & D. J. Cohen (Eds.), *Developmental psychopathology* (Vol. 2, pp. 243–273). New York: Wiley.

Taylor, H. G., Klein, N., & Hack, M. (1994). Academic functioning in < 750 gm birthweight children who have normal cognitive abilities: Evidence for specific learning disabilities. *Pediatric Research, 35,* 289.

Taylor, J. A., & Bell, D. A. (1998). *Gene-gene-environment: New insight into smoking-induced bladder cancer.* Washington, DC: NIEHS.

Taylor, J. A., & Sanderson, M. (1995). A reexamination of the risk factors for the sudden infant death syndrome. *Journal of Pediatrics, 126,* 887–891.

Taylor, M., & Carlson, S. M. (1997). The relation between individual differences in fantasy and theory of mind. *Child Development, 68,* 436–455.

Taylor, M., & Hort, B. C. (1990). Can children be trained to make the appearance-reality distinction? *Cognitive Development, 5,* 89–99.

Taylor, R. D. (1995). Social contextual influence on family relations: Adolescent adjustment and competence in African-American families. In M. L. Maher & P. R. Pintrich (Eds.), *Advances in motivation and achievement* (Vol. 9, 229–253). Greenwich, CT: JAI Press.

Teale, W. H., & Sulzby, E. (1985). *Emergent literacy: Writing and reading.* Exeter, NH: Heinemann Educational Books.

Tebes, J. K., Kaufman, J. S., Adnopoz, J., & Racusin, G. (2001). Resilience and family psychosocial processes among children of parents with serious mental disorders. *Journal of Child and Family Studies, 10,* 115–136.

Telama, R., Yang, X., Laakso, L., & Viikari, J. (1997). Physical activity in childhood and adolescence as predictors of physical activity in young adulthood. *American Journal of Preventive Medicine, 13,* 317–323.

Tellegen, A. (1988). The analysis of consistency in personality assessment. *Journal of Personality, 56,* 621–663.

Terman, L. M. (1925). *Genetic studies of genius.* Stanford, CA: Stanford University Press.

Terman, L. M., & Oden, M. H. (1959). *The gifted group in midlife: Thirty-year follow-up of the superior child.* Stanford, CA: Stanford University Press.

Teti, D. M. (1992). Sibling interaction. In V. B. Van Hesselt & M. Hersen (Eds.), *Handbook of social development* (pp. 201–228). New York: Plenum.

Teti, D. M., Sakin, J. W., Kucera, K., Corns, K. M., & Eiden, R. D. (1996). And baby makes four: Predictors of attachment security among preschoolage firstborns during the transition to siblinghood. *Child Development, 67,* 579–596.

Thelen, E. (1989). Self-organization in developmental processes: Can systems approaches work? In M. Gunnar & E. Thelen (Eds.), *Systems in development* (Vol. 22, pp. 77–117). Hillsdale, NJ: Erlbaum.

Thelen, E., & Smith, L. B. (1994). *A dynamic systems approach to the development of cognition and action.* Cambridge, MA: MIT Press.

Thelen, E., & Smith, L. B. (1998). Dynamic systems theories. In W. Damon (Ed.), *Handbook of child psychology* (Vol. 1, pp. 563–633). New York: Wiley.

Thoma, S. J., & Rest, J. R. (1999). The relationship between moral decision making and patterns of consolidation and transition in moral judgment development. *Developmental Psychology, 35,* 323–334.

Thoman, E. B. (1990). Sleeping and waking state in infants: A functional perspective. *Neuroscience and Biobehavioral Review, 14,* 93–107.

Thoman, E. B., & Whitney, M. P. (1989). Sleep states of infants monitored in the home: Individual differences, developmental trends, and origins of diurnal cyclicity. *Infant Behavior and Development, 12,* 59–75.

Thoman, E. B., & Whitney, M. P. (1990). Behavior states in infants: Individual differences and individual analyses. In J. Colombo & J. Fagen (Eds.), *Individual differences in infancy: Reliability, stability, prediction* (pp. 113–136). Hillsdale, NJ: Erlbaum.

Thomas, A., & Chess, S. (1970). The origins of personality. *Scientific American, 223,* 102–109.

Thomas, A., & Chess, S. (1977). *Temperament and development.* New York: Brunner/Mazel.

Thomas, A., & Chess, S. (1985). The behavioral study of temperament. In J. Strelau, F. Farley, & A. Gale (Eds.), *The biological bases of personality and behavior* (Vol. 1, pp. 213–225). Washington, DC: Hemisphere.

Thomas, A., Chess, S., & Birch, H. G. (1968). *Temperament and behavior disorders in childhood.* New York: New York University Press.

Thomas, J. R., & French, K. E. (1985). Gender differences across age in motor performance: A meta-analysis. *Psychological Bulletin, 98,* 260–282.

Thomas, M. H. (2000). Abstinence-based programs for prevention of adolescent pregnancies. *Journal of Adolescent Health, 26,* 5–17.

Thomas, R. M. (1996). *Comparing theories of child development.* Belmont, CA: Wadsworth.

Thompson, K. P. (1993). Media, music, and adolescents. In R. M. Lerner (Ed.), *Early adolescence: Perspectives on research, policy, and intervention* (pp. 407–418). Hillsdale, NJ: Erlbaum.

Thompson, R. A. (1991). Infant day care: Concerns, controversies, choices. In J. V. Lerner & N. L. Galambos (Eds.), *Employed mothers and their children* (pp. 9–36). New York: Garland.

Thompson, R. A. (1998). Early sociopersonality development. In W. Damon (Ed.), *Handbook of child psychology* (Vol. 3, pp. 25–104). New York: Wiley.

Thompson, R. A. (1999). Early attachment and later development. In J. Cassidy & P. R. Shaver (Eds.), *Handbook of attachment* (pp. 265–286). New York: Guilford.

Thompson, R. A., & Nelson, C. A. (2001). Developmental science and the media: Early brain development. *American Psychologist, 56,* 5–15.

Thompson, R., & Zuroff, D. C. (1998). Dependent and self-critical mothers' responses to adolescent autonomy and competence. *Personality and Individual Differences, 24,* 311–324.

Thompson, S. C., Sobowlew-Shubin, A., Graham, M. A., & Janigan, A. S. (1989). Psychosocial adjustment following a stroke. *Social Science and Medicine, 28,* 239–247.

Thornberry, T. P., Smith, C. A., & Howard, G. J. (1997). Risk factors for teenage fatherhood. *Journal of Marriage and the Family, 59,* 505–520.

Thorne, B., & Luria, Z. (1986). Sexuality and gender in children's daily worlds. *Social Problems, 33,* 176–190.

Thornton, M. C., Chatters, L. M., Taylor, R. J., & Allen, W. R. (1990). Sociodemographic and environmental correlates of racial socialization by Black parents. *Child Development, 61,* 401–409.

Thorogood, P. (1997). *Embryos, genes, and birth defects.* New York: John Wiley & Sons.

Thorp, J. A., & Breedlove, G. (1996). Epidural analgesia in labor: An evaluation of risks and benefits. *Birth, 23,* 63–83.

Thorpe, K. J., Dragonas, T., & Golding, J. (1992). The effects of psychosocial factors on the mother's emotional well-being during early parenthood: A cross-cultural study of Britain and Greece. *Journal of Reproductive and Infant Psychology, 10,* 205–217.

Tilford, C. A., Kuroda-Kawaguchi, T., Skaletsky, H., Rozen, S., Brown, L. G., Rosenberg, M., McPherson, J. D., Wylie, K., Sekhon, M., Kucaba, T. A., Waterston, R. H., & Page, D. C. (2001). A physical map of the human Y chromosome. *Nature, 409,* 943–945.

Time. (1993, Fall). Special issue, September 8–9 poll. *Time,* 10.

Tobin-Richards, M. H., Boxer, A. M., & Petersen, A. C. (1983). The psychological significance of pubertal change: Sex differences in perceptions of self during early adolescence. In J. Brooks-Gunn & A. C. Petersen (Eds.), *Girls at puberty* (pp. 113–134). New York: Plenum Press.

Tolan, P. H., & Loeber, R. L. (1993). Antisocial behavior. In P. H. Tolan & B. J. Cohler (Eds.), *Handbook of clinical research and clinical practice with adolescents* (pp. 307–331). New York: Wiley.

Tom, D., & Cooper, H. (1986). The effect of student background on teacher performance attributions. *Basic and Applied Social Psychology, 7,* 53–62.

Tomada, G., & Schneider, B. H. (1997). Relational aggression, gender, and peer acceptance: Invariance across culture, stability over time, and concordance among informants. *Developmental Psychology, 33,* 601–609.

Tomasello, M. (1992). The social bases of language acquisition. *Social Development, 1,* 67–87.

Tomasello, M., & Akhtar, N. (1995). Two-year-olds use pragmatic cues to differentiate reference to objects and actions. *Cognitive Psychology, 10,* 201–224.

Tomasello, M., & Mannie, S. (1985). Pragmatics of sibling speech to one-year-olds. *Child Development, 56,* 911–917.

Tomasello, M., Strosberg, R., & Akhtar, N. (1996). Eighteen-month-old children learn words in non-ostensive context. *Journal of Child Language, 23,* 157–176.

Tomlinson-Clarke, S. (2001). Education and identity within a psychological and sociocultural context. In N. K. Shimahara & I. Z. Holowinsky (Eds.), *Ethnicity, race, and nationality in education: A global perspective* (pp. 193–210). Mahwah, NJ: Erlbaum.

Torney-Purta, J. (1992). Cognitive representations of the political system in adolescents: The continuum from pre-novice to expert. In H. Haste & J. Torney-Purta (Eds.), *The development of political understanding* (pp. 11–25). San Francisco: Jossey-Bass.

Torney-Purta, J. (1994). Dimensions of adolescents' reasoning about political and historical issues: Ontological switches, development processes, and situated learning. In M. Carretero & J. F. Voss (Eds.), *Cognitive and instructional processes in history and the social sciences* (pp. 103–122). Hillsdale, NJ: Erlbaum.

Torrance, E. P. (1988). The nature of creativity as manifest in its testing. In R. Sternberg (Ed.), *The nature of creativity: Contemporary psychological perspectives* (pp. 43–75). New York: Cambridge University Press.

Torsheim, T., & Wold, B. (2001). School-related stress, school support, and somatic complaints: A general population study. *Journal of Adolescent Research, 16,* 293–303.

Toselli, M., Farneti, P., & Salzarulo, P. (1998). Maternal representation and care of infant sleep. *Early Development and Parenting, 7,* 73–78.

Travillion, K., & Snyder, J. (1993). The role of maternal discipline and involvement in peer rejection and neglect. *Journal of Applied Developmental Psychology, 14,* 37–57.

Treboux, D. A., & Bush-Rossnagel, N. A. (1991). Age differences in adolescent sexual behavior, sexual attitudes, and contraceptive use. In R. M. Lerner, A. C. Petersen, & J. Brooks-Gunn (Eds.), *Encyclopedia of adolescence* (pp. 1018–1021). New York: Garland.

Tremblay, R. E. (2001). The development of physical aggression during childhood and the prediction of later dangerousness. In G. Pinard & L. Pagani (Eds.), *Clinical assessment of dangerousness: Empirical contributions* (pp. 47–65). New York: Cambridge University Press.

Trent, K., & Crowder, K. (1997). Adolescent birth intentions, social disadvantage, and behavioral outcomes. *Journal of Marriage and the Family, 59,* 523–535.

Trice, A. D., & Rush, K. (1995). Sex-stereotyping in four-year-olds' occupational aspirations. *Perceptual and Motor Skills, 81,* 701–702.

Trickett, P. K., & Kuczynski, L. (1986). Children's misbehavior and parental discipline in abusive and non-abusive families. *Developmental Psychology, 57,* 115–123.

Trickett, P. K., & McBride-Chang, C. (1995). The developmental impact of different forms of child abuse and neglect. *Developmental Review, 15,* 331–337.

Trommsdorff, G. (1995). Person-context relations as developmental conditions for empathy and prosocial action: A cross-cultural analysis. In T. A. Kindermann & J. Valsiner (Eds.), *Development of person-context relations* (pp. 113–146). Hillsdale, NJ: Erlbaum.

Tschann, J. M., Adler, N. E., Irwin, C. E., Millstein, S. G., Turner, R. A., & Kegeles, S. M. (1994). Initiation of substance use in early adolescence: The roles of pubertal timing and emotional distress. *Health Psychology, 13,* 326–333.

Tucker, J. S., Friedman, H. S., Schwartz, J. E., Criqui, M. H., Tomlinson-Keasey, C., Wingard, D. L., & Martin, L. R. (1997). Parental divorce: Effects on individual behavior and longevity. *Journal of Personality and Social Psychology, 73,* 381–391.

Turecki, S., & Tonner, L. (1985). *The difficult child.* New York: Bantam.

Turiel, E. (1998). The development of morality. In W. Damon (Ed.), *Handbook of child psychology* (Vol. 3, pp. 863–932). New York: Wiley.

Turner, H. A., & Finkelhor, D. (1996). Corporal punishment as a stressor among youth. *Journal of Marriage and the Family, 58,* 155–166.

Turner Syndrome Society of the United States. (2001). *Resources and research.* Houston, TX: Turner Syndrome Society.

Uauy, R., & Peirano, P. (1999). Breast is best: Human milk is optimal food for brain development. *American Journal of Clinical Nutrition, 70,* 433–434.

Udry, J. R. (1995). Integrating biological and sociological models of adolescent problem behaviors. In R. D. Ketterlinus & M. E. Lamb (Eds.), *Adolescent problem behaviors* (pp. 93–108). Hillsdale, NJ: Erlbaum.

Ullstadius, E. (2000). Variability in judgment of neonatal imitation. *Journal of Reproductive and Infant Psychology, 18,* 239–247.

Ungerer, J. A., Brody, L. R., & Zelazo, P. R. (1978). Long-term memory for speech in 2- to 4-week-old infants. *Infant Behavior and Development, 1,* 177–186.

UNICEF. (1993). *Psychosocial programme: Emergency in former Yugoslavia.* New York: UNICEF.

UNICEF. (2001). *The state of the world's children.* New York: UNICEF.

United Nations. (1998). *Population and development indicators for Asia and the Pacific, 1998.* Bangkok, Thailand: United Nations.

Upchurch, D. M., Levy-Storms, L., Sucoff, C. A., & Aneshensel, C. S. (1998). Gender and ethnic differences in the timing of first sexual intercourse. *Family Planning Perspectives, 30,* 121–127.

Updegraff, K. A., McHale, S. M., Crouter, A. C., & Kupanoff, K. (2001). Parents' involvement in adolescents' peer relationships: A comparison of mothers' and fathers' role. *Journal of Marriage and the Family, 63,* 655–668.

Updegraff, K. A., & Obeidallah, D. A. (1999). Young adolescents' patterns of involvement with siblings and friends. Social Development, 8, 52–69.

Urban Institute. (2000). *Child care patterns of school-age children with employed mothers.* Washington, DC: The Urban Institute Press.

US Census Bureau. (1996). *Household and family characteristics: March 1995.* Washington, DC: US Census Bureau.

US Census Bureau. (1999). *Household and family characteristics.* Washington, DC: US Census Bureau.

US Census Bureau. (2001a). *Home computers and Internet use in the US.* Washington, DC: US Census Bureau.

US Census Bureau. (2001b). *Living arrangements of children.* Washington, DC: US Census Bureau.

US Census Bureau. (2001c). *Overview of race and Hispanic origin.* Washington, DC: US Census Bureau.

US Census Bureau. (2001d). *Population projections of the United States.* Washington, DC: US Census Bureau.

US Census Bureau. (2001e). *School enrollment, 1999.* Washington, DC: US Census Bureau.

US Census Bureau. (2002). *Health insurance coverage: 2000.* Washington, DC: US Census Bureau.

US Department of Commerce. (1996, March). *Who's minding our preschoolers? Current Population Reports.* Washington, DC: US Department of Commerce.

US Department of Education. (1993). *Public school kindergarten teachers' views on children's readiness for school.* Washington, DC: US Department of Education.

US Department of Education. (1995). *Reforming schools, transforming partnerships.* Washington, DC: US Department of Education.

US Department of Education. (1996). *Achievement of U.S. students in science, 1969 to 1994; mathematics, 1973 to 1994; reading, 1971 to 1994; writing, 1984 to 1994.* Washington, DC: US Department of Education.

US Department of Education. (1997). *Dropout rates in the United States: 1995.* Washington, DC: US Department of Education.

US Department of Education. (2001a). Elementary and secondary education: An international perspective. Washington, DC: US Department of Education.

US Department of Education. (2000b). *Implementation of the Individuals with Disabilities Education Act.* Washington, DC: US Department of Education.

US Department of Health and Human Services. (1999). *Child maltreatment 1998: Reports from the states to the National Child Abuse and Neglect Data System.* Washington, DC: US Department of Health and Human Services.

US Department of Heath and Human Services. (2001). *Child maltreatment 1999.* Washington, DC: US Government Printing Office.

US Department of Justice. (1999). *Missing and exploited children's program.* Washington, DC: US Department of Justice.

US Department of Labor. (2001a). *Employment characteristics of families.* Washington, DC: US Department of Labor.

US Department of Labor. (2001b). *Occupational wages in the US: 1999.* Washington, DC: US Government Printing Office.

US State Department. (2000). *International adoptions.* Washington, DC: US Government Printing Office.

Valdez, E. O. (1996). Chicano families and urban poverty: Familial strategies of cultural retention. In R. M. De Anda (Ed.), *Chicanas and Chicanos in contemporary society* (pp. 63–74). Boston: Allyn & Bacon.

Valdez, J. (1994, September 18). Teen pregnancy: Interviews and statistics. *Arizona Republic.*

Van Beveren, T. T., Little, B. B., & Spence, M. J. (2000). Effects of prenatal cocaine exposure and postnatal environment on child development. *American Journal of Human Biology, 12,* 417–428.

van de Vijver, F. J. R., & Willemsen, M. E. (1993). Abstract thinking. In J. Altarriba (Ed.), *Cognition and culture* (pp. 317–342). Amsterdam: North-Holland.

van der Heijden, J. (1996). *World population.* Unpublished data.

Van-Evra, J. P. (1998). *Television and child development.* Mahwah, NJ: Erlbaum.

Van Griffin, K., & Haith, M. M. (1984). Infant visual response to gestalt geometric forms. *Infant Behavior and Development, 7,* 335–346.

van-Laar, C. The paradox of low academic achievement but high self-esteem in African American students: An attributional account. *Educational Psychology Review, 12,* 33–61.

Vandell, D. L., & Corasaniti, M. A. (1990). Child care and the family: Complex contributors to child development. *New Directions for Child Development, 49,* 23–37.

Vandell, D. L., & Wolfe, B. (2000). *Child care quality: Does it matter and does it need to be improved?* Washington, DC: US Government Printing Office.

van IJzendoorn, M. H., Schuengel, C., & Bakermans, J. J. (1999). Disorganized attachment in early childhood: Meta-analysis of precursors, concomitants, and sequelae. *Development and Psychopathology, 11,* 225–249.

Vartanian, L. R. (1997). Separation-individuation, social support, and adolescent egocentrism. *Journal of Early Adolescence, 17,* 245–270.

Vartanian, L. R., & Powlishta, K. K. (1996). A longitudinal examination of the social-cognitive foundations of adolescent egocentrism. *Journal of Early Adolescence, 16,* 157–178.

Vasta, R., Knott, J., & Gaze, C. (1996). Can spatial training erase the gender differences on the water-level task? *Psychology of Women Quarterly, 20,* 549–567.

Vellutino, F. R. (1991). Introduction to three studies on reading acquisition: Convergent findings on theoretical foundations of code-oriented versus whole-language approaches to reading instruction. *Journal of Educational Psychology, 83,* 437–443.

Verbeek, P., Hartup, W. W., & Collins, W. A. (2000). Conflict management in children and adolescents. In F. Aureli & F. B. M. de Waal (Eds.), *Natural conflict resolution* (pp. 34–53). Berkeley: University of California Press.

Verhulst, F. C., & Koot, H. M. (1995). *The epidemiology of child and adolescent psychopathology.* Oxford, England: Oxford University Press.

Verschueren, K., Buyck, P., & Marcoen, A. (2001). Self-representations and socioemotional competence in young children: A 3-year longitudinal study. *Developmental Psychology, 37,* 126–134.

Vigil, J. D. (1988). Group processes and street identity: Adolescent Chicano gang members. *Ethos, 16,* 421–445.

Villani, S. (2001). Impact of media on children and adolescents: A 10-year review of the research. *Journal of the American Academy of Child and Adolescent Psychiatry, 40,* 392–401.

Violato, C., & LeRoy, T. (1995). *Advances in adolescent psychology.* Calgary, Canada: Detselig Enterprises.

Vitaro, F., Tremblay, R. E., & Bukowski, W. M. (2001). Friends, friendships and conduct disorders. In J. Hill & B. Maughan (Eds.), *Conduct disorders in childhood and adolescence. Cambridge child and adolescent psychiatry* (pp. 346–378). New York: Cambridge University Press.

Vitaro, F., Tremblay, R. E., Kerr, M., Pagant, L., & Bukowski, W. M. (1997). Disruptives, friends' characteristics, and delinquency in early adolescence: A test of two competing models of development. *Child Development, 68,* 676–689.

Vogt, C. J. (1999). A model of risk factors involved in childhood and adolescent obesity. In A. J. Goreczny & M. Hersen (Eds.), *Handbook of pediatric and adolescent health psychology* (pp. 221–234). Boston: Allyn & Bacon.

Volling, B. L., & Elins, J. L. (1998). Family relationships and children's emotional adjustment as correlates of maternal and paternal differential treatment. *Child Development, 69,* 1640–1656.

Volling, B. L., Youngblade, L. M., & Belsky, J. (1997). Young children's social relationships with siblings and friends. *American Journal of Orthopsychiatry, 67,* 102–111.

von Hofsten, C. (1983). Catching skills in infancy. *Journal of Experimental Psychology: Human Perception and Performance, 9,* 75–85.

von Kries, R., Koletzko, B., Sauerwald, T., von Mutius, E., Barnert, D., Grunert, V., & von Voss, H. (1999). Breast feeding and obesity: Cross sectional study. *British Medical Journal, 319,* 147–150.

Vygotsky, L. S. (1978). *Mind in society.* Cambridge, MA: Harvard University Press.

Vygotsky, L. S. (1986). *Thought and language* (A. Kozulin, Trans.). Cambridge, MA: MIT Press. (Original work published 1934)

Waas, G. A., & Graczyk, P. A. (1998). Group intervention for the peer-rejected child. In K. C. Stoiber & T. R. Kratochwill (Eds.), *Handbook of group intervention for children and families* (pp. 141–158). Boston: Allyn & Bacon.

Wachs, T. D. (1992). *The nature of nurture.* Newbury Park, CA: Sage.

Wachs, T. D. (1995). Relation of mild-to-moderate malnutrition to human development: Correlational studies. *Journal of Nutrition Supplement, 125,* 2245S-2254S.

Wachs, T. D., & King, B. (1994). Behavioral research in the brave new world of neuroscience and temperament: A guide to the biologically perplexed. In J. E. Bates & T. D. Wachs (Eds.), *Temperament: Individual differences at the interface of biology and behavior* (pp. 307–336). Washington, DC: American Psychological Association.

Wachs, T. D., & Kohnstamm, G. A. (2001). *Temperament in context.* Mahwah, NJ: Erlbaum.

Wagner, K. D., & Ambrosini, P. J. (2001). Childhood depression: Pharmacological therapy/treatment. *Journal of Clinical Child Psychology, 30,* 88–97.

Wakeley, A., Rivera, S., & Langer, J. (2000a). Can young infants add and subtract? *Child Development, 71,* 1525–1534.

Wakeley, A., Rivera, S., & Langer, J. (2000b). Not proved: Reply to Wynn. *Child Development, 71,* 1537–1539.

Waldman, S., & Springen, K. (1992). Too old, too fast? *Newsweek,* 80–88.

Walk, R. D., & Gibson, E. J. (1961). A comparative and analytical study of visual depth perception. *Psychological Monographs, 15* (Whole No. 519).

Walker, K., Taylor, E., McElroy, A., & Phillip, D. (1995). Familial and ecological correlates of self-esteem in African American children. In M. N. Wilson (Ed.), *African American family life: Its structural and ecological aspects* (pp. 23–34). San Francisco: Jossey-Bass.

Walker, L. J. (1984). Sex differences in the development of moral reasoning: A critical review. *Child Development, 55,* 677–691.

Walker, L. J. (1988). The development of moral reasoning. *Annals of Child Development, 5,* 33–78.

Walker, L. J. (1989). A longitudinal study of moral reasoning. *Child Development, 60,* 157–166.

Walker, L. J. (1991). Sex differences in moral reasoning. In W. Kurtines & J. L. Gewirtz (Eds.), *Handbook of moral behavior and development* (Vol. 2, pp. 333–364). Hillsdale, NJ: Erlbaum.

Walker, L. J. (1995). Sexism in Kohlberg's moral psychology? In W. M. Kurtines & J. L. Gerwitz (Eds.), *Moral development* (pp. 83–107). Boston: Allyn & Bacon.

Walker, L. J., & Henning, K. H. (1997). Moral development in the broader context of personality. In S. Hala (Ed.), *The development of social cognition* (pp. 297–327). Hove, England: Psychology Press.

Walker, L. J., & Pitts, R. C. (1998). Naturalistic conceptions of moral maturity. *Developmental Psychology, 34,* 403–419.

Walker, L. J., Pitts, R. C., Henning, K. H., & Matsuba, M. K. (1995). Reasoning about morality and real-life moral problems. In M. Killen & D. Hart (Eds.), *Morality in everyday life* (pp. 371–407). New York: Cambridge University Press.

Walker, N. C., & O'Brien, B. (1999). The relationship between method of pain management during labor and birth outcomes. *Clinical Nursing Research, 8,* 119–134.

Wallace-Broscious, A., Serafica, F. C., & Osipow, S. H. (1994). Adolescent career development. *Journal of Research on Adolescence, 4,* 127–149.

Wallerstein, J. S., & Corbin, S. B. (1999). The child and the vicissitudes of divorce. In R. M. Galatzer-Levy & L Krasu (Eds.), *The scientific basis of child custody decisions* (pp. 73–95). New York: Wiley.

Wallerstein, J. S., & Kelly, J. B. (1975). The effects of parental divorce: Experiences of the preschool child. *Journal of the American Academy of Child Psychiatry, 14,* 600–616.

Wallerstein, J. S., & Kelly, J. B. (1976). The effects of parental experiences of the child in later latency. *American Journal of Orthopsychiatry, 46,* 256–269.

Wallerstein, J. S., & Kelly, J. B. (1980). *Surviving the breakup: How children and parents cope with divorce.* New York: Basic Books.

Wallerstein, J. S., & Lewis, J. (1998). The long-term impact of divorce on children: A first report from a 25-year study. *Family and Conciliation Courts Review, 36,* 368–383.

Wallerstein, R. S., & Goldberger, L. (1998). *Ideas and identities: The life and work of Erik Erikson.* Madison, CT: International Universities Press.

Walsh, P. E., & Stolberg, A. L. (1989). Parental and environmental determinants of children's behavioral, affective and cognitive adjustment to divorce. *Journal of Divorce, 12,* 265–282.

Walsh, P. V., Katz, P. A., & Downey, E. P. (1991, April). *A longitudinal perspective on race and gender socialization in infants and toddlers.* Paper presented at the biennial meeting of the Society for Research in Child Development, Seattle, WA.

Wang, F., Oakland, T., & Liu, D. H. (1992). Behavior problems exhibited by Chinese children from single- and multiple-child families. *School Psychology International, 13,* 313–321.

Wang, J. Z. (2000). Asian gangs: New challenges in the 21st century. *Journal of Gang Research, 8,* 51–62.

Wapner, R. J. (1997). Chorionic villus sampling. *Obstetrics and Gynecology Clinics of North America, 24,* 83–110.

Ward, S., Newcombe, N., & Overton, W. (1986). Turn left at the church, or three miles north: A study of direction giving and sex differences. *Environment and Behavior, 18,* 192–213.

Wasz-Hockert, O., Michelsson, K., & Lind, J. (1985). Twenty-five years of Scandinavian cry research. In B. M. Lester & C. F. Z. Boukydis (Eds.), *Infant crying* (pp. 349–354). New York: Plenum.

Waterman, A. S. (1988). Identity status theory and Erikson's theory. *Developmental Review, 8,* 185–208.

Watkins, D., & Regmi, M. (1999). Self-concepts of mountain children of Nepal. *Journal of Genetic Psychology, 160,* 429–435.

Watkins, J., & Peabody, P. (1996). Sports injuries in children and adolescents treated at a sports injury clinic. *Journal of Sports Medicine and Physical Fitness, 36,* 43–48.

Watson, J. B., & Raynor, R. (1920). Conditioned emotional reactions. *Journal of Experimental Psychology, 3,* 1–14.

Weber-Fox, C., & Neville, H. (1996). Maturational constraints on functional specializations for language processing: ERP and behavior evidence in bilingual speakers. *Journal of Cognitive Neuroscience, 9,* 231–256.

Wedemeyer, N. V., Bickhard, N. H., & Cooper, R. G. (1989). The development of structural complexity in the child's concept of family: The effect of cognitive stage, sex, and intactness of family. *The Journal of Genetic Psychology, 150,* 342–357.

Wegener, D. H., & Aday, L. A. (1989). Home care for ventilator-assisted children: Predicting family stress. *Pediatric Nursing, 15,* 271–376.

Weinberg, R. A. (1989). Intelligence and IQ: Landmark issues and great debates. *American Psychologist, 44,* 98–104.

Weinstein, R. A. (1998). Promoting positive expectations in schooling. In N. M. Lambert & B. L. McCombs (Eds.), *How students learn* (pp. 81–111). Washington, DC: American Psychological Association.

Weiss, B., & Dodge, K. A. (1992). Some consequences of early harsh discipline: Child aggression and a maladaptive social information processing style. *Child Development, 63,* 1321–1335.

Weiss, M. R., & Hayashi, C. T. (1995). All in the family: Parent-child influences in competititve youth gymnastics. *Pediatric Exercise Science, 7,* 36–48.

Wellman, H. M. (1990). *The child's theory of mind.* Cambridge, MA: MIT Press.

Wellman, H. M., & Gelman, S. A. (1998). Knowledge acquisition in foundational domain. In W. Damon (Ed.), *Handbook of child psychology* (Vol. 2, pp. 523–574). New York: Wiley.

Wellman, H. M., & Woolley, J. D. (1990). From simple desires to ordinary beliefs: The early development of everyday psychology. *Cognition, 35,* 245–275.

Wentzel, K. R., & Erdley, C. A. (1993). Strategies for making friends: Relations to social behavior and peer acceptance in early adolescence. *Developmental Psychology, 29,* 819–826.

Werker, J. F., & Tees, R. C. (1984). Cross-language speech perception: Evidence for perceptual reorganization during the first year of life. *Infant Behavior and Development, 7,* 49–63.

Werker, J. F., & Vouloumanos, A. (2001). Speech and language processing in infancy: A neurocognitive approach. In C. A. Nelson & M. Luciana (Eds.), *Handbook of developmental cognitive neuroscience* (pp. 269–280). Cambridge, MA: MIT Press.

Werner, E. E., & Smith, R. S. (1982). *Vulnerable but invincible: A longitudinal study of resilient children and youth.* New York: McGraw-Hill.

Whalen, C. K., & Henker, B. (1991). Therapies for hyperactive children: Comparisons, combinations, and compromises. *Journal of Consulting and Clinical Psychology, 59,* 126–137.

Whalen, C. K., Henker, B., Buhrmester, D., Hinshaw, S. P., Huber, A., & Laski, K. (1989). Does stimulant medication improve the peer status of hyperactive children? *Journal of Consulting and Clinical Psychology, 57,* 545–549.

Wheeler, L., & Kim, Y. (1997). What is beautiful is culturally good: The physical attractiveness stereotype has different content in collectivistic cultures. *Personality and Social Psychology Bulletin, 23,* 795–800.

White, M., & LeVine, R. A. (1986). What is an *Ii ko* (good child)? In H. Stevenson, H. Azuma, & K. Hakuta (Eds.), *Child development and education in Japan* (pp. 55–62). New York: Freeman.

White, S. D., & DeBlassie, R. R. (1992). Adolescent sexual behavior. *Adolescence, 27,* 183–191.

Whitebook, M. C., Howes, C., & Phillips, D. (1989). *Who cares? Childcare teachers and the quality of care in America.* Oakland, CA: Childcare Employee Project.

Whitebook, M. C., Howes, C., & Phillips, D. (1998). *Worthy work, unlivable wages: The National Care Staffing Study.* Oakland, CA: Child Care Employee Project.

Whiting, B. B., & Edwards, C. P. (1988). *Children of different worlds: The formation of social behavior.* Cambridge, MA: Harvard University Press.

Whiting, B. B., & Whiting, J. W. M. (1975). *Children of six cultures: A psychocultural analysis.* Cambridge, MA: Harvard University Press.

Widerstrom, A. H., Mowder, B. A., & Sandall, S. R. (1991). *At-risk and handicapped newborns and infants: Development, assessment, and intervention.* Englewood Cliffs, NJ: Prentice-Hall.

Widom, C. S. (2001). Child abuse and neglect. In S. O. White (Ed.), *Handbook of youth and justice* (pp. 31–47). New York: Kluwer.

Wierson, M., Long, P. J., & Forehand, R. L. (1993). Toward a new understanding of early menarche: The role of environmental stress in pubertal timing. *Adolescence, 28,* 913–924.

Wiese, D., & Daro, D. (1996). *Current trends in child abuse reporting and fatalities.* Chicago: National Committee to Prevent Child Abuse.

Wigfield, A. (1993). Why should I learn this? In M. L. Maehr & P. R. Pintrich (Eds.), *Advances in motivation and achievement* (Vol. 8, pp. 99–138). Greenwich, CT: JAI Press.

Wigfield, A., Battle, A., Keller, L. B., & Eccles, J. S. (2002). Sex differences in motivation, self-concept, career aspiration, and career choice: Implications for cognitive development. In A. McGillicuddy-De Lisi & R. De Lisi (Eds.), *Biology, society, and behavior: The development of sex differences in cognition* (pp. 93–124). Westport, CT: Ablex.

Wigfield, A., & Eccles, J. S. (1989). Test anxiety in elementary and secondary school students. *Educational Psychologist, 24,* 159–183.

Wigfield, A., Eccles, J. S., & Pintrich, P. R. (1996). Development between the ages of 11 and 25. In D. C. Berliner & R. C. Calfee (Eds.), *Handbook of educational psychology* (pp. 148–185). New York: Macmillan.

Wilcox, M. J., Hadley, P. A., & Ashland, J. E. (1996). Communication and language development in infants and toddlers. In M. J. Hanson (Ed.), *Atypical infant development* (pp. 365–402). Austin, TX: Pro-Ed.

Wilcox, M. J., & Terrell, B. Y. (1985). Child language behavior: The acquisition of social communicative competence. In C. S. McLoughlin & D. F. Gullo (Eds.), *Young children in context* (pp. 40–65). Springfield, IL: Charles C Thomas.

Willett, J. B., Singer, J. D., & Martin, N. C. (1998). The design and analysis of longitudinal studies of development and psychopathology in context. *Development and Psychopathology, 10,* 395–426.

Williams, S., & McGee, R. (1991). Adolescent self-perceptions of their strengths. *Journal of Youth and Adolescence, 20,* 325–337.

Williams, T. M. (1986). *The impact of television: A natural experiment in three communities.* New York: Academic Press.

Williamson, L. (1998). Eating disorders and the cultural forces behind the drive for thinness. *Social Work in Health Care, 28,* 61–73.

Willig, A. (1985). A meta-analysis of selected studies on the effectiveness of bilingual education. *Review of Educational Research, 55,* 269–317.

Wilson, B. J., & Smith, S. L. (1998). Children's responses to emotional portrayals on television. In P. A. Andersen & L. K. Guerrero (Eds.), *Handbook of communication and emotion* (pp. 533–569). San Diego, CA: Academic Press.

Wilson, C., & Keye, W. (1989). A survey of adolescent dysmenorrhea and premenstrual symptom frequency. *Journal of Adolescent Health Care, 10,* 317–322.

Wilson, E. O. (1978). *On human nature.* Cambridge, MA: Harvard University Press.

Wilson, R. D. (2000). Amniocentesis and chorionic villus sampling. *Current Opinion in Obstetrics and Gynecology, 12,* 81–86.

Wimmer, H., & Perner, J. (1983). Beliefs about beliefs: Representation and constraining function of wrong beliefs in young children's understanding of deception. *Cognition, 13,* 103–128.

Windass, A. (1989). Classroom practices and organization. In C. Skelton (Ed.), *Whatever happens to little women?* (pp. 38–49). Milton Keynes, England: Open University Press.

Winer, G. A. (1980). Class-inclusion reasoning in children: A review of the empirical literature. *Child Development, 51,* 309–328.

Winsler, A., Diaz, R. M., & Montero, I. (1997). The role of private speech in the transition from collaborative to independent task performance in young children. *Early Childhood Research Quarterly, 12,* 59–79.

Wisniewski, L., & Marcus, M. D. (1998). Childhood obesity. In V. B. Van Hasselt & M. Hersen (Eds.), *Handbook of psychological treatment protocols for children and adolescents* (pp. 179–201). Mahwah, NJ: Erlbaum.

Witkin, G. (1991, April 8). Kids who kill. *U.S. News and World Report.*

Wolf, A. E. (1996, October). Tantrums. *Child,* 42–46.

Wolf, D. P. (1990). Being of several minds: Voices and versions of the self in early childhood. In D. Cicchetti & M. Beeghly (Eds.), *The self in transition* (pp. 183–212). Chicago: University of Chicago Press.

Wolfe, D. A. (1993). Prevention of child neglect: Emerging issues. *Criminal Justice and Behavior, 20,* 90–111.

Wolff, P. H. (1963). Observations on the early development of smiling. In B. Foss (Ed.), *Determinants of infant behavior* (Vol. 2, pp. 113–138). London: Methuen.

Wolff, P. H. (1969). The natural history of crying and other vocalizations in early infancy. In B. M. Foss (Ed.), *Determinants of infant behavior* (Vol. 4, pp. 97–112). London: Methuen.

Wolfner, G. D., & Gelles, R. J. (1993). A profile of violence toward children: A national study. *Child Abuse & Neglect, 17,* 197–212.

Wolfson, A. R., & Carskadon, M. A. (1996). Early school start times affect sleep and daytime functioning in adolescents. *Sleep Research, 25,* 117.

Wolfson, A. R., & Carskadon, M. A. (1998). Sleep schedules and daytime functioning in adolescents. *Child Development, 69,* 875–887.

Wolfson, A. R., Tzischinsky, O., Brown, C., Darley, C., Acebo, C., & Carskadon, M. A. (1995). Sleep, behavior, and stress at the transition to senior high school. *Sleep Research, 24,* 5–20.

Women's Sports Foundation. (1998). *Sport and teen pregnancy.* New York: Women's Sports Foundation.

Wong, D. L., & Perry, S. E. (1998). *Maternal child nursing care.* St. Louis, MO: Mosby.

Woods, E. G. (1995). Effective schooling practices and at-risk youth: What the research shows. *School Improvement Research Series, 17,* 1–21.

Woodward, A. L., & Markman, E. M. (1998). Early word learning. In W. Damon (Ed.), *Handbook of child psychology* (Vol. 2, pp. 371–420). New York: Wiley.

Woodward, E. H., & Gridina, N. (2001). *Media in the home.* Philadelphia: Annenberg Public Policy Center.

Woodworth, S., Belsky, J., & Crnic, K. (1996). The determinants of fathering during the child's second and third years of life: A developmental analysis. *Journal of Marriage and the Family, 58,* 679–692.

Woolley, J. D., & Wellman, H. M. (1990). Young children's understanding of realities, nonrealities, and appearances. *Child Development, 61,* 946–961.

World Health Organization. (1997). *WHO global database on child growth and malnutrition.* Geneva, Switzerland: World Health Organization.

World Health Organization. (1999). *Care of the umbilical cord: A review of the evidence.* Geneva, Switzerland: World Health Organization.

Wright, J. C., Huston, A. C., Vandewater, E. A., Bickham, D. S., Scantlin, R. M., Kotler, J. A., Yelland, N., & Lloyd, M. (2001). Virtual kids of the 21st century: Understanding the children in schools today. *Information Technology in Childhood Education Annual, 12,* 175–192.

Wright, S. C., & Taylor, D. M. (1995). Identity and the language of the classroom. *Journal of Educational Psychology, 87,* 241–252.

Wynn, K. (2000). Findings of addition and subtraction in infants are robust and consistent: Reply to Wakely, Rivera, and Langer. *Child Development, 71,* 1535–1536.

Wynne, E. A. (1997). For character education. In A. Molnar (Ed.), *The construction of children's character* (pp. 63–76). Chicago: The National Society for the Study of Education.

Wyshak, G. (1983). Secular changes in age at menarche in a sample of U.S. women. *Annals of Human Biology, 10,* 75–78.

Wysocki, T., & Green, P. (1997). Self-management of childhood diabetes in family context. In D. S. Gochman (Ed.), Handbook of health behavior research II: Provider determinants (pp. 169–187). New York: Plenum.

Yagel, S., Anteby, E., Hochner-Celnikier, D., Ariel, I., Chaap, T., & Ben-Neriah, Z. (1998). The role of midtrimester target fetal organ screening combined with the "triple test" and maternal age in the diagnosis of trisomy 21. *American Journal of Obstetrics and Gynecology, 178,* 40–44.

Yamamoto, K., Soliman, A., Parsons, J., & Davies, O. L., Jr. (1987). Voices in unison: Stressful events in the lives of children in six countries. *Journal of Child Psychology and Psychiatry, 28,* 855–864.

Yanai, J., Steingart, R. A., Snapir, N., Gvaryahu, G., Rozenboim, I., & Katz, A. (2000). The relationship between neural alterations and behavioral deficits after prenatal exposure to heroin. In S. F. Ali (Ed.), *Neurobiological mechanisms of drugs of abuse* (Vol. 914, pp. 402–411). New York: New York Academy of Sciences.

Yankelovich, S., & White, C. (1989). *The role of Sesame Street among children in poverty.* New York: Children's Television Workshop.

Yee, D. K., & Eccles, J. S. (1988). Parents' perceptions and attributions for children's math achievement. *Sex Roles, 19,* 317–333.

Yenen, S. (1997). *Turkish odyssey.* Ankara, Turkey: Serif Yenen.

Yetman, N. R. (1991). *Majority and minority.* Boston: Allyn & Bacon.

Yi, S. H., & Lee, S. E. (1997). Video game experiences and children's abilities of self-control and visual information processing. *Journal of Child Studies, 18,* 105–120.

Yin, R. K. (1994). Discovering the future of the case study method in evaluation research. *Evaluation Practice, 15,* 283–290.

YMCA. (2000). *Talking with teens: The YMCA parent and teen survey final report.* New York: The Global Strategy Group, Inc.

Young, J. (1996). *Developmental care of the premature baby.* Philadelphia: Balliere Tindall.

Younger, B. A., & Fearing, D. D. (1999). Parsing items into separate categories: Developmental change in infant categorization. *Child Development, 70,* 291–303.

Youniss, J. (1980). *Parents and peers in social development.* Chicago: University of Chicago Press.

Youniss, J., McLellen, J. A., & Strouse, D. (1994). "We're popular, but we're not snobs": Adolescents describe their crowds. In R. Montemayor, G. R. Adams, & T. P. Gullotta (Eds.), *Personal relationships during adolescence* (pp. 101–122). Thousand Oaks, CA: Sage.

Yuille, N. (1997). Children's understanding of traits. In S. Hala (Ed.), *The development of social cognition* (pp. 273–296). East Sussex, England: Psychology Press.

Yung, B. R., & Hammond, W. R. (1994). Native Americans. In L. D. Eron, J. H. Gentry, & P. Schlegel (Eds.), *Reason to hope: A psychosocial perspective on violence and youth* (pp. 133–144). Washington, DC: American Psychological Association.

Yung, B. R., & Hammond, W. R. (1997). Antisocial behavior in minority groups. In D. M. Stoff & J. Breiling (Eds.), *Handbook of antisocial behavior* (pp. 474–495). New York: Wiley.

Zahn-Waxler, C., Radke-Yarrow, M., Wagner, E., & Chapman, M. (1992). The development of concern for others. *Developmental Psychology, 28,* 1038–1047.

Zaiwalla, Z., & Stein, A. (1993). The physiology of sleep in infants and young children. In I. St. James-Roberts, G. Harris, & D. Messer (Eds.), *Infant crying, feeding and sleeping: Development, problems, and treatment* (pp. 135–149). New York: Harvester Wheatsheaf.

Zebrowitz, L., Kendall-Tackett, K., & Fafel, J. (1991). The impact of children's facial maturity on parental expectations and punishments. *Journal of Experimental Child Psychology, 52,* 221–238.

Zebrowitz, L., & Montepare, J. M. (1992). Impressions of babyfaced individuals across the lifespan. *Developmental Psychology, 28,* 1143–1152.

Zeifman, D., Delany, S., & Blass, E. M. (1996). Sweet taste, looking, and calm in 2- and 4-week-old infants: The eyes have it. *Developmental Psychology, 32,* 1090–1099.

Zero to Three. (1997). *Parents speak: Nationwide Survey Among Parents of Zero-to-Three-Year-Olds.* Washington, DC: Zero to Three.

Zeskind, P. S. (1985). A developmental perspective on infant crying. In B. M. Lester & C. F. Z. Boukydis (Eds.), *Infant crying* (pp. 158–186). New York: Plenum.

Zhou, M. (1997). Growing up American: The challenge confronting immigrant children and children of immigrants. *Annual Review of Sociology, 23,* 63–95.

Zigler, E. (1999). Head Start is not child care. *American Psychologist, 54,* 142.

Zigler, E., & Gilman, E. (1998). *The legacy of Jean Piaget.* Mahwah, NJ: Erlbaum.

Zigler, E., & Styfco, S. J. (1998). Applying the findings of developmental psychology to improve early childhood intervention. In S. G. Paris & H. M. Wellman (Eds.), *Global prospects for education* (pp. 345–365). Washington, DC: American Psychological Association.

Zill, N. (1999). Promoting educational equity and excellence in kindergarten. In R. C. Pianta & M. J. Cox (Eds.), *The transition to kindergarten* (pp. 67–108). Baltimore: Brookes.

Zillmann, D. (1982). Television viewing and arousal. In D. Pearl, L. Bouthilet, & J. Lazar (Eds.), *Television and behavior* (Vol. 2, pp. 53–67). Washington, DC: US Government Printing Office.

Zillmann, D., & Gan, S. L. (1997). Musical taste in adolescence. In D. J. Hargreaves (Ed.), *The social psychology of music* (pp. 161–187). New York: Oxford University Press.

Zimmerman, B. F. (1998). Classroom disruption: Educational theory as applied to perception and action in regular and special education. In A. Rotatori & J. Schwenn (Eds.), *Advances in special education* (Vol. 11, pp. 77–98). Greenwich, CT: JAI Press.

Zimmerman, M. A., Copeland, L. A., Shope, J. T., & Dielman, T. E. (1997). A longitudinal study of self-esteem: Implications for adolescent development. *Journal of Youth and Adolescence, 26,* 117–141.

A. C. Nielson Media Research, 275
Aasheim, M., 346
Abbott, S., 354
Abel, E. L., 87
Abella, E. M., 72
Abelman, R., 277
Aber, J. L., 313, 322, 325
Abikoff, H. B., 310
Ablon, J. S., 310
Ablow, J. C., 245
Aboud, F. E., 303, 304, 305
Abrams, C. L., 376
Abrams, S. M., 104
Acebo, C., 421
Achenbach, T. M., 450
Acosta, S., 91
Acredolo, L., 162
Adams, G., 195, 196
Adams, G. R., 335, 395
Adams, H. F., 140
Adams, M. J., 299
Adams, R. J., 144
Adams, W. G., 219, 300, 301
Adamson, L. B., 169
Aday, L. A., 125
Addington, J., 305
Adessa, R., 449
Adler, L., 295
Adler, N. E., 363
Adler, P. A., 386
Administration on Children,
    Youth, and Families, 235
Adnopoz, J., 320
Adolph, K. E., 138
Adoption and Foster Care Analysis
    and Reporting System, 211
Agency for Healthcare Research
    and Quality, 133
Ager, A., 319
Aggleton, P., 449
Aguilar, A., 91
Aharoni, A., 68
Ailey, A., 296
Ainsworth, M. D., 186, 187, 188,
    189, 191, 192, 259
Akbas, S. H., 72
Akhtar, N., 141, 162, 163, 240
Alaimo, K., 287, 367
Alan Guttmacher Institute, 417,
    446, 447
Alberts, D. M., 234
Albright, N. L., 420
Albright, T. E., 420
Alcantara, A. A., 117, 118
Alderman, M. H., 123
Alemmi, B., 124

Alessandri, S. M., 90, 181
Alexander, A., 237
Alexander, J. M., 103
Alfieri, T., 385
Alibhai, M., 371
Allen, L., 328, 442
Allen, M. C., 111, 122, 123, 126
Allen, O., 371
Allen, W. R., 389
Allhusen, V. D., 197
Almeida, D. M., 366
Almeida-Porada, G., 72
Aloise, P. A., 302
Alper, O., 72
Alpert, A., 266
Alsaker, F. D., 363, 364
Altarriba, J., 375
Alvarez, M. M., 366
Alvarez-Huerta, M., 68
Amabile, T. M., 296, 297
Amato, M., 179
Amato, P. R., 261, 264, 266
Ambert, A. M., 392, 394
Ambrosini, P. J., 327
American Academy of Pediatrics,
    126, 140, 219, 287, 454
American Association of University
    Women, 307, 430
American College of Obstetricians
    and Gynecologists, 92
American Heart Association, 351
American Medical Association, 35
American Psychiatric Association,
    309, 311, 324, 326, 328, 369,
    371, 452
American Psychological Associa-
    tion, 276
Ames, N. L., 377
Amsel, E., 375
Anand, K. J. S., 121
Anastasi, A., 294
Anderman, E. M., 377
Anderson, C. A., 406
Anderson, D., 145
Anderson, D. R., 275
Anderson, E. R., 268
Anderson, K. J., 399
Anderson, R. C., 298
Anderson, W. P., 253
Andersson, T., 363
Ando, K., 257
Andrea, R. K., 364
Andres, R. L., 87
Andrews, D. W., 324
Aneshensel, C. S., 441, 442
Angelini, P. J., 445

Anglin, J. M., 164, 237, 298, 299
Angst, J., 324
Ani, C., 217, 287
Anteby, E., 91
Antill, J. K., 366
Antonucci, T. C., 105
Anwar, M., 109
Aoki, W. T., 452
Apgar, V. A., 109
Appel, A. E., 203
Appleton, H., 236
Apter, A., 288
Arawaka, K., 113
Arbreton, A., 378
Archer, S. L., 388
Archibald, A. B., 399
Arcia, E., 308
Arcus, D., 185
Ardelt, M., 261
Arditti, J. A., 267, 269
Arend, R., 194
Argys, L. M., 267
Ariel, I., 91
Aries, E., 249
Aries, P., 11
Arland, T., 263
Arms, K. J., 18
Arnett, J., 398, 444
Arnold, C., 268
Arnold, L. E., 310
Aronoff, H. R., 310
Aronson, J. A., 432
Asendorpf, J. B., 185
Asher, S. R., 270, 271, 327, 332, 333,
    398
Ashland, J. E., 239
Ashley, J., 255
Askan, N., 262
Aslin, R. N., 118, 119, 120, 145, 160
Asnis, L., 327
Association of SIDS and Infant
    Mortality Programs, 126
Astolfi, P., 91
Astone, N. M., 447
Atchinson, J., 419
Atkin, C. K., 277
Atkin, L. C., 180
Atkins, M. S., 256
Atkinson, L., 192
Atkinson, R., 353
Atterbury, J. L., 112
Attie, I., 372
Aube, J., 200
Augoustinos, M., 205, 304
Aunola, K., 391
Aurand, S., 449

Avenevoli, S., 390
Avinoam, B. C., 250
Avis, J., 228
Ayers, M., 398
Aylward, G. P., 9
Azmitia, M., 270
Azuma, H., 261
Azuma, S. D., 90

Baba, Y., 402
Bachman, J. G., 459
Backx, F. J., 422
Bada, H. S., 89
Baddeley, J., 346
Bae, Y., 431
Bagdon, L., 86
Bagwell, C. L., 270, 271, 333
Bailey, D. B., Jr., 214
Bailey, J., 70
Bailey, S. M., 338
Bailey, W. T., 194
Baillargeon, R., 153, 154, 223, 224
Bain, B., 306
Bain, R. P., 71
Baird, A. A., 413
Baird, S. M., 178
Baker, L., 221, 290
Baker, L. S., 234
Bakermans, J. J., 191, 192
Bakke, I., 346
Balcazar, H., 127
Baldo, M., 449
Baldwin, L. E., 299
Bales, D. W., 246
Baley, J., 125
Balle-Jensen, L., 444
Baltes, M. M., 440
Baltes, P. B., 3
Baltimore, D., 61
Bancroft, J., 360
Band, E. B., 319
Bandura, A., 35, 252, 253
Bank, L., 260
Banks, C. A. M., 305
Banks, J. A., 305
Banks, M. S., 119, 144, 146
Barbarin, O. A., 20
Barber, B. K., 391
Barber, B. L., 422
Bard, K. A., 106
Bardin, C., 122
Baris, M. A., 264
Barkley, R. A., 309, 324
Barlow, D. H., 328
Barnard, K. E., 232
Barnert, D., 142

Barness, L. A., 126
Barnett, S. W., 235
Barr, H. M., 87, 88
Barr, R. G., 178
Barrerra, M. E., 145
Barrett, M., 326, 337
Barry, S. M., 405
Bartholomew, K., 186
Bartsch, K., 227
Bates, E., 157, 161, 163, 165, 166, 238
Bates, J. E., 182, 183, 184, 194, 205, 259, 325, 392
Bathurst, K., 313
Battle, A., 432
Bauchner, H., 219, 300, 301
Bauer, C. R., 89, 123
Bauer, D. H., 328
Bauer, P., 157
Bauer, P. J., 221
Bauman, K. E., 395
Baumeister, A. A., 313
Baumeister, R. F., 313, 385
Baumrind, D., 262, 263
Baumringer, N., 311
Bayer, C. L., 391, 392
Beal, C. R., 385, 399
Bear, G. G., 256
Beard, J., 367
Beardslee, W., 424
Beardslee, W. R., 327
Beauchamp, G. K., 120
Beaudry, M., 275
Beautrais, A. L., 142
Becker, S., 88
Beckman, D. A., 86
Beckwith, L., 113
Bedwell, J., 71
Beebe, M. E., 325
Beernink, F., 65
Begley, S., 115
Behnke, M., 90
Behrman, R. E., 405
Beintema, D., 111
Beitel, A. H., 195
Beitins, I. Z., 360
Bell, C., 323
Bell, D. A., 68
Bell, R., 327
Bellinger, D. C., 140
Belsky, J., 105, 192, 194, 195, 197, 198, 200, 201, 203, 204, 205, 263, 274, 325, 360
Bem, S. L., 251, 254
Bemporad, J. R., 326, 327
Benbow, C. P., 312, 430
Bender, B., 7, 10
Bender, M. E., 310
Benedek, E. P., 265
Benes, F., 356, 414
Benjamin, J., 67
Ben-Neriah, Z., 91
Bennett, C., 335
Bennett, D. S., 256
Bennett, V. R., 80
Bennett, W., 425, 426
Benson, B., 392, 446
Benson, J. B., 153, 155
Benson, P., 461

Benson, P. L., 427
Bentz, L. S., 112
Benz, J. J., 179
Berenbaum, S. A., 253, 431
Berendes, H., 140
Berg, K. M., 113
Berg, W. K., 113
Bergstrom, R., 92
Berk, L. E., 229, 230, 334
Berkey, C. S., 142, 372, 373
Berko, J., 239
Berkowitz, M. W., 425
Berlin, M., 192
Berliner, L., 201
Berman, C. M., 13
Berman, S. L., 322
Bernal, M. E., 388
Berndt, T. J., 376, 397
Berry, J. W., 291
Bertenthal, B. I., 119, 145, 214
Best, C. T., 160
Betancourt, L. M., 90
Bettes, B. A., 169
Bezruczko, N., 460
Bhapkar, M. V., 361
Bhatia, T. K., 241
Bickham, D. S., 404
Bickhard, N. H., 264
Biddle, S., 368
Bidell, T. K., 38
Biederman, J., 308
Bier, J. A. B., 124
Bierman, K. L., 398
Bigelow, K. M., 202
Bigler, R. S., 250, 254, 304, 305
Bijur, P. E., 286
Biller, H. B., 105
Bimonte, H. A., 431
Binder, B., 117
Binet, A., 293
Bingol, N., 89
Birch, H. G., 327
Birkimer, J. C., 104
Bithoney, W. G., 144
Bittner, M. T., 321
Bjorklund, D. F., 28, 39, 147, 149, 222, 292, 293, 294, 375
Blaas, J., 68
Black, B., 334
Black, J. E., 117, 118, 285
Black, K. A., 398
Black, M. M., 27
Black-Gutman, D., 304
Blair, R., 413
Blake, J., 332
Blancero, D. A., 403
Bland, K., 201
Blank, M., 223
Blasi, A., 344
Blass, E. M., 120, 146
Blehar, M. C., 189
Blemnfeld, P., 377
Block, J., 458
Bloom, F. E., 117
Bloom, L., 161, 165, 169, 239, 240, 298, 299, 461
Bloom, P., 162
Bloom, S. L., 103

Blue, J. H., 358, 360
Blum, N. J., 140
Blum, R. W., 417
Blumenfeld, P., 378
Blumenfeld, W. J., 449
Blumenthal, J., 414
Blyth, D. A., 363, 377, 379
Boeck, M. A., 371
Boer, F., 274
Bogenschneider, K., 442
Bohannon, J. N., 168
Bohlin, G., 194, 334
Bon-De-Matte, L., 369
Boos, R., 71
Booth, C. L., 194
Booth, D. A., 370
Booth, S., 310
Borke, H., 223
Borman, E. H., 390
Borman, K., 440
Bornstein, M. H., 10, 90, 113, 118, 145, 147, 158, 178, 195, 271, 272, 392
Borstelmann, L. J., 11
Borsting, E., 214
Bosma, H. A., 387
Boston, M. B., 251
Bosworth, P., 386
Botvin, G. J., 385
Bouchard, C., 356, 422
Bourdony, C. J., 361
Bourgeois, J. P., 356
Bouwmeester, H. J., 68
Bowen, F., 394
Bowen, J., 310
Bower, J., 177
Bower, M., 86
Bowers, W. A., 370
Bowker, A., 398
Bowlby, J., 29, 186, 187, 328
Bowlds, M. K., 390
Bowman, L. L., 164
Bowman, M. J., 141
Bowman, P. J., 249
Boxer, A. M., 363, 450
Boyce, W. T., 327
Boyer, D., 445
Brackbill, Y., 99
Brackshaw, E., 276
Bradbard, M. R., 251
Bradley, R. H., 41, 123, 231, 232
Bradley, S. J., 250
Braine, M., 165
Braja, M., 331
Branch, C., 401
Branch, C. W., 304
Brannon, B., 331
Brassard, M. R., 201
Braungart-Rieker, J. M., 183, 192
Braza, F., 252
Braza, P., 252
Brazelton, T. B., 99, 114, 177, 200
Breakey, J., 310
Brederode, M. E., 236
Breedlove, G., 99
Breinlinger, K., 154
Bremer, J., 404, 406
Bremner, G. J., 147

Brendgen, M., 3, 394, 398
Brenner, R. A., 140
Brenner, V., 325
Brent, D., 234
Brent, M. R., 165
Brent, R. L., 86
Bretherton, I., 157
Breunig, K., 264
Bridges, A., 238
Bridges, K., 176
Bridges, L. J., 192
Bridges, M., 266
Brion-Meisels, S., 424
Brisk, M. E., 306
Britner, P., 206
Broadhurst, D. D., 201, 202
Broberg, A., 198
Brodersen, L., 121, 318
Brodsky, A. E., 249
Brodsky, N. L., 90
Brody, G. H., 248, 274, 331
Brody, L. R., 148
Brodzinsky, D. M., 186
Bromley, D. B., 423
Brone, R. J., 370
Bronfenbrenner, U., 22, 40, 41
Bronstein, P., 376
Brook, D. W., 88
Brook, J. S., 88
Brooks, J. B., 181
Brooks-Gunn, J., 41, 261, 313, 360, 362, 363, 365, 366, 372, 390, 393, 409, 442, 443, 447, 452
Brown, A., 248
Brown, A. L., 225, 293
Brown, B. B., 395, 396, 397
Brown, C., 421
Brown, C. F., 265
Brown, E., 147
Brown, J., 218
Brown, J. D., 368, 403
Brown, J. L., 325
Brown, J. R., 240, 274
Brown, K. H., 141
Brown, L. G., 63
Brown, L. K., 80, 417
Brown, M. M., 334
Brown, R. P., 432
Browne, J. V., 124
Bruce, C., 105
Bruce, J., 23
Bruck, M., 227, 300
Brucken, L., 250
Bruene, C. M., 333
Bruner, J. S., 158, 169
Bryan, J. H., 258
Bryant, B. K., 318, 329, 331
Bryden, M. P., 216
Bryk, A. S., 434, 435
Buchanan, A., 258
Buchanan, C. M., 269, 358, 360, 362, 441
Buchanan, C. N., 266
Buchanan-Barrow, B., 337
Bugental, D. B., 259, 329
Buhrmester, D., 274, 310, 397
Buis, J. M., 376
Buka, S. L., 88, 89

Bukoski, W. J., 456
Bukowski, W. M., 3, 333, 395, 398
Bullock, M., 224
Burack, J. A., 311
Burchinal, M. R., 198, 214, 232, 233
Burd, B., 141
Bureau of Labor Statistics, 16
Burgeson, R., 377
Buriel, R., 259, 266
Burnett, J. W., 253
Burns, A., 433
Burns, K. A., 89
Burns, W. J., 89
Burt, M. R., 436
Burts, D. C., 260
Bush, G., 234
Bush-Rossnagel, N. A., 444
Buss, A., 183
Buss, D., 28
Buss, K., 180
Bussey, K., 252, 253, 341
Buster, M., 442
Butler, J., 148
Buyck, P., 245
Byers, J., 86
Byler, P., 234
Byrne, B., 300
Byrne, D., 444
Byrnes, J. P., 285, 373

Caddell, J., 310
Cadwallader, T. W., 402
Cahalan, C., 432
Cahill, T. C., 70, 71
Cairns, R. B., 13, 402
Caissy, G. A., 361, 363
Caldwell, B. M., 41, 232
Calkins, S. D., 273
Callanan, C., 142
Callanan, M. A., 164, 274
Camargo, C. A., 142, 372, 373
Camarota, A., 19
Campaign for Our Children, 445
Campbell, D., 178
Campos, F., 19
Campos, J. J., 22, 139, 145, 176, 193
Campos, M. M., 200
Cantrell, D., 397
Cantu, C. L., 389
Capon, N., 375
Carbone, T., 109
Carlo, G., 258, 335, 391, 424
Carlo, W., 123
Carlsmith, J., 363
Carlson, E. A., 309
Carlson, S. M., 228
Carlson-Luden, V., 157
Carlton, M. P., 234
Carlton-Ford, S., 377
Carossino, P., 107
Carpendale, J., 302
Carpenter, M., 162
Carr, A., 206
Carreras, M. R., 252
Carskadon, M. A., 421
Carson, D. K., 321
Carter, C., 303
Carter, D. B., 261

Carthan, W., 403
Carton, E. R., 327
Cartwright, T., 165
Case, R., 38, 223, 285
Casey, B. J., 356, 414
Casey, D. M., 277
Casey, M. B., 431
Casey, P. H., 123, 144, 232
Casey, R. J., 145
Caskie, G. I. L., 198
Casper, L. B., 442
Casper, L. M., 330, 331
Casper, R. C., 372
Caspi, A., 182, 183
Cassidy, D. J., 225
Cassidy, J., 194
Cassidy, P., 98, 99
Castellanos, F. X., 309
Castex, G. M., 19
Castle, J., 257
Castronova, F. C., 103
Caswell, C., 334
Catalano, R. F., 451
Cauce, A. M., 259
Cauffman, E., 373
Cavell, T. A., 186
Caverly, S., 334
Ceci, S. J., 22, 227
Cellappah, G., 121
Center for Applied Research and
    Educational Improvement, 421
Center for the Evaluation of Risks to
    Human Reproduction, 86, 92
Centers for Disease Control, 86,
    133, 219, 263, 264, 287, 288,
    351, 367, 369, 372, 373, 400,
    415, 416, 417, 418, 421, 441,
    442, 443, 444, 445, 451, 452,
    453, 454, 455, 458
Cernkovich, S. A., 398
Cernoch, J. M., 121
Cerrelli, E. C., 415
Chaap, T., 91
Chacon, M. E., 218
Chaille, C., 433
Chall, J. S., 299
Challela, M., 125
Chan, R. W., 17, 18
Chance, R., 402
Chandler, M., 228
Channiah, D., 419
Chapin, J. R., 403
Chapman, M., 257
Charbonneau, C., 275
Chard, S., 205
Charlesworth, R., 234
Chase, W. G., 226
Chase-Linsdale, P. L., 261, 265, 447
Chasnoff, I. J., 89, 90
Chatman, C., 307
Chatters, L. M., 389
Chaudry, N., 325
Chazan, R. Z., 327
Cheek, N. H., 397
Chen, C., 261, 314, 315, 336, 379,
    380, 452
Chen, E., 452
Chen, M., 314, 432

Chen, S., 193
Chen, W. A., 87
Chen, Y. R., 389
Chen, Z., 292
Chen, Z. Y., 399, 440
Cherlin, A. J., 265, 267, 269
Chess, S., 183, 184, 327
Chi, M. T. J., 226
Child Care Action Campaign, 199
Children Now, 405
Children's Defense Fund, 1, 379
Children's TV Workshop, 236, 237
Chilman, C. S., 249
Chiodo, L. M., 142
Chisholm, J. S., 180
Chisum, G. M., 89
Choi, S., 170
Chomsky, N., 166, 168
Chorpita, B. F., 328
Christensen, K. M., 121
Christenson, P. G., 403
Christiansen, S. L., 448
Christopher, F. S., 260, 277, 441,
    443, 448
Chronis, A. M., 310
Chrousos, G. P., 358, 452
Cicchetti, D., 192, 201, 452
Cillessen, A. H. N., 271
Clark, E. V., 161, 164, 168, 237
Clark, G., 330, 398
Clarke, A. T., 276
Clarke-Stewart, K. A., 197, 200, 232
Claussen, A. H., 29, 193, 218
Clemens, J. D., 87
Clements, D. C., 197
Clewett, A. S., 277
Clifton, R. K., 149, 154, 214
Clingempeel, W. G., 263, 264
Clinton, J. F., 94
Clubb, R., 125
Cnattingius, S., 92
Coatsworth, J. D., 321
Cochran, K. M., 255
Coffman, J., 219, 300, 301
Cohan, M., 105, 448
Cohen, B. M., 413
Cohen, J., 313
Cohen, K. M., 449
Cohen, L. M., 312
Cohen, M. A., 436
Cohen, S. E., 113
Cohen, Y., 417
Cohler, J. J., 450
Cohn, A. H., 206
Cohn, D. A., 270
Coie, J. D., 256, 271, 319, 333,
    334
Colbus, D., 327
Colby, A., 341, 344
Colditz, G. A., 142, 372, 373
Cole, B., 326
Cole, C. F., 236
Cole, E. B., 169
Cole, M., 230
Cole, R. E., 445
Cole, T. J., 142
Coleman, J. M., 319
Coleman, M., 267

Coles, C., 87
Coles, M., 413
Coles, R., 428, 444
Coley, R. L., 261, 447
Colin, V. L., 186, 187, 188, 189, 190,
    191, 195
Coll, C. G., 20
Collaer, M. L., 252, 431
Colletti, J., 403
Collier, J., Jr., 231
Colling, M., 125
Collins, D. L., 414
Collins, K., 178
Collins, W. A., 255, 390, 392, 393,
    394, 399, 440
Collinsworth, P., 313
Coltrane, S., 195
Combs-Orne, T., 105
Comite, F., 360
Commitee on Pediatric AIDS, 86
Compas, B. E., 319
Comstock, G., 236, 275, 276
Conant, C. L., 255
Condon, L. M., 121
Condry, J., 275
Conger, J., 460, 461
Conger, R. D., 206, 259, 261, 264,
    363, 391, 452
Connell, J. P., 192
Conner, R. F., 236
Conners, C. K., 308, 310
Connolly, J. A., 399
Connolly, S. D., 358, 360, 362,
    441
Connor, D. B., 158
Connor, E. M., 86
Connor, R. T., 334
Connor-Smith, J. K., 319
Conroy, M. M., 121
Consortium for Longitudinal
    Studies, 235
Consumer Product Safety
    Commission, 133, 287
Cook, T. D., 236
Cooksey, E. C., 195
Coolbear, J., 192
Coon, K. A., 276
Cooney, G., 248
Cooper, H., 338
Cooper, R. G., 264
Cooper, R. P., 120
Coopersmith, S., 245, 246
Copeland, L. A., 385
Copeland, P., 67
Coplan, R. J., 273
Copstick, S. M., 102
Corasaniti, M. A., 197
Corbin, S. B., 267
Corcoran, J., 447
Cordell, A. S., 248
Coren, S., 216
Corkum, V., 158
Corley, R., 7, 8
Cornelius, S., 390
Corns, K. M., 273
Cornwell, T., 306
Cortez, V. L., 329
Costa, P. T., 419

Costigan, K. A., 182
Cote, J. F., 388
Cotton, S., 366
Couchoud, E. A., 258
Coulton, C. J., 205
Counts, C. R., 364
Coupey, S. M., 369, 370, 418
Courtlandt, C. D., 219
Covington, M. C., 336
Cowan, C. P., 245, 263
Cowan, G., 366
Cowan, P. A., 245, 263
Cowan, R., 87
Cowden, J. E., 285
Cox, B. C., 292
Coy, K. C., 176, 393
Coyle, T. R., 292
Cozby, P. C., 48, 50
Crain, W., 33, 36
Cramer, D. W., 88
Crane, J., 325
Crane, J. P., 71
Cratty, B. J., 116, 117, 135, 138, 213,
    214, 215, 216, 286
Creasy, G. L., 334
Crick, N. R., 256, 319
Criqui, M. H., 264
Crispell, D., 459
Criss, M. M., 259, 392
Crittenden, P. M., 29, 191, 192, 193
Crnic, K., 20, 21, 105, 194, 195, 263,
    325
Crocker, A. C., 367
Crombie, G., 338, 433
Cross, D. R., 158
Crouter, A. C., 274, 275, 393
Crowder, K., 446
Crowe, P. A., 385
Crowell, J., 29
Cryer, D., 198
Csikszentmihalyi, M., 271, 296,
    394, 462, 463
Cuellar, R., 91
Cuffe, S. P., 205
Culp, A. M., 169
Culver, L. C., 260
Cumberland, A., 258
Cumberland, A. J., 334
Cummings, E. M., 206, 266
Cunningham, A. E., 336, 337, 378
Cunningham, F. G., 85, 86, 90, 92,
    103
Cunningham, P. B., 416
Curie, M., 296
Curran, D. J., 18
Curran, J. M., 273
Curry, G. D., 402
Curtis, T., 400
Curtis, W. J., 3
Curtiss, S., 47, 170, 171, 172
Cutler, G. B., Jr., 359, 360
Cutler, G. P., 358
Cyphers, L., 271, 272
Czarnecki, D. M., 87

Dabholkar, A. S., 137
Dacey, J., 354, 365
Dahl, K. L., 301

Dahm, P. S., 166
Daigneault, J. P., 422
D'Air, A., 376
Dainton, M., 14
Dale, P. S., 163, 165, 166, 238
Dalton, M., 456
Daly, K., 105
Damasio, A. R., 167
Damasio, H., 167
Damon, W., 257, 258, 338, 345,
    385, 425, 427
Daniels, D. H., 246
Daniels, M., 8
Daniels, S. R., 371
Danish, S., 368
Danley, K. L., 331
Dannemiller, J. L., 118, 119,
    145
Dansen, P. R., 291
D'Apolito, K., 90
Darby, B. L., 87, 88
Darley, C., 421
Darling, N., 452
Daro, D., 202, 205, 206
Darroch, J. E., 400, 445, 446
Darwin, C., 13, 14, 28, 47
Dasen, P., 291
Datta, L. E., 235
DerSimonian, R., 87, 140
Davey, A. G., 304
Davey, S. G., 288
Davidson, J., 322
Davidson, J. E., 295
Davidson, J. K., 18
Davidson, R. J., 180
Davies, L., 257
Davies, M., 327
Davies, O. L., Jr., 318
Davies, P., 266
Davies, P. S., 357
Davies, P. T., 399
Davies, S., 327
Davies, W. H., 458
Davis, A. C., 257
Davis, B. E., 139
Davis, B. T., 266
Davis, E. C., 442
Davis, J. F., 277
Davis, L. B., 121
Davis, R. W., 68
Dawson, D. A., 332, 453
Day, N. L., 89
Day, R. D., 259, 263
Deak, G. O., 164
Deal, J. E., 259
Deater-Deckard, K., 188, 198
de Benedictis, T., 375
DeBlassie, R. R., 447
DeCasper, A. J., 119, 147
Decavalas, G. O., 89
Deci, E. L., 385
Decker, M. D., 219
DeCorte, E., 314
Dedrick, C. F., 192
Deford, F., 65
DeFries, J. C., 7, 8, 67, 70, 71
Degirmencioflu, S. M., 395
deGraft, J. A., 310

deHass, I., 88
de Houwer, A., 241
DeJonge, C. J., 75, 76
DeJoseph, J., 93
DeKlyen, M., 325
Dekovic, M., 263, 394
Delaney, M., 364
Delany, S., 120
De Lisi, R., 430, 432
Dell, D. L., 447
DeLoache, J. S., 225
DeLongis, A., 14
Delucchi, K., 375
Demaray, M. K., 338
DeMarie-Dreblow, D., 225
Demetriou, H., 257
DeMier, R. L., 125
DeMulder, E., 334
Demuth, K., 298
Denham, S., 334
Denham, S. A., 258
Dent, C. W., 331
Depner, C. E., 269
Deregowski, J. B., 294
DeRoche, E. F., 426
De Rosier, M. E., 333, 335, 365
Derry, P. S., 365
DerSimonian, R., 87, 140
Derzon, J. H., 324
Descartes, R., 231
Deslandes, R., 390
DeVet, K. A., 249
de Villiers, J., 165, 168, 298
de Villiers, P., 165, 168, 298
Devlin, B., 8
De Vos, R. C., 68
DeVries, M., 22, 185, 235
Dewey, M. J., 219
DeWolf, D. M., 260
De Wolff, M. S., 192
Diamond, A., 153, 154, 285
Diamond, L. M., 449
Diamond, M., 250
Diaz, M., 91
Diaz, R. M., 229
Diaz, T., 385
Diaz, V., 89
Dichtellmiller, M., 192
Diehl, S. F., 125
Dielman, T. E., 385
Dietz, T. L., 406
Dietz, W. H., 288
DiGeronimo, T. F., 180
DiGirolamo, A. M., 285
DiLalla, L. F., 229
DiMaggio, P., 230
Dimas, J. M., 319
DiPietro, J. A., 142, 182
Dishion, T. J., 274, 324, 325, 330,
    390, 392
DiVitto, B., 127
Dix, T., 261
Dixon, S., 200
Dode, I., 452
Dodge, K. A., 205, 256, 259, 271,
    319, 325, 333, 334, 392, 416
Doherty, M., 374
Doherty, W. J., 105, 195

Dollaghan, C., 163
Dollberg, S., 88
Don, A., 87
Donahue, M. J., 427, 428
Donaldson, M., 223
Donhowe, J., 121
Donnelly, D. A., 392
Donnerstein, E., 275
Donohue, P. K., 126
Donovan, E. F., 123
Doppler, M., 276
Dorn, L. D., 358, 452
Dornbusch, S. M., 263, 266,
    269, 363, 388, 399, 440,
    452, 459
Doussard-Roosevelt, J. A., 124
Downey, E. P., 303
Downs, A. C., 251
Doyle, A. B., 3, 304, 398
Doyle, L. W., 142
Dragonas, T., 94
Drapeau, S., 275
Draper, P., 360
Dreves, C., 431
Drewett, R. F., 141
Dreyer, B. P., 219
Driscoll, A., 443
Driscoll, M. E., 434
Driscoll, R., 320
Dryfoos, J. G., 376
Dubois, A. F., 441
DuBois-Reymond, M., 442
Dubowitz, H., 206
Dubrow, N., 461
Dubrow, N. F., 322, 331
Duda, J., 368
Duerst, B. L., 443
Dukes, R. L., 388
Dulcan, M. K., 309, 310
Dumas, J. E., 247
Dumka, L. E., 319
Dunbar, K., 375
Duncan, G. J., 313, 409, 442
Duncan, P., 363, 376
Duncan, R. M., 229
Duncan, S., 202, 203
Dunn, J., 7, 9, 228, 240, 255, 257,
    273, 274, 275, 331
DuPaul, G. J., 309
DuPont, S., 389
DuPre, E. P., 308
Durso, F. T., 226
Duseck, J. B., 354
Dusman, A. E., 126
Dvorak, T., 392
Dweck, C. S., 181, 245, 246
Dwyer, C. A., 430
Dwyer, K. M., 331

Eason, E., 100
Easterbrooks, M. A., 194
Easterling, D. V., 102
Eastman, G., 390
Eaton, W. O., 252
Eaves, L., 7, 9
Eaves, L. J., 107, 309
Ebata, A. T., 460, 461
Ebstein, R., 67

Eccles, J. S., 247, 376, 377, 378, 379, 380, 386, 391, 394, 422, 432, 433, 434
Eckenrode, J., 205, 326
Eckensberger, L. H., 345
Eckert, T. L., 309
Eddy, J. M., 325
Edelbrock, C., 450
Edelbrock, C. S., 309
Edelstein, W., 38
Edens, J. F., 186
Edgerton, R. B., 311
Edgeworth, J., 206
Edison, N., 277
Edwards, C. P., 252
Edwards, L., 94
Egeland, B., 192, 263
Egley, A., 402
Ehrenkranz, R. A., 123
Ehrhardt, A. A., 250
Ehri, L. C., 298
Ehrle, J., 195, 196
Ehrlich, A., 249
Eiben, R., 124
Eiberg, H., 64
Eidelman, A. I., 127
Eiden, R. D., 273
Einstein, A., 296
Eisenberg, A., 82, 92, 104
Eisenberg, M., 188, 198
Eisenberg, N., 3, 82, 252, 255, 256, 257, 258, 260, 270, 318, 319, 334, 335, 386, 432, 433
Eisenbud, L., 251
Eklund, R. C., 367
Eland, J., 125
Elardo, R., 41, 231
Elbert, T., 29
Elder, G. H., 261, 363, 452
Elias, S., 72
Elicker, J., 194, 335
Elins, J. L., 274
Elkind, D., 11, 234, 376
Elliot, D. M., 201
Elliot, S. N., 338
Elliot, T. S., 296
Elliott, D. S., 453
Elliott, G., 310
Elliott, J. G., 328
Elman, J., 28
Elo, I. T., 400, 443
ElSohly, M., 89
Ely, R., 240, 428, 432
Emery, R. E., 202, 205, 206, 265
Emes, C. E., 406
Emslie, G. J., 327
Endsley, R. C., 251
Engelsmann, F., 197
Engen, T., 120
Englund, M., 194, 335
Ennett, S. T., 395
Enns, L. R., 252
Enright, M., 148
Ensminger, A. H., 367
Ensminger, M. E., 367
Entwisle, D. R., 434
Epperson, C. N., 104
Epstein, J. L., 380, 397

Epstein, L. G., 86
Erdley, C. A., 398
Erel, O., 274
Erich, W. B., 422
Erickson, J. A., 427
Erickson, M. T., 309
Ericsson, R. J., 65
Erikson, E. H., 31, 32, 44, 47, 176, 180, 386, 387, 397, 443
Eron, L. D., 276, 277, 324
Esbensen, F., 402
Escarce, M. E. W., 100
Espenshade, T. J., 16
Espinosa, C., 389
Espinoza, R. L., 249
Esterberg, K. G., 17
Estell, D., 402
Evans, A. C., 414
Evans, G. W., 41
Evans, J. K., 71
Evans, K., 370
Evans, M. I., 72
Eveleth, P. B., 361
Ewigman, B. G., 71
Ewy, R., 145
Eyler, F. D., 90
Ezzaki, A., 236

Fabes, R. A., 3, 23, 43, 45, 120, 182, 252, 255, 256, 257, 258, 260, 270, 277, 318, 319, 334, 335, 385, 386, 391, 424, 432, 433
Fabris, C., 90
Fafel, J., 29
Fagen, J. W., 148
Fagot, B. I., 147, 250, 260
Fainaru, M., 288
Fainaru, O., 88
Fairchild, H., 275
Falbo, T., 332
Falk, P. J., 17
Fan, X., 314, 432
Fanaroff, A. A., 122, 123
Fang, J., 123
Fantuzzo, J., 235
Fantz, R. L., 118
Farah, M. M., 374
Faraone, S. V., 308
Farber, E. A., 258
Farber, N., 376
Farmer, M., 334
Farneti, P., 113
Farol, P., 414
Farrar, M. J., 225, 240
Farrington, D. P., 450, 453
Farver, J. A. M., 322
Fearing, D. D., 157
Fearnow, M. D., 319
Featherman, D. L., 353
Federal Bureau of Investigation, 406, 451, 452
Federal Interagency Forum on Child and Family Statistics, 414
Federman, J., 276
Fegley, S., 459
Fein, D. A., 413
Fein, G., 198

Feingold, A., 247
Feldlaufer, H., 377
Feldman, D. H., 172, 297, 313
Feldman, J., 103
Feldman, P., 100
Feldman, R., 127
Feldman, R. S., 205
Feldman, S. S., 355
Fellman, V., 124
Fennema, E., 430
Fenson, C., 157
Fenson, L., 163, 238
Fenton, N., 331
Fenton, T., 310
Ferguson, A. E., 124
Ferguson, L. R., 429
Ferguson, R. E., 338
Fergusson, D. M., 88, 142, 268
Ferketich, S., 93
Fernald, A., 119, 160
Fernald, L., 217, 287
Fernandez, T., 71
Fernandez-Collado, C., 277
Ferrell, K. A., 214
Ferron, C., 441
Feshbach, N. D., 275
Fetter, M. D., 396
Feynman, R. P., 293
Fichner-Rathus, L., 74
Field, A. E., 142, 372, 373
Field, T., 104
Field, T. M., 198
Fielding-Barnsley, B. R., 300
Fierman, A. H., 219
Fifer, W. P., 92, 120, 147
Figueredo, A. J., 203, 205
Filsinger, E. E., 120
Finch, M. D., 459
Finch, N. M., 142, 143, 144, 287, 288, 370, 371
Fincham, F. D., 266
Fine, C., 308
Fine, D., 445
Fine, G. A., 403
Fine, M., 267
Finkelhor, D., 392
Finkelman, B., 201
Finkelstein, J. W., 363
Finn, J. D., 434
Finnegan, L. P., 89
Fiscella, K., 445
Fisch, J., 236
Fisch, R., 121
Fischer, J. L., 397, 398
Fischer, K. W., 38, 214
Fischer, M., 309
Fisher, C. B., 45, 370
Fisher, M., 366, 414
Fitch, R. H., 431
Fitzgerald, B., 17
Fitzgerald, H. E., 458
Fitzgerald, M., 376
Fivush, R., 226
Fix, M., 19
Flake, A. W., 72
Flakierska-Praquin, N., 328
Flanagan, C., 377
Flanagan, C. A., 386

Flanagan, P., 447
Flannery, D. J., 401, 402
Flavell, E. R., 228
Flavell, J. H., 9, 228, 302, 423
Flay, B. R., 331
Fleming, J., 125
Fletcher, J. L., 85
Fletcher, J. M., 300
Fleury, J., 200
Flood, M. F., 442
Focus on the Family, 17
Fogel, A., 93, 107, 138, 139
Foltz, C., 375
Fombonne, E., 370, 371, 373
Fondell, M. M., 195
Foorman, B. R., 300
Forbes, G. B., 356
Ford, C. M., 406
Ford, G. W., 142
Forehand, G., 310
Forehand, R., 385, 441
Forehand, R. L., 360
Forrest, D., 144
Forrest, J. D., 443
Forsyth, B. W. C., 27, 90
Foster, C. M., 360
Foster, E. M., 261
Fowler, A. E., 70
Fowler, J., 48
Fowler, W., 231
Fowles, D. C., 325
Fox, G. L., 105
Fox, N. A., 195, 273, 285
Fox, R. A., 261, 325
Frable, D. S., 248
Fracasso, M. P., 195
Frame, C. L., 364
Francis, D. J., 300
Francis, G., 328, 329
Franco, N., 329
Franco, O., 376
Frank, E., 327
Frankel, K. A., 194
Frankel, S. J., 288
Frankowski, B., 376
Franssetto, S., 260
Frary, R. B., 367
Frazier, A. L., 142
Fredrickson, B. L., 181
Freedman-Doan, C., 378, 432, 433, 434
Freeman, M., 394
Freier, K., 89
French, D. C., 324, 325, 330, 333
French, K. E., 252, 286
Freppon, P. A., 301
Freud, S., 29, 30, 31, 44, 296
Freund, L. S., 221, 290
Frey, K. S., 246
Frick, P. J., 324
Friedman, H. S., 264
Friedman, S. B., 414
Friedrich, L. K., 278
Friedrich-Cofer, L. K., 277
Friel, L. V., 442
Frigoletto, F. D., 71
Frisch, R. E., 361, 420
Frith, U., 7

Fritz, A. S., 228
Frolund, L., 181
Frome, P., 432, 433
Frome, P. M., 247, 377
Frone, M. R., 459
Frongillo, E. A., 287, 367
Frosch, D. L., 322
Frost, J. L., 273
Fruehling, J. J., 327
Fry, P. S., 305
Fuchs, M., 89
Fujita, N., 240
Fuligni, A. J., 391, 393, 394, 440
Fulker, D. W., 7, 8
Fultz, J., 260
Furman, W., 271, 399
Furnham, A., 371
Furstenberg, F. F., 265, 267, 269, 400, 442, 443
Futterman, D., 418
Future of Children, 19

Gabriel, S. W., 333
Gaddis, A., 366
Gadow, K. D., 277
Gaffan, E. A., 192
Gagnon, J. H., 443
Gaines, C., 393
Gaithright, J. F., 235
Galambos, N. L., 366
Galbraith, K. A., 392, 446
Gale, J. E., 305
Gallagher, A. M., 432
Gallahue, D. L., 137, 138, 141, 285, 420
Gallant, S. J., 365
Gallup Organization, 337
Galotti, K. M., 102
Gamble, T. J., 235
Gan, S. L., 403
Ganchrow, J. R., 146
Gandhi, Mahatma, 296, 344
Ganong, L., 267
Gant, N. F., 85, 86, 90, 92, 103
Gao, Y., 186
Garbarino, J., 47, 227, 322, 323, 331, 461
Garber, J., 333, 452
Garcia, H. V., 20, 21
Garcia Coll, C. T., 16, 20, 21
Gardner, H., 216, 295, 296, 312
Gardstrom, S. C., 403
Garmezy, N., 320
Garner, P. W., 257
Garrison, W. T., 420
Garrity, C., 264
Garwood, M. M., 192
Gatzanis, S., 327
Gauss, K., 231
Gautier, T., 250
Gauvain, M., 228
Gauze, C., 398
Gaze, C., 429
Ge, X., 261, 363, 452
Geary, D. C., 28
Gecas, V., 390, 397
Geidel, S. A., 113
Geis, H. K., 285

Gekowski, M. J., 148
Gelles, R. J., 202, 203
Gelman, R., 70, 223, 224
Gelman, S. A., 164, 227
Georgieff, M. K., 216, 218
Geotz, D., 327
Geraldson, B., 216
Gershenson, H. P., 445
Gershman, H., 441
Gershoff, E. T., 334
Getz, I., 346
Geva, J., 219, 300, 301
Giannetta, J. M., 90
Gibbs, J., 341, 344
Gibbs, R. S., 85
Gibson, E. J., 145
Giedd, J. N., 356, 414
Gil, A. G., 319
Gilbert-Barness, E., 126
Gillberg, C., 328, 369, 371
Gillette, J., 238
Gillian, D. O., 250
Gilligan, C., 346
Gillman, M. W., 142
Gilman, E., 36, 38
Gilmore, M. R., 447
Ginsburg, H. J., 252
Giordano, P. C., 398
Girnius-Brown, O., 260
Givaudan, M., 180
Gladstein, J., 323
Gladstone, T. R. G., 327, 452
Glass, R. H., 74
Glastris, P., 19
Gleason, J. B., 159, 240, 428, 432
Gleitman, H., 169
Gleitman, L. R., 70, 169, 238
Glick, B., 403
Glover, V., 92
Gnagy, E. M., 310
Goedhart, T., 274
Golan, M., 288
Gold, D., 338, 433
Goldberg, J., 276
Goldberg, M., 196
Goldberg, S., 107, 127
Goldberg, W. A., 105, 194
Goldberger, L., 32, 386, 387
Goldfarb, J., 397
Goldfield, B., 238
Goldin-Meadow, S., 171
Golding, J., 94
Goldman-Rakic, P. S., 356
Goldschmidt, L., 89
Goldsmith, H. H., 180
Goldsmith, R., 377
Goldstein, A. P., 403
Golombok, S., 17
Golub, M., 217
Gomez, C., 178
Goncalves, M., 200
Goncu, A., 158, 159, 182, 230, 231
Gondoli, D. M., 440, 441
Gonzales, N. A., 319
Goodman, G. S., 202, 225, 226
Goodman, M., 394
Goodman, R., 332
Goodman, R. A., 117

Goodman, S., 70
Goodnow, J. J., 259, 260, 366
Goodwyn, S., 162
Goodyear, I., 327
Gopnik, A., 145, 157, 161, 170
Gordis, E. B., 321
Gordon, B., 312
Gordon, L. C., 264
Gordon, R. A., 261
Gordon, R. C., 85
Goring, J. G., 308
Gorman, K., 217
Gorman-Smith, D., 41, 321, 323, 453
Gortmaker, S. L., 124, 288
Goswami, U., 290
Gotlib, I. H., 262
Gottesman, I. I., 8
Gottfredson, D. C., 450, 451
Gottfried, A. E., 313
Gottfried, A. W., 124, 184, 232, 313
Gottlieb, G., 7
Gottman, J. M., 266, 271, 334
Gottwald, S. R., 124
Goubet, N., 154
Goudsmit, J., 86
Gould, E., 118
Gove, F. L., 194
Graber, J. A., 360, 363, 399, 443
Graber, M., 153, 154
Grabill, C. M., 327
Grabowecky, M., 356
Graczyk, P. A., 333
Graham, M. A., 420
Graham, P., 274, 326, 327
Graham, S., 380
Graham, S. A., 164
Granger, R. H., 90
Grant, B., 78
Grant, B. F., 453
Grantham-McGregor, S., 217, 218, 287
Gray, C., 232
Gray, J. A., 328
Gray, M. R., 263, 398
Gray, R. H., 88
Grayson, A., 179
Gredler, G. R., 234
Green, E. H., 256
Green, F. L., 228
Green, J. A., 178
Green, M., 32, 34, 256
Green, P., 420
Greenberg, B. D., 67
Greenberg, B. S., 277
Greenberg, M. T., 325
Greenberger, E., 394, 452, 459
Greene, B., 109, 112, 152, 176
Greene, K., 376
Greene, R. W., 308, 310
Greene, S. M., 397, 398
Greenhill, L. L., 310
Greening, L., 419
Greenough, W. T., 117, 118
Greenspan, N. T., 176
Greenspan, S. I., 176
Greenwald, R. L., 260
Greer, B., 314
Greulich, F., 246

Gridina, N., 275, 276, 281
Griesler, P. C., 335, 394
Griffin, A., 198
Griffin, D. W., 186
Griffin, K. W., 385
Griffin, R. S., 286
Griffith, D. R., 90
Griffith, E. M., 234
Griffith, J. R., 327
Griffiths, M. D., 404
Grimshaw, P. N., 214
Groark, C. J., 45
Groat, H. T., 398
Grolnick, W. S., 305
Grolund, J., 361
Gromisch, D. S., 89
Groome, L. J., 112
Gross, L., 449
Gross, R., 363
Grosvenor, M. B., 143, 144, 217
Grotevant, H. D., 23, 386, 462
Grotpeter, J. K., 256
Gruber, M. L., 277
Gruber, S. A., 413
Grunert, V., 142
Grunseit, A., 449
Grusec, J. E., 255, 259, 260, 261, 263, 269
Guenther, Heidi, 370
Guerin, D. W., 184, 313
Guger, S., 192
Guidubaldi, J., 265
Guis, M., 68
Gullone, E., 371
Gullotta, T. P., 335, 395
Gunnar, M. R., 23, 106, 121, 188, 318
Gunnell, D. J., 288
Guo, S., 125
Guralnick, M. J., 334
Gustafson, G. W., 178
Guthrie, I. K., 3, 182, 258, 318, 319, 334, 335
Gvaryahu, G., 90

Haaland, W., 186
Haan, D., 259, 391
Hack, M., 124, 126
Hackney, R., 334
Hadley, P. A., 237, 239, 334
Hafer, S., 330
Hagan, M. S., 268
Hagen, E. H., 104
Hagen, J., 218
Hageskull, B., 194, 334
Haggerty, R. J., 353
Haith, M. M., 144, 153, 155
Haka-Ikse, K., 443
Hakanen, E. A., 403
Hakuta, K., 306
Hala, S., 228, 302, 423
Hale, L. J., 376
Hale, P. M., 360
Halil, T., 179
Hall, D. G., 164
Hall, G. Stanley, 13, 14, 332
Hall, H., 368
Hall, J. A., 252
Hall, M. J., 38

Halperin, J. M., 256
Halpern, D. F., 428, 429, 431, 432
Halverson, C. F., 228, 250, 251, 254, 259
Hamel, S. C., 89
Hamer, D., 67
Hamilton, C. E., 198, 337
Hammer, L. D., 363
Hammond, M. A., 232, 334
Hammond, W. R., 323, 325
Hampton, R. L., 335
Hanish, L., 45
Hanna, G., 452
Hansen, C., 329
Hansen, D. M., 459
Hansen, K. L., 346
Hansen, W. B., 331
Hardy, J. B., 447
Harel, Y., 286
Hargreaves, D. J., 403
Harkness, S., 176, 271
Harlan, E. T., 184
Harlow, B. L., 88
Harold, R. D., 378
Harpin, V., 121
Harrington, R., 452
Harris, B. G., 94
Harris, D. V., 420
Harris, H. B., 125
Harris, J. F., 226
Harris, J. R., 5
Harris, L. J., 216
Harris, P. L., 228, 319
Harrison, D. D., 72
Hart, B., 169
Hart, C. H., 260
Hart, S. N., 201
Harter, S., 245, 246, 247, 384, 385, 386
Hartup, W. W., 255, 270, 397
Harwood, R. L., 22, 193
Hasemeier, C. M., 361
Hashima, P. Y., 261
Hassold, T. J., 69
Haste, H., 346
Hatfield, R. F., 125
Hathaway, S. E., 82, 92, 104
Hatton, D. D., 214
Haugaard, J. J., 202
Hauser, S. T., 390
Hausfather, A., 197
Haveman, R., 462
Hawkins, A. J., 448
Hawkins, J. D., 451
Hawkins, M., 330, 331
Hay, D. F., 256, 257
Hayashi, C. T., 368
Hayes, D. S., 277
Hayes, R., 102
Hayghe, H. V., 330
Hayne, H., 148, 149
Hayward, C., 363
Haywood, H. C., 229
Hazen, N. L., 334
Heald, F., 323
Health Behavior in School-Aged Children, 367, 369, 420, 421

Healy, R. W., 364
Hearold, S., 276
Heath, A. C., 107, 309
Hechtman, L., 309, 310
Hedges, L. V., 428
Hediger, M. L., 142
Heffer, R. W., 260
Hegyi, T., 109
Heim, S., 29
Heimann, M., 113
Hein, K., 418
Heinemann, R., 332
Heller, W., 252
Helm, P., 361
Helsen, M., 387
Hench, K. D., 360
Henderlong, J., 271
Henderson, C., 326
Henderson-King, D., 247
Henderson-King, E., 247
Hendrick, C., 443
Hendrick, S. S., 443
Henggeler, S. W., 416
Henker, B., 310
Hennessey, B. A., 297
Henning, K. H., 344, 425
Henricson, C., 390
Henry, B., 182
Henry, C. S., 392
Henshaw, S., 445, 446
Heppner, P. P., 253
Hercigonja, V., 322
Herdt, G., 450
Herman, A. A., 88
Herman, P. A., 298
Herman-Giddens, M. E., 361
Hern, K., 309
Hernandez, M., 276
Herold, E. S., 441, 442, 444, 448
Herrmann, D. J., 46
Hershberger, S. L., 450
Hertzler, A. A., 367
Hess, L., 256
Hess, L. I., 364
Hessen, L. D., 373
Hetherington, E. M., 263, 264, 265, 266, 268, 269, 392
Hewett, J. K., 309
Hewitt, M. P., 385
Hewlett, B. S., 261
Hiatt, M., 109
Hickey, P. R., 121
Hickson, F., 304
Hiebert, E. H., 300
Higgins, A., 425, 426
Higgins, D., 256
Higgins, E. T., 385
Hildebrand, D. K., 312
Hill, C. R., 329
Hill, E. J., 400, 448
Hill, J. P., 366, 391
Hill, K. K., 445, 447
Hill, P. T., 19
Hilton, S. C., 447
Hines, M., 252, 429, 431
Hinshaw, S. P., 263, 310
Hiscock, H., 104
Hobar, J. D., 124

Hochner-Celnikier, D., 91
Hochschild, A. R., 16
Hodgeman, J. E., 113
Hodgson, D. M., 182
Hodnapp, R. M., 311
Hodnett, E. D., 102
Hoff-Ginsberg, E., 169, 240, 298
Hoffman, D., 296
Hoffman, H. L., 257
Hoffman, L. W., 200
Hoffman, M. L., 257, 339, 391
Hoffmann, T., 346
Holden, G. W., 203
Holderby, A., 419
Holditch-Davis, B. P., 94
Holland, S. B., 112
Hollander, M., 164, 238
Holliday, M. A., 357
Hollin, C. R., 392
Holmbeck, G. N., 390, 393
Holmes, F., 328
Holzman, C., 26
Holzman, L. H., 299
Homel, R., 433
Hong, H., 178
Honzik, M. P., 328
Hood, L., 239
Hoover, K. R., 388
Hopkins, B., 178, 216
Hopkins, W. D., 216
Hoppenbrouwers, T., 113
Hops, H., 266
Hopwood, N. J., 360
Horn, J. L., 41
Horney, K., 31
Hornick, R., 125
Horowitz, F. D., 43, 45
Hort, B. C., 228
Hort, B. E., 250
Horwood, L. J., 88, 142, 268
Horz, B., 398
Host, P. C., 432
Hou, Q. C., 106
Hovey, J. D., 319
Howard, C., 249
Howard, G. J., 447, 448
Howard, K. I., 353
Howe, M. J. A., 294, 313
Howell, J. C., 402
Howes, C., 197, 198, 233, 270, 271, 273, 337
Hoyenga, K. B., 253
Hoyenga, K. T., 253
Hoyt, C., 180
Hoza, B., 310
Hsu, L. K. G., 369
Hu, S., 67
Hubbard, J. A., 271
Huber, A., 310
Hudson, B., 258
Hudson, J. A., 148, 226
Huesmann, L. R., 276, 277, 324, 453
Huestis, M. A., 89
Huff, C. R., 401, 402
Hughes, F. P., 273
Hughes, S. O., 258
Hunan, M. T., 125
Hunt, C., 376

Hunt, R. H., 119
Hunter, F. T., 158
Hunter, J., 449
Hunter, S. M., 397
Hunziker, J., 260
Hurt, H., 90
Hurtado, A., 22, 92
Hurtado, E. K., 218
Husarek, S. J., 176
Huston, A. C., 236, 251, 261, 275, 276, 277, 278, 313, 366, 404
Hutcheson, R. H., 219
Hutchinson, S., 105
Huttenlocher, P. R., 137, 214
Huttonlocher, J., 239
Hwang, C., 198
Hyde, J. S., 256, 430
Hymel, S., 333, 398
Hynd, G. W., 309

Iedema, J., 387
Imaizumi, S., 90
Imperato-McGinley, J., 250
Ingram, D., 169, 237
Ingram, R., 178
Inhelder, B., 222, 290, 374, 375
Inoff-Germain, G. D., 358
Insabella, G. M., 266
Institute of Medicine, 74, 75
International Association for the Evaluation of Educational Achievement, 430
International Human Genome Sequencing Consortium, 61
Intons-Peterson, M. J., 250
Irizarry, N. L., 194
Irvin, F., 450
Irwin, C. E., 363, 365
Isabella, R. A., 192
Itard, J., 6, 7, 26
Ito, J., 70
Iyengar, S., 327
Izard, C. E., 176, 177, 328

Jack, G., 261
Jacklin, C. N., 252, 256, 429
Jackman, G. A., 374
Jackson, K. M., 319
Jackson-Newsom, J., 274
Jacobs, A., 255
Jacobs, E. H., 309
Jacobs, J. E., 432, 433
Jacobs, P. J., 273
Jacobs, R. A., 7, 29, 230
Jacobs, V. A., 299
Jacobsen, L. K., 71
Jacobson, A. M., 390
Jacobson, J. L., 142
Jacobson, K., 154
Jacobson, S. W., 142
Jacobvitz, D., 309, 310
Jaffe, M. L., 11
Jagnow, C. P., 120
Jahoda, G., 292
Jain, A., 195
James, R., 413
Janigan, A. S., 420

Janowsky, J. S., 431
Jansen, R. C., 68
Janssens, J. M., 263
Jarvie, G. J., 364
Jarvis, P. A., 334, 459
Jason, L. A., 276
Jauregui, M., 91
Jeannin, A., 441
Jelalian, E., 369
Jellinek, M. B., 416, 417
Jellinek, M. S., 287
Jenkins, R., 20, 21
Jenkins, V. Y., 145
Jenni, C. B., 328
Jensen, P. S., 310, 327
Jersild, A., 328
Jessor, R., 450
Ji, G., 332
Jiao, S., 332
Jimenesez, D. P., 364
Jimenez, E., 218
Jing, Q., 332
John, E., 419
John, R. S., 274
Johnsen, M. C., 205
Johnson, A. M., 399
Johnson, C., 91, 259
Johnson, C. A., 331
Johnson, D. E., 23
Johnson, D. L., 232
Johnson, J. S., 168
Johnson, L., 27
Johnson, L. M., 430
Johnson, M. H., 153
Johnson, M. P., 72
Johnson, P., 125
Johnson, S., 433
Johnson, T. R. B., 182
Johnson, V. G., 305
Johnson Institute, 454
Johnston, H. F., 327
Johnston, J. R., 264
Johnston, L. S., 364
Jones, C., 364
Jones, C. P., 169
Jones, D., 286
Jones, D. C., 257
Jones, K. L., 87
Jones, K. P., 420
Jones, M. C., 364
Jones, O. W., 70, 71
Jones, R. E., 74, 75, 77, 80, 82, 83,
    94, 98, 100
Jones, S., 3, 313
Jones, S. K., 226
Jones, S. M., 325
Jones, S. S., 178
Jorgensen, S. R., 447
Joseph, R., 83
Josephs, R. A., 432
Josephson, W. L., 276, 277
Jouriles, E. N., 325
Jovanovic, J., 364, 431
Joyner, K., 449
Joyner-Kersey, J., 296
Juffer, F., 186
Jusczyk, P. W., 119, 160
Jussim, L., 307, 377

Kachur, S. P., 416
Kagan, J., 157, 185, 188, 259, 325
Kagan, S., 345
Kagan, S. L., 235
Kahn, P. H., 345
Kalamas, A. D., 277
Kalkose, M., 192
Kallen, K., 88
Kane, M. J., 293
Kanfer, F., 329
Kapitanoff, S. H., 202
Kaplan, H. B., 385
Kaplan, K. J., 331
Kaplan, K. M., 219
Kaplan, T., 327
Kaplan, W. E., 89
Kardash, C. M., 319
Karlson, H. C., 201
Karoly, P., 329
Karpov, Y. V., 229
Kasari, C., 311
Kashani, J. H., 326
Kaslow, N. J., 326, 327, 452
Kassianos, G. C., 219
Katchadourian, H., 400, 442, 443
Katz, A., 90
Katz, J. R., 273
Katz, L., 266
Katz, P. A., 275, 303, 304
Katzman, D. K., 370
Kaufman, J., 201
Kaufman, J. S., 320
Kaufman, N. L., 300
Kavanaugh, R. D., 228
Kavrell, S. M., 379
Kay, T., 70
Kaye, H., 120
Kayne, H., 287
Kazdin, A. E., 324, 327, 452
Kazuo, G., 193
Kearsley, R. B., 157
Keating, D. P., 441
Kedem, P., 331
Kee, D. W., 48, 50
Keefer, C. H., 200
Keel, B. A., 75, 76
Keenan, M., 70
Kegeles, S. M., 363
Kehoe, E. J., 33
Keil, F. C., 39
Keith, T. Z., 267
Keizer, L. C., 68
Kelch, R. P., 360
Kelder, S. H., 420
Kelleher, K. J., 123
Keller, L. B., 432
Keller, M. L., 443
Keller, R. W., 89
Kellermann, A. L., 374
Kelley, K., 444
Kelley, M. L., 260, 261
Kellman, P. J., 119, 144, 145
Kelly, D. P., 308
Kelly, E. A., 142
Kelly, J. B., 265, 267
Kelly, M., 375
Kemper, A. B., 422
Kendall-Tacket, K. A., 29, 205

Kendler, K. S., 309
Kennard, B. D., 327
Kennedy, C. L., 276
Kennedy, J. L., 309
Kennedy-Hanaway, L., 276
Kennell, J. H., 106, 186
Kenny, M., 354, 365
Keogh, B. K., 308, 312
Kermoian, R., 22, 139
Kernis, M. H., 248, 385
Kerns, K., 87
Kerpelman, J. L., 387
Kerr, M., 395
Kessler, R. C., 327
Kestenbaum, R., 258
Ketterlinus, R. D., 196, 197, 198, 450
Keye, W., 366
Khan, F., 91
Khan, Y., 414
Kiang, L., 91
Kiernan, K. E., 265
Kight, C., 27
Kilbourne, J., 247
Kilbride, P. L., 216
Killeen, M. R., 385
Killen, J. D., 363
Killen, M., 36
Kilmartin, C., 386
Kim, L. A., 319
Kim, Y., 247
Kimball, M. M., 433
Kimmerly, N. L., 195
Kimura, D., 252
King, B., 182, 184
King, M., 227
King, M. L., Jr., 344
King, R. A., 213
King, R. B., 400, 443
Kinney, D., 395, 396
Kinnish, K., 334
Kipnis, D. M., 277
Kippax, S., 449
Kirby, D., 448
Kirschbaum, R. M., 41
Kirsh, S. J., 194, 405
Kiser, L. J., 462
Kitayama, S., 248
Kittler, P. G., 370
Kitzman, H., 326, 445
Klaczynski, P. A., 375
Klahr, D., 375
Klaus, M. H., 106, 186
Klebanoff, M. A., 87
Klebanov, P. K., 313, 442
Kleiber, D., 368
Klein, H., 94
Klein, M. H., 406
Klein, N. K., 124, 126, 218
Klein, P. D., 296
Klein, R. G., 309
Klein, R. P., 360
Kleinman, R. W., 287
Klepp, K. I., 420
Kless, S. J., 386
Kliewer, W., 319, 386
Kline, J., 89
Klinefelter Syndrome & Associates,
    70

Klinger, M., 458
Knafo, D., 399
Knight, D. K., 158
Knight, G., 256, 345
Knight, G. P., 388
Knight, R. T., 356
Knight-Ridder/ Tribune News
    Service, 403
Knoebber, K., 390
Knott, J., 429
Knutson, J. F., 260
Koch, B. J., 363
Koch, G. G., 361
Kochanska, G., 176, 184, 260, 262
Kochenderfer, B. J., 333
Kocijan-Hercigonja, D., 322
Koegel, P., 311
Koenigsberger, M. R., 86
Koeppl, G. K., 334
Koeske, R. D., 226
Koff, E., 363, 420
Kohlberg, L., 194, 249, 253, 338,
    341, 342, 343, 344, 345, 425,
    426
Kohn, A., 260
Kohnstamm, G. A., 185
Koinis, D., 228
Kolb, K. J., 3037
Koletzko, B., 142
Kolko, D. J., 201, 202
Koller, H., 124
Koller, S., 257
Kolvin, I., 327
Konarski, R., 399
Kondo-Ikemura, K., 186
Konlande, J. E., 367
Konner, M., 116, 214
Koolstra, C. M., 276
Koons, A., 109
Koot, H. M., 323
Koper, C. S., 450, 451
Koplas, A. L., 255
Kopp, C. B., 180
Korbin, J. E., 205
Korht, W. M., 420
Korkman, M., 124
Korman, K., 431
Korones, S. B., 123
Korsvik, S., 121
Korte, D., 102, 103
Korzenny, F., 277
Kosorok, M. R., 180
Koss, M. P., 203, 205
Kostelny, K., 322, 331, 461
Kotchick, B. A., 441
Kotler, J. A., 276, 404
Kotlowitz, A., 321, 322
Kowal, A., 274
Kowalski, K. C., 367
Kowatch, R. A., 327
Kozu, J., 257
Kraemer, H., 368, 422
Krager, J. M., 308
Krahenbuhl, G. S., 420
Kramer, C., 434, 436
Kramer, L., 274
Kramer, M. S., 92
Kramer, R., 194

Kramer, S. J., 145
Krasnewich, D., 71
Kratochwill, T. R., 329
Krauss, D. A., 267
Kresnow, M., 416
Kroger, J., 355, 388
Kruger, H. A., 219
Krull, J. L., 127
Krupa, M., 424
Ku, L., 441, 443
Kubey, R., 403
Kucaba, T. A., 63
Kucera, K., 273
Kuchuk, A., 145
Kuczmarski, R. J., 142
Kuczynski, L., 260, 261
Kudlacz, E. M., 106
Kuhn, D., 250, 374, 375
Kuhn, L., 89
Kuint, J., 127
Kumra, S., 71
Kunda, Z., 253
Kundert, D. K., 234
Kunnen, E. S., 387
Kupanoff, K., 242, 258, 335, 391, 393
Kupersmidt, J. B., 335, 394
Kupferminc, M., 88
Kurdek, L. A., 264
Kuroda-Kawaguchi, T., 63
Kurowski, C., 327
Kurtines, W. M., 319, 322
Kurtz, D. A., 389
Kutz-Costes, B., 276
Kwasman, A., 309, 310

Laakso, L., 286
Laakso, M. L., 273
Ladd, G. W., 333, 334
LaGasse, L., 89
Lagercrantz, H., 106
LaGreca, A. M., 328, 396
Laible, D., 258, 335, 391, 424
Laird, R. D., 259, 325, 392
Lamaze, Fernand, 101
Lamb, M. E., 107, 113, 195, 196, 197, 198, 450
Lambert, D. A., 219
Lamberty, G., 20, 21
Lamborn, S. D., 263, 452
Lambros, K. M., 325
Lamke, L. K., 387
Lamon, S. J., 430
Lampert, W. E., 306
Lande, J., 196
Landeros, G., 180
Landers, D. M., 368
Landers-Pott, M., 310
Landry, D. J., 443
Lane, D. A., 71
Lane, K. L., 325
Lang, R., 186
Langendorfer, S., 141
Langer, J., 36, 155
Langlois, J. H., 145, 247, 251
Lansink, J. M., 157
Laosebikan, S., 93
LaPorte, D. J., 365

Lapsley, D. K., 376
LaRoche, C., 197
Larsen, B., 346
Larson, R., 329, 330, 368, 372, 385, 393, 394, 403, 462, 463
Larson, S. K., 142
Lasker, J., 271
Laski, K., 310
Lassen, K., 88
Last, C. G., 329
Laumann-Billings, L., 205, 206
Laursen, B., 255, 391, 393, 394
Lavin, D. R., 424
Lawson, K., 124
Lawton, C., 430
Lawton, M., 368
Leach, P., 140
Leadbeater, B., 375
Leaper, C., 399
Leboyer, Frederick, 101
Leckman, J. F., 127
Ledbetter, J., 403
Lee, C. M., 262
Lee, L. C., 199
Lee, M., 233
Lee, S., 261, 314, 379, 380
Lee, S. E., 406
Lee, V. E., 434, 435
Leeson-Payne, C., 142
LeFevre, M. L., 71
Lefkowitz, M. M., 277, 324
Legano, L. A., 219
Leger, D. W., 179
Legerstee, M., 145
Leggett, E. L., 181
Leiderman, P. H., 200
Leigh, G. K., 391
Leinbach, M. D., 147, 250
Leiter, J., 205
LeMare, L. J., 398
Lemons, J. A., 123
Lenane, M., 71
Lengua, L. J., 327
Lenihan, E. A., 41
Lenneberg, E., 167, 168
Lennon, J., 296
Lento, J., 460
LePage, D. E., 177
Lepper, H. S., 309, 310
Lepper, M. R., 271
Lerner, R. M., 45, 364, 394
LeRoy, T., 323
Lesch, K. P., 67
Leslie, A. M., 228
Lessing, J. B., 88
Lester, B. M., 89, 99, 114, 179
Leve, L. D., 260
Leveno, K. J., 103
Leventhal, E. A., 102
Leventhal, H., 102
Leventhal, J. M., 27, 90
Leveroni, C., 431
Levin, B., 89
Levin, B. B., 405
Levine, A., 390
Levine, J. A., 259
Levine, M. P., 373
LeVine, R. A., 200, 248

Levine, R. J., 87
LeVine, S., 200
Levinger, B., 287
Levinson, E. M., 294
Levinson, R. A., 448
Levitsky, D., 217
Levy, G. D., 157, 251, 303, 389
Levy, J., 252
Levy, S. R., 305
Levy-Storms, L., 441, 442
Lewinsohn, P. M., 363
Lewis, C., 426
Lewis, H. B., 181
Lewis, J., 265
Lewis, L. A., 403
Lewis, M., 90, 181
Lewis, S. M., 447
Lewis, T. L., 118
Lewit, E. M., 234
Leyendecker, B., 195
Li, Q., 67
Liben, L. S., 250, 254, 304
Liberman, A. M., 299
Liberty, C., 292
Lickona, T., 426
Liebergott, J. W., 169
Lieberman, M., 344
Lieberman, P., 159
Liebert, R. M., 275, 403
Liebling, J. A., 124
Liebo, R., 121
Life Sciences Research Office, 143, 287, 367
Lifshitz, F., 142, 143, 144, 287, 288, 370, 371
Lifshitz, J. Z., 142, 143, 144, 287, 288, 370, 371
Liikanen, A., 124
Lilen, L., 125
Lillard, A., 228
Lillo-Martin, D., 171
Lim, S. W., 219
Lin, K. H., 264
Lind, G., 426
Lindberg, L. D., 441, 443
Lindley, A. A., 88
Lindstroem, M., 328
Linebarger, D. L., 275
Lingenfelter, S. G., 93
Lind, J., 178
Linn, M. C., 375, 429
Lipsitt, L. P., 120
Lipworth, L., 92
Lister, G., 142
Little, B. B., 90
Little, J. K., 250
Little, M., 287
Little, S., 333
Liu, D. H., 332
Liu, X., 385
Livesley, W. J., 423
Lloyd, E. E., 369
Lloyd, M., 404
Locke, J., 12, 14
Lockwood, P., 253
Loeber, R., 256, 309, 450
Loeber, R. L., 453
Logsdon, M. C., 104

Lohr, M. J., 396, 447
Lohrmann, B. C., 270
Lollis, S., 398
Long, C., 293
Long, P. J., 360
Lorenz, F. O., 261, 264, 452
Loriaux, D. B., 358
Loriaux, D. L., 360
Lorys, V. A. R., 309
Losoya, S., 3, 334
Loucks, A. B., 420
Louganis, G., 419
Lounsbury, J. H., 378
Lovelace, L., 236
Lovelace, V. O., 278
Low, J. F., 144
Lowry, R., 416
Lozoff, B., 218
Lubeck, S., 235
Lucas, A., 142
Lucas, D., 148
Lucas, F. R., 67
Lucey, J. F., 124
Luckner, A. E., 102
Ludemann, P. M., 147
Luleci, G., 72
Luria, J. W., 141
Luria, Z., 335
Luster, T., 442
Lutzker, J. R., 201, 202, 205
Lye, D. N., 269
Lynch, D. L., 248
Lynch, M. D., 245
Lynch, M. E., 366
Lynskey, M. T., 88
Lysne, M., 389
Lytle, L. L., 420
Lytton, H., 253, 255, 269
Lyytinen, H., 309
Lyytinen, P., 273

Maas, J., 421
Maas, L. C., 413
Macaluso, M., 255
Maccoby, E. E., 43, 188, 252, 256, 262, 265, 266, 267, 269, 271, 329, 392, 429
MacDonald, P. C., 85, 86, 90, 93, 103
MacDonald, V., 310
MacFarlane, A., 121
Macfarlane, J. W., 328
MacIver, D. J., 377, 380
Mackey, M. C., 102
MacKinnon, C. E., 274, 275
MacKinnon, R., 274
Macksoud, M. S., 322
MacKune-Karrer, B., 453
MacLean, P. D., 29
MacMillan, D. L., 308, 312
Macomber, J., 154
Macrae, M., 33
MacTurk, R. H., 158
MacWhinney, B., 164
Madden, T., 389
Madhavan, S., 123
Madon, S., 307, 377
Maes, H., 309
Maes, L. J., 309

Maestas, M. V., 319
Magai, C., 260
Magee, V., 445
Magolda, M. B. B., 388
Magnusson, D., 4, 41, 363, 364
Maier, S. E., 87
Main, M., 191
Majors, K., 270
Makin, J. W., 121
Makogon, T. A., 426
Malatesta, C. Z., 176, 177
Malina, R. M., 356, 357, 422
Malmud, E., 90
Maloney, M. J., 371
Malouff, J. M., 405
Malson, L., 6
Manalo, M., 91
Mander, R., 104, 107
Mandler, J. M., 155, 156, 157, 221, 225
Maney, D. W., 363
Mange, A. P., 8, 63, 65, 67, 70, 71, 72, 75
Mange, E. J., 8, 63, 65, 67, 70, 71, 72, 75
Mangelsdorf, S. C., 192
Maniello, R. L., 125
Manire, S. H., 258
Manlove, J., 447
Mannie, S., 239
Mannuzza, S., 309
Manos, M., 401, 402
Manuel, M., 218
Maratsos, M., 164, 167
Maratsos, R., 113
March, J. S., 310
March of Dimes, 59, 69, 72, 73, 85, 86, 87, 88, 93
Marcia, J. E., 387, 388
Marciano, P. L., 452
Marcoen, A., 245
Marcus, G. F., 164, 238
Marcus, M. D., 287
Margolin, G., 274, 321
Marguglio, M., 420
Margulis, C., 240
Marin, G., 249
Markel, K. S., 459
Market Data Retrieval, 404
Markiewicz, D., 3, 398
Markman, E. M., 161, 163, 164, 165, 228
Marks, S. B., 308
Markson, L., 162
Markstrom-Adams, C., 388
Markus, H. R., 248
Marques-Bruna, P., 214
Marsh, J. S., 422
Marshall, S. K., 441, 442, 444, 448
Marshall, S. P., 430
Marshall, W. A., 356, 361
Marsiglio, W., 105, 448
Martin, C. A., 445, 447
Martin, C. L., 23, 43, 45, 228, 250, 251, 252, 253, 254, 338, 366, 386, 398, 430, 432, 433
Martin, D. C., 87
Martin, J. A., 262

Martin, K., 363, 364, 442, 443
Martin, L. M., 229
Martin, L. R., 264
Martin, N. C., 51
Martin, R. J., 122
Martindale, C., 297
Martinez, G., 443
Martinez, R. O., 388
Martinez, S., 345
Martini, M., 272, 273
Martins, C., 192
Martinson, I., 125
Martorano, S. C., 375
Marusic, A., 322
Masataka, N., 169
Mason, M. A., 268
Mason, T., 334
Massey, C. M., 223
Masten, A. S., 3, 320, 321
Mastrogiannis, D. S., 89
Mateer, C. A., 87
Mathason, L., 429
Matheson, C. C., 198, 273, 337
Matsuba, M. K., 425
Mattel Toy Company, 431
Mattock, A., 147
Masse, L. C., 389
Maughan, B., 7, 9
Maughn, B., 450
Maurer, D., 118, 145
Mauro, J. A., 183
Maxfield, D., 292
Maxfield, M., 203
May, D. C., 234
May, J. V., 75, 76
May, K., 93
Mayes, L. C., 90
Maza, P. L., 89
Mazur, E., 264
McAdoo, H. P., 18, 20, 21
McAnarney, E. R., 447
McBride, A. B., 104
McBride-Chang, C., 205, 300
McCall, R. B., 45
McCarthy, M. E., 158
McCartney, K., 68, 188, 197
McCarton, C., 124
McCaughey, Bobbi, 78
McCauley, E., 70
McClaskey, C. L., 334
McClearn, G. E., 67, 70, 71
McClelland, D. C., 294
McClelland, J. L., 153
McClintic, S., 181, 246
McClish, D. K., 218
McCloskey, L. A., 203, 205
McClurg, P. A., 433
McCormick, M. C., 124
McCormick, S. H., 393, 400
McCoy, J. K., 274
McCracken, C., 259, 263
McCracken, J., 452
McDermott, D., 249
McDonald, R., 325
McDonnell, L. M., 19
McDonough, L., 221
McDougall, P., 333
McElroy, A., 249

McElwain, N. L., 274
McFarlane, J., 94
McGee, R., 368
McGee, R. O., 182
McGillicuddy-De Lisi, A. V., 430, 432
McGlaughlin, A., 179
McGoey, K. E., 309
McGrath, M. P., 258, 260
McGrory, A., 365
McGuigan, W. M., 203
McGuire, J., 371
McGuire, S., 274
McHale, J. L., 192
McHale, S. M., 274, 275, 393
McIntire, D. D., 103
McLaughlin, B., 306
McLaughlin, F. J., 121
McLellan, J. A., 396
McLoyd, V. C., 259, 261, 313, 325
McManus, I. C., 216
McManus, K., 99
McMillan, D., 250
McNellis, D., 71
McPherson, E., 87
McPherson, J. D., 63
McPherson, S. L., 293
McQuiston, S., 420
McQuivey, R. W., 368, 422
McVeigh, B., 3
McVeigh, T., 3, 26
Meadow-Orlans, K. P., 192
Meaney, M. J., 252
Measelle, J. R., 245
Meck, J., 71
Mediascope, 405, 406
Meeus, W., 387
Mehta, P., 300
Meier, M., 324
Meier, R. P., 171
Meisels, S. J., 127, 192
Meister, C., 305
Mellou, E., 297
Melnick, M. J., 422
Melnick, S., 263
Meltzer, D., 94
Meltzoff, A. N., 113, 148, 157, 161
Melzak, S., 204
Mendelsohn, A. L., 219
Mendes, T. M., 360
Mennella, J. A., 120
Menyuk, P., 160, 169
Mercer, L., 333
Mercer, R. T., 93
Merckelbach, H., 328
Mergendoller, J. R., 301
Mergler, N. L., 226
Merikangas, K. R., 327
Merriman, W. E., 164
Merritt, J. A., 179
Merryman, J. D., 157
Mesias, W., 260
Mest, G. M., 311
Metha, A., 452
Meyer, J., 7, 9
Meyer, J. M., 309
Michaels, M., 227
Micheli, L. J., 287

Michelsson, K., 178
Mick, E., 308
Middlemiss, W. A., 261
Midgley, C., 377, 379
Midgley, C. H., 377
Midgley, C. M., 377
Midlam, J. K., 310
Mikus, K., 105
Milgram, N. A., 323
Milich, R., 310
Miller, A. L., 274
Miller, B. C., 392, 400, 442, 446
Miller, C., 386
Miller, C. L., 377
Miller, E., 377
Miller, H. M., 248
Miller, J. G., 194, 424
Miller, J. Y., 451
Miller, K. S., 441
Miller, M. J., 122
Miller, N. B., 263
Miller, P. A., 257
Miller, P. H., 26, 27, 36, 225, 292, 302, 423
Miller, S. M., 252
Miller, T. L., 447
Mills, R., 261
Millstein, S. G., 363, 365, 418
Mimouni, F. B., 88
Minkoff, H. L., 103
Minton, C., 259
Mintz, J., 246
Minuchin, P. P., 338
Mischel, W., 253
Mistry, J., 158, 159, 230, 231
Mitchell, C. M., 442
Mitchell, J. J., 462
Mitchell, S., 232
Miyake, K., 193
Mize, J., 334
Mnookin, R. H., 265, 267, 269
Modell, J., 394
Modzeleskie, W., 416
Moerk, E. L., 168
Moffitt, K. A., 125
Moffitt, T. E., 182, 324
Mohr, J., 64
Mohr, W. K., 235
Moien, M., 103
Mojica, E., 205
Mol, J., 68
Molfese, D. L., 184
Molfese, V. J., 184
Mollen, E., 218
Monahan, S. C., 266
Money, J., 250
Monitoring the Future, 411, 454
Monk, C., 92
Monsour, A., 384
Mont-Reynaud, R., 399
Montefalcon, R., 71
Montemayor, R., 395
Montepare, J. M., 29
Montero, I., 229
Montgomery, R., 270
Montour, K., 4
Monuteaux, M. C., 308
Moodey, A. F., 373

Moon, C., 120
Moon, R. Y., 139
Moore, C., 158
Moore, K. A., 443
Moore, K. L., 75, 80, 81, 82, 83, 84, 400
Moore, M. K., 113
Moore, N. B., 18
Moore, S., 444
Moore, S. G., 100
Moore, S. M., 371
Moorehead, K., 249
Moorer, S. H., 310
Morales, Y., 124
Morch, W., 346
Moreau, D., 326
Moreau, G. F., 441
Morelli, G. A., 200
Morely, M., 432
Morely, R., 142
Morgan, W. P., 368
Morris, K., 86
Morris, M. K., 326
Morris, N., 102
Morris, P. A., 41
Morris, R. J., 329
Morris, T. W., 294
Morrison, F. J., 234
Morrison, G. S., 378
Morrison, P., 320
Mortimer, J. T., 403, 459
Mory, M. S., 395, 396
Moser, J., 327
Mosier, C., 158, 159, 230, 231
Moss, E., 192
Mounts, N., 452
Mounts, N. S., 263
Mowder, B. A., 124
Mozart, W. A., 296
Mruk, C., 246, 247, 248
Mu, X., 314
Mueller, U., 373
Mufson, L., 326
Muller, T., 16
Mulvenon, S., 452
Mumme, D. L., 145, 176
Munakata, Y., 39, 153
Mundfrom, D. J., 123
Munn, P., 255, 274
Munoz, J. M., 252
Munsch, J., 397, 398
Muret-Wagstaff, S., 100
Muris, P., 328
Murkoff, H. E., 82, 92, 104
Murphy, B., 260
Murphy, B. C., 3, 255, 256, 258, 270, 334
Murphy, D. L., 67
Murphy, J. M., 287
Murphy, R., 416
Murphy, W. D., 202
Murray, J. P., 275, 276, 277
Murray, K. T., 184
Murray, L., 158
Musick, J. S., 445
Mussen, P. H., 364
Muuss, R. E., 388
Myers, A., 287

Myers, B. J., 107, 386
Myers, M. M., 92
Myers, N. A., 149
Mylander, C., 171

Nadder, T. S., 309
Nagy, W. E., 298
Nair, P., 27
Nanchahal, K., 288
Napolitano, B., 366
Narasimhan, B., 240
Nash, J. M., 7, 115, 117
Nash, S. C., 250
Nathanieisz, P. W., 97
National Association for the Education of Young Children, 199, 232, 233, 300
National Campaign to Prevent Teen Pregnancy, 411
National Center for Education Statistics, 17, 232, 234, 283, 306, 335, 337, 404, 436, 467
National Center for Health Statistics, 77, 78, 79, 85, 88, 91, 93, 97, 100, 101, 102, 103, 109, 122, 123, 127, 136, 140, 264, 267, 268, 400, 401, 414, 416
National Center for Injury Prevention and Control, 416
National Center on Addiction and Substance Abuse, 457, 458
National Child Abuse and Neglect Data System, 2, 201
National Clearinghouse on Child Abuse and Neglect, 201
National Diffusion Network, 436
National Down Syndrome Society, 69, 70
National Federation of State High School Associations, 422
National Highway Traffic Safety Administration, 454
National Institute on Drug Abuse, 88, 456
National Institute of Mental Health, 326, 370, 371
National Issues Forum, 195
National Mental Health Association, 320
National Middle School Association, 378
National Research Council, 16, 19, 171, 172, 205, 206
National Science Foundation, 431
National Telecommunications and Information Administration, 404, 405
Nativio, D., 125
Naus, M. J., 292
Navaez, D., 346
Neale, D. C., 305
Neale, M. C., 107, 309
Neckerman, H. J., 402
Neher, L. S., 453
Nelson, C. A., 117, 118, 137, 327
Nelson, D. A., 319
Nelson, E. C., 218
Nelson, K., 225, 226, 238

Nelson, K. E., 161
Nelson, S. A., 341
Nelson-Le Gall, S. A., 341
Netley, C., 70
Neuman, M. J., 235
Nevid, J. S., 74
Neville, H., 172
Newberger, E. H., 144
Newcomb, A. F., 270, 271, 333, 398
Newcombe, N., 304, 429, 430
Newcorn, J. H., 310
Newman, A., 329
Newman, J. L., 366
Newman, L. F., 88, 89
Newman, L. S., 423
Newport, E. L., 10, 160, 168, 169, 171, 172
Ng, S., 89
Nguyen, A., 310
Niaz, M., 373
Niccols, A., 192
NICHD, 197, 198
Nicholls, J. G., 337
Nicholson, J., 235
Nicolaisen, I., 354
Nicolson, J. M., 268
Nieman, R. H., 235
Nigg, J. T., 263
Nilzon, K. R., 327
Nimetz, S. L., 337
Ninio, A., 240, 299
Nitz, K., 324
Nitz, K. A., 450
Noam, G. I., 390
Noble, S., 338, 433
Nokes, K., 125
North, A. C., 403
Norton, M. C., 400
Norwood, W. D., 325
Nosphitz, J. D., 213
Nottelman, E. D., 358
Novick, E. R., 436
Nowell, A., 428
Nozza, R. J., 119
NPRIDE, 456
Nsamenang, A. B., 93
Nua Ltd., 406
Nuechterlein, K. H., 320
Nugent, K. J., 99, 114
Nurcombe, B., 327
Nurmi, J. E., 391
Nuttall, R. L., 431
Nyiti, R., 292

Oakes, L. M., 157
Oakland, T., 332
Oates, R. K., 144, 248
Obeidallah, D. A., 331
O'Brien, B., 99
O'Brien, D., 70
O'Brien, M., 169, 255
O'Connell, A. P., 68
O'Connell, B., 161
O'Connell, M., 330, 331
O'Connor, B. P., 392
Oden, M. H., 51
Oei, T. P., 88
Offer, D., 353

Office of Management and Budget, 19, 21
Office of Minority Health, 85
Ogbu, J. U., 249, 294
Ogino, M., 271, 272
Oh, W., 123, 124
Oh-Cha, S. Y., 376
Okamoto, Y., 38
Olds, D., 326, 445
Oleske, J. M., 86
O'Loughlin, M., 375
Olsen, J. E., 391
Olson, C. K., 394
Olson, C. M., 287, 367
Olson, D. R., 374
Olvera, M. C., 180
Olweus, D., 398
O'Neill, D. B., 287
Ong, A., 389
Onyango, A. N., 310
Opler, M., 107
Ordy, J. M., 118
Orenstein, P., 430
Ormel, J., 7, 9
Ornstein, P. A., 292
Ortiz, V., 18
Orwoll, E. S., 431
Osborn, R. W., 102
Osborne, M. L., 140, 256
Osher, Y., 67
Osipow, S. H., 388
Osmond, M., 104
Osofsky, J. D., 169
Oster, H., 120
Ostfeld, B., 109
Ostoja, E., 462
Ostrov, E., 353
Ostrow, L., 327
Otake, M., 90
Otero-Sabogal, R., 249
O'Toole, B. I., 248
Ott, J., 419
Ottolini, M. C., 139
Overpeck, M. D., 140, 142, 286
Overton, W., 430
Overton, W. F., 43, 373, 375
Oviatt, S. K., 431
Owens, R. E., 159, 160, 161, 168, 169, 238, 239, 240
Ozben, T., 72
Ozmun, J. C., 137, 138, 141, 285, 420

Padilla, M. T., 21
Pagano, M., 287
Pagant, L., 395
Page, D. C., 63
Page, R. M., 371
Paglia, A., 192
Pagnini, D. L., 91
Paik, H., 236, 275, 276
Paikoff, D. F., 442
Paikoff, R. L., 358, 360, 362, 390, 393, 400, 441, 443, 452
Palardy, N., 419
Palfrey, S., 219, 300, 301
Palmer, D., 257
Palmer, E. J., 392
Palmerus, K., 327

Palombaro, M. M., 333
Paneth, N., 26, 109
Papadimitrious, A., 361
Papageorgious, A., 122
Papile, L., 123
Papini, D. R., 390
Pardo, C., 322, 331, 461
Parent, S., 192
Paris, S. G., 305, 336, 337, 378
Parke, R. D., 194, 195, 259, 266
Parker, B., 94
Parker, J. G., 270, 327, 333, 335, 365
Parker, K. C. H., 192
Parkhurst, J. T., 398
Parmelee, A. H., 113
Parris, K. D., 388
Parsons, J., 318
Parten, M., 272
Pascal, B., 231
Pasick, P. L., 127
Passell, J. S., 19
Pasupahti, M., 3
Patterson, C., 270
Patterson, C. J., 17, 18, 335, 394
Patterson, D., 69
Patterson, G. R., 324, 325, 330, 390, 392
Paul, R., 166
Paus, T., 414
Pavelski, R., 368, 422
Pavlov, I., 32, 33
Peabody, P., 287
Peacock, A., 144
Pearson, J. L., 429
Peirano, P., 142
Pelham, W. E., 310
Pellegrini, A. D., 28, 252, 272, 310
Pellegrini, D., 320
Peracchio, L. A., 277
Perathoner, C., 90
Perez-Granados, D. R., 274
Perlmann, R. Y., 240
Perner, J., 228, 374
Perris, E. E., 148, 149
Perry, C. L., 420
Perry, D. G., 253, 277
Perry, I., 403
Perry, L. C., 277
Perry, S. E., 74, 77, 79, 83, 98, 101
Perry, T. B., 376, 397
Persell, C. H., 338
Perusse, D., 107
Pescovitz, O. H., 360
Peskin, H., 364
Peters, H. E., 267
Peters, T. J., 288
Petersen, A. C., 359, 363, 366, 379, 429, 460, 461
Peterson, G. W., 127, 259, 263, 391, 392, 440
Peterson, J. L., 266
Peterson, R. E., 250
Pethick, S. J., 163, 238
Petruzzello, S. J., 368
Pettegrew, J., 403
Pettit, G. S., 205, 259, 325, 334, 392
Pettitt, L. M., 326
Peyton, V., 255

Pezaris, E., 431
Phelps, L. A., 364
Phillip, D., 249
Phillips, D., 196, 197, 198
Phillipsen, L. C., 198, 397
Phinney, J. S., 345, 388, 389
Phipps-Yonas, S., 320
PHS, 417
Piaget, J., 9, 35, 36, 37, 38, 44, 47, 149, 150, 151, 152, 153, 154, 155, 220, 222, 223, 224, 229, 255, 256, 290, 297, 305, 338, 339, 340, 341, 373, 375
Pianta, R. C., 337
Picasso, P., 312
Pick, H. L., 45
Pickles, A., 7, 9, 309
Pieniadz, J., 376
Pierce, C. M., 102
Pierson, M., 325
Pinker, S., 164, 238
Pinto-Martin, J., 109
Pintrich, P. R., 376, 377, 378, 379, 380, 434
Pipher, M., 385
Pisoni, D. B., 119, 160
Pittman, J. F., 387
Pitts, R. C., 425
Pitts, T., 368, 422
Pizzini, E. L., 338
Placek, P. J., 103
Plato, 11
Platt-Houston, C., 205
Pleck, J. H., 441
Plewis, I., 179
Plimpton, C. E., 286
Plomin, R., 7, 8, 9, 67, 70, 71, 183, 324
Plumb, N., 106
Plumb, P., 366
Plumert, J. M., 45, 157
Plumlee, T. M., 260
Plunkett, J. W., 127, 192
Podorefsky, D., 424
Poikkeus, A. M., 273
Polce, L. M., 386
Polit, D. F., 332
Pollack, H. A., 287
Pollitt, E., 217, 218
Pollock, L. A., 11
Pomerantz, E. M., 246
Pooler, W. S., 65
Poortinga, Y. H., 291
Pope, A. W., 398
Pope, S. K., 123
Popkin, B. M., 369
Porac, C., 216
Porges, S. W., 124, 142
Portegal, M., 180
Porter, R. H., 121
Posada, G., 186
Posada, R., 186
Posner, J. K., 331
Posner, M. J., 184
Post, J., 235
Post-Gordon, J. C., 405
Poston, D. L., 332
Pott, M., 193

Potts, R., 276
Poulin, F., 271
Poulin, R., 3
Poulin-Dubois, D., 223
Poulton, L., 192
Powell, G. F., 144
Powell, K. E., 416
Power, A. R., 426
Power, F. C., 425, 426
Power, T. G., 258, 259
Powers, B. P., 192
Powers, J., 326
Powers, S. L., 390
Powlishta, K. K., 376
Prandi, G., 90
Pransky, J., 206
Pratt, C. C., 203
Pratt, M. W., 229
Prectl, H. F. R., 111
Preece, A., 14
Preisig, M. A., 327
President's Council on Physical Fitness and Sports, 368, 420, 421, 422
Pressley, M., 299
Price, D. W. W., 226
Price, J., 333, 335, 365
Price, J. M., 460
Prinstein, M. J., 396
Pritzker, S. R., 297
Prodromidis, M., 104
Proffitt, D. R., 145
Prugh, D. G., 41
Pruitt, D. B., 462
Prysak, M., 103
Public Agenda, 411
Public Broadcasting Service, 236
Puck, J. M., 72
Pugh, M. D., 398
Puig-Antich, J., 327
Putallaz, M., 334

Quamina, A., 401
Qi, K., 27, 90
Quatman, T., 386, 399
Quist, J. F., 309

Raboy, B., 17
Racusin, G. R., 320, 327
Radke-Yarrow, M., 257, 260, 321
Raeff, C., 248
Raffaelli, M., 442
Rahn, C. W., 360
Rakic, P., 356
Rakison, D. H., 223
Ramey, C. T., 232, 233
Ramisetty-Mikler, S., 206
Ramsey, P. G., 303
Randolph, S. M., 216
Rao, R., 216, 218
Raphael, T. E., 300
Rapoport, J. L., 71, 414
Rappaport, L., 310
Rasmussen, K. L. R., 13
Rasmussen, P., 277
Rastam, M., 369, 371
Rathus, S. A., 74
Rauch, P. K., 404, 406

Raver, C. C., 235
Ravesloot, J., 442
Ray, G. E., 236
Raymond, D., 449
Raynor, R., 33
Recchia, S., 181, 246
Reder, P., 202, 203
Reene, K., 373
Regal, K., 287
Regimbal, C., 286
Regmi, M., 248
Rehm, L. P., 326
Reichert, P., 372
Reichman, N. E., 91
Reid, J. B., 260, 324, 325, 390, 392
Reid, J. C., 326
Reilly, S., 178
Reimer, R. L., 102
Reinholtz, C., 445
Reinisch, J., 360
Reinisch, J. M., 399
Reis, S. M., 312
Reiser, M., 3
Reisman, J. E., 121
Reissland, N., 113
Remafedi, G., 449
Renoir, P., 296
Renshaw, P. F., 413
Renwick-DeBardi, S., 258
Renzetti, C. M., 18
Renzulli, J. S., 312
Repacholi, B. M., 145, 157
Repinski, D. J., 390
Reppucci, N. D., 206
Rescorla, L., 166
Resnick, G., 436
Resnick, M. D., 459
Resnick, S., 192
Rest, J. R., 342, 344, 346
Reuman, D., 377
Reuter, M. A., 206
Revill, J., 389
Reyes, S., 91
Reynolds, A. J., 460
Reynolds, C. A., 309
Reynoso, B., 91
Reznick, J. S., 163, 238
Rheingold, H. L., 257
Rhode, M., 449
Rholes, W. S., 302
Ricco, R. B., 375
Rice, C., 228
Rice, C. L., 303
Rice, E. P., 397
Rice, M. L., 163, 236, 237
Richard, P., 395
Richards, H., 332
Richards, M. H., 329, 330, 372, 373, 385, 393
Richardson, G. A., 89
Richardson, J. L., 331
Richman, A., 200
Richman, N., 274
Rickards, A. L., 142
Riddle, I., 125
Ridely, M., 61, 67
Rieber, R. W., 38
Rierdan, J., 363

Rieser-Danner, L. A., 145
Rifas-Shiman, S. L., 142
Rijavec, M., 322
Riordan, K., 192
Risely, T. R., 169
Risser, W., 385
Ritchie, W. C., 241
Ritter, J. M., 145
Ritter, P., 363
Ritter, P. L., 399
Rivera, S., 155
Robbins, C., 298
Robert-Guroff, M., 86
Roberts, C. R., 389
Roberts, D. F., 403
Roberts, L. R., 366
Roberts, R. E., 389
Roberts, S. B., 372, 373
Roberts, W., 257
Robertson, A. D., 141
Robertson, J. A., 76
Robinson, A., 70
Robinson, C., 399
Robinson, D. L., 114
Robinson, J., 326
Robinson, J. P., 276
Robinson, M. A., 206
Robson, J. R. K., 367
Roby, P., 27
Roche, A. F., 135
Roche, A. M., 456
Rocissano, L., 239
Rock, S. L., 232
Rocket, H. R., 142
Rockstroh, B., 29
Rodasta, A. L., 405
Rodgers, B. R., 442
Rodgers, J. L., 442
Roeder, K., 8
Roeser, R. W., 377, 378, 434
Roffey, S., 270
Rogers, B., 287
Rogers, B. L., 276
Roggman, L. A., 145
Rogoff, B., 157, 158, 159, 230, 231
Rogosch, F. A., 192
Rohner, R. P., 391
Roker, D., 390
Roloff, D. W., 127
Romero, A., 389
Romney, D. M., 253
Roncarolo, M., 72
Rondeau, N., 394
Roopnarine, J. L., 271
Roosa, M. W., 319, 445, 448
Root, A. W., 359
Roper Organization, 18
Rorvik, D. M., 65
Rose, A. J., 256, 270, 271, 333
Rose, H., 251
Rose, K. J., 359
Rose, S. A., 124, 223
Rose, S. P., 214
Rose, T., 403
Rose-Krasnor, L., 194
Rosen, C. M., 219
Rosen, T. J., 164, 238
Rosenbaum, M. B., 365

Rosenberg, D., 445
Rosenberg, M., 63
Rosenberg, T. K., 326
Rosenblith, J. F., 76, 85, 177
Rosenboom, L. G., 186
Rosenshine, B., 305
Rosenstein, D., 120
Rosenthal, B. S., 434
Rosenthal, D., 444
Rosenthal, D. A., 355, 388
Rosenthal, M. K., 199
Rosenthal, R., 331
Rosewarne, D. L., 304
Ross, H. S., 255
Ross-Leadbeater, B. J., 448
Rosser, P. L., 216
Rossner, S., 288
Rothbart, M. K., 182, 183, 184
Rothbaum, F., 193
Rothenberg, S. J., 91
Rotheram-Borus, M. J., 345, 388
Rothstein, R., 306
Rouse, L. W., 327
Rousseau, J.-J., 12, 13, 14
Rovee-Collier, C. K., 148, 149
Rovet, J., 70
Rowe, D. C., 324, 442, 450
Rowland, T. W., 288
Roy, C., 255
Royce, L., 434, 436
Royer, E., 390
Roysircar-Sodowsky, G., 319
Rozen, S., 63
Rozenboim, I., 90
Ruan, W. J., 142
Rubin, D. L., 376
Rubin, K. H., 185, 194, 273, 333, 335, 365, 398
Rubino, K. K., 445
Rubinstein, E. A., 275
Ruble, D. N., 245, 246, 251, 252, 253, 254, 302, 338, 365, 366, 385, 398, 430
Ruch-Ross, H. S., 445
Rudy, D., 263
Ruff, H. A., 156
Ruffman, T., 374
Runco, M. A., 296, 297, 312
Rush, K., 253
Russ, S. W., 297
Russell, G., 366
Russell, M., 87
Russell, S. T., 449
Rutter, M., 7, 9, 67, 70, 309, 450
Rutter, N., 121
Ruusuvaara, L., 443
Ryan, A. S., 143
Ryan, B. A., 335
Ryan, K., 425
Ryan, N., 327
Ryan, R. M., 305, 385
Ryan, S. A., 365
Rydell, A. M., 194, 334
Rymer, R., 170
Rys, G. S., 256

Saarni, C., 145, 176
Sabo, D. F., 422

Sabogal, F., 249
Sachs, H. C., 139
Sacks, C. H., 301
Sacks, J. J., 219
Sacks, M., 271
Sacks, O., 293
Sadker, D., 338, 433
Sadker, M., 338, 433
Sadler, T. W., 83
Safer, D. J., 308
Saffran, J. R., 160
Saffron, L., 17
Sagi, A., 186, 257
Sagrestano, L. M., 393, 400
Sahin, S., 237
Sakin, J. W., 273
Saklofske, D. H., 312
Sales, B. D., 267
Salihu, H. M., 71
Salisbury, C. L., 333
Salovey, P., 295
Saltzman, H., 319
Salvator, A., 125
Salzarulo, P., 113
Salzinger, S., 205
Sameroff, A. J., 21, 22, 192, 378
Sampaio, R. C., 116
Samples, F., 325
Sampson, A., 287
Sampson, E. E., 248
Sampson, K., 399
Sampson, P. D., 87, 88
Samuels, C. A., 145
Samuels, H. R., 214
Samuelson, L. K., 163
Sanchez, M., 91
Sanchez-Hucles, J., 261
Sandall, S. R., 124
Sandelowski, M., 94
Sanders, K., 389
Sanderson, M., 88
Sandler, I., 327
Sands, H. H., 41
Sandy, S. V., 255
Santa, P., 345
Sargent, J. D., 456
Sargent, K. P., 448
Sarigiani, P. A., 366
Sasse, D. K., 441
Sattin, W., 219
Sattler, J. M., 294, 297
Sauerwald, T., 142
Savin-Williams, R. C., 17, 449, 450
Sawyer, D., 386
Sayers, L. K., 285
Scaer, R., 102, 103
Scafidi, F., 104
Scahill, L., 310
Scanlon, J. W., 124
Scanlon, K. B., 124
Scantlin, R. M., 404
Scaramilla, L. V., 391
Scarr, S., 68, 188, 197, 198
Schaefer, C. E., 180
Schafer, W. D., 195
Schaffer, A., 145
Schaffner, W., 219
Schaps, E., 426

Schatschneider, C., 300
Schauble, L., 375
Schebendach, J., 367
Scheel, K. R., 403
Scheier, L. M., 385
Schena, M., 68
Schepher-Hughes, N., 184
Scher, M. L., 89
Schiff, I., 420
Schiff-Myers, N., 171
Schiller, M., 192
Schleifer, M., 341
Schlottmann, A., 225
Schmidt, M., 334
Schmitt, R. E., 388
Schmidt, W., 71
Schmitt, K. L., 275
Schneider, B., 334, 440, 460
Schneider, B. H., 256
Schneider, K., 178
Schneider, W., 147, 149
Schnoll, S. H., 89
Schoelmerich, A., 22, 186, 195
Schoenhals, M., 460
Schonberg, S. K., 414
Schothorst, P. F., 124
Schrepferman, L., 325
Schroeder, D., 27, 90
Schubert, M. T., 120
Schuele, C. M., 334
Schuengel, C., 191, 192
Schulenberg, J., 459
Schuler, M., 27
Schull, W. J., 90
Schultz, L. H., 424
Schultz, M. C., 169
Schultz, R. T., 341
Schulze, L., 403
Schulze, P. A., 22
Schurch, B., 217
Schuster, B., 246
Schutte, N. S., 405
Schvaneveldt, P., 400
Schwartz, D., 271
Schwartz, E., 166
Schwartz, J. A., 327, 452
Schwartz, J. E., 264
Schwartz, R. H., 103
Schwartz, W., 436
Schwebel, D. C., 45
Scolton, K. L., 194
Scopesi, A., 107
Scott, K. G., 218
Scwartz, C. E., 325
Sealand, N., 442
Sealock, M. D., 450, 451
Searleman, A., 216
Sebald, H., 354, 355
Sebby, R. A., 390
Sedlak, A. J., 201, 202
Seeley, J. R., 363
Seff, M. A., 390, 397
Segall, M. H., 291
Seidenberg, M. S., 167
Seidler, F. J., 106
Seifer, R., 192
Seiffge-Krenke, I., 398, 399

Sekhon, M., 63
Sell, M. A., 236
Sells, C. W., 417
Selman, R. L., 424
Sera, M. D., 246
Serafica, F. C., 388
Serketich, W. J., 247
Sessa, F. M., 390, 440
Sever, I., 331
Severe, J. B., 310
Shacham, S., 102
Shaffer, A., 236
Shagle, S. C., 391
Shankaran, S., 89, 123
Shanley, N., 452
Shapiro, C. J., 310
Shapiro, E. K., 338
Shapiro, L. R., 226
Shapiro, S., 447
Sharer, L. R., 86
Shavinina, L., 10
Shaw, D., 325
Shedler, J., 458
Sheeber, L., 266
Sheehy, G., 353
Sheen, C., 419
Sheffield, E. G., 148
Shenhav, M., 88
Shenker, I. R., 367
Shepard, L. A., 234
Shepard, M., 449
Shepard, S., 3
Shepard, S. A., 258, 334
Shepardson, D. P., 338
Sherman, T., 321
Sherrod, L. R., 353
Sherry, J. L., 405
Shettles, L., 65
Shiang, E., 420
Shields, B. J., 141, 287
Shields, M. K., 405
Shifflett, K., 206
Shin, D., 273
Shipley, C., 293
Shope, J. T., 385
Shore, C., 161
Short, J. L., 453
Shrum, W., 397
Shucard, D. W., 428
Shucard, L. L., 428
Shugart, M., 205
Shulman, S., 331, 399
Shuman, M. D., 373
Shurkin, J. N., 51
Shute, N., 99, 102
Shwe, H., 228
Shyi, C. W. G., 148
Sidebotham, P., 202
Sidis, W. J., 4, 51
Sidora, K. J., 445
Siegel, L., 232
Siegler, R. S., 39, 153, 224, 225, 226, 288, 292, 293, 295
Sienna, M., 308
Sigman, M., 113
Sigmundson, K., 250
Signorella, M. L., 250, 254
Sikes, K., 219

Silber, T. J., 369
Silberg, J. L., 309
Silva, P. A., 142, 182, 183
Silverberg, S. B., 440, 441
Silverman, W. K., 322, 328
Silverthorn, P., 324
Simard, M., 275
Simbruner, G., 120
Simeon, D. T., 218
Simmel, C., 263
Simmons, R. G., 363, 377, 379
Simmons Marketing Research, 406
Simon, H. A., 226
Simon, H. K., 374
Simon, R. L., 452
Simon, T., 293
Simon, W., 443
Simonoff, E., 7, 9, 309
Simons, R. L., 259, 261, 264, 391
Simonton, D. K., 296
Simpson, J. L., 72
Singer, D. G., 277
Singer, J. D., 51
Singer, J. L., 277
Singer, L. T., 125
Singer, R. S., 368
Singh, S., 400, 445, 446
Sirota, L. A., 67
Sitarenios, G., 192
Sizer, F., 143
Skaletsky, H., 63
Skinner, B. F., 33, 168
Skinner, E. A., 318
Skinner, J. S., 420
Skoe, E. E. A., 346
Skuse, D., 178
Slade, A., 273
Slater, A., 147
Slater-Rusonis, E., 323
Slavin, R. E., 305
Slawinski, J. L., 292
Sleep, J., 99
Sleet, D., 416
Sloan, R. P., 92
Slomkowski, C., 255
Slora, E. J., 361
Slotkin, T. A., 106
Slutkin, G., 449
Sluyter, D. J., 295
Small, M. Y., 154, 375
Small, S., 442
Small, S. S., 390
Smallish, L., 309
Smeriglio, V. L., 89
Smetana, J. G., 200, 260, 391, 392, 393, 441
Smith, A. C. M., 71
Smith, B. A., 120
Smith, C. A., 325, 447, 448
Smith, D., 305
Smith, D. W., 186
Smith, F., 301
Smith, G. A., 141, 287
Smith, J. B., 434, 435
Smith, J. D., 219, 430
Smith, L. B., 9, 41, 138, 163
Smith, M., 23
Smith, M. C., 256, 270

Smith, P. K., 252, 256, 272
Smith, R., 322
Smith, R. S., 460
Smith, S. L., 276
Smith, T. A., 202
Smith, T. M., 431
Smokowski, P. R., 460
Smolak, L., 373
Smolin, L. A., 143, 144, 217
Smulders, B., 107
Snapir, N., 90
Snarey, J. R., 345
Snellman, L. W., 121
Snidman, N., 185, 325
Snow, C. E., 240, 245, 299
Snow, C. W., 178, 179
Snyder, E., 253
Snyder, H. N., 260
Snyder, J., 325, 335
Snyder, J. B., 416, 417
Snyder-Keller, A., 89
Soberon, H., 19
Sobkiewicz, T. A., 369
Sobol, A. M., 124
Sobowlew-Shubin, A., 420
Socken, K., 94
Socolar, R. R. S., 261
Soldi, A., 90
Soliman, A., 318
Solis, J., 249
Solis-Camera, P., 261
Sollid, D., 93
Solomon, J., 191
Sonenstein, F. L., 441, 443
Sonis, W. A., 360
Sonnenschein, S., 221, 290
Soriano, F. I., 323, 402
Sosa, B. B., 226
Sotos, J. F., 70
Spangle-Looney, S., 166
Spear, L., 356
Specker, B., 371
Speers, M. A., 144
Speicher-Dubin, B., 341
Spelke, E. S., 154
Speltz, M. L., 325
Spence, M. J., 90, 119
Spencer, M. B., 21, 388
Spencer, M. S., 447
Spencer, P. E., 192
Spergel, I. A., 401, 402
Spetner, N. B., 145
Spielberg, S., 294
Spiller, L. C., 325
Spirito, A., 417
Sprafkin, J., 275, 277, 403
Sprague, J., 324
Sprecher, S., 443
Springen, K., 458, 459
Spritz, B., 194,
Sroufe, L. A., 177, 178, 191, 194, 258, 263, 309, 310, 335
St. James-Roberts, I., 179
St. Laurent, D., 192
St. Peter, C., 325
Stack, D. M., 177
Stafford, F. P., 329
Stafford, L., 391, 392

Stang, H. J., 121
Stangor, C., 250, 251, 254
Stanley, B. K., 266
Stanley, J. C., 312, 430
Stanley-Hagan, M., 265, 268, 269
Stark, A., 123
Stark, K. D., 327
Starsen, M., 368
State v. Michaels, 227
Stattin, H., 391
Status of Women Council, 430
Staub, E. M., 41
Staudinger, U. M., 3
Steele, C. M., 432
Steele, N., 125
Steffe, L. P., 305
Stein, A., 113
Stein, A. H., 278
Stein, D. M., 372
Stein, N. L., 181
Stein, R. E. K., 261
Steinberg, L., 263, 327, 331, 360, 366, 373, 390, 392, 394, 398, 399, 440, 452, 459
Steiner, H., 368, 422
Steiner, J. E., 146
Steingard, R. J., 413
Steingart, R. A., 90
Steinhausen, H. C., 324
Stennies, G. M., 416
Stephens, B. R., 145
Stephens, M. B., 71
Stephens, R., 416
Sterman, M. B., 113
Stern, A. E., 248
Stern, D., 118
Stern, S. B., 325
Sternberg, K. J., 196, 197
Sternberg, R. J., 294, 295
Stetterberg, S. R., 416
Stevens, N., 270
Stevens-Simon, C., 447
Stevenson, D. K., 123
Stevenson, H. W., 261, 314, 315, 336, 379, 380
Stevenson, J. E., 274
Stewart, D., 70
Stewart, S. L., 273
Stiefel, G. S., 127
Stifter, C. A., 183
Stigler, J. W., 380
Stimson, C. A., 257
Stipek, D. J., 181, 234, 246, 378
Stockhammar, T. F., 205
Stokes, G., 444
Stolberg, A. L., 266
Stone, M. R., 397
Stone, R. K., 89
Stoneman, Z., 274
Stores, M., 271
Stott, F. M., 47, 227
Stouthamer-Loeber, M., 450
Straus, M. A., 392
Strauss, C. C., 328, 329
Strauss, R., 105
Strauss, R. S., 287
Strauss, S., 375

Straussner, J. H., 322
Straussner, S. L. A., 322
Strayer, J., 257
Streissguth, A. P., 87, 88
Strelau, J., 182
Striefel, S., 206
Stringer, P., 38
Strober, M., 452
Strom, P., 313
Strom, R., 313
Strom, S., 313
Stromswold, K., 172
Strosberg, R., 163
Strouse, D., 396
Strouse, J. S., 385
Strupp, B., 217
Sturla, E., 250
Styfco, S. F., 235
Su, M., 205
Suber, C. F., 341
Sucher, K. P., 370
Sucoff, C. A., 441, 442
Sudela, K., 125
Sugai, G., 324
Sullivan, K., 228
Sullivan, M. W., 90, 181
Sulzby, E., 301
Sun, Z., 68
Suomi, S. J., 13
Super, C. M., 176, 271
Susman, E. J., 277, 358, 363, 452
Susman-Stillman, A., 192
Susser, M., 89
Sussman, S. Y., 331
Sutton, H. E., 71
Sutton-Smith, B., 182
Swank, P. R., 325
Swanson, J. M., 310
Swarr, A., 385
Swarr, A. E., 373
Sweet, R. L., 85
Swendsen, J. D., 327
Swiber, M. J., 112
Swinford, S. P., 398
Synnevaag, B., 186
Synnott, A., 13
Szagun, G., 257
Szapocnik, J., 319

Taffel, S. M., 103
Tager-Flusberg, H., 70, 228
Takahashi, K., 193
Takeuchi, D., 259
Tal, J., 178
Tamis-LeMonda, C. S., 158, 178, 195, 271, 272
Tamkin, G., 236
Tangney, J. P., 181
Tanner, J. M., 213, 214, 356, 357, 359, 361
Tappan, M. B., 229
Tarrant, M., 403
Tarrant, T., 270
Tascon, M., 186
Tasker, F. L., 17
Tatzer, E., 120
Taubman, B., 140
Taylor, A., 308

Taylor, C. B., 372, 373
Taylor, D. M., 306
Taylor, E., 249, 310
Taylor, H. G., 124, 126
Taylor, J. A., 68, 88
Taylor, K. E., 102
Taylor, M., 164, 228
Taylor, R. D., 308, 309, 310, 379, 380, 381
Taylor, R. J., 389
Teale, W. H., 301
Tebes, J. K., 320
Tees, R. C., 160
Tein, J., 445
Tejani, N., 89
Telama, R., 286
Tellegen, A., 8, 320
Temprosa, M., 123
Terlecki, M., 429
Terman, L. M., 51
Terrell, B. Y., 237
Terry, R., 333
Teti, D. M., 273
Thal, D. J., 163, 165, 166, 238
Thelen, E., 9, 41, 42, 138, 139
Thoma, S. J., 344, 346
Thoman, E. B., 111, 112, 113
Thomas, A., 183, 184, 327
Thomas, C. W., 184
Thomas, D. J., 428
Thomas, J. R., 252, 286, 293
Thomas, K. M., 356, 414
Thomas, M. H., 448
Thomas, R., 125
Thomas, R. M., 27
Thompson, D. N., 376
Thompson, K. P., 403
Thompson, R., 441
Thompson, R. A., 29, 118, 137, 179, 186, 187, 188, 190, 194, 197
Thompson, S. C., 420
Thomsen, A. H., 319
Thornberry, T. P., 447, 448
Thorne, B., 335
Thornton, M. C., 389
Thorogood, P., 85
Thorp, J. A., 99
Thorpe, K. J., 94
Thurman, S. K., 124
Tienda, M., 460
Tilford, C. A., 63
Time, 19
Timischl, W., 120
Tinker, E., 240
Tinsley, B. J., 309, 310
Tjebkes, T. L., 176
Tobin-Richards, M. H., 363
Toda, S., 271, 272
Toharia, A., 197
Tolan, P. H., 41, 321, 323, 453
Tolson, J. M., 395
Tom, D., 338
Tomada, G., 256
Tomasello, M., 162, 163, 239, 240, 255
Tomlinson-Clarke, S., 388
Tomlinson-Keasey, C., 264
Tonner, L., 181

Toomey, J., 327
Torney-Purta, J., 427
Torrance, E. P., 297
Torrey, C. C., 285
Torsheim, T., 318
Toselli, M., 113
Toth, S. L., 192, 452
Tout, K., 195, 196
Trabasso, T., 181
Travillion, K., 335
Treboux, D., 29
Treboux, D. A., 444
Treder, R., 70
Treffers, P. D. A., 274
Treiman, R., 299
Tremblay, R. E., 256, 395
Trent, K., 446
Trevarthen, C., 158
Trice, A. D., 253
Trickett, P. K., 41, 205, 261
Trieller, K., 366
Trien, L., 92
Trommsdorff, G., 257
Truglio, R. T., 236
Truhn, P., 206
Trumble, A., 286
Trumble, A. C., 140
Truwit, C. L., 116
Tschann, J. M., 363
Tucker, C. J., 274, 275
Tucker, J. S., 264
Tucker, K. L., 276
Turecki, S., 181
Turett, K., 309
Turiel, E., 338, 346, 425, 426
Turk, A. A., 452
Turner, C. F., 441
Turner, H. A., 392
Turner, Q., 125
Turner, R. A., 363
Turner Syndrome Society of the US, 70
Turtle, M., 414
Tyson, J. E., 123
Tzischinsky, O., 421

Uauy, R., 142
Udelf, M. S., 118
Udry, J. R., 369, 450
Ugur, A., 72
Ullman, M., 164, 238
Ullstadius, E., 113
Ungerer, J. A., 148
UNICEF, 127, 131, 217, 322
United Nations, 332
Upchurch, D. M., 441, 442
Updegraff, K., 45
Updegraff, K. A., 274, 331, 393
Urban, J., 335
Urban Institute, 330
Urberg, K. A., 395
US Census Bureau, 14, 15, 16, 18, 21, 57, 140, 141, 195, 330, 331, 336, 404, 405, 406, 434, 435
US Department of Commerce, 195, 196
US Department of Education, 234, 307, 349, 378, 430, 435, 436

US Department of Health and Human Services, 202, 203, 205, 209
US Department of Justice, 269
US Department of Labor, 16, 195, 198, 200
US State Department, 23
Uttal, D., 314, 315, 336

Vaden, N. A., 335, 394
Valdez, E. O., 249
Valdez, J., 447
Vallancourt, T., 333
Van Beveren, T. T., 90
VanBrakle, J., 309
Van-Cleve, L., 370
Vandell, D. L., 197, 198, 331
VandenBos, G. R., 419
van der Heijden, J., 332
van der Kamp, L. J. T., 276
van der Voet, H., 68
van der Voort, T. H. A., 276
van de Vijver, F. J. R., 375
Vandewater, E. A., 404
van Engeland, H., 124
Van-Evra, J. P., 275
Vanfossen, B. E., 422
Van Griffin, K., 144
van Houwelingen, A. M., 68
van IJzendoorn, M. H., 191, 192
Van-Kammen, W. B., 450
van-Laar, C., 249
van Tunen, A. J., 68
Varner, M. W., 125
Vartanian, L. R., 376
Vasta, R., 429
Vaughn, L. S., 145
Vega, W. A., 319
Vellutino, F. R., 301
Ventura-Cook, E., 22
Verbeek, A. L., 422
Verbeek, P., 255
Verber, J., 89
Verhoef, H., 200
Verhoeven, H. A., 68
Verhulst, F. C., 323
Verma, U., 89
Verschaffel, L., 314
Verschueren, K., 245
Verter, J., 123
Vibbert, M., 145
Vietze, P. M., 158
Vigil, J. D., 401
Viikari, J., 286
Villani, S., 403
Villarruel, F. A., 442
Violato, C., 323
Vitaro, F., 394, 395
Vitaro, M., 3
Vitiello, B., 310
Vogt, C. J., 369
Vohr, B. R., 124
Vollebergh, W., 387
Volling, B. L., 274
Vondracek, F. W., 388
von Eye, A., 364
von Hofsten, C., 145
von Kreis, R., 142

von Mutius, E., 142
von Voss, H., 142
Votto, N., 27, 90
Vouloumanos, A., 120
Vuchnich, S., 203
Vygotsky, L. S., 38, 44, 157, 169, 229, 305

Waas, G. A., 333
Wachs, T. D., 8, 10, 182, 184, 185, 217, 218
Wachtel, R., 27
Wade, S. M., 125
Wadsworth, M. E., 319
Wagner, E., 257
Wagner, K. D., 327
Wagner, R. K., 294
Wake, M., 104
Wakeley, A., 155
Wakschlag, L. S., 261
Walbek, N. H., 258
Walder, L. O., 277, 324
Waldman, I., 192
Waldman, S., 458, 459
Walk, R. D., 145
Walker, C. E., 285
Walker, H., 324
Walker, J. L., 310
Walker, K., 249
Walker, L. J., 344, 346, 425
Walker, N. C., 99
Walker, R. R., 261
Wall, S., 189
Wallace, C. E., 117
Wallace, I., 124
Wallace-Brocious, A., 388
Wallerstein, J. S., 265, 267
Wallerstein, R. S., 32, 386, 387
Walls, H. C., 89
Walls, H. S., 89
Walsh, P. E., 266
Walsh, P. V., 303
Walters, L. H., 376
Walton, M. N., 319
Wampler, K. S., 259
Wan, C., 332
Wang, F., 332
Wang, J. Z., 192
Wang, X., 401
Wapner, R. J., 71
Ward, S., 430
Ware, H. S., 325
Warren, M. P., 360, 362, 452
Warren, R., 86
Warren-Leubecker, A., 168
Wasik, B. H., 20, 21
Wasserman, A., 334
Wasserman, R. C., 361
Wasserman, S., 154
Wasserstein, S., 328
Wasz-Hockert, O., 178
Waterfield, J., 326
Waterman, A. S., 388
Waters, E., 177, 178, 189, 191
Waterson, R. H., 63
Watkins, D., 248

Watkins, J., 287
Watson, C. M., 386, 399
Watson, J. B., 33
Watson, M. W., 229
Waxmonsky, J., 310
Way, N., 448
Weber, S., 236
Weber-Fox, C., 172
Wedemeyer, N. V., 264
Wegener, D. H., 125
Wehler, C. A., 287
Wehner, E. A., 399
Weikel, W. J., 266
Weinberg, R. A., 45, 294
Weinberg, W. A., 327
Weinert, F. E., 246
Weinstein, R. A., 338
Weiss, B., 259, 452
Weiss, G., 309
Weiss, M. R., 368
Weissberg, R. P., 335
Weisz, J. R., 193, 319
Weitzman, M., 287
Weizman, A., 288
Wellborn, J. G., 318
Weller, A., 127
Wellman, H. M., 181, 227, 228
Wells, K., 310
Welsh, R., 445, 447
Wentzel, K. R., 398
Werker, J. F., 120, 160
Werner, E. E., 460
West, J. R., 87
West, S. G., 327
Westefeld, J. S., 403
Whalen, C. K., 310
Wheeler, B., 125
Wheeler, L., 247
Whitaker, H. A., 117
White, C., 236
White, M., 248
White, R., 419
White, R. D., 447
White, S. D., 447
Whitebook, M., 197, 198
Whiteman, M., 88
Whiteside, L., 123
Whiting, B. B., 252, 256
Whiting, J. W. M., 256
Whitney, E., 143
Whitney, M. P., 111, 112, 113
Widerstrom, A. H., 124
Widom, C. S., 201, 202, 203
Wierson, M., 360
Wiese, D., 202, 205
Wigal, T., 310
Wigfield, A., 376, 377, 378, 379, 380, 386, 432, 434
Wiggins, E., 71
Wilcox, B., 275
Wilcox, M. J., 237, 239
Wilczenski, F. L., 364
Wilkins, D. G., 87
Willemsen, M. E., 375
Willett, J. B., 51
Williams, M. M., 426

Williams, S., 368
Williams, T. M., 276
Williams, V. A., 391
Williamson, L., 370
Williamson, S., 308
Willig, A., 306
Wilson, B. J., 276
Wilson, C., 366
Wilson, D. M., 363
Wilson, E. O., 13
Wilson, J., 266
Wilson, L., 259
Wilson, P., 277
Wilson, R. D., 71, 72
Wilson, S. A., 22
Wilson, S. M., 392
Wilson, S. R., 260
Wimbush, D. D., 259
Wimmer, H., 228
Winborn, R. C., 71
Windass, A., 386
Windle, M., 399
Winer, G. A., 222
Wingard, D. L., 264
Winner, E., 228
Winsler, A., 229, 234
Winslow, E. B., 325
Wisniewski, L., 287
Witkin, G., 415
Witschi, J., 420
Wold, B., 318
Wolf, A. E., 180
Wolf, A. W., 218
Wolf, D. P., 245, 273
Wolfe, B., 197, 198, 462
Wolfe, D. A., 205
Wolff, P. H., 177, 178
Wolfner, G. D., 202, 203
Wolfson, A. R., 421
Wolke, D., 178
Women's Sports Foundation, 422
Wong, D. L., 74, 77, 79, 83, 98, 101
Wood, R. M., 178
Woods, C. H., 250
Woods, E. G., 436
Woods, T., 21
Woodward, A. H., 275, 276, 281
Woodward, A. L., 161, 163, 164, 165
Woodward, L., 99
Woodworth, S., 105, 263, 325
Woody, E., 398
Woolley, J. D., 181, 228
Worden, P. E., 48, 50
World Health Organization, 107, 217
Worsley, K., 414
Wozniak, P., 260
Wright, J. C., 236, 275, 276, 404
Wright, K., 341
Wright, L. L., 89, 123
Wright, S. C., 306
Wright, V., 333
Wu, F., 186
Wylie, K., 63, 155, 156
Wynne, E. A., 425, 426
Wyshak, G., 361, 420
Wysocki, T., 420

Xu, F., 164, 238

Yagel, S., 91
Yamamoto, K., 318
Yanai, J., 90
Yang, X., 286
Yankelovich, S., 236
Yee, D. K., 432
Yelland, N., 404
Yenen, S., 107
Yetman, N. R., 18
Yi, S. H., 406
Yin, R. K., 47
YMCA, 411
Yoerger, K., 324
Yoon, K. S., 377, 432, 433
Yotive, W., 375
Young, A., 125
Young, J., 124
Young, M., 319
Young, M. H., 400
Youngblade, L. M., 200, 274
Younger, B. A., 157
Youniss, J., 271, 396
Yu, A., 306
Yucel, G., 72
Yuille, J., 227
Yuille, N., 302, 423, 424
Yung, B. R., 323, 325
Yurgelun-Todd, D. A., 413

Zahn-Waxler, C., 257
Zaiwalla, Z., 113
Zanjani, E. D., 72
Zanobini, M., 107
Zebrowitz, L., 29
Zeifman, D., 120
Zelazo, P. R., 148, 157
Zelis, K. M., 333
Zelkowitz, P., 122
Zelli, A., 453
Zero to Three, 4
Zeskind, P. S., 179
Zeuhlke, S., 106
Zhou, M., 19
Zhou, Q., 257
Zigler, E., 36, 38, 235, 236, 311
Zijdenbos, A., 414
Zill, N., 4, 266
Zillmann, D., 277, 403
Zimler, J., 292
Zimmerman, B. F., 338
Zimmerman, J., 443
Zimmerman, M. A., 385
Zoller, D., 258
Zonta, L. A., 91
Zook, K. B., 403
Zucker, K. J., 250
Zucker, R. A., 458
Zuckerman, B., 90
Zuckerman, D., 275
Zumbahlen, M. R., 22, 139
Zupan, B. A., 263
Zuroff, D. C., 441

Subject Index

A-not-B error, 153
Aborigines, childhood reasoning in, 291
Abortion, 446
    spontaneous, 84
Abstinence, 445, 448
Abstract concepts, 165
Abuse. *See also* Child abuse
    physical, 201
    sexual, 201, 202, 445
Academic achievement
    cross-cultural studies of, 314–315, 379–380
    effect of change in school environment on, 377–378
    effect of students' working on, 459–460
    family influence on, 314–315, 432–433
    gender differences in, 428–433
    of high school dropouts, 434
    low birthweight and, 124
    and teachers' bias, 306–307, 433
Academic competence, self-perceptions of, 378–379
Acceleration programs, 312
Acceptance, in adolescence, 391
Accidents
    automobile, 219, 414–415, 454
    drowning, 141
    in early adolescence, 367
    in early childhood, 219
    with guns, 373, 415–416
    in infancy and toddlerhood, 133, 141
    in late adolescence, 414–415
Accommodation, 36
Acculturative stress, 319
Achievement. *See* Academic achievement
Acquired Immunodeficiency Syndrome (AIDS).
    See AIDS
Active G-E interaction, 69
Active learning, 305
Actual self, 384
ADHD. *See* Attention-deficit hyperactivity
    disorder (ADHD)
Adolescence, 353. *See also* Early adolescence; Late
    adolescence
    cultural perspectives on, 354–355
    Erikson on, 32
    Hall on, 13
    historical perspectives on, 353–354
    terminology related to, 355
Adolescent egocentrism, 375–376
Adolescent peer culture, 394–397
Adoption, 211
    attachment and, 186
    international, 23
    teen pregnancy and, 446
Adoption and Safe Families Act, 211

Adoption studies, 7, 8–9
African Americans, 19
    academic achievement of, 380
    access to computers of, 404
    alcohol consumption by, 454
    community violence and, 323
    custody arrangements of, 267–268
    day care arrangements of, 196
    discipline by, 259, 260
    ethnic identity of, 389
    family relationships of, 14, 15, 16, 268, 314, 315, 453
    in foster care, 211
    gestation lengths of, 97
    Head Start usage by, 235
    incidence of rubella among, 85
    incidence of sexually transmitted diseases among, 417
    incidence of sickle cell anemia among, 66–67
    IQ scores of, 294
    lack of health insurance among, 141
    low-birthweight births among, 122–123
    moral themes of, 345, 346
    mortality rates for, 127, 414, 416
    motor development of, 216
    obesity among, 287
    onset of puberty in, 361
    popular music and, 403
    reducing prejudice among, 304
    self-esteem of, 249
    sexual practices of, 400
    standards of attractiveness among, 365
    as victims of child abuse, 202
Age of viability, 83
Aggression
    effects of television violence on, 48–49, 276–277
    gender differences in, 252, 256
    hostile, 256
    instrumental, 256
    physical, 256
    relational, 256
    understanding intentions of others and, 319
    of young children, 197, 255–256
AIDS, 417–418, 419, 444
    mothers with, 143
    pediatric, 86
Ainsworth's Strange Situation procedure, 189
Airbags, 219
Alcohol consumption, 83, 84
    accidents involving, 133
    contraceptive use and, 444
    by early maturing adolescents, 363
    by late adolescents, 453–454
    maternal, 87, 311

    sports involvement and, 422
Alpha fetoprotein, 72
Ambivalent attachment, 190, 191
American Psychiatric Association, 450
American Psychological Association, 49
American Sign Language, 171, 172
Amino acids, 61
Amniocentesis, 72
Amnion, 79
Amniotic fluid, 79
Amygdala, 356
Anal stage, 31
Anatolia, birth experience in, 107
Androgens, 252, 431
Anencephaly, 92
Anger. *See also* Aggression
    in boys, 252
    in infants, 180
    in young children, 255
Animism, 222, 223
Anorexia nervosa, 369–370, 371
Antisocial behavior
    in adolescence, 451, 453
    in late childhood, 324–326
Anxiety
    in children coping with disaster, 320
    in infants, 186
    separation, 188
    stranger, 188
Apgar Scale, 109, 126
Apnea, 125
Appearance. *See also* Physical development
    and adolescent's perception of self, 364–365, 386
    in early childhood, 213
    in late childhood, 285
    of neonate, 108–109
    and young child's perception of self, 247–248
Applied developmental research, 45–46
Approval, desire for, 227
Arousal, states of, 111–112
Artificial insemination, 76
Asian Americans
    academic achievement of, 380
    discipline by, 261
    ethnic identity of, 389
    family relationships of, 14, 15
    in foster care, 211
    Head Start usage by, 235
    language acquisition of, 169–170
    maternal age of, 91
    mortality rates for, 127
    population of, 18
    as victims of child abuse, 202

Assessment
  of behavior in neonates, 113–114
  of vision in infants, 118
Assimilated (into majority culture), 389
Assimilation, 36
Associational fluency, 429
Associative play, 272
At-risk newborns, 121–127
Athletic ability. *See also* Physical fitness; Sports
  body build and, 285
  timing of puberty and, 363
Attachment, parent-infant, 185–195
  ambivalent, 190, 191
  assessing patterns of, 188–192
  avoidant, 190, 191
  breast-feeding and, 143
  consequences of, 194
  day care and, 197, 198
  development of, 187–188
  disorganized/disoriented, 190, 191
  effect of child abuse on, 205
  factors affecting, 192
  to fathers, 194–195
  insecure, 325
  role of culture in, 193–194
  secure, 190, 192, 194, 195, 335
  smiling and, 178
Attachment-in-the-making phase, 187
Attachment theory, 29, 187–188
Attention, 35
Attention-deficit hyperactivity disorder (ADHD), 308–310
  antisocial behavior and, 324
Attitudes
  of high school dropouts, 434
  sexual, 441–443
Australian Aborigines, childhood reasoning in, 297
Authoritarian parenting, 262
Authoritative parenting, 263
Authority figures, disobedience of, 427
Autistic children, 302
Automobile accidents, 414–415
  alcohol and, 454
  as cause of death among preschoolers, 219
Autonomous morality stage, 340
Autonomy, 440–441
  behavioral, 440
  emotional, 440
  values, 440
Autosomal recessive disease, 65
Autosomes, 63
Avoidant attachment, 190, 191
Axon, 115
Axon terminal, 115

Babbling, 160
Babinski reflex, 110, 111, 114
Baby blues, 104
Baby signs, 162
Baillargeon and Graber's possible and impossible events, 154
Balance, development of, 214
Balanced polymorphism, 67
Baldness, 67
Bandura's social learning theory, 35

Bar mitzvah, 354, 355
Barney, 277
Bases, 61
Basic developmental research, 45–46
Baumrind's parenting styles, 262–263
Behavior
  antisocial, 324–326, 451
  defiant, 450
  effects of divorce on, 265–266
  hormones and, 362
  influence of parents on, 258–263
  influence of teachers on, 338
  measurement of, 51–53
  problem, of late adolescence, 395, 450–458
  prosocial, 257–258
  risk-taking, 385, 400, 415, 422, 450
  sexual, 441–443
  social, 28, 252
  socialization of, 258
  thrill-seeking, 67
  of very-low-birthweight children, 124
Behavior management strategies, and ADHD, 310
Behavior modification, for antisocial behavior, 325
Behavioral assessment, of neonate, 113–114
Behavioral autonomy, 440
Behavioral measures, 52
Beta thalassemia, 66
Bias
  in clinical interview, 47
  in IQ testing, 293
  of teachers, 306–307, 386, 433
Bicultural, 389
Bilingual children, language development in, 241
Bilingual education, 306
  dropout rate and, 435
Binge drinking, 454
  during pregnancy, 87
Binge eating, 371
Biological factors, 5
  in academic achievement, 431
  in antisocial behavior, 324–325
Biology-based theories of development, 27, 28–30, 166–168, 252–253
Birth. *See* Childbirth; Multiple births
Birth control pills, 444
Birth defects, 59, 73
  genetic counseling and, 72
  infectious diseases and, 85–86
  prevention of, 92
  radiation and, 90
  teratogens and, 83–85
Birth rate, 91, 446
Birth rituals, 107–108
Birthing centers, 101
Blacks, 19. *See also* African Americans
Bladder cancer, 68
Bladder control, in infants, 140
Blended family, 14
Blindness, 308
  attachment and, 192
Blink reflex, 110
Blood types, 68
Bloody show, 98

Blooming, of neuronal connections, 116–117, 137
Body fat, 360, 420
Body image, 365, 368
Body size
  in early childhood, 213
  in late childhood, 285
Bonding, parent-newborn, 106–107, 186. *See also* Attachment
Bowel control, in infants, 140
Bowlby's theory of attachment, 29, 187–188
Boys. *See* Gender differences
Brain
  Broca's area of, 167
  infant, 115, 117, 118
  language-related areas of, 167
  Wernicke's area of, 167
Brain damage
  language development and, 172
  language disorders and, 167
  in premature newborns, 126
Brain development, 29
  in early adolescence, 356
  in early childhood, 213–214
  environmental effects on, 117–118
  inadequate nutrition and, 218
  in infants and toddlers, 135–137
  in late adolescence, 413–414
  in late childhood, 285
  language development and, 167–168
  neonatal sleep and, 113
  progressive events in, 115–116
  regressive events in, 117
Brain organization, academic achievement and, 431
Brain potentials (ERPs), 172
Braxton-Hicks contractions, 98
Brazelton's Neonatal Behavioral Assessment Scale, 113–114
Breast development, 360, 363
Breast-feeding, 124, 141, 142–143
  transmission of HIV through, 86
Breast pumps, 143
Breech presentation, 102, 103
Broca's area, 167
Bronfenbrenner's ecological theory, 40–41
Budongshi, 261
Bulimia nervosa, 370–371

Caffeine, prenatal development and, 87
CAH, 252–253
Capillaries, 79
Car seats, 133, 141
Carcinogens, in cigarette smoke, 88
Caregivers, 16, 38. *See also* Day care; Parents
  attachment and, 186–188, 192
  language acquisition and, 169, 240
  maltreatment by, 201
  self-awareness and, 248
Carriers, 65
Case study, 47
Catching, 215
Categories, children's understanding of, 290
Caucasian Americans
  access to computers of, 404
  alcohol consumption by, 454

childhood reasoning in, 291
custody arrangements of, 267
day care arrangements of, 196
discipline by, 259
early sexual activities of, 400
ethnic identity of, 389
family relationships of, 15, 268, 314
in foster care, 211
Head Start usage by, 235
incidence of autosomal recessive diseases among, 65
lack of health insurance among, 141
maternal age of, 91
maternal smoking among, 88
mortality rates for, 127, 414–415
multiple pregnancies among, 78, 79
popular music and, 403
population of, 18
reducing prejudice among, 304
standards of attractiveness among, 365
suicide rates of, 417
as victims of child abuse, 202
Cause-and-effect relationships, 49–50, 161
Cell body, 115
Census, 48
Centration, 221
Cephalocaudal development, 81, 137
Cerebellum, 167
Cerebral cortex, 136
Cerebral palsy, 59, 123, 124, 308
Ceremonies, in birth experience, 107–108
Cervix, 98–99
Cesarean section, 59, 102–103
Change, measurement of, 50–51
Character education, 426, 427
Chemical hazards, prenatal development and, 90–91
Chicano, 21. *See also* Hispanic Americans
Child abuse, 200–206
    ecological model of, 203–204
    effects of, 205
    foster care and, 211
    incidence of, 201
    preventing, 205–206
    victims of, 191, 202
Child abusers, characteristics of, 202–203
Child care. *See* Day care; Preschool
Child custody, 17, 267, 269
Child development, 4
    biology-based theories of, 27–29, 44
    cognition-based theories of, 35–39, 44
    contextual theories of, 40–43, 44
    critical issues in, 4–11
    diversity of, 21–23
    environment-based theories of, 32–35, 44
    historical roots of study of, 11–13
    influences in contemporary life on, 14–21
    psychoanalytic theories of, 29–32, 44
Child-directed speech, 169
Child labor laws, 354
Child maltreatment, by age of child, 209
Child safety seats, 133, 141
Child support, 267
Childbirth. *See also* Infant; Neonate; Multiple births
    complications of, 102–103

cultural differences in, 107–108
    father's perspective of, 105
    methods of, 100–102
    mother's perspective of, 104–105
    newborn's perspective of, 105–106
    out of wedlock, 268, 446
    parent-newborn bonding after, 106–107
    process of, 97–100
Childhood, early philosophical view of, 12–13. *See also* Early childhood; Late childhood
Childhood depression, 326–327
Children
    of antiquity, 11
    latchkey, 330–331
    medieval, 11–12
    neglected, 333
    only, 331–332
    rejected, 333
China
    adolescents in, 355
    family planning in, 332
Chorion, 79
Chorionic villus sampling (CVS), 71, 72
Chromosomal abnormalities, 69–71
Chromosomes, 61, 62–64
Cigarettes, 83. *See also* Smoking
Civil disobedience, 427
Class inclusion, 222, 224
Classical conditioning, 32–33, 34, 146
Clean-cut attachment phase, 188
Clinical interview, 47
Cliques, 394
Cocaine, prenatal development and, 88–90
Code switching, 241
Codeine, 90
Codons, 61
Cognition-based theories of development, 27, 35–39, 168, 253–254
Cognitive development, 4
    cultural contexts of, 158–159, 291
    early intervention and, 234–237
    gender differences in, 428–433
    influence of parents on, 231–232
    influence of schooling on, 304–307
    moral reasoning and, 426–428
    perception and, 155–157
    preoperational stage of, 220–223
    reaching maturity in, 374–375
    sensorimotor stage of, 149–152
    social context of, 157–158, 229–230
Cognitive techniques, for treatment of phobias, 329
Cohort, 51
Cohort-sequential research design, 51, 53
Color-blindness, 67
Colostrum, 142
Columbine High School, 4
Commitment, 387
Communication
    baby signs as, 162
    crying as, 179
    intentional, 160–161
    nonverbal, 252
    social perspective taking and, 301–302
    by socially competent children, 334
Community violence, 321–323

Compadrazo, 249
Compensation, 290
Competence, feelings of, 246
Compliance, 259
Computers, adolescent use of, 404–406
Concept(s)
    children's understanding of, 290
    identity, 221
    preschoolers' understanding of, 221–222
Concrete operational stage, 37, 38, 288
Conditioned response, 33, 34
Conditioned stimulus, 33, 34
Condom, 444
Conduct disorders, 124
Confidence, in math and science skills, 430
Conflict
    management of by school-age children, 334
    management of by young children, 255
    between parents, 266, 269
    parent-adolescent, 392–394
Congenital adrenal hyperplasia (CAH), 252–253
Conservation tasks, 220–221, 223, 288–290, 297
Constructivist theories of learning, 305
Consumer Product Safety Commission, 287
Contextual theories of development, 27, 40–43, 44
Contingent reinforcement procedure, 120
Continuous development, 9
Contraceptive use, by adolescents, 444–445
Control group, 50
Control parameters, 41
Conventional Level (of moral development), 343, 344
Conversational rules, 239
Cooing, 160
Cooperative learning, 305
Cooperative play, 272
Coping strategies
    in adolescence, 460–462
    emotion-focused, 319
    in late childhood, 319–320
    problem-focused, 319
Cord prolapse, 102
Correlation coefficients, 48
Correlational study, 48–49
Counselors, 325, 327
Couvade, 94
Crack cocaine, 89
Crawling, 138, 139
Creativity, 296–297
Creche, 200
Creeping, 138
Cri du chat syndrome, 178
Crimes, by adolescents, 402, 414–416, 451, 452, 453
Crisis/exploration, 387
Critical periods, 9–10
    for language development, 167–168
    for teratogenic effects, 84
Cross-sectional study, 50, 51
Crowds, 395–396
Crowning, 99
Cruising, 138

Crying, 178–180
Cultural scripts, 230
Culture, 22–23. *See also* Ethnicity; *individual cultural groups;* Race
    academic achievement and, 314–315, 379–381
    adolescent peer, 394–397
    attachment and, 193–194
    beliefs on body shape and, 370
    child-directed speech and, 170
    childbirth and, 100, 107–108
    as context for cognitive development, 230–231, 291, 375
    day care and, 199–200
    dropout rate and, 435
    Erikson on, 32
    infant crying and, 180
    infant mortality and, 127, 131
    language learning and, 298
    morality and, 345–346
    motor development and, 216
    neonatal imitation and, 113
    parenting styles and, 261, 263
    play and, 271, 273
    pregnancy and, 93–94
    resiliency and, 123
    responses to maturation and, 362–363
    scaffolding and, 158–159
    self-awareness and, 248
    Sesame Street variations and, 237
    sexual behavior and, 442
    smiling and laughter and, 178
    as source of stress, 319
    temperamental qualities and, 184–185
    in theory of mind, 228
Culture bias, in IQ tests, 293
Custody, 17, 267, 269
CVS, 71, 72
Cystic fibrosis (CF), 65, 66

D4DR gene, 67
Dance of perception, in newborns, 121
Darwin's theory of evolution, 13
Dating, 398–399
    eating disturbances and, 373
Day care, 195–200. *See also* Preschool
Deaf, 308
    language acquisition by, 171, 172
Deaths
    from child maltreatment, 205
    in early adolescence, 367
    from guns, 373, 415–416
    in infancy, 140
    in late adolescence, 414
    maternal, 447
    in preschool years, 219
Defense mechanisms, 30
Deferred imitation, 113, 148
Defiant behavior, 450
Delinquency, 451. *See also* Violence
Delivery. *See also* Childbirth; Labor
    cesarean, 59
    complications during, 101
    cost of, 59
Demandingness, 262
Dendrites, 115
Dependent variable, 50

Depression
    in adolescence, 399, 452
    childhood, 326–327
    parental, 262
    postpartum, 104
Depth perception, by infants, 145–146
Desires, emergence of, 157
Developing nations, nutrition in, 217
Developmental domains, 4
Diet therapies, for ADHD, 310
Difficult infants, 184
Dilation, of cervix in labor, 98–99
Direct learning, 253
Disabilities. *See also individual disability;* Special needs students
    child abuse and, 202
    physical, 308
Disaster, coping with, 320
Discipline, 259–262
Discontinuous development, 9
Discovery learning, 305
Discrimination, 20, 303
Diseases
    in adolescence, 417–420
    as cause of birth defects, 85–86
    in early childhood, 218–219
    genetic, 71–73
Dishabituation, 147
Disorganized/disoriented attachment, 190, 191
Diversity. *See also* Culture; Ethnicity; Race
    of children's development, 21–23
    ethnic and racial, 18
Divided custody, 267
Divorce, 14, 15, 263–269
Dizygotic (DZ) twins, 8
Domestic violence, 203
Dominant gene, 64
Dominant transmission, 64–65
Dongshi, 261
Donor insemination, 17
Dopamine
    in antisocial behavior, 325
    in thrill-seeking behavior, 67
Double standard, 443
Down syndrome, 59, 69–70, 72, 91, 311
Driving, accidents and, 414–415, 454
Dropping out, 376, 377, 385, 434–436
    prevention of, 436
    teen pregnancy and, 447, 448
Drowning, 133, 141
Drugs, use of, 84, 88, 456–458
    child abuse and, 203
    contraceptive use and, 444
    by early maturing adolescents, 363
    prenatal development and, 86–90
    prevention of, 456
    sexually transmitted diseases and, 417
Dynamic systems theory, 41–43, 138–139
Dysmenorrhea, 365, 366

Early adolescence
    definition of, 353
    eating disorders and disturbances in, 368–373
    family relationships in, 390–394
    gender intensification in, 366
    health concerns in, 366–373

    identity formation in, 386–389
    influence of mass media in, 403–406
    influence of school in, 376–381
    peer relationships in, 394–403
    physical growth in, 356–357
    sexual maturation in, 357–366
    thinking and problem solving in, 373–376
    view of self in, 384–386
Early childhood
    body and motor skill development in, 213–216
    effect of divorce in, 263–269
    emotional development in, 254–258
    gender concept in, 248–254
    health issues in, 216–219
    influence of parents in, 258–263
    influence of television in, 275–278
    language development in, 237–241
    peer and sibling relationships in, 269–275
    self-awareness in, 245–248
    thinking and problem solving in, 220–237
Early maturing adolescents, 363
Easy infants, 184
Eating disorders, 368–371
    in early-maturing girls, 363
Eating disturbances, 371–373
Eclampsia, 102
Ecological models, 41, 203–204
Ecstasy, 456
Ectoderm, 79
Ectopic pregnancy, 77
Education. *See also* Preschool; Schools; Special needs students; Teachers
    character, 426, 427
    mandatory public, 354
    money spent on, 349
    moral, 425–427
    multicultural and multilingual, 305–306
    sex, 448–449
Education for All Handicapped Children Act, 307
Ego, 30, 31
Egocentric speech, 229
Egocentrism
    of adolescents, 375–376
    of preschoolers, 222, 223
Elaboration, 225
Embryo, 76, 78, 79–82
Embryo transfer, 76
Embryonic stage, 76, 78–82
Emergent literacy, 301
Emotion-focused coping strategies, 319
Emotional autonomy, 440
Emotions. *See also specific emotions*
    childhood depression and, 326–327
    in early childhood, 254–258
    in infancy and toddlerhood, 176–182
    influence of school on, 335–337
    in late childhood, 318–321
Empathy, 257
Empirically based theories, 27
Employment. *See* Working
Endocrine system, 358
Endoderm, 79
Endogenous smile, 176
English as a Second Language (ESL), 435
Enrichment programs, 312
Environment, 5

ADHD and, 309–310
brain development and, 115–118, 137
as cause of birth defects, 83–85
in ecological model, 41
growth patterns and, 135
hazards in, 81, 90–91, 140
home, 231–232
influence on genetic expression of, 68–69
least restrictive, 307
Locke's beliefs on, 12
pubertal development and, 360
school, 335–337
temperament and, 185, 186
Environment-based theories of development, 27, 32–35, 44
Epidural block, 99
Episiotomy, 100
Erections, 399
Erikson's psychosocial theory, 31–32
Erikson's theory of adolescent identity formation, 386–387
Erogenous zone, 30, 31
ERPs, 172
ESL, 435
Estrogen, 358, 359
Ethic of care, 346
Ethics
in studying child development, 48–49
in treatment of very low birthweight infants, 125, 126
Ethnic identity, 388–389
Ethnicity, 18. *See also* Culture
academic achievement and, 380–381
alcohol consumption and, 454
birth rates and, 91
contraceptive use and, 444
day care arrangements and, 196
discipline and, 259–260, 261
dropout rates and, 435
incidence of sexually transmitted disease and, 417
low birthweight and preterm births by, 122–123
reading and, 232
recognition of, 303
school enrollment by, 335–336
self-esteem and, 249
sexual behavior and, 400, 441, 442
standards of attractiveness and, 365
stereotyping by, 338
suicide rates and, 416–417
teen pregnancy rates and, 445–446
of victims of child abuse and neglect, 202
views of competence and, 336
Ethological theory, 28–29
Ethology, 13
European Americans. *See* Caucasian Americans
Evocative G-E interaction, 69
Evolution, 13
Evolutionary theories, 28
Exercise. *See also* Physical fitness; Sports
in early adolescence, 351, 367–368
in late adolescence, 420–421
onset of puberty and, 360
during pregnancy, 92
Exogenous smile, 177

Exons, 61
Exosystem, 41
Expansion, 170
Experimental group, 50
Experimental study, 49–50
Experts, young children as, 226
Expressive language, 161
Expressive language style, 238
Extended family, 14, 16
Externalizing problems, 450
Extinction, 33
Extramarital sex, during pregnancy, 94
Eyewitness testimony, from young children, 227

Faces
features of, 28
infants' preference for, 145
Fact, 26
Failure-to-thrive (FTT), 144
False-belief task, 228
False labor, 98
Family. *See also* Family relationships; Parents
academic achievement and, 432–433
of adolescent with chronic disease, 420
blended, 14
childhood depression and, 327
as contributor to antisocial behavior, 325, 453
day care arrangements by, 196
divorce in, 264
effects of television on, 275–276
of gay and lesbian youth, 450
giftedness and, 313
of high-risk infant, 125
of infant who begins to walk, 139–140
low-income, 235
self-esteem and, 249
size of, 202
stress in, 261–262
structure of, 14–18, 196
teenage sexual activity and, 442
violence in, 203
Family and Medical Leave Act, 200
Family planning, in China, 332
Family relationships
change in, 390–394
as predictor of violence, 453
Family therapy, 325
Family time, 411
Fantasy play, 228
Fast mapping, 162
Fathers. *See also* Parents
attachment of infant to, 194–195
child sexual abuse by, 203
influence on peer relationships of, 393
influence on self-esteem of, 249
perspective on childbirth of, 105
teenage, 448
Fears, 184, 328–329. *See also* Phobia
gender differences in, 252
innate, 328
Feeding, of infants and toddlers, 143–144
Feelings, understanding of, 302–303
Fertility drugs, 78
Fertilization, 74–75
Fetal alcohol effects (FAE), 87
Fetal alcohol syndrome (FAS), 87

Fetal distress, 102, 103
Fetal stage, 76, 82–83
Fetal steroids, 97
Fetology, 72
Fetus, 76
diseased, 72
expulsion of, 99–100
growth and change of, 82
ultrasound image of, 71
Fine motor skills
in early childhood, 215–216
in late childhood, 286
Fitness. *See* Physical fitness
Folate, birth defect prevention and, 92
Follicular phase, 74
Food and Drug Administration, 86
Foreclosure, 388
Formal operational stage, 37, 38, 373–375
Formula, 141, 143
Foster care, 211
Fragile X syndrome, 67
Frames of mind, 296
Fraternal twins, 8. *See also* Twins
Freud's psychosexual theory, 30–31
Friendships, 335. *See also* Peer relationships
in early adolescence, 376, 395, 397–398
of young children, 270–271
Frontal lobe, 167, 309
Functional isolation, 218

Gamete intrafallopian transfer, 76
Gangs, 400–403
Gardner's seven frames of mind, 295
Gays, 449
as parents, 17–18
Gender bias, in school, 338, 386, 433
Gender consistency, 250
Gender development, 252–254
Gender differences
in aggression, 256
in antisocial behavior, 324
in brain development, 414
in cognitive abilities and achievement, 428–433
in concerns about weight and eating, 372
in expression of shame, 181
in fine motor movements, 286
in friendships, 398
in importance assigned to physical appearance, 247
in math and science skills, 430–431
in morality, 346
in pubertal development, 360–361
in reaction to computers, 404–405
in self-image, 385–386
in sexual behavior, 441–442
in spatial-visual skills, 429–430
in treatment by teachers, 338, 386, 433
in verbal skills, 428–429
in victims of child abuse and neglect, 202
between young boys and girls, 251–252
Gender identity, 249
Gender intensification, 366
Gender labeling, 249
Gender schemas, 254
Gender stability, 249
Gender stereotypes, 250–251, 433

Gene-environment (G-E) interactions, 68
General Social Survey, 48
Generation gap, 392
Generative learning, 305
Genes, 61, 62–64
    dominant, 64
    influence on development of, 61–69
    recessive, 64
Genetic counseling, 72–73
Genetic diseases, 69–71
    detection of, 71–73
Genetic disorders, gender development and, 250,
        252–253
Genetic factors, 5. *See also* Heritability
    in ADHD, 309
    in childhood depression, 327
    in growth patterns, 135
    in obesity, 288
Genetic Privacy Act, 62
Genetic technology, 71–72
Genetic transmission patterns, 64–68
    dominant, 64–65
    polygenic, 67–68
    recessive, 65–67
    sex-linked, 67
Genie, 166, 170–171
Genital herpes, 417
Genital stage, 31
Genomes to Life Project, 69
Genotype, 64
Germinal stage, 76, 77–78
Gestures, 161, 162
Giardia, 141
Giftedness, 51, 294, 312, 313
Girls. *See also* Gender differences
    participation in sports by, 422
Goal-corrected partnership, 259
Goals
    of adolescents, 467
    of infants, 188
Gonadotropins, 358
Gonorrhea, 417
Grades, emphasis on, 379
Grammar, 168, 170, 238
Gross motor skills, development of, 214–215. *See
        also* Motor development
Growth, of infants and toddlers, 135, 136,
        140–141
Growth charts, 136
Growth hormones, 358
Growth spurt, in adolescence, 356–357
Guns, 374, 415–416

Habituation, 147
Hand signals, 162
Handedness, 216
Head lifting, by infant, 137
Head Start, 235–236
Health
    in early adolescence, 366–373
    growth as indicator of, 135
    of infants, 140–144
    in late adolescence, 417–422
    smoking and, 455
    teen pregnancy and, 447
    of young children, 216–219

Health insurance, 140–141
Healthy People 2010, 123
Hearing, in neonate, 119–120
Helpful behaviors, 257–258
Hemispheres, of brain, 136–137, 214
Hemophilia, 67
Heritability, 8. *See also* Genetic factors
    of temperament, 182
Heroin, prenatal development and, 90
Heteronomous morality stage, 339
Heterosexuals, 449
Heterozygous, 64
Heuristic, 375
High-risk behavior, 385, 400
High-risk infants, 125–127
High school dropouts. *See* Dropping out
Hippocampus, 414
Hispanic Americans, 21
    academic achievement of, 380
    access to computers of, 404
    alcohol consumption by, 454
    birth rates of, 91
    community violence and, 323
    day care arrangements of, 196
    discipline by, 261
    dropout rate of, 435
    ethnic identity of, 389
    family relationships and, 14, 15, 268, 314, 315,
        453
    in foster care, 211
    incidence of rubella among, 85
    lack of health insurance among, 140–141
    mortality rates for, 127, 414
    obesity among, 287
    population of, 18
    self-esteem of, 249
    sexual practices of, 400
    suicide rates of, 417
    as victims of child abuse, 202
History, children in, 11–13
HIV. *See* Human immunodeficiency virus (HIV)
Holland, midwives in, 107
Holophrases, 161
Home Observation for Measurement of the
        Environment (HOME) Scale, 231–232
Home signs, 171
Homicides, in late adolescence, 415–416
Homosexuals, 449. *See also* Gays; Lesbians
Homozygous, 64
Hopi Indians, and menarche, 362–363
Hormones
    fetal development and, 83
    gender development and, 250, 252–253, 431
    puberty and, 356, 358–360, 362
Hospital, births at, 100
Hospitalizations, 133
Hostile aggression, 256
Human Genome Project, 61, 62
Human immunodeficiency virus (HIV), 84, 86,
        88, 417, 418
Huntington's chorea, 64–65, 66
Hyperactivity, 124
Hyponatremia, 141
Hypothalamus, 358
Hypothesis, 43
Hypothetico-deductive reasoning, 373–374

Id, 30, 31
Identical twins, 8. *See also* Twins
Identity, 386
    Erikson's theory of formation of, 386–387
    ethnic, 388–389
    Marcia's theory of formation of, 387–388
Identity achieved, 388
Identity concept, 221
Identity confused, 388
Identity diffusion, 386
Idioms, 299
Illicit drugs. *See* Drugs, use of
Image schemas, 156
Imaginary audience, 376
Imitation
    deferred, 113
    in language learning, 168
Immanent justice, 340
Immigrants
    impact of, 18–19
    language abilities of, 168
Immunity, from breast milk, 142
Immunization, 140
    for rubella, 85
Implantation, 77
Impressions, forming, 423
Imprinting, 28
In vitro fertilization, 76
Incubator, 125
Independent variable, 49
Individual Characteristics Model, 395
Individual differences, 10–11
Individualism, 15
Individuals with Disabilities Education Act, 307
Induced labor, 103
Induction, parental influence through, 391
Inductive reasoning, 260
Infant. *See also* Neonate
    attachment of, 187–195
    cognitive abilities of, 149–159
    day care for, 195–200
    emotional development of, 176–182
    facial features of, 28
    failure-to-thrive, 144
    health and safety of, 140–144
    language skills of, 159–166
    learning and remembering by, 146–149
    low-birthweight, 122–127
    measuring behavior of, 52
    perceptual abilities of, 144–146
    physical development of, 135–140
    premature, 122–127
    preterm, 122
    temperament of, 182–185
    very-low-birthweight, 59
Infant mortality, 100, 127, 131, 184
Infant survival rates, 126
Infantile amnesia, 148, 149
Infertility, 75–76, 93
Information processing, in school-aged children,
        292–293
Information processing theory, 39
Informed consent, 49
Injury, 133, 286–287
Innate fears, 328
Innate morality, 12–13

Innate theories, 166–168
Inner working models, 29
Instrumental aggression, 256
Intelligence(s), 7–8
  breast-feeding and, 142
  Head Start and, 235
  identifying components of, 295
  impact of drug-addicted parents on, 90
  impact of poverty on, 313
  measurement of, 293–294
  multiple, 295
  performance, 295
  Piaget's view of, 36
  triarchic theory of, 294–295
  verbal, 293
Intelligence quotient (IQ), 294. *See also* Intelligence(s)
  limits of, 294–295
  mental retardation and, 310–311
Intentional communication, 160–161
Internal speech, 38
Internal working model, 186
Internalization, 259
Internalizing problems, 450
Internet, 406
Intonation, 160
Introns, 61
Iron-deficiency anemia, 218

Jahara of South America, birth experience of, 107
Jicarilla Apache Indian, birth ceremonies of, 107–108
Jobs. *See* Working
Joint custody, 267, 269
Joint legal custody, 267
Joint physical custody, 267, 269
Jumping, 214
Junior high schools, 377–378, 379
Just community schools, 426, 427
Juvenile, 355

Karyotype, 63, 64, 73
Kilogram kids, 123
Kindergarten, 233–234
Klinefelter's syndrome, 70
Kohlberg's theory of moral development, 341–344, 425
Kwashiorkor, 217

Labor
  controlling pain in, 99
  false, 98
  induced, 103
  initiation of, 97
Lactation consultants, 143
Lamaze childbirth, 101, 102
Language. *See also* Language development
  expressive, 161
  native, 160
  newborn preference for, 120
  receptive, 161
Language acquisition device (LAD), 166
Language development, 28, 38
  in bilingual children, 241
  Down syndrome and, 70
  in early childhood, 220, 237–240
  in infants and toddlers, 159–166
  resilient and fragile aspects of, 171–172

in school-age children, 297–299
  theories of, 166–171
Language processing, 137
Language style
  expressive, 238
  referential, 238
Latchkey children, 330–331
Late adolescence
  behavior problems in, 450–458
  changes in sexuality in, 441–450
  cognitive abilities and achievement in, 428–433
  contraceptive use in, 444–445
  depression in, 452
  developing autonomy in, 440–441
  dropping out of school in, 434–436
  employment in, 458–460
  health and safety issues in, 414–422
  homosexuality in, 449–450
  parenting in, 447–448
  physical development in, 413–414
  pregnancy in, 445–447
  prevention of drug use in, 456
  sex education in, 448–449
  thinking and reasoning in, 422–428
  use of illicit drugs in, 456–458
  vulnerability and resiliency in, 460–462
Late childhood
  effect of family and culture on development in, 312–315, 329–332
  effect of school on development in, 304–307, 335–338
  emotional development in, 318–323
  emotional and psychological disturbances in, 323–329
  intelligence and creativity in, 292–297
  language and literacy development in, 297–301
  moral development in, 338–346
  peer relationships in, 332–335
  physical development in, 285–288
  students with special needs in, 307–312
  thinking and problem solving in, 288–292
  understanding of social world in, 301–304
Late-maturing adolescents, 363
Latency stage, 31
Latino, 19. *See also* Hispanic Americans
Laughter, 178
Lead poisoning, 90, 219, 311
Leading questions, 227
Learning, 5
  constructivist theories of, 305
  cooperative, 305
  cultural contexts of, 158–159
  discovery, 305
  generative, 305
  to learn, 293
  social contexts of, 157–158
Learning-based theories. *See* Cognition-based theories
Learning disabilities, fetal alcohol effects and, 87
Least restrictive environment, 307
Leboyer childbirth, 101–102
Lesbians, 449
  as parents, 17–18
Libido, 30, 31
Lightening, 98
Limbic system, 356, 413

Literacy
  emergent, 301
  in school-age children, 299–301
Living conditions, social competence and, 335
Locke's *tabula rasa,* 12
Long-term memory, 39
  in early childhood, 224–225
  in infants, 147–149
Longitudinal study, 51
  of shyness, 185
Love withdrawal, 260
Low birthweight, 122–127, 140
  cocaine use and, 89
Luteal phase, 74

Macrosystem, 41
Mainstreaming, 308
Malnourishment, 144, 217–218
Manipulative tantrums, 181
Mapping, of words, 162–164
  fast, 162
Marasmus, 217
Marcia's theory of adolescent identity formation, 387–388
Marginal (in majority culture), 389
Marijuana, 456. *See also* Drugs, use of
Marquesas Island, play of children on, 272
Masai tribe, difficult infants in, 185
Mass media, influence of, 403–406. *See also* Television viewing
Masturbation, 399
Mate selection, 28
Maternal age, 91
Maternal stress, 92
Math skills, gender differences in, 430–431
Maturation, 5. *See also* Physical development; Puberty; Sexual maturation
Medication
  for ADHD, 310
  antidepressant, 327
  for antisocial behavior, 325
  in labor, 99
Meiosis, 62, 63
Melatonin, 421
Memory
  in early childhood, 224–225
  in infants, 147
  long-term, 39
  short-term, 39
  strategies for, 291–292
Memory distortions, gender stereotypes and, 250–251
Menarche, 356, 360, 361. *See also* Puberty
  cultural traditions associated with, 362–363
  reactions to, 365, 390
Menstrual cycle, 74
Menstrual phase, 74
Mental illness, 7, 31
Mental retardation, 310–312, 313
  Down syndrome and, 70
  fetal alcohol syndrome and, 87
  fragile X syndrome and, 67
  Klinefelter's syndrome and, 70
  low birthweight and, 124
  radiation and, 90
  spina bifida and, 92

Mental rotation, 429
Mentalistic explanations, 302–303
Mesoderm, 79
Mesosystem, 41
Metacognition, 225, 293
Metacomponents, 295
Mexican Americans, 19. *See also* Hispanic
　　Americans
　　ethnic identity of, 389
　　family relationships of, 16, 453
　　moral themes of, 345, 346
Microencephaly, 90
Microsystem, 41
Middle schools, 378
Midwives, 101, 107
Mindblind, 302
Minimal distance principle (MDP), 298
Minorities. *See* Ethnicity; *individual minority*
　　groups; Race
Miscarriage, 447
　　caffeine and, 87
　　cocaine and, 89
　　maternal age and, 91
Mitosis, 62, 63, 77
Modeling, 35
　　as treatment for phobias, 329
Molding, 99
Monozygotic (MZ) twins, 8
Moral development
　　Kohlberg's theory of, 341–344
　　in late adolescence, 425–426
　　Piaget's theory of, 338–341
Moral domain, 425
Moral education, 425–427
Moral realism, 339
Morality, 338. *See also* Moral development
　　culture and, 345–346
　　gender and, 346
　　innate, 12–13
　　temperament and, 184
Moratorium, 388
Moro reflex, 111, 114
Morphine, 90
Mortality rates
　　of infants, 100, 127, 131
　　of mothers, 100
Motherese, 169
Mothers. *See also* Parents
　　age of during pregnancy, 70, 91
　　with AIDS, 143
　　benefits of breast-feeding to, 142–143
　　changes in during pregnancy, 82
　　as child abusers, 203
　　cultural differences in play of, 271
　　influence on peer relationships of, 393
　　mortality rates of, 100
　　perspective on childbirth of, 104–105
　　stress level of, 92
　　surrogate, 76
　　teenage, 447–448
　　working, 16, 195, 196, 200, 330
Motor development
　　cultural and racial influences on, 216
　　in early childhood, 213–216
　　in infants and toddlers, 137–140
　　in late childhood, 285–286

Motor reproduction, 35
Mr. Roger's Neighborhood, 277
Mruk's matrix of self-esteem, 246–247
Mucous plug, 98
Multicultural education, 305–306
Multilingual education, 305–306
Multiparous women, 98
Multiple births, 77–78
Multiple classification task, 290
Multiple intelligences, 295
Multiple pregnancies, 77–78
Multiracial people, 21
Murders, 415–416
Music, popular, 403
Myelination, 116
　　in adolescence, 414
　　breast milk and, 142
　　in early childhood, 213–214
　　in late childhood, 285

National Association for the Education of Young
　　Children, 199, 233
National Health Interview Survey, 48
National Mental Health Association, 320
National Survey of Children, 48
Native Americans
　　community violence and, 323
　　ethnic identity of, 389
　　in foster care, 211
　　Head Start usage by, 235
　　learning by observation and, 231
　　mortality rates for, 127
　　suicide rates of, 417
　　as victims of child abuse, 202
Natural selection, 13
Naturalistic study, 48
Nature versus nurture debate, 5–11, 68–69
Needs, attachment and, 186
Negative reinforcement, 33
Neglect, 201–202. *See also* Child abuse
　　foster care and, 211
　　incidence of, 201
　　victims of, 202
Neglected children, 333
Neonatal Behavioral Assessment Scale, 113–114
Neonatal intensive care, 124–125, 126
Neonate, 108
　　at-risk, 121–127
　　brain development of, 114–118
　　bonding of, 106–107
　　characteristics of, 108–114
　　perceptions of, 118–121
　　perspective on childbirth of, 105–106
Neo-Piagetians, 38
Nervous system, development of, 83
Neural tube, 80, 115
　　defects of, 72, 92
Neurochemistry, childhood depression and, 327
Neurodevelopmental approaches, 29, 30
Neuronal connections, 116–117, 137, 285, 413
Neurons, 115
New familism, 15
Newborn. *See* Neonate
Niche-building, 69
Nocturnal emissions, 399, 400
Noncustodial parent, 266–267

Nonparental caregivers, 16. *See also* Caregivers
Nonverbal communication, gender differences
　　in, 252
Norepinephrine, 327
Nuclear family, 14
Number concepts, understanding of, 155
Nurse-midwives, 101
Nutrition
　　brain development and, 117
　　in early adolescence, 351, 367
　　in early childhood, 216–217
　　failure-to-thrive and, 144
　　in infants, 141–143
　　in late childhood, 287
　　onset of puberty and, 360, 361
　　prenatal development and, 92

Obedience, 341
Obese, 287
Obesity
　　in adolescence, 369, 420
　　breast-feeding and, 142
　　in late childhood, 287
Object permanence, 152–155
Observation, 253
　　in language learning, 168
　　in studies, 48, 52
Occipital lobe, 167
Onlooker play, 272
Only children, 331–332
Operant conditioning, 33–34, 146–147
Operations, 220
Optic nerve, 118
Oral stage, 31
Organization, in memory, 225, 292
Origin of Species (Darwin), 13
Osteoporosis, 367
Out-of-wedlock births, 268, 446
Overextension, 164
Overregularization, 238
Ovulation, 73–74, 143
Ovum, 62, 73, 75
Oxytocin, 98

Pain, in newborns, 121
Palmar grasp reflex, 110, 111, 114
Parallel play, 272, 273
Parent(s). *See also* Family; Fathers; Mothers
　　academic achievement and, 314–315, 432–433
　　adolescents as, 447–448
　　adoptive, 186
　　autonomy and, 441
　　bonding of with newborn, 106–107
　　as child abusers, 202–203
　　cultural differences in beliefs of, 22
　　depressed, 262
　　divorce of, 263–269
　　effectiveness of, 266
　　ethnic identity and, 389
　　of gifted children, 313
　　influence of in early childhood, 258–263
　　influence of in late childhood, 329–331
　　lesbian and gay, 17–18
　　with mental illness, 325
　　noncustodial, 266–267
　　of preterm infants, 127

relationship of with adolescent, 390–394, 411, 442
school transitions and, 376–377
sibling relationships and, 274
single, 203
as teachers, 231–232
training for, 206
Parenting styles, 192, 262–263
authoritarian, 262
authoritative, 263
following divorce, 266
permissive, 262
uninvolved, 262–263
Parietal lobe, 167
Parity, 92
Partners, in teenage sexual activity, 443
Passive G-E interaction, 69
Passive sentences, 298
Pediatric AIDS, 86
Pedigree analysis, 73
Peer groups, 270. See also Peer relationships
deviant, 400–403
Peer Influence Model, 395
Peer rejection, 333–334, 398
Peer relationships
antisocial behavior and, 325
in early adolescence, 394–403
in early childhood, 43, 248, 270
in late childhood, 332–335
role of parents in, 393
stress in, 318
teenage sexual activity and, 442
Perception
early cognitive development and, 155–157
in infant, 144–146
in neonate, 118–121
spatial, 429
Performance
athletic, 422
test-taking, 430
Performance anxiety, 247
Performance intelligence, 293
Permissive parenting, 262
Personal domain, 425
Personal fable, 376, 444
Personality, 7, 8
anorexia nervosa and, 370
gender differences in, 252
Pesticides, 84
Petting, 400
Phallic stage, 31
Phenotype, 64
Phenylketonuria (PKU), 5
Phobia
school, 328
treatment of, 329
Phonemes, 159
Phonemic awareness, 160, 300
Phonics approach, 301
Physical abuse, 201. See also Child abuse
of pregnant women, 94
Physical aggression, 256
Physical appearance. See Appearance
Physical development, 4. See also Appearance
in early adolescence, 356–357, 361–363
fetal alcohol effects and, 87

in infants and toddlers, 135–140
in late adolescence, 413
in late childhood, 285–288
Physical disabilities, 308
Physical fitness, 286–287, 420–421
Physiological measurement of children's behavior, 51–52
Piaget's theory of cognitive development, 9, 35–38
formal operational stage of, 374
preoperational stage of, 220–224
sensorimotor stage of, 149–152
Piaget's theory of moral development, 338–341
Pitocin, 98, 103
Pituitary gland, 358
PKU, 5
Placenta, 79
expulsion of, 100
Placenta previa, 102
Placental barrier, 83
cocaine and, 89
heroin and, 90
Plasticity, 117, 118, 124
Plato, 11
Play, 271–273
associative, 272
cooperative, 272
emotional development and, 182
fantasy, 228
gender differences in, 252
gender typed, 43, 45, 251
onlooker, 272
parallel, 272, 273
pretend, 273
relational, 157
with same-sex peers, 43, 45
solitary, 272
Pleasure principle, 30, 31
PMS, 365–366
Poisoning
in early childhood, 219
in infants, 141
lead, 219
prenatal, 90–91
Political thinking, 427
Polygenic transmission, 67–68
Pons medulla, 167
Popular music, 403
Popularity, 396, 398
Population, U.S., 18, 57
Positive reinforcement, 33
Possible self, 384
Postconventional Level (of moral development), 343, 344, 425
Postpartum depression, 104
Poverty, 409
discipline and, 261
dropout rate and, 435
intellectual development and, 313
resiliency of low-birthweight children and, 123
self-concept and, 248
stress related to, 321
teenage parenthood and, 448
Power assertion, 259
Practice, scripts and, 230

Pragmatics, 159, 299
Preattachment phase, 187
Precausal reasoning, 221
Precocious puberty, 359–360
Preconcepts, 221
Preconventional Level (of moral development), 341, 344
Prefrontal cortex, 356, 413–414
Pregnancy
cultural influences on, 93–94
hazards to, 83–92
ectopic, 77
men's responses to, 93–94
multiple, 77–78
protective factors for, 92–93
sympathetic, 94
teen, 400, 445–448
Prejudice, 303–304
Premature births, 122–127, 140
Premenstrual syndrome (PMS), 365–366
Premoral period, 339
Prenatal androgens, 252
Prenatal checkups, 93
Prenatal development, 73–83
embryonic stage of, 76, 78–82
fertilization in, 74–75
fetal stage of, 76, 82–83
germinal stage of, 76, 77–78
hazards to, 83–92
ovulation in, 73–74
protective factors for, 92–93
spermatogenesis in, 74
timetables for, 77, 80
Preoperational stage of cognitive development, 36, 37, 220–223
Preschool, 232–234
programs of, 16–17
Pretend play, 228–229, 273
Preterm births, 122
attachment and, 192
Primary circular reactions, 150
Primary motor cortex, 167
Primary prevention, 205
Primary sexual characteristics, 358
Primary somatosensory cortex, 167
Primiparous women, 98
Privacy
in studies, 49
teens' need for, 390
Private speech, 38, 229
Problem-focused coping strategies, 319
Problem solving, 221
active, 151
creative, 151
in early adolescence, 373–376
logical, 288–290
social, 424–425
Prodigies, 296
Projection, 30
Projective measures, 52
Prosocial behavior, 257
effects of television on, 277–278
Prostaglandins, 97, 366
Protein-energy malnutrition (PEM), 217
Proteins, 61
Proximodistal development, 81

Pruning, of neuronal connections, 117, 137
  in adolescence, 413
  in late childhood, 285
Psychoanalysis, 31
Psychoanalytic theories of development, 27,
  30–32, 44
Psychological maltreatment, 201
Psychosexual development, 30
Psychosexual theory, 30–31
Psychosocial crises, 32
Psychosocial moratorium, 387
Psychosocial theory, 31–32
Puberty, 5, 351, 355
  conflicts brought on by, 393
  effects of timing of, 363–364
  environmental influences on, 360
  gender intensification in, 366
  generational differences in, 361
  precocious, 359–360
  process of, 357–359
  psychological reactions to, 364–366
  school transitions and, 377
  sex and race differences in, 360–361
Pubescence, 355
Pubic hair, 360
Public Law 94-142, 307
Puerto Ricans, ethnic identity among, 389. *See
  also* Hispanic Americans
Punan Bah, 354
Punishment, 33, 259
  of adolescents, 392
  gender differences in, 253
  and language development, 168

Questionnaire, 13, 52
Quickening, 82

Race, 18. *See also* Culture; Ethnicity; *individual
  racial groups*
  academic achievement and, 380–381
  birth rates and, 91
  children's understanding of, 303–304
  developmental model encompassing, 20
  discipline and, 259–260, 261
  distribution of gestation by, 97
  dropout rate and, 435
  motor development and, 216
  onset of puberty and, 361
  population increase by, 18
  reading and, 232
  resiliency of low-birthweight infants and, 122–123
  stereotyping by, 303, 338
  teen pregnancy rate and, 445–446
  type of family and, 14–15
Racial stereotypes, 303, 338
Racism, child development and, 20
Radiation, prenatal development and, 90
Random assignment, 49
Random sampling, 49
Rate-limiting component, 42–43
Raven Progressive Matrices Test, 294
Reading
  gender differences in, 428
  learning skills of, 299–300
  teaching of, 301

  to young children, 232
Reading readiness, 300–301
Reality principle, 30, 31
Reasoning
  cultural differences in, 291
  hypothetico-deductive, 374
  inductive, 260
  moral, 425
  postconventional, 425
  precausal, 221
  transductive, 221
Recall, 39
Receptive language, 161
Recessive gene, 64
Recessive transmission, 65–67
Referential language style, 238
Reflective abstraction, 375
Reflex, 146
  in fetus, 83
  in infant, 137
  in neonate, 109–111
Reflexive schemes, 149–150
Rehearsal, 39, 225, 292
Reinforcement, 35
  in language learning, 168
  negative, 33
  positive, 33
  vicarious, 35
Rejected children, 333
Rejection, 333, 398
Relational aggression, 256
Relational play, 157
Religion, 411
Religious thinking, 428
Remarriage, adjustment to, 267–268
Repression, 30
Research strategies, 46–50
  for measuring changes over time, 50–51
Resilience
  in adolescence, 460–462
  in childhood, 320–321
Responsiveness, 262
Retention, 35
Reversible thinking, 290
Rewards
  gender differences in, 253
  in language development, 168
  overuse of, 260
Risk-taking behavior, 385, 400, 415, 450
  sports and, 422
Ritalin, 310
Rites of passage, 354
Rooting reflex, 110, 111, 114
Rousseau's innate morality, 12–13
Rubella, 85
Running, 214

Safety
  community violence and, 322
  of day care, 199
  of infants, 141
  in late adolescence, 414–417
  of schools, 337, 414
  of sports, 287
Savants, 296

Scaffolding, 158, 159, 229
  in language learning, 170
Schematic consistency, 254
Schemes, 36
Schizophrenia, heritability of, 8
School-age children. *See* Late childhood
School phobia, 328
Schools. *See also* Academic achievement
  access to computers in, 404
  adaptation to a change in, 377
  addressing special needs in, 307–312
  dropping out of, 376, 377, 385, 434–436
  influence in early adolescence of, 376–381
  influence in late childhood of, 304–307, 318,
    335–337
  junior high, 377–378, 379
  just community, 426, 427
  length of year in, 380
  middle, 378
  optimum opening time for, 421
  readiness for, 234
  safety of, 337, 416
  status of, 283, 380
  teen pregnancy and, 447, 448
Science skills, gender differences in, 430–431
Scientific method, 43, 45
Scientific reasoning, 43
Scientific theories, 26–27
Scripts, 225–226, 291
  cultural, 230
  social, 443
Seat belts, 219
Second-language learning, 172, 306
Secondary circular reactions, 150
Secondary prevention, 205
Secondary sexual characteristics, 358
Secure attachment, 190, 192, 194, 195, 335
Segregation, 20
Self
  actual, 384
  possible, 384
Self-awareness
  in infants, 181
  self-concept and, 245–246
  self-esteem and, 246–247
Self-concept
  in early adolescence, 384–385
  of young children, 245–246
Self-conscious emotions, 181
Self-consciousness, 385
Self-esteem
  in early adolescence, 385
  matrix of, 246–247
  membership in crowd and, 396
  of minority children, 249
  parental support and, 391
  punitiveness and, 392
  school and, 377
  sports and, 368
  of young children, 246–247
Self-perception, 247–248
Self-reports, 52
Semantic bootstrapping, 238
Semantics, 159, 298–299
Sensitive periods, 10, 117, 118

Sensorimotor schemes, 149
Sensorimotor stage, 36, 37, 149
Sensory register, 39
Sentences, 238–239
    first, 165
    passive, 298
Separated (from majority culture), 389
Separation anxiety, 188, 329
Seriation, understanding of, 290, 291
Serotonin, 327
Sesame Street, 236–237, 277
Sesotho, 298
Severe combined immunodeficiency, 72
Sex, choosing, 65. *See also* Gender differences
Sex cells, 62, 63
Sex chromosomes, 63, 67
    abnormalities in, 70–71
Sex education, adolescent, 448–449
Sex hormones, 358. *See also* Hormones
Sex-linked transmission, 67
Sexual abuse, 201, 202. *See also* Child abuse
    teen pregnancy and, 445
Sexual attitudes, in adolescence, 441–443
Sexual behavior
    in early adolescence, 399–400
    in late adolescence, 441–450
Sexual intercourse, 40, 441, 448
Sexual maturation, 357–366
Sexual orientation, 449. *See also* Gays; Lesbians
Sexual precocity, 445
Sexually transmitted diseases (STDs), 400, 417
Shame, 181
Shaping, 34
Short-term memory, 39
    in infants, 147
Shyness, 185
    anorexia nervosa and, 370
Sibling relationships
    in early childhood, 273–275
    in late childhood, 331
Sickle cell anemia, 66–67
SIDS, 126, 139, 140
Simpatía, 249
Single-parent families, 14
    child abuse and, 203
    day care and, 196
    discipline and, 261
Sitting, 137
Situation cues, 148
Sleep patterns
    of adolescents, 421
    of neonates, 112–113
Slow-to-warm-up infants, 184
Smallpox, 84
Smell, sense of, in neonates, 120–121
Smile
    endogenous, 176
    exogenous, 177
    social, 177
Smoking
    by adolescents, 454–456
    genetics and, 68
    prenatal development and, 83, 85, 88, 89
Social behavior, 28
    gender differences in, 252

Social class. *See* Socioeconomic status
Social cognition, in late adolescence, 423–424
Social-cognitive theory, on development of
    prejudice, 304
Social communicative competence, 237
Social competence, 334–335
Social contexts of early learning, 157–158
Social-conventional domain, 425
Social development
    influence of school on, 335–337
    influence of teacher on, 337–338
Social drinking, 454
Social-emotional development, 4. *See also*
    Emotions; Social development
Social interaction theories of language
    acquisition, 168–170
Social learning theory, 35
    of gender development, 253
Social perspective taking, 301–302 , 424
Social policy, child development and, 22–23
Social position variables, 20
Social responsibility, 425
Social script, 443
Social smile, 177
Socialization, 5
Society for Research in Child Develop-
    ment, 49
Sociobiology, 13
Socioeconomic status. *See also* Poverty
    ADHD and, 310
    discipline and, 261
    dropout rate and, 435
    teacher influence and, 338
Sole legal custody, 267
Sole physical custody, 267
Solitary play, 272
Spanish, 19. *See also* Hispanic Americans
Spanking, 259
Spatial perception, 429
Spatial relationships, 137
Spatial task, 291
Spatial-visual skills, 429
    gender differences in, 429–430
Spatial visualization, 429
Special needs students, 307–312
    with ADHD, 308–310
    gifted and talented, 312
    with mental retardation, 310–312
    with physical disabilities, 308
Speech, 160. *See also* Language; Language
    development
    child-directed, 169
    egocentric, 229
    private, 229
Sperm, 62, 65, 75
Spermatids, 74
Spermatocytes, 74
Spermatogenesis, 74
Spermatozoa, 74
Spina bifida, 59, 92
Spinal cord, 167
Split custody, 267
Spontaneous abortion, 84
Sports. *See also* Athletic ability
    in early adolescence, 367–368

in late adolescence, 421–422
in late childhood, 286–287
Stage theories, 9, 30, 36–38. *See also individual*
    theories
Stages, 9
Standardized achievement tests, 379, 432
Standing, 138
Standing reflex, 114
Static thinking, 221
Status offenses, 451
STDs, 417
Stepfamily, 14, 268
Stepping reflex, 110, 114
Stereotypes
    gender, 250, 251, 432
    racial, 303, 338
Sternberg's triarchic theory of intelligence,
    294–295
Stillbirths
    cocaine use and, 89
    syphilis and, 85
Strange Situation, 189, 190, 191, 192, 197
Stranger anxiety, 188
Street gangs, 400–403
Stress
    acculturative, 319
    in adolescence, 460–462
    adolescent depression and, 452
    from chronic disease, 420
    from community violence, 321–323
    exercise as protective factor for, 368
    from family issues, 261–262, 266, 274–275
    in late childhood, 318–321
    maternal, 92
    obesity and, 288
    onset of puberty and, 360
    resilience in children and, 320–321
    school as source of, 318, 376
Study of Mathematically Precocious
    Youth, 312
Suano, 248
Substance use and abuse, 453–458. *See also*
    Alcohol consumption; Drugs, use of
Sucking reflex, 111, 114
Sudden infant death syndrome (SIDS), 126, 139,
    140
Suicide, 326, 416–417, 452
    sexual orientation and, 449–450
Superego, 30, 31
Surrogate mothers, 76
Survey study, 47–48
Swimming, by infants, 141
Swimming reflex, 111
Symbolic representation, 151, 220
Sympathetic pregnancy, 94
Sympathy, 257
Synapses, 115. *See also* Neuronal connections
Synaptic cleft, 115
Synaptic vesicles, 115
Syntactic bootstrapping, 237
Syntax, 159
    development of, 238, 298
Syphilis, 85
Systematic desensitization, 33

Tabula rasa, 12
Talking, 165–166
Tantrums, 255
    manipulative, 181
    temperamental, 181
Taste, sense of, in neonates, 120
Tay Sachs disease, 66
Teachers, 38
    biases of, 306–307, 386, 433
    in child care centers, 198
    influence of, 337–338
    parents as, 231–232
Teen pregnancy, 400, 445–448
    childhood sexual abuse and, 445
Teenager, 355. *See also* Adolescence; Early
    adolescence; Late adolescence
Telegraphic speech, 165
Television viewing
    by adolescents, 403
    aggression and, 48–49, 276–277
    family life and, 275–276
    physical fitness and, 286
    prosocial behavior and, 277–278
    public, 236–237
    supervision of, 277
Temper tantrums, 180–181, 255
Temperament, 182
    childhood depression and, 327
    infant development and, 184–185
    as predictor of shyness, 185
    sibling relationships and, 274
    structure of, 182–184
    of victims of child abuse and neglect,
      202
Temperamental tantrums, 181
Temperature, newborn sensitivity to, 121
Temporal lobe, 167
Teratogens, 83–85
    mental retardation and, 311
    radiation as, 90
"Termites," 51
Tertiary circular reactions, 151
Tertiary prevention, 205–206
Testosterone, 252, 356, 358, 359
    effect on fetal development of, 83
Tests
    culture fair, 294
    IQ, 293–294
    standardized achievement, 379, 432
Thalidomide, 86
Theory, 26
    attachment, 29
    biology-based, 27, 28–30, 166–168,
      252–253
    cognition-based, 27, 35–39, 168,
      253–254
    contextual, 27, 40–43, 44
    dynamic systems, 41–43, 138–139
    ecological, 40–41
    environment-based, 27, 32–35, 44
    ethological, 28–29
    evolutionary, 28
    information processing, 39
    innate, 166–168
    of mind, 226–228

neurodevelopmental, 29, 30
psychoanalytic, 27, 30–32, 44
psychosexual, 30–31
psychosocial, 31–32
scientific, 26–27
social learning, 35, 253
stage, 9, 30, 36–38
Therapy, psychoanalysis as, 31
There Are No Children Here (Kotlowitz), 321
Thinking
    animistic, 222, 223
    creative, 297
    critical and metacognitive, 441
    cultural influences on, 230–231
    egocentric, 222, 223
    formal operational, 374–375
    about people and relationships, 423–425
    political and religious, 427–428
    preoperational, 220–223
    reversible, 290
    static, 221
Third National Incidence Study of Child
    Abuse and Neglect, 201
Three-mountain task, 222, 223
Thrill-seeking behavior, 67
Throwing, 214–215
Thumbsucking, 150
Tobacco. *See* Smoking
Toddler. *See also* Infant
    brain development in, 135–137
    motor development in, 137–140
    weaning and feeding of, 143–144
Toilet training, 140
Tonic neck reflex, 110, 114
Touch, sense of, in neonates, 120
Toxemia, 447
Tracking, 119
Traditional familism, 15
Transactional perspective, 21–22, 43
Transductive reasoning, 221
Transition, 99
Transmission. *See* Genetic transmission
    patterns
Transverse presentation, 103
Treatment
    for antisocial behavior, 325–326
    for depression, 327
    for phobias, 329
Triarchic theory of intelligence, 294–295
Trisomy 21, 69
Trisomy-X syndrome, 70
Turkey, birth experience in, 107
Turner's syndrome, 70, 431
Twins
    ADHD and, 309
    antisocial behavior in, 324
    childhood depression and, 327
    dizygotic, 8
    fraternal, 8
    identical, 8
    incidence of, 77–78
    monozygotic, 8
    puberty and, 359
    sexual orientation and, 449

Ultrasound, 71
Umbilical cord, 79, 100
Unconditioned response, 33, 34
Unconditioned stimulus, 33, 34
Unconscious, 30
Underextension, 164
Undernourishment, 144, 217, 218
Uninvolved parenting, 262–263
United States
    birth experience in, 107
    malnutrition in, 217–218
    population of, 18, 57

Vaccinations, 219
Values autonomy, 440
Variable
    dependent, 50
    independent, 49
Verbal intelligence, 293
Verbal skills, gender differences in,
    428–429
Vernix caseosa, 109
Very-low-birthweight children, 59, 124
Viability, age of, 83
Vicarious reinforcement, 35
Victor, Wild Boy of Aveyron, 6–7, 10, 26, 32
Video games, 405–406, 433
Violence
    by adolescents, 402, 414–416, 451, 452,
      453
    community, 321–323
    family, 203
    on television, 48–49, 276–277
    in video games, 405–406
Virus, and prenatal development, 86. *See also*
    specific viruses
Vision
    in early childhood, 214
    in neonate, 118–119
Visual acuity, 118
Visual cliff apparatus, 145–146
Vocabulary, 161, 163
    of school-age children, 298
    of young children, 237–238
Vulnerability, in adolescence, 460–462
Vygotsky's theory of cognitive development,
    38, 157

Walking, 138–139
    dynamic systems model of, 41–43
    implications of, 139–140
War, stress from, 322
Water intoxication, 141
Weaning, of infants and toddlers, 143–144
Wechsler Intelligence Scale for Children–Third
    Edition (WISC–III), 293
Weight, adolescent concerns about, 372. *See*
    also Eating disorders; Eating disturbances;
    Obesity
Well-child visits, 140
Wernicke's area, 167
Wet dreams, 399
Whole language approach, 301
Wild Boy of Aveyron (Victor), 6–7, 10, 26, 32
WISC–III, 293

Women. *See also* Mothers; Parents
    multiparous, 98
    primiparous, 98
Word
    deciphering meaning of, 162–165
    first, 161
Working
    by adolescents, 458–460

creative style of, 297
    by mothers, 16, 195, 200, 330
Worthiness, 246
Wynn's possible and impossible events, 156

X chromosome, 63, 64, 65, 67, 70
X rays, 84, 90
XYY syndrome, 71

Y chromosome, 63, 64, 65, 67, 71
Youth, 355. *See also* Adolescence; Early adolescence; Late adolescence

Zone of proximal development, 38, 157, 229
Zygote, 77